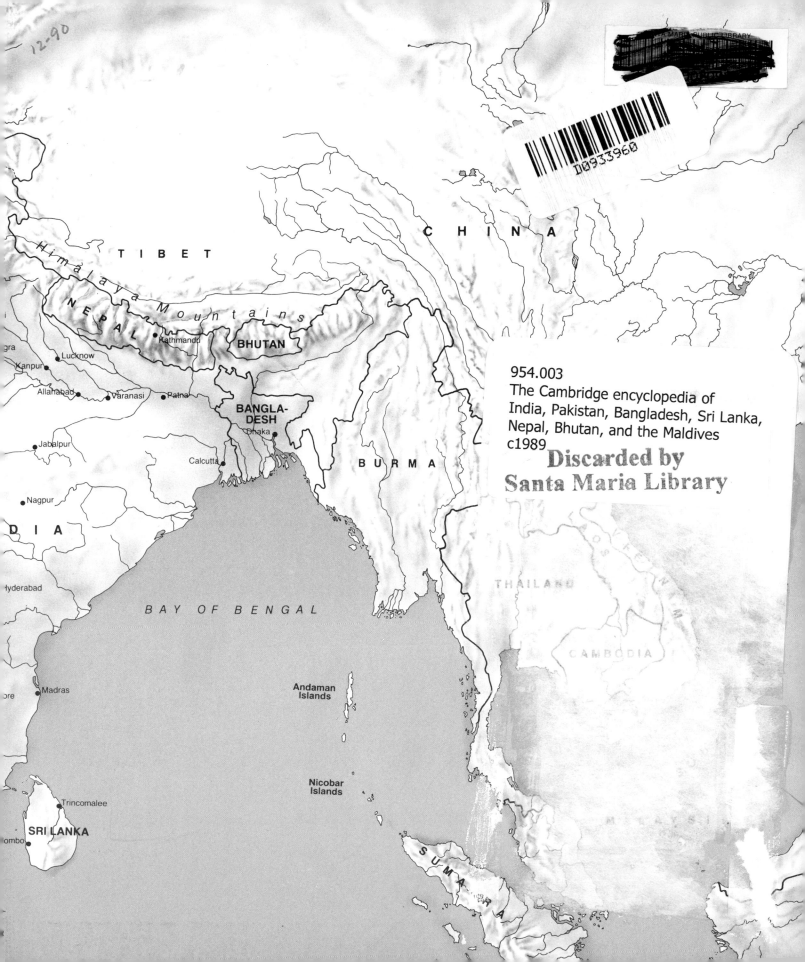

The Cambridge Encyclopedia of India, Pakistan, Bangladesh, Sri Lanka, Nepal, Bhutan and the Maldives

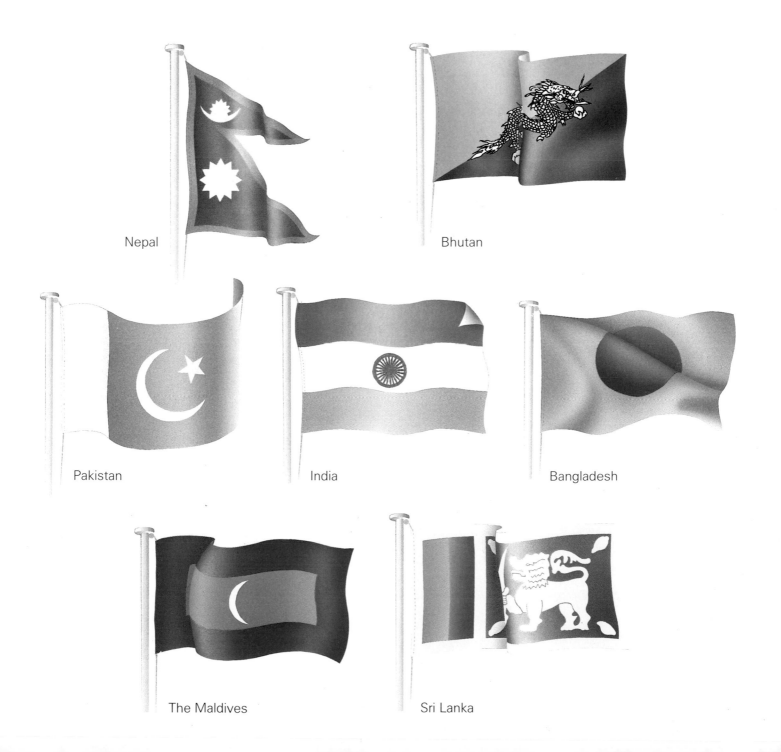

Nepal

Bhutan

Pakistan

India

Bangladesh

The Maldives

Sri Lanka

The Cambridge Encyclopedia of

INDIA

PAKISTAN, BANGLADESH, SRI LANKA, NEPAL, BHUTAN AND THE MALDIVES

Editor
Francis Robinson
Royal Holloway and Bedford New College
(University of London)

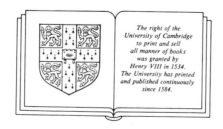

The right of the
University of Cambridge
to print and sell
all manner of books
was granted by
Henry VIII in 1534.
The University has printed
and published continuously
since 1584.

CAMBRIDGE UNIVERSITY PRESS

Cambridge

New York   Port Chester   Melbourne   Sydney

Published by the Press Syndicate of the University of Cambridge
The Pitt Building, Trumpington Street, Cambridge CB2 1RP
32 East 57th Street, New York, NY 10022, USA
10 Stamford Road, Oakleigh, Melbourne 3166, Australia

© Cambridge University Press 1989

First Published 1989

Text setting by Wyvern Typesetting Ltd, Bristol
Colour origination by Spectrum Reproductions, Colchester
Printed in Great Britain by Butler & Tanner Ltd
Maps by Swanston Graphics Ltd, Derby

British Library cataloguing in publication data

The Cambridge encyclopedia of India,
Pakistan, Bangladesh, Sri Lanka
Nepal, Bhutan and the Maldives.
1. South Asia, Social conditions
I. Robinson, Francis
954.05′ 2

Library of Congress cataloguing in publication data

The Cambridge encyclopedia of India,
Pakistan, Bangladesh, Sri Lanka,
Nepal, Bhutan, and the Maldives.
editor, Francis Robinson.
    p.   cm.
Includes index.
ISBN 0–521–33451–9
1. South Asia – Dictionaries and encyclopedias.
I. Robinson, Francis.
DS334.9..C36   1989
954′.003–dc19   88–267737 CIP

ISBN 0 521 33451 9

Contributors

AB   **Dr Aparna Basu**
Delhi University

ABh   **Professor Aghenanda Bharati**
Syracuse University

ABo   **Professor Ashish Bose**
Institute of Economic Growth, New Delhi

AT   **Dr Andrew Topsfield**
Ashmolean Museum, Oxford

BA   **Dr Bridget Allchin**
University of Cambridge

BH   **Dr Barbara Harriss**
London School of Hygiene and Tropical Medicine

BLCJ   **Professor B. L. C. Johnson**
Emeritus Professor, Australian National University

BS   **Professor Brijraj Singh**
Hostos Community College of the City University of New York

BSm   **Professor B. Smith**
Colombia University

CAB   **Dr C. A. Bayly**
University of Cambridge

CMN   **Professor C. M. Naim**
University of Chicago

CR   **Christopher Reynolds**
School of Oriental and African Studies, University of London

CS   **Professor Christopher Shackle**
School of Oriental and African Studies, University of London

DMN   **Professor Daniel M. Neuman**
University of Washington, Seattle

EH   **Professor Edwin Hirschman**
Towson State University, Maryland

FFC   **Professor Frank Conlon**
University of Washington, Seattle

FR   **Dr Francis Robinson**
Royal Holloway and Bedford New College, University of London

FRA   **Professor F. R. Allchin**
University of Cambridge

GJ   **Dr Gordon Johnson**
University of Cambridge

GM   **George Michel**

HT   **Professor Hugh Tinker**
Emeritus Professor, University of Lancaster

IR   **Dr Ian Raeside**
School of Oriental and African Studies, University of London

JDS   **Dr John D. Smith**
University of Cambridge

JH   **Dr John Harriss**
University of East Anglia

JHi   **Professor John Hinnells**
University of Manchester

Contents

Transcription

All diacritics have been dispensed with in transcription from the Devanagari and Perso-Arabic scripts to achieve the simplest possible system yet one which will also give the non-specialist at least an approximate indication of the appropriate pronunciation of South Asian words and personal names.

Devanagari

Vowels:

अ a	उ u	ए e
आ a	ऊ u	ऐ ai
इ i	ऋ ri	ओ o
ई i		औ au

Consonants:

क k	छ ch	ट t	त t	प p
ख kh	छ chh	ठ th	थ th	फ ph
ग g	ज j	ड ड़ d(r)	द d	ब b
घ gh	झ jh	ढ ढ़ dh(rh)	ध dh	भ bh
ङ n	ञ n	ण n	न n	म m
	य y	ल l	श sh	ष s
	र r	व v	स sh	ह h

Nasalization:

   ں n

The inherent vowel is to be omitted where appropriate for Hindi and other modern languages, thus 'Tulsidas: *Ramcharitmanas*', versus Sanskritic 'Krishna', 'Kshatriya', etc.

Perso-Arabic

Vowels:

   a i u e ai o au

Consonants:

ب b	ح h	ز z	ظ z	ل l
پ p	خ kh	ژ zh	ع gh	م m
ت t	د d	س s	غ gh	ن n
ٹ t	ڈ d	ش sh	ف f	ن n
ث s	ز z	ص s	ق q	و v
ج j	ر r	ض z	ک k	ه h
چ ch	ڑ r	ط t	گ g	ی y

Ain and *hamza* have been omitted in transcription. Further conventions have been: the phonetic spelling of the Arabic article in names, the use of *w* after *kh*, the writing of final 'silent h' as *a*, and the writing of the Persian *izafat* as –*e*, thus 'Khwaja Muin ud Din Chishti', 'Siraj ud Daula', 'Jamaat–e Islami', etc.

N.B. Where names have an established form in the Roman script this has been observed. However, when the commonly used form of a name has changed recently, or is in a process of changing, both old and new forms are indicated in the index, for example, Pune and Poona.

Preface

The South Asian region, which comprises the present-day states of India, Pakistan, Bangladesh, Sri Lanka, Nepal, Bhutan and the Maldives, has long been significant in world affairs. For 5000 years it has been one of the main centers of civilization, continually enriching societies beyond its borders and in turn being enriched from outside. Four and a half thousand years ago many millenia of human development reached a striking peak in the Indus valley cities of Mohenjodaro and Harappa. Two and a half thousand years ago South Asia was the cradle of two major world religions, Hinduism, which became wholly identified with India, and Buddhism, which helped to shape the worlds of Southeast and East Asia. Over the past 2000 years there has flourished the high sanskritic civilization of the classical Hindu age and the persianate civilization of the Mughal empire. Since the eighteenth century the region has been the focus of the longest and deepest encounter between an Asian civilization and the West, which came to be entwined with the political struggle between South Asian nationalisms and British imperialism. In this context there were illuminated the qualities of that most remarkable of human beings, Mahatma Gandhi.

Today, more than one out of five members of the human race lives in the region, and each month their absolute number increases by well over a million. This fifth of mankind embraces enormous diversity: every level of human development from stone-age tribesman to Nobel prizewinner; many levels of wealth from mass poverty to comfortable middle class consumerism; the believers of seven major religions – Hinduism, Islam, Buddhism, Sikhism, Christianity, Jainism and Zoroastrianism; the bearers of three racial strains – Aryan, Dravidian and proto-Australoid; and the speakers of languages in two major families, the Aryan and Dravidian, whose multiplicity of forms mean that India alone acknowledges fourteen official languages and 1652 mother tongues.

Since Independence in the mid-twentieth century all South Asian states have striven to achieve greater material prosperity and to spread it more widely amongst their peoples. Success has varied, but there have been triumphs, not just in agriculture's green revolution but also in science and technology. At the same time these states have had to confront the problems of diversity. In regional affairs this has helped to bring about three wars between India and Pakistan resulting in the dominance of India. In domestic affairs it has meant increasingly strong challenges to the political arrangements made at Independence. One challenge has already been successful, leading to the emergence of Bangladesh in 1970. Further challenges in recent years raise a question mark against the future of the region as one of comparative stability.

The aim of this encyclopedia of the countries of South Asia is, as in the case of other Cambridge regional encyclopedias, to make their worlds accessible to as wide a public as possible. At the same time there is the aim of offering new knowledge to the specialist. The fruits of the recent scholarship of sixty-nine leading experts in the field are drawn together; much basic information is presented in tables, charts, figures and maps; and lavish illustration has been used to evoke the distinctive visual qualities of life, landscape and culture. To those who know the region the encyclopedia brings a coverage in one volume which is unique; to those who wish to know it better the means are offered by which they may pursue their interests further. By consulting the index readers will find their way to specific pieces of information. By consulting the contents they will find their way to particular topics. The volume, moreover, is arranged in chapters so that readers may absorb a large chunk of knowledge, say in history or in culture, or even, if they choose, try to embrace the encyclopedia as a whole.

Those who try to grasp the work in this way will note that several substantial themes emerge. There is, of course, the interaction between South Asia and the wider world. On the one hand there have been those great invasions from without, of Aryans, of Muslims, of the British, which have made the region an arena in which great civilizations and different world views have struggled at one moment for ascendancy and at the next for survival. On the other hand, there have been those times when South Asia has been an exporter of influences, of Buddhism, for instance, or of mathematical or mystical ideas, or of its peoples who have come to be over the past century amongst the world's most widespread and successful migrants. Then, there is within South Asia the constant tension between region and center. At times, under the Mauryans, the Mughals and the British, for example, most of the subcontinent was brought under one rule. But the more common condition has been one in which the regions have to a lesser or a greater extent succeeded in asserting their autonomy against the claims of the center. Their success in doing so is manifest in many aspects of South Asian life: language and literature, art and architecture, dance and dress, history and politics. Indeed, the maintenance of a powerful center in Delhi against the demands of regional particularism remains one of the notable features of Indian politics since Independence. A third theme, which was to some extent previewed in the first, is the interaction between South Asian civilization and its pre-industrial world and the forms of modern industrial civilization brought to it from the West. It is a theme which runs through most chapters of the book. In its workings we witness the most fruitful mingling of South Asian 'tradition' and the West in fields as different as politics, religion and the arts; we also witness the assertion of pride in South Asian ways and the practical demonstration of their value in life and thought.

In making of a volume of this kind many debts are incurred. The enterprise has benefited from much counsel from consultant editors. Advice has been offered and services great and small have been rendered by the following: Rukun Advani, Michael Aris, Robert Bradnock, Derek Brown, Frank Conlon, K. M. de Silva, Ben Farmer, Roger Frie, Peter Hardy, Gordon Johnson, Kitsiri Malalgoda, Dan Neuman, Roger Owen, Karl Potter, Leo Rose, Hal Schiffman, Robert Skelton, Rita Townsend, the International Atomic Energy Agency, Pakistan Atomic Energy Commission, Sri Lankan High Commission (London), World Wildlife Trust. The prosecution of the work was much helped by the loan of office space and support services by the history department of the Royal Holloway and Bedford New College (University of London); it was also greatly eased by the enthusiasm and the gifts of the Reference Group in Cambridge University Press. To all of these the editor offers his heartfelt thanks. To Sarah Ansari who worked for five months as assistant editor he owes an especial debt of gratitude. Within the format of the Cambridge regional encyclopedias the final decisions as to contributors and to content have been the editor's alone.

Francis Robinson

LAND

The Swat Valley in northern Pakistan.

Physical structure

Since 1960 new evidence supporting theories of plate tectonics has transformed previously accepted interpretations of global tectonic history. South Asia's own geological origins have both contributed to and been a subject of that re-interpretation.

The subcontinental land mass within which India, Pakistan, Bangladesh, Nepal, Bhutan and Sri Lanka are set falls into three major geological regions with completely distinct origins. The Himalayas and their associated mountain ranges to the west and east not only mark a dramatic northern boundary to the subcontinent, they also comprise a region of recent and continuing tectonic uplift which began less than 130 million years ago. To the south, peninsular India represents one of the oldest and least disturbed large land masses in the world. Its rocks have never been extensively covered by the sea since their formation in the pre-Cambrian period over 3000 million years ago, although they include a number of sedimentary strata deposited by rivers and under glacial conditions. Between the Peninsula and the Himalayas lie the Indo-Gangetic plains stretching from the valley of the Indus River in Pakistan to that of the Brahmaputra in Assam and taking in the deltaic lowlands of Bangladesh.

While Sri Lanka is geologically a part of the Indian peninsula, the Maldives to the south west are coral atolls. These have developed on the easternmost of three submarine ridges beneath the Arabian Sea, themselves associated with volcanic activity, which formed as the ocean floor spread during the last 50 million years.

The distinction between the Indian peninsula (the triangle of mainland India from the Aravalli Mountains southwards and including Sri Lanka) and extra-peninsular India is fundamental both in terms of their origins and their geological structures. Although ancient basement rocks are prominent in the Himalayan ranges, their origins are quite different from those of peninsular India. At the same time, the Indo-Gangetic plains mark both a structural boundary between the peninsula and the Himalayas and are a contrasting geological region in their own right.

The three most important geological regions have only limited correlation with contemporary political units. Pakistan and India share with Nepal and Bhutan sections of the Himalayan ranges and their foothills. Although the greatest part of the Indo-Gangetic plains lie in India, the western portion now lies in the Pakistan provinces of Sind and the Panjab, while the Ganges–Brahmaputra delta in the east now comprises some 90 percent of Bangladesh's surface area. The island state of Sri Lanka is geologically a continuation of the peninsula, the remainder of which lies entirely in India itself. Despite the advances of recent research, the threefold division of the subcontinent remains a valid basis for identifying both the main geological features of the subcontinent and its tectonic history.

The Peninsula

Recent paleomagnetic evidence indicates that the process of sea floor spreading which resulted in the formation of the Maldive Ridge was also responsible for the much more dramatic movement of peninsular India to its present position. This evidence has demonstrated that, as recently as 50 million years ago, the peninsula still lay in the southern hemisphere. It has confirmed the long-known geological and stratigraphical evidence which showed great similarities between the Gondwana series of peninsular rocks in India and similar series in South Africa, South America, Australia and Antarctica.

A great part of the peninsula comprises Archaean rocks. Rocks of this system are the oldest in the world. Although their broad characteristics are well known the details of their origins continue to excite considerable speculation. They are all azoic, highly crystalline, contorted and faulted, and were often formed as plutonic intrusions. However, in detail they are extremely complex, and as they often underlie strata formed subsequently they are commonly referred to as 'basement complex'. Recent advances in geochemistry seem likely to offer the most significant prospect of improving understanding of their formation. Despite the remaining uncertainties, the broad features of the peninsula systems are now well known.

The oldest rocks in the peninsula are the 'high grade' gneissic rocks, a description that applies to the level of metamorphism of the rocks. They are found in five regions. The oldest of these, the charnockites and khondalites of southern and eastern India, have been dated at more than 3100 million years old. The Nilgiri and Palani Hills are among the most striking examples. The Eastern Ghats are a second major belt of gneissic rocks. Rajasthan in the northwest of the peninsula and the Aravalli–Delhi belt both have formations of the Banded Gneiss Complex, while the final group of older metamorphic rocks is found in the Bihar and Orissa regions of the northeastern peninsula.

Between them, these rocks occupy an enormous area of the peninsula, and the charnockites extend into Sri Lanka. There are also some significant 'low grade' Archaean rocks, that is, rock types that have undergone a much lower degree of metamorphism. Most striking among these are the Archaean Greenstone belts, found in several parts of the world and represented in the peninsula by the Dharwar system. According to Windley, it is now believed that there were two ages of Greenstone Belt formation in South India. The larger, well-preserved Dharwar belts were formed in the period 2700–2300 million years ago, while smaller belts, over 3000 million years old, are remnants in the surrounding gneisses. They originated in volcano-sedimentary basins which have undergone some degree of recrystallization.

Greenstone belts around the world contain a range of economic mineral deposits, notably gold, silver and copper. The main gold mining area of India is located on one of the Dharwar system series at Kolar to the east of Bangalore. In peninsular India, the Dharwar system is represented in several isolated exposures outside the Dharwar–Mysore region from which it takes its name. Chota Nagpur, Jabalpur and Nagpur, all in the central peninsula, and the Aravalli region at its northern extremity have important Dharwar–type systems. The former has economically important deposits of manganese ores as well as of the famous marble, but the most

Physical structure.

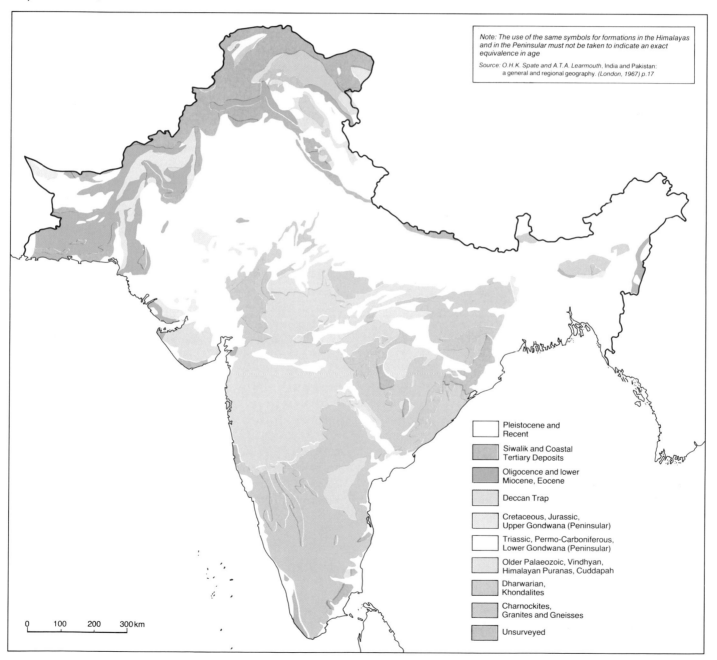

Note: The use of the same symbols for formations in the Himalayas and in the Peninsular must not be taken to indicate an exact equivalence in age

Source: O.H.K. Spate and A.T.A. Learmouth, India and Pakistan: a general and regional geography. (London, 1967) p.17

Pleistocene and Recent

Siwalik and Coastal Tertiary Deposits

Oligocence and lower Miocene, Eocene

Deccan Trap

Cretaceous, Jurassic, Upper Gondwana (Peninsular)

Triassic, Permo-Carboniferous, Lower Gondwana (Peninsular)

Older Palaeozoic, Vindhyan, Himalayan Puranas, Cuddapah

Dharwarian, Khondalites

Charnockites, Granites and Gneisses

Unsurveyed

0   100   200   300km

economically valuable are the iron ore deposits in the Chota Nagpur region.

The peninsula has extensive areas of ancient sedimentary rocks superimposed on the Archaean base. The oldest of these is the Vindhyan series, still dating from the pre-Cambrian period. A stratified formation of sandstones, shales and limestones, often over 4000 m thick, these cover over 100,000 square kilometers. Named after the Vindhyan Mountains north of the Narbada River, these beds stretch from western Bihar in the east to the Aravallis in the west. They comprise two distinct sets of deposits. The lower is marine in origin while the upper is fluviatile. The beds remain almost entirely horizontal and have barely been faulted or folded except on the margins. The Upper Vindhyan beds enclose two diamond bearing horizons, from which the Panna and Golconda diamonds have been mined.

The most important post-Cambrian system in the peninsula is the Gondwana series of sedimentaries. These flat sedimentary strata, some 6000 m in thickness, were fluvial deposits laid down from the start of the Permian period some 250 million years ago. Their basal layers were deposited under proglacial conditions, almost certainly quite near to the southern Polar Circle. The great depths of riverine sediment imply that they were laid down in faulted depressions, and the system shows clear evidence of several changes of climate during its deposition.

There are three main areas of Gondwana rocks in the peninsula; a linear tract along the Damodar valley in West Bengal, an extensive outcrop in Madhya Pradesh along the Mahanadi River, and a series of troughs along the Godavari from Nagpur to the delta. Economically the Gondwana series is the most important in India, containing virtually all India's coal resources (in the Lower Gondwana series) and significant iron ore deposits.

The most recent significant geological formation in peninsular India is the Cretaceous period lava outflow, the Deccan Trap. Covering some 500,000 square kilometers of the northwestern region of the peninsula this overlies both Vindhyan strata and the Archaean basement, moreover the volcanic lava flowed through great rock fissures, spreading to depths of up to 3000 m near Bombay in the west, thinning rapidly eastwards. These lavas were deposited over 60 million years ago, in a process now believed to be directly related to the separation of the peninsula from the African coastline of old Gondwanaland.

The Indo-Gangetic Plains

The origins of the Indo-Gangetic plains lie in the Eocene, some 40 million years ago. They were formed by the deposit of alluvium, notably from the Himalayas, as the peninsula was impelled northwards into the 'Laurasian' land mass. The boundary between the two land masses forms a zone where the Indian plate is being subducted beneath the Asian continental plate, and the alluvium of the plains has been deposited in the resulting trough.

The depth of alluvium varies from less than 100 m to over 5000 m. It is deepest between Delhi and the Rajmahal Hills but underneath the uniformly flat surface the floor of the trough is marked by ridges and troughs of very unequal heights. The boundary zone with the Himalayas is an area of continuing seismic instability.

Throughout the plains there are massive beds of clay and sandy or calcareous silts which correspond to the deposits of today's rivers in the region. A broad distinction is recognized between three categories of alluvium according to their age. The oldest, or Bhangar, dates from the middle Pleistocene, approximately five million years before the present and are found from West Bengal to Uttar Pradesh. The younger deposits, Khadar, dominate the Panjab in Pakistan. In the Ganges delta of Bangladesh, Khadar is confined to the vicinity of the present river channels.

The southern part of Bangladesh and West Bengal emerged from the sea within the last 5000 years, and the active course of the Ganges and Brahmaputra have continued to shift in the present time. The Indus Delta in Pakistan is also a continuation of the Panjab Khadar region and is of very recent origin.

Extra-Peninsular Mountain Ranges

The Himalayas proper dominate the northern flank of the subcontinent. Between 150 and 400 kilometers wide the great Himalayan range stretches 2500 kilometers from northwest to southeast. The associated ranges provide an enclosing front for the western borders of Pakistan and for the northeastern region of India. Highly complex in detail, both its origins and present form are now increasingly well understood.

Although in the central Himalayas there are great areas of metamorphic rocks, these have been dated not to the Archaean period but to the comparatively recent Tertiary. They are now believed to have been created as a result of the crumpling and fissuring process engendered by the subduction of the Indian Plate underneath the Asian Plate.

Conventionally, the main Himalayan ranges, stretching from the Pamirs in Pakistan to the easternmost bend of the Brahmaputra in Assam, have been divided into three main zones: the Outer Ranges or Siwaliks, the Middle Ranges of Panjal and Dhauladhar, and the Inner Himalaya, which is the zone of highest peaks.

Although the Himalayan ranges themselves are of recent geological origin they contain rock series from all major periods. Thus, in the eastern Himalayas there are examples of Archaean basement gneiss, while the Siwalik Ranges along the southern flank comprise a complex set of Tertiary sedimentary deposits. All major periods are represented.

The central core of the Himalayas obtained its characteristic

The Himalayas compared with the Rocky Mountains.

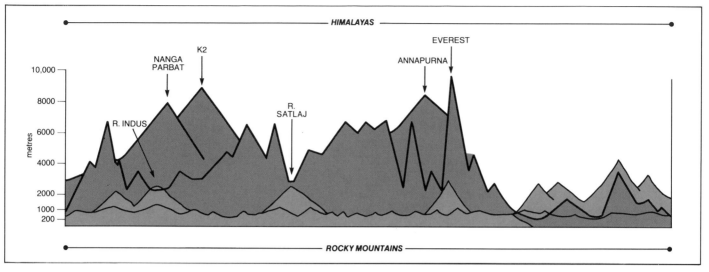

intruded metamorphic rocks in the Tertiary period as a direct result of the great mountain building process itself. Largely crystalline and metamorphic rocks make up this central Himalayan zone, with granites, gneisses, schists and unfossiliferous sedimentaries. In contrast, the outer zone, or Siwaliks, are of very recent geological origin, comprising riverine deposits laid down by rivers emerging onto the plains from the Himalayas. They form the first range of hills from Pakistan to Nepal, having been raised to their present altitude in the latest burst of Himalayan uplift.

The extensions of the Himalayas almost due south from the Pamirs through the western borders of Pakistan are also of Tertiary origin. Permo-carboniferous rocks dominate the Hindu Kush, while to the south of the Khyber Pass are the sandstone ranges of the Safed Koh. Further to the south the Baluchistan borderlands fall into two distinct parts. West of 66° East weak sandstones predominate in an extension of the Iranian plateau. To the east of this line are north–south running anticlines of cretaceous–oligocene limestones.

RWB

Further reading
A. Gansser, *The Geology of the Himalayas* (London, 1964)
D. N. Wadia, *The Geology of India* 3rd edn (London, 1961)
B. F. Windley, *The Evolving Continents* (London, 1986)

Climate

Lying astride the Tropic of Cancer from the equatorial Maldives to the Mediterranean latitude regions of northern Kashmir, the climate of South Asia is dominated by the monsoon. However, while the seasonal wind reversal, which the term 'monsoon' is now widely taken to imply, is a pronounced feature of the subcontinent's climate, there are great climatic variations from region to region. The countries of South Asia include some of the wettest regions on earth as well as both hot and cold deserts. Climatic variations range from the equatorial ocean climates of the Maldivian atolls to the most extreme mountain climates in the world. In order to understand these contrasts, it is necessary first to see South Asia in its wider climatic context.

Climatic system of South Asia
The term 'monsoon' is now accepted to refer to regions which have a seasonal wind reversal of at least 120° with a 40 percent consistency of wind direction in each season. Very large areas, mainly in the Tropics, conform to this pattern. In essence, the principles underlying the Asian monsoon system are now well understood, although in detail it remains highly complex and, in some respects, controversial.

The chief contributing causes are the contrasts between land masses and oceans in their response to changing seasonal levels of received solar radiation. These contrasts have a significant effect on the patterns of change in tropical atmospheric circulation.

Large water bodies rapidly absorb heat and spread it through vertical convection and through horizontal ocean currents. Land

Seasonal wind reversal: the monsoon.

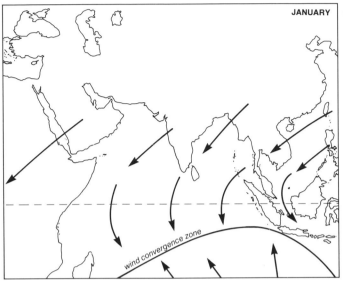 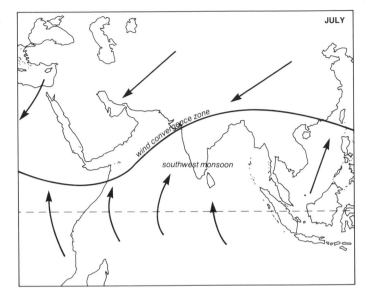

Source: R. Bradnock, Agricultural Change in South Asia. (London, 1984) p.7

masses have no such heat transfer mechanism, with the result that continental land masses heat up much more than oceans and consequently heat the atmosphere above them. In the summer, that heating is responsible for converting the normal sub-tropical high pressure cells into thermal low pressures over land, resulting in a reversal of winter wind patterns.

The winter monsoon over Asia is comparatively simple. High pressure builds over central Asia between latitudes 40°N and 60°N. Most of northern India is protected from the resultant winter or northeast monsoon by the massive bulk of the Himalayas, which prevents the polar air from penetrating to the Indo-Gangetic plains. Indeed, the northeast monsoon is restricted to shallow layers of the atmosphere, with surface northeasterlies replaced by westerlies over 3000 m above sea level. In Pakistan, northern India, Nepal, Bhutan and Bangladesh, these winter westerlies dominate at ground level as well as at high altitude. They are responsible for very important regional climatic characteristics in northern Pakistan and north-western India. Peninsular India and Sri Lanka do experience the northeast winter monsoon, but it is not of polar origin and is generally very weak.

The summer monsoon is both more complicated than the winter monsoon and more significant, as it is the prime source of precipitation almost throughout South Asia. Early theories postulated a relationship between the development of surface low pressures over the Thar desert in the intense early summer heating and the origin of the South Asian monsoon. It is clear that intense summer heating over the northwestern part of the South Asian subcontinent does play a critical role. However, both the timing and the regional contrasts in the arrival of the southwest monsoon, as it is known in South Asia, reflect changes in the upper air wind systems of considerable complexity.

At the end of May, the upper air westerly jet stream which dominates the upper atmosphere system over the Indo-Gangetic plains throughout the winter suddenly collapses and re-forms to the north of the Tibetan Plateau. Meanwhile, an upper air trough formed over the Bay of Bengal moves slowly westwards, assuming position in June at about 75°E. The high level trough brings upper air easterlies to replace the westerly jet stream. This then allows the very humid southwesterlies, which sweep across the Maldives, Sri Lanka and the southern part of the Indian peninsula, to double back and bring rain-bearing winds northwestwards from the Bay of Bengal across the Indo-Gangetic plains to Pakistan.

The intensity of the low pressure belt over northern India, Nepal and Pakistan is increased by the radiation absorbed and then released by the very high mountain mass. This allows the South Asian monsoon to reach depths unheard of elsewhere. Over India, for example, the moist airflow reaches more than 6000 m thick, while the summer monsoon over Japan is only 2000 m thick. The enormous thickness of extremely humid air contributes both to the comparatively high rainfall over much of tropical South Asia and to the extreme intensity of the rain storms which bring much of it.

Mean annual precipitation and season of maximum precipitation.

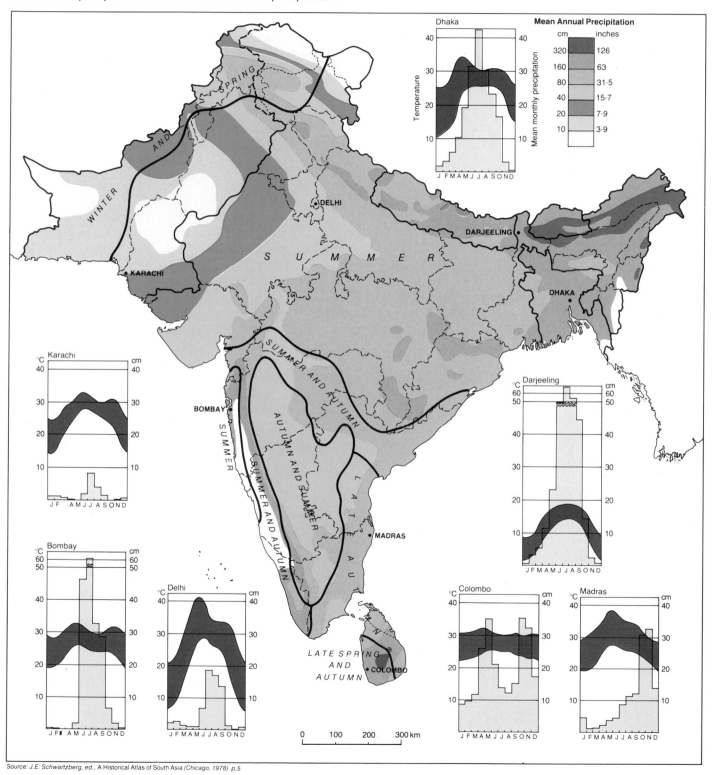

Source: J.E. Schwartzberg, ed., A Historical Atlas of South Asia (Chicago, 1978) p.5

India's summer monsoon often brings floods.

India

India's regional climates range from the desert of Rajasthan to the wettest area on earth, the Shillong Plateau. Despite its tropical latitude, it experiences huge contrasts both of rainfall and temperature from region to region.

India's seasons do not correspond strictly to the temperate progression of winter, spring, summer and autumn, even though the terms are widely used. The distinction between wet and dry seasons is often more important than between hot and cold, and over most of India the normal progression of seasons is cool/dry, hot/dry, less hot/wet, and back to cool/dry.

The precise transition depends on the arrival of the monsoon, although microclimates are affected very strongly by altitude as well. Over the greatest part of India, May is the hottest month with mean maximum temperatures in excess of 40°C from Nagpur to the northern Panjab. Over most of the southern and eastern peninsula, mean maximum temperatures in the hottest month are lower at between 35° and 40°C, and considerably lower at high altitudes as in the western Ghats. Along the west coast, April is the hottest month as the onset of the southwest monsoon winds intensify cloud cover through May in advance of the rains.

Over most of India, January is the coldest month, although much of the central and eastern peninsula enjoys its coolest weather in December. The north–south temperature gradient is reversed from the hot season regime. North of the line from Nagpur to Udaipur the mean minimum temperature in January is below 10°C, while in the extreme south mean minimum temperatures never go below 20°C.

Seasonal and regional contrasts in rainfall are more striking than contrasts in temperature. They reflect two important influences, India's latitudinal spread on either side of the Tropic of Cancer, and the particular form of highland relief. From Bombay southwards, the coastal fringe of the western Ghats intercepts the southwest monsoon winds from May through to October, producing rainfall in excess of 4000 mm. The hills, which run parallel with the coast, produce a marked rainshadow effect, and total rainfall in the interior peninsula rarely exceeds 800 mm until the east coast is reached. Total rainfall increases northeastwards giving totals of over 1600 mm in West Bengal. Assam records some of the highest rainfall totals in the world; over 20,000 mm having been recorded in the Shillong Plateau in one year. Total rainfall diminishes from west Bengal towards the northwest. Delhi receives 600 mm a year on average, and moving further southwestwards into Rajasthan rainfall totals are less 100 mm.

There are some important exceptions to the broad regional climatic patterns described above. Tamil Nadu in southeastern India is in the rainshadow of the western Ghats when the southwest monsoon brings rain to the west coast. It receives most of its rain between October and December, when the northeast monsoon reasserts itself. In contrast, a narrow strip of the submontane region of the Panjab receives winter rain through depressions in the westerlies which prevail across northern India throughout the winter. Finally, the climate of the entire Himalayan region is modified dramatically by altitude. Although precipitation diminishes from east to west in common with the bordering Ganges valley, temperatures drop with altitude producing a vertical transition from semitropical to Arctic conditions within a few miles.

Pakistan

Pakistan's climate is characterized by extremes of temperature and aridity. Temperatures are characteristic of subtropical desert regions, modified in the north and west by altitude. Mean maximum temperatures in parts of Sind exceed 45°C, although the Panjab is somewhat cooler. In winter, the southern coast around Karachi retains some warmth, with mean minimum temperatures of more than 10°C, but minimum temperatures drop sharply northwards. In most of the Panjab mean minimum temperatures are below 5°C in January and at altitude in the northwest frontier very much lower. Even frosts are not unheard of in the low lying Vale of Peshawar.

The south rarely receives more than 200 mm of rain each year, and the wettest regions of the Panjab only have an average annual rainfall of 900 mm. As in the Indian Panjab, winter westerlies are responsible for bringing appreciable amounts of rain to a narrow belt of the northwest frontier, and the Panjab, especially the Vale of Peshawar, although in the rest of Pakistan maximum rainfall follows the general South Asian pattern of peaking between July and September.

Bangladesh

Its much smaller size and greater physical uniformity mean that Bangladesh experiences a much smaller climatic range than its surrounding neighbor, India. It is subject to the same broad monsoonal seasonal pattern that dominates the subcontinent, with three, rather than four, clearly defined seasons.

In the cool dry season, which lasts from November through to March, mean minimum temperatures are between 10°C and 15°C, rising to mean maximum temperatures of between 30°C and 35°C in April, the hottest month. April brings one of the most distinctive features of Bangladesh's climate, the severe northeastern storms. It is now recognized that these originate in the high altitude trough which moves from its winter position over the Bay of Bengal to approximately 75°E in June. These storms are precursors of the main monsoon rains, which move across from the Bay of Bengal northwestwards. Total rainfall diminishes accordingly, from 2400 mm in the southeast to 1600 mm in the northwest. Even in winter, humidity remains above 75 percent, and at the end of the wet season, coastal Bangladesh is particularly subject to cyclonic storms which bring very heavy rainfall and high winds.

Nepal and Bhutan

Both Nepal and Bhutan enjoy climates that are severely modified by their predominantly mountain environment. The broad patterns of climate are dictated by the subcontinental monsoon system and, in particular, their location on the southern flank of the Himalayan ranges. In detail, altitude is the major determinant of microclimates. In the broader valleys such as the Kathmandu Valley, less than 1000 m above sea level, mean minimum winter temperatures are below 5°C, but mean maximum temperatures rise to over 25°C. Precipitation in much of Bhutan is over 4000 mm a year, but there are important valley areas that are very much drier. Over 2400 mm is received in lower lying and southern parts of Nepal, while the driest region in the northwest receives only 800 mm.

Sri Lanka and the Maldives

The location of the Maldives within five degrees of the Equator and Sri Lanka's position slightly to the northeast result in both having a more equable, oceanic climate than much of continental South Asia. However, Sri Lanka is still under the dominant influence of the monsoons. As a result, neither the Maldives nor Sri Lanka has any great variation in temperature throughout the year. Mean monthly minima for Colombo are between 21°C and 23°C while mean monthly maxima hover around 30°C throughout the year. Sri Lanka's central mountains do have an appreciable effect on temperature, though not of course on seasonality.

Sri Lanka's rainfall is particularly strongly affected both by the monsoon pattern and by its physical relief. The southwest monsoon brings the first rainfall peak to the southwestern corner of the island, often referred to as the Wet Zone. Between April and June, Colombo receives over 800 mm of rain, before receiving another peak of 700 mm in November and December from the northeast monsoon. In sharp contrast, the northern and eastern parts of the island have a long dry season induced by the rain shadow effect of the central highlands until the northeast monsoon brings the bulk of its precipitation.

RWB

Further reading

Indian Meteorology Department, *Climatological Atlas of India* (New Delhi, 1981)

S. Nieuwolt, *Tropical Climatology; An Introduction to the Climates of Low Latitudes* (London, 1977)

Y. P. Rao, *The climate of the Indian Sub-continent in World Survey of Climatology* Elsevier (New York, 1981)

Vegetation and soil

The most striking fact about both vegetation and soils throughout South Asia is the extent to which they have been modified by man. Despite the fact that forest is the natural cover for the great majority of the subcontinent, there are virtually no stands of natural forest remaining. Today over 55 percent of India's surface area is cultivated, a figure that rises to over 75 percent in Bangladesh. While deforestation has proceeded over hundreds of years, it is now reaching a point in many areas at which only remnants of forest cover can be seen. Satellite surveys have shown that between 1973 and 1982 India's gross forest cover declined from 17 to 12 percent. In the Himalayan regions of Pakistan, India, Nepal and Bhutan, great swathes of territory are losing their forest cover, and in Bangladesh less than 15 percent is now forested. Nevertheless, as much as 375,000 square kilometers of forest remains in India alone, albeit much of it degraded, and the flora of South Asia remains rich. Inevitably, both vegetation and soils bear evidence of the heavy imprint of man and animals.

Stretching from the Equator to nearly 40°N and from sea level to over 8000 m, South Asia has as wide a range of vegetation cover as anywhere in the world. However, this diversity is under severe threat. Similarly, soils show widespread evidence of man's often malign influence. For this reason, the origins and current distribution of both vegetation and soils can no longer be regarded as purely natural. Soils reflect the characteristics of the underlying geology, tectonic and geomorphological history, climate and resulting weathering processes as well as natural vegetation cover and the activities of man and animals. Not surprisingly, a detailed classification, let alone interpretation, of soil formation in South Asia remains controversial and, despite laborious efforts by the soil survey organizations of the South Asian countries, a great deal remains to be done.

Vegetation

Tropical deciduous forests form the original vegetation cover over most of India between the Himalayas, the Thar desert and the western Ghats. They also extend into all the other countries of South Asia except the Maldives. Indeed, one estimate suggests that over 90 percent of the subcontinent possesses a deciduous forest bioclimate. Their predominantly deciduous nature reflects the lengthy dry season to which all of India is subject. The wide range of climatic environments which was characteristic of India long before man's influence became dominant meant that such forests ranged from tropical semi-evergreen through moist tropical deciduous in areas with between 1300 mm and 1900 mm of rainfall per annum to dry tropical deciduous types in areas with between 900 mm and 1300 mm. Such forests are characteristic of areas with annual mean temperatures above 24°C. Because such areas are also comparatively favorable for cultivation, thousands of square kilometers of previously forested land have been totally cleared and the influence of man is widely believed to have been responsible for the degradation of much of the moist forest to drier types.

Two species of deciduous tree are particularly well known and extensive. Sal (*Shorea robusta*) and teak (*Tectona grandis*) are both very important economically as well as type species. Both are resistant to burning which has helped to enhance their position where man has used fire in his attempt to bring more land into use. While most tropical deciduous forest is highly varied, sal and teak both appear in quite large stands, though this is now often under conditions of artificial propagation.

Sal is particularly common over the northeast of the peninsula but it is found in other parts of the subcontinent. Once dominant in the terai region of Nepal, it is now restricted to the extreme eastern region. Teak's natural distribution is concentrated in the west. However, teak is being widely introduced across the peninsula in response to continuing high demand for its timber which is termite resistant.

On the wetter margins, particularly along the western Ghats at between 500 m and 1400 m to the south of Bombay and in Assam at rather lower altitudes, tropical evergreen rainforest is still found. Characterized by rich species diversity, even these forests are now extensively managed.

As the length of the dry season increases and the absolute rainfall lessens, degraded forests become typical. These are on the drier margins of the peninsula, notably in the northwest and the extreme southeast, are much marked by heavy grazing and in their poorest state are little more than thorn scrub. In areas with less than 750 mm rainfall, xerophytic shrubs become increasingly common. Species such as *Anogeissus pendula*, which forms a dense scrub forest in the Aravallis, and *Prosophis juliflora*, which colonizes sandy tracts in many parts of the south, are two examples of drought-tolerant vegetation.

The pressure on forest resources is threatening a number of well-known species. Indian rose wood, much favored for high quality furniture, is now found in very limited areas of southern India, and the fragrant sandalwood (*Santalum album*) is so valuable that its exploitation is totally controlled by the Government. A far more visible feature of peninsular vegetation are the various palm trees that make a vital economic contribution. Coconut palms (*Cocos nucifera*) fringe most of the west coast and are common also in southern and eastern India. Palmyra palms (*Borassus flabellifer*) are also important in southern India and in Bihar.

Some 40,000 square kilometers of Sri Lanka, its Dry Zone, lies in the dry deciduous belt. With rainfall in the driest parts of the northwest under 700 mm, this is a climatically induced dry deciduous type, but, as rainfall increases to over 2000 mm in the southeast, the original moist deciduous cover has been replaced by secondary cover. This is often scrub jungle and tropical thorn forests. However, there are also semi-evergreen forests in the Dry Zone and the region includes over 1300 species of flowering plants.

The Himalayan forests remain the largest and comparatively least interfered with forest zone in South Asia, although even this is fast changing. Diminishing rainfall from east to west is the chief influence on longitudinal contrasts in forest cover along the Himalayan belt while changes in altitude produce a striking vertical zonation.

Wet hill forest including evergreen oaks and chestnuts predominate between 1000 m and 2000 m in the eastern ranges of India, Bhutan and Nepal, while further to the west are belts of subtropical pine at similar altitudes. The most widespread type, however, is moist temperate forest with pines, cedars, firs and spruce. From the western regions of Nepal, such as the valley of Tila Khola, through to Pakistan, deodars (*Cedrus deodara*) form large stands.

Between 3000 m and 4000 m, alpine forest predominates, with extensive rhododendron cover and widespread birch, juniper and pine. Rhododendron, one of the best known of Himalayan forest trees, is often found in association with other forest types. In Nepal, rhododendrons are most widespread in areas of very heavy rainfall. On the upper stretches of the Rivers Arun and Tamur at above 2500 m lies a zone of almost pure rhododendron. Poplars, such as *Populus ciliata*, are found from Kashmir as far east as Bhutan, while larches, absent from the northwestern Himalayas, are found from eastern Nepal through to Bhutan.

Forested areas and natural vegetation types.

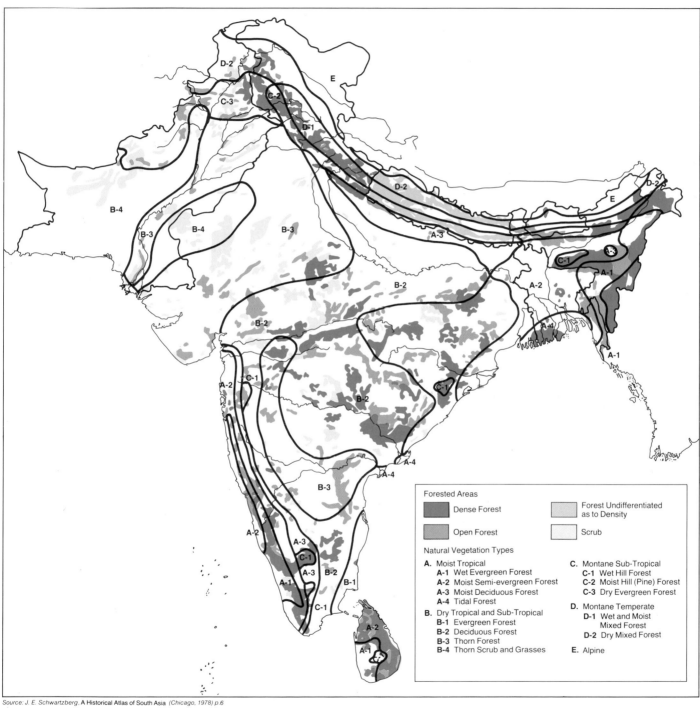

Forested Areas

Dense Forest

Open Forest

Forest Undifferentiated as to Density

Scrub

Natural Vegetation Types

A. Moist Tropical
  A-1 Wet Evergreen Forest
  A-2 Moist Semi-evergreen Forest
  A-3 Moist Deciduous Forest
  A-4 Tidal Forest

B. Dry Tropical and Sub-Tropical
  B-1 Evergreen Forest
  B-2 Deciduous Forest
  B-3 Thorn Forest
  B-4 Thorn Scrub and Grasses

C. Montane Sub-Tropical
  C-1 Wet Hill Forest
  C-2 Moist Hill (Pine) Forest
  C-3 Dry Evergreen Forest

D. Montane Temperate
  D-1 Wet and Moist Mixed Forest
  D-2 Dry Mixed Forest

E. Alpine

Source: J. E. Schwartzberg, A Historical Atlas of South Asia (Chicago, 1978) p.6

21

Rampant rhododendrons in a moist deciduous Himalayan forest.

While forest is by far the most important vegetation cover, India also has some areas of savannah grassland, all biotically induced. The northern edge of the peninsula has *Dicanthium-Cenchrus* grassland while there are also several varieties of coarse grasses occurring along the Terai foothills of the Himalayas. Alpine grasses are common and are important for grazing above 2000 m, but the most distinctive grasslands are the bamboo region of the eastern Himalayas. Bamboo (the *Dendocalamus* species) is found widely throughout India but *Melocanna bambusoides* is a particularly common secondary growth in Assam.

Natural vegetation is very sparse in both Bangladesh and Pakistan, although for different reasons. Pakistan's arid climate restricts the range of plants in many areas to xerophytic, or drought tolerant, shrubs, although, in the wetter hills of the north and northwest, Himalayan and Alpine species are prominent. In Bangladesh, there are few remaining areas of forest. In the eastern districts there are still some 150,000 square kilometers of semi-evergreen forest associated with bamboo jungle, and in the south the tidal Sundarbans have some 6000 square kilometers of mangrove forest which includes six or seven economically important species.

There has been a growing recognition of the dangers to the natural environment throughout South Asia in recent years. Attention is now being paid to the creation of biosphere reserves in order to preserve species and gene pools, and numbers of such reserves have been identified.

Soils

Although it is possible to identify just a handful of the most common soil types that are found throughout South Asia, from the farmer's point of view soil characteristics at a local level are crucially important and vary greatly from place to place.

The largest category of soils are the red soils developed on the ancient archaean rocks of peninsular India. Mainly light, sandy and often gravelly soils, they commonly are easily worked but do not retain moisture. They are not the heavily leached red soils often referred to in the past as laterites, so widely associated with the tropics but now a term much more restricted in its application and used to refer in India and Sri Lanka to very limited areas. With the same geological origins as peninsular India, Sri Lanka soils conform broadly to the red soil pattern. However, in the Wet Zone lowlands, they have been heavily leached and appear as red-yellow podzols.

Over the remainder of peninsular India, black soils, known locally as regur and often referred to as cotton soils, are widespread on the volcanic lavas of the Deccan and in isolated patches further south. Often heavy clays, these soils are potentially rich but often difficult to irrigate.

Along the coastal fringes of India and Sri Lanka and the deltas of the Peninsula, alluvial soils predominate, but these have their widest spread across the Indo-Gangetic plains from Pakistan to Bangladesh. Economically, they are the most important soils in South Asia, providing the basis for settled agriculture for millennia. They vary greatly in quality. In Bangladesh, they are replenished every year by new deposits of silt, itself very rich in plant nutrients. In many areas beyond the reach of floods, they are often poor in organic material. In areas of large scale irrigation such as Sind and the Panjab in Pakistan and Uttar Pradesh in India, they can also

Soil types.

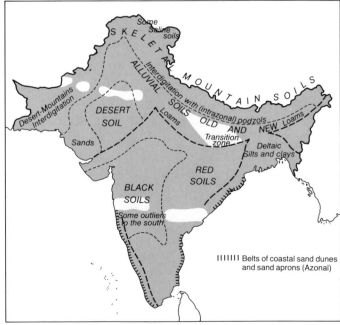

||||||| Belts of coastal sand dunes and sand aprons (Azonal)

Source: O.H.K. Spate and A.T.A. Learmouth, India and Pakistan: a general and regional geography. (London, 1967) p.98

become subject to waterlogging and salinity. While all the soils of Bangladesh derive from river silts, there are very important local contrasts related to the normal depth of flooding and the age of deposition. The slightly higher river levees are covered in coarser silts, ideally suited to jute cultivation, but older silts are often much less fertile. In the Lower Indus plains of Pakistan, the alluvium tends to be coarse and sandy with extensive saline patches.

Soils developed in the mountainous regions of Bhutan, Nepal, India and Pakistan vary greatly according to the underlying rocks, angle of slope and altitude, and the common description of them as skeletal or mountain soils does not do justice to their variety.

RWB

Further reading
O. H. K. Spate and A. T. A. Learmonth, *India and Pakistan: a General and Regional Geography* (London, 1968)
J. D. A. Stainton, *The Forests of Nepal* (New York, 1972)

Fauna

In South Asia as a whole there are well over two thousand species of birds, over five hundred species of mammals and several hundred species of reptiles and amphibians. Yet, despite this diversity, a great number of species are at risk and continue to survive only because of the creation of special reserves and parks.

The diversity of South Asia's species (it has, for example, nearly four times as many species of birds as Europe) is peculiarly at risk because of its adjustment to a predominantly forest environment. The destruction of that environment has removed the essential ecological support system for a great many of the region's best-known species. Felines such as tigers have been reduced from tens of thousands a hundred years ago to hundreds now, and the same story can be told for many other less well-known species. Forest cover has been removed from many parts of South Asia. In the mid 1980s, India had only 12 percent of its area remaining under forest, Bangladesh under 10 percent and Pakistan around 5 percent.

The clearance of the forest has been carried out largely to meet the needs of man and his domesticated animals. The population of South Asia in the middle 1980s had reached one billion, over three quarters of whom were still rural dwellers dependent on agricultural land. India alone had nearly 250,000,000 cattle and 50,000,000 sheep and goats, all of which have steadily eroded the habitat needed by wild species to survive.

Despite these pressures, a remarkable range of species does still exist and recent measures taken by governments in all the countries of South Asia suggest that there are some grounds for hope. All have created national parks, some originally intended to protect single species, others to protect entire ecosystems. Thus, Bhutan, for example, has declared as much as 20 percent of its total area to be a natural reserve. In India, 25,000 square kilometers in fifteen reserves were set aside in 1973 for Project Tiger. These form just part of a much wider program embracing over 250 reserves in total, and there are also big nature reserves in Pakistan, Nepal, Bangladesh and Sri Lanka.

Mammals
South Asia's mammals have always attracted a fascinated interest. Even the comparatively small island of Sri Lanka has one hundred species of mammal, Bangladesh twice as many and India more than twice as many again.

The largest land mammals are the elephants, which until comparatively recently were numerous throughout South Asia. Removal of the forest has destroyed much of their natural habitat. The largest surviving population of elephants in the wild are in northern West Bengal, Assam and Bhutan where there are approximately 6500 remaining. There are a further 200 in the Chittagong Hill Tracts of Bangladesh, 2000 in central India and 6000 in the three south Indian States of Karnataka, Kerala and Tamil Nadu, and further herds in Sri Lanka. There are plans for an elephant reserve on the borders of Bhutan and India covering about 3500 square kilometers.

While elephants are not yet an endangered species, other large South Asian mammals are very much under threat. The One Horned Rhinoceros, the subcontinent's second largest mammal, at one time was found right across the Indo-Gangetic plain. There are now only 1500 left, restricted to three locations in Assam, northern West Bengal and Nepal. Occasionally the smaller Sumatran Rhinoceros is seen in the Chittagong Hill Tracts.

The large felines have also been drastically affected by loss of habitat. Tigers, essentially forest animals that prey on wild pig and deer, are reduced to under 2000 in India and between 600 and 700 in Nepal, Sikkim, Bhutan and Bangladesh. Cheetahs are already extinct, and the only lion species, the Gir, was down to fewer than two hundred until a successful breeding program in the Gir sanctuary in Gujarat resulted in some recovery. South Asia has three species of leopard. In the far north of Pakistan, there are snow leopards in the Khunjerab National Park and in the high Himalayas of Bhutan. The arboreal clouded leopard is still found in northern Assam, Nepal, Bhutan and the Chittagong Hill Tracts of Bangladesh, while India's most famous leopard, the black Panther, it also still found virtually throughout its original range.

Desert and jungle cats are found in Pakistan and northwestern India, as are the bird hunting Caracal. Jungle cats are also found in Sri Lanka. Lynx live at up to 3000 m in the ranges of Gilgit, Ladakh

Fauna

National parks and wildlife reserves of South Asia.

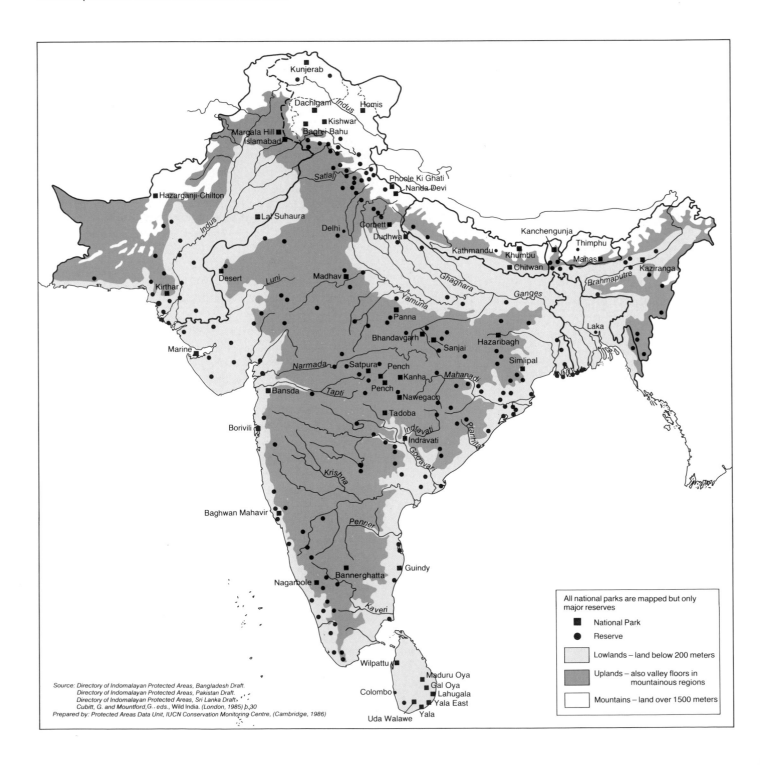

Legend (map key):

All national parks are mapped but only major reserves

■ National Park
● Reserve

Lowlands – land below 200 meters

Uplands – also valley floors in mountainous regions

Mountains – land over 1500 meters

Source: Directory of Indomalayan Protected Areas, Bangladesh Draft.
Directory of Indomalayan Protected Areas, Pakistan Draft.
Directory of Indomalayan Protected Areas, Sri Lanka Draft.
Cubitt, G. and Mountford, G., eds., Wild India, (London, 1985) p. 30
Prepared by: Protected Areas Data Unit, IUCN Conservation Monitoring Centre, (Cambridge, 1986)

Map labels:

Kunjerab, Dachigam, Homis, Kishwar, Margala Hill, Islamabad, Bagh-i-Bahu, Hazarganji-Chilton, Indus, Satlaj, Phoole Ki Ghati, Nanda Devi, Lal Suhaura, Delhi, Corbett, Dudhwa, Kanchengunja, Thimphu, Kathmandu, Khumbu, Manas, Desert, Luni, Madhav, Ghaghara, Ganges, Brahmaputre, Kaziranga, Chitwan, Kirthar, Yamuna, Panna, Laka, Marine, Bhandavgarh, Sanjai, Hazaribagh, Simlipal, Narmada, Satpura, Pench, Kanha, Mahanadi, Bansda, Tapti, Pench, Nawegaon, Tadoba, Borivili, Indravati, Indravati, Pranhita, Godavari, Krishna, Baghwan Mahavir, Penner, Guindy, Bannerghatta, Nagarhole, Kaveri, Wilpattu, Maduru Oya, Gal Oya, Colombo, Lahugala, Yala East, Uda Walawe, Yala

A tiger in Ranthambor nature reserve (Rajasthan); less than 3000 remain in South Asia.

and Tibet. The significance of forest in South Asia's natural fauna is reflected in the continuing importance of the Himalayan region as a home for many remaining species. This is demonstrated by the distribution of the Brown, Black and Sloth Bear. Brown bears are found at high altitudes in the northwestern and central Himalayas, coming down below the snow line in summer. Black bears are quite common at altitudes of up to 3700 m, while Sloth bears, which have a diet of fruit, insects and wild bees, still inhabit Nepal and two reserves in India.

Domesticated ungulates are now often held to be part of South Asia's problem with respect to retaining its diversity of wild life. However, there is a wide range of wild species still at large. The huge Gaur, or Jungle Bison, is one of the most impressive, though restricted to the reserves of Bandipur and Mudumalai in South India and to parts of Nepal. Wild buffalo live in the forests of Assam and Central India, while, in addition to domesticated varieties, there are also wild yaks in Nepal and Ladakh.

There are four South Asian species of wild sheep and five species of wild goat, ranging from the Ibex and Markhor of the western Himalayas, through the Sind Ibex in the deserts of southern

Pakistan to the Nilgiri Tahrs. The Tahrs, which live up to altitudes of 1800 m in the Nilgiris of southern India, are also found living up to 4500 m in the Himalayas.

Gazelles and antelopes have largely disappeared, but some have been successfully reintroduced into reserves. The best known is the Blackbuck, the only true antelope, which is found in a special sanctuary at Velavadar in Gujarat. Chinkara gazelles are still found in deserts, around the Salt Range in Pakistan and open areas of the Deccan.

Deer also used to roam widely across the region, and although they are still common, they too have been seriously affected by loss of habitat. Reserves have made it possible for the large Barasingha or swamp deer to survive in western Nepal, Assam and Madhya Pradesh. The much smaller Muntjac, or barking deer, are found extensively in the lower wooded slopes of the Himalayas and in forests of southern India, while the Musk deer live in the birch woods in the higher forests of the Himalayas.

Perhaps the most famous of South Asia's common wild primates are the various species of monkeys. The two commonest are the Rhesus Macaque and the Common Langur, although there are many related species, some of which are now extremely rare. There are also regional variants. Thus, in the extreme south of India, there are some 800 lion tailed Macaque monkeys left in the rain forests of Kerala, while the Assamese Macaque, the Pig Tailed Macaque of the Naga Hills and the Bonnet Macaque all live in the northern regions of South Asia. The Common Langur, which is found in most South Asian forests, also has its variants: the Nilgiri Langur, the Capped Langur of Assam and the Chittagong Hill Tracts and the Golden Langur of Bhutan. Sri Lanka also has its varieties both of Macaque and Langur monkeys such as the Ceylon Grey Langur and the Bear Monkey. Two main species of Loris, the Slow Loris and the Slender Loris, are two nocturnals that are still common primates of the Lemur family, found in forested areas of the mainland and Sri Lanka.

South Asia has a wide range of carnivores. The most famous and widespread are the various species of mongoose (*Herpestinae*). These range from Sri Lanka to all of the mainland. The three commonest species are small: the Grey Mongoose, the Small Indian Mongoose and the Desert Mongoose. There are also three larger but rare species. Known for their ability to fight effectively even the most deadly of snakes, one of the mongoose species in Assam and Nepal has made crab its chief element of diet.

Civet cats are also widespread from Sri Lanka northwards. Several of the species are omnivorous. In the Himalayas and southern parts of India, otters are found, and in the Sundarbans of Bangladesh they have been trained to help catch fish. There are over two dozen speces of Mustelidae, that is martens, weasels, ferrets and badgers.

Salim Ali (1896–1987) was born in Bombay into the influential Tyabji family. He became interested in nature conservation at an early age and received encouragement from the Bombay Natural History Society with which he developed a life-long association. He started studying for a degree in Zoology but did not complete the course: in his words, this was 'the luckiest thing that could have happened' for it saved him from 'ending up a fossilized bureaucrat'. In 1929–30, after having worked in the Natural History section of the Prince of Wales Museum in Bombay, planning the syllabus of its Nature Study Department, he undertook a course of training in systematic and field ornithology in Berlin. On his return to India, he carried out field surveys of bird life in vast tracts of the subcontinent such as the Hyderabad State Ornithological Survey. In 1976 he received the World Wildlife Fund's J. Paul Getty Wildlife Conservation Prize. The same year he was awarded the Padma Vibhushan by the President of India for continued distinction in ornithology and was nominated to membership of the Rajya Sabha, the upper house of the Indian Parliament. His best-known publications include: *The Book of Indian Birds* (first edition August 1941); *The Birds of Kutch* (1945); his magnum opus, *Handbook of the Birds of India and Pakistan* (ten volumes, 1968–74).

Box 1

Other land-based mammals include many insectivores such as shrews, hedgehogs and moles. Bats, and, most notably in many parts of the region including Sri Lanka, the Flying Fox, are ubiquitous, as are rodents and squirrels. The Indian Scaly Anteater, or Pangolin, is also particularly striking.

The coastal waters and estuaries also have important mammals, including the dolphins and porpoises found in the estuaries of the Indus and Ganges. Gangetic dolphins often move far inland and are tolerant of fresh rather than saline water.

Reptiles

Cobras and Kraits are two of the best known of South Asia's reptiles, but there are well over 200 distinct species or subspecies of snakes alone. The King Cobras, which inhabit the tropical rain forests and may reach lengths of over five meters, are by far the largest poisonous snakes, though both the Rock Python and the Reticulated Python, which have recorded lengths over seven meters and weights over 115 kg, are considerably bigger. Vipers, such as the Himalayan Pit Viper and the Bamboo Viper, and several species of sea snake are further examples of poisonous snakes, though there are many non-venomous species too.

Larger reptiles are also represented, though now in greatly reduced numbers. The Blunt Nosed or Marsh Crocodile (the Magar) is still found in the Terai of Nepal, but the Gharial has only just survived as a result of government action to protect it and the big Estuarine Crocodile is still found from the Ganges to the Mahanadi. All five species of Monitor Lizards, found in both deserts and forests, are endangered, but India retains important breeding beaches for a number of species of turtle. In Orissa, some 300,000 Olive Ridley Turtles breed, as do Green Turtles and Olive Ridley Turtles near Karachi, and Hawksbill Turtles breed in southern Tamil Nadu.

Birds

South Asia has an enormous richness of bird life, and with over 2000 species has more than three times the number of species found in Europe. Their range reflects the region's tropical location and traditionally forested environment, but, although most species originated in the tropical oriental region, a number came from African sources. There are also large numbers of migrants such as ducks, cranes, swallows and fly-catchers which come annually from Central Asia.

Pakistan and northern India are the home of some of the finest birds of prey. Eagles and falcons used to be numerous, and, although there are still over 20 species, systematic hunting has posed a serious threat to their survival. In contrast, the various common species of vulture and of kite are visible in most parts of South Asia. Fishing birds such as egrets are common along any

A peacock in Bandipur tiger reserve (Karnataka); the peacock is India's national bird.

Further reading
S. A. Ali and S. D. Ripley, *Handbook of the Birds of India and Pakistan Together With Those of Nepal, Sikkim, Bhutan and Ceylon*, 10 vols (Bombay, 1968–74)
W. W. A. Phillips, *Manual of the Mammals of Sri Lanka*, Wildlife and Nature Protection of Sri Lanka 2nd edn (Colombo, 1980)
S. H. Praker, *The Book of Indian Animals* 2nd edn (Bombay, 1965)
P. D. Stracy, *Wild Life in India: Its Conservation and Control* (New Delhi, 1964)

Water resources

By definition 'natural resources' only become resources when they are of use to man. In that sense, the technology of use is as important in understanding the availability of natural resources in South Asia as is knowledge of their existence and distribution. Furthermore, the nature of natural resources changes with changing technology, not just with the depletion of existing reserves. For most people in South Asia, the key resource is water. The continuing importance of agriculture as the chief economic activity in all the countries of the region makes the amount and timing of water supply for agriculture the most significant single constraint on economic activity. In addition to its direct role in agriculture, water also contributes to both agriculture and industry as a source of commercial energy through hydro-electricity generation.

The long dry season and variability in the total amount of rainfall have always placed a premium on irrigation in nearly every region of

stretch of water or in irrigated fields from Bangladesh to South India. But while all the countries of South Asia have splendid examples of the largest birds of prey, they also have an enormous diversity of small and colorful birds. Parakeets, woodpeckers and kingfishers abound, various songbirds such as the Indian shama and the famous Indian mynah bird complementing the range. The magnificent plumage of India's national bird, the peacock, symbolizes the color and wealth of the whole subcontinent's bird life.

RWB

Using an archimedes screw to raise water in Rajahmundry (Tamil Nadu).

Water resources

Water resources in South Asian river basins.

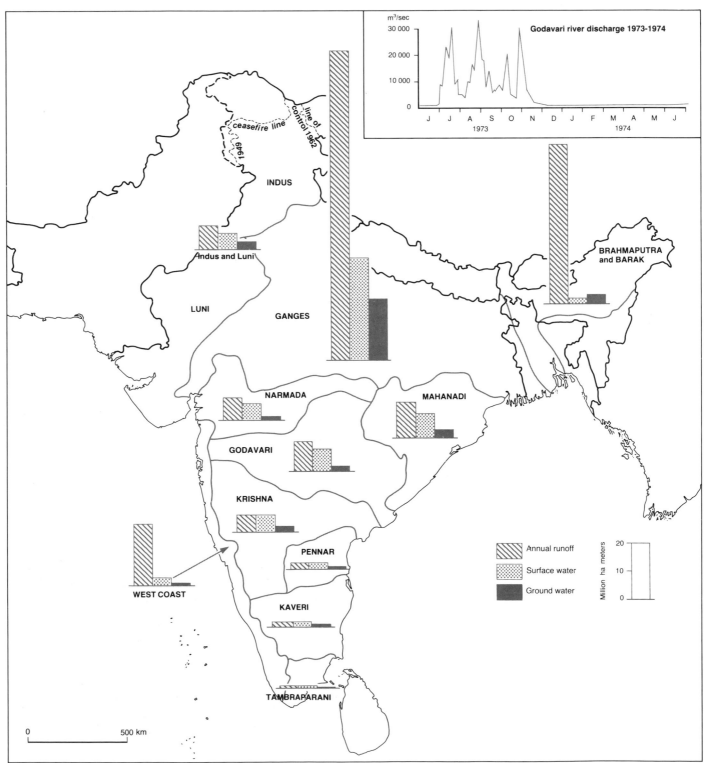

Source: R. Bradnock, Agricultural Change in South Asia (London, 1984) p.7

South Asia. Supplementing rainfall with water from rivers or from under ground has been developed to a fine art in many parts of South Asia over two thousand years. The Iranian system of Karez irrigation, for example, using underground channels is still widely practised in the Baluchistan. The Persian wheel is common in much of northern India, drawing water with bullock power from wells up to 20 m deep, and tanks or small artificial lakes are commonplace in the dry parts of Tamil Nadu, Andhra Pradesh, other eastern regions of India as well as in the Dry Zone of Sri Lanka. Even in the Maldives, it is the presence of shallow layers of fresh water trapped in shallow layers of coral that allows settlement at all on the scattered islands.

Although small-scale irrigation continues to play an important role in many parts of South Asia today, large-scale schemes have done much to transform water use. Two changes in technology, that is, massive dams and associated irrigation systems and pump sets powered with electricity or diesel, have made possible far fuller use of water resources than ever before. Thus, in India alone, more than one third of the cropped area was irrigated by the end of the 1980s. In Pakistan, well over two thirds of agricultural land depended on irrigation. Even Bangladesh, where over a third of the land is flooded annually, irrigation during the dry season has spread to over 20 percent of the cropped area.

As a result of increased demand, many regions of South Asia are experiencing severe pressure on water resources. Locally their scale and availability depends primarily on rainfall and on the water-bearing capacity of underground rocks, but the resources of large regions like Bangladesh and Pakistan depend crucially on river water that originates outside the region.

The extent of pressure on water resources is illustrated by the fact that in India, where the irrigated area rose from under 10 percent in 1947 to over 33 percent in the mid-1980s, virtually half of the total estimated available water was in use. In the late 1980s, 66 million hectare meters (one hectare meter being the volume of water required to cover one hectare of land to a depth of one meter), was tapped from surface water, while 27 million hectare meters came from ground water. However, the regional distribution of these resources was very uneven. Ground water is found very extensively in the alluvium of the Indo-Gangetic plains from Pakistan to Bangladesh, though in Sind and parts of northwestern India some is heavily saline. Elsewhere on the hard ancient rocks of peninsular India and Sri Lanka, ground water is more isolated in occurrence and very restricted in its volume. In some areas ground water use is now faster than replacement.

Pakistan's agriculture depends almost entirely on control of the Indus River system and its major tributaries, which are shared with India. The signing of the Indus Waters Treaty between India and Pakistan in 1960 was necessary to provide the framework for a

Methods of irrigation.

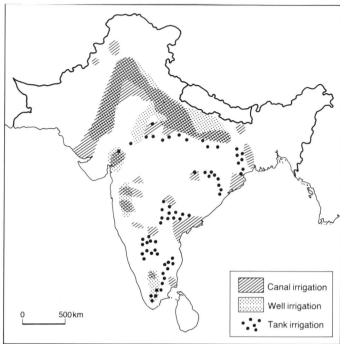

Canal irrigation
Well irrigation
Tank irrigation

0   500 km

Source: R. Bradnock, Agricultural Change in South Asia. (London 1984) p.11

secure irrigation future. Even that was only possible with the construction of massive dams at Tarbela and Mangla in Pakistan and at Bhakra Nangal in India. Conflicts of interest over water resources in South Asia are often sharp. The building of the Farakka

The Tarbela dam on the Indus, finished in the 1970s. It is the largest rock-filled dam in the world and completes Pakistan's vast Indus Basin Scheme. Pakistan's agriculture depends almost entirely on control of the Indus River system.

Barrage across the Ganges in India to divert water down the Hooghly River to Calcutta continues to be a bone of contention between India and Bangladesh, and, within India, there are extensive and protracted disputes between states over water rights which have prevented more rapid exploitation of the resources. At the same time, some of the massive engineering works involved in the development of water resources have caused large scale displacement of previous settlers or interference with the environment on a scale to cause great concern. Both the Kaptai Lake in Bangladesh and the Mahaweli Ganga scheme in Sri Lanka illustrate these problems.

RWB

Further reading
B. L. C. Johnson, *India: Resources and Development* (New York, 1979)
K. L. Rao, *India's Water Wealth* (New Delhi, 1981)

Natural and man-made disasters

South Asia's subcontinental location astride the Tropic of Cancer, surrounded by warm oceans and overlying one of the earth's major plate junctions, ensures that periodically it is subject to violent natural events. Not all such events result in disasters for man. Tropical cyclones, for example, are a frequent occurrence in the Bay of Bengal, striking the coast of South Asia anywhere from southern India to Bangladesh several times a year. Yet whether or not they result in great loss of life depends on precisely where they strike with greatest intensity. Similarly although much of the Himalayan belt passing through India, Bhutan, Nepal and northern Pakistan is one of the great earthquake regions of the world, damage resulting from earthquakes depends on the location of the earthquake relative to man's settlement. Although such events have caused disasters on a number of occasions throughout history, the risk of damage to life has been increasing sharply in this century as population in all countries of the region has grown and economic demands have increased.

Many of the disasters which have overtaken people in South Asia have been the result of the interaction of natural events with man's activity. Increasingly dense settlement in areas prone to flooding, whether in Bangladesh or the Indus Valley, along the banks of the lower Ganges or in lowland Sri Lanka, increases the risk of catastrophic damage. Similarly, famine may be regarded as the result of the interaction of natural causes, notably drought, with human, economic and political factors. But some of South Asia's disasters owe their origin entirely to man's activities. The gas leak at Bhopal in 1984 highlighted the risks of catastrophe from large scale industrial processes inadequately provided with safeguards.

Floods
Several regions are prone to flooding in South Asia, but the effects are not always disastrous. Indeed, at least a third of Bangladesh is flooded every year, and without the annual deposition of rich silts from the Ganges and Brahmaputra Rivers the intensive rice cultivation characteristic of the country would be impossible.

However, disastrous damage has been caused by flooding in several parts of South Asia. Intense local rainfall, characteristic of the extremely moist warm tropical maritime airmasses, can trigger severe local flooding. As much as 500 mm can fall in twenty four hours, making adequate drainage on flat land impossible. Such rainfall may be responsible for devastating floods in themselves, as in Tamil Nadu in 1977, or may simply add to flooding from other sources, as in the Indus plains in 1973 or in Bangladesh in 1974.

A more frequent cause of devastating flooding in South Asia is the inability of the large rivers to cope with increased discharge upstream. The Son-Kosi River system in northern India has become particularly notorious. In September 1984, for example, the Kosi breached its banks in Saharsa District, Bihar, killing two hundred people, making half a million homeless and destroying at least 20,000 hectares of crops. However, the worst floods of this sort in South Asia were those that devastated large tracts of agricultural land in Pakistan's Panjab and Sind in 1973. Major canal headworks and irrigation systems were severely damaged or destroyed, and the death toll reached thousands in just over a week of catastrophic flooding in the late monsoon period. The floods were the result of abnormally heavy rainfall in the lower regions of the Indus system coinciding with snow melt and monsoon rain in the upper reaches of the catchment area.

The scale of such disasters often stretches the imagination. At the end of December 1957, Sri Lanka also experienced catastrophic flooding. In several areas, rainfall in December had been four times the average, and in the last week a series of flood surges damaged numerous irrigation systems, left 250,000 people homeless and caused 125 deaths by drowning. This abnormal rainfall was associated with an intense cyclonic depression of the sort that more frequently causes havoc further north.

Flooding may also come from the sea. Bangladesh is particularly susceptible to such floods, for a rise in sea level of only ten meters would leave three quarters of Bangladesh permanently under the sea. Storm surges, again associated with cyclones, may raise sea level temporarily by up to three meters. As in 1970 this can lead to the inundation of enormous areas under sea water leading not only to loss of life on a colossal scale but also to long-term damage to agricultural land through salinization. Such surges have also wreaked havoc in other parts of South Asia. Some of the atolls of the Maldives have been completely inundated, resulting in total loss of life and destruction of the island habitat. Periodically the east coast of India has also been badly hit, as in the cyclone disaster of Andhra Pradesh in 1978 when perhaps 25,000 people lost their lives.

Cyclones

The most dramatic natural disasters in South Asia have been associated with cyclonic storms. Originating in the late summer over the oceans of southeast Asia when water temperatures exceed 27°C, the critical minimum for tropical cyclones to form, these track across the Bay of Bengal, guided by the Upper Air Easterlies. The Bay acts as a funnel, and if the curved path of the storm brings it across the coast of Bangladesh in the most populated parts of the flat islands devastation can result.

On November 12, 1970 just such a situation occurred. Sea level rose in the very low pressure eye of the storm by over two meters, and the sea surge coincided with very heavy rain and hurricane winds. Wind speeds of up to 240 km/h contributed a tidal wave of up to nine meters in height which struck the islands in the mouth of the

Ganges delta, and the already densely populated region had additional numbers of seasonal migrants. These flat islands, barely rising above the water level, become densely populated as the normal riverine floods recede. In November 1970, the early warning system of cyclones was largely ineffective, and, without the protection of a sea wall or shelter, tens of thousands of people had nowhere to flee. Some estimates put the death toll as high as half a million.

In the 1970s, enormous damage was also caused by cyclones in Tamil Nadu and Andhra Pradesh, emphasizing the risk to which all the coastal districts of eastern India and Bangladesh are exposed. The Krishna Delta was particularly hard hit in December 1977, and, in addition to widespread loss of life, tens of square kilometers of rice and sugar cane were laid waste.

Famines

Famine illustrates particularly clearly the complex links between events in the natural environment and man's influence. Drought is a common phenomenon in many parts of South Asia. The Indian government has identified nearly one third of its territory as 'drought prone', a consequence of the normal variability of rainfall in regions where the average rainfall is only barely adequate for agriculture. However, the severest famines have occurred in regions such as Bengal, Bihar and Orissa where rainfall is normally plentiful enough to allow very dense settlement to develop and where, as a consequence, failure of rains can affect millions of people. In 1770, for example, contemporary estimates suggest that up to ten million

Satellite photographs of the Ganges–Brahmaputra river systems as they flow into the Bay of Bengal in the dry and in the monsoon season. They reveal a continuing process of delta formation. The new islands created are quickly populated, but they are also very susceptible to cyclones such as the one which killed several hundred thousand Bangladeshis on November 12, 1970.

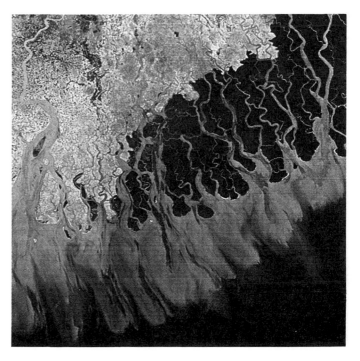

people died in Bengal, a region that includes modern Bangladesh. Over a century later, two years of drought and accompanying scarcity killed over five million in western and southern India.

Although these catastrophic events were related to drought-induced crop failures, they were also the result of actions taken by man which worsened the crisis rather than alleviated it. Subsequent famines have illustrated this relationship even more clearly. The worst famine of modern times was the Bengal famine of 1943. Up to two million people died in a famine that was very largely the result not of climatically induced food shortage but of restrictions on the movement of food and of its marketing. The British Government, anxious in wartime India to prevent the advance of the Japanese, banned the use of country boats in Bengal. These played a vital part in the local movement of foodstuffs and their impounding disrupted food supplies. The failure of the monsoon encouraged traders to hoard stocks, and the poor were simply unable to afford food grains.

There have been major famines in different parts of South Asia in the last two decades, but improvements in communications and in the management of food shortages have prevented the large scale starvation that was such a feature of earlier famines. Maharashtra experienced severe famine conditions in 1965–66, Bihar in 1967, and Maharashtra again in 1974–75, but central government aid, food for work programs and the increasing use of emergency irrigation helped to mitigate the worst effects.

Earthquakes and landslides
Although the entire Himalayan region is on one of the earth's major earthquake belts, the generally sparse population has restricted the number and scale of catastrophic earthquakes in South Asia. Risk, however, is increasing, as more very large dams are built in the earthquake-prone foothills of the Himalayas. Damage to the new Tarbela Dam on the Indus completed in the late 1970s, could pose a major threat in the future. On a local scale, the increasing pressure to settle on all available land has put many at increasing risk in Nepal, Kashmir and the steeper slopes of the mountain ranges from land slips which can destroy both agricultural land and houses.

Industrial disasters
On the night of December 2, 1984, a leak of methyl isocyanate from the Union Carbide pesticide factory in Bhopal left over 2000 people dead and many times that number severely affected by chemical poisoning. It was by far the worst industrial disaster in India and one of the worst in the world. The plant itself had been established to meet a rapidly growing demand at the end of the 1970s for pesticide to meet the needs of increasingly intensive agricultural practices which depended on high levels of chemical fertilizer and pesticide for success. New industries were welcomed by both the Central and State governments as bringing employment, particularly to economically backward states such as Madhya Pradesh. However, as is common in South Asia, low paid workers were not provided with accommodation, and were allowed to defy regulations by building shacks along the perimeter of the factory compound. The juxtaposition of dense settlement and the production of lethal chemicals (combined with inadequate management controls which allowed the deadly gases to build up and then escape) were prime contributors to the catastrophe. However, even this combination would not have caused the disaster without meteorological conditions of complete absence of wind and a temperature inversion which kept the escaping gas close to the ground as it escaped in the early hours of the morning, a time when everybody was asleep and unaware of the danger.

No part of South Asia is beyond the reach of natural disasters. However, as the Bhopal gas leak showed particularly clearly, most disasters are increasingly the result of the interaction of natural and man-induced causes. As the population of South Asia has grown so the number of people at risk from natural and man-induced disasters has also increased. Although some of the worst disasters in the last forty years have clearly identifiable causes, they have often only produced widespread devastation as a result of the apparently chance combination of several unrelated factors. However, as pressure on resources has risen and man's use of land and resources has become more and more intensive, the frequency with which those factors have combined with devastating consequences seems to have increased.   *RWB*

Further reading
R. W. Bradnock, *Agricultural Change in South Asia* (New York, 1983)
I. Burton and R. E. Kates, Eds, *Readings in Resource Management and Conservation* (Chicago, 1965)
B. L. C. Johnson, *Pakistan* (London, 1979)

Area of cross section, Everest to the Kerala coast.

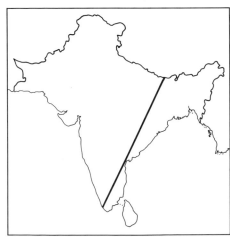

Geographical regions

South Asia's area of over four million square kilometers contains almost endless diversity of physical environment and landscape. This diversity is evident in the contrasts at a subcontinental scale, for example between the deserts of the northwest and the flooded deltas of the east. But it is also often clearly apparent on a very local scale.

Geographical regions are rarely neatly divided from each other. It is even less common for political boundaries to conform to those of geographical regions. The scale on which regional identity is sought has a vital bearing on the pattern of regions discussed. So also does the basis of regional division itself. Purely physiographic regions only infrequently have sharp limits. Similarly, climatic contrasts are generally progressive rather than abrupt. South Asia is no exception to these general principles. Some of the political changes of the last thirty years have brought a greater degree of conformity between geographical regions and major political units. States like Kerala and Tamil Nadu in South India illustrate this trend. However, some of the most important national boundaries created since 1947 cut across natural features and divide otherwise coherent physical regions. The boundary between Pakistan and India, for example, owes little to the nature of geographical regions.

Although national boundaries in South Asia frequently fail to coincide with physical boundaries, each of the countries with the exception of the Maldives has distinct regions within it. Thus, while recognizing the continuity of some important regions across national borders, the regional division outlined below uses the individual countries as the starting point.

India

India has all three of the subcontinent's main physiographic regions represented within its borders. It shares the Himalayas with Pakistan, Nepal and Bhutan, and the Indo-Gangetic plain stretches across both its western border into Pakistan, Nepal and Bhutan, and its eastern border into Bangladesh. Only the peninsula is entirely within Indian territory, though geologically the peninsula of India is part of the same landmass that makes up Sri Lanka. However, these three regions are themselves subdivided into important contrasting areas.

Himalayas

The Himalayas are by far the greatest of all mountain ranges, with 95 peaks reaching a height of over 7500 m. Of recent geological origin, the Indian Himalayas fall into three main sections from Kashmir in the northwest through the central Himalayas of Himachal Pradesh and Kumaon to the eastern ranges of the Kosi and Darjeeling, with an extension of mountainous terrain southwards into the Assam—Burma ranges.

The greatest part of the northernmost great Himalayan ranges, the Karakoram, now lies in Pakistan, separated from the Zaskar ranges running parallel to the south by the Indus River. Cupped between these high peaks and the Pir Panjal to the southwest lies one of the most famous of Himalayan valleys, the Vale of Kashmir. A synclinal trough marked by a faulted edge along its northern flank, the Vale lies at an altitude of about 1500 m. Measuring 135 km long by 40 km wide, it is by far the most fertile and densely populated region of the Himalayas. Its beautiful lakes, a great attraction to tourists from India and abroad, owe their origin to the very recent uplift of the surrounding mountains, which is still continuing.

Cross-section: Everest to the Kerala coast.

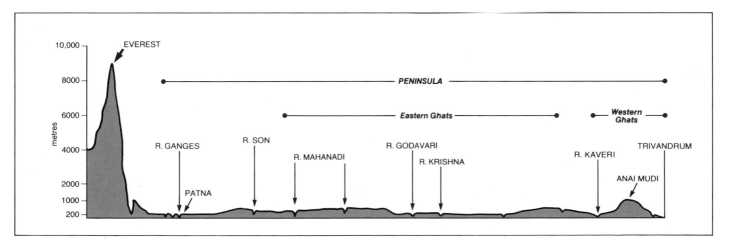

The southern flank of the Himalayas, from the foothills of Kashmir eastwards, is marked by the 6000 m thick Tertiary deposits which now comprise the Siwalik ranges. Massively folded and faulted in the mountain building movements that created the Himalayas themselves, the Siwaliks are marked by series of longitudinal valleys. In the west these are known as 'duns', and although they provide some opportunities for settlement they are on a smaller scale than those offered by the Vale of Kashmir.

The Indian sections of the central Himalayas are separated by Nepal into the western and eastern regions. The west is the source of some of South Asia's greatest rivers, the Ganges rising in India itself, the Indus and the Brahmaputra rising in Tibet. The Satlaj and the Yamuna also rise in the region, flowing through the Siwaliks of the modern State of Himachal Pradesh onto the plains to the south. The crystalline core of the Great Himalayas themselves and the associated ranges to the south show evidence of the tremendous thrusting and folding of the mountain building process, and the speed of uplift has led some of the rivers like the Satlaj to carve deep gorges, sometimes over 1000 m from top to bottom.

To the east of Nepal, the main trend of the central Himalayan range becomes east to west. Directly exposed to the monsoon, the region experiences far higher rainfall than any other part of the mountain chain, producing luxuriant vegetation on the lower slopes. The main rivers cut straight across the east–west parallel ranges, spilling out like the Tista onto the plain as a mountain torrent.

Ganges Plains

Sloping very gently eastwards from the watershed of the Indus to the delta of the Ganges, the alluvial plains form an uninterrupted stretch of almost completely flat terrain. They were formed by the deposition of alluvium in the trough fronting the Himalayas, and the rivers which erode the still-rising mountains to the north continue to leave their sands and silts on the plains below. In the east the alluvium reaches depths of more than 3000 m, gradually becoming shallower towards the north and west. However, on the surface, the only significant contrasts marking out the Upper Ganges plains from the Middle and Lower regions are climatic, rainfall decreasing progressively westwards from the Ganges delta up to the plains of the Panjab.

The plains' monotonous physical appearance is broken only at the margins and in the northwest, where isolated outliers of the ancient rocks of peninsular India penetrate the surface. On the southern flank of the plains, notably to the south of Agra, the alluvium is cut by rivers such as the Chambal into strikingly eroded 'badland', scrub-covered ravines providing ideal shelter for bands of dacoits. On the northern margins, the streams and rivers emerging from the Himalayas have often formed their own detrital cones where they debouch onto the flat plains, creating a confusion of broken rough terrain, as in the *chos* around Rupar.

The present physical appearance of the plains is greatly influenced by man's activity, for they are now one of the most densely populated regions in the world. The Upper Ganges plains were the hearth of Indian culture, settlement spreading eastwards from this core region over three millennia. The original forest cover has now virtually disappeared, and contrasts in soil are a major determinant locally of agricultural potential and hence of regional character. Even the Terai, the swampy and densely forested strip of land running along the northern margins of the plains, has been tamed through the eradication of malaria since 1947 and is now being brought under cultivation.

Irrigation is now one of the chief features distinguishing the Upper plains from the Middle and Lower. The early large-scale canal irrigation projects were on the doab, or interfluve often known as the Doab, between the Ganges and the Yamuna rivers, and subsequently the further development of canal irrigation from the mid-nineteenth century transformed the landscape of many areas of the northwestern plains. Since the early 1960s, the enormous wealth of groundwater trapped in the alluvium has also been extensively tapped, augmenting the agricultural prosperity of the drier northwest while the Lower Ganges plains of eastern Uttar Pradesh and Bihar, which receive much higher rainfall, remain among the poorest regions of India.

The Peninsula

The ancient basal rocks of the peninsula provide striking physical contrasts with the flat alluvial plains to the north. Even though the relief is subdued when compared to the Himalayas, the western Ghats which run parallel with the coast facing the Arabian Sea reach heights of more than 2500 m. Extensive gently sloping plateaus and broad river valleys, which are the hallmark of one of the world's most ancient erosion surfaces, cover great areas of the peninsula. Although a broad regional division is, to some extent, arbitrary, each comprising important subregions, it is possible to distinguish five separate physical regions in the peninsula.

The Aravalli Mountains mark the northernmost outpost of the old Gondwanaland land mass, with their outliers appearing through the Indo-Gangetic alluvium as far north as Delhi. To their west lies the 260,000 km^2 of the Thar desert, sand ridges covering the underlying plain and shading southwards into the equally arid Deccan lavas and traps of the Kathiawar Peninsula and the salt marshes of the Rann of Cutch (Kacch). The southern margin of the region is formed by the Vindhyan and Satpura ranges, which present dramatic south facing scarps overlooking the Narmada and Tapti, respectively, the only two major rivers of peninsular India that flow from east to west. They form both a traditional and a contemporary boundary between the northern and southern regions of the peninsula. To the east, the region contains a series of plateaus and relatively low hills, culminating in the Chota Nagpur and Ranchi plateaus.

The second region is made up of the western Ghats, the hill and mountain chain stretching from north of Bombay to the southern tip of India. The northern half is both lower and generally set further back from the coast than the southern, with heights ranging up to 1000 m inland of Bombay while in the Nilgiris, Palanis and Annamalais of the far south altitudes of over 2500 m are common.

With the exception of the Narmada and Tapti, all of peninsular India's most important rivers rise near the crest of the western Ghats within 40 to 60 km of the Arabian Sea, then flow eastwards across the peninsula to the Bay of Bengal. The interior plateaus comprise the third major region. Deccan lavas cover some 300,000 km^2 of the northern plateau to the south of the Vindhyans, and plateau lands stretch southwards across Telengana in Andhra Pradesh into the Mysore Plateau and the Tamil Nadu plains in the far south.

While the predominant slope is from west to east the series of hills running discontinuously up the eastern flank of the peninsula, often referred to as the eastern Ghats may be regarded as a fourth region. Reaching heights of 1500 m in Orissa the significant hill blocks are cut through by rivers such as the Brahmani and the Mahanadi. Until recently most of these hill masses were isolated, densely forested and malarial, the preserve of scattered tribal groups, but settlement has increasingly made its impact felt.

Finally, the peninsula is fringed by a narrow strip of coastal lowland. The western littoral is hemmed in by the Ghats, and feeling the full force of the southwest monsoon has rainfall commonly over 2000 mm. In contrast the eastern coast is much drier, and slopes much more gently up to the plateaus. Rivers, such as the Kaveri in Tamil Nadu, the Krishna and Godavari in Andhra Pradesh and the Mahanadi in Orissa, have all created large deltas, regions of intensive irrigated rice cultivation that further marks them out from the drier interior.

Pakistan

Pakistan can be divided into three distinct physical regions; the Karakoram and high Himalayas of the far north, the hills and mountains of the western and northwestern frontier from Swat southwards to Baluchistan, and the Indus plains.

The Karakoram are probably much older than the main ranges of the Himalayas to the east. Recent evidence suggests that their highest peak, K2, may in fact be even higher than Mount Everest. A bleak and desolate massif, cut through by the gorges of the Indus, the deepest of which is over 5000 m and less than 25 km wide, the higher reaches are covered in places by extensive snow fields and huge glaciers. To the west are Gilgit and Hunza, themselves transitional to the ranges of the Hindu Kush still further to the west and southwards to the Safed Koh.

The western hills and mountains of Baluchistan and northwest Frontier Province are lower than those to the north but still striking. With the exception of isolated valleys, notably the Kabul River, a semi-desert climatic environment prevails, although the relatively heavy winter rains make intensive agriculture possible in the encapsulated lowlands of Peshawar and Bannu. Further to the south, the hills disappear under the stone and sand deserts of Baluchistan on the Makran coast in one of the world's most desolate landscapes.

The plains of the Indus present a striking contrast both physically and culturally. Until the advent of canal irrigation in the late nineteenth century, the entire plains region was sparsely populated scrub jungle. The lower course of the Indus in Sind receives no tributaries, and the Indus delta could scarcely be more different from the delta of the Ganga on the opposite side of the subcontinent. Recent alluvium, often coarsely grained, dominates the eastern valley, older alluvium the west, but it is the irrigated lands of the east that provide a substantial livelihood. To the north, the plains of the Panjab are equally dependent on the irrigation of the major doabs between the tributaries of the Indus, which has converted the region into one of the most prosperous agricultural regions of South Asia.

Bangladesh

Bangladesh is largely a deltaic region, the chief exception being in the southeast where the Chittagong Hill Tracts rise to some 500 m above sea level. Three major rivers have deposited their silts gradually causing the land surface to extend into the Bay of Bengal: the Ganges and its chief channel in Bangladesh, the Padma, the Brahmaputra and the much smaller Meghna. The extremely low lying nature of the terrain conceals important regional contrasts.

The formation of Bangladesh has been dominated by its rivers, and particularly by the progressive shifting eastwards of the active course of the Ganges and the major shifts in course of the Brahmaputra. Three main regions can be distinguished. In the north is the Barind tract, essentially the doab of the Ganga and Brahmaputra made up of old alluvium, outwash deposited by the Tista as it debouches onto the Plains. Although it is the driest region of Bangladesh, it suffers severe flooding in the rainy season.

On the western flank are the moribund and mature parts of the delta, most of the former being in modern India. Old courses of the Ganges and its distributaries have been long abandoned to become ox-bow lakes or *bhils*. Heavy clayey silt soils make land difficult to work but the lakes provide important sources of fish and game during the wet season. Further east, the rivers are carving their

Geographical regions

A India: the Himalayas at Pahalgam in Kashmir.

B India: the Western ghats near Mahabaleshwar, Satara district, Maharashtra.

C India: the coastline of the peninsula at Kovalam, south of Trivandrum, Kerala.

The physical geography of South Asia.

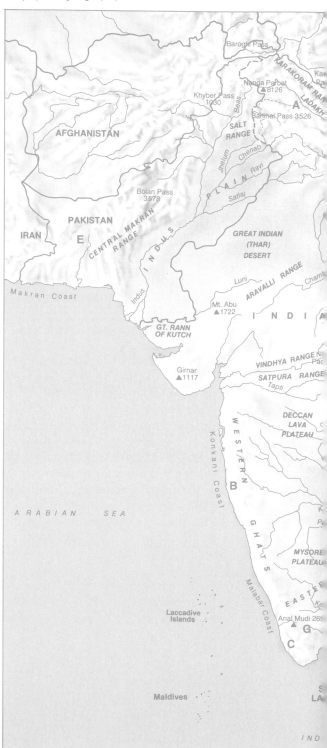

D India: the Ganges plains at Mankapur, Gonda district, Uttar Pradesh.

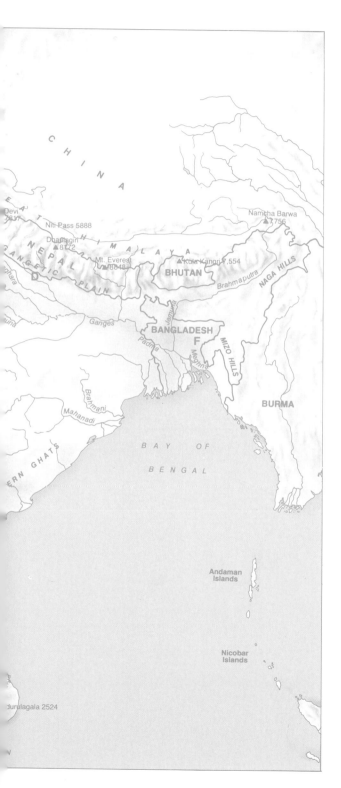

E Pakistan: sand desert in Baluchistan.

F Bangladesh: watery landscape near Dhaka.

G India: the Sirumalai Hills in the south of the peninsula at Dindigul, Tamil Nadu.

37

active courses, and the fresh deposits of silt make agriculture a quite different proposition.

On the eastern flank, the valley of the Meghna and the Surma give rise to one of the most remarkable physical regions of South Asia, where the great depressions, known locally as *haors*, flood to depths of five or six meters every year, yet support a distinctive type of rice cultivation adapted to such conditions. Along the southern flank of Bangladesh lie the Sundarbans, a region of dense mangrove forest and sparse habitation.

Nepal and Bhutan

Nepal stretches some 900 km along the southern flank of the highest ranges of the Himalayas to the south of Tibet. Its width of between 160 and 240 km contains three broadly parallel regions, the Terai, bordering India, the Midland zone and the *Pahar* or hill country proper. Bhutan's 47,000 square kilometers also contain some of the world's great mountains, among them Chomo Lhari in the northwest which reaches 7263 m.

Nepal's Terai, containing the Siwaliks in the foothills and the Mahabharat Ranges, reaching up to 2800 m and running the length of the country, was until recently densely forested and heavily malarial, a great barrier to settlement and especially to the movement of hill people onto the plains. This has now changed, and it has become a densely settled region.

The Midlands have always been the key region of Nepal with the Kathmandu Valley at its heart. The valley itself is an old lake bed, lying at 1350 m above sea level. The great mountain wall of the High Himalayas stretches across the northern flank, with Everest to the northeast of Kathmandu and the peaks of Annapurna and Dhaulagiri to the west overlooking Pokhara.

Sri Lanka and the Maldives

The dominant feature distinguishing Sri Lanka's regions is climatic rather than physiographic, for the island falls into two clearly demarcated rainfall zones, the Wet Zone, essentially in the southwest quadrant, and the remaining Dry Zone. However, this climatic contrast itself reflects the dominant relief feature, that of the central highlands, which cause a pronounced rainshadow effect during the southwest monsoon. Piduratalaga, the highest peak, reaches 2524 m, and the main mass of the central highlands along with a broad sweep from the southwest to the northeast of the island belong to the Khondalite series of rocks found in Tamil Nadu and Orissa. With the exception of the limestones of the Jaffna peninsula, virtually the whole of Sri Lanka comprises crystalline pre-Cambrian rocks. From Piduratalaga and Adam's Peak, the hills descend in three steps of varying width down to the coastal lowlands. The scarps that separate them are often major features, deeply dissected by the rivers that traverse the short distance from the highlands to the coast.

The Maldives could scarcely show a greater physical contrast to Sri Lanka. Its one thousand and nine tiny atolls stretch north–south for nearly 800 km into the Indian ocean, yet the total surface area is less than 300 km^2. Regional contrasts are slight. None of the atolls reaches an altitude greater than 2 m above sea level, occasional beach dunes reaching 4 m. The largest island, Fua Mulaku, is less than 6 km long by 1.4 km wide.

RWB

Further reading

B. H. Farmer, *An Introduction to South Asia* (London, 1983)

R. L. Singh, *India: A Regional Geography* (Varanasi, 1971)

D. E. Sopher, Ed. *An Exploration of India, Geographical Perspectives on Society and Culture* (New York, 1980)

O. H. K. Spate and A. T. A. Learmonth, *India, Pakistan and Ceylon: The Regions 3rd edn.* (London, 1972).

PEOPLES

A mother and child at
Modhera, Gujarat.

Ethnology

A Pathan tribesman.

A Sikh.

A Tamil family.

A Sinhalese woman.

Cultural regions of South Asia.

1 Northern India
2 Eastern Plains
3 Northeast Frontier
4 Himalayan Borders
5 Northwest
6 Western India
7 Tribal Belt
8 South India
9 Sri Lanka and the Islands

0   100   200   300 km

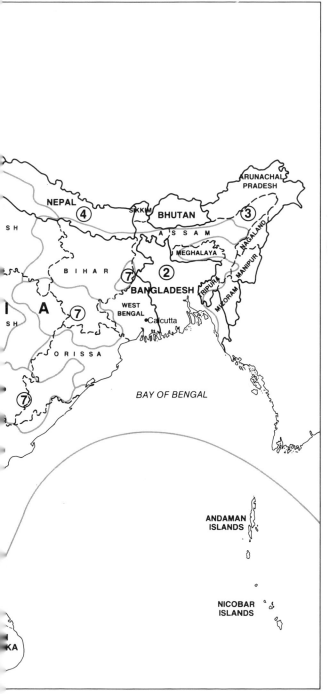

A Nepali woman.

A Konyak Naga tribesman.

A north Indian Muslim.

A Bengali woman.

One member of the human race in every seven now lives in India, which is, after China by a long margin, the second most populous country in the world. With the further addition of the very large populations of Pakistan and Bangladesh, together with the smaller numbers who inhabit the other countries of the region, South Asia as a whole is the home of no less than one-fifth of mankind. In numerical terms, given the present rapid rates of population growth in the area, this will in the near future come to represent a total surpassing one billion (1,000,000,000) human beings.

'Races'

The writings left by all three of the incursive groups who have had most influence in the shaping of modern South Asian social and cultural patterns – the Aryans of the second millenium BC, the Muslims of the medieval period, and the British during colonial times – testify to the historic antiquity of the puzzlement caused to outsiders by the 'dark-skinned' peoples of the subcontinent and their 'strange customs', and there has never been any shortage of attempts to explain cultural differences in terms of physical characteristics. This is as true within South Asia itself as it is of outsiders, for local chauvinists are often quite as ready to cite supposedly scientific racial theories in support of their positions as are, for instance, anti-immigrationist lobbies abroad.

It must, however, be observed that neither archeology nor physical anthropology, although both are scientific disciplines with a distinguished intellectual pedigree in South Asia, have been able to produce more than very tentative suggestions as to the evolution and distribution of racial types within the region's population.

One of the most striking characteristics of this vast population is, after all, its apparent homogeneity. The loose use of the terms 'Indian', 'East Indian', 'Hindu', or their popular equivalents in the world's major languages immediately evokes the picture of a recognizable physical type, most obviously distinguished by a brown pigmentation of the skin, additionally by such secondary physical characteristics as full black hair and typically prominent dark brown eyes. Even a closer observation will show only that the people of South Asia are internally differentiated in physical appearance from one another by regional tendencies rather than by absolute traits. Thus, as might be expected from their geographical location, people in the northwest tend to be relatively light-skinned and heavily built, while those in the northeast tend to exhibit Mongoloid traits, with rounder faces and high cheekbones. Southerners, by contrast, tend to be darker in complexion than people from the north and to be more slightly built.

Since the total population of South Asia by the end of the first millenium BC is reliably estimated to have approached 100,000,000, the exercise of backwards extrapolation from the well-established enormous genetic pool implied by this figure must at best be very speculative. This is particularly the case given the rather scanty evidence from archeological sources. As in all comparably long-inhabited areas of the world, great numbers of microliths have been recovered from prehistoric sites, notably in northwestern Pakistan and throughout peninsular India. Archeologists have not yet, however, been able to discover human remains remotely comparable in age and significance to those found in Africa and in China. Substantial skeletal evidence is available only from the very late Indus Valley sites (third millenium BC), which yield a variety of skull types not markedly different from those in the present local population.

Although physical anthropologists have made significant discoveries about such invisible characteristics of the South Asian population as a whole, such as the markedly low ratio of A-type blood (presumed to be so because it is selected against by smallpox, long endemic to the region), their attempts to construct schemes of racial groups within the population have proved less satisfactory. These schemes tend to rely upon an uneasy mixture of reconstructed prehistory, usually postulating the gradual infiltration of dark-skinned 'Dravidian' primitive stocks by fairer 'Aryan' invaders from the north of heavier build and narrower skulls, with historical extrapolation from modern social attitudes, notably the almost universal association in South Asian society between lightness of skin color and high social status. Such taxonomies are often bolstered with a wealth of anthropometric statistics, but the often doubtful value of these is notoriously illustrated by the pioneering obsession of Risley (1901) with measurements of the nasal index, designed to demonstrate 'scientifically' the racial difference between the fine-nosed upper castes and their squat-nosed menials. Now fortunately largely discredited, such exercises are at best misguided, at worst dangerous.

Except in the special cases of extremely isolated primitive groups (themselves now largely extinct or assimilated) such as the Andaman Islanders or the Veddas of Sri Lanka, the present existence of radically distinct racial types within the South Asian population may therefore be discounted. The internal groupings within the immensely complex societies of the region actually stem far more from cultural factors rather than from the facial or bodily appearance with which these may be associated in popular imagination.

Religions

The most important of cultural determinants, when viewed from a pan-South Asian perspective, is religion. South Asia contains adherents of at least seven major religions – Hindus, Muslims, Christians, Buddhists, Sikhs, Jains and Parsis – not to speak of innumerable subgroups and sects. Religious allegiance implies far more than private belief or chosen place of worship, implying as it

A north Indian Brahmin

does choice of name, costume, diet, role of the sexes, and a vast further range of patterns of group behavior.

Even the present political map of the region is largely determined by religion. The partition of British India in 1947 was effected to secure the separate establishment of the Muslim-majority areas as the new state of Pakistan, from whose split in 1971 the Islamic Republic of Bangladesh was born. The geographically isolated Maldives constitute the third Muslim country of South Asia. The continuing civil conflict between Buddhists and Hindus in Sri Lanka finds some counterpart in the underlying tensions of the societies of the Himalayan kingdoms of Nepal and Bhutan.

In India, the most important country of the region, the professed official commitment to a secular policy is continually taxed by the task of reconciling the legitimate aspirations of a huge Hindu majority with those of its very significant religious minorities. This continuing process should be viewed not simply in terms of the expression in religious terms of the socio-economic tensions inevitably generated in a society embracing one of the largest and poorest sections of mankind, but also in the context of the home of one of the world's oldest and proudest civilizations.

From the aspect of social organization, the most striking charac-

teristic of Hindu culture is the extreme emphasis placed upon the inequality of status which underlies the system of hereditarily separated castes. This is formalized in the well-known classical *varna* class-system of Priests, Warriors, Merchants and Peasants, which relates only vaguely to modern social realities. While caste-membership remains the main determinant of Hindu social identity, the ritually superior Brahmins, with their traditional monopoly of learning and education, face increasing challenges from other groups. While hereditary business-castes continue to dominate the commercial life of the cities, in a still largely peasant-based society it is the locally dominant landowning castes who are increasingly prominent in most regions of the country, and on whose patronage less favored specialist castes must rely.

Unlike their British predecessors, with their minutely compiled tabulations of caste-membership, the census officials of India take cognizance of only two special categories besides general enumerations of the population under the broad headings of religion and language.

The first is that of the Scheduled Castes. In spite of their rescue under the influence of Gandhian idealism from their traditionally polluting association with the disposal of human corpses, the processing of human excrement in a society still unable to meet its needs for flushing toilets, or dealing in the leather-products of the sacred cow, the 'Untouchable' label formerly applied to them is hard to shake off. In spite of the statutory positive discrimination applied to them under the Indian Constitution, the Scheduled Castes still constitute perhaps the world's largest group of both economically underprivileged and ritually discriminated-against human beings, whether engaged in their traditional occupations or employed as landless laborers.

The second group distinguished by the Constitution is that of the Scheduled Tribes, often peripheral groups in Indian society with distinctive lifestyles, although the fierce pressure on environmental resources in South Asia has long since forced the hereditary hunters among them to peasant cultivation. Their modern title of *adivasi* or 'original inhabitants' of South Asia owes more to primitive romanticism than to any convincing corpus of hard data from the physical anthropologists who have accorded these groups considerable attention in their search for primitive ethnic strains in the Indian population. But the major tribal groups have on the whole nevertheless been more successful than the Scheduled Castes in establishing their separate modern identity.

The traditional emphasis of Hinduism upon the ritual justification of social differences and inequalities has had a quite considerable effect upon the attitudes of most other religious groups in South Asia. Even in the case of the Muslims, for instance, whose 25 percent of the total population makes them by far the largest of these groups, the egalitarianism so strictly propounded by Islam tends to be locally modified, by conscious pride in a fair-skinned central Asian lineage, or by the manifestation of social reserve toward groups involved in particularly filthy activities. Similar types of attitude are to be found amongst other South Asian religious minorities also, recruited as they have been almost entirely through conversion rather than immigration.

In one important aspect of social behavior, the social freedom accorded to women, the Muslim societies of South Asia are notably more restrictive than other religious communities. In spite of the prominence of women in public life in several South Asian countries, they tend anyway to be a collectively disadvantaged group, and the remarkable reversal of the normal sex ratio in South Asia, where women constitute a numerical minority of the population, is presumably associated with differential patterns of child-care. The figures are given added point by the markedly low rates of literacy and professional employment for Muslim women, great numbers of whom are subject to restraints imposed by the ideals of the purdah system. Amongst most other religious minorities and many tribal groups, by contrast, women enjoy much greater social freedom.

Regions

Second only in importance to religious identity which, as has been indicated, may embrace a variety of allegiances to castes, tribes and other groups, stand the many large group-identities which relate to geographical location. The great variety of regional environments and regional cultures in South Asia imposes its own pattern, cross-cutting the religious divides, often also the national frontiers the latter have imposed. The increasingly explicit formulation of regional identities is one of the most striking features of modern South Asian societies, and is symbolized on the map by contemporary provincial boundaries, sometimes also by national frontiers, as in the case of Bangladesh.

These social regional identities correspond only in part to clearly defined geographical regions. It is true, of course, that ecological factors will help determine locally possible types of cultivation, dietary preferences and constraints, and differential regional standards of living.

But ecological differences are given sharply added social focus by the extraordinary multiplicity of languages spoken in the subcontinent. At least twenty prominent languages are in use, mostly belonging to the Indo-Aryan group in the north, but also to the indigenous Dravidian family in the south, not to mention a great many more lesser languages current among tribal and other peripheral groups. The prominence given to returns under the heading of language, alongside those for religion, in the censuses of India and other countries in South Asia is thus to a very real extent a reflection of present social realities, with their complex mix of identities, perceived in terms of both religious allegiance and regional loyalty.

The cross-cutting diversity implied by these twin criteria can hardly be fitted precisely within the neat national and provincial boundaries of the map on pp. 40–1, which at best represent adeptly drawn compromises. It is a striking characteristic of modern South Asian society that its expanding cities tend to draw their huge populations from a whole range of different regions. Much is rightly made of the still heavy rural preponderance of South Asian society, some 75 percent of whose people live in the countryside, with its relatively stable regional pattern. But it is the transregional élites of the cities who determine its present evolution, and their vast proletariats who must help determine its future.

The social patterns of South Asia are thus so complex that any attempt to characterize the regional variations among its peoples can only be the product of a series of approximations and compromises between different sets of criteria. The nine zones of inevitably unequal size, described in roughly clockwise progression below, with only casual reference to modern political frontiers, are to be regarded in this light.

Northern India

The Upper Gangetic plain, particularly the Doab region between the Ganges and Yamuna, is the cultural heartland of India, containing not only the historic capital of Delhi, but also some of the holiest centers of Hinduism and many splendid architectural memorials of the Mughal past. The great physical and social variety of the dense population of this area is entirely consonant with its dominant role in the subcontinent's history.

At the basis of its society lie long-settled villages, whose concrete physical separation is socially underlined by strict rules of village exogamy. This is a wheat-growing region whose lands are largely in the control of Jat and Rajput castes, acknowledging the ritual superiority of the Brahmins but commanding the services of an array of specialists and the labor of a rural proletariat of hereditary Scheduled Castes, notably the Chamars traditionally associated with leatherwork. Parallel to this Hindu hierarchy, which continues to dominate the village life of the region, there is a quite substantial Muslim minority, variously fitted into it according to their social status.

The historic political dominance of the Muslims in the towns and cities of the region which rely, as throughout South Asia, upon the base of the agricultural economy, has been largely eroded by political developments, although the specialization of functions which is as characteristic of Indian towns as it is of its villages has allowed some of them a continuing role, and historically imposed attitudes continue to govern aspects of social behavior, notably the rather restricted social role of women.

Religious composition of the main South Asian states, 1981

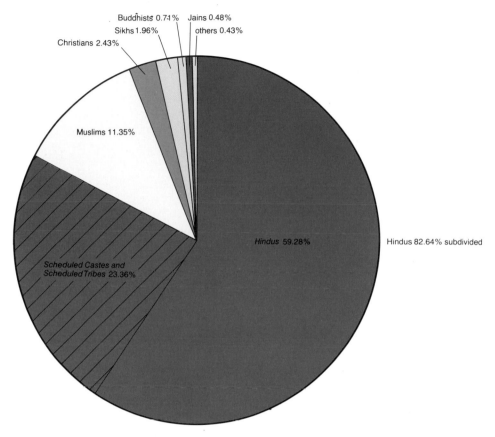

Buddhists 0.71%
Jains 0.48%
Sikhs 1.96%
others 0.43%
Christians 2.43%
Muslims 11.35%
Hindus 59.28%
Hindus 82.64% subdivided
Scheduled Castes and Scheduled Tribes 23.36%

INDIA 684 million

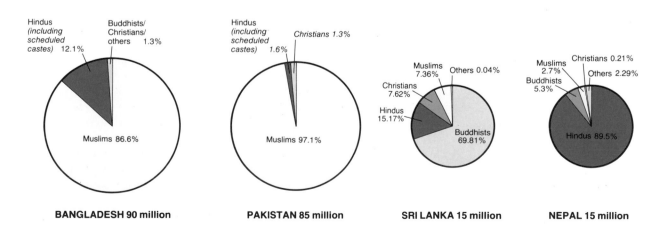

Hindus *(including scheduled castes)* 12.1%
Buddhists/ Christians/ others 1.3%
Muslims 86.6%

BANGLADESH 90 million

Hindus *(including scheduled castes)* 1.6%
Christians 1.3%
Muslims 97.1%

PAKISTAN 85 million

Muslims 7.36%
Others 0.04%
Christians 7.62%
Hindus 15.17%
Buddhists 69.81%

SRI LANKA 15 million

Muslims 2.7%
Christians 0.21%
Buddhists 5.3%
Others 2.29%
Hindus 89.5%

NEPAL 15 million

This is, however, the heartland of Hindi in India, indeed the one region in which the national language is spoken as a natural tongue at all levels of society (albeit in its Urdu form by many Muslims). As such, it acts as the natural center of the huge spread of northern Indian states which have adopted Hindi as their official language.

This central pull finds vivid physical reflection in the enormously variegated population of modern Delhi, the region's natural metropolis. Ambitious politicians, administrators and businessmen are naturally drawn to the capital from all parts of the country, but an immense further variety of people from neighboring areas, ranging from erstwhile princes of Rajasthan to the most destitute laborers from the Scheduled Castes and Tribes of the eastern Hindi areas, continue to fuel its insatiable growth.

The Eastern plains
The increasingly heavy rainfall deposited by the annual monsoons, the nearer their source in the Bay of Bengal is approached, is reflected in a shift from a relatively prosperous wheat-growing region to a vast area dependent upon intensive rice cultivation, with all the social consequences in terms of very high population density implied by that famously productive grain. Over a quarter of the total population of South Asia is concentrated within this region, whose natural richness has been exploited almost beyond its limit.

Ecological pressure and the maintenance of a markedly conservative hierarchy of castes make the intermediate zone of the middle Ganges plain, divided between the eastern Hindi-speaking states of East Uttar Pradesh and Bihar, one of the least developed regions in India, and many of its inhabitants are driven to seek employment elsewhere.

The natural center of this zone lies in Bengal, the vast and densely populated deltaic region, in which the Ganges joins with the outflow of the Brahmaputra. Although now divided between the largely Hindu Indian state of West Bengal and the predominantly Muslim country of Bangladesh, the shared Bengali cultural identity, based upon the Bengali language, is one of the most tenaciously fostered of all in South Asia. Although dominated by the former imperial capital of Calcutta, now sadly reduced in its enormous sprawl to the status of a byword for Third World urban deprivation, this identity rather resembles the more romantic picture of a water-based landscape of scattered hamlets accommodating an astonishing density of rural population, much less differentiated by caste and class differences than is characteristic of the north Indian heartland.

While Bengalis provide a whole set of recognizable stereotypes to other South Asians, whether as eaters of rice and fish, or as the archetypal 'babu' Brahmins of Calcutta, or indeed as the source of the subcontinent's most bewitching female beauties, it is the expansionist pressures invoked by their enormous numbers which is of chief concern to their neighbors. 'Greater Bengal' is a dominant

factor in the cultural attitudes of the much smaller settled Hindu populations to the north, in the Brahmaputra valley of Assam, and to the south, around the Mahanadi delta in Orissa.

The Northeast frontier
The traditional picture of South Asia as a society preserved in stable, even stagnant equilibrium is hardly anywhere more false than in the hilly territories which surround the Bengal plains. In the sharpest possible contrast to the vast cultural uniformity of their low-lying neighbors, these hills, historically a cultural borderland between south and southeast Asia, are home to many of the most fiercely preserved tribal identities in the subcontinent.

This is therefore the zone to which the rough cultural categories adumbrated above are least applicable. Both the formerly head-hunting Nagas, subsequently profoundly influenced by the teachings of Christian missionaries during the British period, and the Mizos have succeeded in securing the recognition of their tribal identities, if at the cost of long guerilla campaigns, within the Indian Union. Lesser tribal groups, whether of animist, Buddhist, or Christian allegiance, continue to maintain their right to often marvellously picturesque separate identity, whether conceived in terms of lifestyle or religion and language, in the face of increased pressure upon their hereditary resources from both parts of Bengal.

The Himalayan borders
The world's highest range of mountains, which fences in South Asia from the north, inevitably imposes profound ecological constraints upon the rather sparsely settled inhabitants of its lower southern slopes. In the same way as the heterogeneous tribal populations of the northeast frontier were incorporated into South Asia largely as the consequence of British Indian 'defence policy', so too are the peoples of the most lofty northernmost strip of this extended zone, which traverses in turn Bhutan, India, Nepal, India again, and finally Pakistan, effectively outposts of the civilization, language, and demanding ecology of the high Tibetan plateau. Apart from the Islamized Tibetan-speakers of Pakistani Baltistan, most of these high-mountain dwellers continue allegiance to the lamaistic Buddhism of their parent Tibetan culture.

In this most acutely ecologically conditioned region, it is the more fertile intermediate valleys which chiefly determine the patterns of society. Ever since the establishment of the Gorkha kingdom of western Nepal in the eighteenth century, the most notable feature of the region has accordingly been the expansion of the Nepali language and the Hindu culture associated with it, at the expense of traditional Buddhist allegiances. Actively encouraged in Nepal, whose famously valorous Gurkha soldiers are often in fact drawn from quite different linguistic and tribal groups, this process has come to be increasingly prominent both in Bhutan and the intermediate Indian corridor.

The Northwest

The valleys and plains of the Indus and its tributaries and the hills and deserts which lie to their west constitute the area of South Asia longest subject to Middle Eastern cultural influences, especially to Islam. The population is largely Muslim, and the bulk of the area lies in Pakistan, where the contrast between the tribal peoples of the hills and the settled inhabitants of the plains has a long history.

The best-known and most dynamic of the tribal peoples are the Pashto-speaking Pathans of the northwest frontier, famous for their continuing martial traditions, embracing the extremes of both hospitality and ruthlessness. A Middle Eastern type tribal society of a different type is represented by the Baluch tribes to their south, with their elaborate system of tribal chiefs.

South Asian social patterns are naturally more marked in the settled areas, though these are collectively distinguished from the neighboring north Indian zone by the predominance of Muslims and consequent lack of elaborate caste-hierarchies. The beautiful northern valley of Kashmir has a quite distinctive ecology, based upon rice-growing, and a quite distinctive social pattern with a Muslim majority long co-existing with a Hindu minority composed almost entirely of Brahmins.

Most of the population live in vast wheat-growing plains of the Panjab, one of the most agriculturally prosperous and productive areas in South Asia, divided since 1947, when a virtually total exchange of population took place, between Pakistan Panjab, almost entirely Muslim, and the smaller Indian Panjab, which is the home of the Sikhs but also has a large number of Hindus. In spite of this divide, a Panjabi cultural identity of formidable confidence characterizes members of all communities. Finally, around the lower Indus lies the very different society of Sind, whose historical isolation has encouraged the survival of more conservative ways, but whose social patterns have been disturbed by the influx of large numbers of Muslim refugees from north India, speaking Urdu rather than Sindhi. These Urdu-speakers constitute a majority of the population of Karachi, so that the greatest city in Pakistan is socially somewhat different in character from its immediate hinterland.

Western India

Geographically separated by deserts and hills from the northern plains, western India rather looks outwards to the Arabian Sea. This is particularly true of Gujarat, whose indented coastline provides many excellent harbors. Although its alluvial soils permit high agricultural productivity, and its capital Ahmadabad is the centre of India's cotton industry, Gujaratis are best known for their skill as businessmen. Besides the many Hindu business castes (the background of Gandhi, Gujarat's most famous son), local commercial opportunities have attracted and encouraged the development of a quite remarkable number of prosperous religious minorities in the region, including Jains, Parsis, and such Muslim sects as the Ismailis, Bohras and Memons.

Many Gujarati businesses are located in Bombay, the colossal city which is India's foremost port and the center of its film industry, also the capital of the Marathi-speaking state of Maharashtra, which constitutes the greatest area of Indo-Aryan speech in southern India, and is thus something of a cultural border-zone between north and south. Socially dominated by the Maratha (Kunbi) farming caste, who once generated one of India's most powerful empires, Maharashtra is also famous for the traditional learning of its Brahmins, and the old capital of Pune (Poona) is better known in India for its Sanskrit than for its colonels.

The long establishment of Goa as the capital of the Portuguese empire of the east has resulted in the continuing existence of strong Roman Catholic Christian traditions in a small coastal enclave to the south of Maharashtra.

The Tribal Belt

The majority of India's tribal population, apart from the special case of the border tribes of the northeast frontier, is to be found in a broken central belt extending along the north–south cultural divide from Gujarat to Orissa.

Some fifty different tribes, speaking a great variety of languages, not only Indo-Aryan and Dravidian but also of the distinctive Munda family, are to be found in this region. Although its hills and scrubby jungles no longer permit the maintenance of old hunting traditions, and most tribespeople exist by marginal agriculture or as hired hands, the distinctive traditions of at least the major tribes – Bhils in Gujarat, Gonds in Orissa and Santals in Bihar – continue to be maintained in the face of pressures to conform to the norms of Hindu society.

Less likely to survive are the southern tribes living in isolated pockets along the western Ghats, all speakers of distinctive Dravidian languages. The best known of these are the picturesque Todas of the Nilgiri Hills, well known as tourist attractions to visitors to Ootacamund.

South India

The four southern states of peninsular India – Kannada-speaking Karnataka, Telugu-speaking Andhra Pradesh, Malayalam-speaking Kerala, and Tamil-speaking Tamil Nadu – have both individually and collectively a powerful sense of their separate regional identity within the country. This identity has these Dravidian languages, quite unrelated to the Indo-Aryan languages of the north, as its most obvious and proudly maintained symbol, but is naturally supported by a whole range of distinctive patterns of social behavior and organization. Clothes are looser, the food much more highly spiced, and women notably more free socially in the south than in the north. Names are naturally quite different, often indeed hardly pronounceable by northerners, castes are differently organized, and marriage preferences differ considerably, since the emphasis of northern Hindu society on marrying out of the family is replaced in the south by a preference for marrying cross-cousins.

Within the south, there are naturally internal differences, not merely between the different language-areas, but also as determined by the physical environment, for example between densely populated fertile coastal areas and the more sparsely cultivated uplands. This is, however, the region least affected by external invasion and cultural incursion through history, and Hindu traditions (in their distinctive Southern forms) remain strong. Only in Hyderabad, now the capital of Andhra Pradesh, did the Muslims succeed in establishing a colonial outpost where northern traditions and the Urdu language have survived the abolition of the Nizam's princely state to any significant extent.

Other minorities have been established from the Middle East by sea. Kerala, one of the most densely populated areas in South Asia, is particularly notable in this regard, with a Christian community claiming foundation by the Apostle Thomas, the Mapilla Muslims who look directly to Arabia for their traditions, and even formerly a small Jewish community in Cochin. Economic pressures are now so great, however, that Keralans are forced to move in the reverse direction in search of employment.

Sri Lanka and the Islands

Though geographically so close to south India, Sri Lanka has a very long tradition of separate cultural evolution, primarily determined by the continuing dominance of Buddhism in the island's culture. The early implantation of the Sinhala language, belonging to the northern Indo-Aryan group and thus unrelated to Tamil and the other Dravidian languages, has also served to underline its separate cultural identity.

Although there are castes in Sri Lanka, the fact that the Sinhalese population is overwhelmingly Buddhist naturally entails an absence of Brahmins, since spiritual authority is vested with the monks. In happier times, when the extreme fertility of the subtropical areas of the 'wet zone' of the island permitted a level of prosperity unusual in South Asia, much was rightly made of the great contribution of pacific Buddhist ideals to the extraordinarily agreeable quality of Sri Lankan life.

More recently, however, demographic pressures and social tensions have come increasingly to the fore, particularly in the increasingly bitter conflict between the Sinhala-speaking Buddhist majority and the Tamils of the northeastern areas, who share their language and much of their culture with their fellow Tamil-speakers in south India.

The other clusters of islands off South Asia each have populations of a very different type. The extraordinarily densely populated Laccadive Islands are inhabited by Malayalam-speaking Muslims. Existing largely by fishing, they can hardly hope for the additional resources available from tourism to their fellow-Muslims in the Maldives, who speak Divehi, closely related to Sinhala.

In the Bay of Bengal, the Nicobar Islands retain their original population, related by race, custom and language to southeast rather than South Asia. The primitive pygmy population of the Andaman Islands, whose devilish skill with the blowpipe so baffled Sherlock Holmes, is now virtually extinct. The islands are now being developed as a settlement area for emigrants from eastern India willing to disregard their depressing fame as the principal penal settlement of the British Raj. *CS*

Further reading
C. von Fürer-Haimendorf, *Tribes of India* (London, 1985)
C. Maloney, *Peoples of South Asia* (New York, 1974)
C. Maloney, Ed., *South Asia: Seven Community Profiles* (New York, 1974)
D. G. Mandelbaum, *Society in India*, 2 vols (Berkeley, 1970)

Demography

Population counts have taken place from time to time in South Asia but the first regular decennial census was carried out in the region by the British in 1881. During the later part of the nineteenth and the early twentieth century, population growth was slow by contemporary standards. It was also erratic chiefly due to recurring mortality crises of which the most frequent were precipitated by famines. Among the worst famines were those in Bombay Presidency and Madras in 1876–78, in the region stretching from the North West Provinces through central India to Bengal and including Madras in 1896–97, and in western and central India in 1899–1900. Severe fluctuations in the death rate were often accompanied by fluctuations in the birth rate as crises disrupted family life. The registration of births and deaths, though established by the late nineteenth century, does not give a full record, but statistical reconstructions reveal that population growth was far from steady, particularly in those provinces of British India which experienced more severe food shortages due to greater climatic irregularities.

From the 1880s, when a Famine Code was introduced by the British, the first 'famine lines' were added to the railway network to assist the movement of food and alleviate mass starvation. In the twentieth century, there was a discernible reduction in famine-induced mortality crises. The only serious famine occurred in wartime when, in 1943, a food shortage in several districts of Bengal was not met by a full implementation of the Famine Code, resulting in some three million deaths. This century, nevertheless, saw the most serious mortality crisis ever, but it was not due to famine. In 1918, the influenza pandemic caused more than seventeen million deaths in the subcontinent. Most areas of the region suffered an actual population decline between 1911 and 1921. In general, the south of the subcontinent fared less badly than the north. The island communities of the Maldives were not spared, but Sri Lanka appeared to suffer relatively less in terms of reduced demographic growth.

Demographic reconstruction and the testimony of the intercensal growth rates indicate that death rates were generally maintained at the high level of over 35 per 1000 in subcontinental India and

Table 1. Growth rates of selected populations of South Asia from 1901 to 1981 (annual percentage average per decade)

	Bangla-desh	India	Maldives	Nepal	Pakistan	Sri Lanka
1901–1911	—	0.6	—	—	—	1.4
1911–1921	—	0.0	−0.2	−0.1	—	0.9
1921–1931	—	1.0	1.3	−0.1	—	1.6
1931–1941	—	1.3	0.2	1.1	—	1.5
1941–1951	—	1.2	0.9	2.5	—	2.8
1951–1961	2.3	2.0	2.5	1.7	2.4	2.7
1961–1971	2.5	2.2	2.6	2.1	3.4	2.3
1971–1981	2.3	2.2	3.3	2.6	3.3	1.7

Note: Censuses were not always taken in the first year of the decade (as in India): these figures therefore refer only approximately to the decade indicated. In the case of Nepal, the earlier figures are thought to be particularly unreliable, and there is no substantial series available for Bhutan. The figures for the Maldives are also largely reconstructed.

around 30 per 1000 in Sri Lanka until the eve of Independence. These figures imply that about one in five infants died before their first birthday, and that those who survived this critical year could expect to live for another forty years. These, of course, represent averages: as is the case today, it was always true that some social groups and residential locations were especially disadvantaged. There is fragmentary evidence from the city of Bombay to indicate that only one in three babies there might have survived their first birthday at the beginning of the twentieth century. Sanitary reports point to appalling environmental conditions emerging in the slums of Calcutta during the same period. Even the British Army stationed in India suffered death rates in excess of 50 per 1000 during the first half of the nineteenth century.

The underlying growth rate of between one half and one percent per annum during the early twentieth century arose from the difference between death rates of about 35 to 40 per 1000 and birth rates of about 40 to 45 per 1000. Birth rates of this order are *not* exceptionally high by world standards: they represent an average of five to six live births to each woman in the course of her life. The fact that women married in their teenage years and that marriage was almost universal meant that low fertility may have been due to long interbirth intervals, possibly resulting from prolonged breast-feeding which is known to reduce the probability of conception.

The second half of the twentieth century started with a dramatic upsurge in growth rates in the region. From 1950 onwards, most countries began to experience growth rates of over two percent per annum. The cause is clear: death rates had begun to fall rapidly while birth rates remained more or less constant, thus widening the gap between the two. The most striking instance of this

Table 2. Estimates of birth rates, death rates, and infant mortality rates around 1980 (per thousand)

	Birth rate	Death rate	Infant mortality rate	Population size (nearest census)
Bangladesh (1980)	41.2	13.1	108	87[a] million
Bhutan (1980–1985)	38.4	18.1	144	1.3 million (estimate)
India (1982)	33.3	11.9	114	684 million
Maldives (1983)	43.1	10.4	77	180 thousand
Nepal (1980–1985)	41.7	18.4	144	15 million
Pakistan (1979)	41.7	9.6	95	85 million
Sri Lanka (1983)	26.2	6.1	34	15 million

[a]The figure of 87 million for the population of Bangladesh was later adjusted by the Government to 90 million.
Note: The figures for Bhutan and Nepal were taken from projections made by the United Nations Population Division. The other estimates are from recent surveys or sample registration schemes in cases where the national vital registration is regarded as incomplete.

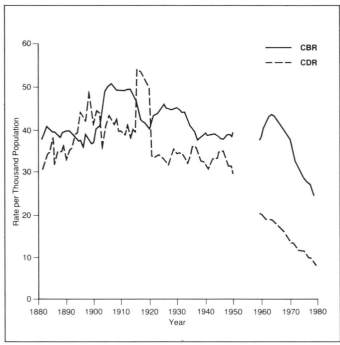

These estimates were reconstructed from vital registration data by T. Dyson, and this figure is reproduced with his kind permission.

Five-year moving averages of adjusted crude birth and death rates in the Indian province of Berar (later part of the state of Maharashtra) 1881–1980.

phenomenon occurred in Sri Lanka. Between 1946 and 1953, the death rate fell from nearly 30 per 1000 to around 13 per 1000. In the space of a few years, malaria, which in the previous decade had accounted for 2000 deaths out of a total of 20,000 deaths a year, had its toll reduced to around 200 by a vigorous mosquito eradication campaign. By 1960, deaths from malaria had reached single figures. But since malaria had accounted for only 10 percent of deaths in the average year, Sri Lanka's falling death rate also indicated a very marked improvement in the general health of the population.

In independent India, the death rate declined from at least 30 per 1000 in the 1940s to just over 20 per 1000 by 1961. The consequent increase in population growth galvanized the government into taking various measures to promote food production in the form of the 'green revolution'. The first health intervention programs were aimed at clearly controllable diseases such as malaria and smallpox. Steps had already been taken against cholera under British rule and progress continued after Independence, but the disease persisted especially in the state of West Bengal. Complete eradication of water-borne diseases requires huge infrastructural outlays, while diseases of poverty and overcrowding, like tuberculosis, require social reform as much as medical intervention for their eradication.

Partly for these reasons, therefore, the precipitous decline in death rates has not continued. In the 1980s, India's death rate is estimated to be still around 12 per 1000, with 100 infants per 1000 dying in their first year of life (in Europe the rate is about 10 per 1000). Fairly similar levels exist in Pakistan. In Bhutan and Nepal, mortality is believed to be higher, with death rates approaching 20 per 1000, while Bangladesh probably lies between these two groups. Contrasts within the region are highlighted if these mortality figures are compared with Sri Lanka's current achievement of a death rate of only 6 per 1000, reflecting an infant mortality rate of only one in thirty. They are also mirrored in the contrasts *within* nations: in India, for instance, the infant mortality rate in the state of Uttar Pradesh is three times that in the state of Kerala.

Until the 1970s, only Sri Lanka had experienced a significant fall in the birth rate. Indeed, it is possible that, for a combination of economic and social reasons relating to post-Independence modernization, birth rates have had a tendency to rise: migrants to urban areas, for instance, became less likely to breast-feed their young. Sri Lanka achieved her quite remarkable fall in the birth rate largely through an increase in the age at which women marry. The 'mean age at first marriage' in the Sri Lankan female population was nearly 24 by 1971 as opposed to between 16 and 19 in Bangladesh, Pakistan and India. Precisely which social or economic factors most influence age at marriage are the subject of current research. One feature which differs substantially from one South Asian country to another is the degree of female education. Census data on basic literacy indicate stark contrasts. In Sri Lanka, for instance, 71 percent of women over ten years old were literate in 1971. In Pakistan and Bangladesh, it was only about 12 percent, while the Indian average was 22 percent although the difference between states was enormous, ranging from over 50 percent in Kerala to under 15 percent in Bihar. By 1981, the position had hardly improved, with 16 percent of women literate in Pakistan, 18 percent literate in Bangladesh and 29 percent in India. The Maldives, however, demonstrate that high female literacy rates alone do not necessarily account for lower birth rates for here birth rates are relatively high.

It was not until the 1970s that serious efforts were made at government level to curb the birth rate through the encouragement of contraception within marriage. In India, the proportion of the national budget devoted to family planning programs increased from less than a half of one percent in the 1960s to 2 percent in the 1970s. The program had a stormy career. The inter-uterine contraceptive device (IUD), promoted during the 1960s, was virtually abandoned in the following decade as a result of unfavorable publicity due to its side-effects. From the mid-1970s, a male and later a female sterilization program was thrust on the population. Misuse of funds for promotional purposes became notorious and illegal coercive measures were sometimes adopted, especially dur-

Family planning is taken very seriously in India; by the 1970s it absorbed two percent of the national budget. India's population grows by over fifteen million a year.

reductions in the 1970s. Both Pakistan and Bangladesh still retain moderately high birth rates. Contraception, although available, has not been as vigorously promoted in these predominantly Muslim countries as in India; similarly, the largely Muslim Maldives have only recently permitted the distribution of contraceptives. Interpreting the social determinants of fertility decline is complex. What little evidence there is would suggest that economically better-off families have been the first to limit their fertility even in countries such as Pakistan and Bangladesh where there is little change in the overall birth rate. But in India, both urban and rural poor are beginning to do the same since children are no longer considered the economic asset that they were in the past.

It is frequently argued that the status of women is a crucial consideration in explaining both fertility and mortality decline. In most parts of South Asia today, men and women have approximately the same life expectation (in the UK and the USA women live longer than men), whereas in the region's recent demographic past men generally used to outlive women. Today, even in Sri Lanka, death rates are still higher for girls than for boys from the age of about six months until their fifth birthday. In India, the difference persists until the age of 35. This phenomenon is thought to reflect the diminished care and respect received by girls in local cultures. Again there are intraregional variations. The southern and eastern states of India are in many ways culturally distinct from other parts of the country and this is reflected in higher survival rates for women. Higher male mortality after the age of 35 may be a reflection of their easier access to westernized aspects of life. With urbanization, a richer diet, tobacco and alcohol have come the circulatory and respiratory diseases that are increasingly responsible for adult male mortality among the poor as well as the rich in the cities.

The rapid growth in South Asian populations that occurred as death rates plunged gave rise to new patterns in the age distributions of the populations. For the first time, the proportion of population below the age of fifteen reached 40 percent; in Britain and the USA, the proportion is nearer to 20 percent. The increase in this proportion placed an added burden on the efforts of national governments to educate their young. It also meant that the population was exceptionally well-stocked with potential mothers, threatening further population increase. Finally, it implied a more rapid supply of potential labor force to work the land at a time when landlessness was increasing, as much an economic as a demographic problem.

For most South Asian countries, the peak in the proportion of youth in their populations occurred in the 1970s. India and Sri Lanka now have less than 40 percent of their populations in the under-fifteen age group. Their falling birth rates can also be seen from the undercutting of their 'age-pyramids', implying fewer children born in the last five years than ten years ago. Bangladesh

ing the suspension of democratic rule in India during the Emergency of 1975–77. Indeed, in some Indian states, the conduct of the program probably lost the Congress Party the 1977 elections. All the same, the adoption of contraception has continued to increase in the early 1980s, to the extent that about 24 percent of couples were reported to be practising birth control by 1982, and India's birth rate has dropped significantly below the 40 to 45 per thousand mark. Contrasts in the rate of decline between individual Indian states are again substantial: Kerala has witnessed a considerable fertility decline through increased contraception and delayed marriage, while Bihar and Uttar Pradesh experienced only marginal

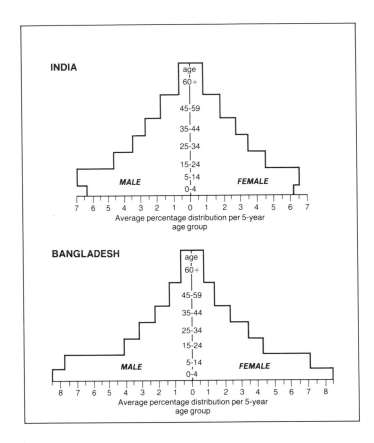

Age pyramids for India and Bangladesh in 1981.

Further reading
R. H. Cassen, *India: Population, Economy, Society* (London and Basingstoke, 1978)
T. Dyson, Ed., *India's Historical Demography: Studies in Famine, Disease, and Society* (London, 1988)
T. Dyson and N. Crook, Eds, *India's Demography: Essays on the Contemporary Population* (New Delhi, 1984)

Urbanization

Recent census figures reveal that no South Asian nation registers more than 28.3 percent of its population as urban, and the estimated regional average is only 23.8 percent (see Table 3). Nevertheless given the size of the national population bases, these proportions represent a very large number of town and city dwellers. India vividly illustrates this phenomenon. In 1981 it had 214 cities or urban areas with 100,000 or more inhabitants, including the well-known metropoli: Calcutta (9,165,650), Bombay (8,227,332), Delhi/New Delhi (5,985,571) and Madras (4,276,635). The 1981 Indian census enumerated 159,727,357 residents in all cities and towns, which total constitutes the fourth highest national urban population in the world, although it represents only 23.3 percent of India's total population. By comparison, the corresponding urban shares of national populations for the UK, USA and Japan were 78.9 percent, 68.9 percent and 68.1 percent, respectively. Statistical analysis of historical patterns of South Asian urbanization suffers from a lack of reliable census materials for pre-modern times. In territories under British colonial rule modern census coverage was uneven and no rigorous definition of 'urban' was employed. From 1901 through 1951 Indian censuses defined as a 'town' all municipalities regardless of population, all civil lines not within municipal limits, and any other place permanently inhabited by 5000 or

and Pakistan are closer to their maximum proportion of youth, as are almost certainly Nepal, Bhutan and the Maldives. All are likely to remain so as long as mortality has scope for further fall while fertility is still high. With large numbers of potential mothers in the population, even vigorous future birth control programs cannot prevent a large number of children being born albeit fewer to each mother. Taking this consideration into account, a future population of well over a billion is inevitable for India alone and at least a billion and a half is likely for the region as a whole before the population stabilizes at zero growth. The absolute size of India's population needs to be emphasized. The 1981 census placed it at 684 million. During the 1980s, India has been adding over 15 million a year to the global total, which is more in absolute number than any other nation including China. The larger of her neighbors both have populations which are verging on 100 million. The demographic history of South Asia, therefore, indicates resilience and variety. It is probable that these qualities will see its populations through to a new growth equilibrium, but the transition will not be an easy one.

NC

Table 3. Urban populations and proportions by state

Country	Year	Total pop.	Urban pop.	Urban %
Bangladesh	1981	87,119,965	13,227,625	15.2
Bhutan	1982	1,162,000	32,000	2.8
India	1981	685,184,692	159,727,357	23.3
Maldives	1977	142,832	29,522	20.7
Nepal	1981	15,022,829	956,721	6.4
Pakistan	1981	84,253,644	23,841,471	28.3
Sri Lanka	1981	14,848,364	3,194,479	21.5
Totals		887,734,358	201,009,175	23.8

Source: United Nations *Demographic Year Book, 1984* p. 175ff. (New York, 1986). Data on Bhutan are based on World Bank, *Bhutan: Development in a Himalayan Kingdom* pp. 137–8 (Washington, 1984). Bhutan urban population calculated from estimated population of towns with at least 5,000 residents.

more persons. Subsequently the Indian census defined as 'urban' all places with municipal corporations, town committees or cantonment boards, and all places having 5000 or more inhabitants with a density of not less than 1000 persons per square mile, 'pronounced urban characteristics' and at least 75 percent of the adult male population employed in pursuits other than agriculture.

This technical definition assumes that urbanization is significant as a process of social and economic transformation in South Asia, as it is in other parts of the world. In the West, along with population aggregation, city growth has been associated with forces of dynamism, modernity and change. Although by no means all of South Asia's urban citizens are participants in the dynamic culture of new ideas and institutions, which tend to remain the preserve of relatively small segments of the population, nevertheless, as urban economic life is increasingly dominated by commerce and industry, South Asian cities have become arenas of innovation and diversity.

South Asian Urban Patterns

Cities and towns of South Asia do not present a uniform picture to the observer. The lush palm-fringed settings of Cochin or Colombo offer a stark contrast to the desert-like surroundings of Jaisalmer or Quetta. The quiet and slow pace of life in a small district town like Karwar in Karnataka is a polar opposite to the bustling congestion of Chandni Chauk in Old Delhi. Recognizing the great diversities of South Asian urban landscapes, it is possible to identify a traditional urban style that characterizes towns and cities which date from pre-modern times. Traditional concerns for security promoted dense settlement patterns and also suited pre-modern transport technologies. Within the traditional urban pattern main roads are often narrow, without footpaths, and often encroached upon by shopkeepers or artisans, while still narrower and crooked side lanes may not be even passable by wheeled vehicles. Apart from lanes and interior court yards, the ground is usually completely covered by

Old and new housing in Bombay.

structures. Densities are limited primarily by the absence of buildings of more than two storeys. Where higher structures exist, as in some neighborhoods of Calcutta and Bombay, as many as 400,000 people per square mile have been recorded. In land use no clear distinction exists between residential, commercial and industrial activities although there may be clustering or segregation of residence by ethnic population and of trade by the particular commodity produced or sold. Until very recently, well-to-do Indians resided in the centers of town while the lower socio-economic classes including 'untouchables' resided in poorer dwellings on the periphery.

During the nineteenth century British rule, either direct or indirect, contributed innovative features to the indigenous morphology such as municipality offices, central market and clock tower. However, the more prominent colonial urban features were the 'cantonments' or 'civil lines', adjacent urban areas, built on a European plan with broad streets and open spaces and separation of residences and businesses. In the era of British rule these areas were the preserve of Europeans reflecting a post-1857 concern for civil security against both rebellion and disease. Today they are occupied by Indian members of business, professional and administrative classes. The British quest for cool retreats from the heat and dust of the plains led to the development of another colonial urban form, the 'hill stations', mountain resort towns in which were recreated many aspects of 'home'. An extension of foreign urban design may be seen also in the spacious symmetry of the vistas, broad roads and lawns of the modern planned cities of New Delhi, Chandigarh and Islamabad. However, such planned cities reflect resource investments which cannot be repeated often in South Asian economies. Most areas of new urban growth in South Asia today reflect compromises between modern attempts at planning or enforcing standards and the seemingly inexorable demands of a vast and growing population for rapid exploitation of urban land.

Colonial urbanization

The growth of cities in the colonial era represented the creation of new arenas of activity and opportunity in administration, commerce and, eventually, industry. The pre-modern cities of the subcontinent have been interpreted by scholars to have been particularly dependent upon political military functions or religious activities. As such, capital cities' fortunes could be hostage to shifting needs of rulers, while religio-cultural cities functioned as centers for authoritative preservation of the traditional order. While these generalizations overstate the static or insecure nature of pre-modern South Asian urbanism, they serve to highlight what are thought to be the main forces behind colonial urbanization. Commencing with the rimland ports of Madras, Bombay and Calcutta, the English East India Company's priorities of promoting commerce meant that

in these new cities security was guaranteed for mercantile interests and a growing diversity of occupational activities. The new cities, requiring merchants, artisans and subordinate administrators, recruited talented individuals from older centers and the countryside. New institutional bases for economic, intellectual and political participation and innovation created opportunities for individuals and enabled emergence of new interest groups which were not defined solely by traditional ascriptive labels of caste or community.

While some cities grew, altered political conditions reduced the fortunes and size of other previously important places. Old political and trading centers, such as Murshidabad and Pune, Thatta, Dhaka and Surat, underwent a decline or stagnation of population and activity. Some experienced renewed growth in the nineteenth century as new networks of communication, transportation and administration developed under British rule; others, passed by the new railroads or possessing harbors that could not accommodate deep draft steamships, slipped back into the status of large villages.

The principal difficulty of many approaches to urban dynamism, whether those of the British Indian censuses or those of modern scholarship, is that they appear to assume that the traditional city was equated with a pre-modern, pre-industrial stage of technology, whereas the modern colonial city belonged to a modern, industrial stage. In fact, industrialization was extremely limited in nineteenth century India. Towns and cities did grow in number and size, yet this appears to have been due less to industrialization and more to shifts which occurred in South Asia's demography and political economy.

In spite of periodic famines and epidemics, rural birth rates rose as those of mortality declined. The gradual growth of commercial and administrative centers and limited industrialization generated rural–urban migration which was reinforced by rural economic insecurity. One facet of this pattern was a male dominant urban sex ratio, which persists. (In 1961 India's urban population contained on average 123 men to every 100 women, with still higher proportions in larger cities.) Most poor rural migrants came only in quest of employment with the expectation that they would return to the countryside. Anxious to maximize income, they accepted substandard living conditions in unsanitary settings which often were hotbeds of disease. The pace of urbanization was thereby checked and in fact, under the impact of a series of plague epidemics the percentage of urban population actually declined in the 1901–11 decade (see Table 4).

It was precisely the threat of plague and other epidemic diseases which required massive investments of infrastructure, water, lighting, sewers and roads in the cities of British India. These costly items were to be funded by local taxation, and hence the institutions of municipal self-government were gradually introduced. The quest

The forty largest cities in South Asia in 1981.

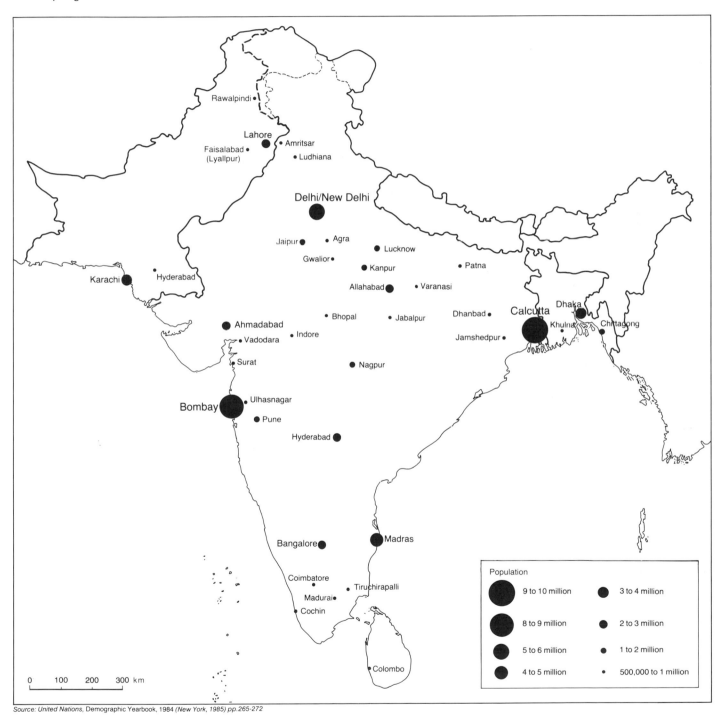

Population

9 to 10 million   3 to 4 million

8 to 9 million   2 to 3 million

5 to 6 million   1 to 2 million

4 to 5 million   500,000 to 1 million

Source: United Nations, Demographic Yearbook, 1984 (New York, 1985) pp.265-272

Table 4. Percentage of population classified urban, 1881–1981

Census year	Bangladesh[a]	India	Nepal	Pakistan	Sri Lanka
1881	n.a.	9.3	n.a.	n.a.	n.a.
1891	n.a.	9.4	n.a.	n.a.	n.a.
1901	n.a.	10.0	n.a.	n.a.	11.6
1911	n.a.	9.4	n.a.	n.a.	13.2
1921	n.a.	10.2	n.a.	n.a.	14.2
1931	n.a.	11.1	n.a.	n.a.	14.6
1941	n.a.	12.8	n.a.	n.a.	14.8
1951	n.a.	17.3	n.a.	10.4	14.9
1961	n.a.	18.0	2.8	13.1	18.0
1971[b]	8.8[b]	19.9	4.0	25.5[b]	22.4
1981	15.2	23.3	6.4	28.3	21.5

(No percentages are reported for Bhutan and the Maldives due to lack of statistical series)
Sources: Kingsley Davis *Population of India and Pakistan* p. 127 (Princeton, N.J., 1951), J. Schwartzberg *A Historical Atlas of South Asia* pp. 113–14 (Chicago, 1978) for post 1941 figures. (Some scholars have offered variant readings of the Indian population figures; however, these appear to reflect reworking of pre-1947 census data to exclude territories no longer within India after 1947.) Pre-1981 Indian figures exclude Sikkim.
[a]For 1881–1941, figures for territories now comprising Bangladesh and Pakistan are subsumed under the India heading. Pakistan figures for 1951–61 include territories which were subsequently incorporated in Bangladesh.
[b]Because of the Bangladesh war in 1971, figures given here are based on general census operations carried out in Pakistan in 1972 and in Bangladesh in 1974, cf. United Nations *Demographic Yearbook 1975* pp. 173–75 (New York, 1976).

for urban improvement introduced new media of information, new impingements of authority, new taxes, and hence, politics. The British raj regarded urban India and its inhabitants as unpleasant problems. Colonial civil servants officials regarded appointments in municipal government to be hardship posts, preferring postings in the countryside, dealing with 'real Indians', that is a peasantry who did not presume to question their benevolent rulers. Education and literacy were urban arts. Cities and towns became seedbeds of religious reform movements and political consciousness. Urban delegates predominated in the early meetings of the Indian National Congress. Calcutta and Pune became centers of militant nationalism. Municipalities served as the classrooms of future nationalist politicians and provided new arenas for the political aspirations of diverse interest groups. Where taxation policy could divide the propertied from non-propertied voters, a proposal to ban cow slaughter or give a particular language official recognition could promote inter-religious or ethnic tensions. Towns and cities became a stage for new communal politics, often extending into the sphere of public violence. Indeed, this pattern continues in contemporary South Asia as may be seen in modern ethnic turmoil in such diverse cities as Peshawar, Karachi, Dhaka, Ahmadabad, Bombay, Jaffna and Colombo.

Although India's freedom struggle grew from urban roots, the later glorification of village life by Gandhi promoted the view of cities as parasitic, dehumanizing institutions. This anti-urban ideology did nothing to hinder urban migration, but probably has predisposed state and central governments to ignore claims of cities to a fair share of government talents and investments. The issue of allocating scarce development resources to cities, when the countryside is poor except in voters, has had profound implications for the daunting social-economic problems faced by modern South Asian cities.

Contemporary urban patterns

World War II and partition increased and redistributed urban populations in India and Pakistan. Karachi, Bombay, Delhi and Calcutta were swamped by refugees. New refugee camps grew into towns and cities. Ulhasnagar outside Bombay which began in 1947 as a collection of tents and shacks in a muddy field, is today a congested city of well over 600,000 inhabitants. Many of South Asia's large urban centers have undergone rapid, mostly unplanned growth in the past half century (see Table 5).

Modern capital cities with their cosmopolitan élite populations present contrasting models of planning, administration, maintenance and health, but non-élite neighborhoods suffer neglect as surely as do the rural towns and cities. Control of growth and overcrowding involves a contradiction between abstract principles of planning and concrete priorities of political management and vote mobilization.

Over much of this century the largest cities have grown at the highest rates. Cities of several million people like Calcutta or Bombay can grow simply by natural increase, yet in the absence of adequate economic opportunity in the countryside migration continues. The city economies are in fact underindustrialized. Labor surplus yields underemployment and the informal sectors of the economy predominate. South Asian cities do not appear able to

Table 5. Capital cities of South Asian states

Country	Capital city	Population
Bangladesh	Dhaka	3,458,602
Bhutan	Thimphu	8,922
India	Delhi	5,585,971
Maldives	Malé	29,522
Nepal	Kathmandu	235,160
Pakistan	Islamabad[a]	77,318
Sri Lanka	Colombo	623,000

Source: United Nations *Demographic Yearbook, 1984* pp. 265–72 (New York, 1985).
[a]Pakistan's new capital after 1963 at Islamabad is adjacent to the urban center of Rawalpindi, pop. 615,392, which served as provisional capital in 1961–63. Before 1961 Karachi was the capital and many government agencies shifted to the new capital only after many years.

Slums outside the Ritz Hotel, Ahmadabad. Between twenty and thirty-five percent of the population of South Asia's major cities live in slums.

generate revenue surpluses to be spent on urban overheads. The overloaded infrastructures of older cities show signs of crumbling. In 'smaller' cities like Bhopal no real infrastructure of urban amenities ever existed for the vast immigrant population. Slums, unauthorized hutment areas, deforestation arising from the quest for cooking fuel, inadequate water supply and nonexistent sewers provide a grim alternative to South Asian rural poverty. Still, at least one thousand people migrate into Bombay every day. For most South Asian urban slum dwellers, the cities, however appalling the conditions, are places of hope and not despair.

FFC

Further reading

R. Bala, *Trends in Urbanisation in India, 1901–1981* (Jaipur, 1986)

A. Bose, *India's Urbanization, 1901–2001* (New Delhi, 1980)

K. Davis, *The Population of India and Pakistan* (Princeton, N.J., 1951)

G. Fox, Ed., *Urban India: Society, Space and Image* (Durham, N. C., 1970)

A. D. King, *Colonial Urban Development: Culture, Social Power and Environment* (London, 1976)

R. Turner, Ed., *India's Urban Future* (Berkeley, 1962)

Internal migration

The common perception of internal migration in South Asia in terms of city-ward migration of adult males is partly due to the lack of adequate data on internal migration. In the absence of details regarding rural/urban residence prior to migration, all that could be obtained from the Censuses was the quantum of *total* migration within the country. Table 6 based on the substantially improved Census of India data of 1961 and 1981 brings out the dominance of rural to rural migration. We shall, therefore, give a greater weightage to this form of migration without denying the importance of increasingly rapid urbanization in recent decades and the crucial role of rural to urban migration in triggering off this process.

In the colonial period, there was considerable discussion about the unique phenomenon of the 'marriage migration' of females caused by the practice of village exogamy in various parts of the subcontinent. Detailed Census data since 1961 confirm the persistence of this deeprooted phenomenon.

It has been pointed out that a distinctive feature of internal migration in the subcontinent is the 'comparative immobility' of the population. On the basis of Census data relating to place of birth and place of enumeration, a statistical measure of immobility can be made. In 1901, only 3.3 percent of the total population of India was enumerated outside the state or province of birth. In 1911, the figure was 3.6 percent, in 1921 3.7 percent and in 1931 it was again 3.6 percent. The 1951 Census of post-Partition India presented data on internal migration, but only for the new state of India (excluding Pakistan). Indian Censuses since then confirm the contention that, if the unit of observation is the state/province, there is considerable immobility of the Indian population. Moreover, the index of immobility has remained fairly constant. So in 1951 only 3 percent of the total population was enumerated outside the state/province of birth, in 1961 3.3 percent, in 1971 3.4 percent, and in 1981 3.6 percent. On the other hand, if persons born outside the place of enumeration are considered as migrants, a very different picture of migration emerges. Considered in this way, the percentage of migrants to total population in 1961 is 30.7 percent and not 3.3 percent, and therefore mobility in India is quite considerable: about one-third of the population was enumerated outside its place of birth.

Five main factors have usually been proposed as contributing to this immobility across state/province boundaries: predominance of agriculture, the caste system which in suppressing social mobility suppressed geographical mobility, early marriage and the joint family, diversity of language and culture, and lack of education.

On the basis of data now available it can be asserted with some confidence that the main factor behind the immobility of the

Table 6: Migration streams in India, 1961 and 1981

	1961			1981		
	Total (percent of migrants)	**Males**	**Females**	**Total** (percent of migrants)	**Males**	**Females**
1. *Short-distance* (Within the district)	67.8	54.4	73.8	61.8	49.4	66.9
Rural to rural	57.6	40.1	65.5	49.0	32.0	56.1
Urban to rural	2.0	2.3	1.8	3.1	3.4	3.0
Rural to urban	6.1	9.0	4.8	7.2	10.5	5.7
Urban to urban	2.1	3.0	1.7	2.5	3.5	2.1
2. *Medium-distance* (Within the State)	21.4	26.8	19.0	26.0	30.9	24.1
Rural to rural	12.1	11.3	12.4	12.7	10.1	13.9
Urban to rural	1.1	1.5	1.0	2.0	2.4	1.9
Rural to urban	4.9	8.8	3.2	6.2	10.7	4.3
Urban to urban	3.3	5.2	2.4	5.1	7.7	4.0
3. *Long-distance* (Between States)	10.8	18.8	7.2	12.2	19.7	9.0
Rural to rural	4.0	5.3	3.4	3.6	4.1	3.4
Urban to rural	0.5	0.8	0.4	0.9	1.2	0.7
Rural to urban	3.6	7.8	1.7	4.1	8.3	2.4
Urban to urban	2.7	4.9	1.7	3.6	6.1	2.5
Total	100.0	100.0	100.0	100.0	100.0	100.0

Source: Computed from Census of India, 1961 and 1981.

population of this region is the lack of economic growth and the comparative stagnation of the economy. The predominance of agriculture in the colonial era meant, in fact, perpetuation of subsistence agriculture. In the 1960s, however, the 'green revolution' in the Panjab (Pakistan) and the Panjab, Haryana and western Uttar Pradesh (India) generated considerable migration of labor to the agriculturally prosperous areas from the depressed ones. Neither the innate love of home nor the caste system, that figured in earlier explanations, could hold back the poor from migrating from eastern Uttar Pradesh to the Panjab in India or from Sind to the Panjab in Pakistan: wage rates in agriculture were never so good and the illiterate migrant relying on family, caste and village networks had access to a unique oral information system regarding the scope for better living conditions in distant places within the country. Remittances home not only meant an improvement on their normal subsistence household economy but brought hope and cheer about future prospects of migration and employment. There is here a close parallel between internal and international migration. The migrations of skilled and semi-skilled labor from the subcontinent to the UK in the 1960s and the Gulf countries in the 1970s are significant developments in international migration but its mechanics are in no way dissimilar to the process of internal migration in the subcontinent. Only the wages offered are much higher and the hopes and aspirations of the potential migrants are heightened by the much better economic situation in the developed or oilrich countries.

Even during the colonial era, the prime centers attracting internal migration were industrial, commercial and port cities (Bombay, Calcutta, Madras) apart from industrial cities (Kanpur, Ahmadabad). Tea plantations in northern Assam and Bengal attracted labor from central India, while in Assam there was an unending migration of agriculturalists from Bengal, particularly from Mymensingh district which now forms part of Bangladesh. The influx of these migrants, who are now classified as international migrants, has caused considerable social and political tension.

It has been argued on the basis of the social and political consequences of internal migration to Assam that the process of modernization, by providing incentives and opportunities for mobility, creates the conditions for increasing internal migration and so the modernization process nurtures the growth of ethnic identification and ethnic cohesion but may also render these two processes antagonistic. Thus, social, cultural and political conflicts are often caused by demographic and economic factors.

But interestingly enough, the reverse of this phenomenon is also true. The partition of India was the culmination of a political process and it caused a tremendous movement of people between India and Pakistan, a movement marked by untold misery and violence, death and destruction. Such migration (which would have been termed internal before partition) became at once international, and was, in fact, one of the greatest such movements in the history of the world. In spite of its short duration, it had long-term consequences for the economy and society of India, Pakistan and Bangladesh. About 15 million people moved across the borders: Hindus and Sikhs came to India from Pakistan (both west and east) and Muslims from India went to Pakistan (both west and east). In 1951, 7.3 million refugees were enumerated in India (4.7 million from west Pakistan and 2.6 million from east Pakistan). The 1951 Census of Pakistan enumerates 7.2 million *muhajirs* (refugees) from India (5.8 million from northwest India, 0.7 million from eastern India and 0.7 million from other parts of India).

The figures from migration of refugees between India and Pakistan cancel each other out. This fact, however, gives a highly misleading picture of the impact of such migration. Take, for instance, the impact of refugee migration on urbanization. According to the 1981 Census of India, 54 percent of the refugees from Pakistan settled down in the urban areas of India: as only 17.3 percent of India's population was urban in 1951 this was a disproportionate share of refugees in urban areas. Thus, Delhi (including New Delhi) became a Panjabi city and Calcutta engulfed the culture of Dhaka in east Pakistan (now Bangladesh). In Pakistan in 1951 roughly 25 percent of refugees from India were enumerated as absorbed in urban areas. Karachi city alone absorbed 616,906 refugees. It is worth noting that the total population of Karachi in 1941 was only 435,887.

The economic impact of the migration of refugees to cities severely strained the utterly inadequate infrastructure of even the biggest cities like Calcutta, Bombay and Delhi. For example, the population of south Dum Dum, a constituent town of the Calcutta agglomeration grew by 138 percent during 1941–51: in the same period Greater Bombay's population increased by 76 percent and Delhi's by 107 percent. No city in India, Pakistan or Bangladesh had the physical and economic infrastructure to cope with the new demands made by displaced persons for residential land, housing, water supply, sewerage and transport. And yet the problem had to be solved on a war-footing as millions of refugees were pouring into the cities. New 'refugee colonies' sprang up in almost all cities affected by partition.

Apart from these efforts to create new townships, the ambitious Dandakarnya Project was taken up in India to resettle displaced persons from east Pakistan. An area of 80,000 square kilometers in the districts of Koraput and Kalanandi (Orissa) and Bastar (Madhya Pradesh) was carved out for agricultural development and to resettle about 20,000 displaced families every year. Unfortunately, ineffective planning and administration contributed to the virtual failure of this project. About 20,000 families were rehabilitated during the period 1969–79.

A settlement project in the Andaman and Nicobar Islands was far more successful than the Dandakarnya Project. Curiously enough, a penal settlement was established by the British in the Andaman

A rickshawallah does a school run in Patna. Rickshawallahs are often migrants from country to city in search of work.

Islands in 1858 but was closed in 1923. In 1956, the Islands were constituted a 'union territory' administered by the Central Government. In order to develop the resources of the Islands, it was necessary to encourage people to migrate there. The India's First Five Year Plan (1951–56) authorized clearance of 20,000 acres of land for settling 4000 agricultural families. Over the years, a threat to the ecology of these islands emerged and a ban was imposed on the cutting down of forests for the settlement of migrants. The latest development in this regard is the preparation of comprehensive development plans for the islands, bearing in mind demographic, economic, social and ecological factors.

In the colonial era the British adopted a policy of colonization of newly irrigated areas in order to relieve the pressure of population on land and also to enhance sources of revenue, surplus food and exportable crops. There were three major settlements in what is now the Panjab province of Pakistan, namely Lyallpur Colony (1892), Shahpur Colony (1902) and Montgomery Colony (1913). These colonies covered approximately 6 million acres of irrigated land; another 4 million were colonized in the 1930s. These areas soon became flourishing agricultural regions. But the period of rapid agricultural growth and buoyant expectations in the canal colony districts proved short-lived. The depression years of the 1930s brought falling revenues, increased indebtedness and land transfers.

The most recent experience of resettlement of agricultural population in rural areas has been in the *terai* (swamp land) region on the foothills of the Himalayas bordering Nepal. Here, after Independence, the government of Uttar Pradesh (India) eradicated malaria, settled hardworking Panjabi (mostly Sikh) migrants and developed the virgin land. Today the terai region is one of the most agriculturally prosperous regions; mosquitoes, tigers and bandits have been contained by the new settlers. However, the very success of this project, based on free enterprise backed by the Government, has given rise to social and ethnic tensions which have ominous potential as in generating acute conflicts between the so-called 'sons of the soil' and the 'outsiders'.

In contrast to the situation in India, Pakistan and Bangladesh, Sri Lanka's small size and comparatively good road and rail transport network has generated considerable rural–urban mobility without rural–urban migration. The strain on the urban infrastructure, therefore, is not as severe in Sri Lanka as it is in the other countries of the region. However, the very lopsided distribution of permanent migrants from India has in recent years led to serious ethnic conflicts which threaten the stability of the country.

In regard to rural settlement schemes in Sri Lanka, the transfer of population from the Wet Zone to the Dry Zone districts should be noted. Current thinking is that the economic benefits of these schemes have not been commensurate with the costs concerned. Moreover, while schemes of land settlement have increased population mobility, village expansion schemes have reduced it. Since most village expansion schemes have been in the Wet Zone, they have induced a large number of people to stay in their villages instead of drifting to the cities or to the major settlement schemes.

As in India and Pakistan, the urban population of Bangladesh has increased very rapidly. According to the 1981 Census, the urban population increased by 401 percent during 1961–81. In a sample survey in rural areas of Matlab *thana* in Comilla District, it was found that at least two-thirds of the rural migrants moved to urban areas. The consequences of such migration seem grim. The enormous gap between the needs and available services in the urban areas coupled with the rising expectations of the people suggest that individual and social tensions in the urban areas of Bangladesh can only grow.

In general, therefore, internal migration in the subcontinent has the potential to contribute to balanced regional development, economic growth and social change, but at the same time it also has the potential to increase social tension, conflict and instability. At the moment it appears that the social and political consequences of internal migration are more significant than the demographic and economic forces which underlie them.

ABo

Further reading

A. Bose, *India's Urbanization, 1901–2001* (New Delhi, 1980)

K. Davis, *The Population of India and Pakistan*, (Princeton, N. J. 1951)

A. S. Oberoi, Ed., *State Policies and Internal Migration* (New York, 1983)

M. Weiner, *Sons of the Soil – Migration and Ethnic Conflict in India* (Delhi, 1978)

External migration

Mass emigration from the subcontinent came after British power was consolidated in the Indian Ocean area. This was mainly of contract laborers under the indenture system. They provided the workforce for the sugar, coffee, tea and rubber plantations created to supply Europe with primary tropical products.

With the abolition of slavery throughout the British Empire in 1833, the former slaves departed from the scene of their bondage and the planters were left with an acute labor shortage. They looked to the teeming millions of India. After reports of gross ill treatment and exploitation, the Government of India laid down codes of practice in 1837 and 1839. Recruitment of the 'coolies' (as they were invariably called) had to be reviewed by district magistrates; they were assembled in government-supervised holding centers and transported to the colonies in special ships. The laborers signed on for a five year term, when they were entitled to a free return passage. The main demand was for male workers but the regulations stipulated that for every one hundred males, forty females had to be engaged: in practice, this was widely evaded.

The planters, accustomed to a slave workforce, endeavored to reduce the condition of the indentured people as near to slavery as was possible. The interests of the workers were supposedly in the care of a 'Protector of Immigrants', but this official was locally appointed and, with some exceptions, bowed to planter pressures. Despite adverse conditions, however, an increasing proportion of the indentured workers chose to remain in the plantation colonies when their five years of bondage ended. Those who attracted notice were promoted as foremen, called sirdars or, following slave custom, drivers. For many years, there were few alternatives to employment on the plantations but gradually some achieved a small degree of independence. They acquired smallholdings or set up as carters and hauliers. Some opened shops for estate workers; often rum shops for heavy drinking became the main outlet for men confined to the squalid 'lines' on the estates.

The natural increase of the Indian population was slow owing to the shortage of women and heavy mortality from disease, yet they steadily increased. In Mauritius, the largest recipient of Indian

Large numbers of Indians migrated throughout the world in the nineteenth and early twentieth centuries to work in plantations and industries owned by Europeans. Here a tea planter in Ceylon (Sri Lanka) stands surrounded by his coolies.

labor, they formed two-thirds of the island population by 1880. In British Guyana also, the numbers of Indian descent gradually overtook those of African origin; while in Trinidad, a society with many ethnic elements, they formed the largest minority. Indentured migration to Fiji began relatively late in 1879 but by 1920 they were overtaking the ethnic Fijians in numbers. The system was also applied to Dutch Surinam, where Indians provided almost all estate labor, to French Réunion, to Jamaica, to the smaller Caribbean islands and to French Martinique and Guadeloupe.

Three territories of great importance for Indian labor migration,

Sri Lanka, Malaya and Burma, made little use of indenture because all were close enough to do without elaborate arrangements. Migration to Sri Lanka before the days of steam was mainly across the narrow Palk strait, while the voyage to Rangoon or Penang was brief and increasingly cheap. Work gangs were enlisted by contractors (*kanganis*), who financed the emigrating party and then made deductions from their wages. In Sri Lanka and Malaya, they were organized on European estates. In Burma, they were employed as harvest gangs cutting paddy and as an urban lumpenproletariat working in the Rangoon docks and the city's rice mills and public utilities such as refuse disposal. The traditional Indian pattern of seasonal labor, followed by periodic reunions with their families at home, long continued.

Another variation on the pattern evolved in East Africa. To build the Uganda railway, 32,000 indentured workers were recruited in northern India, mainly in the Panjab. Many died during the operation; others returned but a third or more stayed on. Their penetration of the interior encouraged others to follow. Many of the railway staff were Indians, but more important was the spread of petty traders (*duka-wallas*) up-country. They supplied carpenters, other tradesmen and increasingly clerks and technicians within the infrastructure of administration and business.

Elsewhere the demands of colonial governments and European business attracted Indians other than laborers. The annexation of Upper Burma in 1886 was fiercely resisted and the task of pacification was taken over from the regular army by military police, specially raised in India and initially numbering 32,000. Their strength was gradually reduced, yet about 1930 was still 11,000. A special Indian artillery force was raised to serve in Singapore and Hong Kong while the original nucleus of the King's African Rifles were Indians. In Burma and Malaya, most of the railway and postal staff were Indians. A feature peculiar to Malaya was the engagement of Jaffna Tamils as government clerks, and eventually as doctors and other professionals.

The Bhojpuris, inhabiting the over-crowded western districts of Bihar and the area around Benares provided the largest source of indentured labor: they formed the bulk of the emigrants to Mauritius, the Caribbean and Fiji. Sri Lanka and Malaya were geographically nearest to south India and their estate labor was drawn from the densely populated Tamil areas, inland and south of Madras. South Africa and Réunion drew heavily on the Tamils, who also went to Burma though many laborers were from the coastal districts of Orissa. Burma's military police consisted of Panjabis with some Gurkhas. The adventurous Panjabis, especially Sikhs, penetrated many lands: some managed to get into North America with its bar on Asian immigration and helped to build the railways and fell trees in the Canadian West. The rural areas around Ahmadabad were closely linked with East Africa; among them the caste called Patel, which produced shrewd business men.

Twentieth-century emigration

The 'Plural Society' was a familiar feature of the colonial structure but the tensions it created were masked until the Whites were confronted by political demands from non-Whites. The first occurred in South Africa where Indians had arrived as indentured workers on the Natal sugar estates. The 'coolies' were closely followed by others termed 'Passenger Indians', merchants, shopkeepers and a few professional people, among them Gandhi, the

'coolie lawyer'. Indian grievances in the Afrikaner republics were cited by Lord Lansdowne as one of the main Boer 'misdeeds'. Yet it was mistreatment in Natal, in particular refusal to recognize Indian marriages as valid, which led Gandhi to launch his first *satyagraha* campaign. Partly in consequence, indentured immigration to Natal was terminated in 1911. Indenture was also ended in Malaya in 1909 mainly because it was unnecessary. A report on Fiji by C. F. Andrews, commissioned by the Indian National Congress, fueled active protest in India. After a long campaign, indenture was totally abolished on January 2, 1920. Shortly afterwards, the leaders of the Kenya Indian community presented a demand for voting rights on a common roll with the Whites. Their claim was strenuously resisted but, as a result, any move towards responsible government for the Kenya Whites was checked.

With the onset of the world depression in 1930, Indians in Burma were made to feel the hostility of the Burmese. They were resented first because the coolies with their squalid living conditions undercut the local 'sons of the soil', and secondly because the Chettiyars, the banking caste from Madras, dominated the apparatus of rural credit. When Burmese peasants did not repay their debts in the slump, their fields were seized. Burmese feeling culminated in an anti-Indian pogrom in May 1930: 7000 became homeless and 33,000 were frightened into returning to India. For economic reasons, similar departures took place in Malaya (193,000 left between 1930 and 1938) and in Sri Lanka (420,000 left between 1930 and 1935). There, the granting of universal suffrage in 1931 provoked the first stirring of Sinhalese nationalism and demands that the estate Indians be denied the vote.

More anti-Indian riots occurred in urban Burma in 1938: then in 1942 disaster overtook the community with the Japanese invasion. The Burma Indians, nervous of a chauvinistic backlash, trekked out to India, a country many had never seen. In 1941, the total population numbered 16,823,798 of whom over a million were Indians. Half of them fled, although many, variously calculated between 10,000 and 100,000, never reached India. In Malaya, only about 4500 were evacuated; the remainder, together with 70,000 Indian soldiers, passed under Japanese rule. An Indian National Army was raised, and was to suffer heavy casualties. The community was hit even harder by conscription of estate laborers to work on the 'Death Railway'. No record was kept of those who perished but an informed estimate suggests that 60,000 died. The postwar Malayan Indian population had shrunk from 15 percent of the total before 1942 to 10 percent. They never fully recovered.

Independence for India and Pakistan in 1947 posed an identity problem for the overseas communities. Were they to identify with the ancestral motherland or with the territories of their adoption? Most produced an ambiguous answer. There was another factor: under the 1948 British Nationality Act, most were citizens of the

Countries with communities drawn from the subcontinent numbering over 40,000 (c. 1980–84).

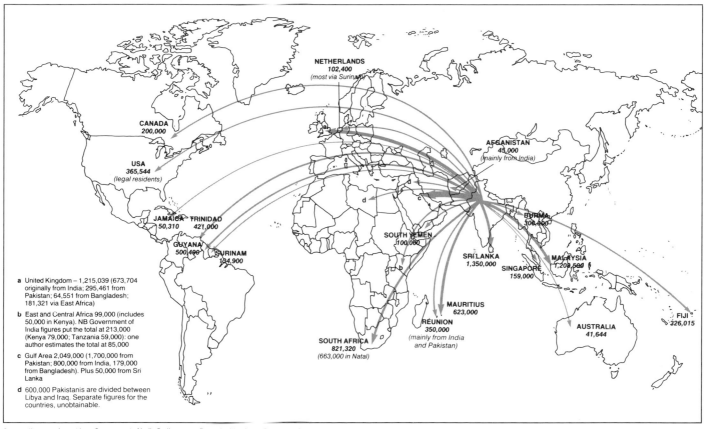

a United Kingdom – 1,215,039 (673,704 originally from India; 295,461 from Pakistan; 64,551 from Bangladesh; 181,321 via East Africa)

b East and Central Africa 99,000 (includes 50,000 in Kenya). NB Government of India figures put the total at 213,000 (Kenya 79,000; Tanzania 59,000): one author estimates the total at 85,000

c Gulf Area 2,049,000 (1,700,000 from Pakistan; 800,000 from India, 179,000 from Bangladesh). Plus 50,000 from Sri Lanka

d 600,000 Pakistanis are divided between Libya and Iraq. Separate figures for the countries, unobtainable.

Source: (figures adapted from Government of India Parliamentary Record, 1980, Arthur P. Helweg, Sikhs in Britain (1986), Muhammad Anwar, Race and Politics (1986), Minority Rights Group Report No.68 (Migrant Workers in the Gulf), Government of South Africa Yearbook, 1985, and other sources)

UK and Colonies. The Colonial Office was deeply suspicious, asserting that independent India intended to recreate the 'Greater India' of nationalist historical myth. Official policies were directed to controlling and minimizing political demands and pressures for increased settlement. Thus, in Kenya, Asian immigration was restricted while European immigrants were encouraged.

The partition of the Panjab at Independence created massive population movements: some of the most enterprising among those dispossessed sought to build new lives overseas. Many were Sikhs, but some were displaced Muslims, particularly from Mirpur on the Kashmir border. Postwar Britain had a labor shortage: people were leaving the old industries, such as textiles and ironworks. Public transport experienced a labor shortage as wage rates were low. In the London area, there was rapid industrial growth. Here were openings for Asians: instead of migration being a phenomenon on the periphery of the British Empire, it now became an integral part of metropolitan society.

Asian immigration, initially on a small scale, went largely unnoticed. The first settlers were mainly Sikhs who left their families behind with the intention of working hard for a period of years, accumulating savings, and returning home. This pattern of temporary settlement, with one member of the family replacing another in the workplace, was halted by immigration legislation in 1962 and 1965. It was now impossible to sojourn in Britain for a period of years; the migrant either had to stay or go, with no chance of a replacement. Almost all stayed and brought wives and families to join them. Gradually, certain areas like Southall in west London and inner Leicester became Indian enclaves. In all the main cities, there were settlers from the subcontinent. By 1981, about three-fifths of those belonging to families from areas now in the Indian republic were born in Britain, as were about two-fifths of the 'Pakistanis' and one-third of the 'Bangladeshis'.

By the 1980s, virtually all members of these communities regarded themselves as permanent residents in Britain. The early attempts at 'assimilation', as when most Sikhs shaved their beards and cut their hair, have been replaced by strong assertions of

After Independence there was considerable South Asian migration to Europe and North America. Here we see Sikhs in Southall, an Indian enclave in west London.

separate cultural identities. The *gurdwara*, the mosque or the Gujarati temple have become the focus for community activity. Earlier community leaders counselled caution in dealing with the police or white people in general in order to avoid trouble. Increasingly, militancy has been recognized as the only way that these communities will secure their rights. Such action can be linked with militant causes in the ancestral homeland: there is strong emotional support for the establishment of a Sikh state (Khalistan) among many British Sikhs as well as substantial financial support.

Asians have suffered during the economic depression of the 1980s, hard hit by the collapse of the textile industry in the north of England and metal manufactures in the Midlands. Increasingly, however, they are building up their own firms, small and large. They also attach great importance to securing the best education for their children. A minority are gaining a hold in the professions, medicine and accountancy in particular. British Asian communities in the 1980s are still in a transitional stage. So many of the young people brought up in Britain find their cultural norms subject to intense pressure from two opposite directions: those of village India and those of the youth culture of the West. Most try to find their own middle way, for example, in marriage practices, but they still suffer from being different from the so-called host community as well as from their relations back home.

In the 1950s and 1960s several newly-independent countries began to put pressure on their Indian communities. The Burma Indians never regained their pre-war position. Then, in 1962, the new military government announced that all foreign residents would be expelled. This applied to all Indians except the handful who had acquired citizenship. They were largely cleared out of Rangoon but elsewhere some managed to stay. East African governments adopted a draconian policy of Africanization which precipitated an exodus of 'British Asians' to the UK. Kenya had an Asian population of 176,613 in 1962: by 1967, some 40,000 had entered Britain and in 1968 barriers were raised against British passport holders. In contrast to the steady pressure exerted in Kenya and Tanzania, General Amin, dictator of Uganda, suddenly announced that the entire Asian population would be expelled and their assets seized. Numbering 80,000 at Ugandan independence, their numbers had already fallen to 50,000 by this time. Their flight following Amin's order was chaotic. Many passed through United Nations camps in Europe: while 6000, mainly the richer and better-qualified, entered Canada, most of the remainder finally ended up in Britain.

In South Africa, the position of the Indian community remains uncertain. They were only accepted as permanent residents after World War II, although still denied political rights and restricted by zoning laws. In 1980, they formed a small group (3.2 percent) beside the Africans (68 percent), Whites (18 percent) and Coloreds (10.5 percent). Concentrated in Natal, they form the second largest group in that province. The overwhelming majority put down English as 'the language of the home': 91 percent live in urban areas. The Whites have endeavored to co-opt them by granting them a separate Assembly, like the Coloreds, sitting separately from the White Assembly where power resides. They were not impressed: at the first election in 1983, only 20 percent of the Indian electorate cast their vote.

Malayan Indians are recognized as citizens but their political and economic role is one of inferiority, despite small numbers holding high positions in education, medicine and the law. By contrast, the Singapore Indians, merely 7 percent of the population, enjoy their full share of the island's prosperity. The Indian community in Sri Lanka suffered intensely. First, the tea estate Indians were deprived of voting rights and most were denied citizenship. Throughout the following years, despite repeated talks between the Government of India and successive Sinhalese premiers, no final settlement was reached. Indigenous Tamils, whose ancestors arrived two thousand years ago or more, regarded this grievous treatment with indifference, not realizing that their turn would come next. In the 1960s, the Jaffna Tamils began to lose the privileges that their superiority in English education had gained. The demand grew for an autonomous Tamil state in the north. Anti-Tamil riots in Colombo and army repression set in train a Tamil exodus to Europe and North America, almost all by clandestine routes. On arrival, they claimed refugee status.

The former sugar colonies moved more slowly towards independence. Only in Mauritius with its overwhelming Indo-Mauritian majority did they at last achieve political power in 1968, although economic power remains a White preserve. In Guyana, although substantially in the majority, the 'East Indians' were denied real power, mainly because their leader, Chedi Jagan, was a declared Communist even if a confirmed constitutionalist. The Colonial Office devised a fancy franchise whereby power was devolved to the supposed moderate Black politician, Burnham. The same kind of device helped to maintain the Fijian chiefly leaders in control, despite an Indo-Fijian majority. The precarious partnership between 'Indian' and Fiji politicians was abruptly terminated in 1987 when Colonel Sitiveni Rabuka staged two military coups which abolished the 1970 constitution and established an all-Fijian government.

In the 1970s and 1980s, new opportunities opened up in widely different circumstances in the Arabian Gulf and North America. With the oil boom came a construction boom in the Gulf. The privileged local Arab population was not interested in laboring and this was overcome by introducing migrants under conditions of servitude resembling indenture. Yet, however much they were exploited, earnings were considerably higher than at home. The largest number were from Pakistan, which also supplied military personnel to the sheikhs. Remittances home in 1980–81 were USA $2580 million to Pakistan, $2293 million to India, $329 million to Bangladesh and $290 million to Sri Lanka. At the same time, there was the extraordinary immigration explosion to North America. Canada was the most important in the 1960s, but was then overtaken by the USA where under the 'Green Card' system a resident's family members enjoy automatic right of admission. The manner in which the USA Census figures are tabulated makes an accurate estimate even more difficult than for Britain, but it would appear that there were approximately 32,000 from the subcontinent in the USA in the early 1970s. A decade later, the number was more than ten times higher. One informed observer has estimated that if 'illegals' are included (and from 1986 those already domiciled can establish themselves legally) the total is 500,000. Virtually all are middle class: some have become leading entrepreneurs, most are in the professions or business, and for only a minority have expectations not been adequately realized.

Denied entry, or discriminated against so often, South Asian emigrants have survived, and, despite adversity, have come through.

HT

Further reading

A. Ali, *Plantation to Politics; Studies on Fiji Indians*, (Suva, 1980)

S. Arasaratnam, *Indians in Malaysia and Singapore* (Oxford, 1970)

N. C. Chakravarti, *The Indian Minority in Burma; the Rise and Decline of an Immigrant Community* (Oxford, 1971)

A. P. Helweg, *Sikhs in Britain* (Oxford, 1979) 2nd edn (enlarged) 1986. [Contains statistics on almost all Indian communities overseas and a bibliographical survey of works on these communities]

H. Tinker, *A New System of Slavery; the Export of Indian Labour Overseas, 1830–1920* (London, 1974); *Separate and Unequal; India and the Indians in the British Commonwealth, 1920–1950* (London, 1976); *The Banyan Tree; Overseas Emigrants From India, Pakistan and Bangladesh* (Oxford, 1977)

M. Twaddle, *Expulsion of a Minority: Essays on Uganda Asians* (London, 1975)

Overleaf The procession passes the Juma Masjid as the Viceroy, Lord Curzon, makes his state entry into Delhi in December 1902. Such processions with their associated durbars were ways in which the British expressed their authority as rulers of India.

HISTORY TO INDEPENDENCE

The sources

Archeological evidence

Recent academic work on South Asian archeology has been concerned to enlarge the categories of evidence available to the researcher. The tendency had been to think of archeology in terms of artifacts – of stone, iron or other metal tools and vessels; of pottery objects and fragments of fabrics; of remains of dwellings and funeral sites. Stress is now also laid on such evidence as animal, plant and organic remains as well as geo-physical features like abandoned river courses, buried soils and dead drainage systems.

Not all these wider categories of evidence have been found in South Asia. There is, for example, an almost total lack of fossil hominids. Nonetheless the map of the subcontinent (with the exception of Sri Lanka where the evidence for prehistoric times is restricted to the later periods) shows a very wide distribution of archeological sites with an extensive range of materials. Indeed, for the Stone Age period the countryside is replete with items, many of them unexamined. The regional character of the archeological evidence is clearly established by the time of the earliest agricultural settlements from at least the sixth millennium BC onwards (when at least four main regions can be described) although it takes on a more unitary character during the centuries of the Indus Civilization. Unfortunately there are as yet inadequate sources relating to the appearance and development of cities in the first millennium BC. Only Taxila has been at all adequately excavated.

The Vedas

Archeological evidence remains important down even to the British period but its value is greatly enhanced when it can be used in association with other historical sources. Before the availability of written evidence (the earlier Indus inscriptions being as yet undeciphered) the Rigveda assumes considerable significance for scholars. This is a compilation made between *c.* 1500 and 1200 BC of sacred hymns and verses. It was handed down orally from generation to generation and gives an early glimpse of religion, agriculture and society in the Panjab and North India. Later religious texts such as the Upanishads, the Puranas and the epics are also of importance.

Inscriptions

The earliest written materials are the proclamations of the Emperor Ashoka (*c.* 272/268 BC to 232 BC) inscribed on tall columns and rocks. These have been recovered at over thirty-five locations near towns, trade routes or religious centers. The actual inscriptions were deciphered early in the nineteenth century and consist either of religious declarations or government statements.

Inscriptions form a most important source for all historical periods from the third century BC. It is estimated that around 100,000 have been found and many have been transcribed and printed. Written on plates of copper, the stone walls of temples or other imperishable materials, the vast majority are to be found in South India. The Chola dynasty alone accounts for more than 10,000. There are also coins which can be particularly valuable for dating the reigns of rulers and for showing the extent of trading zones.

Islamic sources

The centuries of Muslim dominance in India resulted in completely new classes of material becoming available. Most important here is the fact that Muslim élites developed the art of writing chronicles and histories of reigns. Some of the more notable of these include: Barani's *Tarikh-e Firuz Shahi* (about 1358) chronicling part of the Delhi Sultanate; Abdullah's *Tarikh-e Daudi* (early seventeenth century) describing the rule of the Lodi Emperors; and Abul Fazl's *Akbarnama* (1601) covering Akbar's reign. Two Mughal Emperors, Babur and Jahangir, even wrote their own autobiographies. Complementary with these chronicles are the descriptions of Islamic rule in India given by travelers from overseas like Ibn Battuta, Thomas Roe, Bernier and Tavernier.

The Mughal rulers developed a corpus of administrative documentation of great value. This includes: royal firmans (charters); statistical surveys and revenue rules and regulations; court bulletins and newsletters; and collections of letters kept as models of style.

The colonial phase

The European missionaries, adventurers and trading companies that first arrived in South Asia in the sixteenth century brought with them Western techniques of record keeping. Their descendants provided the region with one of the best documented accounts of government in the world. It followed that portions of the records they created are to be found in metropolitan capitals, notably London.

In London the main archive is that of the India Office Library and Records (IOLR). Its collections can be divided into: (a) official records; (b) personal papers of leading officials and other Europeans; (c) materials such as maps, photographs, prints and portraits. The official papers include such categories as records of the early trading stations or 'factories'; despatches and correspondence between Britain and India; day to day records of Indian administration in the form of 'Consultations'; modern departmental files introduced from about the 1880s. There are many official publications and statistical collations.

Outside the IOLR, the Public Record Office houses the records

India has rich records of its modern history. In this letter M. K. Gandhi tells A. H. West at Phoenix Farm, which was the first experiment in communal living that Gandhi established in South Africa, about one of his early campaigns of passive resistance on behalf of peasants in Gujarat. The Government of India has published Gandhi's collected works in over eighty volumes.

of the Cabinet, Foreign Office, War Office and (important for Sri Lanka) the Colonial Office. In Europe there are important collections for the Dutch, French, Portuguese and Vatican connections with the region.

Holdings of government archives for the colonial period within South Asia, be they at the Center or in the districts, are very extensive and mirror the classes of records held in London and elsewhere in Europe. Mention should also be made of personal papers (including those of nationalist leaders and Parties) deposited in various national and local record offices in the region. Among the more notable collections are those in the Nehru Memorial Museum and the National Archives of India, New Delhi, and those in the National Archives of Pakistan, Islamabad.

Recent historians of colonial rule have been much concerned with the Eurocentric nature of their evidence which does not adequately reflect developments in the indigenous sector. The very wealth of the evidence gives the misleading impression that only centralized actions mattered while its reliability is questioned. The tendency, therefore, has been to use existing sources more critically and find new types of evidence like vernacular family records, local newspapers and oral histories.

LC

Further reading

B. and R. Allchin, *The Rise of Civilization in India and Pakistan* (Cambridge, 1982)

A. L. Basham, Ed., *A Cultural History of India* (Oxford, 1975)

D. A. Low, J. C. Iltis and M. D. Wainwright, *Government Archives in South Asia* (Cambridge, 1969)

M. L. P. Patterson, *South Asian Civilizations: A Bibliographic Synthesis* (Chicago, 1981)

J. D. Pearson Ed., *South Asian Bibliography* (Hassocks, Sussex, 1979)

J. D. Pearson, *A Guide to Western Manuscripts and Documents in the British Isles Relating to South and South East Asia* (London, 1988)

Prehistory and the Harappan era

Early prehistory

The Indian subcontinent abounds in archeological remains of every period from the Lower Paleolithic to the early historic. Lower Paleolithic hand axes were discovered in South India and in Sind in the 1860s, only a few years after they had been found in Europe and recognized as tools of early man. Numerous prehistoric sites have been recorded and materials collected since. During the British period and in the early days of independence in India, the attention of the few available professional and amateur archeologists tended to be directed to the many fine monuments of historic times and to later prehistoric sites. This and a dependence upon European models to interpret the later Pleistocene geology and geomorphology, which always play such an integral part in understanding early human cultures, have until quite recently contributed to the lack of progress in understanding the early prehistory of the subcontinent.

During the last three or four decades some progress has been made in understanding the sequential relationships of early cultures, their climatic and environmental setting and their age. Furthermore, in a limited number of cases it has been possible to reconstruct something of the overall culture of a stone age site or a group of sites. In India the Tata Institute of Fundamental Research and the National Physical Laboratory have done much to provide independent physical dates, especially for later prehistoric cultures. In Pakistan an important contribution in this field has been made by the Department of Geology in Peshawar University. A series of climatic fluctuations resulting in periods when climatic and environmental conditions differed markedly from those of the present, and the relationship of the pattern of climatic change in and around the great Indian Desert to that of other deserts of the northern hemisphere, during the terminal Pleistocene and early Holocene was demonstrated in the 1970s by Indo-Australian and Indo-British teams working in northwest India; work on these problems continues in both India and Pakistan.

The fundamental factor in bringing about a more dynamic approach to the study of early man in South Asia has been the recognition in the 1960s of plate tectonics as an important factor in the formation of continents, mountain ranges and plateaus. The collision of peninsular India with mainland Asia is now seen to have been taking place forcefully and dramatically during the last twenty million years, and has created the Himalayas and the Tibetan plateau. It has affected every aspect of the configuration of the landscape, the climate and the environment of early man. This is immediately apparent in the north and northwest of the subcontinent, but less obvious in the south. Almost universally very rapid rates of erosion and deposition have produced archeological situations contrasting in almost every respect with those of northern temperate regions. For example, a Stone Age site in use several hundred thousand years ago may be exposed on a low hill, while a few hundred yards away another of the same period may be buried under more than a hundred feet of silt in a river valley, and exposed by being cut through by the changing course of a stream. In the proximity of the Himalayas, major rivers have had their courses changed radically in historical times, and tool-bearing deposits have been folded or cut by streams to reveal artifacts and fossils.

On the basis of observations of this kind in the river valleys of northern and central India during the 1950s and 1960s, an overall picture of the development of stone technology from the later Lower Paleolithic to the Mesolithic industries of the early Holocene was built up. This may be briefly summarized as follows. The sequence began with a well-developed hand axe tradition based on quartzite, which had already been seen to be widely distributed throughout the subcontinent, far beyond these river valleys. This appeared to have developed locally into a range of prepared core and flake industries with many regional and temporal variants. The distinguishing feature of these industries in peninsular and central India was that they employed a wider range of materials than their predecessors. Although the basic technology was consistent, they appear to use flakes from prepared cores without working them up into traditionally established tool types. Industries with the same basic technology in Sind and the arid regions of the northwest differed in that they produced recognizable tool types, made from flakes, which included points, scrapers of several kinds including distinctive carinated scrapers and simple burins. One of a group of inhabited rock shelters, many with paintings, at Bhimbetka in central India has been carefully excavated and provides some insight into the life of the Late Acheulian and Middle Paleolithic inhabitants. It appears to have been inhabited regularly, perhaps continuously, by people using largely local materials, but also obtaining small quantities of stone for certain kinds of tools from places several days' journey away. This picture has recently been radically extended backward in time in the northern Panjab, Pakistan, through the discovery by the British Archeological Mission to Pakistan, of stone artifacts, a chopping tool and some flakes, in a geological horizon dated by the paleomagnetic method to two million plus or minus two hundred thousand years.

Towards the end of the Pleistocene Era the prepared core and flake technique was augmented, but never totally replaced, by a characteristic Upper Paleolithic technology based on the production of slender parallel-sided blades from cylindrical or prismatic cores and an increasing range of burins. In the Potwar Plateau, Panjab, Pakistan, an Upper Paleolithic working area sheltered by a windbreak has been excavated, and thermoluminescent dating of the overlying loess gives it an age of around 38,000 BC. In central India Upper Paleolithic tools are found in occupation deposits in rock shelters. These are of a similar age, perhaps going back as far as 40,000 BC, and rock paintings of animals are associated with them.

At Pushkar in Rajasthan pallet stones with traces of red ochre and other heavy stone artifacts, which appear to be hammers, are found with Upper Paleolithic blade industries. The combined flake-bead tradition appears to develop locally into a rich and varied series of microlithic industries based on a wide range of fine materials including milky quartz and semi-precious stones such as agate and carnelian. These microlithic tools have a beauty and precision far beyond that demanded by use. They served as parts of composite arrowheads, sickles and other tools. They continue into the Holocene Era and only disappear with the advent of iron in the late second millennium BC. Heavier stone tools like those of the Upper Paleolithic age and also small querns for grinding grain are found with them. The highly developed stone-working tradition of Mesolithic communities overlaps with both the tool-making and bead-making crafts of the early settlements which also continued until replaced by iron, and with stone bead-making which continues to the present day.

Mesolithic communities continued in many parts of the subcontinent, regionally or continentally in parallel with early settlements such as Mehrgarh (see below), and with Harappan and post-Harappan cities. The way of life associated with them has been the subject of much discussion. They probably represent many lifestyles, ranging from hunting and gathering and various kinds of fishing, through combinations of these with forms of simple agriculture and animal husbandry, to that of highly organized trader-pastoralists. At some Mesolithic sites remains of huts and hearths have been found, and there are also burials and shrines of mother goddesses. For all these lifestyles there are parallels in the subcontinent today, or were within the last century. An example of a mixed hunting–agricultural economy is provided by Bagor in eastern Rajasthan which is contemporary with the Harappan period. The inhabitants built permanent dwellings, small quantities of copper were used alongside stone tools, and studies of the animal bones indicate an increasing predominance of domesticated species over wild species. In central Indian rock shelters Mesolithic industries are associated with a whole range of rock paintings or crayon drawings showing animals, people, hunting scenes, lines of dancing figures and many other subjects, a number of which have close parallels in modern folk art. Some are also records of events, showing chariots being waylaid by bowmen, or armed men in the dress of cultures from outside the region but known from documents of the early centuries BC/AD.

The late Upper Paleolithic and Mesolithic cultures of the Indian subcontinent provide the matrix or widespread cultural network of the subcontinent within which the first settlements formed. It was in this context that the sophisticated urbanism of the Mature Harappan culture flourished, and also, later, the early historic cities of the Ganges valley. The so-called 'tribal' communities are in many senses the heirs of the Mesolithic inhabitants, even if they are not always their genetic descendants.

Early agricultural societies

The earliest evidence of the beginning of agriculture in South Asia comes from the western borders. At Mehrgarh at the junction of the Indus plains and Baluchistan hills a settlement has been excavated which shows continuous development from the seventh millennium through to the mature Indus civilization. Already at the beginning of the period barley and wheat were cultivated, and sheep and goats were present alongside many wild animals; but by *c.* 5000 BC humped Indian cattle came to form the most common domesticated species, and were probably recently domesticated, while game animals formed a much reduced element. At the opening of the period there was no pottery, although clay was used to make mud bricks for storehouses and graves. Pottery makes its appearance by *c.* 5000 BC and thereafter increases in frequency until around 3500 BC when the introduction of the potter's wheel led to its mass production. By this time the presence of numbers of compartmented mud-brick storehouses, presumably for grain, suggests a considerable concentration of population. Beads and ornaments of sea shells, turquoise and lapis lazuli indicate long distance trade.

It is probable that other comparably early sites await discovery in the western borders of the Indus system, but as yet there is no definite evidence of related developments elsewhere in South Asia, where Mesolithic groups must have flourished. Recently it has been claimed that in the southern Ganges plains and Vindhya plateau,

The Indus Valley civilization: sites of the mature period.

south of Allahabad, agricultural settlements exploiting rice, cattle, sheep, goats and pigs, arose by the fifth millennium. But the chronology of these settlements still needs confirmation. Should this be forthcoming it will represent an apparently largely independent development to that of the Indus regions.

From around 3500 BC an expansion of agricultural settlements began to take place throughout a great part of the Indus system. The basic crops and domesticated animals remained as in the earlier period; while the stone and bone tools were augmented by increasing use of copper and bronze. Regional varieties of fine painted pottery and terracotta figurines became prominent. A new feature was the exploitation of the Indus floodplains for purposes of agriculture. This no doubt led to an increase in population and in the size of settlements. At Rehman Dheri near Dera Ismail Khan a substantial walled settlement has been excavated. There is also evidence of growing craft specialization.

This process continued during the first half of the third millennium BC, and there is evidence of many new settlements throughout the Indus system. During these centuries a remarkable change began to take place: the regional character of the settlements in various areas (Middle and Lower Sind, West and East Panjab, North Rajasthan) becomes less prominent and a more uniform character begins to emerge. From this period there are more excavated sites and radiocarbon dates, so that the picture assumes a firmer perspective than hitherto. Among the excavated sites Kot Diji in Sind and Kalibangan in North Rajasthan are important. Contemporary settlements have also been excavated at Amri, Mehrgarh, Rehman Dheri and Sarai Khola in Pakistan, Banavali and Mitathal in Haryana and Surkotada in Kacch (Cutch). Other significant features are the discovery at some sites of small stone seals, and the widely distributed use of certain painted motifs on ceramics, already suggesting elements of a common mythology. We may conclude that a process of social and cultural change was taking place which represents the formative period of the Indus civilization and which leads to the full urbanism of the succeeding period. For this reason the terms 'Early Indus' or 'Early Harappan' seem to be preferable to the older term 'Pre-Harappan', still current in some publications, for describing this period.

From c. 3000 BC onward agricultural settlements also began to appear in many parts of South Asia east of the Indus system. These 'cultures' as they are often called seem to have arisen largely independently of the developments in the Indus valley, and in no case did they lead to the formation of cities at that time. Their interest, however, lies in the foundations which they laid for subsequent ages; they may be regarded as the first clear manifestations of local Indian cultural developments, and it may well be that they are already ancestral to the modern cultural and ethnic regions of India.

Indus civilization

In the Indus system the process recorded in the previous paragraphs reaches its culmination in the second half of the third millennium (c. 2500 BC), in the Indus (or Harappan) civilization. Around this time fundamental but as yet incompletely understood changes took place involving the appearance of cities. Among excavated sites Mohenjo-daro and Harappa are the best known, Kalibangan still awaits full publication. Other sites await fuller excavation and research. Many of the new settlements were built directly over the earlier ones, but their area was invariably much larger. The new cities depended upon the same technology and subsistence basis, but on an enhanced scale. Stone tools continued to be made, but copper and bronze became more common. There is much evidence of greater craft specialism. The most important settlements show a remarkable, underlying planning concept with a carefully oriented layout involving a high mound or 'citadel', probably a socio-political and ritual center, and a larger area to the east with evidence of spe-

A street scene in Kalibangan, one of the cities of the Indus civilization.

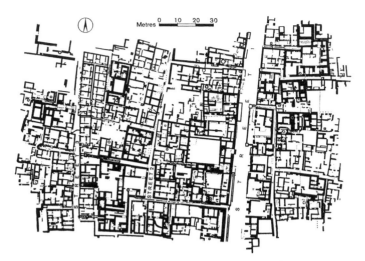

Plan of part of the lower city of Mohenjodaro; one estimate puts its population at 35,000.

cialized craft zones and more general occupation. Monumental architecture occurs in such structures as the Great Bath at Mohenjodaro, the great brick basin or 'dockyard' at Lothal, and the granaries at Harappa.

Not only do many of the settlements show direct continuity of occupation from the previous period, but the extent of the Indus civilization is also almost identical to that of the early Indus, with certain significant variations. There are some peripheral areas in which typical Indus settlements are found among a majority of sites of a provincial type reflecting the continuing early Indus style – perhaps suggesting a colonial situation. In at least one peripheral area the early Indus style continues without any evidence of an 'Indus' intrusion. At Shortughai in northeast Afghanistan a small Harappan trading colony was established, some 500 km from the nearest regular Harappan settlement, and probably linked to the lapis lazuli trade. The total area covered by the distinctive Indus sites is considerably larger than modern Pakistan, and greater than the states of either Egypt or Mesopotamia at their height.

The social and political structure which created and maintained this cultural unity over so large an area and over five or more centuries is still far from clearly understood. But its existence is demonstrated by, for example, the promulgation of a single script (and presumably language) throughout. The distinctive stone seals, bearing carved subjects and in some cases still unread inscriptions, are evidence of this. Indus seals have been found along with imported trade goods in contemporary Mesopotamia. Some bear representations of what appear to be religious symbols or mythological scenes. Occasionally identical scenes are found at widely separated sites. A number of the symbolic motifs appear to derive

from those of the previous period, and some survive into later Indian art, and even into modern times.

There has been considerable discussion regarding the exact cause or causes of the emergence of the Indus civilization. One school of thought has invoked invasion by a people coming from outside, but this seems improbable. Whatever external stimuli there may have been, the cities arose as a result of internal developments within the Indus region itself (and the changes may be no more than a reflection of the emerging lifestyle of the cities). Even more unclear are the exact causes of the breakdown of Indus urban society, somewhere after 2000 BC. Probably they too involved internal as well as external factors. Whatever these were, with the end of the cities, much of their culture and lifestyle remained alive, to be passed down through the Late Harappan culture of the second millennium to later Indian society.

FRA and BA

Further reading

D. P. Agrawal, *The Archaeology of India* (London and Malmo, 1982)

B. and R. Allchin, *The Rise of Civilization in India and Pakistan* (Cambridge, 1982)

G. L. Possehl, *Ancient Cities of the Indus* (New Delhi, 1979)

From the Vedic to the Classical Age, 1500 BC to AD 650

The Vedic Age, 1500 BC to 1000 BC

The Vedic Age began in 1500 BC with the migration of tribes of Indo-European origin, known as Indo-Aryans, from the Iranian plateau into the Panjab, and represented a sharp contrast to the urban culture of the Harappans which had declined in about 1750 BC. The sources for this period are the four *Sanhitas*, or collections of hymns in Vedic Sanskrit, the *Rigveda* for the period between 1500 BC and 1000 BC and the *Sama*, *Yajur* and *Atharva Vedas* for the later period stretching from 1000 BC to 600 BC. The early tribal organization of the Indo-Aryans changed during this later phase when they moved into the Ganges Valley and acquired a clear territorial identity.

The Indo-Aryans were semi-nomadic pastoralists, and first settled down in the region of the Sapta-Sindhu or seven rivers from the Kabul to the Sarasvati (now lost in the desert of Rajasthan) and in the Doab, or plain, between the upper Ganges and Yamuna. They gradually took up agriculture, formed village communities and organized themselves into tribal societies led by a warrior chief (*raja*) who was also the protector of the tribe. Assisted by brahmin priestly families (*brahmanas*) who composed the Vedic hymns, these warrior lineages (*rajanya*) gained the status of rulers. The raja, therefore, was primarily a war leader who, in return for protection, received tribute from his tribe. Tribal assemblies, like the *sabha* and *samiti*, acted as checks on his authority. The term *vish* primarily denoted the tribe which consisted of several villages or *gramas*. Each *grama* was composed of patriarchal extended family units. The economy was based on a mixture of pastoralism and agriculture, with cattle as the main form of wealth as reflected in the terms *gotra* (cowpen), used to describe the endogamous kinship system, and *gavishti* (the search for cows) meaning war.

Intertribal conflicts for hegemony and confrontation with local groups such as the Dasas and the Panis characterized this phase of Aryan expansion. The Dasharajna, or the major battle of the ten kings, was the main political event of this period, in which a confederacy of ten tribes led by the brahmin priest Vishvamitra was defeated by the Bharatas who favored another priest, Vashishtha. It was after the Bharatas, who lived in the region between the Sarasvati and the Yamuna, that the whole of this part of the subcontinent came to be known as Bharatavarsha.

Vedic religion centered around the worship of personified forces of nature and abstract divinities such as Indra, Varuna and Mitra. Offerings were made to them through Agni, the God of Fire, who came to dominate the larger sacrifices as well as domestic rituals. The central ritual of the Vedic religion was the *yajna* (sacrifice) in which the *purohita* (priest) mediated between man and the gods. The chanting of hymns, which had magical significance, and the performance of rituals propitiated the gods, who, in turn, conferred prosperity and valor on the king (the *Yajamana* or performer). The *yajna* acted as a source of legitimation in tribal assemblies. Its performance also involved the redistribution of wealth among the hierarchy of priests and senior tribal leaders, and hence led to a close association between the brahmins and the warrior lineages.

Later Vedic *sanhitas* dealt with a wider geographical region stretching from the Himalayas in the north and the Vindhyas in the south and between the western and eastern seas. The Ganges–Yamuna doab and its surrounding areas were recognized as the Aryavarta (land of the Aryans) and outside it lay the regions of the *mlecchas* (barbarians) and the *vratyas* (people of mixed origin). The sources for this later period include the *Brahmanas* (ritual texts), the *Upanishads* and *Aranyakas* (philosophical texts), the *Shrauta* and *Grihya Sutras* (manuals of *yajna*, domestic ceremonies and social and legal relations) and the epics *Mahabharata* and *Ramayana*. The core of the *Mahabharata* is the conflict between the Kauravas and Pandavas of the Kuru tribe, an event which has been traditionally assigned to 3102 BC, the start of the Kali era, but which is now placed at about 800 BC on the basis of archeological evidence especially from Hastinapura and Indraprastha (Delhi), the two

main settlements associated with the epic. The story of the *Ramayana* takes place in the mid-Ganges Valley (Ayodhya) and central India. Very important, however, in the historical reconstruction of this period have been the Puranas, a group of texts composed in the first half of the first millennium AD. They provide mythical lists of kings for nearly three thousand years starting from the legendary flood which devastated Hastinapura. The two important royal lineages known from these texts are the Suryavamsha (solar) and Chandravamsha (lunar). Vedic literature also refers to many tribes. The most powerful were the Kuru-Panchalas, who occupied the upper doab and Kurukshetra region. They were a large composite tribe incorporating earlier Kurus, Purus and Bharatas. In the northwest were located the Madras, Gandharas, Kekayas and Kambojas. Kashi, Koshala and Videha tribes in the middle Ganges Valley were the rivals of the Kuru-Pancalas. To the east were the Magadha, Anga and Vanga tribes composed of *vratyas* and *mlecchas*. Other semi-Aryan and non-Aryan tribes included the Satvants of central India, the Andhras, Pundras, Shabaras, Pulindas, Mutibas, Vidarbha and Nishada, the last being a generic term for non-Aryans.

The change from a tribal to a territorial identity was indicated by the geographical regions which were now named after the tribe which occupied them. Tribal polity was slowly transformed into a more permanent territorial kingship. Tribute (*bali*) assumed the character of a tax, and royal officials (*ratnin*), in addition to the *purohita* and *senani* (army commander), became a regular part of the rudimentary administrative system. Royal power was symbolized by more elaborate sacrifices and ceremonies like the *ashvamedha*, *rajasuya* (coronation ceremony) and *vajapeya* (sacrifice of drink of strength). The *ashvamedha* or horse sacrifice was closely linked with territorial sovereignty for the king claimed authority over the territory marked out by the horse wandering at will, unchallenged and followed by a body of soldiers. The idea that the king was the owner of all land, together with association of kingship with divinity, helped new political institutions to emerge while the role of the priests was to sustain these beliefs through rituals.

Throughout the period, more and more land was cleared and agriculture expanded. The use of iron and rice cultivation increased, strengthening the agrarian base of the economy. By 600 BC, trade had also become an important economic activity and had stimulated the growth of towns along the rivers, signaling the beginning of the Ganges Valley urbanization, or India's 'second urbanization', by the middle of the first millennium BC. The most important development in the Vedic Age, however, was the emergence of the *varna* order of caste hierarchy. The initial distinction between the Aryan tribes and the non-Aryan peoples of northern India was based on *varna* (colour), the *Arya* and the *Dasa*. The priests the warriors and the people constituted the three main divisions within the Aryan tribes, which later assumed the position of the three *dvija* or twice-born castes. The Dasa and other non-Aryan people, as well as economically less important groups, were brought under the broad category of the shudras who were mainly cultivators and generally expected to serve the three higher varnas. Thus, the caste structure of society emerged from lineage groups into which non-lineage groups had been integrated.

Ritual status was the important element in this fourfold stratification and hence the varna order became a mechanism for integrating new ethnic groups with sub-caste (*jati*) status into the overall caste structure. The jati label became a convenient device to distinguish all occupational and ethnic groups as it referred to birth in an endogamous kinship group and helped to perpetuate hereditary specialized occupations. There was, however, no automatic correspondence between ritual rank and economic status. Wealthy shudras existed and some of the later ruling families such as the Nandas rose from this varna. The idea of purity and pollution operated at all levels and subsequently led to the creation of a fifth category, the untouchables, whose occupations were regarded as impure. Relative purity was maintained by strict rules regarding marriage and commensality. Yet, mixed castes emerged out of *anuloma* (higher caste man with lower caste woman) and *pratiloma* (lower caste man with upper caste woman) marriage. Social mobility was not unknown, especially among the upper castes. Varna, therefore, provided only a broad framework within which variations existed.

Doubts regarding the efficacy of the Vedic religon and Vedic norms of social organization led to non-conformism or asceticism, and the teachings of those who opted out of society came to be incorporated in the *Aranyakas* and *Upanishads* as esoteric texts. Renunciation was now accommodated as the last of the four stages of life (*ashramas*). Questions relating to the universe and to the soul and its relationship with the *Brahman* (universal soul), were raised by Upanishadic philosophers and provided the starting point for various systems of philosophy in later periods. Germs of the doctrine of *Karma* (action) as determining rebirth and caste status can also be traced in Vedic literature.

Continuous interaction between the Aryan and the non-Aryan brought about a two-way process of acculturation and assimilation known as 'Aryanization', even though pre-Aryan elements often determined the nature of this synthesis. The acculturation or 'sanskritization' of the regions beyond Aryavarta was a slow process and continued well into the second half of the first millennium BC. While Dakshinapatha, or the route to the south, was mentioned in later Vedic literature, the extent to which Aryan culture had penetrated the south by the end of this period is still uncertain. Archeological evidence shows that the peninsula remained in the Neolithic–Chalcolithic stage with some traces of post-Harappan

culture appearing in parts of the Deccan. The change to iron technology in southern India took place between 1000 BC and 800 BC. With the appearance of Roman pottery, black and red ware and other written records by the close of the first millennium BC, this part of the subcontinent passed into the early historic period.

Early territorial states: 600 BC to 321 BC

In north India, the Vedic Age was followed by the rise of republics and monarchies known as the *janapadas* (territory of the clan). With considerable political insight, Buddhist and Jain works refer to sixteen *Mahajanapadas* or 'great states' of this period, some of which were represented by older tribes known from Vedic times while others such as the Avanti, Magadha, Anga, Vatsa and Vrijji had come into existence more recently.

The republics (*gana-sanghas*), which marked an intermediate stage between the earlier tribal organization and the development of monarchies, were distributed throughout the Himalayan foothills and in the Panjab. They consisted either of single tribes, such as the Mallas, or were a confederacy like the republic of the Vrijjis. They were governed through a general assembly (*parishad*) by a council of elders, who were representatives of the powerful kshatriya families. One of the elders was elected as chief (raja or *pati*) to preside over the assembly. In the monarchies, the hereditary principle and the concept of divinity came to be attached to the kingship. Elaborate sacrifices for the king's initiation, coronation and consecration, together with other ceremonies such as the *ashvamedha*, tended to preserve the status quo. In contrast, the republics provided an environment in which unorthodox views were able to emerge, leading to the rise of 'heterodox' sects such as Buddhism and Jainism.

The *janapadas* reflected the growth of a stable agrarian economy. Wealthy kshatriyas and landowning *gahapatis* (householders) employed slaves and hired laborers (*dasa-bhritaka*) for cultivation. Concepts of private property and land revenue became important in economic and political organization. Trade which began as part of the internal exchange between *janapadas* soon expanded throughout the Ganges Valley and beyond. Towns (*pura*) emerged on the main highway from Rajagriha (Bihar) to Taxila, of which Kashi (Benares), Vaishali, Ayodhya, Shravasti and Kaushambi in the Ganges Valley were the most notable. Ujjain in the Narmada Valley and Bhrugukaccha at the mouth of the Narmada marked the trade route to the western coast. The needs of expanding trade led to the use of a script (Brahmi) and of coins, which along with the sophisticated northern black polished ware represented three important aspects of the Ganges Valley urbanization. The need for organized commerce resulted in the emergence of guilds (*shreni*) among traders and craftsmen with a system of financing, banking and usury. The *nigama* or merchant towns and guilds, as well as the

From the Vedic to the Classical Age, 1500 BC to AD 650

India in the time of the sixteen Mahajanapadas.

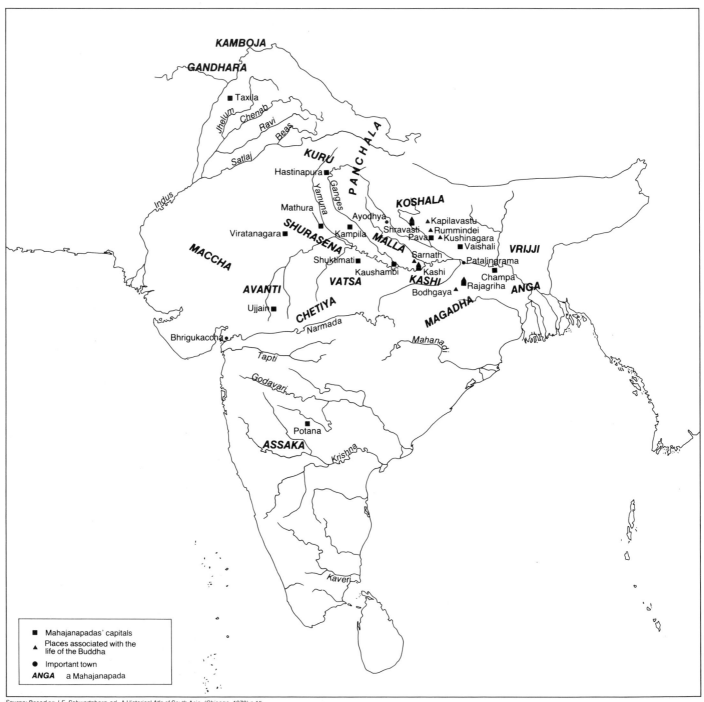

Legend:
■ Mahajanapadas' capitals
▲ Places associated with the life of the Buddha
● Important town
ANGA a Mahajanapada

Source: Based on J.E. Schwartzberg, ed., A Historical Atlas of South Asia. (Chicago, 1978) p.15

janapadas, minted and issued coins, of which the silver-bent bar and the silver and copper punch-marked coins were the earliest in India.

Changing socio-economic conditions in northern India and the inadequacy of orthodox Vedic norms of social order led to the rise of new schools of thought in the sixth century BC. Among them were Buddhism and Jainism which, while they did not negate caste or reject caste society, possessed a reformist zeal that sprang from their stand against brahmin exclusiveness, their belief in equality and their rational approach towards social relations. Both acquired the support of wealthy kshatriyas as well as low caste groups: mercantile groups, for instance, found in them an important avenue of social mobility. Buddhist missionary zeal and royal patronage helped it to spread over India and abroad. By the third century BC Jainism had also reached other parts of the subcontinent through a series of migrations.

Conflict for political hegemony during this period was centered on the Ganges Valley and involved the three kingdoms of Kashi, Koshala and Magadha, and the Vrijjian republic. Magadha ultimately emerged successful and under Bimbisara (543 BC to 491 BC) and Ajatashatru (491 BC to 461 BC) consolidated its pre-eminent position by conquering Kashi and Koshala, breaking the Vrijjian confederacy, and building up a strong administration. Rajagriha, the capital, was strengthened and the foundations of the future city of Pataliputra were laid in Pataligrama on the Ganges. Magadha's geographical position controlling the Ganges Valley and its trade, its access to the eastern coast, and its rich deposits of copper and iron, contributed to its dominance. After a series of mediocre kings, including the Shaishaunaga dynasty, Magadha became vastly more powerful in the fourth century BC under the usurper dynasty of the Nandas. The Greeks knew of the vast army of Mahapadma Nanda, considered to be the first empire-builder in India, and the wealth of the Nandas was mentioned by distant Tamil poets. However, it was only later under the Mauryas that Magadha attained the status of an empire.

The northwest, which had moved away from brahmanical traditions and had become relatively isolated from the rest of northern India, was the scene of a Persian invasion in 530 BC under Cyrus, the Achaemenid emperor who made Gandhara into his twentieth satrapy. A second and much more important invasion under Alexander of Macedon in 327 BC lasted less than two years, during which time the Greeks overran the Panjab and defeated several Indian rulers including Porus (Puru) at the battle of Hydaspes (Jhelum). Alexander was forced to leave when his troops refused to proceed beyond the Beas, thus creating a political vacuum into which Chandragupta Maurya (Sandracottas of the Greeks) stepped.

The state as empire under the Mauryas: 321 BC to 185 BC

The accession of Chandragupta Maurya to the Magadhan throne (*c.* 321 BC) marked the beginning of an important phase in the history of the subcontinent. Literary tradition assigns an important role in the establishment of Mauryan power to Chandragupta's *brahmana* Prime Minister and mentor, Kautilya, also known as Chanakya and recognized as the author of the *Arthashastra*, a famous treatise on political economy. Chandragupta, who conquered Magadha from the Nandas, possessed an army which was estimated at between 400,000 and 600,000. The trans-Indus region was ceded to him in 305 BC by Seleucus Nicator, the Greek lieutenant of Alexander. According to a Jain tradition, Chandragupta later abdicated and migrated with the Jain community to southern India where he died by the rite of *sallekhana* (slow starvation).

Chandragupta's successor, Bindusara (*c.* 297 BC) is credited with the conquest of the south as far as Mysore. The most celebrated of the Mauryas, however, was Ashoka who succeeded Bindusara

Ashoka's edicts were engraved on rock surfaces and polished pillars. This is the capital of a pillar from Sarnath near Benares.

From the Vedic to the Classical Age, 1500 BC to AD 650

Ashoka's empire.

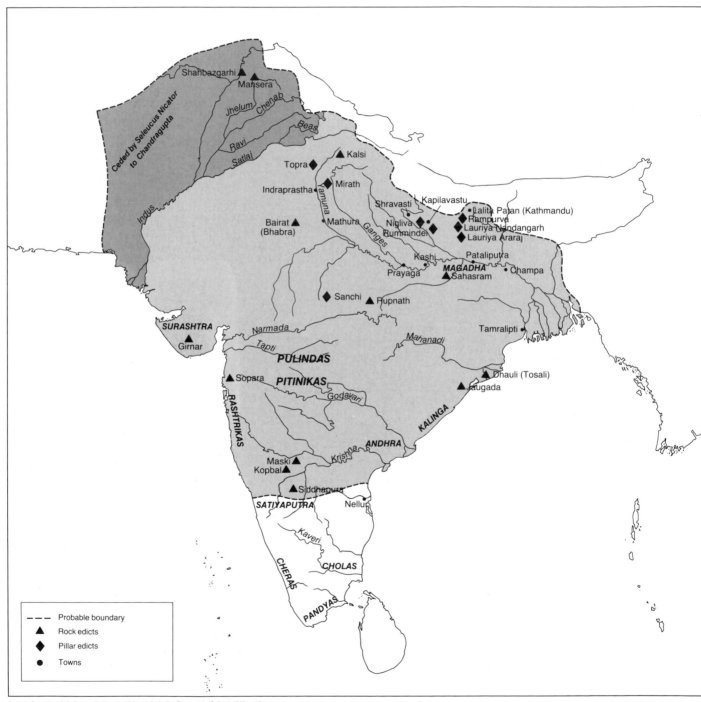

Ceded by Seleucus Nicator to Chandragupta

Indus

Shahbazgarhi
Mansera

Jhelum
Chenab
Ravi
Satlaj
Beas

Kalsi
Topra
Mirath
Indraprastha
Yamuna
Shravasti
Kapilavastu
Lalita Patan (Kathmandu)
Rampurva
Nigliva
Mathura
Rummindei
Lauriya Nandangarh
Lauriya Araraj
Bairat (Bhabra)
Ganges
Kashi
Pataliputra
Prayaga
MAGADHA
Champa
Sahasram

Sanchi
Rupnath

SURASHTRA
Narmada
Girnar
Tapti
Mahanadi
Tamralipti

PULINDAS

PITINIKAS
Sopara
Godavari
Dhauli (Tosali)
Jaugada

RASHTRIKAS
KALINGA

ANDHRA
Maski
Krishna
Kopbal
Siddhapura
Nellur
SATIYAPUTRA

Kaveri
CHERAS
CHOLAS
PANDYAS

Probable boundary
▲ Rock edicts
◆ Pillar edicts
● Towns

Source: Based on C.C. Davies, A Historical Atlas of the Indian Peninsual. (Oxford, 1965) p.13

sometime after 272 BC. His only conquest was that of Kalinga (Orissa). It has been held generally that remorse at the violence and destruction caused by the Kalinga war made Ashoka abandon war and turn to Buddhist teachings. But, it was less Buddhism than a policy of *Dhamma* which Ashoka propagated through his edicts. *Dhamma* or *dharma* was a code of conduct which inculcated social responsibility, ensured human dignity and encouraged socio-religious harmony. It reflected the need to cope with social tensions created by caste, religious loyalties and economic differences. Special officers, called *Dhamma Mahamattas*, were appointed to supervise its implementation. Ashoka emphasized the paternal role of the king, and his edicts show that he paid attention to the welfare of his subjects by building roads and rest houses, planting medicinal trees and setting up healing centers.

Ashoka's edicts, engraved on rock surfaces and polished monolithic pillars, used the Brahmi script and Prakrit language except in the northwest where they were in Greek and the Kharoshthi script. Their distribution marked the extent of his empire which included southern Afghanistan and stretched over the whole of the subcontinent with the exception of the far south which was under the control of the Cholas, Cheras and Pandyas, described in the edicts as friendly border people. The Mauryan empire did not represent a unitary or monolithic state despite the centralized character of its administration. Its four main provinces were under princes of the royal family while other regions were administered by local governors under the supervision of salaried royal officers. Every conceivable sphere of activity, rural and urban, was supervised by these officials. Good communication networks and an espionage system helped the metropolitan state to keep a watchful eye over the whole empire. A regular taxation system and a well-organized revenue department under a *Sannidhatri* (treasurer) and a *Samahartri* (chief collector), ensured a strong fiscal base derived mainly from land revenue and, to a lesser extent, from trade. Shudra cultivators and slaves were used to increase agricultural output, often on state-owned farms. Mining was a state monopoly.

The decline of the empire was not, as often suggested, due to a brahmin reaction to Ashoka's pro-Buddhist policy nor to his belief in non-violence leading to the weakening of the army. A more plausible explanation attributes the decline to pressure on resources as a result of variations in economic development and revenue between regions under direct Mauryan control and less developed areas including tribal zones which were not fully integrated into the state system. In addition, the centralized bureaucracy was held together by loyalty to the king. Its successful working depended on the king's personality; hence, under weak successors, the empire disintegrated.

The Mauryan empire was the earliest expression of the political notion of the state in the subcontinent. It was the culmination of a long process of socio-political formation which had turned a lineage or tribal organization into a state system. Orthodox brahmin tradition looked upon the state as a divine creation while Buddhist and Jain concepts perceived it as the result of a contract meant to contain the chaotic and demoralizing effects of property and material possessions. The ideal of dharma in the sense of the social order and its preservation took precedence over the political notion of the state, and accounted for the continuity of important social institutions over long periods of time.

Period of the small kingdoms: 200 BC to AD 300
The post-Mauryan era was one of dispersed political units. The Shungas (185 BC to 28 BC), who succeeded the Mauryas, were a *brahmana* dynasty and had originally been officials under their predecessors. They belonged to Ujjain in central India which continued to be the main concentration of their power. The Shungas were in turn succeeded by the Kanvas in 28 BC. During this period, however, the main scene of political events shifted to the northwest and the Panjab, which were drawn closer to central Asia in the second century BC. The Bactrian Greeks, who overthrew allegiance to the Seleucids of Syria, crossed the Hindu Kush range and established their rule in northwestern India under Demetrius II (180 BC to 165 BC). The Indo-Greek rulers, known mainly from their coinage, occupied Gandhara, the Panjab and even reached as far as Mathura, and possibly came into conflict with the Shungas and the rulers of Kalinga. Apart from the two main ruling families of Etuthydemus and Eucratides, the most important of the Indo-Greek kings was Menander (Milinda) (155 BC to 130 BC) who ruled the Swat Valley and the Panjab. He is famous for having been converted to Buddhism under the influence of the Buddhist philosopher Nagasena. Heliodorus, the Greek envoy of King Antialcidas of Taxila to the court of one of the later Shungas, became a follower of the Bhagavata (Vaishnava) cult as indicated by the inscribed Garuda pillar erected by him at Vidisha (Besnagar) (*c.* 100 BC).

The Indo-Greeks were replaced by the Scythians (Shakas) in the first century BC, who, in turn, later made way for the Parthians (Pahlavas). The migration of these central Asian tribes into India was itself the result of large-scale movements of nomadic tribes such as the Little Yueh-chi and the Great Yueh-chi caused by the hostility of the Han rulers of China. The Yueh-chi drove the Shakas out of northwestern India into Gujarat and Malwa, and established the second most powerful foreign dynasty in India, the Kushanas, during the first century AD. At its widest extent, the Kushana kingdom touched Benares in the east and Sanchi in the south, with Purushapura (Peshawar) and Mathura as its northern and southern seats of government. Kanishka was the third and most celebrated of the Kushana rulers whose date of accession ranges from AD 78 to AD 248. Both the Indo-Greeks and the Kushanas adopted exalted titles

From the Vedic to the Classical Age, 1500 BC to AD 650

Major powers of the post-Mauryan period.

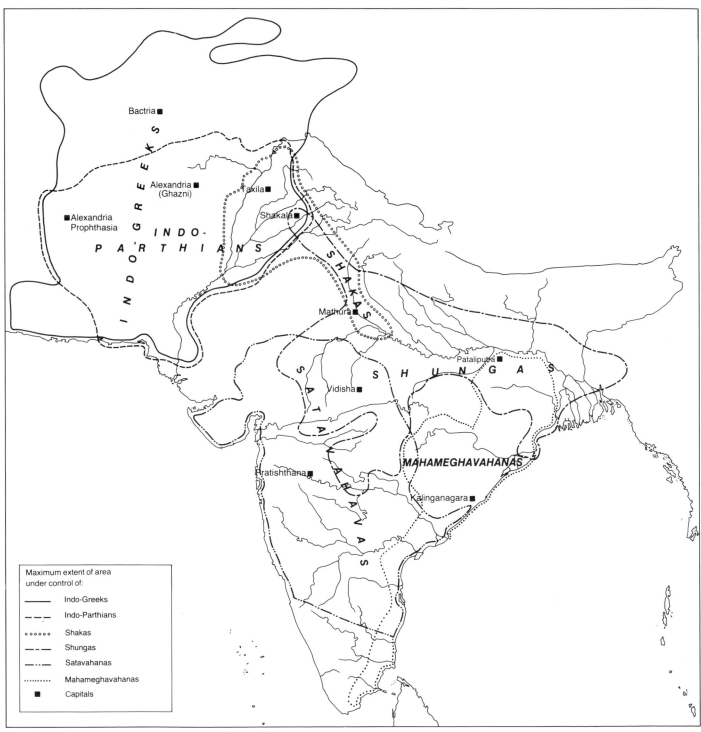

Maximum extent of area
under control of:

——— Indo-Greeks

– – – Indo-Parthians

∘∘∘∘∘∘ Shakas

–·–·– Shungas

–··–··– Satavahanas

·········· Mahameghavahanas

■ Capitals

Source: Based on J.E. Schwartzberg, ed., A Historical Atlas of South Asia (Chicago, 1978) p.20

such as *Shahanushahi* (King of Kings) and *Daiva putra* (Son of Heaven). The Kushana state was, however, a decentralized one, and its fiscal base was derived mainly from control over trade between central Asia and northern India which traveled along the route between Taxila and Mathura.

Tribal republics still occupied parts of the region between the Indus and the Ganges. Notable among these tribes were the Audumbaras, Kunindas and Yaudheyas in the Panjab, the Arjunayanas in the Doab, the Malavas and Shibis in Rajasthan, and the Abhiras scattered in western and central India and later in the Deccan and Andhra Pradesh. The Ganges Valley kingdoms, which continued to be important, were those of Ayodhya and Kaushambi. There were also Naga dynasties like that located in Padmavati near Gwalior. The Andhras (known also as Satavahanas) are listed in the Puranas as successors to the Kanvas. They were, however, a Deccan power whose original home remains a matter of dispute. Records dating from the second century BC to the first century AD locate them in northwestern Deccan with Pratishthana (Paithan) as their political center. In the second century AD, they acquired control over the Krishna Valley, the Andhra heartland. Temporarily displaced from the western Deccan by the Shakas, they regained control over the same region in the second century AD. Gautamiputra Satakarni, the most powerful of their rulers, restruck the silver coins of Nahapana after defeating the Shakas. Satavahana bilingual coins with legends in Prakrit and Tamil and 'ship' coins point to their control over the Deccan and Andhra coasts as well as parts of the Tamil region and also to an interest in maritime trading activities.

The Satavahana kingdom, as the Andhra kingdom later became known, was fairly extensive and was considerably influenced by Mauryan political organization. Yet, power was decentralized in the hands of many subordinate chieftains. Being a brahminical dynasty, the Satavahanas used the symbols of the Vedic sacrificial religion and protection of the *Varnashrama dharma* for legitimizing their power. At the same time, they extended their patronage to Buddhism in order to promote the trade of the region, which continued to provide the second main source of revenue after land. The Satavahanas were succeeded by their feudatories: the Chutus of Kuntala (South Maharashtra); the Ikshvakus of Nagarjunakonda in the Guntur district (Krishna Valley); the Abhiras in the Nasik region; and the Pallavas in Andhra who later became the rulers of the Kanchipuram region in northern Tamil Nadu.

The first written sources for the southernmost part of the peninsula, known as Tamilakam and comprising much of present-day Tamil Nadu and Kerala, date from the third century BC. The earliest corpus of Tamil literature, known as the 'Sangam' works and consisting of anthologies called the *Ettuttogai* (Eight Collections), *Pattuppattu* (Ten Songs) and *Padirruppattu* (Ten Tens), forms the most significant source for the period from 300 BC to AD

The Satavahanas patronized Buddhism to promote trade. This is the chaitya hall of the Buddhist cave temple at Karle on one of the trade routes from the Konkan ports into the Deccan.

200, while the well-known later epics, *Shilappadikaram* and *Manimekala*, also provide useful information. Tamil society and political organization were dominated by the three 'crowned kings' of the Cholas of Uraiyur, the Cheras of Vanji and the Pandyas of Madurai as well as several chiefs called the Velir. The Velir claimed descent from clans which had risen from the sacrificial pit of a northern sage identified with Agastya, a legendary figure believed to have brought Aryan civilization to southern India and regarded as the father of the Tamil language. Warfare among the Cholas, Pandyas and Cheras was frequent and usually followed by the plundering of each others' resources such as the pepper of the Chera region and the pearls of the Pandya coast (Mannar Gulf). Victory over rival kings and over the Velir brought hegemonic status to the conqueror. Lesser chiefs known as the Tiraiyar ruled over Tondainadu (northern Tamil region) with Kacchi (Kanchipuram) as their headquarters.

The 'Sangam' literature provides evidence of a predominantly indigenous non-Aryan culture into which Aryan traditions of the north had already begun to penetrate, as well as evidence of a transition from a tribal to a peasant economy, especially in the river valleys. Apart from pastoralism and agriculture, trade, and external trade in particular, was an important economic activity, consciously encouraged by the ruling families who developed their ports for promoting maritime trade. Kinship was the basis of social organization, with gifts and reciprocity as the chief means of distributing resources. The brahmins were an important high status group, but the varna order had not become established. Brahminical deities were known but *Tinai* (different eco-zones) deities were still important in regular worship. Murugan, the wargod of the hilly tracts, was the most important of the Tamil deities. Buddhism wielded influence in the coastal towns but Jainism was widely accepted in the interior. The decline of Roman trade and the sudden onslaught of the Kalabhra tribe overturned this Tamil socio-political order and created a political vacuum which continued to exist until the end of the sixth century AD.

Urbanization and trade

Despite the fragmentation of political authority and the emergence of dispersed political units, there was an underlying unity which emerged throughout the subcontinent in the period from 200 BC to AD 300 marked by a spurt in internal and external trade and the rise of the mercantile community to a position of unprecedented importance in society. Urbanization, which previously had been centered on the Ganges Valley, now became an all-India phenomenon. The growth of urban centers and organized commerce through guilds (*shrenis*) of traders and artisans such as corn dealers, weavers, potters and leather workers, is attested by the inscriptions of Buddhist monuments in the Deccan (Nasik), central India (Sanchi), the northwest (Taxila) and Andhra (Amaravati–Nagarjunakonda). Guilds were guided by codes of rules (*shreni-dharma*). The merchant guild, for instance, was headed by *shresthi* who was also a financier and the forerunner of the modern Seths of North India and the Chettiyars of the south.

The increasing monetization of the economy was reflected in the large variety of coins minted by both the guilds and by ruling families. Punch-marked coins in silver and copper (*satamana* and *karshapana*) were prevalent all over India. Tribal republics and dynasties in the Panjab, the Doab and the Deccan all issued coins. The coins of the Indo-Greeks, Shakas and Kushanas with their portraits and names of rulers influenced the Satavahanas and later the Guptas, who followed these traditions but indigenized them to a remarkable degree. Coins in gold, such as the *suvarna* and *dinara* based on the Roman denarius, as well as in other metals, such as copper (*masha* and *kakini*), are known from literary and epigraphic sources. Roman coins have been found in many parts of the subcontinent with a significant concentration in southern India, especially in the Coimbatore region where semi-precious stones were mined and near trading stations.

Trade routes opened up the Indian subcontinent to the outside world. The main overland route was the royal highway which linked Taxila with Pataliputra and further on with Tamralipti, the main port in the Ganges delta. Taxila provided access to West Asian routes and to the Black Sea and the Mediterranean as well as the old

Silk Route connecting China with Bactria via central Asia. The Ganges Valley was linked to the western port of Bhrigukaccha (Broach) through Rajasthan and Ujjain. Coastal sea traffic ran from Bhrigukaccha through the southern ports and Sri Lanka to Tamralipti. Southern ports and trading centers such as Muziris (Cranganore on the Kerala coast), Comari (Kanya Kumari), Colchi (Korkai on the Pandya coast), Khaberis or Camara (Kaverippumpattinam, the Chola port) and other ports on the Andhra coast actively participated in external trade. The monsoon winds, believed to have been 'discovered' by Hippalus in the first century BC, enabled direct sailing to the Persian Gulf and South Arabia, making the voyage faster and less dangerous than the coastal route. To southeast Asia, sea voyages followed the coastal route via Burma and Malaya, or made directly for the southern straits of Malacca and China beyond. Merchants from Gujarat, Kalinga and southern India settled in small communities in Burma, Malaya, Cambodia, Sumatra, Java and Bali.

Trade and the growth of towns were of considerable significance in restructuring society. The influx of foreigners as conquerors and traders posed problems of their integration into local society. While foreign ruling families were accepted as 'degraded' kshatriyas in the caste hierarchy, the Yavanas (people of West Asian and Mediterranean origin), who settled in the large ports and trading centers, were assigned shudra status and regarded as *mlecchas*. Changes and adjustments in the organization of society, the important status attained by the vaishyas, and the increasing liberalism of urban life, forced the upholders of traditional law and social order to define social, economic and legal privileges through law books known as the *Dharmashastras*, of which the best-known was that of Manu.

In the sphere of religion, this period was marked by important developments linked to socio-economic changes. A serious schism occurred within Buddhism between the Hinayana (Lesser Vehicle) and the Mahayana (Greater Vehicle) which was mainly the result of the widening of Buddhism's social base. Buddhism in general and Mahayanism in particular found favor with foreign ruling families; Kushana patronage, for instance, encouraged its rapid spread in central Asia. Jainism underwent similar changes with its division into the Svetambara (White Clad) and the Digambara (Sky Clad) sects, each with its own sets of scriptures. Royal patronage and collective participation by merchant and craft guilds resulted in very impressive Buddhist architecture in the form of *stupas* (funerary tumuli), *chaityas* (shrines) and *viharas* (monasteries) at various centers such as Taxila, Mathura, Sanchi, Nasik and Amaravati. Vedic brahmanism, confronted by the growing popularity of heterodox religions, transformed itself by evolving the concept of the trinity (Brahma, the creator; Vishnu, the preserver; and Shiva, the destroyer), the cult of *bhakti* (devotion) and the monotheistic concept of god as manifested in either Shiva or Vishnu. The *avatara* or incarnation theory, which gave several forms to Vishnu to save humanity from evil, and the worship of Shiva in the form of a *linga* (the phallic emblem), were the basic ingredients which helped the expansion of the Puranic religion in subsequent periods by incorporating popular and folk cults. The *Mahabharata* and *Ramayana*, based on stories of secular events, were now turned into religious works by the brahmins. The *Bhagavad-gita*, added to the *Mahabharata*, became the most important sacred book on account of its wide appeal.

The classical age: the age of the Brahminical states AD 300 to *c.* AD 650

The classical age in early Indian history, starting from AD 300, was dominated by the Gupta era which began with the accession of Chandragupta I (*c.* AD 319–20) under whom the dynasty emerged as a great power in the middle Ganges Valley and Magadha with Saketa (Ayodhya) and Prayaga (Allahabad) as its main centers. The Guptas' pre-eminence was achieved through marriage alliances with the Licchavis, an event celebrated in the Gupta coin issues, and with the Vakatakas, an important Deccan dynasty. The conquests of Samadragupta, the successor to Chandragupta I, brought the whole of Aryavarta under his control. The remnants of Kushana power were eradicated and the eastern coastal region as far south as Kanchipuram was overrun although its local rulers were afterwards reinstated.

The conquest of the Shakas of western India by Samadragupta's successor, Chandragupta II Vikramadiya, in the early fifth century AD, completed the establishment of an extensive territorial authority in northern India with access to the trade of the western coast. After Chandragupta II, however, Gupta power declined as the result of the severe blow dealt by waves of Hun invasions in the latter half of the fifth century and the early sixth century AD. The Huns (Hunas in Sanskrit) were a branch of the Ephthalites or White Huns, who swept into the subcontinent from the Oxus Valley. The disruption of central Asian trade caused by the Hun movements destabilized Gupta power leading to dissensions within the family. The Huns were followed by more central Asian tribes including the Gurjaras who replaced the older tribes in Rajasthan, some of their chiefs becoming the ancestors of the Rajput families which ruled North India in the medieval period.

Among the dynasties of the Deccan at this time were the Vakatakas of Vidarbha (fourth to fifth centuries AD), the Vishnukundis of Andhra (fifth to sixth centuries AD) and the Kadambas of Vanavasi, South Karnataka (fourth to fifth centuries AD). The Salankayanas of Vengi (Guntur and Krishna districts) rose to power in the fourth century and were replaced by the Vishnukundis in the following century. Two branches of the Gangas are known to have ruled in Kalinga (Orissa) and southern Mysore. The Pallavas of

---

Major states, dynasties and rulers *c.* BC 550 – *c.* AD 650

Century		
6–4 BC	*Magadhan Ascendancy* (North India)	
	543–491	Bimbisara
	491–461	Ajatashatru
	c. 362–334	Mahapadma Nanda
4–2 BC	*Mauryan Empire* (India except area south of Karnataka)	
	c. 321–297	Chandragupta Maurya
	c. 297–272	Bindusara
	c. 272/268–232	Ashoka
2–1 BC	*Shungas* (Ganges Valley and part of Central India)	
2–1 BC	*Indo-Greeks* (Northwest India)	
	180–165	Demetrius II
	155–130	Menander (Milinda)
1 BC to AD 3	*Satavahanas* (North Deccan)	
	c. 120	Gautamiputra Satakarni
1 BC to AD 3	*Shakas* (West India)	
1 BC to AD 3	*Kushanas* (Northern India and Central Asia)	
	c. 78–248	Kanishka
AD 4–6	*Guptas* (North India)	
	c. 319/20–335	Chandragupta I
	c. 335–376	Samadragupta
	c. 376–415	Chandragupta II
	c. 415–454	Kumara Gupta I
	c. 454–467	Skanda Gupta
AD 4–9	*Pallavas* (Tamil Nadu)	
AD 5–6	*Hunas* (Northwest India and Central Asia)	
AD 7	*Harsha* (North India)	
	606–747	Harshavardhana

Source: A. L. Basham *The Wonder that was India* 2nd edn, pp. xvii–xviii (London, 1967); RC.

Box 2

Kanchipuram maintained close relations with the Gangas and Kadambas. Most of the Deccan and Andhra dynasties performed Vedic sacrifices, called themselves *Brahma-Kshatriyas*, fostered brahminical institutions such as the *Ghatika* (center of learning) and followed the Puranic religions of Vaishnavism and Shaivism. The system of land-grants to brahmins and temples became a regular feature in the establishment and expansion of their agrarian bases.

Northern India after the Guptas was divided into four kingdoms: those of the later Guptas of Magadha (not connected with the earlier Guptas), the Maukharis of Kanyakubja (Qanauj, western Uttar

The Gupta empire.

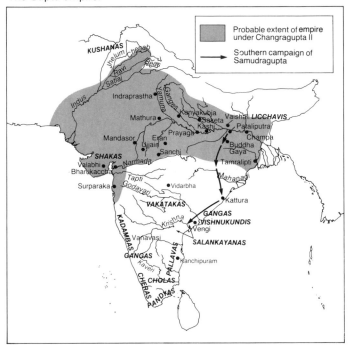

Harsha's empire.

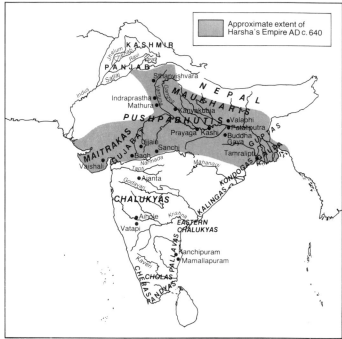

Source: Based on C.C. Davies, A Historical Atlas of the Indian Peninsula. (Oxford, 1965) p.21

Pradesh), the Pushpabhutis of Sthanvishvara (Thanesvar, north of Delhi) and the Maitrakas of Valabhi (in Gujarat). The Pushpabhutis ultimately emerged as the most powerful rulers under Prabhakaravarahana and his more famous brother, Harshavardhana. Under Harsha (AD 606–647), the Maukhari kingdom was united with the Pushpabhutis, and included the Panjab, Kashmir, Nepal and Gujarat. However, his efforts to extend his territory southwards into the Deccan were checked by the Chalukya Pulakeshini II of Vatapi. After the death of Shashanka, the powerful king of Gauda (Bengal), Harsha conquered the eastern region. In addition to his military achievements, Harsha was a playwright and patron of letters. The *Harshacarita*, written by Bana, his court poet, was the first important historical biography in the subcontinent.

Neither the Gupta kingdom nor that of Harsha can be described as centralized states, although in terms of size they were the second and third largest in pre-medieval India. The assumption of impressive titles such as Maharajadhiraja (the great king or king of kings) by the Guptas acknowledged the existence of several smaller centers of power under local chiefs. Local divisions like the *desha* and *bhukti* were in the charge of officers such as the *ayukta* and *kumaramatya* who linked the king's government with the locality. The Guptas initiated a system of land-grants to the brahmins (*agrahara*) and other religious institutions as well as to secular officers instead of salary. This led to an increase in privileges with the tendency for these offices to become hereditary, and played a significant part in

determining later social and political organization, helping in the emergence of landed intermediaries and feudatories (*samanta*).

Gupta patronage of art and literature encouraged the evolution of the classical idiom which became the standard for subsequent creative efforts. Sanskrit had already become the language of the ruling classes. Ashvaghosa's *Buddhacarita* provides the earliest example of Sanskrit *Kavya* (poetry), a style which reached its perfection in the works of the poet Kalidasa, one of the 'nine gems' in the court of Chandragupta II. Gupta sculpture marked the culmination of a quest for spiritualism and the perfection of the sculpting technique after a long search for perspective and three-dimensional expression. In architecture, the formative stages of the *Nagara* and *Dravida* temple styles occurred during the period of Gupta rule. The remarkable paintings of Ajanta and Bagh (fifth to seventh centuries AD) provided inspiration for Buddhist art throughout Asia. The *Puranas* and *Shilpa* texts laid down the beginnings of the formal principles of *Vastu* (architecture), *Shilpa* (sculpture) and *Chitra* (painting) as well as iconography. The classicism of this age was also reflected in the large variety of Gupta coins, mainly of gold, which were of a very high esthetic and technical order.

The Guptas performed Vedic sacrifices to legitimize their rule, and patronized the brahminical religions. Buddhism also received a fair amount of support: its continuing influence was illustrated by the visits of Chinese pilgrims such as Fa Hsien (AD 405–411) in search of Buddhist manuscripts in Indian monasteries. This period also witnessed the crystallization of the main components of later Hinduism, such as bhakti, image worship, the temple as the central institution in social and religious life, Vaishnavism and Shaivism as the two prime brahminical religions, and Tantric worship especially of the Mother Goddess. Six systems of philosophy, the *Nyaya*, *Vaisheshika*, *Sankhya*, *Yoga*, *Mimansa* and *Vedanta*, were evolved, and *Vedanta*, which refuted the theories of non-Brahminical schools, has continued as the basis of all philosophical studies and debates to this day. The Puranas, of which a great many were composed during this period, acquired a religious character, narrating myths relating to Shiva and the *avataras* (incarnations) of Vishnu.

Interest in astronomy and medicine dated back to the period of maritime commerce, when ocean navigation became more frequent. Two basic treatises on medicine by Charaka and Sushruta are also datable to the pre-Gupta times. But under the Guptas mathematics made great progress and the use of the cipher and Indian numerals were later carried by the Arabs to Europe. Aryabhata, the well-known astronomer, and Varahamihira, whose works exhibited considerable knowledge of Greek astronomy, both belong to this period. The life of the *Nagarika* (sophisticated citizen) became the concern of many writers at this time. Vatsyayana, for instance, is famous as the author of the *Kamasutra*, a manual on the art of love remarkable for its sophistication. Legal texts and commentaries of Yajnavalkya, Narada, Brihaspati and Katyayana represented important attempts to formalize judicial procedures by commenting on social problems and property rights.

It was in this classical form that Indian culture was increasingly carried to southeast Asia in the wake of trade and commerce. Chinese annals make increasing reference to Indian trading ventures in this region and attempts to acquire trading interests in Canton. Contacts between India and China became more frequent and embassies from the T'ang emperor reached the court of Harsha. The Malayan peninsula became particularly important for this trade: Takkola (modern Takuapa), the first landing stage leading to the Bay of Bandon, across the mountains and to the Straits of Malacca, played a significant role in its movement. Sri Vijaya (Sumatra) became a naval and commercial power of great importance in the trade relations between India, southeast Asia and China in the centuries following the Gupta period. As a result of these trading links, religious ideas flowed out of the subcontinent and colonized these new regions. Buddhism, for instance, influenced the religious traditions of southeast Asia, as well as China and later Japan. Equally influential was the impact of brahmanical social and religious values, especially on the evolution of the composite cultural patterns of the islands of Sumatra, Java and Borneo, and even of mainland Indo-China. The indianized kingdoms of Funan

India's influence in Southeast Asia to AD 650.

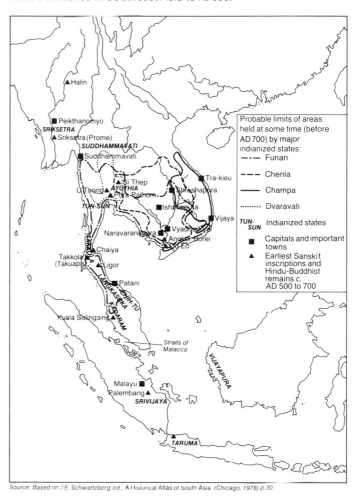

Source: Based on J.E. Schwartzberg, ed., A Historical Atlas of South Asia (Chicago, 1978) p.30

(Kambuja), Champa (Indo-China) and Ayuthia (Thailand) displayed the impact of these cultural influences in varying degrees: the use of Sanskrit in their inscriptions, the concept of the God-King, local versions of the *Ramayana*, and, above all, the influence of classical Indian traditions on their religious art and architecture were some of the most visible effects of this impact.　　　*RC*

Further reading

D. D. Kosambi, *The Culture and Civilisation of India in its Historical Outline* (London, 1965)

R. C. Majumdar, Ed., *The Vedic Age* (London, 1957); *The Age of Imperial Unity* (Bombay, 1968); *The Classical Age* (Bombay, 1970)

R. S. Sharma, *Aspects of Political Ideas and Institutions in Ancient India* (Delhi, 1968)

R. Thapar, *A History of India* Vol. 1 (Harmondsworth, 1982); *Ancient Indian Social History: Some Interpretations* (New Delhi, 1978)

Regional kingdoms and the development of distinctive regional cultures, AD 650 to AD 1250

North India

Regionalism dominates the history of India after the Guptas, with regions peripheral to the Ganges Valley and South India playing a more prominent role than before. The Ganges Valley ceased to produce influential powers after Harsha. A three-way struggle for Qanauj, the city symbolizing control over the Valley, began in the middle of the eighth century between the Gurjara-Pratiharas, the Palas of Bengal and the Rashtrakutas, the first Deccan dynasty to aspire to political dominance over northern India. All three in turn gained control over Qanauj with the Pratiharas enjoying the longest spell of success. The most celebrated of the Pratihara rulers were Vatsaraja (acc. 773), Nagabhata I (793–833) and Bhoja (836–885). Founded by Gopala (c. 750) in Bengal, the Palas acquired control over Qanauj under Dharmapala (770–810). His successor Devapala (810–859) reasserted Pala authority in Bengal and Bihar, and even claimed control over the Deccan. The Palas had commercial interests in southeast Asia.

Among the smaller states which arose on the periphery of these larger kingdoms was Kashmir under Lalitaditya Muktapida in the eighth century. Until the Turkish invasions of the eleventh and twelfth centuries, Kashmir was dominated by factional politics. In the northwestern region of Attock, the Hindu Shahiya dynasty was established by a Brahmana minister of the Turkish Shahiya, who ruled over the Kabul Valley and Gandhara. Later, in the ninth century, this dynasty also seized the Panjab from its Turkish rulers. Along the Himalayan foothills were located smaller states such as Champaka (Champa), Kulutu (Kulu) and Garhwal. Nepal and Kamarupa (known as Assam after the Ahoms of the thirteenth century) lay on the main trade route between India, Tibet and China. Katmandu and Patan in Nepal and Pragjyotisha in Assam were important towns.

The Rajputs

The Rajputs (*Rajaputra*), who rose to power in Rajasthan, were a substantial force in medieval Indian society and politics. Their origin has been a subject of controversy but general consensus inclines towards their having come from abroad. In keeping with Puranic tradition, they acquired solar and lunar lineage connections and kshatriya status. The important Rajput clans claimed descent from a mythical figure who arose out of a vast sacrificial pit near Mt. Abu, and called themselves the *Agni-kula* (Fire Family). Even local chiefs adopted this myth in a bid to gain Rajput status. The Pratiharas of South Rajasthan and Chahamanas (Chauhans) of East Rajasthan (Shakambhari and Ajmer) rose to power on the ruins of the old Pratihara kingdom. The Chaulukyas (Solankis) of Kathiawar had their branches in Malwa, Chedi, Patan and Broach. The Paramaras, feudatories of the Rashtrakutas, became independent at the end of the tenth century with Dhara near Indore in Malwa as their capital. Other Rajput dynasties in western and central India included the Chandellas of Jejakabhukti (Bundelkhand) centered in Khajuraho (tenth to eleventh centuries), the Guhilas of Chitor in Mewar (tenth to eleventh centuries) located south of the Chauhans, and the Kalachuris of Tripuri near Jabalpur. The Tomaras in the Hariyana region including Thaneshvar were also feudatories of the Pratiharas and founded Dhillika (Delhi) as early as 736.

The general tendency in northern India after the seventh century was for local rulers to assert their independence and for fully-fledged monarchies to emerge. Constant internal strife and attention to local affairs minimized contact with the outside world. In the eleventh century, the Rajputs fought among each other incessantly. The Chauhans, who occupied the Tomara kingdom in the region of Delhi, produced the greatest hero of the time in the famous Prithviraja (III), who wooed and won the daughter of the enemy Gahadavala ruler of Qanauj, an event celebrated in the epic poem, the *Prithvirajaraso* of Chand Bardai. He also acquired fame as the valiant Rajput who fought successfully against Muhammad Ghuri in the battle of Tarain (1191), although he died on the same battlefield the following year.

Two new factors which entered the politics of North India during this period were the Arabs and the Turks. The Arab conquest of Sind, described in a local chronicle, the *Chach Nama*, marked the easternmost point of Arab expansion in 712. The Turkish invasions of India by Mahmud of Ghazni between 1000 and 1026 became almost annual affairs, aimed at plundering the fertile plains of the Panjab and the proverbial riches of India's temples. Mathura, Thaneshvar, Qanauj and Somnath were some of the temple towns attacked by Mahmud, who used the loot to enhance the greatness of Ghazni. The Arab and Ghaznavid invasions, however, did not create any awareness of the outside world among Indian rulers, who failed to grasp the significance of further attacks. The later invasion of Muhammad of Ghur, in the last decade of the twelfth century, introduced a new political entity in India, the Delhi Sultanate, which began with the Slave dynasty founded by Qutb ud Din Aibak, his general, in 1206.

Orissa

The regional politics and culture of Orissa evolved when several small principalities and kingdoms, whose centers and distribution

Regional kingdoms and the development of distinctive regional cultures, AD 650 to AD 1250

India AD 1000 to AD 1200.

Source: Based on J.E. Schwartzberg ed., A Historical Atlas of South Asia (Chicago, 1978) p.32

in and around the Mahanadi and Brahmani Valleys had remained unchanged from the sixth to the eleventh centuries, were integrated into a regional state. In the eleventh century, the Somavamshi dynasty united Dakshina Koshala in western Orissa with Utkala (central Orissa), and established the first regional kingdom with its capital at Bhuvaneshvar. In the twelfth century, the eastern Gangas unified their southern homeland, Kalinga, with central and northern Orissa, making most of the rulers of the small principalities their feudatories (*Samanta rajas*). The integration of these areas into a loosely-structured political system was achieved both by conquest and through the royal cult of Jagannatha (Vishnu), which emerged as a result of the great synthesis of the folk deities with Shaiva and Vaishnava gods. This ritual 'royalization' of the deities was sustained by the building of gigantic temples, such as the one at Puri, and the ideological support provided by the brahmins.

Deccan

The first regional kingdom in the Deccan was established by the Chalukyas of Vatapi (mid-sixth to eighth centuries) in the Malaprabha Valley with Aihole and Pattadakal as two other centers of power. Pulakeshini II (610–643), the most successful of these rulers, checked Harsha's advance into the Deccan, conquered Vengi (the lower Krishna-Godavari Valley), where he established the eastern Chalukya branch and waged successful wars against the Pallavas of Kanchipuram. Deccan and Tamil powers now fought against each other for control over the agrarian resources of the Tungabhadra and the Krishna Valleys as well as the trade routes which linked Karnataka, Andhra and Tamil Nadu.

Dantidurga, the founder of the Rashtrakuta kingdom, overthrew Chalukya power in *c.* 753. Rashtrakuta interest in capturing the trade routes to the Ganges Valley continued under Dhruva (780–

Major dynasties and rulers *c.* AD 650–1206 [a]

c. 300–888	*Pallavas* (Tamil Nadu)	
	630–668	Narasimhavaraman Mahamalla
	730–796	Nandivarman II
c. 556–757	*Chalukyas of Vatapi* (West and Central Deccan)	
	610–643	Pulakeshin II
seventh to tenth century	*Pandyas of Madurai* (Tamil Nadu)	
	768–815	Varuguna I
	815–862	Shrimara Shrivallabha
	862–867	Varaguna II
c. 630–970	*Eastern Chalukyas of Vengi* (Andhra Pradesh)	
c. 750–1142	*Palas* (Bengal and Bihar)	
	c. 750	Gopala
	770–810	Dharmapala
	810–859	Devapala
c. 753–973	*Rashtrakutras* (West and Central Deccan)	
	780–793	Dhruva
	793–833	Govinda III
	814–878	Amoghavarsha
	878–914	Krishna II
	914–972	Indra III
	939–986	Krishna III
c. 773–1019	*Pratiharas* (West India and Upper Ganges Valley)	
	773–793	Vatsaraja
	793–833	Nagabhata I
	836–885	Bhoja
	c. 908–942	Mahipala

c. 850–1278	*Cholas of Thanjavur* (Tamil Nadu)	
	984–1014	Rajaraja I
	1014–1044	Rajendra
	1070–1118	Kulottunga I
c. 916–1203	*Chandellas* (Bundelkhand)	
c. 950–1195	*Kalachuris of Tripuri* (Madhya Pradesh)	
c. 973–1192	*Chahamanis* (East Rajasthan)	
c. 973–1189	*Chalukyas of Kalyani* (West and Central Deccan)	
	992–1008	Satyashraya
	1043–1068	Someshvara I
	1076–1126	Vikramaditya VI
	c. 1181–1189	Someshvara IV
c. 974–1238	*Chaulukyas* (Gujarat)	
c. 974–1060	*Paramaras* (Malwa)	
c. 1090–1193	*Gahadavalas* (Qanauj)	
c. 1110–1327	*Hoysalas of Dvarasamudra* (Central and South Deccan)	
c. 1118–1199	*Senas* (Bengal)	
c. 1190–1294	*Yadavas of Devagiri* (North Deccan)	
c. 1197–1323	*Kakatiyas of Warangal* (Andhra Pradesh)	

[a]The dates given for these dynasties are for their periods of importance. In many cases their existence can be traced both earlier and later.

Source: A. L. Basham, *The Wonder that was India* 2nd edn, p. xviii (London, 1967); RC.

Box 3

793), Govinda III (793–833) and Indra III (914–972) despite constant revolts and involvement in wars against the eastern Chalukyas and Cholas. Under Amoghavarsha (814–878), Manyakheta (Malkhed in Andhra Pradesh) became their capital. Krishna III (939–986), in alliance with the Gangas, overran the northern parts of the Chola territories. The sudden decline of Rashtrakuta power enabled their feudatory, Taila, to establish the later Chalukya kingdom in the Deccan by c. 973. From its nucleus in Bijapur, later Chalukya power extended up to the Godavari in the north and over southern Karnataka (Mysore) and Konkan, with Kalyani in Bidar as its headquarters. Beginning in the reign of Satyashraya (992–1008) and lasting until the middle of the twelfth century, the Chalukyas were engaged in a series of campaigns against the Cholas in which both claimed victory. The Kalachuri usurpation under Bijjala, one of the Chalukya feudatories (c. 1156–1167), undermined their power, and, after a brief revival under Someshvara IV (c. 1181–1189), they were overthrown by a feudatory belonging to the Yadava dynasty. The most celebrated of the Chalukyas was Vikramaditya VI (1076–1126), whose achievements are glorified in Bilhana's *Vikramankadevacarita*, the second great historical biography produced in India.

The Deccan was now divided between the Yadavas (Seunas) of Devagiri in the north and the Hoysalas of Dvarasamudra (Halebid) in the south. The Kakatiyas of Warangal, who rose to power in the Telengana region of Andhra Pradesh, were contemporaries and rivals of these Deccan dynasties. The eastern Chalukyas in the heartland of Andhra declined after a long and checkered political career between the seventh and twelfth centuries, giving way to a number of minor ruling families including the Telugu Chodas of Nellur. In the thirteenth and fourteenth centuries, southern India was harrassed by the predatory raids of Malik Ghafur under the Khaljis and the Tughluq invasions. Their devastation of the rich south Indian temples caused the ultimate decline of the three most important ruling dynasties and paved the way for the rise of Vijayanagar in the Tungabhadra region and the Bahmani kingdom in northern Deccan (Gulbarga) in the middle of the fourteenth century.

Tamil Nadu

The Pallavas, who became independent in the Andhra region after the decline of the Satavahanas, had established the first regional kingdom in Tamil country by the seventh century, acquiring a territorial base around Kanchipuram (Palar Valley), south of Madras. The Simhavishnu line of Pallavas built up their power under Mahendravarman I (575–630), Narasimhavaraman Mahamalla (630–668), who defeated the Chalukya Pulakeshin II and destroyed Vatapi, and Nandivarman II (730–796), who successfully faced the hostility of the Chalukyas and the Pandyas of

Madurai. The Pandyas (seventh to tenth centuries) ruled over the Vaigai and Tamraparni Valleys. They allied themselves more often with Chera and Sri Lankan rulers to resist the expansionist moves of other Tamil powers. Varaguna I (768–815), Varaguna II (862–867) and Shrimara Shrivallabha (815–862) were the most successful of the Pandya rulers. Their aspirations to control the lower Kaveri Valley brought them into conflict with the Pallavas. Under the Pallavas and Pandyas a process of agrarian expansion was begun through land grants to brahmins (*brahmadeya*) and temples, with special emphasis on the construction of irrigation works. The Pandyas continued as chief participants in the maritime trade of southern India with Sri Lanka, Arabia and southeast Asia. The imperial Cholas of Thanjavur, who rose to power in the middle of the ninth century after overthrowing the Pallavas, established one of the most powerful regional states of South India with the Kavari delta as its nucleus. The four hundred years of Chola rule (850–1278) achieved the political unification of the Tamil country and the integration of its sub-regions (*mandalams*) into a wider cultural zone. The Cholas adopted the bhakti ideology of the Tamil saints with the temple as the supreme institution of integration and symbol of royal power. Under Rajaraja I (984–1014), Rajendra (1014–1044) and the Chalukya-Chola Kulottunga I (1070–1118), Chola power expanded over the whole of Tamil Nadu, southern Karnataka, Vengi, Venad (South Kerala) and northern Sri Lanka where Polunnaruva was the Chola center. Rajendra's expedition to the lower Ganges Valley acted as a check to the imperial ambitions of Mahipala and was commemorated by the foundation of a new capital, Gangaikondacholapuram. His maritime expeditions to Kadaram and Sri Vijaya in southeast Asia established trading rights and facilities for South Indian merchants in this region and as far as China, where trade missions were sent by Rajaraja and Kulottunga. Nagappattinam at the mouth of the Kaveri developed into the biggest Chola port. But, by the beginning of the thirteenth century, Chola power had declined due to rebellious feudatories, revived Pandya invasions and Hoysala intrusion from South Karnataka.

Kerala

Kerala, known as the land of Parashurama, emerged at the end of the eighth century with the rise of the Kulashekharas of Mahodayapuram. Based in the Periyar Valley, the Mahodaya kingdom laid the foundations of the region's culture with caste as the determining factor in socio-political organization, dominated by a brahmin priestly landowning group and an aristocratic, landowning military class, later becoming the Nayar caste, with a special *sambandham* (marriage relationship) with the brahmins and a system of matrilineal descent. Kerala was constantly subjected to or in alliance with the Pandyas of Madurai (seventh to tenth centuries) and the Cholas of Thanjavur (tenth to twelfth centuries). After the decline of the Mahodaya kingdom in the twelfth century, Venad (Travancore) became the center of political authority.

Medieval Indian society

The early medieval state in India has been characterized as a decentralized feudal polity on the basis of the land-grants, both religious and secular, which created powerful landed intermediaries (*Samantas*) and established a hierarchy of land-rights through service relations and a dependent peasantry. 'Indian Feudalism', however, was not identical with classical European feudalism. More recently, the theory of the segmentary state has been used to describe South Indian kingdoms, especially that of the Cholas, in which ritual sovereignty was emphasized and local government placed in the hands of fairly autonomous 'segments' or entrenched peasant units (*nadu*), the village level sabha or brahmin assembly, and the *ur* or peasant (*velala*) assembly. Another characterization of the medieval Indian state introduces the concept of a lineage polity, with ranking as the crucial factor in integration.

Although regionalism dominates the history of India during this period, two features common to all the regions were the spread of the Puranic religion, through a two-way process of sanskritization of local cults and localization of brahminical social order. The brahmin priestly and landowning group dominated socio-political organization, sharing authority with the kshatriyas, or local ruling families of obscure origins claiming kshatriya status, and fabricating for them impressive genealogical connections and divine descent or providing gotra affiliations. The *brahmadeya/agrahara* and the temple were both citadels of brahmin culture and institutional forces for the integration of various ethnic and economic groups in the varna (caste) hierarchy through ritual ranking.

As far as other religious developments were concerned, Buddhism declined from the seventh century and became increasingly confined to Bihar and Bengal where the Vajrayana form developed under the impact of Tantricism. Under patronage from the Pala rulers, Buddhist universities were established in the region. Buddhist institutions also received support from rulers in southeast Asia such as Balaputradeva, the Sailendra king of Sumatra and Sri Maravijayottungavaraman of Sri Vijaya. Jainism flourished in Gujarat and Rajasthan, where a powerful trading community and royalty together gave patronage to the Svetambara sect. Similarly, in Karnataka, the Digambara sect was supported by the Kalachuris and Gangas, then spread to other parts of southern India. Meanwhile, Shaiva sects grew up in various parts of the subcontinent. An esoteric form of Shaivism, *Pratyabhijnya*, flourished in Kashmir. The non-conformist Pashupata and Kalamukha sects became powerful in Gujarat, Rajasthan, Orissa and the Deccan. In Karnataka, the Vira Shaiva sect, founded by Basava in the twelfth century as a reaction to Jain influence, was inspired by the Tamil

bhakti movement. The bhakti cult of the Shaiva *nayanars* and Vaishnava *alvars* originated in the Tamil region during the Pallava period and was encouraged by the Cholas, under whom Shaivism became the dominant local religion. Often characterized as a social protest, the bhakti movement emanated in an urban context. Bhakti saints defeated Jains and Buddhists in religious debate and helped bring about the decline of the 'heterodox' sects in South India.

The greatest philosophers of the period were Shankara (eighth and ninth centuries) and Ramanuja (twelfth century), well known for the clarity and vigor of their thought. Their teachings were derived from the monism of *Vedanta*. Ramanuja, a Vaishnava reformer based in Srirangam, the holiest of the Vaishnava centers, founded the Srivaishnava sect. He propounded the Vishishtadvaita or qualified monism. The two main aspects of their philosophy were the paths of *jnana* (knowledge) and bhakti (devotion).

Indian influence in Southeast Asia AD 650 to AD 1250.

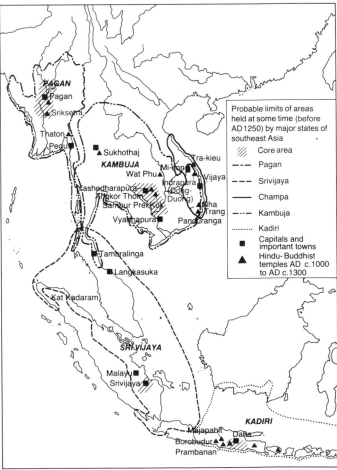

Source: Based on J. E. Schwartzberg, ed., A Historical Atlas of South Asia (Chicago, 1978) p. 36

Regionalism expressed in temple architecture: the Lingaraja temple, Bhubanesvar
(Orissa).

Regionalism expressed in temple architecture: the Udayaswara temple at Udaipur (Rajasthan).

Another uniform feature of the period was the land-grant system, which led to agrarian expansion. Internal trade developed with agrarian surpluses and market centers like the *nagaram* of South India became a part of the local exchange systems as well as long distance trade. Monetization, however, was only partial, reflected in the paucity of coins. Described as the third urbanization, this period saw the revival of trade in which Bengal, Gujarat and South India took the lead. Itinerant merchant organizations, like the powerful supra-regional 'Ayyavole Five Hundred', crossed over to Sri Lanka and countries in southeast Asia where they interacted with local trading groups. They established special centers in South India protected by mercenaries under royal charters. Jewish and Arab traders dominated the western seas and its horse trade, and acquired trading charters from the rulers of Kerala. The Chinese dominated the eastern seas, while the Arabs appropriated southeast Asian commerce by the thirteenth century. South Indian guilds specialized in textiles, spices and gems, and Indian textiles enjoyed an expanding market: Kanchipuram in South India became the biggest textile manufacturing center attracting international commerce. In Rajasthan, individual families of merchants like the Uesavala (later Oswals) conducted organized trade.

Sanskrit was used in official records, formal education and court literature. However, local languages like Tamil took precedence over Sanskrit as demonstrated in the records of the Pallavas and Cholas which are in both Tamil and Sanskrit. Exponents of *bhakti* preferred the vernacular and contributed to the gradual breakaway from Sanskrit which led to the evolution of the present-day languages of the subcontinent; Tamil, which dates from the third century BC, is the main exception to this process. Efforts to translate the *Mahabharata* and *Ramayana* into local languages enriched the vernacular idiom.

Regionalism found its most remarkable expression in the *nagara* and *dravida* styles of temple architecture. The nagara temple tower reflected the dominant trends of development in the regional schools of Orissa, central India, Rajasthan and Gujarat. The dravida style of South India developed under the Pallavas and Cholas, with the storeyed tower of the shrine (*vimana*) rising to great heights and the enclosures and gateways (*gopura*) marking the horizontal expansion of the temple complex.

In the development of sculpture and painting, the norms of the classical idiom of the preceding Gupta age did not prevent dominant local traditions from asserting themselves in the Pala and Sena sculptures of Bengal. The Tamil regional style is represented by the large-scale narrative sculptures of Mamallapuram under the Pallavas and the Chola creations in bronze such as Shiva as Nataraja, the comic dancer, unparalleled in its conception and execution. Under the Chalukyas of Vatapi and the Rashtrakutas, the Deccan produced vigorous and dynamic narrative panels at Badami, Elephanta and Ellora. But then the artists at Ellora gradually moved away from this tradition and introduced what has been called the 'medieval factor' in sculpture and painting, a feature which persisted until the Mughals in northern India and, through Vijayanagar art, to the eighteenth century in the south.

RC

Further reading
R. C. Majumdar, Ed., *The Age of Imperial Kanauj* (Bombay, 1964); *The Struggle for Empire* (Bombay, 1966)
K. A. Nilakanta Sastri, *A History of South India from Prehistoric Times to the Fall of Vijayanagar* 4th edn (Madras, 1976)
R. S. Sharma, *Social Change in Early Medieval India* (New Delhi, 1969); *Indian Feudalism* (Delhi, 1981)

B. Stein, *Peasant, State and Society in Medieval South India* (New Delhi, 1980)
G. Yazdani, Ed., *The Early History of the Deccan*, 2 vols, (London, 1960)

The Delhi Sultanate, 1206 to 1526

Following the assassination of the last great Ghurid Sultan, Muizz ud Din Muhammad, in 1206, his empire disintegrated. The Indian territories became practically autonomous under his Turkish slave lieutenants, of whom Qutb ud Din Aibak at Lahore is traditionally regarded as the founder of the Delhi Sultanate. Strictly speaking, however, the birth of the Sultanate dates from the seizure of power in 1211 by Aibak's own lieutenant Iltutmish, who made Delhi his capital. There was no guarantee at this stage that the North Indian plain would not swiftly revert to being the outpost of an Islamic empire centered beyond the Indus: in 1211–16 Ghur and Ghazna were occupied by the Khwarizmshah Muhammad ibn Takash, who bestowed them on his son Jalal ud Din and might well have endeavored to incorporate the Panjab in his dominions. Nor was it necessarily certain that the infant Delhi Sultanate would triumph over the other heirs of the Ghurids in Sind and Bengal and acquire the whole of Muizz ud Din's Indian legacy. Chengis Khan and the Mongols, by sweeping away the Khwarizmian empire in 1219–22, inadvertently ensured that Muslim India would go its own way; Iltutmish, by denying Jalal ud Din a refuge in the Panjab and by annexing Sind (1228), Bengal (1230) and the Khwarizmian prince's ephemeral conquests east of the Indus (1229), established the Sultanate as Islam's sole protagonist in the subcontinent.

At the outset the Delhi Sultanate was dominated by a corps of Turkish slaves (*mamluks*) who largely provided the military leadership, the provincial governors and the great officers of court. The terms 'Slave dynasty' and 'Slave Sultanate' sometimes applied to the early decades are, however, misleading. Of the thirteenth-century sovereigns, only two were former slaves: Iltutmish himself, whose descendants ruled until 1266, and Balaban, who then founded a new dynasty. Moreover, slave status was only one channel, if at this time the most important one, for recruitment to the ruling élite. The mamluks faced competition both from the growing number of free immigrants (nobles, bureaucrats and soldiers of fortune), who sought asylum in India after the Mongol devastation of central Asia and eastern Iran, and from the emerging Indo-Muslim element. In 1290 Balaban's line in turn was supplanted at Delhi by the Khaljis, leaders of a group of free-born immigrants of Turkish stock. The

The Delhi Sultanate, 1206 to 1526

India in the time of the Delhi Sultanate.

Rulers of India 1206–1526

Sultans of Delhi 1206–1526

Slave Kings

1206–1210	Qutb ud Din Aibak
1210–1211	Aram Shah
1211–1236	Shams ud Din Iltutmish
1236–1237	Rukn ud Din Firuz
1237–1240	Jalalal ud Din Raziyya
1240–1242	Muizz ud Din Bahram Shah
1242–1246	Ala ud Din Masud Shah
1246–1266	Nasir ud Din Mahmud
1266–1286	Ghiyas ud Din Balaban
1286–1290	Muizz ud Din Kayqubad
1290	Shams ud Din Kayumars

Khaljis

1290–1296	Jalal ud Din Khalji
1296	Rukn un Din Ibrahim
1296–1315	Ala ud Din
1315–1316	Shihab ud Din Umar
1316–1320	Qutb ud Din
1320	Nasir ud Din Khusrau Khan

Tughluqids

1320–1324	Ghiyas ud Din Tughluq
1324–1351	Muhammad
1351–1388	Firuz Shah
1388–1389	Tughluq II
1389–1390	Abu Bakr
1390–1394	Muhammad II
1394	Ala ud Din Sikandar
1394–1413	Nasir ud Din Mahmud
	versus
1394–c. 1400	Nusrat Shah

Sayyids

1414–1421	Khizr Khan
1421–1434	Mubarak Shah
1434–1445	Muhammad
1445–1451	Ala ud Din Alam Shah

Lodis

1451–1489	Bahlul
1489–1517	Sikandar
1517–1526	Ibrahim

Sultans of Bengal 1336–1526 (Sultanate ends 1576)

In Eastern Bengal

| 1336–1349 | Fakhr ud Din Shah |
| 1349–1352 | Ikhtiyar ud Din Ghazi Shah |

In Western Bengal and then all Bengal

| 1339–1345 | Ala ud Din Ali Shah |

Line of Ilyas Shah

| 1345–1358 | Shams ud Din Ilyas Shah |

1358–1390	Sikandar Shah I
1390–1410	Ghiyas ud Din Azam Shah
1410–1412	Shihab ud Din Bayazid Shah
1412–1414	Ala ud Din Firuz Shah

Line of Raja Ganesha

| 1414–1432 | Jalal ud Din Muhammad Shah |
| 1432–1436 | Shams ud Din Ahmad Shah |

Line of Ilyas Shah restored

1437–1460	Nasir ud Din Mahmud Shah
1460–1474	Rukn ud Din Barbak Shah
1474–1481	Shams ud Din Yusuf Shah
1481	Sikandar Shah II
1481–1487	Jalal ud Din Fateh Shah

Line of Habashis

1487	Sultan Shahzada Barbak Shah
1487–1490	Saif ud Din Firuz Shah
1490–1491	Nasir ud Din Mahmud Shah
1491–1494	Shams ud Din Muzaffar Shah

Line of Sayyid Husain Shah

| 1494–1519 | Sayyid Ala ud Din Husain Shah |
| 1519–1532 | Ala ud din Firuz Shah |

Sultans of Kashmir 1346–1526 (Sultanate ends 1589)
[Chronology uncertain for the fourteenth century]

Line of Shah Mirza Swati

1346–1349	Shams ud Din Shah Mirza Swati
1349–1350	Jamshid
1350–1359	Ala ud Din Ali Shir
1359–1378	Qutb ud Din Hindal
1378–1394	Shihab ud Din
	Qutb ud Din Hindal
1394–1416	Sikandar But-shikan
1416–1420	Ali Mirza Khan
1420–1470	Zain ul Abidin Shahi Khan
1470–1471	Haidar Shah Hajji Khan
1471–1489	Hasan
1489–1490	Muhammad (first reign)
1490–1498	Fateh Shah (first reign)
1498–1499	Muhammad (second reign)
1499–1500	Fateh Shah (second reign)
1500–1526	Muhammad (third reign)

Sultans of Gujarat 1391–1526 (Sultanate ends 1583)

1391–1411	Zafar Khan Muzaffar I
1411–1442	Ahmad I
1442–1451	Muhammad Karim
1451–1458	Qutb ud Din Ahmad II
1458	Daud
1458–1511	Mahmud I Begra
1511–1526	Muzaffar II

Box 4 *(continued over)*

The Delhi Sultanate, 1206 to 1526

Sharqi Sultans of Jaunpur 1394–1479

1394–1399	Malik Sarvar
1399–1402	Mubarak Shah
1402–1440	Shams ud din Ibrahim
1440–1457	Mahmud Shah
1457–1458	Muhammad Shah
1458–1479	Husain Shah

Sultans of Malwa 1401–1526 (Sultanate ends 1531)

Line of Ghuris

1401–1405	Dilavar Khan Husain Ghuri
1405–1435	Alp Khan Hushang
1435–1436	Ghazni Khan Muhammad
1436	Masud Khan

Line of Khaljis

1436–1469	Mahmud Shah I
1469–1500	Ghiyas Shah
1500–1511	Nasir Shah
1511–1531	Mahmud Shah II

Bahmanid Sultans of the Deccan and their successors 1347–1526 (Sultanate ends 1527)

1347–1358	Ala ud Din Hasan Bahman Shah
1358–1375	Muhammad I
1375–1378	Ala ud Din Mujahid
1378	Daud
1378–1397	Muhammad II
1397	Ghiyas ud Din
1397	Shams ud Din
1397–1422	Firuz
1422–1436	Ahmad I Vali
1436–1458	Ala ud Din Amhad II
1458–1461	Ala ud Din Humayun Zalim
1461–1463	Nizam
1463–1482	Muhammad III Lashkari
1482–1518	Mahmud
1518–1521	Ahmad III[a]
1521–1522	Ala ud Din[a]
1522–1525	Valiullah[a]
1525–1527	Kalimullah[a]

[a]nominal sultans under the tutelage of the chief minister Amir Barid of Bidar.

Imadshahis of Berar 1484–1526 (Sultanate ends 1572)

1484–1504	Fatehullah
1504–*c.* 1529	Ala ud Din

Nizamshahis of Ahmadnagar 1490–1526 (Sultanate ends 1595)

1490–1508	Ahmad I
1508–1553	Burhan I

Baridishahis of Bidar 1492–1526 (Sultanate ends *c.* 1609)

1492–1504	Qasim I
1504–1549	Amir I

Adilshahis of Bijapur 1489–1526 (Sultanate ends 1686)

1489–1511	Yusuf Adil Shah
1511–1534	Ismail

Qutbshahis of Golconda 1512–1526 (Sultanate ends 1687)

1512–1543	Sultan Quli

Faruqi Sultans of Khandesh 1370–1526 (Sultanate ends 1601)

1370–1399	Malik Raja Faruqi
1399–1437	Nasir Kahn
1437–1441	Adil Khan I
1441–1457	Miran Mubarak Khan I
1457–1503	Adil Khan II
1503–1510	Daud Khan
1510	Ghazni Khan
1510	Alam Khan
1510–1520	Adil Khan III
1520–1537	Miran Muhammad I

Dynasties and rulers in the South

1216–1327	Pandyas of Madurai (Tamil Nadu)

Rulers of the Vijayanagar Empire 1339–1526 (Effective rule ends 1646)

1336–1354	Harihara I
1354–1377	Bukka I
1377–?1404	Harihara II
?1404–1406	Bukka I
1406–1422	Devaraya I
1422–1425	Vira Vijaya
1425–1447	Devaraya II
1447–1465	Mallikarjuna
1465–1485	Virupaksa
1485–1486	Praudhadevaraya
1486–?1492	Saluva Narasimha
?1492–1503	Immadi Narasimha
1503–1509	Vira Narasimha
1509–1530	Krishnadevaraya

Source: C. E. Bosworth, *The Islamic Dynasties* revised edn, pp. 186–209 (Edinburgh, 1980); S. Lane-Poole, *The Mohammadan Dynasties* pp. 320–21 (London, 1893); A. L. Basham, *The Wonder that was India* 2nd edn, p. xviii (London, 1967); P. Spear, Ed. *The Oxford History of India* 4th edn, pp. 318–19 (Delhi, 1981); PJ.

Box 4 *(continued)*

'Khalji revolution' further undermined the hold of a tradition that equated slave status with the most essential qualification for military and administrative office, although slaves were by no means eliminated from the political scene, and accelerated the rise of an indigenous Muslim aristocracy.

The three decades following Iltutmish's death in 1236 were critical. His successors, with the qualified exception of his daughter Raziyya who was the first woman to attain sovereignty in the Islamic world, inherited none of his vigor and were mere creatures in the hands of rival factions. Not until the victory of Balaban, who ruled first through Nasir ud Din Mahmud (1246–66) and then as Sultan in person (1266–86), did the Sultanate obtain any degree of stability. The factionalism between mamluk and non-mamluk, and even within the slave élite itself, might well have destroyed the Delhi state, confronted as it now was by an external threat of vast proportions. In 1241 the Mongols, having reduced the trans-Indus territories to obedience, launched their first attack on the Sultanate and sacked Lahore. Thereafter Mongol invasions were an annual event. Nor were they viewed as unwelcome in every quarter. In the 1250s Sultan Mahmud's renegade brother and a number of mamluk grandees were all found at the Mongol imperial court offering submission, and in 1257 the governor of Sind turned his province temporarily into a Mongol protectorate. The Delhi empire was reprieved by the outbreak of civil war within the Mongol empire in 1260–61 and its division into a number of warring khanates, none of which effectively controlled Afghanistan. Early in his reign, Balaban was, thus, able to restore the walls of Lahore; yet the northwest frontier had in reality receded from the upper Indus, where it stood in the time of Iltutmish, as far as the Beah. It is a testimony to this frontier's importance that the founders of the Sultanate's two greatest dynasties were both veteran campaigners against the Mongols: Jalal ud Din Khalji had been governor of Samana and Ghiyas ud Din Tughluq governor of Dipalpur.

The advent of the Khalji dynasty coincided approximately with the occupation of Afghanistan by the Chaghatai Mongols of central Asia and a consequent build-up of Mongol pressure on India. In the reign of Ala ud Din Khalji (1296–1315) their raids penetrated beyond the Panjab and into the provinces of Budaon and Avadh. The Sultan fought an indecisive battle in 1299 with an unprecedentedly large invading force not far north of Delhi, and in 1303 the capital itself underwent a two-month siege. This invasion prompted Ala ud Din to enact various fiscal and administrative measures with a view to averting any repetition of the crisis; but however salutary these proved, the people of Delhi had good reason to be grateful also for the internecine strife which broke out in central Asia c. 1305 and led to another respite from Mongol attacks.

In its other principal task, that of enforcing Islamic rule over the independent Hindu powers, the Sultanate made only fitful progress in the thirteenth century, when many campaigns involved mere plundering raids and the temporary reduction of Hindu fortresses. In the western Panjab the Khokhars, a Hindu tribe severely chastized toward the end of the Ghurid era, had soon recovered their autonomy and were a constant source of disruption. To the south, the independence of the Hindu principalities of Rajasthan was unaffected by Muslim raids. A case in point is the great fortress of Ranthanbor, which had been captured by Iltutmish in 1226: it was abandoned under Raziyya, and although it was attacked in 1248, 1259 and 1291, its definitive conquest had to wait until the reign of Ala ud Din Khalji. Balaban confined himself to more limited objectives such as clearing the forest region around Delhi of Hindu marauders and constructing fortresses there which he garrisoned with Afghan settlers.

In this respect too the Khalji era marked a watershed. A series of expeditions in Ala ud Din's reign conquered Gujarat (1299) and the strongholds of Ranthambor (1301), Chitor (1303), Sevana (1308) and Jalor (1311) in Rajasthan. This enabled the Sultan to launch raids south of the Narmada river, where tribute was exacted from the Yadava kingdom of Devagiri (1307), the Kakatiya kingdom of Tilang (Telengana) (1309) and the Pandya kingdom in the far south (1311). It may well be asked how the empire was able to sustain such efforts at a time when it was called upon to withstand formidable assaults from the northwest. The answer seems to be that regular expeditions against the Hindu states, yielding plunder and tribute, were vital in order to finance the creation and maintenance of large armies for defence against the Mongol threat. The Sultanate genuinely overstretched its resources, and hence brought on its own collapse, only as a policy of profitable raiding was replaced by one of outright annexation: this occurred under Qutb ud Din Khalji (1316–20) and his Tughluqid successors, when garrisons and provincial administrations were established in the Deccan (c. 1318), Tilang and Mabar (c. 1323).

Qutb ud Din was murdered in 1320 by a favorite, who ascended

Silver coin of Ala ud Din Khalji. On obverse – The most mighty sovereign, Ala ud Duniya wa ud Din Abul Muzaffar Muhammad Shah, the Sultan. On reverse – Sikandar the second, right hand of the caliphate, supporter of the commander of the faithful. On margin – This silver [was] struck at the capital, Delhi, in the year 712.

the throne as Khusrau Khan (the only sovereign of Delhi, in fact, who was a Hindu convert). His overthrow in turn by Ghiyas ud Din Tughluq (1320–24), who was apparently a slave commander of Turco-Mongol extraction, was achieved in the teeth of pronounced Indo-Muslim opposition. It comes as no surprise, therefore, to find the Tughluqid dynasty relying for support on non-Indian elements. Tughluq's son and successor Muhammad (1324–51) deliberately sought to attract immigrants from all over the Islamic world in order to broaden his power-base: one of them was the Moroccan Ibn Battuta, who left a lengthy account of his stay in India in the years 1333–47. Muhammad's policy, which was abandoned by his successor Firuz Shah (1351–88), may well have been one factor underlying the extraordinary number of rebellions during his reign.

Muhammad is perhaps the most controversial figure in the history of the Sultanate, a ruler whose generosity and brutally repressive punishments were like a byword in his own day. The significance – and indeed the sanity – of his various projects are still disputed by historians. Yet it seems that his policy was over-ambitious rather than whimsical. In view of the greatly increased size of his empire he attempted from 1327 to establish his capital at the more centrally-situated Devagiri (renamed Daulatabad) in the Deccan and to foster Muslim colonization of the province. He took the offensive against the Mongols, raiding Peshawar and planning an impressive expedition into Afghanistan which in the event had to be abandoned; part of the enormous force raised for this purpose, however, was sent to some unspecified region of the sub-Himalayas (possibly Kashmir), where it was decimated. To facilitate payment of his troops he introduced a token currency, which was greeted with suspicion by his subjects and had to be recalled, and increased the revenue-demand on the Doab cultivators, thereby provoking widespread peasant uprisings.

With the revolts of Muhammad's reign began the first phase in the disintegration of the Delhi Sultanate. First Mabar seceded (c. 1334); then Bengal was finally lost (c. 1335), followed by Tilang (c. 1339). In 1347 the Deccan became independent under its own ruling dynasty, the Bahmanids. The death of Firuz Shah in 1388 and the struggle for the throne among his progeny brought on the second phase. The Sultanate became a tempting prey for the central Asian conqueror Timur (Tamerlane), whose invasion succeeded where his Chaghatai predecessors had failed. Delhi was taken and sacked in 1398, and its hegemony ended. Already Khandesh had become autonomous (c. 1382). Now Sivistan, which had rebelled in Muhammad's day but had been reduced to tributary status by Firuz, fell away. Independent sultanates appeared in Jaunpur (1400), Malwa (1406) and Gujarat (1407). In Rajasthan the Hindu kingdoms of Marwar and Mewar emerged. Even in districts much closer to the capital, small principalities were founded by Muslim amirs at Kalpi and Mahoba and by a Hindu raja at Gwalior. The

Sultanate had shrunk to the point where it was again merely one of a number of Muslim states competing for primacy in the north.

On a superficial view, the Delhi Sultanate had come to embrace a territory of vast extent. Yet its sovereigns presided over a society in which their fellow-Muslims were never more than a minority. Effective rule depended on the possession of a network of strongpoints which dominated the military highways and trade routes. We should judge the government's real power by its capacity to exact the land tax (*kharaj*), particularly in the fertile Doab region which served as the granary of the capital, and to tap the wealth of the flourishing ports of Gujarat and Bengal. The degree of control also varied with the precise relationship between the Sultans, the military and the provinces. Ala ud Din took care to maximize the area under the immediate supervision of the revenue office (*divan*), which in turn would pay cash stipends directly to the troops. This system was still operative, in part at least, in the early years of Muhammad bin Tughluq. But during Firuz Shah's reign it seems that there was a reversion to the earlier arrangements that had obtained, for example, under Balaban: a commander was granted an assignment of revenue (*iqta*) on a specified district, from which he was to raise and maintain a body of soldiers. Such decentralization nurtured the growth of the semi-independent warlords who were politically active under the last Tughluqids and in the Sayyid and Lodi eras. The government's authority over the rural Hindu aristocracy was generally still more tenuous. Even close to the heartlands of the Sultanate there were always regions like Katehr and the Khokhar territory where tribute was obtained only intermittently and the Sultan's writ scarcely ran; and it is clear that the local Hindu chiefs, especially in Rajasthan, retained their positions under Muslim overlordship, so that they were able to reassert themselves when the central control atrophied in the late fourteenth century.

If the provinces south of the Narmada had rejected government from Delhi, the colonization of the Deccan in the Khalji and early Tughluqid periods had nevertheless ensured that it would continue to form part of the Islamic world. The Bahmanid state itself gradually broke up in the fifteenth century, and by the time the Mughals entered India its former territories were disputed among five dynasties: the Baridshahis of Bidar, the Imadshahis of Berar (1484), the Adilshahis of Bijapur (1489), the Nizamshahis of Ahmadnagar (1490) and the Qutbshahis of Golconda (1512). In the far south, however, the Muslim occupation proved far more precarious. Here it was a Hindu power, the newly-created state of Vijayanagar, that profited from the collapse of Muhammad bin Tughluq's authority. It came to embrace a considerable tract, annexing the short-lived Sultanate of Mabar *c.* 1377, and was able for some time to turn the constant wars of the Deccan states to its own advantage. Reaching its peak under Krishnadevaraya

(1509–30), it was finally to succumb to a coalition of its Muslim neighbors in 1565.

The last feeble Tughluqid Sultan died in 1413, and Delhi was occupied by Khizr Khan (1414–21), a former officer of the dynasty whom Timur had appointed as his governor of Multan and Lahore. The new dynasty, the so-called Sayyids, initially acknowledged the overlordship of Timur's successors and eschewed the royal title. They lost Multan to an independent dynasty, the Langahs, in 1440 and were repeatedly threatened by the power of Jaunpur in the east. In 1451 they were replaced by the Lodis, leaders of an Afghan clan that had entered the empire in the time of Firuz Shah Tughluq. Under the more energetic rule of Bahlul Lodi (1451–89), whose power was buttressed by the immigration of Afghan tribesmen in significant numbers, the Sultanate experienced a modest revival, notably with the installation of the Sultan's younger son as client prince of Jaunpur (1479) and its annexation, together with Bihar, by Sikandar Lodi (1489–1517) in the 1490s. But the last of the Lodis, Ibrahim (1517–1526), encountered opposition even from the Afghan chiefs who governed the western Panjab on his behalf, and it was one of these who called for assistance from Timur's descendant, Babur, the ruler of Kabul, and ushered in the Mughal conquest. Ibrahim met the invader at Panipat and was defeated and killed (1526).

PJ

Further reading

A. B. M. Habibullah, *The Foundation of Muslim Rule in India* 2nd edn (Allahabad, 1961)

P. Hardy, 'Dihli Sultanate' *Encyclopaedia of Islam* (Leiden and London, 1954–) new edn in progress

A. M. Husain, *Tughluq Dynasty* (Calcutta, 1963)

K. S. Lal, *History of the Khaljis A.D. 1290–1320* 2nd edn (Calcutta, 1967); *Twilight of the Sultanate*, 2nd edn (New Delhi, 1980)

R. C. Majumdar (General Ed.), *History and Culture of the Indian People*, V; *The Struggle for Empire*; VI; *The Delhi Sultanate* 2nd edn (Bombay, 1967)

T. Raychaudhuri and I. Habib, Eds, *The Cambridge Economic History of India*, Vol. 1, (Cambridge, 1982)

The Mughal empire, 1526 to 1707

Babur, Humayun, the Suris and the establishment of the Mughal empire 1526 to 1556

Babur's victory over the Lodi ruler, Ibrahim, at Panipat gave him control of Delhi and Agra. The Afghans, however, still held several important towns in the Upper Ganges plain. They sought to recover power with the backing of the Sultan of Bengal in the east and the Rajputs to the south of Agra who, under Rana Sanga of Mewar, were themselves threatening to restore their rule over districts further north. Babur reacted to these threats by assigning unconquered territory to his own nobles, and by declaring jihad against the Rana. To emphasize his determination, he renounced wine and took a vow from his army to fight to the death. He crushed the Mewar forces with brilliant leadership and his knowledge of the superior war tactics of west and central Asia in March 1527. Babur then continued his jihad against the Rajputs of Chanderi until June 1528 when Afghan risings in the east forced him to withdraw. In 1529, he defeated a joint army of the Afghans and the Sultan of Bengal at Ghagra near Benares. But this expedition, like the one on his southern borders, remained unfinished. Developments in central Asia and his failing health drew him back to Agra, and then to Lahore where he died in December 1530.

Humayun, his son, inherited a difficult situation. At first he was successful against the Afghans in the east, but he could not match the political and military skill of their new leader, Sher Khan Suri, who had earlier administered his father's revenue assignment (*jagir*) in Bihar and had come to know the region and its magnates well. Humayun was forced to come to an agreement with Sher Khan in 1533 in order to check the activities of Bahadur Khan, the Sultan of Gujarat. Bahadur Shah had captured Malwa; his court had become the center of opposition to Humayun's authority. Humayun conquered Gujarat but his victory was short-lived for, once he had withdrawn to rest in Malwa, his brother, Askari, failed to contain the continued raids of the Gujarati nobles and holders of superior land-rights (*zamindars*) in 1535–36. By the time that Humayun turned eastwards again, Sher Khan had dislodged the Sultan of Bengal and had taken over his capital at Gaur. Humayun captured Gaur, but Sher Khan escaped to Bihar from where he proceeded to disrupt the Mughals' communications with upper India. Humayun was also hampered by heavy rains, Afghan offensives, and, to his great discomfort, opposition from his own nobles to his plans. He was outplayed by his Afghan opponent; and defeats at Chausa in 1539 and Qanauj in 1540 completed the rout.

Humayun confronted a difficult problem with his nobles. The armed clans owed primary allegiance to their respective chiefs. Babur's personality, and the fact that many of them rose to high

The Mughal empire.

Extent of Mughal empire 1530

Extent of Mughal empire 1605

Extent of Mughal empire 1707

Babur's Afghan kingdom showing attempted Mughal expansion

Suri empire

Attempted Mughal expansion

Source: F. Robinson, Atlas of the Islamic World since 1500. (Oxford, 1982) p.59

Rulers of India 1526–1707

Mughal Emperors 1526–1707 (Empire ends 1858)

1526–1530	Zahir ud Din Babur
1530–1540	Nasir ud Din Humayun (first reign)
1540–1555	Suri Sultans of Delhi
	1540–45 Sher Shah
	1545–54 Islam Shah
	1554–55 Muhammad Shah Adil
	Ibrahim ⎱ Dispute
	Sikandar ⎰ succession
1555–1556	Nasir ud Din Humayun (second reign)
1556–1605	Jalal ud Din Akbar I
1605–1627	Nur ud Din Jahangir
1627–1628	Dawar Baksh
1628–1657	Shihab ud Din Shah Jahan I
1657	Murad Baksh (in Gujarat)
1657–1660	Shah Shuja (in Bengal)
1658–1707	Muhi ud Din Aurangzeb Alamgir I

Sultans of Bengal 1526–1576 (Sultanate begins 1336)

Line of Sayyid Husain Shah

1519–1532	Nasir ud Din Nusrat Shah
1532–1533	Ala ud Din Firuz Shah
1533–1539	Ghiyas ud Din Mahmud Shah

Line of Suri Afghans

1539–1540	Sher Shah Sur
1540–1545	Khizr Khan
1545–1555	Muhammad Khan Sur
1555–1561	Khizr Khan Bahadur Shah
1561–1564	Ghiyas ud Din Jalal Shah

Line of Sulaiman Kararani

1564–1572	Sulaiman Kararani
1572	Bayazid Shah Kararani
1572–1576	Daud Shah Kararani

Sultans of Kashmir 1526–1589 (Sultanate begins 1346)

Line of Shah Mirza Swati

1526–1527	Ibrahim I
1527–1529	Nazuk (first reign)
1529–1533	Muhammad (fourth reign)
1533–1540	Shams ud Din
1540	Nazuk (second reign)
1540–1551	Haidar Dughlat (governor on behalf of Mughal Emperor)
1551–1552	Nazuk (third reign)
1552–1555	Ibrahim II
1555–1557	Ismail
1557–1561	Habib

Line of Ghazi Khan Chak

1561–1563	Ghazi Khan
1563–1569	Nasr ud Din Husain
1569–1579	Zahir ud Din Ali
1579–1586	Nasr ud Din Yusuf
1586–1589	Yaqub

Sultans of Gujarat 1526–1583 (Sultanate begins 1391)

1526	Sikandar
1526	Nasir Khan Mahmud II
1526–1537	Bahadur
1537	Miran Muhammad I of Khandesh
1537–1554	Mahmud III
1554–1561	Ahmad III
1561–1573	Muzaffar III (first reign)
1573–1583	Mughal conquest
1583	Muzaffar III (second reign)

Imadshahis of Berar 1526–1572 (Sultanate begins 1484)

1504–*c.* 1529	Ala ud Din
c. 1529–*c.* 1560	Burhan
1568–1572	Tufal (usurper)

Nizamshahis of Ahmadnagar 1526–1595 (Sultanate begins 1490)

1508–1553	Burhan I
1553–1565	Husain
1565–1588	Murtaza
1588–1589	Miran Husain
1589–1590	Ismail
1590–1594	Burhan II
1594	Ibrahim
1594–1595	Ahmad II
1595	Bahadur

Baridi Shahs of Bidar 1526–*c.* 1609 (Sultanate begins 1492)

1504–1549	Amir I
1549–1562	Ali
1562–1569	Ibrahim
1569–1572	Qasim II
1572–*c.* 1609	Mirza Ali
c. 1609	Amir II

Adilshahis of Bijapur 1526–1686 (Sultanate begins 1489)

1511–1534	Ismail
1534–1535	Mallu
1535–1557	Ibrahim I
1557–1580	Ali I
1580–1627	Ibrahim II
1627–1660	Muhammad
1660–1686	Ali II

Box 5 *(continued over)*

The Mughal empire, 1526 to 1707

Qutbshahis of Golconda 1526–1687 (Sultanate begins 1512)

1512–1543	Sultan Quli
1543–1550	Jamshid
1550	Subhan Quli
1550–1581	Ibrahim
1581–1612	Muhammad Quli
1612–1626	Muhammad
1626–1672	Abdullah
1672–1687	Abul Hasan

Faruqi Sultans of Khandesh 1526–1601 (Sultanate begins 1370)

1520–1537	Miran Muhammad I
1537	Ahmad Shah
1537–1566	Mubarak Shah II
1566–1576	Miran Muhammad II
1576–1577	Hasan Shah
1577–1597	Raja Ali Khan or Adil Shah IV
1597–1601	Bahadur Shah

Rulers of the Vijayanagar Empire 1526–1646 (Empire begins 1336)

1509–1529	Krishnadevaraya
1559–1542	Achyuta
1542–c. 1570	Sadashiva
c. 1570–c. 1573	Tirumala
c. 1573–1585	Ranga I
1585	Venkata I
—	Others
1642–1646	Ranga II
(1646, practical end of dynasty)	

Chhatrapati Bhonsles to 1707

1674–1680	Shivaji I
1680–1689	Sambhaji
1689–1700	Rajaram
1700–1707	Tara Bai

Source: C. E. Bosworth, *The Islamic Dynasties* revised edn, pp. 193–210 (Edinburgh, 1980); S. Lane-Poole, *The Mohammadan Dynasties* pp. 320–21 (London, 1893); C. H. Philips, Ed. *Handbook of Oriental History* p. 86 (London, 1951); P. Spear, Ed. *The Oxford History of India* 4th edn, pp. 318–19 (Delhi, 1981).

Box 5 *(continued)*

---

rank under him, had maintained the loyalty of these chiefs. Humayun, however, lacked his father's charisma. While his opponents had some rapport with the locality, he fought under constant fear of the emergence of a rival center of power within his camp. He virtually shared the empire with his brothers, all of whom threatened to use his shaky command over the nobility to their own advantage. Between 1545 and 1555, after his return from Persia, a hardened Humayun asserted his royal authority, eliminated many

of those to whom Babur had given titles and built up the power of his own group of nobles. With his brothers systematically removed from the scene and the nobles' realization of the inadequate resources of Afghanistan, reconquest of India became feasible. Afghan power in India, meanwhile, was in shambles by 1555.

Sher Khan Suri's achievements had been remarkable considering the brief period of his rule. Between 1540 and 1545, he had conquered Malwa and almost the whole of Rajputana, developing a strong central army. His reign was noted for the restoration and construction of roads and fortified lodgings, an improved revenue system, standardized weights and measures, and regularized tariffs on trade. Sher Khan, however, died in an accident during the siege of Kalinjar in May 1545. His son, Islam Shah, tried to keep the empire intact. But, in the course of disputes over succession, palace intrigues and insurrections, he eliminated many of his nobles, forcing others to join hands with the insurgents. On his death in 1554, the empire broke into several parts. Sikandar Sur held the Panjab, Delhi and Agra. Ibrahim held Sambhal and the Doab, while Adil Shah, in power in the east, struggled against both. Bengal and Malwa became independent under Muhammad Khan Sur and Baz Bahadur, respectively. This chaos provided the opportunity for Humayun's re-entry into Hindustan. In June 1555 at Sirhind, the Mughals under Bairam Khan and Prince Akbar crushed Sikandar Sur's defence. But Humayun died in Delhi at the beginning of 1556 before he could recover the whole of his former empire. The young Akbar succeeded him under the regency of Bairam Khan.

Akbar and the consolidation of the empire, 1556–1605

The task which faced Akbar was the reconquest and consolidation of the empire by ensuring control over its borders and, more importantly, by providing firm ground on which it could stand. Until 1560, the teenage emperor was loyally served by the regent, Bairam Khan.

The Mughal victory at Panipat in November 1556, and the subsequent recovery of Mankot, Gwalior and Jaunpur demolished the Afghan threat revived by Hemu, a Hindu general of the Suri ruler, Adil Shah. In the following years, Akbar conquered Ajmer, Gondwana, Bundelkhand and Malwa in central India. The fall of Chitor and Ranthambor in 1567–68 brought almost the whole of Rajputana under his suzerainty. But Mewar refused to yield and later its ruler, Rana Pratap, after his defeat by the Mughals, continued to make raids until his death in 1597 when his son, Amar Singh, took over the mantle of opposition to Mughal rule.

Rajputana opened up to Akbar the routes to Gujarat, whose rich lands proved a strong temptation. Gujarat, once in Mughal hands, had lately become the haven of the refractory Mirzas. Akbar conquered the region at his second attempt in 1573, and celebrated by building a lofty victory gate at his new capital Fatehpur Sikri.

Gujarat gave him clear passage to the Indian Ocean, but Akbar did not show much interest in what was taking place overseas. His encounters with the Portuguese aroused his curiosity only about their religion and painting. The declaration of independence by Daud Karrani, an Afghan vassal in eastern India, brought Akbar back to Patna in 1574. Soon after his return, the Mughals were once more in Gaur, and, with the death of Karrani in 1576, the last Afghan threat had ended.

Akbar, thus, came to command the whole of Humayun's former possessions. He evolved a new pattern of king–noble relationship which suited the needs of a centralized state. The empire was now to be defended by nobles belonging to diverse ethnic and religious groups. Akbar refused to concede special powers, even to Bairam, insisted on assessing the arrears of areas under the command of the old Turani clans who had followed his grandfather from central Asia, and, in order to strike a balance in the ruling class, promoted Persians, Indian Muslims and Rajputs to imperial service. Well-established eminent clan leaders were given charge of frontier areas, while the civil and finance departments were staffed by relatively new, non-Turani recruits. The revolts of the old guard – the Uzbeks, the Mirzas, the Qaqshals and the Atka Khails – between 1564 and 1574, illustrated the intensity of their indignation over these changes. Utilizing the resentment of the Muslim orthodoxy to Akbar's liberal views, they organized their final resistence in 1580, when they were also supported by new elements who feared Akbar's regulations designed to check the strength of his nobles. The rebels proclaimed Akbar's half-brother, Mirza Hakim, the ruler of Kabul, as their king. Akbar crushed the opposition ruthlessly.

The empire expanded further during the 1580s and 1590s, strengthening its grip on its more far-flung corners. Following Mirza Hakim's death and a threatened Uzbek invasion, Akbar brought Kabul under his direct control, and, to demonstrate his strength, ordered the Mughal army to parade through Kashmir, Baluchistan, Sind and the tribal districts of the northwest. In 1598, he wrested Qandahar from the Safavids, which together with Ghazna and Kabul fixed the northwest frontier. These three towns were important for India's overland trade, in particular for securing horses for the Mughal cavalry. In the east, Man Singh consolidated Mughal gains by annexing Orissa, Cooch Bihar and large parts of Bengal. The conquest of Kathiawar, and later of Asirgarh and the northern territory of the Nizamshahi kingdom of Ahmadnagar, ensured a firm command over Gujarat and central India. At Akbar's death in October 1605, the Mughal empire covered the entire area north of the Godavari river, with the exceptions of Gondwana in central India and Assam in the northeast.

Administration of the empire under Akbar

Akbar's principal achievement was the creation of an administrative framework which sustained the empire for about one hundred and fifty years. His experiments extended over twenty years and resulted in a revenue schedule which suited the peasantry but which provided maximum profit for the state. In 1580, he obtained local revenue statistics from the previous ten years, details of productivity and price fluctuations, and then averaged the produce of different crops and their prices. He also grouped together districts which possessed similar agricultural conditions. Area measurement by bamboo linked with iron rings, instead of by hemp rope, introduced definitiveness. Revenue demands, fixed according to the continuity of cultivation and quality of soil, ranged from one third to one half, and were paid in cash. This system, called *zabt*, applied to North India and to Malwa and Gujarat. Earlier practices, such as crop-sharing, still operated in parts of the empire.

Another feature of Akbar's administrative system concerned the organization of the nobility and the army. Every Mughal official held a *mansab*, divided into *zat* (personal) and *sawar* (cavalry), which was expressed in numbers and indicated his rank, pay, armed contingents and obligations. The mansab holders (*mansabdars*) were generally paid in non-hereditary and transferrable jagirs. Over their jagir districts, distinct from those reserved for the emperor (*khalisa*) and his personal army (*ahadis*), the assignees (*jagirdars*) normally had no magisterial or military (*faujdari*) authority. Akbar's insistence on a regular check of the mansabdars' soldiers and their horses demonstrated his efforts to achieve a reasonable balance between their income and their military obligations.

In land revenue administration, Akbar secured support from local powerholders. With the exception of villages held directly by peasants where the community as a whole paid the revenue, in all other cases his officials – largely Hindus at subordinate levels – dealt with the leaders of local communities and the holders of superior land-rights. These zamindars collected revenue from the peasants, paid it to the treasury, keeping a proportion for themselves in return for their services and their zamindari claim over the land. Thus, the zamindar emerged as one of the most important intermediaries in the Mughal system of administration.

Akbar's close relations with important ruling Rajput families, many of whom were integrated into direct state service, were intended to widen the base of his power. For the same reason, he adopted a conscious policy of religious toleration. He abolished the tax on non-Muslims (*jizya*), pilgrimage cesses exacted on Hindus, and the practice of forcibly converting prisoners of war to Islam; he encouraged Hindus to be his main confidants and policy makers. To legitimize his non-sectarian ideas, Akbar sought the ability to interpret religious law by holding lengthy discussions with Muslim learned men (*ulama*) in his famous house of worship (*ibadat khana*) at Fatehpur Sikri. When these efforts proved fruitless, he continued his search in the company of non-Muslim religious experts. In time, he evolved a theory of rulership as a divine illumination incorporating the acceptance of all irrespective of creed or sect. The Mughal empire, thus, benefited from being ruled by a strong and non-sectarian monarch, in full command of a heterogenous but well-knit nobility, with considerable cooperation from the local aristocracy and Hindu clerical castes.

Jahangir and Shah Jahan: the climax of the empire, 1605–58

The reigns of Jahangir and Shah Jahan are noted for political stability, brisk economic activity, beautiful paintings and magnificent buildings. The developments at the end of Shah Jahan's reign, however, did not augur well for the future of the empire. Jahangir's most significant political achievement was the ending of the Mughal–Mewar conflict, following three campaigns and his own arrival in Ajmer in 1613. In addition, the Rajput rulers of Kangra, Kishtwar (in the Himalayas), Navanagar and Kutch (in western India) accepted Mughal supremacy. Bir Singh Bundela was given a high rank and a Bundela princess entered the Mughal harem. Equally important was the subjugation of the last of the Afghan domains in east Bengal in 1612 and Orissa in 1617, and more notably, the incorporation of the Afghans under Khan Jahan Lodi into the nobility. In the Deccan, the rise of Malik Ambar at Ahmadnagar and his alliance with the Adilshahis of Bijapur initially forced the Mughals to retreat. Later, however, two Mughal victories against combined Deccani forces in 1618 and 1620 restrained this threat. But the Deccan expedition was not completed as a result of the rise to power of the Emperor's favorite queen, Nur Jahan, and her relatives and associates. The queen's alleged efforts to secure the prince of her choice as successor to the ailing Emperor, resulted in the rebellion of Prince Shah Jahan in 1622, and later of Mahabat Khan, the queen's principal ally, who had been deputed to subdue the prince. Meanwhile, the loss of Qandahar to Persia in 1622 proved a serious blow to the prestige of the empire.

The Deccan and the northwest border were already facing serious problems by the time that Shah Jahan became emperor in 1628. The Marathas had recently emerged as an important force in the Deccan. While Jahangir had included some Marathas among his nobility, Shahjahan showed better appreciation of the situation. His personal knowledge of Deccan politics, together with the experience gained early in his reign from the rebellion of Khan Jahan, convinced him of the advantages of all-out war against the Nizamshahi kingdom. He conquered it at the second attempt in 1636, leaving part of it to the Sultan of Bijapur who, together with the Sultan of Qutbshahi Golconda, had acceded to Mughal suzerainty. The treaty allowed them to conquer the old Hindu principalities in the south, while the

Mughals regained Qandahar (1638), consolidated and extended their position in the east on the Assam border (1639), and demonstrated their power on the northwest frontier (1646–48). Shah Jahan also had time to complete the most famous of his buildings in Agra and Shahjahanabad (Delhi) where he shifted his capital in 1638.

Early in the 1640s, the Uzbeks of Balkh and Bukhara were reunited and threatened to invade Ghazni and Kabul. In 1646, therefore, Shah Jahan sent a huge army to the aid of the Uzbek ruler who was faced with internal disputes. The campaign cost the Mughals heavily, but it effectively demonstrated their strength, their frontier towns no longer faced the Uzbek threat, and Shah Jahan had reason to celebrate its completion. Setbacks in Balkh, however, provided Iran with a chance to capture Qandahar in 1649, and the city was never recovered. Lack of success in the northwest encouraged Mughal aggression in the Deccan where Shah Jahan insisted on a share of the booty captured by Bijapur further south. The Deccanis and the Marathas were invited to participate in the imperial service, but once they joined the authorities asserted a claim over their *jagirs* in the rich south and coastal tracts.

Shah Jahan's aggressive thrust southwards was designed to meet a threatened crisis of the empire, reflected in recent modifications to the mansab and jagir system. Political unification and the establishment of law and order over wide areas, together with the ostentatious lifestyle of the Mughals, had encouraged the emergence of big centers of commerce and crafts, which were also nourished by the sizeable foreign trade carried out by Asian and European merchants. Lahore, Delhi, Agra and Ahmadabad, linked by road and waterway to other important towns and the key sea ports, were among the leading cities of the world at the time. Grain markets and small townships (*qasbahs*) followed the Mughal system of taxation, increased cash-nexus and commodity production, which, in turn, led to a highly differentiated population in the countryside. The wide acceptability of credit bills (*hundis*) indicated the degree to which money circulated.

But these developments had little bearing on the economic position of peasants and artisans, and, hence, were not necessarily a good index of the strength of the Mughal state. Often prestige and prevailing value system dictated grandiosity. The ranks and resources of Mughal officials were generally overstated. If the *zabt* system suited the empire, it enriched even more local intermediaries who benefited from the rise in prices. There was little effort to revise the revenue schedule. Local élites resisted handing over the full amount of revenue to the treasury; their conflict with the empire, therefore, persisted even after the Mughals had tried to resolve the problem by making them virtually a part of their system. The Mughal state was enormously militarized in this period. The strength of the nobles and their armed contingents rose almost fourfold, in glaring disproportion to the increase in the size of the

Jahangir and his court ride past Akbar's tomb at Sikandra.

empire. In many cases, nobles were posted within the empire with doubled or additional conditonal *sawar* rank. Jahangir had left a treasury that was almost empty and a vastly reduced amount of Crown land. Shah Jahan's reforms in the mansab system, which involved scaling down his officers' obligations, implied the state's formal recognition of its failure to reduce the gap between the assessed revenue (*jama*) and its actual collection (*hasil*). The state's incentive to extend cultivation had its limitations, for society did not allow everyone who invested in land to become a free peasant, let alone a zamindar. The system of administration failed to produce any lasting change in the existing social structure, nor did it encourage the generation of resources independently of dominant caste zamindars and village headmen. In their complete dependence on land revenue collected through rural magnates, the Mughals indirectly nurtured forces which eventually led to the break-up of their empire.

Aurangzeb: further expansion and signs of weakness, 1658 to 1707

The empire under Aurangzeb reached its greatest physical limit, but his reign also witnessed the unmistakable symptoms of its decline. For over a decade, Aurangzeb appeared to be in full control. The Mughals suffered somewhat in Assam and Cooch Bihar, but they invaded the Arakanese, captured Chittagong and succeeded in Bikaner, Bundelkhand, Palamau, Navanagar, the Morang hills and Kumaon. There was the usual display of wealth and grandeur at court.

Soon, however, disturbances in several regions rocked the empire. Jats of the Agra-Delhi region, restless over the size of land revenue demands and aspiring for a greater share of power, rose up in 1669 and 1685. They continued their raids even after their leaders had been captured or slain. In 1672, in Narnaul, peasants and members of the low-born caste of Satnamis clashed with Mughal forces. The empire also experienced problems in the region around Sirhind and Jalandhar inspired by the teachings of the Sikh Guru, Tegh Bahadur. The Guru was executed in 1675, but the movement was not crushed. Organized into a military brotherhood by his son, Guru Gobind, his followers fought against the Mughals and their local allies during the reigns of Aurangzeb and his successors. To the northwest, Pathans plundered the border districts and trading caravans, after declaring war against Aurangzeb in 1667 and again in 1672. Aurangzeb's personal command over these hard fought campaigns, the attempts to win over Pathan leaders (1674–76) and the long tenure of Amir Khan's governorship (1678–98) finally pacified them. However, the deployment of almost the whole of the Mughal armed forces against them helped to reduce pressure on the Marathas in the Deccan. Similarly, Aurangzeb's war in Rajputana (1678–80) relieved this pressure still further.

Aurangzeb valued the Mughal alliance with the Rajputs. Rajput chiefs had obtained high ranks early in his reign despite restraints on their promotions in general. In 1678 he asserted his right to bring Jodhpur under direct control following the death of its ruler, Jaswant Singh, without any male descendant. Later, Aurangzeb favored Jaswant's cousin rather than his posthumous son, and, reacting to the protest of these Rajputs, confiscated Jodhpur and demolished its temples, planning also to partition Marwar. Aurangzeb crushed the opposition and occupied Jodhpur but at the heavy expense of a break with the Rajputs and their supporters in Mewar. Those Rajputs who remained with him were also uncertain of their fortunes. Significantly, no Rajput chief later fought on the side of the Mughals against the Sikhs. Aurangzeb's son, Muhammad Akbar, realized the folly of his father's policy towards the Rajputs and rebelled against him during the Rajput war. Eventually, his flight to the Maratha court at Satara compelled the Emperor to settle his differences with the Rajputs whose contribution to the rise and growth of the Mughal Empire had been so great.

Early in Aurangzeb's reign, the Maratha chief, Shivaji, had established a large principality in the Western Ghats, humiliated both the Bijapur (1659) and Mughal armies (1660–64), and emerged as a hero of the entire Maratha land. After being defeated by Jai Singh, he was forced to visit the Mughal court in 1666. But Aurangzeb failed to take notice of his importance. Shivaji fled from Agra and rallied his resources to the extent that he was able to crown himself in 1674. At his death in 1680, his territory included large parts of Karnataka with a second capital at Jinji on the east coast. His son, Sambhaji, was a weak ruler but the Marathas remained the principal threat to the empire.

On his arrival in the Deccan in 1681, Aurangzeb tried but failed to isolate the Hindu Marathas from Muslim Bijapur and Golconda. These kingdoms had encountered several Mughal offensives after 1656. Bijapur had been forced to part with the Nizamshahi areas ceded to it in 1636, and Golconda had had to pay a huge indemnity to the Mughals. The Marathas, thus, enjoyed their full support. Subsequently, Aurangzeb captured Bijapur (1686) and Golconda (1687) with the objective of defeating the Marathas which he finally felt that he had done with the capture of Sambhaji. Sambhaji was executed in 1689, and his successor, Raja Ram, was forced to flee to Jinji which also fell to the Mughals in 1698. The Mughals had overrun almost the whole peninsula.

The Marathas, under the Peshwas, however, continued to fight. Aurangzeb had no time to make lasting agreements with local holders of power in his newly acquired lands. These lands were rich but difficult to administer. Many of his nobles disapproved of his policy; some dealt secretly with Maratha and Telugu warriors to protect their own jagirs; others contrived easily manageable assignments. All this encouraged factionalism at court, aggravated by

Aurangzeb's efforts to corner the most profitable tracts of land for khalisas; while old nobles sought success for 'their designs', new Deccani elements proved 'unstable in their loyalties'.

The increasing association of Aurangzeb's government with religion further weakened the empire. Sunni Muslim theologians, ignored by Akbar, reasserted their authority, but with a limited influence on state policies at first. Aurangzeb could not resist their pressure. He opposed the pantheistic sufi doctrine of *wahdat ul wujud* (unity in being), sought justification for his power in orthodox religion, and issued ordinances to ensure that the lives of the people and government actions conformed to Islamic law (*sharia*). He tried to overcome the threat posed by the struggles of local elements against the central government by promoting Muslims with zamindaris and additional privileges in and around disturbed areas. He also tried to replace Hindus in local and revenue departments with Muslims. When confronted with strong opposition, he even offended his Hindu allies by destroying their places of worship. He reimposed the tax on non-Muslims (*jizya*) and raised the cry of jihad against the Marathas in order to rally Muslims in defence of his empire. Overall, Aurangzeb failed miserably; while he captured the forts of the Marathas, many of his jagirdars in the north were unable to collect their dues from the villages of their jagirs. In 1707, when Aurangzeb died, serious threats from the peripheries of his empire had begun to accentuate problems at its core. Land was not stripped of its wealth, but the revenue-procuring machine of the Mughal government no longer worked effectively.

MA

Further reading
M. Athar Ali, *The Mughal Nobility under Aurangzeb* (Bombay, 1968)

S. Chandra, *Medieval India: Society, the Jagirdari Crisis and the Village* (Delhi, 1982)

P. Hardy, M. N. Pearson and J. F. Richards, Articles on the Decline of the Mughal Empire, *Journal of Asian Studies*, XXXV, No. 2 (1976)

I. Habib, *The Agrarian System of Mughal India* (Bombay, 1963)

M. Hasan, *Babur, the Founder of the Mughal Empire in India* (Delhi, 1986)

A. R. Khan, *The Chieftains in the Mughal Empire during the Reign of Akbar* (Simla, 1977)

I. A. Khan, *The Political Biography of a Mughal Noble: Mun'im Khan Khan-i Khanan* (Delhi, 1973)

A. J. Qaisar, *The Indian Response to European Technology and Culture, 1498–1707* (Delhi, 1982)

T. Raychaudhari and Irfan Habib, Eds, *The Cambridge Economic History of India, I* (Cambridge, 1982)

J. F. Richards, *Mughal Administration in Golconda* (Oxford, 1975)

S. A. A. Rizvi, *The Religious and Intellectual History of the Muslims in Akbar's Reign* (Delhi, 1975)

The struggle for power and the establishment of British supremacy, 1707 to 1858

Disintegration of the Mughal Empire, 1707 to 1765

The Mughal Empire needed to expand in order to survive, and so Aurangzeb had sought to consolidate his domain by conquering the southern kingdoms of Bijapur and Golconda, and also by emphasizing the Islamic basis of the state as a focus of loyalty. Before his death, the disruptive consequences of these policies had become clear; after his death, the critical nature of the crisis revealed itself. A succession of short-lived emperors allowed faction to become entrenched in their court. The Sayyid brothers seized the reins of state and gathered around themselves a party of Indian-born Muslims and Hindus. They were opposed by nobles of Iranian or central Asian origin who had been Aurangzeb's great commanders. In 1719, the emperor Farrukhsiyar was murdered in the course of these factional disputes which greatly weakened the prestige of the imperial house. Under his successor, Bahadur Shah (1719–48), Delhi never really regained control over events in the provinces. Three great nobles who continued to give obeisance to the throne and even to remit money to the center, nevertheless began to build up their own domains with little reference to it. They were Asaf Jah, Nizam ul Mulk in the Deccan, Mughal India's new frontier, Burhan ul Mulk Saadat Khan, who was also the chief minister of the Empire, in Avadh, and Murshid Quli Khan in its richest province, Bengal.

Two other developments sapped imperial vitality. First the revolt of Hindu landholders throughout India gained momentum as the center was seen to be distracted. Rich and powerful chieftains in Avadh asserted their independence in a series of revolts; the Maratha movement revived in the 1720s and 1730s and overwhelmed the rich central province of Malwa; even in the very environs of Delhi, Jat peasant farmers harried imperial lines and created a state within a state. Then the weakness of Delhi was brutally revealed to the whole of Asia when, in 1739, the Persian despot Nadir Shah invaded India in search of booty, defeated the imperial armies and sacked Delhi, looting from it vast sums of treasure. Delhi's economy recovered from the Persian invasion, but its prestige was further diminished. The provincial dynasts asserted their covert independence more forcefully; imperial mercenary troops of Afghan origin, the Rohillas, created kingdoms for themselves northeast of Delhi and the exodus of soldiers, administrative experts and learned men from Delhi to provincial centers gathered momentum.

In some ways, the decline of the empire was a form of decentralization which had been facilitated by the slow economic growth of

The struggle for power and the establishment of British supremacy, 1707 to 1858

The breakup of the Mughal empire and the emergence of successor states *c.* 1766.

AFGHANISTAN

Qandahar

■ Qandahar

A B D A L I S

Lahore

S I K H S

Kalat

Multan

MUGHALS

Panipat 1761

■ Rampur

Nepal

GURKHAS

■ Kathmandu

AHMADZAIS

BIKANER

Delhi

JATS

Farrukhabad

BANGASH

■ Fyzabad

AVADH

JAISALMER

RAJPUTS

Amber
Jaipur ■ ■ Bharatpur

JAIPUR

Benares

Assam

Sind

K A L H O R A S

MARWAR

Jodhpur ■

MEWAR

S I N D H I A

Allahabad

Bihar

Bengal–Bihar, 1765

■ Murshidabad

Udaipur ■

■ Bhuj

G A E K W A R

H O L K A R

■ Ujjain

M A R A T H A

BENGAL

CUTCH

Junagarh ■

■ Baroda

Maheshwar ■

B H O N S L E

■ Sambalpur

Songarh ■

■ Nagpur

Orissa

C O N F E D E R A C Y

■ Nasik

■ Chanda

Br. Bombay
Poona ■

P E S H W A

NORTHERN CIRCARS

Panipat 1761

Satara ■

THE NIZAM

Golconda ■ ■ Hyderabad

Kolhapur ■

Northern Circars, 1766

Goa

Bednur ■

MYSORE

Ardot ■ ● *Br. Madras, 1763*

Malabar

Seringapatam ■

C A R N A T I C

Calicut ■

COCHIN
Cochin ■

■ Thanjavur
THANJAVUR

■ Madura

TRAVANCORE

Legend

——	Principal political frontiers (approximate) as of 1766
- - -	Frontiers, as of 1766, between vassal and suzerain states, between two vassals of the same power, or between British provinces
(light grey)	Extent of Afghan kingdom
(dark grey)	British possessions
JATS	Dynasty or power
CUTCH	State
Sind	Region
■	Capitals of independent states and major Maratha houses

Source: J. E. Schwartzberg, ed., A Historical Atlas of South Asia *(Chicago, 1978) p.54*

Rulers of India 1707–1858

Mughal Emperors 1707–1858 (Empire begins 1526)

1707	Azam Shah
1707	Kam Bakhsh (in the Deccan)
1707–1712	Shah Alam I
1712	Azim ush Shan
1712–1713	Muizz ud Din Jahandar
1713–1719	Farrukhsiyar
1719	Shams ud Din Rafi ud Darajat
1719	Rafi ud Daula Shah Jahan II
1719	Nikusiyar
1719–1748	Nasir ud Din Muhammad
1748–1754	Ahmad Shah Bahadur
1754–1760	Aziz ud Din Alamgir II
1760	Shah Jahan III
1760–1788	Jalal ud din Ali Jauhar Shah Alam II (first reign)
1788	Bidar Bakht
1788–1806	Shah Alam II (second reign)
1806–1837	Muin ud Din Akbar II
1837–1858	Siraj ud Din Bahadur Shah II

Navvabs of Bengal 1703–1770

1703–1727	Murshid Quli Jafar Khan
1727–1739	Shuja ud Din
1739–1740	Sarfaraz Khan
1740–1756	Alivardi Khan
1756–1760	Siraj ud Daula
1760–1763	Mir Qasim
1763–1765	Mir Jafar
1765–1766	Najm ud Daula
1766–1770	Saif ud Daula

Navvabs of Avadh 1724–1856

1724–1739	Saadat Khan
1739–1754	Safdar Jang
1754–1775	Shuja ud Daula
1775–1797	Asaf ud Daula
1797–1798	Vazir Ali
1798–1814	Saadat Ali
1814–1827	Ghazi ud Din Haidar
1827–1837	Nasir ud Din Haidar
1837–1842	Ali Shah
1842–1847	Amjad Ali Shah
1847–1856	Vajid Ali Shah

Navvabs of Arcot 1707–1858 (Rule begins 1690, ends 1874)

1703–1710	Daud Shah
1710–1732	Muhammad Sayyid Saadatullah Khan I
1732–1740	Dost Ali Khan
1740–1742	Safdar Ali Khan
1744–1749	Anvar ud Din Muhammad
1749–1795	Vala Jah Muhammad Ali
1795–1801	Umdat ul Umara
1801–1819	Azim ud Daula
1819–1867	Azam Jah

Nizams of Hyderabad 1724–1858 (Rule ends 1948)

1724–1748	Mir Qamar ud Din, Nizam ul Mulk Asaf Jah
1748–1750	Mir Muhammad Nasir Jang
1750–1751	Muzaffar Jang
1751–1762	Mir Asaf ud Daula Salabat Jang
1762–1802	Nizam Ali
1802–1829	Mir Akbar Ali Khan Sikandar Jah
1829–1857	Nasir ud Daula
1857–1869	Afzal ud Daula

The Line of Haidar Ali of Mysore 1761–1799

1761–1782	Haidar Ali
1782–1799	Tipu Sultan

Maratha Peshwas 1714–1818

1714–1720	Balaji Vishwanath
1720–1740	Baji Rao I
1740–1761	Balaji Baji Rao
1761–1772	Madhava Rao Ballal
1772–1773	Narayan Rao
1773–1774	Raghunath Rao
1774–1796	Madhava Rao Narayan
1796–1818	Baji Rao II

Line of Holkar to 1858

1728–1765	Malha Rao Holkar
1765–1795	Ahalya Bai
1795–1798	Tukoji I
1798–1811	Jaswant Rao
1811–1834	Malha Rao II
1834–1843	Hari Rao
1843–1886	Tukoji Rao II

Line of the Gaikwar to 1858

1721–1732	Pilaji
1732–1768	Damaji
1768–1771	Govind Rao I
1771	Sayaji Rao I
1771–1789	Fateh Singh
1789–1793	Manaji
1793–1800	Govind Rao II
1800–1818	Anand Rao
1818–1847	Sayaji Rao II
1847–1856	Ganpat Rao
1856–1870	Khande Rao

Box 6 *(continued over)*

The struggle for power and the establishment of British supremacy, 1707 to 1858

Line of Sindhia to 1858

1761–1794	Madhava Rao (Mahadaji Sindhia)
1794–1827	Daulat Rao Sindhia
1827–1843	Janjoki Rao
1843–1886	Jayaji Rao

Sikh Rulers of the Panjab 1792–1849

1792–1839	Ranjit Singh
1839–1840	Kharak Singh
1840–1841	Nao Nehal Singh
1841–1843	Sher Singh
1843–1849	Dalip Singh

British Viceroys and Governors-General 1774–1858

Governors-General of Fort William in Bengal

1774–1785	Warren Hastings
1785–1786	Sir John Macpherson[a]
1786–1793	Lord Cornwallis
1793–1798	Lieut.-Genl. Sir Alured Clarke[a]
1798–1805	Lord Mornington
1805	Lord Cornwallis (second time)
1805–1807	Sir George Barlow[a]
1807–1813	Lord Minto
1813–1823	Lord Moira
1823	John Adam[a]
1823–1828	Lord Amherst
1828	Butterworth Bayley[a]
1828–1834	Lord Bentinck

Viceroys and Governors-General of India

1834–1835	Lord Bentinck
1835–1836	Sir Charles Metcalfe[a]
1836–1842	Lord Auckland
1842–1844	Lord Ellenborough
1844	William Wilberforce Bird[a]
1844–1848	Sir Henry Hardinge
1848–1856	Lord Dalhousie
1856–1858	Lord Canning

[a]temporary appointment.
Source: C. E. Bosworth, *The Islamic Dynasties* revised edn, p. 210 (Edinburgh, 1980); C. H. Philips, Ed. *Handbook of Oriental History* pp. 86–87, 92–93 (London, 1951); M. Hasan, *History of Tipu Sultan* pp. 6, 21, 317 (Calcutta, 1971); *Thacker's Indian Directory, 1909* pp. 61–62 (Calcutta, 1909).

Box 6 *(continued)*

meant the decline of Mughal political culture. On the contrary, new centers of Mughal culture developed, notably Murshidabad, Lucknow, Hyderabad and Faizabad, while the Mughal system of government and the purview of Mughal learned men spread to areas of the south such as Mysore and Tamil Nadu where it had previously not been seen. In Avadh and Bengal, relatively stable 'successor states' to Mughal dominion developed with the dynasts amalgamating the hitherto separate jurisdictions of Governor and Revenue Manager (*divan*) and making them hereditary. However, it must also be noted that the implosion of the Mughal political system increased the possibilities for conflict throughout India. Not only were new regional entities at war, damaging trade and revenue on the fringes even when they enhanced them in the center of their domains, but Hindu merchant and peasant leader, Muslim revenue farmer and noble were increasingly pitted against each other. Out of dynamic and even creative growth, the seeds of severe economic and political conflict in the second half of the century were sown.

The growing presence of the East India Company

Against this background, the European East India Companies, and in particular the English Company, were able to enhance their resources and ambitions. In 1701, the British had received a grant of the territorial revenues of the Twenty Four Pargannas near Calcutta from the Mughal Emperor. This was a sign of their growing importance in the economy of Bengal where their trade now rivalled that of the Dutch Company. English, French and Dutch all brought in silver and copper to pay for their increasing purchases of Bengal cloths and silks. Silver imports helped the smooth functioning of the Mughal revenue system, besides expanding the artisan economy and benefitting the province's Hindu commercial people. Even before 1757, the English Company had begun to hold down prices paid to the weavers by using political power. Company servants, trading on their own accounts to make up for poor official salaries, had gained possession of monopolies in valuable articles such as saltpetre and betel nut. A significant part of the Bengal economy had already become dependent on European trade.

However, it was in South India that the Europeans first began to transform trading initiatives into political power. Here Mughal influence was late in coming. It did not significantly affect Tamil Nadu until after 1704 when Saadatullah Khan, a lieutenant of the Governor of the Deccan and hence of the Emperor, was established as Navvab of Arcot, a town about sixty miles west of the British station of Madras. Power in the south had always been localized and its state forms characterized by 'segmentation': that is, a regional domain containing within itself many smaller and virtually autonomous entities which replicated it but were tied to it by little more than ritual relations. After the decline of the Hindu kingdom of Vijayanagar in the late sixteenth century, local rulers at

areas farther from Delhi's control over the previous century, notably Avadh, Bengal and the northwestern Deccan. Here, Hindu warriors and merchants had grown rich and assertive under the loose aegis of imperial control. They and incoming Muslim families had transformed the rewards of service into more permanent zamindari holdings. Again, the demise of the power of Delhi hardly

Madurai, Jinji and Trichinopoly were virtually free of intervention from outside powers. There was buoyant growth in paddy production and in the export of fine cloths to Europe, the Middle East and southeast Asia. This was sometimes interrupted by warfare such as the conflicts which led to the establishment of Maratha power in the rich rice delta of Thanjavur, or conflicts between local village controling magnates, the poligars (*palaiyyakarars*).

After the death of the Nizam of Hyderabad in 1742, factional conflicts spread into Tamil Nadu with members of the Navayat family from which the first Navvab of Arcot had been drawn, led by Chanda Sahib, facing the Avadh family of Muhammad Ali Vallajah and his supporters. The French under Dupleix who had been involved in Hyderabad politics for some years supported the Navayats, and the British, who feared French interruption of their lucrative Madras trade, supported Muhammad Ali Vallajah. In the course of the long struggle between the two European nations which was not brought to a conclusion until the Peace of Paris in 1763, the British gained a decisive control over their Indian ally, the Navvab of Arcot, supporting him with their armies and privately lending large sums of money to him.

However, if the British achieved a dominant political role in Tamil Nadu before 1763, their power in Bengal had already been decisively augmented in 1757. Maratha invasions and the stagnation of European trade due to war had brought Bengal's Indian summer to an end before the death of the old Navvab Alivardi Khan in 1756. The new, young Navvab, Siraj ud Daula, attempted to assert his authority over the kingdom. But he ran foul of the English Company which had fortified Calcutta against the French and failed to make customary presents to him. Siraj occupied Calcutta and drove the British out. But Robert Clive, who had a large European force based on Madras as a result of the war with the French, determined to seize back the Company's most valuable prize. He was aided by a combination of interests in Bengal society which opposed the attempts of the Navvab to increase his authority: dissident Muslim soldiers, Hindu zamindars of West Bengal and the influential Hindu merchant community which was being damaged by the expulsion of British trade from Bengal. At Plassey, the Navvab was defeated by the plotters and the British placed on the Bengal throne a nominee of theirs, Mir Jafar Ali.

Over the next three decades, British control over the province was formalized. After Plassey, there was a great boom in Company and private European trade. Europeans and their Indian associates (*banians*) made huge fortunes from gifts, presents, monopolies and the looting of Bengal revenues. Attempts by the ruler, Mir Qasim, to halt the expansion of European trade privileges led to his expulsion and defeat alongside his ally, the Navvab of Avadh, Shuja ud Daula, at Baksar in 1764. In 1765, Clive took over the revenue management (*Divani*) of Bengal which was granted by the powerless

The Mughal Emperor, Shah Alam, hands to Clive the formal grant conferring in perpetuity on the East India Company the management of the revenues of Bengal.

Mughal Emperor. From this year dated direct British control in Bengal. Hereafter, a number of unsuccessful and destructive systems of revenue management were employed until, finally, in 1793, Lord Cornwallis fixed the land revenues in perpetuity and established the system of district collectors which became the bedrock of the Indian Civil Service. Despite the terrible famine of 1770–71 and the degeneration of Bengal's once buoyant economy, the new colonial power was able to employ the huge annual $4 million land revenues of Bengal to support its military activities in other parts of the subcontinent. Bengal's upper castes (*bhadralok*) provided a reserve of skilled manpower for subordinate administrative posts within the British system, while Calcutta, which had a population of about 250,000 by 1788, grew to be the largest British bridgehead in Asia.

Expansion of Company power

The desire of the Company to subvent its weak trading position with territorial revenues along with the insatiable appetite for profit of private traders had led to the takeover of Bengal. But elsewhere the British rise to power in India was a more indirect process. Neither the Court of Directors of the East India Company, nor the increasingly concerned British ministries were in favor of unrestrained territorial expansion. In India itself, the Company sought to stabilize its frontiers and provide for the payment of its troops through arrangements which were called subsidiary alliances. Indian rulers were 'protected', ostensibly from outside invaders, by British troops stationed in their territory. In turn, they provided 'subsidies' or tribute to the Company. In this way, the British hoped to prevent their military costs ratcheting ever upwards as trading profits declined in the face of warfare and competition from their own servants' private trade. But the cure was usually worse than the disease. Time and time again, indigenous states were squeezed into defiance or collapsed under the weight of debt created by the rigidities of payment under the subsidy system.

Benares provided the first example of this process. The kingdom of Benares had originated in a revenue contract put out by the Navvab of Avadh. The family asserted its kingly status around the holy city and in 1765 its revenues were finally transferred to the Company following the settlement of Baksar. When Warren Hastings found himself at war with the Marathas and Mysore in 1780 he pushed relentlessly for payment of the Benares tribute and the large sums which remained outstanding as a result of the state's poverty following a series of bad harvests. Pressure from the Governor-General pushed Benares into revolt in 1781, and the

The growth of British power: North India 1750–1860.

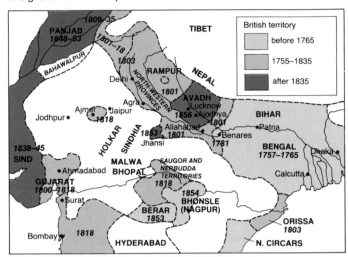

The growth of British power: South India 1750–1820.

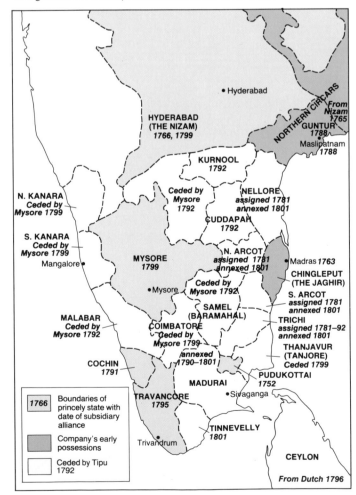

kingdom was virtually annexed after a brief campaign. Pressure of subsidiary payments and local revolt pushed Avadh in the same direction. Again, the province was unable to remit the huge tribute it had incurred after Baksar on a regular basis. British military officers stationed within Avadh and other private traders combined with great revenue farmers and other magnates of Avadh to weaken the Navvab's authority. In the medium term, Lord Cornwallis tried to restrain the forces of expansion by excluding private trade from Avadh and reducing the subsidy. But in the context of the Napoleonic world war, Richard Wellesley, Lord Mornington, decided that Avadh was too 'disorganized' to act as a satisfactory buffer zone for British territories and annexed a large part of its richest districts in 1802.

A similar state of affairs developed in the south. Here Arcot had flourished under British protection. But denied the opportunity to annex the revenues of the rich Maratha state of Thanjavur in 1766, the debts which the Navvab had contracted with British private creditors gradually assumed enormous proportions. During the Mysore and Maratha War of 1779–83, Arcot officials were unable to meet their obligations to support company troops under the subsidiary alliances, so several districts were temporarily assigned to the Company. The same happened in Cornwallis's war against Mysore in 1792–93. Ultimately Wellesley used the excuse of supposedly treasonable correspondence between the Arcot royal family and Mysore to dispossess Muhammad Ali's heir in 1800. The real reason for annexation, however, was the inability of Company authority and the interests of creditors and their Indian agents to co-exist with that of the Arcot state. Pressure on village headmen and the poligar chieftains tended constantly to embroil the Company in costly local wars. The final Mughal successor state Hyderabad remained formally independent after 1802. In fact, it had already lost its richest coastal districts (the Northern Sarkars) to the Company between 1764 and 1784. Its internal administration was distorted by pressure of Company demands for revenue. The court, supported by the British, fought a succession of wars against local chieftains until 1857.

Not all Indian states succumbed to this slow attrition by the fiscal and military demands of the Company. The Marathas, the Sikhs and Mysore all made a bid for continuing independence, building up their machineries of revenue extraction and more modern military forces to face the threat. The Maratha confederacy in western India had originated as a revolt of zamindars and peasant farmers against Mughal rule. In time it took on many of the characteristics of the Mughal state, including considerable autonomy of its regional chieftains (notably Scindia, Holkar and the Gaekwad of Baroda). The nominal chief minister of the Maratha king, the Peshwa, retained authority in Poona, but little power in the Maratha domains which stretched to Agra in the north and the Kannada territories in the south. The Marathas had some success against the British, defeating the Bombay army in 1779 and retaining considerable independence under the great diplomatist Nana Fadnavis (d. 1799). The British feared their modernizing military power, and sought constantly to subject the Peshwa and his subordinates to a subsidiary alliance. In 1802, Wellesley took advantage of a factional conflict within the Maratha realm to conclude such an alliance with the Peshwa in the Treaty of Bassein. This panicked the other Maratha warlords into war with the British. They were defeated in a close-run war. Maratha independence, however, was finally snuffed out in the war of 1816–18, when the British took the excuse of raids by free cavalry soldiers left over from Indian armies (the Pindaris) to discipline the still uncowed chieftains.

Mysore also attempted resistance under its two dynamic sovereigns Haidar Ali and Tipu Sultan. Haidar built a prosperous and militarily powerful domain in the southern Deccan while much of the rest of India was in economic decline. His son, under constant pressure from the British, remodeled the army and administration with an emphasis on Islamic purism. But, unable to match British resources deriving from control of the seaboard and trade, he was fought to a draw by Cornwallis in 1793 and killed in 1799 fighting on the walls of his capital Srirangapatnam. Only the Indian states of the northwest survived the onward march of British conquest. Here the Afghan Durranis had attempted to establish a northwestern successor to the Mughal dominion between 1742 and 1762. But they were unable to maintain their rule in the Panjab against resurgent Sikh warbands (the *misals*) which grew in power after 1762.

Ultimately in 1799 the leader of one of the chief misals Ranjit Singh, took Lahore and established a Sikh state which embraced the whole Panjab and pioneered a revival of trade and agriculture within the framework of a modified Mughal-style revenue machinery. The British were prohibited by lack of resources from intervention in the northwest until the later 1830s. They came to an uneasy agreement with Ranjit Singh in 1802; tolerated the regime of the Talpur Amirs of Sind and encouraged the rulers of both Persia and Afghanistan to hold themselves aloof from first French and later Russian alliance. The Gorkha conquest-state of Nepal which had been founded in the 1790s, was too close to their lands in the North-Western Provinces to survive, and so the Gorkhas were defeated and forced into a subsidiary alliance in 1818 following minor skirmishes over trade privileges and border security.

The East India Company as ruler

British expansion was in part powered by the expansive force of private and Company trade. Certainly, the desire to break into the rich trade monopoly of pepper operated by the southwestern principality of Travancore and the importance to the growing port of Bombay of the raw cotton of Gujarat, used in trade to China, were key considerations leading to the conquest or annexation of these territories. Military and financial needs, however, came to dominate Company strategy. The wars of Wellesley's period alone tripled the Company's debt in London. Stabilization of land-revenues, therefore, became a critical feature of British administration. Equity and economic growth was constantly sacrificed to these considerations. In Bengal, the British made a compact with great landed magnates who were perceived as English-style landlords under the Permanent Settlement of 1793. But the state was excluded from the benefits of agricultural expansion which went to the zamindars. In the south and west, a different system of (*raiyatvari*) settlements became the norm. This involved making compacts for payment of land revenue with 'individual' proprietors on the assumed basis of the value of their fields. It was more appropriate to areas where large territorial magnates did not exist or were too weak to guarantee revenue and agrarian stability. But the early results of the raiyatvari system were no more favorable than those of the Bengal system. Peasants deserted their lands and revenue receipts were falling sharply by the 1830s.

The main reason for this was that the British had squeezed up the land revenues to impossibly high levels. During the later 1820s and 1830s, India also experienced a sharp liquidity crisis. Inflows of bullion into the country slowed; important currency earners, notably indigo which was sold in Europe and raw cotton and opium which were sold in China, were less in demand. Indian merchant houses and peasantry suffered badly, especially when, ironically, the 1830s also witnessed a series of bad famines deepened by the *laissez faire* policies which had now come into vogue among the colonial rulers. Artisans, especially weaving communities, already adversely affected by falling demand for their products and the influx of British-made twist and yarn, suffered rapid impoverishment while the commercial groups who had benefitted from British rule, notably the *bhadralok* (gentry) and entrepreneurs of Calcutta, found themselves squeezed between a declining internal economy and external European competition.

Under the governor-generalship of Lord William Bentinck (1828–36), the authorities in Britain attempted to react to this situation. Since free trade pressure was about to deny the Company its one lucrative area of trade monopoly, the China trade, a policy of military and fiscal retrenchment seemed inevitable. This was what lay behind Bentinck's 'Age of Reform'. The Governor-General cut budgets and wages, in part by introducing Indians into the lower levels of administration where they had been excluded since Cornwallis's time. Bentinck also sought to call a halt to the continuing process of expansion which in 1824–26 had seen the British invasion of Upper Burma in an attempt to stabilize the eastern frontier. British agents were also withdrawn from direct management of the princely state of Hyderabad, though the pressures generated by the subsidiary alliances through its ruthlessly extractive revenue system continued to oppress the peasantry.

Bentinck's years are also associated with social reform in India. It is true that the state finally abolished the practice of widow-burning (*sati*) in 1829, partly in response to the urging of Christian missionaries who had been given a freer hand in India since the revision of the East India Company's Charter in 1813. Macaulay, the historian, drew up his law code in the last years of Bentinck's rule and education and government in the English language was given a notable fillip by decisions against vernacular education. The Grand Trunk Road between Delhi and Lahore was remodeled and the East Yamuna Canal works were begun. But, in truth, the first Age of Reform achieved relatively little. Money was too tight and the government was inhibited from a more direct intervention in Indian social life by fear of Hindu and Muslim reaction.

Indian responses to Company rule

Meanwhile Indian society had thrown up its own responses to the coming of colonial rule. Raja Rammohan Roy (1770–1830) had molded together themes taken from Christianity, Western Deism and Indian monotheism to create a new reformed Hindu faith institutionalized in the Brahmo Samaj (1828), which opposed idol worship, brahminism and 'barbarous customs' such as widow-burning. In Bombay and Madras, intellectuals initiated debating societies for social reform. There were a few conversions to Christianity both in Bengal and Madras, though these were fiercely resisted by a revived Hindu orthodoxy. Equally significant was the trend of reform and change in Hinduism and Islam which drew on earlier traditions. Movements of devotional sectarianism which had continued to emerge even in the eighteenth century now revived in the challenging conditions of colonial India. Satya Narayan in Gujarat established a monotheistic form of the Hindu Vaishnavite cult as did the Raidasis of central India, while the Ramanandis of North India consolidated the gains they had made in previous centuries.

Muslim reformers were equally autonomous and equally active. One tradition of godly reform which emphasized the importance of teaching, a rapprochement between mysticism (sufism) and formal religious learning, and the centrality of the Prophet Muhammad was the tradition of the Muhammadiya associated with Shah Valiullah and his son Shah Abdul Aziz. This school had an ambiguous relationship with colonial rule. Many of its followers refused to serve the British in administrative capacities but held aloof from open opposition. A few, notably Sayyid Ahmad of Rai Bareli who began a war of religion against the Sikhs in the Panjab, were more hostile to British rule. Others such as Dudu Miyan of the so-called Faraizi movement of Bengal concentrated on purist reform among the peasantry.

At the same time, earlier forms of the Islamic high tradition continued to develop. For instance, the rationalistic syllabus of Islamic scholarship which had been formulated by the learned men of Firangi Mahal (*Dars-e Nizamiyya*) at the beginning of the eighteenth century, continued to be consolidated by this Lucknow-based family and to be spread throughout India. Local saint cults and popular Islam, however, retained their vitality, spreading along new lines of communication, and benefitting as much as the purist reformers from the slow spread of the printing press.

The British liked to portray India as stable and acquiescent between 1818 and the Mutiny–Rebellion of 1857. In fact, the subcontinent was constantly in revolt, though revolt remained uncoordinated and was suppressed or accommodated through local concession. The Deccan and central India was in constant turmoil as the power of the central state bore down on local poligars and other magnates. Tribal wars with the Bhils, Kols, Kolis and Santals irrupted as the colonial state and Hindu settlers and capitalists invaded tribal lands. Peasant rebels fought by non-cooperation or by active rebellion against the new revenue systems and outside intrusion. Some groups were completely flattened, but others such as the *mirasidar* landlords of Thanjavur or the *khoti* magnates of the Konkan were able to achieve privileged status within the colonial system. The economic conditions of the 1830s saw a wave of grain rioting and discontent.

Against this background the Rebellion of 1857 was less a squall in a calm sea than once thought. Discontent had gradually been growing in the Bengal army which resented the loss of its privileges and the introduction of lower castes, Sikhs and 'Gurkhas' from Nepal after 1848. The Bengal soldiers' relations among the high caste Bhumihar Brahmin and Rajput peasantry of the north were in

The Mutiny–Rebellion of 1857.

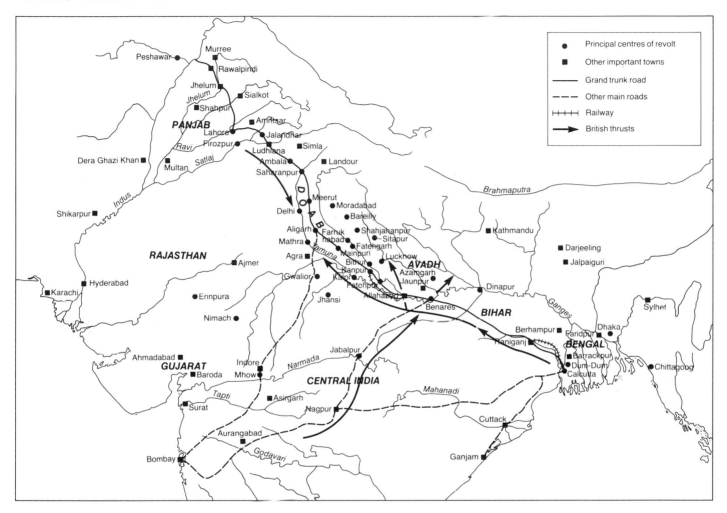

poor economic straits as a result of subdivision of property. The annexation in 1856 of Avadh, a rich revenue bearing princely state, from which many of them hailed, and fear of pollution by the animal grease on the cartridges of the new Lee Enfield rifle sparked a revolt. When the garrison in Meerut and other northern stations mutinied in May and June 1857, the British were too stretched to make an adequate riposte. Their forces were gathered around Calcutta or in the Panjab. Moreover they were wrong-footed by simultaneous revolts among urban mobs, marginal nomadic people (Gujars, Bhattis and Pasis) and among some peasants, particularly the Jats of the Meerut division who had suffered punitively high revenue rates.

The mutinous soldiers gained support from the last Mughal emperor Bahadur Shah at Delhi, from the dispossessed court at Lucknow and even from exiled relations of the old Maratha court such as Nana Sahib at Kanpur. Some large landowners joined the rebellion in support of the Mughal or through the play of local faction or hostility to particular British officers. But the revolt never managed to cut the British lines of communications or strike against the source of British power in the Panjab or Bengal. In November 1857 Delhi was taken by a column from the Panjab after a bloody fight and later in the same month the rebellion at Lucknow was finally broken. As a consequence of the rebellion, the East India Company was abolished and from 1858 the British Crown took over direct administration of the Indian Empire.   *CAB*

Further reading

C. A. Bayly, *Indian Society and the Making of the British Empire* New Cambridge History of India (Cambridge, 1988)

R. Guha, *A Rule of Property for Bengal* (Paris, 1963)

D. Kopf, *British Orientalism and the Bengal Renaissance* (Berkeley and Los Angeles, 1969)

D. Ludden, *Peasant History in South India* (Princeton, NJ, 1985)

P. J. Marshall, *Problems of Empire: Britain and India, 1757–1813* (London, 1968)

P. J. Marshall, *Bengal: the British Bridgehead* New Cambridge History of India (Cambridge, 1988)

E. Stokes, *The English Utilitarians and India* (Oxford, 1959)

E. Stokes, *The Peasant and the Raj: Studies in Agrarian Society and Peasant Rebellion in Colonial India* (Cambridge, 1978)

British Imperialism and Indian Nationalism, 1858–1947

The British Empire in India, after 1858

In its last century, British rule in India had at least five elements, which were also in some senses successive phases. The first, its predominance coming to an end in the late 1870s, was characterized (as in the work and writings of John and Richard Strachey) by optimism about the 'civilizing mission' supposedly undertaken on India's behalf. Technology, public works, education and law were confidently expected to produce a social and economic revolution which would make British rule both welcome and indispensable in India; many thought railways and trade would be sufficient in themselves. The idea of progress united diverse opinions, and allowed such celebrated and different members of the Indian government as Henry Maine and James Fitzjames Stephen to justify conquest and illiberal laws by the need to modernize backward peoples.

The second aspect, prominent in the last twenty years of the nineteenth century, was more pessimistic, doubting the automatic beneficence of British rule and even recognizing, as in J. A. Hobson's *Imperialism* (1902), the link between empire and unequal trade. The case rested upon a 'scientific' examination and categorization of the society, and responded to the apparent failures of policy discovered in poverty, rural unrest and social change. Famines struck in various places between 1860 and 1900, and internal order was threatened at times by agrarian or urban riots, for example over indigo, revenue demands or religious controversy.

The next phase saw a burst of social and political engineering under Lord Curzon (Viceroy from 1899 to 1905), directed toward what was thought of as a loyal rural sector, but also the third element; attempts to isolate and repress political dissent. This was one motive for the partition of Bengal presidency (1905–11) and for increases in executive powers in order to restrict politicians, the press and public meetings (1907–19).

The fourth aspect was a contradiction in British thinking about empire, between a liberal rhetoric and the fact of territorial, economic and intellectual expansion. The contradiction had fashioned the Indian constitution, even before the end of East India

Governor-Generals and Viceroys of India 1858–1947

1858–1862	Lord Canning
1862–1863	Lord Elgin (eighth Earl)
1863	Major-General Sir Robert Napier[a]
1863–1864	Colonel Sir William Denison[a]
1864–1869	Sir John Lawrence
1869–1872	Lord Mayo
1872	Sir John Strachey[a]
1872	Lord Napier[a]
1872–1876	Lord Northbrook
1876–1880	Lord Lytton (first Earl)
1880–1884	Lord Ripon
1884–1888	Lord Dufferin
1888–1894	Lord Lansdowne
1894–1899	Lord Elgin (ninth Earl)
1899–1904	Lord Curzon
1904	Lord Ampthill[a]
1904–1905	Lord Curzon
1905–1910	Lord Minto
1910–1916	Lord Hardinge
1916–1921	Lord Chelmsford
1921–1925	Lord Reading
1925	Lord Lytton (second Earl)[a]
1925–1926	Lord Reading
1926–1929	Lord Irwin (later Lord Halifax)
1929	Lord Goschen[a]
1929–1931	Lord Irwin
1931–1934	Lord Willingdon
1934	Sir George Stanley[a]
1934–1936	Lord Willingdon
1936–1943	Lord Linlithgow
1943–1947	Lord Wavell
1947	Lord Mountbatten

[a]temporary appointment

Source: *Thacker's Indian Directory, 1909* p. 62 (Calcutta, 1909); B. N. Pandey, Ed. *The Indian Nationalist Movement, 1885–1947: Select Documents* pp. 265–66 (New York, 1979).

Box 7

Company government in 1858, into what contemporaries called 'double' government, in which India got the despotism and Britain provided the checks and balance. During and after World War I, however, there came a transition toward two realizations, that Indian independence was unavoidable, and foreign enterprise could not answer India's problems.

Inevitably the fifth and final phase concerned the means and manner of the relinquishment of British suzerainty, not so much fulfilling as bypassing earlier promises that Indians would be 'educated' until, like good Whigs, they could manage a parliamentary system. The main issue was settling the succession between

The British Empire in India *c.* 1900

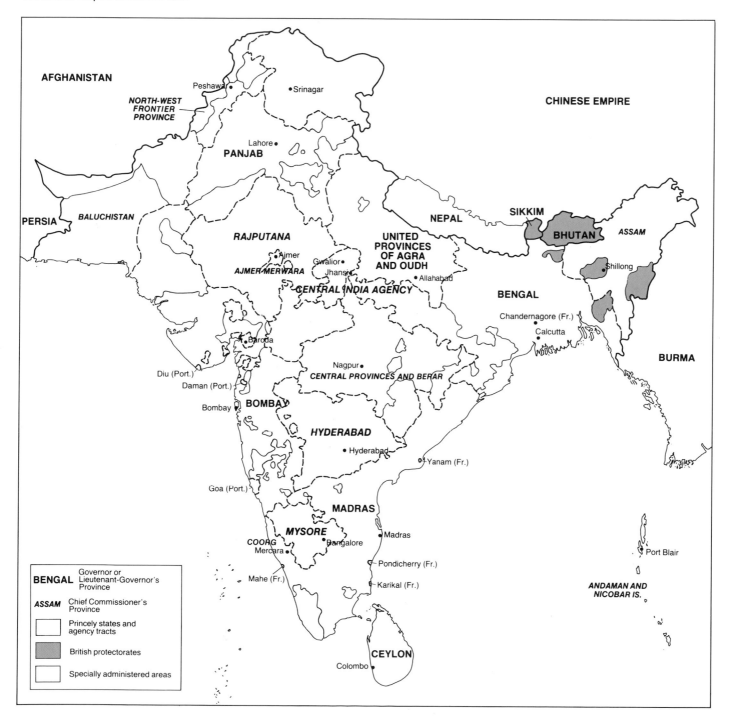

AFGHANISTAN

Peshawar

Srinagar

CHINESE EMPIRE

*NORTH-WEST
FRONTIER
PROVINCE*

Lahore

PANJAB

PERSIA   *BALUCHISTAN*

RAJPUTANA

Ajmer

AJMER-MERWARA

Gwalior

Jhansi

**UNITED
PROVINCES
OF AGRA
AND OUDH**

Allahabad

CENTRAL INDIA AGENCY

NEPAL

SIKKIM

BHUTAN

ASSAM

Shillong

BENGAL

Chandernagore (Fr.)

Calcutta

BURMA

Baroda

Diu (Port.)

Daman (Port.)

Nagpur

CENTRAL PROVINCES AND BERAR

Bombay

BOMBAY

HYDERABAD

Hyderabad

Yanam (Fr.)

Goa (Port.)

MADRAS

MYSORE

COORG

Mercara

Bangalore

Madras

Port Blair

Mahe (Fr.)

Pondicherry (Fr.)

Karikal (Fr.)

*ANDAMAN AND
NICOBAR IS.*

CEYLON

Colombo

BENGAL Governor or
Lieutenant-Governor's
Province

ASSAM Chief Commissioner's
Province

Princely states and
agency tracts

British protectorates

Specially administered areas

parties assumed to represent separate interests or communities.

Two related questions are often raised: how far the Indian administration was subjected to the imperial control of the government of Britain, and whether Indian society was distorted by the influence of British government in India? Military history provides one important strand of evidence for the first of these; trade another. Between the mutiny of 1857 and the crisis of World War I, the Indian army's complement of British troops and hence its cost were maintained at a high level. Moreover, the army became an instrument of British foreign policy, either partly or wholly at Indian expense (the latter when Indian interests were supposedly involved, as in an Afghan war of 1878–80 which led to the creation of British Baluchistan, a Burman war which resulted in the annexation of upper Burma in 1885–86, and an expedition to Tibet in 1903–04). Much is still made, though some commentators dismiss it as relatively unimportant, of the drain of wealth which British government imposed on India, because of the high cost of European administration, stores and loans, in payments made in London. More damaging was the priority given to the army in the spending of Indian revenues.

In the period from c. 1840 to 1914, India also became Britain's most important trading partner, dominant in regard to its cotton exports, vital for many other manufactures, hugely involved in capital investment, and concealing much of Britain's deficit in trade with other industrialized nations. The fact that India was ruled from Britain undoubtedly contributed to the purchase of British machinery and cloth, and the failure of the Indian government to use tariffs to protect the indigenous cotton industry. Britain also introduced economic dogmas which restricted the state's role in economic development: on the whole the government believed that trade would encourage economic growth but that governments should not meddle in trade.

Improvements in long-distance communications, within India and between India and Britain, encouraged centralization and imperial control. Strains soon appeared. Officials were chosen by competition after 1853, the means repeatedly examined to try to ensure recruits of intellectual competence, social distinction, and European race. They became self-conscious about their role and prestige. The Government of India too presented itself as the heir to an indigenous political tradition and the repository of local knowledge. Hence, though India was regarded as a 'possession', its policies ultimately controlled in London to benefit Britain, it was also spoken of as a 'trust', its officials putting forward what they saw as Indian needs. Yet British control weakened in the twentieth century – and one reason was government policy itself.

Much as the Mughals before them, the British made use of existing institutions and local élites which they attempted to incorporate into their systems of rule. This strategy implied a minimum of interference with Indian society, a policy often advocated during British rule. Yet the British could hardly help interfering, partly because of the picture they had of India and the expectations they had of government. Christian belief and ethics convinced them that Indian society was barbarous; therefore they could improve it. Consistently believing in a 'natural' order (redefined from time to time), they tried to marry European ideas of social leadership and the 'gentleman' with supposedly Indian categories of tribe and caste. Racial stereotypes implied Indians were inferior, social theories that India was at a relatively early stage of evolution. Hence officials agreed that India would have to change, even those officials who feared political consequences and argued for protective laws.

At first after 1858, the preference was for aristocratic forms of social and political control. A landowners' association was set up in Avadh as a result of the post-Mutiny 'clemency' of Lord Canning, Viceroy from 1856 to 1862. There was pressure, although it was ultimately unsuccessful, to fix the land-revenue demand permanently in those areas (outside greater Bengal) where the tax was liable to periodic reassessment and payable by village communities or peasant proprietors; the aim was to create an independent landowning aristocracy. Under Lord Lytton (1876–80) these policies were given more symbolic form in a durbar celebrating Queen Victoria under her new title of Empress of India, as if she were a feudal monarch surrounded by her Indian princes and vassals. Such fantasies had their legacy in subsequent durbars, in the honors and precedence systems, in colleges for Princes and education for the scions of great estates, and, as late as the 1920s, in the grandiose development of the capital at New Delhi.

Other officials thought British rule was distorting Indian society. For example, they blamed laws giving individual rights over property, because they claimed that Indians had only understood ownership in terms of communal shares. They worried about contract and market relations where custom had supposedly been supreme. But the only remedy was further legislation, importing other assumptions. The alternative policies, which were to restrict land transfer in the Deccan (1879) and the Panjab (1900), and to 'restore' tenant rights in permanently-settled Bengal and Bihar (1859 and 1885), were clearly designed to benefit dominant but numerous groups of proprietary farmers. Some concern was directed towards under-tenants and laborers too, but legislation tended to reflect the influence of dominant groups. Legal provisions eventually have social repercussions; thus Indians who were given legal privileges were able to consolidate or improve their position in practice.

By the later nineteenth century intervention was inevitable; it was implicit in the administrative systems themselves. After 1858 India was ruled not only under the British Crown but increasingly under a British system of law, provided in a refined and expanding structure of bureaucracy and courts, and embodied in penal, criminal and civil codes (1860–61). Even princely states eventually felt the effects. The numbers of laws and regulations increased as bureaucratic structures were improved and particularly as the British came to discover and to manage knowledge about India. Specialist agencies developed, with their own expertise: Boards of Revenue, departments for excise, irrigation or public works, licensees for monopolies in certain commodities, railway and road boards, the army and police, municipal and district councils; all could cut across existing Indian interests. Also, although seldom with significant results, the British sought improvements in agriculture and commercial crops, and finally even the development of Indian manufactures, for example by assistance to steel makers and buying government stores in India. Thus they interfered with trade not so much by putting British interests first, as by determining, for example, where communications should be improved, or which groups should be protected from the rigor of the market-place.

A second reason for interference was a running budgetary crisis originating with the debt from the military campaigns to quell the Indian uprisings in 1857 and 1858. Financial reforms were repeatedly introduced, beginning in 1859 when James Wilson became Finance Member in the Government of India, but the budgetary problems were never permanently solved, since low taxation was considered politically essential but the expectations and functions of the state continued to expand. The problem was compounded by military costs, by charges for famine relief and capital-intensive works, and by a declining exchange rate between the rupee and sterling. The last was particularly serious for the Indian government because of the proportion of its budget devoted to meeting expenses and servicing debts in England, a problem compounded by the fluctuating value and increasing cost of the land-revenue collections. The solution was therefore the diversification of the sources of government income: particularly, in the twentieth century, a rapid shift towards taxes upon trade, which gave an added acerbity to the Government of India's pleas for fiscal autonomy and differential tariffs. Earlier there was a tendency to set up schemes for user-payment, as in court fees, registration stamps, road cesses, and local board taxes; these gained in significance from the 1870s.

The consequences of such intervention were that, by the start of the twentieth century, and increasingly thereafter, the British faced a society which they could no longer control through the methods they had inherited or developed early in their rule. The changes were essentially a standardization and a generalizaton of institutions, identities and concepts. British policy accordingly became concerned with forging different kinds of alliances. In the nineteenth century, particularly in the period of Gladstonian liberalism represented by most of Lord Ripon's viceroyalty (1880–

The King-Emperor, George V, and the Queen-Empress, Mary, show themselves to their Indian subjects from the ramparts of the old Mughal palace (the Red Fort) at Delhi, 1911.

84), the British had been ready to enter into a limited compact with the Indian educated classes. But what was shown in early attitudes to the Indian National Congress or in another outlet for the Western-educated in 1892 – indirect elections for legislative councils – was that concessions were intended to delineate acceptable attitudes, so as to outlaw more 'extreme' positions, and so as to avoid having to reach agreement on how power might be shared with Westernized Indians. In any case the greatest compact was intended to be with rural élites, even under Ripon; his expansion of local self-government, taking up proposals of 1870, was partly intended to teach a principle of English local government – delegation to the gentry. By contrast, in the twentieth century, the idea that the rulers need only secure the contentment of the rural masses through traditional leaders, gave way to a belief that the masses were being 'stirred up' by political and religious agitators, and even that they should be stirred up by the British in order to re-forge loyalty on a less passive basis. Politics, which became increasingly nationalist, supplanted the land and revenue as preoccupations of the Indian civil servant. The great issues of internal policy in the nineteenth century – pacification, revenue settlement, landholding, famine – declined in importance and glamor in the face of the new challenges of constitutional change and nationalist agitation.

PGR

Further reading

Judith M. Brown, *Modern India. The Origins of an Asian Democracy* (Delhi, 1985)

Neil Charlesworth, *British Rule and the Indian Economy 1800–1914* (Economic History Society; London, 1982)

Dharma Kumar, Ed., *The Cambridge Economic History of India, Vol. 2: c. 1757–c. 1970* (Cambridge, 1983)

B. B. Misra, *The Administrative History of India 1834–1947. General Administration* (London, 1970)

R. J. Moore, *Liberalism and Indian Politics 1872–1922* (London, 1966)

Percival Spear, *The Oxford History of Modern India 1740–1947* (Oxford, 1965)

B. R. Tomlinson, *The Political Economy of the Raj 1914–1947* (London, 1979)

D. A. Washbrook, 'Law, State and Agrarian Society in Colonial India', *Modern Asian Studies* 15, 3, pp. 649–721 (1981)

Political development

In the three decades spanning the time between the mutiny uprising of 1857–58 and the first meeting of the Indian National Congress in 1885, the transformations of British colonial rule, which are discussed in the preceding section, were mirrored in a growing Indian political awareness, the emergence of a self-conscious Indian public opinion, the growth of politics and the appearance of a steadily increasing number of 'public men' of affairs. While Indian participation in public life generally was dominated by a small educated élite, the period formed the seedbed of Indian national consciousness when, for the first time, a substantial number of Indians began to see themselves as a nation. Sharing the opportunities and frustrations presented by British colonial rule, these incipient nationalists searched for a sense of national culture and national interest. However, the very processes of mobilization by which an Indian nationalist consciousness was forged among the educated, predominantly Hindu élite, also stimulated awareness of distinction and differentiation among leaders of less advantageously situated communities and interests. Certain public leaders, particularly among the Muslim élites of northern India, calculating the costs and

benefits of adherence to the British Raj or participation in the nationalist movement, preferred the former over the latter. Thus at the very birth hour of the Indian National Congress and its articulation of an enduring all-Indian nationality, there also emerged a dissenting voice of a counter-nationalism of South Asia's Muslim people which denied the reality of the all-India national identity.

Indian political activity prior to 1858 was limited to occasional episodes of organization in a few localities over specific issues. The Land Owners' Society at Calcutta (1838) was the first attempt of political association which claimed to speak on behalf of an all-India interest group, although in fact it mobilized special interests in defense of the Bengal Permanent Settlement. Resentment against Christian proselytizing and government sponsored social reform stimulated the Dharma Sabha (1830), also at Calcutta, and the founding of Pacheappa's Institution at Madras in 1842. For the handful of Indians who obtained Western education or a knowledge of English, these years saw a schism emerge in Hindu society between those favoring social reform and those who were more concerned with preservation of the ancestral faith. Mobilization of public opinion began to matter in religious reform debates such as the 1843–44 agitation in Bombay over the readmission to caste of a Hindu youth, Shripat Sheshadri, who had dined with Christian missionaries. The remarkable champion of Hindu revivalism in Maharashtra, Vishnubawa Brahmachari (1825–71), clearly appreciated the utility of mobilizing public opinion against missionary activities.

The so-called Lex Loci Act of 1850 (Civil Disabilities Removal Act) which preserved the 'Hindu' family property rights of Christian converts provoked a prolonged agitation among educated Hindus in Bengal and Bombay who objected to the seeming alliance of government with evangelical missions. Although unsuccessful, the Indian agitation directly paralleled a similar campaign among the non-official British community resident in India to hold on to conventional rights and privileges enjoyed as a racial monopoly. If these European agitations hurt Indian sensibilities, they nonetheless offered an instructive model of political mobilization.

In 1851 the forthcoming review of the East India Company's charter stimulated new Indian political activity in the form of political associations. The British Indian Association was launched at Calcutta to petition the British parliament regarding the shortcomings of Company rule. Next the Deccan Association was formed at Poona (1852), but soon waned when its leaders were transferred from the city. A Madras Native Association and the Bombay Association followed. The significance of these early organizations lay primarily in their very existence and in the effort of the British Indian Association to mobilize an all-India constituency. Although these associations' influence upon the parliamentary review was negligible, they established the precedent of making direct appeals to Britain.

Much of the early political activity was conducted by a small, but influential strata of Indian society centered in the coastal port cities, who possessed knowledge of English and some Western style education. These men were the initial products of the 1835 decision to support English medium higher education. Paying their colonial rulers the sincere compliment of imitation, these educated Indians assimilated both a new language and new ideas.

Macaulay had observed in 1833 that 'the public mind of India may expand under our system until it has outgrown that system; that by good government we may educate our subjects into a capacity for better government; that having become instructed in European knowledge, they may in some future age demand European institutions'. Macaulay himself was not sure that such a time would come, and in the period from 1857 to 1885, few Britons in India could conceive of the event. Their post-mutiny mentality left them with little confidence in the desirability or possibility of introducing Westernizing social changes to India and further left them inclined to regard with suspicion all Indians, save for the presumably conservative, traditional élites of princes and rural landed magnates.

Educated Indians, on the contrary, saw a promise of new opportunities and of partnership in the governance of British India. If these men perceived the flaws of colonial rule, they nevertheless sought consultation, participation and collaboration in the Raj, preferring its modification rather than its removal. Loyalty, not sedition, was the watchword of political India.

English education permitted adoption of European ideas and supplied new means of inter-regional contact and solidarity. This was facilitated by the development of transport and communication: roads and railroads, telegraph, cheap post and the press. Centralization and standardization were hallmarks of the British Indian administrative system after 1858. The new universities and educational hierarchies, the new High Courts with their judicial networks, the new law codes and new administrative procedures contributed to an intensification of British rule in the subcontinent and thereby supplied common experiences which shaped the development of Indian political consciousness.

The enormous costs of suppressing the Mutiny had important implications for Indian politics in that the Government of India pursued new financial resources and fiscal strategies. One of these was a gradual introduction of local self-government so that expenditures for improvements could be shifted to local taxpayers. This created new arenas of incipient political activity, initially in the municipalities of large cities and towns – the precise locus of the educated class. Another innovation was the introduction of new forms of taxation which in turn spawned movements of protest. Led

by non-official resident Britons, strong opposition was raised against new License and Income taxes under the slogan of no taxation without representation. The concession of a legislative council, which had limited power to legislate and which included some Indians to balance the presence of non-official Britons, followed in 1861.

Educational policy, which had looked forward since the 1830s to the creation of a useful and educated class of Indians, finally began to bear fruit after the creation of the new universities and the grants-in-aid system for supporting secondary education. The continued expansion of English education in the 1860s and 1870s meant an increased number of educated Indians now existed for whom no suitable jobs were available. In absence of real opportunity in Government service, educated Indians turned in increasing numbers to teaching, law and journalism, professions from which political participation was an easy step.

The Government of India began to view higher education as a wasteful investment. Proposals in 1870 for the curtailment of government aid to colleges in Bengal led to the first attempt of members of the educated classes in India to launch a province-wide agitation; the movement revealed both the growth in numbers of the educated and their capacity to act in a concerted fashion.

The geographical spread of such campaigns reflected a physical expansion of the educated interests. In 1881 three-fourths of the University of Calcutta's graduates were stationed somewhere other than Calcutta, contributing to growth of political consciousness and public life in mofussil towns and provincial cities. However, one must also note that this growth produced tensions as Bengali Hindus, for example, pursued opportunities in northern India where their successes engendered resentment from local élites, particularly among Muslims.

It must be emphasized that politics were not under monopoly control of the educated interests. In municipal and regional politics 'graduates' were often subordinate to the practical dominance of local men of affairs from mercantile and property holding groups whose energies were sometimes turned to more provincial or pragmatic concerns, and sometimes to promotion of narrow interests of religious communities.

Another differentiation that arose grew from conflicts between generations. Younger educated men chafed at the dominance of caste or community elders. It was in the context of such a dispute in Poona over the management of an important temple that a significant new political association was created in 1870. The Poona Sarvajanik Sabha employed a unique device to legitimize its claims of a constituency by requiring that each member obtain an undertaking from at least sixty citizens granting him the right to speak for them in public affairs. The Sabha's birth in temple reform was quickly surpassed in significance by its subsequent activity as the leading association of public opinion in western Maharashtra in which it was distinguished by an active interest in rural as well as urban affairs. In Calcutta also generations and interests came into competition as the older zamindar-dominated British Indian Association found itself rivaled, after 1876, by a new Indian Association promoted by Surendranath Banerjea (1848–1925).

In a sense, the British, having called into being an educated class of Indians, found them an inconvenience and sought to ignore them as surely as if they were illiterate poor of the countryside. Disappointment and resentment were prominent features of the emerging Indian public consciousness. Educated Indians were beginning to demand the rights of British subjects as British subjects, no more, no less. Given their moderate tenor, their political representations could not justify official suppression. British frustration found some satisfaction in dismissing the educated Indians as hybrid Babus who could be ignored for the simple fact that having learned English they could be disregarded as unrepresentative Indians.

Despite Queen Victoria's 1858 proclamation which held out the promise of Indian employment in high office, her Indian government pursued policies which reduced prospects for Indian candidates to its foremost ranks, those of the Indian Civil Service. This stimulated a campaign in 1876–77 in which, for the first time, Indians themselves, without European help, coordinated an all-India agitation. A further significant grievance appeared a year later in 1878 with the passage of Lord Lytton's Vernacular Press Act which sought to gag the Indian language press. Indian responses included formation of new political associations as well as periodic conventions of public men for mutual consultation.

Not all Indians shared the same degree of distaste for Lord Lytton's measures. While many Muslim élites regarded British rule with ambivalence, some sought to find means of building a rapprochement with the new colonial order. Abdul Latif (1828–93) founded the Mahommedan Literary and Scientific Society of Calcutta to assist Bengal's Muslims to catch up with their Hindu neighbors. In 1877 Sayyid Amir Ali formed the Central National Mahommedan Association as a body for English-knowing Muslims who took the view that the best course for overcoming perceived Muslim backwardness was in offering loyalty to the government, and demanding in return preferential treatment in education and government employment.

The 1880s saw an intensification of these developments, called forth, not by further conservative British repressions, but by a liberal policy of encouragement to political India by Gladstone's chosen Viceroy, Lord Ripon.

Conscious of the alienation caused by Lytton's policies, Ripon attempted to introduce measures of reform. He attached great importance to public opinion and sought to enlist it as a counterweight to the conservative bureaucracy. His extension of local self-government was welcomed by Indian opinion which saw this as opening to the introduction of representative institutions and, possibly in the future, national self-government. Surendranath Banerjea suggested in 1882 the convening of a 'national congress' to strengthen the Viceroy's hand by ensuring the availability to the government of Indian opinion. The launching in 1883 of *Voice of India*, a journal of press-extracts revealed a growing sense of unanimity on issues among the educated interest.

The Criminal Jurisdiction (Ilbert) bill, which was introduced at this time, proposed to remove certain anomalies of exemption of Europeans from trial by Indian magistrates in the countryside. While it was not central to Ripon's reforms, it became the target of cumulative resentment in the European community in India, revealing considerable racial animosities which led some to fear eventual open clashes.

The prospects of violence were in fact limited. The period had seen popular agrarian or religious violence shake authority in specific times and places. The so-called 'Blue Mutiny' of 1859–62 had shaken parts of rural Bengal as peasants protested against forced contracts for the cultivation of indigo. Maratha peasant discontent disturbed some Deccan districts in 1875, while earlier in the Panjab the Kuka uprising for purification of Sikhism briefly eroded imperial authority. The closest thing to an outright rebellion had occurred in 1879 when Vasudeo Balvant Phadke, a disenchanted government servant at Poona, planned and led low caste Ramoshis and Mangs against government installations and money lenders. The suppression of all of these rebellions and riots provided a contrast with pre-1857 India, illustrating the point that so long as military force could hold India, the British were set to stay. Yet it was fear of 'another mutiny' which led a retired civil servant, Allen Octavian Hume, to urge the need for a 'safety valve' for Indian opinion. The agitation of non-official Britons against the Ilbert Bill may also have convinced educated Indians of the need for further organization to offer alternative views to the British public.

Ripon's departure in 1884 occasioned a heartfelt outpouring of Indian gratitude. Hume among others encouraged this expression. New political associations, the Madras Mahajana Sabha and the Bombay Presidency Association in effect transferred some of the political initiative away from Calcutta where the very success of political mobilizations had revealed inherent contradictions among a wide array of interests. The attitudes of two Muslim organizations, the Mahommedan Literary Society and the Central National Mahommedan Association, reflected the distance felt by Muslim élites from the educated Hindus.

Hume encouraged a private network of contacts, the Indian National Union to plan an all-India 'national conference' of like-minded public men at Poona in December, 1885. The privacy of the arrangements had the embarrassing side effect that Surendranath

Banerjea was unaware of the plan and announced a National Conference at the same season for Calcutta. The Poona hosts hurriedly altered the name of their organization to the 'Indian National Congress'. Just prior to the meeting, a cholera epidemic forced the movement of the meeting to Bombay where, in December 1885 the new Congress met for the first time. The resolutions of the Congress were couched in total loyalty to the British crown, with a strong sense of the blessings of British rule. The grievances raised reflected the desire of educated Indians to be recognized as legitimate potential partners in the rule of their nation. Important issues included the question of Indian recruitment to the Indian Civil Service, extension of representative government, support for education and promotion of Indian development. Recognizing the limits to consensus, the sponsors avoided questions of social or religious reform which would detract from the goal of informed unanimity with which India could face the British bureaucracy in India and the British parliament and public in London.

If the early sessions of the Congress more resembled those of a debating society than a political party, this was an accurate reflection of the stage which political consciousness had reached in British India. For all its limitations the Indian National Congress represented a valid if incomplete vision of the idea of a common Indian nationality. In 1885 it was the most prominent feature on India's political map, although then the most prominent fact in India's rule remained the bureaucratic colonial state. Congress delegates were predominantly urban and Hindu and they regretted the absence of many representatives from less politically advanced regions of the subcontinent, particularly from the élite Muslim community of North India.

The position of the Muslims varied enormously across India in the period. Whereas in Bengal a Muslim majority was both economically and socially disadvantaged, in upper India Muslims continued to hold a disproportionate share of élite positions. The introduction of local self-government led Muslims to realize that they were a minority. The emergent Hindu politicians potentially could create difficulties for Muslims in such matters as restricting the consumption of beef or the celebration of Islamic festivals. The growth of local politics and public opinion in North India stimulated Hindu demands for government recognition of Hindi in the Devanagari script as against the Urdu language and its Perso-Arabic script.

Upper India had been the heartland of Mughal culture and there members of the old élite, particularly the old service gentry, sought to preserve a measure of their past dominance and culture in the face of foreign rule and the bustling advance of Bengali clerks and local Hindu merchants. Among the Muslim leaders the most significant was Sir Sayyid Ahmad Khan (1817–98) who launched a movement leading to the founding in 1877 at Aligarh of the Muhammadan

Anglo-Oriental College and related educational institutions. The college became a focal point of his modernist interpretation of Islam which emphasized the compatibility of Islam with modern Western knowledge. Its students, mostly young Muslims from well-to-do families of the Urdu-speaking region, could master Western learning in a congenial setting while retaining links to their Islamic legacy. Sayyid Ahmad actively discouraged Muslim participation in the Indian National Congress on grounds that its 'nationalism' was ultimately an expression of Hindu, especially Bengali, interests. His argument that Muslims could best protect their interests by remaining loyal to the British Raj offered an effective counter to claims of the Congress to speak for all India, and served as a functional foundation for the growth of Muslim separatism in succeeding decades. Just as participation of the urban, educated Hindu, élites colored the orientation of the early Congress' image of the Indian nation, so the propagation of the idea of a South Asian Muslim nationality was influentially flavored by the concerns and style of the upper Indian Muslim élite. In both instances many years of political development would be required to broaden these concepts of national identity and purpose.

FFC

Further reading
S. Banerjea, *A Nation in Making: being Reminiscences of Fifty Years of Public Life* (London, 1925)
C. A. Bayly, *The Local Roots of Indian Politics: Allahabad, 1880–1920* (Oxford, 1975)
S. Gopal, *The Viceroyalty of Lord Ripon, 1880–1884* (Oxford, 1953)
P. Hardy, *The Muslims of British India* (Cambridge, 1972)
B. B. Majumdar, *Indian Political Associations and Reform of Legislature (1818–1917)* (Calcutta, 1965)
J. C. Masselos, *Nationalism on the Indian Subcontinent: An Introductory History* (Melbourne, 1972)
S. R. Mehrotra, *The Emergence of the Indian National Congress* (Delhi, 1971)
A. Seal, *The Emergence of Indian Nationalism: Competition and Collaboration in the Later Nineteenth Century* (Cambridge, 1968)

Growth of political organization. The Indian National Congress and the All-India Muslim League 1885–1909
The increasing pressure of the British imperial structure on Indian society and culture in the later nineteenth century was crucial in giving birth to a new kind of politics and a new style of politician on the subcontinent. As the British presence and the imperial linkage with Britain modified many of the sources of power in India, the pathways to power and the skills necessary for successful politics, India's new style politicians recognized that local organization was

SUMMARY

OF

RESOLUTIONS PASSED AT THE

FIRST INDIAN NATIONAL CONGRESS,

Composed of Representatives from Calcutta, Madras, Bombay, Poona, Allahabad, Lahore, Lucknow, Agra, Benares, Ahmedabad, Kurrachee, Surat, Veerumgaum, Ganjam, Masulipatam, Chingleput, Tanjore, Combaconum, Madras, Tinnevelly, Coimbatore, Cuddapah, Anantapoor, Bellary and Umballa,

HELD IN BOMBAY,

On the 28th, 29th and 30th December, 1885.

RESOLUTION I.

Resolved.—That this Congress earnestly recommends that the promised inquiry into the working of Indian Administration, here and in England, should be entrusted to a Royal Commission, the people of India being adequately represented thereon, and evidence taken both in India and in England.

[Proposed by Mr. G. Subramania Iyer, (*Madras*); seconded by Mr. P. M. Mehta, (*Bombay*): and supported by Mr. Norendronath Sen, (*Calcutta*).]

RESOLUTION II.

Resolved.—That this Congress considers the abolition of the Council of the Secretary of State for India, as at present constituted, the necessary preliminary to all other reforms.

[Proposed by Mr. S. H. Chiplonkar, (*Poona*); seconded by Mr. P. Ananda Charlu, (*Madras*); and supported by Mr. J. Ghosal, (*Allahabad*).]

RESOLUTION III.

Resolved.—That this Congress considers the reform and expansion of the Supreme and existing Local Legislative Councils, by the admission of a considerable proportion of elected members (and the creation of similar Councils for the N.-W. Provinces and Oudh, and also for the Punjab) essential; and holds that all Budgets should be referred to these Councils for consideration, their members being moreover empowered to interpellate the Executive in regard to all branches of the administration; and that a Standing Committee of the House of Commons should be constituted to receive and consider any formal protests that may be recorded by majorities of such Councils against the exercise by the Executive of the power, which would be vested in it, of over-ruling the decisions of such majorities.

[Proposed by the Hon. K. T. Telang, c.i.e., (*Bombay*); seconded by the Hon. S. Subramania Iyer, (*Madras*); and supported by the Hon. Dadabhai Naoroji, (*Bombay*).]

RESOLUTION IV.

Resolved.—That in the opinion of this Congress the competitive examinations now held in England for first appointments in various civil departments of the public service, should henceforth, in accordance with the views of the India Office Committee of 1860, 'be held simultaneously, one in England and one in India, both being as far as practicable identical in their nature, and those who compete in both countries being finally classified in one list according to merit,' and that the successful candidates in India should be sent to England for

The founding of the Indian National Congress in 1885 marked the beginning of an organized Indian nationalist movement.

---

not enough. If they wished to speak effectively and authoritatively to their rulers, and to the British parliament and electorate, they needed India-wide organization to prove they had continental rather than merely local or sectional support. The Anglo-Indian agitation against the Ilbert Bill during Ripon's viceroyalty served to underline the efficacy of such organization. In 1885 the first session of the Indian National Congress marked the vital step of continental organization. The founders of Congress had gained their political experience in the politics and professions of the Presidency towns, and many had first met as students in London. They included Pherozeshah Mehta, Badruddin Tyabji, W. C. Bonnerjee, Manmo-

Presidents of the Congress 1885–1947

Year		President
1885		W. C. Bonnerjee
1886		Dadabhai Naoroji
1887		Badruddin Tyabji
1888		George Yule
1889		Sir William Wedderburn
1890		Sir Pherozeshah Mehta
1891		P. Ananda Charlu
1892		W. C. Bonnerjee
1893		Dadabhai Naoroji
1894		Alfred Webb
1895		S. N. Banerjea
1896		Rahimtulla Sayani
1897		C. S. Nair
1898		A. M. Bose
1899		R. C. Dutt
1900		N. G. Chandravarkar
1901		D. E. Wacha
1902		S. N. Banerjea
1903		L. M. Ghosh
1904		Sir Henry Cotton
1905		G. K. Gokhale
1906		Dadabhai Naoroji
1907		Dr Rashbihari Ghosh
1908		Dr Rashbihari Ghosh
1909		M. M. Malaviya
1910		Sir William Wedderburn
1911		B. N. Dhar
1912		R. N. Madholkar
1913		Nawab Syed Mohammad Bahadur
1914		Bhupendra Nath Basu
1915		Sir S. P. Sinha
1916		A. C. Mazumdar
1917		Mrs Annie Besant
1918	(Special Session)	Hassan Imam
1918	(Annual Session)	M. M. Malaviya
1919		Motilal Nehru
1920	(Special Session)	Lajpat Rai
1920	(Annual Session)	C. Vijayaraghavachariar
1921		C. R. Das (in prison)
		Hakim Ajmal Khan (acting President)
1922		C. R. Das
1923	(Special Session)	A. K. Azad
1923	(Annual Session)	Mahomed Ali
1924		M. K. Gandhi
1925		Mrs Sarojini Naidu
1926		S. Srinivasa Iyengar
1927		Dr M. A. Ansari
1928		Motilal Nehru
1929–1930		Jawaharlal Nehru
1931		Vallabhbhai Patel
1932		R. Amritlal

Box 8

1933	Mrs J. M. Sen Gupta
1934	Rajendra Prasad
1935	Rajendra Prasad
1936	Jawaharlal Nehru
1937	Jawaharlal Nehru
1938	Subhas Chandra Bose
1939	Subhas Chandra Bose re-elected but forced to resign; Rajendra Prasad elected instead
1940–1946	A. K. Azad
1946 (July–September)	Jawaharlal Nehru
1946–1947	J. B. Kripalani

Source: B. N. Pandey, Ed., *The Indian Nationalist Movement, 1885–1947: Select Documents* pp. 264–65 (New York, 1979)

Box 8 *(continued)*

han Ghose, Surendranath Banerjea and Romeschandra Dutt; and they were assisted by a former British official, A. O. Hume, who poured time and money into the precarious new organization.

Congress was not a 'party' with a clear ideology, effective organization and finances, and regular recruitment procedures. It was a loose association of influential men in provincial politics who recognized their common need for a national platform. In its earliest decades there was little year-round activity or organization: those men who were locally interested in its survival ran skeleton offices and committees, often just from a lawyer's office. Congress was mainly operative at annual Christmastime gatherings where key issues were debated, resolutions passed, and arrangements for the next year's meeting handed over to an organizing committee. Congress finances were insecure, and its membership was loose and unstable, depending largely on where the session was held, whether local issues generated enthusiasm, or whether disagreements among the leaders drove them to rally delegates to support their particular viewpoint. Delegate numbers fluctuated considerably from 1584 in Poona in 1895 to 243 in Lahore in 1909. Their origins reflected the uneven spread of English education, demonstrating that Congress was not representative of India's complex and regionalized society. It was completely male-dominated. Brahmins attended in a far higher proportion to their numbers in the population than did non-Brahmin Hindus, or members of other religious communities: and Presidency men massively outnumbered those from other provinces. Panjab, for example, provided around 1500 compared with over 4000 from Madras between the foundation of Congress and 1909. Lawyers predominated over other occupational groups, composing well over one-third of the delegates between 1892 and 1909.

Given the delegates' background, their preoccupations and ideals were understandable. They were all patriots, certainly; concerned about the dependent status of India and Indians in the empire. Some felt that the British were destroying a pre-existing national entity; others thought India's experience of imperial rule was creating a new nation; while most were convinced economic nationalists, agreeing that Britain was draining India of her wealth. However, Congressmen were scrupulously loyal to the Raj. They did not wish for radical political or social change, but merely for modifications in government and the structures of political life; for they had prospered from the new education, professions and administration. Even when they began to envisage colonial self-government as a goal in the early twentieth century their aims were moderate, and their concern was more with issues touching their status, professional and political opportunities. They deliberately insulated themselves from social, religious and economic issues (such as the emotive and communally divisive question of cow-killing) which threatened their unity. But in consequence they denied themselves and their organization the popular support which would have been forthcoming on such matters. It was a high price to pay for the semblance of national unity. Congressmen's necessary ambivalence on so many matters showed the problems which would for decades face any party or leader attempting to weld a popular, national movement on the subcontinent.

A similar dilemma for Congress was the choice of tactics. In general Congress politicians opted for studied moderation to maintain their continental credibility. They developed a political style which their rulers would recognize as legitimate – the public meeting, the petition and campaigns in the expanding English and vernacular press. Most of them, out of conviction as well as political calculation, shunned the violence of the tiny groups of terrorists who emerged, particularly in Bengal, the Panjab and the Bombay Presidency, among a younger generation of the educated, who were frustrated at the limitations of Congress politics and enthusiastic for a holy motherland in contrast to Congressmen's secular patriotism. The evidence of the campaign against the ill-judged British partition of Bengal in 1905 suggested that development of a more populist and active style of politics would be the negation of everything Congressmen cherished. In the specific communal and economic context of Bengal, strident educated Hindu opposition to the partition of the Presidency, which included the development of the tactic of economic boycott of foreign goods, *swadeshi*, precipitated communal violence, alienated both Muslims and Hindu landlords, and laid activists open to the Raj's retribution.

However, even Congress' considered self-limitation over political issues and tactics could not always preserve its all-India unity. Although Congressmen shared so much in terms of interests, education, caste and community, they were often divided by personal animosities and the factionalism which focussed on individual leaders and was endemic in provincial and city politics.

Bal Gangadhar Tilak (1856–1920), nationalist leader from Maharashtra.

There in the local arenas of politics still lay the main sources of power to which the new-style politicians aspired: there, in local political groups in district, city or university, or in the network of the legal profession, often in the context of specifically local issues, men made a name for themselves, and attracted allies and clients. Even the giants of continental politics whom the British accepted as in a sense all-India figures, such as Banerjea from Bengal, Mehta from Bombay, and the Maharashtrian rivals, Tilak and Gokhale, had their roots in their localities and had constantly to watch their local power bases. All-India politics and the Congress organization could not be insulated from the controversies and eruptions of passion and partisanship which occurred in the regions. Indeed, control of the local Congress organization became an element in such controversies; and those involved in them could and did use the all-India arena and their trans-continental connections in it to further their local ends. The most obvious, and from the Congress point of view the most damaging, example of this interplay between

local and all-India politics occurred in the first decade of the new century and actually split Congress at its annual meeting in 1907, amidst unedifying and rowdy scenes more redolent of a bazaar fracas than a gathering of India's most educated men. The rift was allegedly between Moderates and Extremists, personified by Gokhale and Tilak, the issues being the ideology, goals and tactics suitable for patriotic politicians at this stage in India's political development. But the two men, and the factions clustered round them, had far more to share as Western educated Chitpavan Brahmins in interests and goals than the issues which divided them. At heart the split was an all-India projection of a local feud, whereby Tilak particularly as the weaker local man tried to boost his position by forging alliances with men from other regions such as Bengal who similarly felt themselves to be locally threatened and wished to shift the balance of power locally with the lever of an all-India alliance. Local factionalism rocked Congress in 1907; but this type of political connection was a ubiquitous aspect of the development of Indian politics and was to plague the all-India and local Congress organization right up to independence and even thereafter.

Although Congress had established itself by the early twentieth century as the main all-India political organization, its achievement was undermined not just by splits among its members, but much more seriously by its failure to attract Muslims. Between 1892 and 1909 under 1000 Muslims attended out of a total of nearly 14,000 delegates. In the light of communal hostility in the decades before independence and the eventual partition of the subcontinent, it is easy to assume that early Muslim wariness towards Congress was natural and inevitable.

This was not so. Muslim aloofness from early Congress politics reflected no fundamental hostility between Muslims and Hindus, but rather the fact that there were few English-educated Muslims in the three Presidencies who could see the relevance of such politics to their interests or were equipped to participate in them. However, in northern India, where Muslims had a proud ancestry as the core of the Mughal empire's culture and bureaucracy, far more were educated in the new style and had positions in public life under the new Raj. Among them developed a considerable suspicion of Congress. In UP (the United Provinces) Muslims were perturbed at evidence of Hindu revivalism and feared that their locally strong position would be undermined by the provincial government's educational and bureaucratic reforms, and the beginnings of elective self-government: while in western UP they were also losing land to Hindu commercial men. They cooperated in defence associations and campaigned for special representation in local elected bodies, and for the retention of Urdu as the language of provincial administration, rather than working with Congress whose goals appeared only to benefit the educated in the Presidencies. One of their most prominent spokesmen and organizers was Sir Sayyid

Those present at the foundation meeting of the All-India Muslim League at Dhaka, December 30, 1906. The League was eventually to lead the movement for Pakistan.

Ahmad Khan, founder of the famous Aligarh College, who urged Muslims to cooperate with the Raj rather than with Congress, as Congressmen's hopes for representative legislatures would only place Muslims in a permanent political minority. Elsewhere Muslims also had reasons for shunning Congress. In Panjab it appeared to support local Hindu money-lending interests to the detriment of the Muslim peasantry: in Bengal the anti-partition campaign suggested that the interests of Muslim peasants and educated men alike would be sacrificed by Congress to those of Hindu educated and landholding men.

Yet the diversity of India's Muslims made it virtually impossible for them to cooperate in a single political organization because their local origins and interests in the different regions were so varied. However, when it became clear that the British were going to concede constitutional reforms in the first decade of the twentieth century, UP Muslims masterminded the creation of the first continental Muslim political organization, the All-India Muslim League, in 1906. This strategy reflected their local fears and was also aimed at warding off the threat of a younger generation of Aligarh students who seemed discontented with Sir Sayyid's strategy. Some historians have interpreted the beginnings of Muslim continental political organization as part of a British plot to 'divide and rule', mainly from the evidence of a visit of a Muslim deputation to the Viceroy, Lord Minto, to voice fears that Muslims as a minority would not receive a proper share of seats under a more democratic electoral system, a visit which preceded the foundation of the League. The deputation included some who were soon leading Leaguers: but their motivation lay in their local experiences rather than being a response to any overt British wish to separate them from Congress. Yet the Viceroy's sympathy indicated that a Muslim body claiming to represent all Muslims would be considered a legitimate political organization of which the rulers would take note. Although the League's founders were assisted by some Bengali Muslims, UP men dominated the new body. Like the early Congress the League was ill-founded and organizationally weak. Its membership of a few hundred was restricted by region and by social and economic background, as members had to be over 25, literate and of reasonable income. If Congress did not represent all India, even less did the League represent all India's Muslims.

As modern political organization developed the British had to respond to its presence. Initially they refused to recognize Congress as the genuine voice of an Indian nation: they visualized India not as a nation but as a conglomerate of peoples and interests, and saw themselves as the guardians of the 'real people' of India, the millions who had no voice in any political organization. Running the empire meant contriving alliances with notables who had followings in town and countryside, and with powerful interest groups: the modern politicians did not fit easily into this role. The Morley–Minto constitutional reforms of 1909, although expanding the consultative processes within the Raj's framework, still worked on this principle that India's different *interests* required representation; and indeed began to formulate at all-India level the principle of communal representation which was to bedevil all-India political development thereafter. Yet Morley as Secretary of State for India had sensed the importance of India's educated politicians and the force of their demands as he discussed reform with Gokhale; and thereafter the imperial rulers gradually began to accept the legitimacy of Congress politics. British strategy was modified, as the new century unfolded, by an acceptance of the more moderate within the ranks of Congress and their sympathizers as suitable allies who should be attracted by constitutional reform into becoming a constructive, stabilizing element in public life. Nevertheless, the British were careful to

127

balance this strategy against continued reassurance of communities and groups who were not aligned with Congress. This stance in turn influenced styles of political organization, convincing many aspiring politicians that the banner of a caste or community would assure them of a hearing from their rulers and so would be a viable base on which to build a following.

Although political organization had stretched across the subcontinent, as Indians became aware of the importance of the provincial and national levels of politics and the need to have organizations appropriate to those levels, Congress and League alike were still very limited in appeal and leverage. Little change could be expected in their position in Indian politics unless they generated far more popular support, or other forces made the British more vulnerable to the new politics and their practitioners.

JMB

Further reading
C. A. Bayly, *The Local Roots of Indian Politics. Allahabad 1880–1920* (Oxford, 1975)

P. Hardy, *The Muslims of British India* (Cambridge, 1972)

G. Johnson, *Provincial Politics and Indian Nationalism. Bombay and the Indian National Congress 1880–1915* (Cambridge, 1973)

J. R. McLane, *Indian Nationalism and the Early Congress* (Princeton, 1977)

F. Robinson, *Separatism among Indian Muslims. The Politics of the United Provinces' Muslims 1860–1923* (Cambridge, 1974)

Watershed of empire: 1909 to early 1920s
In 1921 when the Prince of Wales visited India there was rioting on the streets of Bombay, which compared strikingly with the pomp of the royal Darbar in Delhi a decade before. The intervening years, of World War I and its aftermath, were a watershed for Britain's Indian empire. By the 1920s the old certainties of imperial paternalism were gone. India's place within the empire was open to question: so was the role of Indians in the subcontinent's government. There were clear signs of the beginnings of a more popular politics, being welded into a nationalist movement by a new leader, M. K. Gandhi, who was to become a household name in India and beyond, called 'Mahatma' or 'Great Soul', for the visionary zeal he brought to Indian public life.

World war was one of the most critical influences on the Indian empire in the twentieth century. World War I imposed a great strain on India's economy and administration, as men, money and raw materials were poured into the war effort. India was denuded of European troops, leaving internal security to rest almost totally on Indian loyalty and Britain's informal network of allies with key groups such as the Princes and rural and urban notables who could answer for their supporters and clients.

By 1916–17 increasing government expenditure, rising prices and shortages of essentials began to affect ordinary people, causing outbreaks of violence and disorder: while only a few profited, the manufacturers of cotton, iron, steel, chemicals and other goods which were normally imported. Economic dislocation and public distress were not sufficiently severe to destabilize the imperial structure but they provided the local material out of which much popular politics grew at the close of the war; and during the war persuaded the British that they must strengthen their political alliances to buttress their rule. Yet the political problem lay far deeper than the need to offset distress. The war gave India's politicians in the new political organizations both cause to expand their claims and ideological leverage against their rulers. Indian troops were fighting for the British cause as equals with soldiers from Britain and the white colonies. Britain and her allies spoke of the war as defending the rights of nations and the sanctity of treaties and charters. Consequently Congressmen called in 1915 for an advance towards self-government and asked Britain to declare this to be her goal: democracy and nationalism could not be lauded and defended merely in Europe. To compound the problem for the Raj, a wide range of politicians who had been divided since the 1907 split in Congress and the 1906 foundation of the Muslim League now united behind this demand. The death of an older generation of 'Moderate' leaders allowed their former 'Extremist' opponents to re-enter Congress in 1916, and at that year's session Congress called for a British proclamation that they would give India self-government at an early date. This demand was backed by the emergence of two Home Rule Leagues under B. G. Tilak, former 'Extremist', and the Irish Theosophist, Annie Besant. The Leagues' joint membership reached 60,000, and their use of the press and other populist publicity techniques spread their message far wider than the core membership. The geographical and social spread of their politics contrasted markedly with the restricted range of early Congress support. Even more striking was the new unity cemented between Congress and the Muslim League. The Ottoman Empire's alliance with Germany had perturbed the British, sensitive to the feelings of their Muslim subjects, to whom the Ottoman Sultan was *Khalifa* or spiritual leader of Islam throughout the world. Although Indian Muslims were ambiguous and certainly not unanimous in their attitude to the Sultan and their degree of obligation to him, their concern about the future of Islam in the Ottoman lands and the prospect of further political reform raised by the world war created the context in which rising young Muslim politicians from northern India were able to swing the League into alliance with Congress behind the Lucknow Pact of 1916. Under its terms Congress gained backing for a scheme of constitutional reform, while the Muslims gained acceptance from the Congress, the organization of Indian nationalism, of separate political status through separate electorates

Presidents of the Muslim League and the Muslim League Sessions, 1906–1947

Presidents of the League

1908–1913	Aga Khan
1914–1918	Raja of Mahmudabad
1919	A. K. Fazlul Haque
1920–1930	M. A. Jinnah

In 1931 the office of Permanent President of the League was abolished.

Presidents of the League Sessions (From 1931 also Presidents of the League)

1906	Nawab Salimullah Bahadur
1907	Sir Adamjee Peerbhoy
1908 (Aligarh)	Shah Din
1908 (Amritsar)	Syed Ali Imam
1910 (Delhi)	Sir Ghulam Ali Khan Bahadur
1910 (Nagpur)	Syed Nabiullah
1912	Nawab Salimullah Bahadur
1913 (Lucknow)	Mian Mohammad Shafi
1913 (Agra)	Sir Ibrahim Rahimtulla
1915–1916	Mazharul Haque
1916	M. A. Jinnah
1917	Raja of Mahmudabad
1918 (Bombay)	Raja of Mahmudabad
1918 (Delhi)	A. K. Fazlul Haque
1919	Hakim Ajmal Khan
1920 (Calcutta)	M. A. Jinnah
1920 (Nagpur)	Dr M. A. Ansari
1921	Maulana Hasrat Mohani
1923	Ghulam Mohammad Bhurgri
1924 (Lahore)	M. A. Jinnah
1924 (Bombay)	Syed Riza Ali
1925	Sir Abdur Rahim
1926	Sheikh Abdul Qadir
1927–1928 (Jinnah Group)	Moulvi Mohammad Yakub
1928 (Shafi Group)	Sir Muhammad Shafi
1928 (Calcutta)	Raja of Mahmudabad
1930	Sir Muhammad Iqbal
1931	Choudhury Zafarullah Khan
1933 (Howrah)	Mian Abdul Aziz
1933 (Delhi, Hidayat Group)	Hafiz Hidayat Hussain
1936	Syed Wazir Hassan
1937–1947	M. A. Jinnah[a]

[a]Between 1937 and 1943 M. A. Jinnah presided over eight Muslim League sessions and between July 1944 and December 1947 five League Council meetings.

Source: S. S. Pirzada, Ed. *Foundations of Pakistan: All-India Muslim League Documents: 1906–1947* Vol. 2, pp. 608–9 (Karachi, 1970).

Box 9

in the provincial and all-India legislatures, and a fixed proportion of seats, including extra seats where they were a local minority. Prominent among the UP men who supported the Congress–League alliance which rested on this pact were Mohamed and Shaukat Ali, brothers who rejected the old politics of Aligarh and contrived an overtly religious political style.

Faced with such political developments the British began to re-think their position. They had no intention of making radical concessions, and they made this clear by reinforcing their existing coercive powers with the 1915 Defence of India Act. But they recognized their need of political friends wherever they could find them, and the probable weakness of their existing allies in the face of the revivified Congress and its Muslim allies. For some years they had hoped to attract those they called 'Moderate' among the educated in and out of Congress, and as war progressed this strategy became more appealing and urgent: London, Delhi and the provincial governments began discussing what gestures could be made in recognition of India's war effort. The upshot was the declaration of August 20, 1917, known as the Montagu Declaration after the current Secretary of State for India. British policy was stated to be aiming towards 'increasing association of Indians in every branch of the administration, and the gradual development of self-governing institutions, with a view to the progressive realization of responsible government in India as an integral part of the British Empire'. This was not intended as a charter for self-government or for British relaxation of control in key areas of decision-making: compromise and misunderstanding contributed as much to its wording as did careful thought. Yet it marked a watershed in imperial policy. Never before had anything like 'responsible government' been considered appropriate for a non-white colony. To implement the declaration, Montagu and the Viceroy, Lord Chelmsford, toured India in winter 1917–18, listening to a wide range of public opinion, and prepared a plan of constitutional reform. Somewhat modified by official and parliamentary discussion, this came to fruition in the 1919 Government of India Act, which significantly altered the framework of decision-making and gave Indians a far wider role in government. Provincial and central legislatures were enlarged, and freed from an official majority, and the franchise by which members were elected was considerably widened. Communal electorates, conceded in earlier reforms in 1909, were retained, and the Lucknow Pact became a guide to the distribution of seats. Real change occurred in provincial rather than central government. In the provinces certain subjects were transferred entirely to the control of Indian ministers responsible to the legislature, while others were reserved for the Governor and his Executive Council. The provinces received certain revenue sources to enable them to fund their new responsibilities, although the paucity of their resources became a cause of Indian complaint.

British concern to retain control of crucial areas of public life, to ensure India's role as a vital part of the worldwide imperial enterprise, was manifest in the powers kept in 1919, and in plans to control 'sedition' once the Defence of India Act lapsed at the end of the war. Following the report of the 1918 Rowlatt Commission, the government introduced peace-time legislation against terrorism which deeply offended a wide range of Indian public opinion, not least because it was pushed through the Imperial Legislative Council against the opposition of every Indian member. It was the Rowlatt legislation which gave Gandhi an entrée into Indian politics. An unknown and failing provincial lawyer, he had gone to South Africa in 1893 for a legal case and had stayed over twenty years, building up political skills and a reputation as a protagonist of Indian immigrants who encountered severe racial discrimination. He returned to India during the war, fired with a religious vision of a new India, whose *swaraj* would not be Home Rule as commonly understood, but a moral reformation of a whole people which would either convert the British also or render their Raj impossible by Indian withdrawal of support for it and its modern values. He brought back with him *satyagraha*, 'truth force', or non-violent resistance to injustice, which he had tried out as a popular political technique in Africa, and which he considered the one moral form of conflict because it actually forwarded the goal of moral transformation. At first his ideas and methods were viewed with skepticism by India's educated, though gradually they saw something of his political potential as he used satyagraha in a variety of local causes beyond the restricted range of Congress politics. In response to the Rowlatt legislation he offered the tactic of a nation-wide cessation of work as a protest. Although as a continental satyagraha it failed, it triggered disturbances in the Panjab which were the occasion for the notorious firing on an unarmed crowd in a walled area known as Jallianwala Bagh. Although the government, after enquiry, strongly denounced this show of force by a local army commander, Congress called the government response 'whitewash' and proceeded with its own enquiry: and it was this which gave Gandhi his first real influence in Congress circles. His other spring-board into political prominence was his championship of the pan-Islamic 'Khilafat' movement, and alliance with the Ali brothers, whose cause and treatment by the government he considered religious issues with which Hindus should sympathize if they were to create bonds for their nation over and above purely communal loyalties. In 1920 he suggested a broad-ranging program of *satyagraha*, in the form of non-cooperation with the government as a result of the Panjab and Khilafat causes, and late that year Congress agreed to a modified plan, including non-participation in elections to the new legislatures, withdrawal from government law courts and schools, and a program of *swadeshi*, using goods made in India rather than imports which were primarily from Britain.

The stated goal of non-cooperation was swaraj in one year. But few other than Gandhi thought this a real possibility. There had been no wholesale shift of political thinking or style among Congressmen, no radical conversion to Gandhian idealism. Rather, politicians had made calculations that they had more to gain than to lose by at least a temporary experiment with such unorthodox and populist tactics. Gandhi undoubtedly had support from consider-

Gandhi at the Ahmedabad Congress session in December 1921, two months before he called off the movement of non-cooperation with government.

able numbers of delegates who were new to Congress, particularly among Muslims and men from regions other than the Presidencies where he had organized local satyagrahas. But established Congressmen also voted with him, seeing the strength of his support, the significance of the Khilafat alliance if they wished to pressurize the government, and fearing for their own positions locally and nationally in Congress if they opposed him. In some areas the new franchise seemed so heavily weighted towards the landed and wealthy that they doubted whether it was worth contesting seats under the new constitution. Further, there was no alternative all-India leadership round which potential opponents of Gandhian politics could rally: the old 'Moderate' leaders were gone, and Tilak died on the very day Gandhi launched the new campaign.

Non-cooperation lasted from August 1920 to February 1922, when Gandhi called it off because of a vicious attack on a police station which was the negation of its supposed non-violence. It did not achieve swaraj; and the pressure it exerted on the Raj was limited. The new constitution came into operation after elections in late 1920, though in some areas the poll was extremely low. (Significantly Congressmen did not boycott municipal elections, which were the gateway to the local power they most coveted.) Government courts and schools and the administration continued to function, though the number of pupils dropped, some lawyers retired, and excise revenue dried up in some areas as a result of temperance movements. Imports of cloth also fell; but it was questionable how far this and the decline in student numbers was due to the post-war depression or to the boycott campaign. Ultimately non-cooperation was abandoned because of violence against the government and between Indians, landlord against tenant, Hindu against Muslim, and because Congressmen came to feel that the new strategy would yield few permanent political gains and that working the new constitution might be more productive.

Despite its overall failure, non-cooperation was a watershed in Indian politics. For the first time a truly national and popular political campaign had developed, breaking out of the old molds of Congress and League politics, and involving men and women from all regions and a wide social background, in local styles of protest appropriate to their local situations – from withdrawing from elections and boycotting courts to picketing liquor shops and cutting grass illegally. Gandhian publicity methods had spread a new ideal of nationhood and began to convince people that the Raj was not invincible: if Indians withdrew their cooperation it could not remain. Furthermore, Gandhi's strategy had boosted Congress's significance in Indian politics and helped at least temporarily to make it a more popular and representative body with a new constitution, and to stabilize its finances. Such enlargement of the politically conscious nation and broadening of political techniques, however, raised all the questions early Congressmen had faced in

the late nineteenth century and answered by severe self-limitation of their aims, allies and actions. Non-cooperation demonstrated that in the localities long-standing political grievances, campaigns and leaderships ran at their own pace and in their own way, and only if these dovetailed with all-India campaigns could the latter acquire a popular backing. The material of popular politics was not always amenable to leaders with national aims and strategies. It was a problem Gandhi and Congress were to wrestle with until 1947 – how to construct a genuinely national movement out of the subcontinent's complexities and wide variety of regional and social groups. For the British political calculations could never be the same. Even more now they would need to attract the most amenable of the educated into the new constitution, and watch the areas of strain which might generate widespread distress and hostility like that which followed the war. But by so doing the Delhi government made India and its stability its primary concern, and became increasingly unable to acquiesce in London's demands that India should be a major military and financial contributor to the empire. When tariffs, government expenditure or the Indian army were debated, for example, Delhi now looked to India and its politicians to assess what was politically feasible. Britain could no longer expect the unquestioned outpouring of resources visible in 1914–18: a watershed had been crossed in imperial relations.

JMB

Further reading

C. Baker, 'Non-cooperation in South India', in C. J. Baker and D. A. Washbrook, *South India: Political Institutions and Political Change 1880–1940* (Delhi, 1975)

J. M. Brown, *Gandhi's Rise To Power. Indian Politics, 1915–1922* (Cambridge, 1972)

M. K. Gandhi, *An Autobiography. The Story of my Experiments with Truth* (London, 1966)

G. Minault, *The Khilafat Movement: Religious Symbolism and Political Modernization in India* (Columbia, 1982)

P. G. Robb, *The Government of India and Reform. Policies towards Politics and the Constitution 1916–1921* (Oxford, 1976)

F. Robinson, *Separatism among Indian Muslims. The Politics of the United Provinces' Muslims 1860–1923* (Cambridge, 1974)

B. R. Tomlinson, *The Political Economy of the Raj 1914–1947. The Economics of Decolonization in India* (London, 1979)

Imperialism and nationalism between the wars

The quarter of a century between the two world wars witnessed two major developments in the political history of India. The first involved a re-assessment of India's direct value to Britain and of its position within Britain's larger empire; the second concerned important changes in India's government and a corresponding growth of powerful nationalist movements. Together these developments help to explain a re-alignment of British and Indian interests that, by the mid-1940s, forced fundamental change and led to the political independence of South Asia.

In the later nineteenth century India was of vital importance to Britain. It was an essential market for those British manufactures – especially cotton textiles and heavy machinery – on which the health of the British metropolitan economy then depended. Although India sold much less to Britain in return, it developed, by the export of food and other raw materials, a favorable balance of trade with those countries, especially in Europe and North America, with whom Britain in turn had a trading deficit. The use of this surplus enabled India to balance her account with Britain, and thus both by direct trade and through a complex series of multi-lateral trading settlements, India played a vital part in maintaining Britain's economic position. Further, India was an excellent place for British investment overseas – British capital was lodged with the Government of India, put into Indian railways, and in plantations and business concerns. Additionally, the Government of India, through the army and its superior civilian services, employed a large number of Britons; but above all, India provided Britain with substantial military resources. It was the Indian tax-payer who provided the money to support units of the British army when stationed in India. The Indian army itself, paid for by Indians and outside Parliamentary control, provided the British empire with the military wherewithal to promote and defend wide interests from the Middle East to China, from South Africa to the Pacific.

These imperial concerns played a large part in determining how India was governed. First, it was essential that it be governed easily and at no expense to Britain; then, it had to be governed with imperial responsibilities in mind as well as responding to the domestic needs of Indian peoples. This led to the creation of a single administrative and political system designed to serve British interests while also involving Indian society in the process of government itself. Despite its many shortcomings, government in India became more coherent and centralizing. Locality was linked to province, province to nation, and the whole made technically responsible to Parliament in London. From the blueprint it seemed a good management structure and for many practical purposes, though in constant need of revision, it worked well. Unity was given to a state machinery that overlay some of the diversities of the subcontinent and which allowed it to grapple with the problems of managing such a large and complex area. However, the evolving constitution contained within it the great paradox that increasing efficiency and better control could only be achieved by decentralization of administrative practices, and by the incorporation within the state structure of those social groups who, being separately and independently of importance within Indian society and its

economy, would also be likely to be those most critical of the foreigners' control of it.

Crucial to any understanding of the 1920s and 1930s is an appreciation that Indian nationalism developed within this governmental system. From the mid-1880s, we find Indians in different regions and from different social classes getting together to put common demands to a common government. As the political structures were made more uniform, there were also more opportunities for Indian politicians to try to influence governmental decision-making. Here they were helped not only by constitutional practice but by the spread of literacy in the rulers' language. However weak these connections may have been, politicians began the move from towns and villages into wider political arenas. Here they met and bargained with others similarly placed, and the process speeded up in two important ways: first, Indians experienced, from the very earliest days of their nationalist movements, the benefits of a pragmatic approach to politics, one which stressed the need for alliance and cooperation, which eschewed regional, class or ethnic differences, and which formed the basis for party organization designed to hold firmly together as many groups as possible. (Although, of course, politicians would not always nor in all places find that they could either accommodate each other or contain their conflicting interests.) Secondly, faced with the quite necessary participation by Indians, and powerful Indians at that, within their colonial regime, the British had to take account of them in future political development. Thus constitutional reform had to benefit Indians as much as the British if government was to function at all efficiently. Imperial and national interests became impossibly entangled, and the process of political change developed a momentum of its own. The reforms of 1920 and of 1935 were prompted both by the need to secure better control, for imperial purposes, of the government of India, and to meet as fully as possible the most pressing of Indian political demands. In the end these aims were to prove incompatible with each other.

After 1920 India no longer stood quite where she had been in relation to Britain and within the British empire. The post-war years saw a shift in the pattern of trade. India remained an important market for British goods, but, with the decline of the textile industry and a move in the home economy toward consumer goods and services, it was no longer such a vital one. Indeed, by the late 1930s the balance of trade turned in India's favor as she began to sell more to Britain than she imported from her. The intricate pattern of early-twentieth century international trade also changed and India no longer played so important a part in making up Britain's total trade balance. British investment in India began to decline in significance. British firms in India either stagnated or took on board Indian management or joined up with Indian enterprises. Their importance in the Indian economy was soon overshadowed by the indigenous business giants like the Tatas and the Birlas. India even became a less attractive place for young Britons seeking employment. Already by the mid-1920s the government was worried about the dearth of British candidates for entry into the Indian Civil Service. At the end of World War II there were less than five hundred British senior civil servants and only two hundred British police in the whole subcontinent, and many of them were nearing retirement or had stayed on beyond retirement to help out during the war. But the greatest change could be seen in India's military position. After World War I, the Government of India could no longer muster the resources to keep its army abreast of technological change. In the age of the tank and the aeroplane, the Indian army still boasted the finest cavalry regiment. It remained highly labor-intensive and static. It was equipped to fight a Crimean war and was stationed to repel an Afghan invasion or to assist in the maintenance of domestic law and order. In short, it had lost its imperial role.

These changes had a subtle effect on policies. Just as the constitutional tie between Delhi and London was, in formal legal terms, being tightened, there was a loosening of economic constraints. The Government of India was allowed to have its own tariff policy, and it did impose duties on British goods from Lancashire in a way that would have been unthinkable in the later nineteenth century: cotton manufacturers in Lancashire pulled less weight within British politics now, and, conversely, Bombay manufacturers were of more consequence within India itself. In the 1930s the Government of India stood up far more effectively to demands from London than its predecessors had been able to do. The State Bank was established and Delhi had more say in determining the value of the rupee against the pound – a reflection of the growing disengagement of the two economies and of the greater importance due to Indian rather than British investment. Successive viceroys made it clear to the cabinet, from the Versailles treaties onwards, that if the Indian army was to be used for imperial purposes, then the empire had to pay; and if the army had to be re-organized and re-equipped to keep up this role, then the money to pay for that had to come from outside India as well. Of course, the changes in the economic and imperial relationships between the two countries did not occur suddenly. But, in the thirty years or so before the end of the empire a sufficient divergence of interests was taking place which meant that, if it became difficult for the British to govern Indians, then there would be strong reasons for adjusting the constitutional relationship between the two countries. Britain might not need to retain imperial control in order to continue a mutually beneficial association with South Asia.

Just as imperial circumstances began to change radically, so too did the internal politics of India. From the second decade of the twentieth century, Indians showed a greater capacity for mounting political campaigns and for capturing positions of power within the system itself. The greater control, greater centralization and greater efficiency that lay behind the Montagu–Chelmsford reforms of 1920 and the Government of India Act of 1935, was only achieved by an accompanying decentralization, increased involvement by Indians in the governmental structure and a devolution of real authority to powerful free-standing interests within Indian society. In part this strategy was dictated simply by the scale of the operation: as the British unified and developed their government, they decentralized power as a way of holding on to it. Tighter chains of command would only stand the strain if there was a proper distribution of power within the system. As the center grew more refined, so power was devolved to the provinces and, importantly, to Indians within them. This was sensible given the size and complexities of Indian society. But, the provinces became more important, they were given more political responsibility and they needed resources to play their part. Indians could not be trusted to have views on imperial matters, or internal security, but they could usefully be involved in policy making about irrigation, or education, or the provision of tapped water and street-lighting. It seemed a skilful ploy to divert Indian political energy into the provinces: leave the British in control at the top and let Indians run their local affairs.

But the snag was that if the government were to function adequately it needed to be associated with the more powerful and dynamic Indian social and economic interests. Not unnaturally such groups would not participate unconditionally. Moreover, they would be the very people best placed to exploit the political and economic structure of the Raj to press for further changes in Indian government and greater influence in serious decision-making. Much of the business of politics, therefore, would be striking the right sort of bargains with key groups of Indians in order to achieve their participation at an acceptable political price. The task was complicated because, just as British needs changed over time, so too would the composition and nature of those Indian classes whose support was crucial to the maintenance of the imperial regime.

Before World War I, Indians had begun to put together relatively stable alliances of social interests which were capable both of participating in government and of resisting and agitating against British control of it. To begin with, organizations like the early Congress seemed to be unduly weighted toward the capital cities of the coastal provinces, or to white-collar workers and all-India service élites. But even in the early days such coordinating groups touched a wider geographical area and made connections with dominant banking, industrial or agricultural interests. By 1920, nationalism was becoming both more formidable and more complex. Although the Indian economy as a whole grew pitifully slowly during the late British period, nonetheless there were substantial developments in some regions and in some sectors. Panjab, for example, saw a fast rate of growth in its agrarian economy; Bombay city became one of the leading textile producers of the world; Gujarat thrived in both town and countryside; the Andhra deltas were filled with new rice-fields; a broad belt across northern India eastwards to Calcutta witnessed a significant drive to profitable cash-cropping and some associated industrial development. More importantly, indigenous bankers, farmers and industrialists responded to new demands from both domestic and foreign markets. What was significant about such development was that, patchy though it may have been, economic growth increased social and occupational mobility, led to a significant rise in literacy (particularly in Indian languages), and brought about a heightened cultural and political consciousness. Consequently, political activists emerged in all the main provinces and they gave the nationalism of the 1920s and 1930s its bite.

Of course, given the size and complexity of India it was very difficult to organize and coordinate into a single nationalist movement the energies of the provinces. Besides regional differences there were also religious and cultural incompatibilities, not to mention those of class or of individual temperament. It is important to remember this when assessing the remarkable achievements of the nationalist leaders. The two decades saw not only the entrenchment of the Indian National Congress as the organization of mainstream nationalism – in fact a fairly broad-based alliance of many and diverse political interests – but the establishment or consolidation also of other significant party groupings, much the most important of which was the Muslim League. Although these two parties dominated Indian political discourse other parties which had influence beyond their mere numbers included the Hindu Mahasabha which represented conservative and, some would argue, politically rightwing Hindu communal interests, a plethora of socialist parties, and the Communist Party of India. Some political parties, such as the Unionist Party in the Panjab or the more short-lived Justice Party in Madras, represented pragmatic alliances of local élites anxious to capture and control provincial government. Their influence was limited to their own region, but the Unionists were sufficiently strong to keep the main nationalist parties out of Panjab affairs until the mid-1940s. Moreover, a great deal of political activity went on outside the scope of the larger political parties: the Bombay mill industry, for example, saw several attempts to organize workers, while across in Bengal the frustrations of the young educated élite found an outlet in terrorism. Terrorism also provided a release for other passionate radicals in Panjab and northern India where extremism was often associated with religious reform. Movements of social uplift and of caste organization also flourished. A common factor of many of these movements was that while they provided an opportunity for bringing together groups of Indians on a new and broader basis, they also tended to be socially, religiously or culturally exclusive and so often

sharpened communal antipathies. Furthermore this exclusiveness made it difficult for such organizations to fit easily into the pragmatic and broader alliances of the main parties.

The Indian National Congress undoubtedly owed much of its success to the brilliant leadership provided for it from 1920 onwards by Mohandas Karamchand Gandhi and a relatively small number of other politicians. To begin with these included formidable old leaders, such as Motilal Nehru and Madan Mohan Malaviya from the United Provinces and C. R. Das from Bengal. But as the 1920s progressed and death took its toll from the political establishment there emerged a new generation of politicians who, however acute their political differences, were content to work with Gandhi and to submit to his authority. Prominent among this inner group were Jawaharlal Nehru, who became Congress President in 1936 and was in the end Gandhi's heir-apparent as the statesman best able to maintain unity within Indian nationalism; C. Rajagopalachari, a lawyer from Madras, later to be Governor-General of independent India; Rajendra Prasad from Bihar, independent India's first President; A. K. Azad, a Muslim religious thinker from Bengal, who was Congress President from 1939 to 1946 and independent India's Education Minister from 1947 to 1958; and Sardar Vallabhbhai Patel, who came from Gujarat and whose special forte lay in organization and who, as Home Minister, took India through the trauma of partition and was responsible for the speedy and efficient (some would say too efficient) negotiations with the Indian princes for the integration of their territories into the newly independent Indian state. The Bengali, S. C. Bose, was for a time part of this group, but then unwilling to work with Gandhi after the latter opposed his bid for a second term as Congress President. He was attracted to European Fascism and during World War II he organized with German and Japanese help the Indian National Army in southeast Asia to fight against the British. His disappearance after a plane crash in 1945 removed a gifted though volatile politician from the Indian scene.

At its annual meeting in December 1920, the Congress had adopted a new constitution, largely drawn up by Gandhi, that served it well as a nationalist organization. The main political problem all nationalist leaders faced was how to achieve unity among Indian politicians in order to confront the British. This meant devising ways in which internal rivalries could be contained, neutralized or reconciled. It was important to be as open and receptive as possible in order to achieve the maximum representation of Indian interests, while at the same time there had to be a clear chain of command and effective control if the political organization was to work well in practice. The 1920 Congress constitution went a long way towards attaining these political objectives. Anyone over 21 years of age who agreed to the aims and objectives of the Congress could be a member of it. Earlier there had

Sardar Vallabhbhai Patel.

Jawaharlal Nehru.

A. K. Azad.

C. Rajagopalachari.

M. A. Jinnah.

been great dissension about how to express the aims and objectives of the Congress. Gandhi simplified this with a formula which gave *swaraj*, or independence, as the objective of Congress; but the words used were skilfully ambiguous and could be assented to by the most moderate constitutionalist or the most extreme radical. It was, therefore, very easy to subscribe to the Congress creed and to be a member of the party. But the genius of the 1920 constitution was the way in which it overlay the openness and accessibility of Congress with a hierarchy of committees – from district, to province, to all-India – thus providing a means of discipline and control over what could have been an anarchical and diffuse movement. District committees were responsible to provincial committees, which were now established in each main linguistic region of India. This provided equal opportunities for groups which had previously found it hard to work together locally to participate in Congress affairs. The various provincial committees were represented on, and subordinated to, an All-India Congress Committee, but as this was a body of some 350 people, all policy-making initiatives and day-to-day executive power were conceded to an inner cabinet – the Congress Working Committee. It was this committee, largely influenced by Gandhi even when for long periods he was not technically a member of it, that took charge of Congress affairs and enabled it to function effectively in political negotiations with the British and with other Indian parties.

The Congress' main aim was to force concessions from the British. To this end Gandhi chose carefully the issues on which he was prepared to fight and his campaigns were designed to show the fundamental injustice and immorality of foreign imperial rule. In 1919 he tried (with only limited success) to raise opposition to an Act of the Government of India which would enhance its repressive capacities and give it in ordinary peace-time powers restricting individual rights which it had exercised during the war. Then the rather cavalier way in which the European powers proposed to dismember the Ottoman empire at the peace settlements at Versailles provided a further opportunity to mount an Indian campaign – this time for the protection of Islamic holy places in the Middle East. Indian Muslims felt strongly about this and, moreover, Hindus could offer unconditional support. It was also a canny choice of issue because British counsels were divided: while the cabinet looked for a settlement of a long-standing problem in European diplomacy by simple dismemberment of the Ottoman empire and an increase of European influence in the Middle-East, the Government of India was more sensitive to Muslim feelings, constituted as it was in a country with the largest Muslim population in the world. In fact it was this issue, the Khilafat issue, that provided the resources and energy for Gandhi's capture of the Congress from the old liberal leadership in 1920 and which led into the first non-cooperation movement of 1920–22 (for details and assessment see preceding section). Although that movement ran into the ground in 1922 and had developed too late to have any direct impact on the framing of the new Government of India Act of 1919, the scale and widespread nature of the disorder resulting from non-cooperation was unprecedented and, by presenting a new challenge to foreign rule, marked a political milestone in India's development.

Far greater impact was made by the Congress on British policy during the early 1930s. The British had decided in 1927 to review the working of the government of India and they appointed a commission, under the chairmanship of Sir John Simon, to undertake the task. No Indian was made a member of the commission and consequently the Congress, along with other parties, were outraged at this disregard of Indian opinion in so vital a matter. The Congress response was to devise (under the guidance of Motilal Nehru) a new Indian constitution for India and to demand from the British full Dominion status by December 1929. Although the Viceroy, Lord Irwin, was prepared to discuss matters with the Congress leadership, there was no successful outcome and consequently Gandhi launched the Congress on a campaign of civil disobedience in March 1930 by undertaking a well-publicized march from Ahmedabad to Dandi on the coast where he ceremonially broke the salt law by picking up a lump of natural salt from the sea. For the next four and a half years the Congress and the Government of India were locked

Indians in Madras protest against the Simon Commission to examine the working of government. Indians had been outraged when not one Indian was appointed to the Commission, and wherever it went in 1928–29 it was met with hostile demonstrations.

either in conflict or negotiation as what became the 1935 Government of India Act was hammered out.

However, no matter how skilled the leadership nor how just the issues, the complexities of Indian affairs refused to be simplified out of existence. One problem for the Congress (and, it must be stressed, for the British too) was that the nationalist movement was never wholly at one. This becomes more apparent as one moves from the grand symbolic gesture to the detailed discussions and to the debates on just how the government of India was to be reformed. It was one thing to win concessions from the British – to make the British govern more and more according to Indian needs – but once the shift of power began in a serious way, as it did in 1920, then it became a vital matter as to exactly who would reap the benefit. Interests, particularly of significant minorities, had to be protected; there was a perennial debate about the balance of power between a central government and regional authorities, as well as discussion of the number and size of the provinces themselves. Each constitutional blueprint, however bland and moderate it might seem on the surface, tended in fact to conceal serious political problems. Center-province relationships ran throughout the political discourse of these decades and beyond. The British were clear they needed a unitary state, but size dictated it be some form of federal structure with varying views on where power ultimately should lie. Then, increasingly from the 1920s the position of the Indian princes came to be seen as a serious problem in creating any form of new, geographically rational order. But the main question which persistently refused solution turned upon the nature of communal representation in government.

Although the Congress included among its members many Muslims, and although the Congress leadership made strenuous efforts to meet Muslim demands, significant Muslim interests held aloof from it through the 1920s and 1930s. Some of these, such as those in the Panjab and, to some extent in Bengal also, simply found that their needs were adequately met by concentrating on provincial politics. But others were anxious about their position, especially where they constituted large or exposed minorities of the population. For them, the main vehicle for their demands was not the Congress but the Muslim League. This body never had the large following of the Congress but it faced similar problems of organization, for Muslims were as much divided among themselves, regionally, ethnically, culturally and by class as Indians at large. During the 1920s, however, M. A. Jinnah, a lawyer from Bombay, emerged as the central figure in presenting Muslim demands. In response to the Congress' proposed constitution for India Jinnah published in March 1929 the Muslim League's 'Fourteen Points' which laid down the main conditions for Muslim acceptance of constitutional change. In drawing up this list, Jinnah had to tread carefully between conflicting opinions among Muslim politicians, and his

great achievement was his success in acting as a broker between different Muslim constituencies. Gradually, under his leadership, the Muslim League became the acknowledged representative of Muslim aspirations. The League made articulate a set of demands designed to safeguard the position of Indian Muslims, culminating in the demand for a separate Muslim state approved at its meeting at Lahore in 1940. Key points of difference between the League and the Congress concerned not only the question of communal safeguards but also the distribution of power through a federal system and the claim of the League to be recognized exclusively as the spokesman for Indian Muslims.

One further point needs to be considered. It was almost inevitable that, as the process of government became more successful and more effective, so specifically British interests within it would become more constrained and more limited in their operation. If the evolving government required increasing participation by Indians, and by powerful Indians at that, then no matter how much the British strove to retain control from the heights of the political system they would find it harder to master overall. It became clear after 1920 just how boxed in the British were becoming. The Government of India was inhibited from playing its full imperial role because it found it could not raise more resources in India without also raising the volume of Indian political demand. The reason why it could not afford to spend as much as might be desirable on imperial purposes, such as modernizing the army, for example, was because Indian political élites, friends and critics alike, wanted the money to be spent on other things. Although the successive nationalist agitations in themselves never came near to making government unworkable (except in a few very special districts), nonetheless the need to accommodate a large enough number of the political élite ensured that power was moving inexorably into Indian hands. Even the best Anglo-Indian political friendship, such as that between the British and the Panjab, was bought at a price. The structural weakness of the British position within the strengthening governmental systems of India could still be concealed, at least in the short term; but the underlying trend was clear. When in 1942 Churchill asserted that he was not prepared to meet Indian aspirations halfway, Amery, his Secretary of State, complained that the Prime Minister had not 'the slightest idea of the extent to which we have been kicked out already, or how impossible it is to hold our position indefinitely except on terms which mean we shall certainly be kicked out in the end'. Yet when the end came, the dismissal of the British from the government of India was perhaps the least momentous of the political events which wreaked havoc in the country in 1947.

GJ

Imperialism and Nationalism in South Asia 1858–1947

1858	British Crown assumes direct control of India
1861	Indian Councils Act. Central Legislative Council formed. Legislative Councils also formed in Madras and Bombay. Provision made for similar councils in Bengal, North-Western Provinces and the Punjab. At least half the new members to come from outside the civil service
1882	Ripon's Resolution on Local Self-Government aims to achieve direct election to municipal councils and district boards
1883	Ilbert Bill gives Indian judges the right to try Europeans. European protest brings amendment and nationalist response from Indians
1885	Foundation of Indian National Congress in Bombay
1892	Indian Councils Act enlarges the size and the powers of legislative councils at the center and in the provinces. Some members now elected to provincial councils by local bodies and corporations
1905	Partition of Bengal
1906	Oct: Muslim deputation petitions the Viceroy for separate electorates and weightage in representation to take account of Muslim 'political importance'.

Dec: Foundation of All-India Muslim League at Dhaka |
1908	Congress constitution declares its aim to be the attainment of a 'system of government similar to that enjoyed by the self-governing Members of the British Empire'
1909	Indian Councils Act. Morley–Minto reforms to the legislative councils introduce elections at the center and separate electorates for Muslims in all councils. Officials have a small majority at the center but non-officials (elected and nominated) have majorities in the provinces. Indians now able to sit on provincial and central executive councils and that of the Secretary of State
1911	Coronation Durbar of George V, who announces the reunification of Bengal and the transfer of the capital from Calcutta to Delhi
1913	Muslim League adopts 'self-government suitable to India' as its goal
1915	M. K. Gandhi returns to India from South Africa
1916	Congress and the Muslim League conclude the Lucknow Pact, a joint constitutional scheme for India on the basis of dominion status
1917	Secretary of State, Montagu, announces 'the gradual development of self-governing institutions with a view to the progressive realization of responsible government in India as an integral part of the British Empire' to be the aim of the British in India
1919	Feb: Rowlatt Bills passed enabling government to try political cases without juries

April: Amritsar firing during martial law enforcement in the Punjab; over 300 are killed and 1000 injured

Dec: Indian Councils Act. Montagu–Chelmsford reforms bring territorial constituencies and a measure of provincial autonomy. Provincial government is divided into 'reserved' and 'transferred' areas (diarchy) over the second of which Indian ministers responsible to legislative councils are to have full control |
1920–1922	Congress–Khilafat Committee non-cooperation campaign. Gandhi now leads Congress, its aim becomes the achievement of *swaraj*, its organization is transformed for the purposes of mass mobilization
1922	Motilal Nehru and C. R. Das form the Swaraj Party to wreck the legislative councils from within
1927	Simon Commission appointed to enquire into the working of the Montagu–Chelmsford reforms
1928	Nehru Report proposes a constitution in which India would attain dominion status with full responsible government at the center and in the provinces, and which in character is more unitary than federal. It recommends the abolition of separate electorates for Muslims but an increase in the number of Muslim majority provinces from two to four
1930	Congress declares January 26 Independence Day. Muhammad Iqbal in his address to the Muslim League suggests the formation of a Muslim state within the Indian Federation
1930–1931	Mass Civil Disobedience campaign led by Gandhi

Box 10

1930–1932	Communal Award grants separate electorates to Muslims, Sikhs and Untouchables. Gandhi fasts in protest; Poona pact replaces separate electorates for Untouchables with some reserved seats
1935	Government of India Act gives almost complete autonomy to the provinces. It establishes 'The Federation of India' comprising both provinces and princely states, with a federal central government and legislature for the management of central subjects. The principle of diarchy is abolished in the provinces and transferred to the center
1937	First general elections under 1935 Act. Congress forms governments in seven out of eleven provinces, adding an eighth in 1938
1939	Congress governments resign because Government of India declares war without consulting Indians
1940	Muslim League declares the formation of Pakistan to be its goal
1942	Mar–April: Cripps Mission. Cripps offers dominion status or full independence after the war in return for India's assistance for the duration. The offer is refused
1942	Aug: Quit India movement. Over 60,000 arrested
1945	Simla Conference of all political groups fails to agree over the composition of the Executive Council
1945–1946	Second general elections under the 1935 Act. The Muslim League wins over 90 percent of reserved Muslim seats
1946	Cabinet Mission fails to win agreement from Congress and Muslim League over India's constitutional future
1947	Feb: Britain announces that it will leave India by June 1948; Mountbatten is appointed Viceroy
	June: Mountbatten announces the partition of the subcontinent into India and Pakistan
	Aug: 14 Pakistan wins Independence
	Aug: 15 India wins Independence

Source: Adapted from J. E. Schwartzberg, Ed., *A Historical Atlas of South Asia* p. 70 (Chicago, 1978)

Box 10 *(continued)*

Further reading

C. J. Baker, *The Politics of South India 1920–1937* (Cambridge, 1976)

C. J. Baker, G. Johnson and A. Seal, Eds, *Power, Profit and Politics: Essays on Imperialism, Nationalism and Change in Twentieth-Century India*, reprinted from *Modern Asian Studies*, vol. 15, part 3 (Cambridge, 1981)

M. K. Gandhi, *An Autobiography or The Story of My Experiments with Truth* (London, 1966)

D. A. Low, Ed., *Congress and the Raj: Facets of the Indian Struggle 1917–47* (London, 1977)

J. Nehru, *An Autobiography with Musings on Recent Events in India* (London, 1936 and subsequent reprints)

D. Page, *Prelude to Partition: The Indian Muslims and the Imperial System of Control 1920–1932* (Delhi, 1982)

B. N. Pandey, Ed., *The Indian Nationalist Movement 1885–1947, Select Documents* (Delhi, 1979)

G. Pandey, *The Ascendancy of the Congress in Uttar Pradesh 1926–34. A Study in Imperfect Mobilization* (Delhi, 1978)

S. Sarkar, *Modern India 1885–1947* (Madras, 1983)

B. R. Tomlinson, *The Indian National Congress and the Raj, 1929–42: the Penultimate Phase* (London, 1976)

The Princes and the Raj

Throughout the period of British rule in India it was possible to travel from Bombay to Delhi passing through hardly any districts that were constitutionally or administratively part of the Government of India. At independence in 1947, some two-fifths of the subcontinent, containing between a fifth and a quarter of the whole population, remained in the hands of Indian princely families. Here, social and political relationships based on community and indigenous cultures had survived to a remarkable degree. Princes managed their states as autocrats; they were patrons of the most traditional ways of Indian life and were seen to symbolize the purest of Indian values. The very existence of so much territory lying in uneasy and ambiguous relationship to the developing modern state was bound to cause problems. During the 1920s and 1930s, the princes came to the fore in political discussion and, in the post independence period, individuals from princely families have used their local power and influence to considerable effect. Yet the overall impression must be that, as the twentieth century has progressed, the princes generally have lost ground. During the crucial months of the transfer of power, 1946–48, the princely states were increasingly ignored and then sacrificed as they were incorporated into the newly established India and Pakistan. By the early 1970s their contemporary irrelevance resulted in a loss of formal status, privileges and privy purses. The Princely Derecognition Act of 1971 at last tidied them away into history.

Although princely India is often thought of as a single entity, in fact it was nothing of the sort. To begin with, the Indian states were scattered irregularly through the subcontinent. They also varied

British Imperialism and Indian Nationalism, 1858–1947

The princely states in 1947.

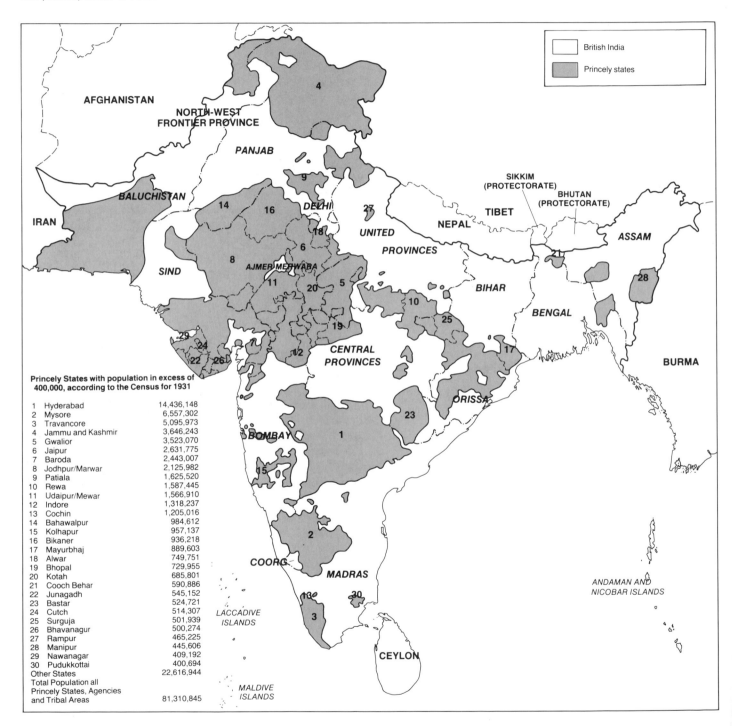

| | British India |
| | Princely states |

Princely States with population in excess of 400,000, according to the Census for 1931

1	Hyderabad	14,436,148
2	Mysore	6,557,302
3	Travancore	5,095,973
4	Jammu and Kashmir	3,646,243
5	Gwalior	3,523,070
6	Jaipur	2,631,775
7	Baroda	2,443,007
8	Jodhpur/Marwar	2,125,982
9	Patiala	1,625,520
10	Rewa	1,587,445
11	Udaipur/Mewar	1,566,910
12	Indore	1,318,237
13	Cochin	1,205,016
14	Bahawalpur	984,612
15	Kolhapur	957,137
16	Bikaner	936,218
17	Mayurbhaj	889,603
18	Alwar	749,751
19	Bhopal	729,955
20	Kotah	685,801
21	Cooch Behar	590,886
22	Junagadh	545,152
23	Bastar	524,721
24	Cutch	514,307
25	Surguja	501,939
26	Bhavanagur	500,274
27	Rampur	465,225
28	Manipur	445,606
29	Nawanagar	409,192
30	Pudukkottai	400,694
	Other States	22,616,944
	Total Population all Princely States, Agencies and Tribal Areas	81,310,845

greatly in size, and hence in importance. Hyderabad was the biggest, with an area of more than 82,000 square miles and a population in 1947 of over 14 million; but the smallest of the states in Kathiawar covered less than three-tenths of a square mile and supported a population of less than 200. There were over 600 individual states, ruled by hereditary families of varying rank and diverse origins, maintaining formal links of different kinds with the imperial overlord. Some had full-blown treaties, similar to those existing between truly sovereign nations; others had only the most scrappy documentation acknowledging their separate identity. Most of the states were small and insignificant. Only 28 of them had populations exceeding half-a-million, and even within this group the largest eight accounted for half the total area, population and revenue. Princely authority was highly localized and culturally extremely diverse. Jat, Rajput, Maratha, Hindu, Sikh and Muslim – all were represented in microcosm in the Indian states. It was unlikely, therefore, that whatever political and economic pressures were brought to bear on princely India in the twentieth century, the princely states could be regarded as a collective or coherent whole: the logic of history, geography and culture told against that.

The Indian states, as they survived into the twentieth century, were the creation of the East India Company's expansion from the later eighteenth century. Once the British had become dominant in Bengal and on the southeast coast, the main aims of their expansion were to secure politically and economically those areas of India which were most densely populated and of most value to them. This involved a steady encroachment up the Gangetic plain and the capture of key producing areas elsewhere. Sometimes this was done by conquest; sometimes by alliance. In the confused political history of the Mughal decline, the Company sought to achieve its objectives partly by administering Indian districts directly and partly by entering into alliances with other Indian rulers. This latter process became more formalized in the closing years of the eighteenth century when the Company caught up many of its more important neighbors in a network of alliances that provided for a common system of defence. Such arrangements offered considerable attractions to some Indian rulers, but they also required such princes to reduce their independent armies and to contribute towards the cost of a defence policy devised and controlled by the British. By 1800, Wellesley had achieved remarkable benefits for the Company, partly through war and partly through alliance with states such as Avadh, Hyderabad and Mysore.

The second decade of the nineteenth century, however, found the Company faced with serious disruptions upon its administrative frontiers and the borders of its allies. It was during this period that the map of central and western India was largely drawn. The British did not have the resources to undertake notable conquest of difficult terrain and of marginal economic areas, however much such regions

Maharaja Jaswant Singh of Marwar, better known as Jodhpur, one of the largest princely states. The Maharaja was head of the Rathor clan of Rajputs.

impinged on the more settled districts of the British and their allies; nor did the Company have the capacity to administer them directly as a coherent whole. The British, therefore, determined to make a settlement that established and stabilized a highly localized political structure. A ring-fence was erected round the area and a network of military communication thrown over it. Small detachments of irregular troops were sent in to pacify the districts. Military intervention was followed up by political arrangements: this involved the instant and pragmatic recognition of any local lordling who could guarantee some stability over however small an area on condition that he accepted British paramountcy and closed his doors to disturbers of the pax britannica. Much of central and western India, and of Rajasthan, once an area of shifting politics, became a fixed mosaic of petty states.

After 1820, the British controlled enough of the subcontinent to overawe the rest. Policy towards the Indian states throughout the nineteenth century was marked by pragmatism and ambivalence. Since, with few exceptions, the states were located in relatively backward areas, and since they were so disjointed and disparate, they posed little threat to British dominance. The British therefore neglected them or intervened within them as circumstances dictated. While recognizing their separate existence, the British still felt able to annex some of them if the need arose. Hence by mid-century there had been a further formal expansion of British territory by the annexations of Avadh, Satara and Nagpur and by conquest in parts of Punjab and Sind.

Following the serious disturbances of 1857–58, the Government of India began also to see positive political possibilities in the Indian states. Canning expressed the feeling most clearly when, in 1859 he noted that many Indian rulers had afforded real aid to restoring order in the mid-Gangetic plain and that they had thus 'served as breakwaters to the storms which would otherwise have swept over us'. More generally, the princes came to be seen as a possible category of support for imperial rule and as a useful conservative block on too hasty a political development. The sweeping reforms of 1920 and 1935, however, brought out all the anomalies and inconsistencies in the very existence of princely India. Montagu, keen to reward Indian rulers for their very real contribution to the war effort, and determined to bring them into closer association with the Raj, consulted representatives of the princes about his proposed constitutional changes, which led to the establishment in 1921 of the Chamber of Princes. This was a deliberative assembly designed to advise the Government of India about the interests of Indian states. It had limited powers and an active membership of about forty. Far from easing political development, the Chamber began seriously to hinder it, for it gave the princes an opportunity to put the intricate matter of their precise relationship with the British onto the political agenda. Montagu's informal discussions, and the debates in the Chamber, also revealed how very divided the princes were over political matters.

At the first round table conference in 1930, Sir Tej Bahadur Sapru, a liberal lawyer from Allahabad, brought the constitutional issues to a head by calling for a federation between British India and the Indian states. The princes took the idea up enthusiastically, but as the decade progressed it became clear that they could not evolve a coherent policy for themselves. Insufficient urgency was put into the discussions and the prospect of a federal structure into which the states would have been incorporated had disappeared by 1939. With the pre-war failure of schemes for federation, the princes were

edged into the wings. The real political battle was seen increasingly as that between the British, the Congress and the Muslim League.

GJ

Further reading
S. R. Ashton, *British Policy towards the Indian States 1905–1939* (London, 1982)
E. M. Forster, *The Hill of Devi* (London and New York 1953 and subsequent reprint)
Sir William Lee-Warner, *The Native States of India* (London, 1910)
V. P. Menon, *The Story of the Integration of the Indian States* (Madras, 1961)
B. N. Ramusack, *The Princes of India in the Twilight of Empire: Dissolution of a Patron–Client System, 1914–1939* (Columbus, Ohio, 1978)

World War II, the partition and the transfer of power

When British rule came to an end in India in 1947, it did so for two reasons. The first was that the relationship between Britain and India had so changed since the early years of the century that there was no longer any need for the British to rule India in order to derive benefits from her Indian connections. The second was that within

The Indian Army played a major role in the defence of the British Empire in World War II as it did in World War I. Here Indian troops show off a Nazi flag captured in the North African campaign at Sidi Omar.

India substantial power had already been conceded to Indian interests and that the ability of the British to manage them easily had been greatly reduced. From the early 1940s, no serious politician ever questioned that India should become more independent: but there was no common view about what this meant, how it was to be achieved and within what timescale. It was not until the end of World War II that the politicians were forced to make decisions about the ending of British rule.

In some respects, British rule in India during the war was outstandingly successful. Despite opposition by some Indian politicians, India was brought fully into the war effort. Over two million additional Indians were recruited into the army, and massive resources were diverted to their support. The economy experienced significant booms, but also shortages and famine. In an attempt to deal with the social and economic repercussions of mobilization for war, there was government intervention on an unprecedented scale. The situation was manageable in the short term, but it could not hold for ever. The government had little difficulty in suppressing Gandhi's bid to force the British out in the 'Quit India' movement of 1942 and it was able to find political allies to keep the machinery going, or to do without the participation of some politicians at all. But those with the closest knowledge of India knew that this situation could not last forever. Most importantly, war-time activity upset the social base on which the Raj rested and also made support uncertain for the main Indian political parties. Lord Linlithgow, retiring as Viceroy in 1943, believed that British rule could go on for another thirty years. But his successor, Field Marshall Wavell, noted that Linlithgow had told him: 'we must be careful that we did not get into a position when we could not get out of India because of the chaos it would cause but were unable to control and administer it if we remained'. Anxieties about the future shape of Indian government haunted other politicians too: for some as worried as the British by the prospect of political collapse, the most important aim was to retrieve intact the strongly centralizing governmental structure which had been evolving during British rule; for others, fears as to which groups might control such a government forced them to press for a more loosely federal scheme of things, or even for the dismantling of the unitary system. Political developments since 1920 at least had ensured a significant transfer of power into Indian hands at least at the local and provincial levels; but there had been no corresponding handover at the center. Here the British had wished to stay and, until the end of the war, managed to stay. If that central government was to remain a strong and effective body with sufficient power to maintain the unity of India, then it mattered vitally who succeeded to the British there.

This was not straightforward, for there were many political interests that had to be accommodated. Foremost among these was the Indian National Congress. This was long-established and well organized. Its support came from town and country alike; it straddled class and religious barriers; it had the largest paid-up membership of any political party in the world. Under the leadership of Gandhi, Nehru, Patel and others, the Congress had run widespread campaigns of civil disobedience and, as a result of its convincing victories in the elections held in the winter of 1936–37, Congressmen were able to form ministries in eight of the eleven provinces of British India.

But the Congress did not have the field to itself. In some regions it did not command much support; for some people it was too Hindu; for others it was too much a party of the socially and economically privileged. Consequently, any arrangement which would ensure its dominance at the national level would be strongly challenged. For a time, in the 1930s, this suited British interests. There were the princes to consider, and then the government chose to worry about its responsibilities toward the so-called untouchables, poor laborers and cultivators whom it saw as lying outside the Congress. But above all, there were the Muslims who looked to the British for a fair deal. In the end all the other divisions in Indian society pale into insignificance beside this one. It is remarkable that this should have been so. Although the All-India Muslim League had been in existence since 1906, putting forward the view that Muslims deserved special political consideration, it must be remembered that they did not form a single community. Although large numbers of Muslims lived in northwestern and northeastern India, they were scattered through the subcontinent and were divided theologically, linguistically, racially and by class. Nevertheless Muslims had in their distinctive religion a potentially unifying force which stressed the need for purity of doctrine and communal self-help. This did not necessarily mean that the differences among the Muslims were removed, nor did it stop them living and working alongside other Indians; but it provided a new context for political activity. A quickening of religious communal awareness, which was always an unpredictable and forceful influence in politics, developed at the expense of other social connections.

What came first was a demand that Muslims must be represented in political institutions only by Muslims, and then that they should be able to protect their community by being given an equal share of power with everyone else. The Muslim predicament was this: overall they made up only a fifth of the population and the danger was that with the development of democratic institutions they would become subordinated to the non-Muslim majority and be lost in Indian society at large. For many people this is a sufficient explanation for the creation of Pakistan.

Taken by itself, the separatist strand in Muslim politics need not have led to partition in 1947. The tactic made some sense where Muslims were an influential minority but in Panjab and Bengal Muslims were a majority of the population. Here special consideration for minorities would only benefit Sikhs and Hindus. What most Muslim politicians in these regions wanted was provincial self-rule with a weak central government. For much of the 1930s Muslim leaders thought this the best way to take care of their interests in India and separatist politics were at a discount.

When the change came, it came quickly. Undoubtedly some Muslim politicians were alarmed by the success of the Congress in the provincial elections. Then there was a determination by a wide range of Muslim leaders to restrict any political advance at the center which might allow the Congress to consolidate its already strong hold on the government. In this the Muslims found ready allies in the princes, other non-Congress groups and in the British. By September 1939, the Muslim League, revived as a prominent party by Mohammad Ali Jinnah, declared itself 'irrevocably opposed' to any federal objective. In March 1940, meeting in Lahore, the League demanded the partition of India and the grouping of regions in which Muslims were numerically in a majority into 'Independent States'. This became the charter for Pakistan.

Even so, it is debatable what the Lahore resolution meant. Certainly it was not a demand for an exclusively Muslim state – rather for a separation of existing provinces in which Muslims were a majority, and perhaps only a scant majority at that. Then, the question of the relationship between this Muslim Raj and the rest of India was also left open. Certainly, the Lahore resolution must be seen as a bargaining counter to be used when constitutional negotiations were taken further with the British and the Congress. But it was also used to bring the Muslim leaders in Panjab and elsewhere into line. Jinnah knew the League would not be able to bargain effectively unless it could win support from the provinces where most Muslims lived – areas where it had been very weak hitherto. Over the next five years the League, which unlike the Congress remained active throughout the war, hammered away at its cause. It succeeded in persuading Muslim leaders in Panjab and Bengal that provincial autonomy would not protect a Muslim position if the British were to give way to Congress at the center of a united government.

So it was that when the British began in earnest to work out a new political deal the position seemed simpler. Princes, Sikhs and all the other special interests were pushed into second place. Now only the Congress and the League counted. 'We have every reason to mistrust and dislike Gandhi and Jinnah, and their followers', Wavell wrote. 'But the Congress and the League are the dominant parties in Hindu and Muslim India, and will remain so. They control the Press, the electoral machine, the money bags; and have the prestige of established parties. Even if Gandhi and Jinnah disappeared tomorrow . . . I can see no prospect of our having more reasonable people to deal with.'

The Viceroy's frustration showed that the question was no longer whether the British would hand over power to Indians: it was one of how this was to be done economically. At the heart of the matter was the question of Pakistan. Was a new state to be created, and if so, what form would it take. The League insisted that partition was the only solution to the political problem since Muslims would not be ruled by the Congress. Moreover, Pakistan must include all the provinces and princely states where Muslims made up a sizeable population. The British did not care for this, mainly on practical grounds, and the Congress would not contemplate it at any price fearing a further balkanization of India if it were to be allowed. The Congress line was tersely summed up by an entry in Wavell's Diary 'no Pakistan, strong Centre, and the Muslims will come to heel all right'. So the parties dug in and communal tempers flared. Each new outbreak of violence made it more difficult to look for a compromise. The League's success in winning seats in the Muslim-majority provinces in 1946 greatly strengthened the case for Pakistan. But in so doing it reduced the politicians' room for maneuver.

The British still hoped that it would be possible to get the Indians to agree on a single successor state. Wavell made several attempts to get the Congress and the League to devise a scheme for an Indian Union. If the League were to accept the need for some central authority to handle at least defence, foreign affairs and communications, then it might be possible to form one federation of Hindu-majority provinces and another of Muslim majority provinces, each with a good deal of autonomy and working together as equals at the center. Such a scheme, although it sounds simple, was capable of great refinement and it reached its most detailed elaboration in the proposals worked out in the summer of 1946 by a delegation of Cabinet Ministers sent out from London to resolve the Indian problem. Failure then to get agreement meant that some form of partition was inevitable.

But where would the line be drawn? Not, surely, around the large territory claimed by the League: more likely around a smaller area inhabited more exclusively by Muslims. In late 1945, Wavell had told the Secretary of State that if the League persisted in its demand then the Government would have to make it clear that large numbers of Hindus and Sikhs could not be included in Pakistan against their will. This would mean that western Bengal, including Calcutta and at least two-fifths of Panjab would be excluded from Pakistan, and the League would be left with what Jinnah himself described as only 'the husk'. Such a plan would have some chance of being accepted by the Congress, which would then inherit a government with strong central authority covering most of South Asia. The League leaders greeted such a scheme with incredulity.

By late 1946 the situation was in total deadlock. No progress toward a constitutional settlement seemed possible. The government decided now to replace Wavell as Viceroy by Lord Mountbatten. Announcing the change in the House of Commons on February 20, 1947 Attlee said that it was the government's intention to hand over power in India by 'a date not later than June 1948'. If by that time a constitution had not been worked out by a fully representative assembly then the Government would make its own decision, in Attlee's words, 'in the best interests of the Indian people'. The idea was to put pressure on the politicians to agree: but the result was to make the parties dig in even more stubbornly, and in effect, by setting a hard and fast timetable, the British made partition that much more likely. The Congress scented victory in that it was the largest party and by accepting a limited Pakistan it would still be the main beneficiary of the transfer of power. The League became desperate to preserve what it could and saw that it must hold out for some sort of Pakistan.

By late 1946 the British government faced the fact that they could not hold India and Mountbatten was instructed to implement whichever proposal would achieve British withdrawal. He approached his task with vigor and with an open mind. He listened to the politicians and leading officials rehearse all the arguments. He concluded that it would only be possible for the British to leave by transferring power to two governments. But this would not give the League what it wanted. As Mountbatten pointed out to Jinnah in April, if he accepted the League's arguments for the partition of India as a whole, then they had also to be applied to Panjab and Bengal. The League was now faced with a stark choice of coming in with the Congress or of accepting a 'truncated' and 'moth-eaten' state, Jinnah's words again. But relations between the two parties were now so bad that as one Muslim Leaguer told Mountbatten 'if your Excellency was prepared to let the Muslim League have only the Sind Desert I would still prefer to accept that and have a separate Muslim state in those conditions than to continue in bondage to the Congress with apparently more generous concessions'. This was a far cry from the grand schemes to protect Muslims at the center of Indian politics.

When it came about, the transfer of power in India really satisfied none of the parties. Partition did not meet the Muslim demand, and it ruthlessly sacrificed the interests of Sikhs, princes and a host of others as well.

In this sudden ending of British rule decisions were made which reflected the precarious position of all the parties involved. Not only the government was losing control. The intransigence of Gandhi and Jinnah and Nehru's radical and often emotional outbursts, show that the instability was hitting the political parties too. They

Congress, Muslim League and Sikh leaders talk with the Viceroy on June 2, 1947.
Clockwise round the table from the left they are: Abdur Rab Nishtar, Sardar Baldev Singh, Acharya Kripalani, Sardar Vallabhbhai Patel, Jawaharlal Nehru, Lord Mountbatten, M. A. Jinnah, Liaquat Ali Khan.

The partition of India.

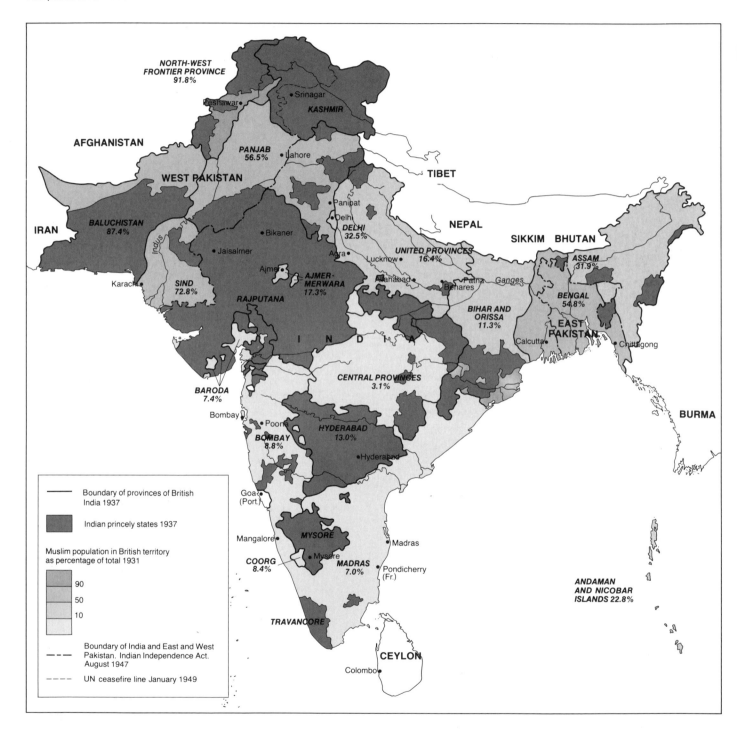

NORTH-WEST
FRONTIER PROVINCE
91.8%

• Srinagar

KASHMIR

AFGHANISTAN

PANJAB
56.5%

• Lahore

WEST PAKISTAN

TIBET

IRAN

BALUCHISTAN
87.4%

• Bikaner

• Panipat

Delhi •

DELHI
32.5%

NEPAL

SIKKIM   BHUTAN

• Jaisalmer

Agra •

UNITED PROVINCES
16.4%

Lucknow •

ASSAM
31.9%

Karachi •

SIND
72.8%

Ajmer •

AJMER-
MERWARA
17.3%

Allahabad •

Patna
Benares •

Ganges

BENGAL
54.8%

RAJPUTANA

I   N   D   I   A

BIHAR AND
ORISSA
11.3%

EAST
PAKISTAN

Calcutta •

• Chittagong

BARODA
7.4%

CENTRAL PROVINCES
3.1%

BURMA

Bombay •

• Poona

BOMBAY
8.8%

HYDERABAD
13.0%

• Hyderabad

Boundary of provinces of British
India 1937

Indian princely states 1937

Muslim population in British territory
as percentage of total 1931

90

50

10

Boundary of India and East and West
Pakistan. Indian Independence Act.
August 1947

UN ceasefire line January 1949

Goa
(Port.)

Mangalore •

MYSORE

• Madras

• Mysore

COORG
8.4%

MADRAS
7.0%

Pondicherry
(Fr.)

ANDAMAN
AND NICOBAR
ISLANDS 22.8%

TRAVANCORE

CEYLON

Colombo •

were finding it hard to keep a grip on their own supporters, and that in itself limited the political choice they could make. In a less fraught situation, they might have worked something out in the summer of 1946, but the tragedy was that all the politicians – British and Indian alike – rushed for fear of a worse collapse; and in cutting through the final difficulties were overwhelmed by the horror of it all.

GJ

Further reading

H. V. Hodson, *The Great Divide: Britain, India, Pakistan* (London, 1969)

A. Jalal, *The Sole Spokesman: Jinnah, the Muslim League and the Demand for Pakistan* (Cambridge, 1985)

N. Mansergh (editor in chief) *Constitutional Relations between Britain and India: The Transfer of Power, 1942–7*, 12 vols (London, 1970–83)

V. P. Menon, *The Transfer of Power in India* (Princeton, 1957)

P. Moon, *Divide and Quit* (London, 1961)

P. Moon, Ed., *Wavell: the Viceroy's Diary* (London, 1973)

Sri Lanka

In Sri Lanka, as in most parts of South Asia, *homo sapiens* made his first appearance around 500,000 BC. Experts in the field believe that the later stone cultures of Sri Lanka began around 10,000 BC and had two distinct phases, the first which lasted, very probably, until about 100 BC and the second which may have ended, in some parts of the island at least, with the introduction of metal about three to four centuries later. The stone-working technology of these early cultures, the Balangoda cultures, appears to continue into proto-historic times. In its mesolithic phase, the Balangoda cultures probably had an island-wide distribution from around 5000 BC to 500 BC. There were isolated survivals until the end of the first millenium AD.

Scholars are still in the process of assessing the significance of recent archeological excavations relating to Sri Lanka's pre-history. Many believe that these finds would change the picture of the island's pre-history quite dramatically and, as is the case with the much better established archeological evidence stemming from excavations in southeast Asia in recent times, available evidence would appear to suggest that domestication of plants may have occurred as early as 15,000 BC to 10,000 BC. Nevertheless, there is no firm evidence as yet of any close link between the mesolithic and neolithic cultures of Sri Lanka and the southeast Asian Hoabinian cultures. If such a link is scientifically established, it would mean that one of the three great external influences on the island's history,

the southeast Asian, has a much longer existence than the present state of our historical knowledge would lead us to believe.

The most important of these external influences, however, has been that of the Indian subcontinent. From the earliest times, Sri Lanka has had a multi-ethnic society. Its main component elements have a common Indian origin, one North Indian and 'Indo-Aryan', the other South Indian and 'Dravidian'. The majority group in ancient times, as it is today, were the Sinhalese, a people of Indo-Aryan origin who first came to the island from northern India about 500 BC. There is little agreement among scholars about the exact location of their original home in India. Little is known about the first South Indian or Tamil settlements on the island. From about the third century BC, there appear to have been trade relations between Sri Lanka and South India. There may have been settlements of Tamils who came as traders and subsequently as invaders, but, until the tenth century AD, these settlements were not very substantial.

Two of the most striking features of Sri Lanka's long and complex recorded history of over two thousand years spring from the island's proximity to India. While its close proximity brought the island within range of a wide variety of Indian influences, its separation enabled it to retain a distinct identity in religion, culture and language. Thus, while Buddhism has virtually disappeared from its Indian homeland, it survives and thrives in Sri Lanka. Again, Sinhala, the language of the majority of the population, has its roots in classical Indian languages, but is spoken nowhere else in the region.

The third external influence on the island was Western colonialism. Few countries of the Third World have felt the influence of Western colonialism for a longer period than Sri Lanka. That influence began with the Portuguese intrusion into the affairs of the island's coastal region in the sixteenth century. By 1600, the Portuguese were well established despite prolonged resistance from the Sinhalese. Within sixty years, they were displaced by the Dutch with the active support of the Sinhalese, and then the Dutch were replaced by the British in 1795–96. Much of the interior remained independent under the Kandyan kings, until 1815–18 when it was absorbed into the British crown colony of Ceylon. For the first time, in several centuries, one power controlled all of Sri Lanka. British rule lasted until 1948.

Ancient Sri Lanka

Two chronicles, the *Mahavansa* (possibly compiled about the sixth century but probably later) and its continuation the *Culavansa* (compiled in the thirteenth century) provide a remarkably full and accurate account of the island's ancient and medieval history. Despite shortcomings inevitable in such works compiled by *bhikkhus* (members of the Buddhist order) and the religious (including

Ancient Sri Lanka.

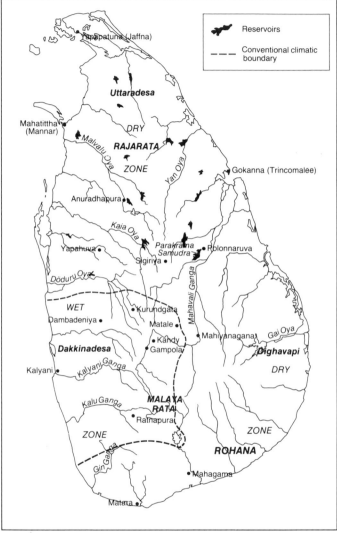

Source: K. M. de Silva, A History of Sri Lanka. (London, 1981) p.15

on the vagaries of the northeast monsoon. As the settlements spread it became necessary to insure against frequent drought. By the first century BC a solution had been devised – a highly sophisticated irrigation system remarkably attuned to the geological and geographical peculiarities of the island's dry zone. Considerable technical expertise met the requirement of rice for the provision and retention of water in fields over long periods of time.

The first five centuries AD form the most creative and dynamic phase in the development of this irrigation system. The construction of canals and channels exhibited a remarkable knowledge of trigonometry and the design of the tanks or artificial lakes a thorough grasp of hydraulic principles. By the third century BC, Sri Lankan engineers had discovered the principle of the valve tower or valve pit to regulate the escape of water from tanks. Some tanks were man-made lakes of prodigious dimensions and demonstrated striking technological sophistication, as did the intricate network of canals which linked them together in bringing water to the paddy lands they were designed to serve.

Two important cores of Sinhalese civilization developed in the north-central regions and control over them gave Sinhalese rulers the resources to extend their sway over the whole island. There was a third core in Rohana the dry zone of the south, and southeast, which was settled almost simultaneously with the north-central plain. In the early years of the island's history the main centers of agricultural settlement were under the control of independent or semi-independent rulers.

With the expansion of population princes began to aspire to rule the whole island. A fifteen-year campaign, waged in the first century BC by Dutthagamini, a Sinhalese prince from Rohana, against Elara, a Chola general from South India who had established himself at Anuradhapura in the north-central plains, dominates the later chapters of the *Mahavansa*. It is dramatized as a decisive confrontation between the champion of the Sinhalese – and Buddhist – cause and a Dravidian invader. The campaign culminated in Dutthagamini's victory. His triumph over Elara was significant for being the first notable success of centripetalism over centrifugalism in Sri Lanka's history.

Despite the growing increase in the power of the ruler at Anuradhapura, however, the problem of control over the outer provinces from the capital was just as intractable in Sri Lanka as it was in the Indian subcontinent. Periodically Rohana asserted its independence or served as a refuge for defeated Sinhalese kings or aspirants to the throne, but it was as frequently controlled by the former and seems never to have rivaled it in economic power or population resources.

Sri Lanka's celebrated mastery of irrigation technology elevated her to the position of one of the great hydraulic civilizations of the ancient world, in a super-league which included China and the

sectarian) biases inherent in them, these chronicles have no rival in any part of India as historical sources.

The political history of the period from the first century BC to the end of the thirteenth century AD forms the backdrop to the development, expansion, and eventual collapse of an intricate irrigation system which was the key to the establishment, consolidation and maturation of Sinhalese civilization in the dry zone of the country. This latter was an extensive plain covering the northern half of the island and stretching southwards along the east coast to a smaller southern plain.

The earliest settlements were on the banks of the rivers of these regions. Rice was the staple crop and its cultivation was dependent

Kingdoms and Rulers of Sri Lanka fourteenth century to 1948

1371–1597	Kings of Kotte (Southwest Sri Lanka)
1521–1594	Kings of Sitavaka (Central Highlands)
1469–1815	Kings of the Udarata or the Kandyan Kingdom (Central Highlands)
? –1620	Kings of Jaffna (North Sri Lanka)
1594–1658	Portuguese Captains-General
1640–1796	Dutch Governors
1798–1948	British Governors
1798–1805	The Hon. Frederick North
1805–1811	Sir Thomas Maitland
1812–1820	Sir Robert Brownrigg, Bart.
1822–1823	The Hon. Sir Edward Paget
1824–1831	Sir Edward Barnes
1831–1837	Sir Robert W. Horton, Bart.
1837–1841	J. A. S. Mackenzie
1841–1847	Sir Colin Campbell
1847–1850	Viscount Torrington
1850–1855	Sir G. W. Anderson
1855–1860	Sir Henry G. Ward
1860–1863	Sir Charles Justin MacCarthy
1865–1872	Sir Hercules G. Robinson
1872–1877	Sir William H. Gregory
1877–1883	Sir James R. Longden
1883–1890	The Hon. Sir Arthur H. Gordon
1890–1896	Sir Arthur E. Havelock
1896–1903	Sir J. West Ridgeway
1903–1907	Sir Henry Arthur Blake
1907–1913	Sir Henry E. McCallum
1913–1916	Sir Robert Chalmers
1916–1918	Sir John Anderson
1918–1925	Sir William H. Manning
1925–1927	Sir Hugh Clifford
1927–1931	Sir Herbert J. Stanley
1931–1933	Sir Graeme Thomson
1933–1937	Sir Edward Stubbs
1937–1944	Sir Andrew Caldecott
1944–1948	Sir Henry Monck-Mason-Moore

Source: K. M. De Silva *A History of Sri Lanka* pp. 569–72 (London, 1981)

Box 11

fertile crescent of West Asia. However, the political system that evolved did not have the rigorous authoritarian and heavily bureaucratic structure which Karl Wittfogel, the theorist of hydraulic civilizations, regarded as the key features of their polities. The Sri Lankan version also demonstrated much greater tolerance, if not ready acceptance of, local autonomy. It was in fact much closer to European feudalism than to ancient China, Wittfogel's classical model of a hydraulic society. While Sri Lanka's hydraulic society had, in common with European feudalism, an obligation to service as a condition of holding land whether from secular authorities or religious institutions, there was the significant difference that in Sri Lankan society the nature of that obligation was also affected by the caste status of the individual. Caste became in time the basis of social stratification. Castes had a service or occupational role as their primary distinguishing function, but in the Sinhalese system, in contrast to the Indian prototype, there was no religious sanction for caste which softened its impact considerably.

The entry of Buddhism to the island around the third century BC which is identified by the *Mahavansa* with the initiative of Devanampiya Tissa who was a contemporary of the Indian ruler, Ashoka, was an even more significant landmark in the island's history than the development of irrigation technology. For Buddhism became in time the state-religion, and the bedrock of the culture and civilization of the Sinhalese. Subsequently the intermingling of religion and 'national' identity has had a profound influence on the Sinhalese, who believe they are 'chosen' people with a divine mission to protect and preserve Buddhism in their island home.

The two great cities of ancient Sri Lanka, Anuradhapura and Polonnaruva are testimony to the wealth and refinement of Sri Lanka's rulers of old. Anuradhapura was a sprawling city and at the height of its glory was one of the great cities of ancient South Asia. Polonnaruva the capital from the eleventh century, was more compact but contained within its boundaries all the characteristic features of a capital city of ancient Sri Lanka, tanks, stupas, palaces and parks and their architectural and sculptural embellishments. It too was a gracious cosmopolitan city.

The flourishing irrigation civilization of Sri Lanka's northern plain was vulnerable to invasion from South India. These assaults began as early as the third century BC but increased in frequency and destructiveness after the sixth century AD. In the fifth and sixth centuries AD a new factor of instability was introduced into politics with the rise of three militantly Hindu states in South India, the Pandyas, Pallavas and Cholas. In this process South India ceased to be the important Buddhist center it had been up to this time.

The Sinhalese contributed to their own discomfiture by calling in Tamil assistance in settling disputed successions and dynastic squabbles. South Indian auxiliaries became, in time, a vitally important if not the most powerful element in the armies of Sinhalese rulers, and an unpredictable, turbulent group who were often a threat to political stability. They were also the nucleus of a powerful Tamil influence in the court. Sri Lanka was drawn into conflicts among these South Indian states and became an integral element in the power politics of that region. More important still, Tamil settlements in the island became sources of support for South Indian invaders.

In the middle of the ninth century the Sinhalese intervened

Buddhism forms the foundation of Sinhalese civilization; it is closely intertwined
with Sinhalese national identity. A standing and a lying Buddha at the Gal Vihara,
Polonnaruva, capital of Sri Lanka from the eleventh century.

directly in South India with disastrous consequences for themselves in provoking the hostility of the rising power of the Cholas. Under Rajaraja the Great (984–1014) the Cholas, having conquered all of South India, extended their control to the north-central plains of Sri Lanka. For seventy-five years this region was ruled as a province of the Chola empire.

The Cholas established their capital at Polonnaruva in the northeast of the dry zone, and nearer the Mahavali, a shift determined as much by reasons of security as it was by economic considerations. They were eventually driven out of Sri Lanka in 1070 by Vijayabahu I, with Rohana serving as his base of operations. Once Vijayabahu regained control of Anuradhapura he followed the Cholas in retaining Polonnaruva as the capital. During his reign of forty years the country recovered from the ravages of the Chola occupation, but he left a disputed succession, and another period of extensive civil war followed, until stability was restored by Parakramabahu I who ruled at Polonnaruva from 1153 to 1186. He unified Sri Lanka under his control, and built a remarkable series of irrigation works and public and religious monuments. The Parakrama Samudra (the sea of Parakrama), with an embankment nearly nine miles long at an average height of forty feet, was the greatest of the irrigation works of ancient Sri Lanka.

The vigorous revival of ancient grandeur under Parakramabahu I eventually exhausted the energies of the Polonnaruva kingdom. After him there was a brief decade of order and stability under Nissanka Malla (1187–96) during which Polonnaruva reached the peak of its development as a capital city. Its architectural features rivaled those of Anuradhapura. But renewed dissension among the Sinhalese, and dynastic disputes attracted South Indian invasions which culminated in a devastating campaign of pillage under Magha of Kalinga. These invasions from South India, and the unparalleled destruction they wrought contributed greatly to creating an image of the Tamils as the implacable historical foe of Sri Lanka and the Sinhalese.

The drift to the southwest

The collapse of the irrigation civilizations of Sri Lanka's dry zone is one of the critical turning points in the island's history. The four centuries from about 1200 to 1600 constitute a period of decline in which we see three main trends. The first and most important of these was the drift of Sinhalese power to the southwest of the island a shift which was as much the cause as it was the result of a fundamental change in the economic resources of the state and in the nature of its revenue system. The change was from an over-whelming dependence on irrigation-based rice cultivation, to rain-fed agriculture, with trade rising higher in the scale of the ruler's priorities than ever before. Cinnamon became one of the main export commodities. This was especially so in the principal Sin-halese kingdom. Muslim settlers in the island largely controlled its export trade. As this trade grew in importance they settled in larger numbers in the coastal areas and in the ports, and then gradually penetrated to the interior.

Second, the invasion of Magha led directly to the formation of a Tamil kingdom in the island for the first time. The core of this kingdom was the Jaffna peninsula in the north of the island. The kingdom of Jaffna had a short but tempestuous history. Its power and influence in the country reached its peak in the fourteenth and early fifteenth centuries when it began a long decline until it succumbed to Portuguese power in the early seventeenth century. Its political status and influence changed dramatically from time to time: for a short period a very powerful kingdom; at others a satellite of expanding Dravidian states in southern India; and at times subjugated by the principal Sinhalese state of the day, and generally acknowledging its suzerainty. Parakramabahu VI (1412–67), the last Sinhalese ruler to bring the whole island under his rule, overran Jaffna in 1450. But Sinhalese control over the north which he thus established was not maintained for long after his death, and Jaffna re-asserted its independence.

The third of these trends was that the central region began to stake a claim to an independent political role of its own. This was the origin of the Kandyan kingdom which became in time the last of the Sinhalese kingdoms of the island.

Political instability was the bane of Sri Lanka's history throughout this period. The result was that when the Portuguese

Sri Lanka under the Portuguese.

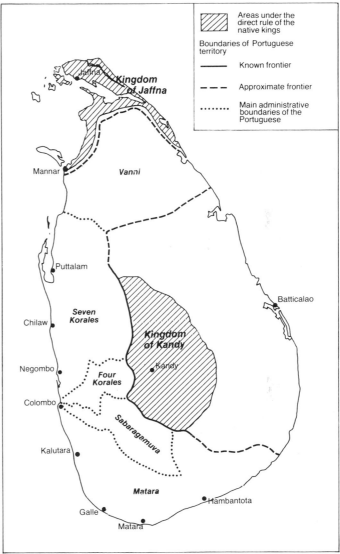

Source: K. M. de Silva, A History of Sri Lanka (London, 1981) pp.17-19

arrived in Sri Lanka in the early sixteenth century they found the island divided into three independent and squabbling kingdoms.

The rulers of these kingdoms were well aware of the seriousness of the threat they faced from the Portuguese, but they felt they could use them for their own purposes. Eventually they ended by having them well entrenched in the island. Yet the choice was not the simple one of survival in the face of the threat of Portuguese domination. It was more complicated for there was also the increas-ing influence of Arab and Islamic power extending either by sea through the Arabian Sea or by land through southern India. Had the Portuguese not prevailed there was the distinct prospect of an

Islamic domination of the island's affairs in which Sri Lanka's Buddhist civilization may have been far more systematically undermined than it was by Christianity. The latter was introduced in all its various forms by or under the aegis of the three Western powers who ruled the country, or parts of it, from around the late sixteenth century to the early part of the twentieth century. Roman Catholicism, Calvinism and Anglicanism, each in turn, enjoyed a special relationship with the ruling power while converts to the orthodox version of Christianity in vogue, especially under the Portuguese and the Dutch, enjoyed a privileged status.

Sri Lanka under the Dutch.

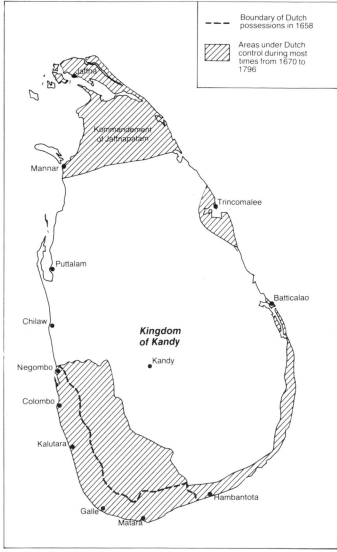

| | Boundary of Dutch possessions in 1658 |
| | Areas under Dutch control during most times from 1670 to 1796 |

Kingdom of Kandy

Jaffna
Kommandement of Jaffnapatam
Mannar
Trincomalee
Puttalam
Batticalao
Chilaw
Kandy
Negombo
Colombo
Kalutara
Hambantota
Galle
Matara

Source: K. M. de Silva, A History of Sri Lanka (London, 1981) pp.17-19

Colonial influences: religion

Although the Portuguese ruled Sri Lanka's maritime regions for a much shorter period of time (1600 to 1658) than the Dutch (1658–1795) they have had a more powerful and lasting influence on the people of the country. Conversions to Roman Catholicism under the Portuguese have stood the test of harassment under the Dutch and indifference under the British. From the second quarter of the nineteenth century onwards Roman Catholics constituted nine-tenths of the Christian community in the island. Today Christians form 6.7 percent of the Sri Lankan population, of which 90 percent are Roman Catholics. Sri Lanka's Christian community is no longer as influential as it was but it is still the largest Christian group in the whole of South Asia in terms of percentage of population, or for that matter in most of Asia save the Philippines.

Calvinism introduced by the Dutch did not, unlike Roman Catholicism, develop any strong roots among the people; it disappeared with few traces remaining almost as soon as the Dutch were replaced in control of the littoral by the British. How Protestant groups who came in under British rule will fare in years to come is still to be seen but those who see signs of their becoming moribund have good reason; their pessimism is based on what happened to Calvinism after the Dutch left.

While the local languages, Sinhala and Tamil, absorbed a number of Portuguese and Dutch words, Portuguese was spoken in the island, and used in schools, until well into the nineteenth century. A Portuguese dialect still survives in some parts of the island, which is explained in part by the fact that Portuguese was the *lingua franca* of maritime Asia up to the middle of the nineteenth century. The Sinhalese of the low country have adopted and still retain Portuguese surnames like de Silva, de Sousa, Fernando, Perera and de Mel even where they have long since given up the Roman Catholicism which was usually linked with such names. The Dutch language disappeared years ago, and so too have Dutch names except among the descendants of the Dutch living in the island who still have Dutch surnames: they form a tiny minority. Curiously, while English first names were very popular, English surnames never were, except among the Tamils of Jaffna, who adopted them under the influence of American missionaries, but these too have now been abandoned in favor of traditional Tamil ones.

Colonial influences: the economy

The rule of the Portuguese, and later, the Dutch, in the littoral marked the beginning of a fundamental change in the island's economic system: the dominance of export trade over the traditional sources of state revenues. Their main interest was in spices, and in particular cinnamon: they monopolized the export trade in cinnamon, and the profits from it became the mainstay of their revenues. Cinnamon lost its primacy as a source of revenue in

Sri Lanka under the British.

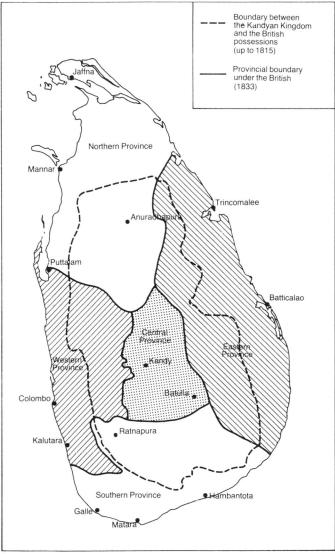

Boundary between
the Kandyan Kingdom
and the British
possessions
(up to 1815)

Provincial boundary
under the British
(1833)

Source: K. M. de Silva, A History of Sri Lanka *(London, 1981) pp.17-19*

British times to coffee, and by the 1840s, there was a remarkable transformation of Sri Lanka's economy through the success of coffee as a plantation crop. The coffee industry reached its peak in the 1870s, and then succumbed rapidly to a virulent leaf disease. Nevertheless, plantation agriculture demonstrated an extraordinary resilience over the three decades from 1880 to 1910 when a pattern was established of an overwhelming dominance of three crops, tea, rubber, and to a lesser extent coconuts, which still widely prevails despite every effort made since independence to broaden the base of the economy and to encourage industrial development.

Labor on the coffee plantations was mainly provided by immigrant Indians. When tea and rubber replaced coffee as the principal plantation crop, a significant change in the pattern of immigration occurred for unlike coffee these required a permanent and resident labor force. South India was once more the source of supply, but the workers came to the island as permanent or semi-permanent residents rather than as seasonal migrants. From this change emerged Sri Lanka's Indian problem in its modern form, the position of these late nineteenth century and early twentieth century migrants in the Sri Lankan polity.

In British times, one far-reaching effect of the development of a capitalist economy on the foundation of plantation agriculture and trade was the growth of a new élite. This was largely an indigenous capitalist class. The traditional élite, especially in the low-country areas was absorbed into this new élite but was soon left far behind by others in the two most important channels of social mobility; the acquisition of a Western education, usually English, and especially participation in capitalist enterprise. The élite as a whole, and in particular its Sinhalese segment, had a fondness for an anglicized lifestyle, which meant emulating the English upper classes. Traces of this still remain.

One notable adverse effect of the growth of plantations was the comparative neglect of traditional agriculture. This was seen from Dutch times when rice, the staple food of the people, began to be imported. It continued under British rule despite the sustained, if not unbroken, effort made from the second half of the nineteenth century to rehabilitate the dry zone of the country through a revival of the ancient irrigation works there. At independence more than half of the country's requirements of rice was imported. After independence traditional agriculture came into its own, as the most dynamic sector of the economy to the point where today the country is very nearly self-sufficient in rice.

Colonial influences: the growth of nationalism

Initially the British encouraged change and reform in Sri Lankan society but they became much more sympathetic to the conservative forces in the island by the last quarter of the nineteenth century. This was due in part to an over-reaction to pressures from the more vocal and assertive section of the élite then seeking a very modest share of political power. Incipient nationalist sentiment among the Sinhalese was religious, in the main Buddhist, in outlook and content. Political overtones in it were perceptible almost from the beginning especially in the appeal to the glories of the ancient past in contrast with the contemporary reality of foreign domination. The nationalist movement developed a more positive political content and ideology in the early twentieth century. Nevertheless, even among the most ardent nationalists faith in the permanence of British rule remained largely unshaken, and nobody in public life at the turn of the century would have believed that Sri Lanka would regain her independence within 50 years. The second principal feature of the reform movement was its restraint, indeed its indestructible moderation. Its third feature was a pervasive pragmatism. Both of these in part at least are a reflection of the continuing influence of British political attitudes which have been powerful factors in Sri Lankan politics throughout the twentieth century. The formation of the Ceylon National Congress in 1919 after many years of debate and negotiation was evidence of the continuing strength of these attitudes rather than any radical departure from them.

There were bolder initiatives in politics in the 1920s some of which reflected the increasing politicization and radicalization of Colombo's working class whose leadership advocated more vigorous expressions of opposition to British rule in imitation of the contemporary policies of the Indian National Congress. Again, it was in this decade that some of the most intractable political problems of contemporary Sri Lanka emerged, many of these developing out of, or complicated by, the increasing prospect of the transfer of a share of political power to Sri Lankan hands. Minority groups, led by the Tamils, were soon engaged in a purposeful effort to secure protection of their interests as the price of their support for this process.

Constitutional reforms introduced in 1931 on the recommendations of the Donoughmore Commission amounted in effect to an assurance of self-government in the near future as an inevitable next step. Equally important was the grant of universal suffrage in 1931. Few events in Sri Lanka's recent history have had so profound an impact on politics and society.

Sri Lanka became the first Asian colony of the British empire and, if one excludes the white settlement colonies which had developed into Dominions, the first colony to enjoy that privilege. The first general election in Britain under universal suffrage was held in 1929; Sri Lanka had its first such general election only two years later. Women got the vote in 1931 for the first time, at 21 years of age, well ahead of many countries among the more mature democracies of the West. In Britain the extension of the franchise followed upon the expansion of educational opportunities, and the growth of political awareness among the masses; in Sri Lanka universal suffrage preceded these developments.

One of the immediate effects of the introduction of universal suffrage was the stimulus it gave to a broad impulse towards social welfare, especially in the last decade before independence: 1936–1947. This included a comprehensive program for restoring the irrigation works of the dry zone, and the settlement there of peasant 'colonists' from other parts of the country. There was also massive investment of resources on education, health and food subsidies. Together these formed the basis of Sri Lanka's mini welfare-state. This welfare policy, to which all Sri Lankan governments since independence have been committed, has narrowed the gap between rich and poor much more effectively than in most Asian and African states, with the result that while Sri Lanka is one of the poorer nations of the world, it nevertheless provides its citizens with a quality of life which much wealthier nations have yet to achieve.

Universal suffrage had an immediate impact on the electorate in the resurgence of nationalism linked with Buddhist revivalism and its associated cultural heritage. Again, the massive rural vote

Don Stephen Senanayake (1884–1952), Sri Lanka's first Prime Minister, 1947–52.

provided a solid political base for this new nationalism. But, although the rural vote swamped the working class vote, universal suffrage did strengthen working class movements to the extent that they could, for instance, play an independent role in politics as a radical force. By the early 1930s Marxists had established themselves in the leadership of the indigenous working class movement. (The Indian plantation workers, by far the larger segment of the working class, had their own leadership.) One other notable feature of this nationalist resurgence was the impetus it gave to the rehabilitation of the heartland of the irrigation civilizations of old, a policy that is associated with the dynamism and vision of Don Stephen Senanayake as Minister of Agriculture and Lands. This has had a lasting influence on post-independence governments of Sri Lanka, and has enjoyed enormous popular support from the Sinhalese masses.

The final phase in the transfer of power began under the leadership of Senanayake who was to become the country's first Prime Minister. In response to the agitation in Sri Lanka the British government appointed the Soulbury Commission in 1944 to examine the constitutional problem. The constitution that emerged from their deliberations was based substantially on one drafted for Senanayake in 1944 by his advisers. It gave the island internal self government while retaining some imperial safeguards in defence and external affairs, but Sri Lanka's leaders pressed, successfully, for the removal of these restrictions, and the island was granted independence on February 4, 1948. The transfer of power was deceptively smooth and peaceful in contrast to the violence which accompanied the process in the Indian subcontinent and Burma.

KM de S

Further reading

S. Arasaratnam, *Ceylon* (Englewood Cliffs, N.J., 1964)
H. W. Codrington, *A Short History of Ceylon* (London, 1947)
K. M. de Silva, 'Historical Survey' in K. M. de Silva, Ed., *Sri Lanka: a Survey* (London, 1976)
K. M. de Silva, *A History of Sri Lanka* (London, 1981)

Nepal from the formation of the State in 1769 to 1951

Following the successive waves of Muslim invasions of India, immigrant Hindu chiefs from Rajasthan made their way to the hills of the central Himalayas in order to escape religious and political persecution. There they carved out principalities for themselves, asserting their rule over indigenous tribes.

Until the middle of the eighteenth century, the territory forming present-day Nepal was divided into as many as fifty principalities. The modern kingdom is a result of the consolidation of these

Prithvinaryan Shah, founder of the modern kingdom of Nepal and king from 1743–1775.

principalities, achieved through military conquest by one of the local chiefs, Prithvinarayan Shah, who became Raja of Gorkha in 1743, and by his successors.

King Prithvinarayan established the present Shah dynasty of Nepal after conquering the three kingdoms of what was then called the Nepal Valley by 1769, and making his capital Kathmandu. By the time he died in 1775, he had incorporated into his kingdom all of the present-day eastern Nepal. He, for the first time, gave the country a single name and a strong central government, and warned his successors to be cautious in dealings with China and British India. Nepal was a 'yam between two boulders' and should never provoke them.

King Prithvinarayan was followed on the throne by a succession of minors which led to the concentration of power in the hands of Regents and Prime Ministers until the 1830s. During this period, the boundary of Nepal was extended from the River Tista on the east to the River Satlaj on the west, far beyond the borders of the kingdom today. However, these territorial ambitions were curbed by war with China in 1792 and war with British India in 1814–16 which reduced Nepal to its present size; the 1815 Treaty of Sugauli cost Nepal one-third of its territory.

Out of this crisis emerged a strongman, Bhimsen Thapa. The succession of two minors within a short interval and the support he received from King Rana Bahadur's thirteen year-old widow, Regent Queen Tripurasundari (1806–32), enabled him to enjoy powers never before acquired by a minister. During his administration from 1806 to 1837, the position of kingship reached its lowest ebb before the Rana period.

The Regent Queen died in 1832. Now King Rajendra Bikram Shah (1816–47) asserted his own position with assistance from the Pande family, which had regained a foothold in the court with the backing of the King's first wife, Senior Queen Samrajyalakshmi. They launched a vigorous campaign blaming Bhimsen solely for the disastrous 1814–16 war. But it was the complete dominance of Queen Samrajyalakshmi in court politics that proved Bhimsen's undoing. In 1837, he was dismissed and died two years later in prison.

The fall of Bhimsen, who had run Nepal almost singlehanded for thirty years, gave King Rajendra an opportunity to assert full royal authority, but he proved too weak to carry on the administration alone. An atmosphere of suspicion and uncertainty developed around the throne with intense rivalry between different factions represented by royal collaterals, royal priests and three other leading families of the time, the Thapas, the Pandes and the Basnyats. During the nine years between the fall of Bhimsen and the rise of Jang Bahadur in 1846, eight changes in the government took place; only one Prime Minister died a natural death.

The power of Junior Queen Rajyalakshmi rose steadily following the death of Senior Queen Samrajyalakshmi in October 1841 and, by January 1843, she had acquired plenipotentiary powers from her weak husband. She was obsessed with the ambition of supplanting Heir Apparent Surendra on the throne with her own son, and when she found in her way the Prime Minister, General Mathbar Singh Thapa, she had him murdered in May 1845 with the help of Jang Bahadur Kanwar. Then General Gagan Singh Bhandari, the queen's favorite, commander-in-chief and member of the government, was murdered on September 14, 1846. His death triggered off the most critical event in Nepal's modern history. Queen Rajyalakshmi summoned all leading court officials to an emergency state council that same night in the Kot or Armory near the Palace. Heated exchanges took place, and the Prime Minister, Fatte Jang Shah, and one of his colleagues were shot dead. A third, mortally wounded, accused Jang Bahadur of killing Gagan Singh. It was a free-for-all until Jang's forces arrived to restore order, and nearly thirty people died. Afterwards Jang was appointed Prime Minister by the queen. Many of Nepal's élite responded to this shift in power by leaving the country. Jang put an end to feuding among the remaining élites by centralizing all effective power in his own hands. His rise restored stability to Nepal and helped to prevent British military intervention. Thus, the 'Kot Massacre' paved the way for the emergence of a strong man to cope with the prevailing chaos.

Rulers of Nepal to 1951

The Shah Dynasty of Kings

1743–1775	Prithvinarayan Shah
1777–1779?	Rana Pratap Singh Shah
1779?–1799	Rana Bahadur Shah
?	Girvan Juddha Bikram
1816–1847	Rajendra Bikram Shah
1847–1881	Surendra Bikram Shah
1881–1911	Prithvi Bir Bikram Shah
1911–1955	Tribhuvan Bir Bikram Shah

The Rana Dynasty of Prime Ministers

1846–1877	Jang Bahadur
1877–1885	Ranoddip Singh
1885–1901	Bir Shamsher
1901	Deva Shamsher
1901–1929	Chandra Shamsher Jang Bahadur Rana
1929–1932	Bhim Shamsher
1932–1945	Juddha Shamsher
1945–1948	Padma Shamsher
1948–1951	Mohan Shamsher

Source: RSL.

Box 12

Nepal.

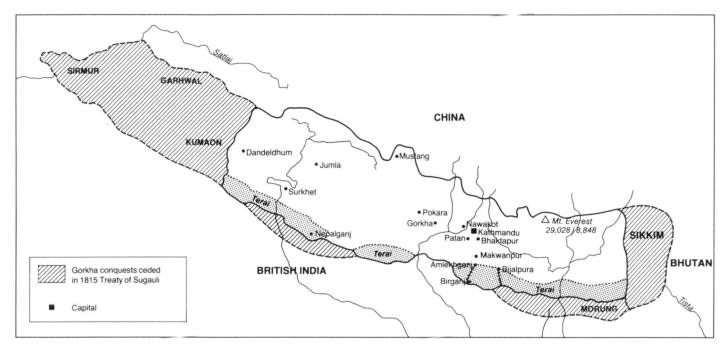

In less than a year, Jang consolidated his position against his royal adversaries by expelling the plenipotentiary queen and her sons to Benares, and, in May 1847, by removing King Rajendra from the throne and putting in his place his son Heir Apparent Surendra. Jang also appointed his own brothers to key government positions and introduced urgently needed reforms. In 1850, Jang paid a visit to Britain and France as the ambassador of his new king. He wished to see for himself the real nature of these European powers. After his return, he introduced a legal code in 1854 and mitigated the severity of punishment for criminal offences. Jang's travels abroad convinced him of the overwhelming might of Britain's military and industrial power. He decided that the safest course for Nepal was friendship with Britain as long as this allowed Nepal to follow its traditional policy of isolation, to exclude foreigners, and to keep contact with the British to the barest minimum. This foreign policy was followed till the very end of the Rana regime in 1951. Nepal assisted the British during the Indian 'Mutiny' uprising of 1857–58 and the two World Wars of the twentieth century.

Jang established a system of hereditary prime ministers with a novel method of agnatic succession regulated by a predetermined roll. He set a pattern of government that lasted for over one hundred years, known as the Rana regime after the name adopted by his family. In August 1856, Jang, maneuvering to gain greater power, temporarily resigned the Prime Ministership in favor of his brother. He was made a Maharaja and obtained a written undertaking from the King that both the monarch and his Prime Minister would abide by the Maharaja's advice in all matters of state policy. They would allow themselves to be disciplined by the Maharaja, if necessary with the help of troops who had instructions to carry out Jang's orders even when in conflict with the commands of the King himself. The Maharaja was also given the power to inflict capital punishment on anyone plotting against him. These rights were made hereditary; while the same agreement provided a predetermined roll of succession for the office of the Prime Minister which was to go to the oldest agnate of the Rana family. This document wrested power from the helpless reigning monarch, King Surendra Bikram (1847–81), and served as the legal basis for the Rana regime for ninety-five years, leading to the institutionalization of the Rana family within the political structure.

Jang's eldest son, General Jagat Jang, should have inherited the office of the Maharaja with absolute powers and the position of Prime Minister should have gone to Ranoddip Singh as the eldest agnate of the family. But after Jang died in 1877, his brothers manipulated King Surendra and had Ranoddip appointed both Maharaja and Prime Minister. Throughout the rest of the Rana period both positions were held by the same person.

Jang's nephew, Bir Shamsher, and his brothers killed Maharaja Ranoddip Singh (1877–85) in November 1885 and Bir was appointed Maharaja and Prime Minister by King Prithvi Bir Bikram Shah (1881–1911). They retained the members of their own family on the roll of succession but removed all the direct descendants of Jang and his other five brothers. Their Shamsher faction of the Rana family remained in firm control of Nepal until 1951.

Maharaja Bir Shamsher (1885–1901) followed the main lines of Jang's foreign policy, but in order to secure British recognition of the legitimacy of his government, and to ward off the threat from the sons of Jang Bahadur and his other brothers who were in exile in India, he was accommodating on the question of Gorkha recruitment into the British Indian Army.

Bir was succeeded by Deva Shamsher but a bloodless coup brought his younger brother, Chandra Shamsher (1901–29) to power three months later. Chandra proved more pro-British than any of his predecessors, assisting the British military expedition to Lhasa under Colonel Younghusband in 1904 and visiting Britain four years later. As a reward for his assistance to Britain in World War I, Nepal received an annual payment of one million Indian rupees in perpetuity. At home, Chandra established the first college in Nepal and introduced social reforms such as the abolition of slavery and of widow burning. He also introduced technical innovations such as electricity in Kathmandu and a short railway line in the terai.

Chandra was succeeded by his brother Bhim Shamsher who was followed in 1932 by another brother Juddha Shamsher (1932–45). Juddha's first problem was a severe earthquake that struck Nepal on January 15, 1934. He successfully managed relief and reconstruction efforts without outside help. Then two months later, he defused a tense political situation by removing several sons and grandsons of Maharajas Bir and Bhim from the roll of succession.

During 1940, a plot to overthrow the Rana government by the Nepal People's Council (*Nepal Praja Parishad*) acting together with King Tribhuvan Bir Bikram Shah (1911–55) was unearthed. Juddha decided not to touch the King but inflicted harsh punishment on all others associated with this organization. Leading members of the organization were executed in January 1941. Several others were sentenced to long terms of imprisonment.

During World War II, Juddha announced that he would retire to a life of prayer once his troops loaned to the British were back in the country. On November 29, 1945, he became the first Rana Prime Minister to relinquish his office voluntarily when he put the Prime Minister's headdress on the head of his nephew, Padma Shamsher (1945–48). But Juddha's forcible suppression of even peaceful efforts to extend civil rights and social reforms inside the country and his opposition to the Indian independence movement proved a hindrance to his successor who is also said to have inherited an empty treasury.

The Rana regime's failure to adjust to post-war changes in the world resulted in its collapse. During the closing years of the 1940s, it was confronted by the withdrawal of the British from India and a Communist government in China. The Ranas proved to be a house divided. Padma did not have the strength to bring about change against the opposition of Chandra's and Juddha's sons who resisted the moderate reforms envisaged in the 1948 constitution and forced Padma's resignation in April 1948.

Padma's successor, Maharaja Mohan Shamsher (1948–51) was the last hereditary Rana Prime Minister. He refused to heed Jawaharlal Nehru's friendly warning that if Nepal did not keep pace with the march of time, it would find itself in serious trouble. By 1950 the situation had deteriorated further. Following the discovery of a plot to assassinate the Prime Minister in September 1950, King Tribhuvan, together with members of the royal family, sought asylum in India. In February 1951, India's firm diplomatic pressure combined with the insurrectionary tactics of the Nepali Congress resulted in King Tribhuvan being restored to the throne. A British-style parliamentary monarchy was adopted, and an interim government formed with an equal representation of the Ranas and the Nepali Congress. Maharaja Mohan remained Prime Minister. This coalition cabinet was supposed to conduct the administration pending elections for the constituent assembly scheduled to be held by the end of 1952. But the Rana–Congress coalition collapsed in November 1951, and King Tribhuvan entrusted the Nepali Congress with the entire charge of the government. Matrika Prasad Koirala, president of the Nepali Congress, now became the first commoner to be Prime Minister of Nepal after 104 years of Rana rule.

RSh

Further reading

R. Shaha, *Heroes and Builders of Nepal* 5th edn (Calcutta, 1970)
R. Shaha, *Essays in the Practice of Government in Nepal* (New Delhi, 1982)
L. F. Stiller, *The Rise of the House of Gorkha* (New Delhi, 1973)
J. Whelpton, *Jang Bahadur in Europe* (Kathmandu, 1983)

Sikkim: internal development and relations with the British

The modern political history of Sikkim commences with the establishment of the Namgyal dynasty in the mid-seventeenth century. The indigenous Lepcha tribal community that inhabited this mid-montane area of the central Himalayas was well-organized along clan lines but not as a centralized polity. Several Tibetan Mahayana Buddhist sects exerted a strong influence over the Lepchas as well as the migrant 'Bhutia' (Tibetan) families from Tibet and Bhutan, but had not established a theocratic-based political system in Sikkim as in those two neighboring hill states. It was in the context of the intense religious/political struggles under-way in Tibet in the seventeenth century that a unified state emerged in Sikkim. The Namgyal family and most of its adherents were political refugees from Tibet who had fled to Sikkim to avoid submission to the Dalai Lama-headed regime based in Lhasa. Indeed, the first consecrated Namgyal ruler, Phuntsog Namgyal, was crowned by three refugee lamas from Tibet in 1642, and established his capital at Gangtok thereafter.

While the Bhutias in Sikkim provided the core support base for the Namgyal dynasty, Phuntsog Namgyal was able to attract cooperation from the key clan leaders in the Lepcha community and also later among the Limbu (Tsongs in Sikkimese) community in eastern Nepal, which formed part of the Namgyal kingdom for 150 years. The political administrative system established by Phuntsog Namgyal reflected the multicommunal character of Sikkimese society. A State Council, consisting of representatives from the twelve main Bhutia clans, was constituted, and provided the officialdom at the royal court. The kingdom was subdivided into twelve *dzongs* (districts) initially headed by Lepcha Dzongpöns (district officers). The second Namgyal ruler revamped the State Council to include representatives from the leading Bhutia, Lepcha and Limbu families. The Court Ministers (*Kajis*) were appointed from the State Council. A broader-based council, called the Lhadé Midé, consisting of all important civil and monastic officials, was summoned at times of national emergencies.

The Namgyal rulers were granted the highest title in the Mahayana Buddhist lexicon – *Chogyal*. *Cho* is religion and *gyal* is king. Thus a Chogyal is a 'religious king', the 'protector of religion', or the 'defender of the faith'. The Namgyal monarch was the head of both the Buddhist establishment and the civil government in Sikkim, and was considered to be a manifestation of Chana Dorje (Vajrapani), one of the Buddhist trilogy.

In the period from 1780 to 1815, Sikkim nearly disappeared as an independent entity due to steady encroachments from both Nepal and Bhutan. It survived, and was reestablished, somewhat reduced in size, after the British–Nepal War of 1814–16, but thereafter was heavily dependent on the British and the Tibetans for its continued existence.

From 1820 to 1885, the Chogyals used complex balance of power strategies, accepting Tibetan and British assistance as deterrents to Nepal and Bhutan, but then seeking to play off the Tibetans against the British in an effort to enhance their own autonomy. It worked as long as no one was particularly interested, but in the 1880s British India and Tibet were trying to work out their own relationship and Sikkim became an issue in dispute. A minor British–Tibetan clash in Sikkim in 1888 led to the Anglo-Tibetan Agreement of 1890 in which Lhasa, in effect, recognized British dominance over Sikkim. Calcutta, unhappy with the games the Chogyal had played, established direct administrative control over Sikkim in 1890 through the appointment of a Political Officer with broad, if unspecified, powers, while the Chogyal was 'temporarily' deprived of all royal powers.

The modernization of Sikkim commenced with the appointment of the Political Officer in 1890, even though the British moved slowly and carefully in reorganizing Sikkim's traditional political system with its intricate devolution of administrative powers and functions. A new State Council was formed, somewhat smaller and less representative than its predecessor under the Chogyal, but with a greater involvement in decision-making. The Dzongpön system was retained, but under careful surveillance by the State Council and the Political Officer. Administrative rules and procedures operative in British India were introduced into Sikkim on a selective basis, and the first modern (Western-style) schools were established.

Perhaps the most important early decision of the British Political Officer in the 1890s was the reversal of the Sikkimese regulation strictly banning Nepali immigration into the country. By 1895,

Sikkim.

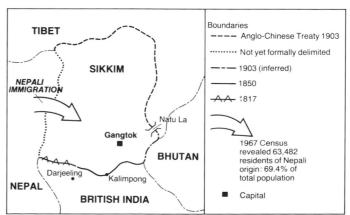

Nepalis were streaming into Sikkim under a well-coordinated settlement program managed by some prominent Nepali families from Darjeeling with long experience at operating under the British. These Nepali landholding families were given the title of Thikadar, the same administrative and revenue-collection responsibilities in southwestern Sikkim that the Bhutia/Lepcha/Kazi families held elsewhere in the country, and representation on the State Council. Within three decades, Nepalis constituted a majority of the population in Sikkim. This had a profound effect upon politics within Sikkim and led eventually, in 1975, to the merger of the country into the Indian Union.

The British gradually allowed the Chogyals to resume a role in the government of Sikkim. In 1905, the Chogyal became the leader of the State Council and then finally in 1918 full internal autonomy was restored to the Sikkim Court. The Chogyal introduced some changes of his own in 1918, appointing three secretaries in the

The Maharani of Sikkim in 1888; she wears the Tibetan head-dress adopted by the Maharanis of Sikkim. 'Her disposition is a masterful one,' declared one visitor, 'and her bearing always dignified.' The Maharaja was entirely under her influence.

Rulers of Sikkim to 1975

The Namgyal Dynasty of Chogyals

1641–c.1670	Phuntsog Namgyal
c.1670–c.1700	Tensung Namgyal
c.1700–c.1717	Chador Namgyal
c.1717–c.1734	Gyurmey Namgyal
1734–c.1780	Namgyal Phuntsog
c.1780–1790	Tendzin Namgyal
1790–1863	Tsugphud Namgyal
1863–1873	Sikyong Namgyal
1873–1914	Thutob Namgyal
1914	Sikyong Tulku
1914–1962	Tashi Namgyal
1962–1975	Palden Thondup Namgyal

Source: W. W. Risley *The Gazetteer of Sikkim* pp. 16–38 (Calcutta, 1894); R. F. Tapsell *Monarchs, Rulers, Dynasties and Kingdoms of the World* p. 424 (London, 1983).

Box 13

Palace, each with jurisdiction over several departments. Later, a private secretariat for the Chogyal was added, headed by a member of the British Indian Foreign Office deputed to Sikkim in this capacity. The disagreements between this British official and the British Political Officer became so disruptive, however, that in 1927 the private secretariat post was abolished.

It was inevitable that the nationalist politics prevalent in India should have an impact on Sikkimese politics, but what is surprising is how long this took to happen. It was only after World War II, when British intentions to withdraw from their Indian empire became apparent even in Gangtok that the various Sikkimese political factions began to organize themselves with post-independence Indian politics in mind. The first political party, the Sikkim State Congress, was formed in December 1947 by members of several 'dissident' Kazi and Thikadari families and their clientele. The Chogyal, seeking to immunize his kingdom from the disruptive developments to the south, sought British recognition of Sikkim's independence, but unsuccessfully. In August 1947, Sikkim ceased being a protectorate of the British Crown and was almost immediately transformed into a protectorate of the newly independent Government of India, with broad internal autonomy exercised under strict Indian supervision thereafter.

LR

Further reading

L. B. Basnet, *Sikkim: a Short Political History* (New Delhi, 1974)

P. Raghunanda Rao, *India and Sikkim, 1814–1970* (New Delhi, 1972)

P. Raghananda Rao, *Sikkim, the Story of its Integration with India* (New Delhi, 1978)

Bhutan: internal development and relations with outside powers to 1952

The small but independent kingdom of Bhutan in the eastern Himalayas occupies a somewhat anomalous position in South Asia. It is the only state in the region without a substantial 'Indian' component in its population, which is made up almost entirely of Tibeto-Burman speaking groups and some recent immigrants from Nepal. Moreover, traditional ties in the past were largely directed northwards to Tibet. Today it is the only country which upholds a form of Lamaist Buddhism as its state religion. And among South Asian countries it has the lowest population density. Located in a range of mountains to which access from the north is made difficult by the main Himalayan range and from the south by dense subtropical forests, Bhutan's geographical isolation is not the only cause of its unique and sovereign status today. Historical and cultural factors can readily be shown to have conspired with geography to ensure its continuing survival.

Prior to the country's unification in the seventeenth century, the eastern Bhutanese speakers of the language known as Tsangla were ruled by clans claiming descent from a refugee Tibetan prince of the ninth century. The western region, inhabited by a composite group known as the Ngalong, was divided into estates ruled by various monastic schools introduced there from Tibet from the eleventh century onwards. The hereditary Buddhist hierarchs who headed these estates enjoyed both spiritual and temporal control over their subjects. In the Bumthang region of central Bhutan, which has its own archaic language affiliated to those of neighboring valleys and to the speech of the northern Monpas in Arunachal Pradesh, there existed a nobility known as the *Dung*. On the peripheries of these important agricultural groups lived very much smaller groups of jungle-dwellers and pastoralists, each distinguished by their own language, dress and customs. The ethnic and linguistic map has hardly changed today.

When the prince-abbot Shabdrung Ngawang Namgyal (1594–?1651), destined to be singly most responsible for unifying the country and giving it its present shape, arrived there as a refugee from Tibet in 1616, he found a land whose multiple barriers had already been partly eroded by a uniform set of religious institutions

Tashicho Dzong, Thimph. The construction of these fortified monasteries in the valleys of Bhutan was the achievement of the Shabdrung Ngawang Namgyal. They were also centers of local government and administration.

Bhutan: internal development and relations with outside powers to 1952

The Nga Chudugma. The seal of the Shabdrung Ngawang Namgyal (1594–?1651), the unifier of Bhutan.

Bhutan.

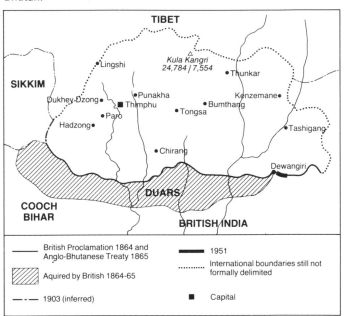

implanted from Tibet, by a common agricultural livelihood capable of yielding profits, and by a network of cultural and trade contacts which had begun to link the main valleys. (The iron chain suspension bridges constructed by the famous saint Thangtong Gyalpo, 1385–1464, had helped to develop these contacts.) The Shabdrung, as he is commonly known by his title, was able to use the monasteries of his own school already founded in the area as a power base from which he extended his control over all the western valleys. He contended successfully not only with rival lamas in the region but also with several Tibetan invasions mounted against him by the Tsangpa and Gelukpa rulers of Tibet. His most visible achievement remains the construction of a series of fortified monasteries (or monastic fortresses, *dzongs*) located in each valley. Those situated in central and eastern Bhutan were built in the 1650s shortly after his death. All these imposing edifices still serve today both as state monasteries and as centers of local government and administration.

The country created by the Shabdrung eventually took its name, Drukyul ('Land of the Thunder Dragon'), from his own school of the Drukpa (a branch of the Kagyüpa, 'School of Oral Transmission'). The Drukpa in turn derived its name from its first monastery in Tibet. 'Bhutan' is really an Indian usage, though now officially and internationally accepted.

The Shabdrung died in about 1651, but until 1705 it was

pretended that he was still alive and in spiritual retreat. During these years successive Regents made protracted and secret attempts to establish a true heir, all of which failed. Ultimately the principle of reincarnation was used (as in the case of Tibet's Dalai Lama) to discover the Shabdrung in a new embodiment. Even then there were difficulties. A compromise solution to the problem of rival claimants was eventually found whereby it was decided that the Shabdrung's body, speech and mind had been reborn in three separate bodies. The 'mind incarnations', known to the British as the Dharma Rajas, came to act as heads of state. The six who achieved recognition in the period 1724 to 1931 were little more than figureheads. The Regents (Deb Rajas of the British records) were their theoretical nominees, but in practice it was usually the strongman of the day who gained office. Until the second half of the nineteenth century, most of the Regents and the often more powerful provincial governors (*pönlop* and *dzongpön*) were fully ordained monks. Those who were not monks were required to abide by a quasi-monastic code of discipline while in office.

At its high point in the eighteenth century the Bhutanese theocracy established relations with the Ahom kings of Assam, the Gorkha kings of Nepal, and with Ladakh and its feudatories in the west. But the most important and difficult relationship continued to be with Tibet. In 1731 the Tibetan ruler Polhané succeeded in imposing suzerainty on Bhutan, and this relationship was in turn formally passed on to Tibet's own overlord, the Ching dynasty of China. Although there is no evidence of either Tibet or China ever

Rulers of Bhutan from the unification of the state

Heads of State[a]

1724–1761	Jigme Dragpa I
1762–1788	Chöeki Gyaltshen
1791–1830	Jigme Dragpa II
1831–1861	Jigme Norbu
1862–1904	Jigme Chhogyal
1905–1931	Jigme Dorji

Regents[b]

1651–1656	Tendzin Drugye
1656–1667	Tendzin Drugdra
1667–1680	Minjur Tempa
1680–1695	Tendzin Rabgye
1695–1701	Gedün Chomphel
1701–1704	Ngawang Tshering
1704–1707	Umdze Peljor
1707–1719	Druk Rabgye
1719–1729	Ngawang Gyamtsho
1729–1736	Mipham Wangpo
1736–1739	Khuwo Peljor
1739–1744	Ngawang Gyaltshen
1744–1763	Sherab Wangchuk
1763–1765	Druk Phuntsho
1765–1768	Druk Tendzin
1768–1773	Sonam Lhundub
1773–1776	Kunga Rinchen
1776–1788	Jigme Singye
1788–1792	Druk Tendzin
1792–1799	Tashi Namgyal
1799–1803	Druk Namgyal
1803–1805	Tashi Namgyal
1805–1806	Sangye Tendzin
1806–1808	Umdze Parop (with Böp Chöda)
1807–1808	Böp Chöda
1809–1810	Tsulthrim Drayga
1810–1811	Jigme Dragpa II
1811–1815	Yeshey Gyaltshen
1815	Tshaphu Dorji
1815–1819	Sonam Drugyal
1819–1823	Tendzin Drugdra

1823–1831	Chöki Gyaltshen
1831–1832	Dorji Namgyal
1832–1835	Adap Thrinley
1835–1838	Chöki Gyaltshen
1838–1847	Dorji Norbu (with Tashi Dorji)
1847–1850	Tashi Dorji
1850	Wangchuk Gyalpo
1850–1852	Jigme Norbu (ruled from Thimpu)
1851–1852	Chagpa Sangye (ruled from Punakha)
1852–1856	Damchö Lhundrup
1856–1861	Kunga Palden (ruled from Punakha) with Sherab Tharchin (ruled from Thimpu)
1861–1864	Phuntsho Namgyal
1864	Tshewang Sithub
1864	Tsulthrim Yonten
1864	Kagyü Wangchuk
1864–1866	Tshewang Sithub
1866–1870	Tsöndrü Pekar
1870–1873	Jigme Namgyal
1873–1879	Kitsep Dorji Namgyal
1879–1882	Chögyal Zangpo
1882–1884	Lam Tshewang
1884–1886	Gawa Zangpo
1886–1903	Sangye Dorji
1903–1905	Choley Yeshe Ngödub

Hereditary Kings of Bhutan[c]

1907–1926	Ugyen Wangchuk
1926–1952	Jigme Wangchuk

[a]'Mental incarnations' of Shabdrung Ngawang Namgyal, the unifier of Bhutan, who are known in the British records as 'Dharma Rajas' and in the Bhutanese records as the 'Shabdrung Thuktrul'.
[b]The effective rulers of Bhutan who are known in the British records as 'Deb Rajas' and in the Bhutanese records as the 'Druk Desi'.
[c]Known as the Druk Gyalpo.

Source: M. Aris *Bhutan: The Early History of a Himalayan Kingdom* pp. 270–74 (Warminster and New Delhi, 1979)

Box 14

having implemented their rule in Bhutan, both occasionally claimed a legitimate right to interfere in local politics, though their attempts were rarely successful.

Beset by constant regional struggles, the theocracy nevertheless succeeded in introducing a uniform ideology and style of government which none opposed, however heavily the state weighed on its subjects. In the field of Buddhist art and scholarship the monks developed a national style that could stand up to the best Tibetan traditions.

British involvement with Bhutan began in the 1770s and 1780s with a number of missions sent by Warren Hastings after a conflict between Cooch Bihar and Bhutan. The sympathetic accounts left by these missions show that they were motivated as much by a desire to extend the frontiers of knowlege as to open a trade route to central

Asia. The British missions of the nineteenth century were by contrast mainly aimed at containing the predatory activities of the border Bhutanese in the frontier regions of Bengal and Assam. While the Bhutan state had won for itself various traditional rights over these areas (known as the *duars*), it seems the center had little control over their exploitation by local officials and raiding parties. But the government benefited too, since the income derived from these areas helped it to maintain the state monks in the capital and provincial dzongs. Furthermore, Indian slaves captured in the plains, or descended from them, were employed both by the state and its taxpayers.

The disastrous mission of 1864 led by Ashley Eden directly resulted in a border war that left Bhutan, despite some initial successes, without any of its eighteen duars. An annual sum was paid by the British, and is still paid by the Government of India, by way of compensation for the sequestration of these lands.

The British defeat of Bhutan did nothing to affect the fortunes of their chief enemy, Jigme Namgyal, the pönlop of Tongsa. Five years later he was enthroned Regent, and after a four-year rule he continued to fill the post with men of his choice until his death in 1881. The period was one of almost continuous civil war. Jigme Namgyal's own son, Ugyen Wangchuk, finally emerged triumphant from these struggles in 1907 when he was elected as Bhutan's first hereditary monarch. His accession was made possible not only by strength of arms but by other factors too. Most Bhutanese were genuinely weary of civil strife. The British offered him strong support (he had acted as mediator during the Younghusband mission to Tibet of 1904). And he had the advantage of illustrious descent from probably the most famous of Bhutanese saints, Pemalingpa (1450–1521).

To counter a Chinese threat from the north the British concluded a treaty with Bhutan in 1911 whereby in exchange for agreeing not to interfere in Bhutan's internal administration, the Bhutanese agreed 'to be guided by the advice of India in regard to its foreign relations'. Just as the events of 1731 had occasionally been seen as incorporating Bhutan within the Chinese empire, so was this treaty sometimes taken to imply Bhutan's inclusion within the British empire. It was renewed in 1949 by the second king Jigme Wangchuk and the newly independent government of India, but the relevant clause now seems to be regarded by both parties as a colonial fragment that is best forgotten.

During the reigns of Ugyen Wangchuk (1907–26) and Jigme Wangchuk (1926–52) no radical changes were introduced to mark a definite break with the past. Both kings consolidated their personal rule by appointing members of their family and trusted confidants to all key posts. The demise in 1931 of the last officially recognized Shabdrung, in circumstances which have never been fully explained, was followed by the appearance of further unsuccessful claimants. The first attempts to introduce a modern army and schools were made, but with little help from the British. It was left to the third king to open the doors to the twentieth century and to achieve international recognition for Bhutan's independence.

MAr

Further reading
M. Aris, *Bhutan: The Early History of a Himalayan Kingdom* (Warminster and New Delhi, 1979)
M. Aris, *Views of Medieval Bhutan: The Diary and Drawings of Samuel Davis, 1783* (London, Washington D.C., and New Delhi, 1982)
M. Aris, *Sources for the History of Bhutan* Wiener Studien zur Tibetologie und Buddhismuskunde, Heft 14, Vienna, 1986
K. Labh, *India and Bhutan* (New Delhi, 1974)
J. C. White, *Sikhim and Bhutan: Twenty-one Years on the North-East Frontier, 1887–1908* (London, 1909)

Maldives

The Maldive Islands have been an independent state since early in the Christian era. The earliest mention is perhaps by Ammianus Marcellinus, who wrote that in 362 the Roman Emperor Julian received embassies *ab usque Divis et Serendivis*. The Serendivi are clearly from Sri Lanka (Seren = Ceylon), the Divi may be from the Maldives, whose name to its own inhabitants is *Divehi Rajje*, 'the island kingdom'. In the ninth century Sulaiman the Merchant describes them as ruled by a queen. The people were probably already Buddhists, as is shown by remains of stupas on various islands, and it seems that the power of the sovereign extended over

The Minaret and Muslim graveyard at Malé in the Maldives.

the whole 500 miles of the group from Minicoy in the north to Addu in the south, and that Malé (which is central) was already the capital. Maldivians have always depended on trade for supplies of grain and textiles, which are not available on the islands, in return for fish, coconut products, ambergris and cowries; these last were used, in huge quantities, as international currency. Recent excavations in Malé testify to regular visits of Chinese traders on their west-bound journeys by the tenth century. In 1153, the Maldive king was converted to Islam, either by Yusuf Shams ud Din of Tabriz or by Abul Barakat the 'Berber', and from this time onwards there is a written history of the sultanate, compiled in Arabic, originally in 1725, supplemented by a few records in Divehi (Maldivian), a language akin to Sinhala.

A lengthy description of the islands is given by the North African traveler Ibn Battuta, who resided there for two separate periods in 1343–44 (when he became Qazi or Chief Justice) and 1346. Though the islands were solidly Muslim by this time, they still happened to be ruled by a queen, and Ibn Battuta commented unfavorably on the latitude allowed to women there.

The Portuguese became involved in Maldivian affairs during their struggle with Mamale of Kannanur in southwest India, who claimed suzerainty over the king of the Maldives, and they occupied Malé from 1558 to 1573, after the then king had become a Christian. They were expelled by the efforts of Bodu Muhammad Takuru-fanu, founder of a new dynasty and the greatest hero of Maldivian history, whose birthplace in a small northern island is kept as a shrine today. The northernmost island of Maliku (Minicoy) remained permanently under the control of Kannanur after this time.

In 1602 the Frenchman François Pyrard of Laval was ship-wrecked on one of the Maldivian islands, whence he was transported to Malé and kept prisoner for five years. He learnt to speak the Divehi language, and his account of the islands, published in France in 1611, after he had managed to escape, constitutes the most extensive description of the country available before the nineteenth century.

After 1645 the Maldivian government sent an annual embassy to the Dutch Governor in Ceylon, and to his successors the British Governors until 1947, but there was never a colonial occupation. A full survey of the islands was made in 1835 by Lts Young and Christopher of the Indian Navy, and in 1887 a British protectorate over the Maldives was declared. A British man-of-war paid an annual visit thereafter, but the islands were unhealthy and generally avoided, except for the Cambridge scientific expedition of 1899–1900 and the American expedition of 1901.

The Maldive kings in the latter part of the nineteenth century fell heavily into debt to resident Borah merchants from Gujarat, and the resulting intrigues in Malé led the British government to some reluctant involvement in Maldivian politics in the early twentieth century. In 1932 the king (the title 'Sultan' was only used in formal contexts) was compelled by his nobles to accept a constitution; he was later deposed and exiled.

During World War II British forces used bases in Maldivian territory.

Rulers of the Maldives to the mid-twentieth century

1573–1584	Bodu Muhammad Takurufanu al Alam
1584–1609	Ibrahim ibn Muhammad
1609–1620	Husain Famuderi
1620–1648	Imad ud Din Muhammad I
1648–1687	Ibrahim Iskandar I
1687–1691	Muhammad Ibn Ibrahim
1691–1692	Muhi ud Din Muhammad
1692	Shams ud din Muhammad al Hamawi
1692–1700	Muhammad Ibn Hajji Ali
1700–1701	Ali
1701	Hasan ibn Ali
1701–1705	Muzhir ud Din Ibrahim
1705–1721	Imad ud Din Muhammad II
1721–1750	Ibrahim Iskandar II
1750–1754	Imad ud Din Muhammad Mukarram
1760–1766	Izz ud Din Hasan Ghazi
1766–1773	Ghiyas ud Din Muhammad
1773–1774	Ghams ud Din Muhammad
1774–1778	Muizz ud Din Muhammad
1778–1798	Nur ud Din Muhammad
1798–1834	Muin ud Din Muhammad
1834–1882	Imad ud Din Muhammad III
1882–1886	Nur ud Din Ibrahim (first reign)
1886–1888	Muin ud Din Muhammad II
1888–1892	Nur ud Din Ibrahim (second reign)
1892–1893	Imad ud Din Muhammad IV
1893	Shams ud Din Muhammad Iskandar (first reign)
1893–1903	Imad ud Din Muhammad V
1903–1935	Shams ud Din Muhammad Iskandar (second reign)
1935–1945	Nur ud Din Hasan Iskandar
1945–1952	Abdul Majid Didi

Source: R. F. Tapsell *Monarchs Rulers Dynasties and Kingdoms of the World* p. 445 (London, 1983).

Box 15

Laccadives

The term 'Laccadive' or 'Lakshadweep' means '100,000 islands' and the name originally included the Maldives also, the modern Laccadives consisting of only 27 islands. They were settled by Hindu people from the Malabar coast of India – the people today (except in Minicoy) speak a form of Malayalam – and the traditional date of the introduction of Islam is 661.

The Chola emperors claimed suzerainty over the Laccadives in the eleventh century, but by 1200 they had fallen into the control of the Muslim rulers of Kannanur. The southern islands of the group remained under nominal control of Kannanur until 1908, though the three northern islands fell into the East India Company's domains in 1799.

The island of Maliku or Minicoy, the largest and most populous of the whole group, lies to the south of the Laccadives proper, and is inhabited by Maldivian speakers who were Buddhists until the twelfth century. It also fell under the sway of the rulers of Kannanur before 1500; however, it remains Maldivian today in language and social organization. The lighthouse, on the direct Aden–Colombo route, was opened in 1885.

Andamans

The Andamans have been settled from antiquity and are mentioned by passing travelers such as I Tsing (672) and Marco Polo (1286), but no detailed information is available until Blair's survey of 1788 for the East India Company. The Andamans were officially colonized by the Company in 1789, but owing to a malign climate the station was closed in 1796. It was reopened in 1858, primarily as a penal settlement, and continued as such until World War II. The original Andamanese, negritos who speak a unique type of language, were severely reduced in number during this period as Indian settlement progressed. Viceroy Lord Mayo was assassinated while visiting the islands in 1872.

The islands were occupied by the Japanese in 1942, and in 1943 were visited by Subhas Chandra Bose (Netaji) who hoped that they might become the first liberated portion of independent India.

Nicobars

The Nicobars have been settled from antiquity by speakers of languages of the Mon-Khmer type, but except for a claim by the Chola emperor Rajendra to have conquered *Nakkavaram* (1050), little is known of them before the arrival of European travelers. Spanish priests arrived there in the seventeenth century, one of whom was still resident when William Dampier arrived in 1688. There are descriptions by Dampier, and in the notebooks of the Swedish naturalist Dr J. G. Koenig who visited in 1778. Numerous attempts were made in the seventeenth and eighteenth centuries to set up Christian mission stations in the Nicobars by the French and especially the Danes, but all succumbed to the climate. In 1869 the British took possession, treating the islands as part of the Andaman dependency. A prison settlement was kept there until 1888.

During the occupation by the Japanese in 1942–45, the unofficial leader of the islanders was an Anglican priest of Indian extraction, John Richardson, who subsequently became a Bishop and presided over a considerable expansion of Christianity in the main island, Car Nicobar.

CHBR

Further reading

Maldives
C. Maloney, *People of the Maldive Islands* (Madras, 1980)
T. Malten, *Malediven und Lakkadiven (Materiale zur Bibliographie)* (Wiesbaden, 1983)
F. Pyrard, *Voyage* 3rd edn (Paris 1619), tr. A. Gray, Hakluyt Society 1st series 76, 77, 80 (London, 1887–1890)

Laccadives
M. Ramunny, *States of our Union: Lakshadweep* Govt. of India, 2nd edn (Delhi, 1979)

Andamans and Nicobars
L. P. Mathur, *History of the Andaman and Nicobar Islands (1795–1966)* (Delhi, 1968)

Opposite **A** India: cartoon by Laxman of the *Times of India* (Bombay), early 1970s. **B** Bangladesh: anonymous cartoon, 1987. **C** Sri Lanka: an election cartoon of 1956 based on a scene from the life of the Buddha where he is confronted by a threat from the powerful forces of death. Here the threat to modern Buddhism is from the UNP government in alliance with USA imperialism, westernization and debauchery. The Prime Minister, Sir John Kotalewala rides the elephant with a belly dancer and directs his spear at the Buddha. The elephant is led by Sir Oliver Goonetilleke, the Governor-General, while J. R. Jayawardene (then minister of agriculture) clings to its tail. **D** Pakistan: cartoon by Jawed Iqbal of the *Daily Jang* (Lahore) 1987. Maulana Noorani, a leading mullah politician, tells the carpenter: 'if the Round Table Conference fails, then make small stools of the round table'.

POLITICS

...we must be cautious—some rich nations are jealous of the progress we have made....

Introduction

The states of South Asia emerged from British colonial rule with a diversity of historical experiences and encounters with British imperialism. The Indian nationalist movement under Gandhi's leadership was a model and a beacon for all the colonial states in Asia and Africa. In Sri Lanka, however, a broad-based confrontational movement against British authority never developed, while Nepal managed to retain its Independence throughout the period of British paramountcy in South Asia.

There was no single British 'impact' upon the several South Asian states, but rather a complex series of interactions with social groups and local political systems, in which the various peoples of the region selected some aspects of Western civilization for emulation, while they rejected or adapted others. Moreover, British rule did not always have 'modernizing' consequences, but sometimes involved reinforcement of aspects of tradition. The British introduced ideas of political equality, judicial rationality, and a secular state which did not interfere in any serious way with the diverse religious practices of the people. On the other hand, caste was recognized in the censuses, in courts of law, and in military recruitment and British courts applied the separate religious laws of the major religious communities in South Asia in important matters relating to marriage, divorce and inheritance.

In fact, the peoples of South Asia have retained a strong sense of continuity with the past through the preservation and even the re-creation of ancient institutions, ideas and practices, while simultaneously accepting many modernizing changes most of which have occurred without displacing existing institutions and practices. Statutory *panchayats* (councils) were introduced at the village level in several South Asian states to recreate presumed forms of local government from the ancient past, some ascriptive caste groups were converted into semi-voluntary caste associations, and Pakistan and Sri Lanka deliberately departed from Western models of the secular state. Islam provided the ideological justification for the creation of Pakistan and has been an integral part of Pakistani nationalism ever since. Islam is, in effect, if not in formal declaration, the state religion of Pakistan and Islamic courts exist to enforce the Muslim personal law (*sharia*). In Sri Lanka, Buddhism also has a prominent place as the predominant religion of the country entitled to special consideration and protection.

The British provided a firmer physical basis for unity on the Indian subcontinent and in the island of Sri Lanka than had ever existed before through such means as the development of modern systems of transportation, communication and bureaucratic control. However, their rule was also associated with the intensification of numerous cultural, linguistic and regional differences among the peoples of South Asia, some of whom felt that they had lost ground in education, in public service, or in income compared with other groups, and who feared dominance by those groups when the British departed. At Independence, the leaders of the Muslim League succeeded in separating the Muslim-majority provinces from India on the grounds that the Muslims had suffered in comparison with the Hindus, who would continue to press their advantage in an independent India. In Sri Lanka, the bases for the later civil war between Tamils and Sinhalese had already been laid in the differential advantage that some Tamils had gained in English education and entrepreneurial activity in relation to the Sinhalese.

Politically, both India and Sri Lanka had experienced the gradual introduction of representative institutions and limited forms of self-government during British rule. India, Pakistan and Sri Lanka also adopted at Independence variants of the British parliamentary system, but with differential success and consequences in the long term.

Of all the expectations held at Independence, the one that has been least fulfilled in the former colonial countries of Asia and Africa has been the belief that Western forms of parliamentarism, democracy and participation in electoral politics and in public life generally could be sustained. Virtually everywhere in Asia and Africa, parliamentary institutions, political parties and elections have been replaced by military-bureaucratic states.

The political history of the South Asian states since Independence presents the full range of experiences characteristic of the former colonial states elsewhere. Broadly speaking, those experiences have encompassed the following types of regimes. India, exceptionally among postcolonial states, has functioned since Independence, save for a two-year period of authoritarian rule between 1975 and 1977, with a full-fledged, highly participatory and competitive federal parliamentary system. Pakistan, in contrast, has undergone several regime changes, alternating between unstable competitive parliamentary systems and military-bureaucratic autocracies.

Bangladesh, after its successful secession from Pakistan with the aid of the Indian army in 1971, began its independent political life with a plebiscitary leadership, which terminated with the assassination of Sheikh Mujibur Rahman and most members of his family in 1975. Since then the country has undergone a succession of military coups none of which has been able to establish a stable and effective political order, although General Zia ur Rahman had developed some popularity and had established a reputation for efficiency and effectiveness during his rule from 1975 until he too was assassinated in 1981. Sri Lanka moved from three decades of parliamentarism to a presidential system modeled on the French type after 1977, but has in the 1980s descended into anarchy and civil war. The Maldives converted from a monarchy to a presidential republic for a brief period in 1953 and then again in 1968 with the inauguration of a second republic. Nepal and Bhutan have retained monarchical forms of government.

It is impossible to avoid the conclusion that, forty years after the departure of the British from South Asia, no one type of regime has become entrenched in any country, with the possible archaic exception of Nepal. Nor is it possible to say that the boundaries of the states of South Asia have now been fixed. One successful secession has already occurred in South Asia, that of Bangladesh which, aside from the partition of Cyprus, has been the only successful secession in the postwar postcolonial world.

Most troubling of all, however, has been the spread and intensification of violence of all sorts throughout South Asia, including state-directed violence against dissident minorities and the entrenchment in some parts of the region of extremely vicious forms of terrorism against wholly innocent groups of peaceful civilians.

PRB

India

Introduction

India arrived at Independence after a long struggle and with a multiplicity of heritages and legacies which influenced its post-Independence course in complex ways. One legacy was the various institutions, ideas, and practices introduced during British rule. A second was the existing social order, the social structure and social conflicts which surrounded and influenced political movements, ideas and practices. A third was the shared experience of those Indians who participated in or identified with the nationalist movement and its great leaders.

Constitution and the colonial legacy

There was a considerable degree of continuity between the Government of India Act of 1935 and the Constitution of India. The government of independent India also decided to retain the characteristic feature of British autocratic rule, the Indian Civil Service (ICS), changed in name only to the Indian Administrative Service (IAS). However, the Constitution adopts in total the Westminster form of parliamentary government rather than the mixed parliamentary-bureaucratic authoritarian system which actually existed in India. Moreover, fundamental rights were included in the Constitution of India, but not in the Government of India Act of 1935.

The Constitution also contains some unique features that reflect a desire to depart from strict British parliamentary practices and to introduce into the charter of the country a program of social and economic reform. Most notable in this respect is the simultaneous presence in the Constitution of lists of both Fundamental Rights of the People and Directive Principles, a combination of protections for the people against the encroachments of state authority with directives to the state to introduce specified reforms to make those rights effective.

Nevertheless, most of the specific features of the Constitution of India and the administrative structure retained or adopted at Independence represented borrowings from abroad, which had to be adapted to the social structure, traditions and practices of an entirely different society.

Social structure: communal and caste bases of Indian politics

It was commonly argued by the British rulers of India that parliamentary democracy was unsuited to a society intensely divided into religious and other communal groupings whose social structure also was imbued with an ideology of hierarchy rather than equality. Indian nationalists, however, argued strongly against such ideas and insisted that Hindu–Muslim communalism itself was a British creation and that, left to themselves, Hindus and Muslims would work together in a secular political order and would divide internally on economic and class, rather than religious lines.

They also argued against the view that caste Hindus and untouchable and other low castes could hardly be expected to work together as equals in a democratic political order, that the former would maintain the rigidity of traditional hierarchies and caste discriminations which would prevent the poor and disadvantaged low castes from participating effectively in politics. At Independence, although the Congress leaders resisted any efforts to create separate electorates for the low castes, the Constitution and government policies instituted mechanisms and procedures to ensure their full participation as equal citizens in the new order. These mechanisms and procedures included reservation of seats in the legislatures and other bodies, the maintenance of a list of low caste groups on a schedule (hence the name Scheduled Castes) entitling them to special privileges and preferential policies of all sorts, the abolition of untouchability and the like.

Divisions among the élite and middle status land-controlling castes in large parts of India also existed at Independence. Backward caste leaders had argued before Independence that their place was insecure under a parliamentary system which the élite castes could turn to their advantage and that they too, like the Scheduled Castes, required special protections.

These issues of Hindu–Muslim communal relations, of the integration of the low castes as effective participants in a democratic political order, and of caste conflict between the backward castes and the élite castes have persisted throughout the post-Independence period up to the present and have posed recurring challenges to the maintenance of an integrated society, an egalitarian politics and non-violent mechanisms of conflict resolution.

Administrative divisions of India.

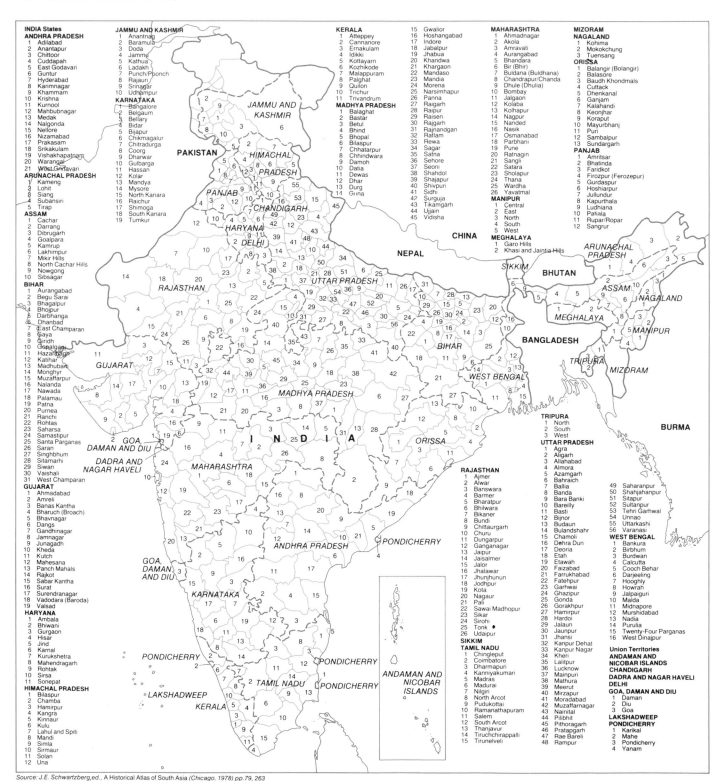

INDIA States

ANDHRA PRADESH
1 Adilabad
2 Anantapur
3 Chittoor
4 Cuddapah
5 East Godavari
6 Guntur
7 Hyderabad
8 Karimnagar
9 Khammam
10 Krishna
11 Kurnool
12 Mahbubnagar
13 Medak
14 Nalgonda
15 Nellore
16 Nizamabad
17 Prakasam
18 Srikakulam
19 Vishakhapatnam
20 Warangal
21 West Godavari

ARUNACHAL PRADESH
1 Kameng
2 Lohit
3 Siang
4 Subansiri
5 Tirap

ASSAM
1 Cachar
2 Darrang
3 Dibrugarh
4 Goalpara
5 Kamrup
6 Lakhimpur
7 Mikir Hills
8 North Cachar Hills
9 Nowgong
10 Sibsagar

BIHAR
1 Aurangabad
2 Begu Sarai
3 Bhagalpur
4 Bhojpur
5 Darbhanga
6 Dhanbad
7 East Champaran
8 Gaya
9 Giridh
10 Gopalganj
11 Hazaribagh
12 Katihar
13 Madhubani
14 Monghyr
15 Muzaffarpur
16 Nalanda
17 Nawada
18 Palamau
19 Patna
20 Purnea
21 Ranchi
22 Rohtas
23 Saharsa
24 Samastipur
25 Santa Parganas
26 Saran
27 Singhbhum
28 Sitamarhi
29 Siwan
30 Vaishali
31 West Champaran

GUJARAT
1 Ahmadabad
2 Amreli
3 Banas Kantha
4 Bharuch (Broach)
5 Bhavnagar
6 Dangs
7 Gandhinagar
8 Jamnagar
9 Junagadh
10 Kheda
11 Kutch
12 Mahesana
13 Panch Mahals
14 Rajkot
15 Sabar Kantha
16 Surat
17 Surendranagar
18 Vadodara (Baroda)
19 Valsad

HARYANA
1 Ambala
2 Bhiwani
3 Gurgaon
4 Hisar
5 Jind
6 Karnal
7 Kurukshetra
8 Mahendragarh
9 Rohtak
10 Sirsa
11 Sonepat

HIMACHAL PRADESH
1 Bilaspur
2 Chamba
3 Hamirpur
4 Kangra
5 Kinnaur
6 Kulu
7 Lahul and Spiti
8 Mandi
9 Simla
10 Sirmaur
11 Solan
12 Una

JAMMU AND KASHMIR
1 Anantnag
2 Baramula
3 Doda
4 Jammu
5 Kathua
6 Ladakh
7 Punch/Poonch
8 Rajauri
9 Srinagar
10 Udhampur

KARNATAKA
1 Bangalore
2 Belgaum
3 Bellary
4 Bidar
5 Bijapur
6 Chikmagalur
7 Chitradurga
8 Coorg
9 Dharwar
10 Gulbarga
11 Hassan
12 Kolar
13 Mandya
14 Mysore
15 North Kanara
16 Raichur
17 Shimoga
18 South Kanara
19 Tumkur

KERALA
1 Atteppey
2 Cannanore
3 Ernakulam
4 Idikki
5 Kottayarn
6 Kozhikode
7 Malappuram
8 Palghat
9 Quilon
10 Trichur
11 Trivandrum

MADHYA PRADESH
1 Balaghat
2 Bastar
3 Betul
4 Bhind
5 Bhopal
6 Bilaspur
7 Chhatarpur
8 Chhindwara
9 Damoh
10 Datia
11 Dewas
12 Dhar
13 Durg
14 Giína
15 Gwalior
16 Hoshangabad
17 Indore
18 Jabalpur
19 Jhabua
20 Khandwa
21 Khargaon
22 Mandaso
23 Mandia
24 Morena
25 Narsimhapur
26 Panna
27 Raigarh
28 Rajpur
29 Raisen
30 Rajgarh
31 Rajnandgan
32 Ratlam
33 Rewa
34 Sagar
35 Satna
36 Sehore
37 Seoni
38 Shahdol
39 Shajapur
40 Shivpuri
41 Sidhi
42 Surguja
43 Tikamgarh
44 Ujjain
45 Vidisha

MAHARASHTRA
1 Ahmadnagar
2 Akola
3 Amravati
4 Aurangabad
5 Bhandara
6 Bir (Bhir)
7 Buldana (Buldhana)
8 Chandrapur/Chanda
9 Dhule (Dhulia)
10 Bombay
11 Jalgaon
12 Kolaba
13 Kolhapur
14 Nagpur
15 Nanded
16 Nasik
17 Osmanabad
18 Parbhani
19 Pune
20 Ratnagin
21 Sangli
22 Satara
23 Sholapur
24 Thana
25 Wardha
26 Yavatmal

MANIPUR
1 Central
2 East
3 North
4 South
5 West

MEGHALAYA
1 Garo Hills
2 Khasi and Jaintia Hills

MIZORAM

NAGALAND
1 Kohima
2 Mokokchung
3 Tuensang

ORISSA
1 Balangir (Bolangir)
2 Balasore
3 Baudh Khondmals
4 Cuttack
5 Dhenkanal
6 Ganjam
7 Kalahandi
8 Keonjhar
9 Koraput
10 Mayurbhanj
11 Puri
12 Sambalpur
13 Sundargarh

PANJAB
1 Amritsar
2 Bhatinda
3 Faridkot
4 Firozpur (Ferozepur)
5 Gurdaspur
6 Hoshiarpur
7 Jullundur
8 Kapurthala
9 Ludhiana
10 Patiala
11 Rupar/Ropar
12 Sangrur

TRIPURA
1 North
2 South
3 West

UTTAR PRADESH
1 Agra
2 Aligarh
3 Allahabad
4 Almora
5 Azamgarh
6 Bahraich
7 Ballia
8 Banda
9 Bara Banki
10 Bareilly
11 Basti
12 Bijnor
13 Budaun
14 Bulandshahr
15 Chamoli
16 Dehra Dun
17 Deoria
18 Etah
19 Etawah
20 Faizabad
21 Farrukhabad
22 Fatehpur
23 Garhwai
24 Ghazipur
25 Gonda
26 Gorakhpur
27 Hamirpur
28 Hardoi
29 Jalaun
30 Jaunpur
31 Jhansi
32 Kanpur Dehat
33 Kanpur Nagar
34 Kheri
35 Lalitpur
36 Lucknow
37 Mainpuri
38 Mathura
39 Meerut
40 Mirzapur
41 Moradabad
42 Muzaffarnagar
43 Nainital
44 Pilibhit
45 Pithoragarh
46 Pratapgarh
47 Rae Bareli
48 Rampur
49 Saharanpur
50 Shahjahanpur
51 Sitapur
52 Sultanpur
53 Tehri Garhwal
54 Unnao
55 Uttarkashi
56 Varanasi

WEST BENGAL
1 Bankura
2 Birbhum
3 Burdwan
4 Calcutta
5 Cooch Behar
6 Darjeeling
7 Hooghly
8 Howrah
9 Jalpaiguri
10 Malda
11 Midnapore
12 Murshidabad
13 Nadia
14 Purulia
15 Twenty-Four Parganas
16 West Dinajpur

RAJASTHAN
1 Ajmer
2 Alwar
3 Banswara
4 Barmer
5 Bharatpur
6 Bhilwara
7 Bikaner
8 Bundi
9 Chittaurgarh
10 Churu
11 Dungarpur
12 Ganganagar
13 Jaipur
14 Jaisalmer
15 Jalor
16 Jhalawar
17 Jhunjhunun
18 Jodhpur
19 Kota
20 Nagaur
21 Pali
22 Sawai Madhopur
23 Sikar
24 Sirohi
25 Tonk
26 Udaipur

SIKKIM

TAMIL NADU
1 Chingleput
2 Coimbatore
3 Dharmapuri
4 Kanniyakumari
5 Madras
6 Madurai
7 Nilgiri
8 North Arcot
9 Pudukottai
10 Ramanathapuram
11 Salem
12 South Arcot
13 Thanjavur
14 Tiruchchirappalli
15 Tirunelveli

Union Territories

ANDAMAN AND NICOBAR ISLANDS

CHANDIGARH

DADRA AND NAGAR HAVELI

DELHI

GOA, DAMAN AND DIU
1 Daman
2 Diu
3 Goa

LAKSHADWEEP

PONDICHERRY
1 Karikal
2 Mahe
3 Pondicherry
4 Yanam

Source: J.E. Schwartzberg,ed., A Historical Atlas of South Asia (Chicago, 1978) pp.79, 263

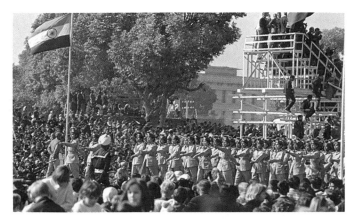

The march past on India's Republic Day which is celebrated on January 26.

Transformation of a nationalist movement into a governing political party

Three quarters of a century of thought and struggle over defining the Indian nation, over freeing the country from alien occupation and over the desirable shape of the social and economic order in a future independent India had provided the nationalist leadership at Independence with a set of ideas and goals that helped to structure their responses to the problems of governing the newly independent country. At the top of all their goals, the *sine qua non* for everything else, was an abiding faith in and determination to preserve the national unity and integrity of the country against all potential internal and external threats to it. The very fact that this first priority, the center of the dreams of the Congress nationalists, had to be sacrificed at Independence itself, with the partition of the country, re-enforced the determination of the leaders never to make such a sacrifice again.

In the process of transforming itself from a mass movement claiming to represent the entire nation into a political party engaged in free and open competition with other parties for dominance in a democratic political system, the Congress leaders had, however, to make a number of changes and compromises in relation to other groups whose demands were neither secessionist nor communal religious. In dealing with internal and external dissident forces, the leaders of the Indian National Congress have followed hegemonic policies of absorption in relation to some groups, have deliberately set out to destroy others, and have adopted tolerant and conciliatory stances in relation to still others.

Scheduled Castes had largely been left out of the Congress during the nationalist movement and its leaders set out to rectify this situation quickly after Independence by such measures as giving Dr Ambedkar, the great untouchable leader, a central role in the Constitution-making process, by seeking to provide other Scheduled Caste persons with positions as ministers in the central and state governments, and by pursuing a variety of preferential policies designed to improve their social standing and ameliorate their economic deprivations.

The Congress had, for the most part, avoided supporting direct class confrontations between the tenants and landlords in British-ruled India in order to preserve maximal unity in the fight against the British themselves. However, once Independence was achieved, the Congress governments in most states moved to expropriate the former princes and landlords through the passage of various land reform measures such as abolition of all intermediaries between the cultivator and the state and legislation placing a ceiling on the amount of land which could be owned.

In relation to political opposition groups, the Congress was prepared to allow free and open competition. This did not, however, stop the Congress from adopting quite ruthless political tactics to defeat such early opposition parties as the Socialists who split from the Congress in 1948 and the left wing of the Communist party, against which the full powers of the state were used in the 1950s and 1960s to displace its leaders from power in Kerala and to imprison its cadres under preventive detention laws elsewhere in the country. The Congress also, from time to time, adopted repressive measures against parties considered to be communal, both Hindu and Muslim.

Gandhi's tactics of non-violent resistance to untruth and injustice, which included a variety of individual and mass protest techniques, had become embedded in Congress ideology and practice. The Congress governments at the Center and in the states since Independence have followed ambiguous policies towards such extra-constitutional, non-violent forms of protest. The Constitution armed the state with several measures, most notably preventive detention, which allowed the government of the day to deal effectively, even in advance, with any protest that threatened to become violent or was too inconvenient for the ruling party to tolerate. The result has been an adaptation of parliamentarism and constitutionalism in India to the particular practices of Indian society through the institutionalization of a process of extra-constitutional confrontation between the state and dissident groups in which both sides use as a matter of course measures that are uncommon in Western parliamentary systems.

Leading ideas of the nationalist élite at independence

At independence, there were two quite different visions of India's future. Gandhi's desires for political decentralization, for a village- and agrarian-oriented economy, for conversion of the Congress into an organization devoted to constructive service for the people rather than towards adversarial party competition for power were either ignored or given a distinctly subordinate place in the thinking and practice of Congressmen who took up the reins of power in 1947 and created a new Constitution for an independent India. These Congressmen and other nationalist leaders shared a rather different vision, consisting of the following principal elements, which differed from Gandhi's views less in the underlying values than in the centralized, state-centered methods to be used to realize them.

First, the nationalist leaders at Independence were determined to declare for all the world to hear and for any internal dissidents who had a different view that India was to be a sovereign independent republic.

Unity was the second assumption of the nationalist élite. The partition experience also led the nationalist leaders, some of whom had been previously sympathetic to some kinds of regional cultural and linguistic demands, to reject sharply in the Constituent Assembly and in the early years after Independence any other potential division that seemed to threaten the country's unity, such as a North–South division implied in the Dravidistan slogan of the Tamil regional nationalist party, the DMK, or even the linguistic reorganization of states, which had been an implicit part of the Congress program since the 1920s.

The disintegration of public order in the Panjab, in Calcutta, and in the national capital of Delhi itself, whose streets were littered with dead bodies during the riots that accompanied partition, re-enforced the determination of the nationalist élite to enforce authority in independent India, to instill discipline in its people and to maintain order at all costs.

The nationalist élite also held the view that India's social and economic progress had been retarded by centuries of British rule, that the country had been kept agrarian, its industrial potential arrested, its people kept backward, illiterate and bound to out-moded forms of agricultural production. Consequently, it was necessary and urgent for the state itself to undertake the modernization of Indian society and to institute economic reforms that would free the country from feudalism and archaic social practices.

Secularism was another widely-shared and deeply-felt value. It involved an assertion that nationalism and the nation, based on the loyalty of individuals to the state before their community, was the basis for modern politics and not religion, the false slogan of the Pakistan élite.

All these leading ideas held by the nationalist élite converged to provide overwhelming justification in their minds of the need for a strong, centralized state. The State was perceived as the instrument which would establish India's sovereign independent presence in the world, would preserve its unity against foreign enemies and internal secessionists, would ensure authority, order and discipline in a society perceived as always on the brink of disorder and violence, would promote economic development through centralized planning which would bring India out of the backwardness of agrarian life and free it of a social order dominated by feudal institutions and practices and by religious superstitions, and would make it possible for Indians also to maintain an effective parliamentary system.

India's political culture: rhetoric versus reality

It became apparent very quickly after Independence, however, that fundamental transformations were occurring in the actual functioning of the institutions and practices borrowed from the West in which adjustments were made that reflected indigenous cultural and behavioral patterns, but without any conscious modeling on its own traditions.

Some observers attempted to encapsulate the process of contradiction and adjustment that was going on by arguing that there were several 'idioms' or 'cultures' in fundamental conflict with each other – a modern or Western idiom, centered in the ideas of the nationalist élite and in institutions in Delhi, a traditional idiom or culture, rooted in the kin, caste and communal relations of village, locality and province, and a 'saintly' idiom characteristically Indian, associated with Gandhi and his disciples involving selfless devotion

Peasants petition the Raja of Mankapur. Morning and evening audiences are held by every prominent politician in India.

to constructive work for the good of society and immune from mimicking of foreign models or from contamination by the archaic superstitions and feudal practices of Indian society.

These useful attempts to categorize the basic contradictions between Indian politics and society, however, left many adjustments, adaptations, and everyday practices unsatisfactorily explained. Little attention, for example, was paid to indigenous traditions of princely rule and their effects upon contemporary political practices, demonstrated every day in the morning and evening durbars or audiences held by every prominent politician in the land, in the duty of prominent people to provide support and protection for their clients, in the responsibility of those political leaders who achieved power and control over public resources to distribute them lavishly to their followers, and in the practice of dynastic succession to leadership in India.

Indian politicians also began early to display, indeed had been practicing at the local levels since the nineteenth century, a strong penchant for opportunistic behavior in pursuit of personal ambition to achieve high office and control public resources for personal advantage and for distribution to their followers. Indian politics have been characterized by an all-pervasive pragmatism which washes away party manifestoes, rhetoric and effective implementation of policies in an unending competition for power, status and profit.

If American political traditions have continued to emphasize the importance of limiting the role of the state while Western Europe has adopted the model of the welfare state and the Socialist countries the model of a socially transforming state, India has adopted the model of the state which exists for its own sake. It is a good in itself and the source of all goods. Of course, no state can serve everybody's interests and the Indian state has not succeeded in doing so since Independence. The contradictions between the foreign models adopted, the Indian traditions which have permeated the actual practices within the Western-derived institutions, and what can actually be achieved in an agrarian society, a caste-dominated social order and a heterogeneous civilization have been of the essence of Indian politics since Independence.

PRB

Further reading

G. Austin, *The Indian Constitution: Cornerstone of a Nation* (Oxford, 1966)

W. H. Morris-Jones, *The Government and Politics of India* 3rd rev. edn (London, 1976)

A. Nandy, *At the Edge of Psychology: Essays in Politics and Culture* (Delhi, 1980)

R. L. Park and H. Tinker, Eds, *Leadership and Political Institutions in India* (Princeton, N.J., 1959)

L. I. Rudolph and S. Hoeber Rudolph, *The Modernity of Tradition: Political Development in India* (Chicago, 1967)

Main outlines of political change from 1947 to the present

Nehru period

Jawaharlal Nehru, the first Prime Minister of India, was not formally selected either by the Congress party organization or by the Congress party in parliament. He was simply the natural choice as the acknowledged leader of the Congress and the designated political heir of Mahatma Gandhi. However, the party organization in the early years after Independence was dominated by Sardar Patel, who was also the most powerful minister in the Cabinet after Nehru and recognized as Nehru's equal in all other respects. Numerous differences developed between Patel and Nehru in the Cabinet and a great struggle for control over the party organization culminated in a victory for Patel's candidate, Purushottamdas Tandon, as party President in 1950. However, after Patel's death in December 1950, Nehru moved quickly to take over the party organization, forcing Tandon to resign the presidency, which Nehru then assumed himself for the next four years. After the overwhelming victory of the Congress under Nehru's leadership in the 1952 elections, there was no longer any doubt about Nehru's supremacy in the party and the government and he remained the unchallenged leader of both until his death in 1964.

Rulers of India since Independence

Head of State

Governor-General

1947–1948	Lord Mountbatten
1948–1950	C. Rajagopalachari

President

1950–1962	Rajendra Prasad
1962–1967	S. Radhakrishnan
1967–1969	Zakir Hussain
1969–1974	V. V. Giri
1974–1977	Fakhruddin Ali Ahmed
1977–1982	Neelam Sanjiva Reddy
1982–1987	Zail Singh
1987–	R. Venkataraman

Prime Minister

1947–1964	Jawaharlal Nehru
1964–1966	Lal Bahadur Shastri
1966–1977	Indira Gandhi
1977–1979	Morarji Desai
1979–1980	Charan Singh
1980–1984	Indira Gandhi
1984–	Rajiv Gandhi

Source: Government of India, Ministry of Information and Broadcasting, *India 1984: A Reference Annual* p. 599 (New Delhi, 1985); R. L. Hardgrave Jr. and S. A. Kochanek *India: Government and Politics in a Developing Nation* 4th edn, p. 77 (San Diego, 1986).

Box 16

Nehru's personality, attitudes and style of leadership influenced profoundly all aspects of the functioning of the Indian political system during the period of his dominance, which were characterized by the following critical features. Nehru asserted effectively and decisively the primacy of the office of the Prime Minister against challenges from the President and from the Congress organization. He was determined also that the Indian National Congress should rule the country and achieve power not only in Delhi but in all the Indian states. In a few cases, the attainment of that goal involved considerable political manipulation and the use of the power of the central government to undermine the positions of opposition parties and dissident Congress factions in states such as Panjab and Kerala. However, from the position of strength which Nehru established for the Congress, he then acted generously towards most opposition parties and their leaders, though not always so towards parties he considered to be of the extreme Right and towards the Communists. In some respects, Nehru himself was the leader of the opposition, for he was constantly haranguing and berating subordinate leaders and the rank and file for not being faithful to Congress ideals and for failing to implement Congress policies.

During the Nehru period, state and central politics were largely autonomous, though the central leadership of the Congress, known as the High Command, often played arbitrating and mediating roles between competing factions in the state Congress parties. Moreover, under Nehru, a strong central government coexisted with strong states and powerful state leaders in a mutual bargaining situation in which ultimate authority existed in Delhi.

Nehru and his Cabinet also exercised firm control over both the civilian and military bureaucracies. Although the élite civil service established by the British was maintained, Nehru and his principal ministers provided clear and firm policy guidance. Similarly, the supremacy of civilian control over the military also was strongly asserted.

Finally, Nehru articulated a clear set of ideological and policy goals which included a commitment to a non-dogmatic form of socialism, to secularism, to economic development through state-directed planning, and to nonalignment in international affairs. Success in achieving specific policies included under these broad goals was often limited, but they provided always a clear social and economic orientation, direction and cohesion to state policies.

Towards the end of Nehru's life, the central party organization, with Nehru's acquiescence, re-emerged as a powerful force, initially in support of Nehru's own desire to gain firmer control of both party organization and government in all the states of the Union. Kamaraj Nadar, former Chief Minister of the state of Tamil Nadu, was elected President of the Congress in 1963 and, along with four other party 'bosses' from different states, took control of the party organization. Upon Nehru's death in 1964, this group, known as the Syndicate, and especially Kamaraj as party president, played the critical roles in the succession to Nehru by Lal Bahadur Shastri and of Mrs Gandhi to Shastri two years later.

The rise of Indira Gandhi

The entire period between Nehru's death in 1964 and the consolidation of power in the country under Mrs Gandhi's leadership in 1971–72 constituted a prolonged succession crisis and struggle for power, with the period of Lal Bahadur Shastri's prime ministership from May 1964 to January 1966 but a brief interregnum between Nehru and Mrs Gandhi, the two dominant leaders of India since Independence. The period is marked by five critical steps in the rise of Mrs Gandhi and the defeat of all her potential rivals.

The first step was her own succession to power in 1966 after the sudden death of Shastri. The 1967 defeat of Morarji Desai in the Congress Parliamentary Party (CPP) was the second critical step in Mrs Gandhi's consolidation of power, which established her pre-eminence against her only serious rival despite severe losses suffered by the Congress in the 1967 elections under her leadership.

Once again, an unexpected death in office, this time of the President of India, Zakir Husain, had the effect of speeding up a struggle that was, in any case, already in progress. The Congress split of 1969 over the Congress nominee for the presidency of India was the third critical point in Mrs Gandhi's consolidation of power. Mrs Gandhi won the battle for the presidency with the election of her candidate, V. V. Giri, against the official Congress nominee, Sanjiva Reddy. However, in the process, she was expelled from the Congress and lost control over the party organization since most of the entrenched state party bosses remained in the Congress (O), while Mrs Gandhi's strength was more in the CPP than in the state party organizations.

In September, 1971, Mrs Gandhi decided to call national, parliamentary elections. The people of India were, in effect, asked to settle the struggle for power that had been going on since Nehru's death, to choose between Mrs Gandhi and her opponents, between the old Congress and the new. The results of the 1971 election were an overwhelming victory for Mrs Gandhi, whose Congress (R) won a two-thirds majority in the Lok Sabha. Mrs Gandhi was now unquestionably the pre-eminent leader of the country.

Shortly after the September 1971 election, the civil war and secessionist movement in East Pakistan began. Mrs Gandhi's attentions had now to be turned to this conflict, which occupied her and the country until December 1971, when the Indian Army invaded East Pakistan, defeated the Pakistan Army in the Third Indo-Pakistan War, and became the critical factor thereby in the foundation of the new state of Bangladesh. With this triumph behind her, the Congress (R) and Mrs Gandhi were able to go to the polls in the March 1972 legislative assembly elections with confidence and gain large majorities in all the major states in the Indian Union. At this point, one can say that the first succession crisis in post-Independence India had been decisively ended in favor of Mrs Gandhi, who now occupied a position of centrality and dominance in the Indian political system that appeared to equal or even surpass that of her father.

Mrs Gandhi established a distinctive strategy of rulership between 1972 and 1975 that was highly personalized and centralized and that involved unprecedented assertions of executive power in the Indian political system. Within the Congress party organization also, Mrs Gandhi established personal control, the dominance of the ministerial wing of the party over the organization, centralized direction of lower units, and authoritarian rather than democratic procedures for recruitment of party officers.

Mrs Gandhi's centralizing actions also transformed the character of center-state governmental relations in the states controlled by the Congress. Unlike her father, who preferred to deal with strong chief ministers in control of their legislative parties and state party organizations, Mrs Gandhi set out to remove every Congress chief minister who had an independent base and to replace each of them with chief ministers personally loyal to her and without an independent base. Even so, stability could not be maintained in the states, factional maneuvering to replace each appointed chief minister continued, the principal difference in such maneuvering now being that the decisions could not be taken in the state capitals but only in New Delhi.

Threats to Mrs Gandhi's dominance and the imposition of the emergency

A personalized strategy of rulership has the effect of focusing attention on the ruler, who receives the blame when things go wrong. In 1973–74, food shortages and rising prices combined with local political grievances to produce major popular demonstrations and movements that turned violent in the states of Gujarat and Bihar and that could not be handled effectively by the chief ministers appointed by Mrs Gandhi in those states. Inside the Congress, a small group of MPs were becoming discontented with Mrs Gandhi's economic policies.

Then, in March 1974, a new and ominous development occurred when Jayaprakash Narayan (JP) took the leadership of the Bihar agitation and offered also to lead a countrywide agitation against corruption and what he considered to be Mrs Gandhi's increasingly authoritarian rule. JP offered a direct, personal challenge to Mrs Gandhi's authority, legitimacy and character from a personal position of moral authority.

In the midst of these and other developments threatening Mrs Gandhi's dominance, the Allahabad High Court precipitated matters by finding Mrs Gandhi's 1971 election invalid on the grounds of corrupt practices in an election petition filed by Raj Narain and decided on June 12, 1975. This event brought new hope and vigor to the opposition, which began to join forces and to plan a mass mobilization campaign to demand the resignation of Mrs Gandhi.

The Emergency

In the early morning hours of June 26, 1975, Mrs Gandhi moved decisively to put an end to all opposition to her continuance in office. All her principal opponents, not only in the opposition but in the CPP itself, were arrested. At her request, the President of India declared an Emergency under Article 352 of the Constitution. Parliament moved swiftly to pass new electoral laws superseding the laws under which Mrs Gandhi was found guilty and her election

Independent India's ruling family: Jawaharlal Nehru, Indira Gandhi and Rajiv Gandhi, grandfather, daughter and grandson in 1950.

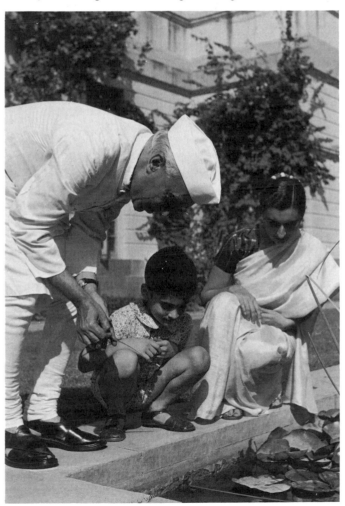

voided. Within a few months, President's Rule was imposed in the two non-Congress-ruled states of Gujarat and Tamil Nadu, thereby bringing the entire country under direct dictatorial rule from Delhi. Parliamentary elections scheduled for March 1976 were postponed and the terms of both Parliament and the state legislative assemblies extended. Mrs Gandhi's young son, Sanjay, came forward as the principal defender of the Emergency, acquiring dictatorial powers himself because of his identification with his mother, which he exercised in an arbitrary, arrogant and capricious manner. Tens of thousands of local-level party workers were jailed and press censorship made it difficult for other-than-local and very limited political protests to be made publicly by regime opponents who were not in jail.

It was not long, however, before considerable discontent at the mass level, though veiled, began to develop as a consequence of specific acts of the Emergency regime. The most notable set of such acts was the sterilization program of birth control introduced at the prompting of Sanjay Gandhi. Discontent also began to develop among Muslims, again as a consequence of one of Sanjay Gandhi's projects, in this case slum clearance and elimination of pavement squatters, accompanied by violent incidents, for the sake of 'beautification of Delhi'. Finally, all those persons who were affected by the demands for increased discipline in the workplace, by the pressures to procure sterilizations, and by freezes on wage increases also became disaffected with the Emergency regime.

The 1977 elections and return to normalcy

The 1977 elections

In the face of these simmering discontents, which were evidently not known to Mrs Gandhi because of the distortions in the flow of information and communication produced by fear and sycophancy among Congressmen and government officials, Mrs Gandhi suddenly announced in December 1977 a call for new parliamentary elections and a relaxation of the Emergency restrictions on the press and the opposition, including the release from jail of most political prisoners. Mrs Gandhi and Sanjay probably believed that the opposition would not have sufficient time to mobilize and gather the necessary resources to fight an effective election campaign in the few weeks available to them.

The results confounded any reasonable expectations that Mrs Gandhi and Sanjay could have had. The Janata party achieved a great victory, winning 270 seats, a bare majority in the Lok Sabha, but the opposition as a whole secured more than two-thirds of the seats, reducing the Congress to 153 seats, only 28 percent of the seats in the House.

The return to normalcy

The Janata government that came to power with Morarji Desai as Prime Minister had promised to restore normalcy if it succeeded at the polls and it set out to do so immediately after taking office. Civil liberties of the people were fully restored, press censorship was eliminated and the independence of the press from government interference re-established and all remaining political prisoners were released. The Janata government restored the main features of parliamentary democracy in India and made the future imposition of an Emergency somewhat more difficult.

The Indian parliamentary system, since its restoration in 1977, has survived the fall of the Janata government in 1979, the return of Mrs Gandhi to power thereafter, the threat to Indian unity posed by the Panjab crisis and the assassination of Mrs Gandhi in 1984, and the return of the Congress to power in 1985 under Rajiv Gandhi with an 80 percent majority in Parliament. It would be foolish to assume either that India, having weathered an authoritarian challenge to its parliamentary regime, is now secure from such a threat in future or to predict the re-establishment of authoritarianism in the future. Political practices since Independence have provided precedents for both types of regimes.

PRB

Further reading

M. Brecher, *Succession in India: A Study in Decision-Making* (London, 1966)

S. C. Gangal, *Prime Minister and the Cabinet in India* (New Delhi, 1972)

H. C. Hart, Ed., *Indira Gandhi's India: A Political System Reappraised* (Boulder, Co, 1976)

J. R. Wood, 'Extra-Parliamentary Opposition in India: An Analysis of Populist Agitations in Gujarat and Bihar' *Pacific Affairs* XLVIII, No. 3 313–334 (Fall, 1975)

Framework of politics; the Constitution and its working

The President

The Constitution of India formally vests virtually all the executive powers of government in the President. In fact, however, it is understood that the President's powers are to be exercised, with only rare exceptions, upon the advice of the Prime Minister and the Council of Ministers. Nevertheless, there have been persistent concerns from the time of the deliberations of the Constituent Assembly up to the prime ministership of Rajiv Gandhi that a President might misuse or abuse – in effect, actually *use* – the powers formally granted to him in the Constitution or that he might, under certain circumstances be in a position to exercise discretionary powers.

The most persistent concerns have centered round the degree of freedom the President may have to select a Prime Minister in an unstable House. Because of such concerns, ever since the 1967 elections and the split in the Indian National Congress in 1969, as a consequence of which the political dominance of the Congress at the Center has not been assured and inter-party political competition for the prime ministership has become more intense, the election of the President has become a highly politicized matter.

However, it was not until Sanjiva Reddy's term of office (1977–82) that the anticipated difficulties surrounding the exercise of presidential discretion in selecting a new Prime Minister and dissolving the House and calling a new election in a divided House arose: in July 1979, after the resignation of Morarji Desai, and a month later after Charan Singh, Desai's successor, also lost his majority. In three instances, precedents were established for the exercise of discretion by the President: in rejecting Morarji Desai's request to form a new government after his initial resignation; in insisting that his successor, Charan Singh, seek a vote of confidence in the Lok Sabha by a specific date; and in his insistence, after Charan Singh's resignation with a recommendation for calling a new election, upon consulting other party leaders before making the decision himself to call a new election. Although all three actions by the President were controversial, none were inconsistent with parliamentary conventions nor did they betray a desire for the exercise of personal power by the President.

Indeed, the exercise of even the limited discretionary powers available to the President has occurred so infrequently that each such exercise has occasioned extensive public comment and some controversy. In 1987, for example, Giani Zail Singh made use for the first time since Independence of the President's power to return a bill to Parliament – the Indian Post Office (Amendment) Bill, authorizing the Post Office to open private mail for intelligence

President Zail Singh and prime minister Rajiv Gandhi. The Indian president has limited discretionary powers, but can function effectively only when he has the confidence of the prime minister.

purposes. The employment of this power and the President's written complaints to the Prime Minister at the same time that he was not even being kept briefed on major issues precipitated a public controversy and much speculation on the President's motives and intentions, including the possibility that he might exercise his formal power to dismiss the Prime Minister. In fact, the constitutional reality is that the President can function effectively only if he has the confidence of the Prime Minister and not vice-versa.

There appear, therefore, to be few real grounds for concern that the President of India represents a potential political counterweight to the Prime Minister, the cabinet, and the elected leadership of the country.

Prime Minister and Cabinet

The framers of the Constitution adopted the conventions of British cabinet government as it had evolved up to that time, including the leading position given to the Prime Minister and the collective responsibility of the cabinet. During the Nehru period, from the time of the death of his chief political rival, Sardar Patel, in 1950, to 1964, the cabinet functioned in conformity with the basic norms of 'Prime Ministerial government', but one in which individual cabinet ministers were still allowed to play important political roles and of whom some were persons with substantial political followings.

Under Nehru's successor, Lal Bahadur Shastri, the Prime Minister's Secretariat emerged as an alternative source to the cabinet of advice, influence and power in the executive branch of government. Following Shastri's example, Mrs Gandhi used the Prime Minister's Secretariat as an independent source of advice, but she enlarged its role significantly. However, the influence of the Secretariat also declined, especially during the Emergency between 1975 and 1977, when Mrs Gandhi came to rely heavily for both policy advice and political counsel upon her son, Sanjay.

The restoration of parliamentary government by the Janata coalition which came to power with Morarji Desai as Prime Minister in 1977 did not succeed in restoring the significance of the Cabinet as an institution. The divisions in his government were too great, the collective responsibility of the Cabinet disintegrated in open warfare, and Desai himself had to resign in July 1979.

The pattern of prime ministerial dominance of a weak Cabinet was restored by Mrs Gandhi after her victory in 1980. After the death of her son Sanjay, in 1981, Mrs Gandhi relied upon other relatives and former retainers of the Nehru household and turned increasingly also to her second son, Rajiv. Rajiv as Prime Minister has continued his mother's pattern of consulting his own personal circle of advisers, irrespective of their position inside or outside the Cabinet.

The close advisers of the Prime Minister may come from the

political sphere, from business, from former school associates, from his immediate family or distant relatives, or from family retainers. Although it is more comparable to the White House staff than to the British Cabinet, the closest parallel is to the Indian institution of the *durbar* which, in one meaning, refers to the inner circle of advisers to the ruler. Members of the inner circle are dependent upon the ruler's favor for their positions. They may receive the ruler's patronage or dispense it on his behalf, but they may also be dismissed or find themselves disregarded and have no recourse for their positions are informal, not institutionalized. Moreover, most members of the inner circle lack an independent political base. The ruler, therefore, depends upon the members of this inner circle but is not dependent upon them. He can change them at will.

The role and powers of Parliament

In principle in India, as in Britain, the Prime Minister is chosen by Parliament and he and his Cabinet are 'collectively responsible' to it, that is, they must retain the confidence of a majority of the members of the lower House of Parliament or resign and give way to an alternative government. On only a few occasions, however, has there actually been a contested election in the ruling parliamentary party in India. In fact, even though the CPP played an important role in maintaining support for Mrs Gandhi in her struggles with her rivals, it is the members of Parliament who have been in the dependent role, following a popular leader to what they have considered their best hope for power for themselves as well rather than actually selecting a leader from among alternatives.

There have, however, been two occasions in the post-Independence period when the persistence of a government in power has depended in fact upon the confidence of the House as a whole: in 1969, after the party split in the ruling Indian National Congress when Mrs Gandhi retained a majority in Parliament and again in July–August 1979 when the ruling Janata coalition split and Morarji Desai lost his majority in Parliament and had to resign. Individual members of Parliament and opposition groups in the Indian Parliament also have played roles that are equivalent in importance to those played by their counterparts in Britain in the question hour, the amendment process and in debate. Equally

The Indian Parliament Building, New Delhi.

important in India, however, have been dramatic gestures, defiance of parliamentary procedure, and other forms of demonstrative behavior designed to express total opposition to government policies. Only during the Emergency was such opposition in Parliament stifled. On the other hand, some of the normal prerogatives of the legislature in India have been encroached upon by the Cabinet on numerous occasions, most notably the very frequent passage of legislation by Ordinance of the President (that is, in effect, by the Cabinet or the Prime Minister's Secretariat).

The Lok Sabha (House of the People) is the lower house and the supreme legislative body in India. Nevertheless, the Rajya Sabha (Council of States) is not without importance. Although the Rajya Sabha does not normally obstruct legislation passed in the Lok Sabha, it has occasionally done so, particularly on constitutional amendments which require a two-thirds majority in both houses. The second important power of the Rajya Sabha is its coequal role with the Lok Sabha as an electoral college, which includes also the state legislative assemblies, for the election of the President of India. The significance of these two powers taken together is that the Rajya Sabha must also be controlled before a government can consolidate its power in Delhi.

The judiciary

The powers of the Indian Supreme Court are comparable to those of its USA counterpart, including broad original and appellate jurisdiction and the right to pass on the constitutionality of laws passed by Parliament. In the exercise of its powers, however, the Court has been at the center of major controversies concerning the constitutional and political order in India. Two such controversies have been especially persistent and have had broad ramifications. One concerns the efforts by the Court to give priority to the Fundamental Rights provisions in the Constitution in cases where they have come into conflict with the Directive Principles, which specify the broad ideological and policy goals of the Indian state and to which the executive and legislature have often given priority. The second concerns the court's powers of judicial review of legislation passed by Parliament, which have on numerous occasions led to stalemates that point to a constitutional contradiction between the principle of parliamentary sovereignty and that of judicial review. Although the contradiction has not been satisfactorily resolved, with the two institutions each asserting an incompatible priority, the Court has retained an imprecisely defined power of judicial review which at its broadest, according to the judgment in the landmark 1973 case of *Keshavananda Bharati* versus *State of Kerala*, prohibits Parliament from passing even constitutional amendments which violate 'the fundamental features' or the 'basic structure' of the Constitution.

During the Emergency, the Court's powers were severely eroded when both Fundamental Rights and judicial review were suspended. The Court even failed to uphold the hallowed common law right of *habeas corpus*. Although many of the Court's powers have since been restored, the executive assertion of the primacy of the Directive Principles has been largely sustained and the principle of judicial review has not been established as firmly in India as it has in the USA.

The Court has become, nevertheless, a centrally important institution in the Indian political system, deeply and directly implicated in the political process in ways which have rarely if ever occurred in the USA. A 1975 decision of the High Court of Allahabad (the highest court in the province of Uttar Pradesh), overturning the election of Mrs Gandhi while she was Prime Minister, was reviewed by the Supreme Court in a judicial process that precipitated the Emergency. When the Emergency ended and the Janata government came to power, the Court passed on the constitutional validity of the following actions of the new government designed to consolidate its power in the country and to keep Mrs Gandhi on the defensive: the dismissal of nine state governments before the end of their terms and the calling of new elections in those states (the Dissolution Case, 1977) and the appointment of Special Courts to try Mrs Gandhi for alleged excesses and criminal acts committed by her during the Emergency (the Special Courts Reference Case, 1978).

Government in the states

In India's federal parliamentary system, the structures and institutions of the central government have their counterparts at the state level. Each state has a Governor who is the official head of state, a bicameral legislature in which the directly-elected lower house is generally called the Vidhan Sabha and the upper house, whose members are elected under a variety of different types of franchises, is generally called the Rajya Sabha, a Chief Minister and his Council of Ministers or Cabinet, and a High Court.

These state institutions, however, have not functioned in the same way as their central models. The politics of the state legislatures have been much more fluid than politics in Parliament and there is often no clear majority in the legislature. As the agents of the central government, appointed by the President acting on the advice of the Prime Minister, it has been common since the late 1960s for the governors to intervene in such situations of instability in the states in ways which clearly indicate that they are following the explicit directives or the tacit desires of the central government rather than simply implementing their constitutional mandate to give formal approval to the decisions of the chief minister and cabinet and to report impartially to the Center the situation in the states.

During the early post-Independence period in some states, a form of 'chief ministerial' government developed, but the more common patterns were cabinet instability and struggles for power even within the ruling Congress parties, which have always been highly factionalized, leading in many states to frequent changes in the office of the chief minister. Two factors have prevented the establishment in most states of governments dominated by the chief ministers: the fluidity of party loyalties and alignments in the legislatures and the unwillingness in the post-Nehru period of the leadership of the ruling party or coalition at the Center to permit strong chief ministers. Increasingly, therefore, many state legislatures have lost their powers to choose the chief ministers and cabinets, a function which has been taken up by the governing group at the Center. The primary activities of the state legislators consist of plotting to overthrow the government of the day and seeking patronage to distribute to followers in their constituencies.

The High Courts in the states, like the Supreme Court, have become involved in issues of Fundamental Rights and in matters of judicial review. Many of the constitutional issues which ultimately reached the Supreme Court were originally adjudicated in the High Courts.

In general, however, there have been marked differences in the actual practices of state and central government institutions.

PRB

Further reading

G. Austin, *The Indian Constitution: Cornerstone of a Nation* (Oxford, 1966)

G. E. Beller, 'Benevolent Illusions in a Developing Society: The Assertion of Supreme Court Authority in Democratic India' *The Western Political Quarterly* XXXVI, No. 4, 513–532 (December, 1983)

B. D. Dua, 'A Study in Executive–Judicial Conflict: The Indian Case' *Asian Survey* XXIII, No. 4, 463–483 (April, 1983)

H. C. Hart, 'The Indian Constitution: Political Development and Decay' *Asian Survey* XX, No. 4, 428–451 (April, 1980)

M. V. Pylee, *Constitutional Government in India* 3rd rev. edn (New York, 1977)

B. Sengupta, *Last Days of the Morarji Raj* (Calcutta, 1979)

The arms of the state; the bureaucracy, the police and the armed forces

Bureaucracy

The British ruled India through a bureaucratic system, whose primary functions were the maintenance of law and order and the collection of revenue. The fear of disorder and disintegration of the new Indian state at Independence, occasioned by the partition of the country, communal violence, and the problems involved in integrating the princely states into the Indian Union caused the leadership of independent India to rely heavily on the existing bureaucratic apparatus and to put aside any ideas of reform. At the highest levels of government in India, in fact, senior officers of the Indian Administrative Service (IAS), especially those in the Prime Minister's Secretariat created under Prime Minister Lal Bahadur Shastri, have at times become more influential than Cabinet ministers. Mrs Gandhi especially relied upon a few senior officers in her Secretariat, who did her political bidding as well as providing her with policy advice. Many of the senior bureaucrats welcomed her Emergency regime. Consequently, when the Janata Government came to power, most of the senior officers closely identified with the Emergency regime were transferred to undesirable postings or suspended from service under charges of corruption. The post-Independence structure of political-bureaucratic relationships has consequently been fundamentally transformed in a direction away from the Weberian ideal type of a rational-legal bureaucratic system to a patrimonial regime in which the political leadership selects officers who are personally loyal, who serve their narrow political interests, and who expect reciprocal preferments in return.

The highest levels of the state administration, as well as of the central government, are staffed by IAS officers. Below the élite all-India services, there are several layers of bureaucracy in both the central and provincial governments, including the higher state civil services as well as vast armies of clerks, peons and messengers at the lower levels. The numbers of government employees in central, state, quasi-government and local bodies quadrupled from approximately four million in 1953 to more than sixteen million in 1983. The pay and emoluments of government servants constitute a major drain on state revenues and resources to such an extent that they constitute a major cause of the deficiency in resources needed to increase public sector capital investment in the economy.

The decision to retain the IAS system of bureaucratic control was associated also with the decision of the Constituent Assembly in favor of a predominantly centralized system of government with federal features. The proponents of an alternative, 'Gandhian', tradition have succeeded from time to time in having institutional reforms enacted to introduce measures of decentralization. In fact, however, the planning process, including the articulation of goals, the allocation of resources, and the systems of bureaucratic control and accountability everywhere in India have remained highly centralized.

Below the IAS level and the level of the senior officers in other branches of administrative service in India, the bureaucracy is generally ineffective and non-cooperative in most areas of policy implementation. Although there remains some doubt about the extent to which corruption has penetrated the IAS officer cadres, there is universal agreement that bribe-taking on a small scale at the lowest levels and extensive, massive corruption at the middle and

Arms of the State: India

Table A

Growth in Strength of Police Force, 1951–1981

Year	Police strength
1951	468,000
1961	526,000
1971	707,000
1981	904,000

Source: Shailendra Misra *Police Brutality: An Analysis of Police Behaviour* p. 73 (New Delhi, 1986).

Table B

Armed Force Levels (Military and Paramilitary), 1986

Force	Number
Armed Forces	1,260,000
Army	1,100,000
Navy	47,000
Airforce	113,000
Paramilitary Forces	255,000
National Security Force	112,000
Border Security Force	90,000
Assam Rifles	37,000
Indo-Tibetan Border Police	14,000
Coastguard	2,000

Source: *The Military Balance, Institute of Strategic Studies, 1986–1987* pp. 154–55 (London, 1986).

Table C

Size of Armed Forces, 1956–1986

Year	Size
1956	400,000
1961	530,000
1966	879,000
1971	980,000
1976	1,055,500
1981	1,104,000
1986	1,260,000

Sources: *The Military Balance, Institute of Strategic Studies, 1964–1965 to 1986–1987* (London, 1964–1986) and W. A. Wilcox *India, Pakistan and the Rise of China* p. 129 (New York, 1964).

Table D

Defense Expenditure, 1951–1986

Year	Defense expenditure in USA $ 100 million[a]	Percentage of Government spending
1951	3.4	22.1
1956	4.1	17.2
1961	n.a.	n.a.
1966	12.6	n.a.
1971	16.6	21.6
1976	28.1	19.6
1981	50.2	18.5
1982	56.8	17.8
1983	56.8	17.1
1984	69.1	19.3
1985	63.3	n.a.
1986	69.6	n.a.

[a]Figures for 1966 to 1986 are in current USA dollars. Since figures vary widely in different issues of *The Military Balance*, whose editors attempt to revise earlier figures on the basis of later information, the figures in this table were taken from the latest available issues of the journal pertaining to each year.

Source: Figures for 1966 to 1986 from *The Military Balance, Institute of Strategic Studies, 1966–1967 to 1986–1987* (London, 1966–1986); figures for 1951 and 1956 from W. A. Wilcox *India, Pakistan and the Rise of China* p. 130 (New York, 1964).

higher levels up to and including at least some IAS officers is endemic and pervasive. In order to serve the needs of the people, therefore, 'middlemen', 'fixers' and 'brokers' have sprung up in the countryside to serve as intermediaries between villagers and bureaucracy to make actually available to the people the agricultural, medical and other services that are supposed to be provided under myriad government programs.

Thus, both at the top and the bottom, the Indian administrative system that has evolved since Independence departs significantly from 'Weberian' criteria of a rational-legal system. The mechanisms, ties, and attachments that make the system work are based rather on personal and social obligations to patrons and clients, kin and caste fellows, on informal connections, and on illegal fee-for-service cash payments. Although they are subordinate at the highest levels to the most powerful political leaders and at the lower levels to powerful local politicians, the higher grades of the Indian bureaucracy dominate routine decision making and, in the frequent absence of ministerial leadership, general policy making in both the central and state governments. They are no longer the élite 'rulers of India' but a vast dominant class, the principal beneficiaries of the benefits and resources produced and distributed through the agency of the Indian state.

Box 17

Police

The central government maintains several large police forces, numbering altogether above 800,000 men and including, among others, the Central Bureau of Intelligence, the Central Reserve Police, the Border Security Force, the Central Industrial Security Forces (who maintain order at public sector industrial enterprises) and the Indo-Tibetan Border Police. The domestic police force proper, however, is under the control of the state governments. In 1981, it comprised 904,000 men (civil and armed), but this figure did not include a number of other special duty police forces.

The administrative structure of the Indian Police Service (IPS) is similar to that of the IAS. It is an all-India service, divided into state cadres. The IPS officers constitute an élite corps whose members fill virtually all the senior state and district police administrative positions. Officers advance from assistant superintendent of police (SP) in a district to district SP and ultimately to a deputy inspector-general or to an inspector-general position in the state capital in charge of an entire branch of state police administration. During the British period and into much of the post-Independence period, the SP was under the control of the district magistrate, but the SPs are now directly responsible for the police administration in their districts to the state inspectors-general and are no longer considered to be subordinate to the district magistrates. Below the IPS cadre is the rank of deputy SP, which is recruited by the state public service commission; below that rank are the inspectors and sub-inspectors, recruited at the district level; and at the bottom are the constables recruited by the district SP. The pay and service conditions of the IPS are comparable to those of the IAS, but the pay and conditions of the constables are wretched, below those of peons in civil administration.

In addition to the ordinary police establishment which carries out the routine police work and maintenance of public order on a daily basis, each state also has a substantial armed police force, known as the Provincial Armed Constabulary, which is a reserve force whose units remain in barracks most of the time, to be called out on special duty to deal with large-scale disturbances to public order.

The Indian police have become increasingly politicized in the past two decades from the local up to the national level. The more powerful district politicians want pliable and responsive SPs and deputy SPs, who in turn require the support and patronage of the politicians. The principal sanctions which the politicians have to influence the police are the power to transfer constables to remote parts of their districts and senior officers to undesirable districts, to protect corrupt police from criminal prosecution, and to influence promotions. At the local level, protection from police victimization and the use of the police to harass one's rivals have become critical elements in the powers of local politicians. Politicians in the districts of India who wish to build a stable political base for themselves,

therefore, must not only be able to distribute money and patronage, but must also be able to control the police. The police in turn must have powerful political allies if they are to be effective and to advance their own careers.

Political involvement of the police in contemporary political controversies reached a peak during and after the Emergency when the police at all levels were called upon to arrest most of the important opposition leaders in the country and to keep under surveillance many others, including leading figures in the ruling Congress (I) itself. After the Emergency, the Janata government replaced senior police officers who had acted partially and, allegedly, overzealously in supporting the Emergency.

The persistence in post-Independence India of Gandhian techniques of mass mobilization and the spread of group violence in communal riots, student agitations, and massive political demonstrations against the government of the day have increasingly involved the police in confrontations with the people. Police firings on unarmed crowds, participation of the police in brutal attacks on minorities and provocative actions against peaceful demonstrators that provoke them to commit acts of violence have become commonplace in contemporary India.

The combination of increased group violence, decline of legitimate political authority in the countryside, politicization of sections of the police, and their involvement in incidents of violence has contributed to an increasingly pervasive Hobbesian state of disorder, unpredictability, and fear of violence among ordinary people in the rural areas of India. The overall contemporary performance of the police in India, therefore, can no longer be considered appropriate to a free, democratic, impartial political order. The police are in fact themselves too often among the more dangerous and disorderly forces in the country.

Military

India has one of the largest military forces in the world and one that has been continuously active since Independence in a wide range of actions, including the fighting of four wars, the takeover of Goa from the Portuguese in 1961, and numerous domestic operations in support of the civil authorities.

The politicization that has so affected the bureaucracy and the police services and which has contributed to a decline in the effectiveness of their performance has not affected the functioning of the Indian military to the same degree.

The British reproduced in India the Anglo-Saxon pattern of civilian control over the military, whose officers were taught that the military must remain a politically neutral arm of the state. The values of senior Congress leaders also fostered military subordination to civilian leadership. In contrast to the pattern in many other developing countries, including neighboring Pakistan where an

The heads of the Indian armed services are all subordinate to the civilian defence minister.

alliance of the civilian and military bureaucrats developed against the politicians, in India an early alliance developed between the politicians and the civilian bureaucracy to control the military. Specific steps taken to reduce military influence and to ensure civilian control included the removal of the Commander-in-Chief from the first Cabinet in independent India, followed by the abolition of the position itself, leaving no overall commander of all the armed forces other than the civilian head of government; the subordination of all three military chiefs to the civilian Defence Minister, who has usually been either a confidant of the Prime Minister or a powerful politician; and, in recent years, the use of the more doubtful practice of appointing only politically acceptable persons as commanders of the several armed forces.

There is an alternative tradition of militarization of politics and of the infusion of nationalism with military values, represented in the nationalist period by Subhas Chandra Bose, the founder of the Indian National Army which fought against the British in Asia during World War II. Since Independence, political leaders have emphasized the indispensability of a strong military for the maintenance of India as a powerful and respected country and have at times introduced into Indian nationalism a military element.

Military leaders have resented the extent of civilian control over their actions, the lack of specialized military knowledge of the civilian leadership, and their own limited role in the making of military policies. Internal discontents also have developed in the Indian army in recent years over pay, status, and declining opportunities for promotion. The potential for military intervention in Indian politics nevertheless remains low. There has never been an attempted coup in India. Even if the will to intervene were present, the obstacles to effective intervention are formidable. The military

itself is too large and divided to imagine the possibility of a united leadership implementing a coup. The conditions which have led to or been used as a justification for military intervention in other Asian and African countries – such as political instability, widespread corruption, absence of electoral legitimacy of the civilian politicians, politicization of the military – have either not been present in India or have not been present in the same combination or have not progressed to the same extent. With the exception of the period just before and during the Emergency, the legitimacy of the political leadership has never been seriously questioned. A coup remains highly unlikely, the subordination of the military to civilian leadership remains firm, and the government in Delhi continues to be led by legitimately elected authority.

The more serious problems concerning the contemporary role of the military in Indian society pertain to the increasing use of the army – on the average 40 to 50 times per year – by the political authorities in domestic disturbances of all sorts, particularly to deal with major incidents of violence. Several paramilitary forces were created in the 1950s and 1960s specifically to handle situations that were beyond the capabilities of the local police. However, the army has had to be called in on several occasions to restore order within these forces themselves. In addition to its use to deal with specific disturbances, the army has also been stationed permanently or for long periods in several Indian states, continuously in Kashmir since 1947 and for long periods since 1983–84 in the troubled states of Assam and Panjab. One long-term danger to the Indian political system, therefore, is of a militarization of politics and a politicization and demoralization of the army arising from its widespread use as a mechanism of political control in a society tending towards anomie.

Further reading

D. H. Bayley, *The Police and Political Development in India* (Princeton, N.J., 1969)

S. P. Cohen, 'The Military and Constitutionalism in India' in Atul Kohli, Ed., *India's Troubled Democracy: An Analysis of Changing State–Society Relations* (Princeton, N.J., 1988)

B. D. Dua, 'Federalism or Patrimonialism: The Making and Unmaking of Chief Ministers in India' *Asian Survey* XXV, No. 8, 793–804 (August, 1985)

D. C. Potter, *India's Political Administrators: 1919–1983* (Oxford, 1986)

R. G. Reddy and G. Haragopal, "The Pyraveekar: 'The Fixer' in Rural India" *Asian Survey* XXV, No. 11, 1148–1162 (November, 1985)

Center-state relations, regionalism, pluralism, and communal tensions and conflicts

Center-state relations

India today is a Union of twenty-four states. The leadership of the Congress and the Constituent Assembly at Independence was firmly in the hands of those who believed in the necessity for a strong, centralized state in India. In the Indian federal system, therefore, there is a considerable array of central powers in relation to the states and numerous unitary features. They include the following: (a) separate lists of legislative powers for the Center and the states, but with a concurrent list in which the Center may claim priority, with residuary powers left to the Union, and with the power held in reserve in emergencies and other situations for the Center to legislate on matters contained in the state list; (b) the power of the Center to create new states and to revise the boundaries of or even eliminate existing federal units; (c) the retention by the Center of control over the most lucrative sources of taxation and the authority to collect certain taxes on behalf of the states and to distribute the revenues among them; (d) the power of the Center to take over the administration of a state and declare President's Rule under specified conditions that have been interpreted very broadly; (e) the power to declare a national emergency that, in effect, may convert the country into a unitary state.

In practice, however, despite strong centralizing drives by Congress governments in Delhi, especially during Mrs Gandhi's leadership, there have been recurring problems in center-state relations and long-term trends that favor regionalism, pluralism and decentralization. The Finance Commissions, for example, which are responsible for the distribution to the states of centrally collected taxes, have done little to rectify regional imbalances among states. The Planning Commission, which was designed to introduce a system of centralized economic planning, has never been able to ensure implementation of its goals by the states and has in general declined in influence during the past two decades. Although the Center has several times used the Emergency provisions of the Constitution, especially during the 1975 to 1977 period, and has often imposed President's Rule on individual states, both of which allow it to exercise considerable direct control over the administration of the states, these measures are symptomatic of an overall weakening of effective central and state government in India rather than indications of permanent centralization.

Moreover, there have been recurring problems arising out of India's enormous cultural diversity. During Nehru's tenure in office, most linguistic, regional, and minority conflicts and controversies were ultimately resolved through pluralistic mechanisms. During Mrs Gandhi's periods in office, however, especially in the 1980s, several issues developed into major challenges to the unity of India and to amicable relations among its major ethnic and religious communities. Some of these problems were exacerbated by the centralizing drives of and the involvement of the central leaders themselves in political manipulation in the states in contrast to the Nehru period when the central government preferred to stand back from such problems as far as possible and adopt arbitrating and mediating roles.

Pluralism and Indian language policies

India's national leaders had to confront several language problems in the first two decades of Independence and what appeared to some of them in the aftermath of Partition to be a real threat of the 'Balkanization' of the country. These problems included especially the official language issue and demands for the linguistic reorganization of the provinces of India whose boundaries, during British rule, did not conform to linguistic divisions. Most of the language conflicts in the Nehru period, some of which became at times bitter and violent, were ultimately resolved through pluralistic solutions.

Controversy over designating an official language for India began in the Constituent Assembly itself, where it was the most divisive issue faced by that body. The Assembly after prolonged debate decided, however, that Hindi in the Devanagari script was ultimately to be the official language of the country, but that English was to be the principal official language for an interim period of fifteen years. As the date for the transition approached, demands came mainly from the southern states for the retention of English, which the élites of those states preferred to Hindi, as the official language of the country. Some violent protests also occurred in the state of Tamil Nadu.

An extended debate in Parliament on the matter in 1963 was followed by the passage of the Official Languages Act, 1963. The Act fulfilled the intentions of the Constituent Assembly by declaring that Hindi would become the sole official language of the country in 1965, but resolved the controversy by continuing the use of English as an associate additional official language for an indefinite period beyond 1965. In 1967, the Official Languages Act was further amended to strengthen the guarantee concerning maintenance of associate official status for English as long as even a single non-Hindi-speaking state so desired.

The principal consequences of the compromise Act of 1963 have been the continued use of English along with Hindi in Parliament and its use as the language for inter-state communication among the non-Hindi-speaking states and between the Center and the non-Hindi-speaking states as well. Although the compromise amounts to a bilingual resolution, in fact there has been a broader multilingual compromise on other matters, most notably concerning the medium of examination for entry into the Indian Administrative Service. For the latter purpose, any of the fourteen

Obliterating an anti-Hindi slogan in Tamil Nadu. Resistance from the south of India has so far blocked attempts to make Hindi the sole official language of the country.

regional languages listed in the Eighth Schedule of the Constitution of India or English may be used.

The first linguistic reorganization of states occurred in the aftermath of a significant movement in the Andhra region of the old Madras province, which led to the appointment of the States Reorganization Commission. Following upon its *Report* published in 1955, the States Reorganization Act was passed in 1956, which led to the reorganization of the boundaries of the southern states to conform more closely to traditional linguistic regions. The bifurcation of Bombay province into the present states of Gujarat and Maharashtra followed in 1960. In 1966, Panjab was reorganized and its several parts distributed among three units: the core Panjabi Suba, the new state of Haryana, and Himachal Pradesh. Several new states also have been carved out in response to tribal demands in the northeastern region of the country from time to time. All the reorganizations except that in the Panjab and in the northeastern region have satisfied the grievances of the principal large language communities of India.

The problems in the northeastern region and in the Panjab, however, have been complicated by the presence of other factors. In the northeast, the issues have been tangled by the presence there of several tribal minorities, whose demands have been secessionist, by the migration of large numbers of people from other provinces of India, particularly West Bengal, to the northeastern states of Assam and Tripura especially, by illegal migrations from Bangladesh as well, and by the presence of large numbers of both Hindus and Muslims among the migrant and local populations.

Panjab crisis
In the Panjab, the majority Sikh community constitutes a separate religious as well as linguistic group. Moreover, the Sikhs have only a

bare majority in the state's population, which they have not been able to transform into the political dominance which leaders of the Sikh political party, the Akali Dal, have sought. Most important, the central government never completed the reorganization of the Panjab, leaving unresolved the controversial issues concerning the status of the former capital city of Chandigarh, the disposition of some disputed territories, and the distribution of river waters among Panjab, Haryana, and the state of Rajasthan.

The failure to resolve the remaining problems associated with the linguistic reorganization of the Panjab has created the most violent single source of domestic conflict in the Indian political system since Independence and has contributed to an embitterment of Hindu–Sikh relations in India generally comparable to the hostilities that affect Hindu–Muslim relations (see below). In the years between 1980 and 1984, the Government of India allowed several extremist Sikh organizations to function with relative impunity in the Panjab, until they took control of the Golden Temple, the central Sikh shrine in Amritsar, from which terrorists moved out freely to engage in murders of Sikhs belonging to rival religious sects and political organizations and of Hindu opponents as well. Many entirely innocent Hindus were also killed at random by terrorists presumed to be Sikh.

In June 1984, Mrs Gandhi ordered the Indian army to clear the Sikh extremists out of the Golden Temple, which was done with great loss of life and damage to the Golden Temple that has created a deep and burning anger among many Sikhs against the Government of India and its leaders. Mrs Gandhi herself was assassinated by two Sikh bodyguards in November 1984. A massacre of thousands of innocent, mostly poor Sikhs, in Delhi, Kanpur and Begusarai followed with the complicity or malign neglect of the authorities, the police and the Congress leaders.

Although the new Prime Minister, Rajiv Gandhi, reached an Accord with the Akali Dal leadership in September 1985, to resolve all the outstanding issues, its provisions have not been implemented and terrorist violence persists. After a period of twenty-one months of governance by the Akali Dal with the support of the Congress, the Panjab was placed under President's Rule in May 1987 and was then under virtual occupation by various police and armed forces sent by the central government to control terrorism.

Demand for regional autonomy and restructuring of center-state relations
Among the by-products of the Panjab crisis has been a demand for restructuring of center-state relations to grant more powers to the states amounting to regional autonomy, with the powers of the Center confined to a restricted range of subjects. The initial demand in the Panjab was formulated in a resolution of the Akali Dal passed at Anandpur Sahib in 1973. Since then, several non-Congress

India in 1954, before the reorganization of the states.

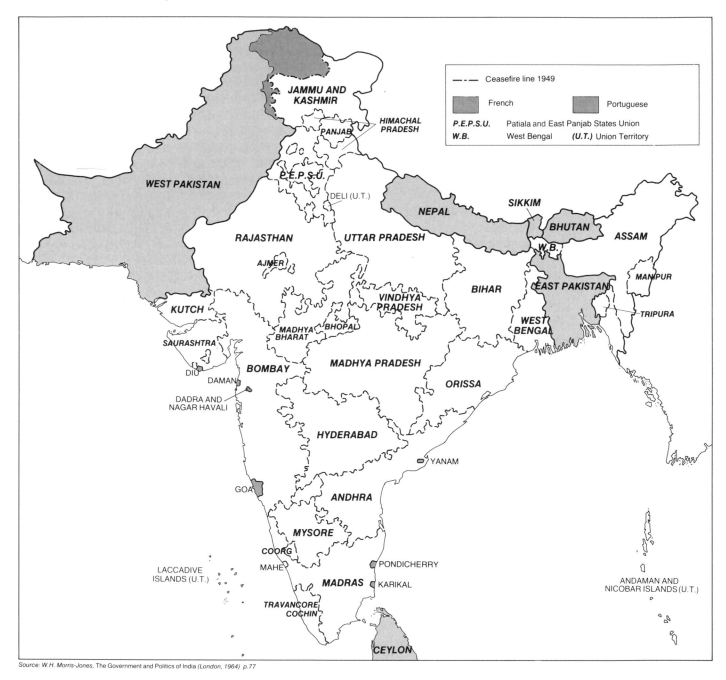

Source: W.H. Morris-Jones, The Government and Politics of India *(London, 1964) p.77*

India after the reorganization of the states on a linguistic basis in 1956 with later changes.

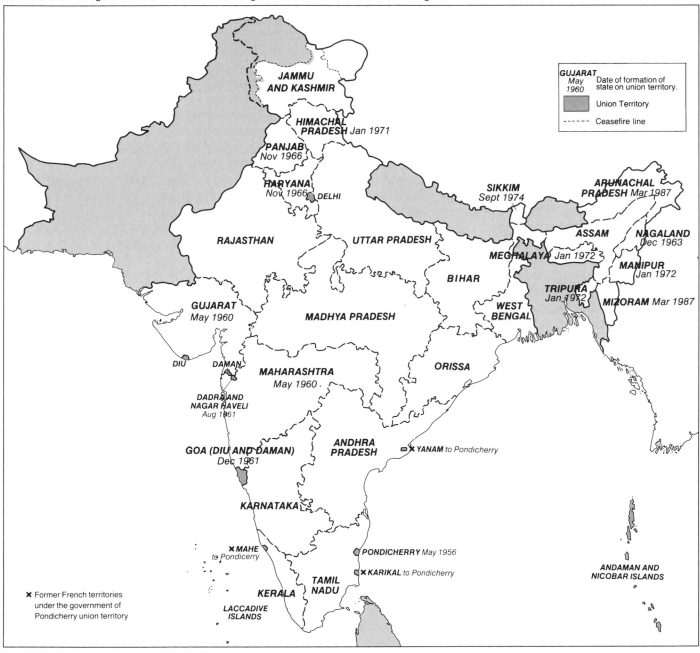

GUJARAT
May
1960
Date of formation of
state on union territory.

Union Territory

Ceasefire line

JAMMU AND KASHMIR

HIMACHAL PRADESH Jan 1971

PANJAB Nov 1966

HARYANA Nov 1966

DELHI

RAJASTHAN

UTTAR PRADESH

SIKKIM Sept 1974

ARUNACHAL PRADESH Mar 1987

ASSAM

NAGALAND Dec 1963

MEGHALAYA Jan 1972

MANIPUR Jan 1972

BIHAR

TRIPURA Jan 1972

MIZORAM Mar 1987

WEST BENGAL

GUJARAT May 1960

MADHYA PRADESH

ORISSA

DIU

DAMAN

MAHARASHTRA May 1960

DADRA AND NAGAR HAVELI Aug 1961

GOA (DIU AND DAMAN) Dec 1961

ANDHRA PRADESH

✕ YANAM to Pondicherry

KARNATAKA

✕ MAHE to Pondicerry

PONDICHERRY May 1956

✕ KARIKAL to Pondicherry

ANDAMAN AND NICOBAR ISLANDS

✕ Former French territories under the government of Pondicherry union territory

KERALA

TAMIL NADU

LACCADIVE ISLANDS

Source: Babulal Fadia, State Politics in India, Vol.1 (New Delhi, 1984), p.63

parties have made similar demands in other peripheral, border, and non-Hindi-speaking states, such as West Bengal, Tamil Nadu, Andhra, Kashmir and Assam. The central government leadership was most reluctant to take up this issue, but ultimately agreed to appoint a Commission on Centre-State Relations, chaired by a retired Supreme Court judge, Mr R. S. Sarkaria, whose appoint-

ment took effect on June 9, 1983. The Commission's report had not been completed as of June 1987.

Persistence of Hindu–Muslim communal divisions

Religious differences between Hindus and Muslims, rather than language, provided the principal sources of political mobilization, conflict and violence between communal groups in the pre-Independence period. Even in the post-Independence period, Hindu–Muslim communal differences have persisted and have continued to provide a major source of violent conflicts and deaths in Indian society. So-called Hindu–Muslim riots – often in fact organized rather than spontaneous affairs – have become recurring, virtually endemic features of the social life of several important towns of western Uttar Pradesh, but many other cities and towns in other states of India have also experienced severe communal riots from time to time. A considerable increase in the number of communal incidents and the number of persons killed and injured in them has occurred since the late 1970s, as indicated in Table 7.

Table 7. Communal incidents in India 1978–82

Year	Number of communal incidents	Number of persons killed	Number of persons injured
1978	230	110	1,853
1979	304	261	2,379
1980	427	375	2,838
1981	319	196	2,613
1982	474	238	3,025

Source: Government of India, Ministry of Home Affairs, *Report, 1982–83* p. 3 (Government of India Press, New Delhi 1983).

Rise of inter-caste conflicts

Inter-caste conflicts, primarily between the élite caste groups, on the one hand, and both the Scheduled Caste and 'backward' castes of intermediate ritual status in Indian caste hierarchies, on the other hand, have increased in number and intensified to the point of extreme violence in several states in recent years, most notably in Gujarat and Bihar. Such conflicts have generally arisen in states which have large populations of backward castes, who often are important landowning castes, but have been behind the élite castes in education, urban employment (particularly in the public services) and political representation. Several states have adopted policies granting preferential treatment to these backward castes to redress the imbalances between them and the élite castes. Resentment on the part of the élite castes, with the lead often taken by students in higher educational institutions whose life chances thereby appear diminished, may then burst forth in violent responses and caste riots. The worst such riots anywhere in India since Independence occurred in Gujarat, in the major industrial city of Ahmedabad and in other areas of the state as well, in 1985, after the Congress government under a backward caste chief minister announced an increase in backward class (Scheduled Caste, Schedule Tribe and backward caste) reservations in universities and

government employment from ten to twenty-eight percent. These riots, which expanded to include Hindu–Muslim killings, violent confrontations between the police and the public, and involvement of the criminal *lumpenproletariat* as well, persisted for five months, led to approximately 275 deaths, and ended only with the resignation of the Congress chief ministers. Although Gujarat represents an extreme case of inter-caste conflict, most states in the country have experienced some forms of confrontation and struggle between backward and élite castes in recent years.

Explaining the rise and resurgence of regional, caste and communal conflicts

Many alternative explanations have been offered for the resurgence of regional and communal and the rise of caste conflicts in the past fifteen years, including the persistence of immutable primordial cleavages in Indian society, their underlying basis in economic or class differences, and specific policies and political tactics pursued by the central and state governments.

Whichever of the competing explanations seems most persuasive, the problems in center-state relations, including those involving regional minorities, have highlighted an important structural problem in the Indian political system. That problem arises from the tensions created by the centralizing drives of the Indian state in a society where the predominant long-term social, economic, and political tendencies are toward pluralism, regionalism and decentralization. Although the same tensions existed in the Nehru years, central government policies then favored pluralist solutions, non-intervention in state politics except in a conciliatory role or as a last resort, and preservation of a separation between central and state politics, allowing considerable autonomy for the latter. From the early 1970s, however, during Mrs Gandhi's political dominance, the central leaders have intervened incessantly in state politics to preserve their dominance at the Center, the boundaries between central and state politics have disappeared in the critical north Indian states especially, and pluralist policies, though not discarded, were often subordinated to short-range calculations of political benefit.

The persistence of Hindu–Muslim conflicts requires another set of explanations. These would include the bitter legacies of partition, the non-responsiveness of some state governments, particularly in north India, towards Muslim minority demands, and the political advantages that some politicians and communal-minded political groups at the local level gain by fomenting communal disorders.

The common link among the three types of conflicts, regional, caste and communal, is their emergence out of a multi-ethnic, multi-cultural society. Such tensions and conflicts require constant political management, pluralist accommodation, and self-denying attitudes on the part of political leaders which would prevent them from extracting political advantage from these situations. During the past fifteen years, however, quite different policies, approaches and attitudes have been dominant.

PRB

Further reading

P. R. Brass, *Language, Religion, and Politics in North India* (London, 1974)
'The Punjab Crisis and the Unity of India', in Atul Kohli, Ed., *India's Troubled Democracy: An Analysis of Changing State-Society Relations* (Princeton, N.J., 1987)
'Pluralism, Regionalism, and Decentralizing Tendencies in Contemporary Indian Politics', in A. J. Wilson and Dennis Dalton, Eds, *The States of South Asia: Problems of National Integration* (London, 1982)
J. Das Gupta, *Language Conflict and National Development: Group Politics and National Language Policy in India* (Berkeley, 1970)
M. Weiner, *Sons of the Soil: Migration and Ethnic Conflict in India* (Princeton, N.J., 1978)

Parties and politics

Indian National Congress

The Indian National Congress, founded in 1885 by a relatively narrowly-based national élite, had gradually become transformed during the Independence movement into a broad-based mass organization which included in its fold a wide range of ideological, social and religious groups. After Independence, as the Congress went through the transformation first into a ruling party, then into a party competing with others for success in free elections, numerous conflicts arose within the party, some groups left the party or were expelled from it, and some groups, such as Muslims and Scheduled Castes gained increased representation within the party. Internal conflicts in the party became particularly intense from 1951, when the electoral process became a primary focus of the Congress organization and a party nomination to contest a legislative assembly or parliamentary seat the primary ambition of most Congressmen.

The Indian National Congress is formally a mass party with a dues-paying membership and with an elaborate, hierarchical organizational structure extending from local to district to state to all-India committees culminating at the top in a Working Committee, the executive committee of the national party, with an elected President as its head.

The formal structure was important in Nehru's days, but more important was an informal structure of factional linkages and conflicts, extending from the local to the national level. Factional

President of the Congress

elected by all the delegates
for a two-year term

Working Committee

Congress president and twenty members:
seven elected by the All-India Congress Committee and
thirteen appointed by the president

All-India Congress Committee

one-eighth of the delegates of each province
elected by the delegates of that province

Annual Congress Session

president, former presidents, and
all delegates
(all members of the Pradesh Congress
Committees are delegates)

Source: Stanley A. Kochanek, *The Congress Party of India* p. xxii (Princeton, N.J., 1968).

The national decision-making structure of the Congress.

conflicts within the Congress ultimately culminated in struggles for control of the state governments themselves, with most states in the country divided between a ministerial wing, the faction which dominated the government and sometimes, but not always, the party organization as well and a dissident wing which struggled to gain control of the party organization in order to use it as a base to gain control of the government.

Factional conflicts in the Congress then and now had little policy content. Moreover, although the Congress organization was in the 1950s and 1960s a highly factionalized, internally competitive party, factional conflict terminated at the highest levels where, from 1950–51 onward, Nehru remained in complete mastery of policy and politics.

Upon the death of Nehru, however, a grand succession struggle developed. Indeed, a formal split in the Congress occurred in 1969 over the issue of selection of the nominee of the Congress for President of India. The wing of the Congress which remained under Mrs Gandhi's leadership became known as Congress (R) – for Ruling – and demonstrated its predominance in the country against the other wing, known as Congress (O) – for Organization – in the

Mrs Gandhi amongst Congress party leaders.

1971 parliamentary elections. A further split in the Congress (R) occurred in 1978 upon the termination of the Emergency after which the Congress of Mrs Gandhi, which once again emerged as the dominant Congress in the country, became known as the Congress (I) for Indira. The Congress had become, in effect, her personal party, dependent upon her populist, sometimes demagogic, leadership rather than on local party organization, to win elections. The Congress organization itself at the provincial and local levels atrophied. The extent to which a great national movement had become converted into a Nehru family patrimony was indicated by the immediate and unquestioning acceptance of Rajiv Gandhi as Prime Minister of the country and leader of the Congress upon his mother's assassination in November 1984.

In most states, particularly in North India and in Maharashtra, the Congress leaders come from the élite – or at least middle status – land-controlling, dominant castes in the countryside. A basic, somewhat paradoxical, coalition was put together early after

Independence and strengthened under Mrs Gandhi, consisting of strong support from the extremes of the social order, from the élite, land-controlling castes at the top, who occupied the leadership positions in the party, on the one hand, and from the low-castes, the poor, and disadvantaged, including many minority groups, on the other hand.

The existence of this formidable coalitional support base combined with the enormous popularity of the Nehru family leaders made the Congress the center of the party system, which scholars came to label a one-party dominant system, to indicate at once the centrality of the Congress in the system and the peripherality of the opposition. It was always obvious, however, that since the Congress itself rarely polled a majority of votes in most states and only once since Independence, in 1984, nearly did so at the Center, Congress dominance was only partly a result of its own support base. Equally important was the disunity of the opposition which, if it could be overcome, as it was in 1977, could lead to the displacement of the Congress from power at the Center.

Non-Congress parties

Radical and revolutionary parties and movements

The Left has been divided into two main streams – Socialist and Communist. Both wings of the Left have suffered from numerous party splits, though the Communists ultimately survived them better. Aside from the usual opportunistic reasons and leadership conflicts that have contributed to or been dominant factors in party splits among most parties in India, there has been a single principal theme which caused divisions in both the Socialist and Communist movements, namely, the stance to be taken towards the ruling Congress. Division on that issue, rather than divisions in the international Communist movement, were principally responsible for the split in the Communist Party of India (CPI) in 1964, which led to the formation of the Communist Party of India (Marxist) (CPM), and for the splintering off from both Communist parties after 1969 of a number of romantic revolutionary and terrorist movements. The CPI throughout most of its post-Independence history has favored a strategy of alliance with the Congress or at least with 'progressive elements' within the Congress, whereas the CPM has favored a more militant policy of opposition to the Congress.

A similar division occurred among the non-Communist Left parties in the 1960s and constituted the principal ideological division between the more militant Socialist party led by Dr Rammanohar Lohia and the less militant Praja Socialist Party. Under Lohia's leadership, the radical Left was principally responsible for creating the conditions that ultimately led to the broad inter-party coalition politics that toppled the Congress in half the Indian states in the 1960s and 1970s and that contributed to the Janata alliance which formed against the Congress during the Emergency. In this latter process, however, the Socialist parties disappeared as organized entities and their various leaders ended up in several political parties which no longer bore a Socialist label.

The Communist movement also experienced two prolonged periods of debate on the question of political tactics, that is, whether to pursue parliamentarism or revolution. The first period, in which the central focus of debate was the famous Communist-led insurrection in the Telengana region of Andhra, the strategy of revolutionary confrontation with state authority was defeated both in theoretical debate and in practice by 1951, after the intervention of the Indian army.

The second debate was inspired by the split from the CPM in Bengal of a local group of party activists who were leading a violent agitation in the Naxalbari subdivision of Darjeeling district. The incidents in Naxalbari were followed by the spread of revolutionary romanticism among numerous Communist splinter groups, using terrorist tactics in widely dispersed pockets of the Indian countryside. Although the Communist parties, particularly the

Jyoti Basu, leader of the Communist Party of India (Marxist) in West Bengal. The communist parties have consistently won just under ten percent of the votes in Lok Sabha elections; their strength is in the states of Kerala and West Bengal.

CPM, were initially shaken by these developments, neither of the two established parties diverged from their essentially parliamentary and reformist paths. Moreover, in the early 1970s, the Indian police and other military forces, including the army in some cases, set out systematically to annihilate these bands of Communist revolutionaries, virtually all of whom were ultimately killed or jailed.

India has been distinctive among non-Communist countries in the extent to which Communist parties have actually held power at the state level. In Kerala, the CPM leads a counter-coalition against a Congress-dominated coalition, with whom it alternates in power. In West Bengal, the CPM has become the dominant party and has been in power at the head of a Left coalition, in which it is overwhelmingly dominant, since 1977.

It is difficult not to conclude on the basis of the history and performance of the radical parties in India since Independence that the prospects for radical change through these parties either in the existing system or through a revolutionary upheaval are quite limited. Factors limiting the ability of the Left parties to introduce more radical change have been the threat of political repression by the Center if the radical parties attempt to do too much too fast, the absence of Left unity, and the fact that one of the leading Communist parties has often been in alliance with the ruling Congress party. Moreover, in most parts of the country, right-wing, centrist and regional forces are much stronger than the parties of the Left.

Right-wing, agrarian and militant nationalist parties

The Swatantra Party. The Swatantra party, which drew together a number of regional parties such as the Ganatantra Parishad in Orissa, the Janata party of the Raja of Ramgarh in Bihar, a coalition of landed groups in Gujarat, some of the former princes in Rajasthan and scattered discontented former landlords in other parts of the country, was formed on an all-India basis in 1959. It was of consequence nationally only in three general elections, in 1962, 1967 and 1972. During its heyday, Swatantra was the leading secular party of the Right offering a full-scale critique of the Congress policies of centralized planning, nationalization of industries, agrarian reform and nonalignment.

Lok Dal. This was a second prominent agrarian-based party, which succeeded in achieving broad support in North India after its foundation in 1969, which played a central role in the Janata coalition against the Congress in 1977, and which emerged as the second largest party in the Lok Sabha in 1980. The Lok Dal began life in Uttar Pradesh under the leadership of a prominent former Congressman, Charan Singh, who left the Congress to form the first non-Congress government in that state in 1967. Charan Singh drew his agrarian supporters together, most of whom came from the so-called backward or middle-status cultivating peasant proprietor castes, into a new political party called the BKD, which emerged as the second largest party after the Congress in that state in its first electoral contest in the 1969 mid-term legislative assembly elections. In 1975, the largest section of the radical Socialists in both Uttar Pradesh and Bihar, consisting primarily of those leaders whose support base came from the backward classes in those states, joined forces with Charan Singh's BKD, which was thereafter called the BLD. In 1977, the BLD in turn merged into the Janata coalition. When that coalition itself fell apart, largely as a consequence of Charan Singh's aspirations to displace Morarji Desai and become Prime Minister himself, the old BLD re-emerged as the Lok Dal.

Jan Sangh. Although considered by its detractors to have been a Hindu communal, even anti-Muslim party with fascist inclinations, members of the Jan Sangh, a significant North Indian party from 1952 until 1977, would vehemently deny such labels and would accept only that they were militant nationalists in a Hindu country which, as such, ought legitimately to draw its symbols of nationalism from the predominantly Hindu traditions of the country. The Jan Sangh was a formidable force in North India not only because of the appeal of its ideology but because it was able to call upon a disciplined body of political workers from a militant Hindu cultural organization known as the Rashtriya Swayamsevak Sangh (RSS), which always provided the most vigorous canvassers at election time. Important RSS persons also always occupied the controlling positions in the Jan Sangh party organization and the leadership postions in its legislative parties as well.

The rise and fall of the Janata coalition

All the leading parties of the non-Communist Left, of the Center and the Right, with the later addition also of some defectors from the Congress, joined forces towards the end of the Emergency to form a new political organization called the Janata party. The program and policies of the Janata party drew primarily from the ideas of Charan Singh and the Socialists for the promotion of agriculture, a self-sufficient peasantry and labor-intensive small-scale industry.

Structurally, the Janata party never succeeded in becoming anything other than a loosely-knit coalition of ambitious political leaders and political parties which attempted to retain their previous organizational and social support bases. In July 1979, the coalition broke apart in a struggle for the prime ministership. Charan Singh became Prime Minister for three weeks only until his resignation and the calling of a new election, which led in 1980 to the return of Mrs Gandhi and the Congress to power.

After the disintegration of the Janata coalition, the political parties which initially joined it either re-formed themselves with new names or disintegrated. The principal remnants of the original Janata coalition today are the Lok Dal (divided since the death of Charan Singh into two separate parties, Lok Dal (A) and Lok Dal (B)), the Janata party led by a former Congressman of moderate Socialist inclinations, Mr Chandrashekar, and the Bharatiya Janata Party (BJP), which consists primarily of former Jan Sangh leaders and members. Many of the former Congress (O) and Socialist leaders and members are in the Janata party led by Chandrashekar, but some of the Congress (O) people have gone over to the BJP.

Regional parties

In several states in India, the largest non-Congress political parties are specific to a single state and have little or no strength outside their home state. The most important such parties are the All-India Anna Dravida Munnetra Kazhagam (AIADMK) and the Dravida

Munnetra Kazhagam (DMK) in Tamil Nadu, the Telugu Desam in Andhra, the Akali Dal in Panjab, the National Conference in Jammu and Kashmir, and the Assam Gana Parishad in Assam. In fact, in all these states in 1987, the non-Congress party was in power, in some cases with the support of the Congress, in other cases independently of Congress support. All these single-state parties are distinguished by their adoption of a regional nationalist perspective, by their political desire for greater regional autonomy of states in the Indian Union, for their focus on issues specific to their states, or for their base within a religious minority.

In the light of the additional fact that in several other states, non-Congress parties are either dominant or equal rivals to the Congress in the state legislative assemblies and sometimes control their state's delegation of MPs to the Lok Sabha as well, the position of the Congress as the dominant party in the country seems much less secure than its 80 percent majority achieved in the Lok Sabha in the 1984 elections would indicate. In West Bengal, the dominant party is the CPM. In Karnataka, the current ruling party is Janata. In Kerala, a CPM-led Leftist coalition returned to power in the aftermath of the March 1987 legislative assembly elections. In Haryana the Lok Dal came to power in alliance with the BJP with a massive majority in the state elections of June 11, 1987. The Congress, in effect, therefore, despite its huge majority in Parliament, was the dominant party in 1987 only in the larger Hindi-speaking states and the adjacent states of Gujarat, Maharashtra and Orissa. In the northeast, in Bengal, in Kashmir, Panjab, Haryana and the entire south, non-Congress parties were dominant.

PRB

Further reading

P. R. Brass, *Factional Politics in an Indian State: The Congress Party in Uttar Pradesh* (Berkeley, 1965)
and M. Franda, Eds, *Radical Politics in South Asia* (Cambridge, Mass., 1973)
S. A. Kochanek, *The Congress Party of India* (Princeton, N.J., 1968)

Electoral politics

The electoral process

As in the British parliamentary system, elections to the Lok Sabha (lower house) of Parliament must be held within five years of the election of the previous parliament, but they may be called by the President upon the advice of the Prime Minister at any time before the expiration of the normal five-year term of the House. The actual mechanics of the election, including the delimitation of constituency boundaries, the setting of specific dates for the polling in different parts of the country, the establishment and manning of polling booths, the allotment of party symbols, the acceptance or rejection of nominations according to the electoral laws and rules, the counting of votes, the publication of the results and the like are all supervised by the Election Commission, a semi-autonomous body whose functions are defined in the Constitution of the country.

Until 1971, when Prime Minister Gandhi called the first mid-term election for the Lok Sabha, the general practice was that a general election included the simultaneous scheduling of polling for both the Lok Sabha and the state legislative assemblies. The call by Mrs Gandhi for a mid-term election in 1971 and the consequent 'delinking' of parliamentary and legislative assembly elections at that time included the clear design to separate the national from the state elections and thereby to capitalize upon the national appeal of Mrs Gandhi against her rivals in the Congress organization and in state politics generally. Since 1971, the general practice has been to

An Indian ballot form. Because the majority of voters are illiterate, parties are identified by symbols.

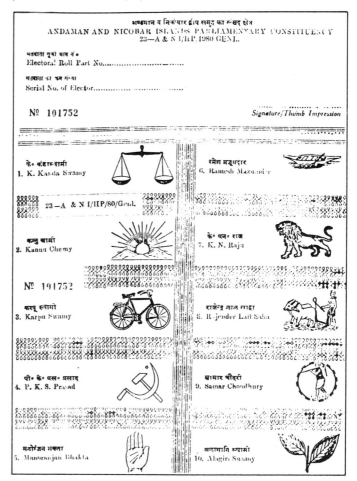

hold parliamentary and state legislative assembly elections separately, although they do sometimes coincide in particular states.

At present, the electoral unit, as in Britain, is a single-member constituency, in which the winning candidate is the person who succeeds in gaining a plurality of votes on the first ballot. The only distinction among constituencies concerns whether they are reserved for Scheduled Castes or Scheduled Tribes or not. In a reserved constituency, only persons from designated low caste or tribal groups may contest, but all adults are eligible to vote. The number of reserved constituencies is proportionate to the total population of Scheduled Castes or Tribes within a state. In the country as a whole, approximately 21 percent of the total Lok Sabha and state legislative assembly seats are reserved.

Most Indian constituencies are overwhelmingly rural, containing only a few small towns, in which each polling booth covers a single village or several adjacent villages. In the urban areas, there will naturally be a large number of polling booths set up in ways familiar in industrialized societies within public buildings such as schools.

Most Indians are still unable to read. Therefore, each party and independent candidate is allotted a distinctive symbol.

Election campaigns

A campaign in a rural constituency requires of a candidate who aspires to success that he visit as many as possible of the hundred or so villages in an assembly constituency and at least a sample of the five hundred or six hundred villages of a parliamentary constituency. Such campaigning, concentrated within the statutory

Voters queue outside a polling station in Teynampet (Tamil Nadu).

three-week period, is an extraordinarily grueling experience, carried out by jeep, by foot, and by bullock cart, with each candidate scheduling perhaps as many as six village visits a day. In the cities, election campaigning involves neighborhood street corner rallies, house-to-house canvassing by the candidates' workers, and parades through the city with the candidate himself riding in a jeep saluting the crowds as he drives through the town.

There are three principal means of communicating the message of a party or of independent candidates during a campaign. Each well-organized party will issue a printed manifesto in both English and the vernacular language, stating the distinctive positions of the party on the major issues of the day. The second means of communication is through public speeches by the candidate and his supporters in the villages and city street corners. The third type of approach to the voters is through private and implicit appeals. The candidates' supporters will, in this respect, depart from the printed manifestoes and public statements of their candidate and will stress ties of caste between the candidate and his brethren, his accomplishments or promises to do things for particular villages and localities, the candidate's probity and his rivals' venality, with emphasis especially on any evidence that can be found or concocted that the candidate's principal rival has had some criminal record or has had some criminal charges filed against him.

Indian voting behavior

A multiplicity of factors affect voter decisions at election time, including appeals to class, community, caste and faction loyalty as well as the personal attractions of popular and charismatic leaders. At the local level, in the countryside, by far the most important factor in voting behavior remains caste solidarity. Large and important castes in a constituency tend to back either a respected member of their caste or a political party with whom their caste members identify. However, local factions and local-state factional alignments, which involve inter-caste coalitions also are important factors in influencing voting behavior.

Issues also matter in India and may sometimes sway many groups of voters in the same direction and create a 'wave' or landslide across large parts of the country. One wave developed in 1967 against the Congress on issues of rising prices, scarcity, and the discontent of government employees and students in North India. A second occurred in 1971–72; first in the parliamentary then the legislative assembly elections, in favor of Mrs Gandhi in the aftermath of her struggles with the old Congress party bosses and her leadership of the country in the Third Indo-Pakistan War which brought about the Independence of Bangladesh. A third swept the Janata coalition into power in 1977 as a consequence of widespread discontent with alleged excesses committed by the government during the Emergency regime. In 1984, a fourth wave arose in sympathy with

Rajiv Gandhi after the assassination of his mother and in response to his appeals for national unity against forces said to threaten the unity and integrity of the country.

Parties and elections

Parties do not dominate electoral politics in India to the same extent as in Western parliamentary systems. There are many localities in India where local notables, often descendants of great landlord or princely families, and other persons with independent bases of local power and support within a caste group, for example, have sufficient independent resources either to contest elections successfully on their own or to bargain for the support of established political parties.

Also, the notion of party loyalty is extremely weak in India in contrast to its prevalence in Western parliamentary regimes. Persons from factional groups defeated in struggles to gain the party nominations for themselves or their allies and supporters in a general election rarely hesitate either to switch their loyalties to another party which offers them a nomination or to contest the election as independents.

Finally, party institutionalization is rare in India. Although the Indian National Congress is one of the oldest political parties in the world and the Communist parties trace their origins back to the 1920s, most other parties in India have had relatively brief existences, sometimes only for a single election, other times for two or three.

Election results, 1952 to 1987

The vote for the Congress

The Congress organization clearly has been the leading political institution in post-Independence India. Since Independence, there has always been one predominant Congress organization in the country, which has always been either in power or has been the largest opposition party in Parliament and which has also always had broader support in most states of the Indian Union than any other party, even though it has never won a clear majority of the popular votes in the country.

The vote for the non-Congress parties

With the exception of the 1977 elections, no single non-Congress party has ever polled even as much as half the Congress vote in the country as a whole. The Election Commission has always made a distinction in publishing the figures for parliamentary elections between 'national' parties and other parties. For a time, there appeared to be a trend toward 'nationalization' of the party system, with the vote for the 'national' non-Congress parties having gone up from the 20 to 30 percent range in the 1950s to the 30 to 40 percent

Main features of Indian elections

Table A

Congress Party results in eight parliamentary elections, 1952–1984

Election	Vote Percent	Seats Number	Percent
1952	45.0	357	73
1957	47.8	359	73
1962	44.7	358	73
1967	40.7	283	54
1971	43.7	352	68
1977	34.5	153	28
1980	42.7	351	67
1984	49.2	401	79

Source: M. Weiner *India at the Polls, 1980: A Study of the Parliamentary Elections* p. 157 (Washington DC, 1980); R. L. Hardgrave and S. A. Kochanek *India: Government and Politics in a Developing Nation* 4th edn, p. 269 (San Diego, 1986).

Table B

Vote shares for the Congress, 'National' opposition parties, and others in parliamentary elections, 1952–1984

Years	Congress	'National' opposition	Other parties and independents	Total
1952	45.00	29.57	25.43	100.00
1957	47.78	25.26	26.96	100.00
1962	44.72	37.85	17.43	100.00
1967	40.73	37.90	21.37	100.00
1971	43.62	34.23	22.15	100.00
1977	34.50	50.17	15.33	100.00
1980	42.68	42.39	14.93	100.00
1984	49.16	31.38	19.46	100.00

Source: P. R. Brass, *Pluralism, Regionalism and Decentralizing Tendencies in Contemporary Indian Politics* in A. J. Wilson and D. Dalton (Eds) *The States of South Asia: Problems of National Integration* p. 242 (London, 1982); Result Sheets, Election Commission of the Government of India.

Table C

Distribution percent by party of votes polled in Lok Sabha elections, 1952–1984

Year	INC/ INCI	NCO/ INCU/ INCJ/ INCS	CPI	CPM	SOC	PSP/ KMPP	SSP	SWA	BJS/ BJP	JNP	JNPS/ LD/ DMKP	Other parties	IND
1952	45.0	—	3.3	—	10.6	5.8	—	—	3.1	—	—	16.4	15.9
1957	47.8	—	8.9	—	—	10.4	—	—	5.9	—	—	7.6	19.4
1962	44.7	—	9.9	—	2.7	6.8	—	7.9	6.4	—	—	10.4	11.1
1967	40.8	—	5.0	4.4	—	3.1	4.9	8.7	9.4	—	—	10.1	13.7
1971	43.7	10.4	4.7	5.1	—	1.0	2.4	3.1	7.4	—	—	13.8	8.4
1977	34.5	1.7	2.8	4.3	—	—	—	—	—	41.3	—	9.8	5.5
1980	42.7	5.3	2.6	6.1	—	—	—	—	—	19.0	9.4	8.5	6.4
1984	49.2	2.1	2.6	6.0	—	—	—	—	7.7	7.0	6.0	11.5	7.9

Sources: V. B. Singh and Shankar Bose *Elections in India: Data Handbook on Lok Sabha Elections, 1952–80*, p. 25 (New Delhi, 1984); R. L. Hardgrave, Jr and S. A. Kochanek *India: Government and Politics in a Developing Nation*, 4th edn, p. 269 (San Diego, 1986).

INC:	Indian National Congress	KMPP:	Kisan Mazdoor Praja Party
INCI:	Indian National Congress (Indira)	SSP:	Samyukta Socialist Party
INCO:	Indian National Congress (Organization)	SWA:	Swatantra Party
INCU:	Indian National Congress (Urs)	BJS:	Bharatiya Jana Sangh
INCJ:	Indian National Congress (Jagjivan Ram)	BJP:	Bharatiya Janata Party
INCS:	Indian National Congress (Socialist)	JNP:	Janata Party
CPI:	Communist Party of India	JNPS:	Janata Party (Secular)
CPM:	Communist Party of India (Marxist)	LD:	Lok Dal
SOC:	Socialist Party	DMKP:	Dalit Mazdoor Kisan Party
PSP:	Praja Socialist Party	IND:	Independent

Box 18 *(continued opposite)*

Table D

Vote shares percent of Congress and its closest competitor, by state,[a] parliamentary elections, 1984

State	Congress (I)	Closest competitor
Andhra Pradesh	42.07	44.10 (Telugu Desam)
Bihar	52.05	13.58 (DMKP/Lok Dal)
Gujarat	53.24	18.64 (BJP)
Haryana	54.95	19.10 (DMKP/Lok Dal)
Himachal Pradesh	67.60	21.84 (BJP)
Jammu and Kashmir	31.38	44.06 (NC-F)
Karnataka	51.62	35.09 (Janata)
Kerala	33.24	19.83 (CPM)
Madhya Pradesh	56.96	30.03 (BJP)
Maharashtra	51.24	12.27 (Congress-S)
Orissa	57.5	32.01 (Janata)
Rajasthan	52.72	23.68 (BJP)
Tamil Nadu	40.43	25.27 (DMK)
Uttar Pradesh	51.37	22.08 (DMKP/Lok Dal)
West Bengal	48.16	35.15 (CPM)

[a]Only the larger states of the Indian Union have been included. Excluded are Manipur, Meghalaya, Nagaland, Sikkim, and Tripura, which elect only one or two seats each to the Lok Sabha.

Source: Government of India, Election Commission, *Third Annual Report, 1985* pp. 93, 97 (New Delhi, 1986).

Table E

Number of seats won by Congress and principal opposition party in 1984–1987 state legislative assembly elections

State	Congress	Principal opposition
Andhra Pradesh	50	202 (TD)
Assam	25	64 (AGP)
Bihar	196	46 (DMKP/LKD)
Gujarat	149	14 (JP)
Haryana	5	58 (DMKP/LKD)
Himachal Pradesh	58	7 (BJP)
Jammu and Kashmir	24[a]	36 (NC-F)
Karnataka	66	139 (Janata)
Kerala	33	36 (CPM)
Madhya Pradesh	250	58 (BJP)
Maharashtra	162	54 (Cong-S)
Orissa	117	21 (Janata)
Pondicherry	15	6 (AIADMK)
Panjab	32	73 (Akali Dal)
Rajasthan	113	39 (BJP)
Sikkim	1	30 (SSP)
Tamil Nadu	62	132 (AIADMK)
Uttar Pradesh	269	84 (DMKP/LKD)
West Bengal	40	187 (CPM)

[a]Congress (I) ally.

Source: Government of India, Election Commission, *Third Annual Report, 1985* pp. 93 and 97 (New Delhi, 1986); *Overseas Hindustan Times*, January 4, 1986; *India Today*, April 15, 1987; *New York Times*, June 23, 1987.

range between 1962 and 1971 to the 40 to 50 percent range in 1977 and 1980, with a corresponding decline in the relative vote shares of the category of 'other parties and independents' (Box 18, Table B). The trend, however, was partly illusory and appears chimerical in the face of the 1984 election results. Except for the Congress and the Communist parties, none of the other 'national' parties has persisted through time. Moreover, the second-place party has changed in every election since 1952, when the Socialist Party came in second with 10.6 percent of the vote (Box 18, Table C). It is also important to note that, in any single parliamentary election, the second-place party is likely to be different in different states. Second, many of the so-called national parties did not have a genuine national spread at all. Finally, even if there was a trend line toward nationalization of the opposition, it was demolished in the 1984 elections when the collective vote share of the 'national' opposition parties was reduced to 31.38 percent, a figure lower than any in the previous five elections.

Regional parties and state party systems

The most important reason for doubting the existence in India of anything that can be called a national party system is the fact that all the Indian states have distinctive party systems. The extent of

Table F

Election data, Indian parliamentary elections, 1952–1984

Year	Electorate (in millions)	Polling stations	Votes polled (in millions)	Turnout (percent)
1952	173.2	132,560	80.7	46.6
1957	193.7	220,478	91.3	47.1
1962	217.7	238,355	119.9	55.1
1967	250.1	267,555	152.7	61.1
1971	274.1	342,944	151.5	55.3
1977	321.2	373,908	194.3	60.5
1980	355.6	434,442	202.3	56.9
1984	375.8	479,214	238.4	63.4

Source: R. L. Hardgrave, Jr and S. A. Kochanek *India: Government and Politics in a Developing Nation* 4th edn, p. 302 (San Diego, 1986).

Box 18 *(continued)*

variation in patterns of party competition and of regional variations in party strength can be seen by comparing the relative strength of the two leading parties in each state in the 1984 parliamentary and the subsequent legislative assembly elections (Box 18, Tables D and E). In 15 states, there were eight different configurations of first and second-place parties. Moreover, it needs also to be kept in mind that, in the state legislative assembly elections, the leading non-Congress parties do much better in the smaller constituencies and in many states, as a result, they emerge as formidable opposition parties or even as the ruling parties, relegating the Congress to the opposition (Box 18, Table E).

In short, both the attempt to nationalize parliamentary elections by delinking them from state legislative assembly elections and the overwhelming Congress dominance that is usually produced in Parliament have failed to erode significantly the distinctiveness of regional political patterns in India or to establish a truly national party system in the country.

Elections and political mobilization

Turnout has increased by nearly 17 percentage points from 46.6 percent in 1952 to 63.4 percent in 1984 (Box 18, Table F). Increasing turnout has also involved political mobilization of new groups of voters. In the legislative assembly elections especially, there has been a process of caste succession in the elections in which candidates both from élite caste groups which were less well represented before and from the larger backward caste groups have entered the electoral arena. Although the processes of political mobilization have affected the lower backward and the lowest castes (Scheduled Castes) as well, there is no firm evidence concerning their actual turnout rates.

The more widespread and politically significant process of political mobilization which has been occurring in many parts of the country has been the increasing mobilization of the middle status backward agricultural castes and the lower backward artisan, service, and smallholding castes. In some states, the backward castes (and some lower backward castes as well) have successfully displaced the previously dominant élite castes in leadership positions in the Congress. In other states, Tamil Nadu being the leading example, the backward castes have dominated the principal opposition to the Congress – the DMK and the AIADMK in Tamil Nadu – and have succeeded in displacing the Congress from power. In still other states, most notably the north Indian states of Uttar Pradesh and Bihar, the old élite castes of Brahmins, Rajputs and Bhumihars have remained dominant in the Congress, which itself has remained the dominant party, while the middle and lower backward castes have been mobilized by the opposition, first by the Socialists in the 1950s and 1960s, then by the Lok Dal in the 1960s and 1970s. Finally, in two other states, Kerala and West Bengal, the lower

backward and even the Scheduled Castes have been mobilized by the CPM. However, electoral politics and political mobilization in most of India remain dominated by the leading land-controlling castes of élite or middle status.

PRB

Further reading

P. R. Brass, *Caste, Faction and Party in Indian Politics*, Vol. II: *Election Studies* (Delhi, 1985)
V. B. Singh and S. Bose, *Elections in India: Data Handbook on Lok Sabha Elections, 1952–80* (New Delhi, 1984)
M. Weiner, *India at the Polls, 1980* (Washington, D.C., 1980)
M. Weiner and J. O. Field, Eds, *Studies in Electoral Politics in the Indian States* 4 vols (Delhi, 1974, 1975, 1977)

Problems and prospects in the working of the system

Problem of the persistence of the present parliamentary system
India is virtually unique among contemporary post-colonial countries in having functioned since Independence, with the exception of the Emergency, with a parliamentary system modeled on the British form of government. India's parliamentary system has evolved from one in which the Cabinet and the Prime Minister were dominant and the President was a figurehead – though potentially important – into a form of prime ministerial government, in which both the Parliament and the Cabinet play a secondary role.

Behind the adopted form of British prime ministerial government, however, there lie two indigenous adaptations: the predominant patrimonial system of the Nehru family and the politics of personal ambition, personal conflict and political opportunism of the Janata coalition. Each of these indigenous adaptations is inherently unstable for the one depends upon the fate of a family and on the fragilities of personal leadership in general, while the second offers the prospect of the disintegration of any central authority in the system.

India's federal system also presents some peculiarities and adaptations of a well-known form of government. Although politics in India are more regionalized than in any other federal polity in the world, reflecting the unrivaled cultural diversity of the country, the system has more unitary features than most federal systems including especially that of the USA.

In the Nehru period, there were some states which developed a sort of Chief Ministerial form of government comparable to the prime ministerial pattern at the Center, while other states developed more in the direction of an unstable factional and coalition politics of personal ambition, patronage and corruption. During Mrs Gandhi's period, most of the states in which the Congress ruled lost their autonomy and came directly under the control of the central leadership. However, underlying the overall pattern of Congress dominance in the states and increasing central control over the state governments was an alternative type of politics, involving the assertion of regional political and social forces and identities.

Although the struggles for power at the Center and between regionalizing and centralizing forces have produced singular adaptations of both parliamentarism and federalism in India, they have also created tensions that have from time to time aroused a desire among some of the participants to change the system to ensure continuity and authority at the Center and the primacy of the central government in relation to the states. A current of opinion favors the adoption of a new form of government of a presidential type which would enhance still further the authority of the central leaders and the Union government to restore order in troubled areas of the country, to eliminate corruption and to increase the pace of economic and social change.

The presidential system most widely favored is not the American type, but the French system as it functioned in the Gaullist period, with its strong executive and unitary pattern of government. The very problems which have produced a desire for stronger central authority have also produced a counter-tendency in the form of demands from several states for greater regional autonomy and in somewhat more feeble, but recurrent proposals from politicians who continue to draw inspiration from the Gandhian tradition for greater decentralization of institutions in India down to the district and village level as well.

Problem of establishing a stable structure of national power: parties, politics and elections

Even during the Nehru period, the Congress faced persistent problems in maintaining its dominance in and control over the several states. Although Mrs Gandhi succeeded twice (in the succession struggle that followed upon Nehru's death and after her defeat in the 1977 elections and her return to power in 1980) in re-establishing the overwhelming dominance of the Congress in the country, she knew very well that that dominance was not secure in the states and that Congress power at the Center was always threatened by the potential disintegration of the party in important states in the Union.

The assassination of Mrs Gandhi and the Panjab crisis converged in 1984 to build support behind the new leader, Rajiv Gandhi, and the Congress won an unprecedented 80 percent majority in the parliamentary elections held in December 1984. Rajiv Gandhi's victory notwithstanding, it is now evident that the political system has become more competitive at the national level with the central leadership of the Congress aware that power can be lost at the Center under certain conditions. Those conditions include the disintegration of the Congress and the rise of opposition forces within

particular states, the occurrence of an incident or incidents that arouse widespread discontent in North India, such as the sterilization campaign during the Emergency or the Panjab crisis in the 1980s, and the development of unity among the important non-Congress parties.

Since the delinking of parliamentary and legislative assembly elections in 1971, a new cycle of consolidation and disintegration of national power has come into being. Each cycle begins with the call for parliamentary elections either by the ruling party or, as in 1979, as a consequence of the disintegration of the governing coalition. So far, every parliamentary election since 1971 has led to a decisive result in favor of one party or another, that is, in favor either of the Congress or the Janata coalition in 1977. The new Prime Minister then dismisses most state governments controlled by the opposition and calls for fresh state legislative assembly elections, which invariably lead to the victory of the ruling party or its allies in the several states. At this very point, when power is consolidated in Delhi and in nearly all the states, the last step in the cycle occurs, namely, the beginning of a new cycle as a consequence of the disintegration of power in state after state either through factionalism in the Congress or through inter-party struggles in the non-Congress coalitions.

The great dilemma at the heart of Indian politics is that it is impossible in such a diverse country within the framework of a federal parliamentary system to maintain a stable structure of national power for long. It is an extremely difficult, prolonged and absorbing task to build national power in the country and it begins to disintegrate at the very point when it appears to have been consolidated.

At this stage, therefore, authoritarian solutions or alternative regimes, which remain always lurking in the background, emerge as a possible resolution to the central political dilemma of Indian politics and make it impossible to say, even forty years after Independence, that a stable parliamentary regime of the Westminster type has been established.

Problem of maintaining the unity of the country

Since Independence, the central leadership has, nevertheless, confronted several major challenges to the unity of the country with skill and success. These have included the integration of several hundred semi-autonomous princely states into the Indian Union in the years immediately after Independence, the linguistic reorganization of the states, the resolution of the official language controversy and the granting of partial official status in many states to minority languages, including Urdu among others.

On the other hand, none of the resolutions has resolved all relevant problems. The integration of the princely states left Kashmir divided and three wars with Pakistan have been fought in which the unresolved international status of Kashmir figured. Within the linguistically reorganized states, minorities and minority language speakers sometimes experience varying degrees of discrimination. Demands for greater regional autonomy, at times bordering on secessionism, have emerged from time to time in many states. In recent years, there has been an increasing polarization of communal hostilities and feelings and a great deepening of distrust between members of the Hindu and Muslim communities.

Despite numerous successes, therefore, in resolving some of the urgent problems threatening the unity of the Indian state since Independence, some of the problems that remain are so severe as to cast doubts on the ability of the central government under a centralized parliamentary system to maintain the unity of the country. Moreover, the remaining problems cannot be considered to be merely the unresolved remnants of old conflicts but reflect a fundamental structural tension in the Indian political system between forces seeking to strengthen further and centralize more decisively the Indian state and regional and other forces demanding further decentralization.

The centralizing and nationalizing measures taken by Mrs Gandhi included the political destruction of the state political bosses, the selection of the chief ministers of the Congress-dominated states by Mrs Gandhi herself in consultation with her small clique of advisors, the increased use of President's Rule in the states, the increased use of central police and intelligence forces to monitor and control regional opposition, populist, demagogic appeals to national categories of voters, such as the poor, the landless and the minorities, and some manipulation of xenophobic and paranoiac nationalism against Pakistan and the American CIA.

The primary dangers in Mrs Gandhi's strategy and its possible revival by Rajiv Gandhi lie in the collisions that inevitably result between these centralizing, nationalizing and militantly nationalist tendencies and the predominant tendencies toward regionalism, pluralism and decentralization. There are two possible strategies that the central government might use to avert these collisions which have become increasingly frequent and violent: reversion to the pluralist policies of the period of Nehru's dominance or a further drastic strengthening of the powers of the central government in an attempt to impose order upon India's diversity. The latter strategy, however, is more likely to lead to the transformation of regional forces into increasingly hostile, potentially secessionist elements threatening the disintegration of the country than to a true resolution of the underlying structural problems.

Problems of order, disorder and violence

The previous two decades have been marked by a decline of authoritative institutions in Indian politics, of which the most threatening to the future stability and peace of the country have been the disintegration of the Congress organization, the ever-declining effectiveness of and the ever-increasing corruption of the bureaucracy, and the demoralization of the police and its direct involvement in the perpetration rather than control of violence.

The Congress has disintegrated as a functioning organization. The party's formal institutions either do not exist any longer at the state and district level or they function only sporadically or at the call of the central leadership.

Since Independence, corruption in the bureaucracy has reached the highest levels of the IAS. Although many IAS officers remain honest and effective and present a facade of efficiency, intelligence and honesty at the top of the administrative hierarchies in Delhi, the state capital and the districts, there is a sharp break in the quality of personnel below the élite senior officers. Moreover, corruption below the élite levels has been institutionalized and affects virtually all departments such that no service can be expected as a right and virtually nothing can be done without payment of an illegal gratuity.

The spread of police violence also has eroded public confidence in the legitimacy of state institutions and in the ability of the Indian state to fulfill the elemental function assigned to it by Hobbes of ensuring the basic security of the people from the fear of violent death. Investigations and other police 'work' are undertaken upon payment of money by private citizens. Since everybody knows very well the methods of police work, people increasingly have taken the law into their own hands. This latter tendency is manifested in the increased display of guns by locally powerful persons, especially politicians, the increased use of violence against one's opponents in politics or otherwise, and the increased incidence of confrontations between police and people.

Conclusions

Despite their evident decay over time within India, the performance of India's political institutions compares favorably in many respects with those of her neighbors or with most other post-colonial societies. Indeed, the Indian political regime is one of the most democratic in the world by most conventional measures of political participation, electoral and party competition, persistence of parliamentary institutions, and diffusion of information.

It is sometimes argued that many of the deviations from accepted standards of parliamentary performance, bureaucratic probity and police honesty which developing countries such as India have been undergoing are stages that every developing or modernizing country, including the USA and Great Britain, have undergone and that such deviations do not necessarily suggest the imminent collapse of India's republican regime. It is, however, equally plausible that India's recent political difficulties are a pre-fascist stage. The point is that India's political system is unique and has to be understood on its own terms and its future is uncertain.

Although the Indian political system shows signs of disintegration, it is unlikely that it will do so, at least not through secessionist movements. The more immediate danger is the further spread of violence, lawlessness and disorder at the local level.

Alternative solutions, however, are available within India's traditions and political philosophies. They would include a move, which would be sanctioned by Gandhian ideas, toward greater decentralization of power to the states, districts and villages of India, a return to the pluralist policies of the Nehru period, and essential reforms of the bureaucracy and the police.

If neither a decisive move toward further centralization and authoritarianism or toward decentralization and pluralism are initiated, the future is likely to bring persisting social disorder and alternating periods of reassertion and decline of authority. It would be folly, however, to be sanguine about the future of India, to consider that the country is only going through a 'stage' in its development, and to fail to recognize that a grave systemic crisis is in progress.

PRB

Pakistan

The independent state of Pakistan, created on August 14, 1947, represented the outcome of a campaign on the part of sections of the Indian Muslim community for a Muslim homeland which had been triggered by the British decision to consider transferring power to the people of India. Although there was a sizeable number of Muslim politicians who were comfortable at the thought of remaining a minority in an independent India, albeit with safeguards to ensure that Muslims would not suffer discrimination, a second group believed that their community would become second-class citizens in a Hindu-dominated state. For them, the partitioning of the subcontinent along communal lines was the only way to protect the rights of the Indian Muslim 'nation'. Under the leadership of Mohammad Ali Jinnah and the Muslim League, the two-nation theory gained sufficient popularity to make Pakistan into a reality.

The establishment of Pakistan, however, did not solve the political problems of the Muslims of British India. Pakistan, in the form in which it was created, survived for only twenty-four years. Explanations of political instability in Pakistan have tended to place great store on the influence of individuals. For instance, it is claimed that the failure of Jinnah to hand power to his successor, Liaquat Ali Khan, before his death on September 11, 1948 was instrumental in bringing about fairly weak political leadership. Unlike Nehru in India, who had not had to wait for Gandhi's death before taking full command but had been sworn in as Prime Minister at independence and benefitted from Gandhi's support when challenged by Sardar

Rulers of Pakistan since Independence	
Head of State	
Governor-General	
1947–1948	Mohammad Ali Jinnah
1948–1951	Khwaja Nazamuddin
1951–1955	Ghulam Muhammad
1955–1956	Major-General Iskander Mirza
President	
1956–1958	Major-General Iskander Mirza
1958–1969	Field Marshal Ayub Khan
1969–1971	Major-General Yahya Khan
1971–1973	Zulfikar Ali Bhutto
1973–1978	Fazl Elahi Chaudhuri
1978–1988	General Zia ul Haq
1988–	Ghulam Isaq Khan
Prime Minister	
1947–1951	Liaquat Ali Khan
1951–1953	Khwaja Nazamuddin
1953–1955	Muhammad Ali of Bogra
1955–1956	Chaudhuri Muhammad Ali
1956–1957	H. S. Suhrawardhy
1957	I. I. Chundrigar
1957–1958	Feroz Khan Noon
1973–1977	Zulfikar Ali Bhutto
1985–1988	Muhammad Khan Junejo
1988–	Benazir Bhutto

Source: *The Statesman's Yearbook 1948–1986/1987*

Box 19

Vallabhbhai Patel, Liaquat found it difficult to establish his own independent authority. Moreover, he inherited only one of the three positions held by Jinnah, that of the Presidency of the Muslim League. The other two went to politicians from East Pakistan: Khwaja Nazimuddin became Governor-General and Maulvi Tamiz ud Din was elected President of the Constituent Assembly. In addition, while Nehru was able to make use of post-independence euphoria to provide India with a constitution, much of the enthusiasm with which Pakistan's citizens had greeted the emergence of the country had already dissipated by September 1948. Bengal and the smaller provinces of Sind and the Northwest Frontier had begun to resent being excluded from decision-making by the groups which dominated politics in the new capital city of Karachi. Thus, Liaquat was still discussing the 'basic principals' of constitution-making at the time of his assassination in 1951.

But the search for the roots of Pakistan's persistent instability has

Administrative divisions of Pakistan.

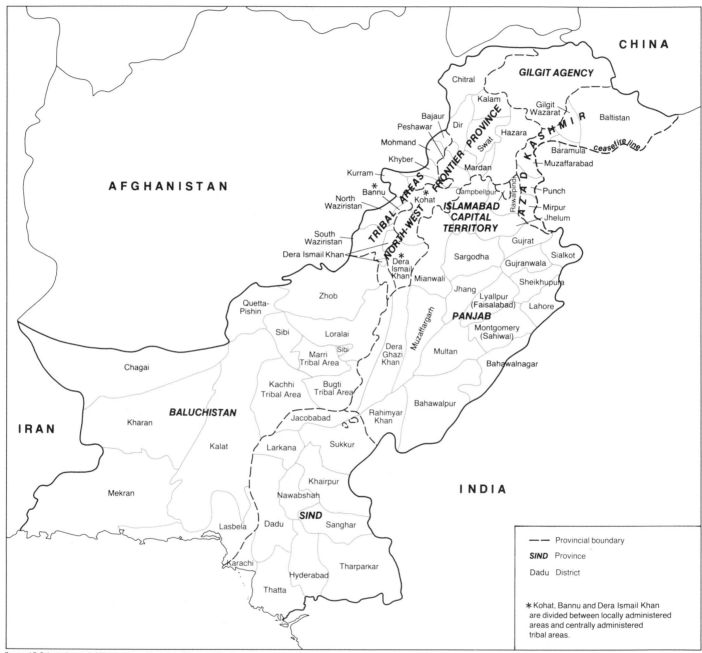

Source: J.E. Schwartzberg, ed., A Historical Atlas of South Asia (Chicago, 1978) p.79

to go much deeper than explanations which center on the absence of a strong leader. They can only be found in the social, economic and political dynamics of the very diverse society that, in 1947, with unexpected suddenness became the new state of Pakistan. Despite Jinnah's claim that they constituted a nation, the Muslims of the subcontinent did not automatically share common objectives. There were serious divisions within the community both before and after partition. Only urban Muslims from the Muslim-minority provinces who migrated to Pakistan after 1947 seemed satisfied with what independence brought them. Those who remained in India found the political equation there inexorably altered. Muslims in the provinces which became West Pakistan took time to accommodate themselves to the immense changes which partition brought about in their political situation. It was only after the emergence of the country's eastern wing as Bangladesh in 1971 that the political aspirations of this section of Pakistanis can be said to have been at least partially fulfilled.

Diversity was initially caused by the movement of over fourteen million people that accompanied partition: Pakistan lost 7.3 million people and in return gained 7.2 million refugees from India. By far the most important of these as an influence on Pakistan's early economic and political development were the Muslims who came from Delhi, the United Provinces (now the state of Uttar Pradesh), the Central Provinces (now Madhya Pradesh), Bombay, Gujarat and the princely states of Bhopal, Hyderabad and Junagadh. A second stream of migrants came from the eastern districts of the Panjab. The majority of these *muhajirs* (refugees) were drawn to the cities and towns of southwestern Pakistan. Since many had decided to migrate in order to benefit from the economic opportunities that

Jinnah's *mazar* or mausoleum in Karachi, which has come to be regarded as a symbol of the unity of Pakistan.

Muslim refugees from India; one in six of the people of West Pakistan was a refugee.

were being opened up for them, it was logical for them to head for the capital. In 1947, however, Karachi was not a big city; it was smaller than Lahore and did not have the infrastructure of a large urban center. Thus, migrants who could not be accommodated by Karachi went to Hyderabad, Sukkur and other towns in its hinterland. By 1951, the year of Pakistan's first census, refugees accounted for 57 percent of Karachi's population, 65 percent of Hyderabad's and 55 percent of Sukkur's. In all, migrants from India constituted 46 per cent of the combined population of the twelve major cities of Pakistan.

The muhajir culture was significantly different from that of the provinces which physically made up Pakistan, and a clash between the two was almost inevitable. While there were important differences within the refugee community, especially between those who came from India's urban areas and those who migrated from eastern Panjab, there were even greater differences separating muhajirs from the population of the Muslim-majority provinces which made up Pakistan. Those who dominated the urban refugee community believed in relatively 'secular' politics and laissez-faire economics; indigenous local leaders, with their ranks reinforced by refugees from East Panjab, sought the establishment of an Islamic state and a state-managed economy.

These differences were highlighted during the first decade of Pakistani politics. Soon after Independence, Jinnah's Muslim League was split into three factions: the muhajirs, the Bengali Muslim Leaguers and the local landed aristocracy and religious leaders. While Jinnah and Liaquat were still alive, the most powerful of these factions was the one dominated by the urban muhajirs. Jinnah kept himself above factional feuds; moreover, his enormous standing in Muslim politics made it difficult for other factions to challenge him. Liaquat, on the other hand, was of smaller political stature; when he assumed Jinnah's political mantle, the other two factions came into their own. The Bengali Muslim Leaguers were much less cohesive than the Liaquat group and plagued by divisions. They suffered a humiliating electoral defeat in 1954 at the hands of the United Front, which was a hastily-constructed opposition group representative of many different interests, and were eclipsed in national politics for good.

The Muslim League's defeat in East Bengal reduced the influence of the Bengali leadership at the center. This marginalization of the Bengalis in Pakistan politics was arrested for a short while when H. S. Suhrawardy, a prominent leader from Bengal, was called upon to become the Prime Minister. Once in office, Suhrawardy discovered that his role was highly constrained by the influence of the groups from West Pakistan who were deeply engaged in an unending game of political musical chairs. He resigned and was replaced by a politician from West Pakistan.

From 1954 to 1958, therefore, the battle for political spoils at the national level was fought between the muhajirs on the one hand and local landed aristocracy and religious leaders on the other. During these years, the pendulum swung widely but, by 1958, it had come to rest on the side of the latter when their representative, Malik Firoz Khan Noon, became Prime Minister. Although the army under General Ayub Khan struck in 1958, before the new Prime Minister had had time to settle in, the advent of military rule did not result in any reduction in the power of the indigenous faction. Rather, under Ayub Khan, it gained even more power at the expense of the muhajir community. Under the command of leaders such as Firoz Khan Noon and Ayub Khan, the Muslim League returned to the organizational state of pre-independence Panjab and Sind when political parties had depended more on official patronage than on broad-based political appeal to gain political power.

A further clash took place on the floor of the Constituent Assembly which for four years debated the Constitution's 'basic principles'. For a state founded on the basis of religion, the definition of basic principles should not have presented a serious problem. But a serious problem it became, and days were spent debating the role of religion in the state and the question of the rights of the federating provinces. The exchange of population between India and West Pakistan had created a religiously homogeneous wing, while East Pakistan retained a sizeable Hindu minority; there could not, therefore, be an easy solution to the question of Islamization. Differences between the western provinces themselves further complicated the discussion. And urban muhajirs, given their more 'secular' approach to politics, made

things even more difficult. Before 1954, they had a formidable presence in the Constituent Assembly which they used to keep at bay those who sought to turn the new country away from the Westminster mold of politics. The solution that was eventually found in the 1956 Constitution accommodated all three groups. The preamble accepted Allah's sovereignty over man; all laws were to conform to the Quran and the Sunnah; and the state would never place on the books a law that was repugnant to either the Quran or the accepted practice of the Prophet Muhammad. This, however, was clearly only a declaration of intent given that the constitution failed to set up mechanisms to determine whether the legislative processes at the center or in the provinces ever produced un-Islamic legislation.

In 1955, the provinces of Panjab, Sind, the Northwest Frontier, Baluchistan, and several princely states were merged to form the administrative unit of West Pakistan. With West Pakistan thus organized into one province, the country acquired two wings. The expectation was that this reorganization would help quicken the process of constitution making. The 'principle of parity' between the two wings of the country laid the groundwork for agreement between East and West Pakistan on the constitution of 1956. The Bengalis gave up their demand for 'one man, one vote' which, with their larger share of the overall population, would have given them a sizeable majority in the National Assembly. In return for this concession, West Pakistan agreed to increase the share of Bengal in the administration and the armed forces. West Pakistan also agreed to provide Bengal with a growing share in the allocation of development resources from the central budget. The question of protecting the rights of the two federating provinces against possible encroachment by the central authority was resolved by incorporating specific provisions which defined subjects of concern to the government and then by dividing them into those of central, provincial and joint responsibilities. Except for the Islamization provision, however, which was the consequence of the earnest pleadings of *ulama* (religious scholars) inside and outside the Constituent Assembly, there was little novelty in the constitution. Pakistan was to remain a member of the British Commonwealth under a President rather than a Governor-General representing the British crown. Members of the central and provincial legislatures were to be elected every five years. Effective power was to rest at the Center in the hands of the Prime Minister who was to be chosen by a simple majority in the national legislature; the provincial chief ministers were to be similarly elected and were to be responsible for the subjects over which the constitution gave them jurisdiction.

Under the new constitution, promulgated on March 23, 1956, General Iskandar Mirza became the President and Chaudhuri Muhammad Ali was chosen as Prime Minister. Ali was a muhajir but from East Panjab. As such, he did not belong to the group of

Arms of the State: Pakistan

Table A

Armed Force Levels (Military and Paramilitary), 1986

Force	Number
Armed Forces	480,600
Army	450,000
Navy	13,000
Airforce	17,600
Paramilitary Forces	164,000
National Guard	75,000
Civil Armed Forces	89,000

Source: *The Military Balance, Institute of Strategic Studies, 1986–1987* p. 165 (London, 1986).

Table B

Size of Armed Forces, 1963–1986

Year	Size
1963	253,000
1966	278,350
1971	392,000
1976	428,000
1981	450,600
1986	480,600

Sources: *The Military Balance, Institute of Strategic Studies, 1964–1965 to 1986–1987* (London, 1964–1986).

Table C

Defense Expenditure, 1963–1986

Year	Defense expenditure in USA $ 100 million[a]	Percentage of Government spending
1963	2.3	n.a.
1966	4.7	n.a.
1971	7.1	n.a.
1976	8.1	17.2
1981	16.5	32.6
1982	22.0[a]	26.7[a]
1983	18.7	35.7
1984	19.6	39.8
1985	20.7	n.a.
1986	n.a.	n.a.

[a]Figures for 1963 to 1985 are in current USA dollars. Since figures vary widely in different issues of *The Military Balance*, whose editors attempt to revise earlier figures on the basis of later information, the figures in this table were taken from the latest available issues of the journal pertaining to each year.

Source: *The Military Balance, Institute of Strategic Studies, 1963–64 to 1986–1987* (London, 1963–1986).

Box 20

urban muhajirs that had dominated Pakistani politics in the early days. He also followed a different route to political power, not that of climbing the organizational ladder within a political party but that of moving sideways from a major institution of the state, as several of his successors were to do. As a prominent member of the bureaucracy, Ali had been involved in organizing the administrative structure of the new state, and had been chosen to head the civil service as its Secretary General. He left the civil service in 1951, when, following Liaquat's assassination in the October of that year, the cabinet was reshuffled and Ali became Minister of Finance. Ali, therefore, was the perfect choice for making the transition from a political system dominated by urban muhajirs to one in which indigenous leaders played an increasingly important role.

This transition was hastened by the formation in 1956 of the Republican Party, which brought together a number of prominent politicians native to West Pakistan who had been kept out of power by the Muslim League. President Iskandar Mirza was the new party's patron. The Republicans successfully challenged Chaudhri Muhammad Ali's Muslim League. Ali resigned and was succeeded by Firoz Khan Noon. But the process of indigenization had proceeded much faster than was acceptable to those who had vivid memories of the way that many leaders of the Republican Party had opposed the creation of Pakistan. The ensuing political turmoil was ended by General Ayub Khan's coup in 1958. The coup, although organized in great secrecy, was not altogether unexpected. The army's direct entry into politics was treated with a sense of relief by large segments of the population who had become tired of politicians' machinations.

The Ayub Khan era

In his autobiography, *Friends not Masters*, General Ayub Khan provided two reasons which motivated him to take over the government reins on October 7, 1958. He was convinced that the growing quarrels between politicians as they prepared for the elections decreed for 1959 by the 1956 Constitution were hurting the country's economic prospects. What he felt was required was a firm hand at the helm, directing the country into less turbulent waters. His were to be those hands; aided by his military colleagues, he felt that he could bring about rapid economic progress. Ayub Khan had also convinced himself that Pakistan could not be governed by the model which had inspired the 1956 Constitution. Accordingly, he spent the first two years of his administration setting up and refining a system which better suited 'the genius of the Pakistani' people. There may have been a third reason for military intervention in politics. By 1958, Pakistan had established itself as an important link in the chain of containment that Eisenhower was erecting around the communist bloc. The Pakistan–United States Mutual Defence Agreement was initialled in 1954 when Ayub Khan was commander-in-chief of the Pakistan army. This was followed by the Baghdad Pact of 1956 which included Iran, Iraq, Pakistan and Turkey in a mutual defence agreement, and by the Southeast Asia Treaty Organization (SEATO) also in 1956 which involved Pakistan with Thailand and the USA. Pakistan's exceptionally fragile political situation in the summer of 1958 made the USA nervous and apprehensive. Some historians believe that this nervousness probably resulted in encouragement being given to Ayub Khan, who was by now a trusted friend of the USA, to establish a military presence in Pakistan's government.

The settlement of refugees, the creation of Basic Democracies, the formation of the Pakistan Muslim League and the move of the country's capital from muhajir-dominated Karachi to the army garrison town of Rawalpindi set the stage for the drafting of Pakistan's second constitution. The task was assigned to a small group of lawyers who produced a document radically different from the 1956 Constitution. The new system of government was to be much more centralized with its executive branch under the full control of an indirectly-elected President who was to be chosen by an electoral college made up of 80,000 Basic Democrats or union councillors. The powers of the central and provincial legislatures were severely restricted; the President could veto any legislation but the legislatures were not given the power to override his veto.

In determining the relations between East and West Pakistan, the new constitution borrowed the principle of parity from its 1956 predecessor. Seats in the National Assembly were to be shared equally between the two provinces while the presence of Bengalis in the administration and military was to be significantly increased. The constitution also contained a clause which made the elimination of economic disparity between the two provinces the cornerstone of the government's economic program.

Having watched with dismay Pakistan's slow descent into political chaos between 1954 and 1958, Ayub Khan concluded that not only was a strong executive fundamental to good government but that the executive could only remain strong if it were protected from the buffeting of political parties. Initially, therefore, the Ayub system did not have any role for political parties. Basic Democrats and members of the national and provincial assemblies were to

represent themselves, not political ideologies or parties. This provision, however, proved impractical.

Not as impractical was Ayub Khan's ambition to distance government from the religious leadership. In handling the question of the role of Islam in government, he displayed the modernizing zeal typical of military men of his time. He saw himself as Pakistan's Kemal Ataturk, influential and powerful enough to cut the cord between the Muslim ulama (learned man) and those responsible for managing the state. The constitution promulgated on March 1, 1962 did not call Pakistan an Islamic Republic. Its preamble, while declaring that sovereignty over the entire universe belongs to Allah alone, did not recognize the Quran and the Sunna (the custom of the prophet) as the sole inspirations for the laws of the land. Despite the fact that the constitution declared that 'no law should be repugnant to Islam', and announced the establishment of an Islamic Advisory Council and an Islamic Research Institute, there were no mandatory provisions relating to laws 'repugnant' to Islam. In making these moves, Ayub Khan displayed the political naïveté which marked his eleven years in office and which also permanently soured his relationship with the country's religious leaders.

With Basic Democrats elected, with the national and provincial assemblies cooperating with the executive branch of government, and with the world calling the basic elements of the system which he had introduced not only a success but a model for other third world countries to follow, Ayub Khan was prepared to make some changes. Two were important but both failed to offer the system any measure of stability. Ayub Khan's first departure was to allow political parties to function. Working with a number of close associates, including Zulfikar Ali Bhutto, he undertook the kind of political engineering that earlier had resulted in the factionalization of the Muslim League and the formation of the Republican Party. Political leaders who were likely to pledge loyalty to Ayub Khan were summoned and presented with a party manifesto which they proceeded to approve. Thus was born the Convention Muslim League with its lineage going back not to Jinnah's Muslim League but to the Unionist Party of Sir Sikandar Hayat Khan during the British period and the Republican Party of Dr Khan Sahib. Old Leaguers, who had not been invited to join, decided to convene their own council which resulted in the formation of the Council Muslim League.

The second departure, the decision to downgrade the importance of Basic Democrats, also struck at the very heart of Ayub Khan's political system. His reason for letting local councils be dominated by the civil bureaucracy rather than remain an independent political force reflected his close relationship with senior civil servants, in particular with members of the élitist Civil Service of Pakistan. Accordingly, when an ambitious rural development plan program was launched first in East Pakistan in 1961 and then in West

President Ayub Khan reviews junior commissioned army officers in May 1965.

Pakistan two years later, funds were put at the disposal of district commissioners rather than at that of elected Basic Democrats.

Ayub Khan's fall

Ayub Khan might have been able to prolong his years in office had he not been weakened by a number of developments both internal and external. The first of these was the presidential election of January 1965 in which opposition parties came together under the umbrella of a hastily-constructed political outfit with the rather unimaginative title of the Combined Opposition Party (COP) and put up Fatima Jinnah as their candidate. Miss Jinnah, sister of Pakistan's founder, was a reluctant recruit; however, having accepted the COP's offer, she proved to be an enthusiastic and tireless campaigner. Much of her support came from interests which had suffered under Ayub Khan. None was more powerful than the merchant and industrial community of Karachi. The loss of their monopoly over the industrial sector, which resulted from the economic policies of the Ayub regime, incited the opposition of this powerful group. Miss Jinnah lost the election, but Ayub Khan's rather narrow margin at the polls shook his confidence in the political system, even one which allowed only limited participation and was managed by the powerful civil bureaucracy.

The second development was also internal. Its seeds had been sown during the early years of martial law. From the time of his coup to the promulgation of the 1962 Constitution, Ayub Khan had shown little respect for the political views of ulama and other religious leaders. They were upset by the treatment given to Islam in the 1962 Constitution and were alienated further by the government's decision to block their efforts to persuade the National Assembly to declare the Family Laws Ordinance of 1961 'repugnant'. These efforts brought Maulana Maududi to political prominence and provided his Islamic fundamentalist political organization, the Jamaat-e Islami (the Islamic Society), with the opportunity to increase the basis of its support. Maududi had

207

founded the Jamaat-e Islami in the East Panjab town of Pathankot in 1941. Small towns like Pathankot had offered a hospitable climate to such an organization. They were not urbanized enough to be distracted by the modernizing influences of professional classes, but were sufficiently distant, in a social sense, from the countryside. The rapid development of the Panjab during the 1930s and 1940s brought migrants from the countryside prepared to be liberated from the influence of *pirs* (sufi saints and their hereditary descendants) and to practice a form of Islam less dependent on continuing allegiance to local religious dignitaries.

After the creation of Pakistan, the pace of economic development quickened and the spatial dispersal of population changed. Farmers and entrepreneurs were drawn into small towns to set up markets and enterprises for the disposing and processing of agricultural produce. This relocation of population reduced the influence of traditional religious leaders and offered religious organizations such as the Jamaat fertile ground for sowing their ideas more widely. Maududi responded to this opportunity and used his cadre of devoted followers to spread his word. The debate in the early 1950s over the 'basic principles' of the constitution provided Maududi with an opportunity to launch his anti-Ahmadiya campaign. Deploring any form of deviation from the fundamentals of Islam, Maududi aimed his wrath at the Ahmadiya community which had been founded by Ghulam Ahmad in the East Panjab town of Qadiyan in the late nineteenth century. Ghulam Ahmad, by claiming prophethood for himself, challenged the cherished belief of Muslims that Muhammad was the last prophet. Pakistan had to be an Islamic state with political authority in the hands of those who understood the true meaning of Islam: since the Ahmadiyas were not, in Maududi's opinion, true believers, he wanted them to be declared non-Muslims and barred from holding prominent positions in government. It irked Maududi to see Muhammad Zafarullah Khan, a devout Ahmadi, function as Pakistan's Minister for Foreign Affairs and act as an influential member of Khwaja Nazim ud Din's cabinet.

Maududi's anti-Ahmadiya campaign attracted a great deal of attention both in Karachi and in the urban areas of the Panjab, turning violent in the spring of 1953. Governor-General Ghulam Muhammad responded by dismissing Nazim ud Din and by inviting General Ayub Khan, commander-in-chief of the armed forces, to restore order. This was Pakistan's first martial law. It brought the army in touch with Maududi and the Jamaat-e Islami. Ayub Khan and his fellow generals saw Maududi as an obscurantist, determined to stop Pakistan from modernizing, but junior officers and soldiers, with an increasing number of them coming from towns in the Panjab, began to develop an appreciation for Maududi's teachings. It was in this context that Maududi found Ayub Khan's later modernizing zeal abhorrent. He focussed on the Family Laws Ordinance and on the government's highly visible family planning efforts and labeled them unacceptable on Islamic grounds. Ayub Khan tried to placate religious opposition but refused to abandon his program for reform. The Jamat was not satisfied by gestures such as the naming of the new capital Islamabad and redoubled its efforts, particularly in the small towns of the Panjab, to remove the President from office.

The third contribution to Ayub Khan's fall was the result of a sudden and, to this date, unexplained departure in his foreign policy. During the first six years of his presidency, Ayub Khan had followed a conciliatory approach towards India. He had refused the temptation offered by India's 1962 war with China to strike in Kashmir, accepting the view of the USA that Pakistan's communist neighbors posed a greater security threat than India. But Ayub Khan's position changed as he began to politicize his political system. Within a year of being re-elected, he was drawn into an armed conflict with India. The issue was Kashmir; from available evidence, it appears that Ayub Khan accepted advice that the time had come for finding a military solution to the problem which had plagued Indo-Pakistani relations for nearly twenty years. He believed that such a move would be popular in the country, particularly with parties such as the Jamaat who had some support in Kashmir. Beginning on September 6, 1965, therefore, the two countries fought a brisk war which lasted for seventeen days. The most important result of this conflict was the open disaffection of many young generals over the conduct of the war. Under these circumstances, Ayub Khan found it increasingly difficult to persist with his political experiment. The 1965 Indo-Pakistan war interrupted the momentum of economic development. The rate of growth in Pakistan's economy had become one of the highest in the developing world. The war not only diverted to military use resources which would otherwise have gone into development, it also resulted in a sharp decline in the flow of external assistance. The nation was asked to tighten its belt and might have been willing to do so had tangible gains been made on the battlefield. But the war ended in a state of confusion, with both sides claiming victory. When the peace agreement was finally signed in the Soviet city of Tashkent, its terms left the impression that advantage lay with India.

The Tashkent Agreement was the turning point in the political life of Ayub Khan's administration. Bhutto, his Foreign Minister, left the government giving the strong impression that what had not been lost on the battlefield had been surrendered at Tashkent. He warned that India sought to convert Pakistan into her satellite by holding out 'inducements of peaceful cooperation'. Bhutto's words echoed for a long time in the ears of those who had always believed that Pakistan had to be extremely vigilant if it was to protect its national integrity. By initially basing his campaign against Ayub Khan on the Tashkent Agreement, Bhutto was able to draw towards himself people who had become disenchanted with the military regime.

The final blow to Ayub Khan's authority came in early 1968 when a near-fatal heart attack put him out of action for several months. The 1962 Constitution had provided for just such an eventuality; in the case of the President's severe indisposition, the task of running the government was to be assumed by the speaker of the National Assembly. The speaker at that time was Abdul Jabbar Khan, a politician from Bengal who had shown exceptional loyalty to Ayub Khan. Had Jabbar Khan assumed the Presidency, it would have provided a test for the constitution during a period of crisis and would have convinced Bengalis that they were not condemned forever to be junior political partners at the national level. Instead, however, while Ayub Khan recuperated slowly, the reins of government were taken up by a small coterie of civil servants.

When Ayub Khan finally returned to office, he found that the political situation had changed quite dramatically. Bhutto had formed the Pakistan Peoples' Party (PPP) with the aim of gaining strong support from a broad spectrum of political opinion. The PPP's manifesto represented the first serious effort on the part of a political organization to obtain mass support on the basis of a well-articulated program rather than on the basis of the aggregated following of individual leaders. Bhutto was correct in his assessment that power would have to be forcibly wrested from the military but that his followers would only take to the streets if they liked the program that was being offered to them. Moreover, he probably understood that discrediting Ayub Khan and his administration would not automatically transfer power to politicians such as himself. If Ayub Khan was forced to leave, he would probably hand over the administration to other generals. Some form of military government would have to intervene between Ayub Khan's demise and Bhutto's own ascendancy.

Bhutto played his cards wisely. Soon after leaving the government he toured the country to get to know the people and to understand their frustrations. He discovered that those most affected by the economic slowdown lived in small towns and rural areas and had been hurt by the sharp decline in agricultural prices. Sensing this mood of unease, Bhutto formulated the program of his political party. His initial impulse had been to use Pakistan's foreign policy as its centerpiece. Now he knew that antipathy towards India, although a common sentiment, was not felt strongly enough by people to risk their livelihood, possibly their lives, by challenging the authority of the government in a violent way. Rather, they could be convinced that Ayub Khan had failed to deliver on the promise to turn Pakistan into a state fashioned on the principles of Islam and also to distribute to the poor the benefits of economic growth that had occurred during his ten years in office. The government's own 'decade of development' campaign, therefore, provided the ideal background for the staging of Bhutto's political offensive. As Ayub Khan, the governors of the two provinces and the ministers of the central provincial governments criss-crossed the country underscoring the remarkable economic progress since 1958, Bhutto and his colleagues followed them, reminding the people how little they themselves had benefitted from all that the government said had been accomplished. Right in the middle of this debate, Mahbub ul Haq, the government's chief economist, announced his 'twenty-two family hypothesis'. In a speech given in Karachi, he regretted the fact that so few of the gains made by Pakistan had been distributed to the people. The principal beneficiaries of the economic miracle were a small group of industrial families including that of Ayub Khan. The 'twenty-two families' slogan was just what Bhutto needed.

Bhutto's campaign against inequality prompted Bengali leaders to demand provincial autonomy. East Pakistan had always felt discriminated against; for instance, it had always argued that the foreign exchange earned from the export of jute (which for a long time was Pakistan's main export earner but was produced only in the country's eastern wing) had been used mostly in the Western Province. Accordingly, the Bengali party known as the Awami League proclaimed a six point program aimed at limiting the powers of the central government to defence, foreign affairs and currency. With this program, agitation against Ayub Khan acquired a new dimension. The pace of the opposition campaign quickened. What had started as an economic campaign in the small towns and villages of West Pakistan now assumed the form of a mass civil disobedience movement. Leader after leader was incarcerated; Bhutto and Mujibur Rahman, the East Pakistani leader, went to jail. But the opposition continued to gain momentum. In the early months of 1969, Ayub Khan summoned opposition leaders after conceding that his 1962 Constitution had to be abandoned in favor of a system that was more representative. He tried hard to reach an agreement, but Bhutto, who by now had emerged as the most important political figure in West Pakistan, refused to cooperate. Having developed a strong constituency for himself in West Pakistan, but with no support whatsoever in East Pakistan, Bhutto did not want a political accommodation in which he would not be the primary figure. Ayub Khan's resignation finally came on March 20, 1969 when General Yahya Khan became President. These developments heralded Pakistan's second spell of military leadership. It lasted for thirty-three eventful months during which the two wings of Pakistan fought a bloody civil war leading to the emergence of the independent state of Bangladesh in December 1971.

The Yahya Khan interregnum

Within a few months of assuming power, Yahya Khan and his military colleagues dismantled the political system erected by Ayub

Khan. Initially, they kept all politicians at bay in the belief that the mission which they had set out to accomplish could be performed only if the military worked alone and without a great deal of close contact with politicians. Even the civil service was assigned a secondary role in the new administration; a number of Ayub Khan's trusted civilians were sent home in keeping with the 'purge' of the civil bureaucracy. Air Marshal Nur Khan, Admiral Abul Ahsan, General Abdul Hamid all wielded much more political power than Ayub Khan had assigned to his military associates. Yahya Khan thus established a semi-military state, creating a precedent which was later followed by General Zia ul Haq. But there was a contradiction in Yahya Khan's approach. At the same time that he militarized politics, he introduced changes which returned the country to parliamentary democracy. Yahya Khan decided to accept Bengal's demand for representation on the basis of population. Once this had been agreed, the preservation of the One Unit of West Pakistan was no longer necessary. The smaller provinces in West Pakistan had never been satisfied with the One Unit arrangement; for them, it had been both an administrative inconvenience and a political nuisance. A One Unit (Reorganization) Committee was established in December 1969 and had divided West Pakistan into the four provinces of Baluchistan, Northwest Frontier, Sind and the Panjab by June 1970. A Legal Framework Order, issued on March 30, 1970, outlined the structure of the new National Assembly and its constitution-making duties. It was to be elected directly by the people, with 162 representatives chosen by East Pakistan and 138 by

National elections in Pakistan, 1970, 1977 and 1988

Table A

General Elections of December 7, 1970

Party	West Pakistan		East Pakistan		Total	
	Number of seats won	Percent	Number of seats won	Percent	Number of seats won	Percent
Awami League	—	—	160	98.8	160	53.3
Jamaat-e Islami	4	2.9	—	—	4	1.3
Jamiat ul-Ulama-i Islam	7	5.1	—	—	7	2.3
Jamiat ul-Ulama-i Pakistan	7	5.1	—	—	7	2.3
Muslim League (3 factions)	18	13.0	—	—	18	6.0
National Awami Party	6	4.3	—	—	6	2.0
Pakistan People's Party	81	58.7	—	—	81	27.0
Others	15	10.9	2	1.2	17	5.7
	138	100.0	162	100.0	300	99.9

Numbers do not add up to 100 due to rounding.

Source: S. J. Burki *Pakistan Under Bhutto, 1971–1977* p. 57 (London, 1980).

Table B

General Elections of March 7, 1977

Party	Number of seats won	percent
Pakistan People's Party	155	77.5
Pakistan National Alliance	36	18.0
Others	9	4.5
	200	100.0

Source: S. J. Burki *Pakistan Under Bhutto, 1971–1977* p. 196 (London, 1980).

Table C

General Elections of November 16, 1988[a]

Party	Number of seats won	percent
Pakistan People's Party	93	45.4
Islamic Democratic Alliance	54	26.3
Muhajir Qaumi Markaz	13	6.3
Jamiat ul-Ulama-i Islam (F)	7	3.4
Independents	27	13.2
Others	11	5.4
	205	100.0

[a]Results of elections held for 205 Muslim seats; total seats in Assembly, 237.

Source: *India Today* (December 15, 1988).

the four provinces of West Pakistan. The Assembly was to be given only 120 days to come up with a new constitution. If the Assembly could not complete the drafting within this time, it would be dissolved and another round of elections held. The President reserved the right to authenticate the constitution so that it did not contravene the five basic principles laid down in the Legal Framework Order. These required Pakistan to be an Islamic state, with a democratic system based on free and fair elections, and stipulated that the country's territorial integrity be preserved for all time to come, that earnest efforts be made to eliminate economic disparity between the two wings of the country, and that the provinces be allowed maximum autonomy without rendering the federal government totally impotent.

Elections under the Legal Framework were held on December 7, 1970 and produced results which few had anticipated. The most important was the emergence of two political leaders with very different mandates. Mujib ur Rahman, whose Awami League won 160 out of 162 seats in East Pakistan, was to negotiate for East Pakistan a degree of autonomy; the 1970 election set the Bengalis on a route which was to take them to complete independence a year later. An entirely different political approach resulted in the triumph of Bhutto's Pakistan People's Party with 81 out of 138 seats in West Pakistan. His political program aimed at the total restructuring of the economy. People were promised socialism: state control over the economy and equal access by all people to basic needs such as food, education, shelter and health care. Neither leader was interested in sitting down for 120 days in the National Assembly in order to draft a constitution.

Events now moved quickly. Bhutto decided to boycott the convening of the National Assembly on March 3, 1971, arguing that he needed first to reach an understanding with Mujib on important constitutional issues. Yahya Khan's response to Bhutto's ultimatum was to postpone the meeting, an action which provoked Mujib to order his followers not to cooperate with the military government. By the first week of March, Islamabad's writ no longer ran in Dhaka and Pakistan's flag had begun to be replaced by that of the Awami League. On March 7, Mujib laid down new conditions for participating in the National Assembly. At this stage, the Awami League announced that it intended to stop short of full secession. This was a risky course for Mujib to take for most East Pakistanis expected him to go the whole distance. However, Mujib's compromise conditions were not accepted and after a couple of weeks of tense negotiations Yahya Khan launched 'Operation Searchlight' against the Awami League. Mujib was arrested and taken to West Pakistan. A number of his close associates, however, escaped to Calcutta where they formed a government in exile. 'Operation Searchlight' lasted until December 17 when, helped by Indian armed forces, the *Mukti Bahini* (Bengali freedom fighters) took Dhaka and established the independent state of Bangladesh.

The Bhutto era

Zulfikar Ali Bhutto had joined Yahya Khan's government as Deputy Prime Minister shortly before the surrender of the Pakistan army to Indian forces in Dhaka. In this capacity, he had traveled to New York to negotiate a peaceful solution to the crisis. A day before the surrender took place, he had stormed out of the meeting of the United Nations Security Council, tearing into shreds the resolution offered by Poland to end the fighting and vowing a 'thousand years war' with India. This extraordinary scene viewed by millions of Pakistanis on television burnished in their minds an image of a remarkable patriot refusing to submit even as his own forces were about to surrender to an invading army. This performance won Bhutto the support even of those who had not voted for him in the December 1970 election. It also won him the admiration of young army officers who felt humiliated by the conduct of the generals. As Bhutto traveled back to Rawalpindi, these officers staged a silent coup against their senior colleagues. Yahya Khan was persuaded to resign the presidency, and Bhutto, upon his return, was sworn in as President and Chief Martial Law Administrator of what was left of Pakistan.

The Bhutto era lasted for five and a half years during which the economy was restructured, the public sector was given a great deal of prominence, Pakistan's approach to the outside world was redefined on the basis of a relationship with India which no longer rested on equality, and a new consensus was developed on constitutional issues between different political players. It was a period of dynamism, but also one of lost opportunities.

With Pakistan now divided into four very unequal parts, there was no easy solution to the problem of power sharing between the center and the provinces. The domination of the Panjab was feared by the smaller provinces. The Panjab had nearly 60 percent of the population and a large representation in the armed forces; it also produced well over half the country's Gross National Product. But the trauma of defeat in East Pakistan helped politicians to agree to a new constitution. Bhutto convened the National Assembly which met in Islamabad on April 4, 1972. By October 1972, only six months after its first meeting, the leaders of the different political parties in the Assembly had signed a constitutional accord. The constitution was authenticated by President Bhutto on April 12, 1973 and came into force on August 14 of the same year with Bhutto stepping down from the Presidency to assume the office of Prime Minister. Thus, Pakistan, on its twenty-sixth birthday, acquired its third constitution which represented a consensus on three matters: the role of Islam in politics, the sharing of power between the federal government and the federating provinces, and the divisions of

Opposite Zulfikar Ali Bhutto, as deputy prime minister and foreign minister of Pakistan, accuses the United Nations Security council on December 16, 1971 of delaying action on the Indo-Pakistan conflict to permit the fall of Dhaka. A few minutes later he stormed out of the meeting vowing a 'thousand years war' with India.

responsibility between the President and the Prime Minister.

Soon after the adoption of the constitution, it became clear to the opposition that Bhutto did not really intend to abide by the consensus which he had reached with them. Opposition governments in Baluchistan and the Northwest Frontier suffered open discrimination; their leaders were frequently criticized for being unpatriotic. Finally, on February 12, 1974, the Baluchistan government was dismissed on the charge of inciting the people of that province to rebel against the central authorities. The government in the Frontier resigned in sympathy with its Baluchi counterpart. On May 24, an amendment in the constitution gave the executive the power to declare illegal any political party found 'operating in a manner prejudicial to the sovereignty or integrity of the country'. This power, exercised with the approval of the Supreme Court, was used to ban the National Awami Party, the only effective opposition to the PPP. The final step towards Bhutto's unstated, but by now obvious, objective of turning Pakistan into a one-party state was another general election which would put the PPP in total command of the National Assembly. Opposition was fragmented and in retreat when, in early 1977, Bhutto announced general elections to be held on March 7, 1977.

The speed with which the opposition organized itself into a fairly cohesive force, given the name of the Pakistan National Alliance (PNA), must have surprised Bhutto. The Alliance was a collection of nine political parties ranging from the Jamaat-e Islami on the right to the National Democratic Party (previously the National Awami League) on the left. The opposition put together a program which seemed attractive to many; it also campaigned hard, drew very large crowds to its public meetings and, on the eve of the election, seemed in a position to capture a significant number of seats in both the national and provincial assemblies. Nobody expected the PNA to win, not even its leaders, but most political observers expected it to improve its position in the legislatures. It was, therefore, with surprise and dismay that the PNA and its supporters heard the results on the morning of March 8. Of the 192 seats contested, only 36 (or 18.8 percent) went to the PNA. The PNA decided to challenge Bhutto on the streets and succeeded in mobilizing a large number of its followers first to confront the police and then the army when the government placed a number of cities

under martial law. Thereafter, events moved on a familiar course: mounting agitation, government concessions, gains in confidence by the opposition, and the imposition of martial law in order to save the country from 'chaos and disintegration'.

History had offered Bhutto the chance of resolving many of Pakistan's outstanding political, social and economic problems. The army's defeat in East Pakistan had removed it as a political force; for the first time in nearly twenty-five years, the generals had been prepared to accept civilian authority. The triumph of the PPP in the 1970 polls had placed on the political map a genuine party with a program which was found attractive by diverse elements within the country. With power placed firmly in Bhutto's hands, it might have been possible to devise a constitutional arrangement in which the smaller provinces could have placed their confidence. And, with popular support behind him, Bhutto's formula of Islamic socialism provided a way of keeping Islamic fundamentalists at bay. Opportunities had also existed in the area of social reform. Bhutto, although a large landlord from Sind, could have brought about changes in land tenure and the pattern of landholdings that were politically difficult for his predecessors to undertake. With the support of urban workers and industrial labor, he could have also improved the situation of the urban poor. With the problem of 'inter-wing' economic disparity resolved by the independence of Bangladesh, the Bhutto government could have addressed itself forcefully to the economy's many structural problems; the momentum of growth generated during the years of Ayub Khan but interrupted during the Yahya Khan period could have been picked up and Pakistan carried across the divide separating poor countries from middle income nations.

In the first few months of his administration, Bhutto had seemed to be moving in the right direction. The military leadership had been changed, the command of all branches of the armed forces being transferred to officers with no significant record of political involvement. The 1973 Constitution represented consensus among the provinces on the difficult issue of sharing power. As Bhutto had traveled the country addressing public meetings, he had taken every opportunity to remind his large audiences that the basic purpose of Islam could be reconciled with the socialist program of his government. The PPP had started to implement parts of its social and economic program, providing more secure rights of employment and compensation. But for reasons which had more to do with Bhutto's personality than with political pressures, this promise of early years quickly soured and the forces which had previously inhibited Pakistan's progress reassembled themselves once again. Perhaps the greatest disappointment of the Bhutto era were the failures to establish the PPP as a vital and dynamic force in Pakistani politics, to govern relations between the federating provinces within the constitutional framework, to define once and for all the place of

Islam in the political and economic structure, and to provide the economy with enough dynamism to push it over the threshold of poverty.

In governing Pakistan in the way that he did, Bhutto lost the backing of the lower middle classes that watched with dismay as the PPP's economic program began to unfold. These classes had played an important role in providing the PPP with its 1970 victory. They expected social reform to strengthen their position vis-à-vis the propertied classes. Instead, they witnessed the rapid encroachment of the state in economic areas of profound interest to them. The decision of the government to bring in labor legislation which affected small shopkeepers and the nationalization of small agricultural businesses hit the economic heart of lower middle class Pakistan. This situation was aggravated further by what was seen by these classes as socially unacceptable behavior on the part of PPP cadres. Local PPP leaders undermined the authority of the civil bureaucracy by allowing the law and order situation to deteriorate. But this affected ordinary people who began to drift back to the Jamaat-e Islami and other religious parties. Bhutto compensated for these defections by bringing big business and landed aristocracy into the fold of the PPP thereby damaging his credibility with a number of his supporters.

Bhutto, more familiar with the officers who had held senior positions during the Ayub Khan period, did not seem to realize that a significant change had occurred in the social make-up of the armed forces. The rapid expansion of the officer corps and the increasing sophistication of the economy resulted in a marked increase in the representation of the middle classes in the middle echelons of the military command. The performance of the PPP government had proved a great disappointment to these officers and they were happy to support General Zia ul Haq's coup; with their support came the backing of the social and economic classes which these officers represented.

Bhutto's pursuit of foreign policy objectives which were unpopular with Pakistan's upper and highly westernized classes also resulted in further loss of political support. His espousal of third world causes, open confrontation with the West, and initiation of a program to develop a nuclear bomb irritated the USA and its allies. This switch in foreign policy orientation was too dramatic for a country that for three decades had remained a close friend of the West. It made Pakistan's élites, even when they were being wooed by the PPP, highly suspicious of Bhutto's intentions; 'Sukarnoization' was definitely not in their interests. Accordingly, when the army moved in on July 5, 1977, large segments of the population, although shocked by these events, were not willing to come out in open support for the PPP and its leader.

The Zia era

Once the army had moved in, General Zia ul Haq, the Chief of Staff who had been raised above more senior generals by Bhutto, became Chief Martial Law Administrator. The following year, 1978, he assumed the Presidency. The objectives of the armed forces' Operation Fair Play, which was the army maneuver that led first to Bhutto's intermittent incarceration and then to his eventual execution, were to restore democracy and hold elections within ninety days. The elections, however, were postponed to allow for the process of accountability by which Bhutto and his associates were to give a full report of their management of the country's economy and polity. This was completed on April 4, 1979 when Bhutto was hanged in Rawalpindi, but the elections, now promised for November 1979, were postponed again as, in Zia's words, they would not have produced the 'positive results' needed to prepare the way for the establishment of a truly Islamic order in Pakistan.

Zia believed that Pakistan's political system had to be Islamized in order to forge national unity and in order to remain in step with the revival of Islam in the neighboring countries of the Middle East, in particular Iran. But he faced a dilemma: in order to turn Pakistan into an Islamic state, national consensus had to develop on the precise definition of such a state. Zia chose to experiment by adopting a number of measures including the amendment of the Political Parties Act of 1962 according to which political parties

A controversial feature of General Zia ul Haq's Islamization program was the redefinition in 1979 of the punishments to be meted out for a major crime (*hadd*). Thus theft came to be punished by the amputation of a limb and the drinking of alcohol on the part of a Muslim Pakistani by whipping numbering eighty stripes. Other major crimes were adultery and the false allegation of adultery.

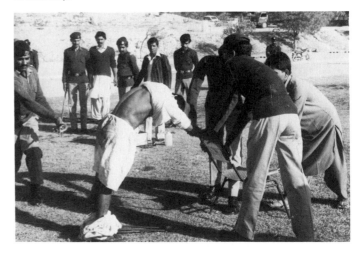

could be denied registration if their manifestoes did not explicitly include Islamic provisions. A twelve-member committee of 'scholars, jurists, *ulama* and prominent persons from other walks of life' was appointed to formulate recommendations for the structure of an Islamic system of government. This committee of wise men failed to reach a consensus on the precise way to Islamize the political structure. But their failure did not deter the government; on March 24, 1981, Zia, on his own authority as Chief Martial Law Administrator, promulgated a Provisional Constitutional Order. The main provisions of this Order concerned the establishment of a Federal Council (*Majlis-e Shura*) 'consisting of such persons as the President may, by order, determine' to 'perform such functions as may be specified in an Order made by the President'. Thus, the Order introduced a system advocated by Islamic scholars such as Maududi, who had long contended that parliamentary democracy was not strictly compatible with the practice followed during the time of the Prophet Muhammad and the four Caliphs who had succeeded him. But the experiment with limited democracy apparently encouraged Zia to take the next step of replacing the Majlis-e Shura with an elected assembly – and thus go beyond the system the followers of Maududi wanted. On November 30, 1984, he announced a national referendum to elicit the peoples' views about his Islamization program. Affirmation by a simple majority of votes cast would act as a mandate for Zia to remain in office for another five years. The referendum was held on December 19 and, according to the results announced by the government, Zia received the mandate which he had sought. Some 62 percent of the 34 million voters were said to have cast their ballots; of these, 98 per cent had said 'yes'. In other words, more than 60 percent of the electorate had voted to keep Zia in office. But, not unexpectedly, the result was contested by the opposition which estimated the turnout of the electorate to have been no more than 10 percent of the total.

Zia then decided to hold general elections on February 25, 1985 for 217 National Assembly seats and on 27 February for 483 seats in the four provincial assemblies. Parties were not permitted to participate and so the opposition boycotted them. Nevertheless, the results, particularly the unexpectedly large turnout of voters in all parts of the country, pleased the government, satisfied many of its critics and persuaded Pakistan's foreign supporters that the ground had been prepared for the restoration of democracy. But, what Zia had given with one hand, he seemed to take away with the other. On March 2, three days after the completion of the electoral process, he promulgated an order which introduced sweeping changes in the 1973 Constitution concentrating political power in the hands of the President; the President's discretion was to be final. Nor did Zia shed his uniform on March 23, 1985 when he picked Muhammed Khan Junejo as his Prime Minister. Junejo, a veteran politician from Sind, had served as a minister in one of Zia's earlier cabinets.

Once sworn in, he displayed a certain amount of public independence, dropping all but one general from the cabinet, and, more important, announcing to the public that democracy and martial law could not co-exist. This assertion of independence and its tolerance by Zia and his military colleagues helped Junejo to establish a political base seemingly distant enough from the military for him to win a unanimous vote of confidence in the National Assembly when it met for its first formal session.

On December 30, 1985, Zia lifted martial law. He went much further than many had expected in returning Pakistan to civilian rule. Martial law courts were closed, the constitution (albeit in its amended form) was restored in full, and human rights were revived without qualification. These changes contained one further surprise: Zia announced that he was staying on as chief of staff of the army. Accordingly, a new pattern of civilian-military relations began to emerge in the weeks following the end of martial law. On January 8, 1986, Junejo announced the revival of the Pakistan Muslim League which, the Prime Minister felt, could aggregate the interests of the groups from which he sought political support. On April 10, 1986, Benazir Bhutto, daughter of Zulfikar Ali Bhutto and co-chairman of the PPP, returned to the country, drawing large crowds as she traveled from one major city to another to ask for support with which to topple Zia from power. People listened with interest but failed to act when Miss Bhutto asked them to challenge the government's authority with force. Agitation began on August 14, 1986 but did not proceed along familiar lines. There was some violence, particularly in the Bhuttos' home province of Sind, but the police were able to restore order. The opposition decided instead to concentrate on persuading the government to hold another election.

In December 1986, Karachi was rocked by ethnic riots that claimed hundreds of lives and destroyed millions of dollars worth of property. The riots saw Karachi's muhajir community battling with Pathans from the Northwest Frontier. Junejo's confidence was shaken; he dissolved his cabinet, dismissed the Governor of Sind and promised to address with greater resolution the problems which had caused the eruption in the first place. The most important consequence of the Karachi riots was to alter the evolving political equation once again in Zia's favor. He consolidated his position in April 1987 by bringing in new officers to command the armed forces.

This system of 'diarchy', with power divided between a military President and a civilian Prime Minister, appeared to have found a solution to one of Pakistan's many problems: the political role of the armed forces. But in May 1988 Zia dismissed Junejo, dissolving the Cabinet, National Assembly and the four provincial assemblies. It was announced that elections would be held within 90 days; they were later put off until November 16.

On August 17 Zia was killed in a plane crash: the political

situation was transformed. The acting President, Ghulam Ishaq Khan, confirmed that elections would take place in November and the military stood aside from the constitutional process. Benazir Bhutto conducted a political and election campaign of notable good judgement, and her PPP emerged as the largest party in the National Assembly with 93 seats as compared with the 54 of the second party, the Islamic Democratic Alliance. At the beginning of December she became, at the age of 35, the first woman premier of a modern Islamic state. She faces the old problems of the political role of the armed forces, the sharing of power between provincial and central government, and the relationship between the state and religion. But there are also pressing new problems: a vast budget deficit, open and violent conflict between ethnic groups, and destabilization caused by the Afghan war in general and its three million refugees in particular. Miss Bhutto's capacity to answer these problems will have much to do with whether or not Pakistan can develop a viable political system.

SJB

Further reading

L. Binder, *Religion and Politics in Pakistan* (Berkeley, 1961)

S. J. Burki, *Pakistan under Bhutto, 1971–1977* (London, 1980)

S. P. Cohen, *The Pakistan Army* (Berkeley, 1984)

A. Hussain, *Elite Politics in an Ideological state: the Case of Pakistan* (Folkestone, 1979)

A. Khan, *Islam, Politics and the State: The Pakistan Experience* (London, 1985)

M. Ayub Khan, *Friends not Masters; a Political Autobiography* (London, 1967)

Bangladesh

The main reasons for the break-up of Pakistan and the emergence of Bangladesh were the lack of Bengali participation in central decision-making processes in Pakistan and the colonial style of economic exploitation of East Pakistan by West Pakistan. Between 1947 and 1951, power rested successively with two non-Bengali leaders, Mohammad Ali Jinnah and Liaquat Ali Khan. After Liaquat's assassination, effective power passed into the hands of a small élite whose support came mainly from senior officers in the Pakistani civil service and army. Largely for historical reasons, such as the recruitment of Muslims from the Panjab to the British Indian Army and the uneven development of Muslim communities in different provinces under the British, the Pakistani army and civil service, in particular the upper levels, were almost wholly manned by non-Bengalis, see Tables 8 and 9. The coup d'état of 1958 was mainly a defensive regrouping of the old élite. By 1970 out of twenty central secretaries, only three Bengalis had attained the rank of acting secretary: similarly, out of thirty-five army officers of the ranks of

Administrative divisions of Bangladesh.

Source: J.E. Schwartzberg, ed., A Historical Atlas of South Asia (Chicago, 1978), p.79

Major-General, Lieutenant General and General, there was only one Bengali.

Throughout the 1950s and 1960s, East Pakistan had a favorable trade balance with foreign countries, while West Pakistan ran a deficit foreign trade balance. Before 1965, East Pakistan earned about 60 percent of the country's foreign currency but received less than 30 percent of imports. In addition, East Pakistan suffered a constant deficit in trade between the two wings of the country, ranging from an annual average of Rs. 162.1 million in the early 1950s to an annual average of Rs. 424.5 million in the 1960s. This pattern of trade clearly suggested a transfer of East Pakistani resources to West Pakistan, with East Pakistan serving as the captive market for West Pakistani industries.

Table 8. Military élite in Pakistan, July 1955 (number of officers)

Service	East Pakistan	West Pakistan	East Pakistan Total (%)
Army	14	894	1.5
Navy	7	593	1.2
Air Force	60	640	8.6

Source: Rounaq Jahan, *Pakistan Failure in National Integration* p. 25 (New York, 1972).

Table 9. East–West Pakistan representation in the higher ranks of the Central Secretariat, 1955

Rank	East Pakistan	West Pakistan	East Pakistan Total (%)
Secretary	—	19	—
Joint Secretary	3	38	7.3
Deputy Secretary	10	123	7.5
Under Secretary	38	510	7.0

Source: Rounaq Jahan, *Pakistan Failure in National Integration* p. 26 (New York, 1972).

Rulers of Bangladesh since Independence

Head of State

President

1971–1972	Sheikh Mujibur Rahman[a]
1972–1973	Justice Abu Sayeed Chowdhury
1973–1975	Mohammadullah
1975	Sheikh Mujibur Rahman
1975	Khandokar Mushtaq Ahmad
1975–1977	Justice Abusadad Mohammad Sayem
1977–1981	Major-General Ziaur Rahman
1981–1982	Abdus Sattar
1982–1983	Justice Abul Fazal Mohammad Ahsanuddin Chowdhury
1983–	Lieutenant-General Hussain Muhammad Ershad

Prime Minister (or equivalent post)

1971–1972	Tajuddin Ahmed
1972–1975	Sheikh Mujibur Rahman
1975	Mansoor Ali
1975–1977	Major-General Ziaur Rahman
1978–1979	Mashiur Rahman
1979–1982	Shah Azizur Rahman
1982–1983	Lieutenant-General Hussain Muhammad Ershad
1984–1985	Ataur Rahman Khan
1986–	Mizanur Rahman Choudhury

[a]Sheikh Mujibur Rahman was elected President of the Provisional Government in absentia; he was still imprisoned in Pakistan. During this period Syed Nazrul Islam was Acting President.

Source: TM.

Box 22

The political leaders of former East Pakistan, now Bangladesh, developed elaborate ideological formulations which challenged the political doctrines propagated by West Pakistanis to legitimize their dominance over East Pakistan. Ultimately, they demanded a central government responsible for defence and foreign affairs, with all taxation powers vested in the provinces, respect for their national language, democracy, secularism and friendly relations with India. The Awami League was their party. It was led by the charismatic Sheikh Mujibur Rahman.

The Awami League received an overwhelming mandate from East Pakistanis in the first national elections held in Pakistan on December 7, 1970 at which the party won 160 out of 162 National Assembly seats allocated to East Pakistan. When the military rulers of Pakistan prepared to annul the election results by force, nationalism in East Pakistan reached its peak. Mujib, declaring that 'the struggle this time is for complete emancipation and independence', launched a country-wide non-cooperation movement. The Pakistan army retaliated with an attack on Dhaka and other towns at midnight on March 25, 1971, and Bangladeshi national resistance began.

This irregular war unfolded in classic fashion: the people of Bangladesh providing the 'vast sea' in which the guerrillas 'swam like fish'. By November 1971, over one hundred thousand guerrillas had forced the Pakistan army to retreat into the relative safety of fortified enclaves. The conflict became locked in stalemate and it took a mighty offensive by Indian armed forces during the eleven-day war of December 1971 to dislodge the Pakistani forces from their strongholds. Bangladesh resistance cost between one and three million lives, and the country suffered property damage estimated at one billion USA dollars.

Abortive democratic and socialist experiment

Despite its traumatic birth, Bangladesh seemed to have a promising political start. On his triumphant return from West Pakistan, where he had remained imprisoned throughout the war, Mujib formed a twenty-three-member Awami League cabinet with himself as Prime Minister. All Indian troops were withdrawn from the country by March 12, 1972. A constituent assembly enacted a constitution which declared 'high ideals of nationalism, socialism, democracy and secularism' as the fundamental principles of state policy and which provided for a unitary parliamentary system. The Awami League government then held general elections on March 7, 1973, which it won overwhelmingly, securing 292 out of the 300 seats in the National Assembly. (See Box 24, Table A.)

In the economic field, socialist reconstruction meant the nationalization of banks, insurance companies and large and medium-sized industries mostly owned by non-Bengalis who had left Bangladesh; low ceilings on private industrial investment; nation-

Sheikh Mujibur Rahman addresses a meeting in Dhaka on March 7, 1971 to protest against the failure of General Yahya Khan, president of Pakistan, to summon the session of the National Assembly which had been elected on December 7, 1970.

alization of the import trade; and the distribution of scarce commodities through licenced dealers.

The holding of elections and the extension of formal government control over the economy, however, did not prevent a sharp drift towards economic and political crisis. Despite massive infusions of foreign aid (2.5 billion USA dollars in the first three years), by the middle of 1974 the cost of living index had risen by 400–500 percent, resulting in starvation and the deaths of thousands of people. Law and order deteriorated as the Awami League seemed unable to counteract mounting left-wing revolutionary opposition.

Political economists interpret this acute crisis in terms of incongruity between the class-character of the Awami League and its socialist goals. They argue that it was the party of the business and professional middle classes which had been growing slowly from the beginning of the present century, suffering from competition first from Hindu middle classes and later from their West Pakistani counterparts. Unstable and impatient for material returns, they exploited nationalized industries, made easy money as 'indenters' smuggling jute, rice and relief goods to India, and simply frittered away their new wealth in non-productive expenditure, thus bringing about a sharp decline in the national economy and fueling revolutionary political activity.

Social anthropologists explain the winner-take-all atmosphere of the post-independence period in terms of Bangladeshi political culture with its emphasis on extreme individualism. They argue that frontier conditions and the economic self-sufficiency of households in the deltaic regions of Bengal under the British led to the flourishing of unrestrained individualism. This remained bridled when the existence of the people as a whole was threatened in 1970–71, but, once the crisis was over, it ran amuck bringing the country to the brink of disaster.

These developments were compounded by the 1971 guerrilla war itself which legitimized violence as a method of securing social and political change and disrupted the pre-liberation consensus in favor of parliamentary government. Organized in two radical parties, the *Jatio Samajtantric Dal* (National Socialist Party) and *Sarbohara* (Proletariat) Party, frustrated ex-'freedom fighters' mounted an armed challenge in order to complete Bangladesh's 'unfinished revolution'. The relationship between the Awami League and the Indian government, culminating in the 25-year Treaty of Friendship between the two countries in March 1972, made the Awami League the butt of anti-Indian feelings aroused in Bangladesh as India emerged, after the break-up of Pakistan, as the predominant power in South Asia. Mujib resorted to one-party presidential rule, but this only increased the vulnerability of the regime.

The 1975 coups and counter-coups

In the early hours of the morning of August 15, 1975, Mujib and most of his family were killed by a group of former guerrillas, now majors in the Bangladesh army, in a surprise attack which was reminiscent of the tactics used against Pakistani officers. The assassination brought the army to the heart of the Bangladeshi political process. Significantly it had suffered sharp divisions since its birth. The first line of cleavage was between 'participants' in the 1971 war (about 8000 men and 200 officers) and the 'repatriates' (about 28,000 men and 1100 officers who had been stranded in West Pakistan during the 1971 crisis). Mujib's decision to give two years' extra seniority and accelerated promotions to those who had fought created resentment within the larger repatriated section of the army. In addition, the experience of fighting in a guerrilla war had politicized those who had taken part. Some now became affiliated to the *Jatio Samajtantric Dal* and formed clandestine *Biplobi Shainik Sangsthas* (Revolutionary Soldiers' Associations). Since most members of the latter were non-commissioned officers and privates,

---

Arms of the State: Bangladesh

Table A

Growth in Strength of Police Force, 1971–1986

Year	Police strength
1971–1972	34,000
1974–1975	40,000
1977–1978	70,000
1985–1986	74,500

Source: TM. *The Bangladesh Revolution* p. 203 (Dhaka, 1980), *Holiday* p. 3 (Dhaka, March 20, 1987).

Table B

Armed Force Levels (Military and Paramilitary), 1986

Force	Number
Armed Forces	91,300
Army	81,800
Navy	6,500
Airforce	3,000
Paramilitary Forces	55,000
Armed Police	5,000
Bangladesh Rifles	30,000
Ansars (Security Guards)	20,000

Source: *The Military Balance, Institute of Strategic Studies, 1986–1987* p. 151 (London, 1986).
Source: TM.

Table C

Size of Armed Forces, 1975–1986

Year	Size
1976	36,000
1981	77,000
1986	91,300

Source: *The Military Balance, Institute of Strategic Studies, 1975–1976 to 1986–1987* (London, 1975–1986).

Table D

Defense Expenditure, 1973–1986

Year	Defense expenditure in USA $ 100 million[a]	Percentage of Government spending
1973	0.6	n.a.
1976	0.5	n.a.
1981	1.5	18.4
1982	2.4	23.6
1983	1.8	19.1
1984	2.6	22.0
1985	n.a.	n.a.
1986	n.a.	n.a.

[a]Figures for 1973 to 1984 are in current USA dollars. Since figures vary widely in different issues of *The Military Balance*, whose editors attempt to revise earlier figures on the basis of later information, the figures in this table were taken from the latest available issues of the journal pertaining to each year.

Source: *The Military Balance, Institute of Strategic Studies, 1973–1974 to 1986–1987* (London, 1973–1986).

Box 23

ideological differences led to a horizontal split between them on the one hand and officers on the other. To this was added conflict between senior and junior officers when the seven 'Majors' killed Mujib without the support of their commanding officers and installed Khandokar Mushtaq Ahmad as President. Major General Ziaur Rahman, the most famous of the liberation war heroes, became the new Chief of Staff of the Army. As the 'Majors' continued to remain outside the command of Army Headquarters, some senior officers led by Brigadier Khalid Musharaf, another 1971 hero, staged a counter-coup on November 3, 1975, removed Ahmad from the presidency and arrested Zia.

Musharaf's move was seen as the restoration of the Awami League–India axis. Consequently, lower ranks in Dhaka cantonment revolted on November 6, and restored Zia to his former position. The failure of the coup did not end dissension within the army. Left wing privates under the *Biplobi Shainik Sangsthas* started killing officers in an attempt to bring about 'uninterrupted' socialist revolution. This development forced the two antagonistic groups of officers ('freedom fighters' and 'repatriates') to unite temporarily under the leadership of Zia who sternly suppressed the opposition.

Political development under Zia

'Young General Zia' (he was forty years old in 1975) proved to be a leader with insight, imagination and initiative. He understood the need for primacy of politics over arms, and could also see that the greatest obstacle to the establishment of a stable civilian political system was the non-professional, politicized and divided army whose feuding factions were prone to make unpredictable forays on government. Zia, therefore, tried to foster unity and professional pride in the armed forces through higher pay, improved training and adequate supplies of arms and ammunition. Simultaneously, he began to reconstruct the country's political structure. First, he advocated reconciliation between the pro-liberation and anti-liberation forces in all sectors of Bangladeshi society. He expressed a linguistic-territorial-*Islamic* nationalism, which he called Bangladesh nationalism, in place of the linguistic-territorial-*secular* nationalism, the Bengali nationalism propounded by Mujib, as it was felt that recognition of Islam was necessary to counteract Indian influence. Zia advocated 'politics of production', a pragmatic economic program seeking solutions to immediate problems of population growth, illiteracy and insufficient food production.

Zia brought various political groups under a Nationalist Front onto his platform of national reconciliation, Bangladesh nationalism and a problem-solving approach in the economic field. He then restored electoral politics and won the Presidential elections held on June 3, 1978 by defeating the Awami League candidate convincingly. Zia soon transformed the Nationalist Front into a political

Parliamentary elections in Bangladesh, 1973 and 1979

Table A

The General Elections of March 7, 1973

Party	Number of seats contested	Number of seats won	Percentage of votes secured
Awami League	300	292	73.2
National Awami Party (pro-Moscow)	223	—	8.6
Jatio Samajtantric Dal (National Socialist Party)	236	1	6.5
National Awami Party (Bhashani)	169	—	5.4
Independent and Others	159	6	6.3
Total	1,087	299[a]	100.00

[a]The election in one constituency was postponed; the seat was later won by an Awami League candidate.

Source: T. Maniruzzaman, *Group Interests and Political Changes: Studies of Pakistan and Bangladesh* p. 145 (New Delhi, 1982).

Table B

The General Elections of February 1979

Party	Number of seats contested	Number of seats won	Percentage of votes secured
Bangladesh National Party	298	207	44
Awami League (Major Faction)	295	39	25
Muslim League/Islamic Democratic League Alliance	265	20	8
Awami League (Minor Faction)	183	2	2
Jatio Samajtantric Dal (National Socialist Party)	240	8	6
Other parties	419	8	6
Independents	425	16	9
Total	2,125	300	100

Source: T. Maniruzzaman, *The Bangladesh Revolution and its Aftermath* p. 226 (Dhaka, 1980)

Box 24

party called the Bangladesh Nationalist Party, which won a large majority in the National Assembly elections of February 1979 (see Box 24, Table B).

Left-wing and anti-repatriate factions in the army remained

disaffected. Their continuing dissent was reflected in about twenty attempted coups against Zia's government. Finally, a group of 'freedom fighting' officers assassinated Zia in Chittagong on May 31, 1981 in a surprise attack similar to the one in which Mujib had been killed. The High Command at the Army Headquarters at Dhaka, however, did not seize power for they were uncertain how the majority of officers and men would react to their takeover. They, therefore, encouraged Vice-President Abdus Sattar to become acting President. As constitutional provisions limited the length of time under an acting President to 180 days, Sattar arranged a Presidential election in November 1981 which, as the Bangladesh Nationalist Party's nominee, he duly won.

Military regime of General Ershad

Force of events brought Zia to power in 1975, but design played the major part in the seizure of power by Lieutenant-General H. M.

Lieutenant-General H. M. Ershad, President of Bangladesh since 1983.

Ershad in a coup on March 24, 1982. By the time that Sattar had been elected President, developments in the Bangladesh army had reached a watershed. Each of the unsuccessful coups during Zia's rule had been followed by severe reprisals resulting in the death and dismissal of suspected dissidents. As 'freedom fighters' were mostly those involved in the coup attempts, their strength in the army steadily decreased. Officers recruited in the post-liberation period resented the monopoly of patriotism claimed by the 'freedom fighters' and had already made common cause with their 'repatriated' counterparts. The unprecedented and universal mourning for Zia gave the High Command the opportunity for a thorough cleansing operation which led to almost the complete removal of officers who had participated in the 1971 war.

Ershad, a repatriated officer who had been appointed Chief of Staff by Zia, saw that the closely-knit repatriated officer corps could easily be mobilized to seize power. With the remnants of the 'freedom fighting' privates demoralized and lacking patrons in the officer corps, the lower ranks as a whole had now become more amenable to the new chain of command. Ershad adopted a twofold strategy to win support. He first drew up a charter of demands including a large increase in salary for defense personnel knowing full well that the government would not accept it. Staff officers spread around the news of its non-acceptance to rouse feelings in the armed forces. Ershad then began to demand a constitutional share of political power for the armed forces which helped to unite them further under his leadership. Sattar was thus forced to hand power over to Ershad while the vast majority of politically-conscious Bangladeshis stood aghast at the way in which power had been seized.

Ershad has remained in power since 1982 primarily by keeping the armed forces satisfied. Formal allocation to defense in the annual revenue budget has increased on average by 18 percent over recent years, while the total yearly budget has increased by 14 percent. (The figures for the growth of the Police, the Armed Forces and defense expenditure are given in Box 23.)

Defense has also received substantial indirect investment through channels such as the Security and Intelligence and Unexpected Expenditure headings. Large proportions of the Housing and Construction, Roads and Highways budgets are spent on the cantonment areas. According to informed estimates, overt and covert defense expenditure has increased by at least 25 percent per year since 1982.

In contrast to the policy followed by previous governments, new pay scales enforced in August 1985 brought about parity of salaries between civilian and military employees. However, defense personnel receive additional allowances and benefits. For officers, these include: service allowances amounting to 12.5 percent of their original pay; free medical treatment; servant allowances; and rations at nominal prices, all of which amount to at least the monthly salary of the highest-ranking civil servant. The benefits enjoyed by lower ranks are proportionally even larger. They receive service allowances amounting to 20 percent of their original pay, free food and accommodation, and allowances for good conduct, efficiency and their children's education. Thus, privates and NCOs get roughly four times the pay received by their counterparts in the civilian sector.

The colonization of civilian posts by military officers, which began in a small way during the Zia regime, has greatly expanded under Ershad. The police service has been virtually taken over by retired military officers, while at least 28 hold senior posts in the Secretariat. Serving or retired members of the armed forces head 14 of the 22 large and lucrative public corporations. Six more are headed by civilians with special connections with Ershad and other senior army generals. Of the 48 heads of Bangladesh missions abroad, one-third are drawn from the defense services.

The substantial share of senior military officers in political power has been the main factor in ensuring their loyalty to Ershad. About 40 percent of his successive councils of Ministers are drawn from the armed services. More importantly, senior military officers act as a 'super cabinet' for Ershad who discusses all important policy measures with them before these measures are formally placed before the Council of Ministers. This practice is still maintained by Ershad although Martial Law was formally lifted on November 10, 1986. Ershad seems to have given a sense of rulership even to the lower ranks by extolling their 'glorious role' in the 1971 war and crediting them with bringing about 'all-round development in the country'.

Since the coup d'état of March 1982, political parties have been demanding the resignation of Ershad and the holding of free and fair elections under a politically neutral caretaker government to restore civilian supremacy in politics. Ershad, however, managed to persuade the Awami League to take part in parliamentary elections held on May 7, 1986 in which the government party 'won' an absolute majority of seats. From reliable accounts, these elections appear to have been 'rigged': even the Awami League leaders have described them as 'ballot robbery'. Ershad was declared President in the presidential election of October 1986 but this was boycotted by all the foremost opposition parties including the Bangladesh National Party and the Awami League. As the foreign press reported and as Ershad himself grudgingly admitted, only two to three percent of the electorate voted in the October 1986 election. Following the example of pre-1971 Pakistan rulers, Ershad, lacking electoral legitimacy, has been trying to gain popularity by raising Islamic slogans.

The greatest obstacle to the continuation of military rule in Bangladesh is the country's political culture. The constructive aspect of this individualistic political outlook is now showing itself in growing resistance to authoritarian military rule through agitations, strikes and mass public meetings. Resentment against the regime is both deep and widespread, particularly among the more educated sections of the population. The two paramount opposition parties, the Awami League led by Mujib's daughter Sheikh Hasina and the BNP organized under Zia's widow Khaleda Zia, are competing with each other in mobilizing popular opposition against army rule. In early 1987, Bangladesh is threatened with increasing polarization between its civilian and military wings: Bangladeshi politics is again at the crossroads.

TM

Further reading

C. Baxter, *Bangladesh: A New Nation in an Old Setting* (Boulder, Co., 1984)

M. F. Franda, *Bangladesh: The First Decade* (New Delhi, 1982)

R. Jahan, *Pakistan: Failure in National Integration* (New York, 1972)

Z. R. Khan, *Leadership in the Least Developed Nation: Bangladesh* (Syracuse, 1983)

T. Maniruzzaman, *The Bangladesh Revolution and its Aftermath* (Dhaka, 1980)

T. Maniruzzaman, *Group Interests and Political Changes: Studies of Pakistan and Bangladesh* (New Delhi, 1982)

C. P. O'Donnell, *Bangladesh: Biography of a Muslim Nation* (Boulder, Co., 1984)

Sri Lanka

Sri Lanka won a reputation for being a stable and competitive democracy during its first thirty years of independence from British rule. This remarkable record was tarnished by increasing ethnic violence which plagued the island after the general elections of 1977 and allegations of fraud in the national referendum of 1982. During this period of political success and then of ethnic crisis, two critical themes emerged in the political system. The first was the re-nationalization of the institutions of government as Sri Lankans tried to transform the political institutions which they had inherited from the British into ones which were culturally more suited to their country. The second was the political system's inability to resolve the serious problems facing Sri Lanka, primarily the economic problems facing the people, and the integration of diverse ethnic groups into one political entity.

From 1947 to 1977, Sri Lanka held eight general elections. From the third general elections in 1956, the governing party has always failed to be re-elected. The highly competitive party system emerged with two major blocks of parties centered around the two

Administrative divisions of Sri Lanka.

Rulers of Sri Lanka since Independence

Head of State

Governor-General

1948–1949	Sir Henry Monck-Mason-Moore
1949–1954	Viscount Soulbury
1954–1962	Sir Oliver E. Goonetilleke
1962–1972	William Gopallawa

President

1972–1978	William Gopallawa
1978–	J. R. Jayawardene (Executive President)

Prime Minister

1947–1952	The Rt. Hon. D. S. Senanayake
1952–1953	Dudley S. Senanayake
1953–1956	The Rt. Hon. Sir John Kotelawala
1956–1959	S. W. R. D. Bandaranaike
1959–1960	W. Dahanayake
1960	Dudley S. Senanayake
1960–1965	Mrs Sirimavo R. D. Bandaranaike
1965–1970	Dudley S. Senanayake
1970–1977	Mrs Sirimavo R. D. Bandaranaike
1977–1978	J. R. Jayawardene
1978–	R. Premadasa

Source: K. M. De Silva *A History of Sri Lanka* pp. 572–73 (London, 1981).

Box 25

largest political parties, the United National Party (UNP) and the Sri Lanka Freedom Party (SLFP). These two parties have directed the post-independence governments of Sri Lanka and have been the primary architects of the changes which have been made in the country.

Re-nationalization of the political system

One of the last legacies of British rule in Sri Lanka was the Soulbury Constitution of 1947 which established a political system modeled on the British system of government. Sri Lankan governments have attempted to adapt the political institutions left by the British to the cultural and social characteristics of their society. This re-nationalization has been a gradual process. Rather than make a radical changeover to a 'Lankan' system of government, the leadership has gradually adapted the system by trial and error. These changes have met the goal of re-nationalizing the political system, but they have

also created new problems. By the 1980s, these new problems threatened the stability of the country's democratic institutions which since independence in 1948 had survived serious economic problems, the assassination of one Prime Minister, and the emergence of severe ethnic conflict.

Re-nationalization meant the imposition of traditional 'Sri Lankan culture'. Unfortunately in this multi-ethnic society, there was no one 'Sri Lankan culture'. The majoritarian system of government established by the British, however, ensured that the Sinhalese Buddhist majority in the country would succeed in asserting itself as the dominant culture. Thus, most of the actions to restore 'traditional culture' involved the restoration of the religion and culture of the largest ethnic group on the island, the Sinhalese, who comprise nearly 70 percent of the population.

One of the first actions of Sri Lanka's Westminster-style government after independence was to deny citizenship to an ethnic minority, the Tamils of Indian origin. These were the children or the grandchildren of Tamil-speaking immigrants who had been brought to Sri Lanka by the British in the late nineteenth and early twentieth century to work on tea plantations. They are not to be confused with the Sri Lanka Tamils who trace their history on the island back as far as the Sinhalese do. The Indian Tamils' existence in the society was seen by many Sri Lankans as a vestige of colonial rule. Through the Citizenship Act of 1948, approximately 800,000 Indian Tamils were denied citizenship and the government attempted to return them to the nation of their ancestors, either India or, in a few cases, Pakistan. As was to be expected, the Indian and Pakistani governments were not receptive to the repatriation of people who, in most cases, had been born in Sri Lanka. The process to determine the citizenship of the Indian Tamils went forward very slowly, and by 1964 the status of very few had been determined. In that year, Prime Minister Sirimavo Bandaranaike and Indian Prime Minister Lal Bahadur Shastri agreed to repatriate 525,000 out of the 975,000 Indian Tamils who then lived in Sri Lanka. Of the remaining 450,000, two-thirds were to be given Sri Lankan citizenship and the status of the rest was to be determined later. In the 1970s, India and Sri Lanka agreed to repatriate one-half of the remaining and grant citizenship to the other half. However, this agreement was never implemented and the final status of the Indian Tamils was not determined until 1986, when the Sri Lankan government agreed to grant citizenship to the last 100,000 of them. Nevertheless, a significant number of Indian Tamils remained in the country with no status; they were supposed to have been repatriated to India, but had refused to leave.

Following the denial of citizenship to the Indian Tamils, the first two Sri Lankan governments, elected in 1947 and 1952, did not try to make other fundamental changes to society or the political system. In 1956, however, a populist coalition of leftist parties led by the SLFP was able to soundly defeat the UNP which had ruled since independence. Their first action after victory was the establishment of Sinhala as the language of government, replacing English which had existed as a link language between the Tamil and Sinhala speakers on the island. The action was very popular among the overwhelming majority of the population which spoke Sinhala, but Tamil speakers, who comprised about 29 percent of the population at that time, were disturbed. The role of the Tamils in Sri Lanka was debated, but unable to command a majority the Tamils could not change the decision; Sri Lankan Tamils, who comprised about 11 percent of the population, were the most vocal. Then, attempts to negotiate the changeover to a Sinhala-only government with the Sri Lanka Tamils came to sudden halt when the popular SLFP Prime Minister S. W. R. D. Bandaranaike was assassinated on September 25, 1959 by a Sinhalese Buddhist extremist. His death led to the collapse of his coalition and a general paralysis of government.

Although Bandaranaike's Sri Lanka Freedom Party was perceived as the anti-Tamil party, the UNP did not try to reinstate English as the language of government when they returned to power in 1965. (They had briefly held the government for three months in 1960 but were unable to obtain a vote of confidence.) In fact, while

Mrs Sirimavo R. D. Bandaranaike, Prime Minister of Sri Lanka 1960–65 and 1970–77.

in power they helped to institutionalize the Sinhala-only policy.

In the 1960s, re-nationalization continued on a new front. A new SLFP government, led by Bandaranaike's widow, Sirimavo, sought in 1960 and 1961 to take over Christian-run schools. These schools had been at the forefront of the development of education on the island and were considered to be the best in Sri Lanka. The takeover effectively weakened the role of the Christian churches at a time when the Christian minority comprised an economic and political élite in the country. The intent was not to harm the Christians but to improve the quality of Buddhist education. After the UNP came to power in 1965, they carried the actions one step further by replacing the Christian Sunday as a public holiday with the Buddhist holy day, the *poya* day.

Until 1970, there was no attempt to change the fundamental structure of government. In this year, the SLFP came together with the Communist Party and a Trotskyite party, the Lanka Sama Samaja Party, to form a 'United Front' coalition government. In 1972, this government promulgated a new constitution which tried to remove alien British elements from the country's institutions. The official name of the country was changed from the English name of Ceylon to the Sinhala name of Sri Lanka. The upper house of the National State Assembly, the Senate, was abolished. It had been loosely modeled on the British House of Lords and was seen to be unnecessary. A number of other institutions borrowed from the British political system were also abolished. Most important, however, Buddhism and Sinhala were given special constitutional status in the new government. The state was to remain secular but the constitution stated that it was the duty of the state 'to protect and foster Buddhism while assuring to all religions the rights granted by'

Arms of the State: Sri Lanka

Table A

Growth in Strength of Police Force, 1951–1981

Year	Police strength
1951	6,439
1961	9,595
1971	11,135
1981	15,933

Source: *The Statesman's Year-Book* for the years, 1953, 1963, 1972–73 and 1983–84.

Table B

Armed Force Levels (Military and Paramilitary), 1986

Force	Number
Armed Forces	21,560
Army	13,900
Navy	3,960
Airforce	3,700
Paramilitary Forces	26,000
Police force	21,000
Volunteer force	5,000

Source: *The Military Balance, Institute of Strategic Studies, 1986–1987* pp. 168, 173 (London, 1986).

Table C

Size of Armed Forces, 1973–1986

Year	Size
1973	12,500
1981	14,840
1986	21,560

Source: *The Military Balance, Institute of Strategic Studies, 1973–1976 to 1986–1987* (London, 1973–1986).

Table D

Defense Expenditure, 1971–1986

Year	Defense expenditure in USA $ 100 million[a]	Percentage of Government spending
1971	0.3	n.a.
1976	0.2	n.a.
1981	0.6	3.8
1982	0.7	7.9
1983	0.8	3.9
1984	1.0	5.1
1985	n.a.	n.a.
1986	n.a.	n.a.

[a]Figures for 1971 to 1984 are in current USA dollars. Since figures vary widely in different issues of *The Military Balance*, whose editors attempt to revise earlier figures on the basis of later information, the figures in this table were taken from the latest available issues of the journal pertaining to each year.

Source: *The Military Balance, Institute of Strategic Studies, 1971–1972 to 1986–1987* (London, 1971–1986).

Box 26

the constitution. These changes were not popular with the Tamils; their feelings of alienation and anger with the government were intensified. Although the constitution promised to protect the ethnic minorities of the country, it offered them no legally-enforceable protection.

An element of economic re-nationalization was added in 1975 when tea, coconut and rubber estates were nationalized. Most of the tea estates were owned by British corporations or individual foreigners. Tea was the main foreign currency exchange earner and an important sector of the economy. Thus, Sri Lanka took back control of part of the economy from the foreign forces that the United Front leadership believed were dominating it.

In 1977, the UNP returned to power in an overwhelming electoral victory. In 1978, the party promulgated a new constitution. This constitution, which differed sharply from its earlier predecessors, was structured around the ideas of the man who was to become the first President under it, Junius Richard Jayawardene. It was modeled on the French system of government and discarded those British trappings which survived in the constitution of 1972. Sinhala was still treated as the official language of government but Tamil was given special status as a 'national language'. This did not satisfy Tamil-speakers as national language status did not appear to carry any special benefits and Sinhala continued to be the official language. The constitution also removed single-member electoral constituencies, and replaced them with a system of proportional representation. It also created a provision for holding referendums.

Parliamentary Elections in Sri Lanka 1947–1977

Party and date of foundation	1947	1952	1956	1960 March	1960 July	1965	1970	1977
UNP (United National Party 1946)	42	54	8	50	30	66	17	139
SLFP (Sri Lanka Freedom Party 1951)	—	9	51[a]	46	75	41	90	8
LSSP (Lanka Samasamaja Party 1935)	10	9	14	10	12	10	19	—
CP (Communist Party 1943)	3	4[b]	3	3	4	4	6	—
BLP (Bolshevik Leninist Party 1947)	5	—	—	—	—	—	—	—
MEP (Mahajana Eksath Peramuna 1956)	—	—	51[a]	10	3	1	—	—
CIC (Ceylon Indian Congress) 1939	6	—	—	—	—	—	—	—
TC (All Ceylon Tamil Congress) 1944	7	4	1	1	1	3	3	—
TULF (Tamil United Left Front) 1973	—	—	—	—	—	—	—	17
FP (Federal Party, 1949)	—	2	10	15	16	14	13	—
Independents	21	12	8	7	6	6	2	1
Others	1	1	0	9	4	6	—	1
Turnout percent	61.3	74.0	71.0	77.6	75.6	82.0	85.2	87.3

[a]Seats won by the Mahajana Eksath Peramuna coalition in which the SLFP was the dominant partner. From 1959 the MEP was a separate party.
[b]Seats won by the Communist Party in alliance with the Viplavakari Lanka Samasamaja Party.

Source: J. Jupp *Sri Lanka: Third World Democracy* pp. 371–72 (London, 1978); and G. P. S. H. de Silva *A Statistical Survey of Elections to the Legislatures of Sri Lanka 1911–1977* (Colombo, 1979).

Box 27

Since the constitution's promulgation, no national elections have been held using proportional representation, although on several occasions it has been used in local elections. In 1982, two national elections were held under the provisions of the constitution. Jayawardene was re-elected to the presidency for a six-year term. In December 1982, a referendum was held on whether parliamentary elections should be held in the following year as required by the constitution or whether the legislature should be given an additional six-year term. Over 54 percent of the voters supported the extension of the term of Parliament to 1989. The referendum, however, was marred by widespread allegations of ballot-rigging which left many dissatisfied with the outcome.

Emerging ethnic and economic problems

Throughout the period following the Sinhala-only legislation in 1956, English was gradually diminishing in importance as a language in the educational system and in government. The onward march of Sinhala, however, was not straightforward; many government officials preferred to carry on business in English and many school subjects continued to be taught in English because of the lack of textbooks in Sinhala or Tamil. In addition, the hostility of the Tamil speakers was growing. They felt discriminated against in the competition for government jobs which carried the highest status in society. They also felt that, as the law, employment and all import-ant economic transactions increasingly required Sinhala, they were steadily becoming second-class citizens.

As a result of this dissatisfaction, in the early 1970s Tamil youths began to rebel. At first, they launched occasional amateurish attacks against government installations or personnel. But by the 1980s, these youths, now called 'tigers', had developed into several well-trained and equipped armies of liberation. Some observers have estimated that there are over 30 tiger groups, of which the largest and most powerful is that of the Liberation Tigers of Tamil Eelam led by Velupillai Prabhakaran. By 1986, the Liberation Tigers had gained control of much of the northern Jaffna peninsula. The main demand of the 'tigers' has been the creation of Eelam, an independent Tamil state, comprising the Northern and Eastern Provinces of Sri Lanka.

The ethnic problem was intensified by anti-Tamil riots which broke out in 1977, 1981 and 1983. The 1983 riots were the severest the country has seen and were accompanied by charges that government troops and police stood by and watched as rioters attacked Tamil homes and businesses. After the riots, the fighting between the government and the 'tigers' escalated into open warfare in the northern and eastern provinces of the country. The government's response to the riots and the increasing violence was to improve the fighting capacity of the army by hiring mercenaries, obtaining arms from western countries, and taking a harder line towards the Tamil leadership. The non-violent and legal Tamil United Liberation

but will not permit them to be combined as one province as most of the Tamil leaders demand.

While the nationalization of the political system progressed, the Sri Lankan economy failed to grow as rapidly as had been expected. The high levels of education and the high value placed upon it by Sri Lankans led many social scientists in the 1950s to expect Sri Lanka to develop very rapidly. Admittedly there were some impressive developments in state and society. The country developed a very effective social welfare system which has elevated health standards and improved the quality of life for most Sri Lankans. Life expectancy at 69 years, and other health standards are high when compared to Third World countries. In addition, an extensive social welfare system from independence to 1979 provided every Sri Lankan with a free measure of rice as well as other social welfare benefits. Accompanying these changes was a drastic drop in the birth rate. Sri Lanka went from a population increase rate of 2.7 percent per year in the 1950s to a rate of 1.7 percent per year in the 1980s. In other words, it went from the second highest rate of increase in Asia to among the lowest in Asia in less than thirty years.

At the same time, however, growth was slow, achieving a *per capita* income of only 330 USA dollars by the mid-1980s. Moreover, the country remained reliant on fluctuating international prices in tea, coconut and rubber for generating foreign currency. It was also unable to establish an industrial base. The UNP government elected in 1977 established a 'Free Trade Zone' but it attracted only a moderate number of multinational corporations. In addition, many of the jobs that were created required low skills levels, and offered few hopes of long-term employment. The sluggish economy combined with the high population growth rates of the 1950s to create a more serious problem, that of high levels of youth unemployment. The Sri Lankan educational system has been very successful in turning out large numbers of well-educated graduates, but the economy has not expanded rapidly enough to create jobs commensurate with their educational level. The consequence is a large pool of educated Sri Lankan youths who have been unable to find employment. This problem helped to create a youth-led insurrection in 1971 which resulted in several thousand deaths, and has continued to lead to a large degree of dissatisfaction among young people on the island. The 1971 insurrection was primarily among Sinhalese youth. However, it is not a coincidence that the Tamil insurrection in the north and east is largely a youth movement. Society's high stress on education and the economy's inability to provide jobs present Sri Lankan youth with a dismal future.

Sri Lanka has a great deal to be proud of in the development of stable democratic institutions and in the provision of a minimum standard of living to most of its population. Severe ethnic tension, however, and continuing economic problems raise questions about the future of the political system and the unity of the state. The re-

A Tamil 'tiger' who fights for the creation of Eelam, an independent Tamil state in the Northern and Eastern Provinces of Sri Lanka.

Front (TULF), the main Tamil political party, was expelled from Parliament after the anti-Tamil rioting of 1983. Serious negotiations between the Tamils (both the TULF and the 'tigers') and the government did not occur until 1985, and only then under pressure from the Indian government which was drawn into the conflict because the 'tigers' had established training and staging bases in the southern Indian state of Tamil Nadu. The main area of disagreement in the negotiations has been over the Tamil demand for autonomy in the Northern and Eastern Provinces. The government has been willing to grant these regions a degree of local autonomy

nationalization process has helped to restore a sense of pride but it has also intensified ethnic tensions and made the resolution of ethnic problems more difficult to achieve.

RCO

Further reading

M. P. Moore, *The State and Peasant Politics in Sri Lanka* (London, 1985)

R. C. Oberst, *Legislators and Representations: The Decentralization of Development Planning in Sri Lanka* (Boulder, Co., 1985)

S. J. Tambiah, *Sri Lanka: Ethnic Fratricide and the Dismantling of Democracy* (Chicago, 1986)

Maldives

After World War II, Muhammad Amin Didi took charge of the country (which was still nominally a monarchy, but with a Regency Committee instead of a monarch) and introduced numerous reforms. In January 1953 he changed the country from a monarchy to a Republic, with himself as first President; but his absences abroad allowed his opponents to overthrow him in September of the same year, and when he tried to return on December 31, 1953 he was attacked and injured in the streets and subsequently died. A nominal monarch was then restored who reigned until 1968, but without power. The government was at first under the control of Ibrahim Ali Didi, with whom the British government came to an agreement to reactivate a wartime base on Gan island in Addu Atoll. The economic and social influences exercised indirectly by the British forces paved the way for a breakaway movement (the 'Suvadive Republic') in the southern atolls, headed by Afif Didi, which was eventually put down but led to bad relations with the British under Ibrahim Ali Didi's successor, Ibrahim Nasir. In 1965, complete severance from Britain was declared, and in 1968 the last king resigned and a second republic was instituted. Gan remained on lease, but the British government gave this up unilaterally in 1976. Nasir was replaced as President in 1979 by Maumun Abdul Gayum, and in 1982 the Maldives rejoined the Commonwealth.

Under Nasir's rule the modernization of the Maldives, begun by Amin Didi, was speeded up, particularly in Malé. The Borahs and the Sri Lankan Moors were expelled, and foreign trade became a government monopoly. A merchant navy was acquired, trading largely with India and the Middle East. The two Government schools in Malé (for boys and for girls) were converted into English-medium schools on the Sri Lankan pattern, with teaching staff brought over from Sri Lanka, and young Maldivians were sent

Administrative divisions of the Maldives.

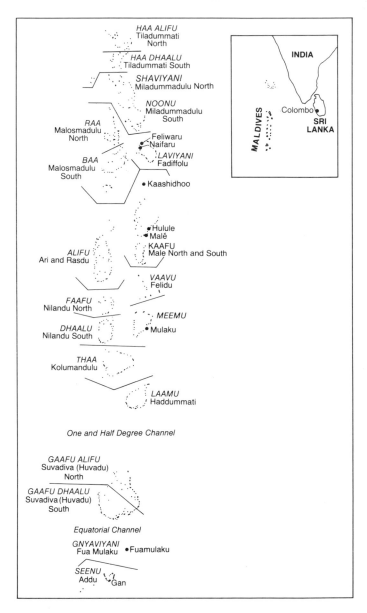

abroad on training courses. The old aristocratic order of society in Malé was thus greatly modified.

In 1972 the government of Sri Lanka suddenly discontinued their bulk purchases of dried fish from the Maldives. This had been the principal Maldivian export for over a century, and was channeled entirely through Sri Lanka, where it formed an essential curry-stuff. One result of this ban was the leasing out of fish-processing rights to a Japanese company, which stationed 'collecting vessels' at various points in the archipelago and purchased fish from Maldivian

Nepal

Administrative divisions of Nepal.

Source: *J.E. Schwartzberg, ed.,* A Historical Atlas of South Asia *(Chicago, 1978) p.79*

fishermen at agreed prices. Another was to give a sudden fillip to the development of tourism, involving regular air communications with the outside world and the introduction of such tourist essentials as alcohol (not available to Maldivians). The unexpected closure of the British post on Gan led to a large influx of Addu people into Malé, and the population of the capital rose from 11,000 in 1967 to an estimated 35,000 in 1987. In order to accommodate these, it has been necessary to drain large areas of shallow lagoon. The past two decades has seen the internal affairs of this republic of atolls increasingly exposed to external forces.

CR

Further reading
M. Adeney and W. K. Carr, 'The Maldive Republic' in J. M. Ostheimer, Ed., *The Politics of the Western Indian Ocean Islands* (New York, 1975)
A. D. W. Forbes and C. H. B. Reynolds, 'The Maldives' in Bernard Lewis, *et al.*, Eds, *Encyclopaedia of Islam*, new edn, vol. VI, fasc. 101–102, pp. 246–47 (Leiden, 1987)

The overthrow of the Rana family regime in 1951 cleared the way for the introduction of programs of political and economic modernization. Over the next 35 years Nepal experimented with a variety of political systems. By 1965, there were representative institutions at both the local and national level, a cabinet led by a Prime Minister, a national court system and modern legal code, a well-organized administrative system, and a Planning Commission. Through all these changes, however, the persistence of traditional Nepali patterns of political and social interaction have given these modern institutions a uniquely Nepali character. The modernization process has not as yet seriously disrupted the basic stability and continuity of the political system inherited from the Ranas.

The 1951 Delhi Compromise, which created the first post-Rana government, was an agreement between the four main political forces that dominated Nepali politics through the 1950s: the monarchy; the political parties; the Rana family; and the Government of India. The governance of Nepal from 1951 to 1959 was essentially an *ad hoc* operation, with the distribution of office and powers largely determined by access to the royal court and the Indian Embassy. The Prime Ministers were usually drawn from the parties, but on the basis of a party's weakness rather than its strength. Power gradually became focused on the monarch, particularly after King Mahendra succeeded to the throne in 1955.

Mahendra sought to build a broader support base for the monarchy through extensive national tours and the dispensation of instant justice and gratuities. But he was only partially successful, as

```
┌─────────────────────────────────────────────────────┐
│                                                       │
│         Rulers of Nepal since 1951                    │
│                                                       │
│                                                       │
│     Head of State                                     │
│                                                       │
│     King                                              │
│     1911–1955    Tribhuvan Bir Bikram Shah            │
│     1955–1972    Mahendra Bir Bikram Shah             │
│     1972–        Birendra Bir Bikram Shah             │
│                                                       │
│     Prime Minister (or equivalent post)               │
│                                                       │
│     1951–1952    M. P. Koirala                        │
│     1953–1955    M. P. Koirala                        │
│     1956         Tanka Prasad Acharya                 │
│     1957         K. I. Singh                          │
│     1957–1959    Subarna Shamsher Rana                │
│                  (as head of the Advisory Council)    │
│     1959–1960    B. P. Koirala                        │
│                  —                                    │
│     1963         Dr Tulsi Giri                        │
│                                                       │
│     1966         Surya Bahadur Thapa                  │
│                  —                                    │
│     1969–1973    Kirtinidhi Bista                     │
│     1973–1975    Nagendra Prasad Rijal                │
│     1975–1977    Dr Tulsi Giri                        │
│     1977–1979    Kirtinidhi Bista                     │
│     1979–1983    Surya Bahadur Thapa                  │
│     1983–1986    Lokendra Bahadur Chand               │
│     1986         Nagendra Parasad Rijal               │
│     1986–        Marich Mansingh Shrestha             │
│                                                       │
│     Source: LER.                                      │
│                                                       │
└─────────────────────────────────────────────────────┘
```

Box 29

the foremost political party, the Nepali Congress, was similarly involved in an intensive campaign to build a national party organization, and with considerable success. Under these circumstances, Mahendra could not ignore the political party demands for a democratic constitution and an elected government. However, he assigned the constitution-making tasks to a committee he had appointed and then, in 1959, bestowed a constitution on the country. It was a model democratic document except in one respect: the King retained the power to declare an Emergency and suspend the constitution at his own discretion.

Parliamentary elections were held under the constitution in early 1959, with the Nepali Congress winning over two-thirds of the seats. An elected government, headed by the Nepali Congress leader, B. P. Koirala, was formed and governed the country with little interference from the Palace for 18 months. A democratic parliamentary system seemed to be firmly in place and the Nepali Congress Ministry moved carefully but forcefully to establish its control over the bureaucracy and to use its status as the governing party to expand its organizational base. By mid-1960, Nepal appeared to be evolving toward a 'dominant party system' modeled after the Congress Party system then extant in India under Nehru's leadership.

These developments aroused concern among the opposition party leaders, some bureaucrats, and finally King Mahendra, but only the last had the capacity to take effective action. In December 1960, Mahendra suddenly declared an Emergency, arrested most Nepali Congress leaders, and suspended the 1959 Constitution. A new constitution, introduced in 1962 and characterized as a 'Partyless Panchayat System', was formulated upon two principles: the 'outlawing' of political parties; and the organization of a governmental structure from the local to the national level based upon *panchayats* (councils) that were supposedly modeled after the traditional Hindu caste system council of elders in Nepal. The local panchayat councils are directly elected, but the panchayat units at the district, zonal and central (Rashtriya Panchayat) levels were initially elected indirectly by subordinate units.

In operation, the 1962 Constitution did not impose any effective limits on the powers of the monarch or the small coterie around the Palace, and even minor decisions on local issues invariably had to be confirmed at the top. The inflexibility and procrastination built into the system eventually antagonized almost everyone, including much of the political élite and bureaucracy that had opted to work within the system. Some important reform programs were introduced, such as land reform and a new legal code, but most of the attention in Nepal was directed toward the vicious infighting within the bureaucracy and panchayats for royal favors. Economic development programs, while formulated in impressive five-year plan packages, were of secondary importance to those in power and, hence, made only limited progress.

With Mahendra's death in 1972 and the succession to the throne of King Birendra, certain changes in style were quickly introduced. Birendra's closest associates were quite different from the group that had surrounded Mahendra, as the new ruler brought into the Palace young Nepalis with graduate degrees in economics and the social sciences. Their objective was to reorganize the administrative and political institutions of the Panchayat system to make them more responsive to economic development demands. They accomplished the reorganization tasks successfully. But the results in economic development terms were negligible, for in the process they lost contact with key elements in the panchayat élite on the national and local level whose cooperation in development tasks was required.

By 1980 it was painfully evident to King Birendra that economic development without political reform was a non-starter, and he began making some adjustments. His first move was to hold a

King Birendra of Nepal.

national referendum in which the public was asked to choose between the panchayat system and a multiparty system. The panchayat system won, but the vote was close to 50–50, thus indicating substantial dissatisfaction in the country. Birendra next introduced direct elections of the Rashtriya Panchayat. The first Assembly election was held on this basis in 1981 and a second in 1986. On both occasions, most candidates identified as Palace nominees were defeated and a random collection of candidates from local élitist families won. In 1981 and 1986, the Rashtriya Panchayat selected the Prime Minister, though on both occasions it was known that the man selected had been 'endorsed' by the Palace.

Politics in Nepal now operate in a vacuum in which certain formalities are followed but decision-making responsibility lies with the King – as much by default as by design. The political parties are still 'outlawed', but function in most respects like legal parties elsewhere, holding national conferences, party worker seminars and organizational drives. The press is still subject to censorship, but in effect all this usually means is that the royal family cannot be criticized but almost anything and anyone else can be. There is a sense in Nepal that the country's overriding problem is not the lack of political development but rather the extremely low rate of economic development combined with a high birth rate. There is broad divergence within the political public on a political model that might improve the rate of economic growth in Nepal as the record

on these matters in countries to the north and south no longer appears particularly inspiring.

LER

Further reading

N. P. Banskota, *Indo-Nepal Trade and Economic Relations* (Delhi, 1981)

M. P. Lama, *The Economics of Indo-Nepalese Co-operation* (New Delhi, 1985)

Ramakant, *Nepal–China and India* (New Delhi, 1986)

L. E. Rose and J. T. Scholz, *Nepal: Profile of a Himalayan Kingdom* (Boulder, Co., 1980)

Bhutan

The establishment of an hereditary monarchical system in the place of the theocratic Buddhist polity in Bhutan in 1907 was the first important step in the direction of the modernization of this previously isolated country. The first two Wangchuk dynasty rulers concentrated on efforts to assert an effective central authority over a disparate collection of monastic and regional élites. On this foundation, the third ruler, Jigme Dorji Wangchuk (1952–72), inaugurated programs directed at fundamental political reform and economic development; his successor, Jigme Singye Wangchuk, has continued and expanded these efforts in all fields.

Jigme Dorji's primary innovation was the establishment of the *Tshogdu* (National Assembly) in 1953, thus introducing the concept of representative government into the Wangchuk system. Initially, the Tshogdu had more the character of an advisory body than a legislative institution. But this changed significantly in 1968 when royal ordinances decreed that decisions of the Tshogdu were final

Administrative divisions of Bhutan.

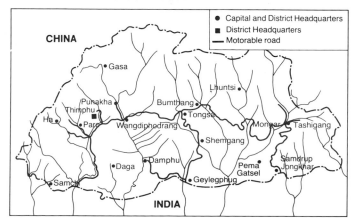

Jigme Dorji Wangchuk, King of Bhutan 1952–72, and his successor, Jigme Singye Wangchuk.

Rulers of Bhutan since *c.* 1950

Head of State

King
1926–1952	Jigme Wangchuk
1952–1972	Jigme Dorji Wangchuk
1972–	Jigme Singye Wangchuk

Prime Minister[a]
| 1958–1964 | Jigme Dorji |
| 1964–1965 | Lhendup Dorji |

[a]Jigme Dorji and Lhendup Dorji were given the rank and title of 'Lonchen', which is usually translated as Prime Minister. No other Bhutanese official before or since has been given either this rank or the responsibilities and functions of a Prime Minister. The King normally serves in this capacity.

Source: LER.

Box 30

and did not require royal approval, and that the Assembly was given the power to remove a reigning monarch (but not the monarchy) by a two-thirds vote. The electoral system for the elected members of the Tshogdu (110 of 150) is based on a limited franchise comprising village elders and heads of families. However, in Bhutan's social structure the results are broadly representative.

Jigme Dorji Wangchuk also established new institutions as consultative bodies on policy matters; the *Lodoi Tsokde* (Royal Advisory Council) and the *Lhungye Shuntsog* (State Council), as well as the *Lhengyel Tsok* (Council of Ministers) as the administrative institution. The King, in effect, acts as his own Prime Minister, and works with these institutions in a very informal and open manner. Most decisions of the Government of Bhutan, thus, are the product of a broad if informal consultative process, but there are no formal constitutional limits on the powers of the King to issue royal ordinances on his own discretion.

A very modest central administrative system had been established by the first two Wangchuk rulers but this has been greatly expanded and modernized since 1950. The Dzongdas (district officers) in the 15 districts in which Bhutan is divided wield a wide range of administrative and political powers (and until the mid-1970s, judicial powers as well), and are the focal points for most development programs. In the 1980s, King Jigme Singye Wangchuk has sought to introduce ambitious decentralization programs in economic planning and administration, but these are still in an early stage of implementation. There has also been a concerted effort since the mid-1970s to expand the judicial system by the establishment of a

Thimkhang Gongma (High Court) at the Center, more responsible *Thimkhangs* (courts) in the districts as well as a legal code that combines modern principles of jurisprudence and Bhutan's traditional customary law.

The introduction of a new political system in the 1950s was accompanied by the abandonment of Bhutan's traditional isolationist foreign policy. Subsequently, Bhutan has exchanged diplomatic relations with several countries other than India, joined the United Nations and numerous other international organizations, and become the recipient of international aid from various bilateral and multilateral sources. Bhutan's close identity with India on security and, in most instances, other international issues continues.

LER

Further reading
R. Rahul, *Royal Bhutan* (New Delhi, 1983)
L. E. Rose, *The Politics of Bhutan* (Ithaca, 1977)

FOREIGN RELATIONS

The leaders of the seven South Asian nations meet in their first-ever summit at Dhaka, December 7, 1985, to launch the South Asian Association for Regional Cooperation (SAARC). From the left: President Zia ul Haq of Pakistan, King Birendra of Nepal, President Ershad of Bangladesh, President Jayewardene of Sri Lanka, Prime Minister Gandhi of India, King Jigme Wangchuk of Bhutan and President Gayum of the Maldives.

Introduction

South Asia is often called the subcontinent, and this is an accurate descriptive term. While South Asia is a subregion of the greater Asian continent, for most of recorded history it has had only limited political, economic and cultural ties to other major Asian societies. Before 1947, for instance, there was virtually no direct interaction between the Sinic cultures of East Asia and the Hindu societies of South Asia. The subcontinent, peripheral to the Asian land mass, was never an integral part of the vital land communication systems that criss-crossed the continent from the Mediterranean and Persian Gulf to the China coast. One of the 'silk routes' ran through the northwest corner of the subcontinent, but South Asian societies were never an integral part of that highly lucrative trading system.

No other region of the world has such formidable natural boundaries as the subcontinent. On the north, for nearly four thousand kilometers, lie the massive Himalayan and Hindu Kush ranges, the highest in the world. While they are not impenetrable, they do complicate crosscultural interactions. The range on the Assam–Burma border to the northeast is less majestic but, if anything, more inaccessible. The mountains separating the subcontinent from Iran, Afghanistan and the Islamic world to the west are much less impressive, but are buttressed by extensive semi-arid hinterlands on both sides of the frontier. Although there have long been commercial ties between South Asia and West Asia, these were of minor importance to both. Nevertheless, the routes along which this commerce passed have played a vital role in South Asian history, for since 2000 BC at least they were used by the wide variety of invading armies that poured into the subcontinent from central Asia.

Economically and culturally, South Asia's most important contacts with the outside world for the last two millenia have been by sea, through the Persian Gulf and the Arabian peninsula to the Mediterranean societies, and through Southeast Asia to China. The more important intrusions of external influences into the subcontinent, Islam from West Asia and modern cultures from Europe, first entered via the sea; while India's cultural exports, Buddhist, Hindu and Islamic, traveled across the waters to southeast Asia.

Thus, the centrality of the subcontinent to broader Indian Ocean geopolitics and economics is evident. It was India's status as the principal entrepôt in a complicated but highly profitable oceanic trade structure that made the western and southern coastal areas of South Asia so vital to a succession of maritime empires, from the West Asian Muslim commercial entities in the eleventh to fourteenth centuries to the Portuguese, Dutch, French and British colonial powers in the sixteenth to eighteenth centuries. India became the 'jewel in the crown' of the vast British empire in Asia in part because of its wealth but in the main because of its role as the fulcrum upon which the British imperial and commercial system in all of Asia was balanced.

As the subcontinent was a vital link in the Indian Ocean's geostrategic and commercial systems and was vulnerable to seaward assaults, it is surprising that none of the Indian littoral states ever emerged for more than brief periods as naval powers. There were a few principalities in the southernmost sections of the subcontinent who did indulge in some profitable ventures overseas, contributing in the process to the 'Sanskritization' of several areas of southeast Asia. But most of the population of the subcontinent had land-bound visions, very limited perceptions of the world beyond the 'black waters', and even less curiosity.

The general principle, thus, has been that the external world occasionally intruded upon South Asia but the reverse has rarely been the case, at least in any structured fashion. This has resulted in a strong sense of exclusiveness in the subcontinent and an evident preference for noninvolvement with the rest of the world. Rather unexpectedly, however, this has not resulted in the kind of virulent xenophobic exclusiveness that is integral to the traditional cultures of other major Asian societies such as China and Japan. Indeed, the subcontinent has generally demonstrated both a receptivity to external influences and a remarkable eclectic ability to accommodate them within indigenous cultures.

It should also be noted that South Asia is comprised of a rich mosaic of religions, languages, races and cultures and is, thus, heterogeneous in character and spirit. These differences define national lines within the region, but often cross national boundaries and affect relations between countries. Hindus are the majority community in India and Nepal, but significant minorities in Bangladesh, Sri Lanka and Bhutan. Muslims are the majority in Pakistan, Bangladesh and the Maldives, and minorities in the other states of the region. Buddhists are the majority community in Sri Lanka and Bhutan, and important minorities in Nepal and India.

The distribution of linguistic–ethnic communities across the state system in South Asia further complicates the problems caused by religious heterogeneity. Bengalis, both Hindu and Muslim, constitute about 98 percent of the population in Bangladesh, large majorities in West Bengal and Tripura in India, and a substantial minority in Assam. Panjabi-speakers form about two-thirds of the population in Pakistan and a majority in the Indian states of the Panjab and Haryana. Urdu, the national language of Pakistan, is probably spoken as a home language by more families in India than in Pakistan. There are a large number of Hindi speakers in Nepal, Nepali-speakers in India and Bhutan, Tamil-speakers in India and Sri Lanka, and Pushtu-speakers in Pakistan and Afghanistan. The fact that English is used as a common language of communication by the élites throughout the subcontinent only partly compensates for

South Asia in international politics 1947–87.

USA
Relations with India
1951 – first major shipment of aid.
1956 – sends most aid to India.
1962 – begins arms sailes.
1965 – imposes arms embargo.
1971 – suspends all future licences for arms shipments.

Relations with Pakistan
1954 – Mutual Defence Assistance Agreement.
1959 – Ankara Agreement.
1965 – imposes arms embargo.
1971 – tilts towards Pakistan.
1981 – Military Sales Agreement.

USSR
Relations with India
1956 – begins economic aid.
1963 – begins military aid.
1971 – Twenty Year Treaty of Friendship and Cooperation.
1970s – major supplier of arms.
1980s – largest external economic partner.

Relations with Pakistan
1961 – begins economic aid.
1966 – mediates between Pakistan and India.
1968 – begins military aid.
1970s/80s – continues economic relationship.

USA
⊗ RCD
✪ SEATO
✪ CENTO
Not a full member.

✪ SEATO (1954-75) members

✪ CENTO (1955-79) members

○ members of Colombo Plan – begun 1950

⊗ members of R.C.D. (Regional Cooperation for Development) begun 1964, out of operation 1979-1984)

⚱ members of the Islamic Conference – begun 1970

NAM member of Non-Aligned Movement – begun 1961

member of British Commonwealth

✱ 1971 Pakistan withdraws from SEATO
1972 Pakistan withdraws from British Commonwealth
1979 Pakistan withdraws from CENTO

Source: J. E. Schwartzberg, A Historical Atlas of South Asia (Chicago, 1975) p.90. Boundaries as of 1987

the fact that at least twenty-three major languages and several hundred minor languages and dialects are spoken throughout the region.

The international relations of the subcontinent since 1947 has been strongly influenced by these two geopolitical factors: first, the comparative isolation of the region from the major areas of great power confrontation in Asia; and second, the bewildering heterogeneity of the South Asian societies. While South Asian states will occasionally seek and accept limited affiliations with external powers on political and security issues, this has invariably been interpreted by them in terms of external support for their position in South Asian disputes, rather than their support of the external power in Asian or global disputes. The heterogeneity of the subcontinent has complicated all efforts to attain *regional* responses on issues, other than pro forma positions either denouncing apartheid and racism or supporting the concept of a new international economy, while disagreeing on most of the specifics. There are, thus, at least as many South Asian foreign policies as there are countries in the region, and the effort to establish a viable regional system which would speak with one voice for the subcontinent has only just begun.

LER

India and its neighbors in the region

The subcontinent had constituted an integrated foreign policy system under British rule, with the areas now comprising India, Pakistan, Bangladesh and Sri Lanka as constituents of the imperial system while Nepal, Bhutan and the Maldives had some form of subordinate relationship. The situation changed drastically in 1947 with the partition of the subcontinent. Thereafter, the region consisted of five national units, India, Pakistan, Nepal, Bhutan, and Sri Lanka with the Maldives added as a sixth in 1965 and Bangladesh as a seventh in 1971. The transformation involved more than just the number of national systems responsible for formulating foreign policy; more importantly, it concerned also their different and, in some cases, antagonistic foreign policy perceptions. It became usual for the different states to work at cross-purposes with each other, both on intraregional issues and on the subcontinent's relations with the external world.

India and the other regional states have usually had quite different perceptions of their interests and how these were best protected and advanced. These differences in perspective are, in part, the inevitable consequence of their different geostrategic environment. India occupies the core of the subcontinent, and its natural concern has been with protecting that core, and the marginal areas, from outsiders. The other states occupy frontier areas between South Asia and adjacent regions. Their strategies for survival in the past had been based upon policies directed at balancing off the neighboring external powers against the dominant power in the subcontinent. After 1947, for reasons that made good sense to each of them, India adopted exclusivistic principles in its regional policies while the other South Asian states busily practiced balancing strategies directed at limiting India's dominant status in the subcontinent.

It was in this general context that India formulated the basic principles of its regional policy in the post-1947 period. Stated precisely, the primary objective of Indian policy in South Asia has been to extract, in some form or another, recognition of India's hegemonic status in the region from both the major external powers and from its neighbors in the region. The British Imperial system, under which the peripheral states in the subcontinent were allowed full autonomy in internal affairs in exchange for accepting British supervision in the conduct of their foreign policy, is considered a realistic model for India to emulate. But even this hegemonistic role has eluded New Delhi since, much to its irritation, all the other South Asian states take divergent positions from the Government of India on some key issues, at times, indeed, primarily in order to be seen voting differently from India.

Another aspect of India's regional policy often not noted is its interest in most instances in maintaining the status quo in the region, in preserving the state system within the subcontinent. Some of India's neighbors, and in particular Pakistan, would take strong exception to this statement and would assert instead that India has been a destabilizing factor in the region. While there are several vivid examples of Indian intervention in the politics of neighboring states, what is striking when one examines the history of the area since 1947 is how rarely India has employed such tactics when the opportunities have been numerous and inviting. A significant exception has been the Indian intervention in the Bangladesh crisis in East Pakistan in 1971, but it may be more correct to argue that New Delhi was seeking to restore a modicum of stability in a highly explosive situation on its northeastern frontier even though its actions resulted in the division of Pakistan into two states.

In pressing its objectives within the subcontinent, India has demonstrated an open mind on the question of an overarching regional system. In the immediate post-independence period, New Delhi showed some interest in the establishment of a regional institution to replace the British Imperial system. But this collapsed in the context of the 1948 Indo-Pakistani war over Kashmir. India lost its enthusiasm for a regional system, and responded rather skeptically to the 1978 Bangladeshi proposal that a renewed effort be made to establish some kind of South Asian system. India's views, however, have become more positive in the 1980s, and it was a strong support force in the formal institutionalization of the South Asian Association for Regional Cooperation (SAARC) in December 1985.

There have been some other significant changes in Indian policy toward its neighbors in the mid-1980s, under the premiership of Rajiv Gandhi. From 1947 to 1985, India adopted 'bilateralism' as the basic principle in its efforts to resolve differences with neighbors which meant that it insisted on dealing with each country separately, on a bilateral basis, on all issues in dispute, even if these were multilateral in character. One example was India's consistent refusal to hold multilateral talks with Bangladesh and Nepal on the Ganges River water question, demanding instead that this issue be considered only bilaterally. Rajiv Gandhi, however, has modified the Indian government's position, agreeing to multilateral talks with regional powers on this as well as several other issues. This is seen as an important step in the process of resolving disputes within the subcontinent.

The northwest frontier: Pakistan and Afghanistan

The northwestern section of the subcontinent has been the most crucial area for India in policy terms. India controls only that portion of the northwest that falls on the Indian side of the ceasefire line in Kashmir; most of this highly strategic area lies in Pakistan and Afghanistan and thus, in the Indian perception, in unreliable hands. It is a dominant theme in the Indian world view that the northwest has been the channel through which innumerable invading hordes have poured into the subcontinent since at least 3000 BC, and could do so again. The ultrasensitivity that Indians display toward Pakistan, thus, not only reflects the tragic interplay of relations between the two states since 1947 but also India's distress over the fact that the most vulnerable area of the subcontinent is beyond its control. Pakistan, as a conduit of external involvement in South Asia, has long been a source of apprehension to New Delhi. The Pakistani security alignment with the USA in the 1950s and again in the 1980s, and its close relationship with China since 1961, has aroused anxiety in India. Nor can New Delhi ignore the possibility of a Soviet–Pakistani 'accommodation' on Afghanistan and other issues in the late 1980s as this portends serious problems for India.

The northwest became an area of Indo-Pakistani confrontation immediately after independence because of the dispute over Kashmir. While New Delhi argued its case there in terms of its secular political principles, that is, keeping religion out of politics, it was the strategic importance of Kashmir that made it difficult for New Delhi to agree to any concessions in resolving the dispute. The division of Kashmir along a ceasefire line in 1949 met India's basic geostrategic requirements, and subsequently it was not interested in

doing anything more than pressing for minor adjustments of the ceasefire line when the opportunity arose in 1965 and 1971.

The Kashmir issue became further complicated for India with the outbreak of a border conflict with China in 1962. The Chinese seizure of some areas of Ladakh contiguous to Xinjiang and Tibet in China as well as to both the Pakistani and Indian sections of Kashmir in the 1959–62 period raised a novel problem for New Delhi, the prospect of Sino–Pakistani collaboration in a war with India over Kashmir. The development of India's relations with the Soviet Union has been strongly influenced by its comparatively weak position in the northwest, first in response to the USA–Pakistan military alignment in the 1950s and then by the Sino–Pakistani security relationship in the 1960s and thereafter.

The 1971 Indo-Pakistan war marked a watershed in both countries' policies toward the northwest. Pakistan learned in persuasive terms about the limits of its own capabilities as well as the limits on external support that it could reasonably expect in a conflict with India. New Delhi attained a greater self-confidence about its role in the subcontinent, and simultaneously a somewhat more tolerant attitude toward the other regional states. The Indo-Pakistani conference held at Simla in 1972 set a basically sensible framework for the resolution of the Kashmir issues under which Pakistan agreed to handle the dispute on a strictly bilateral basis and both sides abjured the use of force. In the latter half of the 1970s, discussions on economic and cultural relations were initiated between the two powers, and with some success. For the first time since 1947, large numbers of Indians and Pakistanis were able to visit the neighboring country and cultural exchanges involving some of the greatest artists and musicians of both countries were arranged, with tumultuous and enthusiastic receptions everywhere.

Afghanistan had played an important role in Indian policy in the northwest since 1947. The Afghan–Pakistani dispute over the boundary as defined by the British, which was the Durand Line dividing the Pathan and Baluchi tribal communities in both countries, led to a relationship that was unfriendly in good days and hostile the rest of the time. India found it useful to encourage Pakistan–Afghan antagonisms as this forced Pakistan into two-front defense scenarios and prevented it from concentrating its forces on the Indian border. But New Delhi did not want their hostility to lead to outright conflict, as this would raise the possibility that the much weaker Afghan army would turn to the USSR for assistance and Kabul would emerge as another Soviet client state. India provided economic and military assistance to Afghanistan and, through Afghanistan, to dissident Pathan political factions in Pakistan until 1971. By the mid-1970s, however, New Delhi no longer considered it necessary to complicate matters for Pakistan and the Indians began to urge a settlement on the basis of the existing Pakistan–Afghan boundary.

The Soviet intervention in Afghanistan in December 1979 introduced a new phase in Indian policy in the northwest and, in particular, in Indo-Pakistani relations. New Delhi was disturbed by this direct insertion of Soviet forces towards South Asia and the government then in office was prepared to take a strongly critical position. Before this could occur, however, an election was held in India in early January 1980 and Indira Gandhi was restored to the prime ministership. Her government's first public statement on Afghanistan was supportive of the Soviets, so profusely, indeed, that it became an embarrassment. Indira Gandhi thereafter sought to take a more nonaligned position, calling for the withdrawal of 'foreign troops' (Soviet troops) from Afghanistan but also demanding the termination of support to the Afghan resistance movement. With slight tilts one way or the other, India has maintained this position on Afghanistan subsequently. It has sought desperately to avoid having the Afghanistan issue affect its relationship with the Soviet Union, and Moscow has generally responded in kind.

India's Afghanistan policy placed it on a very different path from that of Pakistan. In 1980 and 1981 both governments tried to work out some kind of common basis for their Afghanistan policy but with no real success. New Delhi was not willing to recognize that the Soviet intervention in Afghanistan raised legitimate security problems for Pakistan and was not prepared to adjust its policies accordingly. Some preliminary discussions in 1980 on a joint security system collapsed, once again on the old question: security against whom? Pakistan had become the home of two to three million Afghan refugees by 1981, as well as a base for the growing resistance movement. Pakistan could not refuse to respond to the call for help from fellow Muslims. It could and did seek, however, to limit the support extended to the resistance through Pakistani territory in order to reduce the chances of a violent confrontation with the Soviets, but it had to allow the channeling of aid from a wide variety of external sources.

This might not have led to a deterioration in Indo-Pakistani relations if it had not been accompanied by a revival of Pakistan's security relationship with the USA in 1981 and thereafter. India reacted sharply to the agreement between the USA and Pakistan in August 1981 under which the USA agreed to provide $3.2 billion in assistance, equally divided between military and economic aid, over a five year period. New Delhi was particularly aroused by the announcement in September 1981 that the USA would sell forty F-16 fighter aircraft to Pakistan, charging that the USA was introducing an arms race into the subcontinent. This was a rather specious allegation, since India had already come to terms with the USSR and was well advanced in negotiations with France for the provision of much larger numbers of only slightly less sophisticated aircraft. But what really disturbed India presumably was that the options available to Pakistan on security issues, previously very limited, had

expanded substantially and the compulsions on Islamabad to settle its bilateral differences with India on New Delhi's terms had been reduced.

Nevertheless, the negotiation process between India and Pakistan has continued with only short interruptions ever since. In August 1981, when signing the agreement with the USA, President Zia also offered India a no-war pact under which both sides would agree not to use force in the resolution of their dispute. In reply, New Delhi proposed a seven-point treaty of 'peace and friendship' in which both sides not only renounced the use of force against each other, but also set several basic principles under which their relationship would be developed. The first was the principle of bilateralism, which, as defined by India, is interpreted to mean that all disputes between the two states will be settled by them directly rather than by reference to any international forum. The second principle, stated rather ambiguously in the Indian proposed treaty text, sets the definition of a common regional policy as an objective. The third, stated more explicitly, is that Pakistan must avoid any entanglements with external powers that could be defined as a security relationship; for example, its present limited alignments with the USA and China would be barred but probably Pakistan's security relationships with several Arab states would not.

While not included as part of its formal treaty proposal, India has pressed Pakistan for further expansions of their economic relationship, in particular a free trade system between the two countries. There have been some achievements in the economic field as the trade relationship has grown slowly but steadily. In the security and political relationship field, however, there has not been much progress since 1981 despite numerous discussions on the subject by their highest officials. New Delhi is not prepared to accept *just* a no-war pact; Islamabad is not yet ready to surrender its options for security relations with outside powers in exchange for the kind of uncertain security commitments it would receive from India.

Developments in Afghanistan in 1987 and, in particular, the apparent Soviet determination to come to terms with Pakistan on a settlement in Afghanistan, has had a significant impact on Indo-Pakistani relations. New Delhi is obviously concerned about the signs of a more even-handed Soviet posture in South Asia with respect to India's critical relations with both China and Pakistan. Islamabad may now be in a position to play a Soviet card as well as its old China and USA cards in negotiations with India, at least to a limited extent. It is a new game; and while the balance of power is still heavily in India's favor, the advantages of mutual concessions are more obvious.

The Himalayan states
The Government of India inherited the role of the British Imperial Government in the Himalayan 'protectorates' of Nepal, Sikkim,

and Bhutan in 1947, as well as some of the privileges that the British had extracted from Tibet. This latter status did not last long as the new Communist regime in China, ignoring India's protests, invaded Tibet in the winter of 1950–51 and also spoke ominously of the three Himalayan kingdoms having been tributary states of the Qing dynasty before the 'imperialist forces' intervened. While New Delhi quickly recognized China's sovereignty in Tibet, it also moved decisively to establish relationships with the border states on a new treaty basis, though one closely modeled after the British treaties with these states. The general principle applied under these treaties was that the Himalayan states should devise their foreign policies in consultation with India.

Nepal

The Rana family government in Kathmandu had accepted a 'special relationship' with India in a treaty signed in 1950, just a few months before the Ranas were overthrown by a revolution launched by pro-Indian political forces. The new government in Nepal developed an even closer relationship with India than the Ranas had permitted, and it was unclear at times whether the Palace or the Indian Embassy was the seat of government. This began to change in 1955 when King Mahendra succeeded his father on the throne and initiated a gradual process directed at modifying Nepal's client status, in part by strengthening relations with China. Mahendra's objective was to obtain both India and China's recognition of Nepal's neutrality, which necessarily involved a reinterpretation of the Indo–Nepali security relationship that was intrinsic to their 1950 treaty.

The slow downturn in New Delhi–Kathmandu relations in the late 1950s coincided with the deterioration in Sino–Indian relations. The 1962 border war between India and China brought into sharp focus the strategic importance of Nepal and the other Himalayan states. New Delhi sought to mollify Kathmandu by agreeing to some of its less critical demands, but was not prepared to amend or abrogate the 1950 treaty, as Mahendra wanted. King Birendra, who succeeded his father in 1972, has also pressed the neutralization theme by requesting all states, including its neighbors, to recognize Nepal as a 'zone of peace'. India has rejected this proposal, presumably as it would undermine the basic Indian security policy of maintaining the Himalayan crest as the South Asian defense line against China. Even King Birendra's concession that India's recognition of Nepal as a 'zone of peace' would not require an amendment of the 1950 treaty has not yet persuaded New Delhi to give its assent.

Economic factors are also critical to this relationship as Nepal is heavily dependent on India economically and, thus, very vulnerable to Indian pressure. On occasion, New Delhi has used economic tactics, for instance, delaying the transit of exports from India and third countries across the Nepal border, when Kathmandu was suspected of indulging in such dangerous games as playing along with the Chinese. For nearly two decades under Mahendra and Birendra, Nepal sought to devise political and economic strategies that would lessen its dependence on India, but the results were disappointing. These problems continued into the 1980s and have been reinforced by growing dissension over the Nepali and Indian communities resident in the other country who have not been granted full citizenship rights even when born in their country of residence. Rajiv Gandhi and Birendra have maintained an open but friendly dialogue which reflects the greater sense of realism in both Kathmandu and New Delhi on critical security, economic and social issues, but the pressures on both leaders to assume more hardline positions are also evident.

Sikkim

The British had played a more direct role in administration in Sikkim than in Nepal (and also Bhutan), and this characterized Indian–Sikkimese relations after 1947. The Sikkim Court faced an internal crisis in 1948–49 that required Indian intervention to settle. In the 1951 Indo-Sikkim treaty, Sikkim was defined as a 'protectorate' in which India exercised full rights over defense, foreign affairs, and communication. Thereafter, the Indian Political Officer in Gangtok and the Indian official lent to Sikkim to head the administrative system played major roles in the government, sharing executive and decision-making powers with the Chogyal (ruler) of the Namgyal dynasty.

Some aspects of a democratic system were introduced in the 1950s: an elected National Assembly, a broad range of political and personal freedoms, and a political party system. But power was never distributed accordingly. This led to discontent among the political activists who criticized the 'divide and rule' tactics used by the Chogyal to maintain his dominant political position in Sikkim. A political movement demanding full democratization (if necessary, through merger with India) was launched in 1973, reportedly with the support of some Indian officials. India had to intervene again and this time New Delhi decided: firstly, to deprive the Chogyal of his powers and, eventually, his office and titles, and secondly to take steps that led to the formal accession of Sikkim into the Indian Union.

Bhutan

The Buddhist monarchy of Bhutan had maintained a friendly but carefully distanced relationship with British India before 1947. In 1910 Bhutan had signed a treaty with the British under which they agreed to accept guidance on foreign policy, but they never allowed a British official to be stationed in Bhutan on a regular basis. After 1947, Bhutan sought to retain its isolationist policy intact, and India was willing. A treaty was signed between the two states in 1949 which retained the foreign policy guidance clause of the 1910 treaty but also included a provision in which India specifically recognized Bhutan's independence.

The occupation of Tibet by the People's Republic of China in 1950–51 raised some initial concerns in both New Delhi and Thimphu about Beijing's objectives south of the Himalayas, but it was only ten years later that these appeared serious enough to the Bhutanese to elicit a basic restructuring of their foreign policy. In the late 1960s, India became the major, and at that time the only, foreign aid contributor to Bhutan's newly introduced development program. Then in 1962–63, in the context of the Sino-Indian war, Bhutan became the recipient of large-scale military assistance from India. Within a three-year period, Bhutan had abandoned its isolation policy for a full-scale alignment with India on security, political and economic issues.

The Thimphu government sought to move toward a broader range of international relations in the mid-1960s, gaining admission to a number of international organizations and in 1971 the United Nations. India had some reservations on this expansion of Bhutan's involvement in international forums, but on all occasions finally rendered their assistance to Thimphu in these efforts, for example, sponsoring Bhutan's admission to the UN. Bhutan has, on some occasions, demonstrated a measure of independence from India in its votes in the UN and the Non-Aligned Movement, but as a general rule the two governments have formulated their foreign policy in similar terms. New Delhi has demonstrated a greater liberality, or perhaps a greater sense of confidence, in its dealings with Bhutan, over the years agreeing to virtually every concession that a cautious and sensible Thimphu government has sought. By 1984, this included an agreement by New Delhi in direct China–Bhutan talks on their border disputes without India as a participant, and permitting airflights into Bhutan on terms that would no longer give India controls over third country foreigners' access to Bhutan.

Bangladesh

India's critical role in the liberation of Bangladesh from domination by West Pakistani 'colonialists' in 1971 led most Indians to assume that the basis had been set for a close cooperative relationship between the two countries. It did not work out that way, and by 1974 India had become the new 'colonial masters' against whom Bangladesh had to struggle. The two countries had signed a 'Friendship Treaty' and a trade pact in 1972; but the former was too ambiguous to constitute a security alignment while the latter did not cover most of the key economic issues in their relationship.

Security considerations, however, play a comparatively minor role in Indo-Bangladeshi relations. Bangladesh, in contrast to Pakistan, has no illusions about its capacity to contend with India militarily and even the most paranoid Indians find it difficult to transform Bangladesh into a serious problem for Indian security, either on its own or in cooperation with other powers. Nor does Bangladesh have much to offer in the way of base facilities that would attract external powers, given the high price that would have to be paid in terms of Indian hostility.

More serious are several economic and social problems that the two countries share, and argue over. One that goes back to the 1950s involves the distribution of the waters of the Ganges River system supplemented, in Bangladesh, by the Brahmaputra system. These river waters are vital to the economies of both countries, and with the present river control facilities available, are inadequate to meet the need of both in the dry season. For this purpose, India has proposed a link canal between the Brahmaputra and Ganges in order to provide western Bangladesh with the water it requires during the dry season and, thus, allow India to use most of the Ganges waters. Bangladesh has rejected this proposal arguing that the canal would use valuable Bangladesh agricultural land, and that the control points would be in Indian territory. Instead, Dhaka has proposed the construction of huge water reservoir systems in Nepal which could release water as needed, during the dry season. Kathmandu, however, is distinctly unenthusiastic about this proposal, so the dialogue goes on, the situation worsens, and a solution becomes more difficult.

Bangladesh's serious overpopulation problem has also raised several issues in its relations with India. Since 1971, large numbers of Bangladeshis (the figures are disputed) have migrated to India illegally. The Indian government had preferred to ignore this matter until it became the basic issue in the 'sons-of-the-soil' movement in Assam in the 1980s. Bangladesh's massive economic and social problems, thus, have contributed to the growth of social and political unrest in India's northeast. This constitutes a complex problem for New Delhi, both in its relations with Dhaka and with the northeastern area of India.

Sri Lanka and the Indian Ocean

The primary objective of Indian policy toward Sri Lanka has been to limit the island republic's relations with external powers. The government in Colombo, following the pattern of India's other neighbors in the subcontinent, has generally tried to involve a selected group of external powers in Sri Lanka as one means of providing Colombo with a greater range of options in dealing with New Delhi. This worked reasonably well, and without putting undue strains on the Indo-Sri Lankan relationship, up to the mid-1980s. Since 1984, however, the Tamil–Sinhalese communal strife in Sri Lanka, extending as it does into the Tamil areas of India, has seriously complicated the relationship between Colombo and New Delhi and enhanced Indian suspicions of all of Sri Lanka's ties with other states, in and outside South Asia.

India played a major role in the liberation of Bangladesh. Sheikh Mujibur Rahman, leader of the liberation movement, welcomes India's Prime Minister, Indira Gandhi, to Dhaka.

India never took a strong exception to the naval base at Trincomalee that the British retained in Sri Lanka for two decades after independence, as this was not seen as posing any threat to India or its interests in the Indian Ocean. New Delhi was more concerned when Colombo began to expand relations with China in the early 1970s, just when Sino-Indian relations were at their nadir. But it became clear that Sri Lanka understood the limits that geostrategic factors imposed upon its China connection: the rhetoric used to describe their 'friendship' was somewhat excessive but China was never allowed any real access to the island's security system. New Delhi frowned at the rhetoric but noted with approval the lack of real substance to the relationship in strategic, political or economic terms.

After the 1971 Indo-Pakistan war, India became somewhat more assertive in its efforts to limit external involvement in the Indian Ocean. New Delhi strongly advised the Maldives to reject an overture from the Soviet Union for access rights to a former British base in the island republic. In the 1980s, India's primary concern has been with the reported periodic discussions between Sri Lanka and the USA over the Trincomalee port facility. While Colombo and Washington had been very sensitive to New Delhi's position on this issue and both had been disinclined to reach an agreement on the base that would arouse Indian hostility, there was some apprehension in India that Sri Lanka might reverse its position in exchange for the introduction of a USA military assistance program in the context of the Tamil–Sinhalese conflict. This was resolved, to New Delhi's satisfaction, by the July 29, 1987 Indo-Sri Lankan Accord under which India assumed primary responsibility for the re-establishment of peace and security in the Tamil majority areas of a unified, if somewhat decentralized Sri Lankan polity. In exchange, Colombo accepted India's hegemonic status in the region, agreed to avoid any kind of security relationship with third powers, and accepted de facto Indian control over Trincomalee's port facilities. There was some criticism in India of the use of the Indian military to suppress the Tamil 'militants', but also a strong sense of satisfaction that India's dominant role in South Asia had finally been accepted by one of the states in the region that has been most careful to maintain its independent status.

Cartoon in the *Daily Jang* of Lahore drawing lessons for Pakistan from the Indo-Sri Lankan Accord of July 29, 1987, under which India assumed primary responsibility for the re-establishment of peace in the Tamil areas of Sri Lanka. The caption read: 'The need to beware of India'.

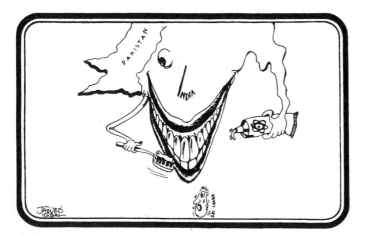

The SAARC system

Proposals for some form of a South Asian regional system were viewed with disdain throughout the subcontinent prior to 1980. Indians tended to view a regional system as an instrument through which the other states would 'gang-up' on India. The other states saw it as yet another channel through which India would exact its dominance. Thus, everyone responded cautiously when, in 1979, Bangladesh proposed the establishment of a regional system. No one wanted to be seen as having sabotaged the proposal, but it was widely assumed that progress would be negligible in view of the apparent lack of enthusiasm in both India and Pakistan.

Very unexpectedly, then, everything moved ahead very well and in early 1987 the Secretariat of the South Asian Association for Regional Cooperation (SAARC) was opened in Kathmandu, with a Secretary General and twelve sub-committees. Care has been used to avoid raising basic security, political and economic issues as areas of competence of the SAARC sub-committees at this early stage of its existence but the annual Heads of States SAARC meetings have become very important channels of bilateral and multilateral negotiation. The participatory states have set aside their original reservations about a regional system and by 1987 had come to view SAARC with considerable enthusiasm.

LER

Further reading

S. S. Bindra, *Indo-Bangladesh Relations* (New Delhi, 1982)

B. S. Das, *The Sikkim Saga* (New Delhi, 1982)

S. Ganguly, *The Origins of War in South Asia: Indo-Pakistani Conflicts since 1947* (Boulder, Co. and London, 1986)

G. Kotturam, *The Himalayan Gateway: History and Culture of Sikkim* (New Delhi, 1983)

M. P. Lana, *The Economics of Indo-Nepal Co-operation* (New Delhi, 1985)

P. K. Mishra, *India, Pakistan, Nepal and Bangladesh* (New Delhi, 1979)

P. R. Rao, *India and Sikkim, 1814–1970* (New Delhi, 1972)

N. Rustomji, *Enchanted Frontiers: Sikkim, Bhutan and India's Northeastern Borderlands* (New Delhi, 1973)

R. Sareen, *Pakistan: The India Factor* (New Delhi, 1984)

A. C. Sinha, *Politics of Sikkim* (New Delhi, 1975)

S. Wolpert, *Roots of Confrontation in South Asia: Afghanistan, Pakistan, India and Bangladesh the Superpowers* (New York, 1982)

India and the world

The British withdrawal from the subcontinent left India with an experienced cadre of indigenous civil servants for internal administrative functions but very few with any background in international political developments. The task of organizing an External Affairs Ministry in 1947 was entrusted to one of the few Indian officials who had held high posts in the British Indian Political Office, the equivalent of a foreign service. More important perhaps, Prime Minister Jawaharlal Nehru had long been interested in international affairs and had some confidence in dealing with the subject.

The catastrophic internal disruptions that accompanied the partition of British India in 1947 compelled the Indian government to concentrate on domestic problems, and not much attention was paid to foreign policy in the first few months of independence. International involvement in the efforts to mediate the Kashmir conflict through the UN provided the first occasion upon which Nehru and his government paid serious attention to foreign policy. And it was in this crisis context that the basic principles of India's foreign policy were first defined in comparatively precise theoretical terms. Thereafter, India has been remarkably consistent regarding the objectives of its foreign policy, if flexible and pragmatic in devising expedient strategies and tactics to achieve these objectives.

Since these early days, the basic objectives of Indian foreign policy have been twofold: first, to exclude or, when that is not feasible, to manipulate the involvement in South Asia of the influential external powers, the USSR, China and the USA, and second to organize the subcontinent into a regional system, formally or informally, that assures India its pre-eminent role in economic, political and security relationships. The conceptual terms used in defining the basic principles of Indian foreign policy, which were 'nonalignment' and 'zones of peace' as part of the process of world disarmament, have stressed universalistic moral values and goals; but as actually employed in specific cases these noble precepts have usually been used selectively to serve India's narrowly conceived regional goals. New Delhi, for instance, can get very enthusiastic about 'zones of peace' in southeast Asia, the Indian Ocean, the western Pacific, or almost anywhere in the world except South Asia. But it repeatedly rejects proposals made by other states in the region for declaring South Asia a 'zone of peace', and in particular a 'nuclear free zone of peace'.

Nonalignment

The definition of nonalignment has also changed in subtle but real ways since the origin of the movement in the early 1950s. Nehru's basic concern at that time was with the prospective division of the world into two 'Cold War' blocs, headed, respectively, by Washington and Moscow. In his view, international peace required a different strategy on the part of the newly independent states of Asia and Africa if they were not to be absorbed into the bipolar blocs as powerless clients. The avoidance of excessive intimacy with either the East or the West became the fundamental goal of Nehru's foreign policy.

Thus, nonalignment, as defined by Nehru, involved a ban on any formal security arrangement with either Cold War bloc, but it did not exclude temporary alignments with either bloc on a specific issue if this served India's interests or could be justified by Nehru's moralistic posturing. He argued that nonalignment allowed a country to evaluate issues on their merit, and every position India assumed on international issues was defended in exactly these terms despite some obvious inconsistencies in policy positions.

Later, in the 1970s, there were some Indians who argued for a 'truly nonaligned' policy which maintained an approximate equidistance between the two superpowers. Nehru had rejected such a policy, arguing that 'leaning to one side' on specific issues was not only unavoidable, it was proper as nonalignment was neither an isolationist or neutralist policy. Indeed, nonalignment was an activist and interventionist policy; a nonaligned government had the responsibility to take positions upon issues in dispute. What was important was not whether they agreed or disagreed with Moscow or Washington but rather whether it was a principled position. Nehru hoped to create an international environment in which as many countries as possible joined the Nonaligned Movement (NAM), in the process transforming the global political balance from a bipolar to a multipolar system in which the newly independent states could have a greater voice.

However, Nehru was also opposed to organizing the NAM into a third bloc, for in his view a tripolar world was only a slight improvement over a bipolar world. He differed from other prominent NAM leaders, Sukarno of Indonesia, Nasser of Egypt, and later Zhou Enlai of China, who were determined to transform the NAM into a coherent and effective power bloc. Nehru perceived the international role of the NAM differently; it was a forum in which the nonaligned states could express their views effectively and achieve a broad consensus on critical issues.

Closely related to Nehru's conceptualization of nonalignment was his 'zone of peace' strategy, which was designed to remove Asia from the Cold War through the exclusion both of the superpowers from Asia and of the Asian states from the Soviet and the Western security systems. The main target of the 'zone of peace' strategy in the 1950s was Southeast Asia, as it was in this region that the interests of the significant external powers converged on an essentially unstructured and potentially explosive basis. India's efforts to arrange a multilateral agreement on the neutralization of Southeast

Asia never made any progress between 1950 and 1980, but both the non-Communist Southeast Asian powers and the Socialist Republic of Vietnam have accepted this concept in the 1980s as the goal toward which they should move.

India's interests in 'zones of peace', meanwhile, had shifted to the Indian Ocean, and New Delhi strongly endorsed the 1971 UN General Assembly resolution requesting the nonlittoral states with military forces in the Indian Ocean, which were the USA, USSR, UK and France, to withdraw them. The Indians welcomed this proposal as it would make India the dominant naval power in the northern Indian Ocean, while Australia and South Africa dominated the southern waters. Indian enthusiasm for the UN resolution remains tempered, however, by the expectation that the other littoral states would soon impose limits on India's navy if the nonlittoral forces were actually removed, as well as by the concern that they would insist on adding 'nuclear free' to the 'zone of peace' provision.

The operating principles of the NAM have also changed significantly since 1970. India led the way in 1971 when the Indira Gandhi government signed a Treaty of Peace and Friendship with the Soviet Union which includes a consultation clause that Nehru would have considered a violation of the basic principles of nonalignment. Subsequently several other 'nonaligned' states have signed formal military alliance pacts with the Soviet Union or somewhat more informal security arrangements with Washington. As a consequence, the factional divisions within the NAM now reflect East–West political alignments. A well-organized and coherent pro-Soviet minority faction argues for an alignment between the NAM and the Socialist bloc, while a badly fractionalized majority supports a variety of positions short of alignment with Moscow.

The Indian government under Nehru was the first of the post-colonial governments to devise policies designed to protect its economy from exploitation by the old imperial powers. Nehru first proposed the total isolation of India and the rest of Asia from the Western-dominated world economy, and the construction of a self-reliant interdependent Asian economic system. He soon recognized that this was not feasible in the world of the 1950s and dropped economic isolationism as an integral aspect of his nonalignment policy. However, his deep suspicions of the political impact of economic interactions with the Western capitalist states became an integral aspect of India's economic policy. Even when India was eager to maximize the transfer of resources from the West to its own economy through both aid programs and private investment, Nehru's preference for state-to-state relations was clearly evident. In foreign private investment, India's restrictive terms were intended to guarantee that the foreign multi-nationals did not dominate the Indian economy; in fact, they deterred them from investing in India at all.

New Delhi accepts the need for massive transfers of resources and technology from the 'North' to the 'South' which is from the 'developed' to the 'developing' countries, but in the cause of self-reliance has adopted policies that discourage this. The results have been large inputs into India through bilateral aid programs and multilateral aid organizations, but minimal private sector investments. One consequence is that India's role in the international economy is very limited. Since 1980, some efforts have been made to revise policies toward foreign private investments and with some encouraging results. But India still has a long way to go before it becomes a significant factor in the world economy.

The China factor

In 1947, India had virtually no relations, political, economic or cultural, with China, and indeed little knowledge or understanding of its giant Asian neighbor. New Delhi moved quickly to establish close relationships, first with the Nationalist regime and then, in

Relations with the People's Republic of China have been a major concern of India's foreign policy. Jawaharlal Nehru with Zhou Enlai, Delhi, January 1, 1957.

The Sino-Indian boundary dispute and the War of 1962.

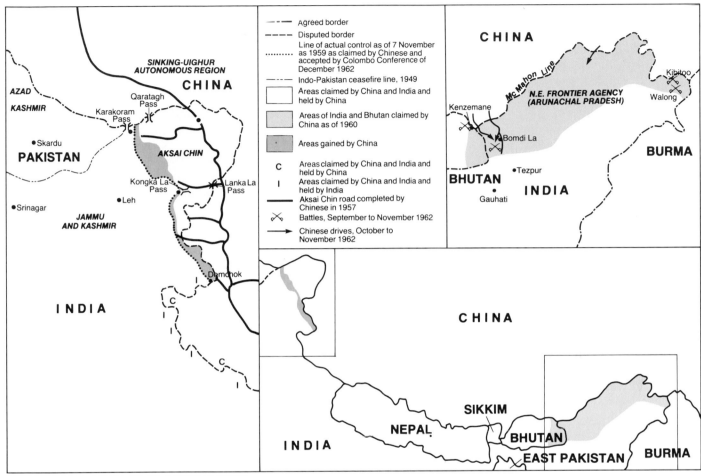

Sources: J. E. Schwartzberg, ed., A Historical Atlas of South Asia (Chicago, 1978) p.88

1949, with the new People's Republic of China (PRC). There was more to this than diplomatic ties with a leading Asian power; far more important was the fact that Nehru's foreign policy, which was directed at excluding Asia from the Cold War, depended upon China's cooperation. The Soviet–PRC military alliance, signed in February 1950, was a major setback for Nehru as China was central to his policy calculations.

In the 1950s, it became a main objective of Indian foreign policy to create the circumstances under which China could, quietly and unobtrusively, be transformed from a member of the Soviet bloc to a participant in the emerging Afro–Asian grouping of states. The 1954 Sino–Indian Treaty, which first proclaimed the five principles (panchshila) of 'peaceful coexistence', was projected as providing the terms for the PRC's relations with its suspicious Asian neighbors and, thus, as an alternative to the Soviet alliance. Nehru took the initiative in introducing the PRC, and in particular Zhou Enlai, to

the non-Communist Third World states at such gatherings as the 1955 Bandung Conference in Indonesia.

By the late 1950s, the Soviet–PRC alliance was badly strained and Beijing was eagerly seeking to expand its involvement in Afro–Asian events. Unfortunately for Nehru's calculations, by 1959 this coincided with a growing crisis in Sino–Indian relations, primarily over their long and difficult high Himalayan border but also over serious differences between Nehru and Zhou on the NAM and their respective roles in it. In late 1962, the border dispute erupted into a short border war in which the Indian army suffered an embarrassing defeat and was left with a strong desire to reverse the decision at some point in the future.

China's victory dominated Indian decision-making on foreign policy in the 1960s, leading to some modifications of basic operating principles. The nonaligned policy was abandoned, at least as far as it applied to China; India cooperated with both the American 'containment of China' policy in South and Southeast Asia and with the separate but supportive Soviet 'containment of China' policy introduced in 1963. Beijing, in response, defined its South Asia policy in confrontationist terms with India into the mid-1970s by encouraging other South Asian states, including Pakistan, to maintain anti-Indian positions. Beijing also provided assistance to some revolutionary tribal and leftist movements in India while New Delhi supported, in collaboration with both the USA and the USSR, Tibetan resistance groups.

The failure of China to intervene in support of Pakistan in the 1965 and 1971 Indo-Pakistan wars reduced New Delhi's apprehensions over the PRC's role in South Asia. For its part, Beijing had decided by the mid-1970s that an overtly anti-Indian policy had become counterproductive because it had persuaded New Delhi to accept a limited security relationship with both the USA (until 1971) and the USSR, while India's victory in the 1971 Indo-Pakistan war had effectively dampened any enthusiasm in South Asia for a China-supported anti-Indian policy.

Beijing decided to try and improve relations with India, and New Delhi responded favorably. In early 1976, ambassadors were exchanged and regular twice-yearly meetings came to be held alternately in Beijing and New Delhi. This has resulted in some expansion of economic and cultural relations, but the border dispute remains unresolved. Beijing has offered to settle the dispute on the basis of the acceptance of the *de facto* border as the legal boundary. This has aroused some interest in India but as yet no agreement, in part because there are still points on the border where the line of control is in dispute. The area involved is small and nonstrategic but the psychological barriers to conceding land to China remain formidable.

'Our Soviet friends'
In the early years of independence, the relationship between India and the USSR was not particularly auspicious as Stalin had very negative views of Nehru, the Indian nationalist leadership and indeed the leaders of all other non-Communist excolonial states. After Stalin's death in 1953, however, and the USA–Pakistan military agreement in 1954, both India and the USSR began to perceive some shared interests. On their pilgrimage to India in 1955, Khrushchev and Bulganin helped to create the basis for what has become, some ups and down apart, a close relationship ever since.

In 1956 the Soviets began an economic aid program centered on large public sector enterprises, although they were reluctant to include a military assistance program that might antagonize the Chinese. They adopted a neutral position in the 1962 Sino-Indian war; the Indians understood the difficulty of their position but were disappointed. However, once the Sino-Soviet split became public in

early 1963, Moscow felt able to introduce a military aid program to India. Then, when the USA suspended military sales to both Pakistan and India during the 1965 Indo-Pakistan war, the USSR became, and has remained, the largest single source of Indian military purchases abroad.

New Delhi was pleased with the course of developments in Indo-Soviet relations in the 1960s, but there were some disturbing aspects as well. In 1965, Moscow began to move toward a more nonpartisan position on Indo-Pakistani issues in an effort to provide Pakistan with policy options other than its China connection and its dependence on its CENTO allies in South Asian security matters. After the 1965 Indo-Pakistan war, the USSR offered its 'good offices' in settling the conflict. At the Tashkent Conference in February 1966, the Soviets took what some Indians characterized as a slightly pro-Pakistani stance by insisting that Indian forces withdraw to the ceasefire line in Kashmir from several strategic points they had occupied during the war.

Also in 1966, the Soviets inaugurated an economic aid program to Pakistan and then, much to India's distress, a military aid program in 1968. New Delhi decided to counter this pro-Pakistani trend in Soviet policy by offering some concessions to Moscow that would enhance the value of its India connection. In 1969, Brezhnev had proposed an Asian mutual security arrangement as part of his China-containment policy. India, like all other Asian states, responded unfavorably to the Brezhnev proposal, but did indicate that it might accept a bilateral treaty with the USSR if, in exchange, Moscow would terminate the arms sales program to Pakistan. In mid-1970 an agreement was reached between the USSR and India on these terms, but the signing of a treaty was delayed at India's request until after the March 1971 elections in India. In August 1971 a Treaty of Peace and Friendship was signed on schedule, although it was presented to the Indian public at that time as necessary in the context of the emerging crisis in Bangladesh.

Since 1971, relations between India and the USSR have been maintained at a friendly level. Both New Delhi and Moscow find it useful to stress the points on which there is a broad convergence of views and interests while playing down some important differences. The Soviet intervention in Afghanistan has been a problem, but one that is usually discussed in private rather than debated in public, with New Delhi reportedly stressing its position that the Soviet forces must withdraw from Afghanistan and Moscow explaining why this is difficult. But perhaps of greater concern to India is Gorbachev's new Asian policy announced in mid-1986, which emphasizes the efforts being made by Moscow to 'normalize' relations with both China and Pakistan. India has concluded that it can no longer assume Soviet support in its disputes with these two neighbors, as Gorbachev implied in his New Delhi visit in November 1986.

Since the mid 1950s India has developed a close relationship with the USSR.
Soviet leader, Mikhail Gorbachev, talks with Indian Prime Minister, Rajiv Gandhi.

By the 1980s, the Soviet Union had emerged as India's largest external economic partner, but on terms that have come to be less attractive, in some respects, to New Delhi. In 1985, India had a large surplus in the 'barter' (rouble-rupee) trade between the two countries, but has found it difficult to find Soviet products other than oil and military equipment that it wants to import. While the voracious Soviet market keeps some highly inefficient Indian industries in operation, the price that India pays in terms of the allocation of resources is considered much too high.

The Indian government, however, is probably more concerned with some of the political rather than the economic consequences of the Indo-Soviet trade system, for Moscow is reported to use Indian firms trading with the USSR as channels of financial support to various groups in India, including opposition parties. This has become such an integral part of the Indo-Soviet political and economic relationship that it tends to be accepted as the norm, but its potential for causing problems in Indo-Soviet relations has been demonstrated in the past and may reappear in the future.

India and the West

The Western powers have posed a perplexing and, at times, controversial problem for India in its loudly proclaimed efforts to avoid identification with the former colonial masters in the post Second World War world. But even Nehru had to recognize that India's political and economic interests, beyond the subcontinent at least, required extensive interaction with the West, and in particular the UK, several Commonwealth countries and the USA. There was no serious debate in India, for instance, over the decision to remain within the Commonwealth, although the monarchical structure of the institution did have to be modified to accommodate India's transformation into a Republic in 1950. And again, during the war with Pakistan over Kashmir in 1948, India did not hesitate in requesting arms from the USA even though Nehru made it clear that he understood the political implications of this Indian initiative for its nonaligned image in the Cold War.

The 1949–54 period was critical for Indian and American efforts to define their relationship in substantive terms. The results, in political policy, were disappointing to both powers as they ended up on different sides in the multilateral strategic balance then evolving in the region. India opted for nonalignment and, according to the standard Indian analysis, rejected inclusion in any USA-sponsored security system. It should be noted, however, that Washington never invited India to join either the Islamic Baghdad Pact in West Asia or SEATO in Southeast Asia. Pakistan was included in both, which led India to conclude that these 'containment of communism' systems would have a negative impact on Indian security in South Asia because of the provision of arms to Pakistan. New Delhi argued, in the 1950s as in the 1980s, that any arms sold to Pakistan will be used against India rather than a Communist power. The USA agreed that there was some basis to the Indian complaint and sought to incorporate restrictions on the use of the weapons supplied to Pakistan, but with minimal success. But in Washington's view, Pakistan's importance to the West Asian security system outweighed these South Asian concerns and justified its inclusion in CENTO.

Another aspect of the Indo-USA relationship in the 1950s, which is often forgotten, is that by 1956 India had become the largest recipient of American economic assistance. The allegation that the USA ignored India and focused its attention in South Asia on Pakistan is not accurate. Indeed, there is some basis to the Pakistani complaint that the USA provided it with direct military assistance but extended indirect military assistance to India through its massive economic aid, as New Delhi used these funds to underwrite both the purchase of military equipment abroad and the capitalization of some defense industries.

The 1962 Sino-Indian War had a serious impact on Indo-USA relations as New Delhi quickly modified its nonaligned policy. During the war, Nehru requested USA airforce assistance in the defense of Indian cities and a USA aircraft carrier was sent into the Bay of Bengal in response. Both the UK and the USA began arms aid assistance to India during the war, and then entered into more formal military assistance agreements with India thereafter. The USA aid program, however, was halted during the 1965 Indo-Pakistani war when Washington suspended arms transfers to both states. This continued as USA policy until 1981, with 'one-time exceptions' sales permitted on occasion, and the USA withdrew as a major source of arms in South Asia. New Delhi was not too disturbed by this, as Pakistan was considered to be more adversely affected than India which had more diverse sources of foreign military equipment.

With the exception of some noisy but short-term differences between Washington and New Delhi, for instance the USA 'tilt toward Pakistan' in the 1971 war, Indo-USA relations in the 1965–81 period were comparatively free of stress. India generally viewed the USA as a neutral factor in South Asia and no great source of complication for Indian policy. The USA saw India as an occasional irritant in broader international issues, but on balance a useful force because of the stabilizing role it played in a non-Communist South Asia.

The Soviet invasion of Afghanistan in December 1979, combined with the overthrow of the Pahlavi dynasty in Iran, revived American concern over Pakistan's security and then, of course, Indian apprehensions over the assertion of an active USA role in the subcontinent. The 1981 military sales agreement between the USA and Pakistan revived Indian fears that this would provide Pakistan with the capacity to 're-do 1965' in Kashmir or to renew armed aggres-

Mrs Gandhi with President and Mrs Nixon at the White House in the autumn of 1971.

sion against India in some other way, supposedly in the context of a USA–China–Pakistan 'axis' in South Asia. However, this time both the USA and India have been careful to keep their relations open and negotiable.

For several reasons, India would prefer not to be tilted unnecessarily in any one direction in its international relations. Economic and industrial development make it essential to diversify international economic relations further; the extensive economic ties with the Soviet Union should be maintained, but greatly expanded interactions with Western Europe, Japan and the United States should be encouraged. Politically, the Rajiv Gandhi government has sought to assume a mediatory role in both Southeast and West Asian disputes and this requires New Delhi to project itself as an autonomous force in global politics. There is, moreover, a concern in India over avoiding a sense of dependence on the Soviet connection at the time that Moscow is eagerly seeking both to normalize relations with Beijing and to reach an accommodation with Pakistan. The improvement of India's relations with Western Europe and the USA, therefore, is critical to both the economic and political–strategic policies of India in the mid-1980s.

LER

Further reading
U. S. Bajpai, *Non-Alignment: Perspectives and Prospects* (New Delhi, 1983)

K. Gopal, *Non-Alignment and Power Politics: A Documentary Survey* (New Delhi, 1983)

S. Mansingh, *India's Search for Power: Indira Gandhi's Foreign Policy, 1966–1982* (New Delhi, Beverley Hills and London, 198)

J. W. Mellor, Ed., *India: A Rising Middle Power* (New Delhi, 1981)

A. S. Mishra, *India's Foreign Policy: A Study in Interaction* (New Delhi, 1982)

B. Sen Gupta, *Nuclear Weapons: Policy Options for India* (New Delhi, London, 1983)

K. Subramanyam, *Indian Security Perspectives* (New Delhi, 1983)

S. Tharoor, *Reasons of State: Political Development and India's Foreign Policy under Indira Gandhi, 1966–1977* (New Delhi, 1982)

R. G. C. Thomas, *Indian Security Policy* (Princeton, N.J. 1986)

Pakistan and the world

Pakistan has had a troubled and difficult history since independence in 1947, so much so that it is sometimes characterized as being in a permanent state of crisis. While this is an exaggeration, Pakistan has yet to establish either the domestic political system or the foreign policy which will provide the sure base required in a complex and politically unstable regional environment. Foreign policy issues intrude forcefully and, at times, in destabilizing forms on internal politics. But, in turn, the Government of Pakistan must carefully heed domestic political factors in formulating external policies. This complicates the tasks that Pakistan faces in defining relations with its neighbors and in devising a foreign policy that can both exploit opportunities available and counter threatening developments.

Pakistan occupies a most important strategic position, namely the frontier area between South Asia, the Southwest Asian countries bordering on the Persian Gulf, and the Central Asian Islamic tribal areas of Afghanistan, the Soviet Union, and Xinjiang province in China. While Pakistan is usually identified as a South Asian state, it could just as reasonably be included in Southwest Asia. And indeed, as a general principle, Pakistanis have preferred to emphasize their ties with the Islamic states to the west rather than with the Hindu majority area in the subcontinent.

There have been, however, some practical limitations on Pakistan's capacity to 'withdraw' from South Asia. Until 1971, half of Pakistan consisted of the eastern wing of the country (now Bangladesh), separated from the western wing by a thousand miles of India. While West Pakistan could reduce economic and cultural ties with the rest of South Asia at limited costs, this was not the case for East Pakistan. One of the chronic complaints of the East Pakistanis that led to the division of the country in 1971 was over the Pakistan government's insistence that the eastern wing adopt exclusivist policies in relations with India. Since 1971, Pakistan's relations with Southwest Asia have expanded economically but have been seriously hampered in political and security matters by crises such as the Iran–Iraq War of the 1980s, which have forced Islamabad to limit involvement in the region.

In the 1980s, it is evident that Pakistan 'belongs' geographically, psychologically, and in terms of its economic and strategic interests, to both South and Southwest Asia. But after an initially hesitant response, Pakistan agreed to join the South Asian Association for Regional Cooperation (SAARC) in 1982, and subsequently has demonstrated increasing enthusiasm for this regional institution. This would suggest that Pakistanis accept that their primary regional affiliation is with South Asia at least as long as Southwest Asia is in near-chaotic condition and thus incapable of providing the support on security issues they feel they require.

Pakistan and South Asia: the India factor

National and subnational conflicts and disputes in the subcontinent, further complicated by the interventionist policies of external powers, have complicated and distorted issues of peace and security in South Asia since 1947. The most destabilizing factor has been the four decades of intermittent Indo-Pakistani conflicts followed by relatively brief interludes in which the two powers try to 'normalize' their relationship. A complex heritage of conflictive imagery has emerged that fosters an aura of mutual distrust between the two countries that is not easily rectified.

The mass slaughters and transfers of population that accompanied independence for both states in 1947 set the tone for their relationship. In Pakistan, elaborate 'Hindu conspiracy' theories were concocted to explain some of the unexpected developments of 1947, for instance, the concurrence of the 'Hindu Congress Party' in the partition of British India and the establishment of the Muslim-majority state of Pakistan. It has become an article of faith in Pakistan that the Hindu leadership accepted partition only as an expedient device to get the British out and, thus, provide the basis for the reunification of the subcontinent into *Akhand Bharat* (united India) under Hindu rule. Statements made by several Congress Party leaders in 1947 expressing the hope that the people of the subcontinent would eventually come to their senses and reunify the country continue to be quoted in Pakistan to prove this point. What is less readily understood in Pakistan is that forty years of dealing with a basically heterogeneous society has made most Indian political leaders very cautious about adding another one or two hundred million Muslims to their already beleaguered political system.

In the late 1940s, it was the dispute over the former princely state of Kashmir that became the primary focus of Indo-Pakistani confrontationist policies, and this continued for two decades. In 1947, Kashmir was ruled by a Hindu princely family within the indulgent confines of the British imperial system in India. While there was a substantial Muslim majority in the state, the Hindu–Sikh community constituted a majority in Jammu district and the Buddhists in Ladakh, complicating ethnographic considerations. Moreover, after independence, Kashmir bordered on both Pakistan and India, and thus the tacit criteria under which other princely states acceded to India or to Pakistan, comprising location, will of the ruler, and will of the people, could not be applied in any reasonable fashion.

In the Pakistani version of developments in the 1947–49 period, Indian military forces intruded into Kashmir in late 1947 to crush a popular uprising of the Kashmiri people against the Hindu ruling family, which then announced the accession of Kashmir to India. At this point, Pakistani troops were sent into Kashmir to protect the Muslim community which led to a bitter and intense war in 1948–49. The dispute was then submitted to the UN Security council, and a ceasefire was arranged under UN auspices which divided Kashmir

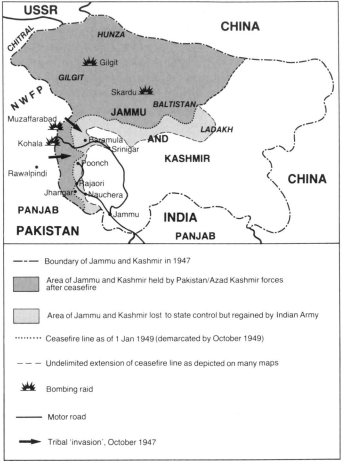

The Indo-Pakistan War 1948.

- - - - Boundary of Jammu and Kashmir in 1947

▨ Area of Jammu and Kashmir held by Pakistan/Azad Kashmir forces after ceasefire

▨ Area of Jammu and Kashmir lost to state control but regained by Indian Army

· · · · · · Ceasefire line as of 1 Jan 1949 (demarcated by October 1949)

– – – Undelimited extension of ceasefire line as depicted on many maps

✹ Bombing raid

——— Motor road

➤ Tribal 'invasion', October 1947

Source: J. E. Schwartzberg, ed., A Historical Atlas of South Asia (Chicago, 1978) p.87

between India and Pakistan. A UN Resolution was adopted calling for the withdrawal of all Pakistani forces and most Indian forces from the state and then the holding of a plebiscite in which the Kashmiris would decide between accession to India or Pakistan (independence was not to be an alternative option). Both Pakistan and India accepted the UN Resolution but failed to abide strictly by its conditions. Military forces were retained in Kashmir under various guises by both states, and India therefore refused to hold the plebiscite. The disagreement between the two governments over responsibility for this failure to honor a UN Security Council Resolution has continued into the 1980s.

Some efforts were made after 1950 to resolve the Kashmir issue on a bilateral basis rather than through the UN. There were several occasions in the 1950s when the two governments discussed this and other issues in dispute at some length, but with no long-term results. These exchanges reached a high point in 1959 when President Ayub Khan proposed a joint defense arrangement with

India, and the resolution of all issues in dispute within the context of this security alignment. But Prime Minister Nehru dismissed the proposal as inconsequential, thus ending for nearly fifteen years all efforts at a peaceful resolution of the Kashmir issue.

In the 1960s, after being frustrated in their efforts to obtain a favorable compromise on Kashmir through negotiation, Pakistan turned to other strategies. In the fall of 1962, Pakistan strongly supported China in the brief but traumatic Sino-Indian War, in part as one form of pressure upon India to make concessions on the Kashmir issue. When this did not produce results, Pakistan then sought to impose a military solution in September 1965. In what was carefully defined as a limited war, that is, limited to Kashmir and to the two sides' military forces stationed there, Pakistan launched 'Operation Gibraltar' in a bold effort to gain control over Kashmir Valley and the main lines of communication between the Valley and India. A quick ceasefire was then to be arranged. India did not play by these rules, but rather launched a counter-offensive on the Pakistan border further south. After an inconclusive but bloody war, a ceasefire was arranged, and then in February 1966 a peace conference was held, under Soviet sponsorship, at Tashkent in Soviet central Asia. The Tashkent Agreement restored the India–Pakistani international boundary and the ceasefire line in Kashmir, but made no significant contribution to the resolution of this irksome problem.

Pakistan, thus, had failed to achieve its objectives in Kashmir through internationally-supervised negotiations in the 1950s or through a military solution in 1965, and has not had an alternative policy that offered much hope. The 1971 Indo-Pakistani War was fought over East Pakistan rather than Kashmir, although heavy fighting did occur along the ceasefire line during the hostilities. The 1972 Simla Conference between India and Pakistan was nominally directed at settling the 1971 'Bangladesh War' but became largely focussed on Kashmir. In the Simla Agreement which emerged, a new 'line of control' replaced the old ceasefire line and both sides agreed not to resort to force in Kashmir. The dispute continues to be an irritant in Indo-Pakistani relations and the arena for occasional small-scale border clashes, which in the mid-1980s occurred mainly in the difficult Siachen glacier area in which the line of control had not been precisely defined. It would appear that Kashmir could still become the excuse for the renewal of hostilities between the two powers but not the real cause.

In the 1980s Pakistan's policy towards India has been strongly affected by the USSR's military intervention in Afghanistan since December 1979 and the perceived need to avoid dangerous confrontations on both the eastern and the northwestern borders. In 1981 President Zia ul Haq launched what was termed a 'peace offensive' directed at a basic improvement in relations with India. He proposed a 'no-war pact' between the two countries as well as expanded

The Indo-Pakistan War 1965.

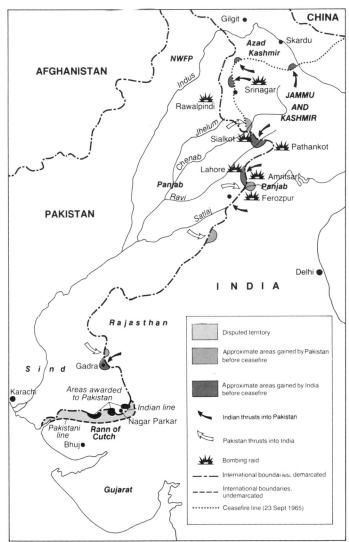

Source: J.E. Schwartzberg, ed., A Historical Atlas of South Asia (Chicago, 1978) p.87

political, cultural and economic relations. India responded positively on economic and cultural issues but insisted upon a more comprehensive security agreement that, as Pakistan interpreted it, would constitute recognition of India's 'hegemonic' status in South Asia and, moreover, oblige other South Asian states to refrain from any form of security relationship with external powers. Pakistanis are still unwilling to accept a treaty with India on such terms as these run counter to the basic strategic principles of its foreign policy.

Nevertheless, Pakistan has continued its efforts to improve relations with India and to reduce the level of tension and hostility in their relationship. Pakistan is also seeking to expand relations with the other South Asian states, both through bilateral agreements and

The Indo-Pakistan War 1971.

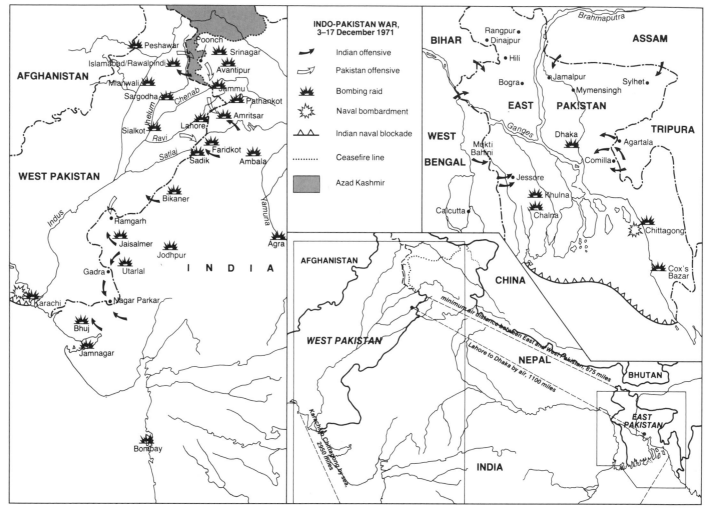

Sources: J. E. Schwartzberg, ed., A Historical Atlas of South Asia (Chicago, 1978) p.89
         T. Hartman and J. Mitchall, A World Atlas of Military History 1945-84 (London, 1984) p.59

an active role in the new regional organization, SAARC. While this remains a supplementary aspect of Pakistan's foreign policy, it does reflect the decision made in the early 1980s to emphasize Pakistan's status as a South Asian state with vital interests of its own in developments throughout the region.

The Islamic connection

A strong sense of identity with the Islamic communities of West Asia had been integral to the Muslim political movement in British India that demanded partition of the subcontinent in 1947. From the beginning, therefore, the new Pakistan government adopted a solid relationship with the international Islamic community as the fundamental principle of its foreign policy. In the 1940s, however,

the West Asian states were in no position to offer Pakistan the economic and strategic support it required; moreover, several Islamic states (Egypt and Syria) usually preferred a close working relationship with India in international politics and were not interested in serving as a deterrent to Hindu expansionism.

The first solid Pakistani achievement in West Asia occurred in the mid-1950s with its adherence to the Baghdad security pact that was sponsored by the USA and UK but included Iran, Turkey and Iraq. The ironic point for Pakistan was that the pact (CENTO after Iraq's withdrawal in 1959) was the consequence of East–West maneuvers in the Cold War rather than an Islamic security system. By the mid-1960s, however, CENTO had been transformed into something more like a regional pact as the American and British role in the security system declined.

President Zia ul Haq of Pakistan talks to India's cricket captain Kapil Dev. In March 1987 the President used the opportunity of a Test series between the two countries to make an official visit and diplomatic overtures.

On the economic side, CENTO was buttressed by the Regional Cooperation for Development (RCD) system established in 1964. In its first decade, the RCD had few accomplishments to its credit, but in the last five years of the Pahlavi dynasty in Iran it did provide the administrative framework for about $750 million in Iranian economic aid which came when Pakistan was in particular need. The RCD quietly disappeared after the Pahlavi dynasty was overthrown and CENTO was disbanded in early 1979. The RCD was revived in 1984, largely on Iran's initiative, and renamed the Economic Cooperation Organization. In the context of the Iran–Iraq War and the USSR's occupation of Afghanistan, Iran sought to restore the old economic relationship with Pakistan and Turkey and, implicitly at least, the security relationship as it applied to Iran's relations with

the Soviet Union but not to the far more difficult question of its relations with Iraq and the Arab states.

Pakistan has benefited greatly from its economic ties with Iran and other Islamic oil-producing states since the 1973 'oil shock' that quadrupled world oil prices. Substantial assistance for Pakistan's economic development and military programs has been forthcoming from several West Asian states, and 2–3 billion more USA dollars have been pumped into the home economy annually by Pakistanis working in West Asia. The Islamic connection, thus, has been the single most-important factor in Pakistan's impressive economic development record since 1976.

The gains for Pakistan from its Islamic connections on critical security issues are less impressive. Pakistanis still play a leading role in the Organization of Islamic Countries (OIC), which still passes strong resolutions critical of the Soviet Union and supportive of Pakistan on the Afghanistan issue. But those same states are busily improving their relations with Moscow, and are not a serious deterrent to confrontations between the Soviet Union and Pakistan. Similarly, while most Islamic countries would nominally side with Pakistan in the event of another Indo-Pakistan war, not one would take strong measures against India. The Islamic states, thus, are useful friends, but do not contribute much to Pakistan's sense of security. In contrast, Pakistan now plays an important role in the defense systems of several Arab states through the 'loan' of some 40,000 well-trained Pakistani officers and men. Presumably, Pakistan expects to obtain some benefits from this informal security system if its difficult relations with India or the Soviet Union should deteriorate further, but there are no public commitments to Pakistan from its Islamic friends and no confidence regarding their response in a crisis.

The USSR and PRC

Pakistan's two giant communist neighbors have been 'enigmas in a puzzle' since the late 1940s. While it was recognized that both posed serious potential threats to the security of the new Islamic Republic, they were also seen as useful balancing forces in the complex geopolitics of South Asia. Despite the harsh denunciations that Moscow and Beijing directed towards Pakistan in the early year, Pakistan tried to keep the lines open to both governments. It was, for instance, the first Muslim country to recognize the new People's Republic of China in January 1950, and thereafter advocated the Republic's admission to the UN despite the complications this evoked in relations between Pakistan and the USA.

Pakistan's decision in the mid-1950s to join the Western-sponsored security systems in West Asia (CENTO) and Southeast Asia (SEATO) was motivated by the perceived need for USA military assistance to counter India's dominant position in South Asia, and an interest in developing security relationships with key states in

Pakistan was host to the four-yearly Islamic Summit in 1974. Among those at prayer are: Yassar Arafat of the PLO, Saddam Hussein of Iraq, Bhutto, Muammar Gaddafi of Libya, King Faisal of Saudi Arabia and the Shaikh of Kuwait. The Islamic connection has been crucial to Pakistan's financial and economic policy since the 1970s.

West and Southeast Asia. Relations with the USSR and PRC deteriorated as a consequence, but within reasonable bounds. In 1955, shortly after joining SEATO, the Pakistani Prime Minister reassured Zhou Enlai at the Bandung Conference that Pakistan would never become involved in conflict between the USA and China.

Developments in the 1960s opened up new opportunities for Pakistan in its relations with both China and Soviet Union. The sudden deterioration in Sino-Indian relations in 1959, culminating in the 1962 border war, unexpectedly raised the prospect of Sino-Pakistani collaboration in South Asia. The two governments commenced serious negotiations in 1961, and in early 1963 signed a border agreement and a trade pact. Sino-Pakistani relations have flourished ever since, with China becoming the primary source of military assistance after USA military aid was cut off during the 1965 Indo-Pakistan War. China's support in Pakistan's conflictual relationship with India is perceived as both critical and reliable, and

Pakistanis refer to China as a firm and faithful friend. Nevertheless, the limits of China's support capabilities are also recognized as these were convincingly demonstrated in the 1965 and 1971 Indo-Pakistan wars when Beijing loudly denounced Indian 'aggression' but took no significant actions in support of Pakistan.

It took a few years longer for Pakistan's relations with the USSR to improve, but this became a possibility when Moscow assumed a more nonpartisan position during and after the 1965 Indo-Pakistan war. In 1966, the USSR signed a pact with Pakistan involving considerable economic assistance and then in 1968 began to provide some military assistance as well. In response, President Ayub Khan introduced 'trilateralism', that is, a balanced relationship with the USA, USSR and China as the basic principle of his foreign policy. Trilateralism did not survive the 1971 Indo-Pakistan war as the Soviets lined up faithfully behind India during the conflict, even though Moscow sought to reinstate a less partisan policy once the war was over.

Throughout the 1970s Pakistan maintained a rather distant if still fairly substantial economic relationship with the USSR. This continued into the 1980s despite the Soviet intervention in Afghanistan and Pakistan's quiet but solid support of the Afghani resistance movement. Relations between Pakistan, the USSR and China have fluctuated around the Afghanistan issue since 1980, with Beijing providing valuable support to the Pakistanis and the Afghan resistance while the Soviets pressure Pakistan to accept a political settlement in Afghanistan that would keep the pro-Soviet government in office. The substantial improvements in Sino-Soviet relations in 1986–87 have had a direct impact on both Pakistan and Afghanistan, and in the process, it is conjectured, has made a compromise political solution of this unusually complex issue somewhat more feasible.

Pakistan and the West

The foreign policy of Pakistan since independence has been dominated by the centrality of India and a perceived need for diversification in sources of external support. Since 1947, however, the relationship with Western powers, and in particular the UK and the USA, has had the highest priority. Until the mid-1950s, Pakistan retained British officials in the highest administrative and military posts, and these 'on loan' bureaucrats and officers were critical to the prompt establishment of an effective government. The British also served as the primary source for military supplies and for the training of military officers and some administrators in specialized fields thereafter; Pakistanis gained access to the broader international economy in the 1950s through their British business connections.

Pakistanis had mixed views on the question of a close relationship with the USA at the time of independence as this was seen as a complication in relations with some powerful neighbors. By 1951, however, a broad consensus had been reached on this issue and the first of a series of overtures were directed to Washington. Working out the terms took several years, but finally in 1954 the USA and Pakistan signed a bilateral military assistance agreement and Pakistan joined the multilateral Baghdad Pact. Then, in 1959, the bilateral Ankara Agreement was signed, detailing in more precise language the obligations of the USA and Pakistan in their security arrangement.

The Pakistanis and Americans have quite different interpretations of the Ankara Agreement. According to the USA, it is committed to assist in the defense of Pakistan only in cases of aggression by a communist power or another state instigated by a communist power. The Pakistanis insist that the USA is obliged to assist Pakistan in a conflict with any power, that is, India. The USA is accused of failing to honor its commitments in the 1965 and 1971 Indo-Pakistan wars, and thus is denounced as unreliable. In

Washington's view, Pakistan initiated the 1965 war through its Kashmir escapade and the 1971 war through its policy in East Pakistan, and the USA was under no obligation to come to its assistance in either conflict.

From 1965 to 1981 both the security and economic relationships between the USA and Pakistan were maintained at low levels and, indeed, in 1979 were totally suspended by Washington because of suspicions about Pakistan's nuclear program. The relationship was revived and expanded, however, in the context of the Soviet Union's military intervention in Afghanistan in December 1979. The 1981 agreement between the USA and Pakistan provided for $3.2 billion in economic and military assistance, and the security relationship was revived on the restrictive terms of the 1959 Ankara Agreement. Pakistan carefully limited its ties to the USA by rejecting any involvement in a broader USA-sponsored Southwest Asian security system and also by denying the USA military the right to establish bases.

The relationship, as delimited, worked out to the general satisfaction of both states and a new multiyear aid program is projected to commence in 1987. Concern in some USA circles over Pakistan's nuclear program is an enduring issue in Washington and a potential complication in their relationship, countered to some extent by Pakistan's supportive role to the Afghan resistance. Pakistan's sensitivity to the unreliability of America in honoring commitments was sharpened by political developments in the USA in early 1987. These have led important segments of Pakistan's political élite to suggest that an accommodation with the USSR may make better sense than the American connection. The Pakistani preference for a maximum diversification of external relations and interest in the trilateralist policy of the 1960s may seem once more to be gaining the upper hand.

LER

Further reading

A. Ali, *Pakistan's Nuclear Dilemma: Energy and Security Dimensions* (Karachi, 1984)

S. Chaudhuri, *Beijing–Washington–Islamabad Entente: Genesis and Development* (New Delhi, 1982)

S. P. Cohen, *The Pakistan Army* (Berkeley, 1984)

T. Eliot, JR., and R. L. Pfaltzgraff, JR., *The Red Army on Pakistan's Border: Policy Implications for the U.S.* (Washington, 1986)

A. Haque, *Trends in Pakistan's External Policy, 1947–1971: With Particular Reference to People's China* (Dhaka, 1985)

A. Rahman, *Pakistan and America: Dependency Relations* (New Delhi, 1982)

L. E. Rose and N. A. Husain, Eds, *United States–Pakistan Relations* (Berkeley, 1986)

L. A. Sherwani, *Pakistan, China and America* (Karachi, 1980)

S. Tahir-Kheli, *The United States and Pakistan: The Evolution of an Influence Relationship* (New York, 1982)

ECONOMIES

A peasant,
Bhojpur district,
Bihar.

Introduction

The economies of the countries in South Asia are among the largest and the poorest in the world. They belong to the group classified by the World Bank as 'low-income countries': their *per capita* income is about 25 percent of the average for all less-developed countries. South Asian countries have, broadly-speaking, followed development policies within a stable institutional structure. They have not attempted radical economic and social reforms as in China and Cuba. For most of the post-war period, they have avoided the extremes of political and economic instability which have characterized many other poorer countries. In terms of performance, they rank somewhere between the economic 'miracles' of South Korea and Taiwan and the recent economic disasters of sub-Saharan Africa.

Heavily dependent on agriculture, India, Pakistan and Sri Lanka, unlike their other South Asian neighbors, have managed to keep the rate of growth of food supply ahead of that of population, thus reducing their dependence on food imports and aid. Since 1970, *per capita* food production has increased in these three countries by about 10, 4, and 25 percent, respectively. All three have also reduced seasonal and to some extent cyclical fluctuations in food production. In Bangladesh, in contrast, *per capita* production has fallen since the mid-1970s, but even so Bangladesh has done rather better than most of the countries in sub-Saharan Africa where production losses have been heavier and yields per acre are continuing to fall. A major reason for the difference in performance in the two continents is that the innovation which has combined higher yielding varieties of cereals and the intensive use of fertilizers and irrigation (the 'green revolution') has not yet been extended to root crops which are the staple foods in Africa.

The development strategies of South Asian countries have stressed the need for industrialization. Industrial development allows for diversification of the economy away from a traditional low-productivity agricultural sector and industrial inputs increase productivity within the land-hungry agricultural sector. A lessening of dependence on the export of primary products is also seen as a way of improving the gains from participating in international trade. Industrial production has advanced most substantially in India and Pakistan, although not as spectacularly as in the newly-industrialized countries of Southeast Asia. In terms of total value added in industrial production, India, which inherited almost the whole of the subcontinent's industrial base at Independence, now ranks third after Brazil and Mexico among the market economies of the less-developed world and produces a wide range of capital goods. In *per capita* terms, however, India still ranks below other Asian countries such as Hong Kong, Singapore, South Korea and Taiwan. Pakistan also produces a large volume of industrial products, although it is much more heavily weighted than India toward consumer goods.

South Asian countries participate in the world economy in ways which vary widely in both degree and composition. As a group, exports have grown in value at a rate higher than that for developing countries as a whole. Manufactured exports have increased faster than total exports. This performance is creditable in the context of a steady deterioration in the terms of trade. Imports have also grown at a relatively faster rate partly because a larger, more sophisticated industrial structure has made South Asia more dependent on fuel imports. All the same, while current account balances have worsened, South Asian debt-service ratios have remained below those of low-income less-developed countries in general and of Latin America in particular. They have, therefore, steered well clear of the debt problems that engulf Brazil, Mexico and Nigeria. India has the most diversified export structure; about 40 percent of India's exports consist of manufactures other than textiles. Manufactured exports from Pakistan and Bangladesh are mainly textiles, which approach half the value of their total exports in both cases. Bangladesh and Sri Lanka are dependent on the export of primary products, jute in the case of the former and tea and rubber in the case of the latter. They stand to gain most from international concessions on primary products such as higher and more stable prices, while Indian and Pakistani interests are more seriously threatened by growing protectionism among OECD countries which discriminates against manufactured exports from low-income countries. In absolute terms, India has so far been the chief recipient of aid in South Asia. In 1984, for instance, India received USA $1.5 billion, compared with $1.2 billion by Bangladesh, $0.7 billion by Pakistan and $0.5 billion by Sri Lanka. In *per capita* terms, however, India receives the least, $2.1 as opposed to $29.5 for Sri Lanka and $12.3 for Bangladesh. India also uses aid more 'effectively' than most other recipient countries in the Third World. The Bangladesh economy, meanwhile, is most dependent on continuous flows of aid and is likely to be badly affected by the inadequate replenishment of International Development Agency funds.

In the forty years since Independence, India has managed to reach a sustained, but not a very high rate of economic growth. In agriculture, the country has managed to keep pace with a very large and rapidly growing population. Notable progress in agricultural research has helped to ease the food situation considerably. India has not managed to reduce the number of the poor, although there is evidence that the proportion of the population living in poverty has stabilized. Persistence of poverty, with a low level of industrial efficiency, has led to growing criticism of economic strategy. Critics argue that growth has been sacrificed to excessive ideological

Table 10. Economic and social indicators, by levels of development, 1984

	Population (millions)	GNP USA dollars[a]	Agricultural output (% total output)	Energy Consumption (Kg/oil[a] equivalent)	Food consumption daily calories[b]	Infant mortality rate
Industrial market economies	733	11,430	3	4,877	3,352	9
High income exporters	19	11,250	2	3,593	3,345	65
Middle income developing countries	1,188	1,250	14	743	2,611	72
Low income developing countries (excluding China and India)	611	190	36	79	2,275	114
Bangladesh	98	130	48	40	1,864	124
India	749	260	35	187	2,115	90
Nepal	16	160	56	16	2,047	135
Pakistan	92	380	24	188	2,205	116
Sri Lanka	16	360	28	143	2,348	37

[a]GNP, energy consumption, and food consumption *per capita*.
[b]Calories Consumption in 1983.
Source: World Bank *World Development Report* (1986)

concern with the reduction of inequality: too many government controls and too large a public sector have led to the development of an inefficient productive structure. As a result, policy is becoming more trade-oriented, more 'open door', with greater scope for financial incentives and with fewer and more selective controls.

Economic and political reasons have made Pakistan rely more heavily on trade and aid. Economic strategy has been more closely oriented towards growth, and there has been much greater tolerance of inequality in the distribution of income and economic power. Most industrial development has been located in the private sector, with a small number of families monopolizing industrial investment. On balance, Pakistan has managed to sustain a higher rate of economic growth than India, even through the rate of population growth has also been higher. But a heavy price has had to be paid for neglecting distributional issues, especially that of regional inequality, which was felt most severely in 1971 with the political dismemberment of East and West Pakistan and the creation of Bangladesh.

The Bangladesh economy remains the poorest and most vulnerable of the larger countries of the region, with the seventh largest population in the world, growing at a rate of 2.5 percent *per annum*. Economic policy has had little impact on poverty, the problems of which are compounded by a lack of necessary infrastructure, a much weaker administrative service than in India and Pakistan, and political instability. The country having little artificial irrigation subjects the economy to a high degree of climatic instability. Industrial growth has been limited, exhibiting low growth of output and very low rates of capacity utilization. Over the years, change of government has led to more emphasis on the private sector. The economy remains highly dependent on imports: its ability to attract commercial credit is poor. The only encouraging developments are

special community-based self-help programs (heralded by the Comilla program) which are being almost forced on the economy by its failure to grow.

Sri Lanka presents a classic example of a 'dual economy', with a modern plantation sector existing alongside a traditional subsistence economy. Its small size and export specialization in primary products has always made it sensitive to changes in international demand. Early attempts at industrialization led the economy into balance of payments problems. The need to contain this deficit resulted in tariffs against imports, then in a growing use of direct controls to support an over-valued exchange rate. Import substitution has given place to a greater emphasis on market forces and on increasing the yield and production of rice. The most significant aspect of the Sri Lankan experience, however, lies in the promotion of social welfare. Its record is outstanding among countries with comparable levels of income. An important contribution to success was Sri Lanka's free rice-ration program which was quite unique and made a very effective impact on poverty while it lasted.

Nepal's economy remains predominantly agricultural, much of it based on small-scale rice production for subsistence or local markets. Its remoteness, together with poor transport facilities, have prevented specialization in plantation or other commercial crops for the international market. The economy is also handicapped by limited educational facilities and shortage of skilled labor. The greatest problem which Nepal faces is demographic pressure on limited and often inaccessible cultivable land: food supply barely keeps pace with population growth. Lately there has been some industrial development with a large part of the textile production based on Indian capital and entrepreneurship. Nepal is also developing as an entrepot for imported synthetic or mixed textiles, destined for the Indian market. The economy is currently

Table 11. Relative rates of growth, 1970–81

	(Average percent per annum)			
	Population	**Gross domestic product**	**Agricultural output**	**Manufacturing output**
Industrial market economies	0.7	2.3	2.2	2.7
High income oil exporters	5.0	2.1	−0.8	n.a.
Middle income developing countries	2.4	3.0	3.1	7.4
Low income developing countries:	1.9	1.0	2.4	4.2
Bangladesh	2.6	1.5	2.5	6.1
India	2.1	1.5	2.8	4.3
Nepal	2.6	−0.5	0.5	n.a.
Pakistan	3.0	1.9	3.1	3.8
Sri Lanka	1.7	3.0	3.9	2.1

Source: World Bank *World Tables* Vol I, 3rd edn (1983).

supported by large inflows of foreign aid; Nepal receives six times more than India in *per capita* terms.

Bhutan and the Maldives both have very small economies. The former shares many of the economic characteristics of Nepal, being physically remote and primarily agricultural. Its staple crop is maize, rather than rice: like much of the Terai and the sub-Himalayan regions, it faces grave long-term problems of environmental degradation. Its main industry is cement-production and forestry. The Maldives requires a wide range of imports to survive. Its main economic activities are confined to the export of fish and fish products and shipbuilding, although tourist interest in the islands has increased in recent years.

PC

Further reading
P. Bardhan, *Political Economy of Development in India* (Oxford, 1984)
P. Chaudhuri, *The Indian Economy: Poverty and Development* (London, 1979)
B. H. Farmer, *An Introduction to South Asia* (London, 1983)
N. Islam, *Development Strategy of Bangladesh* (Oxford, 1978)

The colonial legacy

The impact of colonial rule cannot be calculated precisely in terms of costs and benefits. Both supporters and critics of British rule would agree that the main intended beneficiaries were the poor, the archetypal *raiyat* or tiller of the soil. But, at the end of colonial rule, the average standard of living showed no evidence of all round improvement. Poverty was deep and pervasive, and, although new sources of income had emerged, there had been no structural transformation of the economy to ensure subsequent growth.

In the past, historians would have listed the establishment of law and order, which laid the foundation of orderly economic progress, as the paramount legacy of British rule. Yet, it is by no means clear that the endemic warfare of the pre-colonial period affected the daily lives of millions of villagers, except along routes traversed by armies. The peasant cultivating a smallholding could not distinguish between Mughal or Maratha or British revenue demands except in relation to their level, regularity or inflexibility. Nor did orderly British rule stimulate landlords into productive investment in agriculture. What it did achieve was the creation of an Indian economy, or at least an awareness of it in the minds of those responsible for the formulation and administration of economic policy. It also laid the foundation of an institutional structure without which the modern independent economies of South Asia could not have functioned effectively.

Throughout the period of colonial rule, agriculture remained the main source of livelihood. Three out of four adults worked as agricultural laborers, their low incomes spent on food and other basic necessities. Standards of living were closely tied to agricultural performance. Most evidence shows that agricultural production barely kept pace with population growth during the last hundred years of British rule. This was due to low productivity rather than to rapidly accelerating population growth, which did not take off until the 1920s. The causes of stagnation were many: agricultural technology remained relatively backward; surpluses were not reinvested; the burden of Government revenue demand was heavy; the structure of land rights created and sustained intermediaries less concerned with productive investment than with maximizing rental incomes; the poverty of the masses discouraged investment. Overall, low productivity and lack of sustained increase in output prevented the substantial transfers of agricultural surplus to manufacturing, which had been crucial to the structural transformation of the economies of the West.

'The Ganges Canal, Roorkee (Saharanpur District)' by William Simpson (1863). An important colonial legacy was vast systems of irrigation.

This picture, however, did not apply uniformly. The colonial period saw large increases in the production of cash crops such as cotton, jute, sugarcane, coffee and tea. Production for the market was not a new phenomenon in South Asia. What was new was production directed at meeting the demands of an expanding international economy, whose rapid growth opened up new highly unstable sources of income. Regions which specialized in the production of these higher value crops benefitted considerably, as did farmers who switched to production for the market. All the same, poorer peasants could not afford the levels of investment required for such production. New sources of wealth were therefore unequally distributed among the population. Market instability, now added to climatic uncertainty, introduced a markedly cyclical pattern into the pace of economic growth. Along with an interna-tional market for commodities was created a market for labor.

The greatest achievement of the colonial administration was investment in irrigation systems, especially in northern India, which increased agricultural production in the regions which bene-fitted from them. It also initiated research into higher-yielding varieties of crops. Again, however, the overall benefits were too small in scale and too narrowly diffused to have a positive impact on the overall condition of agriculture. The economy was caught in a 'low-level equilibrium trap' which piecemeal reform could not prise open.

A significant part of the population was engaged also in manufac-turing activities, mainly cotton and silk weaving, some of it high quality for export. Jewellers, swordsmiths and other craftsmen catered for urban luxury consumption. By the end of the colonial

Statistics of the Colonial Legacy

A Population

Year	Millions
1800	186.0
1901	280.7
1931	332.3
1939	382.6

B Estimated death rates

Year	Per thousand
1891–1901	50.0
1921–1931	37.9

C Net domestic product at 1938 factor cost (Rs. billion)

Year	Net domestic product	Agriculture, fisheries, etc.	Mining and manufacturing
1901	22.8	12.9	2.8
1931	27.7	16.8	2.9
1939	30.4	17.7	4.0

D Value of Indian exports

Year	Rs. thousands
1834	79.9
1900	1077.2
1931	1612.0
1939	2135.7

E Indian piecegoods as percent of total exports (= 100)

Year	%
1811–1812	33.0
1850–1851	3.7

F India's share of world manufacturing output (= 100)

Year	%
1800	19.7
1900	1.7
1938	2.4

Sources: A: A. Maddison, *Class Structure and Economic Growth, India and Pakistan since the Moghuls* p. 164 (London, 1972)
B: Dharma Kumar (Ed.), *Cambridge Economic History of India* vol. 2 p. 505 (Cambridge, 1982)
C: A. Maddison, *op. cit.*, pp. 167–8
D: and E: Cambridge, *op. cit.*, pp. 833, 837, 839, 842
F: *Modern Asian Studies*, vol. 19, pt. 3, p. 600 (1985).

Box 31

era, they had been replaced by a small core of modern industry. Modern industrial development began in the 1860s with the establishment of cotton mills in and around Bombay, and received its seal of acclaim with the founding of the Tata Iron and Steel Company in 1907. Its regional spread was limited: almost the whole of the modern industrial sector bequeathed by the colonial regime was located in what became India. Other South Asian countries started life with very little large-scale modern industry. Indian industry consisted mainly of cotton textiles in western India, jute textiles around Calcutta and a coal, iron and steel complex in eastern India. India was nearly self-sufficient in steel at Independence only because demand was very low for a country of its size. The most important aspect of the colonial industrial legacy was its qualitative significance. Parts of the subcontinent emerged with the core of an industrial labor force and familiarity with modern technology, having served an entrepreneurial apprenticeship. Throughout the colonial period, the economy remained dependent on imported manufactured goods. Free trade survived longer in the field of colonial economic policy. Only in the 1920s was the steel industry offered protection which was subsequently extended to certain consumer goods in the following years. The government remained wedded to procurement from Britain.

Government policy on transport, however, proved more significant. Its most important legacy was the railway network, begun in the 1850s and extending to 57,000 km by 1920–21. Demand for railway stock and the railway workshops laid the foundations of modern engineering industry.

Investment in education and health was largely urban-based and inadequate to meet the massive scale of needs. The Government created a system of secondary and higher education, but it failed to improve primary education for the population in rural areas. Health facilities, concentrated in hospitals and medical schools in urban areas, were equally uneven in their impact.

PC

Further reading

B. Chandra, *The Rise and Growth of Economic Nationalism in India* (Delhi, 1966)
N. Charlesworth, *British Rule and the Indian Economy 1800–1914* (London, 1982)
D. Kumar, Ed., *The Cambridge Economic History of India* Vol. 2 (Cambridge, 1982)
Sumit Sarkar, *Modern India, 1885–1947* (Delhi, 1983)
D. R. Snodgrass, *Ceylon: An Export Economy in Transition* (Illinois, 1966)

Agriculture

The South Asian region contains almost a fifth of the world's population and a larger proportion of its poorest people. Land is scarce, and the countries of the region have all experienced food production deficits, although latterly these have been reduced or eliminated in large part through the adoption of new agricultural technology. Between 1970 and 1982, the growth of cereal production outstripped that of population, but not by very much. Performance in terms of this important criterion was less good than in East Asia but better than in most of the remainder of the developing economies. In spite of increased production, however, the distribution of foodgrains is so inequitable that the livelihood needs of many people in South Asia are still not adequately met.

Agriculture now contributes about one-third of gross domestic product (ranging from 24 percent in Pakistan to 56 percent in Nepal); supplies roughly one-third of merchandise exports from South Asia; and employs more than three-quarters of the labor force (ranging from 55 percent in Pakistan to 93 percent in Nepal). The proportion of the labor force engaged in agriculture has not changed very much since the early 1960s.

Crops, livestock and fishing

The most important elements of South Asian agriculture are food-grains, grown both for subsistence and the market. Production of foodgrains in India has increased overwhelmingly by increases in

Table 12. Agriculture in the economies of South Asia

	Structure of production % of GDP in agriculture		Labour force % of labour force in agriculture	
	1965	1984	1965	1980
Bangladesh	53	48	84	75
Bhutan	n.a.	n.a.	95	92
India	47	35	73	70
Nepal	65	56 (1983)	94	93
Pakistan	40	24	60	55
Sri Lanka	28	28	56	53

Source: World Bank *World Development Report* (1986).

yield from 50 million tonnes in 1950 to 154 million tonnes in 1985. Only on the central Deccan plateau has the area given over to foodgrains increased. Elsewhere, the extent of foodgrains has steadily been eroded, for instance by sugarcane and cotton in Gujarat and western Uttar Pradesh, jute in West Bengal and oilseeds in Tamil Nadu.

Chief among the cereals is rice. Tolerant of alkaline and saline conditions, rice is cultivated in intensive multi-cropped mono-culture in the wet, heavy clays of deltas, flood and coastal plains where rainfall exceeds 1250 mm, or on irrigated land. The area under rice cultivation has expanded since Independence although improvements in yield have provided the major motor of growth in

Table 13. Major crops: production in quinquennial averages

Years	Bangladesh	Bhutan	India	Nepal	Pakistan	Sri Lanka
Rice production as milled rice, million metric tonnes						
1961/2–1963/4	—	n.a.	33.0	0.8	10.7	0.6
1964/5–1968/9	—	n.a.	36.6	1.5	13.0	0.8
1969/70–1973/4	10.8	0.2	41.2	1.6	4.3	0.9
1974/5–1978/9	12.1	0.2	47.4	1.5	2.9	1.0
1979/80–1983/4	13.6	0.1	54.6	4.0	3.3	1.4
Wheat, million metric tonnes						
1961/2–1963/4	—	—	11.5[a]	n.a.	4.1	—
1964/5–1968/9	—	—	13.5	0.2[a]	5.4[a]	—
1969/70–1973/4	0.1	0.1[a]	23.4	0.3	7.1	—
1974/5–1978/9	0.5[c]	0.1	29.7	0.4	8.7	—
1979/80–1983/4	1.0	—	38.7	0.5	11.4	—
Millet, '000 metric tonnes						
1961/2–1963/4	—	—	15,338[b]	n.a.	631	n.a.
1964/5–1968/9	—	—	17,401	114[a]	624	17[a]
1969/70–1973/4	0.9	10[b]	17,108	128	609	17
1974/5–1978/9	1.1	5	21,000	132	579	22
1979/80–1983/4	0.5	6	22,268	121	474	15

[a]one year missing from quinquennial average, [b] two years, [c] three years, and [d] four years.

(continued over)

Agriculture

Table 13 *(continued)*

Years	Bangladesh	Bhutan	India	Nepal	Pakistan	Sri Lanka
Maize, '000 metric tonnes						
1961/2–1963/4	—	n.a.	4,424[a]	n.a.	504	9
1964/5–1968/9	—	n.a.	5,413	869[a]	671[a]	13
1969/70–1973/4	2	27[a]	6,033	823	702	16
1974/5–1978/9	2	48	6,089	725	812	24
1979/80–1983/4	1	55	7,205	739	1,013	27
Pulses, '000 metric tonnes						
1961/2–1963/4	—	1	11,188	17	853	5
1964/5–1968/9	—	1	10,613	17	769	6
1969/70–1973/4	266	2	10,673	22	752	7
1974/5–1978/9	228	2	11,738	46	784	17
1979/80–1983/4	216	2	11,337	60	637	27
Roots and tubers, '000 metric tonnes						
1961/2–1963/4	—	19	5,814	238	257	380
1964/5–1968/9	—	26	9,348	341	323	444
1969/70–1973/4	1,546	35	12,187	352	380	533
1974/5–1978/9	1,627	38	15,844	364	481	830
1979/80–1983/4	1,816	33	17,169	399	549	801
Sugar cane, million metric tonnes						
1961/2–1963/4	—	—	n.a.	n.a.	21.2	n.a.
1964/5–1968/9	—	—	108.2[a]	0.2[a]	30.0	0.2[a]
1969/70–1973/4	6.5	—	127.2	0.2	21.6	0.3
1974/5–1978/9	6.5	—	154.2	0.3	27.9	0.3
1979/80–1983/4	6.8	—	162.4	0.5	34.5	0.3
Groundnut, '000 metric tonnes						
1961/2–1963/4	—	—	4,753[a]	—	89[a]	—
1964/5–1968/9	—	—	5,041	—	100	—
1969/70–1973/4	38	—	5,683	—	65	6[a]
1974/5–1978/9	35	—	6,058	—	65	10
1979/80–1983/4	24	—	6,097	—	74	7
Cotton lint, '000 metric tonnes						
1961/2–1963/4	—	—	918	—	348[a]	1[a]
1964/5–1968/9	—	—	1,065[a]	—	495	1[b]
1969/70–1973/4	9	—	1,212	—	651	1
1974/5–1978/9	17	—	1,198	—	546	3
1979/80–1983/4	27	—	1,262	—	756	2
Jute, '000 metric tonnes						
1961/2–1963/4	—	n.a.	1,068	n.a.	1,165	—
1964/5–1968/9	—	n.a.	910[a]	36[a]	1,236	—
1969/70–1973/4	1,099	4.6[a]	1,032	49	1	—
1974/5–1978/9	854	5	1,305	54	1	—
1979/80–1983/4	916	5	1,391	42	1	—
Coffee (green), '000 metric tonnes						
1961/2–1963/4	—	—	56.6[a]	—	—	n.a.
1964/5–1968/9	—	—	67.3[a]	—	—	n.a.
1969/70–1973/4	—	—	84	—	—	10[b]
1974/5–1978/9	—	—	102	—	—	9
1979/80–1983/4	—	—	133	—	—	14

Table 13 (continued)

Years	Bangladesh	Bhutan	India	Nepal	Pakistan	Sri Lanka
Tea, '000 metric tonnes						
1961/2–1963/4	—	—	349	—	—	n.a.
1964/5–1968/9	—	—	391	—	—	222[a]
1969/70–1973/4	24.2	—	429	—	—	211
1974/5–1978/9	33.5	—	535	—	—	209
1979/80–1983/4	39.0	—	588	—	—	200
Tobacco, '000 metric tonnes						
1961/62–1963/4	—	n.a.	342	n.a.	97	4.1
1964/5–1968/9	—	n.a.	345[a]	6[a]	150	6
1969/70–1973/4	38.7	0.8[a]	388	8	99	8
1974/5–1978/9	47.7	1	406	6	70	7
1979/80–1983/4	46.5	1	499	6	71	13
Rubber (natural), '000 metric tonnes						
1961/2–1963/4	—	—	32	—	—	102
1964/5–1968/9	—	—	66[a]	—	—	141
1969/70–1973/4	—	—	109	—	—	144
1974/5–1978/9	—	—	149	—	—	151
1979/80–1983/4	—	—	151[c]	—	—	135

[a] one year missing from quinquennial average, [b] two years, [c] three years, and [d] four years

Sources of statistical material: Bangladesh – Statistical Yearbook of Bangladesh 1975, 1983–84; Monthly Statistical Bulletin of Bangladesh, June 1986; Lloyds Bank Economic Report Bangladesh 1986; FAO Production Yearbooks. Bhutan – FAO Production Yearbook. India – Government of India Economic Summary 1984–85; FAO Production Yearbooks. Nepal – Nepal Statistical Abstracts; FAO Production Yearbooks. Pakistan – Government of Pakistan Agricultural Yearbooks; Government of Pakistan Statistical Bulletins (various); FAO Production Yearbooks. Sri Lanka – Government of Sri Lanka Statistical Abstracts.

production since 1965, especially in the south, on the east coast and on the irrigated loams of the Deccan plateau. Three-quarters of the subcontinent's rice production is in India where it occupies 25 percent of gross cropped area, and, at 61 million tonnes, 38 percent of total foodgrain production in 1985. Since the late 1970s, however, yield increases have tapered off, averaging by the mid-1980s between 2 tonnes per hectare in Nepal and Bangladesh and 3 tonnes in Sri Lanka.

This tapering off is true also of wheat. Wheat is the dominant and highly commercialized *rabi* cereal in northwest India and India alone now produces 80 percent of the subcontinent's wheat. Production comprises, at 45 million tonnes, about 30 percent of India's total foodgrains output. Tolerant of a wider range of soil and moisture conditions than rice, wheat has colonized irrigated land as far south as the Malwa plateau and eastwards into Bihar. High yielding varieties have reduced genetic diversity while resulting in massive yield increases in the Panjab, Haryana, Rajasthan and western Uttar Pradesh. Yields average between 1 tonne per hectare in Bhutan to 2.3 tonnes in Bangladesh, with some parts of India achieving over 7 tonnes per hectare.

Millets comprise 15 percent of foodgrain production. India provides 97 percent of the subcontinent's millet. Of low yields

(typically half to one tonne per hectare), and considered economically inferior to rice and wheat despite nutritional superiority, millets are threatened by the southward march of wheat and by the extension of rice cultivation into the interior wherever there is irrigation. Sorghum, occupying about 20 percent of gross sown area

Ploughing in the Vale of Peshawar, Northwest Frontier Province.

Cropping pattern of India, Pakistan and Sri Lanka.

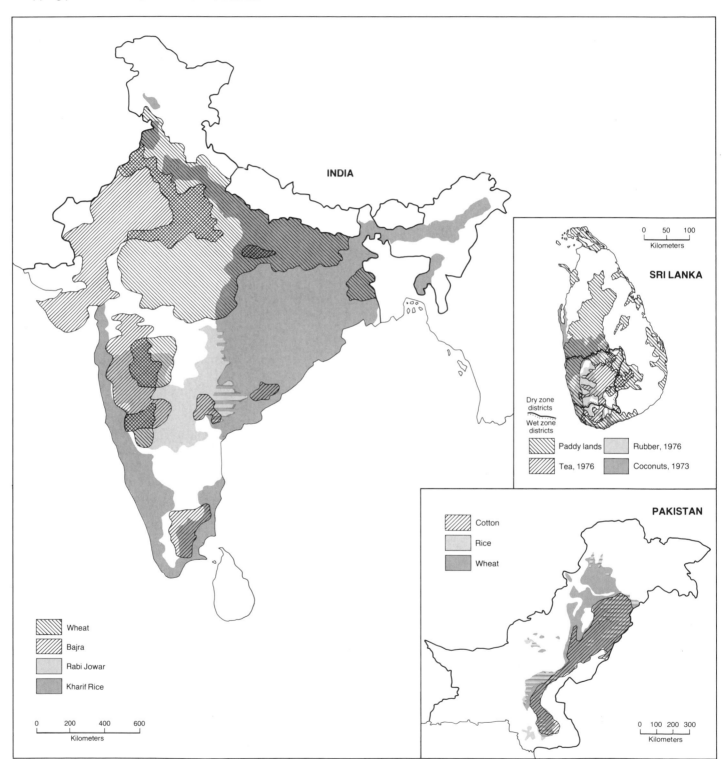

INDIA

SRI LANKA

Dry zone
districts

Wet zone
districts

Paddy lands
Tea, 1976
Rubber, 1976
Coconuts, 1973

0 50 100
Kilometers

PAKISTAN

Cotton
Rice
Wheat

Wheat
Bajra
Rabi Jowar
Kharif Rice

0 200 400 600
Kilometers

0 100 200 300
Kilometers

Area under principal crops.

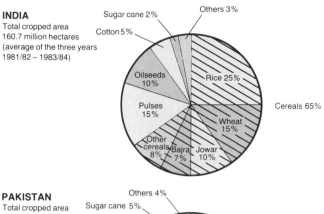

INDIA
Total cropped area
160.7 million hectares
(average of the three years
1981/82 – 1983/84)

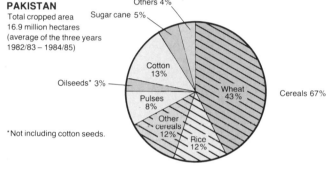

PAKISTAN
Total cropped area
16.9 million hectares
(average of the three years
1982/83 – 1984/85)

*Not including cotton seeds.

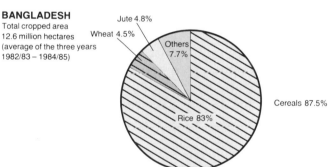

BANGLADESH
Total cropped area
12.6 million hectares
(average of the three years
1982/83 – 1984/85)

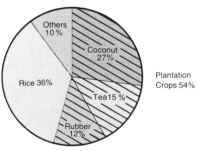

SRI LANKA
Total cropped area
1.7 million hectares
(figures for 1981)

Source: Statistical Abstract India 1984.
Pakistan Statistical Yearbook 1986.
Statistical Yearbook of Bangladesh 1986.
Statistical Abstract of the Democratic Socialist Republic of Sri Lanka 1982.

(g.s.a.), is cultivated in regions of 600 to 1000 mm rainfall. Drought resistant, it is a 3–4 month *kharif* crop except for the south where it can be cultivated in the *rabi/samba* after the northeast monsoon. Pearl millet, another *kharif* crop grown on 7 percent of India's g.s.a., is a low yielding staple in Rajasthan and widely distributed in peninsular India. Ragi commands some 1.5 percent of g.s.a.: a staple of the poor on Karnataka's High Plateau, it is a famine food elsewhere and a rainfed supplement in rice regions.

Maize is a minor foodgrain which has increased from 3 to 5 percent of total grain production since the 1950s. India produces 80 percent, mostly in the north, 10 percent is grown in Pakistan, and 8 percent in Nepal. Maize yields are relatively high for a coarse grain, ranging from 0.5 tonne per hectare in Bangladesh to 1.5 tonnes in Nepal and Bhutan, but it demands both labor and a fertile, well-drained soil. Maize has low status as a cereal, competing with vegetables on the outskirts of towns.

Apart from cereals, South Asia boasts a huge family of pulses: nutritious, nitrogen-fixing legumes providing food for humans and animal feed. Over 90 percent of production is in India. Gram, a rainfed rabi crop comprising 5 percent of g.s.a., is the most important member of this family, and is found in greatest concentration in light soil regions of Uttar Pradesh and Nepal. Although this is the most commercialized of pulse crops, the real price of which is rising, production has stagnated or declined because of the ascendance of irrigated monocropping of cereals. Yields average from 0.5 to 0.8 tonne per hectare. Soya bean, whose cultivation is restricted mostly to Bangladesh with a small amount in Sri Lanka, reaches an average yield of one tonne per hectare.

Table 14. Crops and their names

Common name	Botanical name
Arhar / tur dhal	*cajanus indicus*
Black gram / urad	*phaseolus radiatus*
Chickpea / gram	*cicer arietinum*
Coconut	*cocos nucifera*
Cotton	*gossypium sp.*
Finger millet / ragi / kurakkan	*eleusine coracana*
Gingelly / til	*sesamum indicum*
Green gram / moong	*phaseolus mungo*
Groundnut / peanut / monkeynut	*arachis hypogaea*
Jute	*corchorus sp.*
Lentil / masur	*ervem lens*
Maize	*zea mays*
Paddy / padi / unmilled rice and 1.5 × the weight of rice	
Pearl millet / bulrush millet / bajra / cumbu	*pennisetum typhoideum*
Rice	*oryza sativa* (see also paddy)
Sorghum / jowar	*sorghum bicolor*
Sugar cane	*saccarum officinaru*
Wheat	*triticum sativum*

Table 15. The seasons

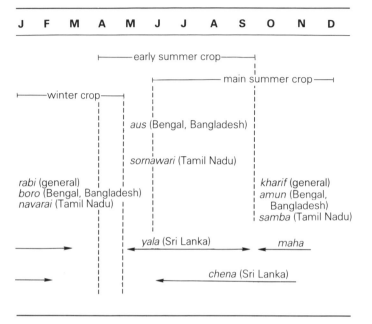

Sugarcane is a highly commercialized industrial foodcrop, demanding of labor, soil nutrients and water. The regional production of India is 80 percent and that of Pakistan, 15 percent. Cultivation is concentrated in Maharashtra and northern Uttar Pradesh. Both acreage and yields are on the increase throughout the subcontinent: average yields currently vary from 22 tonnes per hectare in India to 50 tonnes in Sri Lanka.

Oilseeds occupy about 9 percent of g.s.a. providing edible oil, residues for industrial uses and by-products for feedstuffs and manure. Production is stagnating despite rising prices because of the decline of intercropping in which such crops featured strongly, together with the absence of relatively profitable high yielding varieties. Groundnuts occupy half the total acreage of oilseeds, while sesamaum, mustard, linseed, castor and coconut occupy the rest. India, with 98 percent of the subcontinent's output, is the largest producer of groundnuts in the world. The crop is grown in regions of 500 to 900 mm of rainfall *per annum*, but it is concentrated in southeast India and on the Deccan plateau. Yields are low and vary from 0.5 tonne of groundnuts in pod per hectare in Sri Lanka to 1.2 tonnes in Pakistan.

Fibre crops comprise 6 percent of g.s.a. Cotton is by far the most important. It is a labor-intensive rainfed crop standing 7–8 months in the fields, preferably in heavy soils of regions with between 600 and 850 mm of rain or alternatively in irrigated alluvial soils. Research has resulted in fine long staple high yielding varieties. Average yields of about one tonne of lint per hectare are low. The

expansion of irrigation and subsidized plant protection has greatly increased production in Gujarat, on the Deccan plateau in Karnataka, in both the Panjabs (Pakistan produces 44 percent of the subcontinent's total output) and in southern Tamil Nadu. Jute flourishes in damp soils and moist climates, and hence competes with rice in Bangladesh which accounts for 36 percent of the region's production and boasts the highest average yields of 1.3 tonnes per hectare. Jute cultivation has spread into West Bengal and adjacent states since partition split the productive hinterland in East Pakistan (now Bangladesh) from Calcutta's jute mills.

The livestock economy is indispensable to the cropping system. Three-quarters of the subcontinent's livestock is cattle – an estimated one for every two people. Cattle provide milk, draught, transport, raw materials for fuel, fertilizer, meat, hides and skins for the export-dominated leather industry, and raw material for many other agro-industries. Milk yields are about one-fifth of those in the USA. The economic role of livestock, bullocks in particular, in providing draught power far exceeds their role as suppliers of food. Livestock improvement is constrained by supplies of feedstuffs. The livestock population is increasingly stall-fed on roughages and some industrially-prepared feeds. The great breeding grounds in Haryana and Rajasthan have been threatened by the decline of grazing territories following the expansion of irrigation. Subsidized mechanization of water-lifting, agricultural operations and transport have also reduced demand. Cattle are most densely distributed in relation to cropped areas in the extreme northwest and northeast. Buffalo yield twice the milk of cows, are more versatile but less fertile. Of the 20 percent of livestock that are ovines, goats are the most prolific, hardy and economic since there is a market for their

Table 16. Fishing

Country	Year	Total catch ('000 metric tonnes)	Freshwater (%)	Production *per capita* (kg)
Bangladesh	1951	174.5	85	4.1
	1971	814 (est.)	90	13.0
	1983–4	751	77	7.2
India	1951	752	29	1.6
	1971	1,851.6	37	3.4
	1980	2,423.4 (est.)	36	3.5
Maldives	1974	38	—	295
	1979	28	—	n.a.
	1984	55	—	318
Pakistan	1951	56.3	22	1.6
	1971	155.3	12	2.9
	1985	390.6	18	4.1
Sri Lanka	1984	170	n.a.	11.3

Source: *Statistical Abstract India* 1984; *Pakistan Statistical Yearbook* 1986; *Statistical Yearbook of Bangladesh* 1986; *UN Statistical Yearbook for Asia and the Pacific* 1985.

Bringing in the cotton harvest, Gujarat.

milk as well as their meat and wool. The closure of forests and the privatization of common lands have reduced goat populations. But there are important concentrations in Rajasthan, Maharashtra and Bihar. Sheep are found in the cool dry conditions of the semi-arid tropics, surrounding hills and the Himalayas. Poultry, providers of eggs, meat and manure, are found everywhere, although the quality is low.

Both marine and freshwater fishing play a significant part in the rural economy, and provide employment to large numbers of people. Characterized by very simple technology, production was low at the time of Independence, but there has been appreciable growth since then. Fishing is especially important in Kerala and West Bengal in India; so also in Bangladesh, where it supplies the livelihoods of more than five million people and accounts for 9

percent of the value of exports (1984–85); and in the Maldives, where with tourism and shipping it supplies the base of the economy and provides livelihoods to more than three-quarters of the population.

Irrigation

Rainfall in monsoonal South Asia is highly seasonal and also varies greatly from year to year. Irrigation has, therefore, long been vital to agricultural development either to make cultivation possible or to extend the growing season. About one quarter of India's cropped area is irrigated; in Pakistan the proportion is three-quarters, in Sri Lanka a half, in Nepal a fifth and in Bangladesh a sixth. In precolonial times, rulers were involved in constructing and managing irrigation works, but there were also private wells and, in peninsular

Table 17. Irrigation: Area irrigated by sources ('000 hectares and % of total net irrigated area)

	Bangladesh 1971–1972	1983–1984	% Change ↓	India 1950–1951 ↑	1980–1981	% Change ↓	Pakistan 1950–1951 ↑	1983–1984	% Change ↓
Canals	103 (9)	134 (7)	30 ↑	8,295 (39.8)	15,292 (39.4)	84 ↑	8,206	11,360 (74)	38 ↑
Tanks	—	—	—	3,613 (17.3)	3,198 (8.2)	11 ↓	—	60	—
Wells	—	—	—	5,978 (28.7)	17,734 (45.7)	197 ↑	—	310 (2)	—
Tubewells	48 (4)	667 (35)	1,260 ↑	—	—	—	—	2,950 (19)	—
Traditional lift	417 (36)	322 (17)	30 ↓	—	—	—	—	—	—
Power pumps	418 (36)	667 (35)	60 ↑	—	—	—	—	—	—
Others	181 (15)	130 (6)	28 ↓	2,967	2,581	13 ↓	—	640	—
Total net irrigated area[a]	1,167	1,920	65 ↑	20,853	38,805	86 ↑	—	15,320	—
Total cropped area	—	—	—	131,893	173,324	—	—	20,340	—
% of area irrigated	—	—	—	15.8	22.4	—	—	75.3	—
Cropping intensity	—	—	—	111	128	—	111	128	—

N.B. Comparable data for Sri Lanka are not available.
[a]Net irrigated area means that if two or more crops on a given piece of land are irrigated in the same year from the same source the area is counted only once.
Source: *Statistical Abstract India* 1984; *Pakistan Statistical Yearbook* 1986; *Statistical Yearbook of Bangladesh* 1986.

India and in the dry zone of Sri Lanka, village tanks (storage reservoirs formed often by the construction of an earth dam across the line of an intermittent water course). Under colonial rule, old irrigation systems were refurbished and many new irrigation works were constructed, notably in the Panjab, Sind and the Ganges Valley in the north, as well as in the deltas of the Kaveri, Krishna and Godavari rivers in the south. By the close of the colonial period, just over half of India's total irrigation, some 23.8 million hectares, was provided by public works. The capacity of canal irrigation systems, which were designed principally to supply protection, rather than to permit intensification of cultivation, was determined by the 'run of the river' at barrages where flows were diverted. An important development since Independence has been the construction of massive storage reservoirs, of which the first was the Bhakra–Nangal project in the Panjab, so relaxing the flow constraint. The other important development has been the great expansion of groundwater irrigation.

In India, the irrigated area has more than doubled since Independence, as has the incidence of double cropping. Groundwater irrigation, especially from tubewells, now accounts for a greater share of the irrigated area than do canals, even though there was a 76 percent increase in the canal-irrigated area between 1951 and 1978. Pakistan, where the canal-irrigated area increased by 38 percent between 1951 and 1984, has constructed substantial storage reservoirs at Tarbela on the Indus and at Mangala on the Jhelum. Salinization and water-logging, however, have become serious problems affecting 22 percent and 13 percent of the canal-irrigated areas respectively. Groundwater has become increasingly important, its share in total on-farm water supply rising from 14 percent in 1966–67 to 33 percent in 1979–80. Irrigation has played a part in

increasing the area of double-cropping in Bangladesh (where there was almost no irrigation at Independence) from 30 percent in 1947–48 to 53 percent in 1983–84. Traditional water-lifting devices have given way to low-lift pumps and here too there has recently been expansion of tubewell irrigation. At Independence, Sri Lanka had a number of small irrigation systems, as well as village tanks, almost entirely for paddy. Subsequent large-scale irrigation projects have been the Gal Oya and the Uda Walawe. Under the UNP government elected to office in 1977, rapid development of big schemes on the country's largest river, the Mahaweli Ganga, has been a priority. Irrigated areas have increased two fold since Independence, mostly in the dry zone. In Nepal, estimates of the irrigated area vary from 9 to 20 percent depending on whether the total includes terraced lands watered by small-scale stream diversions. Large-scale projects are limited to the plains of the *terai* (swamp land) bordering India. Further development in this region is vital for the country as the terai constitutes its last frontier for settlement.

Standards of efficiency in the use of irrigation water are low throughout South Asia. Older systems were not designed and constructed to make intensive agricultural production possible or to permit very careful regulation of water flow through them. Too much water is taken out in the upper parts of canal systems and lower reaches are left dry. The delivery of water is often unpredictable, militating against intensive cultivation practices. Irrigation bureaucracies have generally lacked capacity for water management and local level organization is weak, often non-existent. The improvement of irrigation efficiency remains a vital task in agricultural development in South Asia, and will crucially affect the success of projects like Sri Lanka's Mahaweli Scheme.

Organization of agricultural production

Agricultural production in South Asia is generally based on peasant farming except in the case of some commercial crops which are grown on plantations. Peasant production is carried on by people who own at least some of the land, tools and inputs that are required, but who are themselves involved in the work of cultivation, assisted by household members. They produce in the first place to satisfy their own livelihood but their subsistence is based also on the market and almost all peasant households sell some of their produce. Producers of this type may also employ hired labor and hire themselves out as wage workers. The South Asian peasantry is everywhere highly differentiated and characterized by marked inequalities in the ownership of land and other resources.

The top 5 percent of households in a village often own 30 to 40 percent of the land while the lowest 50 percent of households own less than 10 percent. South Asia has a large class of landless agricultural wage laborers, and another large group of peasants who own very small landholdings and who must depend heavily on working for others. Together they make up over half of all rural households. The small group of dominant households which owns the largest share of all agricultural resources varies in character. In regions such as the Pakistan Panjab and eastern Uttar Pradesh and Bihar, the dominant landholders are 'landlords' who lease out part of the land to tenant cultivators. Elsewhere, for example in Tamil Nadu, the dominant group comprises 'rich peasants' who work the land themselves with the assistance of hired labor.

This agrarian structure differs considerably from East and Southeast Asia where operational landholdings have historically been distributed more equitably and production has been dominated by small household producers. It has important implications for the working of the whole agricultural economy of the region. Most agricultural producers lack financial resources for investment in production. South Asian governments have faced difficult choices between allocating resources to programs to assist small producers or encouraging expansion of output in the much smaller number of larger landholdings, thereby risking increasing rural inequality. Now, as in the past, small cultivators often require advances of working capital, whether in cash or kind, to carry on production at all. When they obtain these advances from larger landholders or from agricultural merchants and private moneylenders, they usually pay high rates of interest, committing themselves to selling their product to the supplier of credit often when prices are low after harvest. The proportion of their harvest marketed by the smallest operators is higher than it is among slightly larger operators; they are in the position of having to sell even if they do not have a true surplus, and have to buy back food for themselves at times when prices are higher. This cycle of debt has been a constraint on the expansion of agricultural production. At the same time, the profitability of moneylending, trading in agricultural commodities and land renting has reduced the incentive for larger landholders to invest directly in agricultural production. They control land, labor, commodity and money markets, and influence the prices paid or received by the majority of rural people. The position of laborers and poor peasants in relation to these dominant rural interests is weakened by the pressure of numbers: the supply of rural labor usually ensures that there is little or no upward pressure on wage rates.

The distinctive agrarian structure of South Asia, together with caste divisions, generally inhibits collective action among rural peoples. Images of the village as a 'community' are powerful but the extent of community action over the organization of irrigation or access to common grazing and fuel resources is limited. While there are cases in which community action has been organized by dominant landholders, there are many more accounts of its failure because of manipulation or neglect on the part of its organizers.

There seems to have been a remarkable degree of continuity in the agrarian structure of South Asia. The incidence of landless agricultural workers has increased over the last two centuries and terms of labor contracts have changed from the widespread employment of permanently bonded labor to daily paid casual labor, but a large class of landless people, some of whom were paid cash wages, existed even in pre-colonial times. Inequalities in the distribution of operational landholdings and land titles have not changed greatly from the late nineteenth century. Corporate institutions, although undoubtedly stronger in the pre-colonial period, had already been eroded by eighteenth century developments. Early colonial records in both South India and Sri Lanka comment on the breakdown of irrigation systems as a result of lack of community maintenance.

Much controversy has surrounded the nature of the impact of the more recent development of capitalist production. It is now widely agreed that capital has frequently extended control over agricultural production not through the dispossession of peasant households but through the supply of production and consumption advances. The extent of capitalist organization of production has increased partly as a result of the introduction of modern technology. However, it remains unevenly developed. A process of dispossession is sometimes thought to be taking place as small peasants become increasingly indebted and finally lose the ownership of their land; and the incidence of landless agricultural laborers in the rural labor force has risen from around 28 percent in 1951 to 37 percent in 1981, which would suggest a worsening in the distribution of land ownership. On the other hand survey data and detailed studies from several parts of India show a decline in the incidence of absolute landlessness in the recent past. At the same time, there is evidence of an overall increase in the proportion of households not *operating* any land, together with increasing reliance on wage employment in

The house of a 'landlord', Gonda district, eastern Uttar Pradesh.

agriculture and outside it, a pattern described as 'partial proletarianization'.

The agrarian structure of Pakistan is marked by a particularly high incidence of landlordism and by extensive sharecropping tenancy. In 1960, about 9 percent of landowners held 42 percent of the cultivated area, and, despite the passage of land reform legislation, this concentration remained virtually unchanged in 1972. Statistics of 1976 show that 4.1 percent of owners held 36 percent of the cultivated land while the bottom 71 percent controlled only 25 percent of the area. In 1960, 42 percent of holdings were tenant farmers, occupying 39 percent of the area. The impact of land reforms in 1959 reduced these figures to 34 and 30 percent, respectively, by 1972, although it remains doubtful whether tenants were the main beneficiaries of this change due to the large number of

evictions which followed the reforms. None of Pakistan's land reform legislation has offered effective security of tenure to these cultivators.

The structure of agriculture in Bangladesh is marked by very small landholdings and a high degree of landlessness. Seventy-five percent of rural households are either landless (one-third of the total) or marginal cultivators owning less than 0.8 hectares. Between them, they control less than 24 percent of the total area. In this context, the 10 percent of households owning more than 50 percent of the land enjoy considerable local power and are able to extract surpluses through land renting (especially in the north) and moneylending. They also hold substantial political power and have been the main beneficiaries of state policy towards agriculture since the foundation of Bangladesh.

Table 18(a). Landholding, Bangladesh

Size of holding (hectares)	Distribution of landownership, 1977	
	Holdings percent	Area percent
0	11.1	0.0
0–0.4	47.4	9.3
0.4–0.8	16.4	14.4
0.8–2.0	17.5	33.3
2.0–4.05	5.6	23.3
4.1 and above	1.9	19.7

Types of holding	Holdings percent	Area percent	Area tenanted percent
Owner-cultivator	23.5	10.5	—
Owner-manager	37.7	43.5	—
Owner-cum-tenant	32.0	23.2 (owned)	+ 18.5
Tenant	6.8	0.0 (owned)	+ 4.4
Total	—	77.2 (owned)	+ 22.9

Source: 1977 Land Occupancy Survey of Rural Bangladesh.

Table 18(b). Landholding, Nepal

Size of holding (hectares)	Distribution of landownership		Average size of holding (hectares)
	Holdings percent	Area percent	
0.1–0.4	55.8	11.8	0.2
0.4–2.7	37.8	44.3	1.2
2.7–10.0	5.7	31.6	5.6
10 and above	0.7	12.3	16.5

Source: Asian Development Bank/His Majesty's Government Nepal, *1982: Nepal Agriculture Strategy Study*, 1982.

Table 18(c). Landholding, India

Size of holding (hectares)	Holdings percent		Distribution of operational landholding Area percent	
	1953–1954	1976–1977	1953–1954	1976–1977
Marginal holdings (below 1.0)	39.1	54.6	5.4	10.9
Small holdings (1.0–2.0)	20.9	18.1	10.0	12.8
Semi-medium holdings (2.0–4.0)	19.7	14.3	18.6	19.8
Medium holdings (4.0–10.0)	14.4	10.6	29.3	30.3
Large holdings (10 and above)	5.9	3.0	36.6	26.5

NB. Totals may not always add up to 100 due to rounding.
Source: *Kurukshetra* XXIX, No. 23.

Sri Lanka stands out in relation to other South Asian countries in terms of the organization of agricultural production. Outside the plantation sector, which occupies 50 percent of the total cultivated area, agriculture is based on peasant farming oriented towards wet rice cultivation. It is marked by considerable inequality and sharecropping known as *ande* see Table 18e. In 1982, 42.4 percent of smallholdings were less than one acre in extent, occupying only 8.1 percent of the total area, while 22.1 percent of holdings of more than 3 acres comprised 62.2 percent of the total cultivated area. There is strong evidence of extensive indebtedness. But the dynamics of agrarian change in Sri Lanka appear to be different from those of the subcontinent because of the availability of non-agricultural employment in the wet zone and of land in the dry zone.

The rural population is concentrated in the wet zone of the southwest of the island. Here, because of the diversity of employment opportunities, cereal farming has become a part-time activity. There has been little polarization of landholdings, and old rural élites have been challenged from the 1950s by the emergence of a new political leadership tied to state institutions. The dry zone, in contrast, is much more sparsely populated. It has been the object of government-sponsored settlement schemes since the 1930s. These irrigated settlements, based on smallholdings of not more than 2 hectares, were intended to relieve population pressure in the wet zone and increase food production. Differentiation has emerged, and some of the most striking rural poverty in Sri Lanka is found among the descendants of settlers. Outside the dry zone settlements, the availability of non-irrigated land for shifting cultivation has limited the emergence of absolute landlessness.

In Nepal, small peasants dominate agriculture. In 1961, the bottom 47.6 percent of households accounted for only 10 percent of the land owned while 8 percent owned nearly 40 percent of the land. Almost half of all households farmed plots of less than half a hectare. About 15 percent of the cropped area is operated under various

Table 18(d). Landholding, Pakistan

Size of holding (hectares)	Distribution of land ownership in 1976	
	Holdings percent	Area percent
Marginal holdings (below 2.5)	70.8	24.9
Small holdings (2.5–5.1)	17.5	21.3
Medium holdings (5.1–10.1)	7.6	18.1
Large holdings (10.1–20.2)	2.6	13.2
Very large holdings (20.1 and above)	1.5	22.8

Types of holding 1960[a] and 1972	Holdings percent		Area percent	
	1960	1972	1960	1972
Owner	41	42	38	40
Owner-cum-Tenant	17	24	23	30
Tenant	42	34	39	30

[a]1960 figures are for West Pakistan.
NB. Totals may not always add up to 100 due to rounding.
Source: M. H. Khan *Underdevelopment and Agrarian Structure in Pakistan* Table 3.2 (Boulder, Co., 1981); *Pakistan Census of Agriculture* 1960 and 1972.

Table 18(e). Landholding, Sri Lanka

Size of holding (hectares)	Distribution of operational holdings, 1982[a]	
	Holdings percent	Area percent
0–0.4	42.4	8.1
0.4–0.8	21.9	14.2
0.8–1.2	13.6	15.5
1.2–8.0	22.1	62.2

Type of tenure	Tenure of paddy lands Operators	
	Number	Percent
Ande (sharecropping) cultivators	368,511	28.2
Owner cultivators	840,838	64.4
Owner-cum-Ande	82,994	6.4
Landowners using only hired labor	13,021	1.1
Total	1,305,364	

[a]This evidence is for the 'smallholder' sector. Agricultural holdings of more than 8 hectares are considered as 'estates', where at least one single parcel is of 8 hectares or more, and the land is neither paddy nor chena.
Source: *Census of Agriculture*, 1982: smallholding sector. Ministry of Agriculture and Lands (Colombo, 1987).

tenancy agreements. The average size of holdings in the *terai* bordering India is higher than in the hills and mountains, but inequality of ownership is also greater here. In 1972, according to a sample survey of 17 terai districts, 88 percent of households accounted for less than 15 percent of cultivated land while the top 3.4 percent owned nearly 47 percent of the land. Larger landowners also possess and cultivate the best land, while the majority of small peasants depend on additional sources of income from remittances and small businesses.

Agricultural development in South Asia

The governments of South Asia after Independence, and that of Nepal after the overthrow of the Ranas in 1951, faced similar agrarian problems. They needed to increase agricultural output in order to meet food deficits and to supply raw materials, after a lengthy period during which the level of population growth rose while that of agricultural production declined. Gross output had increased, largely as a result of the expansion of irrigation, but yields of six out of eight of the most important foodgrains had declined during the first half of the twentieth century. Although the record for non-food crops was better, rates of growth of yields were mostly lower in the period immediately preceding Independence than they had been earlier in the century. *Per capita* output and the availability of agricultural materials had seriously deteriorated.

The problem of production was accompanied by problems of acute poverty and attempts at agrarian reform assumed a high priority in independent South Asia. They were accompanied by efforts to create new rural institutions, such as cooperatives, and to mobilize participation in development activity through community development and local government with decentralized planning functions. There were investments in irrigation and the expansion of the cultivated area, and in agricultural research to improve the technical base and the skills of cultivators. These efforts, however, have imposed considerable demands on local administrative capacity. Emphasis has shifted back and forth between, on the one hand, institutional reform and concern to alleviate poverty, and, on the other, attempts to increase output and yields through technological innovations even at the cost of strengthening existing inequalities. More generally, development policies have been criticized for being urban-biased. Import-substituting industrialization during the 1950s and 1960s encouraged allocations of public sector resources which resulted in the relative neglect of agriculture with harmful overall consequences. Rural populations have been able neither to impart sufficient demand stimulus to economic growth, nor to supply agricultural products in sufficient quantities. Even after the marked expansion of agricultural output in India from the late 1970s, general economic performance is still affected by fluctuations in agricultural production.

India

From Independence to the end of the Second Five Year Plan (1956–61), Indian agricultural output grew by about 3 percent per annum. Production was increased principally through the expansion of the cultivated area, and this, in turn, was based on investment in irrigation. Irrigation and power development absorbed 26.8 percent of realized plan expenditure under the first Five Year Plan for 1951–56, and it was at this time that substantial projects like the Bhakra-Nangal Dam on the Satlaj were taken up.

Other notable initiatives in agricultural development in the 1950s were in land reform and the creation of new rural institutions. Support within the ruling Congress party for radical land reform and collectivization along Chinese lines was easily outweighed by the landed interests on which the party relied for the mobilization of political support. The first phase of land reform, intended to abolish the zamindari system which was particularly prevalent in eastern India, was effective. Zamindars were responsible for the payment of land revenue for their estates. The amount that had to be paid to the government had been fixed under the terms of the original settlement, and it was left to the zamindars to extract what they could over and above this from the cultivators. Agents at each stage between the actual occupiers of the land and the zamindars added to the total amount extracted from the producers. Absentee landlordism, rackrenting and illegal exactions were also rife. By 1956 various Zamindari Abolition Acts had removed the zamindars and their intermediaries although the latter were allowed to retain large areas of land as farms. Full land rights came to be vested in hereditary occupancy tenants, and the upper layer of these tenants were the main beneficiaries of zamindari abolition. Their power was enhanced; they became important members of the class of dominant peasants vital to Congress' political organization; subsequently, they opposed moves to implement further tenurial reforms and land redistribution.

Very strong arguments exist in favor of redistributive land reforms in this kind of agrarian structure. Although there is not enough cultivable land for all rural people to have a viable holding, it is held that redistribution of land improves equity at the same time as improving the efficiency of cultivation. This is because of the inverse relationship that has often been observed between operational holding size and yield per unit of land, which probably results from the more intensive application of effort on smaller farms, and the closer supervision of labor. Smaller cultivators, if they are able to apply modern inputs in the same way as larger operators, often do as well or even better than them. Redistribution breaks the power of dominant landholders and reduces constraints on increasing productivity. These arguments have been rehearsed many times in India over the past forty years, and legislation imposing an upper ceiling on individual landholdings has been introduced, the definition of the limit varying over time, from state to state, and according to the quality of the land. This legislation has existed for more than 25 years, yet very little land has actually been redistributed. The reasons for the non-implementation of land reforms lie in the power of dominant landholders who have been able to weaken legislation as it has passed through state legislatures and evade its provisions by registering their land in the names of different family members or by making transfers to dummy purchasers. Perhaps the best that can be said for land reforms over much of India is that they have weakened incentives to maintain very large landholdings. Kerala represents the main possible exception: here land reforms in 1969 eliminated tenants as a class and led to the redistribution of over 35 percent of the net sown area in the State, but again the principal beneficiaries in the long run have been rich peasants.

Zamindari abolition did not remove the problem of sharecropping. This form of tenure can be shown to be economically efficient but it has also been associated with gross exploitation. In eastern India, it has been accompanied by backward agricultural practices where tenants are unable to invest in improved technology, and landlords are not apparently inclined to do so because of successful appropriation of surpluses from indebted cultivators. The extent of land under this form of tenure has always been difficult to determine, because it is easily concealed, but in the 1950s it formed probably at least a quarter of cultivable land and it still lies in the region of 20 percent. The 1951 central government guidelines to the states on land reform legislation included provision for security of tenure and the reduction of rents by setting upper limits. However, the legislation was often anticipated by widespread eviction of tenants. The relatively weak position of sharecropping tenants also enabled dominant landlords to evade legal provisions. This has been the case even in West Bengal where the Communist-led state government gave very high priority to a renewed program of tenancy reform in the late 1970s.

The dominant peasantry also derived most benefit from the institutional innovations of the 1950s, which were supposed to complement land reforms and encourage higher productivity. These included the expansion of agricultural credit cooperatives; programs of community development initiated in 1952, and implemented with the assistance of small teams of officers based in 'blocks' covering one hundred or so villages; and the establishment of local government bodies called *panchayati raj* which were later drawn together in a tiered system. The presidents of village *panchayats* (councils) constituted another council at the 'block' level whose responsibility was to guide 'block' staff according to local needs and opportunities. Finally 'Block Councils' elected or delegated members to serve on district councils. The object of all these measures was to encourage self-help and participation and to promote development on a broad front, encompassing the modernization of agriculture, improved credit, improvements in health, water supplies and literacy.

For all the worthiness of their intentions, these initiatives failed to achieve their objectives. Cooperatives generally became dominated by landlords and rich peasants; community development often amounted to little more than a program of local spending on school buildings, panchayat buildings and sometimes village roads; the system of panchayati raj was tailor-made to provide the means for the political expression of dominant peasant power. The principles of cooperation, community development, local self-government and decentralized planning challenged the existing social order, but supplied no means of overturning it in the context of the unreformed agrarian structure.

At the same time insufficient resources were devoted to raising agricultural production especially during the Second Five Year Plan, and key staff such as village level workers (VLWs) were overburdened with commitments. Under these circumstances and in a period of indifferent monsoons, the Plan's targets became elusive. The 1960s saw a 'new strategy' to increase the rate of growth of agriculture based on the introduction of good seeds and fertilizer, credit facilities and a special team of workers to teach improved methods in particular areas selected for their favorable conditions. Progress, it was hoped, would then spread into the wider community. Such reasoning, however, seemed optimistic even at the time given that the selected districts were relatively well endowed with irrigation and therefore the riskiness of new methods would be higher elsewhere. But these aims gave birth to the Intensive Agricultural District Programme (IADP) inaugurated in 1960–61 and extended as the Intensive Agricultural Area Programme (IAAP) after 1964–65. The arrival in 1965 of new high yielding varieties of wheat and rice, developed at international research institutes in Mexico and the Philippines, respectively, fitted neatly into India's new approach. The 'high yielding varieties' program, launched in 1966, introduced the 'green revolution' to India, although we should not underestimate the contributions made by local, Indian agricultural research.

Assessment of India's 'green revolution' is subject to controversy. Some have disputed the extent to which it has taken place at all, pointing out that the rate of growth of agricultural output in the period after 1965–66 has been lower than in the 1950s; that take-up of the modern varieties has been very patchy; and that real costs of production per unit output have risen. Others refer to the exacerbation of rural poverty and the displacement of labor, to the harmful ecological effects of reduced diversity, to the declining cultivation of pulses and to increased dependence upon agricultural agrochemicals. Yet, the fact remains that the production of foodgrains has increased from 73 million tonnes in 1965–66 to 154 million tonnes in 1984–85, and that India has become self-sufficient in food.

Initially, the 'green revolution' was largely confined to wheat in the northwestern states of the Panjab, Haryana and western Uttar Pradesh where dramatic increases in production were achieved in the later 1960s and early 1970s. This success was due to a variety of factors including the suitability of the early high yielding varieties of wheat, the consolidation of landholdings which came about as a result of reorganization following Partition, and the quality of local irrigation. The 'green revolution' in rice has been less dramatic and took much longer to get under way. By 1976–77, high yielding varieties covered only 25 percent of the rice area in contrast to 70 percent of the wheat acreage. Success in rice so far has been in states where cultivation is most dependent upon irrigation and where more precise control of water, so important for high yielding varieties, is possible. Andhra Pradesh and Tamil Nadu had 57 and 92 percent, respectively, of their total rice areas under high yielding varieties by 1976–77. By contrast, in regions where the monsoon usually supports rice without irrigation, the incidence of high yielding varieties is much lower; less than 20 percent in Bihar, Assam and Orissa and 25–30 percent in West Bengal, Madhya Pradesh and Kerala. These circumstances, together with the absence of any major 'breakthroughs' in the technology of drygrain cultivation (at least until recent developments in sorghum) have encouraged regional differentiation. Irrigated areas in the great river basins such as those of the Indus and Ganges in the north and the Godavari and Kaveri in the south, together with areas assured of rainfall at the foothills of the Himalayas, in the Assam valley and western coastal plains, recorded more than 5 percent per annum growth in their agricultural production between 1962 and 1973. At the other end of the scale, 25 percent of districts located mostly in the regions of the central plateau and around its fringes experienced a decline in agricultural production.

The diversity of agro-climatic and soil conditions requires a considerable range of improved varieties and whole farming system practices. The research system needed to cope with this task is being constructed but suitable high yielding varieties of rainfed rice and of dryland grains have yet to be produced, although there are welcome signs of progress in the northeastern states of India. Meanwhile, new problems have arisen where the 'green revolution' has been successful. Where a particular variety has spread over a wide area, such as the rice type IR 20 in northern Tamil Nadu, the incidence of pest infestation and expenditure on increasingly ineffective plant protection chemicals have risen. Fertilizer requirements may also go up without equivalent increases in yields. In areas where rice is virtually a monoculture, the profitability of cultivation is vulnerable to acute cost squeezes, generating problems over the repayment of loans. The expansion of cheap credit from official credit institutions, designed to supplant private moneylenders, has undoubtedly been an important factor in accelerating agricultural development

Washing the village tractor in Gujranwala district, Panjab (Pakistan).

but it has been heavily subsidized by the state.

In the early 1970s the 'green revolution' was expected to cause social conflict: by the eviction of tenants once landowners were encouraged to invest in production; by its polarizing effects as larger cultivators took advantage of their ability to make use of new inputs; and by changes in the organization of labor in general and of harvest payments in particular. This prognosis, however, was exaggerated. Small operators, admittedly at a disadvantage, have been able to adopt high yielding varieties and increase their incomes, although they still remain close to or below the poverty line. There is also some evidence of benefits accruing to agricultural labor as labor requirements have increased, and real wages have risen, but this latter development depends heavily on the availability of employment outside agriculture. There is no doubt as well that the 'green

revolution' has enhanced the power of the dominant peasantry, especially in the northwest where it has been most successful. Here, mechanization (indicated by the number of tractors per unit area) is far more advanced than elsewhere. There is a good deal of 'reverse tenancy' where smallholders lease out their land to rich farmers, and a new kind of employment of permanent labor has emerged. 'Western-style' capitalist farming is extensive.

Since the mid-1960s, central government has played an increasingly active part in controlling the prices of essential commodities as part of its responsibility for food distribution. The Agricultural Prices Commission fixes desirable wholesale price levels. Its decisions are based on production costs, input prices and trends in the prices of basic non-agricultural goods. In practice, prices are fixed at the discretion of Chief Ministers, often at levels higher than those recommended by the central government. Even so, the overall impact of these decisions on open market prices depends on the proportion which the government decides to procure for 'fair price distribution'.

It is commonly held that the terms of trade between the agricultural and non-agricultural sectors have moved over time towards agriculture. This is most obvious in wheat regions and in areas of long-commercialized irrigated crops, less obvious in rice regions and least obvious in areas of rainfed agriculture. Certain small producers may not benefit from this long-term trend if their marketing is constrained by local mercantile monopolies. The agricultural marketing system is extremely complex, varying by region and by crop from the reasonably efficient and competitive to quite the reverse. Processing agricultural products, in practice bound up with trading, also embraces technology from the primitive to the modern. Certain regions, in particular the northwest and West Bengal, have large enclaves of modern technology which is often state-subsidized.

The strategy for agricultural development over the last twenty years has, therefore, focused on increasing production by technological transformation. The institutional innovations of the 1950s generally remain in place. Land reforms are still on the statute books but now considerations of equity have been given second place in fact, if not in the rhetoric of politics and planning. High levels of rural poverty continue despite the period of modestly good agricultural performance. For instance, measuring poverty by the consumption of food, the rural poor as a proportion of the total population rose from 52 percent in 1960–61 to 70 percent in 1977. Fresh evidence in recent years suggests that the proportion is no longer increasing, but the absolute numbers involved remains remarkably high.

The objective of alleviating rural poverty has featured prominently in the Fifth, Sixth and Seventh Five Year Plans. Small farmers, under the 'Integrated Rural Development Programs' have received subsidized credit for the purchase of productive assets such as milch cows, sheep, bullocks and carts. These efforts are important, but resources devoted to them are small in comparison with the level of need, and show a consistent tendency to 'trickle up' as they are siphoned off by those outside the targeted groups. Rural employment and public works schemes suffer from the same weaknesses, although an exception might be made for Maharashtra's massive Employment Guarantee Scheme which provides a guarantee of employment or benefit for all who register themselves for work.

The balance sheet of agricultural development in India suggests that overall performance has been creditable, particularly in the Sixth Plan period between 1981 and 1985. However, productivity remains low by comparison with countries in East and Southeast Asia. Some evidence suggests that foodgrain consumption per head is actually declining. The tasks facing agricultural research and the spreading and application of the results remains vast. Cultivators and researchers need to communicate more so that research becomes more responsive to cultivators' needs and knowledge. To some extent this has been recognized in the Training and Visit system, which was introduced in India with World Bank assistance from the late 1970s and which is to be extended in the late 1980s. But the emphasis is still on the quicker 'downwards' transfer of technology to farmers. The expansion of irrigation and especially greater efficiency in water management in existing systems remain of critical importance. Nevertheless, the outstanding question is still whether, without reform of the agrarian structure, India can achieve the kind of agricultural performance which has been seen in East Asia.

Pakistan

Many of the problems of Indian agriculture apply to agriculture in Pakistan: a highly uneven distribution of landownership, the small size of most cultivation units, widespread tenancy. Agrarian reform has had an important place in Pakistan's agricultural policy with legislation intended to regulate tenurial conditions introduced in the 1950s. Further measures were introduced in 1972, 1976 and 1977. Tenancy regulations, however, left many loopholes and, instead of providing greater security led to the eviction of tenants on a large scale in Sind and the Panjab. Legislation in 1959 introduced limits on land ownership 'in order to break concentrations of land and wealth, to narrow income inequalities and to encourage more intensive land use and productive investment'. The ceilings of 202 hectares of irrigated land and 495 hectares of unirrigated land were reduced in Bhutto's reforms of 1972, and reduced again in 1977 to 40.6 hectares and 81 hectares, respectively. The impact of these measures is difficult to assess on account of the lack of agricultural census data after 1972. To the extent that the law-enforcing agencies are biased in favor of landed interests, the legal strengthening of the position of tenants has been ineffective. Tenancy has been reduced but the amounts of land made available for redistribution have been very limited: the area redistributed during the Bhutto period was only 2.5 percent of the total farm area. The Bhutto reforms were intended, anyway, to eradicate 'feudalism' and replace it with an agriculture organized around private property and material incentives, not to effect radical structural changes. Very low ceilings would have discouraged the class of agrarian entrepreneurs on whom it was felt that the future of Pakistan's agriculture depended. The effects of a wide range of agricultural policies, therefore, have been to enhance the position of rich farmers and big landowners.

Agricultural production stagnated in the 1950s and a food deficit emerged, prompting planners to give more serious attention to the needs of agriculture. The Second Five Year Plan during the early 1960s achieved a breakthrough when the agricultural growth rate increased to 3.8 percent from the meager 1.8 percent *per annum* of the late 1950s. This shift was achieved mainly as a result of the expansion of irrigation which also supplied the base for Pakistan's 'green revolution' between 1964–69. Encouraged by subsidies on inputs and price incentives, the growth rate increased again to 6 percent *per annum* during the Third Plan period (1965–70). But it fell back to 1.9 percent between 1970 and 1978, apparently because of the inadequate development of agricultural support services. Despite the greater availability of fertilizers, higher yielding seed varieties and water, the agricultural sector experienced diminishing returns because insufficient attention had been paid to the efficiency of their use. Heavy investments were made in big irrigation projects like Tarbela, but additional water supplies were not utilized in the most effective manner: increased water availability on farms far exceeded increases in irrigated area. It was not until the late 1970s that the agricultural growth rate shifted upwards again because of favorable weather conditions, better distribution of inputs and more favorable price incentives. In the 1980s, agricultural production has grown by about 4 percent per annum. The production of wheat, the staple food crop, rose by 236 percent between 1950–55 and 1979–80, more the result of yield than increased acreage. Of the total rice area, 43 percent was under high yielding varieties in the late 1970s.

Table 19. South Asian agriculture: some basic indices

	Bangladesh			Bhutan			India		
	1950–51	1983–84	% change	1974	1984	% change	1950–51	1977–78	% change
Population (m)	42	90	114	1.13	1.4	24	361	684	89
Net sown area (million hectares)	8.3	8.7	5	n.a.	n.a.	n.a.	119	142	20
Total cropped area (million hectares, except where shown otherwise)	10.6	13.3	25	n.a.	96,000 ha	—	132	172	30
Cropping intensity (%)[a]	128	153	20	n.a.	n.a.	—	111	120	8
Gross area irrigated (million hectares)	0.3	1.9	533	n.a.	n.a.	—	23	46	100
Gross area irrigated, as percentage of total cropped area	2.8	14.3	411	—	—	—	17	27	59
Index no. of area under cereals	100	134	34	100	121	—	100	133	33
Index no. of cereals production	100	205	105	100	124	—	100	270	170

	Maldives			Nepal			Pakistan			Sri Lanka		
	1974	1984	% change	1950–51	1977–78	% change	1950–51	1983–84	% change	1950–51	1977–78	% change
Population (m)	0.13	0.17	34	8.1	14.2	75	34	84	148	7.7	14.6	90
Net sown area (million hectares)	n.a.	n.a.	—	1.6	2.3	43	11.6	15.7	35	n.a.	n.a.	—
Total cropped area (million hectares, except where shown otherwise)	3,000 ha	3,000 ha	0	2.0	2.7	35	12.9	20.1	56	0.54	1.1	94
Cropping intensity (%)[a]	n.a.	n.a.	—	125	117	−6	111	128	15	n.a.	n.a.	—
Gross area irrigated (million hectares)	n.a.	n.a.	—	n.a.	n.a.	—	n.a.	15.3	—	0.17	0.5	202
Gross area irrigated, as percentage of total cropped area	—	—	—	—	20	—	n.a.	75	—	31	48	55
Index no. of area under cereals	n.a.	n.a.	—	100	160	60	100	153	53	100	210	110
Index no. of cereals production	100 (1974–76)	119	—	100	117	17	100	263	163	100	625	525

[a]100% = single crop. 111% = 100 acres + 11% cropped the second time in one year.
Source: B. L. C. Johnson, *Development in South Asia* (Harmondsworth, 1983); *Statistical Abstract India* 1984; *Pakistan Statistical Yearbook* 1986; *Statistical Yearbook of Bangladesh* 1986; *UN Statistical Yearbook of Asia and the Pacific* 1985.

Yield and production increases in wheat and rice have been lower than in neighboring northwest India. The production trends of cotton, the staple cash crop and vital foreign exchange earner, have been erratic, although a record crop was achieved in 1985.

Substantial subsidies have been allocated to food and agricultural inputs, and, as in India, most of the benefits have accrued to large farmers. Government policy has also encouraged imports of farm machinery, mainly tractors and threshers, and mostly to the Panjab. The desirability of farm mechanization and its impact on both productivity and the displacement of labor is hotly debated. Access to technology, though not entirely denied to farmers with small landholdings, has clearly been skewed in favor of farmers owning more than 5 hectares of land. In 1972, 2.7 percent of farmers in the 20–60 hectare group held 37.5 percent of all the tractors in the country, while 68 percent of farms with less than 5 hectares held only 9 percent. Ownership of tubewells is more balanced but big farmers again have the greatest share. Disparities in income and wealth among different strata of the rural population have widened, as have regional disparities.

Pakistan, like India, has sought to tackle problems of rural poverty through community programs and recently by means of 'integrated rural development'. The Village Agricultural and Industrial Development Program, begun in 1953, was intended to improve social and economic conditions through community development. Discontinued in 1962 on the grounds that adequate local leadership was lacking, it was succeeded by the Rural Works Program, which, backed by supplies of foodstuffs under USA PL480 Program, aimed to increase employment by creating work opportunities in local infrastructure projects. Considered fairly successful in terms of physical achievements in the late 1960s, this was followed by the Integrated Rural Development Program of 1972–77, designed to improve the social and economic status of farmers of both small and medium acreage through a package of inputs and guidance, and popular participation in the system of rural administration. The same objectives and methods were adopted in the Rural Development Strategy of the Fifth Plan (1978–83). But none of these programs has received more than meager funding; the Rural Works Program's 4.5 percent of public sector development expenditure in 1965–70 being the largest share. The benefits conferred have been again appropriated largely by medium and large acreage farmers. Interventions of this type have little prospect of success in the context of the existing agrarian structure.

Bangladesh

Agricultural policy in Bangladesh has put 'production first' with limited success. Between 1947–48 and 1982–83, the rice area, which constitutes 80 percent of the gross cultivated area, increased by 39 percent, mainly as a result of the expansion of *aus* and *boro* (see

Table 15) cultivation. Production over this period increased by 118 percent. The 'green revolution' has so far only had a limited impact in Bangladesh because the principal high yielding varieties of rice are not suited to the flood conditions of the main rice crop. High yielding varieties occupied 25 percent of the total rice area in 1982–83, but the largest share of them were cultivated in the *boro* (see Table 15) season when 75 percent of the area was under these varieties. Another recent significant development has been the small but fast increasing contribution to national foodgrain supplies made by rabi wheat, which has come about with the spread of tubewells in northern Bangladesh. Production of wheat expanded tenfold between 1970–71 and 1982–83, by which time 96 percent of the wheat acreage was under high yielding varieties.

These developments have mainly benefitted middle and rich peasants. Bangladesh's Integrated Rural Development Programs, involving a two-tier system of cooperatives at village and *thana* (district) level, have generally proved inadequate in the absence of structural reforms. Cooperatives are dominated by richer peasants. Integrated Rural Development Programs have helped to increase agricultural production in selected areas and mainly by richer peasants. Government policy has achieved some increases in production but in a way that has reinforced the power of rich peasants. The agricultural sector has been unable to match increases in population, and the majority of the rural population has come to be caught in the 'Below Poverty Level Equilibrium Trap'. In 1963–64, 5 percent of the rural population were unable to obtain 80 percent of the recommended daily calorie intake. By 1975, this proportion had increased to more than 40 percent, by which time 80 percent of households were estimated to be below the official poverty line. Demographic pressure contributed to the declining average size of landholdings, and both landlessness and tenancy have increased. Bangladesh's rural population is extremely vulnerable to food crises, and a repetition of the famine of 1975 was narrowly averted in 1984 only by prompt imports of food stocks. At the same time, food imports and food aid, together with a policy of procurement at low prices has depressed prices paid to producers. In the 1970s, the internal terms of trade moved against agriculture, the availability of institutional credit was low, and, in practice if not in rhetoric, agriculture was neglected in the allocation of public sector investment.

It is in this context that several non-governmental organizations (such as the Bangladesh Rural Advancement Committee and PRO-SHIKA) have made notable efforts to organize landless men and women. The Grameen Bank has quite successfully pioneered the lending of money for production to those without assets. But these initiatives run counter to the existing power structure and confront enormous obstacles.

Sri Lanka

Sri Lanka has had a food deficit from before the time of British rule. The costs of food imports (equivalent to almost half of all foreign exchange earnings in the early 1970s) on the one hand, and the value of exports of plantation crops on the other, have determined the general state of the economy.

The widespread incidence of ande or sharecropping tenure in Sri Lanka has been considered the fundamental constraint on increasing the country's foodgrain output. Hence, tenurial reforms were implemented in the Paddy Lands Act of 1958. This legislation was intended to give security of tenure and fix rents but, like tenurial reform in other parts of South Asia, it was ineffective, and was so here because the relations between landowners and tenants have generally been embedded in social ties of kinship and patronage. Legislation required tenants to establish their rights in law in a context in which landed interests are powerful. The Paddy Lands Act also set up local Cultivation Committees, elected from among all registered operators of paddy fields in a particular area. The objective was to encourage participation and cooperation in the management of land and water, with inputs and technical facilities being supplied by the new Department of Agrarian Services. These committees were subject to control by local bosses, or had only nominal existence, but the beginning of an infrastructure to service agriculture was established. Redistributive land reforms were not undertaken until the Land Reforms Law in 1972, but the ceiling of 10 hectares adopted with regard to paddy lands meant that very little was affected. In the main, the impact of this piece of legislation was restricted to plantations.

All the same, it is doubtful whether sharecropping tenure has actually been the crucial constraint on paddy production. There is evidence, for instance, which shows that performance is sometimes higher on tenanted lands. More significant have been inefficient technical practices on owner-cultivated and tenanted land, especially the broadcasting of paddy rather than transplanting, and cultivation delays which contribute to the wasteful use of irrigation water so that double cropping has been less extensive than it could have been. Untimely cultivation results from shortages of draught power, only partly relieved by the impact of mechanization; from insufficient labor during peak periods; and from competition between the demands of paddy cultivation and those of *chena* (see Table 15) or rainfed, shifting cultivation. Factors such as the market value of some chena crops and the importance of rainfed food products in local diets, may cause cultivators to give them precedence, and this contributes to the economic inefficiency of Sri Lanka's irrigated settlement schemes in the dry zone. Irrigated settlements remain central to government policy, and the extension of the cultivated area, which has doubled since Independence, has contributed to increasing food production, although the settlement

Table 20. Sri Lanka, index numbers of agricultural production (volume 1962 = 100)

	Coconut	Paddy	Rubber	Tea	Overall
1968	90.3	137.4	142.9	106.1	117.2
1974	79.5	160	126.9	96.3	122.9
1981	87.9	222.6	119.1	99.2	144.2
1984	106.9 (est.)	n.a.	n.a.	101.0	n.a.

Source: *Statistical Abstract of the Democratic Socialist Republic of Sri Lanka* 1982; Lloyds Bank Report 1986.

schemes have been extremely costly. Benefit–cost analyses of the Gal Oya Scheme, the largest until the Mahaweli Development Scheme, showed a negative rate of return. In spite of such inefficiency, successive governments have persisted with this policy for social and political reasons, as well as to reduce food deficits.

For all these difficulties, Sri Lanka has achieved much higher rates of growth of cereal output than other South Asian countries. Yield levels are also higher. An excellent local research system produced a successful generation of improved rice varieties well in advance of the 'green revolution': three-quarters of the rice area was under the local improved variety H4 by 1970. It has continued to supply modern varieties which perform better than those produced by the international agricultural research system. The adoption of these varieties has been encouraged by a policy of subsidizing inputs and credit, rather than by price incentives. By 1979–80, more than 80 percent of the paddy sown was improved varieties, mainly in the *maha* (see Table 15) season when irrigation is most reliable. Yields of the irrigated maha crop are more than double those achieved at the time of Independence.

A tea factory in Sri Lanka. A large proportion of the country's agriculture is devoted to plantation crops for the world market.

The Land Reform Law of 1972 and the Land Reform Amendment Law of 1975 led to the resumption of lands held by public companies and of private landholdings in excess of 50 acres which represented 62 percent of the tea area, 39 percent of the rubber area and 11 percent of the coconut lands. The bigger estates came under the management of state organizations, leaving one fifth of the tea production and one third of the rubber production in the hands of smallholders, and the rest in small private estates. Production on these small units is less efficient than on larger estates but the plantation industry as a whole has for long failed to improve production efficiency. In addition, Sri Lanka's teas have been outflanked by lower cost, low-quality tea, and, consequently, the country's share of the world market has fallen. Tea still accounts for the largest share of the total value of exports (30–40 percent) and the very high world price for tea in 1984 enabled Sri Lanka to reduce its trade deficit by two-thirds. But production has been disappointing and a five year program of reinvestment in tea plantations has been initiated. Rubber is the second most important export. The area under rubber has fallen since Independence but production has increased by replanting with higher yielding clones. Coconut production has suffered from a lack of investment, although there was a sharp increase in output in 1985 after a long period of decline.

Nepal

The agricultural economy of Nepal is characterized by great disparity in landholdings: absentee ownership; high rentals; a system of sharecropping which inhibits productivity; inadequate knowledge of modern production technology and ineffective extension services; lack of timely availability of external inputs and scarcity of institutional credit for tenants and small farmers. Tenancy reforms in 1955 were intended to fix rents and give security, and the 1964 Land Reforms Act reinforced these principles, abolished Zamindari tenure and set ceilings on ownership of holdings. These reforms have had some impact on tenancy conditions but no tangible effect on the uneven distribution of landholdings. Less than one percent of the cultivated area was acquired for redistribution.

Agricultural production has been increased only marginally, and the cropping intensity remains low. The main cereal crops of rice, maize and wheat together account for 86 percent of the total cropped area. Their yields are low and have been declining for the last twenty years. Stagnation in agriculture accompanied by a rapid rise in population has brought about a decrease in *per capita* availability of foodgrains during the last decade. There have been serious food shortages. Population growth has resulted in the use of marginal lands, including areas of low fertility, poor soil types and unfavorable slopes. Forest areas have been denuded; trees and brushwood exploited; pastures have been overgrazed also. These practices have removed vegetation from fragile slopes, accelerating the process of soil erosion.

This picture of agrarian crisis exists despite the high priority that has been given to agriculture in Nepalese development planning. Most planned agricultural development has emphasized infrastructure, but there has also been a trend toward decentralization of rural development activities through the system of non-party elected panchayats, now under the overall charge of the Ministry of Panchayats and Local Development created in 1981. A number of large Integrated Rural Development Programs, financed with the assistance of various foreign donors, have been undertaken but these have stretched Nepal's bureaucratic capacity. There has been too much emphasis on hardware (buildings, infrastructure, vehicles) and not enough attention paid to sustaining these efforts from local resources after project assistance is terminated. The Asian Development Bank in a report of 1982 emphasized Nepal's need for 'a well-defined operational strategy for agricultural development' independent of particular donors.

Bhutan

Bhutan has a range of crops similar to those of Nepal: rice, maize, wheat and potatoes are the main crops, with some barley, buckwheat and millets. A little jute is grown and cardamom is an important foreign exchange earner. The country is far from achieving the goal of self-sufficiency in food laid down in the National Plan, and it currently imports 15,000–25,000 tons of rice every year. Growth in agricultural production has been slow. Only 9 percent of the available land is under cultivation and further increases in food production will be predicated on the more efficient use of irrigation facilities and improvement in farm practices, now being encouraged under recently introduced agricultural credit schemes.

Maldives

With only 3000 hectares of arable land, agriculture is of a very marginal significance in the Maldives. Rice, sugar and wheat flour figure prominently among the islands' imports. A recent FAO report has argued, however, that 70 percent of food needs could be met by a single crop of maize in the north and sweet potato in the south if grown on half of the cultivable area. But self-sufficiency in food is unlikely and transport difficulties inhibit exploitation of the total potential. Efforts have been made to improve coconut, yam, maize and other crops, and to produce locally some of the fruit and vegetables currently imported from Sri Lanka to service the tourist industry.

Growth and fluctuations in agricultural output since Independence

The output of Indian foodgrains is thought to have declined during the century before Independence. Since then, it has kept pace with population increase, a performance at par with that of China. Of the foodgrains, the production of millets and pulses has grown least rapidly. Indeed, millet production has stagnated everywhere except India, while more rapid rates of growth in the production of pulses have only been achieved in Sri Lanka, Nepal and Bhutan where the initial starting points were very low. Bhutan has witnessed a trend toward the replacement of wheat and rice by maize. Wheat production has registered substantial growth in Bangladesh, Nepal and India, the last all the more impressive because production was already substantial at Independence. Rice production has been less

spectacular although the records of Sri Lanka and Nepal are important exceptions. Roots and tubers have experienced an above-average rate of expansion throughout the subcontinent, despite their relative unimportance in terms of agricultural research. With respect to commercial crops, cotton has expanded most, especially in India and Pakistan, while tobacco, sugarcane and groundnuts have only increased production slowly. Plantation crops have also had a chequered recent history. Growth rates of coffee have been highest in Sri Lanka, while those of tea and rubber highest in Bangladesh and India, respectively.

Most of the gains derived from 'green revolution' technology had accrued by 1976. Analyses of growth fluctuations from 1954 to 1980 (omitting the distorting drought years of 1965–67) show that, while the growth rate of wheat has increased since the 'green revolution'

Rice fields in the Paro valley, Bhutan.

Paddy drying in Bihar.

and its instability of output has declined, the growth rate of rice has not increased and production has become more unstable. Similarly, the growth rate of pulses has been negative and combined with increasing instability. Given the lack of evidence for acceleration of growth rates either for cereals or for foodgrains as a whole, gains from wheat production may have been offset by the performance of rice, millets and pulses. Some commentators have attributed increasing instability in production not to specific genotype-environment interactions of high yielding varieties but to irregularities in supplies of fertilizers, pesticides, irrigation and electricity. In reply, others have argued that high yielding varieties achieve their yield potential only with complementary inputs: high yielding varieties cannot be considered in isolation from their institutional setting, and cultivators are thus more vulnerable to market vagaries.

Outlook

With little unused land and ratios of people to land which are already very high, although not as high as in East Asia, the South Asian countries will have to go on seeking increases in output from higher productivity and greater cropping intensity per unit of arable land, water, forest and energy. The achievement of these objectives and of the further goal of improving the livelihoods of the mass of rural people, would be assisted by structural reforms in agriculture, but these do not seem likely to be implemented in the foreseeable future. Reliance will be placed on technical solutions. Fortunately, fertilizer use is still low relative to land, and the marginal productivity of increased fertilizer use is believed to be high given that adequate supplies both of water and of modern seed varieties are available. The prospects for the continuing development of higher yielding seeds seem better in Asia generally than in Africa or in Latin America, in part because of the existence of strong national research systems. The potential for improved use of water is also high, and rests with better management and coordination of existing large and medium scale irrigation projects and a systematic extension of small ones, including those based on the use of groundwater. Alongside these developments there is an urgent need for more diversified employment opportunities, especially in rural areas, in order that rural livelihoods as well as rural production may be improved.

BH and JH

Further reading

V. Ahmed and R. Amjad, *The Management of Pakistan's Economy 1947–1982* (Karachi, 1984)

T. Bayliss Smith and S. Wanmali, Eds, *Understanding Green Revolutions* (Cambridge, 1984)

B. Chattopadhyay and P. Spitz, Eds, *Food Systems and Society in India: Selected Readings* (Geneva, 1987)

Indian Council of Social Science Research, *Alternatives in Agricultural Development* (Delhi, 1979)

B. L. C. Johnson, *South Asia* (London, 1981)

M. M. Khan, *Underdevelopment and Agrarian Structure in Pakistan* (Boulder, Co., 1981)

M. P. Moore, *The State and Peasant Politics in Sri Lanka* (Cambridge, 1985)

U. Patnaik, *The Agrarian Question and the Development of Capitalism in India* (Delhi, 1986)

K. W. Raj, N. Bhattacharya, S. Guha and S. Padhi, Eds, *Essays on the Commercialisation of Indian Agriculture* (Bombay, 1985)

J. E. Schwartzberg, Ed., *A Historical Atlas of South Asia* (Chicago, 1978)

O. H. K. Spate and B. H. Farmer, *India and Pakistan: A General and Regional Geography* (London, 1957)

S. de Vylder, *Agriculture in Chains. Bangladesh: A Case Study in Contradictions and Constraints* (London, 1982)

Energy and mineral resources

The vast majority of the peoples of South Asia live and work in conditions which may be described as pre-industrial. Families living within sight of a nuclear power station still collect cow dung to pat into cakes and dry in the sun for use as domestic cooking fuel. Although the urban housewife may now buy her rice, machine-husked and polished, in a supermarket, her country cousin still pounds the day's needs using a pestle and mortar. Thus, the ways of life and levels of technology to be found in the region range from medieval to ultra-modern. It is true that few are not touched at some point in their daily lives by sophisticated modern technology, but for the most part the industrial revolution has yet to reach them. In India 'living energy', human and animal power, is estimated to account for 39 percent of all energy consumed. The same is probably true for other countries in the region; if Sri Lanka has a slightly lower figure, Nepal and Bhutan would certainly show a higher one. Crops are planted by hand, reaped using sickles, and threshed and winnowed using some form of muscle power. It is common in Bangladesh to see pairs of men swinging baskets on ropes to irrigate their fields, a task more frequently performed in India and Pakistan by livestock harnessed to Persian wheels to raise water from wells or irrigation channels. Ploughs are generally drawn by bullocks, buffaloes and camels. Only the most advanced and prosperous farmers can afford to own or to hire tractors.

Outside agriculture, the contribution of human labor cannot be exaggerated: one will see teams of men and women bearing on their heads baskets of earth at a dam site, or of concrete aggregate for a multistorey building; workers will be crushing road metal with hammers or towing country craft upstream against the current. People everywhere strain under loads of firewood or fodder.

For the very poor there is no choice but to carry it themselves. In cities, porters haul heavy barrows while their brothers pedal cycle-rickshaws. Almost every domestic animal is enlisted in the task of carrying loads or pulling carts. In the forests of India, Bangladesh, Nepal and Sri Lanka, elephants have proved adept toilers in the timber industry, while even sheep on their seasonal migrations from the Himalayas to the plains carry little back-packs of salt or rare herbs.

Increasingly, however, pre-modern village communities are being penetrated by modern forms of inanimate energy. Kerosene led the way, replacing traditional vegetable oils for lighting the home or the shop. Now rural electrification is speeding the process of change, bringing light for those who can afford it, and energy for irrigation pumps, flour and rice mills and small industries. Nevertheless, most rural housewives and small-scale producers of agricultural products still depend on firewood, charcoal or cow dung for

Cow dung is an important source of fuel. Here cow dung cakes dry in a village in Gujrat district, Panjab (Pakistan). The handprints of the women who made the cakes are clearly to be seen.

Table 21. Production of fuelwood and bagasse, 1984

	Fuelwood ('000 cubic meters)	Bagasse ('000 tonnes)
Bangladesh	25,600	2,530
Bhutan	2,946	—
India	218,866	21,628
Maldives	—	—
Nepal	14,875	57
Pakistan	19,388	3,782
Sri Lanka	8,000	73

Source: *United Nations Energy Statistics Yearbook* 1986.

fuel. Another valuable source of energy is bagasse, the crushed sugarcane residue used by farmers to convert cane juice to *gur*.

For the rural family, the collection of firewood has become more difficult. Populations are everywhere growing while forest resources diminish under the relentless pressure of woodcutters, graziers who lop branches for their flocks, and large-scale exploiters of timber. Governments are faced with the problem of conserving precious forests while at the same time meeting the energy needs of their people. In recent years, more positive policies have begun to try and restore the ecological balance. Community forest programs aim to persuade villagers that conservative, sustained yield utilization of their traditional woodland resources must and can be achieved. In Nepal, the situation is particularly aggravated by that country's heavy reliance on forestry as a source of revenue in the past. In the 1950s forests may have covered 60 percent of Nepal; by the 1980s,

the figure was only 30 percent. Deforestation here has also led to the loss of agricultural land through landslides, accelerated soil erosion on steep slopes and the sedimentation of lowland fields. Such problems are shared with India and Pakistan in their Himalayan and sub-montane regions. Chronic over-cutting of forests also takes place in Bangladesh and Sri Lanka.

The use of animal dung to generate methane gas for domestic use as well as to produce nitrogenous liquid manure has been recognized, but the problem remains of designing and developing bio-gas generating plants appropriate in scale and cost to the small farmer household. All the same, India has gone furthest in stimulating interest in this area of energy generation. Family-sized bio-gas plants numbered almost half a million in 1985. Over one hundred larger plants using community sewage were also in use. Bangladesh is promoting five thousand demonstration bio-gas plants under its Third Five Year Plan, and Pakistan already has four thousand units.

The direct use of water power to drive the wheels of flour mills can still be found in Himalayan valleys. Wind power, however, does not seem to have ever been exploited to any great extent. This has been largely for climatic reasons since South Asia experiences light winds and calms for several months of the year. Some potential may exist seasonally in the coastal tracts of Pakistan where houses are built with structures on the roof fixed to funnel the southwest monsoon breezes to lessen the stifling heat inside. On the other hand, the application of the solar-voltaic cell to energizing irrigation pumps does have considerable potential in the region where there is abundant sunshine for much of the year. India again leads the way in this field; but, as with bio-gas, the problem is to design a product affordable and maintainable by a society with limited technological back-up.

Conventional commercial energy resources

Geology, physiography and climate have endowed South Asia with a wide range of energy and mineral resources, but political geography has shared them very unevenly among the countries of the region. India and Pakistan exploit reserves of coal and petroleum. They both have natural gas, as does Bangladesh. Some day Nepal may find natural gas as well, but the prospects of Sri Lanka, Bhutan or the Maldives discovering fossil fuels are minimal. In all countries, except the Maldives, hydro-electricity makes an important contribution to power generation. But, although hydro-electric power is a renewable resource, in many parts of South Asia it cannot be exploited without considerable social and environmental costs. Enforced movement of large numbers of settlers, often tribal peoples, has been a feature of development in India, Bangladesh and Sri Lanka, and the everwidening search for new sources of power has encouraged incentives to be taken in nuclear energy, particularly in India where the nuclear program is most advanced.

Table 22. Consumption of commercial energy by primary sources in '000 tonnes of coal equivalent and kilogram *per capita*, and net imports as percentage of total consumption, 1984

	Total	Solids	Liquids	Gas	Electricity hydro	Electricity nuclear	*Per capita*	Net imports
Bangladesh	5,245	130	1,905	3,099	110	—	53	35
%	100	2.5	36.3	59.1	2.1	—	—	—
Bhutan	16	1	13	—	2	—	12	94
%	100	6.3	81.3	—	12.5	—	—	—
India	176,904	118,550	46,878	4,279	6,729	469	237	7
%	100	67	26.5	2.4	3.8	0.3	—	—
Maldives	12	—	12	—	—	—	69	100
%	100	—	100	—	—	—	—	—
Nepal	268	63	157	—	48	—	17	85
%	100	23.5	58.6	—	17.9	—	—	—
Pakistan	21,291	1,442	7,665	10,566	1,577	40	215	32
%	100	6.8	36	49.6	7.4	0.2	—	—
Sri Lanka	1,934	3	1,674	—	257	—	120	87
%	100	0.2	86.5	—	13.3	—	—	—

Source: *United Nations Energy Statistics Yearbook* 1986.

Almost all the imported energy of the region is in the form of petroleum and its refined products. India is nearest to self-sufficiency in energy thanks to abundant coal, petroleum and hydro-electric resources. Pakistan achieves two-thirds self-sufficiency on the strength of gas, petroleum and hydro-electrical reserves. To reach its more modest level of consumption, Sri Lanka has to import nearly 90 percent of its needs, a figure which will perhaps be reduced somewhat with new hydro-electric schemes coming into production.

India

Coal and lignite provide two-thirds of India's commercial energy output. Most of the country's coal output is of Gondwana coal of which about 21 percent is of coking quality. Much is wastefully used in steam-raising. Gondwana coal, Carboniferous to Jurassic in age, accounts for 99 percent of reserves estimated at 120,105 million tonnes, of which 23 percent of are proven, 37 percent probable and 40 percent possible. At projected rates of consumption, India's coal

reserves are expected to last for over 120 years. The coal seams are preserved in fault-bounded rift-like troughs, countersunk into the more ancient rocks of the northeastern part of peninsular India. From a cluster of small fields at the headwaters of the rivers Son and Narmada in eastern Madhya Pradesh, one line of fields runs due east into the Damodar Valley through southern Bihar into West Bengal. Another runs southeast following the left bank of the Mahanadi River into Orissa. A separate group of fields may be traced southeastwards along the rivers Pench, Wainganga and Penganga, and so to the lower Godavari. Coal of the Tertiary age and of inferior quality is mined in Jammu and Kashmir as well as in the northeastern states of Assam, Meghalaya, Arunachal Pradesh and Nagaland.

Lignite production, 7.8 million tonnes in 1985, is exploited near Bikaner in Rajasthan to produce briquettes for railway engines. More important are the extensive deposits at Neyvali, south of Madras. Here the 3300 million tonnes of reserves provide the basis for power generation and urea manufacture. An annual output of 6.5 million tonnes of lignite is planned in order to support a 600

Table 23. Production and trade in commercial energy in '000 tonnes of coal equivalent, 1984

	Total	Solids	Liquids	Gas	Electricity hydro	Electricity nuclear	Net imports
Bangladesh	3,317	—	108	3,099	110	—	2,251
Bhutan	1	—	—	—	1	—	15
India	174,788	122,559	40,744	4,279	6,737	468	19,352
Maldives	—	—	—	—	—	—	12
Nepal	39	—	—	—	39	—	229
Pakistan	14,398	1,260	954	10,566	1,577	40	8,005
Sri Lanka	257	—	—	—	257	—	2,455

Source: *United Nations Energy Statistics Yearbook* 1986.

Energy and mineral resources

Energy resources of South Asia.

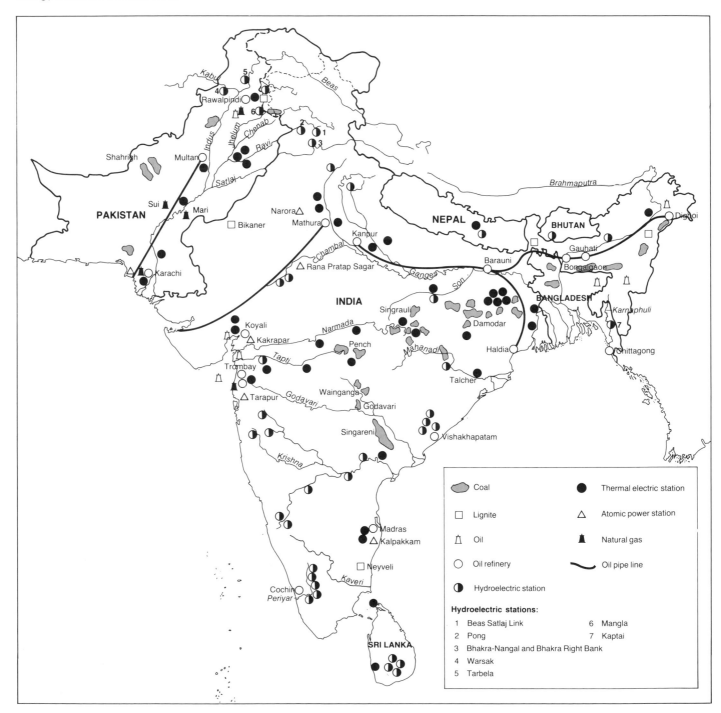

Coal

Lignite

Oil

Oil refinery

Hydroelectric station

Thermal electric station

Atomic power station

Natural gas

Oil pipe line

Hydroelectric stations:

1	Beas Satlaj Link	6	Mangla
2	Pong	7	Kaptai
3	Bhakra-Nangal and Bhakra Right Bank		
4	Warsak		
5	Tarbela		

megawatt power station and a urea plant with a capacity of 1.5 million tonnes.

India has been fortunate in discovering huge petroleum reserves which make the country about two-thirds self-sufficient in crude oil. The earliest fields to be worked, along the Brahmaputra Valley, are still active, but the main focus has moved to Gujarat and the Arabian Sea off the Maharashtra coast where the Bombay High delivers 63 percent of the output. India's refinery capacity is well distributed in twelve refineries serving the most important consuming regions. While Digboi (0.5 million tonnes) serves the local needs of the northeast, a pipeline carries crude from the Brahmaputra Valley via Gauhati (0.85 million tonnes) and Bongaigaon (1.0 million tonnes) to Barauni (3.3 million tonnes) in Bihar. The latter also takes imported crude oil piped from Haldia (2.5 million tonnes) on the Hughli estuary, and pipes products northwest to Kanpur, the industrial center in Uttar Pradesh. Another system of pipelines starts from the deep water port of Salaya on the Gulf of Cutch, in far western Gujarat. It takes imported crude oil to the huge new refinery at Mathura (6.0 million tonnes) and is linked by a branch to the producing fields in Gujarat. Here at Koyali (7.3 million tonnes) local crude oil is refined. In Bombay Harbor at Trombay are two refineries of 5.25 million tonnes and 3.5 million tonnes capacity, soon to be linked to Pune by a product pipeline. The rest of peninsular India is served by refineries processing imported crude, at Cochin (3.3 million tonnes), Madras (2.8 million tonnes) and Vishakhapatam (1.5 million tonnes).

Natural gas makes only a small contribution to India's energy

Table 24. Coal and lignite production and net imports in '000 tonnes, 1984

		Coal	Lignite
Bangladesh	production	—	—
	imports	175	—
India	production	144,970	7,649
	imports	260	—
Nepal	production	—	—
	imports	63	—
Pakistan	production	1,869	—
	imports	578	—
Sri Lanka	production	—	—
	imports	1	—

Source: *United Nations Energy Statistics Yearbook* 1986.

Table 25. Crude petroleum production, trade, refinery capacity and throughput, in '000 tonnes, 1984

	Production	Imports	Exports	Refinery capacity	Refinery throughput
Bangladesh	20	1,004	—	1,500	1,100
India	27,933	14,620	6,760	37,800	35,200
Pakistan	651	4,294	—	6,400	4,800
Sri Lanka	—	1,733	—	2,400	1,700

Source: *United Nations Energy Statistics Yearbook* 1986.

Table 27. Natural gas production, 1984

	Production	Quality (kilojoules per cubic meter)
Bangladesh	90,817	35,064
India	125,405	37,660
Pakistan	309,668	34,805

Source: *United Nations Energy Statistics Yearbook* 1986.

Table 26. Petroleum products production and trade (net imports +, exports −) in '000 tonnes, 1984

		Liquid petroleum gas	Motor spirit	Kerosene	Jet fuels	Diesel	Fuel oil
Bangladesh	Production	6	38	285	4	238	305
	Trade	—	+3	+39	+52	+270	+90
Bhutan	Production	—	—	—	—	—	—
	Trade	+2	+1	+3	—	+3	—
India	Production	844	2,062	3,304	1,332	12,151	7,915
	Trade	+66	−13	+2,658	+64	+2,473	−39
Maldives	Production	—	—	—	—	—	—
	Trade	—	+2	+2	—	+4	—
Nepal	Production	—	—	—	—	—	—
	Trade	—	+13	+39	—	+55	—
Pakistan	Production	67	612	258	474	1,341	1,564
	Trade	—	—	+411	—	+55	+271
Sri Lanka	Production	9	116	148	116	466	658
	Trade	+1	−1	+9	—	+129	−93

Source: *United Nations Energy Statistics Yearbook* 1986.

consumption; indeed, much gas is lost by being 'flared off' at oil well heads. Recently a gas field has been found in South Bassein close to Bombay.

Hydro-electric installed capacity represents about a third of the total generating capacity, and probably about a third of the ultimately feasible hydro-electric potential estimated at 48,000 megawatts. Of this potential, 54 percent is in the Himalayan mountain system which already contains 40 percent of the installed capacity. The mountains provide vast snowfield reservoirs and good sites for harnessing the potential head of water. The extreme seasonality of the monsoon precipitation makes it essential to dam the rivers in order to conserve the summer surplus for use during the dry season when maximum demand from farmers and the need to supply water to the extensive canals that irrigate the plains coincide with urban power demand.

The peninsular river systems flowing to the Bay of Bengal account for 31 percent of the power potential and 20 percent of actual

development of hydro electricity. The Mahanadi, Godavari, Krishna and Kaveri Rivers depend entirely on monsoon rainfall. The rivers draining west to the Arabian Sea have only 13 percent of India's potential but provide 28 percent of the installed capacity. Some of this development, as at Koyna, utilizes the abrupt western slope of the Ghats to generate power using water diverted from eastern flowing rivers. Further, the process is reversed in the case of the Periya which is a western flowing river diverted east into Tamil Nadu. To harness these hydro-electric resources more fully, plans for six new plants have been included in India's Sixth Five Year Plan.

The energy demands of industry, agriculture and the domestic market are growing fast. Thermal super-power stations are regarded as the quickest way of increasing electricity output in order to keep energy production abreast of demand. Thermal stations produced two thirds of the power generated in 1984, with nuclear power stations at Tarapur (Bombay), Kotah in Rajasthan, Madras and Narora (Uttar Pradesh) adding just over two percent. Possessing its own uranium ores, awaiting development in the Singhbhum area of southern Bihar, India can be expected to expand nuclear generating capacity in the future.

Pakistan

Natural gas has become Pakistan's most important indigenous energy source, providing just under half of its energy consumption. Production is mainly from the Sui and Mari fields in the lower Indus Valley. There is a smaller productive field near Karachi. Pipelines link these fields to the cities of Karachi, Lahore, Islamabad and Peshawar. A power station at Gudu, near Sui, is gas fired and will have an ultimate capacity of 639 megawatts. Mari supplies feedstock to fertilizer plants. Altogether, 31 percent of gas is used in fertilizer manufacture, 28 percent for electrical generation, 26 percent for industry and 15 percent for household and commercial purposes.

Medium quality coking coal is mined at Shahrigh, near Quetta, but it is unsuitable for metallurgical use unless blended with better

Table 28. Electricity installed generating capacity in megawatts, 1984

	Total	Thermal	Hydro	Nuclear
Bangladesh	1,289	1,159	130	—
%	100	90	10	—
Bhutan	16	13	3	—
%	100	81	19	—
India	47,690	31,492	15,103	1,095
%	100	66	32	2.3
Maldives	2	2	—	—
%	100	100	—	—
Nepal	178	50	128	—
%	100	28	72	—
Pakistan	5,010	2,325	2,548	137
%	100	46	51	2.7
Sri Lanka[a]	1,016	270	746	—
%	100	27	73	—

[a]1986
Source: *United Nations Energy Statistics Yearbook* 1986; Economist Intelligence Unit, Country Profile, Sri Lanka July 1986.

Table 29. Electricity production, trade and *per capita* consumption, 1984: in million kilowatts per hour, kilowatts per hour *per capita*, and percentages by source

	Total	Thermal (%)	Hydro (%)	Nuclear (%)	Imports	Exports	Consumption per capita
Bangladesh	4,292	79	21	—	—	—	44
Bhutan	30	70	30	—	—	—	26
India	165,440	65	33	2.3	3	65	221
Maldives	11	100	—	—	—	—	64
Nepal	350	10	90	—	80	6	26
Pakistan	21,873	40	59	1.5	—	—	221
Sri Lanka	2,261	7.5	92	—	—	—	141

Source: *United Nations Energy Statistics Yearbook* 1986.

The Meyal oilfields in Attock district, Panjab (Pakistan).

quality coal. Consequently, the new iron and steel plant at Pirri near Karachi, has to import coking coal. Most local coal is of low quality. Some, as at Lakhra, is highly sulphurous and needs special treatment to be suitable for power generation. Other deposits are in North West Frontier Province and Azad Kashmir. Brickmaking is the largest consumer.

Petroleum provides one third of energy consumption but only 13 percent comes from the country's own wells. It has been obtained for many years from fields in the Pothohar Plateau–Salt Range region in northern Panjab. Recent developments have increased output by 31 percent since 1981. Refinery capacity, 6.4 million tonnes, is in two plants at Karachi, one at Kot Adu near Multan (2.0 million tonnes) supplied by a pipeline from Karachi, and one at Rawalpindi, processing local crude oil.

Of the countries of South Asia, Pakistan is the most arid, but is fortunate in being able to harness for power and irrigation three major rivers entering the country on its northern frontiers: the Indus, the Jhelum and Kabul Rivers. Tarbela Dam on the Indus had an installed capacity of 1990 megawatts in 1986, Mangla Dam on the Jhelum had 800 megawatts, and Warsak Dam on the Kabul had 240 megawatts. Whether Tarbela will ever achieve its promise of about 3350 megawatts is now doubtful. The reservoir is fast filling with silt and sand, and an alternative site for utilizing the Indus water is being surveyed at Kalabagh which will have a capacity of 2500 megawatts.

Hydro stations account for over half of electricity production,

thermal stations for two fifths, and only a small contribution from the nuclear power station near Karachi. Proposals for a nuclear station at Chashma on the Indus (600 megawatts) are unlikely to materialize in the near future. Meanwhile, power cuts, the bane of everyday life in Pakistan, are expected to persist into the twenty-first century.

Bangladesh

For the foreseeable future, natural gas will be Bangladesh's most readily accessible source of energy. Production comes from thirteen fields, all in the east of the country. Transmission has proved difficult and costly in the deltaic terrain interlaced by rivers subject to heavy annual flooding. Pipelines supply the cities of Dhaka and Chittagong, two fertilizer plants and a cement works. The problem of transferring the benefits of natural gas to areas west of the Jamuna (Brahmaputra)–Padma (Ganges) Rivers has been overcome by the construction of the East–West Electrical Interconnector to carry gas-generated power across the unbridged Jamuna.

Of the liquid energy consumed, condensate from gas wells contributes six percent, but, despite intensive search, so far no crude petroleum has been found. Bangladesh imports over a million tonnes of crude petroleum annually for its Chittagong refinery, which has a capacity of 1.5 million tonnes. In addition, almost half a million tonnes of refined petroleum products, mainly diesel oil, have to be imported. Bangladesh relies on coal imports. Nevertheless, coal has been located at two sites in the northwest. The deposits are a continuation of the Gondwana coal-bearing structures of West Bengal. At Jamalgonj, reserves estimated at one billion tonnes lie at a presently uneconomic depth of one thousand meters, while the unknown quantities at Parbatipur are at the more reasonable depth of 190–350 meters. Eventually, no doubt, these resources will be developed. Huge deposits of peat in Faridpur, Khulna and Sylhet Districts are likely to take even longer to exploit owing to their situation in low lying water-saturated country.

Of the installed electricity generating capacity of 1159 megawatts in 1984, the hydro plant at Kaptai, on the Karnaphuli, provides some ten percent. Total capacity rose to 1300 megawatts by 1986 but will have to increase substantially to meet future demands, however modest, for only six percent of Bangladesh's technologically-backward, mainly rural population has access to electricity at present. Demand is estimated to be increasing at 11 percent *per annum*. Unless new resources of gas are discovered, prospects for improvement in this sitution are poor. Present known gas supplies up to 1990 are already fully committed.

Sri Lanka

Blessed with a hilly interior enjoying high rainfall for most of the year, Sri Lanka has concentrated development effort on harnessing the Mahaweli River and its tributaries. Hydro-electric power is the country's sole indigenous source of commercial energy, and three-quarters of its installed capacity is hydro. Randenigala, nearing completion, will add 122 megawatts and foreign aid has been arranged for the construction of projects at Samanalawewa (280 megawatts) and Rantambe.

Thermal power generation is by diesel sets, but planning is underway for a large coal-fired station at Trincomalee. Commerce accounts for 43 percent of electricity consumption, local authorities for 24 percent, domestic users for 17 percent and industry for 16 percent.

Nepal

Nepal has no commercial energy resources other than hydro-electricity which provided barely 18 percent of energy consumed in 1984. The remainder came from imported coal and petroleum products from India. There is already a small trade in electricity, 80 million kilowatt hours being imported from India and 6 million kilowatt hours being exported.

While installed hydro-electric capacity rose to 170 megawatts in 1985, the enormous potential of some 83,000 megawatts will require many years and vast capital investment to realize. India and Bangladesh are nearby energy-hungry markets whose needs could ultimately be met by international trade in current generated in Nepal. A 3600 megawatt project at Karauli is under analysis as a potential exporter to India. Meanwhile, a smaller scheme at Kulekhani (60 megawatts) is near completion.

Bhutan

This small Himalayan kingdom has an installed generating capacity of 168 megawatts, three of which are hydro. One joint hydro project is under construction at Chukha (336 megawatts), and the bulk of its output will go most probably to India. Current energy needs are met by imports of petroleum products for 81 percent of energy consumption, and coal for 6 percent. The remaining 12.5 percent is from hydro-electricity.

Maldives

Consisting of a scattered group of coral atolls, the Maldives, not surprisingly, has no commercial energy resources of its own. Its sunshine attracts the tourists whose foreign exchange helps to pay for imports of petroleum products: kerosene for lighting and cooking; diesel oil to fuel two of electrical generating capacity, and, with motor spirit, to power the boats that connect the islands. The only potential for indigenous energy development would seem to lie in solar energy.

Mineral resources

With few exceptions, mineral deposits in the region are confined to peninsula India.

India

India is a leading world producer of iron ore. From its own ores, it manufactured 11 million tonnes of ingot steel in 1985 and exported 21 million tonnes of ore in 1982–83, 41 million tonnes in the boom year of 1980–81. Although iron ore is widespread in peninsula India, in particular in Goa, Karnataka and Madhya Pradesh, some of the world's largest deposits are concentrated in Orissa and southern Bihar. With reserves of over 9300 million tonnes of haematite, the highest grade ore, India is expected to be more than self-sufficient for well over one hundred years. Manganese ore exports from India totaled 436,000 tonnes in 1982–83, from mines in northeast Maharashtra. Chromite, important as a source of a ferro-alloy is found in several parts of the peninsula.

Among non-ferrous metals, India is self-sufficient only in aluminium. Indeed, a situation of over-supply is threatened whenever a plant under construction comes into production. Bauxite is mined around the coastal margins of the peninsula and in its northeastern interior. Expansion in copper ore production promises ultimate self-sufficiency. Current production is 65,000 tonnes but about 45,000 tonnes of metallic copper have to be imported. Ore is

Mineral resources of South Asia.

B	Bauxite (Aluminium)
C	Copper
Ch	Chromite
D	Diamonds
Do	Dolomite
G	Gold
Gr	Graphite
Gy	Gypsum
I	Iron
Il	Ilmenite
L	Limestone
M	Mica

Mg	Magnesite
Mn	Manganese
Mz	Monazite
R	Rubies and other gems
RP	Rock Phosphate
Ru	Rutile
S	Salt
Z	Lead-Zinc ore

An open cut iron ore mine in Goa. India has some of the world's largest deposits of iron ore and is a leading producer.

mined in Bihar and Rajasthan, where also lie the important lead–zinc complexes. Zinc production was 72,800 tonnes in 1985–86 and imports about 30,000 tonnes. Lead production was 15,765 tonnes and imports 35,000 tonnes.

Beach sands in Kerala yield ilmenite and rutile, sources of titanium, and monazite for thorium. As these are regarded as strategic minerals for India, the relevant statistics are not made public. Gold is mined at Kolar near Bangalore at depths of nearly three thousand meters. India's non-metallic minerals include mica, important to the electronics industry, mainly from Bihar, and rock phosphate (apatite and phosphate) from Rajasthan and Uttar Pradesh. Alluvial deposits derived from the ancient rocks of peninsula India have yielded some of the world's most famous diamonds,

like the Koh-e Nur believed to have come from the Krishna District in Andhra Pradesh. A belt of sandstones in Madhya Pradesh currently yields industrial diamonds which meet half of India's needs.

Pakistan

Until now, Pakistan's sole metalliferous mineral of consequence has been chromite, but important copper deposits await development as soon as world prices for the metal improve. Both are found in Baluchistan. At one time, it was hoped that local iron ores could be used in the country's new steel industry, but their quality has proved unacceptable. Pakistan has abundant supplies of limestone

Energy and mineral resources

Table 30. Mineral production (excluding energy sources). Most data are for 1983 or 1984.

	Unit	Bangladesh	India	Nepal	Pakistan	Sri Lanka
Metalliferous						
Bauxite	'000 tonnes	—	2,016	—	2	—
Chromite	'000 tonnes	—	442	—	3	—
Copper ore	'000 tonnes	—	4,152	—	—	—
Gold	kilograms	—	1,988	—	—	—
Ilmenite	'000 tonnes	—	n.a.	—	—	102
Iron ore	million tonnes	—	42.4	—	—	—
Lead conc.	'000 tonnes	—	35.4	—	—	—
Manganese ore	'000 tonnes	—	1,236	—	—	—
Rutile	'000 tonnes	—	n.a.	—	—	6
Tungsten conc.	'000 tonnes	—	53.4	—	—	—
Zinc conc.	'000 tonnes	—	88.7	—	—	—
Non-metalliferous						
Apatite, phosphorite	'000 tonnes	—	868	—	n.a.	13
Barytes	'000 tonnes	—	323	—	21	—
China clay, kaolin	'000 tonnes	3.5	553	—	41	7
Diamonds	'00 carats	—	16	—	—	—
Dolomite	'000 tonnes	—	2,264	—	121	—
Fireclay	'000 tonnes	—	657	—	77	—
Gemstones	Sri Lankan Rupees million	—	—	—	—	706
Graphite	'000 tonnes	—	—	—	—	5.6
Gypsum	'000 tonnes	—	1,039	—	400	—
Limestone	million tonnes	—	45	—	4.6	—
as cement	million tonnes	0.2	—	0.4	—	0.4
Magnesite	'000 tonnes	—	418	—	3,100	—
Mica	tonnes	—	6,282	n.a.	—	—
Pyrites	'000 tonnes	—	64	—	—	—
Rock salt	'000 tonnes	—	4	—	753	—
Sea salt	'000 tonnes	—	7,725	—	224	176
Silica sand	'000 tonnes	—	—	—	111	—
Soapstone	'000 tonnes	—	345	—	17	—
Sulphur	tonnes	—	—	—	884	—

Source: *India: A Reference Annual 1985* (New Delhi, 1986); *Pakistan Economic Survey 1985–86* (Islamabad, 1986); *Bangladesh Third Five Year Plan 1985–90* (Dhaka, 1985); *Sri Lanka: Statistical Pocket Book 1986* (Colombo, 1986); *Far East and Australasia* (London, 1986) Europa Publications.

and gypsum to support its cement industry; dolomite and magnesite for refractories; and rock salt.

Bangladesh

Few countries can be as devoid of mineral wealth as Bangladesh. Composed in the main of deltaic sands, silts and clays, Bangladesh has only a few deposits of hard rock boulders found on its northern borders. Concrete aggregate is normally obtained by crushing kiln-fired bricks by hand. Small reserves of limestone in Sylhet support a cement factory which uses natural gas fuel.

Sri Lanka

Although geologically a detached portion of the mineral-rich plate that constitutes Peninsular India, Sri Lanka does not share its neighbor's wealth. Ilmenite and rutile from beach sands on the northeast coast are a very minor export. Gem stones, for instance, rubies, worth SLRs 874 million in 1985, make up about two percent of exports. Graphite production was worth SLRs 109 million in 1985 exports. Limestones support the cement industry and salt is evaporated from sea water in quantities that vary according to the wetness of the season.

Nepal

A little limestone for cement-making, some mica and the development of magnesite are the sum total of Nepal's interest in mineral extraction at present. A proposal to smelt local iron ore using charcoal as fuel has been abandoned in view of the severe depletion of forest resources.

BLCJ

Further reading
Economist Intelligence Unit (London), *Country Profile*, published
each year, and *Country Report*, published each quarter, for
India, Pakistan, Bangladesh, Sri Lanka and Nepal.
B. L. C. Johnson, *Development in South Asia* (Harmondsworth,
1983)
India: Resources and Development 2nd edn (London, 1983)
Bangladesh 2nd edn (London 1982)
Pakistan (London, 1979)
B. L. C. Johnson and M. le M. Scrivenor, *Sri Lanka: Land, People
and Economy* (London, 1981)

Industry

South Asia has developed a wide ranging industrial base since its
constituent countries achieved their political independence in the
late 1940s. However, industrial activity remains extremely
unevenly distributed both between and within countries. The
Maldives, Bhutan and even the much larger Nepal have very low
levels of industrial activity. In contrast, India now ranks among the
top fifteen industrial countries in the world in terms of gross output.
But even India and Pakistan, which have industrialized much faster
than any other countries in South Asia in the last forty years, have
many areas with no large scale industry at all, and, while both have
developed highly sophisticated industries in some of the large
metropolitan cities, seasonal household industry remains the only
non-agricultural activity in many rural areas.

All the countries of South Asia now see industry as an important
avenue of development. However, not only did they inherit widely
differing industrial bases from the colonial period and marked
contrasts in industrial resources, they have also followed different
strategies in their attempts to encourage industrial growth. In India,
economic planning, espoused in 1951 and practiced in varying
forms ever since, has been a prime tool of government direction.
The Second Five Year Plan (1956–61) identified the creation of a
heavy industrial base under central government ownership and
control as the key to wider industrialization, and, although there has
been significant liberalization since the late 1970s, the government
has retained a very large share in India's industrial ownership and a
tight control over the path of private industrial expansion. By the
mid-1980s the public sector accounted for 70 percent of fixed capital
in the factory sector and approximately 25 percent of both employment and output. At the same time, the government has tried to
foster small scale and cottage-based industry along Gandhian lines.
This is not just in order to stimulate employment and development
in areas too remote from cities or markets for factory industry to
develop rapidly but also to encourage rural self-sufficiency which

Gandhi made an important element of his economic and political
philosophy.

Other South Asian countries have followed different paths.
Although Pakistan has also had a program of formal planning, it has
placed far greater reliance on the private sector and on foreign
collaboration. Sri Lanka's industrial policy has undergone radical
alteration with changes in the political complexion of the Government. From the mid-1950s to the late 1970s, it pursued a path of
socialistic autarky, but since then its industrial strategy has been
based on much greater openness to world trade and inward
investment.

Bangladesh has also undergone fluctuating industrial policies
since 1947. It inherited the weakest industrial base of the three
major mainland South Asian states, which contrasted strikingly
with its seventeenth century position as one of the most admired
manufacturing regions of the world. The muslin industry on which
that reputation had been built had long since disappeared when East
Pakistan was created, and it inherited virtually no industries.
Private capital was encouraged during the Pakistan period, and has
continued to play an important role, though Bangladesh today
remains much less industrialized than India or Pakistan.

India

Until the late nineteenth century, industrial development in India
was actively discouraged by the British colonial government
through a series of measures which made it either impossible or
uneconomic. In the fifty years up to Independence, the factory-
based textile industry, notably cotton and jute, expanded rapidly to
produce for the domestic market, supplementing home spun cotton. India's first iron and steel mill was built at Jamshedpur by the
Tata Company in 1908 making use of Indian capital raised largely in
Bombay. This was followed by the Burnpur plant in 1919
established by the Indian Iron and Steel Corporation, and a comparatively small and specialized mill at Bhadravati in Karnataka. A
widening range of engineering and chemical industries was set up
between then and Independence nearly thirty years later. However,
India's industrial base was still extremely restricted and geographically concentrated very largely in the prominent port cities of
Bombay and Calcutta. The greatest exception to this rule was cotton
textile production where Ahmadabad in Gujarat and the Coimbatore region of Madras had already established themselves as
important cotton textile producing centers.

Since 1947, India's industrial progress has been marked by two
fundamental features: a strengthening of the core industrial base of
heavy industries and a diversifying into wider and wider spheres of
industrial activity. Diversification has taken place increasingly
rapidly in the 1980s and has been matched by efforts to move
industrial activity away from the traditional manufacturing centers.

Industry

Industry in South Asia, 1947.

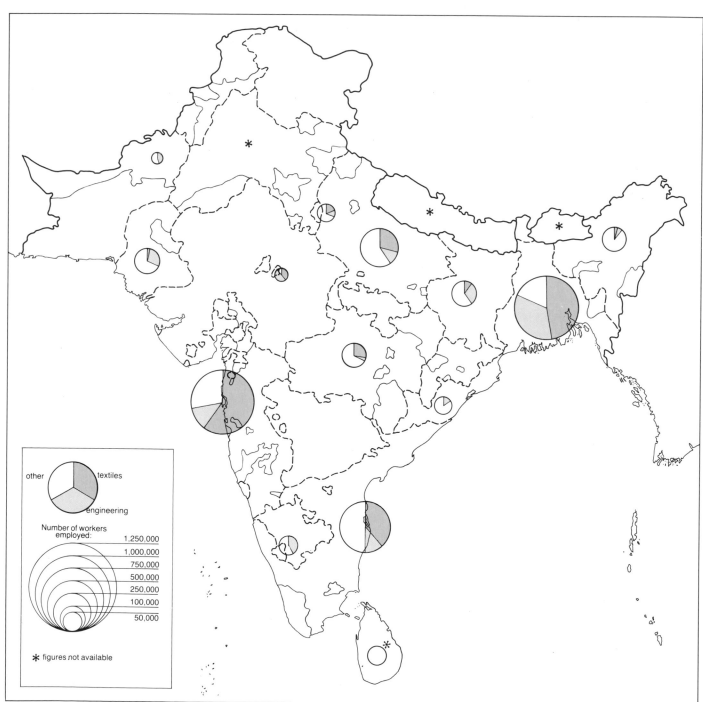

other textiles

engineering

Number of workers
employed:
- 1,250,000
- 1,000,000
- 750,000
- 500,000
- 250,000
- 100,000
- 50,000

* figures not available

Source: Indian Statistical Yearbook 1947

Industry in South Asia, *c.* 1980.

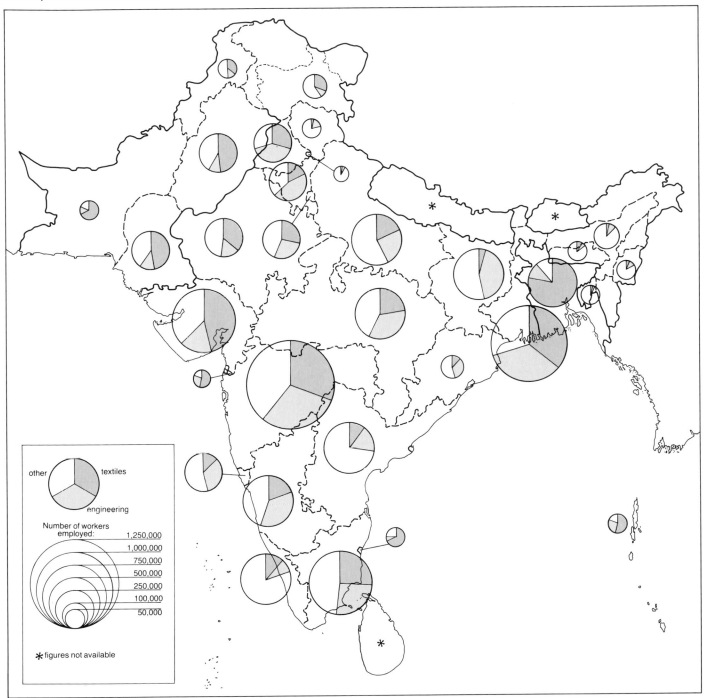

Sources: Indian Statistical Yearbook 1986; 1986 Statistical Yearbook of Bangladesh *(Dhaka, 1986)*; Census of Manufacturing Industries 1979-80 *(Karachi, 1984)*; United Nations
    Statistical Yearbook 1982 *(New York, 1984).*

In terms of employment, food processing industries are both the most important and the most widespread, accounting for over 15 percent of the 8 million people employed in factory industry in 1987. In addition to processing rice, wheat and millets, tea, coffee and sugar all make an important contribution to output. Sugar production has risen to over 6 million tonnes, tea production has doubled since 1950 and coffee production has risen fivefold. However, food processing is also among the least technologically sophisticated industries. Almost equally important as an employer is the cotton textile industry. Although nearly every state has cotton mills, the industry is still heavily concentrated in Bombay, Gujarat, Tamil Nadu and West Bengal, which together have over 70 percent of Indian cotton mills. India ranks third in the world production of cotton goods and in the early 1980s still accounted for 5 percent of the world trade of cotton. Cotton textiles are India's third largest export earner.

Despite the continuing importance of the cotton industry, many of India's cotton mills have suffered from under investment and find it difficult to compete in world markets. Modernization has been very slow in coming and the mill sector has suffered repeated periods of depression. The non-mill sector, on the other hand, has made a significant contribution to total output. Sales of *khadi* (homespun cotton), or hand woven cloth, have increased their 1960 value of Rs. 140 million by nearly tenfold. In the twenty years after 1960 full-time employment in khadi production rose from 200,000 to over 400,000, but it should be noted that this was more than offset by the fall in part-time employment.

Other sectors of India's industrial economy have shown more rapid progress. One of the most striking is the electricity industry which in the mid-1980s accounted for 9 percent of employment but a full 30 percent of invested capital in the factory industrial sector. Part of this growth reflects development not only in the industrial sector itself but also in agriculture. Consumption of electricity has increased thirteen times since the early 1950s and the installed capacity rose from under 5 million kilowatts to 40 million kilowatts in the middle 1980s, pumping irrigation water for agriculture accounting for 20 percent of the total.

The heart of India's industrial strategy has been to expand capital goods industries such as iron and steel and heavy engineering goods. In the late 1950s and early 1960s, three much publicized steel mills at Bhilai, Durgapur and Rourkela were constructed with aid from the USSR, Britain and West Germany, respectively, augmenting production from the plants built previously. All these took advantage of India's extensive local resources of high quality iron ore and of coal, located in the northeastern regions. Subsequently there has been further expansion, notably at Bokaro near Dhanbad, again with Russian help, and at Salem in southern India, where iron ore is also found. The production of steel ingots had risen to 11 million

Iron and steel mills in South Asia.

tonnes by the middle 1980s and of finished steel to over 8 million tonnes. In spite of the many problems that have occurred in its iron and steel industry, India has regarded it as a symbol of progress as well as a serious contributor to its push for industrialization. However, there has been more dramatic expansion in some other industrial fields. Notable among these are the engineering industries and the chemical industries. Between 1970 and 1983, the value of machine tools and mill equipment for cotton textiles, sugar and cement increased eightfold. The production of a range of engineering goods from engines and vehicles to pumps and sewing machines more than doubled in the same period. Increasingly India's engineering base has become more sophisticated. In the middle 1980s, its production of electronic goods, notably radios, televisions and computers started expanding rapidly, and at the top end of the technological scale it was producing high quality electronic equipment for India's own space program. At the same time, nuclear power stations were being constructed, the most recent at Kalpakkam near Madras being entirely Indian designed and built.

While the engineering industry has witnessed both expansion and transformation during the forty years since Independence, the same can also be said for India's chemical industry. A vital stimulus for change has been the development of agriculture. The introduction of high yielding varieties of rice and wheat in the late 1960s greatly increased the demand for chemical fertilizers and pesticides that had already been growing during the previous decade. Originally such fertilizers had to be imported, but, between 1970 and the mid-1980s, production of nitrogenous and phosphatic fertilizers rose from 1 million tonnes to over 8 million tonnes. Production of the basic mineral resources for much of the chemical industry, petroleum and coal, has also expanded rapidly. At Independence India's coal production was under 30 million tonnes a year and crude petroleum was barely discovered. By the middle 1980s, coal production had risen to over 160 million tonnes and petroleum to over 30 million tonnes, providing resources not just for energy but for the wider industrialization which was characteristic of the decade.

Although large-scale factory organization is playing an increasing role in India's development, small-scale industries (units with capital investment of under Rs. 1.5 million) are also important. This importance is not simply a legacy from the past, for small-scale units have multiplied in the last forty years and employment in small-scale industry, at 8 million in 1986, was greater than in factory industry. When the traditional khadi and village industries are added, this rises to over 10 million. A wide range of industrial activity takes place in the small-scale sector, from the manufacture of *bidis* (traditional cigarettes) to handicrafts such as carpet weaving and wood carving. In some regions, notably Panjab and Haryana, small-scale engineering industry has developed rapidly to meet the needs of the booming and increasingly mechanized agricultural sector. At the same time, the Government has reserved some aspects of modern industry for the small-scale sector, and, in cities such as Bangalore, Hyderabad and Delhi, the early 1980s saw a very rapid

In the 1980s the production of electronic goods was a rapidly expanding industry in India.

growth in electronics industries such as television, communications and watch and clock making.

Despite government efforts to achieve balanced regional development there are great contrasts in the levels of industrial activity in different parts of India. This is true even of small-scale units. In the mid-1980s, West Bengal led the field in terms of the number of small-scale industrial units operating with Delhi, Haryana and Panjab between them having nearly 100,000 units, altogether one third of the national total.

Factory industry is even more heavily concentrated in particular regions. Maharashtra, with Bombay dominating its industrial economy, has over 17 percent of the national factory employment. When West Bengal and Tamil Nadu are added the proportion rises to over 40 percent. States such as Orissa, Madhya Pradesh, Assam and Bihar have many regions where industry is totally absent. Thus, the rapid progress toward an industrial economy which is evident in the highly urbanized parts of India is very much slower elsewhere. Since 1977, the Indian government has been making particular efforts to encourage industry to decentralize. An absolute ban has been imposed on new industrial location within the boundaries of cities of one million or more. The policy of fostering industrial estates, which goes back to 1956, has been strengthened significantly by the provision not only of land and buildings but of new financial incentives through both grants and tax benefits.

In the 1980s industrial policy has moved toward a greater openness to inward investment in Indian industry and international cooperation, even though the public sector continues to dominate. This has been evident in several fields, from consumer goods industries such as electrical and electronic goods through to essential items of defense equipment. However, although India has moved a long way down the path toward basic industrial self-sufficiency, great problems of international competitiveness and efficiency remain.

Pakistan

Pakistan inherited an even weaker industrial base at Independence than India. With a much more restricted range of mineral resources at its disposal, industry was almost entirely devoted to processing agricultural produce, notably cotton, sugar and tobacco, alongside some leather- and craft-based industries. There were no large-scale heavy industries, a reflection not only of colonial policy but also of the lack of suitable iron ore and coal resources in close proximity in what became Pakistan. By far the most important resource, natural gas from the Sui field, had already been exploited before Independence. It provided the basic energy needs for the infant textile industry of Karachi in the early 1950s, and very rapid growth took place of spinning yarn and weaving cloth both in the new industrial centers of Karachi and Hyderabad (Sind) as well as in the older textile centers of Lyallpur and Multan. Large-scale textile mills were a comparatively new phenomenon in Pakistan, but the number of spindles and looms grew rapidly. In the first twenty years of Independence, the number of spindles rose from under 200,000 to two and a half million, and there was a similar expansion in the number of looms. By the 1980s, there were four million spindles, and cotton textiles had established themselves as the most important single industry in terms both of employment and of output.

Natural gas serves two vital functions for Pakistan's industry. First it is an important energy source which, even though hydro-electricity and steam powered turbines account for about 85 percent of total generating capacity, makes a significant contribution to electricity generation. Second, it serves as a feedstock for the fertilizer industry. As in India, the advent of the 'green revolution' in agricultural technology of high yielding seeds established a far higher demand for chemical fertilizers and pesticides. Between 1979 and 1983, Pakistan brought an extra fertilizer factory into production each year, raising output of nitrogenous and phosphatic fertilizers to 1.3 million tonnes. This increase is not only important in itself; it symbolizes the continuing role of agro-based industries in the modern Pakistani economy. Sugar and vegetable ghee processing make an important contribution to production for domestic consumption, but both basic foodgrains and more particularly cotton goods and textiles are significant contributors to exports. Agro-based industries accounted for half the total industrial output in 1978 at the start of the Fifth Five Year Plan. At the end of that period, their share had fallen to 46 percent while the share of the newer industries of fertilizer and steel rose to nearly 20 percent.

The Fifth Five Year Plan marked a turning point in other ways. Unlike India, with its very heavy reliance on public sector ownership, which is expressed through the reservation of a wide range of basic industries solely to the public sector and a further category of industries where joint ownership is allowed, Pakistan has always encouraged private industry to invest. After 1978, all industrial fields were opened to private investors, although the basic strategy of supporting exports and building up import substitution industries remained. This is not to minimize the direct role of the government in industrial investment. The Pakistan Industrial Development Corporation was a vital public institution for industrial development, particularly in the field of basic industries. The Fifth Plan represented a renewed commitment to public sector involvement in completing basic industrial projects. The Karachi steel mill, the first in the country and built with Soviet aid, seven cement projects, fertilizer plants and sugar mills all claimed public sector money. Both steel and engineering industries had remained relatively neglected in the early years of Pakistan's development. Small steel rolling mills, largely in Karachi and Lahore, multiplied

but were generally very inefficient and depended heavily on imported pig iron and scrap.

In addition to the fertilizer industry, Pakistan also has a chemical industry of growing importance. Ammonium sulphate is produced at Daud Khel on the Indus using coal from Makerwal and gypsum from the Great Salt Range. Soda ash is used by the glass industry, still comparatively small, and various artificial fibres and plastics are now made locally rather than having to be imported.

Industry in Pakistan is as heavily concentrated in particular regions as in India, even though it did not inherit the same colonial legacy of concentration that characterized India. Karachi has become a dominant industrial center, based on its function as the sole port of significance. Both Panjab and Sind have important industries, but there is considerable concern on the part of the Pakistan government over the lack of industrial development in the two western Provinces of Baluchistan and North West Frontier Province.

Multi-colored block printing on Sindhi Ajrak is a small-scale craft industry in Pakistan.

The export and the processing of jute has played a key role in Bangladesh's economy.

Bangladesh

Of the three paramount countries of mainland South Asia, Bangladesh started its independent existence with the least developed industrial base and the poorest resources. In 1947 it was almost the world's only supplier of jute, but the entire product was processed in Calcutta. Even the craft textile industry had been largely destroyed in the eighteenth and nineteenth centuries, and, although there were a few small cotton textile mills, a cement factory and some works processing agricultural produce for export, industry employed less than one percent of the total population. Even by 1982 there were fewer than half a million industrial employees.

Jute has played a crucial role in Bangladesh's economy, first as an export crop but secondly as the most important raw materal input for agro-processing industry. At the time of partition from India, East Bengal had no jute mills. During the first twenty years of the Pakistan period, 30 jute mills were constructed. In the following period up to 1984, a further 40 mills were added and the total employment in the jute industry had reached 187,000. The total production of jute goods had risen to over half a million tonnes, nearly 90 percent of which was exported. In the same period the number of cotton mills rose from 20 to 58, but production fluctuated greatly. Although at its peak cotton cloth production totaled nearly 90 million yards of cloth in 1979–80, by 1984 it had fallen back to 66 million yards.

As in Pakistan, by far the most important natural resource for industry is natural gas, exploited in Sylhet district. Natural gas provides the energy source for over half of Bangladesh's 3.4 billion kilowatt hours of electricity, while hydro-electricity from the Chittagong Hill Tracts provides 20 percent. However, in Bangladesh too natural gas is an important feedstock for the fertilizer industry, and fertilizer production rose nearly nine times to over 2.4 million tonnes by the mid-1980s.

Some other industrial enterprises were set up close to the time that Bangladesh obtained its independence from Pakistan. The paper mill on the Karnaphuli River in Chittagong, using bamboo as its raw material and built with Japanese assistance, is the largest in Asia. There is a small steel rolling mill in Chittagong, and food processing industries, often on a very small scale, are widely scattered. Shrimps and frogs legs have been valuable exports, though the latter export is diminishing. Very few areas of Bangladesh have a significant degree of industrial activity, and what there is tends to reflect rural needs and opportunities.

Nepal and Bhutan

Although there are historical references to craft industries such as wood carving and cloth making, it is clear that when Nepal opened its frontiers to outsiders in the middle of the twentieth century there was virtually no modern industry. The only exception was the

Biratnagar Jute Mill, established in 1936, which marked the recognition of the need for a new direction for Nepal's rural economy. Food processing followed; rice, sugar and oil mills were established by the end of the 1940s. By 1951, some 65 companies were registered, mainly processing agricultural produce. Not all were successful. Early cotton mills and plywood mills were closed down, and the difficulty of producing efficiently and competitively in the remote and landlocked territory which made up the kingdom was heightened by the almost complete lack of modern transport facilities.

The end of the Rana power in 1951 signaled a new beginning, although a practical start was not made until the First Five Year Plan (1956–57 to 1960–61). This advocated a mixed economy but only allocated Rs. 25 million to industrial development. In subsequent plans, a number of industries have received support and financial backing, especially from the Industrial Development Corporation which was set up in 1957. Rice milling was by far the most important industrial activity, accounting for 60 percent of industrial establishments in Nepal in 1966. Other small-scale industries followed, including flour and oil milling and furniture making. Considerable expansion has taken place since. Nearly 50,000 people were employed in industry by the middle 1970s, and 60,000 by the beginning of the 1980s. Most of this employment was in the central region, and agro-based industries continue to predominate. A recent addition to the income earning economy has been tourism, which promises considerable potential.

Despite the growing sophistication of economic planning and changes in the economic climate, the basis of industry in Nepal is likely to retain a strong rural and agricultural orientation. This is even more true of Bhutan, which has virtually no modern industrial activity.

Sri Lanka and the Maldives

Manufacturing activity grew quite rapidly in Sri Lanka during the 1970s, contributing over 20 percent of the gross national product (GNP) by the end of the decade compared with only 9 percent at the beginning. The basis of Sri Lanka's industrial strategy developed in its first Ten Year Plan in 1959 recognized the lack of industrial raw material resources. The original intention was to import capital goods with income earned from traditional agricultural exports, tea and coconuts. That plan never materialized, but the Government at that time initiated a program of public sector investment. After 1977, when a new government was formed by the United National Party, economic policy reflected free market thinking, with encouragement to foreign investors and the establishment of a Free Trade Zone outside Colombo. Output from Sri Lanka's industries is small compared with that of its South Asian neighbors, but in the mid-1980s it was producing over 600,000 tonnes of cement, refined petroleum, mineral sands, salt and textiles in addition to the traditional craft industries.

The Maldives has three opportunities for economic development, and they have each made a contribution to a rapid rate of growth in the decade from the mid-1970s. These are fishing, shipping and tourism. The World Bank estimates that fish landings could have reached 50,000 tonnes in 1985 and tourist arrivals 100,000. The latter could act as a stimulus to the small traditional manufacturing sector, but the very small population and its highly scattered distribution make it inevitable that manufacturing industry will not play a critical role in the islands' economy.

RNB

Further reading
B. H. Farmer, *An Introduction to South Asia* (London, 1983)
B. L. C. Johnson, *India: Resources and Development* 2nd edn (London, 1983)
B. L. C. Johnson, *Pakistan* (London, 1979)
B. L. C. Johnson and M. le M. Scrivenor, *Sri Lanka* (London, 1983)

Transport and communications

The traveler in South Asia today is frequently struck by the enormous variety of transport in daily use. In the mountainous regions of the far north pack animals such as donkeys and yaks are still often the only means of transporting goods across high passes, supplemented by headloading porters. But headloading is not

Even though modern means of transport have spread into the remotest areas, goods are still commonly carried by bullock cart.

Road network in 1900 and 1980.

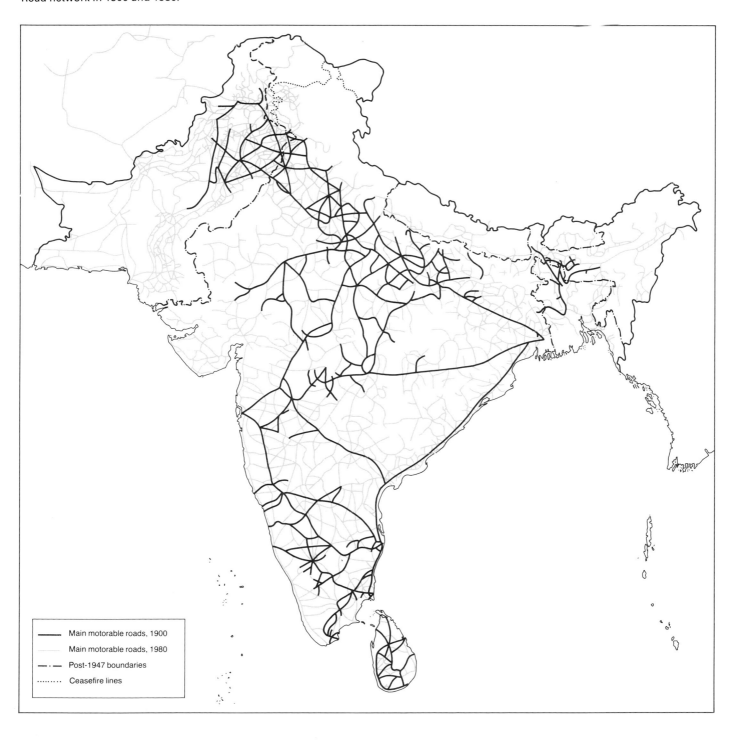

Main motorable roads, 1900
Main motorable roads, 1980
Post-1947 boundaries
Ceasefire lines

restricted to the hills. On the plains too, millions travel on foot. Goods are still commonly carried on the ubiquitous bullock cart. Superficially this may suggest that little has changed over thousands of years. Yet, at the same time, modern communications and means of transport have spread into the remotest areas. India's satellite program, for example, is making it possible to receive television pictures right across the subcontinent. The network of roads and railways, which already straddled South Asia by independence, has been greatly augmented in the past forty years. It carries billions of passengers and hundreds of millions of tonnes of freight every year. Yet, despite the rapid extension of the modern transport system into previously inaccessible regions, some areas remain remote.

The present day political boundaries of South Asia cut across some of the earlier transport routes which have left their mark on contemporary transport networks. This is most strikingly true of the border between India and Pakistan, which divided both the old Grand Trunk Road system of the Mughal Empire and the more modern railway system of the British. However, although some routes have been in use for several hundred years, others have been more ephemeral. The main transport arteries have followed areas of densest population, and the Indo-Gangetic plains have seen the development of transport arteries over three thousand years. The precise nature of the traditional transport in use has often reflected the nature of the local terrain. Thus, in the eastern region of the Gangetic plains, river transport has always played a crucial role which it continues to fulfil.

The relatively easy access provided by the Indus and Ganges plains is in sharp contrast to the much more restricted access elsewhere. Although it is possible to overstate the extent to which the Himalayas acted as a barrier to movement, transport has inevitably been confined to the high passes. Even the main routes, along which many of the people who settled in South Asia from the northwest traveled were constrained by passes through the Hindu Kush and the arid hills to the south. In peninsular India, too, the highest land has tended to be avoided. But mountains have been by no means the only obstacle to easy movement. Dense forest, particularly in regions of malaria such as the *terai* foothills of the Himalayas or the hills of Orissa, have been avoided, and traditional routes followed the narrow coastal fringe or more open plateau lands such as Malwa Plateau.

India

India's modern transport system is amongst the largest in the world. Its railway system is the largest in Asia and the fourth largest in the world. While in most countries of the developed world railway systems have been contracting since World War II, India's has continued to expand. Similarly, the road network has increased dramatically and very few of India's villages are now more than four or five miles from the nearest road and its bus routes.

The first railways were built in the early 1850s, and the basic network was laid out over the next 50 years. Main routes between the colonial cities of Bombay, Calcutta and Madras were broad gauge, with supplementary meter and narrow gauge lines for less important lines. By the start of India's planning era in 1951, India had 54,000 route km of track, of which a bare 388 km was electrified. Most of the locomotives then were still steam powered, often burning wood. In the 35 years since, the overall network has increased to over 60,000 km, nearly 5000 km of which is electrified. Furthermore, there has been considerable modernization of the rolling stock and of the signalling. By the mid-1980s, the number of diesel locomotives had risen from 17 to over 2000 and the number of electric locomotives from 70 to nearly 900. Track improvements now allow considerably faster passenger services, facilitated by computerization of the booking system introduced in the second half of the 1980s. Despite track improvements, however, the services are still slow compared to those in Europe or Japan. Maximum speeds permitted are 120 km per hour, and the great majority of passenger services operate at much lower speeds.

The importance of the railway system to meeting India's transport needs can scarcely be exaggerated. By the mid-1980s, it was carrying 3.6 billion passengers a year, exactly three times the number of passengers carried in 1950. Freight transport had increased threefold from under 93 million tonnes to over 260 million tonnes. In addition to benefitting long-distance transport, Bombay,

India's railway system is the fourth largest in the world. Since Independence the system has been used more and more intensively: diesel and electric locomotives have replaced steam, passenger services have achieved higher speeds, and booking has been computerized.

Rail network in 1900 and 1980.

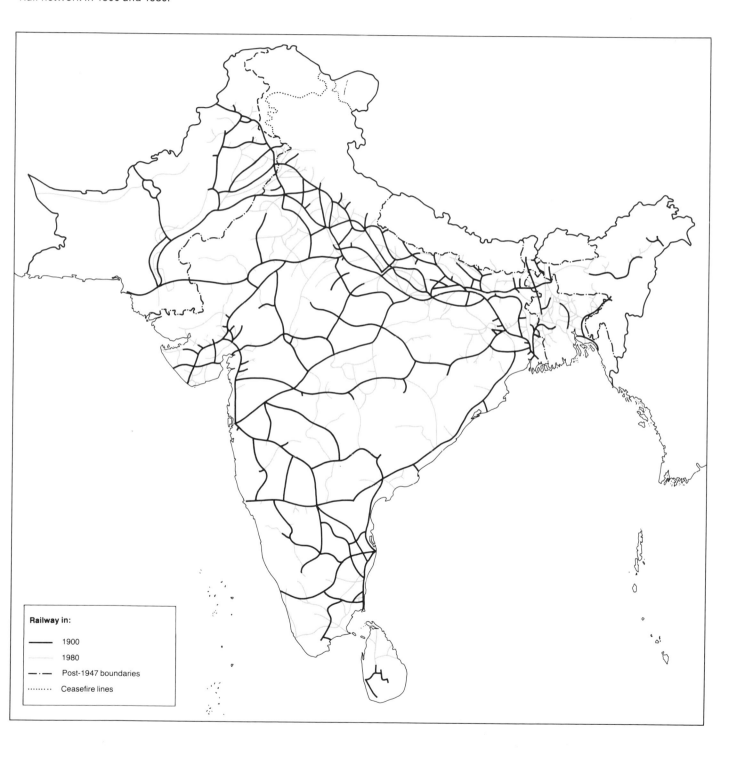

Railway in:

———	1900
———	1980
—·—·—	Post-1947 boundaries
·········	Ceasefire lines

Calcutta and Madras have important commuter services. In Calcutta, these were supplemented in the mid-1980s by the opening of India's first underground railway. The suburban lines in Bombay are renowned for their frequency and at the same time their overcrowding. For 20 of the 24 hours a day, each of the two suburban lines has a train every two minutes, and at peak hours trains carry as many as three times their permitted load of 1500 passengers.

Despite the improvements to track and rolling stock, and even though new lines have been built to fill important gaps in the colonial network which had not been designed to meet the needs of an industrializing independent country, bottlenecks remain and demand continues to exceed capacity. The same is true of the road network. The length of surfaced road increased in the twenty years after 1960 from 263,000 km to nearly 700,000 km, yet over 300,000 of India's 600,000 villages remained without direct connection to the road network. Even though the national highway system has also been greatly improved, its capacity remains low. The number of trucks exceeded half a million in 1980, with more than 150,000 buses, but long-distance travel is made slow and expensive by the poor quality and low load capacity of many of the main roads.

Whereas the railway system is entirely nationalized, there is a greater degree of flexibility in the ownership of buses. In the late 1970s, approximately half the bus routes were operated by public corporations, but in many States a widening deregulation has taken place up to the middle 1980s.

Inland water transport is of comparatively limited significance except locally. There are some 1700 km of waterway used, mainly in the States of Kerala, Andhra Pradesh, West Bengal and Assam. India's merchant shipping fleet has gained rapidly in international significance. It is probably the largest merchant fleet in the developing world and among the top fifteen in the world as a whole. At Independence, India had less than 200,000 GRT of merchant shipping, but, by the early 1980s, this had risen to over six million GRT. Sixteen of the fifty-seven Indian shipping companies engage exclusively in coastal trade, twenty-six in overseas trade and the remainder in both. Among the biggest companies are the publicly-owned Shipping Corporation of India and the privately-owned Scindia Steam Navigation Company and the Mogul Line, which carries mainly Haj pilgrims to Jeddah. In addition to the colonial ports of Bombay, Calcutta and Madras, India has seven major ports and some 160 minor ones along its 6 000 km of coastline. Bombay alone handles about 25 percent of the total traffic passing through the larger ports, and Calcutta, with its outport at Haldia, is the largest handler of bulk cargoes in India.

In common with the expansion of its shipping fleet, air travel has also grown fast. The two largest nationalized airlines, one for external routes and one for internal routes, were joined in the early 1980s by a new private airline for internal routes. Over six million passengers were carried in 1982 compared with threequarters of a million twenty years earlier, and air freight has also increased substantially.

India's communications systems have undergone radical change in the 1980s. An imperial postal service was already well established under the Mughals, but the public service began in 1837. By 1982, there were as many as 140,000 post offices.

Although the first telephone service was introduced in Calcutta as early as 1881, only five years after its invention, it took time for telephones to spread. There were still less than half a million in 1962, a figure which exceeded three million by 1982. Teleprinting was introduced in 1962, telex in 1962 and a limited facsimile service was introduced in Madras in 1969. The commissioning of India's first telecommunications satellite is transforming accessibility to broadcasts, both radio and television, and although in 1982 there were still fewer than two million television sets a revolution had begun.

Pakistan

Partition from India in 1947 left Pakistan with a severed surface transport system. Furthermore much of the railway network that it did inherit had been built for strategic rather than economic reasons. Thus, lines towards the northwest frontier and into Baluchistan served no direct economic purpose, simply a defensive one. Before the Indus plains were incorporated into the region under British rule, they had seen a succession of conquering armies and migrants coming from the northwest. The Panjab had been at the hub of the Mughal empire and the Mughal Grand Trunk roads included the route from Afghanistan to Calcutta, that from Lahore to Karachi and, finally, that from Lahore to Quetta.

In part because of the fragmented and inappropriate nature of the rail network, and in part because of inadequate capital investment in the railways, road transport has always been more important than the railways. In 1976–77, railways accounted for 18 percent of the total passenger km, and, although the total rose from 13 million passenger km, in 1976 to nearly 16 million passenger km in 1983, this represented a fall to 13 percent of the total. Road services also account for a higher proportion of freight than the railways. The problems of the railway are illustrated by the nature of the rolling stock. In 1980 over 250 steam engines were still in use even though they were over 60 years old. Although a railway improvement program is under way, measures have also been taken to relieve pressure on the system by transferring freight to other channels. Most important has been the construction of the Karachi–Multan pipeline, commissioned in the early 1980s and carrying 1000 million tonnes of crude oil per annum. Although, as already stated, road transport is more important than rail, it too suffers serious diffi-

Communications by air.

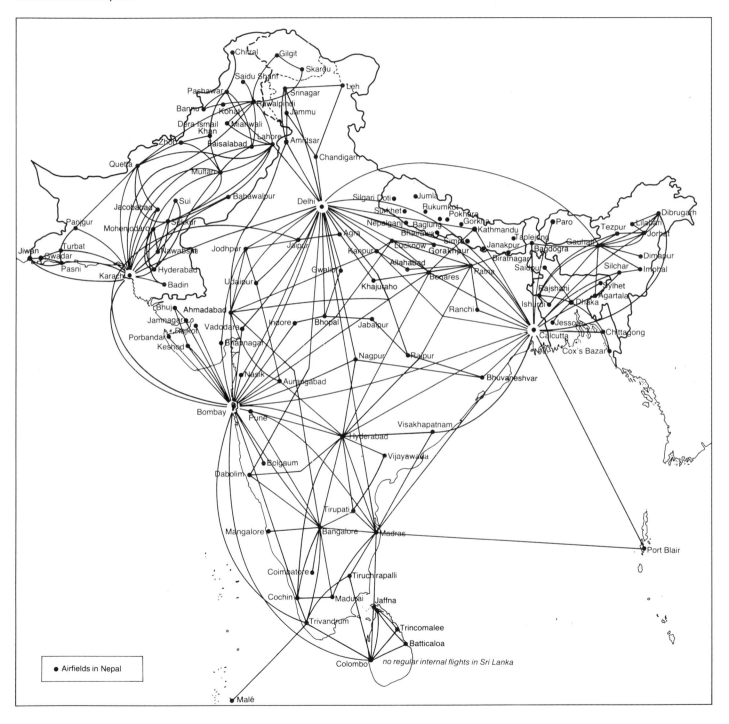

| Airfields in Nepal

no regular internal flights in Sri Lanka

culties. The network of some 30,000 km of surfaced road and 60,000 unsurfaced leaves many areas very sparsely served. Like the Indian road system, there is often a poor or non-existent feeder road network, and even many of the main roads have very low capacities. An improvement program was launched in the Fifth Five Year Plan, leading up to 1983, building some 1300 km of new roads and widening and surfacing a further 6 000 km. This was to enable the system to carry 18 billion tonne km of goods traffic and 90 billion passenger km of traffic.

Unlike Bangladesh and some of the coastal regions of India, the scope for inland waterways in Pakistan is extremely limited. Pakistan's major port, Karachi, has recently been supplemented by the creation of Port Qasim, which, in addition to providing extra capacity for handling bulk cargoes, acts as the main iron ore and coal port for the new Karachi steel mill. Karachi port has also been extended and developed, giving it a capacity in the early 1980s of five million tonnes of dry cargo per annum. Pakistan has a modest merchant shipping fleet of some 50 vessels, with a dead weight tonnage of under 600,000. Over half the ships are more than 15 years old.

By 1976 more than 1.5 million passengers were using Pakistan's domestic airline services. In the following decade it was expected that demand would rise by 20 percent per annum, giving four million passengers by 1983 on domestic routes and nearly two million on international routes. Capacity has been increased steadily to 13 billion seat km in 1981. By far the most important routes are those between Karachi, Lahore and Islamabad. As in India, there are many areas remote from all the main physical means of communication. The mountainous regions of the north and northwest can only be reached on foot or by pack animal, although the opening of the Karakoram Highway has brought the areas through which it passes into regular contact with the outside world for the first time.

Pakistan inherited the same infrastructure of postal and telegraph services as India. It too has experienced rapid growth and significant change. From under 20 million phone calls in 1965, the figure rose to over 150 million in the mid-1980s. Telex traffic rose to over seven million paid minutes in the five year period from 1977, an increase of 35 times. Despite the growing importance of satellite-based communications, traditional channels remained important. The number of post offices for example has risen steadily to nearly 10,000, and there are nearly half a million telephones installed.

Bangladesh

In terms of its physical environment, Bangladesh is unique in South Asia, a uniqueness that has had a telling effect on means of transport. Although, like Pakistan, it inherited a fragmented railway network, comprising some 900 route km of broad gauge and

1800 km of metre gauge, it had an extensive network of navigable waterways totaling over 5000 km perennially navigable and a further 3500 km seasonally navigable. Waterways have always played a vital part in the life of Bangladesh. In 1982, motor launches and steamers carried nearly 50 million passengers, but in many ways these official figures understate the importance of the rivers. The deltaic landscape of Bangladesh is criss-crossed by the distributaries of the Ganges and the Brahmaputra in the west and center and the Meghna in the east. During the wet season from late May to September these rivers flood vast areas. Although they themselves act as vital channels of communication, they also interrupt road and rail systems. Long ferry crossings are necessary, and the ferry terminal points have to move, sometimes many miles, as the floods rise and fall. At their widest, these rivers may be 15 or 20 km across and it is impossible to move across the country without boats.

Thus, the rivers are the greatest obstacles to movement. The

Communications in Bangladesh.

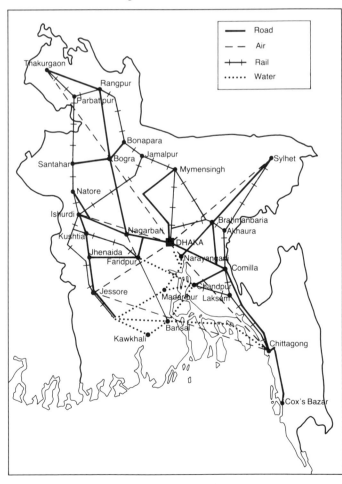

difficulties of movement are further increased by the fragmentary and very low capacity road system. In total, Bangladesh has just over 5000 km of surfaced road, this for an area equivalent to that of England and Wales. Road improvement has been painfully slow. Between 1967 and 1983, a total of 1265 km of new road was surfaced, representing an average of under 80 km a year. This reflects in part the great expense of road building in a country without hard rock and constantly subject to annual flooding which results in a road building cost four times higher in Bangladesh than in Pakistan. The total transport of goods and people is considerably less than in India, which is not surprising in view of the greater poverty of the region. In 1984, nearly three million tonnes of freight was moved by rail, 17 million tonnes in the organized road transport and an estimated 50 million tonnes in the informal road transport sector. Water transport accounted for a further 16 million tonnes. Significant quantities of gas are transported by pipelines notably from Bakhrabad to Chittagong and Titas to Dhaka.

Post and telegraph offices play as important a part in daily life and in communication in Bangladesh as elsewhere in the subcontinent. Although there were over 7500 post offices and over 800 telegraph offices in the country by 1983, there were still only 140,000 telephones serving a population of over 90 million. Indeed, 82,000 of these were in the capital of Dhaka and a further 20,000 in Chittagong; almost three quarters of the total in just two cities. Dhaka's growth in this respect is particularly striking, increasing its share from 44 percent in 1976 to nearly 60 percent in 1983. Moreover, telecommunication is spreading: in 1987 there were 5 million radio receivers and 600,000 television sets.

Given the importance of Bangladesh's inland waterways, it is striking that there are only two large ports handling exports and imports: Chalna particularly specializes in the export of jute and jute products, while Chittagong, by far the larger of the two, has a broader range of activities including the import of crude oil. In 1982, Chittagong handled as much as 82 percent of Bangladesh's imports while Chalna shipped out 64 percent of the country's exports.

In 1971, Bangladesh had only eight small aircraft for its airline. Domestic passenger traffic has remained stagnant at under 350,000 *per annum* although international traffic has increased during the period. Air freight is still very slight.

Nepal and Bhutan
Nepal and Bhutan illustrate perfectly the difficulties of transport and communication in one of the highest mountain regions of the world. Yet, in some respects, the forested and malarial Terai was traditionally as much a barrier to movement in and out of Nepal as the mountain chain of the Himalayas. Movement was almost entirely on foot or with pack animals. These routes have now been supplemented by new roads, such as that from India built in 1956 and the more recent road now opened from Kathmandu to Lhasa, built with help from China.

None of this has yet destroyed the traditional trade over high mountain passes, although the new road linking Pokhara and Kathmandu has provided the alternative of bus transport to the hardy. Trade with Tibet has always provided an important economic outlet for Nepal's agricultural produce in exchange for salt and yaks. This suffered greatly from the political upheaval as China claimed its Tibetan territory, but trade is again increasing slowly. Bhutan is even less well provided with roads, although there is now a link between West Bengal and the old and new capitals of Paro and Thimpu.

Air transport has assumed considerable importance as the only rapid means of transport between the isolated settlements of Nepal, and a number of airstrips have been built with outside help, particularly from the USA and the USSR. Moreover, air transport is also important as a means of connecting Nepal to the Indian tourist circuit, although the kingdom is a prized location not just for tourists from beyond South Asia but also from the subcontinent itself.

Electronic communications are beginning to make an impact, although the number of telephones, televisions and radios per head remains small in comparison with India. Nevertheless, in the 1980s Nepal's internal communications have been sharply improved through the building of a satellite earth station near Kathmandu. This can pick up television pictures from the Far East, the USA and Europe. A World Bank loan and Japanese assistance were also used to set up an automatic telephone exchange, and the Japanese assisted in the building of a medium wave radio network.

Sri Lanka and the Maldives
Internal transport within the Maldives is of necessity almost entirely by boat. In contrast to the scattered atolls of the Maldives, Sri Lanka has a comparatively integrated transport system, in which road and rail each play an important role supplemented by air transport and coastal shipping. Unlike the rest of South Asia, Sri Lanka's railway operates almost entirely on the standard gauge. Routes focus on Colombo, though the network is a minimal link. The main link is northwards to Jaffna via Anuradhapura and northeastwards to the port of Trincomalee, which also has a branch line to Batticaloa. Another line runs east into the hills and one due south to Galle and Matara.

To a significant extent, both the rail and the road pattern reflect the economic functions developed during the colonial period. Both tea and rubber were grown almost entirely for export. Most of this was taken to Colombo for shipment, and the rail system into the hills was designed to facilitate its movement. The plantation estate areas also have the most highly developed road network, a further reflection of the importance of the region economically. Black topped roads now stretch extensively across the island, and in the early 1980s the nationalized bus services covered more than 20 million passenger kilometers, five times the volume of traffic carried by the railways.

As the surface transport system focuses on Colombo, it is not surprising that Colombo is far and away Sri Lanka's most important port. In the early 1980s it handled over 90 percent of the total cargo, while Trincomalee, a magnificent natural harbor used as a naval base by the British, handled just under 150,000 tonnes. Galle on the south coast also handled small quantities of cargo totaling around 50,000 tonnes. Shipping is the lifeline of the Maldives. Malé port offers some facilities for ocean going ships, but a lighterage system has to be used for trans-shipment. All inter-island traffic goes by sea, although the only indication of its scale comes from the fact that 2000 people list their occupations as boatmen. Inter-island communication is by high frequency transceivers, and within islands by means of the 1000 licensed walkie talkies. There is a VHF radio telephone link between tourist resorts and Malé, and a satellite earth station installed with help from Abu Dhabi in 1977 provides external communications.

RWB

Further reading
W. Owen, *Transport and Development* (Washington, 1969)
O. H. K. Spate and A. T. A. Learmonth, *India and Pakistan: a general and regional geography*; with a chapter on Ceylon by B. H. Farmer, 3rd rev. edn (London, 1967)

Trade and tourism

Trade
Foreign trade is important for the economies of South Asia, both as a source of imports and as an outlet for exports. But, while international trade is important, their combined share of world trade is very small. For example, the total value of exports from the five major South Asian economies in the 1980s was less than one percent by value of exports from developed western countries. Except for food, imports are mainly manufactured products, including capital goods and industrial inputs. In the past, exports were the largest outlet for commodities such as jute, rubber, tea and sugar. In spite of growing domestic absorption of some of these commodities, like tea and oilseeds in India, foreign exchange earned through exports plays a strategic role in development. The quantitative significance of trade, however, varies widely between different countries. At the two extremes, exports and imports in Sri Lanka were 27 percent and 37 percent of Gross Domestic Product (GDP) in 1984, while India's exports and imports stood at 6 percent and 9 percent of GDP, respectively. These differences reflect the relative size of the economies, their degree of 'openness' and structural change in the post-independence period.

At independence, roughly 70 percent of imports into India, Pakistan and Sri Lanka consisted of either manufactured consumer goods or inputs for their own manufacturing industries. Demand for capital goods was very low, and even basic industrial inputs all came from abroad. Domestic supply was important for cotton and jute textiles, and iron and steel in India. The main exports were tea, and cotton and jute yarn and manufactured goods from India, raw cotton and jute from Pakistan (the latter from East Pakistan), and rubber and tea from Sri Lanka. The UK and, to a lesser extent, the USA were then the region's most important trading partners. Foreign exchange reserves were fairly healthy, with unspent sterling balances accumulated during World War II.

In absolute terms, India and Pakistan are the most important importers and exporters in South Asia. They are then followed by Bangladesh and Sri Lanka, although trade is relatively more important for Sri Lanka than for any other country in the region. All four countries, together with Nepal, normally run balance of trade deficits of substantial magnitudes. In 1984, Sri Lanka's trading position was the healthiest with a trade deficit of 27 percent as opposed to 60 percent for India, 118 percent for Bangladesh and 127 percent for Pakistan. In the case of Nepal, this ratio was a staggering 294 percent, indicating that the level of imports was about four times that of the country's exports. In every case, the current account deficit for 1984, which included net earnings on service and invisible items, was smaller than the trade deficit, showing that their dependence on the international economy was greater for commodities than for services. This, in turn, reflected the relatively low levels of demand for commercial and financial services in low income countries, rather than a stronger supply position relative to commodity trade. Indeed, while South Asian countries have increased their exports significantly in the past, their demand for imports has consistently outstripped this increase.

The oil price increases of 1974 mark a convenient watershed against which to judge the trade performance of the region. In the previous decade, Indian and Pakistani exports had risen by 2.4 percent and 3.7 percent *per annum*, while for Bangladesh and Sri Lanka export values fell during the early 1970s. Since 1974, these countries have all managed to increase their exports, Pakistan by about 7 percent and the remaining three at around 3 to 3.5 percent each year. In comparison with countries in Latin America and Africa, South Asian economies have been less severely hit by the recession in the world economy. But they have felt the effect of inflation in western economies which has led to increases in the prices of imported manufactured consumer goods, industrial raw materials and machinery. As they are all oil-importing countries, they have also suffered directly from the rise in oil prices with the more advanced economies of the region being more badly affected. Fuel imports now account for over 30 percent of Indian imports, well over 20 percent of imports into Pakistan and Sri Lanka, and just over 10 percent for Bangladesh and Nepal.

In recent years, there have been very substantial increases in the volume of international financial and commercial transactions, made possible by technological progress in the field of electronics and communications. Like most other developing countries, those of South Asia have taken little part in the growth of this trade. Their negative balance of trade in services results from their reliance on the international economy for the more traditional forms of services such as shipping and insurance. In the early 1980s, the region as a whole ran a deficit on shipping, with India's deficit the largest at SDR (Special Drawing Rights) 1.4 million (SDR = USA$ 1.34). For India, this is largely offset by a very substantial positive balance as a result of tourism for which it is the most important market and foreign exchange earner in the region. The other positive item which has helped to make current account deficits smaller than trade deficits is remittances from abroad. These are sums of money sent back by mainly skilled and semi-skilled workers from the subcontinent employed in the Middle East. India and Pakistan earned USA$ 2659 and 2567 millions, respectively in 1984. Indeed, their current account deficits would have been two to three times larger but for these earnings. As oil prices stop rising and demand for foreign labor slackens in the Middle East, the future of these inflows is becoming doubtful. At the same time, South Asian economies have, by and large, kept free of the growing burden of international indebtedness, partly through prudent financial management and partly, as in the case of Bangladesh, through their relative unattractiveness to commercial lenders. In the 1980s, the debt/exports ratio for the major economies of the region have been around 11 to 14 percent of export earnings, in comparison with over 20 percent for certain Middle-East economies and around 50 percent for Chile and Mexico.

A better understanding of the development process in South Asia can be obtained by observing changes in the composition of exports and imports, rather than their levels. In the early 1950s, India exported mostly primary products while imports were mainly manufactured consumer goods. By 1983, only 13 percent of Indian imports consisted of primary products including food, 37 percent of fuel and about 50 percent of machinery and other industrial inputs. Primary exports were down to 30 percent, textiles 14 percent and manufactures and machinery were 38 percent. Other South Asian countries show a similar pattern of reliance on these kinds of imports, with the exception of Bangladesh which depends heavily on imported food products. On the export side, Sri Lanka is still mainly an exporter of primary products. Bangladesh, Pakistan and, to a lesser extent, Nepal rely on textiles for much of their foreign exchange: about half of the total export earnings for Bangladesh and Pakistan come from this source. Nepal, a poorer country, exports large volumes of rice to India where it fetches a higher price. Many commodity movements are unrecorded, making an accurate picture of the pattern and levels of Nepalese trade impossible. Indian and Nepalese sources, for instance, give widely differing values of exports and imports between the two countries.

Bhutan, like Nepal, is landlocked and very reliant on India for markets. According to official figures, Bhutanese exports ran at an average level of USA$ 18 million in the 1980s, while her imports were USA$ 53 million, giving a balance of trade deficit of roughly USA$ 35 million. Her chief imports are fuel, rice and transport equipment, while her main exports are cement, fruit, vegetables and spices (cardamoms) and forestry products. In 1984, the value of exports from the Maldives were USA$ 23 million and imports were USA$ 61 million, leading to a trade deficit of USA$ 38 million which put the country in a relatively better position than either Nepal or Bhutan. The chief export of the Maldives is fish, especially tuna, and her imports cover a wide range of products typical of an underdeveloped and widely scattered island economy, from food and manufactured consumer goods to fuel, machinery and transport equipment.

In addition to changes in the composition of trade, important changes have also taken place in the direction of trade since South Asian countries gained political independence. The reasons are partly political in that they reflect a loosening of political ties with Britain. They are also partly economic, reflecting the declining importance of Britain in the international economy. For all of them,

Loading plantation produce in Colombo harbor.

Britain was the prime trading partner until World War II. Since then, her relative importance has declined both as a market for exports and a source of imports. The gap was initially filled by the USA. But since 1970, this share has also fallen, while trade has grown with the European Economic Community and the developed countries of the Pacific region such as Australia and Japan. Intra-trade between the South Asian economies themselves, however, has remained largely undeveloped. A rough idea of this can be gained for the pattern of trade between the countries which signed the Bangkok Agreement of 1976, that is Bangladesh, India, South Korea and Sri Lanka. In 1980–82, only 2.4 percent of the group's total exports were among its own members, while, within the group, India and South Korea were the main suppliers and accounted for more than 93 percent of the trade.

A shortage of foreign exchange and limited export prospects for a number of primary commodities have led some South Asian countries to develop bilateral trading relationships with the Socialist economies of Eastern Europe, and more recently with China. The most significant of these are between India and the USSR, although their importance has tended to decline over recent years. For these two countries, economic interests have coincided with strong political and strategic ones. Bilateral trading takes the form of barter of selected commodities directly between the countries, the values being adjusted so as to make trade balance. Aid from the USSR and Eastern Europe has also formed part of these relationships. For India, steel and equipment for projects such as the steel mill at Bhilai were paid for by Indian commodity exports. Obviously, the gains from this trade to the countries involved depends on relative prices, and on alternative potential uses of the exported commodities. On balance, South Asian economies have benefited from the barter trade, finding markets for primary exports and simple manufactures, and securing supplies of investment goods and industrial inputs. In relative terms, the volume of trade is small. For example, about 5 to 6 percent of exports from Bangladesh, Sri Lanka and Pakistan went to Eastern Europe in 1984, India's ratio being 15 percent. Its value has also been increasing less rapidly than the region's trade with Western market economies, although the absolute level continues to rise.

The growth and fluctuations in the foreign trade of South Asia have been influenced by domestic policy and changes in the international environment. Both India and Sri Lanka initially followed a policy of import-substitution, emphasizing industrialization aimed at the domestic market and underplaying the possibility of increasing traditional exports. A similar policy was adopted by Bangladesh after independence in 1971. Pakistan, in contrast, maintained a policy which was more favorable to exports, made possible by access to jute and tea from East Pakistan. The need to protect domestic industry and the more urgent need to cope with rapidly worsening balances of payment, however, led to increases in tariff protection in most South Asian countries. Tariff rates in the mid-1970s averaged between 65 and 75 percent in Bangladesh, India and Pakistan, and a little below 40 percent in Sri Lanka. This was accompanied by overvalued exchange rates, which further damaged the competitiveness of exports in world markets. India, in particular, relied heavily on the use of detailed direct control of foreign exchange and investment expenditure through various forms of quantitative controls, licensing of imports and industrial licensing. These policies made possible a substantial increase in industrial production, but also led to the wasteful use of industrial capacity, scarce foreign exchange and low productivity. A much smaller industrial base and greater dependence on the international economy made similar policies untenable in Bangladesh and Sri Lanka. In all three cases, there has been a gradual drift towards greater liberalization and reliance on market incentives. For instance, in 1984–85, the Indian government brought in measures for the liberalization of a large category of imports as well as more selective forms of incentives for export promotion. It has also become more dependent on the private sector, which is also the case in Bangladesh. Pakistan too has used administrative controls for managing the economy but these moved earlier in the direction of encouraging production for exports. The long-term effects of economic liberalization remain to be seen. In the short term, they have led almost uniformly to a deterioration in the foreign exchange position. In addition to changes in fiscal policy, Bangladesh, India and Sri Lanka have set

Table 31. South Asian economies: exports, imports, balance of trade and current account, 1970 and 1984 (Value in millions of USA $)

	1970 Exports	Imports	Balance of trade	Current account	1984 Exports	Imports	Balance of trade	Current account
Bangladesh[a]	321	1,174	−853	−614	934	2,042	−1,108	−521
India	2,026	2,124	−98	−394	9,437	15,002	−5,565	−2,429
Nepal	10.8	12.9	−2.1	n.a.	111	437	−326	−102
Pakistan[b]	535	785	−250	−667	2,592	5,873	−3,281	−1,118
Sri Lanka	339	353	−14	−59	1,454	1,847	−393	+9

[a]1975 figures.
[b]Relates to West and East Pakistan.
Source: World Bank, *World Development Report*, Annual reports; World Bank, *World Tables*, Vol. I, 3rd edn, 1983.

up specific Export Processing Zones (EPZ) to encourage exports of manufactured products. Industrial units setting up in EPZs are given special tax incentives and foreign exchange allowances on condition that production is for the export market. Over the years, a combination of devaluation and floating have also reduced the degree of over-valuation of exchange rates, especially in India and Sri Lanka.

As far as the international economy is concerned, two developments have had particularly significant effects on the trade of the region. First, the economies of the region have suffered from a worsening of the terms of trade due, on the one hand, to inflation, and on the other to falling primary product prices. Primary product prices declined after the Korean War boom until 1970. They reached a peak in the mid-1970s and have declined since then. Between 1974 and 1982, commodity terms of trade for South Asian economies declined at an annual rate varying from 0.5 percent for Pakistan to 7 percent for India. This deterioration was also caused in part by the rise in import prices, in particular oil prices. Potential loss of income from declining terms of trade has been estimated at approximately USA$ 65 million for jute exports and USA$ 408 million for tea during this period alone. In most cases, foreign exchange earnings were maintained through a more than proportionate increase in export volumes. The second factor has been the increasing emergence of protectionism in developed countries in relation to manufactured exports from developing parts of the world. This has led to the erection of tariff and non-tariff barriers. The use of cascading tariffs progressively discourages manufactured products from entering the markets of richer countries, according to the degree of processing involved. To an extent, this tendency has been countered by the setting up of a Generalized Preference System (GPS), which allows tariff concessions on agreed ranges of manufactured imports from the Third World. The positive effects of this system, however, are curtailed by the limited range of commodities that form part of the GPS, as well as by the entry of countries like Greece and Spain into the European Economic Community. A more serious threat to export prospects for the region lies in the increasing

Table 32. South Asian economies, 1983: net expenditure on selected service items (million SDRs, 1 SDR = 1.19 USA $)

	Transport	Travel	Other services	Investment income	Total
Bangladesh	−248	12	40	−76	−272
India	−1,363[a]	958	15	400[a]	10
Nepal	−22	28	73	n.a.	84
Pakistan	−246	33	9	−391	−595
Sri Lanka	−171	60	4	−128	−235

[a]1982
Source: UN ESCAP, *Economic and Social Survey of Asia and the Pacific 1985.*

proliferation and reliance on non-tariff barriers in rich countries which have taken the form of various voluntary agreements imposing informal quotas on a range of competitive exports. It has also taken the form of a Multifibre Agreement (MFA) which is directed at keeping a whole range of traditional and synthetic textiles away from Western markets. Given that the capacity of South Asian economies to import is critically dependent on their ability to earn foreign exchange through exports, growth of trade will depend very much on a move away from protectionism in the developed economies of the world. Otherwise, recent trends towards liberalization of trade and investment policy will have little chance of success.

Tourism

Tourism has emerged as an important economic activity in South Asia. From the so-called hippies of the 1960s, in search of mystic fulfilment, to the luxury package tourists of the 1980s, the subcontinent has come to exert a magnetic hold over people from many other parts of the world, the West in particular. The Taj Mahal, Rajasthani palaces, the imperial splendors of Delhi, Kashmir with its houseboats and waterlilies, and the palm-fringed beaches of Sri Lanka are among the main places on which tourists in their thousands now descend. The cooler part of the year from October to

A tourist bargains in New Delhi's Jan Path. Tourism is an important economic activity in most South Asian states.

March is the favorite time for visiting much of the region, although altitude reduces temperatures in the mountains during the hotter months. Many wealthier South Asians living in the plains or on the coast migrate to hill stations to avoid the heat of the summer. Srinigar (Kashmir) and Murree (Pakistan) have become popular destinations for local honeymooning couples, as has Goa, another center much loved by overseas visitors.

The potential impact of tourism had already been recognized by the time of World War II. Hostilities, however, put a stop to its promotion until 1945 when the Sargent Committee was set up to survey ways of developing tourist traffic. The Committee reported in late 1946 that it was in India's best interests to promote tourism, both external and internal. On the eve of Independence, a fairly large tourist infrastructure existed in the form of hotels and adequate transport and communications, but there was a need for some kind of centralized coordinating organization. Following independence, therefore, India established a Tourist Traffic Branch within the Ministry of Transport in 1949. The country's second Five Year Plan (1956–61) set aside separate funds for schemes to attract more tourists. From this point onwards, increasing amounts of expenditure were allocated to improving tourist facilities. During the 1950s, overseas tourist offices were opened: the first in New York in 1952 followed by others in London, Paris, Frankfurt and Melbourne. In 1967, a separate Department of Aviation and Tourism was created within the Transport Ministry. India now offers visitors a wide variety of different classes of hotel as well as reduced tickets on the railways and for internal air flights.

Other South Asian countries have encouraged tourism to varying degrees. Nepal, after setting up a Government Tourist Office,

opened its doors to tourists in 1952. Since then, it has placed great stress on extending and expanding tourist facilities, laying down an infrastructure of hotels, travel and trekking agencies, international publicity and trained personnel. Sri Lanka has also built up a solid tourist industry although recent ethnic troubles have resulted in a marked decline in the number of overseas visitors. Pakistan has its Ministry of Tourism and Tourist Development Corporation which runs information centers and resthouses in places of interest. As in India, there are travel concessions available to tourists. On the whole, the viability of a tourist industry remains unrealized by the private sector which is reluctant to invest, while the Government, although aware of the importance of generating tourist traffic, has had other spending priorities. Over the past few years, however, greater effort has been made to stimulate tourism throughout the country and in the scenic mountainous region in the northwest in particular. Tourism in Bangladesh remains largely undeveloped, the majority of overseas visitors being Bangladeshis settled abroad. In contrast, the Maldives have actively promoted tourism since the early 1970s, with great emphasis placed on the fine scuba diving facilities offered by the islands' resorts. Even Bhutan, which placed restrictions on tourism in 1974 to safeguard its way of life, now seeks to encourage tourism albeit of the selective, high-price variety: in 1986 the total number of visitors was just under 2500, while the target for the 1990s is only double this figure.

There are two points which should be remembered when assessing tourism as an earner of foreign exchange: first, information is always more readily available on people traveling by air, who are likely to be the wealthier visitors, and second, while it is easy to obtain figures on gross expenditure by tourists, these do not take into account the rather high import content of tourist consumption. So far, India has been the main beneficiary in absolute financial terms since India receives by far the largest number of tourists: in 1981, for instance India received 1.3 million visitors as compared with 370,000 who went to Sri Lanka, 290,000 to Pakistan, 162,000 to Nepal and 49,000 to Bangladesh. Similarly, recorded tourist expenditure in India in 1981 was USA$ 810 million as opposed to USA$ 132 in Sri Lanka, USA$ 128 million in Pakistan and USA$ 8 million in Bangladesh. In terms of relative impact, however, the economic significance of tourism is much greater in the smaller countries of Sri Lanka, Nepal and the Maldives.

About 90 percent of recorded arrivals in India and Sri Lanka in the early 1980s were by air. For Pakistan, it was only 55 percent with as many as 45 percent coming by road or rail, possible poorer workers using the country as a bridgehead for seeking employment in the Gulf and the Middle East. For most South Asian countries, about a quarter of tourists came from Europe and about half from their South Asian neighbors. For Sri Lanka, European arrivals were nearly 70 percent of the total number of tourists, mostly from West

Germany. Rather surprisingly North American proportions were low at about 10 percent for most countries. Less surprisingly those for Africa and Latin America were still lower.

PC

Further reading
V. N. Balasubramanyam, *The Economy of India* (London, 1984)
J. N. Bhagwati and P. Desai, *India: Planning for Industrialization* (Oxford, 1970)
Economic and Social Commission for Asia and the Pacific, 'Trade, Trade Policies and Development', Pt II, *Economic and Social Survey of Asia and the Pacific, 1986* (Bangkok, 1986)
J. Faaland and J. R. Parkinson, *Bangladesh: The Test Case for Development* (London, 1976) (esp. Ch X)
B. Farmer, *South Asia* (London, 1983)
S. R. Lewis, *Pakistan: Industrialization and Trade Policies* (Oxford, 1970)
D. Nayyar, *India's Exports and Export Policies in the 1960s* (Cambridge, 1976)

Savings, investment and foreign aid

South Asian economies, in common with those of other poor countries, face a serious policy dilemma. On the one hand, widespread and persistent poverty requires them to devote resources towards increasing current consumption. On the other, they need to look to the future to ensure that increases in consumption can be maintained at the same time as population grows rapidly. This means investing in all sectors of the economy to increase productive capacity and to introduce more efficient technologies. Such investment needs to be balanced by savings. A tendency for the rate of investment to run ahead of savings leads to excess demand for resources, which in turn creates instability. Such instability, whether it takes the form of inflation or a worsening balance of payments or a black market, in turn endangers the process of capital accumulation itself. As investment increases the level of output, what is crucial for the maintenance of stability is that the rate of investment should not be higher than the marginal rate of savings in the economy.

The more efficient the process of investment, that is, the lower the ratio of capital to output, the more successful is development policy going to be. However, if the relatively poor economies of South Asia were to be restricted solely to domestic savings to finance investment, it is unlikely that they could improve substantially the standards of living of their peoples. They need to attract foreign capital to supplement domestic savings, either as foreign aid from official sources or as loans from the private sector at commercial

rates of interest – multinational firms tending to be more important as sources of technology than of capital. Private loans may come from banks and other financial institutions or as suppliers' credit from commercial firms. Foreign aid is given mostly in the form of loans at concessional rates, on 'soft' terms. It can be either bilateral, that is, from government to government, or multilateral, that is, channeled through international agencies such as the World Bank. Broadly speaking, multilateral aid carries fewer political or economic strings, although it need be by no means unconditional. Nevertheless, multilateral loans from agencies such as the International Development Association have proved to be particularly valuable to poor countries. Apart from being 'soft' loans, they are given for projects most likely to benefit the poor.

Whatever their terms, loans have to be repaid mostly in hard currencies. As is well known, debt-servicing has become an important policy problem for the Third World. There are many reasons for this: deflationary monetary policies in developed countries, their increasing protectionism, the rise in oil prices, and poor economic management in borrowing countries. As donors cut back on aid, borrowers have turned increasingly to private loans at higher commercial rates of interest. Their export earnings are increasingly inadequate as a source of foreign exchange to pay even the interest charges on outstanding loans, as measured by ratios of interest payments to the value of goods and services exported. Although the economies of South Asia have suffered rather less from the debt problem than, for instance, the countries of Latin America, it is still a matter of growing concern.

Tables 33–57 provide details of the trends in savings, investment and foreign capital flows in five of the South Asian economies. Several key points emerge from the tables. First, India and Nepal show the strongest sustained increases in total savings and in their ratios of savings to gross domestic product since the 1960s. For the other three countries there was some setback to the growth of savings in the early 1970s, which was followed by a fairly strong recovery. Second, all five countries show sustained rises in their levels of investment, although savings and investment are both subject to fluctuations from time to time. These fluctuations quite often reflect the effects of internal or external 'shocks', for example poor monsoons, or the oil price increases of the mid-1970s. Mostly, the savings rates have been creditable ones for some of the world's poorest economies to achieve. We have to bear in mind, however, the relatively high ratios of capital to output in these countries which to some extent offset the benefits of investment. The third point to note is that, with the exception of India and Nepal, the gap between domestic savings and investment has tended to increase over time. Bangladesh, Pakistan and Sri Lanka have not been able to reduce their dependence on foreign capital. Fourthly, for all five countries, there have been significant changes in the composition of foreign

Savings, investment and foreign aid

capital. In all cases private capital flows have become more important as donor countries have cut back on the supply of foreign aid. Among sources of aid there has been some shift from bilateral aid to multilateral aid, with the exception of Sri Lanka. The fifth point to emerge from the tables is that the International Development Association has been a particularly important source of aid for Bangladesh and India, and not so in the case of Sri Lanka and Pakistan. This is somewhat surprising in the case of Sri Lanka, given her excellent record in promoting welfare at a relatively low level of *per capita* income. Finally, the debt-burden, which is most usefully measured in the short term by the ratio of interest payments to the value of goods and services exported, has been rising for all five countries, but is especially high for Bangladesh, Pakistan and Sri Lanka.

PC

Table 33. Savings profile of India

Year	Absolute saving (USA $ million)	Annual growth rate of saving (%)	Ratio of saving to GDP[a] (%)	Incremental saving–GDP ratio (%)
1960	5,375.9	—	17.0	—
1965	7,832.8	9.1	15.5	12.9
1970	8,880.0	2.7	16.5	18.1
1975	16,561.1	17.3	19.3	22.7
1980	32,827.1	19.6	20.3	21.7
1981	36,084.7	9.9	—	—

[a]GDP = gross domestic product.
Source: World Tables, 1984; VRP.

Table 34. Investment profile of India

Year	Absolute investment (USA $ million)	Annual growth rate of investment (%)	Ratio of investment to GDP (%)
1960	5,417.9	—	17.2
1965	9,302.8	14.3	18.4
1970	9,792.0	1.1	18.2
1975	18,973.8	18.8	22.2
1980	39,836.6	22.0	24.7
1983	45,943.6	5.1	24.2

Source: World Tables, 1984; VRP.

Table 35. Composition of loan commitments and disbursements to India from different sources (USA $ million)

	1975	1980	1983
Commitments	2,492.0	5,861.9	1,885.2
Official creditors	2,387.8	4,760.4	1,644.7
Multilateral	917.0	3,253.9	1,129.7
World Bank	100.0	555.0	500.1
IDA[a]	817.0	1,948.0	571.8
Bilateral	1,470.8	1,506.5	514.9
Private creditors	104.3	1,101.5	240.5
Suppliers	25.4	16.8	156.2
Financial markets	78.9	1,084.7	84.2
Disbursements	1,793.4	2,532.9	2,764.7
Official creditors	1,682.0	2,251.6	2,073.2
Multilateral	530.6	1,543.6	1,466.5
World Bank	39.3	173.8	470.9
IDA[a]	491.3	651.8	974.1
Bilateral	1,151.4	708.8	606.7
Private creditors	111.4	281.3	691.6
Suppliers	102.7	4.1	51.1
Financial markets	8.7	277.2	640.5

[a]International Development Association.
Source: World Debt Tables, 1983–1984 and 1984–1985; VRP.

Table 36. Foreign economic assistance to India (USA $ million)

	Countries	1960–1961	1970–1971	1982–1983
1	Australia	—	4.7	—
2	Austria	—	2.3	3.8
3	Belgium	—	4.4	4.0
4	Canada	24.5	105.3	43.9
5	Denmark	—	3.2	34.5
6	Finland	—	—	—
7	France	—	20.4	—
8	West Germany	71.3	82.0	184.7
9	Italy	2.9	—	—
10	Japan	11.9	56.7	133.4
11	Netherlands	—	14.0	74.3
12	New Zealand	—	—	—
13	Norway	0.8	3.7	—
14	Sweden	—	9.0	52.3
15	Switzerland	—	4.4	20.3
16	UK	55.4	129.0	145.0
17	USA	347.7	462.6	138.4
18	EEC	—	7.5	86.0
	Total	514.5	910.2	920.5

Source: *Twenty-Five Years of Development Co-operation* A Review, OECD, Nov. 1985, Paris; VRP.

Table 37. India's debt indicators

Indicators (%)	1975	1980	1983
1 DO/XGS	201.4	142.5	—
2 DO/GNP	14.3	10.8	11.4
3 TDS/XGS	12.4	8.6	—
4 TDS/GNP	0.9	0.6	0.7
5 INT/XGS	4.1	3.1	—
6 INT/GNP	0.3	0.2	0.3
7 DO (USA $ million)	12,243.7	17,575.7	21,276.6

DO : Debt outstanding
GNP: Gross national product
XGS : Export of goods and services
TDS : Total debt services
INT : Interest payments
Source: World Debt Tables, 1983–1984 and 1984–1985; VRP.

Table 38. Savings profile of Pakistan

Year	Absolute saving (USA $ million)	Annual growth rate of saving (%)	Ratio of saving to GDP[a] (%)	Incremental saving–GDP ratio (%)
1960	179.2	—	4.8	—
1965	747.6	63.4	12.7	26.11
1970	900.0	4.1	9.0	3.7
1975	673.2	(−) 5.0	5.9	3.7
1980	3,025.	69.9	12.6	18.6
1981	3,697.2	22.2	—	—

[a]GDP = Gross domestic product.
Source: World Tables, 1984; VRP.

Table 39. Investment profile of Pakistan

Year	Absolute investment (USA $ million)	Annual growth rate of investment (%)	Ratio of investment to GDP (%)
1960	428.4	—	11.6
1965	1,263.3	39.0	21.5
1970	1,588.6	5.1	15.8
1975	1,840.2	3.2	16.2
1980	4,378.3	28.6	18.2
1983	5,137.2	3.5	17.8

Source: World Tables, 1984; VRP.

Table 40. Composition of loan commitments and disbursements to Pakistan from different sources (USA $ million)

	1975	1980	1983
Commitments	527.7	1,229.0	1,033.8
Official creditors	509.5	930.5	1,021.7
Multilateral	208.0	570.2	680.2
World Bank	60.0	—	126.7
IDA[a]	38.0	184.8	179.5
Bilateral	301.5	360.2	341.5
Private creditors	18.2	298.6	12.1
Suppliers	5.4	18.8	7.1
Financial markets	12.7	279.8	5.0
Disbursements	867.2	1,209.2	739.5
Official creditors	820.9	902.3	685.7
Multilateral	157.7	326.9	279.6
World Bank	57.2	16.0	39.4
IDA[a]	23.3	73.9	105.2
Bilateral	663.2	575.4	406.1
Private creditors	46.2	306.9	53.8
Suppliers	15.6	45.1	31.3
Financial markets	30.6	261.8	22.5

[a]International Development Association.
Source: World Debt Tables, 1983–1984 and 1984–1985; VRP.

Table 41. Foreign economic assistance to Pakistan (USA $ million)

	Countries	1960–1961	1970–1971	1982–1983
1	Australia	—	1.7	—
2	Austria	—	2.4	—
3	Belgium	—	2.2	—
4	Canada	13.3	40.0	43.2
5	Denmark	—	1.4	—
6	Finland	—	—	—
7	France	—	—	—
8	West Germany	—	55.9	52.3
9	Italy	—	9.0	—
10	Japan	—	43.9	99.1
11	Netherlands	—	3.1	24.8
12	New Zealand	—	—	—
13	Norway	—	—	—
14	Sweden	—	9.5	—
15	Switzerland	—	0.6	2.6
16	UK	14.2	22.7	29.4
17	USA	208.6	166.4	129.8
18	EEC	—	4.2	—
	Total	236.1	363.0	381.2

Source: Twenty-Five Years of Development Co-operation A Review, OECD, Nov. 1985, Paris; VRP.

Savings, investment and foreign aid

Table 42. Pakistan's debt indicators

Indicators (%)	1975	1980	1983
1 DO/XGS	316.6	265.9	248.9
2 DO/GNP	44.5	34.4	31.0
3 TDS/XGS	15.5	17.9	21.9
4 TDS/GNP	2.2	2.3	2.7
5 INT/XGS	6.4	7.5	7.2
6 INT/GNP	0.9	1.0	0.9
7 DO (USA $ million)	5,096.7	8,780.0	9,465.6

DO : Debt outstanding
GNP: Gross national product
XGS: Export of goods and services
TDS : Total debt services
INT : Interest payments
Source: World Debt Tables, 1983–1984 and 1984–1985; VRP.

Table 43. Savings profile of Bangladesh

Year	Absolute saving (USA $ million)	Annual growth rate of saving (%)	Ratio of saving to GDP[a] (%)	Incremental saving–GDP ratio (%)
1960	237.5	—	7.5	—
1965	345.0	9.1	7.9	8.9
1970	534.0	11.0	8.0	8.3
1972	(−)160.5	(−)65.0	(−)3.5	3.2
1975	145.1	(−)14.6	1.0	(−)1.3
1980	452.0	42.3	4.0	11.6
1981	635.1	40.5	—	—

[a]GDP = Gross domestic product.
Source: World Tables, 1984; VRP.

Table 44. Investment profile of Bangladesh

Year	Absolute investment (USA $ million)	Annual growth rate of investment (%)	Ratio of investment to GDP (%)
1960	218.4	—	6.9
1965	502.3	26.0	11.5
1970	756.0	10.1	11.3
1972	216.1	−143.8	4.7
1975	1,149.4	10.4	8.1
1980	1,887.2	12.9	16.7
1983	1,743.1	−2.5	16.4

Source: World Tables, 1984; VRP.

Table 45. Composition of loan commitments and disbursements to Bangladesh from different sources (USA $ million)

	1975	1980	1983
Commitments	859.3	1,068.9	592.7
Official creditors	844.9	1,044.3	597.9
Multilateral	279.2	612.5	442.7
World Bank	—	—	—
IDA[a]	204.6	331.3	231.7
Bilateral	565.7	431.8	137.2
Private creditors	14.4	24.6	12.8
Suppliers	10.3	19.5	12.8
Financial markets	4.1	5.1	—
Disbursements	688.6	619.9	567.9
Official creditors	672.4	603.5	537.9
Multilateral	108.6	306.4	322.1
World Bank	—	—	—
IDA[a]	91.2	155.7	205.4
Bilateral	563.7	297.1	215.8
Private creditors	16.3	16.4	30.1
Suppliers	14.4	8.1	10.8
Financial markets	1.9	8.3	19.3

[a]International Development Association.
Source: World Debt Tables, 1983–1984 and 1984–1985; VRP.

Table 46. Foreign economic assistance to Bangladesh (USA $ million)

	Countries	1960–1961	1970–1971	1982–1983
1	Australia	—	23.7	—
2	Austria	—	—	—
3	Belgium	—	—	—
4	Canada	—	—	87.7
5	Denmark	—	—	22.6
6	Finland	—	—	—
7	France	—	—	—
8	West Germany	—	—	59.3
9	Italy	—	—	—
10	Japan	—	—	160.1
11	Netherlands	—	—	52.3
12	New Zealand	—	—	—
13	Norway	—	—	—
14	Sweden	—	—	20.0
15	Switzerland	—	1.5	3.7
16	UK	—	—	38.6
17	USA	—	—	199.0
18	EEC	—	—	53.8
	Total	—	25.2	697.1

Source: *Twenty-Five Years of Development Co-operation* A Review, OECD, Nov. 1985, Paris; VRP.

Table 47. Bangladesh's debt indicators

Indicators (%)	1975	1980	1983
1 DO/XGS	392.4	325.6	431.4
2 DO/GNP	11.4	30.5	39.1
3 TDS/XGS	16.3	7.0	14.7
4 TDS/GNP	0.5	0.7	1.3
5 INT/XGS	3.8	3.3	6.5
6 INT/GNP	0.1	0.3	0.6
7 DO (USA $ million)	1,612.8	3,521.1	4,184.5

DO : Debt outstanding
GNP: Gross national product
XGS: Export of goods and services
TDS : Total debt services
INT : Interest payments
Source: World Debt Tables, 1983–1984 and 1984–1985; VRP.

Table 48. Savings profile of Sri Lanka

Year	Absolute saving (USA $ million)	Annual growth rate of saving (%)	Ratio of saving to GDP[a] (%)	Incremental saving–GDP ratio (%)
1960	132.7	—	8.8	—
1965	214.6	12.3	11.9	27.8
1970	282.7	6.3	14.2	17.9
1975	215.8	(−) 4.7	7.3	0.1
1980	424.0	19.3	10.5	12.7
1981	427.7	0.9	—	—

[a]GDP = Gross domestic product.
Source: World Tables, 1984; VRP.

Table 49. Investment profile of Sri Lanka

Year	Absolute investment (USA $ million)	Annual growth rate of investment (%)	Ratio of investment to GDP (%)
1960	208.1	—	13.9
1965	215.9	7.7	12.0
1970	378.0	15.0	19.0
1975	460.1	4.3	15.6
1980	1,358.7	39.1	33.8
1983	1,493.7	3.3	28.8

Source: World Tables, 1984; VRP.

Table 50. Composition of loan commitments and disbursements to Sri Lanka from different sources (USA $ million)

	1975	1980	1983
Commitments	285.8	731.6	280.9
Official creditors	256.1	499.0	274.5
Multilateral	59.5	245.2	117.5
World Bank	—	—	—
IDA[a]	29.5	151.5	56.7
Bilateral	196.6	253.8	157.0
Private creditors	29.7	232.7	6.3
Suppliers	29.7	63.8	0.3
Financial markets	—	168.8	6.0
Disbursements	156.8	285.8	373.2
Official creditors	90.1	189.9	280.6
Multilateral	26.0	63.6	109.3
World Bank	5.6	0.4	14.5
IDA[a]	13.6	19.9	60.8
Bilateral	64.1	126.3	171.3
Private creditors	66.7	95.9	92.6
Suppliers	66.7	6.2	1.2
Financial markets	—	89.8	91.4

[a]International Development Association.
Source: World Debt Tables, 1983–1984 and 1984–1985; VRP.

Table 51. Foreign economic assistance to Sri Lanka (USA $ million)

	Countries	1960–1961	1970–1971	1982–1983
1	Australia	—	1.3	9.8
2	Austria	—	—	—
3	Belgium	—	—	—
4	Canada	2.4	6.9	34.6
5	Denmark	—	—	—
6	Finland	—	—	4.1
7	France	—	—	—
8	West Germany	—	—	38.4
9	Italy	—	—	—
10	Japan	—	—	72.4
11	Netherlands	—	—	23.4
12	New Zealand	—	—	—
13	Norway	—	—	—
14	Sweden	—	—	27.0
15	Switzerland	—	—	3.5
16	UK	—	12.6	51.4
17	USA	—	—	—
18	EEC	—	—	13.1
	Total	2.4	20.8	277.7

Source: *Twenty-Five Years of Development Co-operation* A Review, OECD, Nov. 1985, Paris; VRP.

Savings, investment and foreign aid

Table 52. Sri Lanka's debt indicators

Indicators (%)	1975	1980	1983
1 DO/XGS	92.5	100.3	157.0
2 DO/GNP	20.4	33.6	43.5
3 TDS/XGS	21.5	6.3	11.9
4 TDS/GNP	4.7	2.1	3.3
5 INT/XGS	3.2	2.5	6.1
6 INT/GNP	0.7	0.8	1.7
7 DO (USA $ million)	597.4	1,327.4	2,205.0

DO : Debt outstanding
GNP: Gross national product
XGS : Export of goods and services
TDS : Total debt services
INT : Interest payments
Source: World Debt Tables, 1983–1984 and 1984–1985; VRP.

Table 53. Savings profile of Nepal

Year	Absolute saving (USA $ million)	Annual growth rate of saving (%)	Ratio of saving to GDP[a] (%)	Incremental saving–GDP ratio (%)
1960	—	—	—	—
1965	10.5	—	1.8	—
1970	35.4	47.6	4.1	8.8
1975	99.5	36.3	6.3	8.9
1980	194.3	19.0	10.0	18.9
1981	230.2	11.9	—	—

[a]GDP = Gross domestic product.
Source: World Tables, 1984; VRP.

Table 54. Investment profile of Nepal

Year	Absolute investment (USA $ million)	Annual growth rate of investment (%)	Ratio of investment to GDP (%)
1960	—	—	—
1965	35.7	—	6.1
1970	51.7	9.0	6.0
1975	145.7	36.4	9.3
1980	355.8	28.8	18.3
1983	492.8	12.8	20.2

Source: World Tables, 1984; VRP.

Table 55. Composition of loan commitments and disbursements to Nepal from different sources (USA $ million)

	1975	1980	1983
Commitments	16.8	96.8	183.1
Official creditors	16.8	96.8	183.1
Multilateral	16.8	96.8	159.7
World Bank	—	—	—
IDA[a]	—	60.0	46.0
Bilateral	—	—	23.3
Private creditors	—	—	—
Suppliers	—	—	—
Financial markets	—	—	—
Disbursements	9.3	55.2	70.4
Official creditors	9.3	55.2	69.4
Multilateral	6.9	41.2	61.3
World Bank	—	—	—
IDA[a]	2.3	25.0	30.6
Bilateral	2.3	14.0	8.1
Private creditors	—	—	1.0
Suppliers	—	—	—
Financial markets	—	—	1.0

[a]International Development Association.
Source: World Debt Tables, 1983–1984 and 1984–1985; VRP.

Table 56. Foreign economic assistance to Nepal (USA $ million)

	Countries	1960–1961	1970–1971	1982–1983
1	Australia	—	0.9	—
2	Austria	—	—	—
3	Belgium	—	—	—
4	Canada	—	—	—
5	Denmark	—	—	—
6	Finland	—	—	—
7	France	—	—	—
8	West Germany	—	—	—
9	Italy	—	—	—
10	Japan	—	—	—
11	Netherlands	—	—	—
12	New Zealand	—	—	—
13	Norway	—	—	—
14	Sweden	—	—	—
15	Switzerland	—	0.4	11.2
16	UK	—	—	14.7
17	USA	—	—	—
18	EEC	—	—	—
	Total	—	1.3	25.9

Source: *Twenty-Five Years of Development Co-operation* A Review, OECD, Nov. 1985, Paris; VRP.

Table 57. Nepal's debt indicators

Indicators (%)	1975	1980	1983
1 DO/XGS	—	64.0	123.4
2 DO/GNP	2.1	8.9	13.9
3 TDS/XGS	—	1.5	3.0
4 TDS/GNP	0.1	0.2	0.3
5 INT/XGS	—	0.7	1.4
6 INT/GNP	0.1	0.1	0.2
7 DO (USA $ million)	33.7	173.9	346.4

DO : Debt outstanding
GNP: Gross national product
XGS: Export of goods and services
TDS : Total debt services
INT : Interest payments
Source: World Debt Tables, 1983–1984 and 1984–1985; VRP.

Further reading

M. Alamgir, 'Some Analysis of Distribution of Income, Consumption, Saving and Poverty in Bangladesh', *Bangladesh Development Studies* 11 (1974)

M. Alamgir and A. Rehman, *Saving in Bangladesh: 1959–60/1969–70*, Research Monograph, No. 2, Bangladesh Institute of Development Studies (Dacca, 1974)

F. Asmat, *Estimates of Private and Public Savings and Consumption for (West) Pakistan (1959–60 to 1979–80)*, Pakistan Institute of Development Economics, (Statistical Paper Series No. 4) (Islamabad, 1983)

Government of India Planning Commission, Working Group on Savings, *Capital Formation and Saving in India 1950–51 to 1979–80* (Bombay, 1982)

M. I. Khan *et al.*, 'Estimates of Non-Corporate Private Savings in Pakistan: 1949–62', *Pakistan Development Review* IV (1964)

R. N. Lal, *Capital Formation and its Financing in India* (Bombay, 1977)

Marga Institute, *Trade and Investment Based Economic Co-Operation Among Developing Countries of the ESCAP Region: Sri Lanka Study* (Bangalore, 1982)

S. N. H. Nagvi and K. Sarmad, *Pakistan's Economy Through the Seventies* (Islamabad, 1985)

National Council of Applied Economic Research, *All India Household Survey of Income, Saving and Consumer Expenditure, with Special Reference to Middle Class Households* (New Delhi, 1972)

National Council of Applied Economic Research, *Trends in the Indian Economy and Their Relevance for the Future* (New Delhi, 1985)

Opposite Hindus bathing in the Ganges at Garmukteshwar in Meerut district, Uttar Pradesh. Pilgrimages to rivers for bathing are a popular form of Hindu piety. The best known of these is the Kumbh Mela, which takes place every twelve years, when pilgrims from all over India gather at four bathing spots: Allahabad, Hardwar, Nasik and Ujjain.

RELIGIONS

Introduction

South Asia, alongside West Asia and China, formed one of the three nurseries of the great religious traditions of the world which took shape between 800 and 500 BC. While there developed a distinctive monotheistic tradition out of the prophetic visions of the Jews of Palestine, and while Confucius transformed earlier Chinese beliefs and practices into a coherent social and religious system, in South Asia the Upanishads, the seminal works of Hinduism, were composed and both Jainism and Buddhism emerged to challenge the developing Hindu way. Of the three South Asian faiths, Hinduism grew to become the dominant religious tradition of the subcontinent, Jainism although once influential in many parts of the region has been reduced to a few followers, and Buddhism, although similarly reduced, spread not only into Southeast Asia from Sri Lanka but also into East Asia where it helped to shape the worlds of China, Japan, Korea, Mongolia and Tibet. To the West, however, South Asian influences in pre-modern times seem to have been slight and are certainly problematic. Some scholars claim South Asian influences on Jewish heterodox thinkers, Greek philosophers and Muslim sufis, but most dismiss such suggestions out of hand.

South Asia has also been a receiver of religions and religious influences from outside. Small Jewish and Christian communities have flourished for centuries, as have those markedly successful survivors of Iranian Zoroastrianism known as the Parsis. The greatest impact from outside, however, has belonged to the Muslims, who wielded overwhelming power from the twelfth century, and the European Christians who did so from the completion of the British conquest in the nineteenth century. The Muslims changed the religious face of the subcontinent. In the twelfth century they were numbered in thousands; now they form one quarter of the population of the region as well as being one quarter of the Muslims of the globe. The encounter between Islam and Hinduism has had significant results: the long confrontation between the two faiths which remains a major source of tension throughout the region; the development of strands of Islamic thought which have found apparent common ground with the Hindu world in which they move; and the emergence of original movements of reform, such as Sikhism, whose independent character owes much to its founder's explicit rejection of both major religions. The impact of the European Christians was not seriously to change the confessional structure of the region once more, but to raise questions of social and intellectual concern which men of most faiths, and Hindus in particular, felt bound to answer. Thus leading Hindu thinkers from Rammohan Roy, the theist of the early nineteenth century, to Mohandas Karamchand Gandhi, the Mahatma or great soul of the twentieth century, were influenced by their experiences with Christians and Christian thought.

The influences which came from the West in modern times were not restricted to Christian ideas. There were other challenges, for instance, those of secular philosophies, of the modern state, and of the disconnection of religion from political power. The process of response brought about a revival among all the major faiths, introducing a period of great creativity in which religious understandings came to be expressed in new and varied ways. Among Buddhists and Muslims, for instance, for whom colonial rule brought about an end to the association between religion and the state, there developed beliefs and institutions which enabled them to survive quite apart from the structures of the colonial government. Among Hindus and Muslims there developed ways both of embracing and of developing European ideas of nationalism and of socialism. Among Hindus and Muslims again, there developed ideas regarding the appropriate relationship between religion and the state which ranged from a complete disconnection to a complete merging of the two elements. In the latter instance, those Muslims who founded Pakistan pioneered the first Islamic state in modern times which was to be a laboratory in which the relationship between revelation and contemporary requirements might be explored.

An important consequence of this creative response has been that the region has once more become a significant exporter of religions and religious ideas, although this time the main flow is to the West and not to the East as it was over 2000 years ago. Some of these religions and ideas, of course, have traveled with the spread of South Asian communities in the past centuries throughout the world. Thus Hinduism has spread as the British Empire brought new opportunities for trade and work from the Pacific to the Caribbean. So, too, has Sikhism with the migration of Sikhs to Britain, North America and elsewhere. But more significant are those religious ideas generated in India which have influenced men of many different faiths living outside the subcontinent. There are, for instance, those Hindu missionary organizations, such as the Ramakrishna Mission, not to forget many individual holy men whose vogue may only be but brief, that have found followers among the lost souls of the West. There are the Islamic 'modernist' ideas of Muhammad Iqbal and the Islamic 'fundamentalist' ideas of Maulana Maududi which have influenced important Muslim thinkers such as the Egyptian, Sayyid Qutb, and the Iranian, Ali Shariati. There is that outstanding twentieth century example of a Hindu religious life in Mahatma Gandhi which is known and admired throughout the world. The result is that in recent years South Asian religions, and men of faith in South Asia, have come to contribute what might seem to be a disproportionate share both to religious understanding and the growing dialogue among world religions. At the same time, however, and somewhat ironically, within the subcontinent spiritual concerns have come to be emphasized less as religion has been made to serve the ends of state, party, community and vested interest.

FR

Further reading
J. R. Hinnells, Ed., *A Handbook of Living Religions* (Harmondsworth, 1985)
N. Smart, *The Religious Experience of Mankind* (New York, 1969)

Brahmanism

Brahmanism, alternatively called Vedism, designates the earliest religion developed in India by the Indo-European tribes who invaded and settled in the subcontinent. Our knowledge of this ancient religion depends almost entirely on the enormous corpus of Sanskrit texts generated in the period from 1200 BC or before to the middle centuries of the first millennium BC. This corpus of sacred texts is collectively termed the Veda, 'knowledge' or 'wisdom', and forms the authoritative canon for all subsequent forms of orthodox Hinduism. Brahmanism is, then, not only the earliest religion of the subcontinent for which textual records exist; it is also the ancestor of the variety of later religious traditions which go under the name of Hinduism.

The Indo-Europeans came into India from the northwest in waves, perhaps beginning as early as 2000 BC, and quickly became the ruling power in the north. The Indus Valley civilization fell in the face of the superior military capabilities of the invading forces. The oldest surviving texts of the invaders and new settlers of ancient India, including the Rigveda which attained its final redaction *c.* 1200–900 BC, display a religion and a world view indebted in many ways to the Indo-European heritage, and comparable to the early religions of other branches of the Indo-Europeans who settled elsewhere throughout the western world from Iran to Ireland. While there has been some recent scholarship suggesting that the Indo-European invaders assimilated more of the indigenous culture that they found in India than previously imagined, the dominant thinking still maintains that what influence the Indus Valley civilization had on subsequent recorded Indian history and religion was negligible until after the period of Brahmanism.

Brahmanism was first the product of warriors and pastoralists, whose religion was often directed to the attainment of victory over enemies, accumulation of the goods of life (including cattle, which were procured in raids), and the increase of *lebensraum*. Among the chief deities of the Vedic pantheon was the mighty Indra, a thunderbolt-wielding king and warrior whose mythological exploits

include the defeat of the serpent Vritra, the symbol of chaos and obstruction, who had penned up the life-giving cosmic waters. Indra is also known as *puramdara*, the 'fort destroyer', perhaps in reference to his supposed ability to crumble the walled cities of the Indus Valley peoples. In any case, Indra, a powerful conqueror and fierce warrior, is the apotheosis of certain principal values of the Indo-Europeans who came to India. Earliest Brahmanism has thus been called 'agonistic' in that, for these ancient Indians, religion was often war by other means. Prayers and sacrifices unabashedly directed toward the pursuit of military and political power are not uncommon in the Rigveda and other Vedic texts.

Another feature of the early Vedic period was the religious interest in and importance of nature. Many of the deities of Brahmanism are correlated with natural phenomena: Surya, Dyaus, Savitri and Aditya are all connected to the sun; the name of the goddess Ushas means 'dawn'; the god Vayu is also the wind; and the chief deities of the sacrificial cult, Agni and Soma, are also manifested in fire and the soma plant, respectively. Vedic deities often doubled as natural entities and forces, and worship of the gods could often be understood as worship of nature.

Agni, the god of fire, as usually depicted. Agni is the chief messenger between the gods and men; his two faces represent the beneficient and destructive sides of his nature.

But two other traits of Brahmanism, the propensity to tripartition and the theory and practice of sacrifice, are most definitive of the religion.

Tripartition is part of the Indo-European legacy, as has been demonstrated most persuasively by the work of Georges Dumézil and others, and the general Indo-European preoccupation with triads is nowhere manifest more clearly than in ancient India. A tripartite ideology, which categorizes all things and beings into three 'functions' of sovereignty/religion, defense and material prosperity and fecundity, asserts itself in nearly all spheres of Vedic thought. At the most abstract and metaphysical level, the cosmic forces pervading and propelling the universe are divided into three types, corresponding to the three 'functions' of the tripartite ideology. The 'first function' is represented in metaphysical terms by the powers called *rita* (cosmic–moral order) and *brahman* (the religious force that is set into motion by the power of the efficacious word and the sacrificial act). 'Second function' forces, revolving around physically coercive power, include *virya* ('masculine strength') and *kshatra*, the power of warriors and rulers. Finally, there are 'third function' metaphysical forces like *pushti* ('increase') and *shri* ('welfare') which represent the impetus behind all aspects of cosmic fertility and reproduction.

These neuter powers were thought to be realized in the different classes of deities and humans. The cosmos was divided into three spheres of heaven, the atmosphere, and earth, and the thirty-three principal divinities of the Vedic pantheon were assigned to one or another of these cosmic regions. Gods charged with sovereignty and order, such as Mitra and Varuna, who control and manifest the powers of rita and brahman, frequent the heavenly sphere; warrior gods who are deified symbols of physical force, like Indra and his band of storm-troopers, the Maruts, dwell in the atmosphere or middle space; and cultic gods like Agni and Soma, are classified as earthly, and are associated with the powers of prosperity and fecundity.

So too was human society categorized into three interdependent but specialized classes. The later Hindu caste system finds its origin in the Vedic division of society into the three *varnas* (literally 'colors'): Brahmins or priests, Kshatriyas or warriors, and Vaishyas, the agriculturalists or merchants. A fourth varna, the Shudras or servants, was included early on in the classificatory scheme, probably in order to accommodate into Vedic society those who were not Indo-Europeans.

This social system was religiously legitimated in the famous hymn of the Rigveda (10.90) where the origins of the cosmos are depicted as a sacrificial dismemberment of a primeval deity, Purusha. From his head comes the Brahmins, from his arms are produced the Kshatriyas, his loins become the Vaishya, and his feet are made into the Shudras. The hymn is also significant in that it points to the creative power and general importance of the sacrificial ritual in Brahmanism.

The practice and ideology of fire sacrifice forms the centerpiece of Vedic religion. The ritual is divided into two main forms: the *shrauta* ceremonial, performed with three or five fires and up to seventeen priests, and the *grihya* or domestic sacrifice, utilizing one sacred household fire and usually performed by the householder himself. The details and meaning of the shrauta rites comprise the entirety of the earliest Vedic literature. The Veda in the singular is only a collective term for four Vedas: the Rig, Yajur, Sama and Atharva. Each of these four Vedas has survived in several recensions due to the varying practices of different ritual schools, and each Veda is the particular province of one of four different types of sacrificial priest. Every recension of the Veda consists of a Sanhita, in which the ritual formulas or *mantras* are given; a Brahmana, which explains the procedure and meaning of the rites; an Aranyaka or 'forest text', where the more esoteric and secret significances of the sacrifice are detailed; and an Upanishad, where mystical speculations reach their epitome. By the middle centuries of the first millennium BC, ritual guidebooks and encyclopedias called Sutras began to be composed, one type for the shrauta sacrifice and another for the grihya ritual.

The fire sacrifice, with offerings of cakes and butter, or soma (a plant with apparently mind-altering properties), or animals and, perhaps in some instances, humans, was performed to attain a variety of ends. The most spectacular of the supposed effects of the ritual centered around the maintenance of cosmic order. Vedic thought was obsessed by the fear of discontinuity and rupture, and sacrifice was regarded as cosmic glue and medicine: 'With the Agnihotra [the twice daily sacrifice] they healed that joint (which is) the two junctures of day and night, and joined it together. With the [fortnightly] New and Full Moon Sacrifice, they healed that joint (which is) between the waxing and waning lunar half-months, and joined it together. And with the [quarterly] Chaturmasyas they healed that joint (which is) the beginning of the seasons, and joined it together' (*Shatapatha Brahmana* 1.6.3.36). The power of the sacrifice to ensure regularity and continuity in the cosmos is dramatically illustrated in another passage which claims that the sun would not rise if the morning Agnihotra was not performed.

The sacrifice was also thought to have an effect on those who performed it. Not only was the ritual designed to procure for the sacrificer certain material goals in this life (social status, health, prosperity, long life, and descendents) but the sacrifice also served as the womb for the birth of a 'divine self' (a *daiva atman*) and the creation of a place for the sacrificer in the world of heaven. 'The sacrifice becomes the sacrificer's *atman* in yonder world. And, truly, the sacrificer who, knowing this, performs that [sacrifice] comes into existence [in heaven] with a whole body' (*Shatapatha Brahmana*

11.1.8.6). In the later layers of the literature of Brahmanism, this optimistic view of attaining a permanent place in heaven through sacrifice is shaken, first by speculation on the possibility of 'redeath' in the heavenly world as ritually accumulated merit is exhausted, and finally, in the Upanishads, with the notion of continual rebirth on earth impelled by the force of one's past *karma*.

The Veda came to be regarded very early on as sacred and absolutely authoritative due to the claim that it had a transcendental origin. It is called by Hindu religious teachers as early as the third or fourth centuries BC '*apaurusheya*', 'not of humans', and is also designated *shruti*, 'heard' or 'revealed'. Through an elaborate system of techniques for memorizing and reciting the text, the Veda was preserved over the centuries, and even the Vedic ritual survives among a few Brahmins in present-day India. While the doctrines and practices enshrined in the Veda are largely ignored by Hindus, belief in the sacredness of the text remains the touchstone of Hindu orthodoxy.

BSm

Further reading

J. Gonda, Gen. Ed., *A History of Indian Literature* (Wiesbaden, 1975) Vol. 1 fasc. 1: *Vedic Literature (Saṃhitās and Brāhmaṇas)*

J. C. Heesterman, *The Inner Conflict of Tradition: Essays in Indian Ritual, Kingship, and Society* (Chicago, 1985)

B. Lincoln, *Myth, Cosmos, and Society: Indo-European Themes of Creation and Destruction* (Cambridge, Mass., 1986)

L. Renou, *Vedic India* Translated by Philip Spratt (Delhi, 1971)

F. Staal, Ed., *Agni: The Vedic Ritual of the Fire Altar*. 2 vols (Berkeley, 1983)

Buddhism

This important world religion and philosophy is named after the title, the Buddha or Enlightened One, given to its founder, Siddhartha Gautama (*c.* 563–483 BC). According to tradition, Siddhartha was born in Kapilavastu, near the present Indian–Nepalese border. A member of the kshatriya or warrior caste, he was the son of the ruler of a petty kingdom. Raised in a life of sheltered luxury, he married early and had one son. At the age of twenty-nine, he became disillusioned with the worldly life which he renounced to wander as a mendicant. After a period in which he practiced Yoga and engaged in radical asceticism, he gave up these spiritual paths as fruitless and entered on a distinctive course of meditation which resulted in his enlightenment *c.* 528 BC at Bodh Gaya in present day Bihar. After a period of intense inner struggle, the Buddha began to preach. Gathering around himself a body of followers, he organized a monastic community, the *Sangha*, comprised of both monks and nuns. During the annual rainy season the monastic communities settled in fixed retreats, the forerunners of later monasteries. The remainder of the Buddha's life was spent wandering from place to place in the Ganges Valley preaching to monastic and lay followers who later codified his oral teachings. The Buddha died in Kushinagara in what is now Nepal at the age of eighty. The cause of his death was food poisoning.

The Buddha challenged much that the dominant Brahmanic tradition of his day held sacred. He rejected the authority of the priesthood and the Vedic scriptures, and denied the significance of the Vedic gods, sacrificial cult, and caste distinctions. Yet he accepted the Hindu idea that life is cyclical with death followed by rebirth in accordance with the law of *karma* (literally 'deed' or 'action'). Karma is the principle that the nature of one's existence is determined through a natural process as a reward or punishment for one's deeds in past lives. Nonetheless the Buddha denied the Hindu idea of an eternal, unchanging soul (*atman*) which transmigrates, instead maintaining that the individual is comprised only of an ever-changing aggregation of body, consciousness, feelings, perceptions, and predispositions. The heart of the Buddha's teaching was the Four Noble Truths, namely that: life is essentially painful; all such suffering is caused by ignorance and desire; there is an indescribable state beyond suffering called *Nirvana*; the way to attain this ultimate goal of Nirvana is by following an Eightfold Path which can be summarized in terms of perfection of wisdom, morality and meditation.

In simplest terms Buddhist morality involves avoiding evil, doing good and purifying one's mind. Evil is defined as any action which is harmful, whether to yourself or to any other creature, and is believed to be rooted in lust, hatred and delusion. In contrast, the Buddhist ideal is to be detached from the material world and to cultivate the ethical ideals of loving-kindness, compassion, sympathetic joy and equanimity.

The teachings of the Buddha have been codified into a canon of sacred scriptures known as the *Tripitaka* (Sanskrit) or *Tipitaka* (Pali; literally 'Three Baskets'). These were first put into written form in Sri Lanka about the first century BC during the reign of King Vattagamani. Some early schools used Sanskrit as their scriptural language. No complete version of the canon is extant in Sanskrit. However, the full canon survives in Pali, a dialect of Sanskrit. This is used for its scripture by the Theravada Buddhist tradition dominant today in Sri Lanka and much of southeast Asia. Running to about thirty volumes in modern printed editions, the *Tipitaka* is comprised of three major divisions: the *Suttas* or discourses of the Buddha, the *Vinaya* or monastic discipline and the *Abhidamma* or higher scholastic philosophy.

At the time of the Buddha's death, his teachings existed only in

The temptation of Buddha by Mara painted on the wall of a rock temple at Ajanta (Maharashtra) in the fifth century AD. The Buddha sits serene while Mara's daughters dance seductively and his armies assail him.

oral form. Thus his refusal to appoint a successor as head of the Sangha created a potential for disagreement and division within Buddhist community. This threat was early recognized by the community which responded with a series of assemblies intended to reach agreement on correct doctrine and practice. Tradition has identified four such assemblies as major councils.

At the first council, held at Rajagriha shortly after the death of the Buddha, the oral traditions were recited in order to settle on proper monastic discipline and the actual teachings of the Buddha.

A second council was held at Vaishali about a century later. This council was called to respond to the relaxation of ten points of monastic discipline in some circles. Many scholars consider the first great split within Buddhism, that between the *Mahasanghikas* (Great Community) and *Sthaviras* (Elders), to have originated with this council. Although the council temporarily smoothed over the existing points of contention, the tensions continued to smolder. As a result the council was, in effect, reconvened some 37 years later at Pataliputra. Here the issue was certain points of doctrine, such as the nature of saintly perfection, for example, which bore on monastic discipline. The outcome was the formalization of the schism between the majority *Mahasanghikas* and the more orthodox *Sthaviras*. Unlike their more conservative opponents who considered the Buddha to have been but an enlightened human teacher, the *Mahasanghikas* came to regard him as an eternal, transcendent being.

Further internal divisions over the course of time eventually led to the development of the so-called eighteen *Hinayana* (literally 'Little Vehicle') Buddhist schools. The eighteen schools of Hinayana disagreed over such matters as the nature of Buddhist sainthood, the transcendence of the Buddha, what is real, and the precise texts to be recognized as scripturally authoritative, as well as over specifics of monastic discipline.

The third major council was held at Pataliputra during the reign of Ashoka Maurya (r. *c.* 272/268–232 BC). The impetus behind this council was the influx into the order of heretics and monks who were lax in their observance of monastic discipline, a result in part of royal patronage of the Sangha. The council was called by Ashoka to purify the order, and was presided over by an eminent monk, Moggaliputta Tissa. The heretical views were refuted and the offenders expelled by the council. Some consider those expelled to be the forerunners of the *Sarvastivadins*, a school whose scriptures were in Sanskrit and whose thought was distinguished by the idea that all phenomena have a real albeit momentary existence. It is at this council that the *Tipitaka* is supposed to have been completed with the addition of the *Abhidamma* as the third collection of canonical texts.

Buddhist tradition sees Ashoka as the model of a Buddhist monarch. He is presented as a bloodthirsty conqueror who under-

goes a radical conversion, becoming an ardent supporter of Buddhism who based his reign on the Buddhist principles of righteousness, while also patronizing such groups as the Jains and Ajivikas. Ashoka played a crucial role in the spread of Buddhism. According to Buddhist tradition, largely supported by the edicts Ashoka had carved on rocks, pillars and cave walls throughout his empire, Ashoka sent Buddhist missionaries throughout India, into the Himalayan regions, and as far afield as Sri Lanka, and even to Greece. The mission to Sri Lanka, which succeeded in converting the royal court to Buddhism, was headed by Ashoka's son and daughter, Mahinda and Sanghamitta.

The form of Buddhism which became the state religion of Sri Lanka was Theravada, the Way of the Elders. An offshoot from the *Sthavira* movement supported by Ashoka, it emerged in Sri Lanka by the second century BC, a consequence of Mahinda's mission. The position of Theravada was consolidated by King Dutthagamini in the first century AD. It alone of the so-called Hinayana schools survives.

From the time of its introduction until the fifth century AD, Theravada Buddhism prospered in Sri Lanka. A key figure from this period was the fourth to fifth century Buddhist exegete Buddhaghosa who went to Sri Lanka from India. In Sri Lanka he wrote numerous commentaries and *The Path of Purification*, an authoritative compendium of Theravada doctrine.

With the exception of a revival of its fortunes between the twelfth and fourteenth centuries, Buddhism in Sri Lanka underwent an extended period of decline after the fifth century, brought on first by local political upheaval coupled with Tamil invasions from India and, eventually, by European domination of the country beginning in the sixteenth century. Beginning in the second half of the nineteenth century, Buddhism underwent another revival in Sri Lanka. Today over 60 percent of the population of Sri Lanka is Buddhist.

The success of the Ashokan missions to Gandhara and Kashmir made possible the spread of Buddhism to the kingdoms of central Asia and thence, eventually, to China, where its presence is attested by the middle of the first century AD.

The success of these missions also paved the way for the eventual conversion of King Kanishka of the Kushan dynasty in the first or second century AD. The fourth great Buddhist council was held in Kashmir under Kanishka, an active patron of the *Sarvastivadins*, who thrived in the region for nearly 1000 years. At this council the canonical texts of the *Sarvastivadins* were established.

The *Mahasanghikas* are the predecessors of *Mahayana* (literally 'Great Vehicle') Buddhism, one of the most important branches of the religion today, and the form which became dominant in east Asia. The origins and early history of Mahayana are obscure. Whether it first arose in southern or northwestern India has been

The senior monk at the Punakha festival, Bhutan.

much debated. The formative period of Mahayana was between the second century BC and the first century AD. It created new Sanskrit scriptures, among the more important being the *Lotus Sutra* and the *Perfection of Wisdom Sutras*. It developed a concept of divine grace and a devotional (*bhakti*) orientation, worshiping a variety of heavenly manifestations of the Buddha and numerous *bodhisattvas*, or socially oriented saints who are devoted to working for the salvation of others. Some scholars have seen Mahayana as a result of Hinduizing tendencies within Buddhism. Among early Mahayana Buddhists, the philosophers Nagarjuna (second or third century AD) and Vasubandhu (fourth or fifth century AD) are particularly worthy of note.

Still another important form of Buddhism had developed in the north of India by the seventh century AD. Known as Tantrism or *Vajrayana*, it developed side by side a Hindu counterpart also known as Tantrism. Vajrayana developed out of Mahayana under the influence of popular folk magic and religion. An esoteric tradition, it places much emphasis on elaborate and colorful ritual and a system of meditation involving the visualization of both Buddhist deities and demons, as well as the use of mystical chants, gestures and diagrams.

From India, Vajrayana spread throughout the Himalayan regions where it became the dominant form of Buddhism and was influenced by Tibetan shamanism. This type of Buddhism attained the status of official state religion in Bhutan and Sikkim. According to one estimate, 75 percent of the population of Bhutan today is Buddhist, while the number in Sikkim is closer to one third of the populace. Buddhists of this type constitute a significant minority of the population in Nepal as well.

While Buddhism continued to play a role of significance in Sri Lanka and in the Himalayan regions, it fell on hard times in the land of its birth. By the end of the twelfth century AD Buddhism had largely disappeared from India, though it continued to exist in the south and other scattered regions for another two to three centuries. The precise reasons for its disappearance are complex and open to scholarly debate. Three contributing factors seem crucial, however. First, Hinayana seemed to offer little to the laity, and thus found the patronage necessary for its survival ever more difficult to come by. In short, it was no longer a significant spiritual force. Second, from the seventh century AD onward, at the popular level Buddhism had become less and less distinguishable from its Hindu rivals. This was a result of the growing significance of Mahayana devotionalism and the development of Tantrism. Third, the Muslim invasions of India resulted in the large scale slaughter of monks and destruction of the monastic institutions necessary to the vitality and separate identity of Indian Buddhism.

It is only within the last century that Buddhism has begun to undergo something of a resurgence in India. *JPMcD*

Further reading
K. S. Ch'en, *Buddhism: The Light of Asia* (New York, 1968)
H. Nakamura, *Indian Buddhism: A Survey* (Hirakata City, Japan, 1980)
C. Prebish, *Buddhism: A Modern Perspective* (University Park, Pa., 1975)
W. Rahula, *History of Buddhism in Ceylon* M. D. Gunasena (Colombo, 1956)
R. Robinson and W. Johnson, *The Buddhist Religion* (Encino, Cal., 1977)
A. K. Warder, *Indian Buddhism* (Delhi, 1970)

Jainism

There are three and a quarter million Jains in India, just under one half of one percent of the population. Jains are thought of by others as a wealthy, puritanical and inaccessibly exclusive sect, devoted to ascetic practices. Though there is some truth in this stereotype, it fails to recognize the great role Jains have played in the history and imagination of the subcontinent. In ancient times they were largely responsible for establishing vegetarianism as a desirable social practice, and in the recent past they gave Gandhi the basic notion of *ahinsa* (non-violence) which he used so effectively. Today Jains make a disproportionately great contribution not only to industry and commerce, but also to the professions and public life.

The fundamental doctrine of Jainism is that an indestructibly immortal and immaterial 'life' or 'soul' (*jiva*) dwells within every living entity, indeed even within insects and microscopic life. Through passions of desire and hatred, which result in injury to others, the soul is rendered vulnerable to *karma* (the effect of former deeds), conceived as a kind of matter which binds to the soul and defiles it. The result of such defilement is that the soul is forced to suffer, and to be reborn repeatedly. Such suffering will carry on without end unless something drastic is done to interrupt the adhesion of karma to the soul, and to purify it of karma already accreted.

Jainism takes a strikingly austere view of how to purify oneself. One should adopt practices of ahinsa, literally 'non-harming', in every dimension of one's life. One should never cause harm to others by any act of speech, especially by lying. One should never eat meat, nor indeed such vegetables as potatoes or onions, which are thought to harbor microscopic souls. To have possessions at all fosters desire, so one should give up all possessions: in some interpretations, even clothing. One should be celibate, and ideally one should even die through *sallekhana*, a vow to fast until death.

These are stern precepts, and our earliest reliable information on Jainism places it as the creed of a group of self-mortifying, celibate,

A Jain on a personal pilgrimage to the temples of Gujarat sweeps the ground in front of him to avoid harming any form of life.

propertyless male renouncers living in about the sixth century BC, in northeast India in Bihar and southern Nepal. The Jain ascetics, then called *nirgranthas*, the 'unfettered' or 'liberated', were but one such group among the many which burgeoned in the then prevailing atmosphere of philosophical innovation and religious experiment. The nirgranthas were led by Vardhamana, called Mahavira ('great hero'), or the Jina (the 'conqueror' of himself and of karma), whence the terms Jain and Jainism. Mahavira's legendary biography is one of spectacular endurance and self-mortification.

Mahavira was an older contemporary of the Buddha, and the Buddhists for their part regarded the Jains as too extreme in their asceticism. In response the Jains have always regarded other ascetics as too lax, and themselves as holding to the original strict values of the renouncers. There are indeed scraps of evidence to suggest that Jainism did originate before Mahavira, and the Jain practices do seem closest to the ascetic practices which prevailed in that part of India before Mahavira and the Buddha came on the scene. Despite Hindu arguments to the contrary, ancient Jainism owed very little to the Brahmanism of the Vedas and Upanishads.

The nirgranthas were mendicants, supported like other religious mendicants by a charitable laity. At first Jainism offered little to this laity beyond merit leading to a better rebirth, but in medieval times there developed a unique literature, the *sravakacara* texts, which laid down elaborate rules and a great architecture of voluntary vows which a pious layman could undertake. The notions and customs inherent in this literature must have contributed greatly to the Jain laity's puritanical exclusiveness.

But some such exclusiveness must have been inherent very early in Jainism, for Jains have always been schismatic, excluding not only those outside the fold but inside it as well. The first and greatest schism occurred perhaps even as early as the fourth century BC, giving rise to two sects: the Digambaras or 'Sky-clad', so called because their ascetics go naked, and the Svetambaras or 'White-clad', so called because their ascetics wear white. The two sects possess different scriptures, hold slightly different views on cosmological matters, and have never made a serious attempt to come together. The medieval period saw further schisms, some of which are now defunct, and in late medieval and modern times yet further sects proliferated. These latter-day sects differ over such matters as whether to worship images or not. Yet in their devotion to ahinsa, and in their orientation to life around them, Jains of different sects have far more in common than their schismatic history would suggest.

Jains are now spread throughout India, but their greatest concentration is western India: a northern group inhabits Gujarat, Rajasthan, western Madhya Pradesh and Bombay, and a southern group inhabits southern Maharashtra and Karnataka. Jains are one of the few religious groups in India which have more urban than rural members, and a very great many are businessmen. Indeed Jains have probably made the greatest single contribution to the distinctive lifestyle of businessmen (*mahajans*) of all sects in commerce-oriented Gujarat and Rajasthan. Yet not all Jains are merchants, and in the southern group the greatest majority by far are farmers.

Why has Jainism survived in India while Buddhism, evidently more successful in general, nevertheless disappeared in its homeland? The answer perhaps lies in the Jains' very exclusiveness, in their adherence to practices which single them out as unremittingly austere and morally superior. For these practices place them, not at the periphery of Indian life, but at the very center. The social discriminations of caste (the superiority of Brahmins, the inferiority of Harijans, and the fine gradations of castes in between) are predicated on just such practices as vegetarianism, and just such attitudes of exclusiveness, as Jains patented for themselves very long ago. Jains are not Hindus, but they could persevere nowhere better than in Hindu India.

MC

Further reading
M. B. Carrithers and C. Humphrey, Eds, *The Assembly of Listeners: Jains in Society* (Cambridge, *in press*)
P. S. Jaini, *The Jaina Path of Purification* (Berkeley, 1979)
V. A. Sangave, *Jaina Community: a Social Survey.* 2nd edn (Bombay, 1980)

Hinduism

'Hindu' is a term used originally by others to identify natives of the subcontinent. It has come to be used to characterize those Indians who do not explicitly identify themselves with traditions stemming from outside India such as Islam, Christianity, Judaism as well as Buddhism, which though indigenous to India had not been practiced there for many centuries until recently revived. Even this usage of the term is not consistent, however: Jains and Sikhs, for example, are frequently not considered Hindus despite the indigenous origins of their beliefs. There is no organized Hindu church, no recognized leader or leaders of Hinduism, no agreed set of scriptures and no shared doctrines. Thus to speak of Hinduism as a single religion is misleading. Furthermore, if it is thought to be a necessary condition of being religious that there should be belief in a single supreme God, Hinduism cannot even correctly be termed a religion. In India past and present, many sectarian movements have emerged, some theistic, some not.

Indian philosophy
Certain traditional assumptions appear during the first millennium AD to have been characteristic of an Indian view of man and his place in the universe. The three principal human goals (*purushartha*) are material prosperity (*artha*), satisfaction of desires (*kama*), the duties of one's station (*dharma*), and, there is a fourth goal, liberation (*moksha*) from the series of rebirths to which every living being is subject. An ideal life has four stages (*ashrama*): studentship, in which the individual is introduced to the goals and the ways to achieve them; householdership, in which the individual practices

his vocation, procreates his sons and raises them according to his duty; forest-dwelling, in which the individual, after his children have grown, retires to meditate; and the stage of mendicancy (*sannyasa*) where the individual gives up all his possessions and wanders among the populace, dependent on alms.

Types of traditional literature are devoted to each of the four human goals. A general term for a didactic treatise or subject-matter is *shastra*. A number of texts known as *arthashastra* (or, more commonly, *nitishastra*) provide common sense maxims for earning and preserving material possessions, and are supplemented by specific shastras dealing with particular vocations. The *Kamasutra* of Vatsyayana is only the best known of many similar texts which offer counsel in erotics and related matters, including what other traditions would classify under esthetics. *Dharmashastras* teach the proper behavior for those of various stations in a large number of societal situations, dealing especially with family responsibilities and the duties of the several castes.

The literature devoted to the gaining of liberation comprises what has been termed 'Indian philosophy'. Liberation in the present context means deliverance from the round of rebirths which was believed by many Indians of classical times to be the lot of every individual person, animal or god. The mechanism driving this cycle of rebirths was termed *karman* (action, or better, making). According to the theory of *karma* (the effect of former deeds) taught in philosophical literature, each person, animal or god, is a self (*atman*) which has existed without a beginning. This self is the seat of experiences and the agent of actions. Any action, unless done by a suitably knowledgeable person in the spirit of nonattachment to its results, produces traces which accrete to that self and are carried along with it. When the organism with which a self is associated in a given lifetime expires, and perhaps after an interim sojourn in heaven or hell, a certain portion of the traces acquired by that self become operative. This operative portion of one's karmic store is responsible for three features of the next life to come. It determines one's birth, that is, whether one is born next as an animal, human or god, and if human the type of family one is born into; it determines the length of one's coming lifetime; and it determines the experiences one will have in the next life, traces laid down by bad actions having frustrating, perhaps painful results, those laid down by good actions having satisfying, perhaps pleasant results. The operative karma is 'burned off' by the embodiment, life and experiences it produces, but is replaced in the individual's store by the further traces he acquires as he performs actions in the coming life. It is deliverance from this cycle of rebirths that constitutes the highest goal of man.

Systems of Hindu philosophy

The most common term for a philosophical system is *darshana*, literally 'view' or 'vision'. Most systems are maintained to the present day. Hindu philosophy is often classified into six systems: Nyaya, Vaisheshika, Sankhya, Yoga, Purvamimansa and Vedanta. This traditional classification is, however, not particularly old and obscures some of the important similarities and differences among the systems.

Nyaya and Vaisheshika appear to have had their roots in the sciences of debate and medicine, respectively. The speciality of Nyaya is logic and theory of knowledge, while Vaisheshika propounds an atomic theory as the basis of a realistic and pluralistic metaphysics. By the eleventh century, the two systems had explicitly recognized their complementary character. For Nyaya–Vaisheshika, the center of ultimate concern is the self, an eternal substance visited by fleeting qualities and undergoing beginningless and repeated embodiments. Liberation is gained through a scientific investigation of the kinds of entities extant in the universe, and in particular of their causal relations to human experiences. Consciousness is not an intrinsic but only an accidental property of self; therefore, by understanding the causal conditions of experiencing, one can learn to eliminate those conditions through meditation and thus achieve release from rebirth.

Sankhya teaches a fundamental dualism between *purusha*, consciousness, and *prakriti*, the source of the world we know. Prakriti when in contiguity with a purusha transforms itself into mental and material forms familiar to us, and continues to do so as long as the difference between prakriti and purusha is not understood. When this discrimination is achieved, prakriti no longer evolves for that purusha, and liberation ensues. The earliest complete text of Sankhya still extant is Ishvarakrishna's *Sankhyakarikas* (probably fifth century AD). Sankhya treatises are not numerous, and it appears that the system has essentially disappeared as a separate school, perhaps being absorbed into one or more of the Vedanta systems.

Yoga as a philosophical system dates back at least to Patanjali's *Yogasutras* (*c*. third century AD). It essentially shares the metaphysical views of Sankhya. Its principal concern is with the meditative practices leading to higher stages of meditation, the highest of which is liberating. The term 'yoga' comes to mean any kind of spiritual discipline. In the *Bhagavad-gita* several yogas (of knowledge, devotion and ritual activity) are discussed and distinguished, and later on a variety of techniques of self-discipline are taught, for example, repeating God's name (*japayoga*) or a stock phrase (*mantrayoga*), bodily asceticism (*hathayoga*) and so on.

The term '*Purva-mimansa*' ('earlier exegesis') identifies the practice of interpreting scripture according to regular procedures. Vedic exegesis viewed everything in terms of ritual activity: it finds that the Vedas are entirely injunctive in nature, so that those passages that are declarative in form are either reinterpreted as injunctions or are classified as providing ancillary information clarifying the injunctions and making them practicable. Though in early Vedic times liberation was not contemplated, in the seventh century exegetes posited liberation as a goal and entered in philosophical controversies with other schools. They developed a metaphysics and an epistemology resembling Nyaya's but with a few important differences.

The earliest pieces of literature associated with Mimansa philosophy are the *Mimansasutras* of Jaimini (*c.* first century AD) and its commentary by Shabara (*c.* fourth century AD). Although Shabara shows awareness of the kinds of problems other systems have come to discuss by this time, neither of these writers speak of liberation, and thus these texts must properly be thought of as having to do with dharma rather than with moksha.

The two figures who develop Mimansa in philosophy are Kumarila and Prabhakara (both probably seventh century). Although commenting on Shabara's work, at least implicitly they posit liberation as a goal as they controvert the views of other systems that flourished in their period. Kumarila's school is known as the Bhatta, Prabhakara's that of the Guru.

The term *vedanta* literally designates the concluding sections of the Vedic corpus, the Upanishads: it refers to those views which owe their inspiration to the Upanishads. Since the Upanishads are subject to widely varied interpretations the variety of Vedanta systems is not surprising, ranging from mystical idealistic monism to devotional realistic pluralism.

The fundamental texts for all Vedanta systems include, besides the Upanishads themselves, the *Brahmasutra* of Badarayana (*c.* first century AD), a series of aphorisms reflecting Upanishadic teachings, and the *Bhagavad-gita*, a portion of one of the Indian epics, the *Mahabharata*. Vedanta writers frequently comment on some or all of these works. There are many Vedanta systems. Three of the most important are explained below.

Advaita ('nondualistic') Vedanta

The Advaita Vedanta takes as fundamental the Upanishadic identification of the self and Brahman, the single cosmic principle. Generally, Advaitins believe the plurality of things and persons in the empirical world to be the result of cosmic ignorance (*maya* or *avidya*), which projects unreal differences and hides the underlying unity of Brahman. Liberation of an individual self consists of the realization that there is nothing real except the pure consciousness that is Brahman. This realization precludes the acquisition of further karma and eliminates all residues of past actions except for those whose results are operative and so designated to be worked off in the present life. Thus, Brahman knowledge produces a state of liberation while living which ends at that self's death, after which no

further rebirths occur and there is no individual self distinct from the self that is Brahman.

The most famous Advaitin, and India's best-known philosopher, was Shankaracharya (seventh–eighth century AD). Shankara was especially concerned to argue that the path of action and the path of knowledge are incompatible, that both cannot be practiced at once, and that the Upanishads must be understood as having two parts, one enjoining acts on those unprepared for Brahman knowledge, the other providing the understanding of the truth to those prepared for it. In this, he disagreed not only with the Purvamimansaka interpretation of scriptures which finds them exhaustively injunctive in function, but also with various Vedantic predecessors known as Bhedabhedavadins, who believe in a path to liberation combining ritual action and meditation. Meditation for Shankara counts as an action, and anyone who performs actions at all cannot be viewed as liberated.

Vishishtadvaita ('qualified nondualistic') Vedanta

This Vedanta claims as its prime exponent Ramanuja, an enterprising scholar and proselytizer of the twelfth century. While Advaita, though not incompatible with theism, assigns a somewhat inferior status to a personal God, Ramanuja interprets the Brahman of the Upanishads to be a personal God who encompasses the world and the individual selves within Himself as his modes or aspects. Ramanuja is specifically opposed to Shankara's notion that the world and the selves are projections of ignorance and to that extent unreal. For Ramanuja, selves and world are real but partial. Thus, Ramanuja like Shankara views the main message of the Upanishads to be the identity of the self and Brahman, but in Ramanuja's case it is the identity of part to whole. Liberation for Ramanuja is achieved by means of devotion. Soon this was to be interpreted by Ramanuja's followers in a fashion which is typical of the devotional (*bhakti*) period, in which liberation as highest goal is replaced by more worldly ultimate aims, in this case the ideal of servitude (*prapatti*) to the Lord.

Dvaita ('dualistic') Vedanta

Almost completely the creation of Madhva, fourteenth century (who reads the Upanishads in a manner diametrically opposed to Shankara and largely at odds with Ramanuja), is the Dvaita Vedanta. On Madhva's interpretation Brahman is precisely *not* the self, though Brahman is God. Dvaita is, indeed, radical pluralism; there are real and entirely distinct selves and things, all different from each other and distinct from God. Worship of God provides liberation from rebirth to those who are worthy.

These three types of Vedanta are generally cited as the most important ones. There are, however, many other Vedanta systems;

most are fundamentally devotional, and many are associated closely with regional sects.

Devotional sectarianism

While the Godhead was worshipped under various names, there was a growing tendency in classical times to associate the deities so named with one or another of three important gods, Vishnu, Shiva and Brahma. The three are sometimes depicted as three faces of the same statue and are associated in devotional literature as dividing among themselves the three important divine functions of creating (Brahma), maintaining (Vishnu) and destroying (Shiva) the world. However, as time passed, Vishnu and Shiva became the forms of God worshiped as superior by Vaishnavas and Shaivas, respectively.

Other gods are worshipped in shrines and temples, frequently in connection with the specific needs of those who worship. Ganesha, the elephant-headed god, is regularly called on before any task is

Shiva depicted as Lord of the Dance, Nataraja, a Chola bronze, tenth century, Tamil Nadu. The rhythms of Shiva's dance govern the universe. In the left hand he holds fire, symbolic of the inevitable destruction of all that lives; his right hand is raised to bring reassurance; his right foot crushes a squirming dwarf who represents unenlightened man.

begun. Hanuman, the monkey-god who assisted the hero Rama in the epic *Ramayana*, is another popularly found object of devotion. Skanda (Karttikeya) is worshipped in the south as the son of Shiva, and Parvati as Shiva's consort, or sometimes, as in Bengal, the demoness Kali as her dark side. The above are divinities who are drawn from generally-shared higher Sanskritic culture. There are also deities of a more local derivation, such as Shitala, the goddess of smallpox, or in Bengal and Assam, the goddess of snakes.

It is difficult to generalize about much concerned with Indian religions. Although the imagery of Vaishnavism and Shaivism differ frequently, they are also often found together. Although many of the specific subsects of Vaishnavism and Shaivism are regional in orientation, some are pan-Indian. Nothing stated to be Vaishnavism or Shaivism is always or necessarily so: the variations are legion.

Important sects

While Vaishnavism and Shaivism are pan-Indian in the extent of their membership, particular sects falling within them are regionally specific.

Vaishnavism

The earliest recorded Vaishnava sect appears to have been the Bhagavatas of the northwest, who worshipped God under the name of Vasudeva (perhaps related to Krishna). This sect was later systematized into the Pancaratra. There is a close relation between this sect and the *Bhagavad-gita*, which describes devotion as the most available path to liberation.

In South India, there is evidence of Vaishnavism's presence before the end of the first millennium AD. Vaishnavism was spread by two classes of teachers: the Alvars, who composed and sang songs expressing love for Vishnu, and the Acharyas, who carried on discussions aimed at establishing theological and philosophical points. The most famous, though far from the earliest, of the latter was Ramanuja (see above), whose sphere of activity centered at Shrirangam near Tiruchirapalli. South Indian Vaishnavas, whose philosophical persuasion is Vishishtadvaita Vedanta, are known as Shrivaishnavas. The sect divided shortly after Ramanuja's time into the Vadagalai or northern school, which believed in monkey-salvation, required effort on the part of the aspirant and was presented in a literature written in Sanskrit, and the Tengalai or southern school, which believed in cat-salvation, required no effort on the part of the aspirant and was presented in a literature written in local vernaculars such as Tamil and Telugu. The Vaishnavism associated with the Dvaita philosophy is practiced in Mysore and the Malabar coast.

Centering around Vrindaban near Mathura in Uttar Pradesh, the legendary haunt of the cowherd Krishna, one finds followers of the Krishna cult whose philosophical expositions were pioneered by

Vallabha (fifteenth century), whose system is known as Shuddhadvaita ('pure nondualism'). The system identifies Krishna as Brahman and emphasizes joy, love and grace in contrast to Shankara's more austere intellectualism.

Bengal Vaishnavism goes back to the fifteenth and sixteenth centuries and the figure of Chaitanya, whose doctrines are known as Achintya-bhedabheda. Chaitanya was born a Bengali but spent his mature years at Puri and then at Varanasi. His Vaishnavism also celebrates Krishna as the Supreme Self and specifies devotion as the means to enlightenment.

In the central Gangetic plain from the fifteenth to the eighteenth century, Vaishnavism was preached and practised by a number of famous names beginning with Ramananda (fifteenth century?) and Kabir (sixteenth century) born a Muslim according to tradition, and Tulsidas (sixteenth century) author of the *Ramcharitmanas*. In Maharashtra, Namdev (fourteenth century) and Tukaram (seventeenth century) composed oft-repeated songs and prayers which told of the pure love of the devotee for his God.

Shaivism

Especially celebrated in the Shvetashvatara Upanishad, the God Shiva appears to be a descendant of the destructive Vedic God Rudra. Early sects devoted to Shiva include the Shivabhagavatas, known to the grammarian Patanjali (second century BC), the Pashupatas, a group of antinomian ascetics attested in inscriptions going back to the first millennium AD, and the Kapalikas of the seventh century in Maharashtra, likewise famous for demoniacal practices.

Two important philosophical and devotional systems were developed largely in Kashmir and are generally known as Kashmir Shaivism. Their thought resembles Advaita but is also influenced by grammatical philosophy and literary criticism.

In the south, the system known as Shaiva Siddhanta expounded, largely in Tamil, a characteristic metaphysics featuring the three basic principles of the Lord, the individual and fetters. Liberation is through a path with elements of action, discipline, meditation and knowledge. In the Mysore area, there flourishes the Shaiva sect of Lingayats, whose philosophy is known as Virashaivism and somewhat resembles Vishishtadvaita.

Other sects

Various movements are committed to other names and conceptions of the Godhead. One type of worship, known as Shakta or the cult of Shakti, worshipped female divinities that were perhaps originally forms of consorts of the major male gods. This type of movement expresses a general development known as Tantra, which features controlled antinomian practices, including sexual intercourse, as part of spiritual development. Tantric features are found not only in these sects but also in many others, including Buddhism.

In the Rasamandala (Circle of Love) Krishna dances with each of the gopis (cowherds).

Worship

A standard Sanskritic term for worship is *puja*, which basically involves making an offering to God. The contexts for worship are many and varied, ranging from a private meditative offering in the solitude of the forest to singing devotional songs or chanting the names of God in a temple or fair. In any case, worship involves seeing the divine image, and thus the term *darshana* (vision) has a central sense in religion as well as in philosophy.

Popular forms of worship are performed in or near shrines and temples in which an image or symbol of God is displayed. Many of

In contemporary India Hindu gods are often represented in a style known as poster or calendar art. Here Durga-Lakshmi (a composite of the mother goddess and the goddess of good fortune) rides a tiger (Durga's traditional vehicle). She is preceded by Hanuman (popular local deity and beneficent guardian spirit) and followed by Skanda (son of Shiva and the mother goddess). A caption reads: 'Hail to the Mother Goddess'.

them rehearse daily and yearly lifecycles. Thus, a temple may be consecrated to Vishnu or Shiva or a form of one of them, and the duties of the priests of the temple involve waking, feeding, bathing, clothing and providing repose for the deity through appropriate gestures and behavior, often quite literal. These activities are carried out both in private and in public. The worshipper at the temple assists in succoring the deity by providing offerings of food and water, clothes and light, perfume, etc., in the manner of offering hospitality as he would to an honored guest in his house. In return, the devotee has a vision of the Lord who has entered into the image.

An image may be a representation of God, in one of the forms in which he is traditionally held to appear after coming down onto our earth, for instance, the several avatars of Vishnu, the most important of which has become Krishna, the butter-thief, killer of demons, protector of the weak, playful cowherd, amorous consort. Shiva is most famously represented in his dancing form (Nataraj), but is also found as emaciated ascetic, the source of the Ganges and so on.

Not all images worshipped as God are depictions of the god as person. A shrine may display an image of Parvati, Shiva's wife; Lakshmi is worshipped with lights as the bringer of prosperity in a myriad homes at the time of Divali in the fall. Each divinity has his or her respective vehicle, usually an animal, such as the bull Nandi, the vehicle of Shiva. In perhaps their most abstract physical forms, Shiva is worshipped as the *lingam* or phallus, while Vaishnavas find Vishnu in the *shaligrama* stone. Almost anything or anyone may come to be addressed as sacred, both externally and internally. The best-known case is that of the cow, whose sacredness may well be especially due to her economic importance, but most animals are likewise treated as sacred, as well as trees, rivers and lakes, hills and mountains, and indeed even inanimate objects.

Many Hindus go on pilgrimage several times in a lifetime, walking in groups or by themselves to sacred places, their quest culminating in a vision of their Lord. The village temple is a place for individual prayer and meditation, for the priestly round of offerings, and for the everyday lifecycle activities of the people, functioning as the central gathering-place for dramatic and musical events and other celebrations of traditional themes, especially at festival times.

Ritual observances

The force of Hindu traditionalism is evident in the everyday life of an Indian villager. Popular mythology as well as classical literature attests to the prevalent notion of the cyclical nature of creation. For example, Vaishnava tradition has it that the universe is beginningless in extent and that, while each period of the world's maintenance is very long, they are separated by equally long periods of dissolution (*pralaya*) during which nothing happens. Specifically, at the

beginning of a creation the creator god Brahma causes the principle of materiality to evolve in accordance with the karmic propensities attached to the individual selves, propensities which have remained attached though dormant during the interim. The earliest phases of a creative cycle are ones in which the amount of dharma in the world is maximal. As the cycle wears on this amount diminishes, first to three-quarters, then to half, then to a quarter, until finally no dharma remains, the destructive god Shiva terminates the moral chaos that is left and *pralaya* ensues. The final period of a creation, where less than a quarter of dharma remains, is the Kaliyuga in which we now live. Thus, the Hindu looks behind him to times long ago for models of correct behavior, when there was more dharma in the world.

The diminution of dharma signals the gradual breakdown of the social order, as members of the several castes lose their traditional identity and fail to practice the dharma appropriate to their stations. Religious observances constitute reminders to all of their dharma and occasions to rehearse its preservation.

The daily life of a Hindu villager involves frequent reminders of traditional norms. Every home has one or more places within it where puja is regularly carried out, especially by the women. Mealtimes are religious occasions and observed with silent respect. Religious literature is quoted or recited often.

Several times in a year, special occasions arise, frequently involving the services of the family Brahmin priest. Respect for the family is celebrated in the *shraddha* ceremonies, involving offerings for the maintenance of recently deceased ancestors. At the time of pregnancy, birth, investiture into studentship, marriage, attainment to mendicancy and death, various rituals are performed by priests in connection with the event.

Every temple holds a festival at least once a year, sometimes involving processions in which the god's image is led around the village or city or even the surrounding countryside. The most famous is perhaps the festival at Puri in which the cart of Vishnu as Lord of the world ('Juggernaut' that is, *jagannath*) is wheeled around the city. Pilgrims come from all over India for this and similar festivals. Traditionally seven cities were identified as sacred: Varanasi (Benares), Hardwar, Ayodhya, Dwarka, Mathura, Kanchipuram (Conjeeveram) and Ujjain. Other important religious centers for Hindus include Puri and Allahabad for Vaishnavas, and Madurai for Shaivas.

Festivals are fixed by the Hindu calendar, which combines the lunar and the solar, so that it cannot easily be ascertained on which calendar dates to expect them. Important and more or less India-wide occasions for celebration include Divali (Dipavali) in October–November, where lamps are lit and presents exchanged; Dasara (Dussehra), the tenth day of Ashvina in September–October sacred to the mother-goddess, celebrated by Vaishnavas as well as Shaktas;

The cart of Vishnu as Lord of the World 'Juggernaut' (*jagannath*) being wheeled round the city of Puri (Orissa).

Holi in the spring (February–March), in which colored water and powder is thrown about and traditional roles may be reversed; Vasantapancami (February) dedicated to Sarasvati, the goddess of learning, honored with music and dance performances and other cultural events. There are, as well, many regionally specific festivals such as Pongal in the Tamil-speaking area, and Durgapuja in Bengal. *KP*

Further reading
A. L. Basham, *The Wonder That Was India* (New York, 1959)
R. G. Bhandarkar, *Vaishnavism, Shaivism and Minor Religious Systems* (reprinted from *The Collected Works of R. G. Bhandarkar* Vol. IV) (Poona, 1982)
S. N. Dasgupta, *A History of Indian Philosophy* 5 volumes (London 1922–1955; Delhi, 1975)
J. A. Dubois, *Hindu Manners, Customs and Ceremonies* (Oxford, 1925)
D. L. Eck, *Darshan: Seeing the Divine Image in India* (Chambersburg, Pa., 1981)
T. J. Hopkins, *The Hindu Religious Tradition* (Encino, Cal., 1971)
W. D. O'Flanerty, Ed., *Karma and Rebirth in Classical Indian Traditions* (Berkeley, 1980)
K. H. Potter, Ed., *Encyclopedia of Indian Philosophies* 4 volumes, in progress (Princeton, N.J., Delhi, 1970–1981)
P. T. Raju, *Structural Depths of Indian Thought* (Albany, 1985)

Islam

Although Islam differed considerably from the religions of India, it took root and flourished in the subcontinent, over a quarter of whose population are Muslims. The impact of Islam on India commenced in AD 711 when the Arab navies of Muhammad bin Qasim conquered the Indus delta region in Sind. Although this initial contact did not result in significant instances of conversion of Indians to the new religion, it did establish the legal status of non-Muslims in Indo-Muslim states. Comprising but a tiny minority of the population, the Arab conquerors of Sind could not possibly have treated Indians as idolatrous pagans since to do so would have meant, according to Islamic Law, giving the non-Muslim majority the harsh choice of conversion or death. Consequently, there emerged a legal fiction by which all Indian subjects were given a *de facto* status of *zimmi*, or protected peoples, as if they were 'People of the Book' like Christians or Jews. Moreover, once having established their rule in Sind, the Arab rulers confirmed in Sindhi society both the Brahmins in their superior position, and the despised, lowly castes in their inferior position. In short, the initial contact between Arabian Islam and the subcontinent was one in which the former yielded considerably to the realities of Indian religion and society.

The establishment of the Delhi Sultanate (1206–1526) in the Indo-Gangetic plain of North India forever altered the evolution of Islam in the subcontinent. Here it was not Arabs who launched Islam on its long career of political dominance, but Turks hailing ultimately from Central Asia. The character of Islam that pervaded the Delhi Sultanate and its breakaway kingdoms in Bengal and the Deccan was shaped by warrior, slave, and clan institutions inherited

The tomb, with its enclosure, of Ghiyas ud Din Tughluq (r.1320–24) outside Delhi
reflects the Central Asian background and the fortress mentality of the first
centuries of Islamic power in India.

from nomadic Central Asia, combined with a religious zeal born of the Turks' own relatively recent conversion to Islam. As a result, Islam in the early Delhi Sultanate functioned as a colonial ideology identified exclusively with its triumphant Turkish carriers from Central Asia and Afghanistan. This is vividly seen in the writings of court ideologues like Zia ud Din Barani (d. 1358), who strove to preserve the purity of the Turkish race, regarded his fellow Turks as India's natural governing class, and understood Islam not as a universal religion but as, in effect, the tribal cult of the governing class. We see this same sentiment expressed in the architecture of the Delhi Sultans, whose massive mosques, tombs, and military structures generally reflect the 'fortress mentality' of an army of

occupation, and who sought for the most part to replicate in India the architectural styles and forms of their Central Asian homelands.

In addition to associating Islam with Turkish ethnicity, the Turkish ruling class also identified itself with the institutional remnants of the Abbasid Arab Empire. Theoretically subordinate to the authority of Arab Caliphs in Baghdad, whom Sunni Muslims regarded as the legitimate sucessors to the Prophet Muhammad, the Sultans sought cloaks or letters of investiture from the Caliphs that served to give them political–religious legitimacy and to connect them with the wider Islamic world. However, with the destruction of the Caliphate by Mongol invaders in 1258, the Sultans of Delhi became themselves the focus of Islamic authority and functioned as the supreme patrons of Islam, now elevated to the status of state religion. This perception of the court's relationship to Islam is seen in the coinage of the Khalji and Tughluq sultans, and especially in the latter's patronage of scholars and holy men through the extensive construction of shrines and mosques.

With the establishment of the Delhi Sultanate, Iran and Persian culture provided the dominant inspiration for Indo-Islamic civilization. Persian norms in statecraft, ceremony, piety, and literature all flowed eastward as a result of the periodic turmoil in central Asia and Iran that drove large numbers of Muslim soldiers, merchants and artisans, together with learned and holy men, into the Indian subcontinent. These migrants, mainly Iranians or Persianized Turks and Afghans, found service with Muslim states in the subcontinent, especially the Delhi Sultanate and its Mughal successor in North India, or the major provincial dynasties in Bengal, Gujarat or the Deccan. Significantly, both the migrants and those claiming descent from them tended to see themselves as a socially distinct group, known as the *ashraf* (or Muslim élite) typically professing occupations associated with military or bureaucratic service, commerce, piety or scholarship. They also cultivated the Persian language, which was employed by most Indo-Muslim courts, and tended to cluster in the great cities that grew with the advent of Muslim political power, such as Lahore, Delhi, Lucknow, Patna, Dhaka, Ahmadabad and Hyderabad, as well as in the smaller towns also tied to imperial networks. This Persianized Indian ashraf was thus linked with Iran, central Asia and Asia Minor by a shared world of literature and understanding. Except in the case of migrants from post-1500 Iran who typically belonged to the Shia sect, most were Sunni Muslims and adhered to the Hanafi school of Islamic Law. Modes of piety also linked the Indian *ashraf* with the Persian cultural world, since the chief Sufi orders in India, the Chishti, the Suhravardi, the Naqshbandi, the Qadiri and the Shattari, all had their roots in eastern Iran or central Asia.

Indians are known to have converted to Islam from the earliest days of the Arab conquest of Sind, and under the Sultans of Delhi, when Islam enjoyed official patronage, communities of Indian Muslims began to appear. But the great advances in this respect did not occur until the advent of the Mughal dynasty (1526–1858), when communities of Indian Muslims attained to the majority of the population in areas such as western Panjab or eastern Bengal. Curiously enough, this occurred under rulers who did not patronize Islam in a formal way, as did the Tughluq Sultans, but by emperors who adhered to an imperial ideology fundamentally cosmopolitan and secular in nature. Worked out during the brilliant reign of Akbar (1556–1605), and reflected among other ways in that emperor's syncretic architecture (such as at Fatehpur Sikri), this ideology served to integrate Indians into the Mughal cultural and political system at two levels. At the élite level, it absorbed non-Muslim chieftains into its imperial service, transforming potential state enemies into loyal servants. At a lower social level, meanwhile, Mughal imperial ideology sought to expand the Empire's agrarian base, and hence its wealth, by transforming desert or forest lands into arable fields, and the nomadic or forest-dwelling peoples inhabiting those regions into settled farmers of wheat or rice.

In the western Panjab and Sind, shrines of Sufis such as Baba Farid (d. 1265) in Pakpattan, or Baha ul Haq Zakaria (d. 1263) in Multan, played important roles in this process by attracting and integrating pre-agrarian and non-Muslim Jat nomads into their ritual, socio-economic, and political orbits. Descendants of the saints established marriage alliances with the leaders of Jat groups, while the Mughal emperors granted huge tracts of rich land for the support of the ritual ceremonies performed at the shrines. The shrines thus served as mediating agencies at the very point in time that these communities were passing from a life of pastoral nomadism to one of settled agriculture. On the one hand, the shrines mediated between local Jat communities and the Mughal court; on the other hand they mediated between those same communities and an Islamicized divine hierarchy in which Sufi saints played a prominent role.

A similar process operated at the other end of the empire, in Bengal, where Muslim pioneers obtained grants from the Mughals to clear virgin forests so as to expand the empire's area of rice cultivation. These pioneers also constructed mosques that functioned as magnets integrating non-Muslim forest peoples both into an agrarian way of life focused on the mosques, and into a locally structured style of Islam heavily inflected with the culture of saints and saint-veneration. As a result of these processes, by the eighteenth century in both Panjab and Bengal there appeared large communities of Muslim peasants who belonged mainly to the Sunni sect of Islam, reflecting the sectarian affiliation of the saints and pioneers who had carried Islamic culture into the frontiers of Mughal India.

Islam had more limited success in penetrating the countryside in the Deccan Plateau and South India. Since a largely Hindu peasant society was already firmly entrenched in these regions, the coming of Muslim rule did not involve any socio-economic transformation of rural society, as was the case in western Panjab, Sind and eastern Bengal. Nonetheless, the enormous demand of Indo-Muslim courts for consumer goods led to the growth of urban Muslim communities in the Deccan as it did also in Upper India. India's participation in international trade quickened in response to this demand, and there emerged within Indian society new communities of urban Muslim artisans who, like the Muslim peasantry, were generally non-ashraf and Sunni. These communities were defined occupationally, like the Hindu castes (*jatis*) from which most of them originated, and they filled such occupational slots as weavers, dyers, tailors, butchers, perfumers, bangle-makers, paper-makers, tinners, cotton-cleaners or armorers.

Broadly speaking, both the Sunni and Shia ashraf practiced a style of religion informed by adherence to Islamic scripture and scholarship passed on by formally trained learned men. On the other hand Islam as practiced among the non-ashraf cultivating and artisan classes was more often informed by saintly intermediaries and remnants of pre-Muslim local cults. For example, around 1623 the medieval historian Firishta recorded that the people of the Deccan so revered the saint Sayyid Gesudaraz (d. 1422) that one person, on being asked whom he considered the greater personage, the Prophet Muhammad or the saint, replied, with some surprise at the question, that although the Prophet was undoubtedly a great man, the saint was a far superior order of being. Cults focusing on the intercessory powers of Muslim saints were especially popular among women, whose devotional lives generally revolved around their homes and the shrines of Sufi saints, and not at the more male-oriented mosques. Indeed, yet another means by which Islamic culture penetrated rural households was the medium of folk literature composed by Sufis, in which devotional and mystical ideas were woven into songs sung by women while attending to such household chores as grinding meal, rocking infants or spinning thread.

Faced with the practical necessities of governing non-Muslim majorities, Indo-Muslim courts were generally pragmatic in their relations with Hindu society, and some consciously conformed to Hindu conceptions of proper kingship. Accordingly, the discriminatory *jizya* tax, which by Islamic Law had to be collected from protected peoples (zimmi), was in practice either abolished, ignored or collected as part of general taxes unassociated with Islamic Law (an important exception to this was the Emperor Aurangzeb's reimposition of the discriminatory tax in 1679). The outstanding example of the state's conciliatory posture to Indian religions was the Emperor Akbar, who banned activities offensive to Hindus such as cow-slaughter, abolished discriminatory taxes like pilgrim or jizya taxes, admitted Hindu sages into his private audience, appeared in public with his forehead marked as a Hindu and celebrated Hindu festivals. Such postures, however, often placed Muslim courts at odds with the *ulama*, or the learned men employed by the state as Muslim judges, preachers, prayer-leaders, or scholars of Islamic Law. As upholders of the Islamic social vision, many ulama criticized what in their view constituted the state's capitulation to the beliefs and habits of idolatrous infidels. This is seen, for example, in the vicious attacks leveled against Akbar by Abdul Qadir Badauni (d. 1615), or in the attempts of Shaikh Ahmad Sirhindi (d. 1624) to steer Akbar's son, Emperor Jahangir (1605–27), in a direction that would discriminate against Hindus. In the Deccani Kingdom of Bijapur, meanwhile, Sultan Ibrahim II (1580–1627) made similar compromises with Hindu culture, such as in his public devotion to the Hindu goddess Sarasvati, and he too faced admonition from orthodox quarters. The Delhi sultans had also found outspoken critics in the ranks of the ulama, such as the historian Zia ud Din Barani (d. 1358), who called upon the Sultan not only to collect the *jizya* tax, but also 'to overthrow infidelity and to slaughter its leaders who in India are the Brahmans'.

When not making policy recommendations to the state, Muslim intellectuals adopted a much wider spectrum of attitudes toward the Indian environment generally and the Hindu religion specifically, ranging from outright acceptance to outright rejection.

Occupying one end of this spectrum was the Mughal prince Dara Shikoh (d. 1659), who took the extreme view that the study of Hindu scripture was not only compatible with being a Muslim, but was in fact *necessary* for a complete understanding of the Quran. Deeply read in Hindu classical scriptures, the prince reached this conclusion on the conviction that the 'protected book' referred to in the Quran itself (56:77–80) was in fact the Upanishads, protected from Muslims by jealous Hindu sages. Approaching but not reaching this position were those Sufis who experimented with Indian philosophical systems and ascetic practices such as yoga. They did this, however, not in the belief that it was necessary in order to reach a fuller understanding of Islam, which was Dara Shikoh's attitude, but in order to expand their own spiritual experiences.

A more detached position toward Hindu religion and culture was taken by the first systematic Muslim scholar of India's religions, al-Biruni (d. 1050). In effect a premodern sociologist of religion, al-Biruni formulated a conceptual framework that enabled him to view Islam and Indian religions on an equal and non-judgmental basis. Thus he maintained that the educated élites of all religious communities (including Hindus) worship the same god, whom he identified as Allah, whereas the uneducated masses of all religious communities (including Muslims) indulged in the reverence of images, since they required pictorial representations to guide them in their religious gropings. Such intellectualized detachment, however, was highly exceptional, and was perhaps most closely approximated by Akbar's great ideologue and spokesman, Abul Fazl (d. 1602), who believed that all Hindus at some level of abstraction believed in the principle of divine unity. At the folk level, there evolved various forms of syncretic blends of Islam with local cults, as reflected for example in the poetry of Sayyid Sultan, who flourished in Bengal in the late sixteenth century. In his epic poem *Nabi-bagsa*, Sayyid Sultan treated the major deities of the Hindu pantheon such as Brahma, Vishnu, Shiva, Rama or Krishna as successive prophets of God, followed in turn by Adam, Noah, Abraham, Moses, Jesus and Muhammad. Significantly, the poet simply identified the Islamic notion of prophet, or a messenger sent down by God, with the Hindu concept of *avatar*, or an incarnation of God. On the other hand, each avatar/prophet of God was understood in Islamic terms in that he was given a scripture appropriate for his epoch, while time itself was seen in terms of a linear development moving forward to the prophecy of Muhammad, which was the final prophecy and which superceded those of all earlier avatars/prophets. Islam was thus seen as connected to, but also as absolutely superior to, Indian religions.

Occupying the far end of the spectrum of Muslim attitudes toward Indian religions was the strident, exclusivist position adopted by those who saw no connection between Islam and Hinduism at any level, and in fact preached communalism. Shaikh Ahmad Sirhindi, for example, advocated that Muslims indulge in the practice of cow-sacrifice since it would humiliate Hindus and demonstrate the supremacy of Islam, while Zia ud Din Barani simply dismissed Hindus as 'worshippers of idols and cow-dung'.

In the course of their long history of contact with India, then, Muslim intellectuals adopted a great variety of positions respecting the subcontinent and its religious traditions. On balance, however, those adopting a more exclusivist position outnumbered those adopting a more conciliatory one, perhaps because in India Muslims were always a minority and, since the Islamic religion defines itself in terms of a community of believers, Muslims in India were always acutely aware of, and anxious about, their minority status. Thus, to guard against becoming engulfed by India's non-Muslim majority, barriers, both mental and social, were more often erected and maintained than they were dismantled. This conservative tendency also underlay ashraf suspicions of non-ashraf Muslims, as the latter did not claim foreign origin, but had originated from within the rich matrix of Indian society and culture.

RME

Further reading

A. Ahmad, *Studies in Islamic Culture in the Indian Environment* (Oxford, 1969)

R. Eaton, *Sufis of Bijapur, 1300–1700: Social Roles of Sufis in Medieval India* (Princeton, N.J., 1978)

M. Gaborieau, Ed., *Islam et Société en Asie du Sud, Purusartha* 9 (Paris, 1986)

P. Hardy, *Historians of Mediaeval India. Studies in Indo-Muslim Historical Writing* (London, 1960)

S. M. Ikram, *Muslim Civilization in India* (New York, 1965)

B. D. Metcalf, Ed., *Moral Conduct and Authority: the Place of Adab in South Asian Islam* (Berkeley, 1984)

K. A. Nizami, *Some Aspects of Religion and Politics in India in the Thirteenth Century* 2nd edn (Delhi, 1974)

I. H. Qureshi, *The Muslim Community of the Indo-Pakistan Subcontinent 610–1947*, 2nd edn (Karachi, 1977)

Sikhism

Sikhism may be compared in its initial inspiration to many other movements of reform which arose within northern Hinduism under the impact of the religious challenge of Islam in the medieval period, but it is distinguished from them by the success with which it has resisted the general tendency towards reabsorption within mainline Hindu orthodoxy. It is therefore rightly to be regarded as the youngest of the independent religious traditions of India, where the Sikhs (1.8 percent of the population) significantly outnumber the combined totals of all Indian Buddhists and Jains, and significantly outweigh the Indian Christians in political and economic importance. Although still closely linked to its historic homeland in the Panjab, Sikhism has come through successive movements of emigration to assume a considerable presence in other parts of India, not to speak of the substantial communities of Sikhs now established in the UK and North America.

Early Sikhism

Early Sikhism bears the profound imprint of the religious genius of its founder, Nanak (1469–1539), the first Sikh Guru. Born into a Hindu professional family in a village west of Lahore, Nanak was employed as a steward by a local Muslim nobleman until, in about 1500, his life was changed by a profound spiritual experience, and he embarked upon a series of wanderings which led to encounters with religious leaders of all persuasions. Settling down in the Panjab in the last years of his life, he gathered round him the first community of Sikhs (Panjabi for 'disciples').

Much of Guru Nanak's teachings, recorded in the hymns which form the principal inspiration of the Sikh scriptures, find their counterpart in the utterances of other free-thinking reformists of the north Indian Sant tradition preaching excessive devotion to a formless God such as Kabir of Benares (fifteenth century). This is notably the case in the central emphasis of Guru Nanak's theology of salvation, which lies in loving devotion to a non-anthropomorphic God by divine grace alone made manifest as True Guru (*satiguru*) to human awareness. It is also the case in the marked rejection of the claims of both Hindu and Muslim orthodoxies to indicate the true path of salvation, as directly implied by the famous utterance attributed to Guru Nanak on emergence from the vision which transformed his life, 'There is no real Hindu and no real Muslim'.

This formula is, indeed, a direct corrective to the still common misconception that Sikhism is some sort of amalgam of Hinduism and Islam, a view which owes more to the subsequent history of the Sikhs as a minority community in the Panjab subject to frequent pressures from the dominant Muslims and Hindus. While links with local Hinduism have always been strong, and conversions to

Sikhism have predominantly come from Hinduism, the debt to Islam is a very small one, far outweighed in importance by the never-forgotten self-characterization of Sikhism as a 'third force'.

Sikhism's survival and separate development owes much to the emphasis of Guru Nanak's hymns, which are characterized by both great poetic beauty and highly sophisticated internal organization, on the need to practice a disciplined worldliness as an essential precondition for the manifestation of the divine grace. Ascetic practices are set aside in favor of an emphasis upon the triple formula of *nam dan isnan*, literally 'God's Name, charity, bathing', which implies both the centrality of meditative worship and equal necessity of righteous worldly living.

The nuclear Sikh community established in the final period of Guru Nanak's life was already reinforced by this stress upon earning one's bread and sharing any surplus in charity, and shaped in its religious identity by prescribed patterns of daily observance, centered on participation in the congregational singing of hymns (*kirtan*), but beginning with the private recitation before dawn of Guru Nanak's *Japji*. This matchlessly conceived summation of his religious teachings has ever since continued to inspire devout Sikhs.

Later hagiographical tradition is not an entirely reliable guide to many of the details of Guru Nanak's life. But there is no doubt that his careful selection of a trusted disciple to succeed him as Guru did much to avoid the more or less rapid collapse of institutional identity which overtook most of the groups drawn to the charismatic teachings of other Sants. The continuity of leadership provided by the Guruship (whose holders soon came to be selected from within one family) did much to assure the stable evolution of the distinctive institutions of Sikhism, to which increasing numbers of converts came to be drawn from the local Hindu castes, particularly the Jat peasantry.

By the time of the fifth Guru, Arjan (d. 1606), these institutions included a well-established network of the Sikh temples now called *gurdwara* ('abode of the Guru'), used for congregational worship, and to which are attached the voluntarily supported free kitchens open to all (*guru ka langar*). The greatest of these temples was that constructed at Amritsar by Guru Arjan himself, and it was in the Golden Temple, ever since the holiest place of Sikhism, that he installed his compilation of the hymns of his predecessors, vastly expanded by his own prolific writings, known as the 'Original Book' or *Adi Granth* (1604), ever since regarded as the canonical Sikh scripture.

The Khalsa

However pacific in its inner teachings, Sikhism was from the outset never otherworldly. Growing numbers of converts in the Panjab increased the local power of the Gurus, who thus came to be drawn into Mughal politics. Guru Arjan was himself executed at Lahore,

The first page of the Sikh scriptures known as the Guru Granth Sahib. The initial credal statement reads: 'There is one Supreme Being, the Eternal Reality. He is the Creator, without fear and devoid of enmity. He is immortal, never incarnated, self-existent, known by grace through the Guru'. Trans. W. H. McLeod, *Sikhism* (Manchester, 1984).

and the same fate befell the ninth Guru on Aurangzeb's orders in 1675. Although this persecution owed as much to political as to religious factors, the growth of an anti-Mughal militancy among the Sikhs was naturally encouraged, and finally achieved formal sanction in a major reconstitution of Sikhism.

This was effected by the tenth and last Guru Gobind Singh (1666–1708), the warrior-prince who is accorded the same reverence as Guru Nanak, with his foundation of the quasi-military order known as the Khalsa. Admission to the Khalsa is by baptism (*amrit*), and a vow to accept the discipline of the order. This has at its core acceptance of the authority of the Guru, as transferred with the ending of the line of the ten human Gurus to the scriptures, henceforward accorded supreme respect under the title of *Guru Granth Sahib*. The baptismal vows also involve accepting a code of conduct, including observance of the well-known outward marks of orthodoxy called the 'five K's', that is, unshorn hair (*kes*), a comb (*kangha*), a dagger (*kirpan*), a steel bangle (*kara*) and a pair of breeches (*kachh*): dietary restrictions, notably including a strict ban on tobacco; and the adoption of the common titles of Singh ('Lion') and Kaur ('Princess') by all male and female converts, respectively. While Guru Gobind Singh's numerous compositions are not included in the *Guru Granth Sahib*, some do form part of the required pattern of daily private prayers (*nitnem*).

Later developments

With the foundation of the Khalsa and the death of the tenth Guru, the period of Sikhism's primary formation came to an end. While many Sikhs remained content to follow the less demanding old style of devotion, it was the baptized (*amritdhari*) Sikhs who thereafter came to dominate the evolution of the Sikh community. During the heroic age of the eighteenth century, the Khalsa was largely occupied in fighting the Mughal forces and the invading armies of Afghan warlords, until it emerged victorious with the establishment of Sikh rule in the Panjab under Maharajah Ranjit Singh (1799–1838), when the long political challenge of Islam was finally ended.

Although the present appearance of the great Sikh temples owes much to the munificent patronage of Ranjit Singh, the present institutional organization of Sikhism is due to the later initiatives of the Singh Sabha reform movement. This came into being during the colonial period, in the late nineteenth century, and had as its principal objective a re-affirmation of the distinctiveness of the Sikh identity in the face of the twin threat seen to be posed on the one hand by the casual reversion to Hindu practices which had accompanied the years of Sikh power and its aftermath, on the other by the explicit challenge posed by such Hindu reform movements as the actively proselytizing Arya Samaj.

The reformers were largely successful in re-imposing observance of the Khalsa discipline, indeed in expanding it through securing legal recognition of a distinctive ritual for Sikh weddings in the Anand Marriage Act (1909). Attention was next directed towards re-establishing direct Khalsa control over the great temples, many of which had fallen over the years into the hands of Hindu administrators. The mass campaigns of the Akali movement in the 1920s eventually secured reluctant British assent to the Sikh Gurdwaras Act (1925), as a result of which all the important shrines and their immense endowments are controlled by the elected Central Gurdwara Management Committee (SGPC).

The SGPC has since acted as the controlling body within Sikhism, a religion without 'priests' in the accepted sense, since the readers (*granthi*) of the temples are no more than officials paid by committees of lay members. Alternative interpretations of Sikhism have certainly been proposed, but have sooner or later come to be regarded as heretical through their proponents' infringement of the fundamental doctrine of the investiture of the Guruship in the scriptures to the absolute exclusion of all subsequent human claimants. Although the fierce fundamentalism of Jarnail Singh Bhindranvale (1947–84) has come to dominate present-day Sikh thinking about both religious issues and the tense political situation in Indian Panjab from which they are hardly to be divorced, it would therefore seem inevitable that the future development of Sikhism will continue to lie in the hands of the lay members of the Khalsa, founded by the last living Guru to ensure the continuance of the teachings of the first.

CS

Further reading

W. H. McLeod, *The Evolution of the Sikh Community* (Oxford, 1976)

C. Shackle, *The Sikhs* (Minority Rights Group Report No. 65), 2nd edn (London, 1986)

H. Singh, *The Heritage of the Sikhs* 2nd edn (New Delhi, 1983)

Religious revival in modern times

Hinduism

The growth of British power in South Asia from the late eighteenth century presented the greatest challenge to Hinduism since the Muslim invasions six centuries before. Christian religious ideals and modern western rationalist thought not only challenged many of the current practices of Hindu society such as widow-burning, female infanticide, child marriage and untouchability, but also the validity of Hindu scripture, indeed, on occasion the validity of religion itself. One Hindu response was the development of movements for social reform so as to be able to defend Hinduism against Christian influence. Then, alongside these movements there emerged a second response which was a renewal of faith in the gods and the beliefs of the Hindu religious vision. The vigor of these responses, it should be noted, was heightened by the new economic, social and political opportunities that British rule brought to many groups in Hindu society. So, while early Hindu responses were defensive, to the extent of a considerable borrowing from Christian ideas, they came in the late nineteenth century to be increasingly confident, a confidence which was only increased by a pronounced European admiration for the Hindu achievement and by the new pride generated by the Indian nationalist movement. As the twentieth century progressed, Hindu cults became a notable South Asian export to the West.

The first significant response to the British presence came from Rammohan Roy (1772–1833), a Bengali Brahmin of genius who at an early age reached the highest place open to an Indian in the Bengal Civil Service. Rammohan was greatly influenced by his contacts with the British. He studied Christianity with great seriousness, among other things translating the New Testament

Rammohan Roy, a Bengali Brahmin, who led the first Hindu response to western civilization. He died in 1833 while on a visit to England to plead the cause of the Mughal emperor and to oppose a petition to the Privy Council against the abolition of widow-burning.

into Bengali; but while he came to admire its humanity he rejected its doctrine. Concerned to stem the tide of conversion to Christianity, he focused attention on those parts of the Vedas which stressed faith in one supreme Being, thereby offering Hindus a means of abandoning idolatry without necessarily abandoning Hinduism. At the same time he campaigned for the suppression of widow-burning and other social evils. In 1828 he founded the Society of God (*Brahmo Samaj*) to consolidate and to propagate his tenets.

Over the next half century, Rammohan's message was disseminated as the Brahmo Samajists, mainly Bengali government servants, spread through northern India. In 1867 the preaching of the Samaj's leader, Keshab Chandra Sen, helped to inspire the foundation of Bombay city's Prayer Society (*Prarthana Samaj*), which pressed eagerly for social reform, but was not prepared to move as far from mainline Hinduism as its Bengali counterpart had done. Both these organizations contributed much to the formation in 1875 of a third society, the Aryan Society (Arya Samaj) which was founded by Svami Dayananda Sarasvati (1827–1883), and which had as its objective a return to the pure teachings of the *Sanhita* portion of the Vedas. Rejecting caste Dayananda asserted that Brahminhood was not inherited but acquired through learning. Anyone, including women, who studied the Veda and performed the minimum Vedic ritual (*sandhya*), merited the title of 'Brahmin' and had the right to wear the sacred thread of 'twice-born' Hindus (*yajnopavita*). A Gujarati Brahmin who renounced the world at an early age, becoming a *sannyasi*, Dayananda taught his followers to draw a sharp distinction between themselves, the Aryans, and all those who did not follow the Vedic path. The Samaj's geographical stronghold has remained the Panjab, although its influence has spilled over into adjacent parts of Northern India. As a militant and highly articulate response to nineteenth century Muslim as well as Christian proselytism, Dayananda taught a highly structured, pragmatic and unsophisticated doctrine. In his only book, *Satyartha Prakash* (The Light of Truth), he argued against elements in Hinduism which came to be called 'superstitions' by his followers, including idol worship, polytheism and all non-Vedic ritual. But, at the same time, he also rejected the theology of the monistic schools (Vedanta), reserving his special anger for monistic orders, in particular the Advaita Vedanta as propounded by Shankaracharya: the world was not a delusion (*maya*) to him but as real as its creator and the individual soul created by God. Svami Dayananda did not learn English. He taught social concern, and denounced the atrocity of widow-burning, all in the vernacular. He also insisted on strict vegetarianism but since most of his followers were and are Panjabis, from a region not known for vegetarian habits, a schism soon divided the Samaj into a more radical and austere Sanskrit-oriented section and the 'Dayananda Anglo-Vedic' section. Each generated its own schools, colleges and allied institutions which recruited their supporters from different socio-economic groups.

Unique from a crosscultural perspective, the Theosophical movement founded in the late nineteenth century provided a powerful stimulus to Hindu and Buddhist reform and indirectly to early Indian nationalism. It never became a grassroots movement, but has consistently taken its cue from broad, syncretistic and vociferously pro-Indian themes, and these pervade Theosophical writing. Its founders, Mme Helen Blavatsky (1831–91), a Russian, and Colonel Olcott (1832–1907), an American army officer, were succeeded by Annie Besant (1847–1933), an English woman, who was an accomplished orator and founder of the Indian Home Rule League. Theosophical teachings, with their emphasis on fate or destiny (*karma*) and formulated by Mme Blavatsky, are a blend of Tibetan and Theravada Buddhist elements, of advaita monism, and various Christian elements.

An offshoot of the Theosophical Movement was led by Jiddu Krishnamurty (d. 1985), who attracted a large and sophisticated audience, both Indian and Western, to his teachings. His books and sermons have found solid support among members of India's most powerful and influential élites. Though Krishnamurty resented any labels, his teachings drew on Mahayana Buddhist and Hindu advaitic philosophy, which he articulated in English carefully avoiding Sanskritic terms.

Of all Hindu reform movements, that inaugurated by Svami Vivekananda (1862–1902) and named after his guru, Ramakrishna Paramahamsa (1836–86), has probably had the most lasting effect, both in India, if largely in Bengal, and in the West. Vivekananda's simplified and straightforward reading of monistic Vedanta has provided the groundwork for other twentieth century forms of neo-Vedanta. He rejected the austere, scholastic traditional version of Shankaracharya's *mayavada* (the doctrine that the entire empirical universe is a delusion, and that the *brahman*, The Absolute, is the only reality) in favor of social uplift and concern. Unlike Dayananda, Vivekananda did not undergo theological-scholastic training in the primary texts of Hinduism, and his knowledge of Sanskrit remained scanty. He accepted the outlines of scholastic monism, but he saw its inward orientation as counterproductive to social work and reform. Although he seemed to vacillate between these extremes, the latter clearly won the upper hand. He did not really object to his adversaries' criticism that his teachings (preserved in seven substantial volumes) and their results – famine relief, education for boys and girls, care for the sick and the poor – were closer to a Jesuit model than to the highly ecstatic teachings of his master.

As with Theosophy and the teachings of Krishnamurty, Sri Aurobindo's 'integral yoga' has appealed to a western and an English-speaking Indian élite. More at home in English than in his native Bengali, Aurobindo Ghose (1872–1950) joined the nationalist movement after his return from Britain where he had received his higher education. In the following decade, he aligned himself with Hindu political leaders. Jailed by the British, he underwent a transformation not unusual with political detainees in India. Well before his imprisonment, he had already come to identify with a Vedantic worldview, modified by an esthetic vision conceived in England. But in prison, he began practicing and experiencing his own form of meditation, whose power convinced him that his quest and achievement was on a parallel with that of the Upanishadic seers. His esthetic vision of the universe made him reject *mayavada* and declare the world to be as real as its divine essence. He moved to Pondicherry, then a French possession, possibly to avoid a second arrest by the British. There he was subsequently joined by La Mère, formerly Mme Richard, as his divine consort. It was both his writings and his charisma which attracted a growing audience among Indian and foreign seekers. Unlike Ramakrishna and Vivekananda before and Sai Baba afterwards, Sri Aurobindo and his movement did not achieve much grassroots support. The Ashram and the nearby Auroville establishment today provide a dual focus for what his followers regard as his message of 'integral yoga', that is, meditation and study together with pioneering agricultural work. His followers regard his writings, especially his large *Life Divine* and the epic *Savitri*, as great spiritual and literary achievements.

While Mohandas Karamchand Gandhi (1869–1948) may pose many problems for the political scientist, he poses far fewer for the student of religion, to whom he appears as both a charismatic politician and a religious guide. Much of the Mahatma's political and pragmatic terminology is misunderstood on account of its deceptively secular vocabulary. His use of 'trusteeship', the notion that the wealthy hold their property in trust for the less fortunate, makes little sense unless it is seen as anchored in the Hindu axioms of *dharma* (loyalty to the law) and *karma-yoga* (complete renunciation of the fruits of one's actions by offering them to Divinity). Indeed, work performed exclusively as a presentation to the Divine became a teaching central to his seminal role in India's struggle for independence. This coupled with his reading of non-violence (*ahinsa*) and his concept of truth-force (*satyagraha*), identify him as a religious reformer in the Indian template, as much if not more than as a political leader. His vegetarianism, his emphasis on sexual continence (*brahmacharya*), his expansive concern with homeopathic, naturopathic and some aspects of Ayurvedic health care all helped to present him as an ascetic (*sadhu*) to India's masses.

A more recent development has taken place with the emergence of yoga-oriented guru-disciple movements, led by charismatic founders invariably regarded as incarnations of God (*avatars*). Though most of these movements insist on the essential oneness of the teachings of all the gurus, there always exists an implicit or

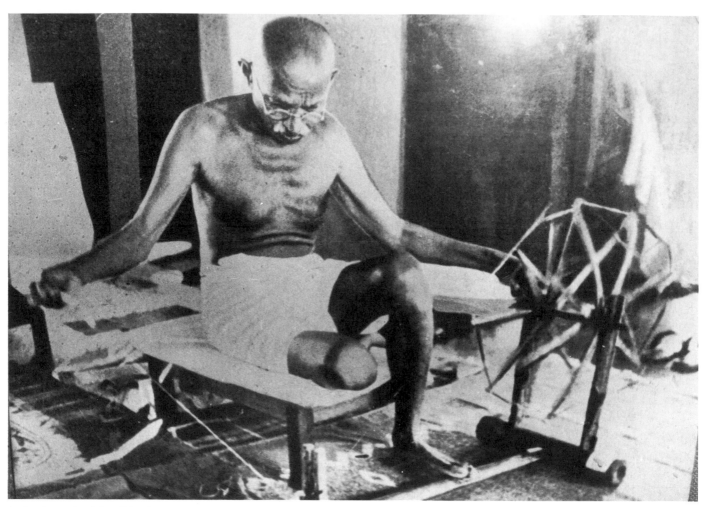

A classic study of Gandhi spinning by the American photographer, Margaret Bourke-White.

explicit understanding of the ultimate superiority of the founder's preaching which is transmitted to his anointed successors. The most spectacular illustration of this development today is the person and following of Satya Sai Baba of Puttaparthi, South India, who was born in 1926 into a non-brahmin Telugu family. Some two to three million people in the subcontinent (Hindu, Muslim and Christian alike) identify themselves as his followers, as do many people of Indian descent in countries such as Trinidad and Guyana, as well as elsewhere in the Americas and Africa. The total number of devotees is estimated to be as high as ten million. In terms of doctrine, there is little difference between the teachings of Sai Baba and those of many other Hindu neo-charismatics. A simple theistic, highly-eclectic type of Hinduism, incorporating certain monistic-immanentistic elements, is aligned with Sai Baba's special emphasis on truth

(*satya*), loyalty to the law (dharma), peace (*shanti*) and love (*prema*). The difference lies in the packaging of these four qualities and the way in which they are solidly centered on Sai Baba, divine incarnation, origin and repository of these virtues. The main factor which distinguishes him from other gurus are the occult powers (*siddhi*) which are seen to rest in him. Not only does Sai Baba seemingly from nowhere distribute consecrated sandalwood ashes (*vibhuti*) to hundreds in a crowd or to individual visitors; he also materializes jewels, gold rings, watches, apricots from banana trees and apples from mango trees. Vibhuti oozes from his picture when worshipped by devotees in places as far apart as Bangalore and San Diego, California. Scientists and doctors have attested to these miraculous feats. Opponents, and there are many, reject them as sleight-of-hand, but criticism only serves to strengthen the convictions of his followers who argue that 'He is God because he acts like God'. While his teachings absorb elements of Tantrism and Shaivite and Vaishnava love of God (*bhakti*), Sai Baba also draws on the spiritual bequest of Shirdi Sai Baba, a saint with a mixed Hindu and Muslim background who died before Sai Baba's birth and whose present incarnation he is thought to be.

Many of these guru-disciple movements, such as those of Rajneesh, of Transcendental Meditation and of Balayogeshvar, the boy-saint of the 1960s, have their support and recruitment bases primarily outside India. The most important of them has been the International Society for Krishna Consciousness (ISKCON) whose members are commonly known as Hare Krishnas and described as the 'only tribe permanently settled on airports' on account of their fund-raising activities there. ISKCON has solid Hindu roots. Founded by A. C. Bhaktivedanta Prabhupada (1896–1977), a Calcutta bullion merchant turned Vaishnava monk, the movement gained a strong foothold in North America in the 1960s. Within fifteen years of Bhaktivedanta's arrival in New York, the organization had spread throughout the West as well as Japan, and then re-entered India to an enthusiastic welcome. Its teachings and practice are firmly based on the Gaudiya Vaishnavism of Sri Chaitanya, a sixteenth century Bengali saint regarded as *avatar* of Krishna by his

Satya Sai Baba who leads one of several recently developed yoga-oriented guru-disciple movements. Sai Baba has several million followers both in the subcontinent and outside.

followers. ISKCON has refused to compromise with western lifestyles, unlike other movements of its kind. The core of devotees live in strictly controlled monastic communes, totally vegetarian and teetotal, and remain celibate until marriage which is usually arranged by the institution. The basic incantation (*mantra*) 'Hare Krishna Hare Rama' is matched by a blend of litany and stylized dancing genuinely expressive to the sound of drums and cymbals (*kirtan*) which is a revival of a celebration virtually defunct in India itself. The movement has built at great expense elaborate shrines with its headquarters in the impressive, though close to kitsch, 'New Vrindavan' in West Virginia, USA. In addition, once the movement had acquired enough wealth, it built large shrines at the key sacred sites of Vaishnavism at Vrindavan, the legendary birthplace of Krishna in Uttar Pradesh, and at Navadvip, the early venue of Sri Chaitanya in West Bengal.

ISKCON is well respected in India which is not the case with other foreign-based movements like Rajneeshism, '3 H O' (that is, Healthy, Happy, Holy), the Sikhism-cum-Trantrism of Yogi Bhajan in California, and even Transcendental Meditation. In spite of, or perhaps because of, ISKCON's high visibility, its aggressive fundraising, and its doctrinal intolerance, Indians acknowledge that this is a successful and imaginative transplant of a movement which had lain dormant since the early seventeenth century. The initially anti-scholastic ISKCON leadership now actively encourages the study of Sanskrit and the doctrinal complexities of Vaishnavism. ISKCON rejects monism and all but the Vaishnava schools of thought and much of its argument is agonistic. It regards the *Bhagavata-purana* as its core scripture, assigning it canonical status by calling it Veda.

Though shared by all neo-Hindu movements, a combination of eclecticism and idiosyncratic representation is epitomized by the Radhasoami Satsang and the Meher Baba Mandali. The first has a strong and affluent following among Panjabis and other North Indians, as well as a western audience which has been increasing recently. The self-consciously idiosyncratic spelling of *soami* for *svami*, the wearing of the Sikh turban by the members of one of its two schismatic groups, the acceptance of the writings of five out of the ten Sikh gurus, and the monotheistic, anti-iconic doctrine culled from the Sikh scriptures and informed in part by regional forms of north Indian bhakti traditions, indicate its eclecticism as does its esoteric meditational technique of *shabad* (sound) and *nam* (the inward repetition of God's name) in *surat-shabad-yoga*. The preceptors of the movement are seen as divine incarnations, through whose aid and mediation salvation can be attained.

Idiosyncratic eclecticism also extends to the founder of the Meher Baba Mandali. Meher Baba (1894–1969) was born a Parsi who encountered and absorbed teachings from Zoroastrianism, Hinduism and Islam. Outwardly, he seemed to be an opulent, moustached businessman to all but his followers until the end of his life, the last forty years of which he spent in total silence, only communicating in writing. His teachings can be described as a simple kind of *advaita* monism without the doctrine of maya, tied to his strong personal identification with God. His large following is middle-class, usually familiar with English, and divided in roughly equal proportions between Indians and non-Indians.

By contrast, the Svaminarayan movement is restricted to Gujarati speakers. Svami Sahajananda (1781–1830), known as Svaminarayana (Lord of the Universe) was probably the first leading Hindu saint-reformer to meet a high ranking Christian cleric in the person of Bishop Heber of the Church of England, and the event is permanently commemorated in the abundant iconography of the movement. The theology of the Svamarayanis centers on the deification of Sajahananda and his main disciple, Gunatitananda, in a complex, highly personalized mystical hierarchy. The teachings are a modified version of the Vallabhacharya tradition tailored to the founders' identities. Their identification with Krishna, Radha and the guided interplay of cosmic forces, follows a Vaishnava idiom. The complex ritual and extreme asceticism of its monastic leaders, who must not ever look at or speak to women at any time, give the movement a distinct character and make it highly visible in western India as well as those parts of the world where large numbers of Gujaratis have settled such as the USA, Great Britain and East Africa.

Svami (Baba) Muktananda's (1908–82) *siddha-yoga* (yoga of spiritual consummation) taught the arousal of the *kundalini*, the coiled-up mystical energy imagined inside the body and blended with the divine energy (*shakti*) visualized as female. He effected this awakening by *shaktipat* (the descent of shakti) through personal initiation of the first generation of his disciples. Muktananda did not know English, but the larger part of his present-day following is not Indian. Siddha-yoga now led by a young Indian woman-disciple, after her brother defected from the diarchic leadership decreed by Muktananda, has well-established centers in India and the West.

In general, therefore, Hindu revivalist reform movements, which stress rural and general social uplift, better living standards, female emancipation and economic progress, de-emphasize individual, contemplative, mystical involvement. Those, on the other hand, which stress the psycho-experimental dimension of yoga, including esoteric and at times tantric elements, and are normally found in urban settings, de-emphasize social and patriotic work and secular ideological involvement. At one extreme of this scale, we must list the Arya Samaj, and perhaps the Ramakrishna Mission, which are focused on reform and social uplift and which view individual mystical pursuit with some misgiving. At the other extreme we should note Sri Ramakrishna himself, and more recently the traditions created by Sri Aurobindo, Meher Baba, Rajneesh, Muk-

tananda and a large number of less-known teachers and their followings.

ABh

Further reading
Amma, *Swami Muktananda: the Saint and his Mission* (Ganeshpuri, 1971)
R. D. Baird, Ed., *Religion in Modern India* (New Delhi, 1981)
F. Daner, *The American Children of Krishna* (New York, 1976)
S. Gambhirananda, *History of the Ramakrishna Math and Mission* (Calcutta, 1924)
K. W. Jones, *Arya dharm: Hindu Consciousness in 19th Century Panjab* (Berkeley and London, 1976)
J. S. Judah, *Hare Krishna and the Counterculture* (New York, 1974)
R. N. Minor, *Sri Aurobindo: the Perfect and the Good* (Calcutta, 1978)
S. B. V. Narasimha, *Life of Sai Baba* (Madras, 1976–80)
C. B. Purdom, *The God-Man* (Meher Baba) (London, 1964)
R. B. Williams, *A New Face of Hinduism: the Swaminarayan Religion* (Cambridge, 1984)

The Buddhist resurgence especially in Sri Lanka

At the beginning of European expansion in South Asia Buddhism survived only in Sri Lanka and the Himalayan region. Sri Lanka came under European pressure early when control over the island's littoral passed on to the Portuguese, and after them the Dutch, pushing the Sinhalese kingdom to the interior. Between the late sixteenth century and the mid-eighteenth, the Sinhalese Buddhist tradition had to be revived three times, with aid from Burma on the first two occasions, and Thailand on the third. On each occasion the revival was supported by royal patronage.

In 1815 revivals of this kind were brought to an end when the British, who had recently captured the littoral from the Dutch, gained power in the interior as well. Buddhists responded in several ways. One was to win the support of the new rulers, but this turned out to be meager and was eventually withdrawn under pressure from Christian missionaries. A second was to restore Buddhist kingship through rebellion, but British power made these attempts increasingly impractical and purely millennial in character. A third was to rely on the oldest form of Buddhist organization, namely, monastic communities depending on the voluntary support of the laity.

Such communities were already in existence in the southern and western parts of the country indicating that the missionary efforts of the Portuguese and the Dutch had only had limited success. But the proliferation of new fraternities also contravened the Buddhist ideal of a unified monastic order. By the mid-nineteenth century the order was riddled with controversies and schisms, a sure enough

Buddhist monks in an alms procession, Sri Lanka.

sign, according to the Buddhist view of history, of the decline of religion. The prognoses offered by non-Buddhists in administrative and missionary circles were even gloomier; they held that Buddhism, unaided by the state and torn by internal dissension, was destined to disappear altogether.

Underneath the apparent symptoms of decay, however, there was a new vitality generated by internal conflict. The new fraternities, both through membership and lay patronage, linked the order to an expanded social base. The multiplication of fraternities led to an increase in the number of monks and monasteries, and to the emergence of new religious centers that rivaled the old one at the last royal capital of Kandy. Competition between fraternities made the monks watchful of the behavior and religious knowledge of one

another, for they had to prove to the laity that they were worthy of support.

Competition for the support of the laity was not confined to different groups of monks. Different groups of missionaries campaigned to win the laity to the Christian side. This wider contest increasingly polarized the two sides. The missionaries conducted the contest on three fronts: education, preaching and the press. The Buddhist response, too, occurred on the same fronts. In the 1860s, monks began to use their preaching and writing skills to counter missionary propaganda; from the 1880s onwards, Buddhist laymen played a prominent role, especially in the field of (lay) education where monks were ill-equipped to compete with the missionaries.

Resulting from its confrontation with Christianity, Buddhism acquired several new features that both imitated and competed with Christian ones. The confrontation also led to the emergence of new leaders who differed markedly from heads of monastic fraternities. Three leaders in particular stood out in succession: Mohottivatte Gunananda (1823–90), who represented Buddhism in a series of public debates with Christians in the 1860s and 1870s; Henry S. Olcott (1832–1907), who combined the presidency of the Theosophical Society with an active involvement in the Buddhist movement after 1880; and Anagarika Dharmapala (1864–1933), who founded the Maha Bodhi Society in 1891.

By the end of the nineteenth century, the Buddhist campaign had reached such momentum that earlier predictions about the imminent collapse of Buddhism were rarely heard. What was heard instead was the expression 'Buddhist revival'. There were parallel developments among the local Hindus and Muslims as well, with the result that conversions to Christianity practically came to an end and the Christian part of the population was frozen at around 10 percent. Buddhists remained the majority (over 60 percent), followed by Hindus (around 20 percent) and Muslims (under 10 percent).

The religious distribution of the population gained renewed significance as the country moved towards independence, with the accompanying need for rulers to command majority support in the electorate. Buddhist organizations which at first had emulated missionary models now evolved in a more political direction. The earliest of these was the All-Ceylon Buddhist Congress, which had its roots in the Young Men's Buddhist Associations begun in 1898, but which gained its political strength and influence in the middle decades of the twentieth century. In political struggles in Sri Lanka since then religion has continued to be a vital issue.

At a less political and more ecumenical level, there was the discovery of coreligionists: new ones in the West, old ones in the East with most of whom contacts had been lost since the decline of Buddhism in India. In a small but lasting way, Buddhism was rekindled in India itself by organizations such as the Maha Bodhi Society, which had been based in Calcutta since 1892. The different national organizations were brought together in 1950 in the World Fellowship of Buddhists. The chief organizer and founding president of the Fellowship was G. P. Malalasekera (1899–1973), who also held the presidency of the All-Ceylon Buddhist Congress from 1939 to 1957.

The World Fellowship of Buddhists held its fourth conference in Nepal, the land of the Buddha's birth, in 1956, the year that marked the 2500th anniversary of Buddhism. By that time several decades of archeological and philological research had uncovered the Buddhist heritage of India which received admiration from many quarters, Buddhist as well as non-Buddhist. The Indian government gave recognition to that heritage with, among other things, an official publication on *2500 Years of Buddhism*. The same year also saw the first mass conversions to Buddhism in India in modern times under the leadership of B. R. Ambedkar (1891–56). Three years later the Dalai Lama arrived in India, and he was followed into exile by some 80,000 Tibetans. That migration created some new Buddhist centers in India and renewed some of the older ones in the Himalayan region. Events that led to the migration also revealed a new challenge to Buddhism (and traditional religions more generally) in contemporary Asia.

KM

Further reading

H. Bechert, 'Buddhist Revival, East and West', in Heinz Bechert and Richard Gombrich, Eds, *The World of Buddhism* (London, 1984)

H. Dumoulin, Ed., *Buddhism in the Modern World* (New York, 1976)

K. Malalgoda, *Buddhism in Sinhalese Society, 1750–1900* (Berkeley, 1976)

Islam

From the establishment of Muslim empire under the Ghaznavids Islam had in large part been associated with power in South Asia. The loss of Muslim power from the eighteenth century, which was accompanied by the loss of Muslim power in the world at large, increasingly seemed to threaten the very existence of Islam in the land: there was the possibility of a steady slide into the maw of Hindu India; this was followed by the possibility of being overwhelmed by the apparently all-conquering culture of the Christian West. Muslim responses to this challenge were influenced in part by movements of revivalist thought and action taking place elsewhere in the Islamic world. They were influenced in much larger part by traditions of Indo-Islamic thought which reached back at least to the time in the late sixteenth century when Shah Abdul Haq and Shaikh Ahmad Sirhindi had attacked the compromises the Mughals were making with Hindu India. Moreover, these responses were all, to some extent at least, both stimulated and shaped by their interactions with the West. The outcome was a most creative period in South Asia's Islamic history in which much use was made of *ijtihad* (individual reasoning) to circumvent the dead weight of the past and to find forms of Islam which could live fruitfully in the present.

The first response came from Shah Valiullah of Delhi (1703–62), the leading thinker of his time who had studied in Medina and sustained in his day the spirit of Abdul Haq and Ahmad Sirhindi. He aimed to consolidate Islam intellectually and to free it from Hindu influence. To help him in the process he appealed to Ahmad Shah of Afghanistan to wage *jihad* or holy war against the rising non-Muslim powers. Valiullah's four sons, the most notable of whom was Shah Abdul Aziz (1746–1824), continued his work, and it was a man from their circle, Sayyid Ahmad of Rai Bareli (1786–1831), who led, in the early nineteenth century, one of the two serious attempts to revive Islam. He strove to rid Islam of Hindu practices, to end belief in the intercessionary power of sufi saints, and to establish an ideal Islamic community. In 1826, following the example of the Prophet, he fled pagan India to establish an Islamic state on the Northwest frontier, and died in 1831 waging jihad against the Sikhs. The second attempt, which took place in Bengal, had similar aims. Known as the Faraizi movement (*faraiz* meaning duties), it was led from 1821 by Haji Shariatullah (1781–1840) who had spent over twenty years in Mecca. Shariatullah's movement, however, differed from that of Sayyid Ahmad in not declaring jihad against the infidel. In Bengal British power was now overwhelming and inner purification seemed the wiser path to follow; only after the death of the founder, when its religious message became more entangled with the economic conflicts of Bengali society, did it follow the path of violence.

The suppression of the mutiny uprising in 1857–58 finally brought home to Muslims throughout South Asia the dominance of British power. The second half of the nineteenth century saw renewed attempts to develop strategies to solve the problem of how to be Muslim in a world where Muslims no longer ruled. Two strategies stemmed from the Delhi world of Shah Valiullah's family. The first was rooted in the Deoband school of *ulama* (Islamic scholars) founded in 1867. They developed a form of Islam based more firmly on the Quran, the *Hadiths* (Traditions) and the *Sharia* (Holy Law), a scriptural Islam which was thereby distinct from the parochial practices of the sufi shrines. It was designed to exist quite apart from the colonial state. As an Islam which men 'willed' on themselves, the sanctions which brought men to obey the Sharia were not those of the state but the human conscience. Moreover, it took the message to the people by making Islamic knowledge as widely available as possible through the recently introduced printing press and translations into the vernacular. In turn it relied on the people for subscriptions to sustain it in its work. Schools connected with Deoband grew up rapidly: in 1880 there were twelve, in 1900 forty, and in 1967 there were 8934. There was, furthermore, an extreme manifestation of the Deobandi thrust in the *Ahl-e Hadiths*, who ignored all medieval scholarship and went just to the Quran and the Hadiths for guidance. Both represented the emergence of a 'protestant' form of Islam, a process found not just in South Asia but elsewhere in the world.

The second strategy was quintessentially the achievement of one man, Sayyid Ahmad Khan (1817–98), and came to be focused on the Muhammadan Anglo-Oriental College at Aligarh which he founded. Sayyid Ahmad, the scion of an old Mughal court family who found service under the British, was determined that his

Sayyid Ahmad Khan, founder of the 'modernist' style of Islamic thought and leading figure in nineteenth century Indian Islam.

Muslim world should come to terms with Western civilization and that the light of Islam should not be dimmed by its encounter with Western learning. Starting from the position that the Quran was genuine revelation, and that the 'word of God' and the 'work of God' could not be in conflict, he used ijtihad to bypass the authority of the medieval schools of law. The Quran and the Hadiths, he argued, should be understood in their linguistic and historical context. What was crucial was to distinguish between the fundamental meaning of revelation and those aspects which merely belonged to the time and place in which it occurred. If, perhaps, he went rather far in his apologetics, his rationalist exegesis of the Quran, his historical scepticism in approaching the Hadiths, and his insistence on ijtihad as the right of all Muslims laid the foundation on which they could deem their faith in harmony with the social, material and intellectual progress of mankind. Many leading Muslim thinkers fell beneath his spell, among whom were Chiragh Ali (1844–95), Muhsin ul Mulk (1837–1907), Altaf Husain Hali (1837–1914), and Amir Ali (1849–1928). They represent the emergence of a 'modernist' form of Islam.

A third strategy was concerned to preserve Islam as it had evolved to the present not so much against the threats of colonial rule as against those of the reformers. This concern to preserve India's custom-laden Islam was crystallized by Ahmad Raza Khan of Bareilly (1856–1921). His solution to the problem of Muslim

Maulana Maududi, the leader of the Jamaat-e Islami, and the establisher of a 'fundamentalist' trend in Indo-Islamic thought. His influence has been felt widely outside India.

guidance in colonial India was to emphasize the uniqueness of the Prophet, whose light he argued partook of the light of God Himself. The Prophet stood at the apex of a hierarchy of saints whose contemporary representatives provided guidance, and the assurance of intercession with God, in every locality. Ahmad Raza and his followers, known as Barelvis, proselytized their cause vigorously, and, although they have not been as successful as the Deobandis in founding schools, they have come to wield great influence among South Asian Muslims.

In the late nineteenth and early twentieth centuries the decline of Muslim power weighed ever more heavily on Muslim minds. In this context the main currents of Indo-Muslim thought, except that of the Barelvis, came to be influenced by pan-Islamic ideas. Having lost their liberty Indian Muslims came to feel a strong emotional attachment to the Ottoman Caliph as the symbolic leader of the Muslim community. The feeling was sharpened by a heightened awareness of decline which was derived in part from the changing structure of power at home, in part from increased travel abroad, but in the main from the growth of the press. At the intellectual level, pan-Islamic theory was developed by the Iranian, Jamal ud Din al-Afghani (1838–97), whose trend of thought was similar to that of Sayyid Ahmad Khan but whose aim was not rapprochement with but resistance to the West. To achieve this aim he sought to unite Muslims around the leadership of the Ottoman Caliphate. Although Afghani visited India several times, it was not until the twentieth century that his influence was to be seen in aspects of the work of Shibli Numani (1857–1914), Abul Kalam Azad (1888–1958) and Muhammad Iqbal (1877?–1938). As a force pan-islamism came to a peak in the Khilafat movement which began in 1919, when Indian Muslims sought to pressurize the British into not imposing humiliating peace terms on Ottoman Turkey. It came to an end in 1924 when the Turks abolished the Caliphate.

The end of the Caliphate knocked away a psychological prop on which Indian Muslims had relied. Now the growing prospect of political independence focused their attention on the challenge of reality. One response was in harmony with Deobandi ideas of the nineteenth century. It was first set out by Azad during the Khilafat movement when he endeavored to show that it was the religious duty of Indian Muslims to defend the Ottoman Caliph against the West. Arguing that the Sharia should be regarded as containing a set of principles rather than precise provisions, and invoking the doctrine of public interest, he used the Quran to justify Muslims joining one category of non-Muslims, the Hindus, to get rid of another, the British. In the 1920s and 1930s his position was developed further by the *Jamiyat ul Ulama-e Hind* (The Association of Indian Islamic Scholars) who in making proposals for India's political future saw the land as a confederation of religio-political communities. The position was brought to its fullest development by the Principal of Deoband, Hasan Ahmad Madani (1897–1959), who argued in his pamphlet *Millat aur Qaum* against the Muslim League demand for a separate Muslim state because the Muslims were but a community (*millat*) within the greater Indian nation (*qaum*). In every case the Sharia was seen as a moral imperative with which government was not concerned. Thus the Muslim reformist strategy which had enabled some Muslims to survive within the colonial state also enabled them readily to embrace the thought of living within a Hindu-dominated India.

A second response stemmed from the modernist strategy of Sayyid Ahmad Khan. It was the achievement of South Asia's greatest Muslim poet of the twentieth century, Muhammad Iqbal, who drew inspiration both from the Islamic tradition and European thinkers such as Nietzsche, Bergson and Renan. At the heart of Iqbal's thinking lay the idea that Islam must keep pace with modern times, and that Muslims must employ their powers of ijtihad to ensure that the Sharia kept pace with modern life. This helped him to reconcile Islam to the modern state in two significant ways. First he linked classical legal theory to the mass base of the modern state by transferring the concept of the consensus (*ijma*) of the Islamic scholars as the force underpinning the law to the people at large, or their representatives. Thus, he created considerable room for legal dynamism should Muslims wish it. Second he built a bridge between the political ideal of a pan-Islamic state and the political realities of the present. Ideally the way to rid the world of evil was to cultivate the innate greatness of the human self which was best done in a community of which Islam offered the best form. Unfortunately this ideal Quranic state had never been achieved in history and was clearly not to be achieved in the present so the most appropriate way forward was for Islam to form the underlying principles of nation-states in the wider Muslim community. In 1930 he proposed that such a state should be the objective of Indian Muslims and should be formed in the Northwest of India. In 1936–37 he pressed his vision on the Muslim League leader, Jinnah, who later admitted that Iqbal had persuaded him. The state of Pakistan which emerged in 1947 was the outcome, in the ideological sense, of the modernist strand in Muslim revivalism.

A third response owed much to the achievement of nineteenth century revivalism but set itself firmly apart from the twentieth century policies of the reformists and modernists. The begetter of this response was Sayyid Abul Ala Maududi (1903–79); it has come to be regarded as an important example of 'fundamentalism' in the Islamic world. In the 1930s and 1940s Maududi became concerned about the dominance of western culture over Muslim intellectuals and the future of Muslims in both a Hindu-dominated nation-state of India and a separate Muslim nation-state of Pakistan. Instead he asserted the superiority of the Muslim way, which was for all mankind. He argued that God alone is sovereign and man has gone astray because he has accepted sovereigns other than God, that all guidance is to be found in the Sharia, that political power is essential to put this law into effect, and that because God's guidance extends to all human activity this state must be all-embracing. The essentials of Maududi's totalitarian polity are set out in the collection of his writings known as *The Islamic Law and Constitution*, which is the most comprehensive statement of the possible nature of the Islamic state in modern times. The irony of Maududi's position is that, while he thought he was restoring the ideal order of the time of the rightly-guided Caliphs, his understanding was fashioned by modern concerns and modes of thought to the extent that he made Islam into an ideology. In 1941 to promote his ideology he formed the *Jamaat-e Islami* (Islamic Society), a vanguard of the righteous. In subsequent decades Maududi and the Jamaat had a continuing influence on both Pakistan and the Islamic world beyond.

Since Independence Muslim revivalism has been expressed in India, as might be expected, in a-political form. The vehicle has been the *Tablighi Jamaat* (Missionary Society), which was founded by Muhammad Ilyas (1885–1944), who hailed from the reformist world of Deoband. It is a simple missionary organization whose annual meetings are said to form the largest gatherings of Muslims in the world after the pilgrimage to Mecca. The Tablighi Jamaat, it should be noted, also has many followers in Pakistan, as it does in Southeast Asia and the Middle East. But, in Pakistan, it exists alongside other strands in the Muslim revival: the Barelvis, the modernists and the Jamaat-e Islami. Here the products of the revival compete to impose their different Islamic understandings on the state. To begin with the modernists had the upper hand. The Muslim Family Laws Ordinance of 1961 is their most striking achievement, and Fazlur Rahman (1919–   ), the director until the late 1960s of the Islamic Research Institute established under the constitution, their most profound thinker. Since the 1970s, however, the ideas of Maududi have come to be more influential on the workings of the state.

FR

Further reading

A. Ahmad, *Islamic Modernism in India and Pakistan, 1857–1964* (London, 1967)

P. Hardy, *Partners in Freedom – and True Muslims; The Political Thought of Some Muslim Scholars in British India 1912–1947* (Lund, 1971)

M. Iqbal, *Reconstruction of Religious Thought in Islam* (London, 1934)

Sayyid Abul Ala Maududi, *The Islamic Law and Constitution*, trans. and Ed. Khurshid Ahmad (Lahore, 1955)

B. D. Metcalf, *Islamic Revival in British India: Deoband, 1860–1900* (Princeton, 1982)

F. Rahman, *Islam and Modernity: Transformation of an Intellectual Tradition* (Chicago, 1982)

Impact of socialist thought

Important electoral victories by communist parties in the Indian states of Kerala and West Bengal since the late 1950s demonstrate the impact which socialist ideas have had in some regions of South Asia. Nevertheless, since the establishment of the Communist Party of India at Tashkent in 1920, South Asian communists have failed to indigenize Marxism to local conditions in any creative way. Rather, they have tended to follow the lead set by Moscow or Peking, applying foreign models of revolutionary strategy, which, to a large extent, helps to explain their limited success. On the other hand, rather more ingenious attempts have been made by thinkers, firmly rooted in the religio-intellectual traditions of the subcontinent, to establish a synthesis between their own philosophical systems and philosophies of socialism. Many dug deep into their religious traditions and discovered arguments which enabled them to absorb and reinterpret aspects of socialist thought within their own philosophical frameworks.

Socialist ideas first found expression during the 1850s in the rationalist and humanist reinterpretation of Hindu ideology carried out by the Sanskrit scholar, Vidyarsagar (1820–91). His Bengali weekly *Samprakash* hailed the formation of the First Workingmen's Association, exposed the oppression of indigo and tea planters, and supported the demand of Calcutta railway workers for an eight hour working day. Some members of the Brahmo Samaj in the late nineteenth century also absorbed elements of socialist thought, albeit selectively, in their ideas. Bankimchandra Chatterjee (1836–94), author of the *Anandamath* and the popular nationalist anthem *Bande Mataram*, was more open in his sympathy for socialist ideas. Situated wholly within the Hindu tradition, he exposed many inequalities which had become institutionalized in Hindu society. In 1879, he published an essay on equality in his magazine *Samya* which drew parallels between socialism and Hindu revivalism. In it, Chatterjee argued for structural change in the rigidly hierarchical orthodox Hindu framework. Similarly, Svami Vivekananda (1862–1902) exhorted young men not to trust the rich and to struggle for the poor: he linked the awaited uprising of the 'shudra class' to socialist revolution in the western world. In the twentieth century, Hindu thinkers continued to reach into their traditions to draw on ideas which, in their view, successfully met the challenges of western radical thought. Rabindranath Tagore (1861–1941), winner of the Nobel Prize for Literature and figure of immense national stature, recognized the appeal of socialism. Opposed to caste distinctions and untouchability, his universalism embraced equality as a fundamental value within the Hindu tradition: socialism, in his opinion, reunified mankind and granted it maximum freedom by seeking to distribute wealth equally.

Hindu modernizers, although aware that the *Dharmashastras* represented a hierarchical tradition in Hindu religious thought, argued that these writings alone did not represent the ultimate truth, and that other sources, particularly the *Bhagavad-gita*, were much better guides to correct human behavior. B. G. Tilak (1856–1920), the nationalist leader, for instance, based his rationalist outlook of a modern interpretation of the doctrine of *karma-yoga* (the philosophy of positive action) which rejected passivity and indolence. He explained the origins of caste distinctions in terms of the division of labor, and believed that, through reform, caste identities could provide the organizational unity necessary for the moral and material improvement of the working-classes. Drawing on the *Bhagavad-gita*, he campaigned for mass protest action and hinted that violence in a righteous cause was morally justifiable. He supported strikes as a legitimate weapon of agitation, exhorted peasants to organize against the payment of rent to the authorities in famine years and enjoined workers to form trade unions. But, like Lala Lajpat Rai (1865–1928), first President of the All-India Trades Union Congress and prominent member of the Arya Samaj, Tilak insisted that Hinduism already embraced socialism in a more refined and truly spiritual manner. Many Hindu thinkers were too committed to basic Hindu values to accept the adoption of violent methods even when they served the nationalist cause. In the opinion of Mohandas Karamchand Gandhi (1869–1948), for instance, socialism could only be achieved by *satyagraha*. Although he came to recognize that there could be no rule of God on the basis of gross economic inequality, he stuck to his original view that the Indian road to socialism had to be non-violent and based on *dharma* (the law of right personal conduct). After Independence, many socialists, including Jayaprakash Narayan (1902–79) and Vinoba Bhave (1895–1982), moved closer to Gandhi's vision through their support for his campaign for *Sarvodaya* (the welfare of all) with its objectives of equality, freedom and peace. They felt that insofar as both socialism and *Sarvodaya* aimed at the withering away of the State and the nature of existing society, there was substantial agreement between them. But, in their understanding and use of class struggle to achieve these goals, they were not prepared to compromise.

Muslim thinkers were first stimulated to examine socialist ideas by the realization that traditional responses to British rule had failed to stave off the collapse of Muslim power. Some began exploring methods of combining the radical ways in which pan-Islamic thinkers used the concepts of *ijtihad* (individual reasoning), *jihad* (holy war) and *ijma* (consensus) with revolutionary socialist strategies in order to restore Muslims to political power. Mushir Husain Qidvai (1887–1937), for instance, attempted to prove by quoting from the Quran and Hadiths that Islam had established a state on 'socialistic' principles: Muhammad's socialism, however, was 'ethical' while 'modern' socialism was 'materialistic'. Even so, Qidvai considered that the very limited socialism already adopted in the modern world had been a boon, and its victory would be 'a triumph of pan-Islamism'. With the victory of the Russian Revolution and Lenin's support for anti-colonial movements, Indian pan-Islamists were encouraged to seek the Bolsheviks' support directly and drew ideologically closer to them. Maulana Barkatullah (1859–1927), a staunch Muslim and member of the Ghadr (Revolutionary) Party, declared himself an irreconcilable enemy of European capitalism in Asia. In India, he argued, the same prerequisites for revolution had matured as those which had existed in Russia in October 1917. In *Bolshevism and the Islamic Body Politik*, he attempted to demonstrate that the 'noble principles of Russian socialism', liberty, equality and international brotherhood, were identical with those of Islam and appealed to Muslims to embrace them enthusiastically. Another pan-Islamic thinker, Maulana Ubaidullah Sindhi (1872–1944), was so impressed by the Russian experience that he prepared a socialist constitution for India.

Other Indian Muslims explored the possibility of reconciling socialist thought with Islam in more philosophical ways. Basing themselves on the dialectical method, they developed a critique of Muslim decline and, through an activist interpretation of Quranic instructions, they impressed upon their fellow-believers the need to take control of their own lives if they wished to make progress. They stressed the need to eradicate religious fatalism which, they considered, had caused Islam to stagnate for so long. A towering figure was Muhammad Iqbal (1877?–1938) who rejected the static world-view which had dominated Muslim thought since the Mongol invasions for a dynamic world-view in which man, and his society, was involved in a constant and creative struggle with nature. Islamic law, therefore, was not an unalterable code but one which, through the ijtihad of a Muslim legislative assembly, could be changed to meet new circumstances. He found similarities between Islam and socialism, for instance, in the emphasis on equality, the rejection of racism and the distaste for monarchy. Nevertheless, in the final analysis, Iqbal criticized socialism for the same reason as he more readily rejected capitalism: he found it rooted in materialism and lacking the vital ingredients of moral and spiritual love.

In the 1940s and early 1950s, Maulana Hifzur Rahman Sihvarvi (1901–62) in India and Khalifa Abdul Hakim (1895–1959) in Pakistan tried to grasp the socialist 'nettle'. On the one hand, they, like Iqbal, repudiated its materialist and therefore amoral nature. On the other hand, they elaborated an Islamic political and economic theory which sought to show how socialist collectivist principles had already been anticipated in Islamic models of state policy. Taking their inspiration from the view of the eighteenth century religious reformer, Shah Valiullah, that a 'pious' economic order was the prerequisite for an 'ethical' order, Maulana Sihvarvi, in particular, recognized in the Quran the right to full employment and economic justice. *Zakat*, the tax on wealth, according to him was instituted to restrict accumulation of riches in a few hands as was the prohibition of usury. In his major work, *Islam Ka Iqtisadi*

Nizam (The Economic System of Islam), published in 1942, he argued for the establishment of cooperative institutions as alternatives to capitalist banking and recommended state control of the main means of production and communication.

Unlike Hinduism and Islam, socialist thought made little significant impact on Sikh religious thinkers. Rather, socialist forms of struggle were combined with traditional Sikh patterns of organization to challenge Government authority on issues such as land rents and community control of gurdwara funds. The Ghadr Party, formed in San Francisco in 1913 and dominated by Sikhs who had acquired radical western ideas abroad, infused this protest with anti-imperialist sentiment. Many Sikhs regarded the Ghadrites as *Sant Sapahis* or warriors for the truth: their aims seemed compatible with the militarist tradition initiated by the tenth and last Guru, Gobind Singh. Similarly, during the 1920s, a left-wing revolutionary terrorist group known as the *Babbar Akalis* (Lion Sikhs) adopted traditional Sikh organizational and cultural symbols to mobilize Sikh peasants in armed action against the authorities. To win support, they drew inspiration from the Sikh Gurus, while drawing practical lessons from the Russian Revolution. Some Sikhs were attracted to socialism by the similarity between its ideas on equality and their own traditions of opposition to the caste system and sympathy for the oppressed. For instance, Sohan Singh Josh (1898–1982), General Secretary of the *Shiromani Akali Dal* (Chief Sikh Party) during the 1920s, became a leading member of the Panjab Communist Party and editor of the communist newspaper *Kirti* (Worker) which interpreted the struggle for socialism as the clash between the powerful and the weak expressed in tales about Guru Nanak's life. Likewise, the tradition of martyrdom as an instrument for mobilizing the *Khalsa* against tyranny was used to create political awareness of colonial oppression among Sikhs.

Buddhist cultural revival in Sri Lanka between 1880 and 1920 combined with the nascent labor movement to produce an economic critique of colonialism as a system based on the exploitation of indigenous people and resources. Only in the 1930s, however, did socialist ideas take an organized form as students educated in England returned to found socialist parties. It was at this point that some poorer groups of Buddhist monks (*bhikkhus*) were attracted to socialism because they perceived in it philosophical similarities with their own faith. Contrary to the passive and non-interventionist outlook of the majority of Buddhist monks, bhikkhus from the Vidyalankara seminar considered it their religious duty not only to demand socio-economic change but also to oppose all measures detrimental to the public good. Some joined the socialist parties; a monk was the first president of the Ceylonese Communist Party. Others, in the 1940s, formed an oppositional political group and brought out a weekly agitational paper which denounced the way that British imperial policies had led to the degeneration of the Buddhist *Sangha* (the religious body which in its true form epitomized democratic, collectivist and egalitarian principles). These bhikkhus called for complete independence and wide-ranging nationalization. They interpreted these demands in terms of their adherence to the great Buddhist virtue of compassion. After independence, the popularity of socialist thought, reflected in considerable support for socialist parties as well as in the development of a welfare state, continued to make headway in the face of opposition from the socio-economic interests of the upper echelons of institutionalized Buddhism.

The need to involve the 'popular masses' of the subcontinent in movements for national independence necessitated the formulation of political strategies which embraced their interests and aspirations. Nationalist leaders, particularly Jawaharlal Nehru (1889–1964) who was much impressed by the successes of the Soviet experiment, harnessed demands for the establishment of a just economic order to the cause of political freedom. Once independence had been achieved, however, the focus shifted from the realm of philosophical thinking into that of political and social action. Nehru, himself ideologically committed to democratic socialism, ensured that the directive principles of the Indian constitution were infused with secular socialist values. The Congress Party stressed considerable state intervention in the economic and agrarian spheres. More generally, centralized planning and some land reform were seen as key elements of state policy in setting countries of the subcontinent on the path of purposeful and accelerated all-round development.

Many leading South Asian politicians have recognized the appeal of socialist ideas in attracting electoral support. In the 1970s, both Indira Gandhi (1917–84) in India and Sirimavo Bandaranaike (b. 1916) in Sri Lanka employed socialist rhetoric in their successful political campaigns. Both India and Sri Lanka were declared 'socialist' republics. In Pakistan, Zulfikar Ali Bhutto (1928–79) in the crucial 1970 elections promised '*Roti, Kapra aur Makan*' (Bread, Clothing and Shelter): 'socialism' became one of the four cardinal slogans adopted by his Pakistan Peoples Party. Similar tactics were used by Mujibur Rahman and Maulana Bhashani to mobilize people in their favor in Bangladesh. However, these leaders subsequently found themselves to be, to varying degrees, prisoners of their own rhetoric.

KHA

Further reading

A. Ahmad, *Islamic Modernism in India and Pakistan 1859–1964* (London, 1967)
W. T. de Bary, Ed., *Sources of Indian Tradition* (London, 1958)
M. Iqbal, *Reconstruction of Religious Thought in Islam* (London, 1934)
B. Josh, *Communist Movement in Panjab 1926–1947* (Delhi, 1979)
U. Phadnis, *Religion and Politics in Sri Lanka* (London, 1976)

Christianity

Christianity has a long history in India. The Thomas Christians of Kerala claim St Thomas the Apostle as their founder. Written evidence is lacking, but in South India it is widely believed, and not only by Christians, that the saint was martyred in Tamil Nadu and buried at Mailapur. There is evidence of Christians in Kerala from the sixth century, when the Nestorian church embarked upon a vigorous policy of missionary work overseas. So Christianity may have been brought to Kerala by priests or traders from Syria: certainly it owed much to Syrian influence. The liturgy of the Thomas Christians was in Syriac, their allegiance was to the Syrian Patriarch of the East, and their doctrine was consequently Nestorian, based upon the proposition that there were two natures, divine and human, in Christ. Some Hindu influence can also be perceived. The Thomas Christians kept aloof from low castes, and were accorded a high social status. The affairs of each church were in the hands of an assembly, or *yogam*, an arrangement similar to the system of management of Hindu temple properties. The community was divided into two endogamous groups: *Thekkumbhagar*, or Southists, and *Vadakkumbhagar*, or Northists. As these names suggest, the origin of this distinction may have been geographical, but each group asserted rival claims to social superiority based on notions of ancestry. The Thomas Christians do not seem to have tried to convert their neighbors: sustained missionary effort began with the Portuguese.

Goa was made an Archbishopric in 1557, and became the center of Portuguese missionary activities in Asia. Eurasians and Indians were trained there for the priesthood. Jesuit missionaries went from Goa to the Mughal court, and engaged in religious debates under Akbar's tolerant encouragement. Some churches were established with small congregations in northern India, and the Jesuits also ministered to various Armenian Christians, most of whom were merchants, while a few held administrative posts in the Mughal empire.

There were many conversions in Goa and its neighborhood, and missionaries were especially active further south. Protection from local potentates may have encouraged the conversion of the whole of the Parava fisher caste of Tamil Nadu and of many of the Mukkuvan fisher caste of Kerala, but their religious devotion impressed successive missionaries. Similarly, in Sri Lanka many converts were made among the Karava fisher caste and the Salagama cinnamon caste. These castes were closely associated with the Portuguese, not only in their economic activities but also in their administration and culture. On conversion most took Portuguese names, and their descendants gained in wealth and social status.

In the era of Portuguese expansion successive Popes granted to the Kings of Portugal rights of *padroado* or patronage to and protection over sees in Asia, and letters from the Vatican were only sent on with the King's countersignature. With the decline of Portuguese power, the Vatican devised other means for missionary expansion. The Congregation *de Propaganda Fide*, which was established in 1622, sent missionaries to areas beyond Portuguese control, under the authority of Vicars Apostolic who were consecrated as Bishops with the titles of sees *in partibus infidelium* (vacant sees mostly in the Ottoman empire). From the Vatican's standpoint this did not infringe the *padroado*, but the Portuguese authorities disagreed.

Propaganda Fide encouraged the training of Indian priests. Mateus de Castro, the first Vicar Apostolic with episcopal rank in India, was an Indian of Brahmin ancestry, and there were two more. But they had difficulties with the Portuguese authorities, and Bishop Mateus also showed bitter hostility to the Jesuits. Thereafter the direction of missionary work was usually entrusted to European members of religious orders, until the end of the nineteenth century. But the ordination of Indian priests continued, and some of the most promising were trained at the Collegio Urbano maintained by *Propaganda Fide* in Rome.

Brahmin converts were relatively few, but early in the seventeenth century the Italian Jesuit Roberto Nobili settled at Madurai, followed a Brahmin way of life and scholarship and eventually converted some Brahmins. This aroused controversy, but he argued that the observance of caste had no religious implications, and his methods were ratified by Pope Gregory XV in 1623.

In matters of doctrine, however, there was no compromise, and at the Synod of Diamper (Udayamperur) in 1599 the Thomas Christians were required to renounce Nestorianism, although the continued use of the Syriac liturgy was sanctioned. Disciplinary changes on the Roman model, such as the celibacy of the clergy, were also imposed. These policies aroused resentment, and in 1653 the authority of the Archbishop of Goa was rejected by a solemn assembly at Mattancheri. Rome then appointed a commission of Italian Carmelites to effect a reconciliation. They had considerable success, and one of the Thomas Christian priests was consecrated Bishop. But some refused to submit, and formed a separate denomination under the Syrian Patriarch of Antioch. This division continued.

When the Jesuits were criticized for compromising with Chinese rites, Nobili's tactics also came under review. Charles Maillard de Tournon was sent to China and India as apostolic delegate to settle these matters, and he ruled that there should be no compromise. What aroused most perturbation was his insistence that missionaries could not refuse to visit sick or dying low castes in their houses. His rulings were finally confirmed by Pope Benedict XIV in 1744,

who declared that all Christians, whatever their birth, should hear Mass and receive Communion in the same church at the same time. The Jesuits claimed that many high castes left the church in protest. Some priests were specially appointed to minister to low castes, and various expedients, such as the provision of special entrances for low castes and the construction of little walls to separate them from high castes in churches, enabled the Jesuits to claim that the policy laid down by Benedict XIV was indeed being followed. But their opponents thought this Jesuitical in the pejorative sense of the term, and after the suppression of the Jesuits in 1773 their successors asked for a ruling from *Propaganda Fide*. The principles laid down by Benedict XIV were reaffirmed, but separate entrances were tolerated for the time being, provided that missionaries tried to eradicate caste prejudices among Christians.

Early in the nineteenth century socio-economic change presented a new perspective. Demands were voiced for low-caste priests. In Kerala there was much opposition from higher-caste Catholics, but in 1836 *Propaganda Fide* ruled that a limited number of low-caste candidates should be trained in the more tolerant atmosphere of Bombay before being ordained to parishes of similar caste in Kerala. When the Carmelite Bishop prevaricated for fear of offending the higher castes, some low-caste congregations transferred their allegiance to the Archbishop of Goa. In Bombay, on the other hand, higher-caste congregations transferred their allegiance to the *padroado* when the Bishop proved sympathetic to low-caste Catholics. The conflict of jurisdictions between *Propaganda Fide* and the *padroado* was deplored by Rome, but it offered opportunities to dissatisfied laymen.

The evangelical revival stimulated Protestant missionary activity in the nineteenth century. Some of the East India Company's chaplains acted as missionaries besides attending to their duty of ministering to British officials and soldiers. Many more missionaries were sent by Anglican and Nonconformist societies. Three functions were soon identified and generally accepted – preaching, teaching and healing – and Christian schools, colleges and hospitals supplemented those of the government and drew some financial support from it. The persistence of caste among converts was opposed by the Baptists in Bengal from the beginning of the nineteenth century and by the Anglican Bishop Daniel Wilson from the 1830s. In South India this prompted some higher-caste Christians to move from the Anglican to the Lutheran church. The American Madurai Mission devised a scheme of 'love feasts', at which Christians of all castes joined with missionaries at meals cooked by low-caste cooks, and other Protestant churches followed this example. However, caste is still observed in an attenuated form among most Christians in South India.

The various denominations made converts, and some Thomas Christians became Protestant as the Mar Thoma Church. But the relatively small number of conversions disappointed many missionaries, and at a Protestant missionary conference in 1855 it was resolved to adopt more conciliatory attitudes towards Hindus and Muslims. At about the same time, Krishna Mohan Banerjea, an Anglican clergyman of Brahmin origin, developed the argument that there was much in Hindu scriptures that was compatible with Christian ideas. Such tendencies culminated in the view elaborated by J. N. Farquhar that Hinduism could be regarded as God's way of preparing India for the Gospel. This was generally accepted at the World Conference of Protestant Missionaries in 1910. The Salvation Army wore Indian dress when they arrived in the late nineteenth century, and in the twentieth century there were various attempts to lessen or remove the western forms which Christianity had acquired. Christian *ashrams* were established, such as Krista Seva Sangh in Maharashtra. There were also Indian Christians who followed the lifestyle of Hindu *sannyasis*, such as the Roman Catholic Brahmabandhab Upadhyay, and the Protestant Sadhu Sundar Singh.

With political independence denominational differences were much criticized as a western irrelevance. Anglican, Methodist and some other Protestant churches were united in 1947 in the Church of South India. A Protestant Church of North India and a Protestant Church of Pakistan were similarly founded in 1970. When the last Portuguese Roman Catholic Bishop of Cochin retired in 1952 the question from which caste to choose his Indian successor seemed a problem, since the Catholics there were divided into two main groups of castes. So the diocese was divided into two sees, each headed by a Bishop of appropriate caste. There remained, however, some suspicion of Christianity as a foreign import, and in 1956 a

committee appointed by the Madhya Pradesh government under M. B. Niyogi, formerly chief justice of Nagpur, criticized the various churches in India as permeated by anti-national, and especially American, tendencies. In the ensuing controversy much evidence was presented to the effect that Christianity had become an authentically Indian religion.

Christians remained a small but growing minority. In 1911 there were estimated to be over three million in India, and in 1941 over seven million, while in 1971 there were over 14 million Christians in India and one million in Pakistan. These increases were greater than those of the total population, Protestants were increasing more than Roman Catholics, and the greatest increase both in numbers and in proportions was in South India. Of the three million Christians in 1911, over two million were Roman Catholics, whereas in 1971 of 14 million Christians some eight million were Roman Catholics. In Sri Lanka, of one million Christians in the mid-1970s, 879,000 were Roman Catholics, while in Pakistan, of one million Christians only 280,000 were Roman Catholics. These figures reflected the long history of Roman Catholic missionary activity in areas such as South India and Sri Lanka.

KB

Further reading

Church History Association of India, *History of Christianity in India* especially vol. i, *From the Beginning up to the Middle of the Sixteenth Century* by A. Mathias Mundadan (Bangalore, 1984); vol. ii, *From the Middle of the Sixteenth Century to the End of the Seventeenth Century* by Joseph Thekkedath (Bangalore, 1982)

F. Coutinho, *Le Régime paroissial des diocèses de rite latin de l'Inde des origines (XVIe siècle) à nos jours* (Louvain, 1958)

M. E. Gibbs, *The Anglican Church in India, 1600–1970* (Delhi, 1972)

Abraham Vazhayil Thomas, *Christians in Secular India* (Cranbury, 1974)

Pope John-Paul II meets nuns on his visit to India in 1986.

Judaism

Judaism has never been a very widespread religion in India, but it has old roots. Accounts by medieval travelers and geographers make it clear that by the thirteenth century there were small settlements scattered along the Malabar coast, and there are grounds for believing that Judaism in this part of India is at least as old as Christianity. There are also scattered Jewish families on the Konkan coast near Bombay who give every appearance of having been settled there for many centuries. The role of India in world trade has ensured a flow of visitors, temporary settlers and immigrants, including Jews from many parts of the Middle East and Europe. Jews were very prominent in the trade of Malabar and in all the trading posts of the European East India Companies. But trade was not their only occupation: in modern times they have played a notable part in manufacture, in administration and in the army. The last wave of immigration, of European refugees from the Nazi genocide, brought numbers of doctors and other professional people.

The origins of the Indian Jews are thus extremely varied, and so are their religious traditions, both native and imported. The minority, descendants of the immigrants of recent centuries and mainly English-speaking, have tended over the generations to discard their more distinctive traditions and have adopted a common ritual, broadly similar to that of other Asian Jewish communities. (There are differences, however, between the rituals of the so-called White Jews or *Paradesi* ('foreigners') of Cochin and those of the more numerous 'Baghdadis' of the northern cities.) The majority, known as Bene Israel ('Children of Israel'), whose ancestral language is Marathi, have gradually come under the influence of other communities, but they have also preserved older customs, evolved during long centuries of relative isolation from outside Jewish contacts. One of their synagogues in Bombay, the Jewish Religious Union, established under British rule, represents Liberal Judaism of the English type and belongs to the World Union for Progressive Judaism.

Both numerically and in terms of wealth and status, the heyday of Indian Jewry was in the last decades of British rule. It is generally agreed that in 1947 there were rather more than 25,000 Jews in India, of whom over 17,000 were Bene Israel, some 6000 were Baghdadis, and between 2000 and 2500 were Malayalam-speaking Cochin Jews. Recent European immigrants numbered only a few hundred. By far the largest presence was in Bombay, but there were also some 4000 Jews in Calcutta, and several smaller communities elsewhere, including Karachi and Pune. These figures may seem insignificant in comparison with other Indian statistics, but it must be borne in mind that the total Jewish population of the world at the time was only about 12 million, and there were well under a million Jews in Palestine. Since independence, emigration has reduced the Jewish population to a small fraction of its former size. It is estimated that there are now only a few thousand Jews left in India and the neighboring countries: with the exception of Bombay, no community consists of more than a few families. On the other hand, there is a considerable presence of Jews of Indian origin in Israel, and religious congregations of Indian Jews exist in England and the USA.

N da L

Further reading
A. Das Gupta, *Malabar in Asian Trade, 1740–1800* (Cambridge, 1967)
W. J. Fischel *et al.*, 'India', in *Encyclopaedia Judaica* vol. 8, cols 1349–1360 (Jerusalem, 1971)
S. Strizower, *The Children of Israel: the Bene Israel of Bombay* (Oxford, 1971)

Zoroastrianism

Zoroastrianism is the oldest prophetic religion. The prophet Zarathushtra, known in the West as Zoroaster (*c.* 1200) lived in northeast Iran. His teaching became the official state religion of successive Iranian Empires, Achaemenids, Parthians and Sasanians, so that between the sixth century BC and the seventh century AD, Zoroastrianism dominated a region stretching from North India to Anatolia. After the Arab conquest of Iran in the seventh century AD, social pressures and persecution dramatically reduced Zoroastrian numbers and forced the stalwarts to retreat to the desert regions. In 936, a faithful few settled on the northwest coast of India where they became known as 'the Persians' or Parsis. There are still some 30,000 Zoroastrians living in Iran, but the numerical center is now India, particularly Bombay. Overseas migration to the Far East, East Africa, Britain and, most recently, to the USA and Canada, means that Zoroastrianism is nowadays practiced in more countries than at any previous time in its history.

Zoroastrian religion
For Zoroastrians, religious duties begin with initiation (*naujote*) which occurs before puberty. Initiation, like most Zoroastrian religious duties, is the same for male and female. It comprises investiture with the sacred shirt (*sudre*) and cord (*kusti*). The sudre should be worn next to the skin at all times, while the kusti is retied five times a day accompanied by prayers which affirm allegiance to the Good Religion of God (*Ahura Mazda*) exemplified in pure thoughts, words and deeds and involving the rejection of evil. Only the children of Zoroastrians can be initiated. The link between religion and race has been strengthened by the acceptance in India of Parsis as a caste.

The home is the traditional focus of worship for the Zoroastrian layperson. However, increased Parsi wealth during the nineteenth centuy resulted in the employment of non-Parsi servants, introducing impurity into the home which made certain rites impossible.

The Bombay high priest invests a young Zoroastrian with the *sudre* (shirt) and Kusti (cord) in the Naupte or initiation ceremony, here performed in the home, before the sacred fire and in the presence of the family priest.

Wealth also facilitated the building of temples, whose place in Zoroastrianism dates back to the fourth century BC. Temples are essentially centers of purity where rituals can be performed involving the housing of an ever-burning fire which is variously interpreted as the Son, Representative or Presence of God. For the layperson, worship involves preliminary purification of the body (through washing) and spirit (through kusti prayers), the recitation of prayers in the sacred Avestan language, and standing in the divine presence. Priests offer 'higher' or 'inner' ceremonies, for instance the prayers of the dead. Non-Zoroastrians are excluded from temples where the fire is burning, for their impurity would defile the sanctity of the place. There are two types of temple. The highest is the *Atash Bahram* or 'Cathedral' Fire Temple, distinguished by the length and complexity of the consecration of the fire it houses. There are eight such temples in India; four in Bombay, two in Surat, one in Navsari and Udwada. The last is a special place of pilgrimage

for it houses the fire which has burned continuously for a thousand years. The more 'ordinary' fire temple, the *dar i Mihr* or *Agiary* (Gujarati – 'House of Fire') is far more widespread; there are more than forty in the city of Bombay alone.

Death is the work of evil in Zoroastrianism, hence all decaying and dead matter represent evil. As earth, fire and water are considered sacred, corpses are instead laid in a *daxma*, or 'Tower of Silence', where they are exposed to vultures to avoid polluting the divine creation. Parsis argue that this method of disposal is quick, hygienic and economic with land. Where there is no daxma in India, Pakistan and Iran, burial is common, although elsewhere in the world cremation is often practiced.

Zoroastrian practice has, on the whole, remained remarkably faithful over the centuries and continents; its interpretation and doctrines, however, have varied. Parsis became the most highly Western-educated section of nineteenth century Indian society with the result that many under Protestant influence rejected 'medieval' priestly traditions as 'corrupt superstitions' in favor of what was presented as the 'pure' teaching of the prophet. Others reacted against this development by finding justification for cherished custom in Theosophy. But, as Theosophy became more Hinduized and moved closer to the Indian nationalist politics of the Home Rule League, Parsis began their own 'Zoroastrianized Theosophy', *Ilm-i Kshnoom* or 'Path of Knowledge' which is still influential today. Since Independence, there have been many different influences at work on Zoroastrians in India: Westernizing and, to some extent, Iranizing influences from overseas; a charismatic and traditional teaching movement, Zoroastrian Studies; Hindu mystical and, to a lesser degree, Sufi influences; new religious movements, notably the cult of the Babas; and tension between traditional centers of authority in Bombay and Gujarat, and smaller but highly educated groups in places such as Delhi who are trying to assert their independence. As numbers decline, there is a growing sense of urgency to identify and preserve the essence of the community and its religion.

JHi

Further reading
M. B. Boyce, *Zoroastrians: Their Religious Beliefs and Practices* (London, 1979)
M. B. Boyce, *Sources for the Study of Zoroastrianism* (Manchester, 1984)
J. R. Hinnells, *Persian Mythology* 2nd edn (London, 1985)
M. Karkal, *Survey of Parsi Population of Greater Bombay, 1982* (Bombay, 1985)
E. Kulke, *The Parsees in India* (Munich and Bombay, 1974)
H. D. K. Mirza, *Outlines of Parsi History* (Bombay, 1974)
K. Mistree, *Zoroastrianism: an Ethnic Perspective* (Bombay, 1982)
P. Nanavutty, *The Parsis* 2nd edn (Delhi, 1980)

SOCIETIES

The lifestyles of the upper middle class and of the poor.

Introduction

Traditional societies everywhere are based on certain first principles which are their unquestioned ideological foundation. Thus, of the 'high' cultures of South Asia, the Buddhist, Hindu, Jain and Sikh ways of life are all based on a notion of moral conduct or righteousness (*dharma*), while Muslims strive to follow the path ordained by God (*sharia*) and Christians to lead their lives in the light of the gospel. Similar deep-seated notions pervade the so-called tribal cultures. These well-established cultural ideologies are expressed in various forms of social organization, such as the caste system, although it is no less possible to regard them as providing justifications for particular societal arrangements. A notable and widespread idea in South Asian cultures generally is that of the inborn character of peoples referred to as *guna* by Hindus or *zat* by Muslims. Inter-personal and inter-group relations are determined by, among other things, this notion of inborn nature. Or they used to be.

A notable break with ideologies of this kind resulted from the South Asian encounter with the West, leading to the colonization of most regions (with the exception of Bhutan and Nepal), from the eighteenth century onwards. The individual rather than the group now became increasingly important, and it was what he/she set out to do, and what he/she achieved, that came to be considered significant rather than who he/she was by birth. Of course, this transformation was not sudden or total, but it did emerge as a critical element in the consciousness of the people educated in the new learning of the West. This transition has been referred to as the change from 'status' to 'contract' as the foundation of social life.

The emergence of individualism, achievement and contract as the bases of social organization represented the forces of modernization and secularization and, as one would expect, were more salient in urban centers than in tribal and peasant villages. But even in the villages new notions of individual property rights took root and brought about changes in agrarian structure. Local self-government was yet another new idea which brought modern politics into the lives of the people. All these ideas and the institutions related to them were fostered by the new learning and protected by new laws.

The gradual growth of new concepts of individual and society generated social reform movements which sought to remove what came to be considered the undesirable aspects of the old ways. Although such movements had clear elements of religious and cultural revivalism, the dominant note was that of westernization. Not only new forms of economic and political activity and of administration were introduced, but also creative life (literature, the performing arts) and leisure time activities (including sports) were affected. In short, South Asia's contact with the West modified old ways of living and generated new ones.

TNM

How people live

Caste and the ordering of Hindu society

An overwhelming majority of the Hindus of South Asia, particularly those living in the rural areas, identify themselves in terms of their *jati* or caste. It has always been so. The implications of caste identity, however, have been changing continuously. Early texts consider the emergence of jati a socially confusing and morally degenerative process resulting from the indiscriminate intermingling of the four *varnas* (colors or major divisions) of Vedic society, that is Brahmins, Kshatriyas, Vaishyas and Shudras. Although these divisions were not rigidly defined, certain rules and conventions obviously governed the choice of spouse and occupation.

Dharma (righteousness) is what sustains the cosmic–moral order (*samsara*). It lifts human activity (*karma*) to the level of righteousness. The three principal goals of human endeavor (*purushartha*) are said to be *dharma*, *artha* (pursuit of economic and political goals) and *kama* (fulfilment of bodily appetites). These are, however, to be so pursued that dharma takes precedence over and includes the other two. A fourth goal, *moksha* or release from the cycle of retribution, is also mentioned but it is usually viewed as a very gradual process. In the meanwhile the emphasis is upon the performance of one's social duties.

In its most concrete connotation dharma is the web of social obligations defined in terms of one's jati and the stage of one's life (*ashrama*). Four such chronological stages were recognized by the ancient law-givers: a preparatory stage of pre-marital youth (*brahmacharya*) was followed by that of the householder (*grihastha*); later in life one was expected to go into retirement for spiritual pursuits (*vanaprastha*); finally came renunciation (*sannyasa*), the complete withdrawal from all social obligations. For the present 'dark age' (*kaliyuga*), the law-givers stressed above all the stage of the this-worldly householder and enjoined domesticity upon him as his dharma. Right conduct, therefore, depended upon observing one's caste and family obligations and was socially sanctioned. This remains the prevailing ideology of Hindu society.

Castes and families are, then, the building blocks of Hindu society. Membership of a caste is by birth: one may lose one's caste identity by being thrown out of one's jati for severe misconduct but one does not thereby become a member of another caste. Castes reproduce themselves through endogamy, that is, marriage within a defined group. Caste occupations are usually hereditary, particularly among artisan and 'service' jatis. Each caste stands below, above or on a par with others in a system of social ranking. While the top and bottom rungs of the social ladder are fairly well defined and occupied by the Brahmin and Shudra castes, there is much competition for the middle positions.

According to traditional caste ideology, which is obviously the brain-child of Brahmins, the key to the rank order lies in the notion of ritual purity. Empirical studies in contemporary rural India have revealed that the acquisition of wealth is generally inadequate to enable a caste to cross the barrier of pollution in attempted upward mobility. Low castes which are not polluting have been, however, known to improve their social rank by collectively adopting some of the crucial elements (for example, vegetarianism, the practice of dowry, Brahminic rituals) of the life-style of higher ranked clean castes: this process has been called 'sanskritization'.

The practice of 'untouchability', severely restricting the social contacts and livelihood opportunities of the lowest castes (usually associated with death and body excrements), against which Mahatma Gandhi launched a countrywide campaign, was declared illegal in the Constitution of independent India. Moreover, the uplift of 'depressed' and 'backward' castes has become the constitutional obligation of the state. The principal instrument employed for this purpose has been protective discrimination. Reservation of 'places' in educational institutions, elective bodies and government service, from the lowest to the highest levels, has enabled the so-called 'scheduled' castes and other notified communities to make considerable socio-economic progress in the last 30 years.

A leading source of social change in caste-bound Hindu society has been electoral politics based on universal adult franchise. While power was traditionally the preserve of clean castes, they are now

Leather workers of the Chamar caste. Chamars are considered 'untouchables': the uplift of such 'depressed' castes is a constitutional obligation of the Indian state.

able to retain it only with the support of the numerically preponderant lower castes who have often chosen to wield it themselves. Caste 'associations' and 'vote banks' have emerged as significant political forces in the assertion of equal rights of citizenship, and have generated considerable tension in the countryside. Legislative measures seeking to alter the traditional patterns of land ownership and land use, though not thoroughly implemented, have been quite broad in scope and have been particularly advantageous to the middle-level peasant castes. Also noteworthy is the emergence of militant movements among the depressed castes in some parts of the country.

Castes have thus become similar to ethnic groups in other plural and socio-economically inegalitarian societies. The forces of politicization, economic development, and secularization have produced a paradoxical situation by simultaneously weakening caste as a ritual status-based group and strengthening it as an ethnic group. A breakdown of the congruence of ritual status and politico-economic power has taken place, but castes are not yet classes.

Of the traditional bases of jati, endogamy remains most widespread, enabling castes to reproduce themselves for objectives which are partly traditional and partly modern. Marriage within the caste (or sub-caste) results in all of a person's kin and relatives by marriage sharing caste membership with him. The smallest kin group within a caste is the household. Households exhibit different forms of familial structure, ranging from the nuclear to the extended, at different points of time. The trend towards nuclearization is becoming gradually stronger. Families often become occupationally and spatially diversified, as individual members move away

The matrimonial advertisements in India's Sunday newspapers illustrate the continuing role of caste in marriage ties.

A Hindu wedding.

Hindu rites of passage

In the past the passage of a Hindu life was marked by several dozen lifecycle rites. Now fewer than ten are generally performed of which the most important concern name-giving, adopting the sacred thread, marriage and death.

The name-giving ceremony takes place on the twelfth day after birth. The baby is dressed in new clothes and placed in a swinging cot. Twelve lamps are lit underneath and a priest pronounces the name chosen by the parents. Those women present then sing songs at which the name is inserted at the appropriate place. For high caste boys this is followed by the thread ceremony. The boy must be aged at least eight and be able to learn sanskrit texts. The occasion is a social one with invited guests who bring suitable presents for a schoolboy and participate in a feast. In the ceremony father and son sit close to the sacred fire. The sacred thread, a loop made of five strands of strong cotton, is placed by a priest over the boy's head so that it hangs from the left shoulder across the chest and down below the right hand. Mantras are chanted. The priest then speaks the following words from the *Rigveda*: 'We contemplate the most radiant luster of the God Savita [the Sun], the sustainer of the Earth, Inter-Space, and Heaven. May he inspire our intellect'. The father whispers this into the boy's right ear; the boy repeats it one word at a time. He is then told to work hard and to do well in his examinations.

Marriage is by far the most important rite. Most marriages are arranged, being seen as an alliance between two families, and the greatest possible congruence is sought regarding language, social status and family tradition. The ceremony begins with the parents of the bride welcoming the groom with presents and formally giving their daughter in marriage to him who with his father receives the bride into her new family. At this time the bride receives gold ornaments, saris and other clothes which become her property. The couple then stand opposite each other, wearing new clothes and garlands, but separated by a silk screen held by the priests of each family. The guests sing songs of blessing and at the end of each verse throw rice at the couple. When the screen is removed bride and bridegroom exchange garlands. After this a sacred fire is lit and they pour ghi onto it praying for wealth, healthy children and a long life while priests chant mantras. They then take seven steps around the fire, the wife following the husband. The first step is for long married life, the second for power, the third for prosperity, the fourth for happiness, the fifth for children, the sixth for the enjoyment of seasonal pleasures, and the seventh for lifelong friendship. Simultaneously the groom repeats a mantra seven times. After the marriage feast the bride goes to her husband's home.

Death brings the last rite. Hindus believe that at the moment of death the soul is trapped in the skull and has to be released through sacred fire so that it may take on some other form. The eldest male relative walks three, five or seven times round the funeral pyre which is constructed so that most of the heat will be directed towards the skull. He lights the pyre and priests chant sacred texts while the body burns. When the skull is broken the mourners disperse. On the third day the ashes are collected and scattered in a river.

Source: V. P. Kanitkar, *Hinduism* pp. 20–27 (Hove, 1985).

Box 32

from hereditary or traditional work. Nevertheless, they retain bonds of ritual obligation (attendance at births, marriages and deaths) and in some cases even joint ownership of some types of immovable property.

A significant development is the pursuit of expanding educational and economic opportunities by individuals within families depending upon personal ambitions and capabilities. The right to inherit and transmit property bestowed on Hindu women through legislation such as the Hindu Succession Act of 1956, though not widely asserted as yet, has resulted in a noticeable 'psychological' change in family life. The gradual strengthening of the aspirations of individuals within households has resulted in a weakening of caste solidarity in certain contexts: kinship loyalties too tend to be increasingly narrowly circumscribed.

TNM

Further reading
L. Dumont, *Homo Hierachicus: The Caste System and its Implications* (Chicago, 1980)

T. N. Madan, Ed., *Way of Life: King, Householder, Renouncer* (Paris, 1982)

D. G. Mandelbaum, *Society in India* (Berkeley, 1970)

'Dhamma', the Buddhist Path

As dharma is the basis of traditional Hindu social organization, so is dhamma of Buddhist society. The Buddha's teaching is often presented as a total repudiation of the established social order. It might be more accurate to say that he sought to recover the pristine purity of the old way of life, which had become degenerate, and to refine it. Thus he said that no Brahmin or outcast was such by his birth but only by his deeds. He, however, questioned external authorities, whether they took the form of a super-human creator or the Vedas, and was against mechanical ritualism (for example, sacrifices) and extremist forms of asceticism. He made moderation, the enlightened 'middle way', the basis of social life for layman and monk alike.

The Buddha is said to have taught that one must avoid the pursuit of both unbridled pleasure and unbounded pain, for both are ignoble and unprofitable. They spring like all evil from ignorance. True knowledge alone could be the basis of a good society. With that the Buddha set in motion, over 2500 years ago, the 'wheel of righteousness' (*dhamma cakka*) and expounded the timeless (*akaliko*) path, which was also for present application (*samditthiko*), and remains so in principle to this day.

True knowledge is based on the four 'noble truths'. The first of these is the centrality of suffering in human life. The second is that suffering arises from the desire for existence, the failure to realize the difference between metaphysical and empirical truth: while the former partakes of the absolute, the latter is concerned merely with probability. Those misled by a false belief in essences (*sattva*) are trapped in the cycle of transmigration (*samsara*) and retribution (*kamma*). The failure to understand that existence is in truth substanceless (*anatta*) and impermanent (*anicca*) results in the craving for pleasure, power and continued life and, consequently, suffering (*dukkha*). The third truth is that suffering can be ended through *nibbana*, that is, the blowing out of desire. The way to such deliverance and therefore tranquillity, the fourth truth, lies in steadfast adherence to the 'noble eightfold path'.

This path consists of the following steps. The first two, called the 'higher wisdom' are right understanding and right mindedness. The following three steps, namely right speech, right action and right livelihood, comprise 'ethical discipline'. Finally, the seeker must cultivate 'mental discipline' through right effort, right mindfulness and right concentration.

Buddhist rites of passage

Buddhists of different cultural traditions practice a variety of rites of passage. However, only a few of those rites have a specifically Buddhist character. Where that character is most evident is in rites solemnizing the transition from home-life to homelessness, that is, from the status of a layman to that of a monk. That transition reenacts the Buddha's own 'great renunciation'.

There is no definite age at which the transition is made. But those who are admitted to the order as novices are generally over eight years of age, while full membership is given only to those over twenty. The granting of full membership involves a more elaborate ceremony than the admission of a novice. But, even as a novice, a monk is clearly distinguishable from a layman by such visible signs as the shaven head and monastic habit. The monk is also given a new name, and commits himself to observing ten precepts, which constitute a more rigorous code than the five precepts of the laity. Both the monks and the laity 'take refuge in the three jewels', the three jewels being the Buddha, his teaching, and his followers.

The recitation of the three refuges and five precepts for the first time, which can be taken as the point at which one becomes a Buddhist, is generally an informal affair in the life of a child. Nor are there obligatory Buddhist rites relating to birth, puberty, and marriage. In old age Buddhists tend to intensify their religious activities in preparation for the hereafter. Death is followed by a series of rites which reflect Buddhist notions of rebirth and merit-transference. The bereaved offer clothing and food to monks and transfer the merit thus obtained to the newly departed. Cremation is the preferred but not universal method of disposing of dead bodies. Bodily relics of the Buddha and his disciples receive the veneration of the faithful. Stupas enshrining relics are a prominent feature of the Buddhist landscape.

Source: KM.

The transition from layman to monk re-enacts the Buddha's own 'great renunciation'.

Box 33

The foregoing was and is a guide primarily for the homeless monks (*bhikkhus*) and nuns (*bhikkhuni*), living in monastic communities (*sangha*) on the outskirts of human settlements. The admissibility of women to the sangha, which are expected to be democratically organized, is one of their notable features. They are maintained on the munificence of the laity. Buddhist countries including Sri Lanka have also known the forest monks, who live in remote solitude and in austerity; in fact, they are considered spiritually superior to the monks of the sangha by people in general.

Monks and nuns alone do not, however, constitute Buddhist societies: there are also the common people (*puthujjana*). The *Admonition to Singala*, attributed to the Buddha himself, spells out the moral basis of everyday life building upon the four cardinal virtues of friendliness, compassion, joy and equanimity.

The *Admonition* first lists the vices that should be avoided: injury to life, stealing, lusts of the flesh, lying. The motives of evil deeds are then enumerated: partiality, enmity, stupidity, fear. The lay followers of the path are advised to avoid squandering wealth, frequenting fairs, drunkenness, gambling, idleness, irregular habits, bad company, enemies, and so on. In a similar vein, lay noblemen are exhorted to serve in diverse ways their parents, teachers, wife, friends, counselors, slaves, servants, ascetics and Brahmins. Above all they should seek the 'triple refuge' – in the Buddha, dhamma and the sangha. Contemporary studies of Buddhist society in Sri Lanka stress continuity and explain gaps between theory and practice as unintended consequences of the original doctrines.

The life of the laity is characterized by prayers at domestic shrines and pilgrimages away from home. The image of the Buddha is much venerated everywhere as are various holy relics. Sarnath in India, where the Buddha preached his first sermon, the Temple of the Tooth in Kandy, Sri Lanka, and other places draw pilgrims from distant places. Elements of Brahminical belief and practice have traditionally been a part of everyday life, for instance in Sri Lanka, where the Buddhist and non-Buddhist elements are fused but not confused; a hierarchy of supernatural powers is recognized, with the Buddha at the top but also including national and local deities, demons and ghosts. Recently ecstatic cults, such as that of a snake-God at Kataragama, have acquired prominence alongside obvious processes of secularization.

Whereas a Buddhist lay person's life is surcharged with an attitude of veneration and piety, there is not much in it by way of ritual pertaining to one's own self. Among South Asian Buddhists there are only two important lifecycle rituals, that is, tonsure or some other ceremony to mark the onset of puberty and cremation or burial. The funeral ceremonies of monks are more elaborate than those of householders. Monks and family elders rather than priests lead or supervise these rites. Marriage is a secular rather than a religious ceremony.

Historically, a very significant happening in Sri Lanka was the establishment of a mutually reinforcing relationship between Buddhism and royal authority. The state and the citizenry became the supporters of the sangha. The long and complex history of this relationship culminated in modern times in the linkage between Buddhism and nationalism in the last quarter of the nineteenth century. Independence in 1948 was followed in 1956 by worldwide celebrations of the 2500th anniversary of the Buddha's death which gave much salience to the place of Buddhism in Sri Lankan culture and politics.

In 1972 the country's Constitution laid it down as a 'duty of the state to protect and foster Buddhism'. A close association between religion, language and the state has resulted in a situation in which the Sinhala speaking Buddhists (67 percent of the population in 1981) have come to be seen as culturally and politically overbearing by linguistic and religious minorities. On their part, the majority are legitimately proud of their historical and cultural achievements which have their main source in Buddhism as a total way of life.

TNM

Further reading
R. F. Gombrich, *Precept and Practice: Traditional Buddhism in the Rural Highlands of Ceylon* (Oxford, 1971)
K. W. Morgan, Ed., *The Path of the Buddha* (Delhi, 1986)
W. Rahula, *What the Buddha Taught* (Bedford, 1967)

The holy law and Muslim life
The constitution of the Muslim societies of South Asia has been a gradual process. The various ways in which Islam was spread throughout India by trade, by conquest and by the word and deed of *sufis* (mystics) produced markedly different Islamic cultures both fascinating and historically significant. Thus, in what is now Bangladesh, sufis employed the idiom of Hindu mythology and cosmology to produce a living culture quite distinct from that in, for instance, Kerala where Islam was brought by Arab traders and sustained by a continuing contact with the Arab lands. No less distinct again are the *ashraf* or high-born who are descended from, or claimed to be descended from, those who entered India largely from Iran or Central Asia to conquer or to serve in the courts of Muslim rulers. They tended to regard themselves as exemplars of Muslim high culture, which was distinct from that of Muslim converts from Hinduism, and which while it borrowed from the Hindu world about it rarely did so with complete ease.

Although culturally and socially different from one another, the Muslim communities of South Asia have all shared a common ideal of becoming true followers of the exalted path which the Quran says, Allah hath ordained as the 'Way-to-be-followed'. *Sharia* (Holy

Muslim rites of passage

Muslim lifecycle rites focus on birth, childhood, marriage and death. Birth is followed immediately by the whispering of the call to prayer into the baby's right ear and the commencement of prayer into the left. Seven days later, in a ceremony called *aqiqah*, the child is given a name and introduced to relatives and close friends. The name itself is usually chosen from those of the Prophet's family, of other prophets mentioned in the Quran, or of great Muslims of the past.

Two ceremonies mark childhood. The *bismillah*, which takes place soon after the age of four, celebrates the beginning of education with the child reciting the *bismillah* formula ('In the name of God the Compassionate and the Merciful') and the first words revealed to the Prophet. Circumcision, which is generally performed on a boy between the ages of seven and twelve, initiates him into manhood.

Marriage, the ceremony is known as *nikah*, is an act of great religious importance. 'When the servant of God marries', declares the Prophet, 'he perfects half of his religion'. Although marriage is a contract and not a sacrament, the bride and groom nevertheless promise to make their marriage an act of obedience to God in accordance with the teachings of the Quran. Great emphasis is placed on the importance of mutual love and respect and the care of children. It is preferred, moreover, that a man cleave to one wife throughout his life, although he may have up to four wives at once on the condition that he treats all of them equally.

When a man is near to death, those at his bedside encourage him to say the confession of faith; just as God was the first word he heard, so it should be the last he utters. After death the body is immediately washed, shrouded and carried to a mosque where the burial service is said. Then the bier will be borne quickly to the grave; the Prophet said that it was good that the righteous should arrive soon at happiness. The body is then buried with the face turned towards Mecca. Muslims are encouraged not to grieve too much; Sunnis mourn for no more than seven days. Death is not the end of life. The separation will only be brief for through God's grace all who truly believe will enjoy life after death.

A young girl at her Bismillah ceremony.

Box 34

Law) was the 'Way' and *din* was the following of the 'Way' and submitting to it was (*islam*). Revealed by God to Muhammad, the Prophet led his followers by personal example (*sunna*). Thus revealed and lived, the sharia is a total and indivisible body of doctrine and practice, including important issues of personal law as well as guidance on the minutiae of the everyday life of common people.

To follow the sharia has been the ideal but it has not always been easy; and those who have claimed to know it have differed among themselves. There have been at one extreme *ulama* (men learned in the sharia and the skills to make it socially useful) who have demanded a rigid and literal adherence to their interpretation of the law. At the other extreme there have stood sufis who had evolved particular methods by which the individual might come to know God which they called *tariqa*. Each follower (*murid*) of a particular method had his own spiritual guide (*pir*). Ideally, the tariqa is not an alternative to the sharia, although in some sufi brotherhoods it has become dangerously close to being so. All of these, it should be noted, came to South Asia from West and Central Asia, but imbibed something of the ethos of medieval Indian egalitarian movements just as they contributed significantly to them. The teachings of Nanak whose followers constituted a new religious community, the Sikhs, show some influence of sufi ideas.

Mediating between the two extreme attitudes to the sharia, there have been ulama and sufis who have sought to strike a balance between sharia and tariqa, between outward adherence to the law and inner search for religious truth. Some displayed a marked responsiveness to changing times, notably to the establishment of British rule in India with its underpinning of Christianity, and to the rise of the Indian nationalist movement with its undertones of

Hindu revivalism. Thus, in the late nineteenth century, the ulama of Deoband responded to the disappearance of the Muslim imperium by creating a form of Islam which would enable Muslims to do without the state and by broadcasting it through a massive expansion of traditional *madrasa* (school) education. Moreover, in the twentieth century, religious scholarship in South Asia has produced as divergent interpretations of Islam as that of Abul Kalam Azad, who supported religious pluralism, and that of Abul Ala Maududi, who advocated a severe fundamentalism.

Sharia, then, is the basic framework, and there are many aspects of social and personal life which reflect it. The unity of God and the finality of the Prophet are generally accepted as the foundation of Islam, so the Ahmadiyyas of India and Pakistan, who acknowledge a modern-day prophet, remain suspect in the eyes of all Muslims although they consider themselves to be Muslims. Apart from these two cardinal precepts, South Asian Muslims adhere in principle, though not always in practice, to the obligations of daily, Friday and Id prayers (*namaz*), *zakat* ('that which is due to the poor'), *roza* or fasting during the month of Ramazan, and *haj*, the pilgrimage to Mecca, which every Muslim who has the means must perform. The Shias, who form about ten percent of the Muslim population of South Asia, place in addition an especial emphasis on the observance of Muharram.

Alongside these 'pillars' of Islam, Muslim communities have many customs and practices which are either survivals from their pre-Muslim past or show the influence of Hindu culture and society. Muslim occupational groups in the villages tend to resemble Hindu castes in being hereditary and observing endogamy. Much more important is the presence of the notion of hereditary status or rank, such as the superiority of the Sayyid (descendants of the Prophet's daughter Fatima) and other high-born (ashraf) families over common people. The Brahminic ideology of ritual purity is, however, rejected explicitly. Birth rituals and marriage ceremonies in many places, for example in the predominantly Muslim Kashmir Valley, exhibit Hindu features. In Bangladesh cultural festivals such as 'Pahela Baisakh', which have a distinctly local character, are being observed. In the Laccadive Islands, a curious blending of Islam and matriliny has occurred. In Pakistan the tribal communities of the northwest have their traditional codes of honor which are as dear to them as the sharia. Cultural synthesis has been notable in the domains of architecture, music and literature, and it is arguable that the Urdu language offers the richest testimony to the creative aspects of the Muslim–Hindu encounter. On the other hand, as South Asian Muslims realized from the early nineteenth century that there was no longer a significant Muslim power to enforce the sharia, a recurrent feature of socio-cultural life came to be revivalist or 'purificatory' movements such as the *tablighi* among the Meos of India.

Revivalist or fundamentalist movements have derived strength not only from a new rigor in adhering to the sharia and a new understanding of it, but also from modernist or secularist tendencies, which may be said to have begun in the late nineteenth century with the innovations that Sayyid Ahmad Khan sought to introduce into Muslim society through western education. His efforts to promote modern rational thought, pragmatism and liberalism were bitterly opposed by many ulama. Recently the state in Pakistan has tried to enforce stricter adherence to aspects of the sharia while in Bangladesh the state has tried to Islamize everyday life through, for instance, the introduction of Arabic words and expressions into Bengali. In India Muslims generally have expressed themselves against the adoption of a common civil code, demanding that sharia continue to be the basis of their family and social life and asserting that the test of the secularism of the Indian state must be that this is permitted.

TNM

Further reading
A. Ahmad, *Islamic Culture in the Indian Environment* (London, 1964)

M. Mujeeb, *The Indian Muslims* (London, 1967)

F. Rahman, *Islam* (Chicago, 1979)

Tribal life

The peoples of South Asia have been categorized in many ways. One of these is to designate some of them as 'tribes' in contrast to 'castes', a practice originating in the colonial period. Today, named tribes, more than 500 in number, constitute anywhere between five and ten percent of the combined populations of South Asian countries: in India alone there are about 52 million tribal people.

Who exactly are classified as tribes depends more upon administrative considerations than sociological criteria. Around the turn of the present century, the British had evolved an approach which attached the greatest importance to religion, social organization and ecology. The tribes were 'animists' rather than Hindus, Muslims or Buddhists; the basis of society was some kind of a descent group (lineage, clan); and the typical habitat of this group was non-urban (often the forest) where a subsistence-level living was eked out. These characteristics were rather arbitrarily fixed as important changes were already afoot even among the remotest tribal areas: for example conversions to Christianity had begun in both the northeast (for example, among the Nagas) and in central India (for example, among the Mundas and the Oraons). Another development of enormous significance was the establishment of the Tata Iron and Steel Company at Jamshedpur (Bihar) in 1908 which brought modern mining and industrial manufacture to the doorstep of the tribal homes.

Although there has been much social change, tribes at different levels of socio-economic development survive in South Asia today. At the one extreme there are small dwindling communities of less than 500 persons; the estimated population of the Jarawas of the Andaman Islands, for instance, is less than 100, and they are still in only limited and intermittent contact with the administration and the neighboring tribes. At the other extreme are the tribes of the northeast, who account for almost the entire population of such Indian states as Arunachal Pradesh, Mizoram and Nagaland, and have adopted highly Christianized and westernized lifestyles, although movements to revive tribal culture are also present.

In striking contrast, the Pakhtuns of the northwest frontier of Pakistan retain their proud cultural traditions in large measure. Strongly patrilineal in character, the organizing principles of Pakhtun society are agnatic rivalry (*tarburwali*), the honor of women (*tor*) and democratic self-governance (within certain limits) through the traditional council of elders (*jirga*). The scope of the jurisdiction of the jirga is wide-ranging and includes matters of religious, family and tribal concern. Decisions are based on a combination of sharia and Pakhtun custom and are strictly enforced.

Among the famous tribal peoples of South Asia, the Todas of the Nilgiri Hills are as celebrated in anthropological literature as the Pakhtuns. Though much affected by the forces of change, this once polyandrous people, whose religion and economy were traditionally centered in the buffalo dairy, manage to continue to grow and live in their original habitat and evolve a cultural synthesis between 'tradition' and 'modernity'. Their ties with other Nilgiri peoples have weakened as the process of their incorporation into the market-centered cash economy and the political institutions of the Indian state has proceeded apace. Their religious orientation also is increasingly toward Hinduism. Symbolic of these changes is a popular temple dedicated to a Hindu goddess and situated near the bazaar in Ootacamund.

The future of the tribal communities of South Asia offers two main alternatives in terms of preferred lifestyles. Those tribes which enjoy advantages of both location and numbers are likely to become modernized without prior absorption into more advanced neighboring communities. This is best illustrated by the Nagas and the Mizos. Those which are 'encysted' both geographically and culturally seem to have a harder road to tread marked by external pressures and internal tensions. Some of these communities, for instance, the Gurungs, the Magars and the Tharus of Nepal, simply seek to include themselves with their neighbors; others, for instance, the Kalash (also called the Kafir) of Pakistan, are similarly destined to become absorbed in the religious culture of the larger society although not in the self-propelled manner of the Nepal communities.

The case of the Santals, who form the largest tribe of South Asia with over three million people, perhaps captures best the contrary pulls of not only 'tradition' and 'modernity' but also of the different roads leading into 'modernity'. Culturally distinct from caste-based Hindu society, the Santals were being gradually dispossessed of their land by rapacious Hindu money lenders, and they broke into open rebellion in 1855–57. While expressing their resentment in such a violent manner, they also strove to emulate high caste customs and practices. This ambivalence has ever since characterized the cultural life of the Santals. Early in the twentieth century they were sucked into newly emergent industrial employment which led to an interest in modern education and a general secularization of lifestyle. Awareness of class interests also has increased alongside a certain degree of politicization. All these processes – Hinduization, secularization, politicization – point to a multiplicity of preferred futures. This indeed is the prospect of most tribes of South Asia.

TNM

Further reading
A. S. Ahmed, *Pukhtun Economy and Society* (London 1980)
A. M. Orans, *The Santal* (Detroit, 1965)
A. Walker, *The Todas of South India* (Delhi, 1986)

The village world
About four-fifths of the people of South Asia live in villages. These rural settlements may be relatively small and socio-culturally homogeneous communities of a few hundred persons, such as the hamlets in Baluchistan or in the hilly areas of Nepal; or they may be quite large and complex, embracing several thousand people of different

A village in Bihar.

cultural, religious and socio-economic backgrounds, such as the villages in the plains of North India or in Bangladesh. The hereditary occupational group and the domestic family (household) are the two main social groups on which village life is based.

The form in which the occupational group-based social organization is best expressed is the Hindu caste system. The nucleus of the society is the land-owning castes of clean ritual status. They exchange grain for the services of specialist castes (for example, blacksmiths, potters, oil-pressers). The grain that one parts with, usually at the time of the harvest, may not always be a 'surplus', but doing so is an obligation and a necessity and the larger landowners have traditionally appeared in the role of patrons of the poorer service and artisan castes. While the patrons generally exploited those who worked for them, they also provided a certain security for the latter by ensuring that they had basic necessities in times of urgent or sudden need such as marriages and deaths.

Although the caste system itself is ideologically Brahminical, the occupational groups comprising it may not all be Hindu but include Muslims and tribals. In an interesting historical development, the social organization of rural Kashmir is characterized by the absence of any Hindu castes other than the Brahmins. Muslim occupational groups, most of them descendants of Hindu converts, provide the services and goods they need. From the Brahmin's point of view these are caste services with strong ritual overtones; from the Muslim's perspective, what binds him to the Brahmin is economic interest. In Sri Lanka the reverse position obtains: although Buddhist, Sri Lankan society is also caste-based, and rural social organization is similar to that of India except that the Brahmin is absent. In Panjabi villages in Pakistan a caste-like social organization prevails although the Brahminic ideology is not present.

In those regions of South Asia where caste is absent as an ideological basis of society, kinship institutions and values provide the bedrock of rural society. Here too 'exchange' plays a pivotal role in establishing and maintaining the bonds of social solidarity. This is generally true of all regions of Pakistan. Thus, in the villages in Panjab, *vartan bhanji* (literally, 'dealings in sweets') is an important institution: it involves the giving of gifts in cash and kind to a household celebrating a circumcision, marriage or another similar event by other members of the village community called a *biradari* ('fraternity'). Those receiving gifts must reciprocate at the appropriate time. Vartan bhanji provides economic assistance in times of need, strengthens social bonds, and enables the big landlords to secure a political following.

All three kinds of ties mentioned above – kin, economic, political – have a tendency to spill over village boundaries. In Bangladesh, for instance, the 'affluent' households of contiguous villages may provide the leaders (*sardars* or *matabbars*) who collectively constitute a decision-making council of elders and bind together a cluster of villages which are referred to as the *samaj* (society). Similarly, a preference for village exogamy, that is marriage outside a defined group, in North India, results in kindreds of recognition which are spread over a much wider area than kindreds of cooperation which may be concentrated in a single village. In short, while the structural discreteness of the South Asian village may not be denied, it is important to recognize the significance of 'extensions'.

The centripetal as well as the centrifugal aspects of village life are also visible in the religious and festive life of the villages. Village level deities and their propitiation are a prominent feature of life in Bangladesh, India, Nepal and Sri Lanka among tribal people, Buddhists and Hindus alike. Thus, smallpox has traditionally been associated in these countries with a village goddess called Shitala. So deeply ingrained has her cult been that after the recent eradication of this scourge, Shitala has been reported to have been provided a new association with tuberculosis in Tamil Nadu (India). In Muslim villages, spiritual leaders (pirs) and other holy men have annual celebrations (*urs*) dedicated to them after their death and shrines are erected at their burial places. Such Muslim shrines and Hindu and Buddhist centers of worship often acquire fame as places where wishes are granted and thus become places of pilgrimage, drawing devotees from far and near. These local cults become the channels of communication for 'high' civilizational ideas to percolate down to the village level and in turn be themselves influenced by them. Besides religious observances, village life is also enlivened by secular gatherings (*melas*), weekly 'markets', cattle 'fairs', wrestling contests, and so on.

While traditional social groupings and institutions survive, although not without alteration, continuing social change adds new dimensions to village life. Such change has become particularly noticeable and significant since the countries of South Asia acquired independence from foreign rule or internal autocracy, both of which had been responsible for the heavy taxation and neglect of the village communities. It was therefore only natural that the national governments would take up rural development as a top priority. The main thrust of the new policies was economic and political, but their social consequences have been far-reaching, although not always in the proclaimed direction.

The basic ideology of the development programs has been that the welfare of common people is the primary responsibility of the state, whether or not they are also seen as the source of legitimate power. Moreover, development is best when brought about with the active co-operation of the people. Thus, the Community Development Program (CDP) in India in the 1950s, or the Integrated Rural Development Program (IRDP) of the 1970s, has been oriented towards the economic uplift of the rural poor. The extensive land and tenancy reforms that came alongside of CDP also sought to alter the agrarian social structure in an egalitarian direction. The concept of village level self-government (*Panchayati raj*) was enshrined in the Constitution itself. The implementation of all these policies has, however, left much to be desired and the rural poor are by common consent far from being the principal beneficiaries of the various programs. The same is more or less true of all other South Asian countries. In Pakistan, the early village AID program, followed by the Basic Democracies policy of the Ayub era (1960s) and the IRDP launched by the Bhutto goernment (1970s), have all benefitted the bigger farmers more than the smaller; the tenants and landless laborers have been neglected. In Sri Lanka, however, distributive justice has received considerable attention.

The unevenness of the benefits of economic development, not only between rural and urban areas but also within rural society itself, combined with increasing politicization, expansion of educational facilities, and the penetration of the remotest and the tiniest of villages by roads and the media (particularly radio and television), has brought about a revolution of rising expectations. Mindless consumerism also is making heavy inroads into the lives of the rural poor. Class antagonisms are replacing traditional rivalries and new forms of violence are emerging. Village in South Asia today is in a state of ferment and radical changes are in the offing.

TNM

Further reading
S. C. Dube, *Indian Village* (London, 1955)
Z. Eglar, *A Punjabi Village in Pakistan* (New York, 1960)
B. Ryan, *Sinhalese Village* (Coral Gables, 1958)
M. N. Srinivas, *The Remembered Village* (New Delhi, 1976)

Urban society
Urban society in South Asia goes back five millennia when its principal locus was in the Indus Valley with later extensions further east and south. Of those proto-historic times only archaeological ruins remain at Harappa (Pakistan), Lothal (India) and elsewhere. Cities of great antiquity with a continuous history, such as Anuradhapura (Sri Lanka), Taxila (Pakistan) and Varanasi (India), each about 2500 years old, bear testimony to town-dwelling as an ancient way of life connected with the practice of religion or affairs of the state.

The towns and cities of today, if not a product of medieval and modern times, bear their imprint. The fortress and the commercial center, and later the colonial trading outpost, emerged as the new foci of urban life, and finally, in the middle of the nineteenth century, arrived the industrial city. Despite this long history, urban populations today do not account for more than about one-quarter of the people of the region: in Bhutan and Nepal 4 percent and 78 percent, respectively, in India and Pakistan 25 percent and 29 percent, with Bangladesh (18 percent) and Sri Lanka (21 percent) falling in between.

Urban lifestyles in contemporary South Asia are pluralist in character. There is a striking persistence of rural forms of social organization. Caste and kinship are important though in many ways altered features of urban life. To give but one example, the very low castes are spatially peripheral people in towns and cities no less than they are in villages and even conversion to non-Hindu religions is of little help. Christian Panjabi sweepers in Karachi are as isolated as any such Hindu group in an Indian city. Kinship ties have been an important channel of recruitment of rural migrants into the industrial labor force. Religious and regional identities are two other primordial bonds responsible not merely for producing exclusive neighborhoods but also for promoting banking, commerce and industry. Parsis, Bohras, and Marwaris are tightly knit communities prominent in modern enterprise.

Traditional bonds and networks alone are not, however, the basis of urban life. Colonial rule produced new patterns of urban settlement with the division of space into cantonments, 'civil lines', and 'old' (often walled) cities, and these are visible even today in Lahore, Delhi–New Delhi, and elsewhere. The consolidation of British rule in India was followed by the emergence of modern educational institutions and hospitals on state and Christian missionary initiatives. The growth of a 'native' middle class, pursuing modern occupations and professions, widened the range of urban activities. A modern capitalist class, conscious of its common interests cutting across primordial loyalties, was prominent in cities like Bombay and Calcutta by the mid-nineteenth century. Lahore was a notable example of a city with its educational and banking institutions built by the new middle class. New social formations never completely displace the old in South Asia, and urban people base their lifestyles on different combinations of old and new elements, a fact which makes the fragmented character of social life salient.

A most regrettable feature of this fragmentation today is the extremely wide contrast in the lifestyles of the rich and the poor. While art galleries, museums, concert halls, cultural festivals and spacious residential suburbs represent the good aspects of urban living, these are overshadowed by the conspicuous consumption which characterizes the lifestyle of the top five percent of the people. Air-conditioned homes, imported limousines, and electronic gadgets of domestic use are more important as symbols of 'high living' than they are functionally. The association of such families with economic offences such as tax evasion renders them suspect in the eyes of the others.

In sharp contrast to these rich suburbs are the slums of every large South Asian city. The squalor, health hazards and over-all degradation of human life makes these settlements, some of which accommodate several hundred thousand people, a matter of serious concern. Outside the slums, there are the destitute pavement sleepers and beggars. Half of the nine million people of Calcutta, a typical 'slumpolis', live on its streets. In this context, the high rate of urban growth, which was as high as 103 percent in Peshawar and 76 percent in Bangalore between 1971 and 1981, is a more significant factor than the relatively low annual rate of urbanization which ranges from 3.5 percent in Sri Lanka to 8.4 percent in Nepal (ignoring Bhutan and the Maldives).

While slums may be localized festering sores, the overall state of ill-health of the South Asian cities is a cause for much serious concern. Urban congestion and decay, environmental degradation, the inadequacy and malfunctioning of public utilities (water, medical care, electric supply, transport), unemployment, crime and other forms of violence are on the increase and affect everybody. Garden cities of a generation ago, for instance Lahore and Bangalore, are fast being converted into jungles of steel and concrete. The contribution of cities like Dhaka and Kanpur to the pollution of the main rivers renders long stretches of them unfit for any purpose whatsoever other than transportation.

Given the stress and strain of urban living, it is not surprising that South Asian cities should witness the emergence of charismatic religious figures and the rise of ecstatic cults. Large sums of money earned from modern secular pursuits are spent lavishly on the construction of grand places of worship and on pilgrimages. A positive development is the emergence of non-governmental voluntary organizations which seek to educate people generally, or specific exploited groups, about their rights and obligations. Social welfare agencies and people's self-help groups have also become quite active. Such developments notwithstanding, unless population pressure does not ease, unless efforts to promote economic growth are not both better informed by distributive justice and accelerated, and unless a considerable improvement in civic sense does not take place, urban living in South Asia will continue to present a mixed picture of progress and decline.

TNM

Further reading
R. G. Fox, Ed., *Urban India, Society, Space and Image* (Durham, N.C., 1970)
S. Hafeez, *Poverty, Voluntary Organizations and Social Change: A Study of an Urban Slum in Pakistan* (Karachi, 1985)
S. Saberwal, Ed., *Process and Institution in Urban India* (New Delhi, 1977)

Status of women
In all South Asian countries today there is a sharply heightened awareness of the need to establish a more egalitarian relationship between men and women. The roots of this awareness lie in modern (Western) conceptions of the autonomy of the individual and the pre-eminence of public as compared to domestic life. South Asian women are thus judged to be not only subordinate to men but also inferior to women in the West. The fact that the first woman head of a modern democratically elected government was Sirimavo Bandaranaike of Sri Lanka (she became Prime Minister in 1960 six years before Indira Gandhi of India), and that Hindu, Buddhist, Christian and Muslim women have played a notable part in national movements, and are today prominent in the professions and public life, is played down as a minority phenomenon. Moreover, it is argued that outstanding public figures such as Mahatma Gandhi, who played a significant role in bringing women into public life, did not really recognize the autonomy of women and continued to look upon them as the helpmates of men. In short, the feminist movement has arrived in South Asia, and is particularly strong in India and Sri Lanka.

In order to present the position of women in South Asian societies in a rounded perspective, it is imperative to pay attention to their cultural backgrounds. There have been several matriarchal societies in India, such as the Garo, the Khasi, and the Nayar, in which women traditionally enjoyed superiority over men in several domains including the economic and the ritual. The processes of modernization have been known to push these societies closer to the patriarchal societies of their Hindu and Christian neighbors. Societies, however, cannot be always judged fairly by the unthinking application of alien standards of status evaluation. Thus, in traditional upper caste Hindu society, the central concern with auspiciousness and purity invest the home with an importance unmatched by any public place: and at home women are not only particularly responsible for the maintenance of purity through the preparation of food but embody in themselves as mothers the supreme value of auspiciousness. Woman is also looked upon as a manifestation of *shakti* or divine power, which, however, is dangerous and needs to be controlled. That these women do not enjoy economic independence is not quite relevant. Among aristocratic Muslim families the power that women exercise behind the purdah through control over information has been documented by sociologists.

The point, however, is that traditional values are being questioned, more in some places than in others, but everywhere. In fact, the status of women in South Asian societies has never been static. The rise of Brahminism would seem to have been restrictive in relation to women, but Buddhism sought to correct this aberration. Islam, though egalitarian in principle, brought with it its own inequalities between men and women, enshrined in the *sharia*, many of which survive till today with the support of tradition-oriented women themselves. The encounter with the West produced considerable uneasiness among the newly educated classes about the status of women. Reformers like Rammohan Roy called

Women in Noorpur village, Meerut district, Uttar Pradesh.

for the abolition of widow-burning (*sati*) and Altaf Husain Hali advocated education for women. It is noteworthy that social reform in India and Sri Lanka throughout the nineteenth century had as its main objective the improvement of the status of women. Women's 'emancipation' and their right to gainful employment and adult franchise became part of the national movement.

Women in general, however, continue to live and work under disadvantageous conditions. If caste or sharia based societies subordinate women to men, so do class based societies. Though women may no longer be excluded from public roles, they are discriminated against in many ways and the gender bias remains deeply entrenched. The relative neglect of female children and discrimination against them, even in the distribution of food at home, is widespread. There is also a lag in the consciousness of women themselves: many new measures of Hindu family law, for instance the right of daughters to a share in ancestral property granted by legislation, have not been widely adopted.

Many social evils remain. The practice of dowry among middle class families has acquired oppressive proportions and cases of so-called 'bride-burning' have been on the increase. Laws protecting women against economic exploitation, prostitution and rape are weak. Since large numbers of women in South Asia work in the unorganized sector, labor laws fail to protect them. It has been observed generally that women have suffered rather than benefitted in the process of economic development. In this respect women in Sri Lanka are better off than in any other South Asian country.

Given the heightened awareness among all sections of society of the need to achieve greater equality with men, particularly among women themselves, the future holds the promise of a better deal for women in South Asia, but it is going to be a hard and long drawn-out struggle.

TNM

Further reading
K. Jayawardena, *Feminism and Nationalism in the Third World* (London, 1986)
J. Liddle and R. Joshi, *Daughters of Independence: Gender, Caste and Class in India* (London, 1986)

The laws under which people live

The general background

Contrary to a widespread popular belief, South Asian laws have never been merely an extension of English law in a different environment. There have always been a large number of indigenous South Asian laws in operation at any one time. At first, modern South Asian laws may appear like borrowed Western legal systems, but by their operation under South Asian conditions of life they have merely contributed to a yet more complex entity clearly dominated by indigenous factors. Now, an appropriate view of South Asian laws cannot avoid the consideration of social reality and of 'living laws'. Studying the official laws alone would be quite fictitious, especially in view of rural realities of life, which we cannot ignore in any South Asian country.

Generally speaking we must distinguish (a) a range of clearly identifiable official legal systems, records of which are available in writing and (b) the somewhat chaotic mass of customary laws, mostly unrecorded and often not officially recognized. The latter, however, continue to determine the lives of most South Asians, even in derogation of official legal provisions. Thus, the laws under which people live in South Asia are only partly those of the official legal system, though such state laws in their various forms tend to claim supremacy.

Since the various, religiously inspired personal law systems of South Asia continue to be of crucial importance, modern national laws, as desirable as they may be politically, are still not readily accepted. This is most clearly shown by the hotly debated issue of a Uniform Civil Code for India (as envisaged by Article 44 of the Constitution of India). The following distinction between traditional and modern legal systems is not as clear-cut as it would appear at first sight. Many facets of traditional South Asian laws are still in full force today, and the beginnings of the modern legal systems of South Asia can be traced back more than 200 years.

The traditional legal systems of South Asia

In South Asia an individual's religious adherence has always had important implications for his legal status. Thus we speak of Hindu, Islamic, Christian, Parsi, Jewish, Buddhist and various forms of tribal law as 'personal laws'. All South Asian countries operate, in effect, a system of concurrent personal laws in addition to a more or less well-developed and comprehensive general legal system, which applies to all citizens uniformly. The borderlines between the various personal laws are not always very clear. Converts may change their religion, but not their way of life. Muslim and Christian law in the subcontinent is subject to much local modification, distinguishing it from classical Islamic law and canon law. The strength of the largely customary personal law systems is often

underestimated. There is much evidence of resentment against undue state interference, because a uniform national law may not pay sufficient attention to local needs and traditions. This fact makes it likely that, much beyond the year 2000, the lives of many South Asians will continue to be determined by the various traditional legal systems.

Hindu law

More than 85 percent of the Indian population is governed by Hindu law, about 15 percent of the population of Bangladesh and of Sri Lanka, as well as about 1 million Hindus of Pakistan. Notably, Nepal is the only surviving Hindu kingdom in the world. Thus both in terms of numbers and because it has influenced the other legal systems in more or less subtle ways, Hindu law is the basic traditional legal system of South Asia. However, there seems to be no such thing as 'Hindu law'. Rather, this collective term comprises a large number of legal systems evolved by Hindus over very many centuries. There is an abundance of written material, from *c.* 1200 BC onwards, about various aspects of Hindu law. Much of this literature has not yet been evaluated specifically for its relevance in legal terms. At any rate, 'law' is, in classical Hindu terms, not a separate entity, but is seen as an integral part of Hindu *dharma*, as an important aspect of human life, which is interlinked with all existence in the cosmic universe.

Classical Hindu law is based on the idea of a pre-ordained order (originally *rita*, later *dharma*), which is not fully self-regulating, but requires the effort of all beings, human and divine. Every Hindu individual is thus placed under an obligation (another level of the operation of dharma) to act in such a way that this order is maintained. Since total harmony remains an ideal, the worldly ruler or king (*raja*) has been placed in a position of authority, requiring him to ensure the smooth functioning of society. The Hindu king is thus the guardian of this order, not the maker of law itself. He does, however, have authority to make administrative rules that promote order, and there is some continuing debate over the exact limits of the powers of the ancient Hindu king.

The theory of the fourfold sources of dharma in *Manusmriti* indicate: that (a) the divinely revealed Vedic hymns (*shruti*), (b) texts that are remembered by the ancient sages (*smriti*), (c) the model behavior of good/learned people (*sadachara*), and (d) individual conscience (*atmatushti*), determine the righteousness of actions. In actual life this order tended to be reversed. The individual Hindu would first examine his conscience, then look to the model of leaders of society, and only then would scriptural authority be sought. Litigation was not encouraged and access to the ruler, in practice, must have been difficult in view of continuous political insecurities. It seems certain that local customary laws determined most issues. If difficult disputes were ultimately brought to a ruler, he was under a duty to find an appropriate solution in consideration of the special facts and circumstances of the case, where these existed, particularly with regard to the customary laws of his subjects. Justice was, thus, sought to be achieved by considering a case on its own merits, not by referring to legislative enactments or binding precedents. There was no legal profession; parties would plead their own case.

Classical Hindu law, then, operates not on the basis of a uniformly binding set of rules, but on a unity of rather broad principles. These are provided, as persuasive guidelines, by the dharma-literature, which we should not, however, see as 'law books', but as handbooks of dharma, that elusive and yet so comprehensive central concept of Hinduism.

In the post-classical period of Hindu law (c. AD 500 onwards) the concept of law as litigation (*vyavahara*) developed. Numerous procedural guidelines for the king and his judicial officers appeared. An increasingly diverse picture of textual evidence led to much confusion in later, medieval times. Specialist writers compiled huge digests (*nibandhas*), collections of legal rules on various topics. These were of little practical use, because it was not clear which rule should be applied. Some texts dealing with property law were given prominence by the British, such as the *Mitakshara* and the *Dayabhaga*, both dating from the eleventh century. Then under medieval Muslim rulers, the development of Hindu law stagnated, but local customary traditions continued to be maintained.

The British soon realized that they could not totally avoid recourse to the indigenous legal systems. The Declaration of 1772 by Warren Hastings appeared to guarantee that Hindus would continue to be governed by Hindu law (and Muslims by Muslim law) with regard to a considerable range of legal topics, mainly in family and religious matters. Gradually, however, the British did interfere and attempted social reforms through law, for example, in the *Hindu Widows' Remarriage Act*, 1856. The early codification of the general law in measures such as the *Indian Penal Code* of 1860 had important implications: from now on very many people in South Asia were, at least in theory, governed by uniform legal provisions. Considerable modifications of traditional Hindu law were introduced by Anglo-Hindu case-law (Anglo-Muhammadan law made a similar impact on Islamic law). The resulting amalgam has been characterized, quite rightly, as a 'bogus' legal system, mainly because it was built on the assumption that the Hindus of South Asia were regulating their lives in accordance with texts like the *Manusmriti*, which was certainly not the case. In the nineteenth and early twentieth centuries there was thus a gradual piecemeal reform of aspects of traditional Hindu law.

Muslim law

Muslim law (*sharia*) made a serious impact on South Asia from c. 1000 onwards. Today the Sunni Muslims of the Hanafi school are dominant, but there are also followers of the Shafii school and a considerable number of Shias.

As Muslim rulers became established in various parts of South Asia, and the Muslim population continued to grow, Muslim law became the second most important personal law in the region. However, the pure sharia law was not applied; the various Muslim laws of South Asia were modified to suit local conditions of life. Thus, many domestic matters of South Asian Muslims continued to be regulated by custom, especially in marriage, adoption and inheritance, and some Muslim communities in South Asia followed what appears to have been customary Hindu law, for example, the Muslim joint families of Kerala.

In those parts of the country where Muslim rulers administered the law, the Islamic criminal law replaced the earlier Hindu criminal law; it was applied till the *Indian Penal Code* of 1860 came into force in 1862. Similarly, the Islamic law of evidence was in operation in most parts of India until the *Indian Evidence Act*, 1872 made it obsolete. The *Muslim Personal Law (Shariat) Application Act*, 1937 further regulated the application of Muslim law in India, and in 1939 the *Dissolution of Muslim Marriages Act* provided statutory grounds for Muslim women to petition for divorce. The traditional Muslim personal laws were thus subject to the same process of gradual state interference as Hindu law.

Buddhist law

Buddhism arose in India, but retreated to the fringes of South Asia. Buddhist law is applied in Bhutan and to some extent in Nepal. It is a personal law in Sri Lanka (Kandyan law) and in Bangladesh, where its position is in doubt. Modern India's neo-Buddhists, close to five million people now, are governed by Hindu law.

Christian law

Christians form about 2.5 percent of the Indian population and constitute small minorities in Pakistan, Bangladesh and Sri Lanka. South Asian Christian laws were codified very early on in the *Indian Divorce Act*, 1869, the *Indian Christian Marriage Act*, 1872, and the *Indian Succession Act* of 1925. All these Acts are still in force in India, Pakistan and Bangladesh. In 1985, India's Supreme Court pointed out the antiquated position of Christian law and the need for reform.

Parsi law

The Parsis are a very small Indian community, mainly concentrated in Bombay and some parts of Gujarat. They have their codified personal law in the *Parsi Marriage and Divorce Act*, 1936, which is as outdated as the Christian law.

Jewish law

There are very few Jews living in India now, mainly in Bombay and parts of Kerala. In theory, at least, they are governed by their own personal law, which remains uncodified.

The modern legal systems of South Asian states

Various forms of co-existence between the traditional, religion-based personal laws and the modern state laws have been developed in the region. There is much tension because of the competing claims of modern unifying tendencies and the desire for the recognition of diversities. Both trends claim to promote better justice.

India

Of all the modern states in the region, India has gone furthest in attempting reforms of traditional laws and in implementing the letter and spirit of its Constitution promulgated on January 26, 1950. A series of Fundamental Rights (Part III) are guaranteed to all citizens. Part IV contains the non-justiciable Directive Principles of State Policy; these have, during the seventies, acquired a more prominent position. Thus, the 42nd Amendment to the Constitution (1976) redrafted the Preamble to make India a 'Sovereign Socialist Secular Democratic Republic', and introduced Article 51A, setting out the fundamental duties of the citizen. The fundamental right to property (Article 31) was abolished by the 44th Amendment in 1978 in order to facilitate the redistribution of assets.

During the present decade, the subtle combination of constitutional provisions, social pressures of various kinds and judicial activism has led to the development of public interest litigation, a movement to bring justice and legal remedies to those who need them most. Modern Indian law has here gone further than its western counterparts, and a growing legal aid movement helps to secure improved access to justice and a higher level of awareness of the rule of law.

The creation of a uniform legal system, apparently in the interest of nation-building, is one of the Directive Principles (Article 44). While the body of general Indian law shows continuous growth, unification of the personal laws has been less easy to achieve. It appears that as a first step the personal law of the majority was subjected to rather far-reaching reforms. The 'Hindu Code' of 1955–56, four Acts of Parliament (*Hindu Marriage Act*, 1955; *Hindu Succession Act*, 1956; *Hindu Adoptions and Maintenance Act*, 1956; *Hindu Minority and Guardianship Act*, 1956), is not, however, a complete codification of Hindu law. Some areas of joint family law are still governed by the ancient shastric law, and, in some respects, Anglo-Hindu law is still valid.

The modern codified law occasionally endorses or saves customary law. In section 7 of the *Hindu Marriage Act*, the traditional diversity of the customary rituals of Hindu marriage solemnization is preserved. Section 29 of the Act expressly recognizes the validity of customary forms of divorce among many low-caste Hindus. Many important reforms have been introduced: section 13 made divorce available to all Hindus on the basis of a large number of fault grounds, and since 1976 also by mutual consent. While the Hindu joint family system was not totally abolished, section 6 of the *Hindu Succession Act* claims to give equal shares to Hindu daughters in cases of intestate succession. Section 14 of this Act has significantly increased the property rights of Hindu widows, much to the dismay of many male Hindus and Sikhs, as a huge amount of litigation vividly demonstrates. The only attempt so far to abolish the traditional obligation system altogether is the *Kerala Joint Hindu Family System (Abolition) Act*, 1975. It is evidently a dismal failure: almost all Hindus in that state continue to arrange their property matters within the context of the joint family, in accordance with traditional legal concepts and not as the modern law requires them to do.

Modern Hindu law also applies to Buddhists, Jains and Sikhs, a fact much resented by the latter, especially because of the implications for property law. Apparently, this extensively secularized, almost de-hinduized, modern Hindu law is intended to serve as a model for the general law of India. Very little difference now exists between the provisions of the *Hindu Marriage Act* and the *Special Marriage Act* of 1954, which is a part of general Indian law and is optionally available to all Indians. It may indeed be seen as a rudimentary Uniform Civil Code, although its provisions are as yet not widely known.

While the other minorities, except the Sikhs, seem unconcerned, Indian Muslims have always viewed the trend towards legal uniformity with some reservation, fearing that their personal law may disappear without trace in a general law. The Shah Bano controversy of 1985 brought such latent tensions to light. In *Mohd. Ahmed Khan* versus *Shah Bano Begum*, the Supreme Court gave effect to sections 125–127 of the *Criminal Procedure Code* of 1973 to the extent that all Muslim husbands were required to pay adequate maintenance to their divorced wives beyond the traditional *iddat* period (three menstrual cycles), namely until the woman's death or remarriage. After much agitation and public unrest, the *Muslim Women (Protection of Rights on Divorce) Act*, 1986, was hurriedly drafted and implemented. The Act appears to give certain rights to divorced Muslim women, but is, in effect, a step away from the goal of legal uniformity and a concession to Muslim fundamentalism.

In 1987, the drafting of a Uniform Civil Code Bill is making some progress, but it would appear that the traditional personal laws, and for good reasons too, will continue to exercise much influence. Most Indians seem unaware of the complex rules in which the official legal system has enmeshed them, and village life largely proceeds along the lines of traditional legal rules.

Women, among them Muslims, protesting against the Muslim Women (Protection of Rights on Divorce) Bill. Through this legislation in May 1986 the Government of India made concessions to Muslim fundamentalism and stepped back from the goal of developing a Uniform Civil Code which is one of the Directive Principles of the constitution.

Pakistan

In this modern state created for Muslims, it is not surprising to see constant efforts to achieve an Islamic legal system. The first Constitution (1956) was based in part on principles designed to achieve an Islamic state, and Pakistan was proclaimed an Islamic republic. While the non-Muslim minority communities voiced some fears then, problems have arisen over the position of minority Muslim groups that stray from orthodoxy. The Ahmadiyyas or Qadianis, who question the doctrine that Muhammad was the last of the prophets, were declared non-Muslims in 1974, and an Ordinance of 1984 made it an offence for them to call themselves Muslims and to refer to their places of worship as mosques. Thus, uniformity and consensus among Muslims remains a problem here, while the small minorities seem to enjoy full constitutional protection.

Islamic principles were established in the *1956 Constitution* to serve as a guide to the state authorities. Article 198 provides that no law should be repugnant to the injunctions of Islam. But confusion over the exact nature of such injunctions, and a volatile political history, have so far prevented the total Islamization of laws in Pakistan. Quite in line with the spirit of reforms in other Islamic countries, the *Muslim Family Laws Ordinance* of 1961 provided far-reaching modern but piecemeal reforms of the Muslim family law. Subsequent Constitutions of Pakistan (1962–73) brought little change, but accommodated a military dictatorship. The *Hudud*

Ordinance of 1979 and similar measures signify a partial return to a classical form of Islamic law. Sharia courts have been introduced since 1980, but there is no comprehensive Islamization of laws as yet. The traditional legal diversity is thus, in essence, being continued, with Islamic personal law clearly of very great importance.

Bangladesh

On Independence and by the operation of the *Bangladesh (Adaptation of Existing Bangladesh Laws) Order*, 1972, the country inherited virtually the legal system of Pakistan as it stood at that time. The *Constitution of the People's Republic of Bangladesh* came into force on December 16, 1972. A new body of case-law is building up, occasionally continuing conceptual confusions of the British period. There is some legislative activity, and there have been calls to develop Bangladesh as an Islamic state, but a full discussion about the future of the legal system has yet to start. Unification of laws may be a solution, but to safeguard the position of minorities will be a tricky task. Islamic personal law is clearly dominant, and custom continues to play an important role in the administration of justice.

Sri Lanka

The country has an extremely hybrid system of laws. There was a great variety of traditional laws, mainly customary: Sinhalese (Buddhist) law; Thesawalamai law, the largely matriarchal Tamil Hindu law; Muslim and Parsi law and some tribal laws. The Portuguese exercised little influence, but the Dutch introduced their own court system in 1659, applying Roman–Dutch law with frequent recourse to Roman–Dutch jurists. The British, in a series of Proclamations from 1799–1801, established a new system of judicial administration, continued the application of Roman–Dutch law, and showed respect for the indigenous laws on similar lines as in India. The Dutch had already codified the Thesawalamai (1707), a Muhammadan code was re-codified in 1806, and piecemeal attempts were made to codify Kandyan (Sinhalese) law. The gradual codification of the general law adopted much of the Indian legislation, for example, the *Indian Penal Code* (introduced 1883). It is significant that custom could override the statutory provisions.

The modern Sri Lankan legal system, within the framework of the 1978 Constitution, is mainly based on legislation that also covers the various personal laws. The ethnic conflict of the 1980s suggests that the legal system has not given sufficient protection to the concerns of minorities.

Nepal

Traditional customary legal systems based on Hindu and Buddhist concepts began to be codified from *c.* 1400 (Code of a Newar king). The most important codification of the 'laws of the country' is the *Muluki Ain* of 1854, published in many later, revised editions, the latest in 1966. The aim of such codifications seems to have been greater control over local and customary laws, so that Nepal appears as a fairly centralized state with the Prime Minister (until 1951), and since then the king, as supreme legislative and judicial authority. The 1967 Constitution makes Nepal a 'monarchical Hindu state'. Modern Nepal, following the first Constitution of 1959, has introduced equality before the law and ceased to recognize the traditional caste hierarchy, without formally abolishing the caste system. Hand in hand with this goes a greater recognition of customary laws, apparently to avoid potentially dangerous minority problems.

Bhutan

The legal system of this Buddhist kingdom is based on a set of codified laws of Buddhist origin, the earliest codification dating from 1652. The modern legal system sees the king as supreme law-making authority and final appellate instance. There is a growing body of legislation to regulate the administration of laws and the operation of the legal system, but respect for the traditional laws remains strong.

Maldives

The Constitution of 1965 establishes a republic with an Executive President. Muslim law is the dominant legal system.

WFM

Further reading

J. D. M. Derrett, *A Critique of Modern Hindu Law* (Bombay, 1970)
  Religion, Law and the State in India (London, 1968)
S. T. Desai, Ed., *Mulla's Principles of Hindu Law* (Bombay, 1982)
M. Hidayatullah, Ed., *Mulla's Principles of Mahomedan Law* (Bombay, 1982)
A. Hoque, *The Legal System of Bangladesh* (Dacca, 1980)
R. Lingat, *The Classical Law of India* (Berkeley and London, 1973)
T. Mahmood, *The Muslim Law of India* (Allahabad, 1982)
  Personal Laws in Crisis (New Delhi, 1986)
H. W. Tambiah, *Principles of Ceylon Law* (Colombo, 1972)

Education

Indigenous education

Most of the countries of South Asia have a tradition of education going back several thousand years. Education was closely tied to religion and was centered round temples, monasteries and mosques. Knowledge was regarded as sacred and passed down from the teacher to his pupils. Apart from religious texts, subjects like mathematics, astronomy, logic and law were taught. The medium in *tols*, Hindu schools of higher learning, was Sanskrit; in *madrasas*, the Muslim equivalent, Persian and Arabic. Teaching was oral and pupils committed to memory what they had learned. Classical education among Hindus was confined to Brahmins, although members of the lower Kshatriya and Vaishya castes were sometimes eligible. Buddhist education was open to all although especially welcomed by powerful rulers and rich merchants. Buddhist monks or *bhikkhus* lived in *viharas* (monasteries) which became centers of learning. The most famous of these were at Nalanda (Bihar), Vikramshila (Bihar) and Takshashila (North West Frontier Province, Pakistan).

At the primary level, Hindu *pathsalas* (schools) were often found in villages. In some regions, these were open to all castes and to girls. They consisted of a single teacher and about a dozen pupils assembled in a temple courtyard, a shed or under a tree. Muslim *maktabs* (schools) were usually attached to mosques, where, as at the pathsala, the curriculum consisted of reading, writing and simple arithmetic.

With the decline of the Mughal Empire in the eighteenth century, educational institutions and teachers started losing court patronage and often had to fall back on their own limited financial resources. The coming of British rule also contributed to the decline of indigenous systems of education, although religious revivalist movements among Buddhists and Muslims, in particular, did help to sustain continuing activity. Indigenous schools survived in Nepal, Bhutan and the Maldives where modern Western education did not penetrate.

Colonial impact

The British were initially pre-occupied with trade and conquest, and, hence, followed a policy of non-interference in education. Then, in the era of Warren Hastings, Governor-General from 1772 to 1786, and over the next four decades, encouragement was given to oriental scholarship for primarily administrative reasons. The Calcutta Madrasa was founded in 1781 and a Sanskrit College at Benares ten years later. The earliest efforts to introduce Western education both on the subcontinent and in Sri Lanka emanated from Christian missionaries.

Table 58. Educational parameters in South Asia

	Literacy rates (1980–1981) (% of total population)			Primary enrollment ratio			Estimated drop out rate before last grade as a percentage of those enrolled	Secondary enrollment ratio			Third level enrollment ratio		
	Total	Male	Female	Total	Male	Female		Total	Male	Female	Total	Male	Female
Bangladesh	20	34	6	62	72	52	80	15	24	6	2.9	4.9	0.8
Bhutan	10	—	—	23	30	16	80	13	5	1	0.3	0.4	0.1
India	36	47	25	79	93	64	59	30	39	20	8.7	12.5	4.7
Maldives	82	82	82	78.5	—	—	—	—	—	—	1.0	—	—
Nepal	19	33	5	91	126	53	—	21	33	9	3.1	4.8	1.2
Pakistan	24	30	10	44	57	31	—	14	20	8	2.0	2.8	1.1
Sri Lanka	85	91	81	103	106	100	9	51	49	54	2.8	3.2	2.4

Source: UNESCO *Statistical Year Book* 1984.

Table 59. Illiteracy in urban and rural areas (latest census or survey data available since 1970)

				Rate of illiteracy						
				Urban areas			Rural areas			Urban–rural
Country	Year	Age group	Total (%)	Total (%)	Male (%)	Female (%)	Total (%)	Male (%)	Female (%)	difference (%)
Bangladesh	1981	15+	60.9	45.5	78.5		83.5	70.9	96.9	22.6
Bhutan	n.a.	—	—	—	—		—	—	—	—
India	1971	15+	39.6	27.6	54.5		72.9	59.4	87.0	33.3
Maldives	1975	5+	12.0	—	—		34.0	—	—	22.0
Nepal	1981	15+	52.6	40.3	67.0		81.3	70.4	92.4	28.7
Pakistan	1981	15+	53.1	43.1	65.3		82.6	73.4	92.7	29.5
Sri Lanka	1981	15+	6.7	4.4	9.2		16.0	10.7	21.4	9.3

Source: *Education in Asia and Pacific* UNESCO, Bangkok, 1986.

In 1813, the East India Company Charter Act enabled the Government to set aside one lakh of rupees (Rs. 100,000) for education. There was no clear directive on how this money was to be spent, and so controversy ensued between the Orientalists, who favored classical Indian education, and the Anglicists, supported by Indians like Rammohan Roy, who advocated Western education. The issue was finally decided by Macaulay's famous Minute and Bentinck's Resolution of 1835. Henceforth, Government funds were to be spent for the promotion of European literature and science.

Colonial education had features common to most of the countries of the region. Mass education was neglected, except in Sri Lanka, since the aim was to create an urban educated élite which could act as interpreters between the rulers and the ruled. It was hoped that education would filter down to the masses, a hope which was frustrated by the hierarchical nature of Indian society and the monopolization of English education by higher castes. Colonial education policy helped to strengthen barriers between the élites and the masses. The English-educated intelligentsia provided the administrators, professionals, political leaders and social reformers who initiated the limited moves towards modernization. In the independent kingdoms of Nepal and Bhutan, education was also the preserve of the few.

Excessive emphasis on examinations dominated high school and university teaching, and encouraged cramming. There was an over-emphasis on the study of languages and the humanities in order to produce the clerks needed by the colonial government. While education expanded under colonial rule, the rate of growth was not even. The impact of English education was first felt by the three Presidencies; educational institutions were clustered around the port cities of Calcutta, Bombay and Madras. Everywhere, literacy and education were more widespread in towns than in villages, and more widespread among men than women and among higher castes, although lower castes involved in trade were frequently more literate than others with higher social rankings.

Structure of education since Independence

All the countries of South Asia have their education systems divided into the familiar primary, secondary and higher levels. Primary education lasts five or six years, the secondary stage again varies from five to six years and the tertiary level is three to four years for the first degree.

Primary education

The number of primary schools and enrollment have increased enormously since the 1950s. Universal primary education is the goal of all countries but only Sri Lanka has been successful. This general failure has been partly due to a more rapid expansion of population than foreseen. There are two main areas of concern in the spread of primary education: the disparity between urban and rural areas, and female education. India has still to bring more than fifty million children into schools of whom two-thirds are girls. In Bangladesh and Nepal, half the girls remain outside the primary system, while in Pakistan two out of three girls of primary school age do not attend. Bhutan has the lowest female primary school enrollment in the world.

Table 60. Primary level schools and enrollment

Country	Institutions	Students enrolled
Bangladesh		
1983	43,472	11,653,106
Bhutan		
1966	83	9,463
1984	141	31,837
India		
1953–1954	40,394	3,889,975
1983	503,741	77,038,922
Maldives		
1977	n.a.	23,544
1982	80[a]	34,090[b]
Nepal		
1954	921	26,186
1983	11,325	1,126,437
Pakistan		
1953/54	40,395	3,889,975
1983	72,053	6,412,000
Sri Lanka		
1953	6,538	1,565,355
1984	9,240	2,156,522

[a]Approximate figure.
[b]The bulk of the enrollment is in maktab schools.
Source: *UNESCO World Survey of Education*, 1961; *UNESCO Statistical Year Book*, 1986; *Educational Statistics of Bangladesh*, Bangladesh Bureau of Educational Information and Statistics (Dhaka, 1984); *Recent Education Development in Nepal*, Ministry of Education and Culture, Nepal, 1984; H. G. Wood *Educational Statistics for Nepal* (Oregon, 1962); *Bulletin of the UNESCO Regional Office for Education in Asia and Pacific*, No. 25, p. 171 (June 1984).

Official statistics often exaggerate enrollment and figures do not always represent actual school attendances. A serious factor which undermines the achievement of universal primary education is the large proportion of children who drop out before completion. The drop-out rate is higher in rural areas than in urban centers, and among girls, on account of the low priority given to education by parents, the employment of children at home and outside, the irrelevance of the school curriculum, and general poverty. Another form of wastage at primary level is grade repetition due to failure in examinations or low attendance. The repetition rate averages around 10 to 12 percent; in Bangladesh in 1983 the rate was as high as 20 percent.

While policies have been formulated for quantitative expansion, qualitative improvement has not received enough attention. Most primary schools, particularly those in rural areas, lack proper buildings, classrooms and basic equipment such as furniture and blackboards. Teachers are often inadequately trained, and absenteeism is another common problem.

Attempts to introduce free compulsory education in India took place as early as 1910–11 when the nationalist leader, G. K. Gokhale, unsuccessfully introduced a Bill in the Imperial Legislature. After 1921, when education became a 'transferred' subject under 'dyarchy', provincial governments introduced legislation aimed at making primary education free and compulsory. Primary education is today free for children aged six to eleven in all the states. It is compulsory everywhere except Nagaland and Himachal Pradesh. Most schools are co-educational.

Universalization of primary education has been an official objec-

A Quran school at Aligarh, Uttar Pradesh.

tive in Pakistan since the country was founded, but less than half the children of school age actually receive it. Latest estimates indicate that there are 11.5 million children in the primary school age, out of whom hardly 6 million attend school. The enrollment rates vary enormously over regions, from 59 percent in Sind to 30 percent in the Federal territories. The physical infrastructure is deficient leading to the twin phenomena of 'ghost' schools and teacher absenteeism. The Sixth Plan (1983–88) envisages a massive expenditure of Rs.7 billion on primary education. Some of the strategies to be adopted for achieving universalization of primary education are the revival of mosque schools and madrasas, the establishment of mohalla schools, the levying of an 'iqra' or elementary education cess of 5 percent on all imports and the commencement of pilot projects integrating education with rural development.

In Bangladesh, primary education is free but not compulsory in government schools where the medium of instruction is Bengali and the curriculum is uniform. In addition to government schools, which form 80 percent of the total, there are government-recognized primary schools and *ibtidai* or traditional Islamic primary schools.

Sri Lanka has the most developed network of primary schools in the region. Education is compulsory and free. A few private schools are permitted to function, while the state assists *pirivenas* or indigenous Buddhist institutions of long standing. Only 320 schools are single-sex and these are in the cities. The medium of instruction is Sinhala, Tamil or English.

Accurate statistics on the number of schools and enrollment of past years in Nepal are not available. Nevertheless, since the beginning of the National Education System Plan in 1971 there has been a tremendous increase in the number of pupils and schools. The number of children in primary schools increased by 41 percent during 1975–85. The largest increase was 54 percent in the Terai region. Schools are either supported by the state or are unaided private institutions. The main problems are how to make primary schools available to inaccessible and remote areas, to certain ethnic groups and to girls, and how to improve physical facilities and the quality of teaching. The provision of free tuition and textbooks in government schools should stimulate education.

A small Department of Education was set up in Bhutan in 1961, and primary schools entirely maintained and controlled by the government were opened across the country. Tuition, board and lodging, textbooks and uniforms are provided free of charge to encourage attendance. A few schools in South Bhutan are run by local communities who provide voluntary labor for public works. The medium of instruction is Dzongkha; Hindi and English are also taught.

In the Maldives, primary education is provided by *Edhurge* or *Kiyavage*, *maktabs* and *madrasas*. The last two are well organized with a wider curriculum than the former where the standard of instruction is low. Up to 1960, instruction in schools was only in Divehi; since then, English has been introduced in government schools in Malé.

Secondary education

The expansion of secondary education has been a common feature in the countries of South Asia (Table 61). One of the prime weaknesses of secondary education in the region is that it has traditionally been looked upon primarily as a preparation for higher education. Despite repeated attempts to diversify and vocationalize education at the secondary level, the bulk of the students still opt for general education.

In India the origins of the system can be traced back to the beginning of the nineteenth century. About 50 percent of secondary schools are privately managed. Lax conditions exist for starting schools with the result that the number of private schools run as

Table 61. Secondary level schools and enrollment

Country	Institutions	Students enrolled
Bangladesh		
1978	8,068	2,387,171
1982–1983	8,809	2,604,293
Bhutan		
1975	n.a.	817
1984	n.a.	5,872
India		
1953–1954	27,558	6,544,209
1983–1985[a]	188,713	39,873,184
Maldives		
1975	n.a.	459
1983	n.a.	2,756
Nepal		
1961	n.a.	41,444
1982: Lower secondary:	2,964	199,678
Secondary:	1,031	170,404
Pakistan		
1953–1954	5,421	1,113,809
1980–1981	8,989	1,440,000
Sri Lanka		
1953–1954[b]	6,538	1,565,355
1984	n.a.	1,382,574

[a]The figures include Higher Secondary, Higher Secondary old pattern, High Schools/Post Basic and Middle Senior Basic Schools.
[b]The figures for 1953–1954 include primary and secondary schools. 1984 data refers to public education only.
Source: *UNESCO World Survey of Education*, 1961; *UNESCO Statistical Year Book*, 1986; *Resume Statistique de l'Unesco*, 1986; *Selected Educational Statistics, 1984–85* (New Delhi, 1986); *Bulletin of UNESCO Regional Office in Asia*, Vol. 1, p. 59, Sept. 1966, and No. 25, p. 187, 1984; *Pakistan, Education*, Government of Pakistan (Islamabad, 1981).

commercial enterprises has grown strikingly. A dual system has emerged consisting of, on the one hand, a small core of good institutions with high fees catering for the élite and, on the other hand, of inferior, ill-equipped schools which employ untrained teachers often without regular salaries. At the plus 2 level, that is classes XI and XII, students can opt for the arts, science or commerce streams. The Basic Education system conceived by Mahatma Gandhi, which was craft-centered and tried to relate education to the child's daily life and work experience, was introduced by the Congress governments in some provinces between 1937 and 1939 and after Independence, but was not successful. The secondary schools continue to be dominated by examinations and act as feeders to colleges.

In Pakistan, as in India, and also Bangladesh and Nepal, the secondary schools are dominated by examinations, and there is a high percentage of failures and consequent wastage. The Sixth Plan proposed to equip secondary schools for vocational education, to redesign the curriculum to provide a wide variety of options, and enable students to select subjects suited to their aptitude. It also aimed to strengthen science and mathematics education, to expand secondary education in the rural areas and to consolidate the agro-technical programs. Emphasis is being placed on the learning of productive skills and agro-technical subjects are compulsory from class VI to X; about 20 percent of total teaching time is devoted to these subjects. At the VI to VIII class level the following subjects have been included: industrial arts, agriculture and home economics (for girls). At the IX and X class level industrial arts, agriculture, home economics (for girls), commerce and a general group of vocational subjects have been introduced.

In Bangladesh secondary education consists of three phases – junior secondary, secondary and higher secondary. There are two public examinations at the end of grades 10 and 12 leading to SSC and HSC, and these are conducted by four autonomous boards. There is a high rate of failure. In 1985 only 45.4 percent passed the SSC and 37.9 percent the HSC examinations, the majority in the second or third division. Failure in English was the most important contributory factor to the high rate of failure. Over 90 percent of the schools are privately managed. Emphasis is being placed on science teaching and scientific equipment is being provided to a large number of secondary schools and madrasas.

Besides the general system, institutions such as *dakhils* in Bangladesh and mosque schools and madrasas in Pakistan, which impart religious instruction to Muslim students, are growing in number in response to recent religious developments. Although figures for Pakistan are not available, Bangladesh shows an increase from 2390 madrasas with 441,400 pupils in 1978 to 2805 such schools with 529,472 pupils in 1983. The numbers of teachers in madrasas rose over the period from 23,839 to 28,743.

In Sri Lanka there existed a fairly developed system of elementary and secondary schools by the end of the nineteenth century. The secondary schools, which were run mostly by missionaries, included post-matriculation courses leading to a university degree. In spite of several attempts at reform, the educational system still shows considerable British influence. The use of Sinhala and Tamil as the media of instruction from 1945 and the introduction of free education in the same year led to a massive expansion of the formal education system under state control. A Curriculum Development Center operates at the national level and is responsible for the development of curricula for all levels of the school system. After completing Junior Secondary School (classes VI to X) students can proceed to Senior Secondary School (classes XI to XII) or to vocational and technical courses.

Secondary education in Nepal is of relatively recent origin. Although the early religious schools provided training through the adolescent years, it was on an ungraded basis, a continuous program without distinctions between primary, secondary and higher education. The first secondary school, as such, was established by Jang Bahadur soon after his visit to Europe in the 1850s, and was modeled on English medium secondary schools in India. Secondary education was restricted by the Ranas to their own children and to the Kathmandu Valley, so that by 1951 there were only seven English secondary schools. The English medium secondary schools were patterned after British education. Indian history was added to the curriculum, but Nepalese history was not included until the late 1950s because of the lack of a textbook. Before 1947 the emphasis was on English. Today the local languages receive more attention; as much as 40 percent of the curriculum time may be devoted to language study, and most pupils study Nepali, Hindi, English, and Sanskrit or Persian. Before the mid-1950s very little attention was given to science. Teaching methods are confined largely to lecturing and rote recitation, often by whole classes. By 1951 there were two Sanskrit schools, by 1961, ten. It is also proposed to develop comprehensive or multipurpose schools. The curriculum is controlled by the SLC (School Leaving Certificate) Board which is appointed by the Ministry of Education and conducts the SLC examination. Nearly two-thirds of those who appear fail.

Secondary education is offered in Bhutan in junior high schools and central schools. Enrollment is restricted and is guided by projected manpower requirements in order to avoid creating a pool of educated unemployed. At the end of the Vth, VIIIth and Xth years of schooling, students take examinations that determine eligibility for subsequent level of education, although this does not necessarily confer entrance. Overall, the education system is closely affiliated to India and the coverage of the Indian secondary school examination has effectively determined the curriculum, choice of textbooks, and so on. The government plans to establish its own

National Board of Secondary Education and Training, and to develop both a secondary school curriculum and an examination system of its own. All schools are government managed.

In the Maldives the modern school system was introduced in 1960. English medium secondary schools exist only in Malé and serve a small élite group. They are geared to the University of London GCE 'O' and 'A' level examinations. There are no trained teachers within the country and so it relies heavily on expatriate teachers who have to be paid high salaries.

Higher education

Higher education has expanded very rapidly throughout South Asia since the 1950s. This expansion had generally been unrelated to manpower needs and its enormous growth has been made possible at the expense of the primary, secondary and technical sectors. Despite the high cost of university and college education, overall performance in terms of quality and output is extremely poor. Drop out and failure rates are very high. In India, about 50 percent of students who enroll fail to sit for their degrees. In some universities in the region, the percentage is as high as 75–80 percent. Of those who do complete their courses, most obtain a third-class degree.

A disproportionate number of students at the tertiary level receive education in the humanities, social sciences and law. In India in 1983–84, 51 percent of male students were enrolled in the arts and sciences, while nearly 75 percent of women opted for these courses. Only 0.68 percent of women were enrolled for engineering and technology, 3.52 percent in medicine and 0.37 percent in agriculture.

Universities have been established by acts of legislatures. They are financed largely by governments; there are no private institutions. Fees do not account for more than 10 percent of the expenditure and private benefactions are small. University Grants Commissions co-ordinate university education and distribute grants. The management of universities follows the British pattern. In Bangladesh, the country's President is Chancellor of all its universities. In Indian universities, this position is held by the Vice-President, Prime Minister or State Governor. The Vice-Chancellor is chief executive and is nominated by the Chancellor. In Sri Lanka, there is a provision that future Vice-Chancellors will be elected by the Senate. Universities have Senates or Courts, Syndicates, Academic Councils, Faculties and Departments.

There are broadly two types of university: the affiliating and teaching type which affiliates colleges, prescribes courses, conducts examinations and also carries out postgraduate teaching and research; and universities which have no affiliated colleges and where all undergraduate teaching is done by the university. The majority of colleges are privately managed. In India, only 15–20 percent of the colleges are government-controlled. In addition,

Table 62. Third level student enrollment

Bangladesh	
1947	1,300
1981	14,500
Bhutan	
1982	244[a]
India	
1953–1954	547,601
1984	852,104
Maldives	
1980	100[b]
Nepal	
1961	311
1983	48,229
Pakistan	
1953–1954	69,565
1980	156,558
Sri Lanka	
1953	4,704
1983	34,725

[a]All students abroad: 200 in India and 44 in other countries.
[b]The figure represents 50 pre-university and 50 university students; all graduate and post-graduate students are in foreign universities.
Source: *UNESCO Word Survey of Education*, 1961; *UNESCO Statistical Year Book*, 1986; *Bulletin of Unesco Regional Office of Education in Asia*, Vol. 1, p. 60, Sept. 1966.

there are professional, medical, engineering and agricultural colleges. Nearly half of these in India are government-managed while in other countries the proportion is even higher. On the whole, regional or local languages are used as the medium of instruction at the under-graduate level and English at the post-graduate level.

India has the oldest and most developed system of higher education in South Asia, and the third largest in the world behind the USA and the USSR. The first college created along modern lines was the Hindu College (later Presidency College), established in Calcutta in 1817. The Universities of Calcutta, Bombay and Madras, founded in 1857, were affiliating and examining bodies modeled on London University. At present there are 130 universities, of which six are managed and financed by the Government of India. There is also a large number of teaching and research institutions outside the university system such as the Indian Institutes of Management, the Indian Institutes of Technology, All India Institutes of Medicine, Indian Institute of Science, the Tata Institute of Fundamental Research and forty research laboratories under the Council of Scientific and Industrial Research.

Pakistan possesses 21 universities to which about 400 arts and science colleges are affiliated. There are also some 100 professional colleges, 4 universities of Engineering and Technology, 3 Agricultural universities, a University of Health Science, an Islamic University and an Open University.

St Stephen's College, Delhi, one of India's élite university institutions.

The University of Dhaka, the oldest university in Bangladesh, started as a teaching institution in 1921. After 1947, it acquired affiliated colleges. Other universities are those at Rajshahi and Chittagong, Jahangirnagar University and the Bangladesh University of Engineering and Technology, both at Dhaka, and the Bangladesh Agricultural University at Mymensingh.

Founded in 1972, the University of Sri Lanka incorporated the University of Ceylon (established 1921), University of Colombo, Vidyalankara University, Vidyodaya University, Ceylon College of Technology, Katubeddi. The five campuses have different specializations.

The Tri-Chandra College in Nepal, started in 1918, was first affiliated to Calcutta and later to Patna University. Tribhuvan University was established in 1960 and remains Nepal's only university. It has 49 affiliated colleges, five of which are Sanskrit colleges. Higher education has hardly developed in Bhutan which has so far only one college affiliated to the University of Delhi. Bhutanese who want higher education have to go abroad. Less than one percent of Maldivians have access to higher education and this is through overseas facilities as the Maldives have no colleges or universities.

Literacy

After gaining independence from colonial rule, educational reform became an uppermost policy goal of South Asian countries. One of the most acute problems was illiteracy. In 1951, literacy was 29 percent for males and 8 percent for females in India, while in Pakistan the equivalent figures were 21 percent and 6 percent. Only Sri Lanka and the Maldives have achieved literacy rates of at least 80 percent; other countries have literacy rates ranging from 10 to 40

percent. Rural literacy rates are everywhere, except Sri Lanka, at least 20 percentage points lower than those for urban areas, and women are more illiterate than men.

Considerable differences in literacy levels exist within countries. In India, for instance, Kerala has the highest number of literates, 70 percent, and Arunachal Pradesh the lowest at 29 percent. Even within Indian states there are significant variations, such as between coastal and northern Andhra Pradesh, or coastal and southern Orissa. These variations tend to reflect socio-economic conditions. In Pakistan, literacy is lowest in Baluchistan (10 percent), then NWFP (16 percent), Panjab (27 percent) and Sind (31 percent). In Nepal, literacy is highest in the Eastern Terai (29 percent). Rates in Bangladesh range from 19 percent in Rajshahi to 25 percent in Chittagong. In Sri Lanka, Gampha district has the highest literacy rate of 94 percent, Colombo comes a close second with 93.8 percent and Jaffna third with 92.9 percent.

Growth of population and literacy in India, 1901–81.

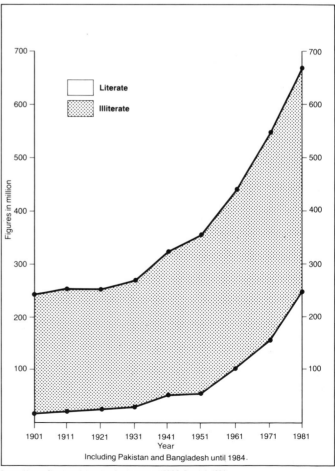

Including Pakistan and Bangladesh until 1984.

Source: Literacy Situation in Asia and the Pacific. India, UNESCO, Bangkok, 1984.

Problems and prospects

The main difficulties facing the countries of South Asia are: the eradication of illiteracy; increasing primary school enrollment and retaining pupils; spreading education among adults; and making secondary education more vocational. Schemes such as the reservation of seats for disadvantaged groups have been initiated in India to reduce these disparities. The investment patterns in education differ from country to country. The percentage of gross national product spent on education is highest in India at 3 percent as is the figure of 9.8 percent of the total budget spent on this sector. Per capita expenditure, however, is highest in Sri Lanka at 7 percent. The intersectional allocation of resources has favored higher education in most countries. India, for instance spent Rs. 55 per primary pupil in 1975–76 compared with Rs. 3664.5 per university student. Sri Lanka, in contrast, spent over 85 percent of its educational budget on primary and secondary education in 1981. Meanwhile, the main problems in higher education are how to cope with escalating numbers of students and balancing quantity with quality. The large number of unemployed university graduates is a cause for concern. Polytechnics and vocational colleges are being started to divert students from courses which have little market value. The 'politicization' of higher education has resulted in campus unrest which has led to frequent closure of universities and disruption of normal academic life.

Since the formal education system is unable to cope with demands, non-formal educational experiments such as Open Universities and correspondence courses are being tried with the aid of radio and television. Education needs to be made more relevant to national development and so curriculum revision and textbook re-writing have been undertaken. But, education problems cannot be solved in isolation. Illiteracy is invariably associated with deprivation and underdevelopment. Vocational education cannot attract students unless jobs are available. Thus, educational progress is closely linked with overall economic growth and social change.

AB

Further reading

Development of Education in Asia and the Pacific (ED-85/ MINEDAP/3)
J. E. Jayasuriya, *Education in Ceylon Before and After Independence, 1939–1968* (Colombo, 1969)
F. E. Keay, *Indian Education in Ancient and Later Times* (London, 1956)
S. Narulla and J. P. Naik, *A History of Education in India* (London, 1951)
Selections from the Educational Records, Pt. I, Ed. H. Sharp, 1781–1839; Pt. II, Ed. J. Richey, 1840–1859 (Calcutta, 1920–22)
UNESCO, *Literacy situation in Asia and Pacific* (Bangkok, 1984)
UNESCO, *Towards Universalization of Primary Education in Asia and Pacific* (Bangkok, 1984)

Health

Systems of medicine

The predominant medical tradition associated with Hindu culture is *Ayurveda*, which may be translated for practical purposes as 'the science of long life'. Its origins are found in the *Rigveda*, where an important curative role is ascribed to physicians who eventually became known as *vaidyas*. Ayurveda emphasizes keeping the basic physiological elements or humors in balance for purposes of avoiding illness. In Ayurveda these elements or humors (*doshas*) are bile (*pitta*), wind (*vata*), and phlegm (*kapha*). In theory, when the three *doshas* are in harmony, a person will enjoy good health. Harmony is achieved by living an unselfish life of moderation with close attention to diet.

Ayurvedic diagnosis and treatment emphasize a holistic approach to the patient. Physical examination and interview are intended to result in a careful identification of both psychological and physical symptoms. Treatment involves giving advice concerning lifestyle, as well as prescription of herbal and synthetic medicines. When

Table 63. Public expenditure on education

Country	Total (USA $)	% of GNP	% of total govt. expenditure	*Per capita* in %	1st level	2nd level	3rd level
Bangladesh (1981)	3,348,107	1.7	8.6	1.0	44.2	29.4	23.4
Bhutan (1978)	26,796	—	—	2.1	22.5	55.9	9.2
India (1981)	44,102,100	3.0	9.6	4.0	36.9	24.2	13.5
Maldives (1978)	1,279	0.6	—	—	—	—	—
Nepal (1982)	839,902	2.5	—	2.0	——48.6——		44.2
Pakistan (1981)	5,601,957	1.9	5.1	4.0	38.9	32.6	19.7
Sri Lanka (1981)	2,485,499	3.0	8.7	7.0	——86.1——		8.7

Source. UNESCO *Book of Educational Statistics.*

387

medicine fails or is deemed inappropriate by the *vaidya*, surgery may be ordered. Long before contact with Arab and Western systems of medicine, Ayurvedic surgeons developed great skill in repairing external wounds.

A second main tradition of Hindu medicine is *Siddha*, which evolved in South India. Siddha is a term implying spiritual accomplishment or perfection. Early in their evolution, Siddha schools were influenced by Ayurveda. Siddha physiology includes the Ayurvedic belief that the basic essences of living things are bile (in Siddha, *pittan*), wind (*vayu*), and phlegm (*kapam*). Siddha, like Ayurveda, holds that mind and body are synergistic in sickness and health. Mind, body, and their social and natural habitats are all the physician's concern. Siddha diagnostic techniques emphasize careful reading of the pulse. Siddha distinguishes between six pulses, three of which are read on the patient's right hand, and three on the left. Each pulse manifests the state of one of the three humors in either its left or right aspect. By diagnosing imbalances in the pulses and their respective humors, the Siddha physician is able to select appropriate remedies and advice.

Unani (literally 'Ionian', or Greek) medicine developed in the Middle East out of Arab contacts with Greco–Roman civilization, and entered South Asia with the successive waves of Muslim invaders discussed elsewhere in this volume. Unani scholarship, physicians and practice were much fostered by the Mughal Emperors, particularly Akbar (r. 1556–1605). Like Ayurveda and Siddha, Unani medicine emphasizes holistic diagnosis and treatment. According to Unani, the body is comprised of seven constituents. These components are *arkan* (the elements out of which all material beings are made), *mizaj* (bodily temperament), *akhlat* (four 'humors' defined as blood, phlegm, yellow bile and black bile), *ada* (anatomy), *ruh* (life force), *quwa* (energy) and *afal* (physiology). As in Ayurveda and Siddha, *Unani* medicine attributes disease to an imbalance of underlying constituents.

Diagnosis also follows lines which are reminiscent of Ayurveda. The Unani physician ascertains mental states through careful examination. In modern Unani, much use is made of case reports to help define and reinforce diagnosis. Unani medical schools have incorporated in their curricula many aspects of Western medical sciences, including surgical techniques, laboratory medicine, and synthetic drugs.

Ayurveda and Unani are widely distributed in South Asia. Unani is the predominant traditional system in Pakistan and is widely practiced in North India and Bangladesh. Ayurveda predominates as a formal traditional system in Bhutan, India (particularly in the north), Nepal, and Sri Lanka. Siddha is the pre-eminent traditional system in South India. A few Ayurveda practitioners are found in the Maldives.

Along with Ayurveda, Siddha and Unani, modern biomedicine plays an important role throughout South Asia. The spread of biomedicine was initially due to the health care needs of East India Company employees and, later, officials of the various British administrations in the Indian subcontinent and Sri Lanka. Medical officers were recruited in the UK to serve army regiments and civil stations. Gradually these medical officers expanded their practice to include patients outside official circles. In the middle of the nineteenth century, the British began establishing medical colleges to train South Asian doctors who could supplement the practice of British physicians. Hospitals and dispensaries (clinics) were also built at district headquarters and in other towns. The expansion of local clinical facilities was, however, painfully slow because the British relied on the limited revenues of municipalities and district boards for the necessary funds. Public health organization was also introduced under British rule, but little was done to set up meaningful local preventive services until health departments were placed under elected ministers after World War I. Even then, progress was slow because of chronic revenue problems exacerbated by the world recession of the 1930s.

Development of modern health services continues to be a paramount goal of South Asian governments. Their main objective has been to provide village-level health care including clinical, preventive and family-planning services utilizing both Western and traditional medicine. Because of sluggish economic development and rapid population growth, the ratio of people to trained health workers has remained high.

With a variety of scarce curative and public preventive resources available, where do people in South Asia turn for help in case of illness? Various surveys of patterns of care suggest certain characteristics. When real income and physical proximity permit, South Asians readily consult practitioners of biomedicine, whether these be physicians, paramedics or pharmacists, especially if patients believe their symptoms are curable by chemotherapy or surgery. This is apparently true not merely of persons who are Western-educated, but also of villagers whose exposure to Western culture is minimal. Some elements of biomedical treatment are also available from Ayurvedic, Siddha and Unani practitioners, many of whom use synthetic drugs marketed in South Asia by multinational companies. Often practitioners of indigenous medicine prescribe these drugs as panaceas regardless of their toxic side-effects. For example, Chloramphenicol, which can produce bone marrow depression, is widely used in South Asia for trivial infections.

For less specific symptoms and those of chronic nature such as rheumatic complaints, people in South Asia often prefer traditional systems of medicine. In addition to practitioners of Ayurveda, Siddha and Unani, people also consult a wide variety of shamans who specialize in identifying illness with specific divine beings and spirits and placating them by means of rituals which are intensely meaningful and often satisfying to a distressed client. The strength of traditional systems of medicine lies in their considering a broken heart as much within their purview as some physical malady.

The availability of the various systems of medicine in South Asia is very uneven. Because registration of practitioners is haphazard, accurate estimates of their numbers and distribution are not available. Generally, biomedical practitioners and their well-qualified traditional counterparts are found mainly in urban areas to the detriment of rural health. Most government medical officers also have their headquarters in towns and their tours in rural areas are often cursory.

Public health

South Asian public health has been dominated by infectious diseases, principally cholera and other enteric diseases, malaria, filariasis, tuberculosis, smallpox and plague. Of these, smallpox is now effectively eradicated, the last South Asian case having been reported in Bangladesh in 1975. Plague cases are rare. A newly-recognized public health problem is posed by cancers related to common exogenous exposures.

Without proper treatment, cholera can be a devastating disease. Severely infected cholera patients present with profuse diarrhoea, vomiting, agonizing muscular cramps, suppression of urine and general collapse. Death may ensue in a matter of hours. Enervating sub-clinical infection is common in parts of India and Bangladesh. Persons with sub-clinical infections can be carriers for several years. Infection with the cholera bacillus is commonly transmitted by faecal contamination of water and food. The principle endemic foci of cholera are the delta areas of West Bengal and Bangladesh. Foci are also found in the deltas of the Godavari, Kistna and Kaveri Rivers on the east coast of India.

In the nineteenth century, cholera epidemics repeatedly swept out of the Gangetic delta along routes traveled by pilgrims and spread through South Asia and beyond. A potent source of infection in the Middle East was the Haj pilgrimage undertaken by Muslims from India. In the endemic cholera areas of India and Bangladesh, surveillance has limited outbreaks for the most part to sporadic peaks in incidence.

Environmental sanitation is the key to cholera control. Currently, vaccines protect only about 50 percent of persons who receive them, and the duration of protection (3–6 months) is relatively short. In recent years, new approaches to treating cholera and controlling its spread have been successfully field tested by the International Centre for Diarrhoeal Disease Research in Bangladesh. These new approaches involve inexpensive oral rehydration and sometimes adjuvant antibiotics. This therapy can be administered on an outpatient basis. In the absence of effective environmental sanitation, treating cholera patients with oral rehydration and anti-biotics may be a more cost-effective approach to controlling the spread of cholera than mass immunizations.

Other common enteric infections include chronic diarrhoea of various causes and intestinal parasites. In non-cholera diarrhoeas, Shigella and non-cholera vibrios are the most commonly-found pathogens, but, in many cases, the precise aetiology cannot be identified. Of the parasitic infections, hookworm (ancylostomiasis) is the most prevalent, particularly in Bangladesh, Assam, West Bengal, Malabar, Travancore and South Kanara. Sri Lanka is also widely infected. Hookworm is severely debilitating because the larvae, which often penetrate the skin of the feet, migrate to the small intestine, hatch, and ingest blood. Severe chronic anemia may result. Enteric infections produced by ascariasis and entamoeba histolytica are also common.

While cholera outbreaks have been localized for the most part, malaria remains a grave public health problem in much of South Asia. The following numbers of reported malaria cases are cited by the World Health Organization for the latest reporting year (1984): Bangladesh (31,787), Bhutan (18,356), India (2,023,462), Nepal (28,208), Pakistan (73,996), Sri Lanka (149,470). Because of under-reporting, these numbers grossly underestimate malaria prevalence. Realistic incidence rates cannot be calculated.

Malaria plasmodia are inoculated into humans by the bite of the female Anopheles mosquito. Acute malaria can kill a person within one or two weeks of a primary attack. Chronic symptoms include enlargement of the spleen, hepatic fibrosis, recurrent fever, and anemia. Chronic malaria is very debilitating and a severe impediment to millions of persons in South Asia who try to eke out a livelihood in labor-intensive occupations.

Malaria eradication efforts have focused on environmental control and insecticidal spraying. Since the Anopheles mosquito lays eggs in or near relatively still bodies of water, environmental measures have focused on draining such bodies of water, and spraying them with oil or DDT. Since its introduction in 1944 as an insecticide, DDT has become a main line of attack in malaria eradication campaigns. Its principal advantage is its residual effect, especially when sprayed on the surfaces of houses where mosquitos settle during their nocturnal feeding. Malathion, another insecticide, is also widely used. Malaria eradication is now confronted with the problem of DDT and malathion-resistant mosquitos.

Like malaria, filariasis is transmitted by mosquito vectors. Filariasis is prevalent in coastal South Asia from Pakistan, through India, Sri Lanka to Bangladesh. Infection is caused by filariae, small nematode worms, the larvae of which are inoculated by mosquito bite. Infective larvae cause an antibody-mediated response in regional lymph glands. As a result, infected areas such as the breasts, scrotum, and groin, may become grossly enlarged. Elephantiasis of these areas and the legs can develop in chronic

A mobile dispensary in operation.

cases. Adult worms may cause abscesses. Other symptoms include fever, headaches, anorexia, and vomiting. Chemotherapy is effective but unavailable to many people.

Tuberculosis is widely-distributed in South Asia, as it is in many developing nations. Prevalence surveys in various areas of the subcontinent have revealed proportions of positive skin tests as high as 80 percent. Historically, tuberculosis has been associated with poverty, and overcrowding. Infection results in necrosis of the lungs, fever, weakness and general wasting. Modern drugs, for example, isoniazid and rifampicin, when properly administered, can result in complete cure. BCG (*bacille de Calmette et Guerin*)

vaccine derived from mycobacterium tuberculosis provides partial immunity, and is widely used.

The importance of interactions between infection and nutrition in South Asia must be stressed. Bacterial infections such as tuberculosis often result in nitrogen imbalances and decreases in serum protein levels. In the South Asian nations, tuberculosis is often associated with the onset of protein malnutrition diseases, especially kwashiorkor. Viral infections such as measles, influenza and chickenpox also seem to precipitate nitrogen depletion and protein imbalance. Moreover, histologic studies of the intestinal mucosa of people from northeast India and Bangladesh have revealed that parasitic infections of the intestines cause deformities which impede the absorption of nutrition. In general, 'intestinal hurry' related to diarrhoea limits absorption.

The obverse of the causal relationship between infection and nutrition also holds. Protein and vitamin-deficient people are at increased risk of tuberculosis, measles, influenza and upper respiratory infections, and their resulting symptoms tend to be more severe than those of patients whose diets have been adequate. Protein malnutrition manifested in kwashiokor is associated with multiple infections, among which fatal bronchopneumonia is common. Deficiencies in vitamins A and C lead to increased susceptibility to most infections as do deficits of B-complex vitamins. An exception to the interaction of B-complex vitamins and risk of infection may be thiamine deficit, which has been shown in some studies to be antagonistic to viral, but not bacterial infections.

A final public health problem which is drawing increasing attention in South Asia and other third world countries is cancer caused by preventable exposures. The reported incidence in some urban areas of lung, oral, esophageal and laryngeal cancers is high.

Table 64. Approximate health-related indicators for South Asia with national income group comparisons

Country	Population per physician 1965	1981	Daily calorie supply *per capita* Total 1965	Total 1985	Crude death rate per 1,000 population 1965	1985	Infant mortality rate per 1,000 live births 1965	1985
Bangladesh	8,400	9,700	1,964	1,899	47	40	153	123
Bhutan	n.a.	18,200	2,904	2,571	43	43	184	133
India	4,880	3,700	2,100	2,189	45	33	151	89
Maldives	n.a.	n.a.	n.a.	n.a.	n.a.	n.a.	n.a.	n.a.
Nepal	46,200	28,770	1,931	2,034	46	43	184	133
Pakistan	3,160	2,910	1,747	2,159	48	44	149	115
Sri Lanka	5,800	7,460	2,155	2,385	33	25	63	36
Low income nations	8,390	5,770	2,046	2,339	43	29	127	72
Middle income nations	11,240	5,080	2,357	2,731	40	32	104	68
Industrialized nations	860	530	3,114	3,417	20	13	23	9

Source: The World Bank, *World Development Report* 1987.

Smoking can elevate a person's risk of getting lung cancer to a level up to about 25 times higher than that of a non-smoker. For other smoking-related cancers the approximate relative risks for heavy smokers versus non-smokers are: laryngeal cancer 10, oral cancer 6 and esophageal cancer 5. Although smoking among women in South Asia is relatively uncommon, it is widely prevalent among males. In Europe and North America, the prevalence of male smoking is around 30 percent, while it is over 70 percent in parts of Bangladesh, over 80 percent in some Nepalese regions, and around 45 percent in Sri Lanka. Domestic consumption of tobacco crops in India and Pakistan also suggests wide smoking prevalence. The chewing of betel quid mixed with tobacco and lime is also common and has been shown to exacerbate the risk of oral and laryngeal cancer due to smoking. Recently, the World Health Organization has given high priority to the reduction of smoking and the chewing of tobacco in developing nations.

While smoking-related cancers are primarily a male health problem in South Asia, relatively high cervical cancer incidence among women is causing concern. Cervical cancer is a sexually-transmitted disease associated with poverty, particularly in urban areas. Recent information from Indian cancer registries indicates that the average annual recorded cervical cancer incidence in Bombay is 19 per 100,000 population, while in Bangalore it is 22 and Madras, 32. Because of underregistration these figures underestimate the cervical cancer problem. By comparison, the average of the annual incidence figures for cervical neoplasms reported by the 11 regional cancer registries in the UK is about 12 per 100,000.

Although acute and chronic morbidity remain common in the South Asian nations, the secular declines in most of their death rates show that overall health conditions have improved considerably. The causes of declining South Asian mortality have been debated, but it now seems clear that sustained improvements in public health depend on rising standards of living, including consistently adequate nutrition. Immunization, environmental control and various treatments may be medically proven, but people's compliance with preventive measures and access to therapy depend upon whether they have the material means and education to make rational choices.

SR

Further reading

R. H. O. Bannerman, J. Burton and C. Wen-Chieh, Eds, *Traditional Medicine and Health Coverage: A Reader for Health Administrators and Practitioners* (Geneva, 1983)
India, Health Survey and Development Committee, *Report* 4 Vols (Delhi, 1946)
C. Leslie, Ed., *Asian Medical Systems: A Comparative Study* (Berkeley, Cal., 1976)
P. E. C. Manson-Bahr, F. I. C. Apted, *Manson's Tropical Diseases* 18th edn (London, 1982)
United Nations, Department of International Economics and Social Affairs, *Determinants of Mortality Change and Differentials in Developing Countries: The Five-Country Case Study Project* Population Studies No. 94 (New York, 1986)
World Health Statistics Quarterly (Geneva)

Social welfare

Throughout South Asia live individuals and families who do not have the capacity or the means to take care of their own needs. Many have no opportunity for work or if they do work do not earn enough to survive; some are physically disabled; many are children, women or old people who have no family or whose families are themselves unable to help. Traditionally, the South Asian family was responsible for its poor or handicapped members, a responsibility often justified by religious beliefs. Hindu religious teaching, for example, stresses the virtue of helping family members in need and promises rewards to the giver in the next world. '*He who keeps his wealth for himself, without allowing his relatives and others to share it goes to Hell. He who is strong enough to work and does not support his family, the Brahmins and the unfortunate is dead though he be alive.*' (Krishna: *Bhagavat-purana* X, 45, 7) Thus sons were expected to look after parents in their old age and families to take in kin when they needed assistance. In Islam, support of social welfare in cash and kind was exalted as a virtue, ranking only next to prayer, and Buddhism stressed obligations to care for family members, thus bringing merit to the giver as well as social and economic support to the relative in need. Even today in South Asia the family holds the primary responsibility for kin in need.

Some formal welfare services were provided in early times by government and religious groups. One duty of Muslim rulers was to support orphans. Early Sinhalese kings in Sri Lanka built hospitals and assigned Ayurvedic physicians to serve groups of villages. In India under King Ashoka (272/268–232 BC) *gopas*, or social workers, were appointed. Under Ashoka's successors training programs for handicapped people and government supported charity and relief services were provided.

However, it was not until the British took over the administration of most of South Asia that personal social welfare services as known in the West were initiated. Voluntary and religious groups offered aid along the lines of that provided by Christian missionaries from the West. In India, for example, *Arya Mahila Samaj* (Aryan Women's Association) and many others established services for the poor, the handicapped, for children and for women. Mohandas Karamchand Gandhi's efforts to organize the Harijans (untouchables) in the 1920s served as a self-help model that has become a significant guide to later welfare work. British governments also responded directly to some welfare needs by establishing such programs as Workmen's Compensation Schemes to aid injured workers and training schools for social workers. In South Asian countries that were never under direct British administration such as the Maldives and Bhutan, however, the social welfare system was and is based largely on bonds of family and kinship.

Welfare since World War II

When most of South Asia achieved independence from colonial rule after World War II, governments seized the opportunity to respond to a broader range of social welfare needs by expanding their role in planning, co-ordination and funding. Most governments shifted the emphasis of welfare concerns and activities, particularly in dealing with unemployment and poverty, away from the idea that poverty is an individual or family problem best ameliorated by charity to the conception that poverty is a symptom of a weak national economy. Most developed series of five-year plans, usually aided by international agencies such as the World Bank, focused on development of the economy. The creation of jobs was seen as the way to improve in the long run the social and economic welfare of all, by raising income and closing the income gap between rich and poor. Table 65 shows that this gap is real; it also shows that the income gap is closing slowly.

Sri Lanka took an unusual direction in the early post-war period, however, based on the idea that social welfare needs should be met first by re-distributing wealth among the whole population rather than developing services for subgroups of those most in need. Thus, following an ideology of egalitarianism, the government provided basic social welfare services to all, irrespective of need, in the form of universal and free health and educational services, subsidized housing and transportation, and universal food subsidies. Expenditures on rations of free rice for everyone along with other low cost, subsidized foods in some years accounted for as much as 20 percent of total government budget and the total welfare package as much as 48 percent. This strategy accompanied a reduction in the income gap between rich and poor. However, the large costs and other political and ideological changes have led to a cutting-back of universal services since 1977 such that by 1981 only 23 percent of Sri Lanka's budget went toward the universal welfare package.

All South Asian countries recognize both that reducing levels of poverty and unemployment through broad social development programs is a long-term strategy and that there may always be people not drawn into the mainstream of the economy who will need special services. Thus, most South Asian governments continue to plan and co-ordinate personal welfare services for the individuals and families most in need. In some cases services are provided directly by central or local governments funded by government revenues but much more commonly direct services are offered by non-governmental organizations financed privately, sometimes with the aid of government grants. India, for example, has as many as 10,000 such non-government organizations and Sri Lanka 4000. Thus central government expenditures on social welfare are small. Families and voluntary groups bear most of the financial burden.

Table 65. Distribution of total income among top 5% and bottom 10% of the population

		1960–1963 (%)	1964–1969 (%)	1970–1974 (%)	1975–1977 (%)
Bangladesh	Top 5%	18.3	16.7	14.6	n.a.
	Bottom 10%	6.9	7.9	6.9	n.a.
India	Top 5%	26.7	26.3	n.a.	22.2
	Bottom 10%	4.1	6.7	n.a.	7.0
Nepal	Top 5%	n.a.	n.a.	n.a.	35.3
	Bottom 10%	n.a.	n.a.	n.a.	4.6
Pakistan	Top 5%	n.a.	20.3	n.a.	17.8
	Bottom 10%	n.a.	6.4	n.a.	8.0
Sri Lanka	Top 5%	26.4	n.a.	18.2	18.6
	Bottom 10%	4.5	n.a.	7.5	7.3

Source: The World Bank: *World Tables* (3rd edn), 1983.

Mother Teresa, a winner of the Nobel Peace Prize, whose Missionaries of Charity care for the homeless and dying, young and old, in urban India.

Personal social welfare services

Disabled and handicapped persons

Poverty, malnutrition and poor, or poorly distributed, health services in most of South Asia partially explain the large numbers of people who are blind, deaf, mentally retarded or physically handicapped. Estimates are that 9 percent (or about 8.7 million) of the population of India are handicapped, the majority of whom are blind. In Nepal 3 percent of the population is blind. Pakistan estimates 3.7 million handicapped and Sri Lanka about 280,000 or 2 percent of the population. Across all of South Asia disabled people are cared for by their families. In Sri Lanka, for example, 80 percent of all handicapped people rely only on their families for aid and that proportion is probably much higher in Bangladesh which recently had or planned the completion of 28 institutions for the handi-

capped to serve a population of about 95 million. Where formal services do exist, as in India, they are usually in the form of training schools rather than preventive or rehabilitative programs; few trained handicapped persons, however, actually go on to employment. The institutions that are available tend to be unequally distributed so that minority groups and residents of rural areas are poorly served.

Children and youth

All South Asian countries have relatively young populations, with about 40 percent of the population under age 15, and this fact along with poverty and ill health means that many of those in need of aid are children. Most countries, through non-governmental organizations, offer some services dealing with basic issues of child survival. For example, in Bangladesh there are a few orphanages and other programs for abandoned children who might otherwise become beggars and, in Pakistan, social welfare centers care for lost or kidnapped children while arrangements are made to return them home. Following a strategy for longer-term benefits to children, Sri Lanka and India, for example, have provided food supplements, in some cases offered in schools, but these programs are known to miss the neediest children who may not attend school or to be skewed toward urban or linguistic-religious majority groups. Organizations in Pakistan, India and Sri Lanka have begun to establish day care centers and crêches so that mothers can work and thus support their children.

More recently a shift away from 'single issue' programs for children is exemplified by India's Integrated Child Development Services (offered in about 1500 communities) in which a package of services including supplementary nutrition, immunizations, health check-ups and referrals, nutritional, health and other education is directed specifically toward the poorest families. All of these formal services for children, however, take limited responsibility for aid compared to families and local communities.

Old people

Formal services for elderly people are meager throughout South Asia since populations are young but with recent increases in life expectancy, up to age 69 in Sri Lanka, the proportion of older people is increasing. This fact along with increased numbers of working adults migrating to seek education and employment suggests that traditional family support for the elderly is likely to weaken. Generally families or local caste or religous organizations care for old people. Sri Lanka and India have a few cottage-type homes for indigent old people, provided by voluntary organizations, sometimes with government aid, and such organizations as Mother Teresa's Missionaries of Charity in India provide care for homeless and dying in urban India.

It is only elderly people who have been employed in government or large urban industrial companies whose old age is at least partially secure because they benefit from pension or lump-sum retirement schemes to which the worker and sometimes the employer have contributed. The bulk of the South Asian old people who live in rural areas and who have been self-employed or worked as casual laborers rely on their children or the village community for needed help.

Poor and unemployed

Poverty underlies most welfare problems in South Asia, sometimes causing distress (poverty causing poor nutrition and in turn poor health of mothers and children, for example) and sometimes limiting what families can do to help (preventing families from giving care to the old). The proportion of people living below the poverty

Table 66. Gross national product *per capita*, 1983 (USA $)

Bangladesh	130
Bhutan	n.a.
India	260
Maldives	n.a.
Nepal	170
Pakistan	390
Sri Lanka	330

Source: The World Bank: *World Bank Atlas*, 1985.

line in India is estimated at 48 percent and it can be shown that all South Asian countries are, on the average, very poor (see Table 66). Until recently those who could not provide for themselves were the responsibility of kin or the local community. Sri Lanka is unusual in providing public assistance to people who are destitute, granting only enough for a minimum subsistence, a payment that often carries with it public stigma. Elsewhere public maintenance support is scattered or non-existent although some governments have created work programs, for example in India, which provides minimum guaranteed work for one person in the poor family.

Most, governments have followed strategies designed to make permanent changes in employment patterns by reducing both unemployment (estimated to be 27 million people in India in 1980, for example) and underemployment (common in Sri Lanka where well educated young people often hold low-level jobs) by training and self-help programs. India's Integrated Rural Development Program, targeted toward the poorest rural families who are often marginal farmers and landless laborers, is designed to improve skills and provide technology (pumps, wells, fertilizer, for example) along with welfare services such as education and nutrition. In 1981–82 2.8 million Indian families were participating in this program. While such programs have been initiated in many places in South Asia they have not yet succeeded in shifting primary responsibility for the poor away from the family and local community.

Recent trends in social welfare

'Social welfare' now means at least two different things in South Asia. To central governments it means, largely, the secure life that comes from an adequate and predictable income, one that allows families to care for themselves. While this condition is a long-term goal, governments have generally chosen to work to this goal through large-scale economic development programs. To voluntary organizations who handle most personal welfare services 'social welfare' has also changed, from the idea of providing 'charity' to the unfortunate to the idea that poor families and handicapped people can be helped to help themselves, bringing permanent improvements to their lives.

The Sarvodaya Shramadana Movement in Sri Lanka exemplifies

this latter approach to personal social welfare, one that echoes Gandhi's earlier work with the Harijans and that is modeled on a similar program in India. At least 300,000 volunteers across the country have helped 2000 villages to organize integrated community development programs having as one goal to increase self-reliance and local control so that villagers, especially the very poor, can provide for their own needs. Work in a village usually begins with a 'work camp' combining Sarvodaya volunteers and local villagers who may build a road or a school playground. Village needs are discussed, raising the consciousness of participants about these issues, then volunteers and community groups choose and carry out educational and service projects. A common choice is to build a pre-school center or crèche to free mothers for work. Local women are formally trained to run these centers and then employed in them, paid by the central organization. Community kitchens and mothers' groups, usually associated with pre-school centers, provide health and nutrition education and have sometimes succeeded in taking action to bring government services such as immunization programs to the village, thus saving mothers long walks to the clinic. Again with support of international agencies, Sarvodaya has established such programs as a recent one in which young women are being trained to manufacture, install, repair and maintain simple water pumps, providing them with jobs for the future as well as better water supplies and thus better health for their communities.

NW-M

Further reading

J. Dixon and Hyujng Shik Kim, Eds, *Social Welfare in Asia* (London, 1985)

N. Ratnapala, 'The Sarvodaya Movement: Self-help rural development in Sri Lanka' in Phillip Coombs, Ed., *Meeting the Basic Needs of the Rural Poor: The Integrated Community-Based Approach* (New York, 1980)

Sports and games

Traditional

Traditional sports and games are popular all over South Asia. As in the past, they are enjoyed by both rich and poor. Chess is perhaps the best known of traditional pastimes indigenous to the subcontinent. It is thought to have originated there in the sixth century AD, spread then to China in the east and to Persia, Arabia and Europe in the west. Known as *chataranga* after the four (*chatar*) component parts (*angas*) of an India army (chariot, elephant, horse and foot-soldier), early Indian chessmen were miniature reproductions of these figures, ranging from the elaborately-carved ivories of the wealthy to fairly crude representations produced cheaply for common use. Backgammon (*chaupar*), originally from Persia, became popular in many parts of the subcontinent where its board has also been adapted for other games played with dice and cowries (small shells). Dice-playing, using a number of dice marked with dots and each with a specific name, goes back to Vedic times at least when religious epics referred to the harm which the gambling associated with dice-halls (*sabhas*) had on domestic life. Card games were popular in South Asia long before the sixteenth century when European cards were first imported: although the earliest set of Indian cards so far known dates from 1501, the wide variety of mythological themes present on indigenous playing cards indicates that they enjoy a long pre-Mughal tradition. Bridge, admittedly a more recent western import dating from the period of British rule, has become a passion for many middle-class South Asians, and it is not really very surprising that one of the leading professional bridge-players in the world, Zia Mahmud, comes from Pakistan.

Fairs, usually associated with religious festivals or related to the seasonal cycle of the agricultural calendar, often provide the setting for many traditional sports which include horse, camel, even elephant-racing, and animal-fighting, such as cock-fighting and bear-baiting. One of the most popular of the sports played on these occasions is wrestling. Wrestling is believed to have flourished in India as early as 1500 BC and is mentioned in classical epics such as the *Rigveda*, the *Mahabharata* and the *Ramayana*. It is 'loose' in style, beginning with wrestlers separated and free to seize any grip of their choice, save that of taking hold of their opponents' clothing. Victory is secured by throwing an opponent onto his back. Mughal sponsorship of regular wrestling competitions encouraged the emergence of professionals who still fight for the title of 'Rustam', the name of a legendary Aryan hero-wrestler. During the nineteenth century, wrestlers, such as Sadika who became champion in 1840, acquired great fame. Families specialized in producing champion wrestlers: for instance, the brothers, Gama and Imam Baksh, and their descendants, Bholo, Aslam and Akram, have been outstanding practitioners of free-style wrestling during the twentieth cen-

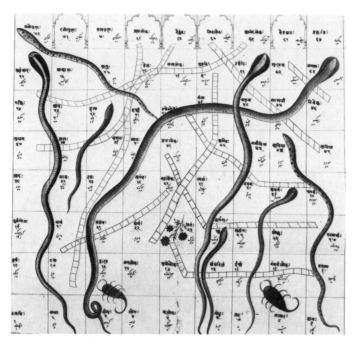

Snakes and Ladders as played in northern India in the eighteenth century. Each square is numbered and labeled with its attribute, for instance, heaven, grief, bad company, and various sins and pleasures, in Persian and Hindi.

symbol of time spent in the subcontinent: extravagant hunts were almost obligatory for viceroys and distinguished British visitors. The pursuit of carnivorous game with spears, regarded by princely families as a test of manliness, became the notorious sport of pig-sticking. The countryside, teeming with game, was a shooting paradise. Since Independence, wealthy families have continued to indulge in these activities: many endangered species, notably the tiger, are now protected, but duck-shooting in particular remains very popular. Archery remains the national sport of Bhutan where nearly every village holds regular archery contests.

Another traditional South Asian sport 'inherited' by the British was polo. First played in Persia, this sport was introduced into the subcontinent by Muslim conquerors in the thirteenth century. Known as *chaugan* after the Persian for 'stick' or 'mallet', or *polo*, the Balti word for 'ball', it was originally a way of training cavalry units for it tested the value of a man and strengthened the bonds of friendship. Polo became very popular among the nobility. Mughal rulers were often painted watching or participating in polo matches, and it was a subject often chosen by poets of the time. The first Europeans to play polo were tea planters in Assam during the first half of the nineteenth century. Then, in the early 1860s, the famous Calcutta Polo Club was established. The sport soon spread back to Britain as well as to North and South America. Nowadays, polo in South Asia is usually associated, on the one hand, with the rich, and, on the other, with the military at whose academies it is often played. There are, however, still some places, notably in the northwestern-most part of the subcontinent in the valley of the River Indus, where polo remains the activity of ordinary people, and it is here that the most agile polo ponies continue to be bred.

Besides the martial sports of wrestling, archery, hunting and polo, there are other more peaceful traditional South Asian pursuits. Pigeon-flying remains a much-loved pastime. Few pigeon-fanciers can today match the twenty thousand birds owned by the emperor Akbar, but traditional contests still take place from the rooftops of many South Asian towns and cities, in which owners use their own birds to try and 'hi-jack' pigeons belonging to their 'rivals'. Kite-flying is another sport well suited to the flat rooftops of South Asia. Throughout much of the Panjab, for instance, the festival of Basant towards the end of February signals the start of the kite-flying season. The kites themselves are normally 'diamond' in shape and constructed from paper fixed onto a strung bow of light material. Competing fliers coat the string with a mixture of glue and powdered glass (*manjha*) in order to sever the strings of other people's kites. There then follows a frantic chase to retrieve falling or fallen kites. Other traditional children's games include spinning-tops, 'yo-yos' and hobby horses. Everywhere, boys spend hours running along while controlling circular metal hoops with bent lengths of wire: similarly, there are many simple games played by

tury, both in British India and in Pakistan. *Kabaddi*, a team version of tag wrestling requiring agility and strength, is another much-loved game which is played in many parts of the subcontinent and is often the subject of friendly rivalry among competing villages.

Sports associated with hunting or *shikar* enjoy a long tradition throughout South Asia. On the whole, however, it has been the upper classes who have been able to afford the 'luxury' of hunting for pleasure. Archery, practiced out of necessity by the less well-off, became a sport for rajas and princes who sought to display their skill by shooting at different kinds of target. The catching and training of falcons was another sport often associated with Indian rulers: the Mughal emperor Akbar is said to have been very fond of hawking, and the general Mughal love of the sport was reflected in the many portraits which were made of favorite royal birds. Hunting took place by order of rank, first the king, then the princes, next the nobles and so on in turn. Methods of hunting included the Mughal practice of constructing a circular stockade into which game was driven by beaters; sometimes men themselves formed the solid enclosure within which animals were trapped. Later, the British, as new members of India's élite, enthusiastically followed in this tradition of hunting. Tiger-hunting, long the sport of kings, became an obsession with their British successors. Tiger skins became a

children which involve variations on the theme of throwing up and catching small pieces of stone either in the palm or on the back of the hand.

Modern

The consolidation of British political power in the subcontinent led to the introduction of Western sports which took firm root in urban areas. While lacking many of the resources available in the West, sport forms an important and integral part of national life in South Asia. Both cricket and hockey are regarded as national sports. As early as 1721, a cricket match was played in Cambay in western India between the officers and men of a British ship. Cricketing records in the three Presidencies of Bengal, Bombay and Madras date from the eighteenth century: the Calcutta Cricket Club is known to have existed by 1792. The first club formed by Indians was the Orient Cricket Club in Bombay in 1848. Its membership consisted of Parsis who enjoyed close social and commercial relations with the British. Upon its dissolution in 1850, another Parsi club, the Young Zoroastrians, was established. During the 1880s, the first match between the Parsis and Europeans in Bombay was followed by two tours to England in 1886 and 1888. Meanwhile, other communities had begun to form their own teams: Bombay's Hindus set up the Union Cricket Club in 1866 while its Muslim population responded by forming the Mohammadan Cricket Club in 1883. In 1906, Hindus competed with the Parsis and the Presidency (Europeans) in a triangular tournament. By 1912, this tournament had become quadrangular with the entry of a Muslim team. Pitches were uneven, gear was crude but already tremendous enthusiasm for the sport existed. In 1926, an England representative side, made its first tour to India, although English tours had been taking place since 1889–90. Some Indians played cricket for England during this period. Prince Ranjitsinhji, a Cambridge blue, was a leading figure in English cricket around the turn of the twentieth century. His impact on Indian cricket was great for his success abroad gave impetus to the sport at home as well as encouraging Englishmen to take Indian cricketers more seriously: in the words of a cricket commentator of the day, 'here was . . . a "black man" playing cricket not as a "white man" but as an artist of another and superior strain'. In 1934, in honor of his influence, the Ranji Trophy became the national championship for which teams from all over British India competed. It remains the major tournament in independent India, while the main prize in Pakistan has become the Qaid-e Azam Trophy. Since 1947, the communal element in cricket sides has disappeared. Clubs are now organized either on territorial bases or sponsored by private companies and government departments.

On the international level, India and Pakistan are both established world-class cricketing nations. India, at first no real match for England and Australia away from home, proved from the outset hard to bear on its own pitches where it scored victories against visiting teams. Pakistan had a very auspicious start in world cricket by winning matches against England at the Oval in 1954 and Australia at Karachi in 1956. In 1986, India followed up its 1983 World Cup victory by finally gaining its first series win in England. Sri Lanka acquired full international cricketing status only recently.

A notable feature of South Asian cricket particularly at the international level is the strong association of certain families with the sport, for example the four Muhammad brothers who all represented Pakistan. Test matches draw vast numbers of spectators. On occasions, for instance at Calcutta during the West Indies' 1966–67 tour, overcrowding combined with heightened passions have led to serious rioting. In the late 1960s and early 1970s, the Indian test side was notable for the strength of its spin bowlers, who included Prasanna, Bedi, Chandrasekhar and Venkataraghavan. Nowadays, South Asian teams enjoy a reputation for fine batsmen, in particular Gavaskar who has scored the highest number of runs and centuries in test cricket, and world-class all-rounders such as Imran Khan of Pakistan and Kapil Dev of India.

Another sport, initially associated with the British but today a 'national sport' in India and Pakistan, is hockey. Hockey was introduced and popularized by the British Army. Like cricket, it was first played by Indians who maintained close contacts with the British, in this case Christians belonging on the whole to the Eurasian community. The railways, manned by Eurasians, were noted for their very good hockey sides. Again like cricket, first-class hockey has developed strong commercial connections: many teams are sponsored by private companies. Internationally, India and Pakistan have dominated the sport at World Championship and Olympic level. In the 1932 Olympics, for instance, commentators voted the performance of the Indian hockey team as the most outstanding exhibition of skill in any sport. While most players throughout the world now use the short-toed stick developed in the subcontinent, the South Asian style of play, featuring short controlled passes and clever stick-work, differs from the European tendency to hit the ball about the field more. The advent of artificial all-weather pitches in international competitions in recent years, which favors the European style of play, means that South Asian sides are now facing a serious challenge from a number of European countries and from Australia in particular.

Volleyball which requires little outlay in terms of equipment and facilities is played in towns and villages in many parts of South Asia, while football is especially popular in Bangladesh and the Indian state of West Bengal. India has produced world-class badminton players such as Prakash Padukone who won the British Open in 1980 and international tennis stars such as Ramanathan Krishnan and the Amritraj brothers. Pakistan, meanwhile, reigns supreme in

Jahangir Khan, one of Pakistan's outstanding squash-players, unbeaten in the world for over five years in the 1980s.

international squash. Despite the fact that, at the time of independence, only two hundred or so players regularly played squash in a handful of courts, Pakistan has produced a succession of world-beaters. One family in particular has dominated the sport, on both the national and international level. Hashim Khan, who earned his living as a marker under the British, emerged at the rather advanced age of thirty-five to take seven British Open titles during the 1950s. Succeeding members of the Khan family, such as Azam, Roshan, Mohibullah, Qamar Zaman and most spectacularly Jahangir, have maintained the high standards set by Hashim. Other sports, such as athletics, have received a boost since India provided itself with improved facilities for national competition as a result of its holding the Asian Games in 1982.

Women in South Asia play many of the same sports as their male counterparts. Playing sport during the first half of the twentieth century was regarded as a sign of modernity and so westernized South Asian women took up sports such as badminton, tennis and table tennis which they played either at mixed clubs or at clubs run by women's associations. The spread of convent schools and women's colleges encouraged team games such as hockey, volleyball and cricket. Nowadays, women's cricket is taken very seriously in India and Sri Lanka where international fixtures draw large crowds. Even in the predominantly Muslim countries of the region, where the visibility of female sport has been reduced in recent years as a result of pressure from orthodox religious groups, middle class urban women have resisted attempts to ban female participation in sport.

SA

Opposite Opaque cobalt blue glass with polychrome silt decoration, the cap made from a Dutch coin mounted in silver. West India or Deccan; eighteenth century. Two sides of the bottle are decorated with floral designs, and two with the figures of the legendary lovers Laila and Majnun. Immortalized by the Persian poet Nizami and others, the lovelorn Majnun (i.e. one possessed by a *jinn* or spirit) spent his life alone in the desert after Laila's father refused to allow their marriage. He is traditionally shown emaciated and dressed in rags, often with birds nesting in his matted hair.

CULTURE

Introduction

As a primary area of cultural achievement and inspiration, fully on a par with the three other focal centers of the Eurasian landmass, in China, in the Middle East and in Europe, South Asia must stand to the fore of any consideration the patterns which have governed the development of human civilization from the beginnings of recorded time down to the global culture of the present. Any serious attempt at understanding South Asian culture as a whole must take account not only of the rich interplay between high cultures and still vital and varied folk-traditions, but also of important external influences which have gone into its shaping.

South Asia in the context of world culture

South Asia is fully comparable in time-depth of civilization to China. Historical contact between the two was discouraged by the formidable geographical barrier of the Himalayas, which was effectively overcome only by the powerful missionary impulses of early Buddhism. This resulted in an enduring South Asian influence on the shaping of the culture of pre-revolutionary China, an influence which continues to be evident in the culture of both Tibet and Japan.

In the intermediate territories of Southeast Asia, the continuing patterns of historic influence from their powerful neighbors determine the cultural frontier between Vietnam on the one hand and Burma and Thailand on the other. In the latter, the direct impress of South Asian culture is still clearly to be seen, whether in religion and iconography, or in loan-words and scripts. Although the once much greater spread of South Asian cultural influence in Southeast Asia has been overlain by the subsequent extension of Islam, it still dominates the Hindu civilization of Bali.

South Asia in world culture.

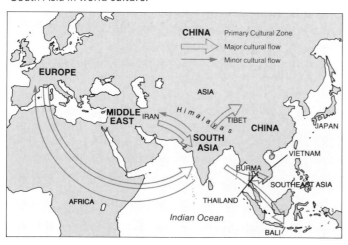

To the West, the cultural relationship between South Asia and the Middle East has been much closer and much less one-sided throughout recorded history. Whatever the connections between the ancient civilization of the Indus Valley and the contemporary cities of the Euphrates, the ease of sea-communication between the two zones and the historic role of Iran as a readily traversable land-bridge have ensured the continuance of mutually transmitted cultural influences of enormous historical importance.

The predominant influence has been from west to east, since South Asian culture as we know it would not have come into being without the Aryan invasions of the second millenium BC and the later influx of the Muslims from AD 1000. But the reverse process is hardly negligible, since it gave the world its greatest game and the numerical system which underlines all contemporary science and technology, through the transmission of chess and of the zero-based number-writing of India to the Arabs.

Although direct contact between Europe and South Asia was established as early as the fourth century BC by the armies of the world-conqueror Alexander, and later continued through the spice-trade maintained between Rome and South India, their geographical separation for long entailed indirect contact via the Middle East. Only with the developments of naval technology achieved in the fifteenth century, and so rapidly exploited by Vasco da Gama and his successors was direct contact on an unprecedented scale made possible, and an ever-closer cultural interlinking between Europe and South Asia finally formed.

Since European technological superiority eventually resulted in British political control of South Asia, the predominant influence was naturally again from west to east, as South Asian culture was subjected to the third of the massive invasions which have gone into its making. The continuance of this pattern even after 1947 has been ensured by the central role of the USA in the English language-based global culture to which South Asia is so closely linked.

Once again, however, the traffic has been far from one way. Indian religio-philosophical ideas made their influential way westwards, first often through the Persian translations earlier commissioned by the Mughals to satisfy their own curiosity, subsequently directly from Sanskrit. The discovery of Sanskrit itself vastly expanded European cultural consciousness, not simply through the re-writing of the history of civilization necessitated by the proving of its relationship with Greek and Latin, but also in the great range of insights opened up by the ancient Indian high culture. Modern linguistics is hardly conceivable without reference to the impact made by the Sanskrit grammarians in the nineteenth century, and the Western sexual revolution of the twentieth might have been much less interesting without the influence of innumerable popularizations of the ingenious *Kamasutra*. Although the artistic impact of South Asia was generally felt rather later, its effects are

Painted ivory chessmen probably from Rajasthan, nineteenth century. The game of chess originated in India.

clearly to be seen in the public buildings of the West, whether palaces or cinemas, to be increasingly heard in a huge variety of both serious and popular music, and to be savored in the immense repertoire of South Asian culinary styles.

The internal context of South Asian culture

Sensitive visitors to any South Asian country today will be immediately impressed by the enormous diversity of the lifestyles being simultaneously pursued in the same city or region. The natural first reaction is to explain this in terms of gross inequalities of income. But it soon becomes apparent that both rich and poor are themselves equally differentiated by varying allegiance to whole sets of only partially compatible cultural norms. Given the basic rules governing human social existence, this allegiance is most obviously manifested in language, dress and food. These fundamental choices will, however, determine in their turn more sophisticated selections, whether of films, music or books.

While the choice provided by the naturally plural societies of most South Asian countries is no more a free one for their citizens than it is for the culturally conditioned individuals of any other society, it is nevertheless still one of exceptional range. The influence of three great high cultures, namely those of Sanskritic civilization, of the Persian-based Muslim empires, and of the English-based British empire, continues to dominate India. It does so, moreover, whatever the acknowledgment due to local traditions in helping to determine the cultural profile of one of the world's

largest polities, and however great the direct appeal of these folk-cultures, whether in literature, music, dance, food or dress, to a West endlessly hungry for new sources of ethnic inspiration. A similar profile, with appropriate local modifications, characterizes the other countries of South Asia.

South Asian culture continues to reflect the diversity appropriate to the subcontinent which contains a quarter of humanity, and will doubtless continue to be more easily grasped in its parts than fully appreciated in its diverse whole.

CS

Further reading
Basham, A. L., *The Wonder That Was India* (London, 1971)
Lannoy, R., *The Speaking Tree: a Study of Indian Culture and Society* (London, 1971)

Languages

From the linguistic viewpoint, as in so many other respects, South Asia is both a region united by many common patterns of historical development within stable external boundaries, and an area of astonishing local variety and often blurred internal frontiers. Outsiders have always been impressed by the sheer number of languages spoken in South Asia. But it is equally important to bear in mind the widespread historical preference for the cultivation of pan-South Asian languages invested with enduring cultural prestige, notably of Sanskrit as the classical language of ancient India and of Persian as the cultural language of the Muslim period. Even in the contemporary period, English similarly continues to dominate the élite culture of most South Asian countries and to exert a common influence on most South Asian languages, although the increasing role being given to language in South Asia as a marker of national and regional identity second only in power to religion has entailed some shift away from traditional patterns of language use towards a greater emphasis upon the regional languages.

Indo-Aryan languages

The dominant languages of South Asia, in terms of both historical influence and present geographical spread, are the Indo-Aryan languages which form the most easterly branch of the Indo-European family. Although they are thus fundamentally similar in structure and ultimately related in vocabulary to most of the languages of Europe, the long separate evolution of the Indo-Aryan languages in South Asia since their introduction by the Aryan invaders of the second millennium BC has resulted in their having many distinctive features, largely attributable to the influence of the indigenous languages assimilated by the Aryans. These include the well-known phonetic distinction between dental consonants and the corresponding retroflex sounds (as heard in the characteristic 't' and 'd' of Indian English), besides a great deal of their vocabulary.

Although Old Indo-Aryan is first recorded in Vedas, it is best known in classical form as Sanskrit, which as codified in the grammar of Panini (fifth century BC) continued to be virtually unchallenged as the dominant learned language of South Asia until about AD 1000, long after it had ceased to be spoken. The early history of most of the modern Indo-Aryan languages is obscured by this long dominance of Sanskrit, which even today continues to provide most of them with their learned vocabulary, although Persian and more recently English have also been fertile sources of loan-words.

These common cultural influences from the three great pan-South Asian languages, all members of different branches of Indo-European, have served to reinforce the basic familial relationship of the Indo-Aryan languages, whose virtually unbroken geographical spread across the whole of the north involves the existence of complex chains of overlapping dialects, belying the apparent neatness of modern political boundaries or the separate appearance of the different scripts which so conspicuously distinguish the major languages in their written form.

The first records of New Indo-Aryan in the north hardly pre-date the eleventh century AD, and many of the modern languages are scarcely recorded before the sixteenth century. The use of Persian by the ruling Muslim élite and the continuing prestige of Sanskrit entailed the general restriction of the Indo-Aryan languages to popular verse literatures of largely religious inspiration throughout the medieval period. Only with the British establishment of provincial schemes of vernacular education in the nineteenth century did they come to assume their modern standardized forms. This lengthy process, involving endless decisions as to correct usage in spelling, grammar and vocabulary, is still not entirely complete, especially in the case of some of the outlying languages.

As British rule was gradually extended westwards from Bengal to the Panjab, particular encouragement came to be given to the widely understood lingua franca of the Delhi region, whose incorporation of huge numbers of Persian loan-words with a notably simple Indo-Aryan grammatical structure made it an obvious choice as a partial successor, alongside English, to Persian, whose prestige effectively collapsed with the end of Muslim political power. Although for a while this lingua franca, known as Khari Boli to linguists, and formerly as Hindustani to the British, successfully occupied this role, it came to be split during the nineteenth century along religious grounds. Its cultural link with Persian was enthusiastically exploited by the Muslims, who continued to draw upon Arabic and Persian vocabulary to make Urdu the prime language of South Asian Islam. The contemporary cultural revival among the Hindus of North India, however, found its linguistic expression in Hindi, a heavily Sanskritized version of Hindustani which uses the Nagari script instead of the Perso-Arabic, and which has come to absorb the medieval Hindi cultural heritage created in quite other literary dialects.

Thus it is that Hindi as the national language of India and Urdu as the national language of Pakistan, while still virtually the same at the level of everyday speech, are hardly mutually intelligible in their formal usage, given their different scripts and learned vocabularies. Similar nationalistic considerations underlie the careful distinction of Nepali from Hindi, although their intrinsic relationship is quite close.

The huge geographical extent of the bloc of 'Hindi-speaking' states in North India, that is, the states in which Hindi has official status, obscures the pattern of intermediary dialects which link the Delhi-based standard to the independently recognized Indo-Aryan

Languages of South Asia by numbers of speakers.

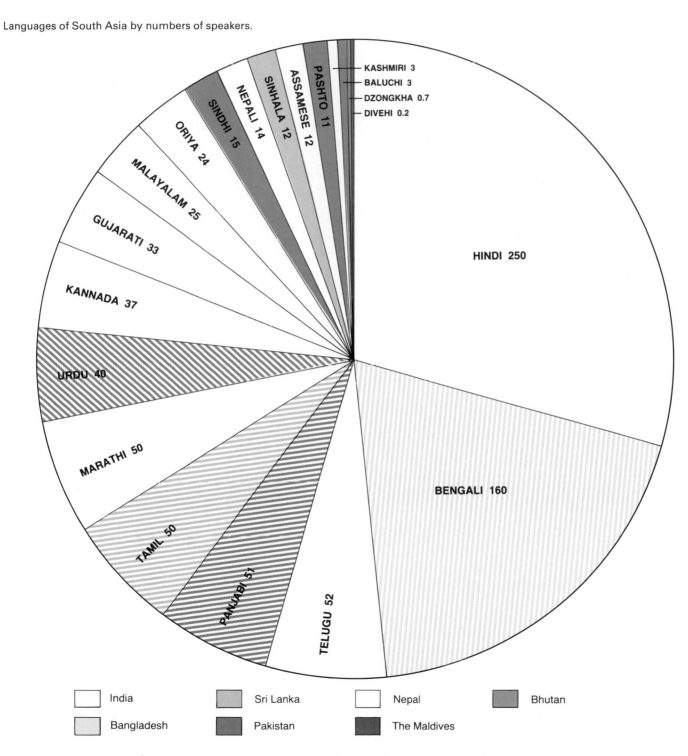

KASHMIRI 3
BALUCHI 3
DZONGKHA 0.7
DIVEHI 0.2

HINDI 250

BENGALI 160

TELUGU 52

PANJABI 51

TAMIL 50

MARATHI 50

URDU 40

KANNADA 37

GUJARATI 33

MALAYALAM 25

ORIYA 24

SINDHI 15

NEPALI 14

SINHALA 12

ASSAMESE 12

PASHTO 11

India   Sri Lanka   Nepal   Bhutan

Bangladesh   Pakistan   The Maldives

● *The numbers (in millions of speakers) based where possible on official figures for 1981 are to be regarded as approximations only. All state languages in India are officially recognized by Schedule VIII of the Constitution.*

Principal languages of South Asia.

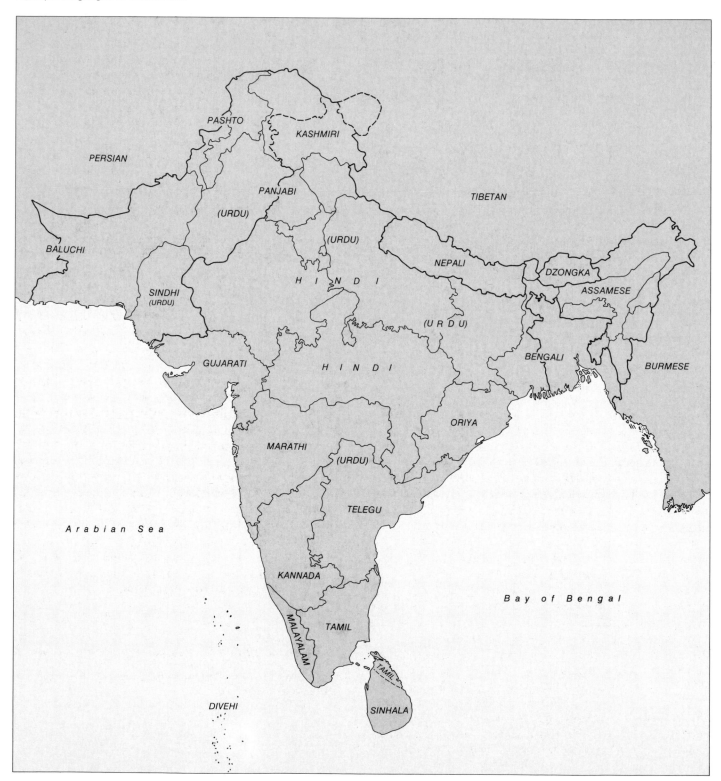

languages of the periphery. By far the most important of these in terms of historical cultivation and numbers of speakers is Bengali, now the official language of Bangladesh, which together with Assamese to the north and Oriya to its south forms a distinctive eastern subgroup within the Indo-Aryan languages, characterized by many grammatical simplifications. The languages bordering the Hindi–Urdu area on the west are more heterogeneous in character. Although the shared survival of the Sanskrit neuter gender suggests a superficial connection between Marathi and Gujarati, the latter is equally close to Hindi. Across the border in Pakistan, where the extra-territorial cultural dominance of Urdu is still very marked, Sindhi is separately characterized by many more individual phonetic and grammatical characteristics than Panjabi, which is heavily influenced by Urdu in Pakistan and by Hindi in India. In the northern mountains several quite distinct languages, collectively assigned to the Dardic subgroup, are spoken, but only Kashmiri has been seriously cultivated.

Indo-Aryan was exported far beyond its homelands in the north when the Gypsy migrations to the near east and Europe brought their Romany dialects as far west as Ireland. In more recent times, the export of indentured labor from India to other parts of the British empire in the nineteenth century resulted in substantial numbers of Hindi-speakers settling in Mauritius and Fiji, while the twentieth century diaspora has resulted in the settlement of speakers of Panjabi, Gujarati, Bengali, Hindi and Urdu in many parts of the western world, notably the United Kingdom and North America.

Within South Asia, the effects of a much older migration are still to be seen in Sri Lanka, where Indo-Aryan was brought from the north under the inspiration of early Buddhist missionary expansion. Pali, a language of the middle Indo-Aryan period dating back to the fourth century BC, is still the scriptural language of southern Buddhism, both in Sri Lanka and in Southeast Asia, and has greatly influenced the evolution of Sinhala, an Indo-Aryan language long completely cut off from its distant relatives in the north and now the national language of Sri Lanka. Its only immediate congener is Divehi, the national language of the Maldives.

Apart from English itself, the only other Indo-European languages seriously established in South Asia belong to the Iranian branch, which is quite closely related to Indo-Aryan. Nowadays the most important is Pashto, the eastern Iranian language of the Pathans of the northwest frontier, which straddles the border between Afghanistan and Pakistan. Baluchi is much closer to Persian and crosses the Pakistan–Iran boundary to the south.

Dravidian and other language groups
Indo-Aryan aside, the most important language group in South Asia is formed by the Dravidian languages, whose four main modern representatives are now confined to peninsular India and northern Sri Lanka, but whose once much greater extent is indicated by the survival of related languages among the tribes of central India, and more dramatically by the survival of the distant Brahui of Pakistani Baluchistan. The distinctive sound-system and grammatical structure of the Dravidian languages, which favor the addition of suffixes rather than the characteristic Indo-European system of grammatical inflexion, have prompted attempts to establish remote historical connections with other Asiatic language groups. These must be regarded as largely unproven, however, and are certainly of lesser significance than the already noted influence of Dravidian in the early formation of Indo-Aryan or the long and continuing reverse influence of Indo-Aryan upon the Dravidian languages, which have been long subject to the cultural dominance of Sanskrit.

The oldest documentation for the Dravidian languages is represented by the outstanding literature of classical Tamil, dating from the early centuries AD, and reflecting in its preference for local vocabulary a partial exception to the general subordination to Sanskrit, which has continued to characterize Tamil in both Indian Tamil Nadu and northeastern Sri Lanka, besides the sizeable overseas communities of Tamil-speakers in the countries of the Indian and Pacific Oceans. Malayalam, effectively a dialect of Tamil until the fourteenth century, is less purist, and the same is true of Kannada and the less closely related Telugu, both well recorded from about AD 1000. In modern times, the distinctive character of the Dravidian languages and their long cultivation, not to speak of the general absence of the Persian influence so important in the history of the north, has come to play a crucial part in the formulation of South Indian cultural identity.

Other language groups are of much less significance, in spite of the great interest for linguists of the isolated Burushaski of northern Pakistan or the tribal Munda languages of eastern India. The border-regions naturally contain representatives of adjacent groups, languages of the Southeast Asian Mon-Khmer group in the Nicobar Islands and Assam, and the long string of Tibeto-Burman languages spoken along the northern and eastern frontiers from Ladakh to Chittagong. Only in Bhutan, however, does the dialectal form of Tibetan called Dzongkha have official status.

CS

Further reading
C. Shackle, Ed., *South Asian Languages: a Handbook* (London, 1985)
M. C. Shapiro, and H. F. Schiffman, *Language and Society in South Asia* (Delhi, 1981)
G. A. Zograph, *Languages of South Asia: a Guide* (London, 1982)

Scripts

The great diversity of the languages of South Asia is visually reflected in the almost equal variety of the scripts in which they are written. Quite without parallel elsewhere in the modern world, this proliferation of alphabetic writing-systems in current use serves to underline the separate identities of the region's major national, regional and religious groups, for whom a distinctive script so often continues to provide a powerful cultural emblem.

Indigenous South Asian scripts

Given the early disappearance from use of the still undeciphered semi-pictographic script of the Indus Valley seals with the destruction of Harappan civilization, the continuous history of writing in South Asia effectively begins with the Brahmi script, first recorded in the Prakrit inscriptions of Ashoka (third century BC). Reflecting the sophisticated powers of phonetic analysis uniquely achieved in the ancient world by the grammarians of India, the Brahmi script was superbly designed to record the distinctive features of the Indo-Aryan sound-system. Its essential principles, which proved equally adaptable with slight modification to the writing of Dravidian languages, characterize all subsequent indigenous South Asian scripts.

Written from left to right, like the Greco-Roman-based alphabets of Europe, South Asian scripts are distinguished by an intrinsic phonetic sophistication, based upon the principle of a one-to-one equivalence between sound and symbol. Full sets of symbols for both vowels and consonants are provided, and are alphabetically arranged in scientific order. The vowel-letters are, however, used only to indicate vowels at the beginning of words or following another vowel, while vowels following a consonant, other than the

Brahmi script from Ashoka's first pillar edict, Lauriya Nandangarh, c.242 BC.

Vowels:

अ a	आ ā	इ i	ई ī
उ u	ऊ ū	ऋ ṛ	
ए e	ऐ ai	ओ o	औ au

Consonants:

क k	ख kh	ग g	घ gh	ङ ṅ
च c	छ ch	ज j	झ jh	ञ ñ
ट ṭ	ठ ṭh	ड ḍ	ढ ḍh	ण ṇ
त t	थ th	द d	ध dh	न n
प p	फ ph	ब b	भ bh	म m
य y	र r	ल l	व v	
श ś	ष ṣ	स s	ह h	

Additional sounds, not found in Sanskrit, are indicated by adding a dot to the appropriate consonant, e.g.:

| क़ q | ज़ z | ड़ ṛ | ढ़ ṛh | फ़ f |

Consonants with vowels are written as, e.g.:

क ka	का kā	कि ki	की kī
कु ku	कू kū	कृ kṛ	
के ke	कै kai	को ko	कौ kau
कं kaṁ	काँ kāṁ		

Examples of common conjunct consonants include:

| क्त kta | क्र kra | क्ष kṣa | ज्ज jja | ज्ञ jña |
| त्त tta | त्र tra | द्ध ddha | र्क rka | श्च śca |

The principles of Nagari spelling are illustrated in such familiar words as:

| कर्म 'karma' | टेलीफ़ोन 'telephone' | ब्राह्मण 'Brahman' |
| संस्कृत 'Sanskrit' | सिनेमा 'cinema' | हिन्दुस्तानी 'Hindustani' |

Numerals:

| १ 1 | २ 2 | ३ 3 | ४ 4 | ५ 5 |
| ६ 6 | ७ 7 | ८ 8 | ९ 9 | ० 0 |

Example of Hindi in Nagari script:

१९४१ के व्यक्तिगत सत्याग्रह की समाप्ति के बाद विनोबा यहां रहने लगे। तब से यह स्थान परंधाम आश्रम, पवनार, के नाम से प्रसिद्ध हो गया है। स्वावलम्बी खेती, खादी, गो-पालन और लोकनागरी-लिपि के प्रकाशन के कई प्रयोग यहां होते रहे हैं। वर्धा से पवनार आते हुए रास्ते में नालवाड़ी नामक एक हरिजनों की बस्ती बसी हुई है। विनोबा १९३३ से करीब १० साल तक वहां रहे। वर्धा जिले के गांवों की सेवा का कार्य वहां से चला।

The Nagari script (as used for Hindi).

	Nagari	Gurmukhi	Gujarati	Bengali	Oriya
a	अ	ਅ	અ	অ	ଅ
ā	आ	ਆ	આ	আ	ଆ
kā	का	ਕਾ	કા	কা	କା
i	इ	ਇ	ઇ	ই	ଇ
ki	कि	ਕਿ	કિ	কি	କି
ī	ई	ਈ	ઈ	ঈ	ଈ
kī	की	ਕੀ	કી	কী	କୀ
u	उ	ਉ	ઉ	উ	ଉ
ku	कु	ਕੁ	કુ	কু	କୁ
ū	ऊ	ਊ	ઊ	ঊ	ଊ
kū	कू	ਕੂ	કૂ	কূ	କୂ
ṛ	ऋ		ઋ	ঋ	ଋ
kṛ	कृ			কৃ	କୃ
ē	ए	ਏ	એ	এ	ଏ
kē	के	ਕੇ	કે	কে	କେ
ai	ऐ	ਐ	ઐ	ঐ	ଐ
kai	कै	ਕੈ	કૈ	কৈ	କୈ
ō	ओ	ਓ	ઓ	ও	ଓ
kō	को	ਕੋ	કો	কো	କୋ
au	औ	ਔ	ઔ	ঔ	ଔ
kau	कौ	ਕੌ	કૌ	কৌ	କୌ
ka	क	ਕ	ક	ক	କ
kha	ख	ਖ	ખ	খ	ଖ
ga	ग	ਗ	ગ	গ	ଗ
gha	घ	ਘ	ઘ	ঘ	ଘ
ṅa	ङ	ਙ	ઙ	ঙ	ଙ
ca	च	ਚ	ચ	চ	ଚ
cha	छ	ਛ	છ	ছ	ଛ

	Nagari	Gurmukhi	Gujarati	Bengali	Oriya
ja	ज	ਜ	જ	জ	ଜ
jha	झ	ਝ	ઝ	ঝ	ଝ
ña	ञ	ਞ	ઞ	ঞ	ଞ
ṭa	ट	ਟ	ટ	ট	ଟ
ṭha	ठ	ਠ	ઠ	ঠ	ଠ
ḍa	ड	ਡ	ડ	ড	ଡ
ḍha	ढ	ਢ	ઢ	ঢ	ଢ
ṇa	ण	ਣ	ણ	ণ	ଣ
ta	त	ਤ	ત	ত	ତ
tha	थ	ਥ	થ	থ	ଥ
da	द	ਦ	દ	দ	ଦ
dha	ध	ਧ	ધ	ধ	ଧ
na	न	ਨ	ન	ন	ନ
pa	प	ਪ	પ	প	ପ
pha	फ	ਫ	ફ	ফ	ଫ
ba	ब	ਬ	બ	ব	ବ
bha	भ	ਭ	ભ	ভ	ଭ
ma	म	ਮ	મ	ম	ମ
ya	य	ਯ	ય	য	ଯ
ra	र	ਰ	ર	র	ର
la	ल	ਲ	લ	ল	ଲ
va	व	ਵ	વ	ব	ଵ
ça	श	ਸ਼	શ	শ	ଶ
ṣa	ष		ષ	ষ	ଷ
sa	स	ਸ	સ	স	ସ
ha	ह	ਹ	હ	হ	ହ
ṛa	ड़	ੜ		ড়	ଡ଼

Scripts of South Asia.

commonest vowel -a (regarded as intrinsic), are indicated by signs added around the consonant-letter. The only drawback to this elegant system occurs in the writing of groups of consonants, where the absence of the intrinsic -a is typically indicated by special amalgamations of the consonant-letters, called 'conjuncts'.

Although the huge variety of historically attested alphabets has been much reduced by the spread of modern educational systems, eleven scripts of indigenous origin remain in officially encouraged use in all the countries of South Asia other than Pakistan and the Maldives.

The dominant script in the Hindu heartlands of the north has for at least the last thousand years been Nagari, also called Devanagari ('the script of the city of the gods'). This is used for writing Hindi, Nepali and Marathi, and its religious associations are powerfully reinforced by its general use for writing Sanskrit. To the west of the Nagari area, Gujarati has its own mercantile-based running script, while Panjabi is written in India in the Gurmukhi script sacred to the Sikhs. The cultural independence of the northeast is symbolized by the Bengali script (also adapted for Assamese), which has come to be a symbol of national identity in Bangladesh. The separate Oriya cultural identity is underpinned by a quite different-looking script, whose letters' circular appearance superficially suggests a southern origin.

The southern scripts (which include the independently evolved Sinhala script) derive their distinctive appearance from the technical demands imposed by the traditional incising of characters with a stylus on palm-leaves for subsequent inking-in, as opposed to the use of a pen with Indian ink on paper or birch-bark. Each of the four

	Tamil	Malayalam	Kannada	Telugu	Sinhalese		Tamil	Malayalam	Kannada	Telugu	Sinhalese
a	அ	അ	ಅ	అ	අ	ja	ஜ	ജ	ಜ	జ	ජ
ā	ஆ	ഓ	ಅ	ఆ	ආ	jha		ഝ	ಝ	ఝ	ඣ
kā	கா	കാ	ಕಾ	కా	කා	ña	ஞ	ഞ	ಞ	ఞ	ඤ
i	இ	ഇ	ಇ	ఇ	ඉ	ṭa	ட	ട	ಟ	ట	ට
ki	கி	കി	ಕಿ	కి	කි	ṭha		ഠ	ಠ	ఠ	ඨ
ī	ஈ	ഈ	ಕೀ	కీ	ඊ	ḍa		ഡ	ಡ	డ	ඩ
kī	கீ	കീ	ಕೀ	కీ	කී	ḍha		ഢ	ಢ	ఢ	ඪ
u	உ	ഉ	ಉ	ఉ	උ	ṇa	ண	ണ	ಣ	ణ	ණ
ku	கு	കു	ಕು	కు	කු	ta	த	ത	ತ	త	ත
ū	ஊ	ഊ	ಉ	ఊ	ඌ	tha		ഥ	ಥ	థ	ථ
kū	கூ	കൂ	ಕೂ	కూ	කූ	da		ദ	ದ	ద	ද
ṛ		ഋ	ಋ	ఋ	ඍ	dha		ധ	ಧ	ధ	ධ
kṛ		കൃ	ಕೃ	కృ	කෘ	na	ந	ന	ನ	న	න
e	எ	എ	ಎ	ఎ	එ	pa	ப	പ	ಪ	ప	ප
ke	கெ	കെ	ಕೆ	కె	කෙ	pha		ഫ	ಫ	ఫ	ඵ
ē	ஏ	ഏ	ಏ	ఏ	ඒ	ba		ബ	ಬ	బ	බ
kē	கே	കേ	ಕೇ	కే	කේ	bha		ഭ	ಭ	భ	භ
ai	ஐ	ഐ	ಐ	ఐ	ඓ	ma	ம	മ	ಮ	మ	ම
kai	கை	കൈ	ಕೈ	కై	කෛ	ya	ய	യ	ಯ	య	ය
o	ஒ	ഒ	ಒ	ఒ	ඔ	ra	ர	ര	ರ	ర	ර
ko	கொ	കൊ	ಕೊ	కొ	කො	la	ல	ല	ಲ	ల	ල
ō	ஓ	ഓ	ಕೋ	కో	ඕ	va	வ	വ	ವ	వ	ව
kō	கோ	കോ	ಕೋ	కో	කෝ	ça		ശ	ಶ	శ	ශ
au	ஔ	ഔ	ಔ	ఔ	ඖ	ṣa	ஷ	ഷ	ಷ	ష	ෂ
kau	கௌ	കൗ	ಕೌ	కౌ	කෞ	sa	ஸ	സ	ಸ	స	ස
ka	க	ക	ಕ	క	ක	ha	ஹ	ഹ	ಹ	హ	හ
kha		ഖ	ಖ	ఖ	ඛ	ḷa	ழ	ഴ	ಳ		
ga		ഗ	ಗ	గ	ග	ḷa	ள	ള	ಳ	ళ	
gha		ഘ	ಘ	ఘ	ඝ	ṛa	ற	റ		ఱ	ෟ
ṅa	ங	ങ	ಙ	ఙ	ඞ	ṇa	ன				
ca	ச	ച	ಚ	చ	ච	kṣa	க்ஷ			క్ష	
cha		ഛ	ಛ	ఛ	ඡ						

Scripts of South Asia (*continued*)

---

major Dravidian languages (Telugu, Kannada, Malayalam and Tamil) has its own script. All are collectively characterized by adaptations needed to record distinctively Dravidian features, such as the distinction between short and long *e* and *o*. The Tamil script is further distinguished by its adherence to archaic spelling norms, which renders it a partial exception to the general rule of symbol-sound correspondence.

The north–south division of South Asian scripts is reflected in their early adaptation, with the spread of Buddhism, to write other languages quite unrelated to Indo-Aryan or Dravidian. The heavily-inked appearance of the northern-derived script used for Tibetan, including Dzongkha in Bhutan, thus contrasts sharply with the southern-derived scripts evolved for the languages of Buddhist southeast Asia, such as Burmese, Thai and Cambodian.

Perso-Arabic scripts
Semitic writing-systems, with their characteristic right-to-left direction, first appeared in South Asia with the Aramaic-derived Kharoshthi used in some Ashokan inscriptions. The most enduring challenge to the indigenous systems, however, was presented by the

Letters of the alphabet (independent forms):

ا	a, ā	ب	b	پ	p	ت	t	ٹ	ṭ
ث	s	ج	j	چ	c	ح	h	خ	x
د	d	ڈ	ḍ	ذ	z	ر	r	ڑ	ṛ
ز	z	ژ	zh	س	s	ش	ś	ص	s
ض	z	ط	t	ظ	z	ع	'	غ	gh
ف	f	ق	q	ک	k	گ	g	ل	l
م	m	ن	n	ں	ṁ	و	v, ū, o, au		
ه	h	ی	y, ī	ے	e, ai				

The vowels are normally very precisely indicated, e.g.:

سر [sar, sir, sur]   میل [mīl, mel, mail]

Numerals:

| ۱ | 1 | ۲ | 2 | ۳ | 3 | ۴ | 4 | ۵ | 5 |
| ۶ | 6 | ۷ | 7 | ۸ | 8 | ۹ | 9 | ۰ | 0 |

Example of Urdu calligraphy:

هم اسے رسولِ مقبول صلى الله عليه وسلم كا ارشاد وگرامى بهى ہے كہ ہميں علم حاصل كرنا
چاہیے اس جستجو میں جاہے ہمیں چین ہى کیوں نہ جانا پڑے ۔ میری خوش نصیبی کہ میں کى جانب
پى آئى ۔ اسے كى افتتاحى پرواز كے موقع پر خیر مقدم كے ایک وفد كے ہمراہ ۱۷ مارچ
فروری ۱۹۴۲ كے دوران ہفتہ بھر كے لیے مجھے چین جانے كا اتفاق ہوا۔

Scripts of South Asia (continued)

cursive Arabic script, slightly adapted for writing Persian, which was introduced by the Muslim conquests.

Although much less well suited, especially in its very shorthand notation of vowels, than the derivatives of Brahmi to recording the sounds of South Asian languages, the cultural prestige of the Perso-Arabic script and its intimate association with Islam have ensured its establishment (with minor modifications) as the recognized medium for writing Urdu. The script's cursive origins are emphasized by a continuing preference for the reproduction of professional calligraphy over the use of moveable type, in sharp visual contrast to the indigenous scripts. It has been variously adapted to write Sindhi, Pashto, Kashmiri and all the local languages of Pakistan.

Roman script

The Roman alphabet is intrinsically as ill-fitted as the Perso-Arabic script to writing South Asian languages. In spite of imperial efforts to promote, for instance, the use of romanized Urdu as an official medium for the pre-1947 Indian Army, the Roman script has become indigenized only in a few peripheral areas subject to intensive Christian influence, such as Portuguese Goa or the areas of later missionary activity in the northeast. Given the very limited

An Indian banknote indicates its value in many different scripts.

distribution of Konkani or Naga, the visual prominence of the Roman script in South Asia is linked principally to the continuing prestige of English.

Numerals

An interesting contrast to this characteristic partial replacement of indigenous alphabetic systems by imports from West Asia and from Europe is provided by the decimal numerical notation which represents one of India's greatest contributions to world civilization. Originally derived from abbreviations of Indo-Aryan number-names, these numerals traveled westwards with the Arabs, who called them *hindisa* ('Indian numerals') and retained the convention of writing them from left to right against the norms of the Perso-Arabic script. From this source they were received by Europe as the familiar 'Arabic numerals', whose universal symbols are coming increasingly to supplant those traditionally associated with the various South Asian alphabets.

A further twist to this complex pattern of cultural diffusion is provided by the Divehi script used in the Maldives, which is written in the Semitic right-to-left direction and employs the Arabic numerals as the first nine letters of its alphabet.

CS

Further reading

A. H. Dani, *Indian Palaeography* (Oxford, 1963)
D. Diringer, *The Alphabet*, 3rd edn, Ed. R. Regensburger, pp. 257–313 (London, 1968)
H. M. Lambert, *Introduction to the Devanagari Script* (London, 1953)

Literature: all-South Asia languages

Sanskrit

During the second millennium BC (according to the most widely accepted account), a very numerous people speaking an Indo-European language migrated into the Indian subcontinent from the northwest. Their name for themselves was *arya*, a word indicating nobility, and they called the peoples they encountered *dasyu* 'barbarian' and *dasa* 'slave'. These invading Aryans set about subjugating the indigenous population and establishing themselves and their culture as supreme, and in the course of the centuries they became dominant throughout the entire land. Their language too, termed 'Old Indo-Aryan' by scholars, spread widely, to the extent that the great majority of northern Indians today speak languages which are descended from it. The Dravidian languages of the south are linguistically unrelated, but they too have been heavily influenced by Indo-Aryan, especially in the matter of Sanskrit vocabulary.

'Sanskrit' is the general name for that form of the Old Indo-Aryan speech which came to be used for literary purposes. Strictly defined, the name refers only to the later form of the language, in which the classical literature was composed; but it is taken here to include also the earlier form, the language of the Vedas or 'Vedic'. Taken together, Vedic and Sanskrit literature constitute an enormous textual corpus. There are works relating to four major religions (Brahmanism, Buddhism, Jainism and Hinduism); there are epics, including the *Mahabharata*, the world's longest poem; there are numerous technical literatures, among them significant bodies of texts dealing with grammar, phonetics, lexicography, poetics, philosophy in its various schools, ethics, medicine and astronomy; there is a large quantity of epigraphic material; and there is a tradition of *belles lettres* extending over many centuries and giving rise to hundreds of works of prose, poetry and drama.

The chronology of Sanskrit literature is notoriously uncertain. The earliest Vedic literature, belonging as it does to the stage where prehistory becomes history, is inevitably difficult to date; but it is remarkable that the problems of absolute dating do not in general become much easier until well into the AD era: even of the great Kalidasa we can manage no more than to say 'probably fifth century AD'. Relative dating is generally more straightforward, and allows a coherent historical picture to emerge, but it is a history with unusually few firm dates.

Literature and 'oral literature'

The very word 'literature' implies writing, and it is therefore worth stressing the large oral component in Sanskrit literature. The earliest surviving texts, the hymns of the *Rigveda*, were originally oral compositions, as was the *Mahabharata*. At a later date many types of text made use of popular stories – religious myths, romances and fables, for instance – that must have originated in oral versions. The various technical literatures, though clearly the product of the pen rather than the tongue, were designed to serve a system of instruction that was (and in some cases still is) predominantly oral: texts were thus composed either in the very terse *sutra* style or else in verse form (generally using the simple *shloka* or *anushtubh* meter), in each case for mnemonic convenience. Even the more obviously 'literary' literature was created with oral performance very much in mind, as is attested by the convention according to which it is divided into the *drishya* or 'that which is to be seen' (drama), and the *shravya* or 'that which is to be listened to' (poetry and literary prose). The idea that one might read to oneself is absent, and there is noticeably less interest than in many parts of Europe and the Far and Middle East in developments relating to the appearance of the written word, such as calligraphy or shaped poems. Even where a text is holy, as is the case with the Vedas and the *Bhagavad-gita*, it is specifically in chanting or recitation that the holiness manifests itself, not in the physical book itself (unlike Christian reverence for the Bible and Muslim reverence for the Quran).

Vedic literature

The ancient Aryans worshipped a large pantheon of gods with many different characteristics: Indra the dragon-slaying warrior, drinker of the intoxicating Soma; Varuna the kingly guardian of the cosmic order and judge of human doings; Agni the god of fire, divine intermediary between gods and men at the sacrificial ritual; gods of sun, storm, sky, earth; and many others beside. The earliest surviving texts are hymns to these deities, in the collection called the *Rigveda-sanhita*, the earliest parts of which are thought to date from around 1200 BC, but which certainly took several centuries to reach its full form. It is a large collection (1028 hymns), and a very rich and varied one. The language in which it is composed is very archaic when compared to the later Sanskrit, and there are not a few difficulties of interpretation; yet many of the hymns have a remarkable immediacy of impact, and are made approachable by the directness and simplicity of their expression. The *Rigveda-sanhita* contains much fine poetry (not all of it explicitly religious); some of the later hymns contain vivid speculations on the problems of existence.

During the later period of the composition of the *Rigveda-sanhita*, other Vedic texts began to be created. The primary function of the *Rigveda-sanhita* was the provision of liturgical texts for use by the *hotar*, one of the chief priests at the sacrificial ritual; in the course of time parallel *sanhitas* were developed for the other two main classes of celebrants (*adhvaryus* and *udgatars*). These, the *sanhitas* of the

There was neither the non-existent nor the existent then;
there was neither the air nor the sky which is beyond it.
What stirred? Where? In whose protection?
Was there water, unfathomably deep?

Who truly knows, who will here proclaim
whence it was produced, whence is this creation?
The gods came later, with the creation of this universe;
so who knows whence it has come into being?

Whence this creation has come into being,
whether it was founded by him or not,
the one who in the highest heaven surveys it,
only he knows; or perhaps he does not know.

Rigveda-sanhita 10.129.1,6–7

Yajurveda and the *Samaveda*, are of less literary interest than the earlier Rigvedic collection, from which they borrowed much material. A fourth *sanhita*, that of the *Atharvaveda*, seems initially to have been unconnected with the ritual, consisting largely as it does of charms and magic spells for good and ill.

Initially interspersed among the liturgical *sanhita* collections but later separated out from them, a second class of Vedic texts began to take shape early in the first millennium BC: the Brahmanas. These are essentially expositions of the meaning of the sacrificial ritual, and their primary aim is to establish complex symbolic equivalences between elements of that ritual and elements of the real world (including the world of the gods). The Brahmanas are not, and were never intended to be, 'literature' in the narrower sense; but in developing a prose style and conventions for the conduct of arguments they were to be extremely influential. They also contain the first surviving real narratives known in India, for one way to establish the cosmic meaning of an element of the sacrifice is to tell a story about it. Firm favorites are the story of Shunahshepa in the *Aitareya-brahmana* and the story of King Pururavas and the nymph Urvashi in the enormous *Shatapatha-brahmana*; the *Jaiminiya-brahmana* too is a particularly rich source of such tales.

In time, the conviction that the sacrifice was central to maintenance of cosmic order and divine favor began to be tempered by a new emphasis on esoteric and mystical knowledge, especially knowledge of the identity between the self (*atman*) and godhead (*brahman*). These ideas begin to appear in the latest phase of the Brahmana literature and are the particular concern of the texts called *Upanishads*, which grew out of the Brahmana tradition towards the end of the first half of the first millennium BC; they constitute the last works of the Vedic canon.

The epics

In the sixth century BC orthodox Brahmanism was directly challenged by two teachers propounding heterodox ideas: Gautama the Buddha and Mahavira the founder of Jainism. However, by the time their followers came to assemble the holy texts of the two new faiths Sanskrit had ceased to be the living speech of the common people, and middle Indo-Aryan vernaculars were chosen instead: Pali by the Buddhists and Ardhamagadhi by the Jains. (At a later period, though, Sanskrit texts were composed by members of both sects.)

There was yet a third new force active in Indian religion in the middle of the first millennium BC; but where Buddhism and Jainism were specific anti-brahmanical doctrines, the gradual emergence of Hinduism resulted mainly from the merging of Brahmanism with elements of popular religion, in particular the religion of the Kshatriya or warrior class. The first tangible evidence of this process is the great Sanskrit epic, the *Mahabharata*.

As it stands now, this gargantuan work consists (in the vulgate version) of approximately 100,000 stanzas, or about eight times the size of the *Iliad* and the *Odyssey* put together. But textual study clearly reveals that this vast bulk has been achieved through centuries of inflation and conflation, and that the original poem consisted of about 3000 stanzas in a single pre-classical meter (*trishtubh*). This poem told of a struggle for supremacy and inheritance between two sets of cousins, the Pandavas and the

Then the violent Bhima, remembering the acts of family-
hostility committed by the Kauravas,
leaped down from his chariot on to the ground, fixing his
eye eagerly upon Duhshasana.

Drawing his sharp sword with its excellent blade, and
treading upon the throat of the writhing man,
he cut open his breast as he lay on the ground, and drank
his warm blood.
Then, having quaffed and quaffed again, he looked up and
spoke these words in his excessive fury:

'Better than mother's milk, or honey with ghee, better than
well-prepared mead,
better than a draught of heavenly water, or milk or curd, or
the finest buttermilk,
today I consider this draught of the blood of my enemy
better than all of these!'

With these words he rushed forward once more, bounding
on in exhilaration after his drink;
and those who saw him then, they too fell down,
confounded with fear.

Mahabharata 8.61.5–8

Kauravas, with the divine Krishna (a 'new' god wholly unknown to the Vedas) siding with the former. Implicit in the story, but made explicit by later additions to it, was the further idea that the Pandavas were incarnate gods, the Kauravas incarnate demons; so that the conflict was a sort of earthly replay of the ancient cosmic battles between good and evil that are frequently spoken of in Vedic texts.

The process of assimilating this tale to Brahmanism took hundreds of years and hundreds of thousands of words. The additions were made mainly in the simple *shloka* or *anushtubh* meter, in an equally simple form of Sanskrit that was to become a standard style for later religious narrative-cum-instructional texts such as the Puranas. They contained elaborations of the main story and numerous new substories, but also many lengthy didactic passages, of which the best-known by far is the *Bhagavad-gita*. The process of inflation probably did not end until around 400 AD, by which time Brahmanism had absorbed and set its own mark on the religious ideas of the epic, and Hinduism had come into being.

The second great Sanskrit epic is the *Ramayana*, which tells the story of the divine Rama's banishment from his kingdom and his battle with the demon Ravana. About a quarter the size of the *Mahabharata*, it is said to be the work of one man, the sage Valmiki. With the exception of the first and last books and some other passages, scholars have tended to agree that single authorship is a real possibility; the text has certainly been added to, but not on the same scale as the *Mahabharata*, and it is thought that the process was much shorter and was over well before the larger epic achieved its final form. The style of the *Ramayana*, though in general comparable to the *Mahabharata*'s typically oral formulaic character, also contains passages of a more literary quality, so that it has often been seen as a transitional text standing at the threshold of the classical Sanskrit *belles lettres* tradition. This certainly fits in well with the Indian perception of the *Ramayana* as the *adikavya*, the first literary poem.

Panini and classical Sanskrit literature

The various technical literatures of Sanskrit have their origin in the *vedangas* or 'limbs' of the Vedas. These were six disciplines whose aim was to ensure the correct pronunciation and understanding of the Vedic texts and the correct performance of the Vedic rituals: phonetics, grammar, etymology, metrics, ritual practice and astronomy. Of these, the study of grammar was to have very far-reaching effects on the development of Sanskrit literature. In about the sixth century BC the famous grammarian Panini wrote a description of the Sanskrit language which many linguists even today feel has never been surpassed for accuracy, economy of expression and theoretical richness. By the third century BC, when the emperor Ashoka had many inscriptions carved, forms of middle Indo-Aryan had replaced

Sanskrit as the language of natural speech; and yet Sanskrit continued to be used for works of learning and literature until well into the Muslim period, and indeed has never fallen wholly out of use. Classical Sanskrit literature is thus written entirely in what would normally be thought of as a dead language, one whose lifespan was artificially and massively extended by Panini's codification of its grammar. It is a literature of courtly esthetes.

> The grammar-books all say that 'mind' is neuter,
> And so I thought it safe to let my mind
>   Salute her.
> But now it lingers in embraces tender:
> For Panini made a mistake, I find,
> In gender.

Subhashitaratnakosha 478, tr. John Brough.

The nature of any literature is largely determined by the nature of the language it is written in, and this must be especially true when the language is maintained only through literary use. A major feature of the Sanskrit language is its ability to form compound words, and classical authors took such compounds to extremes. They could use compounds to create large numbers of synonyms (a king is a lord-of-men, a protector-of-the-people, a supporter-of-the-earth, etc.), thus avoiding frequent repetition of common words; and they could indulge in verbal pyrotechnics by building long alliterative compounds, as when Banabhatta describes the river Mandakini as *tvangat-tunga-taranga-tarat-taralatara-tara-tarakam* 'with the stars twinkling brightly across her high-surging waves'. The history of classical Sanskrit literature is in general a story of ever-increasing reliance on such effects. What follows is a selection of some of the best-known authors and works forming part of that history; it must be emphasized that space forbids even a mention of many others with just as good a claim to be thought of as major contributors to the Sanskrit literary tradition.

The earliest extant classical works are those of the Buddhist author Ashvaghosha (first or possibly second century AD), a fact which in itself suggests the loss of earlier, brahmanically-orientated texts. From his hand we have two poetic texts, the *Saundarananda*, a story of conversion to Buddhism, and an incomplete 'Life of the Buddha' (*Buddhacharita*), also an incomplete drama telling another conversion-story. Ashvaghosha's style is at once simple and ornate: he favors straightforward syntax reinforced with descriptive compounds. A century or two later came the *Jatakamala* of Arya Shura, a collection of Buddhist birth-stories (*jatakas*) in a similarly easy style. The dramatist Bhasa, also dated to the third or fourth century AD, was the author of thirteen plays, many of them based on the *Mahabharata* and the *Ramayana* stories: by later standards sometimes crude, these works are nonetheless lively testaments to the vigor of the Sanskrit drama at a relatively early date.

There has never been any real dispute over who was the greatest Sanskrit poet and playwright: Kalidasa (probably fifth century AD), in whose work the elegant courtly style reaches maturity without straying into excessive complexity. His major works are the two court-epics *Kumarasambhava* ('Birth of the War-god') and *Raghuvansha* ('The dynasty of Raghu'), the well-loved narrative poem *Meghaduta* ('The cloud-messenger'), and the three plays *Malavikagnimitra*, *Vikramorvashiya* and *Abhijnanashakuntala* (often known simply as *Shakuntala*), all of which deal with the separation of star-crossed lovers and their final reunion. Kalidasa's works remain firmly within the bounds imposed by the conventions he inherited, but they illustrate what can be achieved in even a rigorously conventional style. His plays may have the compulsory happy ending demanded by tradition, but they are well-structured and well-characterized; his poetry may deal with standard themes and images, but it does so with real freshness and vitality of expression.

When, in the forest of their meditation,
The holy hermits saw the untimely spring,
Their minds were hard-pressed to resist temptation,
To keep their thoughts from Love's imagining.

When Love came there, his flower-bow ready stringing,
With fair Desire, his consort, at his side,
The forest creatures showed the passion springing
In every bridegroom's heart towards his bride.

From the same flower-cup which his love had savoured
The black bee sipped the nectar as a kiss;
While the black doe, by her own consort favoured,
Scratched by his antlers, closed her eyes in bliss.

The elephant with water lotus-scented
Sprayed her own lord, giving of love a token;
The wheel-drake, honouring his wife, presented
A half-chewed lotus-stalk which he had broken.

Kalidasa, *Kumarasambhava* 3.34–37, tr. John Brough.

Those who followed Kalidasa were often less restrained in their use of the Sanskrit language. In the field of the courtly epic the major later authors were Bharavi, Magha and Bhatti, all of whom took as their themes stories from the *Mahabharata* or the *Ramayana*. In their works, and those of other minor authors in the genre, cleverness takes over from elegance: unusual grammatical forms are paraded, ambiguous language used to produce stanzas with more than one interpretation, and other such devices. Similar developments took place in the drama, leading to the barely comprehensible intricacies of Bhavabhuti (though it should be said

that other dramatists, such as Harsha and Vishakhadatta, succeeded in avoiding these excesses). A style of narrative prose began with Dandin's mildly ornate *Dashakumaracharita*, but soon succumbed to the same stylistic extremism in Banabhatta's (admittedly brilliant) *Harshacharita*.

No end-date can be cited for classical Sanskrit literature, which continues to be produced by small numbers of enthusiasts even to the present day. But by the time of the establishment of Muslim rule in North India the artificiality of writing courtly literature in a dead language was becoming evident, and creative authors began instead to express themselves in the various vernaculars.

JDS

Further reading

J. Brough, *Poems from the Sanskrit* (Harmondsworth, 1968)
M. Coulson, *Three Sanskrit Plays* (Harmondsworth, 1981)
J. Gonda, *Vedic Literature* (Wiesbaden, 1975)
A. B. Keith, *A History of Sanskrit Literature* (Oxford, 1920)
A. B. Keith, *The Sanskrit Drama* (Oxford, 1924)
S. Lienhard, *A History of Classical Poetry Sanskrit-Pali-Prakrit* (Wiesbaden, 1984)
W. D. O'Flaherty, *The Rig Veda* (Harmondsworth, 1981)
J. D. Smith, 'Old Indian: the Two Sanskrit Epics', in A.T. Hatto (gen. Ed.), *Traditions of Heroic and Epic Poetry* Vol. 1 (London, 1980)

Persian

Persian was brought to India as the main administrative and literary language of Islam by the Turkish warlord, Mahmud of Ghazna (998–1030), in whose court much early literary Persian talent had come to be concentrated. Throughout the succeeding centuries of its rule over even greater areas of South Asia, the Muslim élite

South Asia in the world of Persian culture.

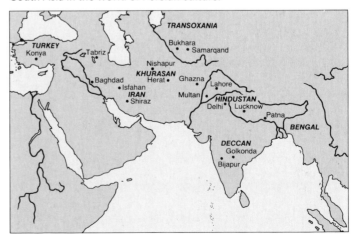

remained highly conscious of its integral membership of the cultural world of eastern Islam, having Persian as its lingua franca and the cultivation of Persian literature at the heart of its civilization. Ties with other parts of this world, stretching at its greatest extent from Istanbul to Bengal, were continually reinforced by immigration from Iran and central Asia, and the integration of indigenous talent (whether from Muslim converts or special Hindu groups such as the Kashmiri Pandits or the Kayasths) into the élite culture of Indian Islam was facilitated by a command of Persian.

This twin pattern, necessarily involving a continued emphasis on the cultural supremacy of Iran over India, endured until the collapse of Muslim political supremacy in South Asia in the eighteenth century, rapidly followed in the nineteenth by the removal of Persian from its long role as the dominant pan-South Asian language in favor of its modern successors, whether English, Urdu or Hindi. Similar contractions elsewhere have reduced the once vast extent of Persian to its present territory in Iran, Afghanistan and Soviet Tajikistan.

Persian and Indo-Persian

The former spread of Persian as a lingua franca was certainly aided by its very simple grammar. Although its debt to Arabic extends beyond both script and a huge number of loan-words to incorporate some inflectional pattern, there are, for instance, no genders nor even separate words for 'he, she, it', and the simple inflexion of nouns and verbs makes classical Persian a language more comparable to English than, for instance, to Hindi, let alone the formidably complex classical Sanskrit.

In northern India, the diffusion of Persian was further facilitated by the Indo-European heritage which it shares with the quite closely related Indo-Aryan languages. As is illustrated by the later history of English in South Asia, however, intrinsic simplicity of linguistic structure may belie innumerable subtleties of pronunciation and idiom. Persian was, after all, an acquired language for all but the most recently arrived South Asian Muslims, and it came to be transmitted in an increasingly old-fashioned 'Indian accent', disagreeable to Iranian ears.

When account is also taken of the stylistic crudities of its less sophisticated practitioners and the fantastic complexities achieved by its most elaborate authors, it is not surprising that chauvinistic Iranian taste should generally have disparaged the vast literary heritage of Indo-Persian, whose bulk much surpasses the Persian literature produced in Iran itself. Although continuing to refer of necessity to the indispensable Persian histories of medieval South Asia, Western writers too, in their search for the 'real India', have similarly felt able to disregard Indo-Persian literature, which consequently remains one of the most seriously underappreciated of the great literatures of Asia.

Classical Persian literature

The range of classical Persian literature is most easily outlined by reference to its classical canon, almost entirely the work of Iranian writers and substantially formalized by the late fourteenth century, since the early Indo-Persian writing which pre-dates this formulation played little part in its making.

As in Iran, central Asia and Turkey, the schoolboys of Muslim India for centuries began their formal study of Persian with the *Gulistan* ('Rose-garden') of Saadi of Shiraz (d. 1291), whose interspersion of cynical prose anecdotes with gnomic verses provides a bewitching introduction to the ambiguities of even the simplest Persian style. Thence they would proceed to the collected poetry (*divan*) of Hafiz (d. 1389), also from Shiraz, and the acknowledged master of the *ghazal*, the premier Persian poetic genre. This is a short lyric of self-contained rhymed couplets which collectively blend the themes of a love-poem with those of a drinking-song, through an elaborately defined poetic vocabulary drawing exclusively upon Iranian landscape for its scenic reference (as in the famous antithesis between *gul* 'the rose' and *bulbul* 'the nightingale'). The equivocal evocativeness of the ghazal is further enhanced by repeated reference to Sufi doctrines of mystical adoration, not to speak of exploitation of the ambiguities inherent in the absence of grammatical gender in Persian.

Talented students were thereafter faced with a dazzling array of examples for future emulation, whether of elaborate formal prose (*insha*) or of the carefully defined classical genres of poetry. Prime models for the technically demanding courtly ode of praise (*qasida*) were provided by Anvari (d. 1191) and Khaqani (d. 1199), or for the narration of romantic themes in elaborate rhymed couplets (*masnavi*) by Nizami (d. 1200). Besides these, the enormously prestigious *Divan* and *Masnavi* of Jalal ud Din (d. 1273), the founder of the 'whirling' Mevlevi dervishes known in India as Maulana-e Rum ('Our Lord of Turkey'), provided continual inspiration to the many poets who were drawn to the practice of Sufism rather than to service at court, not to speak of those who combined both.

Early Indo-Persian literature

The first Muslim courts in South Asia attracted a number of talented poets to Lahore in the eleventh and twelfth centuries. But it is the period of the Delhi Sultanate's glory around 1300 which marks the zenith of early Indo-Persian literature, which was inspired equally by the power of the Sultans and the spiritual authority of Khwaja Nizam ud Din Auliya (d. 1325), the patron saint of Muslim Delhi.

A passionate concern with historiography marks one of the most significant contrasts between Indo-Persian and Sanskrit literature. A fine early example of the Persian histories which chronicle the expansion of Muslim power is the *Tarikh-e Firozshahi* by the conservative cleric Barani (d. *c.* 1358). An equally popular genre of Indo-Persian prose writing were the conversations of Sufi saints (*malfuzat*) recorded by their disciples, and much is to be learnt from the attractive *Favaid ul Fuad* compiled by Nizam ud Din's disciple, Amir Hasan (d. 1328), who was also a mystic poet.

> Rare was the mine which yielded that gem,
> Who for this single verse gave up his soul:
> 'All those whom Resignation's dagger slays
> 'By Unseen power are ever new made whole.'

From Amir Hasan, celebrating the death of a noted Sufi through the ecstasy provoked by hearing a famous Persian verse. [Persian text from Lawrence, op. cit., p. 23]

The Persian literature of the Sultanate is, however, dominated by his friend and co-disciple Amir Khusrau (1253–1325), the one Indian-born poet to be generally regarded on the same footing as the Iranian masters. His purely poetic achievement, which has earned him the title of Tuti-e Hind ('The Parrot of India'), is astonishing enough in terms of both the quantity and the quality of his ghazals and his numerous masnavi poems, which embrace both the classic romantic themes and elaborate courtly histories. Since he was also the author of manuals of formal prose and a noted innovator in Hindustani music, it is hardly surprising that his name should in one way or another be invoked as a father-figure in the discussion of almost every aspect of Indo-Muslim culture.

The Mughal period

The early successes of the conquering Muslim armies brought Persian as a colonial language to all regions of the subcontinent except the extreme south, and local Sultans encouraged the cultivation of many regional traditions of Persian poetry and historical writing. But the early masterpieces of Amir Khusrau and his contemporaries were only matched as a result of the lavish patronage of the Mughal emperors and the contemporary rulers in the Deccan, whose shared enthusiasm for Persian literature encouraged the flowering of both indigenous and imported genius.

The proudly remembered central Asian origins of the first Mughal emperor Babur (d. 1530) are reflected in the choice of his native Turki for his vivid autobiography, although the *Baburnama* was soon made more widely available through Persian translations. Babur's personal literary talent is reflected in the Persian memoirs composed by later generations of the imperial family, including the delightfully naive *Humayunnama* by his daughter, the princess Gulbadan, and the ironically self-justificatory *Tuzuk* of her great-nephew, the emperor Jahangir (d. 1627).

The determining influence of royal whim which characterizes the Mughal heyday of Indo-Persian literature was never more obvious

Abul Fazl presenting the manuscript of the official record of Akbar's reign to the emperor himself.

than during the long reign of Akbar (1556–1605). The erratic brilliance of the illiterate emperor emerges equally from the panegyrics of the poet-laureate Faizi (d. 1595), the official record of the *Akbarnama* by his brother, the court historian Abul Fazl, and even such critical histories as the *Muntakhab ut Tavarikh* by Badauni, whose orthodoxy was outraged by his enforced employment in the translation from Sanskrit into Persian of Hindu texts on which Akbar set much store. Continued later by Akbar's great-grandson, the ecumenically minded prince Dara Shikoh (d. 1659), these versions not only inspired superb illustrations in the miniatures of the imperial artists who gave the translators' text its finished form, but also later played a crucial part in disseminating the contents of sacred Hindu literature in Europe, before western scholarship finally came to terms with the complexities of the Sanskrit originals in the nineteenth century.

During the formative period 1560–1660 itself, however, the attention of contemporary observers of the Indo-Persian literary scene was drawn to more immediately spectacular developments. These stemmed from the attraction of the munificent patronage of the Mughals and the sovereigns of the Deccan to generations of ambitious Iranian talent, including such poets as the young genius Urfi (d. 1591), the lyrical Naziri (d. 1612), the elaborate prose-writer Zuhuri (d. 1615), or the epigrammatical Saib (d. 1677). In collaboration with such local masters as Ghani of Kashmir (d. 1611), these poets created in the favorable conditions of the Muslim courts of South Asia, which were then the America of Persian literature, the excitingly new idiom known as the *sabk-e hindi* or 'Indian style'.

The term should not be taken to imply any adaptation of Iranian norms to take account of Indian themes (which seldom appear in Indo-Persian art-literature after Amir Khusrau's time). The 'Indian style' in fact refers to an extreme exploitation of the material of the classical tradition in a baroque intellectual fashion, involving the fantastic elaboration of traditional imagery. It thus reflects the artificial brilliance of Indo-Muslim courtly culture at the point of its imminent collapse, rather than the realities of the South Asian scene. Subsequent political and literary developments, not to speak of its intrinsic difficulty, have done much to obscure the achievements of writers in the 'Indian style'. But its ultimate master, Bedil of Patna (d. 1721), whose unbelievable exploration of the furthest reaches of Persian style is best glimpsed in the stunning prose and elaborate verses of his spiritual autobiography, the *Chahar Unsur*, continued to have a wide following in Afghanistan and central Asia, and a considerable influence upon the subsequent development of Urdu poetry in India.

So long by this world made so slender and doubled am I;
Now make me an anklet to wrap round the foot of a fly.

A typically exaggerated couplet from a ghazal of Bedil [Persian text in A. Ghani, op. cit., p. 139].

The death of Indo-Persian

The policies of orthodox Islamization followed by Aurangzeb, during whose reign (1658–1707) the post of poet-laureate was abolished, had already affected the cultivation of Persian literature before the wars of the eighteenth century destroyed the political and cultural supremacy of the Muslims in South Asia. The British were for a while content to exploit the Indo-Persian heritage of their Mughal predecessors, and found much of their most immediate access to the culture and institutions of their new subjects through the helpful medium of Persian-speaking informants. But the official use of Persian by Britons to rule Indians in the Company's realms became increasingly artificial, and was finally abolished in 1835.

Even the shaken Muslim élite itself kept little faith with its Persian heritage. Its decline is largely evoked in the Urdu poetry which came to replace Persian as the voice of courtly Indo-Muslim culture in the eighteenth century, and as the medium of the prose literature in which the future destiny of the Muslims of South Asia was to be so fiercely argued in the nineteenth.

Among the few figures which stood out against this general trend was Ghalib (1797–1869), now regarded as the greatest Urdu poet, but in his own aristocratic estimation rather to be remembered for his resurrection of the most chaste tradition of Indo-Persian poetry, and who distracted himself from the horrors of the Mutiny uprising of 1857 in Delhi by composing the Persian prose memoir *Dastanbu*, which achieves the difficult feat of avoiding the use of any Arabic loan-word. An heroic achievement on a quite different later scale is marked by the huge energy put into his Persian poetry, under the influence of pan-Islamic ideas, by Iqbal (1877–1938), who is similarly remembered in Pakistan for his Urdu verse, but whose majestic re-creation of Dante's *Divine Comedy* in his *Javednama* represents the epic swan-song of Indo-Persian literature.

CS

Further reading

A. Ghani, *Life and Works of Abdul Qadir Bedil* (Lahore, 1960)
M. Iqbal, *Javid-nama*, trans. A. J. Arberry (London, 1966)
B. B. Lawrence, *Notes from a distant flute: Sufi literature in pre-Mughal India* (Tehran, 1978)
R. J. Rypka *History of Iranian Literatures* (Dordrecht, 1968)
A. Schimmel, *Islamic Literatures of India* (Wiesbaden, 1973)

English

The literatures of India, Pakistan and Sri Lanka written in English share a common ancestry, but they have developed in diverse directions and show little mutual interaction.

India

The earliest Indian practitioners of English prose, like Rammohan Roy, used English to plead the case of a Western education for India and the reform of Indian society. They were followed by others in the nineteenth century whose examination of Indian history, philosophy and economy established them as leading thinkers and nationalists.

The tradition of using English prose for nationalistic and scholarly purposes was effectively carried on in the first half of the twentieth century by M. K. Gandhi (*Hind Swaraj*) translated from Gujarati by the author in 1910, besides numerous articles), Rabindranath Tagore (*The Religion of Man* 1930), S. Radhakrishnan (*The Idealist View of Life* 1932), and Jawaharlal Nehru (*An Autobiography* 1936). Nevertheless, the fact that English was an imported language had adverse consequences for Indo-English poetry and fiction. In the nineteenth century, poets like Henry Louis, Vivian Derozio and Michael Madhusudan Dutt found their desire to give voice to their Indian sentiments smothered by the influence of the British Romantics, only Toru Dutt succeeding, in 'Our Casuarina Tree', in capturing nostalgia for a lost home and childhood; and no novelist was successfully able to adapt a foreign literary genre to the realities of Indian life. The best, like Bankim Chandra Chatterjee, turned from English to their mother tongues. In the first half of the twentieth century Aurobindo Ghose (*Savitri* 1950–51), although truly original and ambitious with his subject matter, wrote in a style at once archaic and inflated, while the lyrically gifted Sarojini Naidu was never able to free herself from the influence of British poetry of the 1880s and 1890s. Only Tagore achieved distinction, and won the Nobel Prize in 1913, for his English translation of *Gitanjali*.

The next generation of Indian writers had, therefore, no authentic tradition to draw on. Novelists like Mulk Raj Anand chose the path of social realism, while the experimental Raja Rao tried in *Kanthapura* (1938) to Indianize English by recreating in it the rhythms and structure of a Kannada folktale; *The Serpent and the Rope* (1960) is based on *Advaita* philosophy and contains many poetic evocations of India. The equally experimental G. V. Desani (*All About Mr. Hatterr* 1948) plays with language and mixes styles to create a comic fantasy. Fantasy is not absent in R. K. Narayan (*The Maneater of Malgudi* 1961), but it is as the creator of the fictional Malgudi, and as a sharp and comic observer of middle-class life, that he is best known. Several later novelists like Bhabani Bhattacharya, Manohar Malgonkar and Chaman Nahal have found their subjects in Indian history, and Arun Biswas in the alienation that the westernized Indian experiences. While history, politics and social change also interest women novelists like Kamala Markandaya and Nayantara Sahgal, the best like Ruth Prawer Jhabvala and Anita Desai deal with the East–West encounter or pose existential questions. Jhabvala is also internationally known as the scriptwriter for Ismail Merchant and James Ivory's films.

Modern Indo-English poetry, which began in the 1950s, thanks partly to the encouragement provided by P. Lal's Writers' Workshop, soon shook off the influence of Eliot and Auden in favor of a quest for an Indian identity and a poetic idiom in which it could be expressed. India is the subject of this poetry, but the poets view it ironically, bitterly or surreally. Nissim Ezekiel writes to come to terms with his environment, Jayanta Mahapatra meditates on his home State of Orissa. A. K. Ramanujan is concerned with his Hindu heritage and family relationships, Arun Kolatkar with a dialogue between agnostic modernism and superstitious Hinduism. R. Parthasarathy and Adil Jussawalla are concerned with the problems of returning home after a long stay abroad, Kamala Das with her sexuality, Keki Daruwalla with violence and Gieve Patel with belonging to an India minority. Arvind Krishna Mehrotra is playful, surrealistic and disciplined, and Pritish Nandy exuberant, violent, and sometimes deeply moving.

Nirad C. Chaudhuri, outstanding writer of non-fiction prose, whose second volume of autobiography, *Thy Hand Great Anarch!: India 1921–1952* was published in 1987.

Nirad C. Chaudhuri is India's greatest living writer of non-fiction prose. He is erudite, provocative, and writes an English which constantly calls attention to its perfection. His earliest work, *The Autobiography of an Unknown Indian* (1951), is also his most well-known book. Several journalists and civil servants have written informatively and wittily about their experiences, but no prose writers possess the caliber of those of pre-Independence days.

Indo-English dramatists' achievement is representative neither of India's rich dramatic tradition nor of the vitality of regional and folk drama. Before 1947 the best drama in English consisted of a few plays of Tagore which the author had translated into English. In recent years the work of Pratap Sharma, Asif Currimbhoy and Gurcharan Das has had some success on the stage, but the best drama available in English remains Girish Karnad's translations from Kannada of his *Tughlaq* (1972) and *Hayavadana* (1975).

Pakistan

Although Ahmad Ali (*Twilight in Delhi* 1940) opted for Pakistan in 1947, there was a dearth of creative writing in that country for a decade and a half following its establishment. Before creative writing could begin the new nation had to forge a sense of its identity; this task was undertaken by scholars who investigated Pakistan's history, sociology and economics, studied Islamic law, theology and philosophy, and produced biographies of Muhammad Ali Jinnah.

A scene from *My Beautiful Laundrette*; script by the Pakistani playwright, Hanif Kureishi.

Unfortunately, just as creative writing began to appear in collections like Shahid Hosain's edition of *First Voices: Six Poets from Pakistan* (1965), the downgrading of the role of English in education and in government, and the loss of democracy, acted as a curb on development. Some of the best writers migrated to the West. Of those remaining, Bapsi Sidhwa has achieved recognition with *The Crow Eaters* (1978), a comic novel about the Parsis, while *The Bride* (1982) offers a darker vision of the fate of women.

Poetry has thrived better, in part perhaps because its need for social comment is less pressing, and in part because it enables politics to be treated more obliquely. Maki Kureishi is lucid, musical and occasionally profound. Daud Kamal is exploratory and cerebral, and G. Allana is mystical. Taufiq Rafat's shorter poems are often anthologized, but his best work consists of his translation (1982) of the Panjabi mystic poet Bullhe Shah.

The most significant Pakistani writing in English comes from Pakistanis living abroad. The playwright Hanif Kureishi achieved striking success with the film script of *My Beautiful Laundrette* (1986), which deals with the themes of homosexuality and race relations in Britain. Alamgir Hashmi is an experimental, iconoclastic and modern poet; the half dozen collections of his works published in the last decade exhibit a steadily maturing talent. Zulfikar Ghose's three-part novel *The Incredible Brazilian* (1972–79) was followed by *A New History of Torments* (1983) and *Don Bueno* (1983). Set mostly in South America, these works have complex themes and use fairytale elements.

Salman Rushdie is, like Ghose, influenced by Gabriel Garcia Marquez, but is different from both. The comic and brilliantly inventive *Midnight's Children* (1982), winner of the Booker Prize, combines memory, satire and a feel for detail with an interpretation of India's history since Independence, and excels at the recreation of a variety of regional inflections and accents. *Shame* (1984) is set in Pakistan. The humor and fantasy work less well, but political satire remains sharp. Rushdie's work has proved tremendously popular in India, a country with which he identifies more than with Pakistan.

Sri Lanka

In nineteenth-century Sri Lanka James Alwis translated Sinhala works into English, and in the 1920s Ananda Kentish Coomaraswami gained a reputation with treatises on ancient Hindu art. Somewhat later Jinadasa Vijayatunga published a novel (*Grass for my Feet* 1935) as well as collections of verse, the painter George Keyt brought out *Poems* (1936), and M. J. Tambimuttu became well known as editor of *Poetry London*.

At Independence Sri Lanka had the highest standards of English in South Asia. Its replacement by Sinhala as the official language in 1956, and the economic hardships and political violence in the years that followed, caused a number of English teachers and writers to migrate and raised fears that English writing in Sri Lanka was doomed. But it has proved remarkably resilient.

The posthumous publication in 1984 of Patrick Fernando's *Selected Poems* establishes him as Sri Lanka's leading English poet. The poems, several of which were written in the 1950s and 1960s, reveal a man of wide culture attuned to nature and happiest in the recesses of his private world. His successors have charted different courses. The bilingual Lakdasa Wikkamasinha is ironical and denounces colonialism, Michael Ondaatje and Peter Scharen capture, in different ways, the memories of their Sri Lankan experiences from abroad, while Yasmine Goonaratne, also an expatriate, is concerned with exile, 'resonance . . . depth and echoes', and occasionally uses indigenous poetic forms to express contemporary tensions. Anne Ranasinghe uses poetry to understand her German past. Other poets include Ashley Halpé, Jean Arasanagam, and, among the younger writers, Praema Da Norman, Manel Abhayaratne, Alfreda de Silva, Eustace Gunawardena, and Rajan Perera.

Sri Lankan poetry has variety and energy, but lacks so far an identifiable tradition. However, in fiction a set of common concerns, if not a tradition, is discernible. These concerns can be defined as an attempt to convey what it is like to live in rural areas. The theme of social realism, found in Leonard Woolf's *The Village in the Jungle* (1913), still regarded by some as a Sri Lankan classic, receives further treatment in Punyakante Wijenaike's *The Waiting Earth* (1966) and the novella *Giraya* (1971). Both works use standard English to capture a local sensibility. Wijenaike has been followed by James Goonewardene (*A Quiet Place* 1969), the Sinhala playwright Ediriwira Sarachchandra, whose *Curfew and a Full Moon* (1978) deals with the impact of the 1971 insurgency on academic life, Hubert Weerasooriya, who sets *The Tamil Lady and the Sinhala Lawyer* (1982) in the period just after Independence, R. B. Tammita, who deals, in *The House to Let* (1982), with life at the turn of the century, and Dagmar Jayawardene, whose posthumous *Pale Hands* (1983) is a study of rural life in the colonial period. M. Chandrasoma (*Out Out Brief Candle* 1981) and Raja Proctor (*Waiting for Surabiel* 1981) combine Sri Lankan history with a commentary on social mores. Novelists writing on themes other than social include Arthur C. Clarke and Mark Bartholomeuz.

The best of Sri Lankan writing is to be found in short stories, partly because several literary periodicals in the country provide the short-story writer with a readier access to the reading public, and partly also perhaps because the short story has proved more suitable for capturing vignettes of an island society. Most novelists – such as Mark Bartholomeuz, James Goonewardene, Raja Proctor, Jinadasa Vijayatunga and Punyakante Wijenaike – are also short-story writers; some, like Vijayatunga, Wijenaike and Proctor, have published more than one collection; a few, like Wijenaike, write in Sinhala as well as in English. Chitra Fernando's stories are well crafted and show a concern for feminist issues. A representative sample of Sri Lankan stories has been collected by Yasmine Goonaratne in *Stories from Sri Lanka* (1979).

E. F. C. Ludowyck's farce *He Comes from Jafna* is still popular on the stage, and Lucien de Zoyza's *Fortress in the Sky* (1956) is sometimes revived. Ernest MacIntyre's *The Education of Miss Asia* (1971) deals with political upheaval. The recent violence between Sinhalese and Tamils has stirred the conscience of Sri Lankan writers in English, but it is too early to say how it will affect literary activity.

Bangladesh has not yet produced significant literature in English, and creative writing in English is not much practiced in Nepal, Bhutan or the Maldives.

PS

Further reading

J. B. Alphonso-Karkala, *Indo-English Literature in the Nineteenth Century* (Mysore, 1970)

Journal of Commonwealth Literature (1965–   )

Journal of South Asian Literature (formerly *Mahfil. A Quarterly of South Asian Literature*) (1963–72)

M. K. Naik, *A History of Indian English Literature* (New Delhi, 1982)

R. Obeyesekere and C. Fernando, Eds, *An Anthology of Modern Writing from Sri Lanka* (Tucson, Arizona, 1981)

R. Parthasarathy, Ed., *Ten Twentieth-Century Indian Poets* (New Delhi, 1976)

A. Singh, V. Rajiva and I. M. Joshi, Eds, *Indian Literature in English, 1827–1979: A Guide to Information Sources* (Detroit, 1981)

K. R. Srinivasa Iyengar, *Indian Writing in English* 3rd edn (New Delhi, 1983)

Literature: regional languages

North and center: Hindi

In the modern context, the term 'Hindi' usually designates India's national language, which shares with Urdu a basis in the Khari Boli dialect of the Delhi region. In the medieval context, however, the term covers a spectrum of dialects including (from west to east) Rajasthani, Braj Bhasha, Bhojpuri, Avadhi and Maithili; and it is as the vehicle of the major revered texts of North Indian Hinduism, from Gujarat and Panjab in the west to Bihar in the east, that the importance of these forms of Hindi survives in the modern age.

Early beginnings

Among surviving examples from the thirteenth century, when Hindi first emerged from its Apabhransha antecedents, are the ballads and heroic chronicles of the bards of Rajasthan. Some folk epics and poems such as the *Dhola Maru* and the tale of Lorik, still current today, derive from oral versions from this period. The attribution to the Persian poet Amir Khusrau of a collection of Hindi verses suggests that a seminal tradition of sophisticated versification in Hindi existed by *c.* 1300, and serves to remind us also that the interweaving of Hindu and Islamic traditions was a prominent feature of the early literature of Hindi. This eclectic tendency is seen most clearly in the Sufi romances written in Avadhi from the fourteenth century, and culminating later in the *Padmavat* (*c.* 1540) of Malik Muhammad 'Jayasi'; such works are complex allegorical romances, incorporating both Islamic and yogic symbolism.

More recognizably 'Hindu' preoccupations were to inform the mainstream literary traditions of Hindi as they moved towards their period of maturity in the fifteenth and sixteenth centuries. Vernacular poetry found an important new role in expressing the sentiments and theologies of devotional religion (*bhakti*), which saw an unprecedented popular advance at this time. While often resting on well-established theological and mythological bases, the new wave of bhakti was also typified by a directness and an unorthodoxy which was to re-draw the priorities of religious thought and practice.

The Sants

Nowhere was this new consciousness more prominent than in the striking verse of the 'Sant' poets, whose monism found no room for brahminical orthodoxy or the traditional stratifications of Hindu society. The Sant tradition is most fully represented by the great mystic poet Kabir, who flourished in Benares in the fifteenth century. A Muslim weaver by birth, and connected by tradition with the great Hindu theologian Ramananda, he dismissed as mischievous folly the dogma and external observances of both Hinduism and Islam, insisting that the true search for God must be an inner one, accompanied by contemplation on the divine Name. The commonplace attribution to Kabir of a syncretistic intention is, however, ill-founded. Kabir's verse is preserved by various distinct recensions, including one within the Sikh tradition; he is best known for his rough-hewn and often derisive couplets, called *sakhi* ('witness'), still to be heard on many lips today.

Vaishnava poetry

The so-called *nirgun* theological stance of the Sants, based on a conception of the divine as being 'without qualities' (that is, fully transcendental and formless), is contrasted with the *sagun* approach of devotees of Vishnu, envisaged as a qualified and benevolent deity.

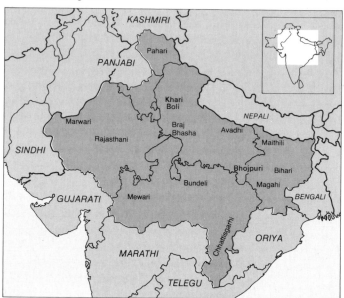

Hindi-speaking area.

Vaishnav tradition ascribes to the gods Rama and Krishna the fully divine nature of Vishnu himself, of whom they are incarnate forms; while fueled by a widespread popular following, this manifold tradition rests on mythologies inherited from classical sources, suitably transmogrified in order to accommodate the priorities of an intensely emotional style of devotional religion.

The greatest poet of Rama-bhakti was Tulsidas (1532–1623), the glory of his age and indeed of the whole of Hindi literature. Of the dozen works ascribed to him it is the *Ramcharitmanas*, the 'Hindi *Ramayana*', upon which his reputation principally rests; woven into its narrative fabric of Rama's defeat of the demonic king Ravana is a wide-ranging body of spiritual and moral teaching which has made this text the unrivalled 'Bible of Northern India'. The supremacy of the *Ramcharitmanas* has been underpinned by its constant use as the textual basis of the *Ramlila*, a vastly popular tradition of dramatic enactment of the Rama story in a 'miracle play' setting which bridges the gap between classical text and folk-tradition. Tulsi presents not only an ideal model for Hindu society but also a devotional theology firmly based on orthodox *smarta* Hinduism. For Tulsi, the name 'Rama' designates not merely the epic hero as a living symbol of righteous action, but also the divine principle itself, transcending the traditional nirgun/sagun taxonomy. The language in which the *Ramcharitmanas* is so skilfully composed (largely in alternating quatrains and couplets, well suited to prolonged recitation) is Avadhi, the dialect of Rama's 'home country' of Ayodhya.

The traditions of Krishna-bhakti have as their starting point the vivid and sensual stories of the divine cowherd-prince Krishna

Gopala. A huge body of literature to Krishna was written in Braj Bhasha, the language of Krishna's earthly home of Braj (between Delhi and Agra); and from the sixteenth century on, this dialect became the literary language *par excellence* over the whole Hindi-speaking area. Antecedents such as the lyrics of the fourteenth century Maithili poet Vidyapati provided models for a vast outpouring of devotional and theological Krishnaite literature, based on puranic traditions but also incorporating new developments such as a fervently reverential attitude to a Radha made divine as Krishna's consort. A typical poetic form was the *pad* or lyric hymn, whose most highly valued examples are found in the *Sursagar* attributed to the blind poet Surdas. Though it now seems unlikely that Surdas composed more than a small proportion of this voluminous anthology, his reputation as the exemplar of Krishna devotees, guaranteed by an efficient sectarian hagiography which connects him with the sect of Vallabhacharya (1479–1531) and with a group of eight poets known as the *ashtachhap*, is secure in the popular memory. Early manuscripts of the *Sursagar* have a high proportion of poems on the perennial theme of 'love in separation' (*virah*), here appearing as a plangent lament in the mouths of Krishna's *gopis* or cowgirl lovers, but some of Surdas's most famous poems, such as the delicate and subtle celebrations of Krishna as a divine child, may in fact be the work of later generations.

Among Surdas's contemporaries was Mirabai, a Rajput princess whose poems (transmitted variously in Braj Bhasha, Rajasthani and Gujarati guise) bear the impress of an ardently felt personal longing for Krishna as lover. Raskhan, a Muslim convert to Krishna-bhakti, is principally remembered for his rhythmic quatrains treating of the gopis. Nanddas, allegedly another member of the *ashtachhap* group,

> I have told you the story as best I am able
> though at first I had chosen to keep it well hid;
> When I saw the extent of your heart-felt devotion
> I recited the story of Ram.
>
> It is not to be told to the false or perverse folk
> who pay no attention to Hari's pure sport;
> nor yet to the covetous, wrathful or lustful
> who adore not the Lord of the world.
>
> Let it not be disclosed to a harmer of Brahmins
> though he be of the rank of the lord of the gods.
> None but they are deserving of Ram's sacred story
> who cherish communion with saints.
>
> Those who serve well the Brahmins are fit for this story,
> intent on their teachers' feet, righteous of heart;
> and to him above all will this story be joyful
> who loves Ram as he loves his own soul.

From the *Ramcharitmanas* of Tulsidas.

wrote elegant adaptations of puranic Krishnaite material. The tradition of *rasik* poets, 'connoisseurs of the spirit' who spurned the generalities of puranic Krishna-mythology the better to concentrate on the love-sports of Krishna and Radha, was represented by Hit Harivansh and Svami Haridas, both closely associated with temple traditions.

Riti poetry

Mythological themes were maintained in *riti* poetry, though with reduced concentration on their devotional aspect, as popular subject matter in a style of poetry which exploited the full armory of rhetorical conceits inherited from Sanskrit poetics. This loosely defined genre of Braj Bhasha verse, dubbed riti or 'mannerist' poetry, was given a scholarly basis by the brilliant Keshavdas, whose major works *Rasik-priya* (1591) and *Ram-candrika* (1600) have as their formal basis the Krishna and Rama stories, respectively. Keshav's large output, typical of its age, includes panegyrics to royal patrons, moralistic verse, technical treatises on poetics, and elaborate classifications of the various different categories of hero and heroine.

This so-called riti tradition found its master in Biharilal, whose exquisite *Satsai* or 'Seven centuries' of piquant couplets were written under the patronage of the court of Jai Singh in the first half of the seventeenth century. Bihari's verse, less self-consciously academic than Keshav's, has remained popular to this day. Following chronologically the major traditions of bhakti poetry (which it in no way superseded), it represented a return to a naturally catholic cultural view in which Hindu and Muslim elements complement one another.

The traditions of devotional, courtly and rhetorical verse which evolved during this 'classical' period continued to develop up to the nineteenth century, often under the patronage of the courts of Orcha, Gwalior, and of the kingdoms of Rajasthan. But these developments were typified by the elaboration of existing themes rather than the cultivation of new ones; and no major change of direction took place until the early eighteen-hundreds, when the influence of Western culture began to be felt.

The nineteenth century: a period of transition

The nineteenth century saw experimentation with various new styles and forms, whose spread was aided by the development of vernacular printing. Although the old literary conventions were long to be maintained in the realm of poetry, where Braj Bhasha and its rarefied, other-worldly themes still reigned supreme, the evolution of a middle-class readership educated on the Western pattern generated a demand for a more pragmatic literature. This need was met by the development of prose literature, hitherto a rarity, written in a Sanskritized style of the Khari Boli dialect (upon which base a

Persianized style had already developed as 'Urdu').

Because of the British presence in Calcutta, it was through Bengal (and the intermediary of Bengali literature) that the first impact of English literature fell on Hindi. The experimental use of Khari Boli prose under British auspices at Fort William College was later developed by the short-lived but prolific writer Harishcandra of Benares (1850–1885). Dubbed 'Bharatendu' ('moon of India'), Harishcandra pioneered Hindi essay-writing, journalism and drama both through his own work and through patronage of other writers, and helped to imbue literature with a new political and social purpose; his creative leadership alleviated the adverse effect of policies adopted in the 1830s, in which English and Urdu were adopted as the vehicles for education and administration, respectively.

Illustration of poems by Surdas, Mewar (Rajasthan) c.1720. The blind poet is depicted in the bottom right-hand corner.

Twentieth-century literature

The modern tradition of narrative prose in Hindi owes more to Western literature than to its own antecedents, the fables and fantasies which gained a wide readership with the development of the printing press. Yet a concern for the maintainance of Hindu values often underlay the polemical didacticism of the early twentieth-century novels; and this concern anticipated the social consciousness pervading the fiction of Prem Chand (1880–1936), whose work laid the foundation for the modern Hindi novel and short story. Prem Chand excelled in the close observation of character, particularly in the rural settings which predominate in his best stories and in his masterpiece, the novel *Godan* (1936). His language exploits both ends of the stylistic spectrum available to the writer of modern Hindi by embracing both Sanskrit loan-words and the Perso-Arabic vocabulary which continues to hold a natural place in the modern language. Prem Chand's neo-Dickensian concentration on the evils of society, with untouchability a specific target, reflects the ethical position of Gandhism which dominated northern India in the years before Independence; and if his idealism may strike later readers as somewhat naive, there can be no doubt that Prem Chand's finger lay surely on the pulse of the turbulent times in which he wrote.

These developments in fiction were paralleled in poetry by a new style pioneered by Mahavir Prasad Dwivedi. Themes of nationalism and social reform denoted a clear break with the figurative Braj Bhasha poetic tradition, and an interest in symbolic nature poetry showed the influence of the English Romantics on poets such as Shridhar Pathak (1859–1928) and Maithilisharan Gupta (1886–1964). The modern treatment of the Krishna legend in the epic

Prem Chand who laid the foundations of the modern Hindi novel and short story.

poem *Priyapravas* (1914) which brought recognition to Ayodhyasinh Upadhyay 'Hariaudh' (1865–1941) is typical of the recasting of traditional themes favored in this 'Dwivedi period'. The rational and didactic nature of this poetry was too contrived for it to achieve lasting success, and its interest is now mainly historical.

Chhayavad

More enduring was the subsequent style called *Chhayavad* or 'reflexionist' poetry, whose humanist lyrics often bore a mystical impress, and which came to dominate Hindi poetry in the 1920s and 1930s. The three originators of this style, Jayshankar Prasad (1889–1937), Sumitranandan Pant (1900–77) and Suryakant Tripathi 'Nirala' (1896–1961), were of a generation much influenced by the lyricism of the Bengali poet Rabindranath Tagore, the English version of whose *Gitanjali* had won the Nobel Prize in 1913: here we see again the formative influence of modern Bengali literature on the development of its younger Hindi cousin. In works such as Prasad's epic *Kamayani*, and in the individualistic verse of Nirala, Hindi poetry in the modern idiom came of age. Love lyrics couched in sensuous, Sanskritized language often allowed of a religio-mystical interpretation, especially in the verse of a latecomer to the *Chhayavad* style, the poetess Mahadevi Varma (1907–87); Mahadevi's expressions of fervent longing for a distant lover recall the *virah* poetry of Mirabai. During this same period, Harivanshray 'Bachchan' won a large following through his recitations of lyric verse less intellectually demanding than those of his *Chhayavad* contemporaries.

The years which saw the mature works of the *Chhayavad* poets and of Prem Chand were marked also by a broad expansion of literary activity in fiction, poetry, drama and other genres. Much writing, as in the fiction of the Marxist Yashpal (1907–76), has a political motivation, while psychological observation is to the fore in writers such as Jainendra Kumar (b. 1905). The popularity of the drama as a written form continued to grow, unperturbed by the absence of a modern stage tradition; and the short story, representing less of a challenge in terms of its formal structure than the novel, proved a particularly suitable genre for the growing circle of writers and readers. Many of the most creative writers, such as Sachchidanand Vatsyayan 'Ajneya' (1911–87), resist classification under any one school; and the labels 'progressive' and 'experimentalist', which are sometimes applied to the writing of the 1940s and 1950s, respectively, obscure the diversity of the literature of this period.

Trends since Independence

The idealism characterizing much fiction of Prem Chand's time rang hollow after the disappointments of Independence, which failed to provide the hoped-for panacea for society's ills; much post-1947 writing shows a mood of frustration at the general resistance to social change. While the injustices of Indian society as portrayed by

As for visions

As for visions – I dreamt last night
Of fire:
Who knows if it was of Love's sacrament
Or a crematory pyre?

Fate sends no omens,
Speaking with a double tongue.
We read what has been written:
We do not comprehend.

The soothsayer hears the dream
And interprets. He is sure
The client is greatly blessed
Who saw Fire the night before.

S. H. Vatsyayan 'Ajneya'.

Prem Chand always implied the possibility of change and reform, no such corollary applies with the near-anarchic disorder of rural life as portrayed in a novel such as Shrilal Shukla's *Rag darbari* (1968). But the proliferation of Hindi writing continued unabated, many writers such as Mohan Rakesh (1925–72) and Upendranath Ashk (b. 1910) establishing their reputations over several different genres. An important post-Independence development was the emergence of a so-called *ancalik* or 'regional' style of narrative; this is exemplified by the novel *Maila ancal* (1954) of Phanishvarnath 'Renu', which with its Maithili dialogue and its descriptive style is strongly redolent of its remote setting in eastern Bihar.

Hindi today is actively promoted as the vehicle of the great literary heritage of the medieval age, as a mouthpiece for the concerns of contemporary Hinduism and Indian nationalism, and, for a small élite, as the medium of literary composition and experimentation; and it has a broad base in the proliferation of popular romantic fiction, the written counterpart of the vastly influential world of the Hindi film.   *RSn*

Further reading
R. A. Dwivedi, *A Critical Survey of Hindi Literature* (Delhi, 1966)

J. S. Hawley, *Sūr Dās: Poet, Singer, Saint* (Seattle, 1984)

R. S. McGregor, *Hindi Literature from its Beginnings to the Nineteenth Century* (Wiesbaden, 1984)

G. Roadarmel, *A Death in Delhi and other Stories* (Berkeley, 1972)

D. Rubin, *A Season on the Earth: Selected Poems of Nirala* (New York, 1976)

K. Schomer, *Mahadevi Varma and the Chhayavad School of Modern Hindi Poetry* (Berkely, 1983)

R. O. Swan, *Munshi Premcand of Lamhi Village* (Durham, N.C., 1969)

C. Vaudeville, *Kabír* (Oxford, 1974)

North and center: Urdu

The language now called Urdu took on its special characteristics soon after the arrival of the Muslims in North India in the eleventh century. Growing out of the Shauraseni Prakrit in the eastern Panjab and western Uttar Pradesh and marked by a ready acceptance of Perso-Arabic lexicon, morphology and script, its earliest names were *hindi* ('of India') and *hindavi* ('of Indians'). Urdu did not originate in Muslim army camps, although 'Urdu' in Old Turkish meant 'military camp' (cf. English 'horde'). But its spread into areas further south and east was doubtless due to the military campaigns of central Asian, Afghan and Iranian fortune-hunters. The name Urdu is not much older than the eighteenth century. It was perhaps originally an abbreviation of such phrases as *zaban-e urdu-e mualla* or *urdu ki zaban*, lit., 'the language of the royal camp', wherein *urdu* referred to the densely settled area adjacent to the Red Fort in Delhi which was totally razed in 1858. Other earlier names for this language were *dakani* ('of the south') and *rekhta* ('mixed; fallen'); the latter also described any verse that employed Urdu and Persian in some combination. During the nineteenth and twentieth centuries this language was sometimes also referred to as *hindustani*, but its close identification with the political aspirations of a vast majority of Indian Muslims left urdu as its exclusive name.

Though purely linguistically Urdu can be described as a synthesis of non-Indian and Indian, or 'Islamic' and 'Hindu', elements, a review of its literary traditions and social conventions reveals the prevalence of a more particularistic attitude. One expression of it was the twin concepts of *markaz* ('[the normative] center [of language and culture]') and *ahl-e zaban* ('[the normative] speakers of a language') which dominated the thinking of the Urdu literati

Urdu-speaking area.

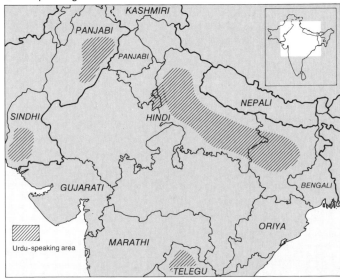

during the eighteenth and nineteenth centuries. The eighteenth century writers of Delhi, for example, claimed for themselves the status of ahl-e zaban and denigrated the dakani literature of the south. They felt dakani was not refined enough, a charge that was in turn made against their language by the writers of Lucknow in the nineteenth century. In both cases, 'refined' implied a more rigorous adherence to the normative rules of Arabic and Persian. More importantly, the same attitude also shaped the construction of the history of Urdu literature, for only the Perso-Arabic genres were included in its ambit. Thus the verses in Indic genres of such medieval writers as Kabir and Jaisi were excluded, though they were no more linguistically different from contemporary Urdu than were those in a Persian genre, and therefore included, of Vajhi and Nusrati. These guidelines will be followed here, and also in regard to the inauthenticated poems attributed to Amir Khusrau (d. 1325) and the scattered verses of some early Sufis.

Urdu literature first flourished in the sixteenth and seventeenth centuries at the courts of Golconda and Bijapur in South India, where at least one ruler, Muhammad Quli Qutb Shah (1581–1611), was himself a talented poet. Two features mark this dakani literature. First, there is a stark preponderance of narrative poems (*masnavi*), reflecting perhaps a continuation of the Iranian royal patronage of this genre; the topics of these substantially long poems include Persian and Indian romances, imaginary or real adventures of the royal patrons, and mystical allegories. Second, there is a kind of eclecticism concerning literary conventions; Indian and Persian themes and motives are freely used, even combined in the same poem. In lyrics (*ghazal*), the female gender of the beloved is just as often explicitly indicated, following the Indian norm, as it is not, as in the Persian practice. Again in lyrics, some Deccan poets express the intensity of love's suffering in a feminine voice (Indian) whereas others follow the Persian convention of a masculine lover. A similar eclecticism is also evident in their language: they freely use Prakrit, Dravidian, Persian and Arabic words, often disregarding the norms of the original language.

By the end of the seventeenth century, Mughal hegemony had destroyed the independent kingdoms of the Deccan. The next flowering of Urdu poetry took place further north in Aurangabad. Two poets of that region, Vali Muhammad Vali (1667–*c*. 1725) and Siraj ud Din Siraj (1715–1763), are historically important. Their poetry was closer to the conventions of Persian and their language to the speech of Delhi. Consequently, they were more accessible and acceptable to the literati of Delhi, who had till then mostly used Persian for creative expression. When the latter turned their attention to Urdu in earnest, they rejected much of the eclecticism of dakani and consciously set out to produce in Urdu a poetry which conformed rigorously with the values and conventions of Persian. As Delhi slowly lost political power, various regional capitals,

particularly, Lucknow, Patna, Rampur and Hyderabad, became havens of security and patronage for Urdu poets. This expansion, however, did not create different regional styles; instead, certain uniform linguistic and literary standards of excellence were adopted. This period, lasting till the final establishment of the English colonial rule in 1858, may be called the 'classical period' of Urdu literature.

The major works of the preceding 'dakani period' had been epic poems and verse romances (masnavi); during the 'classical period', ghazal (lyric) became the dominant genre. It was a major achievement for poets such as Muhammad Taqi Mir (*c*. 1723–1810) and Asadullah Khan Ghalib (1797–1869) to develop individual voices in a genre that already had centuries of established traditions in Persian. Mir is the supreme poet of the passion of love in Urdu, while Ghalib commands affection and respect by his witty and subtle intellectuality. (Ghalib, beside writing major poetry in Persian, also contributed to the development of Urdu prose by publishing his letters which charm with their directness.) At Lucknow, under the patronage of a predominantly Shia high society, *marsiya* (elegy) or, as commonly understood in Urdu, 'elegies on the martyrs of Karbala' gained much prominence, and Babar Ali Anis (1802–74) gave this minor genre the power and drama of epic poetry. Other outstanding achievements of this period were the satires of Muhammad Rafi Sauda (1707–81) and the topical verse of Vali Muhammad Nazir (1740–1830).

Another noteworthy feature is the large number of *tazkiras* written by poets. These 'biographical dictionaries' in Persian mark the first attempts at periodization and critical assessment of Urdu poetry. The poets of this period regarded themselves as craftsmen; they learned their craft from master poets (*ustad*), then brought their literary wares to general attention in expectation of titles, appointments, and honoraria. They competed with each other at poetic assemblies (*mushaira*) or in some patron's salon. In literary achievement, they showed less concern for any absolute originality of thought than for a perfect expression of what was already known. And they were not concerned with 'issues'.

A concern with 'issues' is the most prominent aspect of the literature produced after the final dissolution of the Mughal/Muslim power in 1858 and the establishment of the English colonial rule. For the next seven decades, almost all major Urdu writers were also keenly involved in the movements of religious or political reform of the traditional élites among Indian Muslims. The second half of the nineteenth century was dominated by Sayyid Ahmad Khan (1817–98) and his associates in the so-called 'Aligarh Movement'. A man of enormous energy and diverse interests, Sayyid Ahmad Khan wrote prodigiously on religious, social and political issues and introduced Indian Muslims to modern education; he also helped them develop a literary taste which preferred moral seriousness to formal esthetics.

Muhammad Iqbal, philosopher, political leader and the most important Urdu poet of the twentieth century.

Among his close associates, Altaf Husain Hali (1837–1914) wrote, on the one hand, a powerful long poem 'The Ebb and Tide of Islam' which seared the conscience of Indian Muslims, and on the other, a book of literary criticism which rejected much of the 'classical' heritage as not being socially useful. Nazir Ahmad (1836–1912) published a number of popular novels on such topics as the necessity to educate women and children and the marriage of widows. Even those who differed from Sayyid Ahmad Khan on some issues remained true to his main concern: the sorry state of the Muslim gentry of India. Akbar Husain Akbar (1846–1921) wrote brilliant satirical verse challenging the anti-nationalist position of Sayyid Ahmad Khan and making fun of what he considered merely facile modernization, while Shibli Numani (1857–1914) sought to revive the Persian and Urdu literary heritage and classical Islam through a number of scholarly treatises. Muhammad Husain Azad (1830–1910) wrote the first detailed history of Urdu literature. An inimitable stylist, Azad wrote about poets as cultural heroes, filling his pages with equal parts of nostalgia and analysis. Complementing these were the historical novels of Abdul Halim Sharar (1860–1926), which invoked the past glory of Islam.

Beginning with Halim and Azad, this period also saw the rapid development of *nazm*, a poem requiring no formal restrictions except that it be continuous and thematic in contrast to the ghazal, which was preferably atomistic and non-topical; in other words, a modern poem in either rhymed, blank or free verse. The most notable nazm poet, indeed the most important Urdu poet since Ghalib, was Muhammad Iqbal (1877?–1938), who was also the last major Persian poet of South Asia. Poet, philosopher and political leader, Iqbal is also known as the spiritual founder of Pakistan. Political activism and mystical rapture, glorification of the past and condemnation of religious orthodoxy, anti-Imperialism and Islamic-socialism, Iqbal gave expression to these diverse even contradictory themes in finely wrought poems, which are as much notable for their language and music as for their elevated thought.

Mulla Vajhi (d. 1659) of Golconda wrote the first substantial work, a mystical allegory in rhymed prose, but he had no notable followers for 150 years. Continuous creative expression in Urdu prose began in 1801 at the College of Fort William, Calcutta, with translations of Persian and Indian story literature. Conceived as textbooks for Englishmen in India, they employed a deliberately simple language. This was in marked contrast to the short tales (*qissa*) and lengthy story-cycles (*dastan*) that were composed at Lucknow some years later and told, in ornate style, fantastic tales of romance and magic. A similar difference in language is visible between the novels of Nazir Ahmad (see above) and the semi-picaresque tales of Ratan Nath Sarshar (1846–1903). Both, however, were reformist in intent; the former adopted a more didactic posture, while the latter worked through a colorful mixture of naturalism and broad humor. An erratic writer, Muhammad Hadi, also known as Mirza Rusva (1858–1931) is remembered for one novel, *Umrao Jan Ada*, the story of a courtesan of Lucknow in the 1850s, told with a remarkable lack of sentimentalism.

The Urdu press started in the 1830s, and by the end of the century large numbers of newspapers and magazines were being published. With magazines came short stories, and the credit for being the first to explore that genre is usually given to Sajjad Haidar 'Yildarim' (1880–1943). But the foremost practitioner of that art, and of the novel, during this span of time was Prem Chand (1880–1936), whose real name was Dhanpat Ray Srivastava. Until 1924, Prem Chand primarily wrote in Urdu; later he wrote exclusively in Hindi, but had his works translated into Urdu under his own supervision. He was the first to delineate in Urdu fiction the socio-economic concerns of the rural poor and urban middle classes.

In 1936 a group of writers from different Indian languages launched what is usually referred to as the 'Progressive Movement' (*taraqqi-pasand tahrik*), which profoundly influenced all Indian literatures for at least the next two decades. Imbued with ideas of 'socialist realism and progress', it attracted some of the best writers in Urdu, appealing to the iconoclastic and revolutionary fervor of the time. It declined in influence after India and Pakistan gained freedom in 1947, and eventually lost to 'modernism' (*jadidiyat*) which had in fact begun in Urdu at roughly the same time. The latter is marked by a fondness for experimentation in form, by social concern without ideological bombast, and by a pronounced interest in the psychology of the individual. A third literary trend that made its appearance in the fifties identified itself with Islam, but failed to make any significant impact.

Coming to individual writers, three poets dominated this period: Faiz Ahmad Faiz (1911–84), who identified himself with the 'Progressives', and N. M. Rashid (1910–75) and 'Miraji' (Muhammad Sanaullah, 1912–49), who were claimed as their own by the 'modernists'. Miraji also wrote brilliant criticism and songs (*git*), and translated French and Sanskrit poetry into Urdu. Sardar Jafri (b. 1912) wrote 'Whitmanesque' free-verse in Urdu and also contributed to the formation of a literary-critical attitude that gave social good precedence over formal esthetics. Majruh Sultanpuri (b. 1919), however, used the traditional form and symbols of the ghazal to express his 'progressive' fervor. Saadat Hasan Manto (1912–55), the greatest talent in Urdu short-story writing, left a legacy of nearly two dozen collections. He wrote about the fears and neuroses of the urban middle-class and yet made his readers share the humanity of the pimps and whores and other denizens of the society's lower depths. Other important short-story writers were Krishan Chandar (1914–77), Ghulam Abbas (1909–82), Rajinder Singh Bedi (1915–84) and Ismat Chughtai (b. 1915). The only notable novelist of that generation was Aziz Ahmad (1913–78), who is better known in the West as a cultural historian of Muslim South Asia. A younger writer, Qurratulain Haidar (b. 1928), has written the finest novels in Urdu so far. Like Aziz Ahmad, she too mostly writes about the Muslim upper classes and the cataclysmic changes that political and economic upheavals have caused in their lives. Her most ambitious novel, *Ag Ka Darya*, presents a panorama of Indian history, peopled by certain human types who come together, interact, then separate in subtle variations. Another remarkable work, *Kar-e Jahan Daraz Hai*, is a fictionalized history of her family in two massive volumes. Muhammad Hasan Askari (d. 1978), a man of remarkable erudition, translated Stendhal and Flaubert into Urdu and wrote pioneering literary studies that made Urdu readers become aware of the metaphysical underpinnings of their classical heritage.

Urdu literature still flourishes in India, but with much greater vigor in Pakistan. Lahore and Karachi, not Delhi and Lucknow, are now the major centers of creative activity. There are also a few major writers living abroad in Europe and North America. Of the more important contemporary writers mention must be made of the following: Abdullah Husain and Mumtaz Mufti (novel), Intizar Husain, Anvar Sajjad, and Khalida Husain (short story), Nasir Kazmi, Zafar Iqbal and Bashir Badr (*ghazal*), Munir Niyazi, Zahid Dar, Saqi Faruqi, Shahryar and Kishvar Nahid (*nazm*), and Vazir Agha, Salim Ahmad, Shamim Hanafi and Shams ur Rahman Faruqi (criticism). In addition, Jamil Jalibi deserves special notice for single-handedly attempting the most detailed and analytical history of Urdu literature, of which three volumes have already appeared.

CMN

Qurratulain Haidar, writer of much admired novels in Urdu.

Further reading

D. J. Matthews, C. Shackle and S. Husain, *Urdu Literature* (London, 1985)

M. Sadiq, *Twentieth Century Urdu Literature* (Karachi, 1983); *A History of Urdu Literature* 2nd edn (Delhi, 1984)

A. Schimmel, *Classical Urdu Literature: From the Beginning to Iqbal, A History of Indian Literature* (Ed. Jan Gonda) vol. viii, fasc. 3. (Wiesbaden, 1975)

Northwest: Sindhi, Baluchi, Panjabi, Siraiki, Kashmiri, Pashto

The ruins of Mohenjodaro or of Taxila still bear witness to the ancient status of the northwest as the former home of major centers of cultural diffusion. Since the increasing dominance of Islam from the eleventh century onward, however, the region has come in more recent times to assume the typical characteristics of a border-zone, whose long subjection to powerful external influences, principally from west Asia but also from northern India, has both enriched and inhibited the development of local cultural resources. While their vital character, owing much to folk-traditions, fully reflects the vigorously preserved local identities of the area, the literatures of the regional languages of the northwest still tend to be more restricted in size and scope than those produced in other parts of South Asia, whose history has permitted a fuller and more stable realization of local patterns of cultural evolution.

Literary languages of the Northwest.

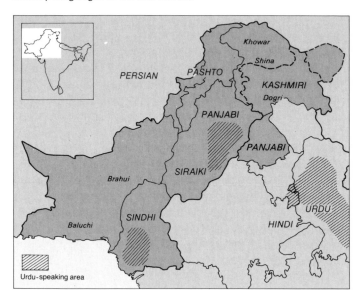

Local languages and folk-literatures

The area of the Indus valley, and of the plains and the mountains and deserts which surround it on either side, collectively constituting the whole of Pakistan besides the immediately adjacent parts of India, is both geographically and socially one of the most varied in South Asia. The local languages are similarly diverse. Those which have significant literatures include, besides Sindhi and Panjabi (to which the overlapping Siraiki of the Multan region should be added), the Dardic subgroup of Indo-Aryan represented by Kashmiri, and the Iranian Pashto. The many other languages which might be added to this list, such as Baluchi, Brahui, Dogri, Shina or Khowar, are only to be disregarded on the basis of their very recent literary cultivation, in most cases hardly preceding the Partition which formally divided the region.

The classic literatures of all the principal regional languages are composed almost entirely in verse which derives much of its most distinctive inspiration from the still vital resources of their respective folk-traditions. This may be seen formally in the general adoption of easy-going metrical patterns which owe more to the rhythms of local songs than to elaborate classical standards, or thematically in the continued drawing upon locally based legends, whether in extended narrative or more allusively in lyrical poetry. To these should be added the powerful poetic connotations invested in local words referring to key symbolic terms, whose reference to physical objects or emotional concepts does much to reinforce the bond felt by contemporary local audiences with their own literary heritage.

External influences

Conversely, however, no account of these literatures can neglect the role played in their development by culturally prestigious languages not themselves native to the region. By far the most significant was Persian, whose official status throughout the Muslim period is reflected in the very high proportion of loan-words borrowed by all the local languages, and in their continuing use of forms of the Perso-Arabic script throughout Pakistan and Kashmir. Similarly, while the provincial quality of most of the Persian writing so prolifically produced by local authors may have ensured its deserved present oblivion, much of the classic literature in local languages (so often of Sufi inspiration), is hardly to be understood without reference to the pervasive spell of the literary genres, themes and symbolism of classical Persian poetry. Although Persian lost this historic role in the nineteenth century, it has found its natural successor in Urdu, which continues (under a thin veneer of English) to dominate most local literatures.

The predominance of this Perso-Urdu influence is naturally most evident in the literatures of the majority Muslim communities of the region. The countervailing force of northern Indian culture long operated with such effect upon the local Hindu communities (until their diaspora in 1947) as virtually to confine their literary production to Sanskrit and to Hindi, although Kashmiri does have a small but important Hindu literature. Substantial divergence from the dominant cultural pattern is accordingly to be noted chiefly in the case of the Sikhs, for whom the cultivation of Panjabi in their sacred Gurmukhi script has now come to form an important part of their cultural identity in India.

Early literatures

Rather little poetry has been reliably preserved from much before the early seventeenth century in most of the languages, whose unlearned character was anyway generally unfavorable to the establishment of accurate manuscript traditions.

Much of the earliest poetry is, however, of outstanding quality. Kashmiri literature begins gloriously with the quatrains (*vakh*) of the ascetic poetess Lal Ded (d. *c.* 1376), which combine the most everyday references to Kashmiri life with the technicalities of Shaivite yoga to give extraordinary depth to her message of mystical devotion. Lal Ded's continuing popularity in Kashmir is rivalled only by that of Shaikh Nur ud Din (d. 1438), founder of the heterodox Rishi order: although his brief verses (*shrukh*) are of lesser poetic power, they enjoy a particular status among the Muslims of the Valley. Kashmiri also provides an unusually early instance of secular poetry in the touching love-lyrics (*lol*) attributed to the sixteenth century Habba Khatun, the peasant-girl who became the last queen of independent Kashmir.

By far the most substantial and best preserved early local

literature is that collected in the Sikh scriptures, the *Adi Granth* (1604). This has as its primary inspiration the 974 compositions of Guru Nanak (1469–1539), the founder of Sikhism and a poet of exceptional beauty and power. Although Guru Nanak, like Kabir and other poets of the North Indian Sant tradition, used a mixed language (in his case, a mixture of Old Panjabi and Old Hindi), his expression, imagery and forms are adapted from the folk-tradition, and thus comparable to those of later Panjabi poets. This is particularly true of his hymns (*shabad*), made up of verses with interspersed refrain, originally composed to the accompaniment of his faithful follower, the Muslim minstrel Mardana. Here the convention of the folk-lyric which casts the poet as a village girl pining for her absent partner is adapted with great beauty to the expression of yearning for the Lord, and expanded with great power by the incorporation of novel theological ideas. A similar abundance of keenly observed local reference distinguishes Guru Nanak's short verses (*shlok*), which are often marked by a characteristically Panjabi mordant humor, while his poetic originality is equally evident in his adaptation of the stanzaic forms of the folk-ballad (*var*) to the vivid exposition of systematic theology (as in the well-known *Asa ki var*), or of the folk-genre which describes a girl's suffering through twelve months of absence from her beloved (as in his *Tukhari Barahmaha*).

> I wept: the whole world wept for me, the forest-birds wept
> too.
> My body's pain, which kept me from my Lord, alone wept
> not.

Guru Nanak, evoking local folk-lyric.

The compositions of the later Sikh Gurus included in the *Adi Granth* seldom match the vivid originality of Guru Nanak's poetry, and anyway tend increasingly towards Hindi rather than Panjabi.

Among the other contributions to the Sikh scripture, the Panjabi verses attributed to the Muslim, Shaikh Farid (fifteenth century?) have a special importance as the earliest record of Panjabi Sufi literature as well as their own gloomy power.

Later classics

A much greater body of literature survives from the later pre-modern period (*c.* 1600–1900), almost all of it being of Persian-influenced Muslim inspiration, since apart from the naive seventeenth century prose hagiographies (*janamsakhi*) of Guru Nanak, most Sikh writing until the end of the nineteenth century abandons Panjabi for Hindi.

The greater part of the preserved literature in all languages is the work of prosy Muslim divines, whether cast in the form of doggerel or of rhymed prose, as in the case of Akhun Darveza (d. 1638),

important for his establishment of a standard literary Pashto transcending dialectal divides. But it also includes much magnificent poetry, often of Sufi inspiration, whose authors continue to assume ever greater importance as symbols of local cultural identities in Pakistan.

Of these identities, that of the Pathans is both the most distinct socially and the most subject to Persian influence culturally. Thus the classic oeuvre of the Khatak chieftain Khushhal Khan (1613–89) reflects the martial and homoerotic preoccupations of Pathan society through adaptations of the classic Persian genres of the *ghazal* and *rubai* to the metrics of Pashto folk-poetry. Similar aspirations, if at a lower creative level, to classical status are detectable in the Pashto *divan* of the great Afghan warlord Ahmad Shah Durrani (d. 1772). Local reverence is, however, rather given in the Pashto-speaking areas of Pakistan to the mystical poetry of Rahman Baba (d. 1706).

The works of numerous local Sufi poets of the Indus plains survive principally in the form of the *kafi*, a short rhythmic lyric with interspersed refrain, in which the dominant folk-tradition of the female invocation of an absent beloved is adapted (often with quite abstruse reference to arcane Sufi sources) to the emotional requirements of musical *qavvali* performance, whether historically at the shrines of the saints, or nowadays in concert or on tape.

In the Panjab proper, the acknowledged master of the kafi is Bullhe Shah (1680–1758), whose combination of ecstasy with sardonic asides recalls Guru Nanak. His reputation can, however, hardly compare with the colossal status accorded in Sind to his Qadiri confrère and contemporary Shah Abdul Latif (1689–1752). His large *risalo* not only incorporates lyrics drawing upon almost every emotional and narrative resource of local folk-traditions on the one hand, and vast reference to both Muslim and Hindu religious life on the other, but also exploits the Sindhi language in a fashion never achieved by his few predecessors or emulated by his many successors.

Serious rivalry to Shah Abdul Latif's status in Sind is presented only by the more directly ecstatic lyrics of Sachal Sarmast (1739–1826), who composed both in Sindhi and in Siraiki. The summation of Siraiki Sufi poetry was, however, achieved by Khwaja Ghulam Farid (1845–1901), whose magically expanded re-conjuring of the

> Where the desert-grasses twist, my love,
> Ever-shifting shapes exist, my love.
> The crickets creak, the pigeons coo,
> The foxes howl, hyenas mew,
> The geckoes puff, the lizards whoo,
> The snakes and serpents hiss, my love.

Khwaja Ghulam Farid, reflecting the local scenery of the deserts of Bahawalpur.

traditional themes of the *kafi* within the physical setting of the deserts of Bahawalpur, which provided much of his inspiration, has ensured him a continuing popularity.

All the languages have rich traditions of folk-narrative, ranging from the heroic, through the historical and topical, to the lyrical re-telling of romantic legends. In spite of their continuing popularity in the bazaars, very few of the more elaborate versions of these verse-tales have achieved an artistic standard notably higher than that of the broadsheet balladier, however ambitious their approximation to the Sufi-inspired Persian *masnavi*.

To this general rule, however, Panjabi provides at least two outstanding exceptions. The long *Hir* (1766) by Varis Shah (whose original 6000-odd lines are much expanded in bazaar editions) re-tells the well-known local romantic legend of the love of Ranjha for Hir in such a way as to encapsulate almost every possible reference to both the material and ideological components of contemporary Panjabi culture, as Ranjha in turn becomes the helpless passenger of the villainous boatman Luddan, herdsman in service of Hir's father to secure illicit meetings in the river-glades with her, and finally pseudo-yogi to reclaim Hir from her forced marriage. Throughout the poem, still continually recited in its affecting special tune, the full resources of Panjabi vocabulary are drawn upon to dazzlingly ironic effect.

> At dawn, when birds called travellers to reveille,
> And when the staffs to churn the milk were plied,
> And folk arose and rushed to rush and wash away
> All traces of the beds they'd occupied,
> Did Ranjha to the river wend his way,
> To find the ferry on the other side,
> Where, Varis, Luddan slumped and gross he saw,
> Like sacks of honey in a grocer's store.

Varis Shah, describing Ranjha's encounter with the villainous boatman Luddan.

Besides the local legends of Hir, Sassi or Sohni, the poets of the Perso-Panjabi tradition were also drawn by the classic tales of the Middle East and the most prominent local rival to Varis Shah's *Hir* is represented by the immensely long *Saif ul Muluk*, deriving from one of the tales of the *Arabian Nights* and composed in masnavi form by Mian Muhammad (1828–1906), which continues to enjoy an enormous vogue in northern Panjab and Azad Kashmir.

Modern literature

While the traditional sources of poetic inspiration were largely defunct by 1900, the subsequent literary development of the region along the Western-inspired lines pursued to such effect in other parts of the subcontinent was much inhibited in the northwest by the cultural dominance of Urdu. Thus it is that the poetry of such modern father-figures as Ghulam Ahmad Mahjur (1885–1952) in Kashmiri or Rahat Zakhili (d. 1963) in Pashto bears the heavy imprint of the Panjabi-born Iqbal (d. 1938) whose preference for Urdu continues to be followed by the majority of his talented Muslim Panjabi compatriots.

Rather few writers in the local languages of Pakistan have seriously challenged the formidably reinforced Iqbalian example, certainly not those in the numerous subregional dialects and languages now being promoted. Sindhi, it is true, constitutes a partial exception, segregated by its individual script and historically confirmed in its separate identity by early writers like the polymath Qalich Beg (1853–1929), not to speak of the powerful heritage of Shah Abdul Latif, freshly exploited by such poets as Shaikh Ayaz (b. 1923).

As yet, it is only the Sikhs who, reverting under the inspiration of their religio-cultural renaissance to the literary cultivation of Panjabi, have succeeded in establishing a modern local literature fully able to compare in range of poetry and prose with other South-Asian models. Owing much of its initial impetus to the immense output in poetry, novels, tracts and scholarship of Bhai Vir Singh (1872–1957), this Sikh-inspired Panjabi literature has been fur-thered by such figures as the prolific popular novelist Nanak Singh (b. 1897), much indebted to Prem Chand, or Panjabi's premier poetess Amrita Pritam (b. 1919) and its short-lived Hindu Chat-terton, Shiv Kumar Batalvi (1937–73), in whose lyrics past themes receive the modern twist needed to secure enduring relevance and appeal.

CS

Further reading

B. B. Kachru, *Kashmiri Literature* (Wiesbaden, 1981)

D. N. Mackenzie, trans., *Poems from the Divan of Khushal Khan Khattak* (London, 1965)

W. H. McLeod, Ed. and Trans., *Textual Sources for the Study of Sikhism* (Manchester, 1984)

A. Schimmel, *Sindhi Literature* (Wiesbaden, 1974)

C. Shackle, trans., *Fifty Poems of Khawaja Farid* (Multan, 1983)

C. F. Usborne, Trans., *The Adventures of Hir and Ranjha* (London, 1973)

Northeast: Bengali, Assamese, Oriya

Origins

The literatures of the northeast in Bengali, Assamese and Oriya are branches of a single tree whose trunk would scarcely be discernible were it not for the discovery, in 1907, of the *Charyapadas*, a unique collection of Buddhist mystic songs. The manuscript containing them was found in Nepal, brought there, perhaps, by Buddhists fleeing oppression in Bengal. Bengali scholars agree that they are written in a form of Old Bengali; but the Assamese and Oriyas also trace the origins of their languages to these same songs.

There are no other texts to represent the period of Buddhist ascendancy (the Pala kings in Bengal, the Bhauma kings in Orissa), but some of the oral literature of the region has roots in Buddhist values. The famous Baul songs of Bengal, for example, which were an inspiration to Rabindranath Tagore and are still being composed today, invoke the equality of all castes and a formless deity detached from any mythology.

The Hindu kings

The Hindu Sena kings in Bengal (eleventh to twelfth centuries) gave courtly patronage not to Bengali but to Sanskrit, and it was under Lakshmanasena that the celebrated *Gitagovinda* of Jayadeva was written. The various kingdoms of Assam, however, developed a tradition of patronage that lasted right until the British annexation of the region in 1826. Much of pre-modern Assamese literature took

Literary languages of the Northeast.

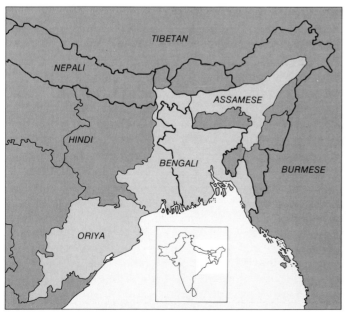

the form of officially commissioned translations of Sanskrit works for the edification of the masses: works such as Madhava Kandali's translation of the *Ramayana* (fourteenth century), the translations and dramatizations of the *Bhagavata-purana* by the great Vaishnava teacher Shankaradeva (sixteenth century), and the translation of the *Dharma-purana* by Kavichandra Dvija (eighteenth century). By then the Ahom kings of eastern Assam, who came originally from north Burma, ruled the whole of the Brahmaputra valley. They adopted Hinduism in the second half of the seventeenth century, and switched to writing their *Buranjis* (historical chronicles) in Assamese rather than in Ahom (a form of Thai). The *Buranjis* are the only pre-modern historical writing in the whole northeast, and are Assam's most original literary achievement.

Orissa held out as an independent Hindu kingdom until 1568, long enough to develop a remarkable literary culture that was truly proletarian. The villages of Orissa are distinguished even today by their libraries of palm-leaf manuscripts, many of them illustrated. The most original genres were the *brata-kathas* or votive tales (comparable to the Bengali *mangal-kabya* but written in prose), and the *chautisas* – ballads in which the stanzas are alphabetically ordered. The outstanding poet was Sarala Dasa, author of the Oriya *Mahabharata*, who flourished during the period of stability that the fifteenth century Solar dynasty brought to Orissa. His epic was not a translation, but a fresh creation, with many local elements.

The Muslim conquests

In 1202 Turki invaders conquered Nadiya, the center of medieval Bengal, and over the next two centuries the region was disrupted to such an extent that no Bengali text can be confidently assigned to this period. But the indigenous *laukik* religious cults and various kinds of folk poetry continued to develop, and historians of Bengali literature accept that Muslim rule, wherever it stabilized, facilitated the emergence of Bengali because it displaced Sanskrit. Sultan Husain Shah, who ruled over almost the whole of Bengal from 1493 to 1519, and his son Nusrat Shah are remembered as promoters of Bengali literature, and under their rule several of the *mangal-kabyas* were composed. These poems, designed for performance in villages rather than for reading, describe the birth of the indigenous deities (Manasa, Chandi and others), how they consolidated their position in the Hindu pantheon, and how human beings started to worship them. The greatest is the *Chandimangal* of Mukundaram Chakrabarti, who wrote at the end of the sixteenth century when Mughal rule brought a second period of unity and relative stability to Bengal. Mukundaram was a conscious artist, not a mere mouthpiece for an oral tradition, and had a gift for lively social observation.

Mughal culture in the seventeenth and eighteenth centuries brought about a weakening of Brahminical influence and the consequent decline of traditional Hindu literature, with Persian and Urdu becoming languages of state; but it also produced poets who were able to unite Hindu and Islamic traditions. Chief among them were Daulat Kazi and Sayyid Alaol, who wrote, among other things, Vaishnava *padas*, and found patronage in the Arakan kingdom of Lower Burma where Bengali became a favored court language.

Orissa, despite repeated Muslim attacks from the late sixteenth century on, never absorbed the Perso-Arabic influences (or the conversions to Islam) that affected Bengal. The old Orissa kingdom broke up into innumerable semi-independent principalities. In some of these, literature flourished: the Bhanjas, who ruled the south Orissa state of Ghumasar, were themselves poets; and Upendra Bhanja (1670–1720) became one of the great names of Oriya literature. In his poems, the ornate versification, wordplay and eroticism of advanced Sanskrit *kavya* were adapted to Oriya and taken to a new extreme.

Vaishnavism

As a source of literary inspiration, Vaishnava or, to be more precise, Krishnaite religion and mythology established itself in the northeast with the *Gitagovinda* of Jayadeva. In Orissa the *Pancha Sakha* (the Five Friends), who wrote at the end of the fifteenth century under the last of the Solar kings, introduced a distinctive strand of Vaishnavism into the complex fabric of religion in Orissa. They were more idealistic than Sarala Das, whose Shaktism had emphasized the darker side of human nature, and they translated the *Ramayana* (Balarama Dasa) and the *Bhagavata* (Jagannatha Dasa). Under their influence, Orissa's national deity Jagannatha became identified with Vishnu as well as the Buddha. This was very different from the Guriya Vaishnavism of Chaitanya (1486–1530); but Orissa was not able to resist for long his Neo-Vaishnava *bhakti* religion. In 1510 Chaitanya settled at Puri, attracted by the Vaish-navism of the *Pancha Sakha*: he encountered Brahminical resistance at first, but soon won many converts including Balarama Dasa. The Krishnaite songs of Vidyapati, who wrote in Maithili (an eastern Hindi dialect), became as popular in Orissa as in Bengal, and *padas* on the love of Radha and Krishna were soon being written and sung throughout the northeast.

Neo-Vaishnavism, promoted in Bengal by Chaitanya's disciples and carried into Assam by Shankaradeva, did not prove as enduring as the Shaiva-Shaktism that lies behind the worship of the Mother Goddess (especially Durga) in Bengal today; but as a literary force its influence was profound. It was the romantic, musical Vaishnava tradition that made it possible for the genius of Rabindranath Tagore to emerge at the end of the nineteenth century. It also produced a medieval Bengali masterpiece, the *Shrikrishnakirtan* of Baru Chandidas, a delightful cycle of lyrics in which the Radha-Krishna theme is given an unusually down-to-earth treatment.

Élite versus popular literature

Most of the pre-modern literature of the region was popular in the sense that it was written in the vernacular for the pleasure or edification of those who did not know the learned languages – Sanskrit, and (later) Persian and Arabic. Works such as the Bengali *Ramayana* of Krittibas (early fifteenth century) became embedded in the lives of the common people. There was also a great mass of oral or bardic poetry and song, such as the famous *Mymensingh-gitika*, secular ballads collected in the eastern part of Mymensingh District (now in Bangladesh) and published in 1923. But Upendra Bhanja's ornate school of Oriya poetry, the sophisticated Muslim Bengali poets of the court of Arakan, and the brilliant Bharatchandra Ray (1705–60), court-poet of the Maharaja of Nabadvip (Nadiya), pointed toward much higher spheres. Bharatchandra's *Annadamangal* was an elegant fusion of medieval *mangal-kabya*, Sanskrit *purana* and Mughal history. A hundred years later, Michael Madhusudan Datta (1824–73) wrote an epic poem based on the *Ramayana* which absorbed a host of western romantic and classical influences as well as medieval Bengali and Sanskrit sources. In the 1930s, the 'Kallol' group of writers (named after a leading literary magazine of the day) addressed readers who had added European and American Modernism to their literary diet. By then the battle for the vernacular as a means of sophisticated literary expression had been won, but at a cost of cutting off literature from the lives of villagers. Rabindranath Tagore's call, in a fine late poem (No. 10 in *Janmadine*, 1941), for 'a poet who shares in the lives of the peasants . . . who is close to the soil' can be taken as an expression of nostalgia for a world in which vernacular literature belonged to the people.

Bengali dominance

The modern literature of the northeast is dominated by Calcutta. Whereas in the pre-modern period the numerically dominant Bengali-speaking region could not necessarily claim superiority in literary achievement, the growth of Calcutta put the English-educated urban Hindu élite, the 'bhadralok' or 'babu', at the forefront of literature. The Assamese and Oriyas had to fight hard against Bengali dominance. In the early period of British rule, Bengalis ran the administration; in 1836 Bengali was imposed on the schools and courts of Assam, and in Orissa partition between Bengal, central Provinces and Madras ensured an equivalent imposition of Bengali, Hindi or Telegu. In both regions mission-aries and enlightened British linguists such as John Beames (District Magistrate of Balasore) joined forces with intellectuals who, because they had been educated in Calcutta, had seen what the Bengalis were achieving and wanted the same. In the early 1870s Assamese and Oriya finally received official recognition, and their modern literary revival began in earnest. Bengali literary influence,

A discourse between the sage Kashyapa and Garuda from an Assamese manuscript of the *Dharma-purana*.

however, remained strong: many leading modern writers of Assam and Orissa can be compared to one or other of the great modern Bengali writers. For example, Radhanatha Raya (1848–1908) was heavily influenced by Madhusudan Datta, adapting his Bengali blank verse to Oriya, and in the 1920s there was a 'Sobuja' (Green) group of Oriya poets who took their lead from Pramatha Chaudhuri's journal *Sobujpatra*, to which Tagore contributed. But Bengali writers met their equal in Phakirmohana Senapati (1843–1918), author of numerous novels and stories and a superb autobiography, and translator of the whole *Ramayana* and *Mahabharata* into modern Oriya.

The great names

There are many figures from the fascinating Calcutta-based Bengali Renaissance who are remembered for introducing modern literary forms. Prose literature was the chief product of Western influence: some of the earliest writers of Bengali prose were missionaries – the Portuguese in the eighteenth century, and the Baptist William Carey in the early nineteenth century. The stumbling prose that Carey and his associates devised for biblical translation or for *Digdarshan* (The Compass), the first periodical to be published in Bengali, attained mandarin confidence in the writings of the great social reformer Ishvarchandra Bidyasagar (1820–91), and vivid colloquialism in Pyarichand Mitra's pioneering novel *Alaler gharer Dulal* (The Pampered Son of a Rich Family). There were pioneer dramatists too: Michael Madhusudan Datta, who wrote two farces and a tragedy as well as epic poetry and sonnets, and Dinabandhu Mitra (1829–74), famous for the political crisis that was caused by *Nildarpan*, his play about indigo exploitation. By the end of the nineteenth century a vigorous theatrical scene had developed in

Calcutta, and though Bengal has so far not produced a playwright of international standing (unless we count Tagore, who turned his back on the Calcutta stage), there have been great Bengali actors (Girish Ghosh, Binodini Dasi, Shishir Bhaduri).

With the extension of literacy and the growth of film and television, many Bengali writers have acquired enormous readerships: Saratchandra Chattopadhyay (1876–1938), for example, whose novels have been translated into most Indian languages, or Bibhutibhushan Bandyopadhyay (1899–1950), or in recent times 'Shankar', whose witty novels about contemporary Calcutta have, like Bibhutibhushan's novels of village life, reached a world audience through the films of Satyajit Ray. Bengali literature is also impressive for its journalistic and periodical writing, for its short stories, and for the cosmopolitan eclecticism of its leading Modernist poets. A poet like Jibanananda Das (1899–1954) speaks for modern humanity, not just for himself or his immediate society.

Bengali writers of world class, however, are so far probably three

---

A strange darkness

A strange darkness came upon the world today.
Those who are most blind now see.
Those whose hearts lack love, lack warmth, lack pity's
  stirrings,
Without their fine advice, the world today dare not make a
  move.
Those who yet today possess an abiding faith in man,
To whom still now high truths or age-old customs
Or industry or austere practice all seem natural,
Their hearts are victuals for the vulture and the jackal.

A poem by Jibanananda Das, translated by Clinton B. Seely.

in number. Madhusudan Datta is remembered as much for his reckless lifestory as for his poetry, but his *Meghnadbadh Kabya* is fully comparable to the classical European epics that were his model. Bankim Chandra Chatterjee (1838–94) applied a formidable intellect schooled in French rationalism to the creation of a new sense of nationhood, writing masterly essays as well as complex historical novels. Above all, Rabindranath Tagore (1861–1941) pulled Bengali into the category of the major literatures of the world. Completing a process that had been started by the great reformer and Indian representative of the Enlightenment Rammohan Roy (1774–1833), whose Hindu reform movement the Brahmo Samaj lies behind the tolerance, rationalism and universalism of the best political leaders of the subcontinent, Tagore created in his

Rabindranath Tagore, winner of the Nobel prize for literature in 1913 and a renaissance figure in Bengali culture, in a sketch by an admirer, the film director, Satyajit Ray.

songs, poems, stories, novels, plays, essays, letters, dance-dramas, his university at Santiniketan and even in his mysterious paintings, a world as rich and vast as Shakespeare's, which foreigners are only now beginning properly to explore.

Bangladesh

The Muslims of Bengal were much slower to embrace English education and the modernizing impulse than the Hindus, and the nineteenth century was therefore a barren period for Muslim Bengali writers, with the exception of the prolific Musharraf Husain, a novelist respected by Bankim Chandra. The foremost Muslim Bengali writer of the twentieth century is undoubtedly Nazr ul Islam (1899–1976) though pre-senile dementia after 1941 finished his career, but his west Bengal origins and the Hindu–Muslim syncretism of his outlook (comparable to the syncretism of pre-Modern Muslim Bengali writers) show how misleading it is to construct a separate literary history for 'East Bengal' or 'Muslim Bengal'. With the founding of East Pakistan and Bangladesh, however, Dhaka has begun to rival Calcutta as a literary center. There are two main reasons for the liveliness of literary culture in present-day Bangladesh. First, the Bengalis of Bangladesh have had to fight for their language. 'Ekushey', February 21, 1952, when demonstrators for the recognition of Bengali as the state language of East Pakistan were shot by the police, is etched into Bangladeshi consciousness. Secondly, Bengali in Bangladesh is much less subject to the English and Hindi influences that are besieging Calcutta. Arguments about whether Bengalis in Bangladesh should give priority to the Bengali, the separate Bangladeshi, or the Muslim parts of their make-up will continue (accounting for the various trends in Bangladeshi literature today). But with writers as good as Shamsur Rahman and Al Mahmud (poetry), Hasan Azizul Haq (short stories), Anis uz-Zaman (criticism), and Selim al Din (plays), Bangladesh already has much to contribute to Bengal, the subcontinent and the world beyond.

WR

Further reading

B. Bose, *An Acre of Green Grass, A Review of Modern Bengali Literature* (Calcutta, 1948)

M. E. Haq, *Muslim Bengali Literature* (Karachi, 1957)

M. Mansinha, *History of Oriya Literature* (New Delhi, 1962)

A. Roy, *The Islamic Syncretistic Tradition in Bengal* (Princeton, N.J., 1983)

S. N. Sarma, *Assamese Literature* (Wiesbaden, 1976)

D. Zbavitel, *Bengali Literature* (Wiesbaden, 1976)

West: Marathi, Gujarati, Konkani

Gujarati and Marathi are closely related languages, yet their literatures have always been distinct except in that they both draw on the common stock of Hindu culture. Konkani, a collection of spoken dialects, has had until the twentieth century no accepted literary form.

Early literature

The earliest Gujarati literature arose within the dominant Jain culture that was fostered by the Solanki kings of Patan and survived the Muslim conquest of Gujarat in 1299 in the Jain monasteries with their huge manuscript libraries or *bhandaras* which are still not fully explored. The earliest datable works in Gujarati are from the beginning of the fourteenth century when the popular tales that had until then circulated orally began to be written down. Mostly these are narrative poems, called *ras* or *phagu*: tales of separated lovers and celebrations of spring when the sap stirs in both man and nature, which are rounded off by a Jain moral often somewhat perfunctorily tacked on at the end.

In a parallel but very different genre, the earliest Marathi literature is also the product of sectarian propaganda written under the Yadavas, the last Hindu kings of Devgiri, modern Daulatabad, which fell to Muslim power in 1296. The works written by the Mahanubhavas in the last years of the thirteenth century were little known outside the sect, whereas *Jnaneshvari* (*c.* 1290) is arguably the greatest work of Marathi literature. *Jnaneshvari* is an immense verse expansion of the *Bhagavad-gita*, which advocated the way of

bhakti devotionalism, a personalized religion which rejects many of the rituals and formulae of brahminical Hinduism. Written, supposedly by Jnandev at the age of 19, in the simple *ovi* meter which is employed for so much later Marathi literature, this work of 8896 verses is divided into the same 18 *adhyayas* or cantos as the *Gita*. It impresses by the vividness of its imagery and the cumulative power of its extended similes, although only a devotee might have the stamina to read it right through to the end.

In a secular vein, one of the most important works of old Gujarati is a pseudo-historical poem called *Kanhadade Prabandha* which narrates an episode in the conquest of Gujarat by the Muslims, the resistance and ultimate fall of the fort of Jalor to Ala ud Din in 1310. It is a bardic poem composed in the mid-fifteenth century by one Padmanabh who was attached to the court of the Songiri Rajput barony of Jalor. There are some earlier and many later examples of such heroic tales, but none so unified or so well crafted. The Rajput setting reminds us that, up to the sixteenth century at least, the cultural center of Gujarat was in the north around the old capital of Patan and included much of southern Rajasthan. Similarly, Marathi at the time of Jnandev and the early Mahanubhavas was centered on the upper Godavari around Paithan (ancient Pratishthana) and the Yadava fort of Devgiri near Aurangabad.

With few exceptions, of which the bardic verse of Gujarati and Rajasthani is an important one, early Indian literature consists of religious verse and divides into two broad strands, of *bhakti* and of *purana*. Bhakti, deriving ultimately from ninth century Tamil devotionalism addressed to Vishnu and Shiva, is an outpouring of individual emotion taking as its goal whatever form of the deity is locally dominant and is expressed in short hymn-like poems. In Gujarati, bhakti's chief exponents were Mirabai (*c.* 1500–50), a Rajput princess, and Narsimh Mehta (1500–80), a poor brahmin from Junagadh in Saurashtra. The verse of both is addressed to Krishna in the temple at Dwarka, and Narsimh is also the author of many poems that verge on the puranic tradition by narrating episodes of the Krishna story personalized to the extent of writing himself into the plot as witness, lover or messenger. The poems of both contain repeated references to certain events of their own lives: in Mirabai's case, her persecution by her brother-in-law the Rana of Chitor and her flight to Dwarka, in Narsimh's his flouting of Brahminical conventions and the ways in which Krishna intervened to save him from disgrace. Narsimh may have been associated with the beginnings of the *Vallabha sampradaya*, a devotional sect founded by Vallabhacharya at Krishna's birthplace in Vrindavan at the beginning of the sixteenth century and which later spread south and found many adherents among Gujarati Vaishnavas. It was for this sect that the last Gujarati bhakti poet, Dayaram (1767–1852), composed his passionately sensuous verse in which the devotion of the soul to god, as exemplified in the amorous sport of the cowgirls

Literary languages of the West.

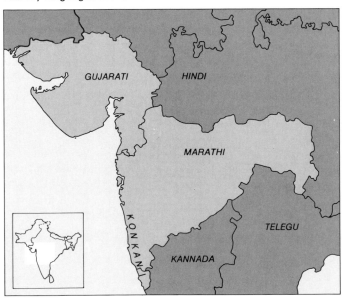

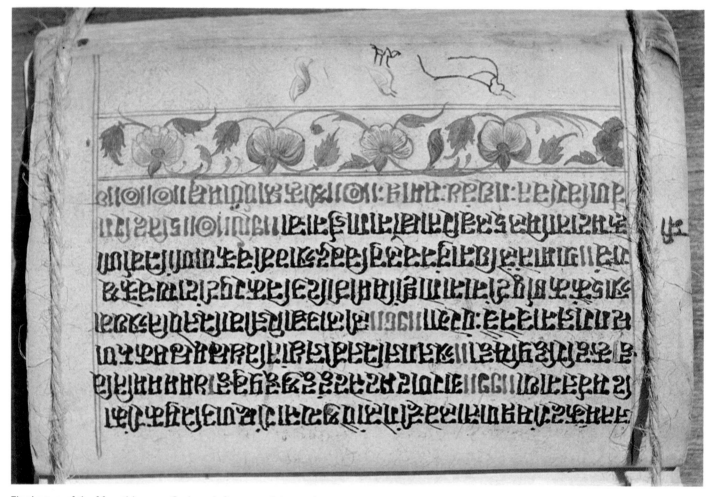

Final page of the Marathi poem *Gadyaraja* from an eighteenth century manuscript.

with Krishna, becomes more sexual than soulful.

Marathi's tradition of bhakti poets begins with a Jnandev, who may be the same as the author of *Jnaneshvari*, and culminates in Tukaram (1608–49), the shudra poet whose verse so appealed to Christian missionaries that he was called by one 'a naturally Christian soul'. All of these Marathi bhakti poets were devotees of the god Vitthal of Pandharpur, a town on the Bhima at the edge of the Maratha country. Whatever the original form of the temple and its image, about which there is much debate, it is now firmly identified with the Vishnu/Krishna tradition.

The puranic poets tell the stories of the *Mahabharata* and the *Ramayana*, the puranas and especially for Vaishnavas the *Bhagavata-purana* for their own age. In Gujarat the supreme exponent of the genre is Premanand (*c.* 1649–1714) with works such as *Nalakhyana*, *Okhaharana* and *Sudamacaritra*. He also related epi-sodes from the life of Narsimh Mehta in *Hundi* and *Kumvarbainu Mameru*, probably the most widely known and best-loved long poem in the whole of Gujarati literature with its humor, its common touch and its marvellous pace. In the same genre, Marathi has Eknath (1548–1600) with his *Eknathi Bhagavata*, his *Rukmini Svayamvara* and the *Bhavartha Ramayana*. Then there is Shridhar who early in the eighteenth century narrated all the old stories in simple flowing *ovi* verses that remain the versions to which the unsophisticated Marathi reader turns first. A refinement of this genre was provided by the learned poets, who, from the seventeenth century onwards, retold these same tales in Sanskrit meters, with a profusion of Sanskrit word borrowings and using every rhetorical trick that it is possible to reproduce in Marathi or Gujarati.

Konkani is the language of the Konkan, the strip of land between the western Ghats and the sea. In the northern part, this language has for centuries been a somewhat nasal dialect of Marathi, in the southern part it is influenced by Kannada, and it is only in the territory of Goa itself that a distinct literary language has developed. In the early centuries of Portuguese rule, the literature is almost entirely Christian doctrine and apologetics written by Jesuits and printed in roman script, the most celebrated being the *Doutrina Christam* of Thomas Stephens published in 1622, an exposition of Christianity in traditional question and answer form. Stephens, known in Goa as Thomas Estevao, also wrote a Konkani grammar, but his major work was the *Christa-purana*, a summary of the Bible with emphasis on the New Testament, which is in Marathi *ovi* verse with only a few Konkani forms. None of these Christian works were known outside Goa until the end of the nineteenth century when they were discovered by scholars and recognized as having uniquely preserved an early state of the language.

Popular literature has been constantly nourished by the undercurrent of folktales and folksongs, traditional tales and fables that go back to sources such as the Sanskrit *Panchatantra*. In Maharashtra from the eighteenth century there is a flourishing tradition of *lavanis*, erotic love-songs often incorporated in popular dramatic entertainments called *tamasha*, and of *povadas*, celebrations of the martial exploits of the heroes of the Maratha kingdom.

The Marathi *bakhars*, which chronicle the feats of Maratha arms, represent almost the only substantial body of prose writing in north Indian literature. The historiography of Gujarat during the same period was left to Muslim writers but their works, of which the *Mirat-e Ahmadi* (1761–65) is the prime example, were written in Persian. Muslims and Parsis, though they spoke their own special brands of Gujarati, contributed only marginally to Gujarati literature before the nineteenth century.

Literature in the nineteenth and twentieth centuries

The firm establishment of British rule transformed the literatures of Gujarati and Marathi. Western style schools and colleges, the founding of literary and debating societes, the performance of Shakespeare plays by student drama groups all helped to create an entirely new literature in the years between 1830 and 1870. School textbooks were needed and a suitable prose had to be developed. By the 1870s, the recipients of the new learning were writing essays and plays, short stories and novels inspired by Dickens and Scott, lyric poetry in the manner of the English romantics. In Gujarati, the first modern poet, Dalpatram, worked in close collaboration with an enthusiastic scholar-civil servant, A. K. Forbes. His son, Nanalal was the greatest lyric poet of nineteenth century Gujarat. In Marathi, new authors were encouraged by a prize fund derived from the *dakshina* money once doled out to Brahmins. By the end of the century, each language had turned out a major novelist. Govardhanram Tripathi's *Sarasvatichandra* which came out in four parts

between 1887 and 1901 still ranks as *the* great Gujarati novel, though with its great length and Sanskritic vocabulary it could never be popular. Hari Narayan Apte's twenty odd novels written between 1885 and 1915 still represent one of the most distinguished contributions to Marathi prose fiction. Over this same period, there were great polemicists in Agarkar, Lokamanya Tilak and N. C. Kelkar, who were also national figures. There also grew a theatrical tradition which is generally recognized as the leading one in India. On foundations which combined western models, the Sanskrit playwrights and the indigenous folk-theatre of *tamasha* and puranic 'miracle-play', the four great dramatists Deval, Gadkari, Khadilkar and Kolhatkar created plays, many of them musicals, which were both major artistic events and primary vehicles of social and political propaganda. In Gujarat, drama was left to Parsi troops performing farces and never attained the same status.

In the twentieth century, Gujarati and Marathi literature has continued to exploit western genres, although the occasional poet has harked back to the ballad and the bhakti hymn. So much is now published each year that it would be invidious to mention names. In 1976, for instance, about 4700 stories were published in Marathi in 176 weekly or monthly magazines; 88 short-story collections were published in book form. One name, however, that must be mentioned is that of M. K. Gandhi who wrote even-handedly in both English and Gujarati. The simple style that he favored had a radical effect on the cumbersome, heavily Sanskritic Gujarati of the late nineteenth and early twentieth centuries. The period between the world wars is often called the Gandhian era of Gujarati and indeed of Marathi and other Indian literatures. The period since Independence has seen literature tackling the themes of the ills of urbanization, the continued sufferings of the rural poor, and the loss of idealism after the simple certainties of the nationalist movement. Marathi continues to maintain its lead in drama, both in the vigor of its professional and amateur theatre and in the power of its dramatists. Vijay Tendulkar, for instance, is known all over India. Gujarati's strength is lyric poetry and Umashankar Joshi, the elder statesman of Gujarati literature, is one of the few poets to have had much work translated into English. Modern Konkani literature, which began only with the end of Portuguese rule in Goa, is almost exclusively poetry and much of that written by established Goan Marathi poets like B. B. Borkar. It is still uncertain whether Konkani can grow to maturity beneath the shade of Kannada and Marathi.

IR

Further reading

M. K. Gandhi, *An Autobiography: The Story of my Experiments with Truth* (London, 1966)

K. M. Munshi, *Gujarat and its Literatures* 2nd edn (Bombay, 1954)

V. G. Pradhan and H. W. Lambert, Trans., *Jnaneshvari* (2 vols, London, 1967–69)

I. Raeside, Trans., *The Rough and the Smooth* (Marathi short stories) (Bombay, 1966)

S. G. Tulpule, *Classical Marathi Literature* J. Gonda, Ed., *A History of Indian Literature* IX.4 (Wiesbaden, 1979)

South: Tamil, Kannada, Telugu, Malayalam

Each of the major languages of South India, Tamil, Kannada, Telugu, and Malayalam is associated with a long literary history and a large and varied body of literature. While certain common trends are apparent in the literary histories of all four languages, Tamil stands apart for at least two reasons. First, Tamil has the longest continuous literary history of all India's regional languages, with the earliest extant works in Tamil dating from about the second century

Literary languages of the South.

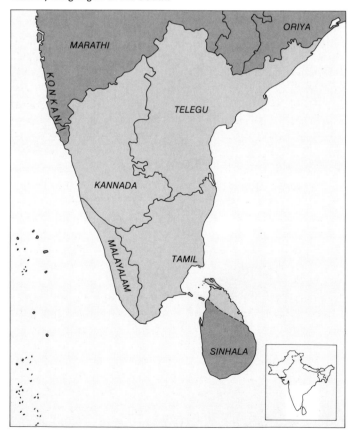

AD. Second, the earliest corpus of polished Tamil literary works grew to maturity in an artistic environment that was largely free of Sanskritic influence. In contrast, the earliest existing works in Kannada and in Telugu, which belong, respectively, to the ninth and eleventh centuries, were inspired by Sanskrit prototypes. Since early classical Tamil poetry flourished in a region encompassing present-day Tamil Nadu and Kerala, and as Malayalam emerged as a language clearly distinct from Tamil only relatively late, early Tamil poems should also be considered part of the literary pre-history of Malayalam.

Until the nineteenth century when the influence of Western literary models began to redirect the course of Indian literary history, the standards for high literary art in each of the four languages usually followed precedents set by the earliest works. Thus, for later generations of Kannada and Telugu poets, Sanskrit works continued to be vital reference points, whereas later generations of Tamil poets tended to extend and develop literary conventions found in early Tamil poems, though they certainly were not blind to Sanskrit literary traditions. In Malayalam, some genres tend to follow classical Tamil models and other Sanskrit models. This pattern applies as much to the language of literature as it does to theme and source of inspiration. All four literary traditions distinguish a formal, 'literary' style of language from the freer, more variable language of colloquial speech. In Kannada, Telugu, and the Sanskritic branch of Malayalam literature, high literary style is associated with a highly Sanskritized diction. In the case of Tamil, however, the stylistic model for polished literature is the language of the earliest Tamil poems, sometimes referred to as *centamil* or 'pure' Tamil, which contains a comparatively low proportion of Sanskrit loan-words.

Not all literary works written in the regional languages of south India before the nineteenth century, however, were modeled directly on Sanskrit prototypes or classical Tamil poems. From very early times, songs, tales, ballads and other largely anonymous literary works must have existed alongside more polished works, although it is only recently that this wealth of folk literature has been collected and recorded. It would also be a distortion to imagine that folk literature and classical literature are entirely distinct literary realms. While it is true that some genres closely conform to an ideal of classical purity and erudition, others, bearing the unmistakable stamp of folk literature in diction, in rhythmic structure and in motifs, have nonetheless achieved a lasting place in the literary canon. In fact, all four literatures can be mapped over a continuum with genres favoring a highly ornate, formal style and precisely defined conventions clustered at one end and genres employing a freer, more colloquial style and folk-inspired motifs at the other. It is, therefore, appropriate to think of literary history as a process of interplay between great and little traditions, keeping in mind that the two great traditions of Sanskrit and classical Tamil come into play in the case of Tamil and Malayalam.

Pre-modern literature

Tamil

The earliest literary corpus in Tamil is composed of eight anthologies of solitary verses, ranging in length from three to about forty lines in the older poems, and a collection of ten longer poems. These poems are known as 'sangam literature' after a legendary literary academy or sangam said to have been patronized by the Pandya kings. These poems and the *Tolkappiyam*, a prestigious normative work on grammar and poetics, show that poets of the age shared a grammar of precisely defined and highly formalized literary conventions that have no direct parallel in Sanskrit or in other Indian literatures. The poetic universe of classical Tamil is divided into two realms, called *akam* ('interior') and *puram* ('exterior'). Akam poems deal with the phases of erotic love expressed in images drawn from five typical Tamil landscape settings. Puram poems deal primarily with the public lives of warriors and kings.

The latest poems included in the sangam corpus are thought to have been composed approximately in the fifth to sixth century, by which time other kinds of texts had become established on the literary scene. One of the great masterpieces of early Tamil literature is the long narrative poem *Silappatikaram* (fifth century?) which incorporates akam and puram themes as well as themes associated with an ancient goddess cult. Its author, Ilanko, like the authors of many other early Tamil texts, is thought to have been a Jain, but unlike the authors of some other roughly contemporary narratives, he was no proselytizer, and thus *Silappatikaram* has come to be regarded as a distinctively Tamil 'epic', free from any sort of parochial sectarianism.

Also roughly contemporary with late classical poetry are didactic works composed of short aphoristic verses. Best known is *Tirukkural* by Tiruvalluvar (fifth century?) which touches upon a wide range of topics concerning household life, renunciation, statecraft and the protocol of romantic love and marriage. It too is celebrated for its nonsectarian spirit.

The poets of the late classical poems are roughly contemporary with the earliest saint-poets of Tamil Vaishnavism and Shaivism, who lived between the sixth and ninth centuries, and composed thousands of devotional poems which were later canonized within Tamil Vaishnava and Shaiva sectarian traditions and incorporated in temple liturgy.

Between the tenth and the early nineteenth centuries, Tamil literary compositions comprised a great variety of genres, some closely related to classical Tamil predecessors, some structurally or thematically reminiscent of Sanskrit literary works, and some

suggesting a kinship with folk genres. Genres such as *kovai*, *arruppatai*, *kalampakam* and *parani*, show affinities with early Tamil poems of love and war. Also composed during this period were Tamil puranas. Some are fairly close renderings of Sanskrit *mahapuranas*, but also included among Tamil puranic literature are *sthalapuranas* ('place puranas'), mythological 'histories' of sacred places in the Tamil country, many of which are the sites of important temples. Another designated 'purana' is the great twelfth century hagiography of the Tamil Shaiva saints, the *Tiruttontar Puranam* by the Chola court poet Sekkilar. Most celebrated of all long narrative poems of this period is Kamban's (tenth century? twelfth century?) rendering of the Rama story titled *Iramavataram*. Kamban was obviously familiar with Valmiki's *Ramayana*, but his work also reflects a sensibility that was deeply influenced by Tamil *bhakti* (devotional) as well as by Tamil literary and folk-traditions.

From the seventeenth century poets began to employ a diction relatively close to spoken Tamil and created works which, through the use of music and other means, were designed to appeal to a wide audience. *Ramanatakam* by Arunachala Kavirayar (1712–79) and *Nantanar Charittirakkirttanai* by Gopalakrishna Bharati (c. 1795–1896) are two important examples of such works.

Kannada

It is fitting that the very first text available in Kannada, *Kavirajamarga* (ninth century), is a free rendering of Dandin's *Kavyadarsha*, a Sanskrit work on poetics, because the relationship between early literature in Kannada and Sanskrit literature is a close one. The 'Sanskrit connection' is evident in the works of the three great tenth century poets, Pampa, Ponna and Ranna, all of whom were Jains and who are known collectively as 'the three gems'. All three wrote works in a form called *champu*, borrowed from Sanskrit, which includes alternating sections of verse and prose. Pampa is the author of *Adipurana*, a narration of the successive births of the first Jain *tirthankara*, and also *Vikramarjunavijaya*, a telling of the *Mahabharata* story containing allusions to contemporary events. During the eleventh century one finds a Kannada rendering of the *Panchatantra* by Durgasimha and also Nagachandra's *Ramachandracharita-purana*, the first extant Kannada *Ramayana*, which was modeled after a Jain version in Sanskrit by Vimalasuri.

But pre-modern Kannada literary history is not entirely dominated by Sanskrit. Virashaiva saints, most of whom lived during the twelfth and thirteenth centuries, composed poems called *vachanas* which expressed their dedication to Shiva and often their contempt for Brahminical Hinduism. They broke with the conventions favored by more classically minded poets, employed the language of spoken Kannada and eschewed the rules of meter. Among the most influential *vachanakaras* were Basavanna, Allama Prabhu, and the woman saint, Mahadevi. The literature of bhakti in Kannada also includes the less iconoclastic Shaiva poetry of Harihara (thirteenth century), and later devotional songs of the Vaishnava Haridasas. Best known among the latter is Purandaradasa (sixteenth century) who is remembered for his contribution to the development of south Indian classical music.

A catalogue of Kannada literature from the time of 'the three gems' until the nineteenth century reveals a sometimes parallel, sometimes oscillating development of highly stylized, classical genres such as the champu, and works that are much closer in form and spirit to folk literature and which appealed to a much wider audience, such as the dramatic genre called *yakshagana*.

Telugu

Sanskritization is even more extensive in the history of Telugu literature. The *adikavi* ('original poet') of Telugu literary tradition is Nannaya (eleventh century), who wrote a partial translation of the *Mahabharata*. A thirteenth century poet, Tikkana, translated most of the remaining portion of the text, and Errana, a poet of the fourteenth century, completed the translation. Beginning with Nannaya, for about 500 years Telugu poets devoted their creative energy largely to the translation of Sanskrit classics.

The first Telugu *Ramayana* appeared in the thirteenth century, and Shrinatha, who explored both highly Sanskritized and more popular styles, rendered a number of Sanskrit *kavyas* into Telugu. Many Sanskrit dramas also served as models for Telugu works during the fourteenth century, but in general Telugu poets transformed their models into champus. Especially honored among the Telugu literary classics based on a Sanskrit prototype is Potana's (1450–1510) rendering of the *Bhagavata-purana*.

The reign of the Vijayanagar king Krishnadevaraya (1509–1529) is referred to as the golden age of Telugu literature. The king, himself the attributed author of a number of works in Sanskrit and Telugu, provided patronage for poets who produced a large literary corpus, including the retelling of stories from the Sanskrit epics, puranic works on local deities, and praise poems. The poets of this period are especially noted for their cultivation of the *prabandha* genre.

Three other genres that stand out in Telugu literary history are the *shataka*, the devotional lyric and·yakshagana. A shataka ideally should contain 100 verses each with the same refrain. As early as the thirteenth century, Telugu poets began composing shatakas on a great variety of subjects. There are shatakas on religious themes, didactic shatakas, philosophical and biographical shatakas and shatakas intended primarily to tell a story. The father of the devotional lyric in Telugu is Annamacharya (1424–1503), a devotee of Venkateshvara. The songs of another Telugu poet-musician, Tyagaraja (1767–1847), a devotee of Rama who lived in Tiruvaiyaru, near Thanjavur in Tamil Nadu, continue to be a

mainstay in the repertoire of South Indian classical music. Thanjavur and Madurai (also in Tamil Nadu) became centers for literary activity in Telugu after the military defeat of Vijayanagar in 1565. Poets of the so-called 'Southern School' flourished here under the Telugu Nayak rulers of the sixteenth and seventeenth centuries, composing *prabandhas*, lyric poems, biographical poems and yakshagana plays.

Malayalam

Tamilizing and Sanskritizing trends in early Malayalam literature are well represented by the genre called *pattu* in the case of the former and by the champu and *samdeshakavya* ('messenger poem') in the case of the latter. The earliest and perhaps the most famous pattu poem is the *Ramacharitam* (probably late twelfth or early thirteenth century). While the subject of this poem is closely modeled after Valmiki's *Ramayana*, the style is deeply rooted in classical Tamil poetry. The earliest Malayalam champu is *Unniyachicharitam* (thirteenth century). However, the genre really came into its own somewhat later, the most famous Malayalam champu being *Ramayanachampu*, attributed to Punam (fifteenth century). The Sanskritizing trend in early Malayalam literature is also represented by messenger poems, which take as their model Kalidasa's *Meghaduta*. The language of many Sanskritizing genres can really be considered a hybrid of Sanskrit and Malayalam. In local tradition this style is known as *manipravalam* ('rubies and coral'), and literary works composed in this idiom are compared to a necklace strung alternately with these gems.

Both the pattu and the champu are far removed from colloquial Malayalam and from the indigenous meters found in ballads and other genres of folk literature. Beginning around the fifteenth century, some poets attempted to bring about an accommodation between highly refined 'art' literature and a more colloquial and accessible idiom. Cherusseri's *Krishna Gatha*, a poem modeled on incidents from the *Bhagavata-purana*, is an outstanding early example of this trend. Even more influential are the works of Ezhuthachan (sixteenth century), who favored the *kilippattu* ('parrot song'), so named because by convention these poems are presented as the narration of a parrot or other bird. Most important among Ezhuthachan's works are his *Ramayanam*, largely based upon a fourteenth century Sanskrit work called *Adhyatma Ramayana*, and his *Bharatam*.

Genres closely associated with dramatic performance occupy a very important place in Malayalam literature. Sanskrit and to some extent Malayalam champus were used as scripts for a type of performance called *kuttu*. Traditionally, a *kuttu* is performed in a special hall adjacent to a temple by a solo, hereditary performer called a *chakyar*. Another kind of poem composed for performance by a solo singer-actor is the *tullal*. A tullal performance, however, is much freer and more popular in appeal than a kuttu. The text is less Sanskritized and often comical; and music and dance is employed to a much greater extent. The great master of this genre was Kunchan Nambiar (b. 1705), known for his earthy, satirical wit and credited with sixty-four tullal scripts.

Full-scale drama is also found in Kerala. *Kudiyattam*, a performance tradition which employs Sanskrit dramas for its scripts, dates from the ninth century. Though the primary script for kudiyattam is in Sanskrit, the Vidusaka (Brahmin-jester), a stock character in these plays, speaks his lines in Malayalam and *manipravalam*. Certain conventions of kudiyattam were later adopted by *kathakali*, the well-known dance-drama of Kerala whose scripts, called *attakkatha*, are fully in Malayalam.

Modern literature

Innovations in education which accompanied British rule in India had a profound effect on literature. By the second half of the nineteenth century writers in all the main Indian languages were exploring imported genres such as the novel, short story, topical essay, biography and autobiography. In an environment where the vast majority of traditional literary genres were in verse, it is striking that so many modern Indian writers have embraced prose as their medium; although poetry, in many cases in new forms inspired by Western poetry, continues to be cultivated.

In South India, as elsewhere, some of the earliest works belonging to the new literary environment were translations of English and to a lesser extent other European classics. Since Bengali was in the vanguard of the westernizing trend, Bengali works were also translated. By the end of the nineteenth century original novels, short stories and other non-traditional forms were cultivated in all the significant South Indian languages. A few writers stand out as pioneers. In Tamil, Subramania Bharati (1882–1921) and V. V. S. Aiyar (1881–1925) were the first truly modern writers and are credited with transforming Tamil into a modern literary language. Bharati, a political activist and spokesman for social reform, was primarily a poet and essayist, while V. V. S. Aiyar is remembered for his short stories. Rao Bahadur K. Viresalingam Pantalu (1847–1919) made a similar contribution to Telugu. A committed social reformer, he developed a simple prose style and wrote not only the first Telugu novel, but also short stories, dramas, biographies, farces and literary criticism. Three outstanding literary figures of the early twentieth century for Malayalam are the poets Kumaran Asan (1873–1924), Vallathol Narayana Menon (1879–1958), and Ulloor Parameswara Iyer (1877–1949). Known as 'the great trio' of modern Malayalam poetry, each in his own distinctive way forged a bridge between Malayalam's literary heritage and the contemporary social environment. In the field of modern Malayalam prose, the

greatest early figures are the novelists Chandu Menon (d. 1899) and C. V. Raman Pillai (d. 1922).

Literary output during the twentieth century has been extensive and only a few prominent names are mentioned here. In Tamil, Puthumaipittan and Mauni are known for their short stories. In the field of modern Kannada literature, Masti is acknowledged as a master of the short story, while K. S. Karant is highly honored for his novels. In Telugu, the poet Sri Sri is remembered for the leading role he played in the progressive poetry movement. In Malayalam, the volatile poet Chengampuzha (1914–48) stands out as a model for self-styled progressive Malayali poets, while among Malayali writers of prose, the names Basheer and Takazhi are especially well known.

Traditional literature has not been left entirely by the wayside in

Cover of a recent translation into English of three stories by the Malayali writer, Vaikom Muhammad Basheer.

present-day South India. Folk ballads are performed by professional balladeers at village temple festivals; the hymns of the *bhakti* saints are sung in the major Hindu temples; and nowadays the study of learned classical literature is pursued in colleges and in university literature departments. At the same time, forms of writing inherited from the West enjoy a very large readership. Short stories and serialized novels are standard fare in many popular periodicals which flourish in the cities and towns of South India along with less widely read literary journals dedicated to writing of a more serious cast. 'Literature' in present-day South India thus encompasses many different kinds of texts, both oral and written, traditional and modern, and this is only fitting in this complex and multilayered cultural setting.

NCu

Further reading
K. Chaitanya, *A History of Malayalam Literature* (New Delhi, 1971)
Encyclopaedia Britannica 15th edn S.v. 'South Asian Peoples, Arts of', by (in part) A. K. Ramanujan.
K. M. George, *A Survey of Malayalam Literature* (London, 1968)
R. S. Mugali, *History of Kannada Literature* (New Delhi, 1975)
G. V. Sitapati, *History of Telugu Literature* (New Delhi, 1968)
V. Zvelebil, *Tamil Literature* (Weisbaden, 1974)

Sinhala
The existence of Sinhala poetry is attested as early as the seventh century AD, but the earliest surviving literature (apart from inscriptions) dates from the tenth century. The literature is almost entirely

Sinhala.

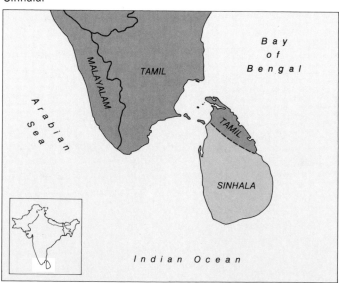

Buddhist in character, secular literature before the twentieth century being confined to a few poems of one particular *genre*.

Many of the earliest surviving works are in prose. Verse nearly always precedes prose, and it is probable that these prose works were a new development in a continuing literary tradition, while earlier poetic works were becoming unintelligible at a time of rapid linguistic change. The earliest works in verse now surviving belong to the early thirteenth or late twelfth century, to Polonnaruwa times when the capital was still situated in the dry zone. They are difficult to understand without the old commentaries which have come down with them. The prose works of the thirteenth century, on the other hand, are fairly readily intelligible today. This is because the literary language became fixed at that period in a mold which still prevails. There is a 'diglottic' situation today in Sinhala (as also in Tamil), where the language of writing differs to a considerable extent from the language of speech. Whether this was so in the twelfth century we have no means of knowing, but the literary standard of that century became fixed as a norm which has not yet been abandoned.

Most of the early prose works were collections of Buddhist tales; such are *Ama-vatura*, *But-sarana*, *Pujavaliya* and *Saddharma-ratnavaliya*, all written before 1300; the last-named is a Sinhala version of the Pali *Dhammapada-atthakatha*. There is also the collection of 547 Jataka stories (stories of previous births of the Buddha), the *Pansiya-panas-jataka-pota*, compiled in the fourteenth century. Most poetry was versified jataka stories; the earliest full poem is *Kav-silumina*, a versification of the *Kusa-jataka*. It is non-rhyming, in obscure meters and not readily intelligible today.

After 1400, when the center of the kingdom had moved from the dry zone to the southwest, a new style of poem arose, of regular pattern and rhyme, and in this style were composed the *sandesa* or message poems, which are purely secular in character, and are copies of the Sanskrit model of Kalidasa's *Meghaduta*; although nominally concerned with the taking of a message, usually by a bird, the message is in fact unimportant and the interest of the poem lies in the lengthy descriptions of the route by which the messenger must travel across Sri Lanka. A number of famous sandesas were written in the fifteenth century, *Sala-lihini*, *Gira*, *Parevi*, *Hamsa* and *Tisara* being the best known; similar poems continued to be written up till the twentieth century. The author of *Sala-lihini-sandesa*, Sri Rahula, is the most famous of classical Sinhalese poets; he also wrote a *mahakavya* or heroic poem called *Kavya-sekharaya*, based on the Sattubhasta jataka. Other fine poems of this epoch are *Buduguna-alamkaraya* and *Guttilaya*. Of collections of Buddhist stories in prose at this time, the best known is *Saddharma-alam-karaya*, a Sinhala version of the Pali *Rasavahini*. Historical works were also written.

After the European powers appeared in Sri Lanka in the sixteenth century, Sinhala literature declined rapidly. The last significant classical poet was Alagiyavanna, who held a post in the Portuguese administration; he versified the *Kusa-jataka* story once more. Of prose works, *Saddharma-ratnakaraya* belongs to this period; but when the coastal areas were occupied by the Dutch after 1650, and the independent Sinhalese kingdom practically confined to the inland areas centered on Kandy, Sinhala literature became more 'popular' in character. The poems of that period are not in general highly prized today, though there was something of a revival in the late eighteenth and early nineteenth century, centered on the south-coast town of Matara. This revival was inspired by Välivita Saranankara (1698–1778) who sought to recover the classical Sinhalese heritage, and in fact reshaped the literary language into a copy of the older mold, thus preventing, perhaps, the normal development of the language while simultaneously preserving its older works into the modern period.

After the British had established political control over the whole island in 1815, Sinhala literature came to a standstill, and the Buddhist ethos which had always infused it became overlaid by secularism and traces of Protestant Christianity (the Christianity which had been established in the island in Roman Catholic form since Portuguese times not having affected literary style to any extent). The rise of journalism after 1860 provided a stimulus for the creation of a quite different kind of literature, which was nevertheless still written in the old literary style. Gradually, but rather slowly, the possibilities of a modern European-type literature that was also genuinely Sinhala (and this really meant of Buddhist inspiration) took hold, and the first Sinhala book which can be called a novel appeared in 1905. It was not until 1944 that a novel of the kind that would be acceptable today was published, by Martin Wickramasinghe (1891–1976), the undoubted founder of modern Sinhala literature. He has been followed by Gunadasa Amarasekara (b. 1929), Siri Gunasinghe (b. 1931), K. Jayatilaka (b. 1926), Simon Navagattegama (b. 1941), Ediriwira Sarachchandra (b. 1914), Mahagama Sekera (1929–76), G. B. Senanayake (1913–85), A. V. Surawira (b. 1930) and others. All these novelists also write short stories.

Sarachchandra has also led the way towards drama as a literary form. There had been no classical Sinhala drama, so he followed the tradition of *nadagam* plays (masques of Tamil origin) on Sinhala themes, starting with *Maname* in 1956; others such as Sugatapala de Silva (b. 1928) have followed with satirical productions, often reflecting modern politics. Poetry has always survived as a popular art form, but a new literary life has been given it in recent years by poets such as Monica Ruwanpatirana (b. 1946) and Parakrama Kodituwakku (b. 1943), whose works also show satirical overtones.

Apart from Sinhala literature, in medieval Sri Lanka works were

Cover of an edition of the collected short stories of Martin Wickramasinghe, the founder of modern literature in Sinhala.

also composed in Pali, the classical language of southern Buddhism, and at the present day Tamil literature flourishes among the Tamil community in Sri Lanka.

CHBR

Further reading

C. H. B. Reynolds, Ed., *An Anthology of Sinhalese Literature up to 1815* (London, 1970)

C. H. B. Reynolds, Ed., *An Anthology of Sinhalese Literature of the Twentieth Century* (London, 1987)

Nepali

Nepali literature is that written in Nepali, the Indo-Aryan language that has become over the last two centuries the national language of Nepal. The literature is extensive and of great interest, but it has yet to be studied in depth. It is therefore still almost totally inaccessible in the West.

Royal inscriptions in Nepali and its related dialects found in the western part of Nepal date back as early as the thirteenth century, but literature does not begin to develop distinctively until the beginning of the nineteenth century. Works written before this time consist mainly of royal panegyrics, religious poetry and manuals in various sciences, such as astrology and medicine.

With the rise of the kingdom of Gorkha and the conquest of the Nepal Valley by King Prithvinarayan Shah in 1769, the Nepali language, also known as Gorkhali, Parbatiya, and Khas-kura, spread rapidly, becoming the language of government and administration, and the chief lingua franca of the country. Literary activity increased dramatically, and vigorous poetic and prose styles developed. A chief example of the prose of this period is the *Dibyopadesha* (*Divine Counsel*) attributed to King Prithvinarayan Shah himself. Between 1769 and 1846 (the beginning of the Rana regime) many of the great works of Sanskrit literature were translated including large sections of the *Mahabharata*, various puranas, and the major works of story literature, such as the *Hitopadesha*, and the *Brhatkathamanjari* of Kshemendra. A distinctive development of the period was the composition of native histories or chronicles (*vamsavali*) that joined dynastic lists, temple records, and religious myth into an important branch of native historiography.

The most important poet of the nineteenth century was Bhanubhakta Acharya (1814–68). He is considered by most native critics to be the most important figure in Nepalese literary history and his *Ramayana*, written between 1841 and 1853, the single most important poetic work in the language. He commands a position in Nepali literature similar to that of Tulsidas in medieval Hindi, and his verses are universally acclaimed by Nepali speakers.

In the early part of the twentieth century, despite the political isolation imposed by the Rana regime (1846–1951) outside influences began to make themselves felt, particularly through the works of British, Continental and Indian writers. Printing was introduced, and the publishing of Western-style books, newspapers, journals, began. The novel, short story, the modern essay, the modern play became forms with which Nepali writers began to experiment. Among writers of importance one should mention Motiram Bhatta and Lekhnath Paudyal, considered by many to be the two most important poets of this period; Girishvallabh Joshi, whose novel *Bircaritra* is an imaginative early work; Shri Guru Prasad Mainali, whose novels and short stories paint a clear picture of traditional Nepali life; Pushkar Shamsher, and Shri Bhavani Bhikshu, both well-known short-story writers. The two most outstanding literary figures of the century, however, are unquestionably Bal Krishna Sama who is generally recognized as one of the most versatile and creative writers of his time, and Lakshmi Prasad Devkota. Since Bhanubhakta, Devkota has influenced the course of Nepali literature, perhaps more than any other figure. His early work, *Muna Mada* (1936), is one of the most popular and influential pieces of twentieth century Nepali poetry. Stifled and unable to work under the Rana regime, Devkota left Nepal for Varanasi, returning only in 1948 just a few years before the end of the regime. Despite his short life, his output was immense, most of it of the highest artistic quality.

Contemporary literary activity is highly varied and rich, with many writers concerned with the present climate of political and social change. Among authors of note may be mentioned the poet, Mohan Koirala, and the novelist Parijat.

TR

Further reading

T. Riccardi, Jr., *A Nepali Version of the Vetalapancavimsati* (New Haven, 1971)

D. Rubin, *Nepali Visions, Nepali Dreams* (New York, 1980)

Nepali.

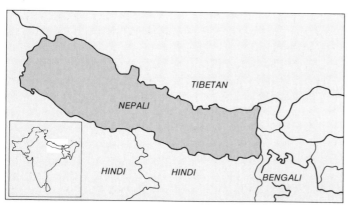

Music

Classical music

In generating limitless variations of melody as spiritual pathway and esthetic expression – produced both through purely melodic unmetered sections as well as the bounded structure of often complex metered compositions – India's classical music system retains its fundamental purpose and principle of sound production born centuries and perhaps millenia ago.

Indeed as early as the Vedas, the impact of sound – verbal or musical, manifest or not – on human affairs was underlined as supremely important in the governance of the cosmos. The correct chanting by priests, of the *Rigveda* and the singing of the *Samveda* was believed fundamentally necessary to maintaining order in the Universe, and by extension, the human world.

Music in South Asia has always exhibited the tendencies of being both other and this worldly. Often considered a means of self realization and salvation rather than mere self expression, this view of music as mode of enlightenment is sometimes over emphasized at the expense of understanding it as a product of South Asian culture; musical sound shaped by the structure of South Asian society, history, ideas and knowledge.

Continuity with the past in South Asia remains a central idea and a foundation for contemporary musical practice. Such continuity has been achieved until very recently through a largely aural system of musical transmission, since notational systems, insofar as they existed were essentially solfege systems used only as a mnemonic for, but not a basis of performance. Even without musical scores, however, the evidence of early recordings demonstrates that South Asian musical traditions have not been restricted by an unvarying orthodoxy. Rather they have remained adaptive and resilient even as the context of musical performance radically changes, as it has during the last century.

What is today the generic term for music in South Asia (*sangita*) referred originally also to dance and drama with which music was inextricably associated. Thus the earliest text dealing with music explicitly is the great treatise on dramaturgy the *Natyashastra* (third to fourth century AD) which includes six chapters on music. Although music is now conceptually and in practice distinct from dance and drama, the classical forms of each remain closely related with much borrowing of terminology, meter and meaning.

Other major texts, important as sources of authenticity and continuity are the *Brihaddesi* (eighth to ninth century AD) in which *rags* (see below) are first named and discussed and then the great *Sangitratnakara* (thirteenth century) which is a systematized compendium of excerpts of earlier treatises and contemporary music practice.

Beginning in the thirteenth century, with the establishment of the Delhi Sultanate, Islamic hegemony in the north is commonly believed to be associated with the evolution of two distinct styles of musical practice in India: The *Hindustani* of the north and the *Karnatak* of the south. Although the Hindustani system is considered different from the Karnatak by virtue of the presence of Persian and Turkic features in the former – musicians from Persia and central Asia were associated with courts in the North at least until the late seventeenth century – some scholars believe that the Karnatak system also absorbed Persian and Turkic musical ideas. We know that as recently as the sixteenth century, musicians were being exchanged between the Hindu court of Vijayanagar and the contemporaneous Muslim Bahmani courts.

Today the two main classical styles in South Asia correspond geographically to the linguistic areas of Indo-Aryan based languages in the north and Dravidian based languages in the south. Although analytically both can be considered two variants of one underlying system, the two systems are considered in India to be distinct constituting separate theory systems, histories, compositions and performers.

Common to both systems are the fundamental concepts of pitch (*svara*), melody type (*raga* known as *rag* in the north and *ragam* in the south) and meter (*tala*, *tal* in the north and *talam* in the south). Both also use similar types of performance ensembles with a vocalist or instrumentalist as soloist, a drummer as rhythmic accompanist and a drone provided by a tanpura. In the case of a vocal soloist, a melodic accompanist on an instrument is also present.

Hindustani music

Hindustani music is usually traced back by its practitioners to the Delhi Sultanate period with Amir Khusrau (AD 1253–1325) as one of the earliest historical personalities. Although traditionally considered the inventor of the *sitar* and the *tabla*, and as well as several rags and other musical genres, the actual evidence for these assumptions is unclear. Along with his close friend and mentor, the great Chishti Saint Nizamud Din Auliya (AD 1236–1325), Amir Khusrau is responsible for having legitimized the practice of musical performance in the context of orthodox Islamic ambivalence towards music, and also championing Indian as opposed to 'foreign' Persian, Arabic and central Asian music.

The zenith of Hindustani music is associated with the great Tansen, one of the jewels of the court of the Mughal emperor, Akbar (r. 1556–1605). A vocalist and an instrumentalist, most Hindustani musicians today trace their musical descent from Tansen. Contemporary musical practices, however, are more directly related to a later descendant of Tansen's, Niyamat Khan (popularly known as Sadarang) and his nephew Adarang who are said to have introduced the *khayal* vocal genre, during the reign of Muhammad Shah Rangile (1719–48). Masit Khan, also considered an eighteenth century descendant of Tansen, introduced a style of sitar playing, the compositional form of which is still basic to sitar performances and known as Masitkhani Gat.

Hindustani musical performance is based on a composition which is set to a meter and from which extemporized variations are generated. The composition is usually a relatively short tune which is said to embody the essence of the rag (mode or melody type) in which it is composed. The rag is constructed out of a scale and patterns of melody within the scale as well as pitches which are emphasized or not depending on the rules of the rag. Accordingly, different rags can have exactly the same scale but are rendered distinctive due to the manner in which the pitch material of the scale is utilized.

A performance begins with an *alap*. For *dhrupad* (four part composition) and in instrumental genres, the alap is elaborate and characterized by the absence of any metered accompaniment. Following the alap, pulsed sections, which are considered subsections of the *alap*, are performed in *dhrupad* and instrumental genres and are called *jor* (instrumental) or *nom-tom* (dhrupad). Sitar and sarod performance practice also includes a *jhala*, which is an alternating pulsed and melodic section often repeated within the composition itself later in the performance. In the vocal khayal the alap is typically non-existent or short and sometimes extended into the metered section.

Once the alap is ended the composition proper is performed. The composition is set to a recurring rhythmic cycle (*tala*) (most often 12 or 16 beats but also 7, 10 as well as many other possibilities) and is provided by the drum (*pakhavaj* for dhrupad, and *tabla* for almost everything else). Improvization assumes a rondo-like form, with elaborations moving from the composition followed by the return to and recurrence of all or part of the composition.

Hindustani vocal music is performed in three major and several minor styles. The oldest and most austere is a four part composition known as dhrupad. Dhrupad is also performed on the stick zither *bin* (or *rudra vina* as it is sometimes known). The main classical vocal form today is the two part composition known as khayal (pers. imagination), usually followed at the end of a concert by a light classical form known as *thumri*. In addition to the ubiquitous *tanpura*, providing the drone there is also a melodic accompanying instrument, either the bowed sarangi or the keyed harmonium, which provides a melodic 'echo' to the main vocal line.

Texts of most compositions are devotional, although these can take on a remarkably wide range of manifestations ranging from abstractly spiritual to the highly erotic.

Most instrumental compositions in the north (referred to as *gat*), although sometimes based on vocal models, are a largely separate repertoire in the north and are performed mainly on either the sitar or the sarod. They include compositions which are inherited through family lineages along with more recent compositions. In this century several other instruments including the flute, sarangi and shahnai have also developed solo performance traditions.

Karnatak music

What is performed today as Karnatak music is derived most immediately from three outstanding composers of the eighteenth century, known collectively as the Trinity: Tyagaraja (1759–1847), Svami Shastri (1763–1827) and Dikshitar (1775–1835). The Trinity, although not themselves patronized by the courts, spent most of their lives within a few miles radius of Tanjore, which became the focal point of musical patronage in the south after the fall of Vijayanagar (1565). Subbaraya Shastri (1803–62), son of Svami Shastri continued a discipular line which extends into the present. Dikshitar's younger brother and disciple Balasvami (1786–1858) was one of the early proponents of the western violin. Tyagaraja is revered both as the supreme artist and a saint, and epitomizes the ideal of musicianship in the south. Most of his immediate disciples were not professional musicians but devotees and it is only after the succeeding generation that professional musicians received Tyagaraja's compositions.

Karnatak performance practice tends to give greater emphasis to the actual composition than is the case for *Hindustani* music. The fixed and memorized composition along with its memorized variations are longer and constitute proportionately much more of a given performance than in the north. It is not uncommon to have approximately a dozen distinct 'pieces' performed in a Karnatak concert in contrast to the at most four or five in a Hindustani performance.

Improvization, rather than moving away from and then returning to the composition as is the Hindustani case, tends rather to improvize on the composition itself; variations both memorized and improvized are based directly upon the composition.

Karnatak music includes three major performance genres as well as some minor ones: the *varnam* an advanced étude-like composition often performed as the first item of a performance. The *kriti*, which is the classical compositional form most often associated wth the eighteenth century Trinity, is devotional in its textual material; and the *ragam-tanam-pallavi* a somewhat more abstract musical form embodying extensive unmetered sections along with a new or borrowed compositional line characterized by rhythmic variation in the pallavi section. The ragam-tanam-pallavi is in principle the centerpiece of a Karnatak performance, although a *kriti* will often assume this role in actual practice.

Despite the series of contrasts one can make between the two systems, they share analogous structural units. For example, the Karnatak *alapana* is in many respects equivalent to the Hindustani alap: both function as the expositional structure of a raga.

Musicians

Hindustani musicians are often associated with one or another *gharana* or stylistic and hereditary school of musicians. Originally composed of hereditary lineages of Muslim musicians evolving in the late nineteenth century, gharanas, usually named after the ancestral urban home of the lineage, came to represent the core of stylistic traditions distinguished from one another on the basis of some difference in compositional repertoire, rag interpretation and other aspects of performance practice.

A comparable institution to the named gharana does not exist in the Karnatak tradition, but lineages of discipular descent remain important there. For example, Svami Shastri's son's line includes Vina Dhannam (1867–1938) whose non-kin disciples and actual descendents are important musicians today.

Instruments

South Asia's instrumentarium reflects the diversity and aesthetic emphasis characteristic of Indian civilization itself. Ancient theorists had as early as the *Natyashastra* divided instruments into the four categories of wind, strings, drums and other percussion instruments (idiophones). Major instruments in the Hindustani tradition include the plucked stringed *sitar, sarod, tanpura* and *vina*; the bowed *sarangi* as well as the western violin; the oboe-like *shahnai*, and the two major drums, the *tabla* and *pakhavaj*.

The most important instruments in the south are the *vina*, played alone, the violin played solo or as accompaniment to a vocalist, and the flute also played as a solo or accompanying instrument. There is also a parallel but somewhat separate tradition of the oboe-like *nagasvaram* and its drums (*tavil*).

Major instruments in the Hindustani tradition of classical music:
(a) table (b) bayan (c) pakhavaj (d) rudra-vina (e) shahnai (f) tanpura (g) sarod (h) sarangi (i) sitar.

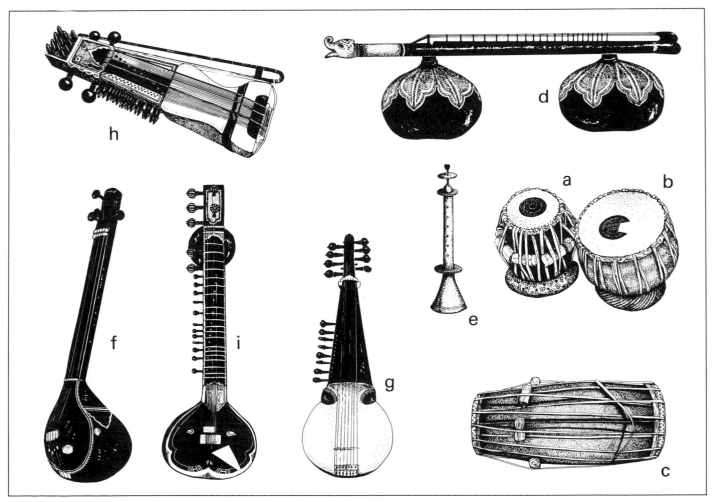

Experimenting with new instruments follows an old tradition in South Asia. Today one can hear the saxophone, clarinet and mandolin in the south and the slide guitar in the north.

Musical culture today

The twentieth century has seen the introduction of new technologies directly affecting performance. A musical tradition which had relied almost exclusively on oral transmission and prodigious memory can now be captured with the economy of a cassette; and performances which were limited to an élite audience of the privileged few are now amplified to hundreds and thousands and broadcast to millions. Economic and political changes have radically altered the structure of musical patronage, moving music from court to concert stage and from the nobility to the bourgeoisie. Music education has shifted from the master-disciple system to institutionalized classroom training.

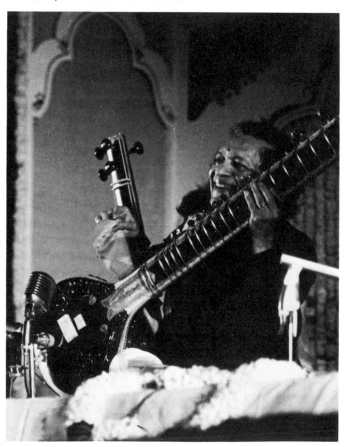

Ravi Shankar, a leading international exponent of Indian classical music, in performance with the sitar.

The musical ramifications of these social and cultural changes are not well understood as yet in detail. Examples are changes in the technique and musical role of the drums and voice, as these are amplified; the choice of repertoire and duration of performances before large and heterogeneous audiences; the crystallization of modes and compositions preserved in recordings; the copying of successful but formerly protected musical techniques and compositions through recordings.

DN

Further reading

N. Jairazbhoy, *The Rags of North Indian Music* (Middletown, 1971)
D. Neuman, *The Life of Music in North India (Detroit, 1980)*
H. Powers, *et al.*, 'India' in the *New Grove Dictionary of Music and Musicians* (London, 1980)
B. Wade, *Khyal, Cambridge Studies in Ethnomusicology* (Cambridge, 1984)

Popular music

Popular music in South Asia as elsewhere in the world reflects the feelings of ordinary people; it does not just represent entertainment but forms an essential element in many of the activities of daily life. It consists mainly of folk songs and devotional music. Much overlapping between these elements has taken place; and, more recently, a third element has been introduced in the form of music influenced by developments in the West. There are also strong underlying connections with the classical traditions of the region.

Folk songs have their own special meaning or message, and usually take their inspiration from historical events, well-known legends or important rituals in the lifecycle. Their structures vary from area to area and from caste to caste. Kashmir's *gulraz*, for instance, is a 'folk tale' which can boast as many as one thousand verses. The *Pandyani* is a legendary narrative set to music in the Indian state of Madhya Pradesh. Love epic poems such as Hir Ranjha, Sasu-Panhun and Sohan-Mahiwal are sung in a specific mode (*sur*) and have their own distinctive style of presentation. In Sind (Pakistan), sur forms the basis of the musical presentation of Shah Abdul Latif's famous *Risalo*, known as *Shah jo Rago*, and represents a synthesis of Sindhi classical and folk traditions. Folk songs are also 'functional' in that the people who perform such music believe that it serves a vital purpose in the wider framework of their combined existence. Women in northern India, for instance, will sing to propitiate the smallpox goddess. Similarly, harvest songs are not simply a way of giving thanks to God but are also a means of ensuring that the following year's harvest will be good. They are usually sung to the accompaniment of drone instruments, usually from the lute family, or to percussion instruments. In the

Panjab, the harvest season is the time of the *bhangra* when men dance and women sing. In Baluchistan (Pakistan), rain songs have great importance. Construction workers on Bombay building sites, fishermen hauling in their nets on the beaches of Kerala and women grinding wheat in Uttar Pradesh sing to ease the tedium of monotonous tasks. Ritual songs form a central feature of the lives of many village women especially at the time of weddings and births; special songs are sung on the birth of a son which is a highly auspicious event in a patrilineal society.

Devotional music in the subcontinent is characterized by the desire to attain religious ecstasy by singing intensely rhythmic, repetitious songs which name God and invoke his grace. Songs associated with the Hindu *bhakti* cult have close links with classical styles of singing. Hindu *bhajans* are often based on ancient religious stories and, like many folk songs, are performed with a leader and a chorus. Christians also sing bhajans in their churches but substitute words about Christianity. Muslims have a special kind of congregational religious music known as *qavvali* which is a combination of chanting, clapping and singing. Its theme is usually based on the concept of a personal relationship with God which in turn is modeled on the anguish of unrequited love felt by a man for his earthly beloved. There are qavvalis, such as those written by Amir Khusrau (AD 1253–1325), which are secular but the ambiguity of reference which is basic to the poem means that the two forms cannot be completely separated. Qavvali is often performed on Pakistani television. In parts of India, Hindus also sing qavvalis, taking as their subject the exploits and glories of Krishna. The harmonium, a portable handpumped organ first imported by European missionaries in the nineteenth century, has become the mainstay of the qavvali vocalist. In contrast to the ecstasy generated by the qavvali and its close relation, the *birha*, is the elegeic *marsiya* which South Asian Shias perform during the Muslim month of Muharram. *Kafis*, or sufi poems often set to classical *rags*, are important throughout northern India.

Traveling cinemas and the availability of relatively inexpensive transistor radios have brought the musical culture of the larger towns and cities of South Asia to the countryside. Film music, which dominates the airways of the region and commands a huge market in terms of the sale of cassettes, blends South Asian classical, folk and devotional music with Western influences, most noticeably the use of a large orchestra albeit including both Indian and Western instruments. It retains its South Asian feel especially in vocal technique and the ornamentation of the melody line. Indeed, the spread of the mass media provides traditional popular music with new channels of communication; the wedding of folk music with mass media techniques has made many popular folk music styles much better known outside their own regions. Changing musical tastes have resulted in the growing popularity of band music.

A qavvali vocalist and his harmonium in performance by the tomb of Amir Khusrau at Nizamuddin in Delhi.

Marching bands using European instruments are nowadays in great demand since they play popular film tunes. However, members of these bands are often from the same low status groups or castes which provided village musicians in the past. Thus, while these changes have spurred efforts to conserve more traditional forms of popular music, they must also be seen as the most recent link in a long chain of developments in which popular music has learnt to respond to changing society.

SA

449

Dance and dance-drama

Indian dance forms can be traced back as early as 2500 BC. Archeological remains at Mohenjodaro and Harappa (2500 to 1500 BC) and literary descriptions in the Vedas (1000 to 500 BC) are convincing proof of a vibrant tradition of dance in the subcontinent. Dance was associated with worship and ritual and thus considered sacred; the divine Dances of the Gods are the themes of many myths and legends. Solo dance was highly stylized, collective dance of tribal and rural communities was related to agriculture and the lifecycle. Although Pali Buddhism established in 500 BC, concentrated on the spiritual aspects of life, dance and music were not neglected. Epic poems such as the *Ramayana* and the *Mahabharata*, together with the Puranas, formed the subject of many dances. In southern India, Tamil poets in their writings such as the *Silppadhikaram*, reflect the beauty and importance of dance.

Between the second century BC and the ninth century AD, many theoretical works were written on dance. The earliest and most famous was the *Natyasastra* attributed to Bharata. Its text consists of thirty-six chapters dealing with all aspects of music, dance and drama. Five chapters are devoted specifically to movements of the body. They give a descriptive account of the ways in which movements of the upper and lower limbs, chest, waist, hip, knee and foot can be used on their own or together. They outline a kinetic language of communication with a defined grammar, in which the eyes and the hands play the most important part. The text also describes in vivid terms cadences of movement (*karanas*), which comprise the 'alphabet' on which all dance movements are constructed, and more extended sequences called 'garlands of movement' (*angahara*). Underlying the whole work is the theory of esthetics popularly known as *rasa*. According to this theory, artistic creation emerges from a deep internalized experience of 'wholeness' where differentiations are lost and which is similar to the meditational state of yoga. Artistic expression seeks to give concrete form, through symbols, myth and artistic archetypal characters, to this experience. The content and form of art is impersonal; diversity is analogous to the different colours of a rainbow which together make up a white light. Life is divided into emotional states such as love (*sringara*), compassion (*karuna*), heroism (*vira*), anger (*raudra*), disgust and hatred (*vibhatsa*), laughter and humor (*haysa*) and wonder and amazement (*adbhuta*), which are known as the different rasas or dominant *bhavas*. Through this spectrum of emotional states, the work of art sets out to evoke in the mind of the spectator, reader or listener, a state of internalized harmony and wholeness similar to the initial experience of the artist. This final stage of the artistic experience is relish or rasa, now used in the singular and also known as *ananda*. All forms of contemporary classical Indian dance subscribe to the theory of rasa; it provides the fundamental unity and unbroken continuity which can be discerned in all periods, regional styles and individual improvization, and which governs content, form and technique.

Many other theoretical texts on dance have been written all over the subcontinent, some as late as the nineteenth century. Important among these works are Nandikesvara's *Abhinaya Darpana* (sixth–seventh century); *Sangita Ratnakara* (eleventh century); Jaya Senapati's *Nrittaratnavali* (Andhra Pradesh, thirteenth century); *Hasta Muktavali* (Assam); *Balarama Bharatam* and *Hasta-laksandipika* (Kerala, seventeenth century); Kumbha's *Nritya Ratnokosha* (Rajasthan, fifteenth century); Meheshwar Mahapatra's *Abhinaya Chandira* (Orissa, seventeenth century); *Govind Sangita Lila Vikasa* (Manipur, eighteenth century); and Muhammad Shah's *Sangita Malika* (eighteenth to nineteenth centuries).

Classical dance forms

Five dance forms are known as classical or art-dance on account of their sophisticated degree of stylization: Bharata Natyam, Orissi, Manipuri, Kathak and Kathakali. At one level, they are united by the theory of rasa and the fundamentals of form and technique. At another level, each is distinctive as a result of connections with the rural and folk forms of dance in the region to which it belongs. They share the pan-Indian myths of Shiva, Krishna, other divinities of the Indian pantheon, and archetypal Indian heroes and heroines. All draw heavily on Sanskrit literary epics such as the *Ramayana* and *Mahabharata*, as well as on poetic and dramatic compositions in regional languages. All are divided into pure dance (*nritta*) and mime (*nritya*), sometimes called expression (*abhinaya*); they possess their own grammars of movement which are made up of strong open movements (*tandava*) and soft restrained lyrical movements (*lasya*).

The use of hand gestures in the Kathak school of classical dance.

Proper nouns

(1) Vishnu: In Kathak gestures indicate the attributes of the subject described. In this case the arms are raised to the head with the hands resting on the back of the head, palms facing outwards and fingers pointing upwards, denoting the crown of Vishnu.

(2) Shiva: There are two gestures. In the first the right hand is held on the head, palm facing outwards, and the left hand in the second makes the movement of tying the hair of Lord Shiva in a knot on the head.

Nouns

(1) Trees:  Both hands are held in front of the chest, palms facing towards each other, the first fingers slightly back, fingers pointing upwards. Then the hands are moved forwards, crossing each other two or three times.

(2) Birds: The hands are held with palms facing inwards, and the four fingers are stretched straight pointing in opposite directions. The thumbs of each hand are interlocked and the hands are then moved in a circular fashion round and round with the fingers fluttering.

(3) Woman: This gesture indicates the pulling of the veil over the face. The hand is held just a little above the right side of the forehead, and as if holding the tip of the veil is brought down a little towards the right eye. It is then lifted into the first position.

(4) Flower:  There are two gestures. The right hand is held forward to the right at chest level, palm up, and then changed to the second gesture.

(5) Peacock:  With the palms of the hands facing outwards the hands are taken from one side to the other in a large circle over the head. At the top the wrists touching, the palms facing outwards, the fingers pointing upwards, the hands are held side by side.

(6) Half-moon: The hand is raised up to face level to the right.

(7) Face: The right hand is held to the left of the face with the base of the palm at eye level. It is then brought slowly round the face under the chin to the right side of the face, so that the fingers point at the level of the right eye. All the time the thumb points upwards.

Verbs

(1) Hear: The right hand, with palm facing outwards, is placed at ear level; the first finger points to the right ear and then the hand is moved sideways with the finger pointing outwards.

(2) Speak: The right hand is raised to the lips, with the palm facing up, then the hand is brought forward a little away from the lips.

(3) Give: There are two gestures. In the first the hand is held at the chest with the back of the hand facing outwards. In the second the hand is moved forwards with the palm up. Then the hand is moved diagonally downwards with the fingers pointing down and the open palm still facing upwards.

(4) Touch: The right hand is placed near the chest and moved forwards in a downwards action, as if touching an object.

Adjectives and Adverbs

(1) Beautiful:  The right hand is held near the lips with the palm facing outwards, and is moved horizontally from the lips to the side and back again.

(2) Sorrowful:  The right hand is raised to the right eye with the palm facing upwards and with the third finger and thumb touching at the lips. They hold a tear and bring it down from the eye, then the hand is lowered and the tear flicked away by third finger and thumb.

Source: E. Bhavnani, *The Dance in India: The Origin and History, Foundations, The Art and Science of the Dance in India – Classical, Folk and Tribal* pp. 102–105. (Bombay, 1965)

The different techniques of each style emerge from different basic positions, emphasis on the use of some parts of the body and not on others, and selective articulation of lower and upper limbs, torso, waist and neck. The nature of floor contacts, choreography, elevations, pirouettes and jumps are similarly distinctive. Their repertoire is governed either by the structure of North Indian (Hindustani) or South Indian (Karnatak) music. Musical accompaniment invariably comprises a vocalist, a drummer either on the double barreled drum (*mridanga*, *madalam* or *pakhavaj*) or

Indirani Rehman in a pose from the Orissi form of classical Indian dance.

the pair of drums (tabla), and a cymbal player who recites the mnemonics. There is also usually one stringed instrument either bowed or plucked. Pure dance movements are carried out to the melodic musical line in any given *raga* and metrical cycle (*tala*), while mime is performed to a poetic line set to a melodic line in any given metrical cycle. In each section, the skill of the dancer lies in his or her ability to improvise on the musical phrase and metrical cycle, and to interpret through gesticulation and mime the poetic line in order to communicate the basic states of love and emotion and thus to evoke the state of joy (*ananda*).

The classical dance called Bharata Natyam has its origins in southern India: its main centers nowadays are still in the south at Madras and Tanjore. Its poses and movements are captured in the sculpture of the tenth–eleventh century, principally in the temples of Brahedesvara and Chidambaram. However, it received its thematic and musical content from musicians at the Thanjavur courts of the eighteenth and nineteenth centuries. Essentially a solo dance, it has close affinities with the traditional dance-drama form called *Bhagvata Mela* performed only by men, and with folk operettas called *Kuruvanjis* performed exclusively by women; the word 'Natyam' itself means a combination of dancing and acting. A body of technique stems from the fundamental position of out-turned thighs, flexed knees and out-turned feet close together, similar to the *demi-plié* of classical western ballet. Foot contacts, of the whole foot, toe, heel and toe–heel combinations are utilized throughout in order to maintain this basic stance; exceptions are limited to two or three sequences with an erect posture. The torso is used as one unit, without being broken up into the upper chest and the lower waist. Straight lines, diagonals and triangles are the basic motifs for executing movements and in floor choreography. Bharata Natyam is also characterized by terse, clean lines with few changes of level; elevations and pirouettes are restrained. The basic unit of movement is the *adavu*. Recitals begin with a number danced to abstract mnemonics called the *alarippu*, literally the temple flower or oleander used as an offering at the beginning of devotional worship. This is followed by pure dance performed to the musical composition *Jatisvaram*. Notes of the melodic line set to a metrical cycle are interpreted through the dancer's movements. A number called *shabdam* introduces mime for the first time; here emphasis is on interpretation. *Varnam* comes next and is one of the most beautiful and highly elaborate dance conceptions, composed of emotional acting and rhythmic cadences. It is by far and away the most difficult and challenging section of the whole dance during which the performer closely follows the structure of the music comprising the *pallavi*, *anupallavi* and *charnam*. Each line is interpreted in mime prefixed and suffixed by passages of pure dance performed to mnemonics and the melodic line. The third phase, *charanam*, builds up to a crescendo where the melodic line is sung by the vocalist in its solfa passages first and then followed by the singing of the words of the poetic line on the same melodic line. The dancer interprets both. The recital concludes with the *tillana*, another pure dance number with intricate rhythms and statuesque postures, followed by lyrical compositions (*padams*) to which mime is performed.

Orissi, from Orissa, is a close parallel of Bharata Natyam. It developed from the musical play (*Sangita, Nataka*) and the dances of gymnasiums known as *akharas*. Sculptural evidence relating to this dance can be traced back to the second century BC in the Rani Gumpna caves. Inscriptions, manuscripts and other records dating from the twelfth century speak of the prevalence of the style in the context of ritual temple dances and of village entertainments. The dance was performed by women called *maharis* in the temple of Jagannath. Later, men dressed as women, known as *gotipua*, performed these dances in the courtyard of the temple. Present day Orissi as a solo form evolved out of all these traditions and has been revived during the last two decades. Its technique is constructed round a basic motif in which the human body takes the thrice-deflected (*tribhanga*) position of Indian sculpture: the lower limbs are in a *demi-plié* while the upper torso is broken into two units of the lower waist and upper chest working in counter opposition. The basic unit of movement is called the *arasa*. Several arasas are strung together to form a pure dance design, recalling sculptural poses in Orissan temples. Movements are performed to a melodic line set to a metrical cycle. Other numbers are performed to poetry, principally the verses of the twelfth century poetic work, the *Gita Govinda*. The performance begins with an invocation (*mangala-charana*) which pays obeisance to a particular deity, principally Ganesa. This is followed by the *batu*, a pure dance number performed to mnemonics, and then the *pallavi*, a musical composition akin to the *jatisvaram* of Bharata Natyam. Pieces of lyrical poetry are interpreted through mime in subsequent numbers. The performance concludes on an ecstatic note with a dance called *moksha* (liberation), again a pure dance number.

Manipuri is a lyrical dance form from the eastern region of India. Although many forms of ritual, magical, community and religious dance were known to Manipur before the advent of the Vaishnava faith in the eighteenth century, the dance known as *Jagoi* and dance-dramas called Rasa are attributed to the creative genius of King Bhagyachandra. In technique, Manipuri is quite different from Bharata Natyam and Orissi. Feet are in front, not out-turned; knees are relaxed, slightly bent forward but not flexed sideways; there is no out-turned position of the thighs. The torso is relaxed with the upper chest and wrist moving in opposition. The whole body is turned into an imaginary figure of eight or similar to the English letter 'S'. The arms move as a unit, with no sharp angles. The fingers of the hands also move in circles, semi-circles and curves, gradually folding and unfolding. The primary unit of movement is

known as the *chali* or the *pareng* on which the dance is built. Five different types of ballet, with well-conceived structuring of *corps de ballet* and solo *pas de deux* revolving around the theme of Radha, Krishna and the Gopis (milkmaids), comprise the large part of the classical repertoire of Manipur. The second group of dances are known as the *Sankirtanas*. They follow a more vigorous technique with jumps and elevations but no leg extensions, and are performed generally by men to typical Manipur drums (*pung*), cymbals (*kartals*) and clapping. A large variety of intricate rhythmic patterns are played on these instruments. The *Nata Sankirtana* often precedes the Rasa. Throughout there is an alternation of pure dance and mime, the latter most restrained and refined with a placidity close to southeast Asian dance. The ritual dances of Manipur are a group apart: the most significant among them are the Maiba and Maibi dances of priests and priestesses before village deities. They often culminate in trances. Lai Haroba, for instance, is spread over many days; its ritual pattern is rigorous and different sections all fall into a dexterous pattern of floor choreography and physical movement performed to a repetitive melody on a bowed instrument called the *pena*. The main dancers are Khamba and Thoibi, supposedly counterparts of Shiva and Parvati.

Kathak from northern India is an urban sophisticated style full of virtuosity and intricate craftsmanship. Commonly identified with the court traditions of the later Navvabs of northern India, it is an amalgam of several folk-traditions, the traditional dance-drama forms prevalent in the precincts of the temples of Mathura and Vrindaban known as the Krishna and Radha *lilas*, and the sophisticated court milieu of Mughal and Indian princes. While its origins are old, its present format is attributed to the genius of Navvab Vajid Ali Shah (died 1887) and the hereditary musician-dancer Pandit Thakar Prasadji. Its contemporary repertoire was evolved by a few families of traditional dancers over the past hundred years. In technique, Kathak is two-dimensional, always following a vertical line with no breaks and deflections. The footwork is the most important part of the dancers' training. They are taught numerous rhythmic patterns with varying emphasis so that the hundred odd ankle bells can produce a fantastic range of sound and rhythm. Straight walks, gliding movements, fast pirouettes, changing tempos and metrical patterns constitute the beauty and dexterity of the style. As in other dance forms, the Kathak performer begins with an invocation (*amad*) and entry (*salami*) followed by an exposition of slow delicate movements of the eyebrows, eyes, lateral neck and shoulders. Next comes the presentation of rhythmic patterns known as *tukras* and *toras*. Time-cycles can be repeated, adding complexity to the presentation. Pirouettes, arranged in groups of three, six, nine, twelve and so on, normally mark the finale. The pure dance sections are followed by short interpretative pieces performed to a repetitive melodic line. Mime is performed to lyrics of Hindi and Brajbhasa well-known to villagers and townspeople alike. The dancer is free to improvise in the pure dance sections; it is common for there to be a healthy competition between the dancer and the percussionists. In the mime portions, again the range of improvisation on the poetic line is the test of a good dancer. Accompaniment consists of a vocalist, a drummer either on the pakhavaj or tabla, and an instrumentalist who plays the repetitive melodic line known as the *nagma*. Other instruments can be added for embellishment.

Kathakali, from Kerala, is a classical dance-drama. Unlike the other four, it is dramatic rather than narrative in character. Different roles are taken by different characters; the dancers are all men or were until recently. Kathakali takes epic mythological themes as its content and portrays them through an elaborate dramatic spectacle which is characterized by an other-worldly quality, supernatural grandeur, stylized large-sized costumes to give the impression of enlarging human proportions, and mask-like facial make-up which is governed by a complex symbolism of color, line and design. Character types, such as heroes, anti-heroes, villains, demons, sages and kings, all have a prescribed make-up and costume governed by the association of green with good, red with valor and ferocity, black with evil and primitiveness, and white with purity. Combinations of these colors suggest the exact character type and his particular mood in the play. Kathakali, however, is dance-drama and not drama because the actors do not speak their lines. The dramatic story is carried forward through a highly evolved vocabulary of body movements, hand gestures and eye movements. The vocalist recites and sings the lines of the dramatic piece. The actor on stage portrays the meaning with the freedom to improvise and interpret. While, therefore, he follows the broad framework of the written dramatic script which is being sung, he makes departures and deviations like dancers in any of the other styles. Similarly, mime is interspersed with pure dance sequences. During the last one hundred years, many poets have written Kathakali plays which represent as much a literary genre as a theatrical spectacle. In technique, Kathakali follows the basic motif on a rectangular position reminiscent of a full *grand-plié* with the important difference that the weight of the body rests on the outer soles of the feet and not on the flat feet. Floor patterns follow the same rectangular motif. Pure dance sequences comprise units called the *Kala samas*, which resemble the *adavu* of Bharata Natyam, the arasa of Orissi, the *tukra* or Kathak and the *chali* and *parenga* of Manipuri. In mime, Kathakali depends more than any other dance style on the elaborate language of hand gestures which has been developed to the highest degree of finesse and subtlety.

While Kathakali is the most developed and sophisticated of Indian dance-drama forms, there are many others which follow the same principles with varying techniques. The Yaksagana of Mysore is a well-known dance-drama form, as is the Kuchipudi of Andhra Pradesh and its off-shoot, Bhamakalapam, which also emerged in Andhra Pradesh in the seventeenth and eighteenth centuries. Kuchipudi was originally performed only by men but during the last few decades women have become exponents of this style. In thematic content, it revolves around Krishna and his consort Satyabhama. Its repertoire has close affinities with Bharata Natyam. It draws its literary inspiration from a work called *Krishna Lila Trangini*. In technique, Kuchipudi accepts the basic out-turned feet and knees position, again similar to Bharata Natyam but less chiseled, an erect torso and straight diagonal lines in movements. There is frequent use of changing levels in place and in space. Men dancers are considered accomplished when they can play the role of Satyabhama successfully. Other favorite numbers include the *desavatara* and *tarangam*.

Folk dance

Whereas classical dances tend to be subject to a definite order and a complicated system of gesture language, footwork and body movements, folk dance is generally much more spontaneous. Its primary impulse is rhythm; its roots lie in religious and seasonal festivals, and hence it is often guided by songs glorifying nature, expressing traditional occupations and offering devotion to deities. The vast majority of folk dances are performed by groups of people, usually consisting of either men or women. Certain basic dance patterns exist. These have been described in medieval Sanskrit literature and consist of the *pindi* (group), the *shrinkhala* (chain), *lata* (creeper) and *bhedyaka* (the separate movement of each dancer away from the group). Even more basic is the *rasak* or rasa, referring to a circular dance. There are two kinds of rasa dance: the *Talai-rasa*, with rhythmic clapping of hands, and the *Danda-rasa*, in which each dancer marks the rhythm with a pair of sticks.

In Gujarat, the festival of Nava-ratri (Nine Nights) is celebrated with the folk dance, Rasa Garba, in honor of the goddess Jagadamba or Nataji. Women form a circle round a pot containing a flame, sing songs in praise of the goddess, and mark a beat with their hands and feet. Another circular dance, the Ghumar, is very popular in Rajasthan where it is performed at festivals and weddings to the accompaniment of song, drums and cymbals. Equally popular is the Ger, performed by men and women, in which the rhythm is struck with colored sticks with bells attached at one end. The Panjab is famous for the energetic dances of its menfolk. Jhumar is a circular dance involving the use of sticks in which the tempo is steadily increased. Bhangra is a much-loved harvest dance which requires its male dancers to leap high into the air and shout out in time with the music of pipes, drums and other percussion instruments such as the *chimta* or iron tongs. Further to the northwest, the Khattak dance is performed by male Pathans. Originally part of the preparations for

Dancers perform a Ladakhi folk dance at Leh.

war against rival tribes, nowadays any joyous event provides the occasion for this dynamic dance. The performers move in circles within the larger circular formation, flourishing handkerchiefs and swords. War dances are still prevalent in some districts of Bengal. In the Birbaum district, for instance, young men circle and dance to the drum and the gong. Aspects of fighting, such as throwing the spear and flourishing the sword, are rendered in rhythmic unison, as are feats of acrobatic skill and balance. In Assam, the most popular folk dance, the Bihu, celebrates the Assamese New Year and advent of the spring season.

Circular folk dances with sticks and hand claps have developed their own regional pattern in southern India, but they basically remain similar in form to the Danda-rasa and Talai-rasa of North India. The Dasara (or harvest) festival of Mysore is inaugurated by the Mandi Kamba dance in which each man carries a long decorated pole. Kolata, the circular dance with sticks, is popular with peasants during the harvest period. Also known as Kolattam, it is also performed by women in Tamil Nadu as is Kummi, another circular hand-clapping dance in a six-beat rhythm accompanied by a song sung in chorus. Pinnal Kolattam is a group dance which combines the weaving of ribbons and the play of sticks. It too is performed by women. Folk dance in Kerala is associated with two great festivals, the Tiruvatira or spring festival, and the Tira-Onam or harvest festival. The Kaikotti-kali is linked with the first, and since Tiruvatira is a special festival for women, this dance is not performed by men. Women move in a circle, stepping in a wide stance with knee bends and rhythmic gestures, followed by varied steps and hand claps. Kaikotti-Kali is also performed during the second festival along with Kummi, Charatu-kuth Kali (a dance in which colored cords are wound and unwound on a pole) and Kol-Kali (a stick dance performed by men).

KV

Further reading
R. Devi, *Dance Dialects of India* (Delhi, 1972)
Mohan Khokar, *Traditions of Indian Classical Dance* (New Delhi, 1979)
K. Vatsyayan, *Classical Indian Dance in Literature and the Arts* (New Delhi, 1968); *Indian Classical Dance* (New Delhi, 1974); Traditions of Folk Dance (New Delhi, 1986)

Architecture

A survey of architecture in the Indian subcontinent inevitably focuses on surviving brick and stone monuments, mostly religious, royal or military constructions. With the exception of prehistoric remains, these monuments span a period of more than two thousand years. They are built in a large variety of techniques and styles, testifying to considerable diversity of climate and materials. Yet there is a consistency of architectural forms, evidence of an underlying conceptual basis for much building practice. Both religious and royal architecture were provided with manuals (*shastras*); these codified procedures form both designing and building.

Domestic architecture in ephemeral materials is difficult to examine, since mud, bamboo, timber and thatch cannot survive the severe monsoonal climate of the subcontinent. Vernacular forms are known in masonry imitations which pervade much of monumental architecture. There is also the evidence of present-day practice, though much of this is rapidly disappearing under the impact of concrete modernism.

Architecture in the subcontinent also absorbed foreign traditions which, in time, were blended with indigenous techniques. Islamic and European architectures were ultimately Indianized; forms unknown elsewhere in Islamic lands or the British empire evolved in the subcontinent. It is, perhaps, this continuously evolving tradition that emerges as the principal theme of this region's architecture.

Architecture of the Harappa culture
Excavations at Mohenjodaro and Harappa (Pakistan) provide evidence for a protohistoric civilization that flourished in the Indus valley region in the second–first millennia BC. Though written records of this culture have not yet been satisfactorily deciphered, there is abundant architectural evidence. This manifests a remarkable uniformity in building materials (standardized bricks throughout) and typologies (houses, baths, granaries). Thus is suggested a high degree of cultural homogeneity. The uniformity of associated finds, especially pottery and steatite seals with animal motifs, confirms that this was a highly ordered civilization. Significantly, Harappa period sites are among the earliest known settlements with a distinctly urban character.

At the principal site of Mohenjodaro, an elevated zone may have functioned as a citadel. Streets, regularly laid out in a grid, divided the town into blocks. Houses consisted of rooms opening off a central court; water was conducted in channels and drains. The largest feature was a rectangular, brick-lined tank, possibly for ritual bathing. A group of square platforms nearby is usually identified as a granary.

Architectural sites.

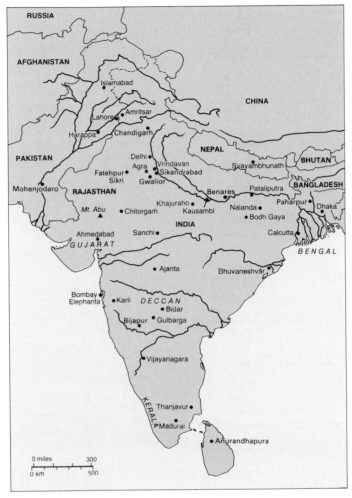

subcontinent were influenced by Achaemenid practice from neighboring Persia.

Ashoka was a great patron of Buddhism and Jainism, and many religious structures were erected during his reign. The most characteristic architectural form of this era was the *stupa*. Originally a funerary mound, the stupa came to serve as a commemorative monument of the Buddha or Mahavira, as well as a symbol of cosmic order.

The most completely preserved stupa is that at Sanchi; this dates from the third to first centuries BC. Here, an unadorned, stone-faced hemispherical mound, 36.6 m (120 ft) in diameter, has an umbrella-like finial at the summit. This finial indicates the position of a casket buried deep within the mound which contained relics of important Buddhist teachers. It also suggested the symbolism of the column passing through the mound, a metaphor for the cosmic pillar separating earth and sky. Other early stupas are found throughout the subcontinent. Examples at Svayambhunath and Anuradhapura, though remodeled innumerable times, preserve similar schemes to that at Sanchi.

Of particular interest at Sanchi are the timber-like stone railings and gateways. Stoneposts and rails also defined a paved pathway around the stupa. (Proceeding in a clockwise direction, devotees circumambulated the stupa as an act of devotion.) In the first century AD, four gateways at the cardinal directions were added. Posts and architraves of these gateways (*toranas*) were completely covered with finely sculptured Buddhist narratives, episodes from the life of the Master, and a host of ornamental themes.

Another significant architectural form evolved under Buddhist patronage was the apsidal-ended *chaitya* hall. This sanctuary was obviously wooden in origins, since it employed a curved vault supported by horseshoe-shaped ribs with a similarly shaped window

The stupa at Sanchi. Note the timber-like stone railings and gateways.

After the middle of the first millennium BC, when the Harappa culture disintegrated, there is a gap in monumental architecture. While this period is characterized by the evolution of Brahminic religions and the emergence of Buddhism and Jainism, architectural evidence is restricted to fragmentary remains of fortified settlements, as at Kaushambi.

Buddhist stupas and monasteries

The first phase of religious architecture in the subcontinent is linked with the beginnings of Buddhism and Jainism. While both religions date back to the sixth–fifth centuries BC, the period of Gautama and Mahavira, no structures are preserved from this era. It was not until the reign of Ashoka in the third century BC, that religious architecture in stone was initiated. Judging from the remains of Ashoka's capital at Patilaputra (eastern India), and the series of columns inscribed with this king's edicts, the earliest artistic traditions in the

above the entrance. Though no timber examples survive, rock-cut versions date back to the second century BC. At Karle, for instance, the chaitya hall was excavated into volcanic trap. Here, the façade was penetrated by the horseshoe-shaped vault; teak ribs were inset into the stone vault. Rock-cut columns defining a central aisle have pot-like bases and capitals; animals with riders are seen above. The devotional focus was a monolithic stupa, complete with an umbrella-like finial (in wood).

Buddhist communities were housed in regularly laid out monasteries (*viharas*). These invariably grouped small cells around a square court; an enlarged cell in the middle of the wall opposite the entrance functioned as a shrine. Both rock-cut and brick viharas are preserved in the subcontinent, the latter only incompletely. At Ajanta, viharas and chaityas were both excavated into the vertical face of a curved ravine. The viharas dating from the fifth century AD are superbly executed, with finely decorated columns and doorways. Sculptured and painted images of the Buddha and his attendants were incorporated into the architectural decor, together with lively scenes illustrating Buddhist legends. The chaityas from this period are also adorned with Buddhist icons; the votive stupa becomes a background to a seated image of the Master in the teaching posture.

The largest monastic establishment in the subcontinent was at Nalanda. This celebrated Buddhist university, known even in China, flourished until about the ninth century, after which Buddhist traditions declined. A number of brick viharas at Nalanda are arranged in a row; these faced temples raised on stepped platforms and approached by long flights of steps. A similarly organized temple, laid out on a stepped plan and raised on a series of receding platforms, is partly preserved at Paharpur.

But the most celebrated shrine of Buddhism was that at Bodh Gaya, the site of the Master's enlightenment beneath the bodhi tree. The present brick structure, though much renovated, is essentially sixth to seventh century in form. Here, a tall pyramidal tower was covered with arch-like motifs; these were ornamental versions of the chaitya window. Miniature towers are seen at the four corners.

Hindu and Jain temples

With the emergence of devotional Brahminical cults in the first centuries of the present era, a new religious architecture was rapidly evolved in stone. Here were housed rituals that focused on worshipping the divine image as a royal personage – waking the deity, dressing him or her, offering cooked foods – and auspiciously 'viewing' (*darshana*) the image. Accordingly, temples were designed with small 'womb chambers' (*garbhagrihas*) to house cult icons and attendant priests; adjoining the sanctuaries were larger halls (*mandapas*) for devotees, performances of music and dance, and recitations of sacred texts. Halls and sanctuaries were axially aligned, generally in an east–west direction.

Temple forms were dominated by cave and mountain images suggesting the mythical abodes of the gods. Sanctuaries were invariably massive and unadorned, as in a cave. Towers, rising over the sanctuaries, were provided with multi-storeyed or curved contours; some superstructures were even termed 'peaks' (*shikharas*). Temple plans were laid out on geometric diagrams (*mandalas*) that symbolically replicated the structure of the universe. Divinities located in the squares of the plan included Brahma the creator god.

Inheriting the rock-cut traditions of Buddhist and Jain architecture, some of the earliest Hindu sanctuaries were also excavated. One of the finest examples is the sixth century Shiva temple at Elephanta. Here, a columned hall on a stepped plan was provided with large-scale wall panels depicting aspects of the god; these were dominated by an immense triple-headed image of Shiva. A small detached shrine housing a phallic emblem (*linga*) of the god was also located within the hall.

In time, structural techniques in temple architecture prevailed. The earliest examples were simple combinations of towered sanctuaries and columned porches. Soon, porches were expanded and columned halls added; sanctuaries were surrounded by enclosed passageways. Outer elevations were dominated by molded basements, and walls ornamented with niches filled with sculptures of divinities, their consorts and attendants. Superstructures, of ever-increasing height, imitated the walls beneath or introduced arch-like emblems; ribbed fruit motifs and pot finials were positioned at the summits. Doorways, columns and ceilings were embellished with guardian figures, foliation and jewelled motifs. Thus did temple architecture and sculpture evolve into increasingly ambitious and elaborate schemes.

By the tenth to eleventh centuries, religious architecture for both Hindu and Jain cults reached a climax. A survey of the different regions of the subcontinent demonstrates a series of stylistic variants. At Thanjavur, for example, the Brihadeshvara temple was dominated by a single soaring pyramidal tower divided into diminishing storeys; a dome-like capping form is seen above. The outer walls of the sanctuary and its adjoining hall had regularly placed projections framed by pilasters; sculpture panels were set into niches.

In contrast, at Khajuraho and Bhubaneshwar, temples were provided with clusters of curved towered forms, in imitation of a mountain range. Figural ornamentation on basements and walls displayed a total integration of sculpture with architecture. The marble Jain temples at Abu provide an even more striking example of architectural sculpture. Almost every column, bracket, lintel and ceiling panel here was encrusted with carved decoration.

Temple traditions in much of the subcontinent were interrupted by the Muslim invasions from the twelfth century onwards. Thereafter, temples either repeated earlier modes, or adopted features from contemporary Islamic architecture. A sixteenth century shrine at Vrindaban, for example, successfully incorporated arched and vaulted forms of Mughal period mosque architecture.

In southern India, however, where the Muslim impact was later and less disruptive, temple architecture continued to develop. Characteristic was the temple complex contained within a series of concentric enclosure walls. Madurai, one of the most impressive establishments of the seventeenth century, was an immense cluster of shrines, columned halls, colonnaded corridors, kitchens, stores, stables, tanks and wells. At the core were sanctuaries dedicated to the god and his consort. The most dominant features were the towered gateways (gopuras) in the middle of the enclosure walls. These lofty structures had brick towers completely covered with fully modeled, brightly painted plaster figures; these vividly depicted the entire heavenly pantheon.

But other temple styles were also evolved, particularly in peripheral zones, such as Kerala and Bengal, where the impact of vernacular traditions predominated. The high rainfall zone of Kerala was responsible for tiers of sloping tiled roofs with which many temples were provided. In Bengal, an absence of stone promoted the use of brick and terracotta. The most popular forms here were hut-like forms, with vaulted roofs and curved cornices that imitated bamboo and thatch construction.

Islamic mosques and tombs

Entirely new architectural forms and techniques accompanied the introduction of Islam into the subcontinent. The mosque, domed mausoleum and tomb complex (*dargah*) were the principal forms. Masonry arches, domes and vaults, and the restriction of decorative themes to calligraphy, geometric designs and stylized foliation, were characteristic features. These were mostly derived from building practice in central Asia, from where most of the invaders came. Timurid period architecture is probably the most important single source for the subcontinent's earliest Islamic styles.

Indigenous practice, however, soon affected these imported techniques and ornament. Arched profiles and domes were achieved by corbelled stonework without voussoirs; geometric and foliate motifs were enlivened with a deeply modeled naturalism derived from temple art.

Delhi preserves the first substantial Islamic architecture in the subcontinent. At the end of the twelfth century, the mosque here was partly constructed of columns from dismantled Jain temples. Its layout was typical, with a large courtyard surrounded by colonnades. The western (*qibla*) wall was provided with an arched niche (*mihrab*), and covered with sculptured calligraphy and arabesque ornament. The nearby minaret, known as the Qutb Minar, served as a tower from which to call the faithful to prayer and

Some of the twelve towered gateways (gopuras) of the temple complex at Madurai (Tamil Nadu).

as a monument to the new Islamic state.

Tomb architecture of the Delhi sultanates usually consisted of a single square domed chamber. Tapering walls were adorned with arched niches in different colored stonework; turrets and pavilions were often added at the corners. Lotus and pot-like finials upon the domes were inspired by temple architecture.

With the emergence of independent Islamic states in the fifteenth century, regional variations of mosque and tomb architecture were achieved. In Gujarat, for example, mosque architecture adopted the elaborately ornamented columns, corbeled domes and double- and triple-storeyed spaces of contemporary Jain temple architecture. In Bengal, brick techniques prevailed, and curved cornices imitated vernacular hut styles. An ornate terracotta ornamentation covered building surfaces.

In the Deccan, there were further stylistic variants. At Gulbarga, the Jami Masjid was completely roofed over with domed and vaulted bays. At Bidar, the theological college (*madrasa*) was purely central Asian in form, complete with corner minarets, bulbous domes and colored tiles. At Bijapur, the Gol Gumbad had one of the largest domes in the world; this was ingeniously supported on a net of intersecting pointed arches.

Islamic architecture in the subcontinent reached its climax under Mughal patronage in the sixteenth to seventeenth centuries. The great Friday Mosques (*Jami Masjid*) of the Mughal capitals at Lahore, Delhi, Agra and Fatehpur Sikri were superbly executed in red sandstone and white marble. The large courts of these mosques were entered through monumental gateways provided with highly ornamented arched doorways. Prayer chambers on the western side of the courts were sumptuously ornamented; walls, arches and domes were carved in relief and also inset with differently colored stones.

But perhaps the greatest contribution of the Mughals was the development of the tomb garden; this was brought to a peak of perfection unknown elsewhere in the Islamic world. Here, the domed tomb of the ruler was set within a garden, regularly divided by paths and water courses into plots. The most popular garden scheme had four squares (*charbagh*) with the tomb in the middle, as in the mausolea of Humayun and Akbar at Delhi and Sikandra,

The Taj Mahal, the high point in the development of the garden tomb. The skilled craftsmen involved in the construction were drawn from throughout the Islamic world of the time: the draughtsmen and calligraphers came from Shiraz, the clerk of works from Qandahar, the finial makers from Samarqand, the dome builder from Ottoman Turkey, the stone and flower cutters from Bukhara, the masons from Delhi and Multan, the inlayers from Multan, and the garden designer from Kashmir.

respectively. But Shah Jahan's mausoleum for his wife at Agra, known popularly as the Taj Mahal, unusually placed the tomb at one end; detached minarets were added at the four corners recalling ancient Indian practice (compare with the Bodh Gaya temple).

Mughal period domes were raised on cylindrical drums and were slightly bulbous in profile. Calligraphy and geometric ornament, often in polychrome stonework, covered the principal façades; interiors were dominated by great domes that rose over the cenotaphs. The Taj Mahal, executed entirely in white marble, was the masterpiece of the series. Its overall design is characterized by a striking simplicity; and yet the ornamental treatment is sumptuous.

During the later Mughal period, mosques and tombs continued to be erected, though on a smaller scale. Contemporary temple architecture, however, was greatly influenced by this style. Even the celebrated Sikh sanctuary at Amritsar derives from later Mughal architecture.

Forts and palaces

Warfare was a constant feature in much of the subcontinent's history. Cities were frequently fortified, and sites with natural defences were converted into citadels. Massive walls with projecting bastions, and defensive gateways with barbican enclosures are known at both Hindu and Islamic sites. Chitorgarh and Gwalior are typical examples dating from the twelfth century, both sited on flat-topped hills. Vijayanagar, the fourteenth to fifteenth century Hindu capital, is conceived as a gigantic citadel with concentric rings of fortifications. The capitals of Islamic states were invariably provided with protective walls; these were often laid out in a circle, as at Ahmadabad and Bijapur.

Though palace architecture has a long history, few remains predate the Islamic era. The finest Hindu examples are seen in southern India (Vijayanagar) and central India (Datia) where Islamic-styled elements are blended with indigenous features. In Rajasthan, palaces were erected by local rulers in a picturesque style, partly affected by contemporary Mughal architecture.

The Mughal capitals were each provided with fortified royal zones in which public and private apartments were laid out in garden settings. These apartments were mostly columned pavilions, originally provided with gorgeous hangings and carpets. Service buildings, too, were incorporated into palace designs, especially stores, kitchens, stables, prisons, treasuries, tanks and wells.

Indigenous features also appeared, such as pyramidal and multi-storeyed towers, columns with ornately fashioned brackets, and angled eaves and corner turrets. At Fatehpur Sikri, the most completely preserved palace city of the Mughals, a variety of unusual building types testify to a considerable inventiveness. One of the most fascinating structures is the Divan-e Khas; within its single chamber, a temple-like column supports a throne from which the emperor could look down on assembled visitors.

European architecture

By the beginning of the sixteenth century, the Portuguese were established at ports on the western coast; the Dutch, French and British followed soon after. At Goa, the Portuguese built a remarkable series of Baroque churches, in the manner adopted by them for colonial settlements. Related to contemporary developments in Europe, these cathedrals were exuberantly ornamented with gilded woodwork carved by local craftsmen.

In the eighteenth century, the subcontinent was increasingly brought under British control. Buildings designed by British engineers were erected all over the subcontinent, mostly in the neoclassical mode that was currently fashionable in Europe. Churches were invariably provided with classical façades and tall pointed spires; civic buildings also displayed classical features. Though military architecture of cantonments was generally more austere, the 'palaces' of the Viceroys were ambitious projects, such as Government House in Calcutta.

Gothic revivalism was popular in Victorian period architecture of the subcontinent. Churches, law courts, post offices and art galleries were often built with pointed arches, spires and steeply angled roofs. But there was also an intrusion of Islamic domes, arches and ornamental features. The finest illustrations of this original style, once known as 'Indo-Saracenic', are seen in the offices, railway stations and university buildings of Bombay. This mingling of European styles with indigenous features was by no means restricted to British buildings; palaces of local rulers were also imaginatively hybrid in style.

Neoclassical modes triumphed in the present century. The Victoria Memorial in Calcutta, one of the most potent symbols of British presence, was provided with an Italian Renaissance dome. Lutyens, the designer of the new capital at Delhi, adopted a neoclassical approach with symmetrically disposed axes to create a strict geometric layout. The city was dominated by a ceremonial avenue leading to the Viceroy's House (now Rashtrapati Bhavan). Here, Lutyens created a new imperial subcontinental style in which elements from both Buddhist and Islamic traditions (the dome-like form of Sanchi stupa, pavilions of Mughal palace architecture) are blended with neoclassical arches and colonnades. Baker's Council House (now Parliament House) was a more conventional neoclassical exercise; Shoosmith's Garrison Church, which demonstrated the beginnings of more experimental architectural forms, was without influence.

Lutyens' new imperial subcontinental style. The dome of the Viceroy's House (now Rashtrapati Bhavan) is reminiscent of the Buddhist stupa at Sanchi.

Modern architecture

With Le Corbusier, who designed the new capital of the Panjab, and Louis Kahn, who worked on both Islamabad and Dhaka, the architecture of the subcontinent became part of a worldwide modernist movement. Le Corbusier's High Court and Secretariat at Chandigarh are among the finest examples of his highly individual style. Here, concrete was used to create recessed sun-breaks; building masses with unusually shaped superstructures were disposed in monumental spaces. In contrast, Kahn made special use of brick construction with arched and circular openings.

Inevitably, the new generation of architects from the subcontinent were influenced by Le Corbusier and Kahn; the first schools of architecture were, in fact, started by their students. Among the new architects, Correa and Doshi have adapted modernist forms to local climatic and social requirements. Concrete and brick remain favored materials, and an expressive use of architectural forms dominate many new structures. Vernacular forms and materials are once again influencing architectural practice, testifying to the vitality of this humble yet pervasive indigenous tradition.

GM

Further reading

P. Brown, *Indian Architecture: Buddhist and Hindu Periods; Islamic Period* 3rd edn (Bombay, 1965)

S. Crowe and S. Haywood, *The Gardens of Mughal India* (London, 1972)

P. Davies, *Splendours of the Raj: British Architecture in India, 1660–1947* (London, 1985)

J. Fergusson, revised by James Burgess, *History of Indian and Eastern Architecture* 2 volumes (London, 1910)

L. Frederic, *The Art of India: Temples and Sculptures* (London and New York, 1959)

S. Huntington, *The Art of Ancient India* (New York and Tokyo, 1985)

S. Kramrisch, *The Hindu Temple*, 2 volumes (Varanasi, 1976)

M. Meister and M. A. Dhaky, Eds, *Encyclopedia of Indian Temple Architecture* (New Delhi, 1983–)

D. Mitra, *Buddhist Monuments* (Calcutta, 1971)

S. Nilsson, *European Architecture in India, 1750–1850* (London, 1968)

O. Reuther, *Indische Palaste und Wohnhauser* (Berlin, 1925)

A. Volwahsen, *Living Architecture: Islamic Indian* (London, 1970)

Sculpture

Sculpture has been a favored medium of artistic expression in the Indian subcontinent from early times, and has enjoyed a very close relationship with architecture. This relationship is particularly evident in many cave temples which are often little more than gigantic sculptures carved out of the rock. Similarly, north Indian temples of the medieval period are so profusely decorated with sculpture that their architectural construction is thoroughly obscured. With very few exceptions, most sculptures now viewed as individual pieces in museums were originally part of larger religious and architectural schema to which the sculpture contributed and from which it, in turn, gained esthetic meaning. While it is obvious that most sculpture had religious significance, the spiritual quality frequently claimed for Indian sculpture was only nominal and its expression was very often surprisingly earthbound and sensuous, especially in the case of the work produced by early schools dating from before the fifth century AD. It is also important to remember that even though religious in inspiration, the sculpture was itself non-sectarian with only iconographical rather than stylistic distinctions between Hindu, Buddhist and Jain images.

The stylistic quality which has come to be most strongly associated with Indian sculpture is its marked plasticity of form. This style was already evident during the period of the Indus Valley civilization (*c.* 2500–1800 BC). Sculpture from this period was notable for its sensitive and naturalistic modeling that set it apart from work produced in centers in the West with which it was closely linked. The following fifteen hundred or so years were characterized by a variety of rural cultures that produced little of what are called 'works of art'. It was only in the third century BC with the rise of the Maurya dynasty that the rebirth of Indian art took place. A splendid series of sculptures, most of the capitals of monolithic columns, were erected roughly from Delhi to Patna in the modern state of Bihar to the east. These columns and carved capitals displayed great technical virtuosity. The sandstone from which they were constructed was very competently handled and painstakingly finished so that the surface of the stone acquired a high gloss without the application of any external polish. However, the style of these sculptures, in spite of this common technique, was hardly uniform. In some cases, it exuded a tense and restless power; in others, a full repose.

The surprising naturalism and confident technique of this new phase of Indian sculpture has led to the belief that Maurya art was either a result of foreign influences, most probably from Persia, or that it marked the end of an indigenous development, whose earlier examples had been in perishable materials, notably wood. Evidence, however, is still inconclusive: foreign influences were certainly present, but it is equally obvious that these had been

Torso from Harappa, third millenium BC, notable for its naturalistic modeling.

Mauryan sculpture. Interment of relics on a stupa railing from Bharhut, second century BC.

veneration. This style of sculpture was almost the opposite of Maurya art, consisting of cubical forms with sharp angular outlines and flat surfaces marked by precisely incised decoration. In the course of time, its hard and rigid form began to relax, finally culminating in works of marked volume with smooth flowing contours and soft and sensuous surfaces.

These developments took place in many parts of the subcontinent, notably in western India in the work adorning the cave temples at Bhaja (c. mid-second century BC) and at Karle (late first century BC), both in Maharashtra. Several cave temples at Udayagiri-Khandagiri in the eastern state of Orissa show a similar evolu-

Gandhara sculpture. Seated Buddha, second century AD.

drastically transformed, a process which can be repeatedly observed, to a greater or lesser extent, in other periods of Indian art.

Maurya sculpture, the result of imperial patronage, passed out of existence with the fall of the Maurya dynasty in the early part of the second century BC. It was followed by what is referred to as early Indian sculpture, whose various schools existed all over the subcontinent, each characterized by a distinctive regional flavor. Their subject matter was often Buddhist, illustrating episodes from the life of the Buddha or Buddhist legendary tales known as *Jatakas*. Their use of ornaments, such as the lotus flower and its derivatives, was connected with the water cosmology which emphasized the waters as the substratum of all existence and thus worthy of

tion. An extremely important school flourished in southern India between the second century BC and the third century AD , centered on Amaravati in modern Andhra Pradesh. Its outstanding characteristic was vigorous movement, producing work of unparalleled vivacity and complexity.

In northern India, in contrast, the narrative relief tradition gradually faded away and there was a new emphasis on the individual icon as an object of worship. Whereas the Buddha had earlier been represented by aniconic symbols such as the tree (representing the tree of enlightenment), or the wheel (a solar symbol associated with universal law which the preaching of sermons by the Buddha had set in motion), at Mathura in Uttar Pradesh during the first century AD the Buddha came to be portrayed in anthropomorphic form, however idealized that form was. The images themselves emphasized physical rather than spiritual power and were dependent on an earlier tradition of the depiction of Yakshas or folk deities who presided over the fertility of

Relief sculpture on a railing pillar from the Stupa at Amaravati (Andhra Pradesh). Second century AD.

Girl playing with balls, Solanki period, eleventh century, from Nagda (Rajasthan). This fine sculpture served as an inclined bracket beneath the eaves of the temple porch. The models for such sculptures were often ladies of high birth.

nature. The other great school in the north of the subcontinent at this time extended over the ancient province of Gandhara which consisted largely of the Panjab in Pakistan and eastern Afghanistan. While the Gandhara school to a great extent shared subject matter and iconography with its counterparts elsewhere, its style was unique. It stressed a much more naturalistic concept of form, ultimately of Roman and Greek origins; and accordingly a different type of Buddha image emerged which radiated sentimental piety. A feature unique to this school was its display of the muscular structure of the human body beneath flowing drapery which required much care in the rendering of the fabric and its folds. Gandhara was also known for relatively large amounts of narrative relief sculpture, but these were generally simple in composition, lacking the complexities of pieces done in other more centrally-located schools.

A new phase in the development of Indian sculpture coincided in the fourth century AD with the rise to power of the Gupta dynasty in north India. The earthy idioms of earlier schools which had seemed to display innocent pleasure in the joys of life, were drastically transformed into a new vision which became decidedly contemplative and spiritual. The body lost its earthiness; soft flesh dissolved and was now rendered more abstractly. This change was most conspicuous in the treatment of the Buddha whose image during this period was perfectly expressive of the compassionate master, who, having transcended pain and pleasure, meditated serenely on the inner world of the spirit. Nor was this contemplative manner confined to the image of the Buddha. Rather, it was a common feature of the period, also found in the images of Hindu divinities whose representations became increasingly present.

An extremely important center of this new style was, once again, Mathura, which produced images of singular grace, but still with the strength and vitality associated with earlier sculpture from the site. Splendid images of the Buddha from Mathura number among the outstanding masterpieces of Indian art. Sarnath near Benares (Varanasi) in Uttar Pradesh, whose artistic traditions stretched back to the third century BC, was the home of another important and influential tradition, characterized by an even more abstract rendering of surface which transfused figures with a luminous and ethereal insubstantiality. Among the most important were the powerful work at Udaygiri in Madhya Pradesh; the graceful idiom characterized by superb ornament of Nachna Kuthara and Bhumara, also in Madhya Pradesh; the Gujarat version with its heavier and more markedly naturalistic forms; and the magnificent sculptures decorating the cave temples of Ajanta and Elephanta in Maharashtra. No similar flowering seems to have taken place in southern India at this time.

Following the decline of the styles of the Gupta period in the sixth century AD, the next two centuries witnessed the evolution of what is

Copulating couple from the Sun Temple, Konarak mid-thirteenth century. Temples of the medieval period are adorned with large quantities of sculpture.

loosely termed the medieval period of Indian sculpture which extended roughly until the thirteenth century in northern India and until the nineteenth century in the south. The early stages of this style in northern India are unclear, but it was well in place by the ninth century. Sculpture of this period was characterized by very conventional treatment of the human body. Contours became more angular, rhythms more staccato, and the modeling of the body was increasingly encrusted with ornament. Temple architecture of this period required large quantities of sculpture to adorn its walls, so that the amount of sculpture produced was vast with a corresponding decline in general quality. By the eleventh century, the style had become, for the most part, dry and mechanical, although exception-

Parvati, consort of Shiva, eleventh century, from Truvenkadu (Tamil Nadu). The elegance and sophistication of medieval bronzes from Tamil Nadu is without rival elsewhere in South Asia.

ally fine works were still produced.

As in earlier periods, a variety of regional idioms developed, extending from the school of Kashmir, which continued to exhibit memories of the school of Gandhara, to the relatively conservative idioms of eastern India in which the marked linearity of central India and Gujarat was avoided. There were many important north Indian centers, of which Osian in Rajasthan, Khajuraho in Madhya Pradesh and Bhubaneswar and Konarak in Orissa were especially productive. Bronze sculpture seems to have gained in importance during this period and superb examples are available from Nalanda and Kurkinar in Bihar and from Kashmir. Exquisite ivories of Kashmiri workmanship have also been discovered during the last twenty years, preserved for the most part in Himalayan monasteries.

Artistic activity, after a considerable lapse of time, gained momentum in south India during the medieval period. The sculpture of Mahabalipuram near Madras in Tamil Nadu, which dates from the seventh century, is elegant and assured, unlike the hesitant contemporary work of the north. By the ninth century the south had developed a style of high esthetic achievement. A tendency towards hardness set in during the subsequent centuries, but productivity was prodigious, particularly from the fifteenth century onward. Vast amounts of sculpture were needed to decorate the towering gateways (*gopuras*) of great temple complexes, and much of this work was conventional and of indifferent quality. The medieval period in Tamil Nadu was also remarkable for bronze sculpture which can hardly be rivaled by any other part of the subcontinent for elegance and sophistication. The region of Karnataka had its own styles ranging from the almost rude strength and power of the caves of Badami (sixth to seventh centuries AD) to the virtuoso workmanship of the richly detailed sculptures of Halebid and Belur (twelfth century AD). Maharashtra too had its own powerful array of work found most notably in the cave temples of Ellora (seventh century AD onwards).

PCh

Further reading

P. Chandra, *The Sculpture of India 3000 B.C. – 1300 A.D.* (Cambridge, Mass., 1985); 'South Asian Peoples, Arts of', *Encyclopaedia Britannica* fifteenth edn pp. 184–197 (1974)

A. K. Coomaraswamy, *History of Indian and Indonesian Art* (New York, 1927)

J. C. Harle, *The Art and Architecture of the Indian Subcontinent* (Harmondsworth, 1986)

Painting

Given the Indian genius for the decorative use of color and line, it is likely that painting flourished in some form at all periods of the subcontinent's history. The only surviving evidence from ancient times consists of prehistoric pictures in rock shelters and the decorated pottery of the Indus Valley and other early sites. Little more remains from the great age of Indian classical painting, culminating in the Gupta and early post-Gupta periods. We know from literary sources that temples, palaces and houses commonly contained wall-paintings, often in special picture halls (*chitrashala*). Painting on wood or cloth was also practiced by amateurs as well as professionals, being one of the polite arts enjoined on the cultivated urban class by the *Kamasutra*. Extant technical treatises (*shilpashastra*) provide details of traditional pictorial theory and methods. Yet the ravages of the climate, pests and Muslim iconoclasm have destroyed all paintings on wood, cloth or palm-leaf before *c*.AD 1000, while the impermanence of secular buildings in India accounts for the loss of all palace murals before the sixteenth century.

The earliest and most important wall-paintings are found in the Buddhist rock-cut caves of Ajanta in the western Deccan (second century BC to late fifth century AD). The walls, ceilings and columns of these monastic and temple halls were covered at different times with complex narrative compositions of *Jataka* stories and other Buddhist themes, together with a wealth of floral and animal decoration. Even in their damaged state, the Ajanta paintings are one of the glories of world art, evoking a timeless universe in which graceful, aristocratic men and women live in harmony with an abundant and exuberantly depicted nature. This delight in worldly life suggests that they were mostly the work of professional artists accustomed to secular as well as religious commissions. The serenity and compassion of spiritually developed beings is also movingly conveyed.

The technique used at Ajanta is a form of tempera on a plaster ground attached to the rock walls by a clay underlayer. The pronounced outline drawing has a vigor and sinuous fluency rarely found in later Indian painting. A form of spatial recession is used, as well as modeling and highlights to accentuate volume. Even the earliest paintings (Caves 9–10) reveal the compositional and drawing skills of an already mature style. The later phases (Caves 16–17, 1–2), dating from the late fifth or possibly early sixth centuries, appear to stand at the end of the stylistic development under the Gupta and Vakataka dynasties. The outline drawing starts to become excessively mannered, prefiguring a movement in the following centuries away from naturalistic modeling, spatial depth and dynamic composition, toward a flatter, linear mode and an adherence to hieratic formulae.

Wall-painting from the Buddhist rock-cut caves of Ajanta (Maharashtra). This depicts a Bodhisattva, Cave 1, second half of the fifth century.

Ajanta no doubt represented only one provincial variant of a widespread tradition. Fine remains of wall-paintings in a related style were formerly visible at the Buddhist caves of Bagh, not far to the north, while other fragments are found at various Deccani and southern sites of the sixth to ninth centuries, including the Hindu Cave 3 at Badami (Karnataka); the rock-face painted with celestial maidens at Sigiriya (Sri Lanka); temples at Panamalai, Kanchipuram and a ninth century Jain cave at Sittanavasal (Tamil Nadu); and the Kailasa temple and Jain caves at Ellora (eighth to ninth centuries). At Ellora the linear idiom of the later western Indian style is becoming more evident, with its angular rhythms and faces turning towards the profile, with a protruding further eye. In the south, the early eleventh century frescoes of dancers and musicians in the Rajarajeshvara Temple, Thanjavur, retain some naturalistic verve, but by the later Vijayanagar period, at Hampi and Lepakshi (*c.* 1540), a more decorative, two-dimensional treatment is well established, continuing in the seventeenth to eighteenth centuries in a more rigid idiom under the Nayaks of Tamil Nadu and in the floridly ornate temple and palace murals of Kerala.

The relatively late development of the arts of the book in India was due both to the scarcity of suitable materials and the earlier reliance on the oral transmission of religious texts. The oldest surviving manuscript illustrations, from the eleventh to twelfth centuries, are small depictions of Buddhas and auspicious deities on the palm-leaf pages and wooden covers of *Mahayana* texts from the scriptoria of the great monasteries of eastern India under Pala rule. These images, which preserve in miniature something of the linear grace of Ajanta, are normally unrelated to the sublimely metaphysical texts which they accompany, but perform a magical, protective function. After the destruction of the monasteries by the invading Muslim Turks in the late twelfth century, the Pala style continued in Nepal, where it was already well established. From the fourteenth to nineteenth centuries, however, the Nepalese manuscript tradition was secondary to the finer and more expansive art of religious scroll-paintings on cloth (Sanskrit: *pata*; Newari: *paubha*; Tibetan: *thangka*). This art also derived from Indian antecedents and was influenced at later times by Indian (Mughal-Rajput) as well as Tibetan painting styles. Further west, the quality of the vanished Buddhist pictorial art of Kashmir can be glimpsed in temple wall-paintings in Ladakh and Western Tibet (just as, at an earlier period, the lost mural art of Gandhara can be surmised from related examples in Afghanistan and Central Asia).

The Muslim Sultans who dominated northern India from the thirteenth century maintained an exclusively Persian court culture. By the fifteenth to sixteenth centuries illustrated manuscripts in provincial Persian idioms were being produced at centers in Malwa and Bengal, and probably also in Delhi, Jaunpur, Gujarat and the Deccan. Literary evidence suggests that mural traditions also flourished under the Delhi Sultanate. Most surviving Sultanate manuscripts show few stylistic concessions to their Indian origins, but some later examples, such as the *Nimatnama* (*c.* 1500), an illustrated cookery book compiled for the sybaritic Ghiyas ud Din Khalji of Mandu, reveal a synthesis of the contemporary Shiraz manner with unmistakably Indian elements (particularly the female figures), borrowed from the newly renascent Hindu manuscript tradition.

During the early Sultanate period the indigenous art of book illustration had been kept alive chiefly by the mercantile Jain community of western India. Wealthy laymen would seek religious merit by commissioning illustrated manuscripts of the Jain scriptures, describing the lives and deeds of the Tirthankaras or the

monk Kalaka. These were presented to temple libraries, where, especially in Gujarat and Rajasthan, they have been preserved in large numbers. The earliest manuscripts, from the eleventh century onwards, were on palm-leaf, but from the late fourteenth century paper (introduced by the Muslims from central Asia) was increasingly used, making possible a less narrow format and more opulent decorative schemes. The repetitive production of a few stereotyped series gave rise to a dry and conservative style, characterized by wiry, nervous drawing and a bright but limited palette with dominant red (later blue) backgrounds. No sense of spatial depth remains, and architecture and natural forms are schematically treated. In the fifteenth century, however, a liberating influence appears, for example in the 1451 *Vasanta Vilasa* scroll, a secular poem celebrating the amorous delights of spring, while in the 1439 *Kalpasutra* from Mandu a new clarity and vitality of line again give a hint of the incipient stylistic revolution under Hindu patronage.

In the fifteenth to sixteenth centuries the resurgence in North India of Vaishnava devotional (*bhakti*) cults, particularly that of the cowherd god Krishna in the Mathura region, had given rise both to a flowering of vernacular poetry and a regeneration of the stagnant manuscript tradition. The tiny surviving group of manuscripts in the new style is often called after its classic and most polished example, the *Chaurapanchashika* series at Ahmadabad. More revealing of the playful energy of the style is a dispersed series of the *Bhagavata-purana*, by several hands; other texts illustrated included the new genre of *ragamala*, or depictions of musical modes. In these works the attenuated pictorial language of the western Indian style was revitalized by bold, curvilinear drawing, greater compositional freedom and a deployment of vivid color schemes to emotional rather than merely hieratic effect. The attribution and dating of the *Chaurapanchashika* group are disputed, but it is likely that the still independent Rajput courts, such as Gwalior and Chitor in the early sixteenth century, were leading centers of patronage. Less refined work was also produced for the Vaishnava merchant class of the Delhi-Mathura region, and the style may well have had a still wider dissemination. It is in any case certain that a number of the Indian painters who later joined the emperor Akbar's studio had been trained in the style, while its fundamental influence on the early seventeenth century Rajasthani schools in Mewar and elsewhere is equally clear.

The growing dominance of the Mughal court under Akbar (1556–1605) and his successors brought revolutionary changes to painting, as to most other aspects of Indian cultural life. From this period book-painting or individual miniatures replaced wall-painting as the most vital form of the art, in a progressive flowering at numerous greater or lesser courts, both Muslim and Hindu, which lasted until well into the nineteenth century. Painters' names were for the first time often recorded in inscriptions, and the fuller historical record

A lady worshipping the lingam. An illustration to the musical mode *Bhairavi ragini*, Rajasthan (?), *c.*1525–30.

synthesis of Persian technique and Indian natural vigor, with a growing influence of Western naturalism from European prints which were now reaching the Mughal court. The most ambitious project of the new studio was a series of 1400 large cloth-paintings illustrating the *Hamzanama*, a rambling adventure story-cycle, which took fifteen years to complete (*c.* 1562–77). In the later decades of Akbar's reign there followed a steady stream of more conventional and highly accomplished illustrated manuscripts of Persian poetic classics, of Hindu religious epics in the Persian translations commissioned by Akbar, and above all of the official histories of Akbar's reign and of the lives of his Timurid ancestors. The mature Akbari style is seen at its best in such series as the Victoria and Albert Museum *Akbarnama*, with its dramatic, densely peopled scenes of life at court, in camp and on the hunting and battlefields. These illustrations were generally the work of two or even three separate artists: after a master had outlined the composi-

An illustration to the *Akbarnama*, *c.*1600, in which Akbar is seen trying to restrain an elephant pursuing another elephant across a bridge of boats which is collapsing. The outline was drawn by Basavan.

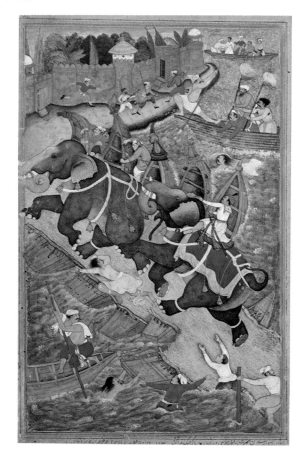

reveals more clearly than before the role of individual royal patrons in shaping their artists' styles.

Although the Mughal emperors shared the Central Asian cultural background of the earlier Sultans, they differed from them in their inquisitive outlook and eclectic tastes. Babur (d. 1530), the founder of the empire, shows in his Memoirs an original mind and a highly observant eye. The more bookish Humayun (1530–56) was driven into temporary exile in Persia, but profited from the great patron Shah Tahmasp's conversion to pious orthodoxy by taking the Safavid painters Mir Sayyid Ali and Abd us Samad into his own service. The youthful Akbar received some training in the Persian style from these masters, but its delicate refinement failed to satisfy his ardent temperament. With typical enthusiasm, he assembled a large studio of native artists from different parts of his rapidly expanding empire, placing them under the direction of the Safavid masters and himself supervising their productions. Within a few years an integrated and dynamic illustrative style resulted from the

tion, an assistant would perform the coloring and another specialist might insert the facial portraits. Among the most gifted painters were the volatile Daswanth, who died early by his own hand, and Basavan, who excelled in naturalistic techniques deriving from European models.

In his quasi-mystical search for the inner truth of man and the world, Akbar had encouraged the art of portraiture, a genre foreign in its realism both to Indian art, with its timeless world of ideal types, and the Islamic tradition, with its prohibition of the depiction of living beings. This revolution in Indian painting, with its secular viewpoint and dispassionate observation of the world, was further advanced by the esthete and connoisseur Jahangir (1605–27). A more selective patron than his father, he reduced the imperial studio to an élite group of the finest masters. Instead of copiously illustrated manuscripts he demanded individual pictures of the highest quality, which were mounted in lavishly decorated borders and collected in albums. The focus of Mughal art changed from wide-scale scenes of crowded action to sober, exquisite portraits of courtiers, standing singly against a plain colored background or grouped statically in the formal solemnity of the darbar. Jahangir's favored artists accompanied him in court or camp, ready to take a portrait or to record the birds, animals and flowers which caught the Emperor's eye. Mansur, who specialized in such natural history studies, received an honorific title ('Wonder of the Age'), as did the outstanding portrait artist Abul Hasan. Other masters included Bishn Das and Manohar (son of Basavan), while the highly gifted Govardhan also excelled in genre scenes of holy men.

In the reign of Shah Jahan (1627–58), a lover of jewels and monumental architecture, this refined style hardened into a magnificent but cold vision of courtly pomp, as seen in the Windsor *Padshahnama*, though more sympathetic genre scenes of ordinary life were still painted for the royal albums. Fine work continued to be produced early in Aurangzeb's reign (1658–1707), but after *c.* 1680 that Emperor's pious distaste for the arts caused a dispersal of painters to provincial courts. Under his many and often short-lived successors Mughal painting declined into a vapid repetition of conventional portrait and harem themes. Some pleasingly informal court scenes were produced for the effete Muhammad Shah (1719– 48), whose passive attitude led to the Persian sack of Delhi in 1739 and a further exodus of imperial artists. Provincial Mughal styles began to flourish in the now virtually independent kingdoms of Avadh and Bengal, but from the early nineteenth century both these and the surviving Delhi tradition became strongly Europeanized as the British strengthened their hold on northern India.

During the early Mughal period, analogous and equally brilliant developments were taking place in the independent Muslim Sultanates of the Deccan. The Sultans had untypically joined forces to overthrow the last Hindu stronghold of Vijayanagar in 1565. In the following decades distinctive styles of painting grew under their patronage, combining the Persian and Turkish elements of their own court culture with indigenous Indian influences and, later, a discreet awareness of European conventions. By temperament the Sultans were esthetes and hedonists, without the sterner martial virtues and imperial ambitions of the Mughals (who were thus able first to dominate and later annexe their kingdoms). Deccani portraits and poetical manuscripts have an intimate and playful atmosphere, with a superb refinement of line and subtle richness of color. Although they were always few in number, their general quality was exceptionally high. Ahmadnagar, where the earliest of the schools developed, also became in 1600 the first of the Deccani kingdoms to succumb to Mughal expansion. At Bijapur, some of the finest Deccani portraits were painted for Ibrahim Adil Shah (1580– 1627), an outstanding connoisseur, musician and poet. From the 1630s more sober Mughal influences affected portraiture at Bijapur and at Golconda under Abdullah Qutb Shah (1626–72) and Abul Hasan Qutb Shah (1672–87). Both cities fell to Aurangzeb's armies in 1686–87, but painting of good quality continued for the Mughal nobility occupying the Deccan. By the mid-eighteenth century the now independent kingdom of Hyderabad had become an important center for portraiture and *ragamala* painting in a sometimes floridly romantic style. Its influence reached many smaller Deccani courts and as far south as Thanjavur under Maratha rule.

The other important centers of painting in the Mughal period were the numerous Rajput courts of Rajasthan, central India and the Panjab Hills. In the early seventeenth century the boldly painted mythological, poetical and *ragamala* series from Mewar and the Malwa and Bundelkhand regions are in stiffer, formalized versions of the earlier *Chaurapanchashika* style. However, through their close connections with the Mughal court the Maharajas soon acquired a taste for a sub-imperial style of painting, which was to modify and revitalize indigenous traditions, especially at Bundi, Kotah and Udaipur. The new art of portraiture also became established at all the major Rajasthani courts in the later seventeenth century, in some cases, as at Amber and Jodhpur, in an initially strong Mughal idiom, which was assimilated within one or two generations to local conventions rooted in the robust rhythms and coloring of folk-painting. At Bikaner the refined Mughal-Deccani style practiced by immigrant Muslim artist families in the late seventeenth century was similarly absorbed. Mughal technique was thus constantly transformed by Rajput poetic vision; at Kishangarh in the mid-eighteenth century the hard contemporary Mughal manner became an expressive vehicle for scenes of the eternal love-sports of Krishna and Radha. Vigorous local sub-styles also flourished at many minor courts (*thikanas*), such as Deogarh in Mewar. A final general decline occurred only after the mid-nineteenth century, when under British influence the Maharajas

Deccani paintings of the Mughal period, although few in number, are of exceptionally high quality. Ibrahim II Adil Shah of Bijapur holding castanets, Bijapur c.1615.

bold and sometimes quirkish results. Following the dispersal of Delhi artists in 1739, however, a further wave of Mughal influence transformed the Pahari styles. Traditional Vaishnava and poetical subjects were now treated with a softer palette and a distinctively mellifluous use of line, based in Mughal technique but surpassing it in expressive power. Originally associated with the court of Guler, the new style was quickly spread to other courts by itinerant members of artist families, among whom the descendants of Pandit Seu were particularly influential. One of the most gifted of these was Nainsukh, who painted portraits of unusual intimacy and insight for his princely patron, Balwant Singh. The mature phase of the style, and with it the final flowering of the Hindu pictorial tradition, took place at the court of Raja Sansar Chand of Kangra (1775–1823), for whom several superb mythological series were painted. Comparable styles also flourished at Garhwal and other courts, but by 1800 the Pahari manner was everywhere degenerating into a facile sentimentality. Within a few years, the Hill kingdoms were conquered by the plains-dwelling Sikhs, who themselves patronized portraiture in an enervated Pahari manner until the British annexation of the Panjab in 1849.

While court art was in decline, painting at the village and bazaar level retained its perennial vitality. Although few folk paintings earlier than the nineteenth century survive, the regional traditions which they embody are in many cases probably centuries old. Early literary sources mention traveling picture-showmen who exhibited cloth-paintings of heaven and hell (*Yamapatas*), much like the painted scrolls used for similar purposes in Bengal up to modern times. Other important folk-traditions associated with narrative performances are the long Rajasthani cloth-paintings (*par*) illustrating the epic of Pabuji and the so-called 'Paithan' paintings of Maharashtra, illustrations on paper to various epic narrative cycles. Coarse but vigorous bazaar styles of mythological painting also developed around important temples to cater for the pilgrim trade, as at Puri (Orissa) and in the Kalighat district of Calcutta. The latter tradition lasted for about a century until it was undermined first by mass-produced wood-cuts and later by lurid chromolithographs (still ubiquitous today). The recent commercial marketing of folk-paintings, such as the wall-designs of the Brahmin and Kayasth women of Mithila in a reduced paper format, has mostly had an unfortunate effect.

In the late eighteenth and nineteenth centuries Company painting, comprising a variety of semi-Westernized local styles, was much patronized by British residents and visitors, albeit mainly at

began to embrace Western academicism and the novel art of photography.

Rajput painting in the Panjab Hills underwent a separate development whose beginnings are still obscure. The farouchely confident late seventeenth century Basohli illustrations of erotic themes have no obvious antecedents. A strongly Mughal style was practiced for a time at Mandi, but generally the imperial conventions of portraiture were rapidly assimilated to indigenous Pahari (Hill) idioms, as at Kulu, Mankot and Mandi, with impressively

The late seventeenth and eighteenth centuries saw much patronage of painting fusing Mughal and indigenous traditions at the many courts of Rajasthan. This is a posthumous picture of Rao Durjan Sal of Kotah hunting lions, Kotah (Rajasthan), 1778.

Radha and Krishna in a grove. Kangra (Panjab Hills), 1785. Painting at the court of Raja Sansar Chand of Kangra (1775–1823) marks the final flowering of the Hindu pictorial tradition.

the cruder bazaar level. Its subject matter was the picturesque aspect of Indian social life, embodied in standardized series of illustrations of native trades and castes, popular festivals, modes of transport and Mughal monuments. In the better examples, European conventions of modeling, spatial recession and muted coloring were adapted to existing styles, sometimes to striking effect. The southern centers of production included Madras, Thanjavur, Trichinopoly and Madurai; in the north, at Murshidabad, Calcutta, Patna, Benares, Delhi and Agra, the Company schools were the impoverished successors of earlier Mughal traditions. In a few cases, however, gifted artists working for discerning patrons produced such fine works as Shaikh Zain ud Din's bird studies for Lady Impey, the Calcutta domestic views of Shaikh Muhammad Amir of Karraya and the portrait paintings of Ghulam Ali Khan and other Delhi artists for William Fraser and Colonel Skinner.

In the later nineteenth century European art schools were established in the major cities of British India. Oil painting also came into favor at the princely courts, the sentimental renderings of mythological subjects by Raja Ravi Varma of Travancore (1848–1906) being especially popular. The attempt to recreate an authentic Indian style by Abanindranath Tagore (1871–1951) and his fol-

In this example of Company painting a nautch party is being held in a European house, Delhi, c.1820.

'Man eating Jalebee' by Bhupen Khakhar, Baroda (Gujarat), 1977.

lowers at the Calcutta Art School, through an eclectic study of the Ajanta and miniature traditions as well as Western and Japanese painting, gave rise to an influential but anemically literary manner.

A stronger originality was shown in the darkly agitated ink and water-color drawings by Rabindranath Tagore (1861–1941) in his old age; in the boldly simplified Bengali folk-based style of Jamini Roy (1887–1972); and in the Gauguinesque studies of villagers by the half-Hungarian, Paris-trained painter Amrita Sher-Gil (1912–41). Since Independence many of the leading movements of international modernism have been experimented with in India and Pakistan, from a modified social realism to abstract work sometimes based on Rajput color values or Tantric imagery. In his eclectic facility the prolific M. F. Husain (b. 1915) is in some ways a characteristic figure. In recent years the Baroda-based figurative painters Bhupen Khakhar (b. 1934) and Gulam Shaikh (b. 1937) have, in their different ways, successfully integrated diverse Western and traditional elements in original and highly colored interpretations of Indian urban life.

AT

Further reading

M. Archer, *Company Drawings in the India Office Library* (London, 1972); *Indian Popular Painting in the India Office Library* (London, 1977)

W. G. Archer, *Indian Paintings from the Punjab Hills* 2 vols (London, 1973)

D. Barrett and B. Gray, *Painting of India* (Geneva, 1963; repr. London, 1978)

M. C. Beach, *The Grand Mogul: Imperial Painting in India 1600–1660* (Williamstown, 1978)

G. Kapur, *Contemporary Indian Artists* (New Delhi, 1978)

J. P. Losty, *The Art of the Book in India* (London, 1982)

C. Sivaramamurti, *South Indian Painting* (New Delhi, 1968)

G. Yazdani, *Ajanta* 4 vols (Oxford, 1931–55)

M. Zebrowski, *Deccani Painting* (London, 1983)

Decorative arts

Although very few examples of pre-Mughal decorative arts survive, Roman sources confirm that South Asian textiles, hardstone-carvings and metalwork were highly prized in the ancient world. South Indian bronze images of the tenth century AD show that metalcasting techniques had by then reached an extraordinary level of sophistication, both in technical and esthetic terms, and the continuation of these skills, passed from generation to generation by the caste system of inherited occupations, is evident in both ritual and domestic metalwork from medieval times to the present day. The survival of the dowry system has also contributed to the continuous production of jewelry in gold, silver and base metals, in traditional styles that must have seen little change over several hundred years. Similarly, the embroidered and appliqué textiles of rural South Asia

Hanging for the side of a bed. Quilted and embroidered cotton. Gujarat; early
twentieth century.

undoubtedly have a long history, albeit an undocumented one.
More widely known are the fine textiles, such as the muslins of
eastern India that the Romans called 'woven winds', and Hindu and
Buddhist texts, as well as sculptures and wall-paintings, attest to the
early existence of fine painted, printed and tie-dyed fabrics, and
possibly also more sophisticated silk brocades.

With the advent of Islam in South Asia, all the arts received a
great stimulus from the introduction of a new decorative repertoire
and a different use of several craft techniques. Indian steel had long
been exported to the Middle East for the manufacture of flexible,
watered blades: now, new styles of arms augmented the Indian
punch-dagger and sword-types such as the *khanda* and *pata*. Luxury
domestic metalwork, such as the inlaid 'bidri' ware of the Deccan
also attained great elegance during the Mughal period, and metal
engraving, which was known but apparently little-used in pre-
Muslim South Asia, became an area of extreme virtuosity. Enamel-
ing was listed as an Indian craft in the *Ain-e Akbari* (completed *c.*
1604) but was probably introduced by the Muslims under European
influence, and high-quality glass production also began, a craft
which already existed in India in a cruder form. Jade carving, which
came to epitomize the Mughal courtly arts, was unknown before the
Jahangiri period, although the raw material, from Khotan in central
Asia, is known to have been brought to India in Akbar's time.
Jahangir possessed several Timurid jades, and he encouraged the

setting-up of jade workshops, which reached their peak under Shah
Jahan. Although jade had been neglected, there had long been a
tradition in India of carving both rock-crystal, mainly for religious
images, and, at Cambaya, hardstones such as agate, for bowls and
beads. Linked to the jade carvings was the use of applied or inlaid
precious stones, a feature of the later Mughal jades which had been
pioneered during the sixteenth century by the Ottoman Turks.

Perhaps even more significant than the technical innovations was
the new range of decorative motifs imposed upon the crafts by the
arts of the Muslim invaders. Foremost among these was the floral
arabesque, and the closely-linked animal-inhabited foliate scroll,
which came particularly to dominate carved and inlaid decoration in
several media. The Perso-Arabic script itself, which plays such a
prominent part in Islamic art, began to be used in South Asia mainly
as architectural decoration.

While the crafts and their decoration in traditional Hindu society,
particularly in the south of India, were inseparable from temple
ritual and its domestic equivalent, the arts of the Muslim north and
Deccan reflected the new courtly society cultivated there. Worship
in Islam demands few material accompaniments and consequently
most Islamic decorative arts have a secular basis. The Muslim
courts, especially that of the Mughals, emulated to a large extent the
connoisseurship of their European contemporaries. French,
English and Italian craftsmen are known to have worked for the

Turban ornament. Gold, set with gemstones, the stem enamelled in translucent green. Mughal; early eighteenth century.

ivory-inlaid fall-fronted cabinets of Sind, as well as the wholly Christian ivory carvings made for them in their original base of Goa. The 'East India trade' in Indian objects made specifically for the European market flourished from the seventeenth century to the nineteenth century, and included ivory furniture and boxes, and cotton hangings embroidered in silk or hand-painted with the coveted fast dyes of South India. These are all adaptations of indigenous crafts to commissions by new patrons, the British, Dutch and Portuguese. Ivory carving had flourished in South and East India and Sri Lanka from very early times, and was used for ornamental combs, handles, plaques and even throne- and bed-legs: now European prototypes were called in as models for the chairs, boxes, writing-desks, tables, mirrors and even chess-sets ordered by the eighteenth century colonists. Western India had its own tradition of painted and lacquered wood, as well as the magnificent mother-of-pearl-inlaid pieces made in Gujarat in the seventeenth century, and exported to other Muslim countries rather than to Europe.

While foreign influences, whether from the invading Mughals or colonizing Europeans, stimulated much of the finest South Asia craftsmanship in the post-medieval period, it was the British who precipitated its decline in the nineteenth century. As well as the detrimental competition from English cotton cloth, the deadening influence of the Victorian trade catalog penetrated into all branches of the arts and led to a period of emulation of a poorly understood decorative repertoire. The setting-up of the Schools of Art, run by the British, exacerbated this tendency and undermined the traditional hereditary craft system. Sir George Watt, writing in 1902, records that at least 50 percent of the silversmiths in South Asia were

Casket. Ivory with silver gilt mounts. The lock and handle set with sapphires. Kotte, Sri Lanka, *c.*1558.

Mughal Emperors in the seventeenth century, and they brought with them techniques such as cameo-carving and pietra dura inlaying, while embassies brought new and intriguing artifacts, as well as influential paintings and engravings from European courts. The traditional practice of keeping wealth in the form of precious stones took on new esthetic connotations as prized gems were admired for their beauty and frequently carved and worn as ostentatious jewels.

Europeans had been a force in South Asia since Vasco da Gama landed in 1498. The Portuguese presence is reflected in the sixteenth to seventeenth century embroidered coverlets of Bengal, which often depict European ships and soldiers, the carved ivory caskets of Sri Lanka and South India, and the seventeenth century

taking their designs from European trade catalogs, and no doubt the same was true of other media. If creativity had declined, technical standards at least were maintained by the Colonial Exhibitions of the mid-nineteenth to early twentieth century, for which virtuoso pieces were specially made. After this final expression of the tradition of patronage, the crafts in South Asia went into a decline from which, with very few exceptions, they have not recovered. Rural and domestic crafts too have suffered from the influx of ready-made goods into the local markets, but a new awareness of folk-tradition has helped, through craft museums and local handicraft boards, to revitalize some of the vast range of South Asia's indigenous skills.

RCr

Further reading
No good overall survey of South Asian decorative arts exists, but several exhibition catalogs cover most aspects. The most useful are as follows.

Metropolitan Museum, *India: Art and Culture 1300–1900* (New York, 1985)
Victoria and Albert Museum, *The Indian Heritage* (London, 1982)
Sir George Watt, *Indian Art at Delhi* (Calcutta, 1903)

Food and culture

Nearly half of South Asia's people eat rice (or its derivatives) as their staple food while the other half depends on wheat, barley, maize or millet. Rice (or a poor substitute like millet) is cooked either by boiling or by grinding and steaming to convert it into a pancake. Cereals are ground into flour to make unleavened bread. Only in the extreme west and the northwest may a slight fermentation of the dough be encouraged to let the bread 'rise' slowly.

For the dominant Hindu food system, the classical scheme of three *gunas* (strands of nature) remains important, classifying foods as superior or 'good' (*sattvik*), middling or excitable (*rajasik*) and inferior or 'dull' (*tamasik*). Superior foods are sweet, soft, wet and fresh, while the middling are sour, dry, bitter, and hard-to-digest, and the inferior are unclean, stale, spoiled, and cause disease. Clarified butter (*ghi*) is thus superior, spices middling and forbidden meat inferior. However, observances vary by caste, sect and region.

People classify their food and drink as high, middle and low. Those ranked high are expected to eat only superior, refined, exclusive, and ritually pure foods. They receive cooked foods only from those equal or higher, but can give foods to all. Giving is superior to receiving; it announces moral and social superiority. Moral quality, ritual purity and auspiciousness, thus, rank Hindu

foods, regulating their acquisition, processing, cooking, feeding, eating, and storage everyday within houseolds. Religious sects and temples also follow similar rules to regulate their food exchanges.

Food is a critical component of all important Hindu rites of passage and religious ceremonies. Auspicious and happy ceremonies (for example, at birth and marriage) call for elaborate cuisine while the inauspiciousness (such as at death) imposes prohibitions, restraints and even absence of cooking. Marriage feasts particularly reflect one's caste status, social prestige and lineage honor, making such occasions a sensitive social affair. Domestic fasts and festivals revolve around the cooking and offering of special foods, intended to obtain health and prosperity.

The Muslim food system in South Asia is culturally very distinct, and ideologically opposed to that of the Hindus. Muslims eat meat frequently but forbidden products include carrion, pork, blood, and animals not slaughtered in the name of God. *Ramazan* is the month-long period of daytime fasting and piety, alms-giving and sharing of cooked and uncooked foods. Muslim marriages are characterized by honor and hospitality, with emphasis on Muslim brotherhood and feasting.

Whether Hindus, Jains, Sikhs, Buddhists or Muslims, women play a critical role in everyday food handling, cooking, and feeding within households. They remain the major guardians of South Asian culinary culture by spending a significant part of their lives around the domestic hearth as kitchen-helpers, wives and daily cooks, and as trainers as mothers and mothers-in-law. Women also run the complex and full calendar of domestic hospitality, rituals,

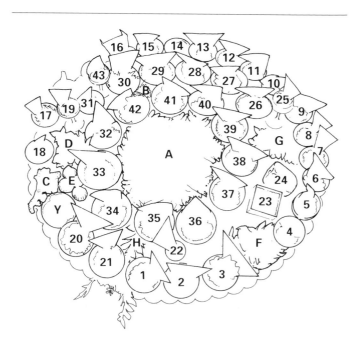

Spices used in South Asian cooking*
1 Cardamom pods, 2 Cumin seeds, 3 Ginger, 4 Mustard, 5 Lindi Pipar, 6 Kamal Kakri, 7 Nilafang root, 8 Gokharu, 9 Amba Haldi (a type of turmeric root), 10 Onion seeds, 11 Fleabane, 12 Tymol seeds, 13 Sugar candy, 14 Edible gum, 15 Ganthera, 16 Dill seeds, 17 Mulla padi, 18 Sesame seeds, 19 Crushed red chillies, 20 Garlic, 21 Cloves, 22 Poppy seeds, 23 Saffron, 24 Capsicum, 25 Peppercorns, 26 Harde, 27 Godavaj, 28 Black salt, 29 Mustard seeds, 30 Nilafang root, 31 Ispaghol gul, 32 Asgan, 33 Vavaring, 34 Lindi Pipar, 35 Badyan Phul, 36 Melon seeds, 37 Salep roots, 38 Shah Jira (similar to caraway seeds), 39 Andarjan, 40 Hing (asafoetida), 41 Vakumba, 42 Manjoo Phulo, 43 Caraway seed.

A Red chillies, B Coriander leaves, C Ginger, D Mint leaves, E Garlic, F Green chillies, G Mint leaves, H Curry leaves, X Fennel seeds, Y Dried crushed chilli.

* Several of these spices have no readily recognizable English name. They are for the most part roots, twigs, calyxes, seeds, pods etc., of plants found on the subcontinent. This particular selection has a Gujarati emphasis.

fasts, festivals, and feasts, intended for the welfare of the entire family.

The subcontinent's cuisine shows Iranian and Central Asian influences in the north (as in *mughlai* dishes), with Lucknow and Delhi as its culinary centers. The south emphasizes rice and lentil preparations (*idli*, *sambhar*, *dosa*) and the east rice and fish-curry. Aromatics, that is spices, herbs and seasonings, constitute the heart of South Asian cooking. Turmeric, coriander, cumin, fenugreek, ginger, fennel seed and cardamoms are widely used. Salt, peppers and herbs (mint, coriander leaves, thyme) season the foods. Though 'Indian curry' epitomizes this cuisine to the West, it is not an authentic dish.

As meal and diet, foods also employ long-standing Ayurvedic (Indian medical) scheme of health and well-being. This means retaining a balance between the three humors (*tridosha* – phlegm, bile and wind) by elaborate manipulation of 'hot', neutral and 'cold' foods in everyday diet. Thus, for example, while suffering from cold, the South Asian avoids 'cold' (for example, radishes, yogurt, unboiled milk) foods to regain his humoral equilibrium. A whole culinary alchemy exists, however, to render hot food neutral or cold (or vice-versa).

At present, the food system is undergoing noticeable social change, especially in urban surroundings. The intricate ritual rules of cooking, commensalism, meat-eating and sectarian feasts and fasts are being simplified, at times even dropped. Modern education, occupational diversity, rapid transportation and distant migrations have generally worked to relax traditional restrictions both regional and sectarian. Roadside food stalls, tea and coffee shops and railway platform food vendors join growing numbers of restaurants to feed people of diverse religions and social ranks. Nowadays even the orthodox Hindu faces change.

RSK

Further reading
M. Jaffrey, *A Taste of India* (New York, 1986)
R. S. Khare, *The Hindu Hearth and Home* (Durham, N.C., 1976)
R. S. Khare and M. S. A. Rao, Eds, *Food, Society and Culture: Aspects in South Asian Food System* (Durham, N.C., 1986)

Dress

Observing the *dhoti* in eleventh century India, the Arab scholar al-Biruni remarked in some surprise that the Hindus 'use turbans for trousers'. His comment embodies the division that has existed at least from the beginning of the Christian era to the present day, between the 'draped' tradition of the indigenous costume and the tailored garments of a succession of settlers and invaders, notably the Kushans, the Muslims and the British. Eastern and southern regions, least penetrated by foreigners, have tended to retain the classical styles of simple draped garments more than the north and west, which were closer to the homelands of central Asian and Muslim invaders and became the cultural and administrative centers of the empires they created, and in which tailored garments still tend to predominate. Within this generalized geographical division, considerations of class, religion and occupation, as well as locally available materials, have always affected regional styles of dress.

Sculptures dating from around the first century AD show both men and women in single draped garments tied around the hips, usually with nothing worn above the waist but a profusion of jewelry. The extreme simplicity of clothing in the early period is in contrast to the extravagant and complicated hairstyles worn by both sexes at the time, often incorporating flowers, strings of jewelry and ropes of fine textiles, and also to the abundance of gold jewelry worn as necklaces, armlets, bangles and anklets. Tight tailored bodices, very like the *choli* of today, are occasionally depicted in the Ajanta frescoes (first to fifth century AD), but 'body-shaped' garments took a firm hold in the northwest with the invasions of central Asian peoples such as the Kushans (first century AD) who came from a colder, horse-riding environment where trousers, top-coats and boots were a necessity. The harsh climate in the Panjab Hills and the Himalayan foothills necessitated, in any case, a quite different wardrobe from the draperies of the plains and the south, and local wool, a material spurned by the rest of South Asia, supplied the material for tailored garments and shawls, as it does today.

Tailored clothing extended its influence in the region with the establishment of Islam in the north in the twelfth century AD. Manuscripts of the Sultanate period show the costume of the contemporary Muslim ruling class to be a round turban, a long tunic with sash at the waist, a tight, thin collarless shirt underneath, and tight *pajamas*: a marked contrast to the dress of Hindus shown in the same manuscripts, who wear the *dhoti* and nothing else, and go bare-headed, often with their hair pulled back into a bun. Women's dress in Sultanate painting approaches surprisingly closely to present-day western Indian usage: a short bodice, a large, light cloth that covers the head and falls down the back, and a skirt-like garment wrapped around the waist and pleated at the front. The Muslim convention of

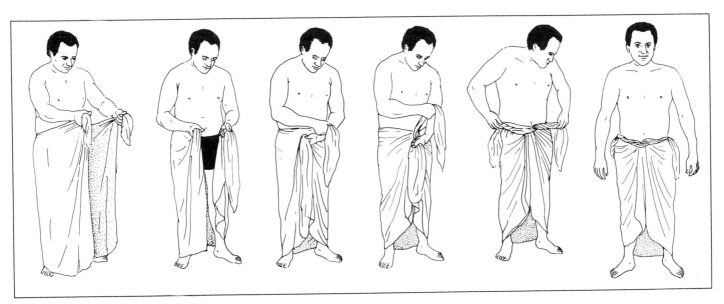

One way of tying the Indian dhoti.

female modesty had a strong impact on northern Indian society, and led to the introduction not only of veils to cover the face in public, but also the division of houses into male and female living quarters, a practice now widespread among both Hindus and Muslims.

Hindu–Muslim synthesis was encouraged by the first Mughal emperors, especially Akbar (r. 1556–1605), who incorporated the powerful Rajput states into his empire and adopted several of their fashions, notably the flat Rajput turban (*pag*). The quintessentially Mughal garment, the *jama* or side-fastening thin coat, was probably an adaptation of the indigenous Indian *angarkha* (Sanskrit 'body-protector'), but the tight *churidar* ('with bangles' that is, gathered at the ankle) pajama worn with it was a Muslim innovation. This combination may still be seen on formal occasions in Rajasthan today, although a more usual formal outfit consists of pajama and Europeanized tight jacket with stand-up collar.

The British came to South Asia in the seventeenth century, but their influence on dress, apart from isolated curiosities like the 'Frank hat' of Jahangir's time, only really dates from the nineteenth century. Military costume in particular became very influential, especially among the local rulers, and tight, front-buttoned coats and riding-breeches, from which sprang the Anglo-Indian 'jodhpurs', were frequently seen. Perhaps the most enduring legacy of British rule, however, is the collared shirt, as opposed to the traditional round-necked *kurta* or side-fastening *angarkhi*, which now increasingly accompanies the native dhoti or *lungi*.

Today, Muslims of both sexes generally tend to wear trousers (*shalwar* or pajama) and a loose shirt (*kamiz* or *kurta*), while Hindus favor the wrapped dhoti and shirt for men, and *sari*, or skirt with head-cover (*orhni* or *dopatta*) for women, although the distinction becomes very blurred in areas of greatest Muslim influence, such as the Panjab, where Hindu women habitually wear tight trousers and a long shirt. The sari is mostly worn in the Gangetic plain, central and southern India and Sri Lanka, in a variety of local styles, usually with an accompanying bodice (choli). Quite how ancient the sari is in its present form is not clear, but by the tenth century the women of eastern India were already wearing a single large cloth that covered both the upper and lower body, leaving the sides bare, and this is more or less the Bengali fashion today. The eastern regions favor white cotton saris with a coloured border, while some southern areas, as well as the urban upper classes all over South Asia tend toward highly decorative silk and brocaded cloths. In the western states of Rajasthan and Gujarat, women wear skirts, bodices and *orhni* in a range of materials from coarse block-printed cotton to the popular modern silk 'georgette'. Muslim women wear the same, but with a long apron-like bodice rather than the short choli.

Costume in the mountainous regions of Nepal and Bhutan is influenced by both the harsh climate and the proximity of Tibet and China. While Nepalese dress tends towards the Indian style, with women in saris and men in front-buttoning jackets and trousers or lungis, Bhutanese men favor the Tibetan cross-over robe (*ko*), which is ankle-length but usually worn hitched up by a belt at the waist, over knee-length felt boots, and the women wear a simple wrapped cloth (*kira*) from the arm-pit to the ankle, held in place by brooches and topped by a short jacket.

While women cover their heads with a sari end or an orhni, male

Early Indian fashion was expressed on the head: male and female hairstyles from Barhut.

headgear is frequently a significant feature which may identify the wearer's home town or district, occupation and social status. The men of eastern and southern India tend to go bare-headed or wear the small white 'Congress' or 'Gandhi' cap as do many male Pakistanis. The Nepalese favor the multi-colored striped 'Gorkha' cap. Western and central regions, however, boast a spectacular variety of turbans. As well as regional differences particular turbans may be worn at different times of the year. Cultivators and herdsmen tend to wear large loose turbans (*safa*) while businessmen sport colorful, tightly-bound narrow ones (pag).

Outside the mainstream of Hindu, Muslim or British fashion, the numerous tribes of South Asia have maintained their own traditions of dress, although these have been severely eroded during the later twentieth century. Similarly, adherents of religious sects, such as the Jain monk with his two white cloths or the ascetic emulating the god Shiva with matted hair and ash-smeared face, have remained untouched by shifts of secular fashion.

RCr

Further reading

R. Alkazi, *Ancient Indian Costume* (New Delhi, 1983)
S. N. Dar, *Costumes of India and Pakistan: a Historical and Cultural Study* (Bombay 1969)
G. S. Ghurye, *Indian Costume* (Bombay, 1951)

One way of tying and draping the classical South Indian sari (length: 5½ to 6 yards, width: 42 inches). Underneath the sari (1) a flared petticoat is worn and gathered with a tie-string. The decorative end of the sari, held in the right hand (10, 11), is known as the pallau.

Cinema

Indian cinema has been a determining influence on the development of South Asian culture during the twentieth century. This is in part due to the enormous influence on society of the large number of popular films produced from Bombay and other regional centers. In a wider context, however, the critical acclaim received by such directors as Satyajit Ray at Western film festivals makes it one of the region's most visible exports to the rest of the world.

From its pioneering days, which hardly post-date the development of film-making in Europe and North America, the Indian film industry rapidly evolved into the principal form of entertainment during the closing decades of the Raj displacing Parsi theatre which had held sway for around a century. Indian cinema achieved its apotheosis in a remarkable replay of the golden years of Hollywood during the Fifties and Sixties. During this period it also spawned secondary industries in Pakistan and other South Asian countries, which were only to founder later in the face of the universal challenge of television and video.

In spite of these general constraints, common perhaps to cinema the world over, Indian film represents a unique and extraordinary combination of many of the distinctive elements of South Asian culture, in which stories of the Hindu gods, the language and manners of high Mughal culture, the traditions of popular theatre and the social themes which concerned sensitive Indian opinion in both the pre- and post-Independence periods, came to be blended in a particularly fascinating manner.

An overview

The first motion picture, exhibited in India in 1896, marked the beginning of an industry which was subsequently to dominate

483

Indian commerce, indeed Indian life. Its unprecedented popularity prompted entrepreneurs to mount large-scale operations touring small towns and rural areas exhibiting newsreels, 'topicals', documentaries, opera, travel and sport. The more enterprising among them invested in theaters, creating empires which held sway for up to thirty years. Pioneers also appeared in the more artistic areas of the industry. At the vanguard of the rising film-makers was Dhundiraj Govind Phalke, commonly known as Dadasaheb. His Brahmin priestly background having prompted him to try his hand at mythological films, he made his first film *Raja Harishchandra* (1913). Its overwhelming success with audiences across the length and breadth of India resulted in a genre which remains immensely popular to this day.

In the next twenty years Phalke produced more than a hundred films including mythological features, documentaries, magic shows and legion other shorts. Distribution was largely handled by Phalke himself with the launching of traveling companies. Rural showings attracted hordes of people who arrived not merely for entertainment but for a profound religious experience. During showings of *Lanka Dahan* (*The Burning of Lanka*, 1917) and *Krishna Janma* (*The Birth of Krishna*, 1918) audiences prostrated themselves when the actors made their screen appearance as gods and many referred to their cinema outings as pilgrimages.

British censorship

In spite of its phenomenal impact, however, by 1927 Indian-made material still constituted only 15 percent of the total number of films exhibited in India and theaters were being increasingly monopolized by films from the USA. Socially conscious audiences began to feel the need for selective viewing, fearing that public standards were threatened by the deviation from social mores and traditional attitudes of foreign idols. Thus began the move towards censorship.

The initiative was greeted enthusiastically by the British government, piqued at the rise in popularity of USA films. Ingeniously, they urged censorship with a view to reducing the intake of American films by instituting the nebulous concept of 'Empire Films'. Echoing Gandhi's sentiment that India had to 'unlearn' Western ideology, the British questioned whether undesirable influences were not most powerfully reinforced by American films. Thus a number of ground rules were laid for film censorship, which included restrictions on criminal, sexual and socially undesirable behavior but in practice, at least in the earlier stages, laid greatest stress on politics and restraint on offending foreign governments. An amusing by-product of this drive resulted in a puritanical screen depiction of love which forbade kissing, a taboo which exists to this day and which when disregarded proves to have sensational pulling power. Even in the absence of the kiss, however, the portrayal of

Nutan in Sujata (1959).

romance was hardly puritanical. A variety of standard symbols quickly evolved such as crashing waves, thunder, lightning, and a torn female garment indicating premarital sex or rape, often echoed in the storyline by pregnancy. Excessive exposure of the body in a sexual context was frowned upon. The effects of these restrictions are still by and large apparent in Indian cinema, although social changes are clearly discernible in today's cinematic themes and symbols.

In spite of the underlying aims of censorship and the 'Empire films' impetus, outlets in urban areas continued to be monopolized by English language films until the Forties when the Indian film industry boomed, eventually becoming Hollywood's closest competitor. The fifties were undoubtedly the golden age of the Indian cinema with such productions as *Devdas* (1955), *Sahib, Bibi aur Ghulam* (1956) and *Sujata* (1959). By the Fifties Indian films were exported all over Asia, including the Far East, Iran, the Arab Middle East and Egypt, finding markets even in the UK, Africa and the USA.

This widespread popularity created large spin-off industries, most importantly the popular music business and publishing which capitalized on the popularity of the stars by producing magazines such as *Filmfare*, *Star and Style* and *Stardust*, which included star interviews, film reviews and gossip columns run by Hedda Hopper prototypes such as Devi and Nita, and *Picturepost* which ran synopses of current films. Such publications appeared in many languages and film items became popular in virtually all but the specialist nationals. In recent years the video boom has taken over, effectively undermining the primary success of the industry off which it feeds.

The genres mushroomed and to the mainstream Bombay studio product, were added art films, realistic film noir and international productions. Despite the artistic and international status of artistic movies with their focus on low profile stars, unglamorous themes and stark settings, the popular Hindi film remained to the forefront of the industry with its own unique adaptation of traditional costume, glamorization of rural location, local custom and elaborately choreographed song and dance routines. The musical scores and lyrics were key ingredients to the overall success of each film, providing advance publicity, making hits and attracting mass audiences.

The advent of sound

The late thirties witnessed a highly professional and organized film-production structure. Each film, subtitled in up to four languages enjoyed increased sales. Theaters who could afford it hired interpreters for the benefit of those who could not read. The coming of sound therefore was a mixed blessing. On the one hand it proved advantageous to the Indian film-maker, highlighting the alienness of English-language films and automatically threatening their monopoly. On the other, it created internal problems. Well-established exhibitors went out of business when they discovered that installation of the appropriate sound equipment would be too expensive. The Indian film lost its universality as producers chose one script language to the exclusion of others while the actors, often Anglo-Indian, could not speak Indian languages. One way of overcoming this problem was to remake films in a number of languages. This proved to be the basis of the regional language industries, which today account for a far larger output than the Bombay-based Hindi mainstream, with Telugu films, followed closely by Tamil films, leading production.

A more substantial factor in the popularization of sound was the introduction of musical sequences. Sometimes as many as sixty in a single film, they succeeded in surmounting language barriers. In the early days these were mostly hymns and traditional lyrics but very soon they included classical music, tightly composed *ghazals* and popular *gits* (songs). Actors therefore had to offer the additional skill

of singing thus creating a hitherto absent selection criterion. Among the earliest of the singing stars were K. L. Saigal (Hindi/Urdu) Kanan Devi (Bengali) and the female impersonator Bal Gandharv (Hindi), whose records continued to sell years after their film careers had come to an end. Soon, however, sound-recording techniques became more sophisticated, giving birth to a related industry – that of film music. Suddenly the field was alive with music directors, composers and lyricists who like the early script-writers, were largely drawn from the stage classical music and literary establishments, although they were soon to form the popular music industry. The most distinctive and enduring of these artists were the famous 'playback' singers who provided the vocals for films. A new lease of life was thus given to actors whose film careers had come to an end, such as Talat Mahmud and actress-turned-singer Nurjehan, still Pakistan'a leading film singer an amazing fifty years later. Unlike their Western counterparts these behind-the-scene artists were given a high professional profile with full billing on screen and disc. They made frequent appearances on stage and radio and later television. Today video distributors stock compilations of their hits.

The Maharashtrian sisters Lata Mangeshkar and Asha Bhonsle made their debut in the Forties, the former going on to win an unbeaten place in the *Guinness Book of Records* as the world's most recorded artist. Often contracted for a formidable dozen films at a time, and in their heyday singing as many as five to eight lyrics per film, Mangeshkar and Bhonsle were essential to the overall success of every Hindi film and for years formed an effective cartel against new female voices. The versatile Muhammed Rafi, also established in the Forties, similarly provided the male vocals for around 95 percent of Hindi films for over twenty years, while Mukesh, Manna Dey, Mahendra Kapoor and Hemant Kumar played a rather more limited part. Kishore Kumar shot to the top after providing the vocals for Dev Anand's spectacular, *Guide* (1965).

Today there is a proliferation of singers mostly imitators of the above mentioned greats. During the seventies a number of Pakistani *ghazal* and film singers including Nurjehan, Mehdi Hassan, Iqbal Bano, Runa Laila and Ghulam Ali toured India and left a distinctive impact on performance styles.

The incredible success of film music popularized many specialized forms such as *qavvali*, *mujra* and *thumri* in stylized film versions which soon became standard. Thus performers in the traditional forms received more popularity and attention than they had done since the days of court patronage.

The stars

By the fifties film stars had gained respect and a bona fide celebrity status, dictating trends in clothes, hair and make up as well as styles of speech and modes of behavior. Inevitably, stars became associ-

Nargis and Raj Kapoor, two of the great stars of the Indian cinema, in Mehboob Khan's *Andaz* (1949).

to play female parts and this marked the rise of A. Salunke, who became an integral part of the Phalke operation for many years to come, starring sometimes dually as female and male lead. However, it was not long before women from the Anglo-Indian community modeling themselves on Hollywood stars entered the industry. With the coming of the Talkie the singing star was much in demand. The industry acquired a glamorous image and very soon became a magnet to young women from all backgrounds.

During the first two decades actors adopted a dramatic acting style under the influence of folk theater, Parsi stage norms and the mime of Indian dance. Later this was considerably modified but many actresses retained gestures and facial expressions reminiscent of old performance traditions. Conversely, actresses of serious talent such as Nargis and Nutan adopted an understated and more realistic acting style under the direction of some of the most superb films noir directors anywhere in the world, including Bimal Roy, Guru Dutt and Raj Kapoor. Another outstanding actress was the tragedienne, Meena Kumari, whose roles overlapped into her personal life providing an exciting scenario for avid gossip-seeking journalists and fans. Tragic and intriguing though her life was, today's stars, many second and third-generation actors reflect a far more progressive, international lifestyle, providing ever more spicy material for the increasingly more predatory film columnists. Sadly, none of the younger crop of media conscious stars, often highly trained or drawn from the large modeling industry, have achieved the degree of fame earned by their predecessors in terms either of mass following or of longevity. The acting careers of women such as Vyjayanthimala and the leading trio mentioned above straddled an entire generation. Male actors apeared to have even longer career spans. The male triad of the fifties was formed by Dilip Kumar, Raj Kapoor (of the well-known Kapoor dynasty of stars) and Dev Anand, all of whom arrived on the scene in the forties and still command vast audiences whether as producers, directors or actors.

Within five years of Independence, the Indian film industry had achieved its heyday, not only as a consequence of colossal international markets but also of a unique coming together of a mass audience enthusiastic about cinematic escape. Those associated with films received boundless adulation, immense sums of money were poured into the complex for modern industrial production of 'artistic' material and film-stars began to command fantastic sums of money. The more popular stars had the pick of roles, frequently becoming contracted to do three to five films simultaneously. Throughout the fifties and sixties, Bombay was by numerical criteria the largest film center of the world. Accordingly, star lifestyle came to reflect the halcyon years of Hollywood half a generation earlier. The stars lived in the highly desirable Bandra and Juhu Beach areas of Bombay and had to disguise themselves in scarves and heavy dark-glasses before venturing out for fear of being

ated with particular roles and these celluloid persona began to overlap with reality. No doubt memories of Nargis in *Mother India* (1957) contributed substantially to her win in the Lok Sabha elections in the early seventies. On her death, her husband, Sunil Dutt, also a star of considerable standing, took over her seat, while Dilip Kumar was elected Mayor of Bombay. The Rajiv Gandhi election of 1984 witnessed a number of stars winning Parliamentary seats, among them Vyjayanthimala, a darling of the fifties and sixties film-going public with many awards to her credit, and Amitabh Bachhan, known to audiences in his film alter-ego of a rebellious, angry young man fighting the injustices of society. In Andhra Pradesh Ramarao and in Tamil Nadu M. G. Ramachandran (MGR) have held sway for a number of decades and are afforded virtually the status of prophets.

Yet the earliest predecessors of these much fêted figures began humbly. In the twenties the theater world was regarded as socially dubious and fear of provoking the prejudice experienced by its actresses deterred women from working in films. Women of reasonable background apart, Phalke found that even prostitutes refused offers of starring roles. He solved the problem by finding a male star

mobbed. Fan mail, posters and fashion magazines all bore testimony to their far-reaching charisma. Fans in rural areas sometimes walked as many as 12 miles to make sure they saw a Rajesh Khanna or Sharmila Tagore movie. This continued until the late seventies when the advent of video in more affluent homes, coinciding with the increased government-financed installation of television sets had a near-disastrous effect on the large screen. Audiences became more selective about the cinema faced with a substantial diet of old and recent cinema classics, and the industry faced sudden decline. As stringent budgetary cuts were introduced the megastar became a thing of the past. The multi-starrer, featuring a number of starlets with perhaps a name or two from the seventies, became more economic but not conducive to creating the same degree of charismatic magnetism as in the old days.

Development of genres

By the late forties, the Indian cinema had started to establish its own distinctive character. The genre called the 'social' no longer concentrated overtly on contemporary social issues but rather focused on romance, although script and song-writers continued to introduce social and political comment into their material. A sub-text to the majority of these films reinforced family values with heavy emphasis on the concept of duty thrusting women into focal roles to bear the onus of propagating these traditions.

Socio-political issues were often referred to through emblematic characters as for example in Guru Dutt's masterly production *Pyasa* (1957) where the love-hate conflict of the young intellectual with his language and culture in the wake of British colonialism is skilfully portrayed through the poet Vijay and his relationships with a glamorous but unattainable co-student representing materialistic Western values and the contemptuously regarded prostitute Gulab, representing the motherland, who is the sole cause of his ultimate success and symbolic resurrection. The fifties saw these contemporary themes overtaking all other genres in popularity whether Muslim spectaculars of the *Mughal-e Azam* (1960) type or the contemporary films such as *Chaudhvin ka Chand* (1961) and *Mere Mahbub* (1964), proved to have their own particular appeal.

Muslim contribution

Predictably, Muslim films dealt with Indian Muslims and were the forum for the portrayal of many social institutions of the exotic upper and lower classes of this community. Emphasis was always laid on their prayer and costume, their quaint linguistic customs and mannerisms, their extraordinary courteousness and perhaps most importantly their *mushairas* (poetry gatherings) and their tendency to reel off couplets at any given moment.

Much of the language of the pre-sixties socials particularly in moments of intense drama, was a high-flown poetic version of that which is today called Urdu, as distinct from Hindustani or Hindi. This must in part have been due to the many literary figures from among the Muslim communities involved in script writing such as K. Abbas, Shakil Badayuni and Saadat Hasan Manto. Interestingly enough the Pakistani film, officially in Urdu, uses an up-to-date colloquial language and rarely produces films of such a historical or poetic nature.

In the main the Pakistan film industry consisted of veterans from India who had chosen to migrate to Pakistan during Partition. The industry never quite measured up to its Indian progenitor since the problem of drawing stars from Muslim families did not allow filmmakers much choice in casting. Audiences too, were far more limited and the import of English language films far more widespread. Budgets were therefore notably smaller and facilities inadequate. The acting scene was for many years dominated by brothers Santosh and Darpan and their wives Sabeeha and Nayyar Sultan. Shamimara, now turned director-producer, and Zeba both enjoyed short bursts of fame and success but the most enduring name in the last twenty-five years has been Bangladesh-born Shabnam who came to prominence in the early sixties.

Social and political impact on genre

In 1966, following the Indo-Pakistan war of September 1965, Manoj Kumar, a popular but unremarkable screen idol proved his talents as producer, director and script writer, inventing the patriotic '*Jai Javan, Jai Kisan*' genre. Taking up Prime Minister Shastri's slogan in praise of the soldier and the farmer, he guaranteed the success of his film *Upkar* (1967) by exhibiting it within eighteen months of the conflict. The film follows the life of a patriotic farmer who takes up arms against his country's enemies and is gratified to see that his village demonstrates powerful solidarity faced with national crisis. This appealed powerfully to emotions freshly exposed to the massive, highly organized dose of war propaganda and the theme was repeated successfully on many occasions.

Ever in search of innovations the industry went through several fashion phases dictated by the Western world, the sixties saw bewigged stars in skimpy costumes, singing jazz-like songs and emulating cabaret acts. In the seventies, following an experimental phase featuring serious themes starring serious young graduate actors, came the Bombay 'masalas' – films with a smattering of everything, including romance, crime, comedy sub-plots, action, melodrama and music. In terms of plot and storyline, these films were less predictable, featuring the anti-hero typified most effectively by Amitabh Bachhan. This was a departure from the established formula of a clearly structured piece centered on a romantic couple, upright and socially responsible, linked to a comedy sub-plot, often associated with an archetypal villain of the piece. The arrival of the 'masala' coincided effectively with the coming of the new style of realistic acting as Filmalaya and other acting school graduates arrived on the scene, such as Sanjeev Kumar, Jaya Bhaduri and Amitabh Bachhan. However, what was to be an admirable achievement in the case of such consummate popular film-makers as Manmohan Desai, Bimal Roy and G. P. Sippy, was to degenerate into a series of violent films, lacking a strong plot or emotional theme and resulting in repeated box-office disasters in an industry made increasingly infirm the popularization of video and the widespread accessibility of television. In despair the film-makers yet again looked West for inspiration and turned their hand to extended action films, combining heavy familial mother-son devotion with Indiana Jones and Rambo-style adventure and revenge. This trend was strongly discernible in Pakistani films which further developed the vigilante-type hero in the eighties.

In the early to mid-eighties the effect of women's lobbies such as 'women against violence' has contributed to the emergence of the women's revenge genre, featuring gang-rape and subsequent revenge. Sadly, however, sexploitation movies such as *Bad Nasib* (1986) and *Adam Khor* (1986) have also resulted. While purporting to make social comment or to promote patriotic values, these are often an excuse to provide a vehicle for the portrayal of women, sometimes schoolgirls, being subjected to humiliation in sequences leading up to violent rape. A new venture is the made-for-video film displaying a style which is recognizable as a combination of the television play technique and the commercial film, with a slower pace, less lavish settings, a studio atmosphere and a sub-art feel. These also tend to concentrate on problems specific to women.

1985 saw the overt presentation of the anti-British Raj theme in the form of *Mard* which was to be Amitabh Bachhan's come-back to the screen and 1986–87 is tending towards portrayal of terrorism, covertly Sikh and Pakistani, against India. A parallel development in Pakistan is the patriotic film set in pre-Independence India but depicted as a Muslim holy war, with strong anti-Hindu and pro-Sikh allusions.

International picture

Co-operative film-making efforts with the Western world began in India as early as 1926 with Franz Osten and Himansu Roy's *Light of Asia*, starring Devika Rania, and other collaborations followed. The first Indian Film Festival in 1952 considerably raised the Indian profile in film-making circles all over the world including Europe, Russia and the USA. Indian film-makers were regularly invited to exhibit their films in the most prestigious international gatherings and began to make a reputation for themselves. One of the most impressive talents in the field for many years, was Satyajit Ray who began his career with *Pather Panchali* (1955). Bengal had long boasted a rich literary and theatrical tradition and now a number of highly imaginative film-makers emerged from the region among

A scene from *Pather Panchali* (1955), the first film of Satyajit Ray, the Bengali film director who has since won much international acclaim. The film, which is of the masterpiece of the same name by the Bengali novelist, Bibhutibhushan Banerji, portrays the life of a Brahmin household seen through the eyes of the two young children of the family.

them Ritwik Ghatak who described *Meghe Dhaka Tara* (1960) as his most 'ambitious' film. The 'art' movement in Indian cinema began to take a steady hold with film-makers from other parts of the country making worthy contributions. Then, in the early sixties, the USA-based duo Ismail Merchant and James Ivory began to produce films in India and won critical acclaim on an international scale.

By this time, the Indian art film, with Satyajit Ray at the vanguard, was receiving greater attention than ever before. New talents became established, among them Shyam Benegal (*Ankur*, 1974) and Kumar Shahani (*Tarang*, 1985). Other impressive achievements in various official Indian languages are seen at regular intervals. Sadly, owing to an unstable political situation, Pakistan has not quite fulfilled the promise shown by its film-maker Saeed Dehlavi in *Blood of Hussain* (1982).

The Sri Lankan, Nepalese and Bangladeshi cinemas, far smaller than those of India or Pakistan, are generally dominated by one or two big stars and producers and do not enjoy the same degree of international popularity as their neighbors although often similar in content to their commercial mainstream. However, a recent initiative from Pakistan has produced a number of collaborations with Sri Lanka, Nepal, Bangladesh. Primarily of the vigilante action type, these productions are set in exotic locations and feature a combination of stars from each country involved.

There has in recent years been a sharp escalation in video exports, which appear, in spite of frequent episodes of piracy, to gross substantial sums for distributors. These films, primarily Panjabi, Urdu (Pakistani), and Hindi, are the staple viewing for large numbers of Asian immigrants all over the world. The growing fascination with pop culture in the 1980s has resulted in several Indian commercial films being shown on British television including a season of highly acclaimed films noir featuring some of the great talents of the genre. In spite of the number of these popular productions, however, most films which cross international barriers to be viewed by culturally diverse audiences and connoisseurs are art films. It is through these that the worldwide reputation of the Indian cinema continues to be built.

SH

The press

From the beginning, the newspaper press of South Asia has been in conflict with government. The very first Governor-General, Warren Hastings, imprisoned the first editor, James Augustus Hicky, and shut down the first newspaper, Hicky's *Bengal Gazette*, in 1780, thus setting an example followed by many of his successor-politicians. The East India Company ran its settlements with a stern hand in the eighteenth century; local governors censored, revoked licenses, seized presses, and even deported editors. The early newspapers in India could either be timid and profitable or bold and short-lived. Those early papers were written for local British residents only. They relayed official announcements, commercial and shipping news, local trivia and gossip, and, most important, news from 'home' via the most recent arrivals.

The first Indian-owned and Indian-language paper (also called *Bengal Gazette*) appeared in 1818. Some of the early 'vernaculars' were socio-religious, such as Rammohan Roy's *Sambad Kaumudi* (1821). Others were primarily commercial, such as the *Bombay Samachar* (1822), which presented business news to Gujarati merchants and, as South Asia's oldest living newspaper, does so still. These small and amateurish Indian journals were often the spare-time product of some clerk, schoolteacher, or job printer. Like their English counterparts, they addressed small and particular audiences.

Broader and sturdier newspapers developed around the mid-nineteenth century, assisted by the repeal of censorship laws (1835), the Crown's takeover of British India (1858), the linking of India's cities by telegraph (1850s, followed soon by Reuters' agency), and the opening of a reliable Indo-European cable (1870). By this time a third category of newspaper had grown, which was run by Indians and written in English for the graduates of the new European-type schools and universities. Usually these papers sharply criticized the imperial order of things and preached Indian nationalism and freedom. Political leaders often published their own mouthpiece journals: the *Bengalee* of Surendranath Banerjea, the *Kesari* of B. G. Tilak, and the *Comrade* of Mohamed Ali. Occasionally the Government would be irritated enough to pass a restrictive press law or arrest a few editors, but they soon let up; the British were preaching the virtues of liberty and democracy, and practicing autocracy made them uneasy. By the time of Mahatma Gandhi a large network of papers could be relied on to support and publicize the Gandhian program and the nationalist movement, with the *Bombay Chronicle* perhaps the most prominent. But other papers opposed Congress-type nationalism, such as *Dawn*, the Muslim League paper in New Delhi, and *Justice*, the voice of the anti-Brahmin movement in Madras.

Independence changed many things for the press. What remained of the British papers in India, like the *Statesman* and the *Times of India*, were gradually 'Indianized'. Papers which had been propelled by patriotic zeal found it difficult to switch to a commercial basis, and some (such as the *Bombay Chronicle*) succumbed to rising costs and tougher competition. South Asian officials were disappointed to find their ex-comrades of the press treating them as antagonistically as if they were British. Reporters were disappointed to find their ex-comrades in government treating the press as contemptuously as had the British.

The newly-independent nations generally accepted the principle of a free press, but with qualifications against irresponsible or incendiary journalism. Thus, Article 19 (1) of the Indian constitution, which guarantees freedom of speech and press, is vitiated by 19 (2), which allows 'reasonable' restrictions 'in the interests of the security of the State, friendly relations with foreign states, public order, decency, morality, or in relation to contempt of court, defamation, or incitement to an offence'. Most other nations enacted similar provisos. In practice, this has usually meant that a free press was welcome until it became too critical of the regime.

But governments need not censor papers or arrest editors in order to work their will on the press. Official and public sector advertising is a vital source of revenue to most papers, and to some even the largest source. Newsprint, both foreign and domestic, is usually distributed by government quota. Large staffs of public information officials see that editors have plenty of official-version materials available. Moreover, many newspapers are units of farflung commercial or industrial empires whose interests often require government permits and cooperation. Therefore, it takes a brave (and secure) editor and proprietor to risk official wrath.

These and other press problems were scrutinized by India's first Press Commission, whose incisive 1954 report led to the appointment of a Press Council and a Registrar of Newspapers. Pakistan and Sri Lanka have had their own Press Commissions. The most dramatic clash of press and government in South Asia came when Prime Minister Indira Gandhi issued her 'emergency' decree, June 26, 1975. Editors were among those arrested and held in 'preventive detention' for nineteen months. A new censorship law was rushed through the Lok Sabha, and censors stationed in news rooms to read and rule on articles.

The group or 'chain' of newspapers, published in different languages or different cities, has become the large newspapers' answer to the fragmented audience: they take the paper to the people by printing it in their city, in their language. By 1980 three groups had attained national prominence in India, those of the *Times of India*, the *Statesman*, and the *Indian Express*. The *Times of India*, which traces its roots back to 1838, had grown into a group of eleven dailies, some in Hindi and Marathi, published in New Delhi and Ahmadabad as well as Bombay. The *Statesman*, begun in Calcutta by Robert Knight in 1875, started a Delhi edition in 1930. The *Indian Express*, begun as a small daily in Madras in 1932, was acquired by a remarkable industrialist, Ramnath Goenka, who in the next half-century built it into a nationwide chain of ten connected daily editions, along with popular Tamil and Marathi journals.

The English-language journals have retained their national prominence, but the greatest growth of the press since independence has been in Hindi and the regional languages. A mass press in the regionals was stimulated by the formation of linguistic states in India in the 1950s and 1960s.

Newspapers in what is now Pakistan go back to 1845 in English (the *Kurrachee Advertiser*) and 1850 in Urdu (Lahore's *Koh-e Nur*), but few colonial-era journals lasted long into the Islamic Republic. Instead, the two leading papers were those which moved from Delhi to Karachi at the time of Independence: *Dawn*, in English, and *Jang* in Urdu. Most of the new papers were connected with various political factions, which often meant trouble with authorities. For instance, President Ayub Khan's government passed restrictive press laws and seized eleven dailies, which it operated through the National Press Trust. In 1979 General Zia ul Haq imposed censorship and shut down *Musawat*, a paper formerly controlled by deposed President Z. A. Bhutto.

East Pakistan had no daily papers until independence when *Azad*, a substantial Muslim League journal, moved from Calcutta to Dhaka. The English-language *Bangladesh Observer* was founded in 1949. *Ittefaq* (b. 1955) was a supporter of the Awami League and became the largest newspaper in independent Bangladesh. The press supported the new nation, but some grew critical of the performance of President Mujib ur Rahman; he responded by instituting censorship in 1974 and shutting down twenty dailies in 1975, shortly before his assassination.

The first newspaper in Sri Lanka, apart from a government gazette, was the *Colombo Journal* of 1832, replaced two years later by what became the *Ceylon Observer*. This journal became a frequent and vigorous critic of the government under a series of able British editors during the next century. In 1923 it was bought by D. R. Wijewardene, a Cambridge-educated lawyer who added it to his *Ceylon Daily News* (founded 1918). Wijewardene's group, called 'Lake House', later added Sinhala and Tamil papers, and at the time

Table 67(a). Daily newspapers

	Number of daily newspapers		Estimated circulation (1,000s)		Number per 1,000 inhabitants	
	1965	1982	1965	1982	1965	1982
Bangladesh	30[a]	30	365[a]	542	7[a]	6
India	522	1,087[b]	6,323	13,033[b]	13	20[b]
Maldives	1[a]	2	n.a.	1	n.a.	6
Nepal	16	29	28	110	3	7
Pakistan	95	106	1,839	1,095[bc]	35	14[bc]
Sri Lanka	13	24	440	1,681	39	111

[a]figures for 1975
[b]figures for 1979
[c]decrease partly due to loss of East Pakistani newspapers after the creation of Bangladesh in 1971.
Source: United Nations *Statistical Yearbook* 1981 (New York, 1983). United Nations *Statistical Yearbook* 1983/84 (New York, 1986).

Table 67(b). Distribution of all kinds of newspapers in India by language

	1959		1981	
	Number of newspapers	Circulation in thousands	Number of newspapers	Circulation in thousands[a]
Assamese	10	53	71	249
Bengali	326	923	1,463	3,299
English	999	3,997	3,583	11,039
Gujarati	326	1,159	696	2,540
Hindi	875	3,553	5,329	13,984
Kannada	126	470	611	1,888
Kashmiri	—	—	1	n.a.
Malayalam	131	80	766	4,127
Marathi	272	1,054	1,098	2,883
Oriya	38	99	255	415
Panjabi	76	183	407	1,028
Sanskrit	10	7	30	11
Sindhi	—	—	62	38
Tamil	231	2,125	804	4,502
Telugu	170	663	546	1,556
Urdu	398	1,047	1,299	2,254
Bilingual	435	766	1,506	1,020
Multilingual	238	238	350	177
Others	80	132	267	92
Total	4,738 [sic]	17,270 [sic]	19,144	51,102

[a]Only 37 percent of newspapers furnished circulation figures for 1981, in the main the larger newspapers.
Source: Minister of Information and Broadcasting, Government of India, *Annual Report of the Registrar of Newspapers for India 1960* p. 76 (New Delhi, 1962) and *Press in India 1982* pp. 16, 32 (New Delhi, 1982).

Table 67(c). Distribution of all kinds of newspaper in Pakistan by language

	1959 Number of newspapers	1981 Number of newspapers
Arabic	1	2
Baluchi	1	3
Brohi	—	1
English	223	320
Gujarati	12	8
Persian	3	1
Panjabi	2	3
Pushto	15	3
Saraiki	—	1
Sindhi	69	74
Turkish	1	—
Urdu	784	1,124
Total	1,282 [*sic*]	1,540

Source: Federal Bureau of Statistics, Government of Pakistan, *Statistical Pocket Book of Pakistan 1962* p. 164 (Karachi, n.d.) and *Statistical Pocket Book of Pakistan 1982* p. 196 (Karachi, n.d.).

of independence dominated the newspaper field. Only the group based on the *Times of Ceylon* (b. 1846 as the *Ceylon Times*) could compete.

In 1963, Prime Minister Sirimavo Bandaranaike, stung by press opposition, appointed a Press Commission, which dutifully warned of the dangers of press domination by capitalists and recommended nationalizing the 'Lake House' group. Mrs Bandaranaike pushed this through in 1973. The *Times* group, facing bankruptcy, was nationalized in 1979. As the older groups sagged, a new one entered the field, headed by M. D. Gunasena. His Sinhala paper, *Dawasa*, was successfully launched in 1961, and in 1964 he founded a new English daily, the *Sun*.

Nepal came late to the press, but newspapers grew rapidly after 1960. The government passed restrictive press laws in 1965 and 1973, enabling officials to ban all criticism of government and the royal family. In Bhutan the only newspapers are weekly government bulletins in English, Nepali, and Dzongkha. The Maldive Islands, independent since 1965, have three daily newspapers, one in English, one in Divehi (or Maldivi) and one bilingual.

Besides the dailies a wide variety of other periodicals issue from the presses of South Asia: small weekly newspapers which acquaint remote towns and villages with the outside world, substantial periodicals of international reputation like the *Economic and Political Weekly* and *India Today* and an immense variety of specialized publications, ranging from *Blitz*, the hard-hitting Leftist news magazine, to the many on films and film stars, including the elegant *Illustrated Weekly of India* and *Akhbar-e Jahan*, a women's magazine with the largest circulation in Pakistan.

EH

Further reading

India, *Report of the Press Commission* (New Delhi, 1954)
India, *The Press in India* (regular report of the Registrar of Newspapers)
M. N. Krishna, *Indian Journalism* (Mysore, 1967)
G. T. Kurian, Ed., *World Press Encyclopedia* (New York, 1985)

Publishing

Origins

The printed word was introduced to South Asia by the Portuguese. St Francis Xavier's *Doctrina Christam* (*c.* 1557), an exposition of the Apostles's creed, inaugurated a slow trickle of missionary literature in Roman letters and, fairly quickly, indigenous scripts. Several 'Doctrinas' in Tamil (Cochin and Quilon, 1578–79) are testimony of missionary efforts, and the Word gradually became more readily available over the following century, largely in southern India. A Danish missionary, Bartholomew Ziegenbalg, established the country's first printing press in Tranquebar in 1712, where he published Martin Luther's *Catechism* in Tamil translation.

Printing crept east to Madras and north along the Coromandel coast in the wake of European trading companies. The requirements of trade necessitated a shift towards secular and reference works, such as grammars and dictionaries, particularly in the nineteenth century with the transition from trade to empire. The earliest printing press in Bengal, at Hughly, published the first book to appear in Bengali characters, *A Grammar of the Bengali Language* (1778) by a civil servant of the East India Company, N. B. Halhed. His contemporary, Warren Hastings, decided to procure translations of Hindi, Persian and Sanskrit literature, a task which was initiated by Charles Wilkins' *Bhagawed Geeta* (1785) and furthered more illustriously by Sir William Jones and the Asiatic Society. The establishment of a Mission Press at Serampore near Calcutta by

Table 68. Books published in South Asia in 1980

	Total	National language	English	Other
Bangladesh	542	420 (379 Bengali, 41 Bengali/English)	122	—
India	11,562	1,276 (Hindi)	5,145	5,141
Nepal	43	43 (Nepali)	—	—
Pakistan	1,279	740 (Urdu)	297	242
Sri Lanka	2,352	1,519 (1,032 Sinhala, 487 Tamil)	584	249

Source: *Statistical Yearbook of the United Nations*, 1982.

The title page of the translation into Tamil of St Francis Xavier's *Doctrina Christam*. Published in 1578 it is the earliest example of printing in an Indian script.

William Carey in the first years of the nineteenth century coincided almost exactly with the foundation of Fort William College where Company officials were taught the languages and customs of India. Within the next thirty years an astonishing 212,000 items in forty different languages issued from this press, including Wilkins' *A Grammar of the Sanskrita Language* (1808) in the Devanagari script as well as textbooks for use by students of the College.

With the growth of mission schools and educational institutions in the decades that followed, the demand for texts increased apace. The earliest commercial publishing ventures seem to have begun around 1815 to meet this need, with some of the texts, such as translations of the *Ramayana* and the *Mahabharata*, spilling over into a market of general readers. Charles Metcalf's repeal in 1835 of an oppressive press ordinance (1823) promoted publishing in the vernacular, and neither a short-lived Press and Registration of Books Act following the Uprising of 1857 nor Lytton's brief attempt to suppress seditious literature with the Vernacular Press Act of 1878 (later repealed by Ripon in 1881) proved serious impediments to the irresistibility of a newly commercialized technology.

Publishing today

The early need for educational texts, along with the promotion of English after 1835, symbolizes the dominant trends in South Asian publishing today. The vast majority of Indian books, for instance, are produced for school and university students, with the largest number of titles in any one language appearing in English.

India's vast population, diversity of languages and increasing literacy ensure a high level of publishing activity, currently reckoned at being the world's eighth highest. Given the present literacy percentage of thirty-five, the average number of titles published each year per million literate people is seventy-five, higher than the Asian average; the average number of English titles per million is as high as 360, higher than the world average. In spite of estimates that there are over 10,000 private Indian publishers, fewer than thirty have adequate capital, marketing facilities and editorial expertise to function as proper publishers. Less than a dozen of these currently achieve a turnover of Rs. 20,000,000. Even these, more often than not, are run with both eyes on the balance sheet and a Nelsonian disregard for product quality, resulting in overnight closures when profits seem insufficient. The overall situation is made worse by the inefficiency of central and state governments which monopolize the school textbook market, comprising about seventy percent of India's entire book market. Since roughly eighty percent of the country's schools are government funded, these are compelled to buy substandard albeit cheap material published by dozens of government publishing agencies scattered through the land. Even with academic and general titles, the private publisher is largely dependent for sales on the sporadic release of government funds to central, state and university libraries. When, in the late 1970s and early 1980s, library funds were withheld, publishers were forced to reduce print-runs.

Despite such market difficulties and the disproportionate rise in the cost of paper in relation to those of typesetting and printing, a reasonable amount of good quality scholarly work has appeared since Independence, increasingly so over the past decade and largely under indigenous imprints (the Foreign Exchange Regulation Act of 1973 limiting foreign holdings). The vast reading public, which looks for literature in local languages, in particular in Bengal, Kerala and Maharashtra, has considerably greater access to reasonably priced titles that are sometimes marketed by low-profit co-operatives. The bulk of the country's general and scholarly work, however, continues to appear and proliferate in English. The 1960s, when American aid subsidized Indian reprints of largely unwanted American books, and the late 1970s, which saw a paucity of funds and shrinkages, now seem distant enough for a little optimism.

The features of contemporary publishing outlined for India are not significantly different, if scaled down in proportion to population, for Pakistan, Bangladesh and Sri Lanka. The differences between India and these countries in terms of educational policy, population/literacy rates, élite culture and purchasing power are not significant enough to disturb similarities in the volume and pattern of publishing. Their bookmarkets are, once again, almost exclusively for schools, universities and prescribed texts, with English titles taking seventy to eighty percent of the market share. The one visible difference in publishing evolution has been that whereas India's size has produced several hundred libraries – all of which have come to sustain a few indigenous academic and general book publishers – this has not occurred in the smaller countries of the subcontinent where scholars tend either to be published in the West or, increasingly, in India. Bookshops and book importers, rather than viable indigenous publishers, characterize the 'publishing arenas' in Pakistan, Bangladesh and Sri Lanka.

RA

Further reading

B. S. Kesavan, *History of Printing and Publishing in India* Vol. I (Vol. II, forthcoming) (New Delhi, 1986)

D. N. Malhotra and N. Kumar, Eds, *Publishing in India Since Independence: Essays in Honour of O. P. Ghai* (New Delhi, 1982)

Radio and television

Broadasting made a slow and uncertain start in South Asia. It was not until 1926 that after much deliberation the Government of British India gave the Indian Broadcasting Company a licence to establish radio stations and to broadcast. Government placed certain restrictions on the broadcasts and reserved the right to insist that official information was included in the transmissions. The information could be anything from weather reports to propaganda. The Company, however, was an independent commercial organization. Its revenue came from radio licenses. Partly because radio did not catch on very fast and partly because many set owners did not buy licenses the Indian Broadcasting Company survived for less than four years. It went into voluntary liquidation in 1930.

In May 1932, the Government of India committed itself to operating a broadcasting service and formed the Indian State Broadcasting Service. In 1936 it was redesignated All India Radio. At Partition the stations which were in Pakistan were handed over to the Government of that Country. Today radio and television throughout South Asia have three common features. All broadcasting organizations are controlled by their governments. A shortage of receivers has severely limited their penetration of rural areas. Television services all have an urban bias in spite of government protestations to the contrary. Government control has led to accusations that programs are dull and unimaginative and that news and current affairs output lacks credibility.

In India, there have been two Broadcasting Commissions to look into these charges. The first, the Chanda Commission, was set up by Mrs Indira Gandhi when she was Information and Broadcasting Minister in 1964. In its report the Commission said: 'It is not possible in the Indian context for a creative medium like broadcasting to flourish under a regiment [*sic*] of departmental rules and regulations'. The Commission recommended that Radio and Television should be run by two autonomous public corporations. In 1970, by which time Mrs Gandhi was Prime Minister, the government told Parliament that it did not intend to relax its control over broadcasting. The second Commission on Broadcasting was set up by the Janata government in 1977. Known as the Verghese Commission it too criticized the cumbersome administration of the two broadcasting organizations which as departments of the government of India have to cope with all the rigors of government administrative and accounting procedures. The Verghese Commission proposed the founding of an autonomous National Broadcasting Trust.

The Janata Information and Broadcasting Minister, Mr Lal Krishan Advani, introduced a bill to set up the trust. Inevitably the bureaucracy fought to retain its control of the broadcasting media.

It was not unsuccessful. The bill, for instance, did not accept the Commission's suggestion that the new trust should have independent auditors, the Comptroller and Auditor General of India being given that responsibility. This defeated in part the purpose of the new proposals which was to develop a flexible administrative system. However, the Janata Government fell before the bill was passed; All India Radio and the television service, Doordarshan, remained departments of the government of India. Subsequently, the hold of bureaucracy has tightened with the government adopting the practice of appointing members of the Indian Administrative Service, not professional broadcasters, as Director Generals of both All India Radio and Doordarshan. In Pakistan, corporations were set up to run radio and television but the Secretary of the Information and Broadcasting Ministry is Chairman of both and they are totally controlled by the government.

Lack of faith in the news and current affairs output of the government-controlled media appears to be the main reason for the widespread habit of listening to foreign radio stations, in particular those of neighboring states.

In Bangladesh All India Radio is the most widely listened to foreign station, in much of India that title goes to the Sri Lanka Broadcasting Corporation and in some parts of India to Radio Pakistan. The BBC is the most widely listened to non-South Asian station throughout the region. In India, for instance, BBC research estimates that there are thirty-five million listeners to the Hindi service alone. Indians also listen to the BBC in Urdu, Bengali, Tamil, Nepali and English. It is a clear indication of the lack of credibility of the government-controlled media that the number of listeners to the BBC increases at times of crisis. Sixteen percent of the listeners to the BBC Urdu service started tuning in during the 1965 Indo-Pakistan war. Many reports in the foreign press spoke of the very high numbers of listeners to the BBC during the agitation against the Bhutto government in Pakistan in 1977 and again during the trial of the former Prime Minister. A BBC survey in northern India found that twenty-two percent of the audience of the Hindi service had started listening during Mrs Gandhi's Emergency (1975–77), and that twenty-six percent started during the unstable Janata Government (1977–79). Most of the available evidence also points to a remarkable increase in the numbers of listeners to the BBC Bengali service during the civil war in the then East Pakistan.

For many years government control also led to drab programing, but there have been significant changes in this in recent years. In particular the decision to transmit commercially sponsored programs mainly made by independent producers on Doordarshan has led to a series of popular and imaginative soap operas. These new programs have, according to Doordarshan's audience research department, achieved something which at one stage was unthinkable, a gradual decline in the popularity of the Hindi films shown on

television. In Pakistan, President Zia ul Haq's Islamization program has inevitably affected broadcasting. Eleven percent of Radio Pakistan's programs are classified as religious, and much of the educational broadcasting is religious too.

In Bangladesh there is a marked emphasis on nationalism and on Bengali culture in the television programs.

Spread of radio and television

In India, Pakistan, Bangladesh and Sri Lanka radio can be heard throughout almost the entire country. The spread of television is more limited. The installation of a large number of low power transmitters between 1982 and 1985 spread Doordarshan's signals to 70 percent of the population. In Pakistan, television signals reach 80 percent of the population but the difficulty and expense involved in reaching the more sparsely populated areas is illustrated by the fact that television can only be seen in 34 percent of the area of Pakistan.

This is in sharp contrast to the flat and geographically much smaller Bangladesh where 8 percent of the country is within range of television transmitters. Sri Lanka, a latecomer to television, has done nearly as well, transmitting its television programs to 84

A scene from *Buniyaad*, a soap opera produced for Indian television by Ramesh Sippy. In 104 episodes *Buniyaad* depicted the life of a Panjabi family through seven decades and at the same time the changes in Indian life and values. The series came to an end in 1987.

percent of the geographic area of the island. The more remote countries present a very different picture. In Bhutan, for instance, a study prepared for UNESCO by Namedia, the Media Foundation of the Non-aligned movement, found that the electronic media was 'of little relevance'. In Nepal, a much larger country in size and population, only 55 percent of the population can hear the government-controlled radio. This is of course in part a reflection of the difficulty of transmitting a signal in mountainous terrain. Television in Nepal is still in its infancy. The Maldives do have a radio station but they have no facilities for producing television programs.

The main constraint on listening and viewing in South Asia, however, is not transmission but receivers. In the sixties the transistor radio did widen the market for receivers by reducing their price and making them more durable. But the figures for India, which has its own radio industry, show that the much vaunted transistor revolution still has a long way to go. All India Radio estimates that there are only 45 million radio sets in a country with a population of about 750 million. There is, of course, a great deal of family listening in India. There are some community sets, and radio can often be heard in tea shops and other places where the public gathers. Nevertheless radio listening in India is still not nearly as widespread as it is in developed countries. The figures are rather worse for the other countries in the region.

Radio, television and development

None of the governments of South Asia have grappled with the problem of producing cheap, durable and widely available television and radio receivers. This has inevitably reduced the effectiveness of the large investments they have made in transmission and production facilities. Because the shortage of receivers is most marked in the rural areas the role of the electronic media in education and development has not been very significant so far.

As far back as 1975 India conducted an experiment in using

Table 69. Radio receivers and television sets in South Asia 1986–7

	Radio receivers	Number of population per receiver	Television sets	Number of population per set
Bangladesh	5,000,000	15	600,000	145
Bhutan	n.a.	—	n.a.	—
India	45,000,000	15	5,200,000	132
Maldives	n.a.	—	n.a.	—
Nepal	1,500,000	10	6,000	2,500
Pakistan	1,600,000	53	850,000	99
Sri Lanka	n.a.	—	n.a.	—

Source: All figures were supplied by the respective governments to Namedia Foundation Research and Publication Center, Delhi, 1986, except the figures for Radio Receivers in India which came from All India Radio Audience Research, 1987.

television transmitted by satellite for rural education and development known as SITE. Two thousand four hundred villages in six states were covered and programs were transmitted in the local language of each area. The experiment, although widely applauded at the time, has not spread very far. India now has its own satellite but there are still only seven Post SITE Centers, as they are called, and they only transmit 'Specific and Development Oriented Programmes' for just 35 to 40 minutes per day. India has a long way to go before it makes full use of its own INSAT satellite as a tool of development education.

The limited availability of television sets in the villages of South Asia has also affected the content of television programs. Because most of the sets are in the politically vocal cities and towns the programs have a very strong urban bias. This bias is strengthened by the demands of advertisers whose markets are in the cities and towns. Most of the products advertised are beyond the means of the majority of Indians, which has led to concern about the effects of television advertising. Many fear that it will lead to dangerous discontent among those who are outside the market for consumer goods. Nevertheless, all the main television organizations are becoming more rather than less dependent on advertising revenue.

Radio has been able to play a much more active role in rural development. Some of the stations of All India Radio have very effective agricultural programs. An official survey in Pakistan found that farmers get more than sixty percent of their information about agriculture from radio. Language places its own limitations on the effectiveness of both radio and television. This problem is particularly acute in India. All India Radio broadcasts in sixty different languages or dialects. While this is a considerable achievement, it obviously places severe constraints on transmission and production resources. This is dramatically illustrated by the small All India Radio station in Kohima (Nagaland) whic has to broadcast in twelve different dialects. Doordarshan's National Network Television Program, which monopolizes the peak viewing hours in the evening, only transmits programs in Hindi and English. Neither are understood by the majority of Indians. The transmissions in Hindi are resented in many non-Hindi speaking areas of the country. In the southern state of Tamil Nadu the government has refused to allow the Madras station to transmit the national news in Hindi. It transmits its own Tamil news bulletin.

The picture which emerges from a survey of television and radio in the subcontinent is of media whose full potential as tools of development is still far from realization. Their political potential has also not been realized. Governments cling tenaciously to control of the media because they want to use them for promoting their political message. Their lack of subtlety in putting over that message undermines the credibility of the messenger.

MT

Further reading
P. C. Chatterji, *Broadcasting in India* (New Delhi, 1987)
H. R. Luthra, *Indian Broadcasting* (Publishing Division, Ministry of Information and Broadcasting, Government of India, 1986)

Science and technology

Up to 1800

Indian science before the nineteenth century was characterized by the assumption that truth lay in the real world with all its diversity and complexity. It was the scientist's responsibility, whatever his discipline, to formulate generalizations, but, at the same time, always to be aware of this reality, conscious of the exceptional nature of each specific instance. This attitude permeated all traditional Indian science and made it an exercise quite different from scientific enterprise in the West.

Linguistics was the first Indian science to be systematized in a rigorous way. Like all other arts and sciences belonging to the Indian tradition, it had its beginnings in the Vedic period when the basic elements and categories of study were established. Sanskrit language and its grammar were first formalized in Panini's *Ashtadhyayi* as early as the fifth century BC. In its four thousand aphorisms (*sutras*), Panini captured Sanskrit as spoken at the time and also managed to explain the way in which it deviated from the Sanskrit of the Vedas. Patanjali (second century BC) produced the earliest existing commentary on Panini's work. In the *Mahabhashya*, he emphasized that valid utterances were not manufactured by the linguist as the potter produced pots. Rather they were established through repeated use. Therefore, it was the duty of the linguist to lay down general rules (*utsargasutras*) and exceptional rules (*apavadasutras*) to enable people to learn larger and larger collections of correct expressions. Following on from Patanjali, grammarians as late as the nineteenth century provided further refinements and simplifications of Panini. The Sanskrit grammar *Siddhanta Kaumudi* (c. 1600), for instance, became very popular on account of its simplicity. Grammars were written for other Indian languages which applied the Panini model, specifying the transfer rules from Sanskrit as well as the specific morpho-phonemic rules (*sandhi*) of the languages concerned. Grammars for Prakrit languages continued to be written in this way until the eighteenth century: similarly, Krishnadas' grammar for Persian, commissioned by the Mughal emperor Akbar in the sixteenth century, was modeled on the style of the Prakrit works.

Mathematics and astronomy were two more important sciences which belong to the Indian tradition. Indian mathematics traces its origins to the famous *Shulvasutras* of Vedic times. Supposedly written to help the accurate construction of various kinds of sacrificial altars, these sutras laid down the basic geometrical properties of plane figures such as the triangle, rectangle, rhombus and circle. Basic astronomical categories were established in the *Vedanga Jyotisha* texts, but rigorous systemization of Indian astronomy began with the work of Aryabhata (b. AD 476). His *Aryabhatiya* is a concise text of 121 verses containing separate sections on astronomical definitions; mathematical procedures in arithmetic, geometry, algebra and trigonometry; methods of determining the mean and the true positions of the planets at any given moment; and descriptions of the movement of the sun and the moon along with the calculation of their eclipses. After Aryabhata there followed a stream of famous astronomers with their equally famous texts. In turn, they too gave rise to a host of commentaries and refinements by later astronomers and became the cornerstones of flourishing schools all over the subcontinent.

The most striking feature of this long mathematical tradition was the efficiency with which complicated problems were handled and solved. Already by the time of the Shulvasutras, mathematicians knew the theorems of plane geometry. They had also developed a sopisticated theory of numbers which included the concepts of zero and negative numbers, and were able to devise simple algorithms by using place-value notations. In other words, they had acquired all the basic concepts and procedures taught in present-day secondary schools. By the eleventh century AD, Indian mathematicians could solve sophisticated algebraic problems such as second order Diophatine equations. By the fourteenth century, indefinite series for sine and cosine functions had been written down for trigonometry as had high level approximations and recognition of its irrational character. The reason for these great advances lay in the explicitly computational nature of Indian science. The objective was not to find absolute truths but methods of solving specific problems. To this end, Indian mathematicians created simple algorithms which gave approximate solutions to immediate problems but they also evolved theories of error and recursive procedures in order to keep these approximations under control. Indeed, this methodology has persisted into the twentieth century as demonstrated by the impressive mathematical discoveries achieved by Ramanujan using the traditional Indian approach.

Another major science which fell within the classical tradition was medicine. It too had its beginnings in the Vedas, especially in the *Atharvaveda* in which a large amount of early medicinal lore was collected. The systemization of Indian medicine took place between the fifth century BC and the fifth century AD in the form of the *Charaka Sanhita*, *Sushruta Sanhita* and *Ashtanga Sangraha*, the so-called *Brihat-trayi* texts which are still popular today. This was followed by a long period of intense activity during which attempts were made to refine the theory and practice of medicine and to bring more and more information into the stream of systematic medicine. Like other Indian sciences, the remarkable feature of Indian medicine was its pragmatic attitude towards scientific theorization. The medicinal texts, while providing a theoretical framework for approaching the problem of finding an appropriate cure for a particular patient, never tired of reminding the practitioner that he was not bound by theory and that he constantly had to observe all the specific features presented by each case. For the *Charaka Sanhita*, the most desirable intellectual accomplishment of a doctor was the possession of *Yukti*, the capacity of the trained intellect to identify the right course of action despite the complexity of phenomena with their multiple causes. The attitude of Ayurveda towards theoretical generalizations was clearly revealed in the insistence of the *Sushruta Sanhita* that the physician had to rely on what was established in tradition based on actual practice rather than acting exclusively on his own theoretical reasoning. This attitude toward theory gave the medical texts a refreshing openness and a surprising keenness of observation. Nothing that might have had an effect on health escaped the observation of physicians: they worried about the differing aspects of the seasons, soils and waters, and, in the therapeutic sections, they combined their theoretical understanding with folk practices which tradition had proved successful. The fact that Indian scientists, given their theoretical attitude, had to be open to the world ensured that folk-traditions and the sciences remained closely bound up with each other.

The same pragmatic attitude and operational simplicity influenced Indian technologies. Indians had mastered the techniques of crop rotation, irrigation, manuring and seed selection from very early times. Their technical ingenuity in solving evolving simple procedures sophisticated enough to take advantage of the full complexity of the local situation and yet fitting into a large and impressive system can best be seen in the tank irrigation of southern India and Sri Lanka. Much of southern India was dotted with these tanks. An eighteenth-century estimate indicated that there were more than 38,000 tanks in the region which later became the state of Mysore. Similarly in the nineteenth century, a British expert estimated the number of tanks in Madras Presidency to be over 50,000. From what is known of the political circumstances of the time, it is clear that these tanks were constructed and maintained by local effort. However, together they formed a closely integrated system so that the outflow from ones at higher levels supplied others lower down the chain.

The South Asian capacity for performing vast tasks through small, simple and dispersed techniques was illustrated by metallurgy. Small furnaces were used for smelting and refining iron and making steel. They were of rather rough external construction, but the internal proportions needed to be exact and so furnaces could be demolished and reconstructed in order to correct some minor error in the angle of blast. These sophisticated furnaces were produced by ironsmiths in a matter of a few hours without the help of complicated instruments and worked efficiently by the standards of those times: two units of charcoal were sufficient to produce one unit of crude iron. Processes of steel making were equally efficient. Steel was prepared by direct carbonization of iron in closed crucibles which contained green leaves, wood and charcoal. The process took only a few hours compared with the days taken by corresponding European techniques. Large amounts of iron and steel were produced, as much as half a ton of iron per furnace during a week's operation. On the basis of nineteenth century information, it has been estimated that the total number of furnaces throughout South Asia in the later part of the eighteenth century could have been well over 10,000, together producing some 200,000 tons of iron annually.

Textiles represented the great industrial enterprise of pre-British times. Up to 1800, South Asia was the world's leading producer and exporter of textiles. Yet this production was almost entirely based on techniques which operated at the level of the individual or the family. Spinning was an activity in which all parts of the subcontinent participated. Small simple spinning wheels or *charkhas* were so efficient that, until the early decades of the nineteenth century, a widowed mother could maintain her family in reasonable comfort by spinning for a few hours a day. Weaving was a relatively more specialized activity. However, the number of people belonging to weaver castes was second only in size to those from agricultural castes. Different regions of the subcontinent specialized in different kinds of techniques and fabrics.

Thus, the subcontinent had developed locally-specific techniques in agriculture, irrigation, metallurgy and textiles, as well as in other areas such as building and construction, sculpture, pottery, glass-making and even the production of luxuries like ice. This is perhaps why most historians agree that India of pre-British times was not only an agricultural but also an industrial society.

JKB

Further reading

K. V. Abhayankar, Ed. and Trans., *Patanjali's Vyakarana Mahabhasya: Ahnikas 1,2* (Poona, 1967)

C. Alvares, *Homo Faber* (Delhi, 1979)

K. Bhishagratna, Ed. and Trans., *Sushruta Sanhita*, 3 vols (Varanasi, 1967)

B. Datta and A. N. Singh, *A History of Hindu Mathematics* Parts 1 and 2 (Bombay, 1962); Part 3 revised by K. S. Shukla, *Ind. J. History of Science* 18, 39–108 (1983)

Dharampal, *Indian Science and Technology in the Eighteenth Century* (New Delhi, 1971)

K. V. Sarma and B. V. Subbarayaopa, *A Source Book of Indian Astronomy* (Bombay, 1985)

S. C. Vasi, Ed. and Trans., *The Ashtadhyayi of Panini*, 2 vols, (Allahabad 1891)

Jantar Mantar, the observatory built by Raja Sewai Jai Singh II at Jaipur between 1718 and 1734.

The nineteenth century

In the early nineteenth century the realization among Indians that their historic institutions for technology and learning were being enfeebled, was coupled to the perception that the European advantage lay in superior technique and powerful organization. These two ideas had enormous practical consequences for the development of science and technology in the two hundred following years. Tension arose between the creation of new institutions which would resemble and imitate centers of advanced research and learning elsewhere, and the desire to assert a unique cultural nationalism through science and technology, a tension between a worldly science and an indigenous science.

Foreigners in India simultaneously pressed for the scientific study and greater extraction of India's resources, as well as for the direct transfer of European science and technology. Despite the efforts of the scholarly Asiatic Society (founded in 1784), few knew about historic Indian scientific achievements. Following Macaulay, some preferred to disregard those capabilities as moribund. By 1850, the commercial demand for English-educated staff resulted in college students writing essays on Kepler's astronomy or the blessings of steam navigation. Public caution toward foreign science and technology was being forced to change.

Despite the fact that chemistry, astronomy, and Western medicine were taught and studied, and modern geology and botany were practiced, there was little active research in India until after the imposition of British rule in 1858. Research in Europe itself was only just becoming a coherent group-activity, with commitment to the publication of scientific papers. New scientific journals and intellectual magazines discussing science (*Calcutta Review, Modern Review*), the apparatus of the educated person of the nineteenth century, were being established in India with official blessing. The need of the Raj was for European experts who could be attracted to settle in India so comparatively good salaries and positions were considered necessary. Mainly working from government departments, universities, and medical schools, these people continued to contribute to European science.

But the government's greatest need was caused by a crisis in administrative expansion, the solution to which required more 'scientifically-minded' Indians who could study abroad, and then work for government or private companies. But these same individuals had to accept colonialist ceilings on their upward advancement, even where their technical abilities were judged equal or superior to foreigners. Ironically, technically well-trained Indians were thus attracted more to the well-paid administrative service than to research. Even the rapid creation of the bureaucratic and scientific Surveys for Geology, Zoology, Botany in the 1870s, scientific departments in universities at Calcutta, Bombay, and Madras, and new government departments of Forestry, Irrigation, and Agriculture before the end of the century did not accommodate the demand for employment among Indians trained for technical scientific work. The top positions went largely to Europeans. This demand spilled over into the private plantation agriculture (cotton, indigo, jute, tea), the military, and British-Indian industry where the employment scope was similarly limited. When unsatisfied, this demand was inevitably inserted into the nationalist political movement, and also served to accelerate the growth of private Indian industry. Indian scientific representation on important government policy committees, however, remained very limited. These patterns held true not only for the economic frontiers of India such as East Bengal, but also for separate territories such as Sri Lanka: all were subject to the same policies and thinking in London, and to the limitations of the colonial administration.

The first sign of a comprehensive Indian effort occurred in 1876 with the founding of the Indian Association for the Cultivation of Science (in whose Calcutta laboratories C. V. Raman did experiments which led to his Nobel Prize in Physics in 1930 for discovery of what came to be known as Raman-spectra). By the late nineteenth century the traditional study of Indian astronomy, mathematics, and chemistry were declining because they no longer enjoyed official patronage, and their intellectual ties with other cultures were also broken. Though their strength varied, the transmission of these indigenous sciences was relegated in the twentieth century to

ayurvedic medicine, to astrology, and to the technical base of trades and handicrafts such as metallurgy or textile dyeing – and of course retained their living roots in unofficial and simplified 'folk theories' of causation. So while it is correct to say that South Asian societies had long traditions and scientific institutions, during the nineteenth century science and technology experienced their most profound change – the consequences of which had to be worked out during the twentieth century.

The twentieth century

Developments in this century are neatly cut in half by the achievement of Independence, which had the effect of releasing a pent-up demand for a thoroughly organized science and technology. Until that time (1947) South Asian societies were dotted with small individually-run research institutions, rooted in the (often heroic) achievements of their founders. This was also usual for Europe and North America in the nineteenth century, and this pattern simply worked itself through South Asian colonial restrictions. Some organized new research institutions. Sir J. C. Bose (1858–1937), working on bio-chemistry, founded the Bose Institute, Sir C. V.

C. V. Raman, Nobel prizewinner and discoverer of the 'Raman effect', the quantum theory of the diffusion of light.

Raman (1888–1970) founded the Raman Institute (using his Nobel Prize funds) and astrophysicist M. N. Saha (1893–1956) founded the Saha Institute of Nuclear Physics. Others worked in university departments, and there were a famous few who worked in isolation and had no institutional influence, such as physicist S. N. Bose (1894–1973), after whom the Bose-Einstein Statistics and the Boson particles are named; and the self-taught mathematician S. Ramanujan (1887–1920), who eventually went to Cambridge University before his premature death. These individuals have been seen as symbolic reflections of the nationalist struggle, because their work was always conducted in the lonely heroic mode, against the indifference or mistrust of surrounding society and against inhibitions of the colonial system. Other segments of the public, ironically, perceived local science to be so fully identified with the colonial system that they viewed it as just another foreign force.

Three related processes had important consequences in South Asia before Independence. The first was the rise of an indigenous capitalist class of industrial entrepreneurs, relying on indigenous expertise; the second was South Asia's dramatic inclusion in war zones and industrial war efforts; and the third was the discovery of alternate paths of scientific and technological development in the Japanese, German, Soviet and American models. Each of these processes served to gradually decrease its dependence upon British authority in science and technology. Added to this change was the increasing employment of locally-trained South Asians in technical positions in railways, hospitals, telegraph and telephones, radio, cinema, and every type of manufacturing. This experience of relying on themselves had profound consequences.

From the Imperial point of view, there were charges that the technical establishment in India was too costly, and benefits were not being transferred to other colonies. If the empire was fused together through practical science and technology, it was argued, it could better withstand the attacks on it, including internal convulsions such as Indian nationalist political demands in the 1920s and 1930s. Also there were questions raised when major famines in 1900 and 1944 seemed to prove that practical research was not being done: could not all pure research be done at home and only applied research done in India? Such views were uninformed: there was a lot of research on practical subjects like forestry, fisheries, and agriculture beginning in 1900, especially in what was called economic botany or plant industry, and its results were indeed slowly transferred from India or Ceylon to the Caribbean, Africa and Australia in the form of new plant varieties. But such transfers simply did not fuse the empire together: they drew South Asia into an entirely more complicated set of international relationships thus preparing India and Ceylon for the end of British rule in 1948.

RSA

After Independence

The sudden emergence of Pakistan, and later of Bangladesh, removed little from India's scientific community and left these new nations little of value (except talent) because these areas had always been the hinterland of science and technology. Pakistan rushed to recreate some elements which had been lost to India, and in many ways to establish a structure which resembled the Indian one – including a government-controlled Council of Scientific and Industrial Research, and an Atomic Energy Commission with its Institute of Nuclear Science and Technology. All the old crop and commodity research and development (for instance, jute, tea, cotton, sugar and rice) were also maintained. Both in scientific output and technological development, India continued to dominate the region because of its headstart, and its sheer size. Two million people have post-graduate degrees in science and technology in India and about 75,000 were publishing in their fields in 1976 (half of them in foreign journals) compared to the USA with 142,000 scientists publishing, the UK with 25,000 and Japan with 14,000. India also became one of the top ten most industrialized nations in the world, thereby leaving its neighbors far behind. Science and technology are cultivated not only as economic policy, but also as cultural policy, to weld the disparate social elements of the South Asian nations together using science as a public philosophy. The

H. J. Babha, father of India's nuclear program.

growth of a mature scientific community coupled with nationalist (occasionally parochial) sentiment caused a re-examination of South Asia's entire technical and scientific history. Some serious research on old records was done for the first time. One popular conclusion was that a once superior tradition had been lost in colonialism and internal indifference.

But the old ambivalence toward 'modern' technology and science persisted. Its alien 'Western' origins offended some, and the tension between practical orientation (to serve the poor) and more theoretical work (in mathematics, for example, in which people had already excelled) was largely unresolved. Each of the South Asian countries was affected, and each had to find a way to link its scientists and technologists to distant centers of science while simultaneously attempting to solve practical problems.

In the post-Independence period there appeared a number of scientists and technologists who became organizers of entire government systems of research: these include, for example, S. S. Bhatnagar (1895–1955, chemist) who developed the vast Council of Scientific and Industrial Research, H. J. Bhabha (1909–66, physicist) who after founding the Tata Institute of Fundamental Research, developed the Department of Atomic Energy and secured enactment of all necessary legislation, and V. Sarabhai (1919–71, physicist) who, while Chairman of the Atomic Energy Commission, nurtured what eventually became India's Department of Space. They each had the necessary personal and political connections to initiate major funding commitments within the Five Year Plans by which India was regulated. New organizations were created as needed, such as the Department of Electronics. What is remarkable is not simply the size of each of these public systems, but also the growth in interaction between them, and interaction with medical research, agricultural research, defense production, electronics. Many new journals and specialist associations were created. Although criticized for being inadequate, the fact remains that this interaction was stimulated by the force of national policy, as well as

Abdus Salam of Pakistan, Nobel prizewinner in physics.

The Indian Space and Research Organization's APPLE satellite. Weighing 675 kg. it was India's first three axis body stabilized satellite to be placed in geostationery orbit for communications experiments. In 1975 India's first satellite was launched and in 1980 the first wholly Indian-made rocket and satellite were launched.

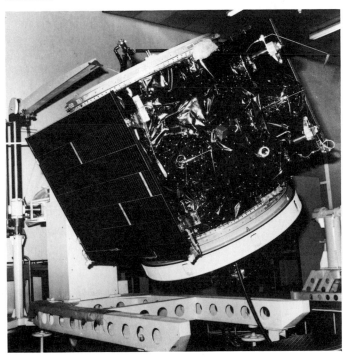

Nuclear power stations and nuclear research in South Asia.

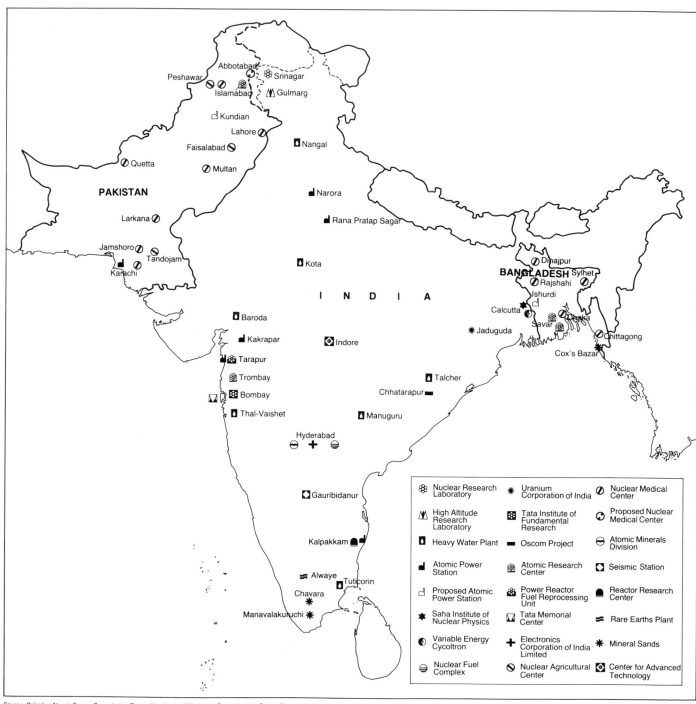

Legend

- 🕸 Nuclear Research Laboratory
- 人人 High Altitude Research Laboratory
- Heavy Water Plant
- Atomic Power Station
- Proposed Atomic Power Station
- Saha Institute of Nuclear Physics
- Variable Energy Cycoltron
- Nuclear Fuel Complex
- ✳ Uranium Corporation of India
- Tata Institute of Fundamental Research
- Oscom Project
- Atomic Research Center
- Power Reactor Fuel Reprocessing Unit
- Tata Memorial Center
- Electronics Corporation of India Limited
- Nuclear Agricultural Center
- Nuclear Medical Center
- Proposed Nuclear Medical Center
- Atomic Minerals Division
- Seismic Station
- Reactor Research Center
- Rare Earths Plant
- ✳ Mineral Sands
- Center for Advanced Technology

Source: Pakistan Atomic Energy Commission; Europa Yearbook 1987, *Atomic Energy in India Today*, Dept. of Atomic Energy, Government of India

Part of the vast petrochemical complex at Baroda (Gujarat) which has been designed and built by Indian engineers.

by new economic possibilities. The undeveloped condition for science and technology in 1947 was made infinitely richer and more complex forty years later in 1987. Similarly, the institutional and public-media support for science and technology has increased greatly. This richness and public support had led to some remarkable achievements.

Nevertheless, some scientists decided to work abroad, where they achieved their reputation: for example, in chemistry (C. Ponnamperuma of Sri Lanka), or in pharmacology (Y. Subba Row of India). Nobel Prizes were awarded to H. G. Khorana of India in medicine (1968) to Abdus Salam of Pakistan in physics (1979) and to S. Chandrasekhar in Physics (1983) for work they had done largely in Europe and North America.

In addition to the very considerable modern intellectual contribution from South Asia to international science, there have been technological developments which both extended scientific research capabilities and emboldened engineers and technologists. The underground explosion of a nuclear bomb in India in 1974 was a watershed event, in part because certain kinds of international cooperation were subsequently terminated, so that India had to become technologically more self-reliant. It also had a shock-effect among the general public, raising both their anxiety and their self-esteem. Before it, experiments using high altitude balloons and construction of a very large radio telescope in the hills of South India had enhanced understanding of space and the behavior of elementary particles. After the nuclear explosion, the first Indian satellite

503

was lifted into orbit in 1975 on a Soviet rocket, and an Indian rocket launched a satellite in 1980 from the rocket range near Madras. Commissioned in 1981, a variable energy cyclotron was built at Calcutta, while near Madras, the first Indian-designed and built CANDU-type nuclear reactor was commissioned in 1983 and a fast-breeder reactor planned immediately afterward. Meanwhile, computer design and building proceeded so far that 'super-computer' abilities were established by 1985 where twenty years before none existed. Pakistan also built CANDU-type nuclear reactors for research and electricity, and Bangladesh planned a nuclear reactor. Officials in smaller neighboring countries like Sri Lanka and Nepal have had a vision of the technological future which differed little from the vision in India, the region's largest economy. But they have seldom had the resources to follow the same path.

Pakistan most clearly, and Sri Lanka and Bangladesh to a lesser extent, have followed a path of significant state investments in science and technology capabilities, including collaboration with other nations. In Pakistan's case, as in India's, such investments were also made due to strategic considerations. A sort of military-industrial complex has been established which can design, manufacture, and even export sophisticated armaments, and the same talents provide the high-technology impetus for a modern industrial state.

But the very unfavorable population to land and resource ratios in South Asia persist, and the question is regularly asked as to whether these expensive high-tech capabilities have been applied to the mundane problems facing most of the population, half of which lives below officially-defined poverty levels. Do technologies and technology-transfer simply address such problems, or do they, as in the case of the sudden accident at the Bhopal chemical plant of Union Carbide in 1984 killing thousands of people, also exacerbate problems (however unintentionally)? And has the limited scope for research been inhibiting creativity rather than setting it free? Are exceptional South Asian scientists still well advised to study and work abroad? These questions are not academic, but are regularly faced by Prime Ministers and Presidents as well as poor people ploughing in their fields. How they are resolved will occupy South Asians for much longer than the remainder of the twentieth century.

RAn

Further reading

R. S. Anderson, *Building Scientific Institutions in India: Saha and Bhabha* (Montreal, 1975)

D. M. Bose, *A Concise History of Science in India* (New Delhi, 1971)

S. Goonatilake, *Aborted Discovery: Science and Creativity in the Third World* (London, 1984)

A. Kapur, *India's Nuclear Option: Atomic Diplomacy and Decision Making* (New York, 1976)

A. Nandy, *Alternative Sciences: Creativity and Authenticity in Two Indian Scientists* (Delhi, 1980)

S. Visvanathan, *Organizing for Science: The Making of an Industrial Laboratory* (Delhi, 1984)

Select glossary

advaita   'allowing no second' i.e. monism.

ahinsa   non-violence towards man or beast.

AIADMK   All-India Anna Dravida Munnetra Kazhagam; Dravidian Progressive Party founded by M. G. Ramachandran in the early 1970s.

Akali Dal   reform group to bring *gurdwaras* q.v. under the control of the orthodox Sikh community; it subsequently entered politics demanding a separate Sikh state.

ashraf   the 'well-born' amongst South Asian Muslims.

ashram   spiritual retreat; place where a Hindu devotee or religious community lives.

aus   early summer crop in Bengal and Bangladesh.

Barelvis   followers of the Muslim movement led by Ahmad Raza Khan of Bareilly.

bhadralok   the 'respectable people' in Bengal; mainly but not exclusively from the higher Hindu literate castes.

Bhagavad-gita   the most famous ethical text of classical Hindu India.

bhakti   devotion to a personal god.

bhikkus   Buddhist monks.

Biplobi Shainik Sangstha   Revolutionary Soldiers Association (Bangladesh).

BJP   Bharatiya Janata Party; fragment of the Janata Party after the disintegration of the Janata coalition q.v.

BKD   Bharatiya Kranti Dal; agrarian party formed by Charan Singh in the late 1960s.

BLD   Bharatiya Lok Dal; name given to Charan Singh's BKD q.v. after it merged with the radical socialists in 1974.

boro   winter crop in Bengal and Bangladesh.

Brahma   the creator who with Vishnu q.v. and Shiva q.v. forms the Hindu trinity.

brahmacharya   studentship, the first of the classical stages of Hindu life.

brahmin   the priestly or highest *varna* q.v. of Hindu society.

Brahmo Samaj   movement formed in Bengal by Rammohan Roy to reform Hinduism.

CENTO   Central Treaty Organization established under the Baghdad Pact, 1955.

chena   main summer crop in Sri Lanka.

choli   short, tight blouse worn by Hindu women.

Congress (O)   'Organization' Congress; section of the Indian Congress Party dominated by entrenched state party bosses after the split in 1969.

Congress (R)   'Ruling' Congress; Mrs. Gandhi's section of the Indian Congress Party after its split in 1969.

CPM   Communist Party of India (Marxist); split from the CPI q.v. in 1964.

CPI   Communist Party of India.

CPP   Congress Parliamentary Party.

Dasara   Hindu festival in September–October sacred to the mother-goddess.

daxma   a Zoroastrian 'Tower of Silence' where bodies are exposed to vultures.

Deccan   'South', a term used sometimes for the whole Indian peninsula, but more often for its northern and central parts.

Deoband   small town in Saharanpur district (Uttar Pradesh) famous for its *madrasa* q.v. which is regarded by some as the second most important traditional university of the Muslim world after al-Azhar in Cairo.

dharma   the duties of one's station in Hindu life.

dhoti   loin cloth.

Divali   Hindu festival in October–November when lamps are lit and presents exchanged; often known as the Hindu 'Christmas'.

DMK   Dravida Munnetra Kazhagam, the Dravidian Progressive Federation founded in 1949.

DMKP   Dalit Mazdoor Kisan Party formed in October 1984 from the Lok Dal, the Democratic Socialist Party and the Rashtriya Congress and led by Charan Singh.

Ganesha   elephant-headed god of Hinduism, son of Shiva q.v. and Parvati q.v., cheerful, benevolent, a remover of obstacles.

ghi   clarified butter.

gurdwara   a Sikh temple; lit 'the door of the Guru'.

guru   a religious teacher; spelled with a capital G one of the 'ten Gurus' or founders of Sikhism.

Hadiths   the words and deeds of the Prophet Muhammad based on the authority of a chain of transmitters.

haj   Muslim pilgrimage to Mecca.

Hanuman   monkey god of Hinduism, a beneficient guardian spirit and very popular god in the villages.

Harijans   lit. 'children of God', the name given by Mahatma Gandhi to the untouchables of the Hindu caste system. Since 1935 they have been known officially as 'scheduled castes'.

Hinayana   the 'Lesser Vehicle', one of the great divisions of Buddhism.

Holi   a Hindu spring festival in which caste restrictions are forgotten as neighbours scatter red powder and squirt coloured water over each other.

IAS   Indian Administrative Service, the successor of the ICS q.v. in independent India.

ICS   Indian Civil Service, the highest ranks of the bureaucracy under British rule.

ijma   'consensus', traditionally that of qualified legal scholars on a point of Islamic law.

ijtihad   'individual reasoning' to establish the ruling of the *sharia* q.v. on a point of Islamic law.

Indra the war-god of Vedic times.

IOLR India Office Library and Records; the archives of the East India Company and the British Indian government in London.

IPS Indian Police Service.

ISKCON International Society for Krishna q.v. Consciousness whose members are commonly known as 'Hare Krishnas'.

jagir an assignment of land revenues.

Jamaat-e Islami 'Islamic Society' founded by Maulana Maududi in 1941.

Jamiyat ul Ulama-e Hind 'Association of Indian *Ulama*' founded in 1919.

Janata Coalition Indian political party founded to fight the general elections of 1977.

Jan Sangh Indian political party founded in 1951 to rebuild India and to remove foreign cultural influences.

jihad 'holy war' either (1) a spiritual struggle against one's baser instincts, or (2) a military struggle against non-Muslims.

Kali a cult title of Durga, wife of Shiva q.v., and particularly popular in Bengal.

karma the effect of former deeds, performed either in this life or in a previous one, on one's present and future condition.

kharif autumn crop.

Krishna hero and god, eighth and most important incarnation of Vishnu q.v.

kshatriya the warrior or second *varna* q.v. of Hindu society.

Lakshmi wife of Vishnu q.v. and goddess of good fortune.

Lok Dal party led Charan Singh from the break up of the Janata Coalition in 1979 to the foundation of the DMKP in 1984.

Lok Sabha lower house of the Indian Parliament.

madrasa a Muslim school for *ulama* q.v.

Mahayana the Great Vehicle, one of the three great divisions of Buddhism.

maktab a Muslim primary school.

Majlis-e Shura 'Federal Council' established in Pakistan in 1981.

mansab an official Mughal rank offering both personal status and military responsibilities and supported by revenue assignments.

mantra a verse or phrase believed to have magical or religious efficacy.

misals Sikh war-bands of the eighteenth century.

Mukti Bahini East Pakistan guerillas who fought to win the state of Bangladesh in 1971.

Muslim League the main Muslim political party in British India founded in 1906.

National Conference regional party of Jammu and Kashmir with its base primarily amongst the Muslim majority of the state.

nirvana the condition of final bliss in Buddhism.

panchayat lit. 'council of five', council traditionally involved in regulating the affairs of a village or a caste.

Panchayati Raj system of local government introduced in India in 1959.

Parvati wife of Shiva q.v.

pir a sufi master able to lead disciples along a path of spiritual development.

pönlop provincial governor in Bhutan.

PPP Pakistan Peoples' Party founded by Z. A. Bhutto.

puja Hindu worship.

puranas sacred texts of Hinduism.

raiyat cultivator, peasant.

Rajya Sabha the upper house of the Indian Parliament.

Ramazan Muslim month of fasting.

RSS Rashtriya Swayamsevak Sangh, a militant Hindu organization founded in 1925.

sadhu a Hindu holy man.

Sangha lit. 'Society', the Buddhist order.

sannyasa a Hindu who has renounced the world, the fourth of the classical stages of a Hindu life.

sant saint.

sari seamless cloth which forms the main part of an Indian woman's dress.

satyagraha 'truth-force', 'soul-force'; Gandhian passive resistance.

SEATO South East Asia Treaty Organization.

shaivism following Shiva q.v. as the highest Hindu god.

Shiva the destroyer, who with Brahma q.v. and Vishnu q.v. forms the Hindu trinity.

shudra the lowest *varna* q.v. of Hindu society.

SLFP Sri Lanka Freedom Party.

SP Socialist Party (India) founded in 1971.

stupa a mound commemorating the Buddha's death.

sufism Islamic mysticism.

sunna received custom in Islam, especially that associated with Muhammad.

sutra an aphorism, or text consisting of aphorism, a religious text.

Swatantra 'Freedom' Party founded in India in 1959.

Tablighi Jamaat Muslim missionary society.

Telegu Desam Telegu party founded in Andhra Pradesh in 1982.

ulama plural of *alim*, a learned man, in particular those learned in Islamic legal or religious studies.

UNP United National Party (Sri Lanka).

vaishnavism following Vishnu q.v. as the highest Hindu god.

vaishya the third *varna* q.v. of Hindu society.

varna lit. 'colour'; one of four classical divisions of Hindu society.

Vishnu the sustainer, who with Brahma q.v. and Shiva q.v. forms the Hindu trinity.

zamindar a landholder.

Maps

Tables

Index

NOTE. References in italics denote illustrations; there may also be textual references on these pages.

Acknowledgements

The publishers gratefully acknowledge the help of the many individuals and organizations who cannot be named in collecting the illustrations for this volume. In particular they would like to thank the picture researcher Callie Crees; Professor Paul R. Brass; Dr Lionel Carter, Librarian, Centre of South Asian Studies, Cambridge; Dr Helen Kanitkar, SOAS, University of London; Ann and Bury Peerless, Slide Resources and Picture Library; and the staff of Cambridgeshire Libraries.

Every effort has been made to obtain permission to use copyright materials; the publishers apologise for any errors and omissions and would welcome these being brought to their attention.

11 © P. Jones-Griffiths/MAGNUM; 18, 190, 247, 253, 393 R.K. Sharma/Fotomedia; 22, 41*tr, br* C. von Fürer Haimendorf/SOAS, University of London; 25, 27*l*, 455 Gerald Cubitt; 26 Nirmal Ghosh/Fotomedia; 27*r*, 31, 36C, E, F, G, 301 Robert Bradnock; 29, 135*br*, 203*r*, 291 Government of Pakistan; 36B, 39, 40, 53, 269, 281, 304, 312, 331, 339, 340, 348, 351, 363B, 365, 366, 367, 390 Ann & Bury Peerless Slide Resources & Picture Library; 36A, D, 41*tl, bl*, 43, 57, 59, 171, 172, 257, 272, 284, 302, 323, 371, 375, 382, 449, 466, 498 Photo by Paul R. Brass; 51, 185, 194 *The Hindu*; 61 Royal Commonwealth Society Library; 64 Heidi Larson; 66–7 Viscount Scarsdale & the Trustees of the Kedleston Estate Trusts/Barrie & Jenkins; 69 *Collected Works of Mahatma Gandhi, vol. XIV*, Navajivan Trust; 72, 77, 81, 92 Archaeological Survey of India; 91, 150, 459, 468 Douglas Dickins; 97, 111 From H. Beveridge, *A Comprehensive History of India*, 1919; 105, 415 Chester Beatty Library & Gallery of Oriental Art; 119, 124, 261, 337*t*, 396, 426, 433 By permission of the British Library; 126 By permission of J. S. Tilak; 127 By courtesy of Dr. Muhammad Saleem Ahmad; 130 Publications Division, Government of India; 135, 244 Nehru Memorial Museum & Library; 136, 175 Hulton-Deutsch Collection; 141 The Brooklyn Museum; 142 The Trustees of the Imperial War Museum, London; 145 Popperfoto; 154, 214, 254, 369 Dean Press Images; 155 From D. R. Regmi, *Modern Nepal*, 2nd ed., 1975. By permission of the Syndics of Cambridge University Library; 160 From J. C. White, *Sikhim & Bhutan*, 1909. By permission of the Syndics of Cambridge University Library; 161, 232, 330 © Michael Aris; 162 From B. J. Hasrat, *History of Bhutan*. By permission of the Syndics of Cambridge University Library; 164 Christopher Reynolds; 167A LAXMAN in *Times of India*; C Centre of South Asian Studies, University of Cambridge; D, 242 *Daily Jang*; 177 T. S. Ashok/Fotomedia; 178, 462 Philip Davies: private collection; 183 Pramod Pushkarna/*India Today*/Fotomedia; 190, 247, 253, 393 R. K. Sharma/Fotomedia; 191, 224, 299, 314, 349, 360, 379 PANA/Fotomedia; 203*l* Stephens' Collection from the Cambridge South Asian Archive, Centre of South Asian Studies; 207, 212, 233 Associated Press; 218 Rashid Talukder; 221 Government of Bangladesh; 227 Willi Hansen/Alfa Press/Dean Press Images; 231, 241, 248 Fotomedia; 265, 286, 293 B. L. C. Johnson; 277 Robert Harding Picture Library; 283 Francis Robinson; 300 Embassy of Pakistan; 328, 399, 401, 470, 473, 474, 475*t*, 476, 477 By courtesy of the Board of Trustees of the Victoria & Albert Museum; 355, 463, 465*c* Courtesy of the National Museum, New Delhi; 337*b* Museum of Modern Art, Oxford; 346 City of Bristol Museum & Art Gallery; 353 Ami Chand & Sons/D. Lelyveld; 354 Islamic Foundation, Leicester, U.K.; 362 J. R. Hinnells; 363*t* ITC Ltd.; 386 Jyoti M. Banerjee/Fotomedia; 398 Stephen J. Line; 417 By courtesy of Chatto & Windus; 418 National Film Archive, London/Mike Laye, photographer; 422 Formerly the Nasli & Alice Heeramaneck Collection, Museum Associates Purchase, Los Angeles County Museum of Art (M.71.1.11); 423 Amrit Rai; 427 By courtesy of Urdu Markaz; 434 Satyajit Ray; 436 Ian Raeside; 441 Edinburgh University Press/George Mackie, artist; 443 Martin Wickramasinghe Trust; 448 Dayanita Singh/Fotomedia; 452 Press Information Bureau, Government of India; 457 Christopher Tadgell; 460 John Ayling; 464*l* Indian Museum, Calcutta; *r* National Museums of Scotland; 465*l*, 472 Courtesy of the Trustees of the British Museum; 467 By courtesy of Thanjavur Art Gallery, Tamil Nadu; 475*b* Courtesy of Bhupen Khakhar & James Kirkman/photo by Timothy Hyman; 479 Women's Cultural Group, Wandsbeck, R.S.A.; 484 National Film Archive, London; 486 Courtesy of Iqbal Khan/Nasreen Kabir; 488 National Film Archive, London/Satyajit Ray; 492 By permission of the Houghton Library, Harvard University; 494 Ramesh Sipi; 499, 500, 501*r* Government of India; 501*l* Abdus Salam; 503 By courtesy of Indian Petrochemicals Corporation Ltd.